Carter Lang

AMERICAN CONSTITUTIONAL LAW: STRUCTURE AND RECONSTRUCTION

CASES, NOTES, AND PROBLEMS

Sixth Edition

■ ■ ■

Charles A. Shanor

Professor of Law
Emory University

AMERICAN CASEBOOK SERIES®

WEST
ACADEMIC
PUBLISHING

American Casebook Series is a trademark registered in the U.S. Patent and Trademark Office.

© West, a Thomson business, 2001, 2003, 2006
© 2009, 2013 Thomson Reuters
© 2017 LEG, Inc. d/b/a West Academic
      444 Cedar Street, Suite 700
      St. Paul, MN 55101
      1-877-888-1330

West, West Academic Publishing, and West Academic are trademarks of West Publishing Corporation, used under license.

Printed in the United States of America

ISBN: 978-1-68328-071-2

To Susan
and
Amanda, Rick, and Leigh

PREFACE

AMERICAN CONSTITUTIONAL LAW: STRUCTURE AND RECONSTRUCTION
(SIXTH EDITION)

This book began nearly 20 years ago with the arrival of the latest edition of the constitutional law casebook I had been using. Already bloated at 1100 pages, it had just become 300 pages worse. I knew it would drive students to the outlines, but found no better casebook on the market. So I began assembling my own materials.

Editing and organizing the core cases, I tried not to shred them to snippets, hide them among cites to marginal cases, bury them under references to academic commentators, or order them eccentrically. My priority was to let the Justices speak who authored the opinions, concurrences, and dissents. Terse notes, providing context and perspective, came next, along with problems encouraging students to apply the cases in sophisticated and innovative ways—much as they would be required to do as lawyers. Finally, I added more user-friendly transitional materials, some longer notes, the epigrammatic case quotes that open each chapter, and relevant images adding a touch of humor, human interest, or perspective.

This fifth edition includes cases and materials through the October 2016 Supreme Court Term. At about 770 pages of text, it is about 40 pages shorter than the previous edition, despite the new cases. The areas of the book affected by changes are diverse: separation of powers, Congress' powers, state privileges and immunities, substantive due process, and equal protection. This edition benefits from diligent purging of typographical errors and draconian reduction of bloat.

Despite my efforts, some students will complain that the material is difficult. All I can say is that I hope the result—a deeper understanding of and ability to work within the fundamental legal framework of the Constitution of the United States of America—is worth the effort.

I appreciate the confidence and suggestions of colleagues, here and elsewhere, who have supported this book and I thank Emory Law School for funding research assistants over the years, editions, and supplements. My assistant, Marianne D'Souza, helped greatly to make this edition better and cleaner than the last one, including the Table of Cases and the Index. All errors of substance or style, of course, are mine alone.

Charles A. Shanor
Emory University School of Law
September 25, 2016

Summary of Contents

―――――

Table of Contents

Table of Cases

The principal cases are in bold type. Cases cited or discussed in the text are roman type. References are to pages. Cases cited in principal cases and within other quoted materials are not included nor are cases included that are referred to without full citation.

The Constitution of the United States

Preamble

We the People of the United States, in Order to form a more perfect Union, establish Justice, insure domestic Tranquility, provide for the common defence, promote the general Welfare, and secure the Blessings of Liberty to ourselves and our Posterity, do ordain and establish this Constitution for the United States of America.

Article I

Section 1. All legislative Powers herein granted shall be vested in a Congress of the United States, which shall consist of a Senate and House of Representatives.

Section 2. [1] The House of Representatives shall be composed of Members chosen every second Year by the People of the several States, and the Electors in each State shall have the Qualifications requisite for Electors of the most numerous Branch of the State Legislature.

[2] No Person shall be a Representative who shall not have attained to the Age of twenty five Years, and been seven Years a Citizen of the United States, and who shall not, when elected, be an Inhabitant of that State in which he shall be chosen.

[3] [Representatives and direct Taxes shall be apportioned among the several States which may be included within this Union, according to their respective Numbers, which shall be determined by adding to the whole Number of free Persons, including those bound to Service for a Term of Years, and excluding Indians not taxed, three fifths of all other Persons.] The actual Enumeration shall be made within three Years after the first Meeting of the Congress of the United States, and within every subsequent Term of ten Years, in such Manner as they shall by Law direct. The Number of Representatives shall not exceed one for every thirty Thousand, but each State shall have at Least one Representative; and until such enumeration shall be made, the State of New Hampshire shall be entitled to chuse three, Massachusetts eight, Rhode Island and Providence Plantations one, Connecticut five, New York six, New Jersey four, Pennsylvania eight, Delaware one, Maryland six, Virginia ten, North Carolina five, South Carolina five, and Georgia three.

[4] When vacancies happen in the Representation from any State, the Executive Authority thereof shall issue Writs of Election to fill such Vacancies.

[5] The House of Representatives shall chuse their Speaker and other Officers; and shall have the sole Power of Impeachment.

Section 3. [1] [The Senate of the United States shall be composed of two Senators from each State, chosen by the Legislature thereof, for six Years; and each Senator shall have one Vote.]

[2] Immediately after they shall be assembled in Consequence of the first Election, they shall be divided as equally as may be into three Classes. The Seats of the Senators of the first Class shall be vacated at the Expiration of the Second Year, of the second Class at the Expiration of the fourth Year, and of the third Class at the Expiration of the sixth Year, so that one third may be chosen every second Year; [and if Vacancies happen by Resignation, or otherwise, during the Recess of the Legislature of any State, the Executive thereof may make temporary Appointments until the next Meeting of the Legislature, which shall then fill such Vacancies.]

[3] No Person shall be a Senator who shall not have attained to the Age of thirty Years, and been nine Years a Citizen of the United States, and who shall not, when elected, be an Inhabitant of that State for which he shall be chosen.

[4] The Vice President of the United States shall be President of the Senate, but shall have no Vote, unless they be equally divided.

[5] The Senate shall chuse their other Officers, and also a President pro tempore, in the Absence of the Vice President, or when he shall exercise the Office of President of the United States.

[6] The Senate shall have the sole Power to try all Impeachments. When sitting for that Purpose, they shall be on Oath or Affirmation. When the President of the United States is tried, the Chief Justice shall preside: And no Person shall be convicted without the Concurrence of two thirds of the Members present.

[7] Judgment in Cases of Impeachment shall not extend further than to removal from Office, and disqualification to hold and enjoy any Office of honor, Trust, or Profit under the United States: but the Party convicted shall nevertheless be liable and subject to Indictment, Trial, Judgment, and Punishment, according to Law.

Section 4. [1] The Times, Places and Manner of holding Elections for Senators and Representatives, shall be prescribed in each State by the Legislature thereof; but the Congress may at any time by Law make or alter such Regulations, except as to the Places of chusing Senators.

[2] The Congress shall assemble at least once in every Year, and such Meeting shall be on the first Monday in December, unless they shall by Law appoint a different Day.

Section 5. [1] Each House shall be the Judge of the Elections, Returns, and Qualifications of its own Members, and a Majority of each shall constitute a Quorum to do Business; but a smaller Number may adjourn from day to day, and may be authorized to compel the Attendance of absent Members, in such Manner, and under such Penalties as each House may provide.

[2] Each House may determine the Rules of its Proceedings, punish its Members for disorderly Behaviour, and, with the Concurrence of two thirds, expel a Member.

[3] Each House shall keep a Journal of its Proceedings, and from time to time publish the same, excepting such Parts as may in their Judgment require Secrecy; and the Yeas and Nays of the Members of either House on any question shall, at the Desire of one fifth of those Present, be entered on the Journal.

[4] Neither House, during the Session of Congress, shall, without the Consent of the other, adjourn for more than three days, nor to any other Place than that in which the two Houses shall be sitting.

Section 6. [1] The Senators and Representatives shall receive a Compensation for their Services, to be ascertained by Law, and paid out of the Treasury of the United States. They shall in all Cases, except Treason, Felony and Breach of the Peace, be privileged from Arrest during their Attendance at the Session of their respective Houses, and in going to and returning from the same; and for any Speech or Debate in either House, they shall not be questioned in any other Place.

[2] No Senator or Representative shall, during the Time for which he was elected, be appointed to any civil Office under the Authority of the United States, which shall have been created, or the Emoluments whereof shall have been increased during such time; and no Person holding any Office under the United States, shall be a Member of either House during his Continuance in Office.

Section 7. [1] All Bills for raising Revenue shall originate in the House of Representatives; but the Senate may propose or concur with Amendments as on other Bills.

[2] Every Bill which shall have passed the House of Representatives and the Senate, shall, before it become a Law, be presented to the President of the United States; If he approve he shall sign it, but if not he shall return it, with his Objections to the House in which it shall have originated, who shall enter the Objections at large on their Journal, and proceed to reconsider it. If after such Reconsideration two thirds of that House shall agree to pass the Bill, it shall be sent together with the Objections, to the other House, by which it shall likewise be reconsidered, and if approved by two thirds of that House, it shall become a Law. But in all such Cases the Votes of both Houses shall be determined by Yeas and Nays, and the Names of the Persons voting for and against the Bill shall be entered on the Journal of each House respectively. If any Bill shall not be returned by the President within ten Days (Sundays excepted) after it shall have been presented to him, the Same shall be a Law, in like Manner as if he had signed it, unless the Congress by their Adjournment prevent its Return in which Case it shall not be a Law.

[3] Every Order, Resolution, or Vote, to Which the Concurrence of the Senate and House of Representatives may be necessary (except on a question of Adjournment) shall be presented to the President of the United States; and before the Same shall take Effect, shall be approved by

him, or being disapproved by him, shall be repassed by two thirds of the Senate and House of Representatives, according to the Rules and Limitations prescribed in the Case of a Bill.

Section 8. [1] The Congress shall have Power to lay and collect Taxes, Duties, Imposts and Excises, to pay the Debts and provide for the common Defence and general Welfare of the United States; but all Duties, Imposts and Excises shall be uniform throughout the United States;

[2]   To borrow money on the credit of the United States;

[3]   To regulate Commerce with foreign Nations, and among the several States, and with the Indian Tribes;

[4]   To establish an uniform Rule of Naturalization, and uniform Laws on the subject of Bankruptcies throughout the United States;

[5]   To coin Money, regulate the Value thereof, and of foreign Coin, and fix the Standard of Weights and Measures;

[6]   To provide for the Punishment of counterfeiting the Securities and current Coin of the United States;

[7]   To Establish Post Offices and Post Roads;

[8]   To promote the Progress of Science and useful Arts, by securing for limited Times to Authors and Inventors the exclusive Right to their respective Writings and Discoveries;

[9]   To constitute Tribunals inferior to the supreme Court;

[10]   To define and punish Piracies and Felonies committed on the high Seas, and Offenses against the Law of Nations;

[11]   To declare War, grant Letters of Marque and Reprisal, and make Rules concerning Captures on Land and Water;

[12]   To raise and support Armies, but no Appropriation of Money to that Use shall be for a longer Term than two Years;

[13]   To provide and maintain a Navy;

[14]   To make Rules for the Government and Regulation of the land and naval Forces;

[15]   To provide for calling forth the Militia to execute the Laws of the Union, suppress Insurrections and repel Invasions;

[16]   To provide for organizing, arming, and disciplining, the Militia, and for governing such Part of them as may be employed in the Service of the United States, reserving to the States respectively, the Appointment of the Officers, and the Authority of training the Militia according to the discipline prescribed by Congress;

[17]   To exercise exclusive Legislation in all Cases whatsoever, over such District (not exceeding ten Miles square) as may, by Cession of particular States and the Acceptance of Congress, become the Seat of the Government of the United States, and to exercise like Authority over all Places purchased by the Consent of the Legislature of the State in which the Same shall be, for the Erection of Forts, Magazines, Arsenals, dock-Yards, and other needful Buildings;—And

[18] To make all Laws which shall be necessary and proper for carrying into Execution the foregoing Powers, and all other Powers vested by this Constitution in the Government of the United States, or in any Department or Officer thereof.

Section 9. [1] The Migration or Importation of Such Persons as any of the States now existing shall think proper to admit, shall not be prohibited by the Congress prior to the Year one thousand eight hundred and eight, but a Tax or duty may be imposed on such Importation, not exceeding ten dollars for each Person.

[2] The privilege of the Writ of Habeas Corpus shall not be suspended, unless when in Cases of Rebellion or Invasion the public Safety may require it.

[3] No Bill of Attainder or ex post facto Law shall be passed.

[4] No Capitation, or other direct, Tax shall be laid, unless in Proportion to the Census or Enumeration herein before directed to be taken.

[5] No Tax or Duty shall be laid on Articles exported from any State.

[6] No Preference shall be given by any Regulation of Commerce or Revenue to the Ports of one State over those of another: nor shall Vessels bound to, or from, one State be obliged to enter, clear, or pay Duties in another.

[7] No money shall be drawn from the Treasury, but in Consequence of Appropriations made by Law; and a regular Statement and Account of the Receipts and Expenditures of all public Money shall be published from time to time.

[8] No Title of Nobility shall be granted by the United States: And no Person holding any Office of Profit or Trust under them, shall, without the Consent of the Congress, accept of any present, Emolument, Office, or Title, of any kind whatever, from any King, Prince, or foreign State.

Section 10. [1] No State shall enter into any Treaty, Alliance, or Confederation; grant Letters of Marque and Reprisal; coin Money; emit Bills of Credit; make any Thing but gold and silver Coin a Tender in Payment of Debts; pass any Bill of Attainder, ex post facto Law, or Law impairing the Obligation of Contracts, or grant any Title of Nobility.

[2] No State shall, without the Consent of the Congress, lay any Imposts or Duties on Imports or Exports, except what may be absolutely necessary for executing it's inspection Laws: and the net Produce of all Duties and Imposts, laid by any State on Imports or Exports, shall be for the Use of the Treasury of the United States; and all such Laws shall be subject to the Revision and Controul of the Congress.

[3] No State shall, without the Consent of Congress, lay any Duty of Tonnage, keep Troops, or Ships of War in time of Peace, enter into any Agreement or Compact with another State, or with a foreign Power or en-

gage in War, unless actually invaded, or in such imminent Danger as will not admit of delay.

Article II

Section 1. [1] The executive Power shall be vested in a President of the United States of America. He shall hold his Office during the Term of four Years, and, together with the Vice President, chosen for the same Term, be elected, as follows:

[2] Each State shall appoint, in such Manner as the Legislature thereof may direct, a Number of Electors, equal to the whole Number of Senators and Representatives to which the State may be entitled in the Congress; but no Senator or Representative, or Person holding an Office of Trust or Profit under the United States, shall be appointed an Elector.

[3] [The Electors shall meet in their respective States, and vote by Ballot for two Persons, of whom one at least shall not be an Inhabitant of the same State with themselves. And they shall make a List of all the Persons voted for, and of the Number of Votes for each; which List they shall sign and certify, and transmit sealed to the Seat of the Government of the United States, directed to the President of the Senate. The President of the Senate shall, in the Presence of the Senate and House of Representatives, open all the Certificates, and the Votes shall then be counted. The Person having the greatest Number of Votes shall be the President, if such Number be a Majority of the whole Number of Electors appointed; and if there be more than one who have such Majority, and have an equal Number of Votes, then the House of Representatives shall immediately chuse by Ballot one of them for President; and if no Person have a Majority, then from the five highest on the List the said House shall in like Manner chuse the President. But in chusing the President, the Votes shall be taken by States, the Representation from each State having one Vote; A quorum for this Purpose shall consist of a Member or Members from two thirds of the States, and a Majority of all the States shall be necessary to a Choice. In every Case, after the Choice of the President, the Person having the greater Number of Votes of the Electors shall be the Vice President. But if there should remain two or more who have equal Votes, the Senate shall chuse from them by Ballot the Vice President.]

[4] The Congress may determine the Time of chusing the Electors, and the Day on which they shall give their Votes; which Day shall be the same throughout the United States.

[5] No person except a natural born Citizen, or a Citizen of the United States, at the time of the Adoption of this Constitution, shall be eligible to the Office of President; neither shall any Person be eligible to that Office who shall not have attained to the Age of thirty five Years, and been fourteen Years a Resident within the United States.

[6] In case of the removal of the President from Office, or of his Death, Resignation or Inability to discharge the Powers and Duties of the said Office, the Same shall devolve on the Vice President and the Con-

gress may by Law provide for the Case of Removal, Death, Resignation or Inability, both of the President and Vice President, declaring what Officer shall then act as President, and such Officer shall act accordingly, until the Disability be removed, or a President shall be elected.

[7]   The President shall, at stated Times, receive for his Services, a Compensation, which shall neither be increased nor diminished during the Period for which he shall have been elected, and he shall not receive within that Period any other Emolument from the United States, or any of them.

[8]   Before he enter on the Execution of his Office, he shall take the following Oath or Affirmation: "I do solemnly swear (or affirm) that I will faithfully execute the Office of President of the United States, and will to the best of my Ability, preserve, protect and defend the Constitution of the United States."

Section 2. [1] The President shall be Commander in Chief of the Army and Navy of the United States, and of the militia of the several States, when called into the actual Service of the United States; he may require the Opinion, in writing, of the principal Officer in each of the Executive Departments, upon any Subject relating to the Duties of their respective Offices and he shall have Power to grant Reprieves and Pardons for Offenses against the United States, except in Cases of Impeachment.

[2]   He shall have Power, by and with the Advice and Consent of the Senate, to make Treaties, provided two thirds of the Senators present concur; and he shall nominate, and by and with the Advice and Consent of the Senate, shall appoint Ambassadors, other public Ministers and Consuls, Judges of the supreme Court, and all other Officers of the United States, whose Appointments are not herein otherwise provided for, and which shall be established by Law; but the Congress may by Law vest the Appointment of such inferior Officers, as they think proper, in the President alone, in the Courts of Law, or in the Heads of Departments.

[3]   The President shall have Power to fill up all Vacancies that may happen during the Recess of the Senate, by granting Commissions which shall expire at the End of their next Session.

Section 3. He shall from time to time give to the Congress Information of the State of the Union, and recommend to their Consideration such Measures as he shall judge necessary and expedient; he may, on extraordinary Occasions, convene both Houses, or either of them, and in Case of Disagreement between them, with Respect to the Time of Adjournment, he may adjourn them to such Time as he shall think proper; he shall receive Ambassadors and other public Ministers; he shall take Care that the Laws be faithfully executed, and shall Commission all the Officers of the United States.

Section 4. The President, Vice President and all civil Officers of the United States, shall be removed from Office on Impeachment for, and Conviction of, Treason, Bribery, or other high Crimes and Misdemeanors.

Article III

Section 1. The judicial Power of the United States, shall be vested in one supreme Court, and in such inferior Courts as the Congress may from time to time ordain and establish. The Judges, both of the supreme and inferior Courts, shall hold their Offices during good Behaviour, and shall, at stated Times, receive for their Services a Compensation, which shall not be diminished during their Continuance in Office.

Section 2. [1] The judicial Power shall extend to all Cases, in Law and Equity, arising under this Constitution, the Laws of the United States, and Treaties made, or which shall be made, under their Authority;—to all Cases affecting Ambassadors, other public Ministers and Consuls;—to all Cases of admiralty and maritime Jurisdiction;—to Controversies to which the United States shall be a Party;—to Controversies between two or more States;—between a State and Citizens of another State;—between Citizens of different States;—between Citizens of the same State claiming Lands under the Grants of different States, and between a State, or the Citizens thereof, and foreign States, Citizens or Subjects.

[2] In all Cases affecting Ambassadors, other public Ministers and Consuls, and those in which a State shall be a Party, the supreme Court shall have original Jurisdiction. In all the other Cases before mentioned, the supreme Court shall have appellate Jurisdiction, both as to Law and Fact, with such Exceptions, and under such Regulations as the Congress shall make.

[3] The trial of all Crimes, except in Cases of Impeachment, shall be by Jury; and such Trial shall be held in the State where the said Crimes shall have been committed; but when not committed within any State, the Trial shall be at such Place or Places as the Congress may by Law have directed.

Section 3. [1] Treason against the United States, shall consist only in levying War against them, or, in adhering to their Enemies, giving them Aid and Comfort. No Person shall be convicted of Treason unless on the Testimony of two Witnesses to the same overt Act, or on Confession in open Court.

[2] The Congress shall have Power to declare the Punishment of Treason, but no Attainder of Treason shall work Corruption of Blood, or Forfeiture except during the Life of the Person attainted.

Article IV

Section 1. Full Faith and Credit shall be given in each State to the public Acts, Records, and judicial Proceedings of every other State. And the Congress may by general Laws prescribe the Manner in which such Acts, Records and Proceedings shall be proved, and the Effect thereof.

Section 2. [1] The Citizens of each State shall be entitled to all Privileges and Immunities of Citizens in the several States.

[2]   A Person charged in any State with Treason, Felony, or other Crime, who shall flee from Justice, and be found in another State, shall on demand of the executive Authority of the State from which he fled, be delivered up, to be removed to the State having Jurisdiction of the Crime.

[3]   No Person held to Service or Labour in one State, under the Laws thereof, escaping into another, shall, in Consequence of any Law or Regulation therein, be discharged from such Service or Labour, but shall be delivered up on Claim of the Party to whom such Service or Labour may be due.

Section 3. [1] New States may be admitted by the Congress into this Union; but no new State shall be formed or erected within the Jurisdiction of any other State; nor any State be formed by the Junction of two or more States, or Parts of States, without the Consent of the Legislatures of the States concerned as well as of the Congress.

[2]   The Congress shall have Power to dispose of and make all needful Rules and Regulations respecting the Territory or other Property belonging to the United States; and nothing in this Constitution shall be so construed as to Prejudice any Claims of the United States, or of any particular State.

Section 4. The United States shall guarantee to every State in this Union a Republican Form of Government, and shall protect each of them against Invasion; and on Application of the Legislature, or of the Executive (when the Legislature cannot be convened) against domestic Violence.

Article V

The Congress, whenever two thirds of both Houses shall deem it necessary, shall propose Amendments to this Constitution, or, on the Application of the Legislatures of two thirds of the several States, shall call a Convention for proposing Amendments, which, in either Case, shall be valid to all Intents and Purposes, as part of this Constitution, when ratified by the Legislatures of three fourths of the several States, or by Conventions in three fourths thereof, as the one or the other Mode of Ratification may be proposed by the Congress; Provided that no Amendment which may be made prior to the Year One thousand eight hundred and eight shall in any Manner affect the first and fourth Clauses in the Ninth Section of the first Article; and that no State, without its Consent, shall be deprived of its equal Suffrage in the Senate.

Article VI

[1]   All Debts contracted and Engagements entered into, before the Adoption of this Constitution, shall be as valid against the United States under this Constitution, as under the Confederation.

[2]   This Constitution, and the Laws of the United States which shall be made in Pursuance thereof; and all Treaties made, or which shall be made, under the Authority of the United States, shall be the supreme Law of the Land; and the Judges in every State shall be bound thereby,

any Thing in the Constitution or Laws of any State to the Contrary notwithstanding.

[3]   The Senators and Representatives before mentioned, and the Members of the several State Legislatures, and all executive and judicial Officers, both of the United States and of the several States, shall be bound by Oath or Affirmation, to support this Constitution; but no religious Test shall ever be required as a Qualification to any Office or public Trust under the United States.

Article VII

The Ratification of the Conventions of nine States shall be sufficient for the Establishment of this Constitution between the States so ratifying the Same.

ARTICLES IN ADDITION TO, AND AMENDMENT OF, THE CONSTITUTION OF THE UNITED STATES OF AMERICA, PROPOSED BY CONGRESS, AND RATIFIED BY THE LEGISLATURES OF THE SEVERAL STATES PURSUANT TO THE FIFTH ARTICLE OF THE ORIGINAL CONSTITUTION.

Amendment [I] [1791]

Congress shall make no law respecting an establishment of religion, or prohibiting the free exercise thereof; or abridging the freedom of speech, or of the press; or the right of the people peaceably to assemble, and to petition the Government for a redress of grievances.

Amendment [II] [1791]

A well regulated Militia, being necessary to the security of a free State, the right of the people to keep and bear Arms, shall not be infringed.

Amendment [III] [1791]

No Soldier shall, in time of peace be quartered in any house, without the consent of the Owner, nor in time of war, but in a manner to be prescribed by law.

Amendment [IV] [1791]

The right of the people to be secure in their persons, houses, papers, and effects, against unreasonable searches and seizures, shall not be violated, and no Warrants shall issue, but upon probable cause, supported by Oath or affirmation, and particularly describing the place to be searched, and the persons or things to be seized.

Amendment [V] [1791]

No person shall be held to answer for a capital, or otherwise infamous crime, unless on a presentment or indictment of a Grand Jury, except in cases arising in the land or naval forces, or in the Militia, when in actual service in time of War or public danger; nor shall any person be subject for the same offence to be twice put in jeopardy of life or limb; nor shall be compelled in any criminal case to be a witness against himself, nor be deprived of life, liberty, or property, without due process of law; nor shall private property be taken for public use, without just compensation.

Amendment [VI] [1791]

In all criminal prosecutions, the accused shall enjoy the right to a speedy and public trial, by an impartial jury of the State and district wherein the crime shall have been committed, which district shall have been previously ascertained by law, and to be informed of the nature and cause of the accusation; to be confronted with the witnesses against him; to have compulsory process for obtaining witnesses in his favor, and to have the Assistance of Counsel for his defence.

Amendment [VII] [1791]

In Suits at common law, where the value in controversy shall exceed twenty dollars, the right of trial by jury shall be preserved, and no fact tried by jury, shall be otherwise re-examined in any Court of the United States, than according to the rules of the common law.

Amendment [VIII] [1791]

Excessive bail shall not be required, nor excessive fines imposed, nor cruel and unusual punishments inflicted.

Amendment [IX] [1791]

The enumeration in the Constitution, of certain rights, shall not be construed to deny or disparage others retained by the people.

Amendment [X] [1791]

The powers not delegated to the United States by the Constitution, nor prohibited by it to the States, are reserved to the States respectively, or to the people.

Amendment [XI] [1798]

The Judicial power of the United States shall not be construed to extend to any suit in law or equity, commenced or prosecuted against one of the United States by Citizens of another State, or by Citizens or Subjects of any Foreign State.

Amendment [XII] [1804]

The Electors shall meet in their respective states and vote by ballot for President and Vice-President, one of whom, at least, shall not be an inhabitant of the same state with themselves; they shall name in their ballots the person voted for as President, and in distinct ballots the person voted for as Vice-President, and they shall make distinct lists of all persons voted for as President, and of all persons voted for as Vice-President, and of the number of votes for each, which lists they shall sign and certify, and transmit sealed to the seat of the government of the United States, directed to the President of the Senate;—The President of the Senate shall, in the presence of the Senate and House of Representatives, open all the certificates and the votes shall then be counted;—The person having the greatest number of votes for President, shall be the President, if such number be a majority of the whole number of Electors appointed; and if no person have such majority, then from the persons having the highest numbers not exceeding three on the list of those voted for as President, the House of Representatives shall choose immediately, by ballot, the President. But in choosing the President, the votes shall be taken by states, the representation from each state having one vote; a quorum for this purpose shall consist of a member or members from two-thirds of the states, and a majority of all the states shall be necessary to a choice. And if the House of Representatives shall not choose a President whenever the right of choice shall devolve upon them before the fourth day of March next following, then the Vice-President shall act as President, as in the case of the death or other constitutional disability of the President.—The person having the greatest number of votes as Vice-President, shall be the Vice-President, if such number be a majority of the whole number of Electors appointed, and if no person have a majority, then from the two highest numbers on the list, the Senate shall choose the Vice-President; a quorum for the purpose shall consist of two-thirds of the whole number of Senators, and a majority of the whole number shall be necessary to a choice. But no person constitutionally ineligible to the office of President shall be eligible to that of Vice-President of the United States.

Amendment XIII [1865]

Section 1.   Neither slavery nor involuntary servitude, except as a punishment for crime whereof the party shall have been duly convicted, shall exist within the United States, or any place subject to their jurisdiction.

Section 2.   Congress shall have power to enforce this article by appropriate legislation.

Amendment XIV [1868]

Section 1.   All persons born or naturalized in the United States, and subject to the jurisdiction thereof, are citizens of the United States and of the State wherein they reside. No State shall make or enforce any law which shall abridge the privileges or immunities of citizens of the United States; nor shall any State deprive any person of life, liberty, or property, without due process of law; nor deny to any person within its jurisdiction the equal protection of the laws.

Section 2.   Representatives shall be apportioned among the several States according to their respective numbers, counting the whole number of persons in each State, excluding Indians not taxed. But when the right to vote at any election for the choice of electors for President and Vice President of the United States, Representatives in Congress, the Executive and Judicial officers of a State, or the members of the Legislature thereof, is denied to any of the male inhabitants of such State, being twenty-one years of age, and citizens of the United States, or in any way abridged, except for participation in rebellion, or other crime, the basis of representation therein shall be reduced in the proportion which the number of such male citizens shall bear to the whole number of male citizens twenty-one years of age in such State.

Section 3. No person shall be a Senator or Representative in Congress, or elector of President and Vice President, or hold any office, civil or military, under the United States, or under any State, who having previously taken an oath, as a member of Congress, or as an officer of the United States, or as a member of any State legislature, or as an executive or judicial officer of any State, to support the Constitution of the United States, shall have engaged in insurrection or rebellion against the same, or given aid or comfort to the enemies thereof. But Congress may by a vote of two-thirds of each House, remove such disability.

Section 4. The validity of the public debt of the United States, authorized by law, including debts incurred for payment of pensions and bounties for services in suppressing insurrection or rebellion, shall not be questioned. But neither the United States nor any State shall assume or pay any debt or obligation incurred in aid of insurrection or rebellion against the United States, or any claim for the loss or emancipation of any slave; but all such debts, obligations and claims shall be held illegal and void.

Section 5. The Congress shall have power to enforce, by appropriate legislation, the provisions of this article.

Amendment XV [1870]

Section 1. The right of citizens of the United States to vote shall not be denied or abridged by the United States or by any State on account of race, color, or previous condition of servitude.

Section 2. The Congress shall have power to enforce this article by appropriate legislation.

Amendment XVI [1913]

The Congress shall have power to lay and collect taxes on incomes, from whatever source derived, without apportionment among the several States, and without regard to any census or enumeration.

Amendment [XVII] [1913]

[1] The Senate of the United States shall be composed of two Senators from each State, elected by the people thereof, for six years; and each Senator shall have one vote. The electors in each State shall have the

qualifications requisite for electors of the most numerous branch of the State legislatures.

[2]   When vacancies happen in the representation of any State in the Senate, the executive authority of such State shall issue writs of election to fill such vacancies: *Provided,* that the legislature of any State may empower the executive thereof to make temporary appointments until the people fill the vacancies by election as the legislature may direct.

[3]   This amendment shall not be so construed as to affect the election or term of any Senator chosen before it becomes valid as part of the Constitution.

Amendment [XVIII] [1919]

Section 1.   After one year from the ratification of this article the manufacture, sale, or transportation of intoxicating liquors within, the importation thereof into, or the exportation thereof from the United States and all territory subject to the jurisdiction thereof for beverage purposes is hereby prohibited.

Section 2.   The Congress and the several States shall have concurrent power to enforce this article by appropriate legislation.

Section 3.   This article shall be inoperative unless it shall have been ratified as an amendment to the Constitution by the legislatures of the several States, as provided in the Constitution, within seven years from the date of the submission hereof to the States by the Congress.

Amendment [XIX] [1920]

[1]   The right of citizens of the United States to vote shall not be denied or abridged by the United States or by any State on account of sex.

[2]   Congress shall have power to enforce this article by appropriate legislation.

Amendment [XX] [1933]

Section 1.   The terms of the President and Vice President shall end at noon on the 20th day of January, and the terms of Senators and Representatives at noon on the 3d day of January, of the years in which such terms would have ended if this article had not been ratified; and the terms of their successors shall then begin.

Section 2.   The Congress shall assemble at least once in every year, and such meeting shall begin at noon on the 3d day of January, unless they shall by law appoint a different day.

Section 3.   If, at the time fixed for the beginning of the term of the President, the President elect shall have died, the Vice President elect shall become President. If the President shall not have been chosen before the time fixed for the beginning of his term, or if the President elect shall have failed to qualify, then the Vice President elect shall act as President until a President shall have qualified; and the Congress may by law provide for the case wherein neither a President elect nor a Vice President elect shall have qualified, declaring who shall then act as President, or the manner in which one who is to act shall be selected, and such person shall act accordingly until a President or Vice President shall have qualified.

Section 4. The Congress may by law provide for the case of the death of any of the persons from whom the House of Representatives may choose a President whenever the right of choice shall have devolved upon them, and for the case of the death of any of the persons from whom the Senate may choose a Vice President whenever the right of choice shall have devolved upon them.

Section 5. Sections 1 and 2 shall take effect on the 15th day of October following the ratification of this article.

Section 6. This article shall be inoperative unless it shall have been ratified as an amendment to the Constitution by the legislatures of three-fourths of the several States within seven years from the date of its submission.

Amendment [XXI] [1933]

Section 1. The eighteenth article of amendment to the Constitution of the United States is hereby repealed.

Section 2. The transportation or importation into any State, Territory, or possession of the United States for delivery or use therein of intoxicating liquors, in violation of the laws thereof, is hereby prohibited.

Section 3. This article shall be inoperative unless it shall have been ratified as an amendment to the Constitution by conventions in the several States, as provided in the Constitution, within seven years from the date of the submission hereof to the States by the Congress.

Amendment [XXII] [1951]

Section 1. No person shall be elected to the office of the President more than twice, and no person who has held the office of President, or acted as President, for more than two years of a term to which some other person was elected President shall be elected to the office of President more than once. But this Article shall not apply to any person holding the office of President when this Article was proposed by the Congress, and shall not prevent any person who may be holding the office of President, or acting as President, during the term within which this Article becomes operative from holding the office of President or acting as President during the remainder of such term.

Section 2. This article shall be inoperative unless it shall have been ratified as an amendment to the Constitution by the legislatures of three-fourths of the several States within seven years from the date of its submission to the States by the Congress.

Amendment [XXIII] [1961]

Section 1.   The District constituting the seat of Government of the United States shall appoint in such manner as the Congress may direct:

A number of electors of President and Vice President equal to the whole number of Senators and Representatives in Congress to which the District would be entitled if it were a State, but in no event more than the least populous state; they shall be in addition to those appointed by the states, but they shall be considered, for the purposes of the election of President and Vice President, to be electors appointed by a state; and they shall meet in the District and perform such duties as provided by the twelfth article of amendment.

Section 2.   The Congress shall have power to enforce this article by appropriate legislation.

Amendment [XXIV] [1964]

Section 1.   The right of citizens of the United States to vote in any primary or other election for President or Vice President, for electors for President or Vice President, or for Senator or Representative in Congress, shall not be denied or abridged by the United States or any State by reason of failure to pay any poll tax or other tax.

Section 2.   The Congress shall have power to enforce this article by appropriate legislation.

Amendment [XXV] [1967]

Section 1.   In the case of the removal of the President from office or of his death or resignation, the Vice President shall become President.

Section 2.   Whenever there is a vacancy in the office of the Vice President, the President shall nominate a Vice President who shall take office upon confirmation by a majority vote of both Houses of Congress.

Section 3.   Whenever the President transmits to the President pro tempore of the Senate and the Speaker of the House of Representatives his written declaration that he is unable to discharge the powers and duties of his office, and until he transmits to them a written declaration to the contrary, such powers and duties shall be discharged by the Vice President as Acting President.

Section 4.   Whenever the Vice President and a majority of either the principal officers of the executive departments or of such other body as Congress may by law provide, transmit to the President pro tempore of the Senate and the Speaker of the House of Representatives, their written declaration that the President is unable to discharge the powers and duties of his office, the Vice President shall immediately assume the powers and duties of the office as Acting President.

Thereafter, when the President transmits to the President pro tempore of the Senate and the Speaker of the House of Representatives his written declaration that no inability exists, he shall resume the powers and duties of his office unless the Vice President and a majority of either the principal officers of the executive department or of such other body as Congress may by law provide, transmit within four days to the President pro tempore of the Senate and the Speaker of the House of Representatives their written declaration that the President is unable to discharge the powers and duties of his office. Thereupon Congress shall decide the issue, assembling within forty-eight hours for that purpose if not in session. If the Congress, within twenty-one days after receipt of the latter written declaration, or, if Congress is not in session, within twenty-one days after Congress is required to assemble, determines by two-thirds vote of both Houses that the President is unable to discharge the powers and duties of his office, the Vice President shall continue to discharge the same as Acting President; otherwise, the President shall resume the powers and duties of his office.

Amendment [XXVI] [1971]

Section 1. The right of citizens of the United States, who are eighteen years of age or older, to vote shall not be denied or abridged by the United States or by any State on account of age.

Section 2. The Congress shall have power to enforce this article by appropriate legislation.

Amendment [XXVII] [1992]

No law, varying the compensation for the services of the Senators and Representatives, shall take effect, until an election of Representatives shall have intervened.

AMERICAN CONSTITUTIONAL LAW: STRUCTURE AND RECONSTRUCTION

CASES, NOTES, AND PROBLEMS

Sixth Edition

I

INTRODUCTION

A. A BRIEF OUTLINE OF THE CONSTITUTION'S TEXT

"[W]e must never forget that it is a constitution we are expounding."

—CHIEF JUSTICE JOHN MARSHALL
McCullouch v. Maryland (1819)

JUSTICE FELIX FRANKFURTER once advised a law clerk for JUSTICE HUGO BLACK: "The problem with your judge is that he thinks you can understand the Constitution by reading it." NOT reading the Constitution, however, is even worse.

Supporters of political positions and citizens who believe they have been treated unfairly frequently support their positions with references to the Constitution. If they oppose a governmental action, saying it is "unconstitutional" appears to add weight and legitimacy to their arguments. Refutations arguing that challenged actions are "constitutional" may neutralize such claims and deflect attention from the action's lack of wisdom. Often, neither side's claims are checked against the document itself, despite its brevity.

READ the Constitution. While it is not a particularly exciting exercise, the text will provide you with a critical starting point for making constitutional arguments.

The Constitution is divided into articles, sections, and clauses. You might outline the Constitution's articles and sections as follows:

Preamble: General Purposes of the Constitution

Article I: Congress

§ 1: Vests legislative powers in the Senate and House.

§ 2: House of Representatives: members chosen every two years; prescribes qualifications for members; requires census for apportionment; gives House power to initiate Impeachments.

§ 3: Senate: members have six year terms; prescribes qualifications; Senate gets power to try Impeachments.

§ 4: Provides for Senate and House elections.

§ 5: Notes independence of each house's rules, requires journals by each.

§ 6: Members and Senators; certain privileges; can hold no other office.

§ 7: Bills passed by Congress to President; veto override by 2/3 vote.

§ 8: Enumerates Congress' powers: tax, spend, regulate commerce, coin money, create inferior federal courts, declare war, etc.; make "Necessary & Proper" laws to carry out Congress' powers.

§ 9: Restricts powers of Congress: no ex post facto laws or bills of attainder, certain taxes barred, no titles of nobility.

§ 10: Restricts state powers: can't make treaties, coin money, tax exports (unless necessary for inspection laws), keep troops, or engage in war.

Article II: President

§ 1: Establishes President and Vice President, length of terms, electors and election, qualifications; removal, compensation, and oath of office.

§ 2: President's powers: Commander-in-Chief, grant pardons, make treaties, appoint officers, fill Senate vacancies.

§ 3: President's duties: State of the Union Address, convene Congress, receive Ambassadors, commission officers; "take Care that the Laws be faithfully executed."

§ 4: Sets impeachment standard.

Article III: Judiciary

§ 1: Vests judicial power of the U.S. in Supreme Court and inferior courts Congress creates; hold office during good behavior.

§ 2: Establishes jurisdiction of Federal Courts, cases for Supreme Court original and appellate jurisdiction; provides jury trials for crimes.

§ 3: Establishes crime of and punishment for treason.

Article IV: State Relations

§ 1: Provides for Full Faith & Credit among states.

§ 2: Confers Privileges & Immunities among state citizens, provides for extradition and fugitive slaves.

§ 3: Sets rules for addition of new states and power for governing territories.

§ 4: U.S. guarantees states "a Republican Form of Government" and protects them from invasion.

Article V: Amendments to the Constitution: sets procedures for amending the Constitution.

Article VI: Constitution's Effects

§ 1: Pre-existing debts are good against the US.

§ 2: Supremacy of the Constitution, laws "made in pursuance thereof," and treaties.

§ 3: Government officials bound by oath to support the Constitution; no religious test for office.

Article VII: Ratification of the Constitution: Nine states necessary.

The Amendments

There are 27 Amendments to the Constitution. The first ten, the Bill of Rights, were adopted in 1791, shortly after the Constitution was ratified; several important Amendments (13, 14, and 15) were adopted following the Civil War; the latest Amendment was ratified in 1992.

The text does not answer many questions neatly. Some items that seem clear may in fact be less so upon reflection. For example, the Constitution requires that the President be at least 35 years old. Is the relevant date the nomination, the election, or the swearing-in? If the President dies and the Vice President is not 35 at the time of the President's death, can the Vice President assume office? If not the Vice President, who? Do the 12th and 25th Amendments answer these questions?

The Constitution also contains a number of provisions that, even on cursory consideration, are ambiguous. Most of this course is devoted to such provisions, including the provisions of the original Constitution that allocate powers to the legislative, executive, and judicial branches of government, those that coordinate Federal and State governmental powers, and those that require "due process of law" and "equal protection of the laws."

Preliminary Exercises

1. **Ambiguity**. Find examples in the Constitution of (a) maddeningly vague language, (b) modifiers like "exclusive" which may imply non-exclusivity elsewhere, and (c) different uses of the same word or phrase in different parts of the document. What benefits and disadvantages do you see to such ambiguities in the Constitution?

2. **Basic Political Science**. Where in the document do you find "checks and balances," "separation of powers," "federalism," and "individual rights," terms that are widely used in discussions of the Constitution? What do these terms mean to you, based on your reading of the document and your college political science background (if any)?

3. **Democracy**. The United States is often referred to as a democracy. Does the Constitution support this popular view?

4. **Political Hot–Button Issues**. How does the Constitution deal with military issues? Slavery and other racial issues? Crime and punishment?

B. A BRIEF HISTORY OF THE CONSTITUTION
AND ITS INTERPRETATION

I–1. "The Signing of the Constitution" by Thomas P. Rossiter. Independence National Historical Park.

The Declaration of Independence identified a number of ideals the American colonists believed to be "self-evident" and listed a number of specific grievances against England and King George III. The first agreement uniting the states, the 1777 Articles of Confederation, provided for a Congress with various powers, including the authority to conduct foreign affairs. READ the Articles of Confederation, reproduced as Appendix A at the end of this book.

Independence was achieved following a war led by General George Washington, whose personal begging, borrowing, and pleading held the colonies together during military hostilities. Following the end of the war in 1781, the states reverted to semiautonomous status: trade barriers were erected among them, and local uprisings (like Shay's Rebellion) disrupted public order. Many decried the demise of the "civic virtue" which had carried the colonies through the war; others concluded that structural changes were needed in the framework of the central government if the states were to progress economically and attain prominence among the nations of the world.

In the summer of 1787, a "Constitutional Convention" comprised of delegates from each state met in Philadelphia to discuss how to reform the Articles of Confederation. George Washington chaired the Convention. James Madison played a formative role and took extensive notes. Though chartered to reform the Articles, the Convention proposed an entirely new constitutional structure.   Indeed, the work of the Convention and the subsequent ratification of the Constitution might be called "unconfederational."

Much debate at the Convention centered on how much central government should be strengthened relative to the state governments. Creation of a bicameral legislature was the "Great Compromise" of the Convention; each state would be represented equally in the Senate (pleasing the small states), while state population would determine representation in the House (pleasing the large states).

Because of concerns about how Congress' legislative power would be wielded, Article I was drafted to give specific limited powers to Congress and to preclude Congress from doing certain things that the English Parliament had done.   Article I also imposed some limits on state power. Debate about executive power focused more on whether to have a unitary or divided executive branch, rather than on the exact powers of the presidency.   The result was Article II, granting "all executive power" to a President designated "Commander-in-Chief" and directed to "take care" to enforce the law.   The creation of a Supreme Court was discussed in technical terms; attention focused upon what "Cases and Controversies" could be heard by that court and by "such inferior courts as the Congress may from time to time ordain and establish."   Though delegates at the Convention disagreed vehemently about slavery, the word was not mentioned in the Constitution.   Several provisions elliptically alluded to this Southern institution, but the tensions between the North and the South over slavery were left unresolved.

The Constitution of the United States was submitted to the states for ratification on September 17, 1787.   During the following months, it was hotly debated within the individual states.   Supporters of the Constitution were called Federalists; opponents were called Antifederalists.   The arguments of Federalists Madison, Hamilton, and Jay, explaining the Constitution and urging its adoption, originally appeared in newspaper articles that were later collected as The Federalist Papers.   Although produced for advocacy rather than pure description, The Federalist Papers remain a frequently-used source of information for discerning the "original intent" of the Constitution's framers.

One of the most serious criticisms made of the Constitution by the Antifederalists was the absence of a bill of rights, for most state constitutions at that time guaranteed citizens certain rights and freedoms.   The Constitution received the last required state ratification in mid–1788, but was not put into operation until early 1789. Two large states, New York and Massachusetts, ratified the Constitution, but called for adoption of a bill of rights in their ratification resolutions.   Rhode Island ratified the Constitution in 1790 only after being threatened by the other states with isolation and trade sanctions.

George Washington was inaugurated as the first President of the United States on April 30, 1789.   John Jay became the first Chief Justice of the

United States Supreme Court (1789–95). The First Congress passed legislation establishing the new government, including the Judiciary Act of 1789.

James Madison introduced a Bill of Rights in Congress on June 8, 1789, as a series of amendments to the Constitution. READ excerpts of his speech introducing the Bill of Rights, reproduced as Appendix B. These twelve amendments, with some modifications, were adopted by Congress and sent to the states for ratification under one of the procedures set up in Article V (passage by 2/3 of each house of Congress and ratification by 3/4 of the state legislatures). Ten of these twelve provisions received the necessary ratifications in 1791.[1] In general, the Bill of Rights limited the national government's power.[2]

After adoption of the Bill of Rights, the text of the Constitution remained virtually unchanged until after the Civil War.[3] The functioning Constitution did change, however, mainly as a result of active interpretation by the Supreme Court.[4] Under CHIEF JUSTICE JOHN MARSHALL's leadership from 1801 to 1835, the Supreme Court established its authority to invalidate federal laws as unconstitutional and to review state law for conformity to federal law. *See Marbury v. Madison* and *Martin v. Hunter's Lessee* (Ch. II). Additionally, the Marshall Court rendered several decisions that expansively interpreted the powers of Congress. *See McCulloch v. Maryland* and *Gibbons v. Ogden* (Ch. IV). Finally, the Marshall Court limited the powers of the states, primarily by using the contracts clause of Article I, § 10 to invalidate state infringements on contractual expectations, rather than by applying the Bill of Rights to the States. *Barron v. Mayor and City Council of Baltimore*, 32 U.S. (7 Pet.) 243 (1833). CHIEF JUSTICE MARSHALL greatly enhanced the stature of the Supreme Court, writing over 1,000 opinions himself, most of them for a unanimous Court.

From 1836 to 1864, the Court was led by CHIEF JUSTICE ROGER TANEY. The Taney Court did not reverse the precedents of the Marshall Court, but it did emphasize states' rights and limits on national powers in cases the Marshall Court might have decided differently. More importantly, the Taney Court became known for the worst decision in the history of the Supreme Court. In *Dred Scott v. Sandford* (Ch. VII), the Court held that a slave was not a "citizen" entitled to invoke judicial processes, and that a federal statute

---

[1] An eleventh, prohibiting certain congressional pay raises, was ratified nearly 200 years later as the Twenty–Seventh Amendment.

[2] Most of the Bill of Rights provisions have been applied to the states as requirements of Fourteenth Amendment due process during the Twentieth Century. See infra, Ch. VIII.

[3] The Eleventh Amendment (1795) restricted suits against states in federal court, in reaction to the Court's decision in *Chisholm v. Georgia*, 2 U.S. (2 Dall.) 419 (1793). The Twelfth Amendment (1804) changed the Electoral College system to avoid problems that had arisen in the election of 1800.

[4] The other branches of government also placed glosses on the Constitution. For example, President Thomas Jefferson doubled the size of the United States by purchasing Louisiana from France, even though the Constitution did not expressly authorize presidential purchase of territory.

compromising slavery matters (the Missouri Compromise) was unconstitutional. Rather than "settling" the slavery issue, as Taney had planned, the decision inflamed the abolitionists, removed the issue of slavery from processes of political compromise, and helped precipitate the Civil War.

Following the Civil War, three new amendments were added to the Constitution. These amendments abolished slavery, established citizenship rights for the former slaves, required the states to provide certain privileges and immunities, equal protection of the laws, and due process of law, granted the former slaves the right to vote, and gave Congress the power to enforce these rights. These amendments, but most importantly the Fourteenth Amendment, ratified under duress by the southern states,[5] transformed the relationship between the United States and the states into a more nationalistic mold.

During the last quarter of the nineteenth century and the first third of the twentieth century, the Constitution was amended through a number of "Progressive Era" amendments and interpreted in a number of "Regressive Era" decisions by the Supreme Court. The Sixteenth, Seventeenth and Nineteenth Amendments empowered Congress to "lay and collect taxes on incomes," provided for direct popular election of Senators, and granted the right to vote to women.[6] The Court's interpretations narrowed the reach of the Fourteenth Amendment, eviscerated the Privileges or Immunities Clause, constrained the scope of the Thirteenth and Fourteenth Amendment powers of Congress, and construed the Equal Protection Clause to permit apartheid ("separate but equal"). *See The Slaughter House Cases* (Ch. VII), *The Civil Rights Cases* (Ch. VII), and *Plessy v. Ferguson* (Ch. IX). Subsequently, the Court transformed the Due Process Clause of the Fourteenth Amendment into a tool for protecting property interests. For example, it invalidated state legislation that guaranteed minimum standards of employment. *See Lochner v. New York* (Ch. VIII).

During the Great Depression, the Court's view of the Constitution conflicted with that of President Franklin D. Roosevelt, who was elected with large majorities in 1932 and 1936. Court decisions in 1935 and 1936 invalidated New Deal legislation, such as the Railroad Retirement Act, the National Industrial Recovery Act, and the Agricultural Adjustment Act. *See, e.g., A.L.A. Schechter Poultry Corp. v. United States*, 295 U.S. 495 (1935). Infuriated, President Roosevelt referred to the Justices as "nine old men." In February 1937, he proposed a plan to prevent "hardening of the judicial

---

[5] The unusual process by which the Fourteenth Amendment was adopted is extensively surveyed by Bruce Ackerman in WE THE PEOPLE: TRANSFORMATIONS (1998), at 99–252. In a nutshell, the story is one of dubious conformity to the requirements of Article V. The text of the Fourteenth Amendment received a 2/3 vote from a Congress that had excluded representatives from the southern states (Democrats who would have blocked passage). State ratification followed dissolution of the governments of the southern states, establishment of military rule pursuant to the Reconstruction Acts of 1867, and creation of new state governments. Readmission to the United States was predicated on their legislatures ratifying the Fourteenth Amendment.

[6] The Eighteenth Amendment, prohibiting the "manufacture, sale, or transportation" of alcohol, was repealed fifteen years later by the Twenty–First Amendment.

arteries" by appointment of a new Justice for each Justice who had not resigned or retired within six months after reaching age seventy, thus allowing for an expansion of the Court from nine to as many as fifteen Justices. In March and April, 1937, the Court reversed earlier restrictions on state labor legislation and upheld the National Labor Relations Act. *See West Coast Hotel v. Parrish* (Ch. VIII) and *NLRB v. Jones & Laughlin Steel Corp.*, 301 U.S. 1 (1937). The Senate Judiciary Committee forcefully rejected the Roosevelt "court-packing" plan in June 1937.

From 1937 to 1941, President Roosevelt appointed many new Justices to the Court to replace those who had died or retired. Without any explicit amendment of the Constitution, these appointees (Hugo Black, Stanley Reed, Felix Frankfurter, William O. Douglas, Frank Murphy, James Byrnes, and Robert Jackson) transformed constitutional law. The Court stopped reviewing economic legislation, whether state or federal, hence facilitating a broader construction of congressional power in the federal system. *See Wickard v. Filburn* (Ch. IV). It also began to consider civil liberties issues in terms of broader theories of political power, *United States v. Carolene Products* (Ch. IX), though this development occasionally seemed in tension with granting broad authority to the federal government. *See Korematsu v. United States* (Ch. IX). When the Court perceived tension between the political branches of the federal government, it was willing to reexamine basic precepts of constitutional theory. *See Youngstown Sheet & Tube v. Sawyer* (Ch. III).

In 1953, President Eisenhower appointed former California Governor Earl Warren as Chief Justice. Warren's mission on the Court was equal justice. Under Warren's leadership, the Court reversed *Plessy v. Ferguson* in *Brown v. Board of Education* (Ch. IX), expanded constitutional protections accorded criminal defendants, reevaluated political fairness in *Baker v. Carr* (Ch. II), enhanced First Amendment protections (speech, press, and religion), and recognized a right of privacy in *Griswold v. Connecticut* (Ch. VIII).

Earl Warren's successor, Warren Burger, was appointed by President Nixon in 1969 to lead a counter-revolution of the Warren Court's jurisprudence, especially in the criminal procedure area. The counter-revolution never came. Though the Burger Court sometimes refused to extend Warren Court decisions, it seldom took a position flatly at odds with its predecessor. Indeed, the right of privacy established in *Griswold* was extended in *Roe v. Wade* (Ch. VIII). The Burger Court declined to apply disparate impact theory to racial matters under the Equal Protection Clause. *See Washington v. Davis* (Ch. IX). One of the most far-reaching decisions of the Burger Court invalidated over 200 federal statutes containing "legislative vetoes." *See INS v. Chadha* (Ch. III).

When Warren Burger resigned in 1986, President Reagan selected Associate Justice William Rehnquist as Chief Justice. He and Republican President George H.W. Bush made five appointments from 1985 through 1992 (Sandra Day O'Connor, Antonin Scalia, Anthony Kennedy, David Souter, and Clarence Thomas). Next, Democratic President Clinton in 1993 and 1994 appointed Ruth Bader Ginsberg and Stephen Breyer. The

Rehnquist Court moved in some new directions. Federalism issues, for the first time since the New Deal, assumed prominence as the Court restricted the reach of federal legislation. *See generally* Chapter IV. New life was breathed into the Privileges or Immunities Clause by *Saenz v. Roe* (Ch. VII), *Roe v. Wade* was reaffirmed but reinterpreted in *Planned Parenthood v. Casey* (Ch. VIII), liberty protections were extended to homosexuals in *Lawrence v. Texas* (Ch. VIII), affirmative action was reexamined (Ch. IX), and equal protection was applied, controversially, in the 2000 presidential election (*Bush v. Gore*, Ch. IX).

In 2005, President George W Bush appointed John Roberts to serve as Chief Justice and Samuel Alito to fill the vacancy created upon the resignation of Justice O'Connor. President Obama appointed Sonia Sotomayor, the first Hispanic member of the Court, and Elena Kagan, who filled the vacancy created upon Justice Stevens' retirement. With the death of Justice Scalia in 2016 and the Senate's refusal to consider any nominee submitted with President Obama in his final year in office, one position remains vacant. Decisions of the Roberts Court (or Kennedy Court, as he has most frequently been the swing justice) have continued to be controversial. See, e.g. *NFIB v. Sibelius* (Ch. IV), *Obergefell v. Hodges* (Ch. VIII), and *Fisher v. University of Texas* (Ch. IX) Whoever is appointed, one fact will remain: each term of court will bring new decisions in which the Court reshapes previous interpretations of the Constitution.

More Preliminary Exercises

1. **Articles and Constitution.** Find at least three ways in which the Constitution differs from its predecessor, the Articles of Confederation (reproduced as Appendix A).

2. **Madison's Proposal and Bill of Rights.** Find at least three ways in which the first ten amendments to the Constitution differ from James Madison's proposal (reproduced as Appendix B).

3. **Significance of Differences.** Are the Articles and Madison's proposal relevant to interpreting the Constitution? Construct an argument concerning the meaning of a provision in the Constitution from different language in the Articles and in Madison's proposal.

C. CONSTITUTIONAL PRINCIPLES

Support (indeed reverence) for the Constitution is a defining characteristic of the increasingly diverse people of the United States. Yet most Americans have not read the Constitution as recently or as carefully as you. Nor have they read even the short systematic history of the Constitution's interpretation that you have just finished. What does it mean for an American citizen to say that he or she is "attached to the principles" (even if not the text or history) of the United States Constitution? The following case shows the importance of that attachment as well as its ambiguity.

SCHNEIDERMAN v. UNITED STATES
320 U.S. 118 (1943).

Mr. JUSTICE MURPHY delivered the opinion of the Court.

*** Petitioner came to this country from Russia in 1907 or 1908 when he was approximately three. In 1922, at the age of sixteen, he became a charter member of the Young Workers (now Communist) League in Los Angeles and remained a member until 1929 or 1930. *** [E]arly in 1925 he became a member of the Workers Party, the predecessor of the Communist Party of the United States. That membership has continued to the present. His petition for naturalization was filed on January 18, 1927, and his certificate of citizenship was issued on June 10, 1927 *** Since 1934 he has been a member of the Party's National Committee. *** When petitioner was naturalized in 1927, the applicable statutes did not proscribe Communist beliefs or affiliation as such. They did *** forbid the naturalization of disbelievers in organized government or members of organizations teaching such disbelief. Polygamists and advocates of political assassination were also barred. *** Applicants for citizenship were required to take an oath to support the Constitution, to bear true faith and allegiance to the same and the laws of the United States, and to renounce all allegiance to any foreign prince, potentate, state or sovereignty. And, it was to 'be made to appear to the satisfaction of the court' of naturalization that immediately preceding the application, the applicant 'has resided continuously within the United States five years at least, *** and that during that time he has behaved as a man of good moral character, attached to the principles of the Constitution of the United States, and well disposed to the good order and happiness of the same.' Whether petitioner satisfied this last requirement is the crucial issue in this case.

*** The claim that petitioner was not in fact attached to the Constitution and well disposed to the good order and happiness of the United States at the time of his naturalization and for the previous five year period is twofold: First, that he believed in such sweeping changes in the Constitution that he simply could not be attached to it; Second, that he believed in and advocated the overthrow by force and violence of the Government, Constitution and laws of the United States.

In support of its position that petitioner was not in fact attached to the principles of the Constitution because of his membership in the League and the Party, the Government has directed our attention first to petitioner's testimony that he subscribed to the principles of those organizations, and then to certain alleged Party principles and statements by Party Leaders which are said to be fundamentally at variance with the principles of the Constitution. *** Said to be among those Communist principles in 1927 are: the abolition of private property without compensation; the erection of a new proletarian state upon the ruins of the old bourgeois state; the creation of a dictatorship of the proletariat; [and the] denial of political rights to others than members of the Party or of the proletariat. *** Those principles and views are not generally accepted—in fact they are distasteful to most of us— and they call for considerable change in our present form of government and society. ***

The constitutional fathers, fresh from a revolution, did not forge a political strait-jacket for the generations to come. Instead they wrote Article V and the First Amendment, guaranteeing freedom of thought, soon followed. Article V contains procedural provisions for constitutional change by amendment without any present limitation whatsoever except that no State may be deprived of equal representation in the Senate without its consent. This provision and the many important and far-reaching changes made in the Constitution since 1787 refute the idea that attachment to any particular provision or provisions is essential, or that one who advocates radical changes is necessarily not attached to the Constitution. As JUSTICE HOLMES said, 'Surely it cannot show lack of attachment to the principles of the Constitution that (one) thinks that it can be improved.' Criticism of, and the sincerity of desires to improve the Constitution should not be judged by conformity to prevailing thought because, 'if there is any principle of the Constitution that more imperatively calls for attachment than any other it is the principle of free thought—not free thought for those who agree with us but freedom for the thought that we hate.' *** The Government agrees that an alien 'may think that the laws and the Constitution should be amended in some or many respects' and still be attached to the principles of the Constitution within the meaning of the statute. Without discussing the nature and extent of those permissible changes, the Government insists that an alien must believe in and sincerely adhere to the 'general political philosophy' of the Constitution. Petitioner is said to be opposed to that 'political philosophy'. ***

With regard to the constitutional changes he desired petitioner testified that he believed in the nationalization of the means of production and exchange with compensation, and the preservation and utilization of our 'democratic structure *** as far as possible for the advantage of the working classes.' *** None of this is necessarily incompatible with the 'general political philosophy' of the Constitution as outlined above by the Government. It is true that the Fifth Amendment protects private property, even against taking for public use without compensation. But throughout our history many sincere people whose attachment to the general constitutional scheme cannot be doubted have, for various and even divergent reasons, urged differing degrees of governmental ownership *** either with or without compensation. And something once regarded as a species of private property was abolished without compensating the owners when the institution of slavery was forbidden. Can it be said that the author of the Emancipation Proclamation and the supporters of the Thirteenth Amendment were not attached to the Constitution? ***

The concept of the dictatorship of the proletariat *** may be taken to describe a state in which the workers or the masses, rather than the bourgeoisie or capitalists are the dominant class. *** There are only meager indications of the form the 'dictatorship' would take in this country. It does not appear that it would necessarily mean the end of representative government or the federal system. *** The 1928 platform of the Communist Party of the United States, *** advocated the abolition of the Senate, [and] of the Supreme Court, and of the veto power of the President.*** These would indeed be significant changes in our present government structure—changes which it is safe to say are not desired by the majority of the people in this country—but whatever our personal views, as judges we cannot say that a person who advocates their adoption through peaceful and constitutional means is not in fact attached to the Constitution— *** and it is conceivable that 'ordered liberty' could be maintained without [those institutions]. The Senate has not gone free of criticism and *** unicameral legislature is not unknown in the country. It is true that this Court has played a large part in the unfolding of the constitutional plan (sometimes too much so in the opinion of some observers), but we would be arrogant indeed if we presumed that a government of laws, with protection for minority groups, would be impossible without it. ***

If any provisions of the Constitution can be singled out as requiring unqualified attachment, they are the guaranties of the Bill of Rights and especially that of freedom of thought contained in the First Amendment. We do not reach, however the question whether petitioner was attached to the principles of the Constitution if he believed in denying political and civil rights to persons not members of the Party or of the so-called proletariat, for on the basis of the record before us it has not been clearly shown that such denial was a principle of the organizations to which petitioner belonged. *** The party's 1928 platform demanded the unrestricted right to organize, to strike and to picket and the unrestricted right of free speech, free press and free assemblage for the working class. ***

*** [T]he Government asserts that the organizations with which petitioner was actively affiliated advised, advocated and taught the overthrow of the Government, Constitution and laws of the United States by force and violence. *** Apart from his membership in the League and the Party, the record is barren of any conduct or statement on petitioner's part which indicates in the slightest that he believed in and advocated the employment of force and violence, instead of peaceful persuasion, as a means of attaining political ends. To find that he so believed and advocated it is necessary, therefore, to find that such was a principle of the organizations to which he belonged and then impute that principle to him on the basis of his activity in those organizations and his statement that he subscribed to their principles. The Government frankly concedes that 'it is normally true *** that it is unsound to impute to an organization the views expressed in the writings of all its members, or to impute such writings to each member ***.' But the Government contends, however, that it is proper to impute to petitioner certain excerpts from the documents *** because those documents were official publications carefully supervised by the Party, *** and because petitioner was not a mere 'rank and file or accidental member of the Party', but 'an intelligent and educated individual' who 'became a leader of these organizations as an intellectual revolutionary.' ***

With commendable candor the Government admits the presence of sharply conflicting views on the issue of force and violence as a Party principle. *** [W]e would deny our experience as men if we did not recognize that official party programs are unfortunately often opportunistic devices as much honored in the breach as in the observance. On the basis of the present record we cannot say that the Communist Party is so different in this respect that its principles stand forth with perfect clarity, and especially is this so with relation to the crucial issue of advocacy of force and violence, upon which the Government admits the evidence is sharply conflicting. *** [A] court in a denaturalization proceeding *** is not justified in canceling a certificate of citizenship by imputing the reprehensible interpretation to a member of the organization in the absence of overt acts indicating that such was his interpretation. So uncertain a chain of proof does not add up to the requisite 'clear, unequivocal, and convincing' evidence for setting aside a naturalization decree. Were the law otherwise, valuable rights would rest upon a slender reed, and the security of the status of our naturalized citizens might depend in considerable degree upon the political temper of majority thought and the stresses of the times. Those are consequences foreign to the best traditions of this nation, and the characteristics of our institutions. ***

Mr. JUSTICE RUTLEDGE, concurring.

*** Immediately we are concerned with only one man, William Schneiderman. Actually, though indirectly, the decision affects millions. If, seventeen years after a federal court adjudged him entitled to be a citizen, that judgment can be nullified and he can be stripped of this most precious right, by nothing more than reexamination upon the merits of the very facts the judgment established, no naturalized person's citizenship is or can be secure. *** If this is the law and the right the naturalized citizen acquires, his admission creates nothing more than citizenship in attenuated, if not suspended, animation. He acquires but prima facie status, if that. Until the Government moves to cancel his certificate and he knows the outcome, he cannot know whether he is in or out. And when that is done, nothing forbids repeating the harrowing process again and again, unless the weariness of the courts should lead them finally to speak res judicata.

No citizen with such a threat hanging over his head could be free. *** Such a citizen would not be admitted to liberty. His best course would be silence or hypocrisy. This is not citizenship. *** It may be doubted that the framers of the Constitution intended to create two classes of citizens, one free and independent, one haltered with a lifetime string tied to its status. *** If every fact in issue going to the right to be a citizen, can be reexamined, upon the same or different proof, years or decades later; and if this can be done de novo, as if no judgment had been entered, whether with respect to the burden of proof required to reach a different decision or otherwise, what does the judgment determine? What does it settle with finality? If review is had and the admission is affirmed, what fact is adjudicated, if next day any or all involved can be redecided to the contrary? ***

Mr. CHIEF JUSTICE STONE, dissenting.

*** [A]t the time of petitioner's naturalization, the statutes of the United States excluded from admission into this country 'aliens who believe in, advise, advocate, or teach, or who are members of or affiliated with any organization, association, society, or group, that believes in, advises, advocates, or teaches: (1) the overthrow by force or violence of the Government of the United States *** '. The statutes also barred admission to the United States of 'aliens who *** knowingly cause to be circulated, distributed, printed, published, or displayed *** any written or printed matter *** advising, advocating, or teaching: (1) the overthrow by force or violence of the Government of the United States *** '. *** The evidence makes it clear beyond all reasonable doubt that petitioner, up to the time of his naturalization, was an alien who knowingly circulated or distributed, or caused to be circulated or distributed, printed matter advocating the overthrow of the Government by force or violence. *** [T]he trial court was justified in finding that petitioner, in 1927, was not and had not been attached to the principles of the Constitution. *** I shall assume that there are such principles and that among them are at least the principle of constitutional protection of civil rights and of life, liberty and property, the principle of representative government, and the principle that constitutional laws are not to be broken down by planned disobedience. I assume also that all the principles of the Constitution are hostile to dictatorship and minority rule; and that it is a principle of our Constitution that change in the organization of our government is to be effected by the orderly procedures ordained by the Constitution and not by force or fraud. ***

Perusal of the record can leave no doubt of petitioner's unqualified loyalty to the Communist Party. *** There is abundant documentary evidence of the character already described to support the court's finding that the Communist Party organizations, of which petitioner was a member, diligently circulated printed matter which advocated the overthrow of the Government of the United States by force and violence, and that petitioner aided in that circulation and advocacy. *** It would be little short of preposterous to assert that vigorous aid knowingly given by a pledged Party member in disseminating the Party teachings, *** is compatible with attachment to the principles of the Constitution. *** It would be difficult also to find as a fact that petitioner behaved as a man attached to the principles of the Constitution. The trial judge found that he did not. *** Yet the Court's opinion seems to tell us that the trier of fact must not examine petitioner's gospel to find out what kind of man he was, or even what his gospel was; that the trier of fact could not 'impute' to petitioner any genuine attachment to the doctrines of these organizations whose teachings he so assiduously spread. It might as well be said that it is impossible to infer that a man is attached to the principles of a religious movement from the fact that he conducts its prayer meetings, or, to take a more sinister example, that it could not be inferred that a man is a Nazi and consequently not attached to constitutional principles who, for more than five years, had diligently circulated the doctrines of Mein Kampf. *** A man can be known by the ideas he spreads as well as by the company he keeps. And when one does not challenge the proof that he has given his life to spreading a particular class of well-defined ideas, it is convincing evidence that his attachment is to them rather than their opposites. ***

Notes

1. **Constitutional Attachment**. Is your attachment to the Constitution (assuming you are attached) based on substantive principles or on procedure? May Congress make membership in the Nazi Party, al Qaeda, or the Ku Klux Klan a bar to naturalization? A basis for citizenship revocation?

2. **Priorities**. Abraham Lincoln wrote that "[t]here is something back of [the Constitution and the Union] entwining itself more closely about the human heart. That something is the principle of 'liberty to all'—the principle that clears the path for all—gives hope to all—and, by consequence, enterprise and industry to all." Lincoln went on to refer to the Declaration of Independence as an "apple of gold" and to say: "the Union and the Constitution are the picture of silver subsequently framed around it. The picture was made, not to conceal or destroy the apple; but to adorn, and preserve it." Do you agree, or are there aspects of the Constitution that are inconsistent with the Declaration? Should the Declaration serve as a source of constitutional values?

3. **Supreme Court Decision-making**. *Schneiderman* was "one of the decade's most ideologically divisive cases." JUSTICE FRANKFURTER sent a note to JUSTICE MURPHY suggesting this headnote to his draft opinion:

> The American Constitution ain't got no principles. The Communist Party don't stand for nothin'. The Soopreme Court don't mean nuthin'. Nuthin' means nuthin', and ter Hell with the U.S.A. so long as a guy is attached to the principles of the U.S.S.R.

At a later conference on the case, Frankfurter explained that his strong feelings came from his own experience as a naturalized citizen, saying "[i]t is well known that a convert is more zealous than one born to the faith." Where then is Frankfurter's dissent from the Court's opinion?

4. **War and Constitutional Law**. Several cases in this book are widely cited as evidence that "during war, the law is silent." Is *Schneiderman*, decided during World War II, consistent with this maxim? Is there any part of the document that says that free speech or other rights should be restricted in war? On the question when is there war and what do the courts have to say about this issue, see Chapter III D.

5. **Citizenship and the Constitution**. Under the Constitution, how does a citizen of the United States differ from a resident alien? Does citizenship by naturalization differ materially, after *Schneiderman*, from birthright citizenship?

D. OVERVIEW OF THIS BOOK

The United States Constitution has significance far beyond its interpretation by the United States Supreme Court: governmental officials are confronted almost daily by the grants and limits upon their power embodied in the Constitution; citizens are regularly affected in their dealings with government officials by the Constitution's grants of rights; political discourse is often shaped by constitutional interpretations; other nations have used the Constitution as a model.

This set of materials, however, primarily concerns the "Constitutional Law" articulated by the Supreme Court. Is this focus appropriate? I think so, for two reasons. First, these materials are designed for use primarily by law students, who will be building constitutional arguments for clients or advising governmental officials primarily from judicial opinions. Second, the Supreme Court's stock in trade—written opinions providing reasoned justifications for decisions reached—provides appropriate material from which to develop a sophisticated understanding of constitutional law.

In organizing these materials, I have chosen a traditional structure. Chapter II examines the sources of and limits upon the Supreme Court's power to interpret the United States Constitution. Chapter III considers the Constitution's distribution of national powers between Congress and the President. Chapter IV focuses on the constitutional framework of Congress' Article I powers and the limits of these powers. Chapter V investigates the limits federalism imposes on the states. Chapter VI examines the Supreme Court's invalidation of state discrimination against and burdens on interstate commerce.   Chapter VII sets out the genesis of the Reconstruction Amendments, the state action requirement built into the Fourteenth Amendment, and the Court's destruction of the privileges or immunities clause of the Fourteenth Amendment. Chapter VIII looks at both procedural and substantive applications of the due process clauses of the Fifth and Fourteenth Amendments. Chapter IX explores the theory and practice of "equal protection of the laws" under the Fourteenth Amendment. Finally, Chapter X explores Congress's power to "enforce" the Fourteenth Amendment. Appendix C contains review problems keyed to the book's chapters.

How does this book differ from other basic constitutional law casebooks? Most importantly, its theory is that less is more.   Neither voluminous collateral case citations nor extensive references to scholarly works facilitate the learning of constitutional law. Rather, they get in the way. I have tried to keep two goals firmly in mind: teaching students how to read constitutional law cases and providing practice in applying these cases to new circumstances. Another difference, as the subtitle indicates, is that this book focuses on the structure of the Constitution and its reconstruction, by amendment and by judicial interpretation. My book does not cover the First Amendment, just as earlier constitutional law casebooks excised the constitutional law aspects of criminal procedure. The First Amendment and criminal procedure are for other courses, other books.

II

JUDICIAL POWER TO ENFORCE
THE CONSTITUTION

"It is emphatically the province and duty of the judicial department to say what the law is. Those who apply the rule to particular cases, must of necessity expound and interpret that rule. *** So if a law be in opposition to the constitution; if both the law and the constitution apply to a particular case, so that the court must either decide that case conformably to the law, disregarding the constitution; or conformably to the constitution, disregarding the law; the court must determine which of these conflicting rules governs the case. *** If then the courts are to regard the constitution; and the constitution is superior to any ordinary act of the legislature; the constitution, and not such ordinary act, must govern the case to which they both apply."

—CHIEF JUSTICE JOHN MARSHALL
Marbury v. Madison (1803)

The power of the federal judiciary and ultimately the Supreme Court to invalidate federal and state legislation is an awesome power. Parts A and B of this chapter consider the scope of the Supreme Court's power to interpret the Constitution. Part C looks at the tools Supreme Court justices use to interpret the Constitution. Part D examines various limits to the Court's exercise of the power of interpretation.

A. INVALIDATION OF FEDERAL LAWS

A brief word is in order to set the stage for the next case in this book, *Marbury v. Madison* (1803). Chief Justice Marshall's opinion was written in politically turbulent times. Marshall, as Acting Secretary of State for Federalist President John Adams, had signed the commissions of Marbury and other justices of the peace whose positions had been created by the Federalist Congress just before Republican Thomas Jefferson took office on March 4, 1801. This was the first changeover from one party to another since the adoption of the Constitution, and President Jefferson was not happy about appointment of "midnight judges" by his political opponents. In this context, it is hardly surprising that he refused to deliver the commissions and claimed that they were void. The Republican Congress elected with Jefferson subsequently repealed "midnight legislation" enacted by the Federalists, but left the justice of the peace appointments intact. Congress also abolished the 1801 and 1802 terms of the Supreme Court, so as to avoid having the Court (headed by Federalist Marshall) consider the constitutionality of its legislation. *Marbury*, one of the best-known decisions of the United States Supreme Court, took up the constitutionality of Jefferson's refusal to deliver Marbury's commission (and an act of the First Congress) at the next term of Court, in 1803.

As you read the following case, credited with establishing the power of judicial review, focus on the logic and ramifications of the decision. How are the issues in the opinion organized? Was the outcome as inevitable as CHIEF JUSTICE MARSHALL's opinion makes it seem?

MARBURY v. MADISON
5 U.S. (1 Cranch) 137 (1803)

At the December term, 1801, William Marbury *** moved the court for a rule to James Madison, secretary of state of the United States, to show cause why a mandamus should not issue commanding him to cause to be delivered to them respectively their several commissions as justices of the peace in the district of Columbia. This motion was supported by affidavits of the following facts; that notice of this motion had been given to Mr. Madison; that Mr. Adams, the late president of the United States, nominated the applicants to the senate for their advice and consent to be appointed justices of the peace of the district of Columbia; that the senate advised and consented to the appointments; that commissions in due form were signed by the said president appointing them justices, &c. and that the seal of the United States was in due form affixed to the said commissions by the secretary of state; that the applicants have requested Mr. Madison to deliver them their said commissions, who has not complied with that request; and that their said commissions are withheld from them; that the applicants have made application to Mr. Madison as secretary of state of the United States at his office, for information whether the commissions were signed and sealed as aforesaid; that explicit and satisfactory information has not been given in answer to that inquiry, either by the secretary of state or any officer in the department of state; that application has been made to the secretary of the Senate for a certificate of the nomination of the applicants, and of the advice and consent of the senate, who has declined giving such a certificate; whereupon a rule was laid to show cause on the 4th day of this term. This rule [was] duly served *** [and the questions argued by the counsel for the relators were,]

1.   Whether the supreme court can award the writ of mandamus in any case.

2.   Whether it will lie to a secretary of state in any case whatever.

3.   Whether in the present case the court may award a mandamus to James Madison, secretary of state. ***

MR. CHIEF JUSTICE MARSHALL delivered the opinion of the court.

At the last term ***, a rule was granted in this case, requiring the secretary of state to show cause why a mandamus should not issue, directing him to deliver to William Marbury his commission as a justice of the peace for the county of Washington, in the district of Columbia. *** The peculiar delicacy of this case, the novelty of some of its circumstances, and the real difficulty attending the points which occur in it, require a complete exposition of the principles, on which the opinion to be given by the court, is founded. ***

In the order in which the court has viewed this subject, the following questions have been considered and decided.

1st.   Has the applicant a right to the commission he demands?

2ndly. If he has a right, and that right has been violated, do the laws of his country afford him a remedy?

3rdly. If they do afford him a remedy, is it a mandamus issuing from this court?

The first object of inquiry is,

1st.   Has the applicant a right to the commission he demands?

His right originates in an act of congress passed in February 1801, concerning the district of Columbia. *** [T]he 11th section of this law, enacts "that there shall be appointed ***, such number of discreet persons to be justices of the peace as the president of the United States shall, from time to time, think expedient, to continue in office for five years. ["] *** [I]n compliance with this law, a commission for William Marbury as a justice of peace for the county of Washington, was signed by John Adams, then president of the United States; after which the seal of the United States was affixed to it; but the commission has never reached the person for whom it was made out.

In order to determine whether he is entitled to this commission, it becomes necessary to inquire whether he has been appointed to the office. For if he has been appointed, the law continues him in office for five years, and he is entitled to the possession of those evidences of office, which, being completed, became his property. ***

[The Court then considered whether Marbury had been appointed.]

The appointment being the sole act of the President, must be completely evidenced, when it is shown that he has done every thing to be performed by him. *** The last act to be done by the President, is the signature of the commission. He has then acted on the advice and consent of the senate to his own nomination. The time for deliberation has then passed. He has decided. His judgment, on the advice and consent of the senate concurring with his nomination, has been made, and the officer is appointed. This appointment is evidenced by an open, unequivocal act; and being the last act required from the person making it, necessarily excludes the idea of its being, so far as it respects the appointment, an inchoate and incomplete transaction. *** The commission being signed, the subsequent duty of the secretary of state is prescribed by law, and not to be guided by the will of the President. He is to affix the seal of the United States to the commission, and is to record it. ***

[His] is a ministerial act which the law enjoins on a particular officer for a particular purpose. *** It is therefore decidedly the opinion of the court, that when a commission has been signed by the President, the appointment is made; and that the commission is complete, when the seal of the United States has been affixed to it by the secretary of state.

Where an officer is removable at the will of the executive, the circumstance which completes his appointment is of no concern; because the act is at any time revocable; and the commission may be arrested, if still in the office. But when the officer is not removable at the will of the executive, the appointment is not revocable, and cannot be annulled. It has conferred legal rights which cannot be resumed. *** Mr. Marbury, then, since his commission was signed by the President, and sealed by the secretary of state, was appointed; and as the law creating the office, gave the officer a right to hold for five years, independent of the executive, the appointment was not revocable; but vested in the officer legal rights, which are protected by the laws of his country.

To withhold the commission, therefore, is an act deemed by the court not warranted by law, but violative of a vested legal right.

This brings us to the second inquiry; ***. If he has a right, and that right has been violated, do the laws of his country afford him a remedy?

The very essence of civil liberty certainly consists in the right of every individual to claim the protection of the laws, whenever he receives an injury. One of the first duties of government is to afford that protection. In Great Britain the king himself is sued in the respectful form of a petition, and he never fails to comply with the judgment of his court. ***

The government of the United States has been emphatically termed a government of laws, and not of men. It will certainly cease to deserve this high appellation, if the laws furnish no remedy for the violation of a vested legal right. If this obloquy is to be cast on the jurisprudence of our country, it must arise from the peculiar character of the case.

It behooves us then to inquire whether there be in its composition any ingredient which shall exempt it from legal investigation, or exclude the injured party from legal redress. ***

Is it in the nature of the transaction? Is the act of delivering or withholding a commission to be considered as a mere political act, belonging to the executive department alone, for the performance of which entire confidence is placed by our constitution in the supreme executive; and for any misconduct respecting which, the injured individual has no remedy. That there may be such cases is not to be questioned; but that every act of duty, to be performed in any of the great departments of government, constitutes such a case, is not to be admitted. ***

It follows then that the question, whether the legality of an act of the head of a department be examinable in a court of justice or not, must always depend on the nature of that act. If some acts be examinable, and others not, there must be some rule of law to guide the court in the exercise of its jurisdiction. In some instances there may be difficulty in applying the rule to particular cases; but there cannot, it is believed, be much difficulty in laying down the rule.

By the constitution of the United States, the President is invested with certain important political powers, in the exercise of which he is to use his own discretion, and is accountable only to his country in his political character, and to his own conscience. *** The subjects are political. They respect the nation, not individual rights, and being entrusted to the executive, the decision of the executive is conclusive. *** But when the legislature proceeds to impose on that officer other duties; when he is directed peremptorily to perform certain acts; when the rights of individuals are dependent on the performance of those acts; he is so far the officer of the law; is amenable to the laws for his conduct; and cannot at his discretion sport away the vested rights of others. *** [W]here a specific duty is assigned by law, and individual rights depend upon the performance of that duty, it seems equally clear that the individual who considers himself injured, has a right to resort to the laws of his country for a remedy.

If this be the rule, let us inquire how it applies to the case under the consideration of the court. ***

The question whether a right has vested or not, is, in its nature, judicial, and must be tried by the judicial authority. If, for example, Mr. Marbury had taken the oaths of a magistrate, and proceeded to act as one; in consequence of which a suit had been instituted against him, in which his defence had depended on his being a magistrate; the validity of his appointment must have been determined by judicial authority. So, if he conceives that, by virtue of his appointment, he has a legal right, either to the commission which has been made out for him or to a copy of that commission, it is equally a question examinable in a court, and the decision of the court upon it must depend on the opinion entertained of his appointment. That question has been discussed, and the opinion is, that the latest point of time which can be taken as that at which the appointment was complete, and evidenced, was when, after the signature of the president, the seal of the United States was affixed to the commission.

It is then the opinion of the court,

1st. That by signing the commission of Mr. Marbury, the president of the United States appointed him a justice of peace, *** and that the appointment conferred on him a legal right to the office for the space of five years. 2ndly. That, having this legal title to the office, he has a consequent right to the commission; a refusal to deliver which, is a plain violation of that right, for which the laws of his country afford him a remedy.

It remains to be inquired whether 3rdly. [he] is entitled to the remedy for which he applies. This depends on, 1st The nature of the writ applied for, and, 2ndly The power of this court.

1. The nature of the writ. ***

[T]o render the mandamus a proper remedy, the officer to whom it is to be directed, must be one to whom, on legal principles, such writ may be directed; and the person applying for it must be without any other specific and legal remedy. *** The province of the court is, solely, to decide on the rights of individuals, not to inquire how the executive, or executive officers, perform duties in which they have a discretion. Questions, in their nature political, or which are, by the constitution and laws, submitted to the executive, can never be made in this court.

But, if this be not such a question; *** what is there in the exalted station of the officer, which shall bar a citizen from asserting, in a court of justice, his legal rights, or shall forbid a court to listen to the claim; or to issue a mandamus, directing the performance of a duty, not depending on executive discretion, but on particular acts of congress and the general principles of law? ***

It is not by the office of the person to whom the writ is directed, but the nature of the thing to be done that the propriety or impropriety of issuing a mandamus, is to be determined. Where *** he is directed by law to do a certain act affecting the absolute rights of individuals, in the performance of which he is not placed under the particular direction of the President, and the performance of which; the President cannot lawfully forbid, and therefore is never presumed to have forbidden; as for example, to record a commission, or a patent for land, which has received all the legal solemnities; or to give a copy of such record; in such cases, it is not perceived on what ground the courts of the country are further excused from the duty of giving judgment, that right to be done to an injured individual, than if the same services were to be performed by a person not the head of a department. *** This, then, is a plain case of a mandamus, either to deliver the commission, or a copy of it from the record; and it only remains to be inquired,

Whether it can issue from this court.

The act to establish the judicial courts of the United States authorizes the supreme court "to issue writs of mandamus, in cases warranted by the principles and usages of law, to any courts appointed, or persons holding office, under the authority of the United States."*

---

* Section 13 of the Judiciary Act of 1789 provides:

That the Supreme Court shall have the exclusive jurisdiction of all controversies of a civil nature, where a state is a party, except between a state and its citizens; and except also between a state and citizens of other states, or aliens, in which latter case it shall have original but not exclusive jurisdiction. And shall have exclusively all such jurisdiction of suits or proceedings against ambassadors, or other public ministers, or their domestics, or domestic servants, as a court of law can have or exercise consistently with the law of nations; and original, but not exclusive jurisdiction of all suits brought by ambassadors, or other public ministers, or in which a consul, or vice consul, shall be a party. And the trial of issues of fact in the Supreme Court, in all actions at law against citizens of the United States, shall be by jury. The Supreme Court shall also have appellate jurisdiction from the circuit courts and courts of the several states, in the cases herein after specially provided for; and shall have power to issue writs of prohibition to the district courts, when proceeding as courts of admiralty and maritime jurisdiction, and writs of mandamus, in cases warranted by the principles and usages of law, to any courts appointed, or persons holding office, under the authority of the United States.

The secretary of state, being a person holding an office under the authority of the United States, is precisely within the letter of the description; and if this court is not authorized to issue a writ of mandamus to such an officer, it must be because the law is unconstitutional, and therefore absolutely incapable of conferring the authority, and assigning the duties which its words purport to confer and assign.

The constitution vests the whole judicial power of the United States in one supreme court, and such inferior courts as congress shall, from time to time, ordain and establish. This power is expressly extended to all cases arising under the laws of the United States; and consequently, in some form, may be exercised over the present case; because the right claimed is given by a law of the United States.

In the distribution of this power it is declared that "the supreme court shall have original jurisdiction in all cases affecting ambassadors, other public ministers and consuls, and those in which a state shall be a party. In all other cases, the supreme court shall have appellate jurisdiction."

It has been insisted, at the bar, that as the original grant of jurisdiction, to the supreme and inferior courts, is general, and the clause, assigning original jurisdiction to the supreme court, contains no negative or restrictive words; the power remains to the legislature, to assign original jurisdiction to that court in other cases than those specified in the article which has been recited; provided those cases belong to the judicial power of the United States.

If it had been intended to leave it in the discretion of the legislature to apportion the judicial power between the supreme and inferior courts according to the will of that body, it would certainly have been useless to have proceeded further than to have defined the judicial power, and the tribunals in which it should be vested. The subsequent part of the section is mere surplusage, is entirely without meaning, if such is to be the construction. If congress remains at liberty to give this court appellate jurisdiction, where the constitution has declared their jurisdiction shall be original; and original jurisdiction where the constitution has declared it shall be appellate; the distribution of jurisdiction, made in the constitution, is form without substance.

Affirmative words are often, in their operation, negative of other objects than those affirmed; and in this case, a negative or exclusive sense must be given to them or they have no operation at all.

Cannons of Construction

It cannot be presumed that any clause in the constitution is intended to be without effect; and therefore such construction is inadmissible, unless the words require it. ***

When an instrument organizing fundamentally a judicial system, divides it into one supreme, and so many inferior courts as the legislature may ordain and establish; then enumerates its powers, and proceeds so far to distribute them, as to define the jurisdiction of the supreme court by declaring the cases in which it shall take original jurisdiction, and that in others it shall take appellate jurisdiction; the plain import of the words seems to be, that in one class of cases its jurisdiction is original, and not appellate; in the other it is appellate, and not original. If any other construction would render the clause inoperative, that is an additional reason for rejecting such other construction, and for adhering to the obvious meaning.

To enable this court then to issue a mandamus, it must be shown to be an exercise of appellate jurisdiction, or to be necessary to enable them to exercise appellate jurisdiction.

It has been stated at the bar that the appellate jurisdiction may be exercised in a variety of forms, and that if it be the will of the legislature that a mandamus should be used for that purpose, that will must be obeyed. This is true, yet the jurisdiction must be appellate, not original.

It is the essential criterion of appellate jurisdiction, that it revises and corrects the proceedings in a cause already instituted, and does not create that case. Although, therefore, a mandamus may be directed to courts, yet to issue such a writ to an officer for the delivery of a paper, is in effect the same as to sustain an original action for that paper, and therefore seems not to belong to appellate, but to original jurisdiction. Neither is it necessary in such a case as this, to enable the court to exercise its appellate jurisdiction.

The authority, therefore, given to the supreme court, by the act establishing the judicial courts of the United States, to issue writs of mandamus to public officers, appears not to be warranted by the constitution; and it becomes necessary to inquire whether a jurisdiction, so conferred, can be exercised.

The question, whether an act, repugnant to the constitution, can become the law of the land, is a question deeply interesting to the United States; but, happily, not of an intricacy proportioned to its interest. It seems only necessary to recognize certain principles, supposed to have been long and well established, to decide it.

That the people have an original right to establish, for their future government, such principles as, in their opinion, shall most conduce to their own happiness, is the basis on which the whole American fabric has been erected. *** This original and supreme will organizes the government, and assigns, to different departments, their respective powers. It may either stop here; or establish certain limits not to be transcended by those departments.

The government of the United States is of the latter description. The powers of the legislature are defined, and limited; and that those limits may not be mistaken, or forgotten, the constitution is written. To what purpose are powers limited, and to what purpose is that limitation committed to writing, if these limits may, at any time, be passed by those intended to be restrained? The distinction, between a government with limited and unlimited powers, is abolished, if those limits do not confine the persons on whom they are imposed, and if acts prohibited and acts allowed, are of equal obligation. It is a proposition too plain to be contested, that the constitution controls any legislative act repugnant to it; or, that the legislature may alter the constitution by an ordinary act.

Between these alternatives there is no middle ground. The constitution is either a superior, paramount law, unchangeable by ordinary means, or it is on a level with ordinary legislative acts, and like other acts, is alterable when the legislature shall please to alter it.

If the former part of the alternative be true, then a legislative act contrary to the constitution is not law: if the latter part be true, then written constitutions are absurd attempts, on the part of the people, to limit a power, in its own nature illimitable.

Certainly all those who have framed written constitutions contemplate them as forming the fundamental and paramount law of the nation, and consequently the theory of every such government must be, that an act of the legislature, repugnant to the constitution, is void.

This theory is essentially attached to a written constitution, and is consequently to be considered, by this court, as one of the fundamental principles of our society. It is not therefore to be lost sight of in the further consideration of this subject.

If an act of the legislature, repugnant to the constitution, is void, does it, notwithstanding its invalidity, bind the courts and oblige them to give it effect? Or, in other words, though it be not law, does it constitute a rule as operative as if it was a law? This would be to overthrow in fact what was established in theory; and would seem, at first view, an absurdity too gross to be insisted on. It shall, however, receive a more attentive consideration.

It is emphatically the province and duty of the judicial department to say what the law is. Those who apply the rule to particular cases, must of necessity expound and interpret that rule. If two laws conflict with each other, the courts must decide on the operation of each.

So if a law be in opposition to the constitution; if both the law and the constitution apply to a particular case, so that the court must either decide that case conformably to the law, disregarding the constitution; or conformably to the constitution, disregarding the law; the court must determine which of these conflicting rules governs the case. This is of the very essence of judicial duty.

If then the courts are to regard the constitution; and the constitution is superior to any ordinary act of the legislature; the constitution, and not such ordinary act, must govern the case to which they both apply.

Those then who controvert the principle that the constitution is to be considered, in court, as a paramount law, are reduced to the necessity of maintaining that courts must close their eyes on the constitution, and see only the law.

This doctrine would subvert the very foundation of all written constitutions. It would declare that an act, which, according to the principles and theory of our government, is entirely void; is yet, in practice, completely obligatory. It would declare, that if the legislature shall do what is expressly forbidden, such act, notwithstanding the express prohibition, is in reality effectual. It would be giving to the legislature a practical and real omnipotence, with the same breath which professes to restrict their powers within narrow limits. It is prescribing limits, and declaring that those limits may be passed at pleasure.

That it thus reduces to nothing what we have deemed the greatest improvement on political institutions—a written constitution—would of itself be sufficient, in America, where written constitutions have been viewed with so much reverence, for rejecting the construction. But the peculiar expressions of the constitution of the United States furnish additional arguments in favour of its rejection.

The judicial power of the United States is extended to all cases arising under the constitution. Could it be the intention of those who gave this power, to say that, in using it, the constitution should not be looked into? That a case arising under the constitution should be decided without examining the instrument under which it arises?

This is too extravagant to be maintained.

In some cases then, the constitution must be looked into by the judges. And if they can open it at all, what part of it are they forbidden to read, or to obey?

There are many other parts of the constitution which serve to illustrate this subject.

It is declared that "no tax or duty shall be laid on articles exported from any state." Suppose a duty on the export of cotton, of tobacco, or of flour; and a suit instituted to recover it. Ought judgment to be rendered in such a case? ought the judges to close their eyes on the constitution, and only see the law.

The constitution declares that "no bill of attainder or *ex post facto* law shall be passed."

If, however, such a bill should be passed and a person should be prosecuted under it; must the court condemn to death those victims whom the constitution endeavours to preserve?

"No person," says the constitution, "shall be convicted of treason unless on the testimony of two witnesses to the same overt act, or on confession in open court."

Here the language of the constitution is addressed especially to the courts. It prescribes, directly for them, a rule of evidence not to be departed from. If the legislature should change that rule, and declare *one* witness, or a confession *out of* court, sufficient for conviction, must the constitutional principle yield to the legislative act?

From these, and many other selections which might be made, it is apparent, that the framers of the constitution contemplated that instrument, as a rule for the government *of courts*, as well as of the legislature.

Why otherwise does it direct the judges to take an oath to support it? This oath certainly applies, in an especial manner, to their conduct in their official character. How immoral to impose it on them, if they were to be used as the instruments, and the knowing instruments, for violating what they swear to support?

The oath of office, too, imposed by the legislature, is completely demonstrative of the legislative opinion on this subject. It is in these words, "I do solemnly swear that I will administer justice without respect to persons, and do equal right to the poor and to the rich; and that I will faithfully and impartially discharge all the duties incumbent on ***, according to the best of my abilities and understanding, agreeably to the constitution and laws of the United States."

Why does a judge swear to discharge his duties agreeably to the constitution of the United States, if that constitution forms no rule for his government? If it is closed upon him, and cannot be inspected by him?

If such be the real state of things, this is worse than solemn mockery. To prescribe, or to take this oath, becomes equally a crime.

It is also not entirely unworthy of observation, that in declaring what shall be the *supreme* law of the land, the *constitution* itself is first mentioned; and not the laws of the United States generally, but those only which shall be made in *pursuance* of the constitution, have that rank.

Thus, the particular phraseology of the constitution of the United States confirms and strengthens the principle, supposed to be essential to all written constitutions, that a law repugnant to the constitution is void; and that *courts*, as well as other departments, are bound by that instrument. ***

Notes

1. **Preliminary Matters.** Consider these separate components of the Court's opinion.

> • How can one distinguish political matters from cases involving individual rights?

> • Why is mandamus appropriate rather than money damages?

> • Do you agree with CHIEF JUSTICE MARSHALL's presentation of the issues concerning the merits of the case before he considers the whether the Supreme Court has jurisdiction? Why he order the issues as he did?

> •   When you read the language of §13 of the Judiciary Act and the language of Article III, are you convinced that the Supreme Court has no jurisdiction over this case?   Can you read §13 so that it would be constitutional?

> • Did Marbury's lawyer make a dumb error by filing his writ of mandamus in the Supreme Court rather than a state (or lower federal) court?

2. **Reasons for Judicial Review.** Are you convinced that judicial review of acts of Congress is logically compelled? Which of the following rationales for the power of the Supreme Court to declare acts of Congress unconstitutional do you

find convincing: oath of office, judicial role, Supremacy Clause, All Writs provision, written constitution?

3.   **Other Reasons for Judicial Review.** What other factors would convince you that judicial review is part of the constitutional framework?

> • The intent of the Framers? *See, e.g.*, Federalist No. 78 ("No legislative act, therefore, contrary to the Constitution, can be valid ***. The courts were designed to be an intermediate body between the people and the legislature, in order, among other things, to keep the latter within the limits assigned to their authority. A constitution is, in fact, and must be regarded by the judges, as a fundamental law. It therefore belongs to them to ascertain its meaning ***.").

> • Subsequent practice over the last 200 years?

> • Necessity? Consider the alternative of having no judicial review.

4.   **The "Countermajoritarian Difficulty."**   "We the People" select our President, our Senators, and our Representatives. We never vote on Supreme Court Justices or other federal judges. This is profoundly undemocratic. Why should unelected judges overturn the will of the people? Are your concerns lessened because the President nominates judges and the Senate confirms them? When may a judge be removed from office? Is undemocratic judicial power better if the judicial function is relatively mechanical?   Does other nonmajoritarian components of the Constitution (e.g. supermajoritarian requirements) alleviate the "countermajoritarian difficulty"?

5.   **Thoughts on Applying the Constitution.**

> • "The government of the United States has been emphatically termed a government of laws, and not of men." CHIEF JUSTICE MARSHALL in *Marbury*.

> • "[W]hoever hath an absolute authority to interpret any written or spoken laws, it is he who is truly the Law-giver ***, and not the person who first wrote or spake them." Gray, NATURE AND SOURCES OF THE LAW (2d ed. 1924).

> • "We are not supreme because we are infallible, we are supreme because we are final." JUSTICE ROBERT A. JACKSON.

6.   **Executive and Legislative Interpretation of the Constitution.** What role, if any, do the other branches of government have in interpreting the Constitution? Thomas Jefferson's view was that "nothing in the Constitution has given [the Court] a right to decide for the Executive" whether a law is unconstitutional and that "the Executive, believing the law to be unconstitutional, was bound to remit the execution of it ***." Andrew Jackson considered it "as much the duty of the House of Representatives, of the Senate, and of the President to decide upon the constitutionality of any bill or resolution which may be presented to them for passage or approval as it is of the supreme judges when it may be brought before them for judicial decision." Conversely, Franklin Roosevelt sent legislation to Congress which would not pass muster under regressive (in Roosevelt's view) decisions of the Supreme Court, saying "no one is in a position to give assurance that the proposed legislation will withstand constitutional tests *** [but I] hope your committee will not permit doubts as to constitutionality, however reasonable, to block the suggested legislation."

7.   **Conflict Concerning Constitutional Interpretation.** A more troubling issue is that of disagreements between the judiciary and the other branches over constitutional issues.   Must the other branches follow the Supreme Court's interpretations, or do the Court's decisions only bind the parties and litigants who follow? Abraham Lincoln, speaking about the Supreme Court's *Dred Scott* decision, said: "[We] propose resisting it and to have it reversed if we can, and a new judicial rule established upon this subject." Further, Lincoln opined that "if the policy of the Government upon vital questions affecting the whole people is to be irrevocably fixed by decisions of the Supreme Court, *** the people will have ceased to be their own rulers." The most sweeping challenge by a President to the Supreme Court's authority was that attributed to Andrew Jackson concerning *Worcester v. Georgia*, 31 U.S. (6 Pet.) 515 (1832), in which the Marshall Court held Georgia had no legislative authority over Cherokee Nation lands: "John Marshall has made his decision. Now let him enforce it."

8.   **The Court's View of its Power.** Perhaps not surprisingly, the Court's view of its power is: "[*Marbury*] declared the basic principle that the federal judiciary is supreme in the exposition of the law of the Constitution." *Cooper v. Aaron*, 358 U.S. 1 (1958). The Court's statement was made in response to claims by Governor Faubus and other Arkansas officials that they were not "bound" by *Brown v. Board of Education*, 347 U.S. 483 (1954). More recently, in response to the argument that a federal statute overturned the requirement established in *Miranda v. Arizona*, 384 U.S. 436 (1966), that police inform suspects of their constitutional rights, CHIEF JUSTICE REHNQUIST wrote: "Congress retains the ultimate authority to modify or set aside any judicially created rules of evidence and procedure that are not required by the Constitution. But Congress may not legislatively supercede our decisions interpreting and applying the Constitution." *Dickerson v. United States*, 530 U.S. 428 (2000). Seven members of the Court agreed that *Miranda* "announced a constitutional rule" and that there was "no justification for overruling" it.   JUSTICE SCALIA, dissenting for himself and JUSTICE THOMAS, claimed that "[W]hat [*Dickerson*] will stand for, whether the JUSTICES can bring themselves to say it or not, is the power of the Supreme Court to write a prophylactic, extraconstitutional Constitution, binding on Congress and the States. *** This is not the system that was established by the Framers, or that would be established by any sane supporter of government by the people."

9.   **Constitutional Amendments.** Many Supreme Court interpretations of the Constitution have been unpopular. A few have been reversed through the amendment process. *See* Amendments 11, 13, 14, 16, 19, and 26. Should the difficulty of the amendment process set forth in Article V affect the Supreme Court's willingness to reinterpret the Constitution to bring it in line with modern conditions? What role, if any, should the Supreme Court have in determining the constitutionality of amendments overturning its decisions?

B. INVALIDATION OF STATE LAWS

The power of the federal courts to invalidate state laws and to nullify actions of state and local officials as unconstitutional is discussed in the following case. Are the sources of this authority the same as or different from those used in *Marbury*? Is the power exercised in this case more or less controversial than that exercised in *Marbury*?

MARTIN v. HUNTER'S LESSEE
14 U.S. (1 Wheat.) 304 (1816)

[The Court of Appeals of Virginia held that land escheated under Virginia law was not affected by a 1794 treaty confirming British land titles. The United States Supreme Court reversed but the Court of Appeals of Virginia refused to obey the Supreme Court. The basis for its refusal was that "the appellate power of the supreme court of the United States does not extend to this court under a sound construction of the constitution of the United States; that so much of the 25th section of the act of congress, to establish the judicial courts of the United States, as extends the appellate jurisdiction of the supreme court to this court, is not in pursuance of the constitution of the United States."

The underlying dispute was a classic case of disputed titles to property. Lord Fairfax, when he died in 1781, devised the Northern Neck of Virginia, claimed through charters and grants from Kings Charles II and James II (affirmed by the Virginia Assembly in 1736) to Denny Fairfax, an English subject and resident. In 1783, the United States and Great Britain signed a treaty of peace and in 1794 entered into a treaty of amity, commerce, and navigation. Between these two treaties, Virginia passed a statute in 1789 that provided in part: "[T]he patents or grants of land from the crown of England, under the former government, shall be, and are hereby declared null and void; and that all lands thereby respectively granted shall be held in absolute and unconditional property, to all intents and purposes whatsoever, in the same manner with the lands hereafter granted by the commonwealth, by virtue of this act." On April 30, 1789, the Governor of Virginia conveyed the land to David Hunter, who leased it to the plaintiff, who sued to eject Denny Martin (Fairfax).]

STORY, J., delivered the opinion of the court.

*** The constitution of the United States was ordained and established, not by the states in their sovereign capacities, but emphatically, as the preamble of the constitution declares, by "the people of the United States." There can be no doubt that it was competent to the people to invest the general government with all the powers which they might deem proper and necessary; to extend or restrain these powers according to their own good pleasure, and to give them a paramount and supreme authority. As little doubt can there be, that the people had a right to prohibit to the states the exercise of any powers which were, in their judgment, incompatible with the objects of the general compact; to make the powers of the state governments, in given cases, subordinate to those of the nation, or to reserve to themselves those sovereign authorities which they might not choose to delegate to either. The constitution was not, therefore, necessarily carved out of existing state sovereignties, nor a surrender of powers already existing in state institutions, for the powers of the states depend upon their own constitutions; and the people of every state had the right to modify and restrain them, according to their own views of the policy or principle. On the other hand, it is perfectly clear that the sovereign powers vested in the state governments, by their respective constitutions, remained unaltered and unimpaired, except so far as they were granted to the government of the United States. ***

The appellate power is not limited by the terms of the third article to any particular courts. The words are, "the judicial power (which includes appellate power) shall extend *to all cases*," &c., and "in all other cases before mentioned the supreme court shall have appellate jurisdiction." It is the *case*, then, and not *the court*, that gives the jurisdiction. ***

If the constitution meant to limit the appellate jurisdiction to cases pending in the courts of the United States, it would necessarily follow that the jurisdiction of these courts would, in all the cases enumerated in the constitution, be exclusive of state tribunals. How otherwise could the jurisdiction extend to *all* cases arising under the constitution, laws, and treaties of the United States, or to *all* cases of admiralty and maritime jurisdiction? If some of these cases might be entertained by state tribunals, and no appellate jurisdiction as to them should exist, then the appellate power would not extend to *all*, but to *some*, cases. If state tribunals might exercise concurrent jurisdiction over all or some of the other classes of cases in the constitution without control, then the appellate jurisdiction of the United States might, as to such cases, have no real existence, contrary to the manifest intent of the constitution. Under such circumstances, to give effect to the judicial power, it must be construed to be exclusive; and this not only when the *casus foederis* should arise directly, but when it should arise, incidentally, in cases pending in state courts. This construction would abridge the jurisdiction of such court far more than has been ever contemplated in any act of congress.

*** [I]t is plain that the framers of the constitution did contemplate that cases within the judicial cognizance of the United States not only might but would arise in the state courts, in the exercise of their ordinary jurisdiction. With this view the sixth article declares, that "this constitution, and the laws of the United States which shall be made in pursuance thereof, and all treaties made, or which shall be made, under the authority of the United States, shall be the supreme law of the land, and the judges in every state shall be bound thereby, any thing in the constitution or laws of any state to the contrary notwithstanding." It is obvious that this obligation is imperative upon the state judges in their official, and not merely in their private, capacities. *** They were not to decide merely according to the laws or constitution of the state, but according to the constitution, laws and treaties of the United States—"the supreme law of the land."

A moment's consideration will show us the necessity and propriety of this provision in cases where the jurisdiction of the state courts is unquestionable. Suppose a contract for the payment of money is made between citizens of the same state, and performance thereof is sought in the courts of that state; no person can doubt that the jurisdiction completely and exclusively attaches, in the first instance, to such courts. Suppose at the trial the defendant sets up in his defence a tender under a state law, making paper money a good tender, or a state law, impairing the obligation of such contract, which law, if binding, would defeat the suit. The constitution of the United States has declared that no state shall make any thing but gold or silver coin a tender in payment of debts, or pass a law impairing the obligation of contracts. If congress shall not have passed a law providing for the removal of such a suit to the courts of the United States, must not the state court proceed to hear and determine it? *** Suppose an indictment for a crime in a state court, and the defendant should allege in his defence that the crime was created by an *ex post facto* act of the state, must not the state court, in the exercise of a jurisdiction which has already rightfully attached, have a right to pronounce on the validity and sufficiency of the defence? *** [U]nless the state courts could sustain jurisdiction in such cases, this clause of the sixth article would be without meaning or effect, and public mischiefs, of a most enormous magnitude, would inevitably ensue.

It must, therefore, be conceded that the constitution not only contemplated, but meant to provide for cases within the scope of the judicial power of the United States, which might yet depend before state tribunals. It was foreseen that in the exercise of their ordinary jurisdiction, state courts would incidentally take cognizance of cases arising under the constitution, the laws, and treaties of the United States. Yet to all these cases the judicial power, by the very terms of the constitution, is to extend. It cannot extend by original jurisdiction if that was already rightfully and exclusively attached in the state courts, which (as has been already shown) may occur; it must, therefore, extend by appellate jurisdiction, or not at all. It would seem to follow that the appellate power of the United States must, in such cases, extend to state tribunals; and if in such cases, there is no reason why it should not equally attach upon all others within the purview of the constitution.

It has been argued that such an appellate jurisdiction over state courts is inconsistent with the genius of our governments, and the spirit of the constitution. That the latter was never designed to act upon state sovereignties, but only upon the people, and that if the power exists, it will materially impair the sovereignty of the states, and the independence of their courts. We cannot yield to the force of this reasoning; it assumes principles which we cannot admit, and draws conclusions to which we do not yield our assent.

It is a mistake that the constitution was not designed to operate upon states, in their corporate capacities. It is crowded with provisions which restrain or annul the sovereignty of the states in some of the highest branches of their prerogatives. The tenth section of the first article contains a long list of disabilities and prohibitions imposed upon the states. Surely, when such essential portions of state sovereignty are taken away, or prohibited to be exercised, it cannot be correctly asserted that the constitution does not act upon the states. The language of the constitution is also imperative upon the states as to the performance of many duties. It is imperative upon the state legislatures to make laws prescribing the time, places, and manner of holding elections for senators and representatives, and for electors of president and vice-president. And in these, as well as some other cases, congress have a right to revise, amend, or supercede the laws

which may be passed by state legislatures. When, therefore, the states are
stripped of some of the highest attributes of sovereignty, and the same are
given to the United States; when the legislatures of the states are, in some
respects, under the control of congress, and in every case are, under the
constitution, bound by the paramount authority of the United States; it is
certainly difficult to support the argument that the appellate power over the
decisions of state courts is contrary to the genius of our institutions. The
courts of the United States can, without question, revise the proceedings of
the executive and legislative authorities of the states, and if they are found to
be contrary to the constitution, may declare them to be of no legal validity.
Surely the exercise of the same right over judicial tribunals is not a higher or
more dangerous act of sovereign power.

Nor can such a right be deemed to impair the independence of state
judges. It is assuming the very ground in controversy to assert that they
possess an absolute independence of the United States. In respect to the
powers granted to the United States, they are not independent; they are
expressly bound to obedience by the letter of the constitution; and if they
should unintentionally transcend their authority, or misconstrue the
constitution, there is no more reason for giving their judgments an absolute
and irresistible force, than for giving it to the acts of the other co-ordinate
departments of state sovereignty. ***

It is further argued, that no great public mischief can result from a
construction which shall limit the appellate power of the United States to
cases in their own courts: first, because state judges are bound by an oath to
support the constitution of the United States, and must be presumed to be
men of learning and integrity; and, secondly, because congress must have an
unquestionable right to remove all cases within the scope of the judicial
power from the state courts to the courts of the United States, at any time
before final judgment, though not after final judgment. As to the first
reason—admitting that the judges of the state courts are, and always will be,
of as much learning, integrity, and wisdom, as those of the courts of the
United States, (which we very cheerfully admit,) it does not aid the
argument. It is manifest that the constitution has proceeded upon a theory of
its own, and given or withheld powers according to the judgment of the
American people, by whom it was adopted. We can only construe its powers,
and cannot inquire into the policy or principles which induced the grant of
them. The constitution has presumed (whether rightly or wrongly we do not
inquire) that state attachments, state prejudices, state jealousies, and state
interests, might some times obstruct, or control, or be supposed to obstruct or
control, the regular administration of justice. Hence, in controversies between
states; between citizens of different states; between citizens claiming grants
under different states; between a state and its citizens, or foreigners, and
between citizens and foreigners, it enables the parties, under the authority of
congress, to have the controversies heard, tried, and determined before the
national tribunals. No other reason than that which has been stated can be
assigned, why some, at least, of those cases should not have been left to the
cognizance of the state courts. In respect to the other enumerated cases—the
cases arising under the constitution, laws, and treaties of the United States,

cases affecting ambassadors and other public ministers, and cases of admiralty and maritime jurisdiction—reasons of a higher and more extensive nature, touching the safety, peace, and sovereignty of the nation, might well justify a grant of exclusive jurisdiction.

This is not all. A motive of another kind, perfectly compatible with the most sincere respect for state tribunals, might induce the grant of appellate power over their decisions. That motive is the importance, and even necessity of *uniformity* of decisions throughout the whole United States, upon all subjects within the purview of the constitution. Judges of equal learning and integrity, in different states, might differently interpret a statute, or a treaty of the United States, or even the constitution itself: If there were no revising authority to control these jarring and discordant judgments, and harmonize them into uniformity, the laws, the treaties, and the constitution of the United States would be different in different states, and might, perhaps, never have precisely the same construction, obligation, or efficacy, in any two states. The public mischiefs that would attend such a state of things would be truly deplorable; and it cannot be believed that they could have escaped the enlightened convention which formed the constitution. What, indeed, might then have been only prophecy, has now become fact; and the appellate jurisdiction must continue to be the only adequate remedy for such evils.

There is an additional consideration, which is entitled to great weight. The constitution of the United States was designed for the common and equal benefit of all the people of the United States. The judicial power was granted for the same benign and salutary purposes. It was not to be exercised exclusively for the benefit of parties who might be plaintiffs, and would elect the national forum, but also for the protection of defendants who might be entitled to try their rights, or assert their privileges, before the same forum. Yet, if the construction contended for be correct, it will follow, that as the plaintiff may always elect the state court, the defendant may be deprived of all the security which the constitution intended in aid of his rights. Such a state of things can, in no respect, be considered as giving equal rights. ***

On the whole, the court are of opinion, that the appellate power of the United States does extend to cases pending in the state courts; and that the 25th section of the judiciary act, which authorizes the exercise of this jurisdiction in the specified cases, by a writ of error, is supported by the letter and spirit of the constitution. We find no clause in that instrument which limits this power; and we dare not interpose a limitation where the people have not been disposed to create one. ***

Notes

1.   **Text of § 25 of the Judiciary Act of 1789:**

> That a final judgment or decree in any suit, in the highest court of law or equity of a State in which a decision in the suit could be had, where is drawn in question the validity of a treaty or statute of, or an authority exercised under the United States, and the decision is against their validity; or where is drawn in question the validity of a statute of, or an

authority exercised under any State on the ground of their being repugnant to the constitution, treaties or laws of the United States, and the decision is in favour of their validity, or where is drawn in question the construction of any clause of the constitution, or of a treaty, or statute of, or commission held under the United States, and the decision is against the title, right, privilege or exemption specially set up or claimed by either party, under such clause of the said constitution, treaty, statute or commission, may be re-examined and reversed or affirmed in the Supreme Court of the United States upon a writ of error. [But] no other error shall be assigned or regarded as a ground of reversal in any such case as aforesaid, than such as appears on the face of the record, and immediately respects the before mentioned questions of validity or construction of the said constitution, treaties, statutes, commissions, or authorities in dispute.

What policy choices do you see embedded in this legislation? Is the scope of this grant of authority sufficient for modern America? Compare the text of § 25 of the Judiciary Act of 1789 with its current form, codified in 28 U.S.C. § 1257:

Final judgments or decrees rendered by the highest court of a State in which a decision could be had, may be reviewed by the Supreme Court by writ of certiorari where the validity of a treaty or statute of the United States is drawn in question or where the validity of a statute of any State is drawn in question on the ground of its being repugnant to the Constitution, treaties, or laws of the United States, or where any title, right, privilege, or immunity is specially set up or claimed under the Constitution or the treaties or statutes of, or any commission held or authority exercised under, the United States.

2. *Martin* **and Federalism.** Does *Martin* threaten the independence of state government? Does it square with the Tenth Amendment? One way of reading *Martin* would be to say that the Court found substantive power to flow to the federal authority because of the Supremacy Clause and the Court's location at the apex of the federal and state judicial systems. Another way of viewing the case is that the Court left tremendous responsibility and discretion concerning enforcement of substantive law, at least in the first instance, in the hands of decentralized state courts. If Hunter's Lessee had prevailed over Martin, might not Congress have responded by centralizing enforcement of federal rights in federal courts?

3. **Policy.** "I do not think the United States would come to an end if we lost our power to declare an Act of Congress void. I do think the Union would be imperiled if we could not make that declaration as to the laws of the several states." OLIVER W. HOLMES, JR., COLLECTED LEGAL PAPERS 295–96 (1920).

4. **Bird's Eye View of the Court's Exercise of its Authority.** Before John Marshall (1789–1801), the Supreme Court did not invalidate any federal or state laws. Under Marshall (1801–1835), it overturned only one federal statute (in *Marbury*) and invalidated 18 state laws. The Taney Court (1836–1864) overturned only one act of Congress (in *Dred Scott*) and 21 state laws. Contrast the Warren Court (1953–1969), which overturned 25 acts of Congress and 150 state laws, and the Burger Court (1969–1986), which invalidated 34 federal and 192 state laws (counting *Chadha* as one federal law rather than the 212 actually affected). The Rehnquist and Roberts Courts' constitutional invalidations to date

are more comparable to the Warren and Burger courts than to the Marshall and Taney courts. Does this prove: (a) that the Court has become more aggressive in expanding the reach of the Constitution, or (b) that Congress and the states are sloppier in writing laws (and write more of them)?

5. **Discretionary Review by the Supreme Court.** The Supreme Court currently receives more than 7,000 petitions to review lower court cases each year. The Court grants plenary review (with oral arguments) to about 80 cases per Term. Rule 10 of the Rules of the Supreme Court stipulates that "review on a writ of certiorari is not a matter of right, but of judicial discretion." Four of the nine Justices must agree for the Court to hear a case (grant the writ of certiorari). The reasons for granting review are (1) to resolve conflicting rulings (among the circuit courts, among state courts of last resort, between a circuit court and a state court of last resort, or between a state court or lower federal court and the Supreme Court) and (2) to decide questions of substantial public importance. If you are a lawyer who believes a ruling against your client was wrong, what do you tell her about taking her case to the Supreme Court? Is review more or less likely to be granted if the ruling was the first appellate ruling on a particular statutory or constitutional issue? Assume you are a law clerk for a Justice who thinks an issue is important but your Justice likely would be in the minority on the merits of the case. Should you urge the Justice to vote against granting review?

6. **Questions and Problems.**

(a) Could Congress constitutionally abolish the federal courts other than the Supreme Court? What do you think of Justice Story's statement that "the whole judicial power of the United States should be, at all times, vested, either in an original or appellate form, in some courts created under its authority"?

(b) A District Court Judge, upon issuing a preliminary injunction against implementation of a state constitutional provision passed by a voter referendum, said that "the issue is not whether one judge can thwart the will of the people; rather, the issue is whether the challenged enactment complies with our Constitution and the Bill of Rights." Do you agree? Should federal judges treat state referenda any differently than state judicial opinions (the facts of *Martin*)?

(c) Suppose that a federal judge rules a state statute unconstitutional and enjoins the local officials who were parties to that litigation from enforcing the statute. Subsequently, in a state court action involving different parties, a state court judge rules that the statute is not unconstitutional and may be enforced by the local officials involved in the second suit. How should our judicial system deal with this unseemly divergence of interpretations?

7. **Story and Interpretive Method**. In addition to serving on the Supreme Court, where he wrote *Martin* and other decisions, Justice Joseph Story wrote the leading constitutional law treatise of his era, a work that was influential through the middle of the nineteenth century. Story has by some been viewed as the leading exponent of the "plain meaning" school of constitutional interpretation, a precursor to the textualist and originalist modes that are dominant today in many court opinions (as discussed in the following section of this book). Others see him as a purposivist (in the terminology infra, a non-originalist) whose background principle was to invigorate the national government. See if you can

find strands of both methodologies in Story's opinion. What interpretive method would describe John Marshall's opinion in *Marbury*?

C. SOURCES AND METHODS OF JUDICIAL DECISIONS

1. INTRODUCTION TO INTERPRETIVE ISSUES

Marbury, *Martin*, and innumerable subsequent cases confirm the judiciary's *power* to void federal statutes and state laws as unconstitutional. The *substance* of the judiciary's exercise of this power in connection with separation of federal powers, federalism's allocation of power between the federal and state governments, and the protection of individual rights is the focus of the remainder of this book.

First, however, it is worthwhile to assess the *interpretive techniques* used by Supreme Court justices and other interpreters of the Constitution. Examining how judges go about saying what the Constitution means is critical to understanding the difficulty of their task and to becoming better constitutional law advocates.

There are many nuanced schools of constitutional interpretation, though all arguably fit into two camps: *originalists* (or *textualists*) and *non-originalists* (or *purposivists*). Members of the former camp see themselves as "agents" of the constitutional founders, while members of the latter see themselves as "partners" of those who drafted or ratified constitutional provisions. The former believe the Constitution should be interpreted through the text and intent of the Framers; the latter interpret the Constitution in to address the needs of contemporary society.

Which approach is better? Justice Antonin Scalia argued that "Originalism [is] more compatible with the nature and purpose of a Constitution in a democratic system. A democratic society does not, by and large, need constitutional guarantees to insure that its laws will reflect 'current values.' Elections take care of that quite well. The purpose of constitutional guarantees *** is precisely to prevent the law from reflecting certain changes in original values that the society adopting the Constitution thinks fundamentally undesirable." Scalia, "Originalism: The Lesser Evil," 57 U. CIN. L. REV. 849 (1989); Antonin Scalia, A MATTER OF INTERPRETATION: FEDERAL COURTS AND THE LAW (Princeton University Press 1997).

On the other hand, former Justice William Brennan, a leading non-originalist, argued that "Current Justices read the Constitution in the only way that we can: as twentieth-century Americans. We look to the history and the time of the framing and to the intervening history of interpretation. ***[T]he genius of the Constitution rests not in any static meaning it might have had in a world that is dead and gone, but in the adaptability of its great principles to cope with current problems and current needs." Brennan, "The Constitution of the United States: Contemporary Ratification," 27 S. TEX. L. REV. 433 (1986). Has Justice Brennan forgotten that Article V provides a means for updating the Constitution by Amendment? Has Justice Scalia forgotten how difficult it is to amend the Constitution? *See also* Stephen Breyer, ACTIVE LIBERTY (Knopf, 2005).

Those who reject rigid borders around constitutional interpretation techniques are often called *pragmatists*. Pragmatists utilize components of various schools of constitutional interpretation to reach decisions. A pragmatist uses textual leanings, historical glosses, and philosophical arguments to argue for a particular reading of the Constitution. The pragmatist argues that flexibility, provides a better way to reach decisions than any one technique affords.

Lastly, scholars who think, like the cartoon below, that all interpretive modes are window-dressing for personal preferences have been called *realists*.

*"Do you ever have one of those days when every-
thing seems unconstitutional?"*

II–1. "Do you ever have one of those days when everything seems unconstitutional?" © The New Yorker Collection 1974 Joseph Mirachi from cartoonbank.com. All rights reserved.

The following paragraphs touch on a few highlights of constitutional interpretation issues.

Textualism. Textualism has historical roots in "the plain meaning rule" from Blackstone's canons of interpretation in the COMMENTARIES ON THE LAWS OF ENGLAND (1765). Blackstone's first canon was, "[w]ords are generally to be understood in their most usual and most known signification" and "[i]f words happen to be still dubious, we may establish their meaning from the context." A mid-twentieth-century Justice, Hugo Black, was a textualist in his reading of the First Amendment. Black was fond of saying "[n]o law means NO LAW" in broadly upholding freedom of speech and religion. Such literal reading of the words of the Constitution may be supplemented by structural textualism, in which the meaning of particular words may be clarified by examining their relationship to other provisions of the text. *See McCulloch v. Maryland*, 17 U.S. (4 Wheat.) 316 (1819). Obviously, since we have a written Constitution, few justices will ever admit to deciding cases contrary to the text of the Constitution. The problem, as we saw in the introductory exercises, is that many textual provisions are ambiguous or the facts of a modern case do not fit neatly into the textual framework of the Constitution.

Originalism. The primary benefit of ferreting out the original intention of the Framers is that, at least in theory, judicial decision-making becomes less subjective. The Justice's role is merely to implement the desire of the drafters and ratifiers of the Constitution. The majority and dissenters both draw extensively upon such materials in the next case, *District of Columbia v. Heller*. But historical materials are often incomplete or indeterminate. There were no tape recorders present at the Constitutional Convention, and the notes of those who were there sometimes differ as to what went on during the deliberations. James Madison, the most detailed note-taker, avoided making his notes of the deliberations available after adoption of the Constitution in part to avoid prejudicing those who would be implementing and interpreting the Constitution. THE FEDERALIST PAPERS, a collection of 85 essays on the proposed Constitution frequently used as a source of original intent, were written by supporters of the Constitution after the Convention. They were never meant to serve as an objective reading of the document, but rather to advocate its ratification. One might well imagine James Madison, John Jay, and Alexander Hamilton skirting the edges of difficult topics and sugar-coating the most controversial components of the Constitution in order to improve its chances of ratification!

Purposivism. Purposivists also trace their origins to Blackstone, whose third rule counseled looking to the "subject matter" or mischief that the law addresses, and whose last canon urged consideration of "the reason and spirit" of the law. A purposivist may start interpreting the Constitution not by focusing on the text, but by considering the values, concepts, and principles behind the text. This school of interpretation in the Supreme Court traces its origins to a statutory case, *Holy Trinity Church v. U.S.*, 143 U.S. 457 (1892), in which the Court conceded that the conduct charged as criminal was within the literal meaning of the statute, but where the Court decided Congress would not have intended this result. The Warren Court is viewed as being largely purposivist, though the leading purposivist case is probably the post-Warren *Roe v. Wade.* Even "pro-choice" scholars sympathetic to protecting abortion access for women often concede that the Constitution lacks language or original intention to support this outcome.

Natural Law. An early discussion of the proper role of natural law in constitutional interpretation occurs in *Calder v. Bull*, 3 U.S. (3 Dall.) 386 (1798). Excerpts from JUSTICE CHASE's opinion concern how natural law might trump constitutional provisions:

[A]lthough its authority should not be expressly restrained by the Constitution, or fundamental law, of the State *** [t]here are acts which the Federal, or State, Legislature cannot do, without exceeding their authority. There are certain vital principles in our free Republican governments, which will determine and over-rule an apparent and flagrant abuse of legislative power; as to authorize manifest injustice by positive law; or to take away that security for personal liberty, or private property, for the protection whereof of the government was established. An ACT of the Legislature (for I cannot call it a law) contrary to the great first principles of the social compact, cannot be considered a rightful exercise of legislative authority. *** A law that punished a citizen for an innocent action, or, in other words, for an act, which, when done, was in violation of no existing law; a law that destroys, or impairs, the lawful private contracts of citizens; a law that makes a man a Judge in his own cause; or a law that takes property from A and gives it to B *** The Legislature *** cannot change innocence into guilt; or punish innocence as a crime; or violate the right of an antecedent lawful private contract; or the right of private property.

JUSTICE IREDELL concurred in the decision, but objected to use of natural law in a political system organized under a written constitution. He wrote:

It is true, that some speculative jurists have held, that a legislative act against natural justice must, in itself, be void; but I cannot think that, under such a government, any Court of Justice would possess a power to declare it so. *** If *** the Legislature of the Union, or the Legislature of any member of the Union, shall pass a law, within the general scope of their constitutional power, the Court cannot pronounce it to be void, merely because it is, in their judgment, contrary to the principles of natural justice. The ideas of natural justice are regulated by no fixed standard: the ablest and the purest men have differed upon the subject; and all that the Court could properly say, in such an event, would be, that the Legislature (possessed of an equal right of opinion) had passed an act which, in the opinion of the judges, was inconsistent with the abstract principles of natural justice.

Natural law was mainly honored in the breach during the early years of the republic. Slavery and the conquest of the Native American population are particularly poignant examples. Take, for example, *The Antelope*, 23 U.S. (10 Wheat.) 66 (1825). In this case the narrow issue was whether federal law prohibiting the slave trade required forfeiture of slaves whom the owners said were bound for Brazil or Cuba, when the slaves were found in United States waters only because pirates had seized the ship and brought it into U.S. waters. CHIEF JUSTICE MARSHALL argued it was irrelevant that the slave trade was "contrary to the law of nature" and "[t]hat every man has a natural right to the fruits of his own labor." The slaves were returned to their Spanish and Portuguese owners. Marshall noted that the case was one in which "the sacred rights of liberty and of property come in conflict with each other." As for the American Indians, Marshall said, "Conquest gives a title which the Courts of the conqueror cannot deny *** [however] opposed to natural right, and to the usages of civilized nations ***." *Johnson and Graham's Lessee v. William M'Intosh*, 21 U.S. 543 (1823) (involving land initially conveyed to plaintiff by American Indians but subsequently granted to defendant by the U.S.).

In modern times, pure natural law has not been brought directly into constitutional decision-making. However, many Supreme Court justices have undoubtedly interpreted vague constitutional text in accordance with their own notions of justice. Words such as "due process" and "equal protection" clearly facilitate importation of philosophical notions of justice.

Precedent. Supreme Court Justices use interpretive techniques within a framework of precedent. The Supreme Court almost never overturns a previous decision concerning statutory construction. If the Court was "wrong" in determining what Congress intended, Congress can simply pass a statute amending the interpreted legislation to overturn the Supreme Court's construction. The Court has been more willing to overturn its decisions construing the Constitution, but precedent may save a decision once made that the Court might not adopt were it writing on a clean slate. In 1966, the Supreme Court held that the police must provide warnings to suspects of their constitutional rights to remain silent, have a lawyer, and so forth. This decision, *Miranda v. Arizona*, 384 U.S. 436 (1966), had many critics, including several members of the Court. Nevertheless, in *Dickerson v. United States*, 530 U.S. 428 (2000), the Court refused to overturn *Miranda*. CHIEF JUSTICE REHNQUIST wrote:

> Whether or not we would agree with *Miranda's* reasoning and its resulting rule, were we addressing the issue in the first instance, the principles of *stare decisis* weigh heavily against overruling it now. "While stare decisis is not an inexorable command," 'particularly when we are interpreting the Constitution, *Agostini v. Felton*, 521 U.S. 203 (1997), 'even in constitutional cases, the doctrine carries such persuasive force that we have always required a departure from precedent to be supported by some 'special justification.'

The following excerpts from *Planned Parenthood v. Casey*, 505 U.S. 833 (1992), discuss the Court's use (or lack of use) of precedent in interpreting the Constitution. Which side of the debate appeals to you most and why?

JUSTICE O'CONNOR, joined in this portion of the opinion by JUSTICES KENNEDY and SOUTER, wrote:

> Although *Roe* [*v. Wade*] has engendered opposition, it has in no sense proven 'unworkable,' representing as it does a simple limitation beyond which a state law is unenforceable. *** For two decades of economic and social developments, people have organized intimate relationships and made choices that define their views of themselves and their places in society, in reliance

on the availability of abortion in the event that contraception should fail. *** No evolution of legal principle has left *Roe*'s doctrinal footings weaker than they were in 1973. ***

The underlying substance of [the Court's] legitimacy is of course the warrant for the Court's decisions in the Constitution and the lesser sources of legal principle on which the Court draws. That substance is expressed in the Court's opinions, and our contemporary understanding is such that a decision without principled justification would be no judicial act at all. *** The Court must take care to speak and act in ways that allow people to accept its decisions on the terms the Court claims for them, as grounded truly in principle, not as compromises with social and political pressures having, as such, no bearing on the principled choices that the Court is obliged to make. *** Despite the variety of reasons that may inform and justify a decision to overrule, we cannot forget that such a decision is usually perceived (and perceived correctly) as, at the least, a statement that a prior decision was wrong. *** Where *** the Court decides a case in such a way as to resolve the sort of intensely divisive controversy reflected in *Roe* and those rare, comparable cases, its decision has a dimension that the resolution of the normal case does not carry. It is the dimension present whenever the Court's interpretation of the Constitution calls the contending sides of a national controversy to end their national division by accepting a common mandate rooted in the Constitution.

The Court is not asked to do this very often, having thus addressed the Nation only twice in our lifetime, in the decisions of *Brown* and *Roe*. But when the Court does act in this way, its decision requires an equally rare precedential force to counter the inevitable efforts to overturn it and to thwart its implementation. *** A decision to overrule *Roe*'s essential holding under the existing circumstances would address error, if error there was, at the cost of both profound and unnecessary damage to the Court's legitimacy, and to the Nation's commitment to the rule of law. It is therefore imperative to adhere to the essence of *Roe*'s original decision, and we do so today.

CHIEF JUSTICE REHNQUIST, joined by JUSTICES WHITE, SCALIA, and THOMAS in dissent, wrote on this point as follows:

Instead of claiming that *Roe* was correct as a matter of original constitutional interpretation, the opinion *** contains an elaborate discussion of stare decisis. This discussion of the principle of stare decisis appears to be almost entirely dicta, because the joint opinion does not apply that principle in dealing with *Roe*. *Roe* decided that a woman had a fundamental right to an abortion. The joint opinion rejects that view. *Roe* decided that abortion regulations were to be subjected to 'strict scrutiny' and could be justified only in the light of 'compelling state interests.'

The joint opinion rejects that view. *Roe* analyzed abortion regulation under a rigid trimester framework, a framework which has guided this Court's decision making for 19 years. The joint opinion rejects that framework. *** Erroneous decisions in such constitutional cases are uniquely durable *** It is therefore our duty to reconsider constitutional interpretations that 'depar[t] from a proper understanding' of the Constitution. ***

Apparently realizing that conventional stare decisis principles do not support its position, the joint opinion advances a belief that retaining a portion of *Roe* is necessary to protect the 'legitimacy' of this Court. *** This is strange, in that under the opinion's 'legitimacy' principle the Court would seemingly have been forced to adhere to its erroneous decision in *Plessy* because of its 'intensely divisive' character. *** The rule of *Brown* is not tied to popular opinion about the evils of segregation; it is a judgment that the Equal Protection Clause does not permit racial segregation, no matter whether the public might come to believe that it is beneficial. ***

Finally, JUSTICE SCALIA, joined by CHIEF JUSTICE REHNQUIST and JUSTICES WHITE and THOMAS, wrote as follows:

The Court's reliance upon stare decisis ***insists upon the necessity of adhering not to all of *Roe*, but only to what it calls the 'central holding.' It seems to me that stare decisis ought to be applied even to the doctrine of stare decisis, and I confess never to have heard of this new, keep-what-you-want-and-throw-away-the-rest version. *** The Imperial Judiciary lives. *** [T]he American people love democracy and the American people are not fools. As long as this Court thought (and the people thought) that we Justices were doing essentially lawyers' work up here—reading text and discerning our society's traditional understanding of that text—the public pretty much left us alone. Texts and traditions are facts to study, not convictions to demonstrate about. ***

Foreign Law. The use of foreign and international law by Supreme Court Justices to assist in interpreting the United States Constitution has caused controversy. A leading case airing this issue is *Roper v. Simmons*, 543 U.S. 551 (2005), in which the Court held that the death penalty for offenders under 18 violated the 8th Amendment's prohibition against "cruel and unusual punishment." JUSTICE KENNEDY'S opinion for the Court stated:

Our determination that the death penalty is disproportionate punishment for offenders under 18 finds confirmation in the stark reality that the United States is the only country in the world that continues to give official sanction to the juvenile death penalty. *** Article 37 of the United Nations Convention on the Rights of the Child, which every country in the world has ratified save for the United States and Somalia, contains an express prohibition on capital punishment for crimes committed by juveniles under 18. *** Parallel prohibitions are contained in other significant international covenants. *** [O]nly seven countries other than the United States have executed juvenile offenders since 1990: Iran, Pakistan, Saudi Arabia, Yemen, Nigeria, the Democratic Republic of Congo, and China. Since then each of these countries has either abolished capital punishment for juveniles or made public disavowal of the practice. In sum, it is fair to say that the United States now stands alone in a world that has turned its face against the juvenile death penalty. *** The opinion of the world community, while not controlling our outcome, does provide respected and significant confirmation for our own conclusions. *** It does not lessen our fidelity to the Constitution or our pride in its origins to acknowledge that the express affirmation of certain fundamental rights by other nations and peoples simply underscores the centrality of those same rights within our own heritage of freedom.

JUSTICE O'CONNOR'S dissent staked out a middle ground:

Because I do not believe that a genuine *national* consensus against the juvenile death penalty has yet developed, and because I do not believe the Court's moral proportionality argument justifies a categorical, age-based constitutional rule, I can assign no such *confirmatory* role to the international consensus described by the Court. *** Nevertheless, I disagree with JUSTICE SCALIA'S contention, that foreign and international law have no place in our Eighth Amendment jurisprudence. ***[T]his Nation's evolving understanding of human dignity certainly is neither wholly isolated from, nor inherently at odds with, the values prevailing in other countries. *** [A]n international consensus of this nature can serve to confirm the reasonableness of a consonant and genuine American consensus. The instant case presents no such domestic consensus, however, and the recent emergence of an otherwise global consensus does not alter that basic fact.

Finally, JUSTICE SCALIA, CHIEF JUSTICE REHNQUIST and JUSTICE THOMAS dissented as follows:

I do not believe that the meaning of our Eighth Amendment, any more than the meaning of other provisions of our Constitution, should be determined by the subjective views of five Members of this Court and like-minded foreigners, *** Though the views of our own citizens are essentially irrelevant to the Court's decision today, the views of other countries and the so-called international community take center stage. *** Unless the Court has added to its arsenal the power to join and ratify treaties on behalf of the United States, I cannot see how this evidence favors, rather than refutes, its position. *** It is interesting that *** the Court is quite willing to believe that every foreign nation-- of whatever tyrannical political makeup and with however subservient or incompetent a court system--in fact *adheres* to a rule of no death penalty for offenders under 18. *** More fundamentally, however, the basic premise of the Court's argument-that American law should conform to the laws of the rest of the world--ought to be rejected out of hand. *** In many significant respects the laws of most other countries differ from our law--including not only such explicit provisions of our Constitution as the right to jury trial and grand jury indictment, but even many interpretations of the Constitution prescribed by this Court itself. The Court-pronounced exclusionary rule, for example, is distinctively American. *** And let us not forget the Court's abortion jurisprudence, which makes us one of only six countries that allow abortion on demand until the point of viability. *** The Court's special reliance on the laws of the United Kingdom is perhaps the most indefensible part of its opinion. It is of course true that we share a common history with the United Kingdom, *** [but] we should [not] look *** to a country that has developed, in the centuries since the Revolutionary War--and with increasing speed since the United Kingdom's recent submission to the jurisprudence of European courts dominated by continental jurists--a legal, political, and social culture quite different from our own. *** The Court should either profess its willingness to reconsider all these matters in light of the views of foreigners, or else it should cease putting forth foreigners' views as part of the *reasoned basis* of its decisions. To invoke alien law when it agrees with one's own thinking, and ignore it otherwise, is not reasoned decisionmaking, but sophistry. *** Foreign sources are cited today, *not* to underscore our "fidelity" to the Constitution, our "pride in its origins," and "our own [American] heritage." To the contrary, they are cited *to set aside* the centuries-old American practice--a practice still engaged in by a large majority of the relevant States--of letting a jury of 12 citizens decide whether, in the particular case, youth should be the basis for withholding the death penalty. What these foreign sources "affirm," rather than repudiate, is the Justices' own notion of how the world ought to be, and their diktat that it shall be so henceforth in America.

Notes

1.   **The Politics of Judicial Appointments.**   Supreme Court appointments have become important issues in recent Presidential elections.   For example, Presidential Candidate Richard Nixon promised that, as President, he would appoint "strict constructionists" to the Court.   As a Senator of the opposite party and ideology of the President, how would you go about exploring a nominee's interpretive approaches and possible substantive decisions?

2.   **Precedent.**   Why should there be different rules of precedent for "blockbuster cases" and "ordinary constitutional cases"?   How should the Justices determine which cases fit in which category?   Arguably, the Court's overruling of

Swift v. Tyson, 41 U.S. 1 (1842), in *Erie Ry. v. Tompkins*, 304 U.S. 64 (1938), which shook the foundations of federal jurisdiction, was as important as *Brown* and *Roe*. Yet no special rule of precedent appears in *Erie*.

3. **Opinions and the Judicial Function.** "The judicial power of the United States is limited by the doctrine of precedent." *Anastasoff v. United States*, 223 F.3d 898 (CA 8, 2000), vacated 235 F.3d 1054 (2000). Alexander Hamilton in Federalist No. 78 concluded: "to avoid an arbitrary discretion in the courts, it is indispensable that they should be bound down by strict rules and precedents, which serve to define and point out their duty in every particular case that comes before them." Precedent is a touchstone of the distinction between the judicial and the legislative power ("the judge's duty to follow precedent derives from the nature of the judicial power itself"). Madison even thought (overly optimistically) that constitutional precedents would accrete until "[the Constitution's] meaning on all great points shall have been settled by precedent"! Is overruling precedents unconstitutional? Who would enforce such a rule?

4. **"Making" versus "Interpreting".** JUSTICE SCALIA says constitution writing involves use of foreign law, but that post-ratification foreign law is irrelevant to judicial interpretation of the United States Constitution. What theories of constitutional interpretation are consistent with use of post-ratification foreign law? What theories of interpretation are inconsistent with such use?

5. **Historical Use of Foreign Law.** In *U.S. v. Smith*, 18 U.S. 153 (1820), the defendant argued that Congress' definition of piracy by reference to "the law of nations" was too vague, but the Court cited Grotius and other international law scholars to find piracy was "robbery on the seas." JUSTICE LIVINGSTON'S dissent complained that "it is not perceived why a reference to the laws of China, or to any other foreign code, would not have answered the purpose as well [as reference to commentators]." In *Dred Scott v. Sandford*, 60 U.S. 393 (1857), the Court cited Roman Law in considering the legal consequences of slavery. Later in the 19th century, the Court referred to the practices of "civilized nations" in *Reynolds v. U.S.*, 98 U.S. 145 (1878), when it held that state law banning polygamy did not interfere with the free exercise of religion. In the early 20th century, *The Paquette Habana*, 175 U.S. 677 (1900), held that Spanish fishing vessels off the U.S. coast during the Spanish-American War were not subject to the rule of capture, because of "the practice of civilized nations" (including Japan). JUSTICE FULLER'S dissent said it was unnecessary to look beyond the English rule at the time of the revolution. *O'Malley v. Woodrough*, 307 U.S. 277 (1939) held that an income tax on judicial salaries was constitutional, referring to decisions of "English-speaking courts." In his dissent, Justice Butler said that such cases construing other nations' statutes had nothing to do with the U.S. Constitution's prohibition on not diminishing federal judges' compensation (Article III, § 1). Finally, in the mid-20th century, JUSTICE FRANKFURTER frequently referred to the practices of "English-speaking peoples." For example, his opinion for the Court in *Wolf v. Colorado*, 338 U.S. 25 (1949) contains a table comparing English-speaking countries' practices on use of illegally obtained evidence.

6. **Clause-Specificity**. *Roper v. Simmons* is consistent with a long line of Eighth Amendment cases that refer to foreign norms. *See, e.g., Trop v. Dulles*, 356 U.S. 86 (1958) (revoking citizenship cruel and unusual punishment when

only 2 of 84 countries surveyed allow it as a penalty for desertion); *Coker v. Georgia*, 433 U.S. 584 (1977) (capital punishment for rape cruel and unusual); *Enmund v. Florida*, 458 U.S. 782 (1982) (no capital punishment for felony murder); *Thompson v. Oklahoma*, 487 U.S. 815 (1988) (no capital punishment for juveniles under 16; JUSTICE SCALIA'S dissent said that 40% of the states and the federal government treated juveniles as adults and "We must never forget that it is a Constitution <u>for the United States of America</u> that we are expounding."); and *Atkins v. Virginia*, 536 U.S. 304 (2002) (a "national consensus" is supported by an international practice of not sentencing the mentally retarded to the death penalty; JUSTICE SCALIA and JUSTICE REHNQUIST object to reliance on the views of foreign countries). Conversely, the Court has made almost no use of foreign law to interpret the Equal Protection Clause, the First Amendment, separation of powers, or federalism. Consider, as you read materials involving various clauses in this book, whether divergent interpretive approaches are appropriate for different clauses.

7. **Congress and Judicial Interpretation of the Constitution**. HR 3799, introduced February 11, 2004, provided in part: "In interpreting and applying the Constitution of the United States, a court of the United States may not rely upon any constitution, law, administrative rule, Executive order, directive, policy, judicial decision, or any other action of any foreign state or international organization or agency, other than the constitutional law and English common law." Is this bill constitutional?

2. INTERPRETIVE CHOICES: THE SECOND AMENDMENT

In 2008, more than two centuries after ratification of the Bill of Rights, the Supreme Court for the first time looked carefully at whether the Second Amendment guarantees a citizen an individual right to carry firearms. As you read this opinion, consider what difference the answer makes since firearms were widely owned by individuals in the United States before the decision. What does the Court say about the ability of the District of Columbia to regulate firearms? Whether the decision applies to state laws and local ordinances is covered in Chapter VIII.

DISTRICT OF COLUMBIA v. HELLER
554 U. S 570 (2008)

JUSTICE SCALIA delivered the opinion of the Court.

*** The District of Columbia generally prohibits the possession of handguns. It is a crime to carry an unregistered firearm, and the registration of handguns is prohibited. *** District of Columbia law also requires residents to keep their lawfully owned firearms, such as registered long guns, "unloaded and dissembled or bound by a trigger lock or similar device" unless they are located in a place of business or are being used for lawful recreational activities. ***

The Second Amendment provides: "A well regulated Militia, being necessary to the security of a free State, the right of the people to keep and bear Arms, shall not be infringed." In interpreting this text, we are guided by the principle that "[t]he Constitution was written to be understood by the voters; its words and phrases were used in their normal and ordinary as distinguished from technical meaning." *** Petitioners and today's dissenting Justices believe that it protects only the right to possess and carry a firearm in connection with militia service. Respondent argues that it protects an individual right to possess a firearm unconnected with service in a militia, and to use that arm for traditionally lawful purposes, such as self-defense within the home.

The Second Amendment is naturally divided into two parts: its prefatory clause and its operative clause. The former does not limit the latter grammatically, but rather announces a purpose. The Amendment could be rephrased, "Because a well regulated Militia is necessary to the security of a free State, the right of the people to keep and bear Arms shall not be infringed." Although this structure of the Second Amendment is unique in our Constitution, other legal documents of the founding era, particularly individual-rights provisions of state constitutions, commonly included a prefatory statement of purpose. *** [W]hile we will begin our textual analysis with the operative clause, we will return to the prefatory clause to ensure that our reading of the operative clause is consistent with the announced purpose.

1. Operative Clause.

a. "Right of the People."   The first salient feature of the operative clause is that it codifies a "right of the people." The unamended Constitution and the Bill of Rights use the phrase "right of the people" two other times, in the First Amendment's Assembly-and-Petition Clause and in the Fourth Amendment's Search-and-Seizure Clause. The Ninth Amendment uses very similar terminology ("The enumeration *** of certain rights, shall not be construed to deny or disparage others retained by the people"). All three of these instances unambiguously refer to individual rights, not "collective" rights, or rights that may be exercised only through participation in some corporate body.

Three provisions of the Constitution refer to "the people" in a context other than "rights"-the famous preamble ("We the people"), §2 of Article I (*** "the people" will choose members of the House), and the Tenth Amendment (*** those powers not given the Federal Government remain with "the States" or "the people"). Those provisions arguably refer to "the people" acting collectively-but they deal with the exercise or reservation of powers, not rights.   Nowhere else in the Constitution does a "right" attributed to "the people" refer to anything other than an individual right.

What is more, in all six other provisions of the Constitution that mention "the people," the term unambiguously refers to all members of the political community, not an unspecified subset. *** This contrasts markedly with the phrase "the militia" in the prefatory clause. As we will describe below, the "militia" in colonial America consisted of a subset of "the people"-those who were male, able bodied, and within a certain age range. Reading the Second Amendment as protecting only the right to "keep and bear Arms" in an organized militia therefore fits poorly with the operative clause's description of the holder of that right as "the people."

We start therefore with a strong presumption that the Second Amendment right is exercised individually and belongs to all Americans.

b. "Keep and bear Arms." We move now from the holder of the right-"the people"-to the substance of the right: "to keep and bear Arms."

Before addressing the verbs "keep" and "bear," we interpret their object: "Arms." *** Some have made the argument, bordering on the frivolous, that only those arms in existence in the 18th century are protected by the Second Amendment. We do not interpret constitutional rights that way *** [T]he Second Amendment extends, prima facie, to all instruments that constitute bearable arms, even those that were not in existence at the time of the founding.

We turn to the phrases "keep arms" and "bear arms." *** The phrase "keep arms" was not prevalent in the written documents of the founding period that we have found, but there are a few examples, all of which favor viewing the right to "keep Arms" as an individual right unconnected with militia service. *** "Keep arms" was simply a common way of referring to possessing arms, for militiamen *and everyone else.* *** [A]s now, to "bear" meant to "carry." When used with "arms," however, the term has a meaning that refers to carrying for a particular purpose-confrontation. *** [I]t in no way connotes participation in a structured military organization. From our review of founding-era sources, we conclude that this natural meaning was also the meaning that "bear arms" had in the 18th century. ***

c. Meaning of the Operative Clause. Putting all of these textual elements together, we find that they guarantee the individual right to possess and carry weapons in case of confrontation. This meaning is strongly confirmed by the historical background of the Second Amendment. We look to this because it has always been widely understood that the Second Amendment, like the First and Fourth Amendments, codified a *pre-existing* right. The very text of the Second Amendment implicitly recognizes the pre-existence of the right and declares only that it "shall not be infringed." ***

Between the Restoration and the Glorious Revolution, the Stuart Kings Charles II and James II succeeded in using select militias loyal to them to suppress political dissidents, in part by disarming their opponents. *** These experiences caused Englishmen to be extremely wary of concentrated military forces run by the state and to be jealous of their arms. *** This right has long been understood to be the predecessor to our Second Amendment. *** And, of course, what the Stuarts had tried to do to their political enemies, George III had tried to do to the colonists. In the tumultuous decades of the 1760's and 1770's, the Crown began to disarm the inhabitants of the most rebellious areas. *** There seems to us no doubt, on the basis of both text and history, that the Second Amendment conferred an individual right to keep and bear arms. Of course the right was not unlimited, just as the First Amendment's right of free speech was not. Thus, we do not read the Second Amendment to protect the right of citizens to carry arms for *any sort* of confrontation, just as we do not read the First Amendment to protect the right of citizens to speak for *any purpose.* Before turning to limitations upon the individual right, however, we must determine whether the prefatory clause of the Second Amendment comports with our interpretation of the operative clause.

2. Prefatory Clause.

The prefatory clause reads: "A well regulated Militia, being necessary to the security of a free State ***."

a. "Well-Regulated Militia." In *United States* v. *Miller*, 307 U. S. 174, 179 (1939), we explained that "the Militia comprised all males physically capable of acting in concert for the common defense." *** Petitioners take a seemingly narrower view of the militia, stating that "[m]ilitias are the state- and congressionally-regulated military forces described in the Militia Clauses (art. I, §8, cls. 15-16)." Although we agree with petitioners' interpretive assumption that "militia" means the same thing in Article I and the Second Amendment, we believe that petitioners identify the wrong thing, namely, the organized militia. Unlike armies and navies, which Congress is given the power to create ("to raise ... Armies"; "to provide ... a Navy," Art. I, §8, cls. 12-13), the militia is assumed by Article I already to be *in existence*. Congress is given the power to "provide for calling forth the militia," §8, cl. 15; and the power not to create, but to "organiz[e]" it-and not to organize "a" militia, which is what one would expect if the militia were to be a federal creation, but to organize "the" militia, connoting a body already in existence, *ibid.*, cl. 16. This is fully consistent with the ordinary definition of the militia as all able-bodied men. *** Finally, the adjective "well-regulated" implies nothing more than the imposition of proper discipline and training.

b. "Security of a Free State." The phrase "security of a free state" meant "security of a free polity," not security of each of the several States *** It is true that the term "State" elsewhere in the Constitution refers to individual States, but the phrase "security of a free state" and close variations seem to have been terms of art in 18th-century political discourse, meaning a "'free country'" or free polity. Moreover, the other instances of "state" in the Constitution are typically accompanied by modifiers making clear that the reference is to the several States- "each state," "several states," "any state," "that state," "particular states," "one state," "no state." And the presence of the term "foreign state" in Article I and Article III shows that the word "state" did not have a single meaning in the Constitution.

There are many reasons why the militia was thought to be "necessary to the security of a free state." First, of course, it is useful in repelling invasions and suppressing insurrections. Second, it renders large standing armies unnecessary-an argument that Alexander Hamilton made in favor of federal control over the militia. Third, when the able-bodied men of a nation are trained in arms and organized, they are better able to resist tyranny.

3. Relationship between Prefatory Clause and Operative Clause

We reach the question, then: Does the preface fit with an operative clause that creates an individual right to keep and bear arms? It fits perfectly, once one knows the history that the founding generation knew and that we have described above. That history showed that the way tyrants had eliminated a militia consisting of all the able-bodied men was not by banning the militia but simply by taking away the people's arms *** The debate with respect to the right to keep and bear arms, as with other guarantees in the Bill of Rights, was not over whether it was desirable (all agreed that it was) but over whether it needed to be codified in the Constitution. During the 1788 ratification debates, the fear that the federal government would disarm the people in order to impose rule through a standing army or select militia was pervasive in Antifederalist rhetoric. *** [T]he threat that the new Federal Government would destroy the citizens' militia by taking away their arms was the reason that right-unlike some other English rights-was codified in a written Constitution. *** [S]elf-defense had little to do with the right's *codification;* it was the *central component* of the right itself.

***

Our interpretation is confirmed by analogous arms-bearing rights in state constitutions that preceded and immediately followed adoption of the Second Amendment. *** We now address how the Second Amendment was interpreted from immediately after its ratification through the end of the 19th century. *** Blacks were routinely disarmed by Southern States after the Civil War. Those who opposed these injustices frequently stated that they infringed blacks' constitutional right to keep and bear arms. Needless to say, the claim was not that blacks were being prohibited from carrying arms in an organized state militia. ***

We now ask whether any of our precedents forecloses the conclusions we have reached about the meaning of the Second Amendment. *** *Miller* *** upheld against a Second Amendment challenge two men's federal convictions for transporting an unregistered short-barreled shotgun in interstate commerce, in violation of the National Firearms Act. It is entirely clear that the Court's basis for saying that the Second Amendment did not apply was *not* that the defendants were "bear[ing] arms" not "for ... military purposes" but for "nonmilitary use." Rather, it was that the *type of weapon at issue* was not eligible for Second Amendment protection: "In the absence of any evidence tending to show that the possession or use of a [short-barreled shotgun] at this time has some reasonable relationship to the preservation or efficiency of a well regulated militia, we cannot say that the Second Amendment guarantees the right to keep and bear *such an instrument.*" "Certainly," the Court continued, "it is not within judicial notice that this weapon is any part of the ordinary military equipment or that its use could contribute to the common defense." Beyond that, the opinion provided no explanation of the content of the right.

This holding is not only consistent with, but positively suggests, that the Second Amendment confers an individual right to keep and bear arms (though only arms that "have some reasonable relationship to the preservation or efficiency of a well regulated militia"). *** *Miller* stands only for the proposition that the Second Amendment right, whatever its nature, extends only to certain types of weapons. ***

We may as well consider at this point *** *what* types of weapons *Miller* permits. *** We think that *Miller*'s "ordinary military equipment" language must be read in tandem with what comes after: "[O]rdinarily when called for [militia] service [able-bodied] men were expected to appear bearing arms supplied by themselves and of the kind in common use at the time." *** We therefore read *Miller* to say only that the Second Amendment does not protect those weapons not typically possessed by law-abiding citizens for lawful purposes, such as short-barreled shotguns. ***

Like most rights, the right secured by the Second Amendment is not unlimited. *** Although we do not undertake an exhaustive historical analysis today of the full scope of the Second Amendment, nothing in our opinion should be taken to cast doubt on longstanding prohibitions on the possession of firearms by felons and the mentally ill, or laws forbidding the carrying of firearms in sensitive places such as schools and government buildings, or laws imposing conditions and qualifications on the commercial sale of arms. ***

It may be objected that if weapons that are most useful in military service *** may be banned, then the Second Amendment right is completely detached from the prefatory clause. *** It may well be true today that a militia, to be as effective as militias in the 18th century, would require sophisticated arms that are highly unusual in society at large. Indeed, it may be true that no amount of small arms could be useful against modern-day bombers and tanks. But the fact that modern developments have limited the degree of fit between the prefatory clause and the protected right cannot change our interpretation of the right.

We turn finally to the law at issue here. As we have said, the law totally bans handgun possession in the home. *** The handgun ban amounts to a prohibition of an entire class of "arms" that is overwhelmingly chosen by American society for that lawful purpose. The prohibition extends, moreover, to the home, where the need for defense of self, family, and property is most acute. Under any of the standards of scrutiny that we have applied to enumerated constitutional rights, banning from the home "the most preferred firearm in the nation to 'keep' and use for protection of one's home and family," would fail constitutional muster. *** We must also address the District's requirement (as applied to respondent's handgun) that firearms in the home be rendered and kept inoperable at all times. This makes it impossible for citizens to use them for the core lawful purpose of self-defense and is hence unconstitutional. ***

[A] 1783 Massachusetts law forbade the residents of Boston to "take into" or "receive into" "any Dwelling House, Stable, Barn, Out-house, Warehouse, Store, Shop or other Building" loaded firearms, and permitted the seizure of any loaded firearms that "shall be found" there. *** [W]e would not stake our interpretation of the Second Amendment upon a single law, in effect in a single city, that contradicts the overwhelming weight of other evidence regarding the right to keep and bear arms for defense of the home. *** [Moreover these laws] are akin to modern penalties for minor public-safety infractions like speeding or jaywalking. *** The District law, by contrast, far from imposing a minor fine, threatens citizens with a year in prison (five years for a second violation) for even obtaining a gun in the first place.

[The Court rejected JUSTICE BREYER'S "interest balancing" approach:] A constitutional guarantee subject to future judges' assessments of its usefulness is no constitutional guarantee at all. *** The Second Amendment *** is the very *product* of an interest-balancing by the people ***. And whatever else it leaves to future evaluation, it surely elevates above all other interests the right of law-abiding, responsible citizens to use arms in defense of hearth and home. *** Assuming that Heller is not disqualified from the exercise of Second Amendment rights, the District must permit him to register his handgun and must issue him a license to carry it in the home. ***

We are aware of the problem of handgun violence in this country, and we take seriously the concerns raised by the many *amici* who believe that prohibition of handgun ownership is a solution. The Constitution leaves the District of Columbia a variety of tools for combating that problem, including some measures regulating handguns. But the enshrinement of constitutional rights necessarily takes certain policy choices off the table. *** [I]t is not the role of this Court to pronounce the Second Amendment extinct. ***

JUSTICE STEVENS, with whom JUSTICE SOUTER, JUSTICE GINSBURG, and JUSTICE BREYER join, dissenting.

The question presented by this case is not whether the Second Amendment protects a "collective right" or an "individual right." Surely it protects a right that can be enforced by individuals. But a conclusion that the Second Amendment protects an individual right does not tell us anything about the scope of that right.

Guns are used to hunt, for self-defense, to commit crimes, for sporting activities, and to perform military duties. The Second Amendment plainly does not protect the right to use a gun to rob a bank; it is equally clear that it *does* encompass the right to use weapons for certain military purposes. Whether it also protects the right to possess and use guns for nonmilitary purposes like hunting and personal self-defense is the question presented by this case. The text of the Amendment, its history, and our decision in *United States* v. *Miller*, 307 U. S. 174 (1939), provide a clear answer to that question.

The Second Amendment was adopted to protect the right of the people of each of the several States to maintain a well-regulated militia. *** [T]here is no indication that the Framers of the Amendment intended to enshrine the common-law right of self-defense in the Constitution. *** The view of the Amendment we took in *Miller*-that it protects the right to keep and bear arms for certain military purposes, but that it does not curtail the Legislature's power to regulate the nonmilitary use and ownership of weapons-is both the most natural reading of the Amendment's text and the interpretation most faithful to the history of its adoption. ***

The preamble to the Second Amendment makes three important points. It identifies the preservation of the militia as the Amendment's purpose; it explains that the militia is necessary to the security of a free State; and it recognizes that the militia must be "well regulated." In all three respects it is comparable to provisions in several State Declarations of Rights that were adopted roughly contemporaneously with the Declaration of Independence. Those state provisions highlight the importance members of the founding generation attached to the maintenance of state militias; they also underscore the profound fear shared by many in that era of the dangers posed by standing armies. ***

The Court today tries to denigrate the importance of this clause of the Amendment by beginning its analysis with the Amendment's operative provision and returning to the preamble merely "to ensure that our reading of the operative clause is consistent with the announced purpose." That is not how this Court ordinarily reads such texts, and it is not how the preamble would have been viewed at the time the Amendment was adopted. ***

"The right of the people"

The centerpiece of the Court's textual argument is its insistence that the words "the people" as used in the Second Amendment must have the same meaning, and protect the same class of individuals, as when they are used in the First and Fourth Amendments. *** But the Court *itself* reads the Second Amendment to protect a "subset" significantly narrower than the class of persons protected by the First and Fourth Amendments; *** the Court limits the protected class to "law-abiding, responsible citizens." But the class of persons protected by the First and Fourth Amendments is *not* so limited; for even felons (and presumably irresponsible citizens as well) may invoke the protections of those constitutional provisions. *** In the First Amendment, *** it is only the right peaceably to assemble, and to petition the Government for a redress of grievances, that is described as a right of "the people." These rights contemplate collective action. While the right peaceably to assemble protects the individual rights of those persons participating in the assembly, its concern is with action engaged in by members of a group, rather than any single individual. *** Similarly, the words "the people" in the Second Amendment refer back to the object announced in the Amendment's preamble. They remind us that it is the collective action of individuals having a duty to serve in the militia that the text directly protects and, perhaps more importantly, that the ultimate purpose of the Amendment was to protect the States' share of the divided sovereignty created by the Constitution. ***

"To keep and bear Arms"

Although the Court's discussion of these words treats them as two "phrases"-as if they read "to keep" and "to bear"-they describe a unitary right: to possess arms if needed for military purposes and to use them in conjunction with military activities. *** When each word in the text is given full effect, the Amendment is most naturally read to secure to the people a right to use and possess arms in conjunction with service in a well-regulated militia. *** And the Court's emphatic reliance on the claim "that the Second Amendment ... codified a *pre-existing* right," is of course beside the point because the right to keep and bear arms for service in a state militia was also a pre-existing right. *** The proper allocation of military power in the new Nation was an issue of central concern for the Framers. The compromises they ultimately reached, reflected in Article I's Militia Clauses and the

Second Amendment, represent quintessential examples of the Framers' "splitting the atom of sovereignty." *** The history of the adoption of the Amendment thus describes an overriding concern about the potential threat to state sovereignty that a federal standing army would pose, and a desire to protect the States' militias as the means by which to guard against that danger. *** As we explained in *Miller:* "With obvious purpose to assure the continuation and render possible the effectiveness of such forces the declaration and guarantee of the Second Amendment were made. It must be interpreted and applied with that end in view." ***

The Court's reliance on Article VII of the 1689 English Bill of Rights-which, like most of the evidence offered by the Court today, was considered in *Miller*-is misguided both because Article VII was enacted in response to different concerns from those that motivated the Framers of the Second Amendment, and because the guarantees of the two provisions were by no means coextensive. Moreover, the English text contained no preamble or other provision identifying a narrow, militia-related purpose. *** The Court suggests that by the post-Civil War period, the Second Amendment was understood to secure a right to firearm use and ownership for purely private purposes like personal self-defense. While it is true that some of the legislative history on which the Court relies supports that contention, such sources are entitled to limited, if any, weight. ***

The key to [*Miller*] did not, as the Court belatedly suggests, turn on the difference between muskets and sawed-off shotguns; it turned, rather, on the basic difference between the military and nonmilitary use and possession of guns. Indeed, if the Second Amendment were not limited in its coverage to military uses of weapons, why should the Court in *Miller* have suggested that some weapons but not others were eligible for Second Amendment protection? If use for self-defense were the relevant standard, why did the Court not inquire into the suitability of a particular weapon for self-defense purposes? ***

JUSTICE BREYER, with whom JUSTICE STEVENS, JUSTICE SOUTER, and JUSTICE GINSBURG join, dissenting.

*** [T]he District's regulation, which focuses upon the presence of handguns in high-crime urban areas, represents a permissible legislative response to a serious, indeed life-threatening, problem. *** [C]olonial history itself offers important examples of the kinds of gun regulation that citizens would then have thought compatible with the "right to keep and bear arms," whether embodied in Federal or State Constitutions, or the background common law. *** Boston, Philadelphia, and New York City, the three largest cities in America during that period, all restricted the firing of guns within city limits to at least some degree. *** Furthermore, several towns and cities (including Philadelphia, New York, and Boston) regulated, for fire-safety reasons, the storage of gunpowder, a necessary component of an operational firearm. Even assuming, as the majority does, that this law included an implicit self-defense exception, it would nevertheless have prevented a homeowner from keeping in his home a gun that he could immediately pick up and use against an intruder. ***

This historical evidence demonstrates that a self-defense assumption is the *beginning*, rather than the *end*, of any constitutional inquiry. That the District law impacts self-defense merely raises *questions* about the law's constitutionality. *** I turn now to the final portion of the "permissible regulation" question: Does the District's law *disproportionately* burden Amendment-protected interests? Several considerations, taken together, convince me that it does not.

First, the District law is tailored to the life-threatening problems it attempts to address. *** Second, the self-defense interest in maintaining loaded handguns in the home to shoot intruders is not the *primary* interest, but at most a subsidiary interest, that the Second Amendment seeks to serve. *** Third, irrespective of what the Framers *could have thought,* we know what they *did think.* Samuel Adams, who lived in Boston *** thought that the protection was *consistent* with local regulation that seriously impeded urban residents from using their arms against intruders? *** Fourth, a contrary view, as embodied in today's decision, will have unfortunate consequences. The decision *** will leave the Nation without clear standards for resolving those challenges. And litigation over the course of many years, or the mere specter of such litigation, threatens to leave cities without effective protection against gun violence and accidents during that time.

As important, the majority's decision threatens severely to limit the ability of more knowledgeable, democratically elected officials to deal with gun-related problems. *** The majority says that that Amendment protects those weapons "typically possessed by law-abiding citizens for lawful purposes." This definition conveniently excludes machineguns, but permits handguns, which the majority describes as "the most popular weapon chosen by Americans for self-defense in the home." But what sense does this approach make? *** I am similarly puzzled by the majority's list *** of provisions that in its view would survive Second Amendment scrutiny. These consist of (1) "prohibitions on carrying concealed weapons"; (2) "prohibitions on the possession of firearms by felons"; (3) "prohibitions on the possession of firearms by ... the mentally ill"; (4) "laws forbidding the carrying of firearms in sensitive places such as schools and government buildings"; and (5) government "conditions and qualifications" attached "to the commercial sale of arms." Why these? Is it that similar restrictions existed in the late 18th century? The majority fails to cite any colonial analogues. ***

At the same time the majority ignores a more important question: Given the purposes for which the Framers enacted the Second Amendment, how should it be applied to modern-day circumstances that they could not have anticipated? Assume, for argument's sake, that the Framers did intend the Amendment to offer a degree of self-defense protection. Does that mean that the Framers also intended to guarantee a right to possess a loaded gun near swimming pools, parks, and playgrounds? That they would not have cared about the children who might pick up a loaded gun on their parents' bedside table? That they (who certainly showed concern for the risk of fire) would have lacked concern for the risk of accidental deaths or suicides that readily accessible loaded handguns in urban areas might bring? Unless we believe that they intended future generations to ignore such matters, answering questions such as the questions in this case requires judgment-judicial judgment exercised within a framework for constitutional analysis that guides that judgment and which makes its exercise transparent. One cannot answer those questions by combining inconclusive historical research with judicial *ipse dixit*.

The argument about method, however, is by far the less important argument surrounding today's decision. Far more important are the unfortunate consequences that today's decision is likely to spawn. *** [T]he decision threatens to throw into doubt the constitutionality of gun laws throughout the United States. ***

Notes

1. **Interpretive Issues.**

(a) The dissenting view previously was called the "collective rights" view of the Second Amendment. Why does JUSTICE STEVENS disavow that label?

(b) Consider whether the majority or dissent gets the better of textual interpretation, drafting history, and judicial precedent arguments.

(c) What role, if any, does consequentialism (whether guns make citizens more or less safe) play in the arguments of either the majority or the dissents?

2. **The Stakes.** The majority proffers a long list of permissible regulations. If much regulation is permissible, what differences remain between the majority and the dissent?

3. **Theory after *Heller*.** What is the test for gun control regulations after *Heller*? Rationality? Undue burden? Strict Scrutiny? What approach does JUSTICE BREYER urge? What is JUSTICE SCALIA'S alternative?

4. **Applications of *Heller*.** Can private businesses bar firearms on their premises? Can public schools bar guns? Could D.C. bar possession of mace or a missile launcher? If carrying a gun for self-defense is a constitutional right, but prohibiting concealed guns is a valid regulation, does this make sense?

5. **Suicide.** Over fifty percent of handgun deaths are suicides. Suicide attempts are more successful when committed with handguns than with other methods. Should the Court have considered these facts?

6. **Judicial Philosophy.** The majority argues that the Constitution confers a federal right to gun ownership for self-defense and hunting. The dissent says individual states and communities should determine their own gun policies. Are these views typical of liberals and conservatives? Did the majority abandon conservative principles of judicial restraint and federalism?

D. LIMITS ON THE JUDICIAL POWER

Parts A and B of this chapter demonstrated the broad expanse of the Supreme Court's power to interpret the Constitution. Part C explored the substantial flexibility Supreme Court justices exercise in interpreting the Constitution. At this point, the student might reasonably perceive that the Supreme Court has limitless authority, via constitutional interpretation, to impose its views on American society, displacing democracy with a judicial dictatorship.

Such a perception would be erroneous. First, as explored earlier in *Marbury*, the Court only has the power of judgment; it cannot impress its decisions against the will of elected officials and the people. Second, as explored below, Congress and the Court impose limits on the exercise of federal judicial power. Finally, a constitutional provision, the Eleventh Amendment, imposes limits on cases Congress may authorize courts to hear See infra Chapter IVD2.

1.   CONGRESSIONAL LIMITS

The Constitution gives Congress an active role in the work of the federal courts. When Congress passes legislation, it often leaves interpretation of what it wrote to the courts and expects that its statutory commands will be enforced through lawsuits. Conversely, repeal of a statute removes the judicial work of interpreting and enforcing that statute. Congress also has the power to tax and spend, a power that includes expanding or contracting the budget of the judicial branch of government. This power is modestly limited by language in Article III, § 1 that prohibits the diminution of compensation paid to judges. Would budget cuts eliminating all law clerk and secretarial assistance for federal judges diminish judicial compensation? Would increased federal income taxes unconstitutionally reduce judicial compensation?

A more judiciary-specific role for Congress appears in Article I, § 8, cl. 9, which allows Congress the power to "constitute Tribunals inferior to the supreme Court." This is reinforced by Article III, § 1, which vests the federal judicial power "in one supreme Court, and in such inferior Courts as the Congress may from time to time ordain and establish." Over the past two centuries, Congress has greatly expanded the number of federal judges and has regularly revised the geographic jurisdiction of the federal district and appellate courts.

Article III, §2 gives the Supreme Court "appellate Jurisdiction, both as to Law and Fact, with such Exceptions, and under such Regulations as the Congress shall make." Can Congress simply exclude from Supreme Court jurisdiction cases or questions which Congress does not want the Court to hear? Congress occasionally has threatened to restrict judicial jurisdiction to avoid having its statutory policy choices challenged in the courts. Generally, Congress has not followed through on these threats and the Supreme Court has not been forced to consider such efforts. Which, if any, of the following hypothetical federal laws would be constitutional?

(a)   "Notwithstanding any other provision of law, the United States District Courts shall not have jurisdiction over any case that challenges the constitutionality of any state or federal law relating to school busing."

(b)   "The Supreme Court shall not have jurisdiction to review any case arising out of any State statute which relates to voluntary prayers in a public school or public building; nor shall its jurisdiction extend to any case relating to placement by any State official of the Ten Commandments in a public place or building."

(c) "No court in the United States shall have jurisdiction to review any claim that the federal statutory prohibition on abortions is unconstitutional."

One specific restriction on congressional power to exclude cases from the reach of the courts appears in Article I, § 9, cl. 2: "The privilege of the Writ of Habeas Corpus shall not be suspended, unless when in Cases of Rebellion or Invasion the public Safety may require it." The following materials examine (a) the interplay between exceptions to federal jurisdiction and suspension of habeas corpus and (b) the extent to which Congress, through legislation, may reverse judicial decisions.

a. Exceptions to and Suspension of Habeas Corpus

Some factual background is helpful to reading the next case, *Ex Parte McCardle*. Habeas corpus is "[a] writ employed to bring a person before a court, most frequently to ensure that the party's imprisonment or detention is not illegal." BLACK'S LAW DICTIONARY 728 (8th ed. 2004). The writ of habeas corpus was implemented in § 14 of the Judiciary Act of 1789, which allowed the federal courts, including the Supreme Court, to issue the writ to free those held "in custody, under or by colour of the authority of the United States." In the aftermath of the Civil War, Congress perceived this authorization of the writ to be too narrow because state prisoners could not obtain federal habeas corpus relief. For example, a freed former slave held under color of state law in violation of the rights recently granted under the Thirteenth Amendment would have been dependent on southern state courts to obtain release.

In February of 1867, the Reconstruction Congress passed an act which for the first time provided federal courts with the power "to grant writs of habeas corpus in all cases where any person may be restrained of his or her liberty in violation of the Constitution or of any treaty or law of the United States." Less than a month after passing this legislation, Congress adopted the Military Reconstruction Act, which divided the South into districts subject to military command. On November 12, 1867, McCardle, an unreconstructed white southerner who edited the *Vicksburg Times*, was arrested by Major General Alvin Gillem and held for trial for the nonmilitary offenses of disturbing the peace, inciting to insurrection and disorder, libel, and impeding reconstruction.

McCardle filed a petition for habeas corpus under the 1867 Act. His petition was denied and he appealed to the Supreme Court. McCardle claimed that suspension of his right to a jury trial under martial law was unconstitutional, that application of the Reconstruction Act to his editorials violated the First Amendment, and that the Reconstruction Act's placement of ten states under military jurisdiction was unconstitutional. The Supreme Court denied a motion by the United States to dismiss McCardle's appeal. Oral arguments on the merits were concluded on March 9, 1868. Three days later, Congress, fearing the Supreme Court would hold the Reconstruction

Act unconstitutional in its ruling on McCardle's appeal, passed legislation, (vetoed by President Andrew Johnson, whose veto was quickly overridden). This new legislation stated, "so much of the [1867 Act] as authorizes an appeal from the judgment of the circuit court to the Supreme Court of the United States, or the exercise of any such jurisdiction by said Supreme Court on appeals which have been or may hereafter be taken, be, and the same is, hereby repealed."

EX PARTE McCARDLE
74 U.S. (7 Wall.) 506 (1869)

The CHIEF JUSTICE delivered the opinion of the court.

The first question necessarily is that of jurisdiction; for, if the act of March, 1868, takes away the jurisdiction defined by the act of February, 1867, it is useless, if not improper, to enter into any discussion of other questions.

It is quite true, as was argued by the counsel for the petitioner, that the appellate jurisdiction of this court is not derived from acts of Congress. It is, strictly speaking, conferred by the Constitution. But it is conferred "with such exceptions and under such regulations as Congress shall make."

It is unnecessary to consider whether, if Congress had made no exceptions and no regulations, this court might not have exercised general appellate jurisdiction under rules prescribed by itself. For among the earliest acts of the first Congress, at its first session, was the act of September 24th, 1789, to establish the judicial courts of the United States. That act provided for the organization of this court, and prescribed regulations for the exercise of its jurisdiction.

The source of that jurisdiction, and the limitations of it by the Constitution and by statute, have been on several occasions subjects of consideration here. *** [W]hile "the appellate powers of this court are not given by the judicial act, but are given by the Constitution," they are, nevertheless, "limited and regulated by that act, and by such other acts as have been passed on the subject." The court said, further, that the judicial act was an exercise of the power given by the Constitution to Congress "of making exceptions to the appellate jurisdiction of the Supreme Court." "They have described affirmatively," said the court, "its jurisdiction, and this affirmative description has been understood to imply a negation of the exercise of such appellate power as is not comprehended within it."

The principle that the affirmation of appellate jurisdiction implies the negation of all such jurisdiction not affirmed having been thus established, it was an almost necessary consequence that acts of Congress, providing for the exercise of jurisdiction, should come to be spoken of as acts granting jurisdiction, and not as acts making exceptions to the constitutional grant of it.

The exception to appellate jurisdiction in the case before us, however, is not an inference from the affirmation of other appellate jurisdiction. It is made in terms. The provision of the act of 1867, affirming the appellate jurisdiction of this court in cases of habeas corpus is expressly repealed. It is hardly possible to imagine a plainer instance of positive exception.

We are not at liberty to inquire into the motives of the legislature. We can only examine into its power under the Constitution; and the power to make exceptions to the appellate jurisdiction of this court is given by express words.

What, then, is the effect of the repealing act upon the case before us? We cannot doubt as to this. Without jurisdiction the court cannot proceed at all in any cause. Jurisdiction is power to declare the law, and when it ceases to exist, the only function remaining to the court is that of announcing the fact and dismissing the cause. And this is not less clear upon authority than upon principle.

Several cases were cited by the counsel for the petitioner in support of the position that jurisdiction of this case is not affected by the repealing act. But none of them, in our judgment, afford any support to it. They are all cases of the exercise of judicial power by the legislature, or of legislative interference with courts in the exercising of continuing jurisdiction.

On the other hand, the general rule, supported by the best elementary writers, is, that "when an act of the legislature is repealed, it must be considered, except as to transactions past and closed, as if it never existed." And the effect of repealing acts upon suits under acts repealed, has been determined by the adjudications of this court. The subject was fully considered in *Norris v. Crecker*, and more recently in *Insurance Company v. Ritchie*. In both of these cases it was held that no judgment could be rendered in a suit after the repeal of the act under which it was brought and prosecuted.

It is quite clear, therefore, that this court cannot proceed to pronounce judgment in this case, for it has no longer jurisdiction of the appeal; and judicial duty is not less fitly performed by declining ungranted jurisdiction than in exercising firmly that which the Constitution and the laws confer.

Counsel seem to have supposed, if effect be given to the repealing act in question, that the whole appellate power of the court, in cases of habeas corpus, is denied. But this is an error. The act of 1868 does not except from that jurisdiction any cases but appeals from Circuit Courts under the act of 1867. It does not affect the jurisdiction which was previously exercised. ***

Notes

1.   **Holding.** Did the Court hold (a) that Congress' power to regulate federal court jurisdiction (including access to the Supreme Court) is plenary or (b) that Congress' withdrawal of its power by repeal of the Act of 1867 was permissible because there was another avenue for Supreme Court review? Which holding is more consistent with *Marbury*? What would you do after the Supreme Court's decision if you were McCardle's lawyer?

2.   **Limits on Habeas Petitions Today.** In *Felker v. Turpin*, 519 U.S. 989 (1996), the Court considered the constitutionality of the Antiterrorism and

Effective Death Penalty Act of 1996, which placed severe limits on second and subsequent habeas petitions and permitted such petitions only after a special appellate panel granted a motion for leave to file the petition. Referencing *McCardle*, the Court unanimously held that Congress had not infringed on the judicial power to hear cases on an "original" writ of habeas corpus and that the limits on second and later writs did not unconstitutionally cause "suspension of the writ." The following case discusses suspension of the writ of habeas corpus in more detail.

3.   **Background on Habeas Corpus in the "War on Terrorism."** Following the attacks on the World Trade Center and Pentagon on September 11, 2001, President George W. Bush issued a Military Order which precluded "any remedy *** or proceeding *** in any court" over alien enemy combatants captured and detained by the United States in military actions against al Qaeda and the Taliban. The Supreme Court held that this order did not preclude statutory habeas as to detainees held in Guantanamo Bay, Cuba. *Rasul v. Bush*, 542 U.S. 466 (2004). Congress responded with the Detainee Treatment Act of 2005, which provided that "no court *** shall have jurisdiction to hear or consider *** an application for a writ of habeas corpus filed by or on behalf of an alien detained *** at Guantanamo Bay, Cuba." In *Hamdan v. Rumsfeld*, 548 U.S. 557 (2006), the Court held that this provision did not apply to cases pending on the date of enactment. Legislation repudiating *Hamdan*, the Military Commissions Act of 2006 (MCA), removed jurisdiction over pending and future habeas cases by alien detainees, at Guantanamo and elsewhere. Part of the MCA read, "[n]o court, justice, or judge shall have jurisdiction to hear or consider an application for a writ of habeas corpus filed by or on behalf of an alien detained by the United States who has been determined by the United States to have been properly detained as an enemy combatant or is awaiting such determination." It also limited non-habeas actions by detainees [Except for a limited appeal to the D.C. Circuit following a military commission trial, "no court, justice, or judge shall have jurisdiction to hear or consider any other action against the United States or its agents relating to any aspect of the detention, transfer, treatment, trial, or conditions of confinement of an alien who is or was detained by the United States and has been determined by the United States to have been properly detained as an enemy combatant or is awaiting such determination."] The MCA provided it would "take effect on the date of the enactment of this Act, [October 17, 2006], and shall apply to all cases, without exception, pending on or after the date of the enactment of this Act." The case in which the Supreme Court addressed the constitutionality of the MCA's limit on habeas at Guantanamo Bay follows.

BOUMEDIENE v. BUSH
553 U.S. 723 (2008)

JUSTICE KENNEDY delivered the opinion of the Court.

Petitioners are aliens designated as enemy combatants and detained at the United States Naval Station at Guantanamo Bay, Cuba. *** [They] present a question not resolved by our earlier cases relating to the detention of aliens at Guantanamo: whether they have the constitutional privilege of habeas corpus, a privilege not to be withdrawn except in conformance with the Suspension Clause, Art.I, §9, cl.2. We hold these petitioners do have the habeas corpus privilege. Congress has enacted a statute, the Detainee

Treatment Act of 2005 (DTA) that provides certain procedures for review of the detainees' status. We hold that those procedures are not an adequate and effective substitute for habeas corpus. Therefore § 7 of the Military Commissions Act of 2006 (MCA), operates as an unconstitutional suspension of the writ. ***

In *Hamdi v. Rumsfeld,* 542 U.S. 507 (2004), five Members of the Court recognized that detention of individuals who fought against the United States in Afghanistan "for the duration of the particular conflict in which they were captured, is so fundamental and accepted an incident to war as to be an exercise of the 'necessary and appropriate force' Congress has authorized the President to use." After *Hamdi,* the Deputy Secretary of Defense established Combatant Status Review Tribunals (CSRTs) to determine whether individuals detained at Guantanamo were "enemy combatants," as the Department defines that term. *** All are foreign nationals, but none is a citizen of a nation now at war with the United States. Each denies he is a member of the al Qaeda terrorist network that carried out the September 11 attacks or of the Taliban regime that provided sanctuary for al Qaeda. Each petitioner appeared before a separate CSRT; was determined to be an enemy combatant; and has sought a writ of habeas corpus in the United States District Court for the District of Columbia. ***

In deciding the constitutional questions now presented we must determine whether petitioners are barred from seeking the writ or invoking the protections of the Suspension Clause either because of their status, *i.e.,* petitioners' designation by the Executive Branch as enemy combatants, or their physical location, *i.e.,* their presence at Guantanamo Bay. ***

That the Framers considered the writ a vital instrument for the protection of individual liberty is evident from the care taken to specify the limited grounds for its suspension *** The Clause *** ensures that, except during periods of formal suspension, the Judiciary will have a time-tested device, the writ, to maintain the "delicate balance of governance" that is itself the surest safeguard of liberty. The Clause protects the rights of the detained by affirming the duty and authority of the Judiciary to call the jailer to account. *** [W]e seek guidance as well from founding-era authorities addressing the specific question before us: whether foreign nationals, apprehended and detained in distant countries during a time of serious threats to our Nation's security, may assert the privilege of the writ and seek its protection. *** [T]he analysis may begin with precedents as of 1789, for the Court has said that "at the absolute minimum" the Clause protects the writ as it existed when the Constitution was drafted and ratified. *** The Government points out there is no evidence that a court sitting in England granted habeas relief to an enemy alien detained abroad; petitioners respond there is no evidence that a court refused to do so for lack of jurisdiction. *** Recent scholarship points to the inherent shortcomings in the historical record. *** We decline, therefore, to infer too much, one way or the other, from the lack of historical evidence on point.

Drawing from its position that at common law the writ ran only to territories over which the Crown was sovereign, the Government says the

Suspension Clause affords petitioners no rights because the United States does not claim sovereignty over the place of detention.

Guantanamo Bay is not formally part of the United States. And under the terms of the lease between the United States and Cuba, Cuba retains "ultimate sovereignty" over the territory while the United States exercises "complete jurisdiction and control." Under the terms of the 1934 Treaty, however, Cuba effectively has no rights as a sovereign until the parties agree to modification of the 1903 Lease Agreement or the United States abandons the base. *** [W]e take notice of the obvious and uncontested fact that the United States, by virtue of its complete jurisdiction and control over the base, maintains *de facto* sovereignty over this territory. ***

The Framers foresaw that the United States would expand and acquire new territories. *** [T]hroughout most of our history there was little need to explore the outer boundaries of the Constitution's geographic reach. When Congress exercised its power to create new territories, it guaranteed constitutional protections to the inhabitants by statute. *** The Government's formal sovereignty-based test raises troubling separation-of-powers concerns *** The necessary implication of the argument is that by surrendering formal sovereignty over any unincorporated territory to a third party, while at the same time entering into a lease that grants total control over the territory back to the United States, it would be possible for the political branches to govern without legal constraint.

Our basic charter cannot be contracted away like this. The Constitution grants Congress and the President the power to acquire, dispose of, and govern territory, not the power to decide when and where its terms apply. Even when the United States acts outside its borders, its powers are not "absolute and unlimited" but are subject "to such restrictions as are expressed in the Constitution." Abstaining from questions involving formal sovereignty and territorial governance is one thing. To hold the political branches have the power to switch the Constitution on or off at will is quite another. The former position reflects this Court's recognition that certain matters requiring political judgments are best left to the political branches. The latter would permit a striking anomaly in our tripartite system of government, leading to a regime in which Congress and the President, not this Court, say "what the law is." *Marbury*.

These concerns have particular bearing upon the Suspension Clause question in the cases now before us, for the writ of habeas corpus is itself an indispensable mechanism for monitoring the separation of powers. *** [T]he outlines of a framework for determining the reach of the Suspension Clause are suggested by the factors the Court relied upon in *Eisentrager*. ***

> "(a) is an enemy alien; (b) has never been or resided in the United States; (c) was captured outside of our territory and there held in military custody as a prisoner of war; (d) was tried and convicted by a Military Commission sitting outside the United States; (e) for offenses against laws of war committed outside the United States; (f) and is at all times imprisoned outside the United States."

Based on this language from *Eisentrager,* and the reasoning in our other extraterritoriality opinions, we conclude that at least three factors are relevant in determining the reach of the Suspension Clause: (1) the citizenship and status of the detainee and the adequacy of the process through which that status determination was made; (2) the nature of the sites where apprehension and then detention took place; and (3) the practical obstacles inherent in resolving the prisoner's entitlement to the writ.

Applying this framework, we note at the onset that the status of these detainees is a matter of dispute. The petitioners, like those in *Eisentrager,* are not American citizens. But the petitioners in *Eisentrager* did not contest, it seems, the Court's assertion that they were "enemy alien[s]." *** The records from the *Eisentrager* trials suggest that, *** there had been a rigorous adversarial process to test the legality of their detention. The *Eisentrager* petitioners were charged by a bill of particulars that made detailed factual allegations [and] they were entitled to representation by counsel, allowed to introduce evidence on their own behalf, and permitted to cross-examine the prosecution's witnesses.

In comparison the procedural protections afforded to the detainees in the CSRT hearings are far more limited, and, we conclude, fall well short of the procedures and adversarial mechanisms that would eliminate the need for habeas corpus review. Although the detainee is assigned a "Personal Representative" to assist him during CSRT proceedings, the Secretary of the Navy's memorandum makes clear that person is not the detainee's lawyer or even his "advocate." The Government's evidence is accorded a presumption of validity. The detainee is allowed to present "reasonably available" evidence, but his ability to rebut the Government's evidence against him is limited by the circumstances of his confinement and his lack of counsel at this stage. And although the detainee can seek review of his status determination in the Court of Appeals, that review process cannot cure all defects in the earlier proceedings.

As to the second factor relevant to this analysis, the detainees here are similarly situated to the *Eisentrager* petitioners in that the sites of their apprehension and detention are technically outside the sovereign territory of the United States. As noted earlier, this is a factor that weighs against finding they have rights under the Suspension Clause. But there are critical differences between Landsberg Prison, circa 1950, and the United States Naval Station at Guantanamo Bay in 2008. Unlike its present control over the naval station, the United States' control over the prison in Germany was neither absolute nor indefinite. *** Guantanamo Bay, on the other hand, is no transient possession. In every practical sense Guantanamo is not abroad; it is within the constant jurisdiction of the United States.

As to the third factor, we recognize, as the Court did in *Eisentrager,* that there are costs to holding the Suspension Clause applicable in a case of military detention abroad. Habeas corpus proceedings may require expenditure of funds by the Government and may divert the attention of military personnel from other pressing tasks. While we are sensitive to these concerns, we do not find them dispositive *** The Government presents no credible arguments that the military mission at Guantanamo would be compromised if habeas corpus courts had jurisdiction to hear the detainees' claims. ***

We hold that Art. I, § 9, cl. 2, of the Constitution has full effect at Guantanamo Bay. If the privilege of habeas corpus is to be denied to the detainees now before us, Congress must act in accordance with the requirements of the Suspension Clause. ***

In light of our conclusion that there is no jurisdictional bar *** the question remains whether there are prudential barriers to habeas corpus review under these circumstances. *** In cases involving foreign citizens detained abroad by the Executive, it likely would be both an impractical and unprecedented extension of judicial power to assume that habeas corpus would be available at the moment the prisoner is taken into custody. If and when habeas corpus jurisdiction applies, as it does in these cases, then proper deference can be accorded to reasonable procedures for screening and initial detention under lawful and proper conditions of confinement and treatment for a reasonable period of time. *** Here, as is true with detainees apprehended abroad, a relevant consideration in determining the courts' role is whether there are suitable alternative processes in place to protect against the arbitrary exercise of governmental power. ***

Although we hold that the DTA is not an adequate and effective substitute for habeas corpus, it does not follow that a habeas corpus court may disregard the dangers the detention in these cases was intended to prevent. *** Certain accommodations can be made to reduce the burden habeas corpus proceedings will place on the military without impermissibly diluting the protections of the writ. *** We make no attempt to anticipate all of the evidentiary and access-to-counsel issues that will arise during the course of the detainees' habeas corpus proceedings. We recognize, however, that the Government has a legitimate interest in protecting sources and methods of intelligence gathering; and we expect that the District Court will use its discretion to accommodate this interest to the greatest extent possible.

* * *

In considering both the procedural and substantive standards used to impose detention to prevent acts of terrorism, proper deference must be accorded to the political branches. *** Within the Constitution's separation-of-powers structure, few exercises of judicial power are as legitimate or as necessary as the responsibility to hear challenges to the authority of the Executive to imprison a person. Some of these petitioners have been in custody for six years with no definitive judicial determination as to the legality of their detention. Their access to the writ is a necessity to determine the lawfulness of their status, even if, in the end, they do not obtain the relief they seek. ***

JUSTICE SOUTER, concurring in the judgment.

*** After six years of sustained executive detentions in Guantanamo, subject to habeas jurisdiction but without any actual habeas scrutiny, today's decision is no judicial victory, but an act of perseverance in trying to make habeas review *** mean something of value both to prisoners and to the Nation.

CHIEF JUSTICE ROBERTS, dissenting.

Today the Court strikes down as inadequate the most generous set of procedural protections ever afforded aliens detained by this country as enemy combatants. *** And to what effect? The majority merely replaces a review system designed by the people's representatives with a set of shapeless procedures to be defined by federal courts at some future date. *** [T]his decision is not really about the detainees at all, but about control of federal policy regarding enemy combatants. ***

To what basic process are these detainees due as habeas petitioners? We have said that "at the absolute minimum," the Suspension Clause protects the writ "'as it existed in 1789.'" The majority admits that a number of historical authorities suggest that at the time of the Constitution's ratification, "common-law courts abstained altogether from matters involving prisoners of war." If this is accurate, the process provided prisoners under the DTA is plainly more than sufficient-it allows alleged combatants to challenge both the factual and legal bases of their detentions. *** The Court objects to the detainees' limited access to witnesses and classified material, but proposes no alternatives of its own. *** What it does say leaves open the distinct possibility that its "habeas" remedy will, when all is said and done, end up looking a great deal like the DTA review it rejects. ***

So who has won? Not the detainees. The Court's analysis leaves them with only the prospect of further litigation to determine the content of their new habeas right, followed by further litigation to resolve their particular cases, followed by further litigation before the D.C. Circuit-where they could have started had they invoked the DTA procedure. Not Congress, whose attempt to "determine-through democratic means-how best" to balance the security of the American people with the detainees' liberty interests, has been unceremoniously brushed aside. Not the Great Writ, whose majesty is hardly enhanced by its extension to a jurisdictionally quirky outpost, with no tangible benefit to anyone. Not the rule of law, unless by that is meant the rule of lawyers, who will now arguably have a greater role than military and intelligence officials in shaping policy for alien enemy combatants. And certainly not the American people, who today lose a bit more control over the conduct of this Nation's foreign policy to unelected, politically unaccountable judges.

JUSTICE SCALIA, dissenting.

*** The writ of habeas corpus does not, and never has, run in favor of aliens abroad; the Suspension Clause thus has no application. *** America is at war with radical Islamists. *** The game of bait-and-switch that today's opinion plays upon the Nation's Commander in Chief will make the war harder on us. It will almost certainly cause more Americans to be killed. That consequence would be tolerable if necessary to preserve a time-honored legal principle vital to our constitutional Republic. But it is this Court's blatant *abandonment* of such a principle that produces the decision today. The

President relied on our settled precedent in *Johnson v. Eisentrager,* when he established the prison at Guantanamo Bay for enemy aliens. *** Had the law been otherwise, the military surely would not have transported prisoners there, but would have kept them in Afghanistan, transferred them to another of our foreign military bases, or turned them over to allies for detention. Those other facilities might well have been worse for the detainees themselves. ***

The writ as preserved in the Constitution could not possibly extend farther than the common law provided when that Clause was written. The Court admits that it cannot determine whether the writ historically extended to aliens held abroad, and it concedes (necessarily) that Guantanamo Bay lies outside the sovereign territory of the United States. Together, these two concessions establish that it is (in the Court's view) perfectly ambiguous whether the common-law writ would have provided a remedy for these petitioners. If that is so, the Court has no basis to strike down the Military Commissions Act, and must leave undisturbed the considered judgment of the coequal branches. ***

Eisentrager *** *held* beyond any doubt-that the Constitution does not ensure habeas for aliens held by the United States in areas over which our Government is not sovereign. *** The Court would have us believe that *Eisentrager* rested on "[p]ractical considerations," such as the "difficulties of ordering the Government to produce the prisoners in a habeas corpus proceeding." Formal sovereignty, says the Court, is merely one consideration "that bears upon which constitutional guarantees apply" in a given location. This is a sheer rewriting of the case. *Eisentrager* mentioned practical concerns, to be sure-but not for the purpose of determining *under what circumstances* American courts could issue writs of habeas corpus for aliens abroad. It cited them to support *its holding* that the Constitution does not empower courts to issue writs of habeas corpus to aliens abroad *in any circumstances.* ***

What drives today's decision is neither the meaning of the Suspension Clause, nor the principles of our precedents, but rather an inflated notion of judicial supremacy. *** Our power "to say what the law is" is circumscribed by the limits of our statutorily and constitutionally conferred jurisdiction. *** Today the Court *** breaks a chain of precedent as old as the common law that prohibits judicial inquiry into detentions of aliens abroad absent statutory authorization. And, most tragically, it sets our military commanders the impossible task of proving to a civilian court, under whatever standards this Court devises in the future, that evidence supports the confinement of each and every enemy prisoner.

The Nation will live to regret what the Court has done today. I dissent.

Notes

1.   **Separation of Powers.** The DTA and the MCA were passed by large margins in Congress and signed into law by the President. The majority says that, ever since *Marbury v. Madison*, it has been the Court's duty within the

federal government to interpret "what the law is" in order to prevent constitutional abuses. JUSTICE SCALIA's dissent sees the application of judicial review to this case as an abuse of judicial authority and a failure to accord proper deference to the other two branches of government. Which side is correct?

2. **Safety, Justice, and Practical Concerns.** While the Justices split on their interpretation of the law, they also disagreed about the practical implications of the decision. The majority stresses the length of time of the detainees' incarceration without the opportunity for full judicial review, while Justice Scalia's dissent points out that allowing habeas corpus will inevitably lead to detainees being freed and greater danger to the U.S. and its citizens. Whose argument is more convincing? How should a government balance access to justice with security concerns?

3. **Sovereignty and the Constitution.** What is the difference between the majority and dissent's views concerning sovereignty? Should the rights and powers of the Constitution flow to all places in which the U.S. exerts control over property and detainees? *See Munaf v. Geren*, 553 U.S. 674 129 (2008).

4. **Where There's a Right There's a Remedy?** *Marbury v. Madison* stands for the proposition that the courts have the ability to remedy constitutional violations. In *Boumediene*, the remedy is straightforward: invalidate the statute that conflicts with the Suspension Clause. What does this remedy do for the individual who brings the habeas action? Boumediene gets a hearing before a judge on his petition. Does it seem likely he will have a sympathetic forum? If the habeas court decides someone is wrongfully detained at Guantanamo Bay, can a court order him released into the United States? If you think the answers to these last two questions are "yes," you would be wrong. *See Latif v. Obama*, 666 F. 3d 746 (C.A.D.C. 2011), cert denied 132 S. Ct. 2741 (2012) and *Kiyemba v. Obama*, 561 F. 3d 509 (D.C.C.A. 2009), cert denied 563 U. S. 954 (2011).

b. *Reversal of Judicial Decisions*

MILLER v. FRENCH
530 U.S. 327 (2000)

JUSTICE O'CONNOR delivered the opinion of the Court.

The Prison Litigation Reform Act of 1995 (PLRA) establishes standards for the entry and termination of prospective relief in civil actions challenging prison conditions. If prospective relief under an existing injunction does not satisfy these standards, a defendant or intervenor is entitled to "immediate termination" of that relief. And under the PLRA's "automatic stay" provision, a motion to terminate prospective relief "shall operate as a stay" of that relief during the period beginning 30 days after the filing of the motion (extendable to up to 90 days for "good cause") and ending when the court rules on the motion. The superintendent of the Pendleton Correctional Facility, which is currently operating under an ongoing injunction to remedy violations of the Eighth Amendment regarding conditions of confinement, filed a motion to terminate prospective relief under the PLRA. Respondent prisoners moved to enjoin the operation of the automatic stay provision of § 3626(e)(2), arguing that it is unconstitutional. *** We must decide whether *** that provision violates separation of powers principles.

This litigation began in 1975, when four inmates at what is now the Pendleton Correctional Facility brought a class action on behalf of all persons who were, or would be, confined at the facility against the predecessors in office of petitioners (hereinafter State). After a trial, the District Court found that living conditions at the prison violated both state and federal law, including the Eighth Amendment's prohibition against cruel and unusual punishment, and the court issued an injunction to correct those violations. *** The Court of Appeals affirmed *** as to those aspects governing overcrowding and doublecelling, the use of mechanical restraints, staffing, and the quality of food and medical services, but it vacated those portions pertaining to exercise and recreation, protective custody, and fire and occupational safety standards. This ongoing injunctive relief has remained in effect ever since, with the last modification occurring in October 1988 ***.

In 1996, Congress enacted the PLRA. As relevant here, the PLRA establishes standards for the entry and termination of prospective relief in civil actions challenging conditions at prison facilities. Specifically, a court "shall not grant or approve any prospective relief unless the court finds that such relief is narrowly drawn, extends no further than necessary to correct the violation of a Federal right, and is the least intrusive means necessary to correct the violation of the Federal right." The same criteria apply to existing injunctions, and a defendant or intervenor may move to terminate prospective relief that does not meet this standard. *** The PLRA also requires courts to rule "promptly" on motions to terminate prospective relief, with mandamus available to remedy a court's failure to do so.

Finally, the provision at issue here, § 3626(e)(2), dictates that, in certain circumstances, prospective relief shall be stayed pending resolution of a motion to terminate. Specifically, subsection (e)(2), entitled "Automatic Stay," states:

"Any motion to modify or terminate prospective relief made under subsection (b) shall operate as a stay during the period—

"(A)(i) beginning on the 30th day after such motion is filed ***; and

"(B) ending on the date the court enters a final order ruling on the motion."

As one of several 1997 amendments to the PLRA, Congress permitted courts to postpone the entry of the automatic stay for not more than 60 days for "good cause," which cannot include general congestion of the court's docket.

On June 5, 1997, the State filed a motion under § 3626(b) to terminate the prospective relief governing the conditions of confinement at the Pendleton Correctional Facility. In response, the prisoner class moved for a temporary restraining order or preliminary injunction to enjoin the operation of the automatic stay, arguing that § 3626(e)(2) is unconstitutional as both a violation of the Due Process Clause of the Fifth Amendment and separation of powers principles. *** [The Court of Appeals decided PLRA violated the separation of powers, but did not reach the due process claim. The Supreme Court likewise did not address the due process claim, but remanded for "further proceedings consistent with this opinion."] ***

The Constitution enumerates and separates the powers of the three branches of Government in Articles I, II, and III, and it is this "very structure" of the Constitution that exemplifies the concept of separation of powers. While the boundaries between the three branches are not "'hermetically' sealed," the Constitution prohibits one branch from encroaching on the central prerogatives of another. The powers of the Judicial Branch are set forth in Article III, § 1, which states that the "judicial Power of the United States shall be vested in one supreme Court and in such inferior Courts as Congress may from time to time ordain and establish," and provides that these federal courts shall be staffed by judges who hold office during good behavior, and whose compensation shall not be diminished during tenure in office. As we explained in *Plaut v. Spendthrift Farm, Inc.*, 514 U.S. at 218–219 (1995), Article III "gives the Federal Judiciary the power, not merely to rule on cases, but to decide them, subject to review only by superior courts in the Article III hierarchy."

Respondent prisoners contend that § 3626(e)(2) encroaches on the central prerogatives of the Judiciary and thereby violates the separation of powers doctrine. It does this, the prisoners assert, by legislatively suspending a final judgment of an Article III court in violation of *Plaut* and *Hayburn's Case*, 2 Dall. 409 (1792). According to the prisoners, the remedial order governing living conditions at the Pendleton Correctional Facility is a final judgment of an Article III court, and § 3626(e)(2) constitutes an impermissible usurpation of judicial power because it commands the district court to suspend prospective relief under that order, albeit temporarily. ***

Hayburn's Case arose out of a 1792 statute that authorized pensions for veterans of the Revolutionary War. The statute provided that the circuit courts were to review the applications and determine the appropriate amount of the pension, but that the Secretary of War had the discretion either to adopt or reject the courts' findings. Although this Court did not reach the constitutional issue in *Hayburn's Case*, the opinions of five Justices, sitting on Circuit Courts, were reported, and we have since recognized that the case "stands for the principle that Congress cannot vest review of the decisions of Article III courts in officials of the Executive Branch." *Plaut*. As we recognized in *Plaut*, such an effort by a coequal branch to "annul a final judgment" is " 'an assumption of Judicial power' and therefore forbidden."

Unlike the situation in *Hayburn's Case*, § 3626(e)(2) does not involve the direct review of a judicial decision by officials of the Legislative or Executive Branches. Nonetheless, the prisoners suggest that § 3626(e)(2) falls within *Hayburn's* prohibition against an indirect legislative "suspension" or reopening of a final judgment ***. In *Plaut*, we held that a federal statute that required federal courts to reopen final judgments that had been entered before the statute's enactment was unconstitutional on separation of powers grounds. *** We concluded that this retroactive command that federal courts reopen final judgments exceeded Congress' authority. The decision of an inferior court within the Article III hierarchy is not the final word of the department (unless the time for appeal has expired), and "[i]t is the obligation of the last court in the hierarchy that rules on the case to give effect to Congress's latest enactment, even when that has the effect of overturning the judgment of an inferior court, since each court, at every level, must 'decide according to existing laws.' " But once a judicial decision achieves finality, it "becomes the last word of the judicial department." And because Article III "gives the Federal Judiciary the power, not merely to rule on cases, but to decide them, subject to review only by superior courts in the Article III hierarchy," the "judicial Power is one to render dispositive judgments," and Congress cannot retroactively command Article III courts to reopen final judgments.

Plaut, however, was careful to distinguish the situation before the Court in that case—legislation that attempted to reopen the dismissal of a suit seeking money damages—from legislation that "altered the prospective effect of injunctions entered by Article III courts." We emphasized that "nothing in our holding today calls ... into question" Congress' authority to alter the prospective effect of previously entered injunctions. Prospective relief under a continuing, executory decree remains subject to alteration due to changes in the underlying law. This conclusion follows from our decisions in *Pennsylvania v. Wheeling & Belmont Bridge Co.*, 13 How. 518 (1852) (*Wheeling Bridge I*) and *Pennsylvania v. Wheeling & Belmont Bridge Co.*, 18 How. 421 (1856) (*Wheeling Bridge II*).

In *Wheeling Bridge I*, we held that a bridge across the Ohio River, because it was too low, unlawfully "obstruct[ed] the navigation of the Ohio," and ordered that the bridge be raised or permanently removed. Shortly thereafter, Congress enacted legislation declaring the bridge to be "lawful structur[e]," establishing the bridge as a "'post-roa[d] for the passage of the mails of the United States,'" and declaring that the Wheeling and Belmont Bridge Company was authorized to maintain the bridge at its then-current site and elevation. *Wheeling Bridge II*. After the bridge was destroyed in a storm, Pennsylvania sued to enjoin the bridge's reconstruction, arguing that the statute legalizing the bridge was unconstitutional because it effectively annulled the Court's decision in *Wheeling Bridge I*. We rejected that argument, concluding that the decree in *Wheeling Bridge I* provided for ongoing relief by "directing the abatement of the obstruction" which enjoined the defendants' from any continuance or reconstruction of the obstruction. Because the intervening statute altered the underlying law such that the bridge was no longer an unlawful obstruction, we held that it was "quite plain the decree of the court cannot be enforced." *Wheeling Bridge II*. *** When Congress altered the underlying law such that the bridge was no longer an unlawful obstruction, the injunction against the maintenance of the bridge was not enforceable.

Applied here, the principles of *Wheeling Bridge II* demonstrate that the automatic stay *** does not unconstitutionally "suspend" or reopen a judgment of an Article III court. [It] does not by itself "tell judges when, how, or what to do." Instead, [it] merely reflects the change implemented by §

3626(b), which does the "heavy lifting" in the statutory scheme by establishing new standards for prospective relief. *** Accordingly, if prospective relief under an existing decree had been granted or approved absent such findings, then that prospective relief must cease, unless and until the court makes findings on the record that such relief remains necessary to correct an ongoing violation and is narrowly tailored. The PLRA's automatic stay provision *** requir[es] the court to stay any prospective relief that, due to the change in the underlying standard, is no longer enforceable, i.e., prospective relief that is not supported by the findings specified ***.

By establishing new standards for the enforcement of prospective relief in § 3626(b), Congress has altered the relevant underlying law. The PLRA has restricted courts' authority to issue and enforce prospective relief concerning prison conditions, requiring that such relief be supported by findings and precisely tailored to what is needed to remedy the violation of a federal right. We note that the constitutionality of § 3626(b) is not challenged here; we assume, without deciding, that the new standards it pronounces are effective. *** Although the remedial injunction here is a "final judgment" for purposes of appeal, it is not the "last word of the judicial department." *Plaut.* The provision of prospective relief is subject to the continuing supervisory jurisdiction of the court, and therefore may be altered according to subsequent changes in the law. ***

The entry of the automatic stay under § 3626(e)(2) helps to implement the change in the law caused by §§ 3626(b)(2) and (3). *** The entry of the stay does not reopen or "suspend" the previous judgment, nor does it divest the court of authority to decide the merits of the termination motion. Rather, the stay merely reflects the changed legal circumstances—that prospective relief under the existing decree is no longer enforceable, and remains unenforceable unless and until the court makes the findings required ***.

For the same reasons, § 3626(e)(2) does not violate the separation of powers principle articulated in *United States v. Klein*, 13 Wall. 128 (1872). In that case, *Klein*, the executor of the estate of a Confederate sympathizer, sought to recover the value of property seized by the United States during the Civil War, which by statute was recoverable if Klein could demonstrate that the decedent had not given aid or comfort to the rebellion. In *United States v. Padelford*, 9 Wall. 531 (1870), we held that a Presidential pardon satisfied the burden of proving that no such aid or comfort had been given. While Klein's case was pending, Congress enacted a statute providing that a pardon would instead be taken as proof that the pardoned individual had in fact aided the enemy, and if the claimant offered proof of a pardon the court must dismiss the case for lack of jurisdiction. *Klein*. We concluded that the statute was unconstitutional because it purported to "prescribe rules of decision to the Judicial Department of the government in cases pending before it."

Here, the prisoners argue that Congress has similarly prescribed a rule of decision because, for the period of time until the district court makes a final decision on the merits of the motion to terminate prospective relief, § 3626(e)(2) mandates a particular outcome: the termination of prospective relief. As we noted in *Plaut*, however, "[w]hatever the precise scope of *Klein*, later decisions have made clear that its prohibition does not take hold when Congress 'amend[s] applicable law.'" The prisoners concede this point but contend that, because § 3626(e)(2) does not itself amend the legal standard, *Klein* is still applicable. As we have explained, however, § 3626(e)(2) must be read not in isolation, but in the context of § 3626 as a whole. Section 3626(e)(2) operates in conjunction with the new standards for the continuation of prospective relief; if the new standards *** are not met, then the stay "shall operate" unless and until the court makes the findings required ***. Rather than prescribing a rule of decision, § 3626(e)(2) simply imposes the consequences of the court's application of the new legal standard.

Finally, the prisoners assert that, even if § 3626(e)(2) does not fall within the recognized prohibitions of *Hayburn's Case*, *Plaut*, or *Klein*, it still offends the principles of separation of powers because it places a deadline on judicial decisionmaking, thereby interfering with core judicial functions. *** Respondents' concern with the time limit, then, must be its relative brevity. But whether the time is so short that it deprives litigants of a meaningful opportunity to be heard is a due process question, an issue that is not before us. We leave open, therefore, the question whether this time limit, particularly in a complex case, may implicate due process concerns. *** In this action, we have no occasion to decide whether there could be a time constraint on judicial action that was so severe that it implicated these structural separation of powers concerns. The PLRA does not deprive courts of their adjudicatory role, but merely provides a new legal standard for relief and encourages courts to apply that standard promptly. *** [T[his provision does not violate separation of powers principles. ***

JUSTICE SOUTER, with whom JUSTICE GINSBURG joins, concurring in part and dissenting in part.

*** Congress has the authority to [impose] new conditions precedent for the continuing enforcement of existing, prospective remedial orders and requiring courts to apply the new rules to those orders. If its legislation gives courts adequate time to determine the applicability of a new rule to an old order and to take the action necessary to apply it or to vacate the order, there seems little basis for claiming that Congress has crossed the constitutional line to interfere with the performance of any judicial function. But if determining whether a new rule applies requires time (say, for new factfinding) and if the statute provides insufficient time for a court to make that determination before the statute invalidates an extant remedial order, the application of the statute raises a serious question whether Congress has in practical terms assumed the judicial function. In such a case, the prospective order suddenly turns unenforceable not because a court has made a judgment to terminate it due to changed law or fact, but because no one can tell in the time allowed whether the new rule requires modification of the old order. One way to view this result is to see the Congress as mandating modification of an order that may turn out to be perfectly enforceable under the new rule, depending on judicial factfinding. If the facts are taken this way, the new statute might well be treated as usurping the judicial function of determining the applicability of a general rule in particular factual circumstances.[3] Cf. *United States v. Klein.*

Whether this constitutional issue arises on the facts of this action, however, is something we cannot yet tell ***.

Notes

1.   **Legislative Alternatives.**   Usually, if the Supreme Court rules an act of Congress unconstitutional, the legislators simply go back to the drawing board and rewrite the problematic part to comport with the Court's decision. But *Plaut,* discussed in *Miller,* involved judgments finalized before Congress acted. Moreover, Congress prospectively adopted, rather than repudiating, the statutes of limitations periods held appropriate in the Court's earlier decisions. What was going on in Congress to produce this response to the Supreme Court?

2.   **Less Judicial Review for Prisoners?**   *Ex Parte McCardle, Miller v. French,* and *Felker v. Turpin* all upheld limitations on judicial review in prisoner cases. Does the Court just not want to hear prisoners' allegations of unfairness and mistreatment? In *Lauf v. Shinner,* 303 U.S. 323 (1938), the Court upheld the Norris–LaGuardia Act's preclusion of federal court injunctions in labor disputes. The statute was designed to keep conservative judges from stopping strikes by workers and their unions. While the Court had held other New Deal statutes unconstitutional, it accepted this restriction on federal court jurisdiction.

3.   **Problem.**   In *Employment Division v. Smith,* 494 U.S. 872 (1990), the Supreme Court said that "generally applicable, religion neutral laws that have the effect of burdening a particular religious practice need not be justified by a compelling governmental interest" under the Free Exercise clause of the First Amendment. The Court found that religion-neutral laws need only be "rational," and that the plaintiff, a member of the Native American Church, was not protected from discharge for "work-related misconduct" when he engaged in sacramental use of the drug peyote. In response to the decision, Congress passed the Religious Freedom Restoration Act (RFRA), which provides that "[g]overnment may substantially burden a person's exercise of religion only if it demonstrates that application of the burden to the person (1) is in furtherance of a compelling governmental interest and (2) is the least restrictive means of furthering that compelling governmental interest." RFRA requires the courts to apply the compelling interest test, even though before *Smith* the Supreme Court had not rigorously applied a compelling interest test. Argue from the cases you have read thus far whether RFRA is constitutional. The Court's decision in *City of Boerne v. Flores,* infra Ch. X, decided on other grounds, won't help you at all.

---

[3] The constitutional question inherent in these possible circumstances does not seem to be squarely addressed by any of our cases. Congress did not engage in discretionary review of a particular judicial judgment, cf. *Plaut* (characterizing *Hayburn's Case*), or try to modify a final, non-prospective judgment. Nor would a stay result from the judicial application of a change in the underlying law, cf. [*Wheeling Bridge II*]; *Plaut* (characterizing *Klein*). Instead, if the time is insufficient for a court to make a judicial determination about the applicability of the new rules, the stay would result from the inability of the Judicial Branch to exercise the judicial power of determining whether the new rules applied at all. Cf. *Marbury v. Madison* ("It is emphatically the province and duty of the judicial department to say what the law is").

2. THE "CASE OR CONTROVERSY" LIMIT

One might assume that the Supreme Court would not limit its own power to decide matters brought to it.   Such an assumption would be erroneous. The Supreme Court has frequently found the exercise of the federal judicial power to be outside its power to decide "Cases" and "Controversies" under Article III.   When the Court finds a matter "nonjusticiable" under Article III, the suit is thrown out of the federal court system.   Whether it might be brought in state court is a matter of state law.

Justiciability encompasses a range of different problems that fall generally within the following broad "hornbook" categories:

• **Advisory Opinions.**   The Court in its early history responded negatively to President Washington's request for an opinion concerning various legal issues arising from the United States' neutrality in a war between France and England.   The Justices declined the invitation to render advice on the grounds that the three branches were "in certain respects checks upon each other; that they were judges of "a court in the last resort; and that extrajudicial decisions of questions did not square with the Article II power of the President to call on the heads of executive departments for opinions. What advantages/disadvantages do you see to advisory opinions?

•   **Standing.** This component of justiciability focuses on whether the plaintiff is a proper party to bring a legal action.   This issue occurs in a remarkably large number of cases involving attempts to enforce modern statutes and will be explored in *Laidlaw*, the next case.

• **Ripeness.** A controversy is not ripe if it is premature; the Court views it as inadequately developed factually.   Further actions, such as by a federal agency adopting a particular rule that harms (or fails to harm) particular individuals, may make a case ripe that previously was not ripe.

•   **Mootness.** A case that has become irrelevant because the dispute between the parties has ended is said to be moot.   An otherwise moot case may be adjudicated, however, if there is a continuing controversy concerning damages from no longer continuing conduct or if, in the Court's words, the controversy is one "capable of repetition, yet evading review." Some aspects of mootness are discussed in *Laidlaw*.

• **Political Questions.** When the Constitution entrusts a discretionary decision to Congress or the President, rather than to the Court, the decision is said to be a political question.   When you read *Baker v. Carr* later in this section, think about whether the formulation of the test for what is a political question squares with the political question discussion in *Marbury*.

The Supreme Court has said the justiciability doctrines "define with respect to the Judicial Branch the idea of separation of powers on which the Federal Government is founded" and that these doctrines demonstrate "concern about the proper—and properly limited—role of the courts in a democratic society." *Allen v. Wright*, 468 U.S. 737 (1984). Nevertheless, the Court acknowledged that justiciability is "more than an intuition but less than a rigorous and explicit theory."   Most of the discussion about justiciability ultimately comes back to whether the Court (1) is overusing justiciability doctrines to avoid deciding cases it would rather avoid (because of the controversial nature of the substantive question, the difficulty of the issue, or the poor quality of the factual setting or advocacy in the case presented) or (2) is ignoring justiciability considerations to decide matters best left to another forum (one of the political branches of the government).

As you read the following materials, consider why the Court would limit the judicial power. Is it seeking the best possible advocacy in cases heard by the federal courts? Is it trying to differentiate the judicial power in principled ways from the legislative and executive powers in Articles I and II? Is the Court avoiding issues that might arouse criticism of it?

a. *Standing and Mootness*

FRIENDS OF THE EARTH v. LAIDLAW ENVIRONMENTAL SERVICES, INC.
528 U.S. 167 (2000)

JUSTICE GINSBURG delivered the opinion of the Court.

This case presents an important question concerning the operation of the citizen-suit provisions of the Clean Water Act. Congress authorized the federal district courts to entertain Clean Water Act suits initiated by "a person or persons having an interest which is or may be adversely affected." To impel future compliance with the Act, a district court may prescribe injunctive relief in such a suit; additionally or alternatively, the court may impose civil penalties payable to the United States Treasury. In the Clean Water Act citizen suit now before us, the District Court determined that injunctive relief was inappropriate because the defendant, after the institution of the litigation, achieved substantial compliance with the terms of its discharge permit. The court did, however, assess a civil penalty of $405,800. *** The Court of Appeals vacated the District Court's order. The case became moot, the appellate court declared, once the defendant fully complied with the terms of its permit and the plaintiff failed to appeal the denial of equitable relief. ***

In 1972, Congress enacted the Clean Water Act (Act), also known as the Federal Water Pollution Control Act. *** Under § 505(a) of the Act, a suit to enforce any limitation in a [pollution] permit may be brought by any "citizen," defined as "a person or persons having an interest which is or may be adversely affected." Sixty days before initiating a citizen suit, however, the would-be plaintiff must give notice of the alleged violation to the EPA, the State in which the alleged violation occurred, and the alleged violator. "[T]he purpose of notice to the alleged violator is to give it an opportunity to bring itself into complete compliance with the Act and thus *** render unnecessary a citizen suit." Accordingly, we have held that citizens lack statutory standing under § 505(a) to sue for violations that have ceased by the time the complaint is filed. The Act also bars a citizen from suing if the EPA or the State has already commenced, and is "diligently prosecuting," an enforcement action.

The Act authorizes district courts in citizen-suit proceedings to enter injunctions and to assess civil penalties, which are payable to the United States Treasury. In determining the amount of any civil penalty, the district court must take into account "the seriousness of the violation or violations, the economic benefit (if any) resulting from the violation, any history of such violations, any good-faith efforts to comply with the applicable requirements, the economic impact of the penalty on the violator, and such other matters as justice may require." ***

In 1986, defendant-respondent Laidlaw Environmental Services (TOC), Inc., bought a hazardous waste incinerator facility in Roebuck, South Carolina, that included a wastewater treatment plant. *** Once it received its permit, Laidlaw began to discharge various pollutants into the waterway; repeatedly, Laidlaw's discharges exceeded the limits set by the permit. *** On April 10, 1992, plaintiff-petitioners Friends of the Earth (FOE) and Citizens Local Environmental Action Network, Inc. (CLEAN) (referred to collectively in this opinion, together with later joined plaintiff-petitioner Sierra Club, as "FOE") took the preliminary step necessary to the institution of litigation. They sent a letter to Laidlaw notifying the company of their intention to file a citizen suit against it under the Act after the expiration of the requisite 60–day notice period ***. On June 9, 1992, the last day before FOE's 60–day notice period expired, [the State] and Laidlaw reached a settlement requiring Laidlaw to pay $100,000 in civil penalties and to make "every effort" to comply with its permit obligations.

On June 12, 1992, FOE filed this citizen suit against Laidlaw ***, alleging noncompliance with the permit and seeking declaratory and injunctive relief and an award of civil penalties. Laidlaw moved for summary judgment on the ground that FOE had failed to present evidence demonstrating injury in fact, and therefore lacked Article III standing to bring the lawsuit. In opposition to this motion, FOE submitted affidavits and deposition testimony from members of the plaintiff organizations. *** [T]he District Court *** found that Laidlaw had gained a total economic benefit of $1,092,581 as a result of its extended period of noncompliance with the mercury discharge limit in its permit [but] concluded, however, that a civil penalty of $405,800 was adequate. *** The court declined to grant FOE's request for injunctive relief, stating that an injunction was inappropriate because "Laidlaw has been in substantial compliance with all parameters in its NPDES [National Pollutant Discharge Elimination System] permit since at least August 1992." *** The Court of Appeals assumed without deciding that FOE initially had standing to bring the action, but went on to hold that the case had become moot *** because "the only remedy currently available to [FOE]—civil penalties payable to the government—would not redress any injury [FOE has] suffered." *** According to Laidlaw, after the Court of Appeals issued its decision ***, the entire incinerator facility in Roebuck was permanently closed, dismantled, and put up for sale, and all discharges from the facility permanently ceased. ***

The Constitution's case-or-controversy limitation on federal judicial authority, Art. III, § 2, underpins both our standing and our mootness jurisprudence, but the two inquiries differ in respects critical to the proper resolution of this case, so we address them separately. *** In *Lujan v. Defenders of Wildlife*, 504 U.S. 555, 560–561 (1992), we held that, to satisfy Article III's standing requirements, a plaintiff must show (1) it has suffered an "injury in fact" that is (a) concrete and particularized and (b) actual or imminent, not conjectural or hypothetical; (2) the injury is fairly traceable to the challenged action of the defendant; and (3) it is likely, as opposed to merely speculative, that the injury will be redressed by a favorable decision. An association has standing to bring suit on behalf of its members when its members would otherwise have standing to sue in their own right, the interests at stake are germane to the organization's purpose, and neither the claim asserted nor the relief requested requires the participation of individual members in the lawsuit.

Laldlaw contends first that FOE lacked standing from the outset even to seek injunctive relief, because the plaintiff organizations failed to show that any of their members had sustained or faced the threat of any "injury in fact" from Laidlaw's activities. In support of this contention Laidlaw points to the District Court's finding, made in the course of setting the penalty amount, that there had been "no demonstrated proof of harm to the environment" from Laidlaw's mercury discharge violations.

The relevant showing for purposes of Article III standing, however, is not injury to the environment but injury to the plaintiff. *** Focusing properly on injury to the plaintiff, the District Court found that FOE had demonstrated sufficient injury to establish standing. For example, FOE member Kenneth Lee Curtis averred in affidavits that he lived a half-mile from Laidlaw's facility; that he occasionally drove over the North Tyger River, and that it looked and smelled polluted; and that he would like to fish, camp, swim, and picnic in and near the river between 3 and 15 miles downstream from the facility, as he did when he was a teenager, but would not do so because he was concerned that the water was polluted by Laidlaw's discharges. Curtis reaffirmed these statements in extensive deposition testimony. *** Other members presented evidence to similar effect. ***

These sworn statements, as the District Court determined, adequately documented injury in fact. We have held that environmental plaintiffs adequately allege injury in fact when they aver that they use the affected area and are persons "for whom the aesthetic and recreational values of the area will be lessened" by the challenged activity.

Our decision in *Lujan v. National Wildlife Federation*, 497 U.S. 871 (1990), is not to the contrary. *** We held that the plaintiff could not survive the summary judgment motion merely by offering "averments which state only that one of [the organization's] members uses unspecified portions of an immense tract of territory, on some portions of which mining activity has occurred or probably will occur by virtue of the governmental action." *** Nor can the affiants' conditional statements—that they would use the nearby North Tyger River for recreation if Laidlaw were not discharging pollutants into it—be equated with the speculative " 'some day' intentions" to visit endangered species halfway around the world that we held insufficient to show injury in fact in *Defenders of Wildlife.*

Los Angeles v. Lyons, 461 U.S. 95 (1983), relied on by the dissent, does not weigh against standing in this case. In *Lyons*, we held that a plaintiff lacked standing to seek an injunction against the enforcement of a police chokehold policy because he could not credibly allege that he faced a realistic threat from the policy. *** Here, in contrast, it is undisputed that Laidlaw's unlawful conduct—discharging pollutants in excess of permit limits—was occurring at the time the complaint was filed. ***

Laidlaw argues next that even if FOE had standing to seek injunctive relief, it lacked standing to seek civil penalties. Here the asserted defect is not injury but redressability. Civil penalties offer no redress to private plaintiffs, Laidlaw argues, because they are paid to the government, and therefore a citizen plaintiff can never have standing to seek them.

Laidlaw is right to insist that a plaintiff must demonstrate standing separately for each form of relief sought. But it is wrong to maintain that citizen plaintiffs facing ongoing violations never have standing to seek civil penalties.

We have recognized on numerous occasions that "all civil penalties have some deterrent effect." More specifically, Congress has found that civil penalties in Clean Water Act cases do more than promote immediate compliance by limiting the defendant's economic incentive to delay its attainment of permit limits; they also deter future violations. *** To the extent that they encourage defendants to discontinue current violations and deter them from committing future ones, they afford redress to citizen plaintiffs who are injured or threatened with injury as a consequence of ongoing unlawful conduct.

The dissent argues that it is the availability rather than the imposition of civil penalties that deters any particular polluter from continuing to pollute. This argument misses the mark in two ways. First, it overlooks the interdependence of the availability and the imposition; a threat has no deterrent value unless it is credible that it will be carried out. Second, it is reasonable for Congress to conclude that an actual award of civil penalties does in fact bring with it a significant quantum of deterrence over and above what is achieved by the mere prospect of such penalties. A would-be polluter may or may not be dissuaded by the existence of a remedy on the books, but a defendant once hit in its pocketbook will surely think twice before polluting again.

We recognize that there may be a point at which the deterrent effect of a claim for civil penalties becomes so insubstantial or so remote that it cannot support citizen standing. The fact that this vanishing point is not easy to ascertain does not detract from the deterrent power of such penalties in the ordinary case. *** In this case we need not explore the outer limits of the principle that civil penalties provide sufficient deterrence to support redressability. Here, the civil penalties sought by FOE carried with them a deterrent effect that made it likely, as opposed to merely speculative, that the penalties would redress FOE's injuries by abating current violations and preventing future ones ***

Satisfied that FOE had standing under Article III to bring this action, we turn to the question of mootness.

The only conceivable basis for a finding of mootness in this case is Laidlaw's voluntary conduct—either its achievement by August 1992 of substantial compliance with its permit or its more recent shutdown of the Roebuck facility. It is well settled that "a defendant's voluntary cessation of a challenged practice does not deprive a federal court of its power to determine the legality of the practice." "[I]f it did, the courts would be compelled to leave '[t]he defendant *** free to return to his old ways.'" *** [T]he standard we have announced for determining whether a case has been mooted by the defendant's voluntary conduct is stringent: "A case might become moot if subsequent events made it absolutely clear that the allegedly wrongful behavior could not reasonably be expected to recur." The "heavy burden of persua[ding]" the court that the challenged conduct cannot reasonably be expected to start up again lies with the party asserting mootness. *** [T]here are circumstances in which the prospect that a defendant will engage in (or resume) harmful conduct may be too speculative to support standing, but not too speculative to overcome mootness. Furthermore, if mootness were simply "standing set in a time frame," the exception to mootness that arises when the defendant's allegedly unlawful activity is "capable of repetition, yet evading review" could not exist. *** Standing admits of no similar exception; if a plaintiff lacks standing at the time the action commences, the fact that the dispute is capable of repetition yet evading review will not entitle the complainant to a federal judicial forum. ***

Standing doctrine functions to ensure, among other things, that the scarce resources of the federal courts are devoted to those disputes in which the parties have a concrete stake. In contrast, by the time mootness is an issue, the case has been brought and litigated, often (as here) for years. To abandon the case at an advanced stage may prove more wasteful than frugal. This argument from sunk costs [to the judicial system, not the litigants] does not license courts to retain jurisdiction over cases in which one or both of the parties plainly lacks a continuing interest, as when the parties have settled or a plaintiff pursuing a nonsurviving claim has died. *** The effect of both Laidlaw's compliance and the facility closure on the prospect of future violations is a disputed factual matter. *** These issues have not been aired in the lower courts; they remain open for consideration on remand. ***

JUSTICE STEVENS, concurring. [omitted]

JUSTICE KENNEDY, concurring.

Difficult and fundamental questions are raised when we ask whether exactions of public fines by private litigants, and the delegation of Executive power which might be inferable from the authorization, are permissible in view of the responsibilities committed to the Executive by Article II of the Constitution of the United States. *** In my view these matters are best reserved for a later case. ***

JUSTICE SCALIA, with whom JUSTICE THOMAS joins, dissenting.

The Court begins its analysis by finding injury in fact on the basis of vague affidavits that are undermined by the District Court's express finding that Laidlaw's discharges caused no demonstrable harm to the environment. It then proceeds to marry private wrong with public remedy in a union that violates traditional principles of federal standing—thereby permitting law enforcement to be placed in the hands of private individuals. Finally, the Court suggests that to avoid mootness one needs even less of a stake in the outcome than the Court's watered-down requirements for initial standing. I dissent from all of this.

Plaintiffs, as the parties invoking federal jurisdiction, have the burden of proof and persuasion as to the existence of standing. *Lujan v. Defenders of Wildlife*, 504 U.S. 555, 561 (1992) (hereinafter *Lujan*). The plaintiffs in this case fell far short of carrying their burden of demonstrating injury in fact. The Court cites affiants' testimony asserting that their enjoyment of the North Tyger River has been diminished due to "concern" that the water was polluted, and that they "believed" that Laidlaw's mercury exceedances had reduced the value of their homes. These averments alone cannot carry the plaintiffs' burden of demonstrating that they have suffered a "concrete and particularized" injury. *** Typically, an environmental plaintiff claiming injury due to discharges in violation of the Clean Water Act argues that the discharges harm the environment, and that the harm to the environment injures him. *** "All available data *** fail to show that Laidlaw's actual discharges have resulted in harm ***

The Court finds these conclusions unproblematic for standing, because "[t]he relevant showing for purposes of Article III standing *** is not injury to the environment but injury to the plaintiff." This statement is correct, as far as it goes. *** [But] Ongoing "concerns" about the environment are not enough, for "[i]t is the reality of the threat of repeated injury that is relevant to the standing inquiry, not the plaintiff's subjective apprehensions," *Los Angeles v. Lyons*, 461 U.S. 95, 107, n. 8 (1983). *** By accepting plaintiffs' vague, contradictory, and unsubstantiated allegations of "concern" about the environment as adequate to prove injury in fact, and accepting them even in the face of a finding that the environment was not demonstrably harmed, the Court makes the injury-in-fact requirement a sham. If there are permit violations, and a member of a plaintiff environmental organization lives near the offending plant, it would be difficult not to satisfy today's lenient standard.

The Court's treatment of the redressability requirement—which would have been unnecessary if it resolved the injury-in-fact question correctly—is equally cavalier. As discussed above, petitioners allege ongoing injury consisting of diminished enjoyment of the affected waterways and decreased property values. They allege that these injuries are caused by Laidlaw's continuing permit violations. But the remedy petitioners seek is neither recompense for their injuries nor an injunction against future violations. Instead, the remedy is a statutorily specified "penalty" for past violations, payable entirely to the United States Treasury. *** That holding has no precedent in our jurisprudence, and takes this Court beyond the "cases and controversies" that Article III of the Constitution has entrusted to its resolution. *** The new standing law that the Court makes—like all expansions of standing beyond the traditional constitutional limits—has grave implications for democratic governance. ***

Article II of the Constitution commits it to the President to "take Care that the Laws be faithfully executed," Art. II, § 3, and provides specific methods by which all persons exercising significant executive power are to be appointed, Art. II, § 2. *** [T]he question of the conformity of this legislation with Article II has not been argued—and I, like the Court, do not address it. But Article III, no less than Article II, has consequences for the structure of our government, and it is worth noting the changes in that structure which today's decision allows.

By permitting citizens to pursue civil penalties payable to the Federal Treasury, the Act does not provide a mechanism for individual relief in any traditional sense, but turns over to private citizens the function of enforcing the law. *** The availability of civil penalties vastly disproportionate to the individual injury gives citizen plaintiffs massive bargaining power—which is often used to achieve settlements requiring the defendant to support environmental projects of the plaintiffs' choosing. Thus is a public fine diverted to a private interest.

To be sure, the EPA may foreclose the citizen suit by itself bringing suit. This allows public authorities to avoid private enforcement only by accepting private direction as to when enforcement should be undertaken—which is no less constitutionally bizarre. ***

Finally, I offer a few comments regarding the Court's discussion of whether FOE's claims became moot by reason of Laidlaw's substantial compliance with the permit limits. I do not disagree with the conclusion that the Court reaches. *** Laidlaw's claimed compliance is squarely within the bounds of our "voluntary cessation" doctrine, which is the basis for the remand. *** [W]hat is required for litigation to continue is essentially identical to what is required for litigation to begin: There must be a justiciable case or controversy as required by Article III. *** Because the requirement of a continuing case or controversy derives from the Constitution, it may not be ignored when inconvenient, or, as the Court suggests, to save "sunk costs."

It is true that mootness has some added wrinkles *** [b[ut it is inaccurate to regard this as a reduction of the basic requirement for standing that obtained at the beginning of the suit. A genuine controversy must exist at both stages. *** The "voluntary cessation" doctrine is nothing more than an evidentiary presumption that the controversy reflected by the violation of alleged rights continues to exist. Similarly, the fact that we do not find cases moot when the challenged conduct is "capable of repetition, yet evading review" does not demonstrate that the requirements for mootness and for standing differ. ***

By uncritically accepting vague claims of injury, the Court has turned the Article III requirement of injury in fact into a "mere pleading requirement"; and by approving the novel theory that public penalties can redress anticipated private wrongs, it has come close to "mak[ing] the redressability requirement vanish." The undesirable and unconstitutional consequence of today's decision is to place the immense power of suing to enforce the public laws in private hands. I respectfully dissent.

Notes

1. **Some Basic Points.**

    • What are the Constitution's textual commands about standing? About citizen suits as an alternative to federal prosecution?

    • Is standing now, as JUSTICE SCALIA charges in his *Laidlaw* dissent, merely a matter of pleading?

    • What is Congress' role on issues of standing?

    • How does mootness differ from standing?

    • What are the political or policy results of these doctrines? Should these results affect the Court's assessment of standing and mootness issues?

2. ***Lujan* and *Laidlaw*.** *Lujan v. Defenders of Wildlife*, 504 U.S. 555 (1992), held that plaintiffs who might at some future date visit endangered species halfway around the globe did not have standing to seek enforcement of the Endangered Species Act. JUSTICE SCALIA wrote the majority opinion, which concluded that absence of definite plans to visit those remote locations, demonstrated for instance by obtaining a ticket to travel there, doomed the plaintiffs' standing. The Court also rejected the plaintiffs' claims that they suffered a "procedural injury"; a plaintiff cannot force the Executive Branch to follow statutory procedures absent a specific interest in the outcome of such procedures. Finally, the opinion discussed whether an injury was "redressable" since agencies that might have funded projects endangering wildlife abroad were not joined and, at any rate, only funded portions of overseas projects. The redressability portion of the opinion lacked a majority rationale. Are the distinctions between *Lujan* and *Laidlaw* principled?

3. **Taxpayer Standing**. Suppose I pay taxes and don't like the purpose for which my taxes are spent. Can I challenge the constitutionality of the government expenditure? *Frothingham v. Mellon*, 262 U.S. 447 (1923), held that a federal taxpayer had no standing because his "interest in the moneys of the Treasury *** is shared with millions of others; is comparatively minute and indeterminable; and the effect upon future taxation, of any payment out of the funds, so remote, fluctuating and uncertain, that no basis is afforded for an appeal to the preventive powers of a court of equity." An exception was carved to allow taxpayer standing to challenge congressional expenditures allegedly in violation of the Establishment Clause, *Flast v. Cohen*, 392 U.S. 83 (1968). In *Hein v. Freedom from Religion Foundation*, 551 U.S. 587 (2007) taxpayers claimed that President's Faith-Based and Community Initiatives program conferences violated the Establishment Clause. The Court distinguished *Flast* on the ground that "executive discretion" is different from "congressional action" and criticized

Flast's failure to recognize that standing "has a separation-of-powers component, which keeps courts within certain traditional bounds vis-a-vis the other branches, concrete adverseness or not." JUSTICE KENNEDY'S concurrence stressed *Flast's* ""narrow exception" to the rule against taxpayer standing," while JUSTICES SCALIA and THOMAS opined that "*Flast* is wholly irreconcilable with the Article III restrictions on federal-court jurisdiction." JUSTICES SOUTER, STEVENS, GINSBURG, and BREYER dissented on the basis that "there is no [separation of powers] difference between a Judicial Branch review of an executive decision and a judicial evaluation of a congressional one." Taxpayer standing to challenge state taxation has also been rejected, *DaimlerChrysler Corp. v. Cuno*, 547 U.S. 332 (2006), but municipal taxpayers generally are accorded standing to challenge illegal use of local funds. Standing, as understood under *Flast*, took another hit in *Arizona Christian School Tuition Organization v. Winn*, 131 S. Ct. 1436 (2011) when the Court held (5-4) that a challenger to a tax credit (as opposed to a governmental expenditure in *Flast*) lacked standing.

4. **Prudential Standing**. *Elk Grove Unified School District v. Newdow*, 542 U.S. 1 (2004), presented the substantive issue of whether public school recitation of the words "under God" in the Pledge of Allegiance was impermissible religious indoctrination in violation of the First Amendment. Ducking this issue, the Court held that "prudential standing considerations precluded a decision on the merits. These factors were that the "realm of domestic relations" is involved; peculiarities of California custody law; the divergence of maternal and paternal views on "under God" in the Pledge of Allegiance; Newdow's ability to explain his views to his daughter; competence of other government institutions to deal with the substantive issue; adverse effects on "a young child *** at the center of a highly public debate;" and Newdow's attempts to "dictate to others what they may and may not say to his child respecting religion." Did the Court use "prudential standing" to avoid a controversial issue? Should matters of "great national significance" invoke different justiciability principles than less important cases?

5. **Individual Standing and Federalism.** Individuals have standing to challenge a federal statute on the ground that it interferes with the powers reserved to the states under the Tenth Amendment because federalism secures individual liberties by diffusing sovereign power. The individual need not rely on vicarious assertion of the state's interests in its own sovereignty. *Bond v. U.S.*, 564 U. S. 211 (2011).

6. **Problems.**

    (a) A good friend of yours is concerned that she and others may develop skin cancer because of the "ozone hole" in the atmosphere and inadequate steps taken by the United States to ban the production of substances responsible for creating the hole. Your friend, who has unlimited financial resources to pursue the issue in court and a passionate commitment to this environmental issue, asks you whether there are any barriers (other than the usual expert testimony to prove probable skin damage) to her successful prosecution of such a suit. Advise her about justiciability issues. Reconsider this issue after reading the next case.

    (b) Suppose a state legislature adopted a variant of the Confederate Flag as the state flag. Who, if anyone, would have standing to object to this decision? *See Coleman v. Miller*, 885 F. Supp. 1561 (N.D. Ga. 1995).

(c) A contractor's association, most of whose members are nonminority contractors, files a suit which claims an ordinance violates the Equal Protection Clause of the Fourteenth Amendment by requiring that 10% of the money spent on city contracts be "set aside" for minority business enterprises. Would the association have to show (1) that members' bids for work were rejected because of the set aside, (2) that members would have bid for such work but were deterred because of the set aside program, or (3) only that the program placed its nonminority members on an unequal footing in the bidding process? *See Northeastern Florida Chapter of Associated General Contractors v. Jacksonville*, 508 U.S. 656 (1993). If the city later changes its setaside program to permit nonminority businesses to qualify for the 10% "set asides," would the association lose its standing? Or would the case be moot? What is the difference, if any? *See Adarand Constructors, Inc. v. Slater*, 528 U.S. 216 (2000).

(d) After the Line Item Veto Act became effective, but before it was used by the President to veto specific items for which Congress had appropriated money, several Members of Congress who had voted against the Act brought suit against the Secretary of the Treasury challenging its constitutionality. The Act contained a provision saying "[a]ny Member of Congress or any individual adversely affected by [this Act] may bring an action *** on the ground that any provision *** violates the Constitution." How should the courts rule on the plaintiffs' standing? *See Raines v. Byrd*, 521 U.S. 811 (1997). Would Members of the House or Senators have standing to challenge legislation which called for sampling rather than actual counting of persons in the decennial census? *See Department of Commerce v. United States House of Representatives*, 525 U.S. 316 (1999); *see also Utah v. Evans*, 536 U.S. 452 (2002) (Utah has standing to challenge allocation of representative to North Carolina through "imputation" by the Census Bureau and the Secretary of Commerce; a court could order the Secretary to "recalculate the numbers and to recertify the official census result").

MASSACHUSETTS v. EPA
549 U.S. 497 (2007)

JUSTICE STEVENS delivered the opinion of the Court.

A well-documented rise in global temperatures has coincided with a significant increase in the concentration of carbon dioxide in the atmosphere. Respected scientists believe the two trends are related. *** Calling global warming "the most pressing environmental challenge of our time," a group of States, local governments, and private organizations, alleged *** that the Environmental Protection Agency (EPA) has abdicated its responsibility under the Clean Air Act to regulate the emissions of four greenhouse gases, including carbon dioxide. *** To ensure the proper adversarial presentation, *Lujan* holds that a litigant must demonstrate that it has suffered a concrete and particularized injury that is either actual or imminent, that the injury is fairly traceable to the defendant, and that it is likely that a favorable decision will redress that injury. *** Only one of the petitioners needs to have standing to permit us to consider the petition for review. *** [T]he party seeking review here is a sovereign State and not, as it was in *Lujan*, a private individual. *** That Massachusetts does in fact own a great deal of the "territory alleged to be affected" only reinforces the conclusion that its stake in the outcome of this case is sufficiently concrete to warrant the exercise of federal judicial power. *** Congress has moreover recognized a concomitant procedural right to challenge the rejection of its rulemaking petition as arbitrary and capricious. Given that procedural right and Massachusetts' stake in protecting its quasi-sovereign interests, the Commonwealth is entitled to special solicitude in our standing analysis. ***

The harms associated with climate change are serious and well recognized. Indeed, the NRC Report itself-which EPA regards as an "objective and independent assessment of the relevant science"-identifies a number of environmental changes that have already inflicted significant harms, including "the global retreat of mountain glaciers, reduction in snow-cover extent, the earlier spring melting of rivers and lakes, [and] the accelerated rate of rise of sea levels during the 20th century relative to the past few thousand years *** These rising seas have already begun to swallow Massachusetts' coastal land. *** Remediation costs alone, petitioners allege, could run well into the hundreds of millions of dollars.

EPA does not dispute the existence of a causal connection between man-made greenhouse gas emissions and global warming. At a minimum, therefore, EPA's refusal to regulate such emissions "contributes" to Massachusetts' injuries. *** Even leaving aside the other greenhouse gases, the United States transportation sector emits *** more than 6% of worldwide carbon dioxide emissions. To put this in perspective: Considering just emissions from the transportation sector, which represent less than one-third of this country's total carbon dioxide emissions, the United States would still rank as the third-largest emitter of carbon dioxide in the world, outpaced only by the European Union and China. Judged by any standard, U. S. motor-vehicle emissions make a meaningful contribution to greenhouse gas concentrations and hence, according to petitioners, to global warming.

While it may be true that regulating motor-vehicle emissions will not by itself *reverse* global warming, it by no means follows that we lack jurisdiction to decide whether EPA has a duty to take steps to *slow* or *reduce* it. *** The risk of catastrophic harm, though remote, is nevertheless real. That risk would be reduced to some extent if petitioners received the relief they seek. We therefore hold that petitioners have standing to challenge the EPA's denial of their rulemaking petition. ***

CHIEF JUSTICE ROBERTS, with whom JUSTICE SCALIA, JUSTICE THOMAS, and JUSTICE ALITO join, dissenting.

*** Apparently dissatisfied with the pace of progress on [global warming] in the elected branches, petitioners have come to the courts claiming broad-ranging injury, and attempting to tie that injury to the Government's alleged failure to comply with a rather narrow statutory provision. I would reject these challenges as nonjusticiable. *** [A] State asserting quasi-sovereign interests as *parens patriae* must still show that its citizens satisfy Article III. Focusing on Massachusetts's interests as quasi-sovereign makes the required showing here harder, not easier. The Court, in effect, takes what has always been regarded as a *necessary* condition for *parens patriae* standing-a quasi-sovereign interest-and converts it into a *sufficient* showing for purposes of Article III. *** [T]he status of Massachusetts as a State cannot compensate for petitioners' failure to demonstrate injury in fact, causation, and redressability.

When the Court actually applies the three-part test, it focuses, as did the dissent below, on the State's asserted loss of coastal land as the injury in fact. If petitioners rely on loss of land as the Article III injury, however, they must ground the rest of the standing analysis in that specific injury. *** The very concept of global warming seems inconsistent with this particularization requirement. Global warming is a phenomenon "harmful to humanity at large," and the redress petitioners seek is focused no more on them than on the public generally-it is literally to change the atmosphere around the world.

If petitioners' particularized injury is loss of coastal land, it is also that injury that must be "actual or imminent, not conjectural or hypothetical," "real and immediate," and "certainly impending." As to "actual" injury, the Court observes that "global sea levels rose somewhere between 10 and 20 centimeters over the 20th century as a result of global warming" and that "[t]hese rising seas have already begun to swallow Massachusetts' coastal land." But none of petitioners' declarations supports that connection. *** The Court's attempts to identify "imminent" or "certainly impending" loss of Massachusetts coastal land fares no better. One of petitioners' declarants predicts global warming will cause sea level to rise by 20 to 70 centimeters *by the year 2100.* ***

Petitioners' reliance on Massachusetts's loss of coastal land as their injury in fact for standing purposes creates insurmountable problems for them with respect to causation and redressability. *** First, it is important to recognize the extent of the emissions at issue here. Because local greenhouse gas emissions disperse throughout the atmosphere and remain there for anywhere from 50 to 200 years, it is global emissions data that are relevant. According to one of petitioners' declarations, domestic motor vehicles contribute about 6 percent of global carbon dioxide emissions and 4 percent of global greenhouse gas emissions. The amount of global emissions at issue here is smaller still; § 202(a)(1) of the Clean Air Act covers only *new* motor vehicles and *new* motor vehicle engines, so petitioners' desired emission standards might reduce only a fraction of 4 percent of global emissions. *** In light of *** a 150-year global phenomenon, and the myriad additional factors bearing on petitioners' alleged injury-the loss of Massachusetts coastal land-the connection is far too speculative to establish causation.

Redressability is even more problematic. *** As the Court acknowledges, "developing countries such as China and India are poised to increase greenhouse gas emissions substantially over the next century," so the domestic emissions at issue here may become an increasingly marginal portion of global emissions, and any decreases produced by petitioners' desired standards are likely to be overwhelmed many times over by emissions increases elsewhere in the world. ***

The Court's sleight-of-hand is in failing to link up the different elements of the three-part standing test. What must be *likely* to be redressed is the particular injury in fact. The injury the Court looks to is the asserted loss of land. *** The realities make it pure conjecture to suppose that EPA regulation of new automobile emissions will *likely* prevent the loss of Massachusetts coastal land. ***

Notes

1. **Important Cases?** Standing is a prerequisite to forcing the EPA to look at an issue of great national and international significance. Is forcing the EPA to decide the issue of regulating greenhouse gases an appropriate role for the Court? Or a role for political processes and actors?

2. **Standing Doctrine Application.** Who has the better of the arguments on injury, causation, and remedy? On the injury prong, why would the Court focus so much on property damage, rather than the public health or environmental concerns that underlie statutes like the Clean Air Act?

3. **Injury Components.** In *Spokeo v. Robins*, 136 S. Ct. 1540 (2016), the Court held that an injury in fact must be both (1) concrete and (2) particularized. Statutory violations alone are not enough for standing – an Article III court must consider whether harm was sufficiently concrete and particularized to satisfy constitutional minimum standards. The case was remanded for reconsideration of whether there was a constitutionally sufficient "concrete" harm.

4. **Generalized Grievances.** In *Lance v. Coffman*, 549 U.S. 437 (2007), the Court dismissed an election challenge on standing grounds, stating that "[t]he plaintiffs here are four Colorado voters. *** The only injury plaintiffs allege is that the law-specifically the Elections Clause-has not been followed [in an election in which they voted]. This injury is precisely the kind of undifferentiated, generalized grievance about the conduct of government that we have refused to countenance in the past. It is quite different from the sorts of injuries alleged by plaintiffs in voting rights cases where we have found standing. Because plaintiffs assert no particularized stake in the litigation, we hold that they lack standing to bring their Elections Clause claim." How do the plaintiffs in *Baker v. Carr* and *Vieth v. Jubelirer*, which follow, differ from the plaintiffs in *Lance*?

b. Political Questions

BAKER v. CARR
369 U.S. 186 (1962)

MR. JUSTICE BRENNAN delivered the opinion of the Court.

*** Between 1901 and 1961, Tennessee has experienced substantial growth and redistribution of her population. *** [T]he complaint alleges that *** "because of the population changes since 1900, and the failure of the Legislature to reapportion itself since 1901," the 1901 statute became "unconstitutional and obsolete." Appellants also argue that, because of the composition of the legislature effected by the 1901 Apportionment Act, compactness redress in the form of a state constitutional amendment to change the entire mechanism for reapportioning, or any other change short of that, is difficult or impossible ***. [T]hey seek a declaration that the 1901 statute is unconstitutional [under the equal protection clause of the Fourteenth Amendment] and an injunction restraining the appellees from acting to conduct any further elections under it. They also pray that unless and until the General Assembly enacts a valid reapportionment, the District Court should either decree a reapportionment by mathematical application of the Tennessee constitutional formulae to the most recent Federal Census figures, or direct the appellees to conduct legislative elections, primary and general, at large. ***

Of course the mere fact that the suit seeks protection of a political right does not mean it presents a political question. *** Rather, it is argued that apportionment cases, whatever the actual wording of the complaint, can involve no federal constitutional right except one resting on the guaranty of a republican form of government, and that complaints based on that clause have been held to present political questions which are nonjusticiable.

We hold that the claim pleaded here neither rests upon nor implicates the Guaranty Clause and that its justiciability is therefore not foreclosed by our decisions of cases involving that clause. *** [W]e deem it necessary first to consider the contours of the "political question" doctrine. ***

We have said that "In determining whether a question falls within (the political question) category, the appropriateness under our system of government of attributing finality to the action of the political departments and also the lack of satisfactory criteria for a judicial determination are dominant considerations." *** The nonjusticiability of a political question is primarily a function of the separation of powers. Much confusion results from the capacity of the "political question" label to obscure the need for case-by-case inquiry. Deciding whether a matter has in any measure been committed by the Constitution to another branch of government, or whether the action of that branch exceeds whatever authority has been committed, is itself a delicate exercise in constitutional interpretation, and is a responsibility of this Court as ultimate interpreter of the Constitution. ***

It is apparent that several formulations which vary slightly according to the settings in which the questions arise may describe a political question, although each has one or more elements which identify it as essentially a function of the separation of powers. Prominent on the surface of any case held to involve a political question is found a textually demonstrable constitutional commitment of the issue to a coordinate political department; or a lack of judicially discoverable and manageable standards for resolving it; or the impossibility of deciding without an initial policy determination of a kind clearly for nonjudicial discretion; or the impossibility of a court's undertaking independent resolution without expressing lack of the respect due coordinate branches of government; or an unusual need for unquestioning adherence to a political decision already made; or the potentiality of embarrassment from multifarious pronouncements by various departments on one question.

Unless one of these formulations is inextricable from the case at bar, there should be no dismissal for non-justiciability on the ground of a political question's presence. The doctrine of which we treat is one of "political questions," not one of "political cases." *** The cases we have reviewed show the necessity for discriminating inquiry into the precise facts and posture of the particular case, and the impossibility of resolution by any semantic cataloguing.

But it is argued that this case shares the characteristics of decisions that constitute a category not yet considered, cases concerning the Constitution's guaranty, in Art. IV, § 4, of a republican form of government *** *Luther v. Borden*, 7 How. 1, though in form simply an action for damages for trespass was, as Daniel Webster said in opening the argument for the defense, "an unusual case." The defendants, admitting an otherwise tortious breaking and entering, sought to justify their action on the ground that they were agents of the established lawful government of Rhode Island, which State was then under martial law to defend itself from active insurrection; that the plaintiff was engaged in that insurrection; and that they entered under orders to arrest the plaintiff. The case arose "out of the unfortunate political differences which agitated the people of Rhode Island in 1841 and 1842," and which had resulted in a situation wherein two groups laid competing claims to recognition as the lawful government. The plaintiff's right to recover depended upon which of the two groups was entitled to such recognition *** Clearly, several factors were thought by the Court in *Luther* to make the question there "political": the commitment to the other branches of the decision as to which is the lawful state government; the unambiguous action by the President, in recognizing the charter government as the lawful authority; the need for finality in the executive's decision; and the lack of criteria by which a court could determine which form of government was republican.

But the only significance that *Luther* could have for our immediate purposes is in its holding that the Guaranty Clause is not a repository of judicially manageable standards which a court could utilize independently in order to identify a State's lawful government. ***

We come, finally, to the ultimate inquiry whether our precedents as to what constitutes a nonjusticiable "political question" bring the case before us under the umbrella of that doctrine. A natural beginning is to note whether any of the common characteristics which we have been able to identify and label descriptively are present. We find none: The question here is the consistency of state action with the Federal Constitution. We have no question decided, or to be decided, by a political branch of government coequal with this Court. Nor do we risk embarrassment of our government abroad, or grave disturbance at home if we take issue with Tennessee as to the constitutionality of her action here challenged. Nor need the appellants, in order to succeed in this action, ask the Court to enter upon policy determinations for which judicially manageable standards are lacking. Judicial standards under the Equal Protection Clause are well developed and familiar, and it has been open to courts since the enactment of the Fourteenth Amendment to determine, if on the particular facts they must, that a discrimination reflects no policy, but simply arbitrary and capricious action.

This case does, in one sense, involve the allocation of political power within a State, and the appellants might conceivably have added a claim under the Guaranty Clause. *** But because any reliance on the Guaranty Clause could not have succeeded it does not follow that appellants may not be heard on the equal protection claim which in fact they tender. *** The right asserted is within the reach of judicial protection under the Fourteenth Amendment. ***

MR. JUSTICE DOUGLAS, MR. JUSTICE CLARK, and MR. JUSTICE STEWART, concurring [omitted.]

MR. JUSTICE FRANKFURTER, whom MR. JUSTICE HARLAN joins, dissenting.

*** A hypothetical claim resting on abstract assumptions is now for the first time made the basis for affording illusory relief for a particular evil even though it foreshadows deeper and more pervasive difficulties in consequence. The claim is hypothetical and the assumptions are abstract because the Court does not vouchsafe *** guidelines for formulating specific, definite, wholly unprecedented remedies for the inevitable litigations that today's umbrageous disposition is bound to stimulate in connection with politically motivated reapportionments in so many States. *** [I]t conveys no intimation what relief *** would not invite legislatures to play ducks and drakes with the judiciary. *** To charge courts with the task of accommodating the incommensurable factors of policy that underlie these mathematical puzzles is to attribute, however flatteringly, omnicompetence to judges. ***

The present case involves all of the elements that have made the Guarantee Clause cases non-justiciable. It is, in effect, a Guarantee Clause claim masquerading under a different label. But it cannot make the case more fit for judicial action that appellants invoke the Fourteenth Amendment rather than Art. IV, § 4, where, in fact, the gist of their complaint is the same—unless it can be found that the Fourteenth Amendment speaks with greater particularity to their situation. *** [W]here judicial competence is wanting, it cannot be created by invoking one clause of the Constitution rather than another. ***

[Appellants] invoke the right to vote and to have their votes counted. But they are permitted to vote and their votes are counted. *** Their complaint is simply that the representatives are not sufficiently numerous or powerful—in short, that Tennessee has adopted a basis of representation with which they are dissatisfied. Talk of "debasement" or "dilution" is circular talk. One cannot speak of "debasement" or "dilution" of the value of a vote until there is first defined a standard of reference as to what a vote should be worth. What is actually asked of the Court in this case is to choose among competing bases of representation—ultimately, really, among competing theories of political philosophy—in order to establish an appropriate frame of government for the State of Tennessee and thereby for all the States of the Union. ***

Dissenting opinion of MR. JUSTICE HARLAN, whom MR. JUSTICE FRANKFURTER joins. [omitted]

Notes

1. **The Factors**. Generations of law students have memorized and mechanically applied the six factors listed in *Baker v. Carr*: The case itself concludes that only one factor—"judicially manageable standards"—was relevant because state officials were involved, not a coequal branch of the federal government. Because "manageable standards" issues exist in many cases, not just those labeled political questions, isn't this very different from CHIEF JUSTICE MARSHALL's notions of political questions? Consider the other *Baker* factors. Isn't *any* exercise of judicial power against a coequal branch in some sense a decision which "upsets a political decision already made," demonstrates a "lack of respect," and holds "the potentiality for embarrassment"? Finally, given what you know of the Constitution's text, the notion of a "textually demonstrable commitment of the issue to a coordinate political department" could potentially sweep out from judicial review all matters contained in Articles I and II. Is the real issue whether the text, structure, and history of the Constitution make a particular decision by a political branch of government final and nonreviewable?

2. **Reapportionment and Standing.** Do blacks in a majority-white electoral district have standing to challenge the parameters of the district in which they live? Do whites in a majority-black district have standing to challenge the parameters of the district in which they live? *See* Ely, *Standing to Challenge Pro-minority Gerrymanders*, 111 HARV. L. REV. 576 (1997) (yes; not because of "segregation" or any "expressive harm"; rather, "filler people" are an "identifiable class separated out for disadvantage.")

3. **Application of the Political Question Doctrine.** Since *Baker*, only two Supreme Court cases discussing the political question doctrine have concluded that there was a political question. *Gilligan v. Morgan*, 413 U.S. 1 (1973), dismissed a complaint that Kent State student protesters had been killed because of negligent training of the National Guard on the ground that military training is left by the Constitution entirely to the elected branches of government. *Nixon v. United States*, 506 U.S. 224 (1993), held that it was a political question whether the Senate had violated its Article I impeachment power by convicting a federal judge based on a fact-finding report by a Senate committee.

(a) Does *Gilligan* bar a claim of negligent actions by military personnel that cause civilian deaths?

(b) *Nixon* focused on the language concerning impeachment trials ("The Senate shall have the sole Power to try all Impeachments."). Would *Nixon* come out differently if the Senate had tossed a coin ("heads you're guilty, tails you're innocent")?

(c) Think about other candidates in Articles I and II for "overcoming the strong but rebuttable presumption of judicial review" established by *Marbury*. Consider Presidential nominations and conduct of foreign affairs, Congress' power to control the militia and to declare war, the President's veto of a bill, Senate action on appointments, and treaty-making and ratification.

(d) Assume a high government official impeached from office for adultery seeks reinstatement, asserting adultery is not a high crime or misdemeanor under Art II, § 4. Does the official's suit present a political question?

4.   **The Guarantee Clause Reconsidered.** What does the Guarantee Clause mean? Some scholars argue state constitutional referenda are unconstitutional on the theory that the clause calls for a "republican form of government" rather than direct democracy in the states. Try to formulate and counter this argument. Should *Luther* bar a suit challenging a state referendum on this ground? See JUSTICE O'CONNOR's opinion in *New York v. United States*, 505 U.S. 144, 184 (1992), in which she argues that the "limited holding" of *Luther* has undergone a "sweeping metamorphosis" into the notion that the Guarantee Clause is in all circumstances off limits to judicial interpretation. *See* Mayton, "Direct Democracy, Federalism, & the Guarantee Clause," 2 GREEN BAG 2d 269 (1999).

5.   **Justiciability Choices.** On August 2, 1990, Iraq invaded Kuwait. President Bush immediately sent troops to the Persian Gulf. The United States took other steps, including participation in a blockade of Iraq, which was approved by the United Nations Security Council. On November 8, President Bush increased the number of Persian Gulf troops to 230,000 to provide "an adequate offensive military option" against Iraq. Congress was not asked for and did not take action "to declare war" on Iraq. Several Members of Congress filed suit to enjoin the President from going to war without a Congressional declaration of war. Is this suit justiciable? *See Ange v. Bush*, 752 F.Supp. 509 (D.D.C. 1990) and *Dellums v. Bush*, 752 F.Supp. 1141 (D.D.C. 1990). Congress later authorized military action against Iraq, but never formally declared war.

VIETH v. JUBELIRER
541 U.S. 267 (2004)

JUSTICE SCALIA announced the judgment of the Court and delivered an opinion, in which THE CHIEF JUSTICE, JUSTICE O'CONNOR, and JUSTICE THOMAS join.

Plaintiffs-appellants *** challenge a map drawn by the Pennsylvania General Assembly establishing districts for the election of congressional Representatives, on the ground that the districting constitutes an unconstitutional political gerrymander.[7] In *Davis v. Bandemer,* 478 U.S. 109 (1986), this Court held that political gerrymandering claims are justiciable, but could not agree upon a standard to adjudicate them. ***

The facts, as alleged by the plaintiffs, are as follows. The population figures derived from the 2000 census showed that Pennsylvania was entitled to only 19 Representatives in Congress, a decrease in 2 from the Commonwealth's previous delegation. Pennsylvania's General Assembly took up the task of drawing a new districting map. At the time, the Republican Party controlled a majority of both state Houses and held the Governor's office. *** Plaintiffs, registered Democrats who vote in Pennsylvania, [seek] to enjoin implementation of Act 1 *** [on the ground that] the legislation ***

---

[7] The term "political gerrymander" has been defined as "[t]he practice of dividing a geographical area into electoral districts, often of highly irregular shape, to give one political Party an unfair advantage by diluting the opposition's voting strength."

constituted a political gerrymander, in violation of Article I and the Equal Protection Clause of the Fourteenth Amendment. With regard to the latter contention, the complaint alleged that the districts created by Act 1 were "meandering and irregular," and "ignor[ed] all traditional redistricting criteria, including the preservation of local government boundaries, solely for the sake of partisan advantage." *** Political gerrymanders are not new to the American scene. *** It is significant that the Framers provided a remedy for such practices in the Constitution. Article 1, § 4, while leaving in state legislatures the initial power to draw districts for federal elections, permitted Congress to "make or alter" those districts if it wished.

The power bestowed on Congress to regulate elections, and in particular to restrain the practice of political gerrymandering has not lain dormant. In the Apportionment Act of 1842, Congress provided that Representatives must be elected from single member districts "composed of contiguous territory." Congress again imposed these requirements in *** 1862, and in 1872 further required that districts "contai[n] as nearly as practicable an equal number of inhabitants". In the Apportionment Act of 1901, Congress imposed a compactness requirement. The requirements of contiguity, compactness, and equality of population were repeated in the 1911 apportionment legislation*** Today, only the single-member-district-requirement remains. ***4

In *Baker v. Carr,* 369 U.S. 186 (1962), we set forth six independent tests for the existence of a political question:

> [1] a textually demonstrable constitutional commitment of the issue to a coordinate political department; or [2] a lack of judicially discoverable and manageable standards for resolving it; or [3] the impossibility of deciding without an initial policy determination of a kind clearly for nonjudicial discretion; or [4] the impossibility of a court's undertaking independent resolution without expressing lack of the respect due coordinate branches of the government; or [5] an unusual need for unquestioning adherence to a political decision already made; or [6] the potentiality of embarrassment from multifarious pronouncements by various departments on one question.

These tests are probably listed in descending order of both importance and certainty. The second is at issue here, and there is no doubt of its validity. "The judicial Power" created by Article III, § 1 *** is the power to act in the manner traditional for English and American courts. One of the most obvious limitations imposed by that requirement is that judicial action must be governed by *standard,* by *rule.* Laws promulgated by the Legislative Branch can be inconsistent, illogical, and ad hoc; law pronounced by the courts must be principled, rational, and based upon reasoned distinctions.

---

4 The States, of course, have taken their own steps to prevent abusive districting practices. A number have adopted standards for redistricting, and measures designed to insulate the process from politics.

Over the dissent of three Justices, the Court held in *Davis v. Bandemer* that *** such cases *were* justiciable. The *** six-Justice majority could not discern what the judicially discernable standards might be. *** As the following discussion reveals, no judicially discernible and manageable standards for adjudicating political gerrymandering claims have emerged. Lacking them, we must conclude that political gerrymandering claims are nonjusticiable and that *Bandemer* was wrongly decided.

We begin our review of possible standards with that proposed by JUSTICE WHITE's plurality opinion in *Bandemer* because, as the narrowest ground for our decision in that case, it has been the standard employed by the lower courts. The plurality concluded that a political gerrymandering claim could succeed only where plaintiffs showed "both intentional discrimination against an identifiable political group and an actual discriminatory effect on that group." As to the intent element, the plurality acknowledged that "[a]s long as redistricting is done by a legislature, it should not be very difficult to prove that the likely political consequences of the reapportionment were intended." However, the effects prong was significantly harder to satisfy. Relief could not be based merely upon the fact that a group of persons banded together for political purposes had failed to achieve representation commensurate with its numbers, or that the apportionment scheme made its winning of elections more difficult. Rather, it would have to be shown that, taking into account a variety of historic factors and projected election results, the group had been "denied its chance to effectively influence the political process" as a whole, which could be achieved even without electing a candidate. ***

Appellants take a run at enunciating their own workable standard based on Article I, § 2, and the Equal Protection Clause. *** To satisfy appellants' intent standard, a plaintiff must "show that the mapmakers acted with a *predominant intent* to achieve partisan advantage," which can be shown "by direct evidence or by circumstantial evidence that other neutral and legitimate redistricting criteria were subordinated to the goal of achieving partisan advantage." *** [A]pplying a "predominant intent" test to *racial* gerrymandering is easier and less disruptive. The Constitution clearly contemplates districting by political entities, see Article I, § 4, and unsurprisingly that turns out to be root-and-branch a matter of politics. *** By contrast, the purpose of segregating voters on the basis of race is not a lawful one, and is much more rarely encountered. Determining whether the shape of a particular district is so substantially affected by the presence of a rare and constitutionally suspect motive as to invalidate it is quite different from determining whether it is so substantially affected by the excess of an ordinary and lawful motive as to invalidate it. Moreover, the fact that partisan districting is a lawful and common practice means that there is almost *always* room for an election-impeding lawsuit contending that partisan advantage was the predominant motivation; not so for claims of racial gerrymandering. Finally, courts might be justified in accepting a modest degree of unmanageability to enforce a constitutional command which (like the Fourteenth Amendment obligation to refrain from racial discrimination) is clear; whereas they are not justified in inferring a judicially enforceable constitutional obligation (the obligation not to apply *too much* partisanship in districting) which is both dubious and severely unmanageable. For these reasons, to the extent that our racial gerrymandering cases represent a model of discernible and manageable standards, they provide no comfort here.

The effects prong of appellants' proposal replaces the *Bandemer* plurality's vague test of "denied its chance to effectively influence the political process," with criteria that are seemingly more specific. The requisite effect is established when "(1) the plaintiffs show that the districts systematically 'pack' and 'crack' the rival party's voters,[7] *and* (2) the court's examination of the 'totality of circumstances' confirms that the map can thwart the plaintiffs' ability to translate a majority of votes into a majority of seats." This test is loosely based on our cases applying § 2 of the Voting Rights Act, to discrimination by race. But a person's politics is rarely as readily discernible and *never* as permanently discernible—as a person's race. Political affiliation is not an immutable characteristic, but may shift from one election to the next; and even within a given election, not all voters follow the party line. *** These facts make it impossible to assess the effects of partisan gerrymandering, to fashion a standard for evaluating a violation, and finally to craft a remedy. ***

Assuming, however, that the effects of partisan gerrymandering can be determined, appellants' test would invalidate the districting only when it prevents a majority of the electorate from electing a majority of representatives. Before considering whether this particular standard is judicially manageable we question whether it is judicially discernible in the sense of being relevant to some constitutional violation. Deny it as appellants may (and do), this standard rests upon the principle that groups (or at least political-action groups) have a right to proportional representation. But the Constitution contains no such principle. It guarantees equal protection of the law to persons, not equal representation in government to equivalently sized groups. It nowhere says that farmers or urban dwellers, Christian fundamentalists or Jews, Republicans or Democrats, must be accorded political strength proportionate to their numbers.[9]

Even if the standard were relevant, however, it is not judicially manageable. To begin with, how is a party's majority status to be established? *** [T]o think that majority status in statewide races establishes

---

[7] "Packing" refers to the practice of filling a district with a supermajority of a given group or party. "Cracking" involves the splitting of a group or party among several districts to deny that group or party a majority in any of those districts.

[9] The Constitution also does not share appellants' alarm at the asserted tendency of partisan gerrymandering to create more partisan representatives. Assuming that assertion to be true, the Constitution does not answer the question whether it is better for Democratic voters to have their State's congressional delegation include 10 wishy-washy Democrats (because Democratic voters are "effectively" distributed so as to constitute bare majorities in many districts), or 5 hardcore Democrats (because Democratic voters are tightly packed in a few districts). Choosing the former "dilutes" the vote of the radical Democrat; choosing the latter does the same to the moderate. Neither Article I nor the Equal Protection Clause takes sides in this dispute.

majority status for district contests, one would have to believe that the only factor determining voting behavior at all levels is political affiliation. That is assuredly not true. *** We turn next to consideration of the standards proposed by today's dissenters. *** [T]he mere fact that these four dissenters come up with three different standards *** goes a long way to establishing that there is no constitutionally discernible standard. *** We conclude that neither Article I, § 2, nor the Equal Protection Clause, nor (what appellants only fleetingly invoke) Article I, § 4, provides a judicially enforceable limit on the political considerations that the States and Congress may take into account when districting. ***

JUSTICE KENNEDY, concurring in the judgment.

*** Where it is alleged that a gerrymander had the purpose and effect of imposing burdens on a disfavored party and its voters, the First Amendment may offer a sounder and more prudential basis for intervention than does the Equal Protection Clause. The equal protection analysis *** works where race is involved since classifying by race is almost never permissible. *** The First Amendment analysis concentrates on whether the legislation burdens the representational rights of the complaining party's voters for reasons of ideology, beliefs, or political association. *** Finally, I do not understand the plurality to conclude that partisan gerrymandering that disfavors one party is permissible. *** The ordered working of our Republic, and of the democratic process, depends on a sense of decorum and restraint in all branches of government, and in the citizenry itself. Here, one has the sense that legislative restraint was abandoned. *** Still, the Court's own responsibilities require that we refrain from intervention in this instance. The failings of the many proposed standards for measuring the burden a gerrymander imposes on representational rights make our intervention improper. If workable standards do emerge to measure these burdens, however, courts should be prepared to order relief.

JUSTICE STEVENS, dissenting.

The central question presented by this case is whether political gerrymandering claims are justiciable. *** [A]s is apparent from our separate writings today, we share the view that, even if these appellants are not entitled to prevail, it would be contrary to precedent and profoundly unwise to foreclose all judicial review of similar claims that might be advanced in the future. *** The plurality reasons that the standards for evaluating racial gerrymanders are not workable in cases such as this because partisan considerations, unlike racial ones, are perfectly legitimate. Until today, however, there has not been the slightest intimation in any opinion written by any Member of this Court that a naked purpose to disadvantage a political minority would provide a rational basis for drawing a district line. *** Purely partisan motives are "rational" in a literal sense, but there must be a limiting principle. *** The rational basis for government decisions must satisfy a standard of legitimacy and neutrality; an acceptable rational basis can be neither purely personal nor purely partisan. *** [I]f the only possible explanation for a district's bizarre shape is a naked desire to increase partisan strength, then no rational basis exists to save the district from an equal protection challenge. ***

JUSTICE SOUTER, with whom JUSTICE GINSBURG joins, dissenting.

*** For a claim based on a specific single-member district, I would require the plaintiff to make out a *prima facie* case with five elements. First, the resident plaintiff would identify a cohesive political group to which he belonged*** Second, a plaintiff would need to show that the district of his residence paid little or no heed to those traditional districting principles whose disregard can be shown straightforwardly: contiguity, compactness, respect for political subdivisions, and conformity with geographic features like rivers and mountains. *** Third, the plaintiff would need to establish specific correlations between the district's deviations from traditional districting principles and the distribution of the population of his group. *** Fourth, a plaintiff would need to present the court with a hypothetical district including his residence, one in which the proportion of the plaintiff's group was lower (in a packing claim) or higher (in a cracking one) and which at the same time deviated less from traditional districting principles than the actual district. *** Fifth, and finally, the plaintiff would have to show that the defendants acted intentionally to manipulate the shape of the district in order to pack or crack his group. *** The harm from partisan gerrymandering is *** a species of vote dilution: the point of the gerrymander is to capture seats by manipulating district lines to diminish the weight of the other party's votes in elections. To devise a judicial remedy for that harm, however, it is not necessary to adopt a full-blown theory of fairness, furnishing a precise measure of harm caused by divergence from the ideal in each case. ***

JUSTICE BREYER, dissenting.

*** [There is] at least one circumstance where use of purely political boundary-drawing factors can amount to a serious, and remediable, abuse, namely the *unjustified* use of political factors to entrench a minority in power. By entrenchment I mean a situation in which a party that enjoys only minority support among the populace has nonetheless contrived to take, and hold, legislative power.   By *unjustified* entrenchment I mean that the minority's hold on power is purely the result of partisan manipulation and not other factors [such as] sheer happenstance, the existence of more than two major parties, the unique constitutional requirements of certain representational bodies such as the Senate, or reliance on traditional districting criteria. ***

Notes

1.   **Plurality, not Majority**. Does JUSTICE KENNEDY tell you where he might draw the line (and form a majority)? When might he find find a political gerrymandering case justiciable?

2.   **Different Tests**.   How strong is the argument that the case is nonjusticiable because the Justices differ on the test for finding a political gerrymandering violation?

3.   **Politics and Race**. What, if anything, distinguishes judicial resolution of racial gerrymandering and political gerrymandering? Is it ease of identification, permanence of classification, frequency of occurrence, need for resolution, or "normal political fights" versus "impermissible racial marginalization"?

4.   **Followup Issues**. The Elections Clause provides: "The Times, Places and Manner of holding Elections for Senators and Representatives, shall be prescribed in each State by the Legislature thereof ***." An Arizona initiative placed redistricting authority in an independent commission. Ruling on a suit by the Arizona legislature, the Court held that "the Legislature" in the Elections Clause includes lawmaking by referendum. *Arizona State Legislature v. AIRC*, 135 S. Ct. 2652 (2015). And in *Evenwel v. Abbott*, 136 S. Ct. 1120 (2016), the Court held that a state may draw legislative districts based on total population; *Baker's* "one person, one vote" requirement does not require "one citizen, one vote." The Court declined to say whether a "one citizen, one vote" rule would also satisfy *Baker*.

III

THE DISTRIBUTION OF NATIONAL POWERS

The powers delegated by this Constitution are appropriated to the departments to which they are respectively distributed: so that the Legislative Department shall never exercise powers vested in the Executive or Judicial, nor the Executive exercise powers vested in the Legislative or Judicial, nor the Judicial exercise the powers vested in the Legislative or Executive Departments.

> —James Madison
> Introducing the Bill of Rights,
> June 8, 1789

This chapter examines the relationship between the powers of Congress (set forth primarily in Article I) and the powers of the President (generally outlined in Article II). Political scientists often refer to the relationship between the political branches of the federal government in terms of "separation of powers" and "checks and balances." These words hide important differences in meaning and emphasis: "separation of powers" suggests noninvolvement of branches that do not possess a specified power, while "checks and balances" signifies division and dispersion of a as well as the separation specified power between the branches.

Purposes. The purposes behind separation of powers and checks and balances generally identified by courts and commentators are (1) prevention of tyranny and (2) efficiency of administration. Most authorities lay heavy emphasis on the former.

   • **Prevention of Tyranny**. Federalist No. 47 stressed that the "accumulation of all powers, legislative, executive, and judiciary, in the same hands *** [is] the very definition of tyranny." Such concentration, which had been common in England's administration of the North American colonies, was a substantial reason for the American Revolution. Separation of powers facilitates the rule of law since different entities make, administer, and interpret the law. During the early years of the United States, the greatest fear was of overreaching legislative power; in recent decades, the focus has often been on the growth of executive power. Only occasionally, as with the *Brown* and *Roe* decisions, does the public seem concerned about overreaching judicial power. The checks and balances in the Constitution have also been viewed as tools for limiting the size and power of the federal government, since a broad consensus is required to change the status quo.

• **Efficiency**. The three-part federal structure was originally seen as a move towards efficiency, a repudiation of the congressional hegemony created under the Articles of Confederation. The framers sought to establish a strong executive to conduct foreign and military affairs more effectively at the federal level. Ironically, a modern complaint is that separation of powers creates inefficiency in governing, and other democracies have adopted parliamentary systems for that reason.

Approaches. Academic commentary stresses two dominant modes of analyzing separation of powers issues under the Constitution.

• **Formalism** demands adherence by each branch to the powers granted that branch. Congress can make laws only if it follows specified procedures. It may not enforce the laws it makes. Conversely, the President enforces laws but may not make them.

• **Functionalism** commands fidelity to the purposes of the distribution of powers. For the functionalist, the Constitution's distribution of powers is violated only if one branch of the federal government aggrandizes its power at the expense of another branch.

In a nutshell, the formalist takes separation of powers as a command of the Constitution's text and structure; the functionalist views such separation as a component of fulfilling the Constitution's goals.

There are problems with this dichotomy, both theoretical and practical. Theoretically, there is a lack of clarity or definition to the formalist distinction between making, executing, and adjudicating; there is a lack of understanding in the functionalist approach as to precisely how separation of powers facilitates the goals discussed above. Moreover, it is not altogether clear that this dichotomy is coherent: the cases use it sparingly, and both schools share concerns over both separating functions and avoiding power imbalances among the three branches of the federal government. Practically, the dichotomy leads to different results, not merely at the margins, but with respect to core aspects of whether operations of the federal government are constitutional.

Federal agencies pose a classic example of diverging formalist and functionalist results. The Constitution does not mention, even generically, agencies like the FTC, FAA, EEOC, NLRB, and EPA. Created by Congress, these agencies generally are subject to varying levels of Presidential control, but they are not "departments" of the Executive Branch like the Department of Justice, the State Department, and the Department of Defense. Furthermore, these agencies frequently combine rulemaking (lawmaking), prosecution of violators (law execution), and claim resolution (adjudication).

A pure formalist would conclude that such agencies are unconstitutional: the Constitution does not permit a "fourth branch" of the federal government, much less a fourth branch that combines Article I, II, and III powers. The formalist responds to the complaint "This is how the federal government has done business for nearly a century," with the response that authorization of fourth branch agencies requires constitutional amendment. The functionalist, on the other hand, argues that these agencies are creative tools for delivering federal goods, services, and regulations that are not clearly prohibited by the Constitution. Some functionalists argue that the Constitution only mandates separation of powers at the apex of the federal government: the President, the Congress, and the Supreme Court. Separation of powers restrictions do not apply to such agencies, they argue: broad rules crafted by Congress as well as congressional oversight and budgetary controls, varying degrees of Presidential control over personnel, and judicial review, although restrained, provide ample controls over exercise of governmental power by such agencies.

The cases below demonstrate that the Supreme Court's decisions concerning the distribution of federal powers take place within a wide variety of contexts and contain differing mixes of formal and functional components. As you will see, the cases in this chapter include the President's authority to initiate policy, both domestic and foreign; the President's ability to "veto" parts of legislation; Presidential privileges, including confidentiality and immunity from suit; the roles of Congress and the President (and even the courts) in appointing and removing federal officials; "legislative veto" by Congress or parts of Congress.

The following case is widely perceived to be the Supreme Court's most important decision concerning the relationship between executive and legislative powers. Part B of this chapter examines executive powers, both in domestic and foreign affairs contexts, and explores executive privileges. Part C deals with the powers of Congress relative to the President. Finally, Part D considers separation of powers issues among the Congress, the President, and the Court in times of war. The powers of Congress as they relate to state power are reserved for later chapters.

A. THE FRAMEWORK

Harry Truman's popularity plummeted between the start of the Korean War and early 1952. At that time, Truman believed a union-management dispute between the steel mills and the Steelworkers' Union threatened the nation's ability to press forward in Korea. Truman, however, refused to use the injunctive powers granted to him under the Taft–Hartley Act (which Congress had passed over his veto) to halt a proposed strike, because he perceived that management intransigence, not union recalcitrance, caused the steel crisis. On April 9, 1952, he seized the steel mills and designated management to keep them operating for the United States. Management feared the President would try to solve the labor-management dispute by unilaterally raising wages.

President Truman was promptly sued by Youngstown Sheet & Tube Company, which argued that his action was unconstitutional. The Court's decision to grant certiorari was made only hours before a planned announcement that the parties, under the pressure of Truman's seizure of the mills, had reached a settlement. When the parties learned of the Court's action, bargaining ceased: management perceived that it had nothing to lose by awaiting a Supreme Court decision. After the Court's ruling (only two months after the seizure of the mills), the union struck for fifty-three days; neither a steel shortage nor any noticeable impact on the war effort materialized.

In light of this brief history, do you think the Court was too hasty? Was the Administration's position, described by the justices, excessive? Incidentally, Truman's memoirs show him to be unrepentant: "[We cannot] separate the economic facts from the problems of defense and security. [The President,] who is Commander in Chief and who represents the interests of all the people, must be able to act at all times to meet any sudden threat to the national security." 2 H.S. TRUMAN, MEMOIRS: YEARS OF TRIAL AND HOPE 478 (1956).

YOUNGSTOWN SHEET & TUBE CO. v. SAWYER
343 U.S. 579 (1952)

MR. JUSTICE BLACK delivered the opinion of the Court.

We are asked to decide whether the President was acting within his constitutional power when he issued an order directing the Secretary of Commerce to take possession of and operate most of the Nation's steel mills. The mill owners argue that the President's order amounts to lawmaking, a legislative function which the Constitution has expressly confided to the Congress and not to the President. The Government's position is that the order was made on findings of the President that his action was necessary to avert a national catastrophe which would inevitably result from a stoppage of steel production, and that in meeting this grave emergency the President was acting within the aggregate of his constitutional powers as the Nation's Chief Executive and the Commander in Chief of the Armed Forces of the United States. The issue emerges here from the following series of events:

In the latter part of 1951, a dispute arose between the steel companies and their employees over terms and conditions that should be included in new collective bargaining agreements. Long-continued conferences failed to resolve the dispute. On December 18, 1951, the employees' representative, United Steelworkers of America, C.I.O., gave notice of an intention to strike when the existing bargaining agreements expired on December 31. The Federal Mediation and Conciliation Service then intervened in an effort to get labor and management to agree. This failing, the President on December 22, 1951, referred the dispute to the Federal Wage Stabilization Board to investigate and make recommendations for fair and equitable terms of settlement. This Board's report resulted in no settlement. On April 4, 1952, the Union gave notice of a nation-wide strike called to begin at 12:01 a.m. April 9. The indispensability of steel as a component of substantially all weapons and other war materials led the President to believe that the proposed work stoppage would immediately jeopardize our national defense and that governmental seizure of the steel mills was necessary in order to assure the continued availability of steel. Reciting these considerations for his action, the President, a few hours before the strike was to begin, issued Executive Order 10340. The order directed the Secretary of Commerce to take possession of most of the steel mills and keep them running. The Secretary immediately issued his own possessory orders, calling upon the presidents of the various seized companies to serve as operational managers for the United States. *** The next morning the President sent a message to Congress reporting his action. Twelve days later he sent a second message. Congress has taken no action.

Obeying the Secretary's orders under protest, the companies brought proceedings against him in the District Court. Their complaints charged that the seizure was not authorized by an act of Congress or by any constitutional provisions. ***

III–1. "We're Waiting to Hear from the Principal" by Silvey Jackson Ray/The Kansas City Star, 1952.

The President's power, if any, to issue the order must stem either from an act of Congress or from the Constitution itself. There is no statute that expressly authorizes the President to take possession of property as he did here. Nor is there any act of Congress to which our attention has been directed from which such a power can fairly be implied. Indeed, we do not understand the Government to rely on statutory authorization for this seizure. There are two statutes which do authorize the President to take both personal and real property under certain conditions. However, the Government admits that these conditions were not met and that the President's order was not rooted in either of the statutes. The Government refers to the seizure provisions of one of these statutes (§ 201(b) of the

Defense Production Act) as "much too cumbersome, involved, and time-consuming for the crisis which was at hand."

Moreover, the use of the seizure technique to solve labor disputes in order to prevent work stoppages was not only unauthorized by any congressional enactment; prior to this controversy, Congress had refused to adopt that method of settling labor disputes. When the Taft–Hartley Act was under consideration in 1947, Congress rejected an amendment which would have authorized such governmental seizures in cases of emergency. ***

It is clear that if the President had authority to issue the order he did, it must be found in some provisions of the Constitution. And it is not claimed that express constitutional language grants this power to the President. The contention is that presidential power should be implied from the aggregate of his powers under the Constitution. Particular reliance is placed on provisions in Article II which say that "the executive Power shall be vested in a President *** "; that "he shall take Care that the Laws be faithfully executed"; and that he "shall be Commander in Chief of the Army and Navy of the United States."

The order cannot properly be sustained as an exercise of the President's military power as Commander in Chief of the Armed Forces. The Government attempts to do so by citing a number of cases upholding broad powers in military commanders engaged in day-to-day fighting in a theater of war. Such cases need not concern us here. Even though "theater of war" be an expanding concept, we cannot with faithfulness to our constitutional system hold that the Commander in Chief of the Armed Forces has the ultimate power as such to take possession of private property in order to keep labor disputes from stopping production. This is a job for the Nation's lawmakers, not for its military authorities.

Nor can the seizure order be sustained because of the several constitutional provisions that grant executive power to the President. In the framework of our Constitution, the President's power to see that the laws are faithfully executed refutes the idea that he is to be a lawmaker. The Constitution limits his functions in the lawmaking process to the recommending of laws he thinks wise and the vetoing of laws he thinks bad. And the Constitution is neither silent nor equivocal about who shall make laws which the President is to execute. The first section of the first article says that "All legislative Powers herein granted shall be vested in a Congress of the United States" ***

The President's order does not direct that a congressional policy be executed in a manner prescribed by Congress—it directs that a presidential policy be executed in a manner prescribed by the President. The preamble of the order itself, like that of many statutes, sets out reasons why the President believes certain policies should be adopted, proclaims these policies as rules of conduct to be followed, and again, like a statute, authorizes a government official to promulgate additional rules and regulations consistent with the policy proclaimed and needed to carry that policy into execution. The power of Congress to adopt such public policies as those proclaimed by the order is beyond question. It can authorize the taking of private property for public use. It can makes laws regulating the relationships between employers and employees, prescribing rules designed to settle labor disputes, and fixing wages and working conditions in certain fields of our economy. The Constitution did not subject this law-making power of Congress to presidential or military supervision or control.

It is said that other Presidents without congressional authority have taken possession of private business enterprises in order to settle labor disputes. But even if this be true, Congress has not thereby lost its exclusive constitutional authority to make laws necessary and proper to carry out the powers vested by the Constitution "in the Government of the United States, or in any Department or Officer thereof." *** [T]his seizure order cannot stand. ***

MR. JUSTICE JACKSON, concurring in the judgment and opinion of the court.

*** Just what our forefathers did envision, or would have envisioned had they foreseen modern conditions, must be divined from materials almost as enigmatic as the dreams Joseph was called upon to interpret for Pharaoh. A century and a half of partisan debate and scholarly speculation yields no net result but only supplies more or less apt quotations from respected sources on each side of any question. They largely cancel each other. ***

The actual art of governing under our Constitution does not and cannot conform to judicial definitions of the power of any of its branches based on isolated clauses or even single Articles torn from context. While the Constitution diffuses power the better to secure liberty, it also contemplates that practice will integrate the dispersed powers into a workable government. It enjoins upon its branches separateness but interdependence, autonomy but reciprocity. Presidential powers are not fixed but fluctuate, depending upon their disjunction or conjunction with those of Congress. We may well begin by a somewhat over-simplified grouping of practical situations in which a President may doubt, or others may challenge, his powers, and by distinguishing roughly the legal consequences of this factor of relativity.

1. When the President acts pursuant to an express or implied authorization of Congress, his authority is at its maximum, for it includes all that he possesses in his own right plus all that Congress can delegate. In these circumstances, and in these only, may he be said (for what it may be worth), to personify the federal sovereignty. If his act is held unconstitutional under these circumstances, it usually means that the Federal Government as an undivided whole lacks power. A seizure executed by the President pursuant to an Act of Congress would be supported by the strongest of presumptions and the widest latitude of judicial interpretation, and the burden of persuasion would rest heavily upon any who might attack it.

2. When the President acts in absence of either a congressional grant or denial of authority, he can only rely upon his own independent powers, but there is a zone of twilight in which he and Congress may have concurrent authority, or in which its distribution is uncertain. Therefore, congressional inertia, indifference or quiescence may sometimes, at least as a practical

matter, enable, if not invite, measures on independent presidential responsibility. In this area, any actual test of power is likely to depend on the imperatives of events and contemporary imponderables rather than on abstract theories of law.

3. When the President takes measures incompatible with the expressed or implied will of Congress, his power is at its lowest ebb, for then he can rely only upon his own constitutional powers minus any constitutional powers of Congress over the matter. Courts can sustain exclusive Presidential control in such a case only by disabling the Congress from acting upon the subject. Presidential claim to a power at once so conclusive and preclusive must be scrutinized with caution, for what is at stake is the equilibrium established by our constitutional system.

Into which of these classifications does this executive seizure of the steel industry fit? It is eliminated from the first by admission, for it is conceded that no congressional authorization exists for this seizure. *** Can it then be defended under flexible tests available to the second category? It seems clearly eliminated from that class because Congress has not left seizure of private property an open field but has covered it by three statutory policies inconsistent with this seizure. *** This leaves the current seizure to be justified only by the severe tests under the third grouping, where it can be supported only by any remainder of executive power after subtraction of such powers as Congress may have over the subject. In short, we can sustain the President only by holding that seizure of such strike-bound industries is within his domain and beyond control by Congress. ***

The Solicitor General seeks the power of seizure in three clauses of the Executive Article, the first reading, "The executive Power shall be vested in a President of the United States of America." Lest I be thought to exaggerate, I quote the interpretation which his brief puts upon it: "In our view, this clause constitutes a grant of all the executive powers of which the Government is capable." If that be true, it is difficult to see why the forefathers bothered to add several specific items, including some trifling ones. ***I cannot accept the view that this clause is a grant in bulk of all conceivable executive power but regard it as an allocation to the presidential office of the generic powers thereafter stated.

The clause on which the Government next relies is that "The President shall be Commander in Chief ***." But just what authority goes with the name has plagued Presidential advisers who would not waive or narrow it by nonassertion yet cannot say where it begins or ends. It undoubtedly puts the Nation's armed forces under Presidential command. Hence, this loose appellation is sometimes advanced as support for any Presidential action, internal or external, involving use of force, the idea being that it vests power to do anything, anywhere, that can be done with an army or navy.

That seems to be the logic of an argument tendered at our bar—that the President having, on his own responsibility, sent American troops abroad derives from that act "affirmative power" to seize the means of producing a supply of steel for them. *** Assuming that we are in a war de facto, whether it is or is not a war de jure, does that empower the Commander-in-Chief to seize industries he thinks necessary to supply our army? The Constitution expressly places in Congress power "to raise and support Armies" and "to provide and maintain a Navy." This certainly lays upon Congress primary responsibility for supplying the armed forces. Congress alone controls the raising of revenues and their appropriation and may determine in what manner and by what means they shall be spent for military and naval procurement. ***[T]he Constitution did not contemplate that the title Commander-in-Chief of the Army and Navy will constitute him also Commander-in-Chief of the country, its industries and its inhabitants. He has no monopoly of "war powers," whatever they are. ***

The third clause in which the Solicitor General finds seizure powers is that "he shall take Care that the Laws be faithfully executed ***." That authority must be matched against words of the Fifth Amendment that "No person shall be *** deprived of life, liberty, or property, without due process of law ***."

The Solicitor General lastly grounds support of the seizure upon nebulous, inherent powers never expressly granted but said to have accrued to the office from the customs and claims of preceding administrations. The plea is for a resulting power to deal with a crisis or an emergency according to the necessities of the case, the unarticulated assumption being that necessity knows no law. *** The claim of inherent and unrestricted presidential powers has long been a persuasive dialectical weapon in political controversy. ***

The appeal, however, that we declare the existence of inherent powers ex necessitate to meet an emergency asks us to do what many think would be wise, although it is something the forefathers omitted. They knew what emergencies were, knew the pressures they engender for authoritative action, knew, too, how they afford a ready pretext for usurpation. We may also suspect that they suspected that emergency powers would tend to kindle emergencies. Aside from suspension of the privilege of the writ of habeas corpus in time of rebellion or invasion, when the public safety may require it, they made no express provision for exercise of extraordinary authority because of a crisis. I do not think we rightfully may so amend their work, and, if we could, I am not convinced it would be wise to do so, although many modern nations have forthrightly recognized that war and economic crises may upset the normal balance between liberty and authority. Their experience with emergency powers may not be irrelevant to the argument here that we should say that the Executive, of his own volition, can invest himself with undefined emergency powers. ***

In view of the ease, expedition and safety with which Congress can grant and has granted large emergency powers, certainly ample to embrace this crisis, I am quite unimpressed with the argument that we should affirm possession of them without statute. Such power either has no beginning or it has no end. If it exists, it need submit to no legal restraint. I am not alarmed that it would plunge us straightway into dictatorship, but it is at least a step in that wrong direction.

As to whether there is imperative necessity for such powers, it is relevant to note the gap that exists between the President's paper powers and his real powers. The Constitution does not disclose the measure of the actual controls wielded by the modern presidential office. That instrument must be understood as an Eighteenth–Century sketch of a government hoped for, not as a blueprint of the Government that is. Vast accretions of federal power, eroded from that reserved by the States, have magnified the scope of presidential activity. Subtle shifts take place in the centers of real power that do not show on the face of the Constitution.

Executive power has the advantage of concentration in a single head in whose choice the whole Nation has a part, making him the focus of public hopes and expectations. ***

The executive action we have here originates in the individual will of the President and represents an exercise of authority without law. No one, perhaps not even the President, knows the limits of the power he may seek to exert in this instance and the parties affected cannot learn the limit of their rights. We do not know today what powers over labor or property would be claimed to flow from Government possession if we should legalize it, what rights to compensation would be claimed or recognized, or on what contingency it would end. With all its defects, delays and inconveniences, men have discovered no technique for long preserving free government except that the Executive be under the law, and that the law be made by parliamentary deliberations.

Such institutions may be destined to pass away. But it is the duty of the Court to be last, not first, to give them up.

MR. JUSTICE DOUGLAS, concurring.

[The] legislative nature of the action taken by the President seems to me to be clear. *** The President might seize and the Congress by subsequent action might ratify the seizure. But until and unless Congress acted, no condemnation would be lawful. The branch of government that has the power to pay compensation for a seizure is the only one able to authorize a seizure or make lawful one that the President had effected. That seems to me to be the necessary result of the condemnation provision in the Fifth Amendment. *** Today a kindly President uses the seizure power to effect a wage increase and to keep the steel furnaces in production. Yet tomorrow another President might use the same power to prevent a wage increase, to curb trade unionists, to regiment labor as oppressively as industry thinks it has been regimented by this seizure.

MR. JUSTICE FRANKFURTER, concurring.

*** The question before the Court comes in this setting. Congress has frequently—at least 16 times since 1916—specifically provided for executive seizure of production, transportation, communications, or storage facilities. In every case it has qualified this grant of power with limitations and safeguards. This body of enactments *** demonstrates that Congress deemed seizure so drastic a power as to require that it be carefully circumscribed whenever the President was vested with this extraordinary authority. ***In any event, nothing can be plainer than that Congress made a conscious choice of policy in a field full of perplexity and peculiarly within legislative responsibility for choice. In formulating legislation for dealing with industrial conflicts, Congress could not more clearly and emphatically have withheld authority than it did in [the Taft–Hartley Act of] 1947. ***It cannot be contended that the President would have had power to issue this order had Congress explicitly negated such authority in formal legislation. Congress has expressed its will to withhold this power from the President as though it had said so in so many words. ***

MR. CHIEF JUSTICE VINSON, with whom MR. JUSTICE REED and MR. JUSTICE MINTON join, dissenting.

*** Plaintiffs do not remotely suggest any basis for rejecting the President's finding that any stoppage of steel production would immediately place the Nation in peril. Under [Plaintiff's] view, the President is left powerless at the very moment when the need for action may be most pressing and when no one, other than he, is immediately capable of action. *** A review of executive action demonstrates that our Presidents have on many occasions exhibited the leadership contemplated by the Framers when they made the President Commander in Chief, and imposed upon him the trust to "take Care that the Laws be faithfully executed." With or without explicit statutory authorization, Presidents have at such times dealt with national emergencies by acting promptly and resolutely to enforce legislative programs, at least to save those programs until Congress could act. ***

The broad executive power granted by Article II to an officer on duty 365 days a year cannot, it is said, be invoked to avert disaster. Instead, the President must confine himself to sending a message to Congress recommending action. Under this messenger-boy concept of the Office, the President cannot even act to preserve legislative programs from destruction so that Congress will have something left to act upon. *** Faced with the duty of executing the defense programs which Congress had enacted and the disastrous effects that any stoppage in steel production would have on those programs, the President acted to preserve those programs by seizing the steel mills. There is no question that the possession was other than temporary in character and subject to congressional direction—either approving, disapproving or regulating the manner in which the mills were to be administered and returned to the owners. The President immediately informed Congress of his action and clearly stated his intention to abide by the legislative will. No basis for claims of arbitrary action, unlimited powers or dictatorial usurpation of congressional power appears from the facts of this case. ***

Notes

1. **Constitutional Theory.** There is no majority rationale in *Youngstown*. Each of the opinions adopts a very different methodology for assessing the constitutionality of the seizure of the mills.

(a) Under JUSTICE BLACK's formalist approach, does the President's power depend at all on whether Congress has or has not acted? Does JUSTICE DOUGLAS solve this problem?

(b) Under JUSTICE JACKSON's functionalist approach, how does the Court decide which zone fits any particular action of the President?

(c) What do you think of the uses of history by JUSTICE FRANKFURTER and the dissenters?

(d) Do you agree with the Court that, whatever the substantive outcome of the case, this is a proper decision for the Supreme Court to be making? Why or why not?

2.   **Fluctuating Powers Approach.**   JUSTICE JACKSON's concurrence breaks the actions of the President into three categories: (1) Where the President acts in accord with the express or implied authorization of Congress, (2) Where the President acts in the absence of any Congressional declaration on the matter, and (3) Where the President acts in direct contradiction to the express or implied will of Congress. The President's powers fluctuate with each category, being the greatest in the first category and the least in the third category. Although JUSTICE JACKSON wrote only for himself in his concurrence, his approach appears to be the one accepted by today's Court, *see Dames & Moore v. Regan*, infra. JUSTICE REHNQUIST, author of the Court's opinion in *Dames & Moore*, was JUSTICE JACKSON's clerk at the time *Youngstown* was decided.

B. EXECUTIVE POWERS, PRIVILEGES, AND IMMUNITY

1. EXECUTIVE POWERS

The *Youngstown* framework is theoretically applicable to the entire range of authority problems that might arise between the Executive and Legislative branches of the federal government. In fact, as the following cases demonstrate, other factors besides this framework may play important roles in the outcomes of specific separation of powers cases. One important consideration seems to be whether the context is domestic or foreign affairs.

a. Domestic Affairs

CLINTON v. CITY OF NEW YORK
524 U.S. 417 (1998)

JUSTICE STEVENS delivered the opinion of the Court.

The Line Item Veto Act (Act) was enacted in April 1996 and became effective on January 1, 1997. The following day, six Members of Congress who had voted against the Act brought suit in the District Court for the District of Columbia challenging its constitutionality. *** We determined, however, that the Members of Congress did not have standing to sue because they had not "alleged a sufficiently concrete injury to have established Article III standing," *Raines v. Byrd*. *** Less than two months after our decision in that case, the President exercised his authority to cancel one provision in the Balanced Budget Act of 1997, and two provisions in the Taxpayer Relief Act of 1997. Appellees, claiming that they had been injured by two of those cancellations, filed these cases *** We now hold that these appellees have standing *** and, reaching the merits, we agree that the cancellation procedures set forth in the Act violate the Presentment Clause, Art. I, § 7, cl. 2, of the Constitution.

We begin by reviewing the canceled items that are at issue in these cases.

Section 4722(c) of the Balanced Budget Act. Title XIX of the Social Security Act authorizes the Federal Government to transfer huge sums of money to the States to help finance medical care for the indigent. In 1991, Congress directed that those federal subsidies be reduced by the amount of certain taxes levied by the States on health care providers. In 1994, the Department of Health and Human Services (HHS) notified the State of New York that 15 of its taxes were covered by the 1991 Act, and that as of June 30, 1994, the statute therefore required New York to return $955 million to the United States. *** New York turned to Congress for relief. On August 5, 1997, Congress enacted a law that resolved the issue in New York's favor. Section 4722(c) of the Balanced Budget Act of 1997 identifies the disputed taxes and provides that they "are deemed to be permissible health care related taxes and in compliance with the requirements" of the relevant provisions of the 1991 statute.

On August 11, 1997, the President sent identical notices to the Senate and to the House of Representatives canceling "one item of new direct spending," specifying § 4722(c) as that item, and stating that he had determined that "this cancellation will reduce the Federal budget deficit" *** and that "[t]his preferential treatment would have increased Medicaid costs, would have treated New York differently from all other States, and would have established a costly precedent for other States to request comparable treatment."

Section 968 of the Taxpayer Relief Act. A person who realizes a profit from the sale of securities is generally subject to a capital gains tax. Under existing law, however, an ordinary business corporation can acquire a corporation, including a food processing or refining company, in a merger or stock-for-stock transaction in which no gain is recognized to the seller; the seller's tax payment, therefore, is deferred. If, however, the purchaser is a farmers' cooperative, the parties cannot structure such a transaction because the stock of the cooperative may be held only by its members; thus, a seller dealing with a farmers' cooperative cannot obtain the benefits of tax deferral.

In § 968 of the Taxpayer Relief Act of 1997, Congress amended § 1042 of the Internal Revenue Code to permit owners of certain food refiners and processors to defer the recognition of gain if they sell their stock to eligible farmers' cooperatives. The purpose of the amendment, as repeatedly explained by its sponsors, was "to facilitate the transfer of refiners and processors to farmers' cooperatives." ***

On the same date that he canceled the "item of new direct spending" involving New York's health care programs, the President also canceled this limited tax benefit. In his explanation of that action, the President endorsed the objective of encouraging "value-added farming through the purchase by farmers' cooperatives of refiners or processors of agricultural goods," but concluded that the provision lacked safeguards and also "failed to target its benefits to small-and-medium-size cooperatives." ***

The Line Item Veto Act gives the President the power to "cancel in whole" three types of provisions that have been signed into law: "(1) any dollar amount of discretionary budget authority; (2) any item of new direct spending; or (3) any limited tax benefit." It is undisputed that the New York case involves an "item of new direct spending" and that the Snake River case involves a "limited tax benefit" as those terms are defined in the Act. It is also undisputed that each of those provisions had been signed into law pursuant to Article I, § 7 of the Constitution before it was canceled.

The Act requires the President to adhere to precise procedures whenever he exercises his cancellation authority. In identifying items for cancellation he must consider the legislative history, the purposes, and other relevant information about the item. He must determine, with respect to each cancellation, that it will "(i) reduce the Federal budget deficit; (ii) not impair any essential Government functions; and (iii) not harm the national interest." Moreover, he must transmit a special message to Congress notifying it of each cancellation within five calendar days (excluding Sundays) after the enactment of the canceled provision. It is undisputed that the President meticulously followed these procedures in these cases.

A cancellation takes effect upon receipt by Congress of the special message from the President. If, however, a "disapproval bill" pertaining to a special message is enacted into law, the cancellations set forth in that message become "null and void." The Act sets forth a detailed expedited procedure for the consideration of a "disapproval bill," but no such bill was passed for either of the cancellations involved in these cases. ***

In both legal and practical effect, the President has amended two Acts of Congress by repealing a portion of each. *** There is no provision in the Constitution that authorizes the President to enact, to amend, or to repeal statutes. *** The President *** may initiate and influence legislative proposals. Moreover, after a bill has passed both Houses of Congress, but "before it become[s] a Law," it must be presented to the President. If he approves it, "he shall sign it, but if not he shall return it, with his Objections to that House in which it shall have originated, who shall enter the Objections at large on their Journal, and proceed to reconsider it." Art. I, § 7, cl. 2. His "return" of a bill, which is usually described as a "veto," is subject to being overridden by a two-thirds vote in each House.

There are important differences between the President's "return" of a bill pursuant to Article I, § 7, and the exercise of the President's cancellation authority pursuant to the Line Item Veto Act. The constitutional return takes place before the bill becomes law; the statutory cancellation occurs after the bill becomes law. The constitutional return is of the entire bill; the statutory cancellation is of only a part. Although the Constitution expressly authorizes the President to play a role in the process of enacting statutes, it is silent on the subject of unilateral Presidential action that either repeals or amends parts of duly enacted statutes.

There are powerful reasons for construing constitutional silence on this profoundly important issue as equivalent to an express prohibition. *** Familiar historical materials provide abundant support for the conclusion that the power to enact statutes may only "be exercised in accord with a single, finely wrought and exhaustively considered, procedure." *Chadha.* Our first President understood the text of the Presentment Clause as requiring that he either "approve all the parts of a Bill, or reject it in toto." What has emerged in these cases from the President's exercise of his statutory cancellation powers, however, are truncated versions of two bills that passed both Houses of Congress. They are not the product of the "finely wrought" procedure that the Framers designed.

At oral argument, the Government suggested that the cancellations at issue in these cases do not effect a "repeal" of the canceled items because under the special "lockbox" provisions of the Act,[31] a canceled item "retain[s] real, legal budgetary effect" insofar as it prevents Congress and the President from spending the savings that result from the cancellation. The text of the Act expressly provides, however, that a cancellation prevents a direct spending or tax benefit provision "from having legal force or effect." That a canceled item may have "real, legal budgetary effect" as a result of the lockbox procedure does not change the fact that by canceling the items at issue in these cases, the President made them entirely inoperative as to appellees. Section 968 of the Taxpayer Relief Act no longer provides a tax benefit, and § 4722(c) of the Balanced Budget Act of 1997 no longer relieves New York of its contingent liability. Such significant changes do not lose their character simply because the canceled provisions may have some continuing financial effect on the Government. The cancellation of one section of a statute may be the functional equivalent of a partial repeal even if a portion of the section is not canceled.

The Government advances two related arguments to support its position that despite the unambiguous provisions of the Act, cancellations do not amend or repeal properly enacted statutes in violation of the Presentment Clause. First, relying primarily on *Field v. Clark*, 143 U.S. 649, the Government contends that the cancellations were merely exercises of discretionary authority granted to the President by the Balanced Budget Act and the Taxpayer Relief Act read in light of the previously enacted Line Item Veto Act. Second, the Government submits that the substance of the authority to cancel tax and spending items "is, in practical effect, no more and no less than the power to 'decline to spend' specified sums of money, or to 'decline to implement' specified tax measures." Neither argument is persuasive.

In *Field v. Clark*, the Court upheld the constitutionality of the Tariff Act of 1890. That statute contained a "free list" of almost 300 specific articles that

---

[31] The lockbox procedure ensures that savings resulting from cancellations are used to reduce the deficit, rather than to offset deficit increases arising from other laws. ***

were exempted from import duties "unless otherwise specially provided for in this act." Section 3 was a special provision that directed the President to suspend that exemption for sugar, molasses, coffee, tea, and hides "whenever, and so often" as he should be satisfied that any country producing and exporting those products imposed duties on the agricultural products of the United States that he deemed to be "reciprocally unequal and unreasonable ***." The section then specified the duties to be imposed on those products during any such suspension. The Court provided this explanation for its conclusion that § 3 had not delegated legislative power to the President:

> Nothing involving the expediency or the just operation of such legislation was left to the determination of the President. *** [W]hen he ascertained the fact that duties and exactions, reciprocally unequal and unreasonable, were imposed upon the agricultural or other products of the United States by a country producing and exporting sugar, molasses, coffee, tea or hides, it became his duty to issue a proclamation declaring the suspension, as to that country, which Congress had determined should occur. He had no discretion in the premises except in respect to the duration of the suspension so ordered. But that related only to the enforcement of the policy established by Congress. As the suspension was absolutely required when the President ascertained the existence of a particular fact, it cannot be said that in ascertaining that fact and in issuing his proclamation, in obedience to the legislative will, he exercised the function of making laws. ***

This passage identifies three critical differences between the power to suspend the exemption from import duties and the power to cancel portions of a duly enacted statute. First, the exercise of the suspension power was contingent upon a condition that did not exist when the Tariff Act was passed: the imposition of "reciprocally unequal and unreasonable" import duties by other countries. In contrast, the exercise of the cancellation power within five days after the enactment of the Balanced Budget and Tax Reform Acts necessarily was based on the same conditions that Congress evaluated when it passed those statutes. Second, under the Tariff Act, when the President determined that the contingency had arisen, he had a duty to suspend; in contrast, while it is true that the President was required by the Act to make three determinations before he canceled a provision, those determinations did not qualify his discretion to cancel or not to cancel. Finally, whenever the President suspended an exemption under the Tariff Act, he was executing the policy that Congress had embodied in the statute. In contrast, whenever the President cancels an item of new direct spending or a limited tax benefit he is rejecting the policy judgment made by Congress and relying on his own policy judgment. Thus, the conclusion in *Field v. Clark* that the suspensions mandated by the Tariff Act were not exercises of legislative power does not undermine our opinion that cancellations pursuant to the Line Item Veto Act are the functional equivalent of partial repeals of Acts of Congress that fail to satisfy Article I, § 7. ***

The statutes [cited by the government] all relate to foreign trade, and this Court has recognized that in the foreign affairs arena, the President has "a degree of discretion and freedom from statutory restriction which would not be admissible were domestic affairs alone involved." *United States v. Curtiss–Wright Export Corp.*, 299 U.S. 304, 320 (1936). *** The Line Item Veto Act authorizes the President himself to effect the repeal of laws, for his own policy reasons, without observing the procedures set out in Article I, § 7. The fact that Congress intended such a result is of no moment. *** Congress cannot alter the procedures set out in Article I, § 7, without amending the Constitution.

Neither are we persuaded by the Government's contention that the President's authority to cancel new direct spending and tax benefit items is no greater than his traditional authority to decline to spend appropriated funds. The Government has reviewed in some detail the series of statutes in which Congress has given the Executive broad discretion over the expenditure of appropriated funds. *** The critical difference between this statute and all of its predecessors, however, is that unlike any of them, this Act gives the President the unilateral power to change the text of duly enacted statutes. None of the Act's predecessors could even arguably have been construed to authorize such a change. ***

[T]he profound importance of these cases makes it appropriate to emphasize three points. First, we express no opinion about the wisdom of the procedures authorized by the Line Item Veto Act. *** Second, although appellees challenge the validity of the Act on alternative grounds, the only issue we address concerns the "finely wrought" procedure commanded by the Constitution. *Chadha.* *** [W]e find it unnecessary to consider the District Court's alternative holding that the Act "impermissibly disrupts the balance of powers among the three branches of government." Third, our decision rests on the narrow ground that the procedures authorized by the Line Item Veto Act are not authorized by the Constitution. The Balanced Budget Act of 1997 is a 500–page document that became "Public Law 105–33" after three procedural steps were taken: (1) a bill containing its exact text was approved by a majority of the Members of the House of Representatives; (2) the Senate approved precisely the same text; and (3) that text was signed into law by the President. The Constitution explicitly requires that each of those three steps be taken before a bill may "become a law." If one paragraph of that text had been omitted at any one of those three stages, Public Law 105–33 would not have been validly enacted. If the Line Item Veto Act were valid, it would authorize the President to create a different law—one whose text was not voted on by either House of Congress or presented to the President for signature. Something that might be known as "Public Law 105–33 as modified by the President" may or may not be desirable, but it is surely not a document that may "become a law" pursuant to the procedures designed by the Framers of Article I, § 7, of the Constitution. ***

JUSTICE KENNEDY, concurring.

*** I write to respond to my colleague JUSTICE BREYER, who observes that the statute does not threaten the liberties of individual citizens, a point on which I disagree. *** To say the political branches have a somewhat free hand to reallocate their own authority would seem to require acceptance of two premises: first, that the public good demands it, and second, that liberty is not at risk. The former premise is inadmissible. The Constitution's structure requires a stability which transcends the convenience of the moment. The latter premise, too, is flawed. Liberty is always at stake when one or more of the branches seek to transgress the separation of powers. *** The law establishes a new mechanism which gives the President the sole ability to hurt a group that is a visible target, in order to disfavor the group or to extract further concessions from Congress. The law is the functional equivalent of a line item veto and enhances the President's powers beyond what the Framers would have endorsed.

It is no answer, of course, to say that Congress surrendered its authority by its own hand; nor does it suffice to point out that a new statute, signed by the President or enacted over his veto, could restore to Congress the power it now seeks to relinquish. That a congressional cession of power is voluntary does not make it innocuous. *** Separation of powers helps to ensure the ability of each branch to be vigorous in asserting its proper authority. *** By increasing the power of the President beyond what the Framers envisioned, the statute compromises the political liberty of our citizens, liberty which the separation of powers seeks to secure. The Constitution is not bereft of controls over improvident spending. Federalism is one safeguard, for political accountability is easier to enforce within the States than nationwide. The other principal mechanism, of course, is control of the political branches by an informed and responsible electorate.

JUSTICE SCALIA, with whom JUSTICE O'CONNOR joins, and with whom JUSTICE BREYER joins *** concurring in part and dissenting in part.

*** In my view, the Snake River appellees lack standing to challenge the President's cancellation of the "limited tax benefit," *** [T]he New York appellees have standing to challenge the President's cancellation of an "item of new direct spending"; but *** I find the President's cancellation of spending items to be entirely in accord with the Constitution. ***

The Presentment Clause *** no more categorically prohibits the Executive reduction of congressional dispositions in the course of implementing statutes that authorize such reduction, than it categorically prohibits the Executive augmentation of congressional dispositions in the course of implementing statutes that authorize such augmentation— generally known as substantive rulemaking. *** [L]imits are established, however, not by some categorical prohibition of Art. I, § 7, which our cases conclusively disprove, but by what has come to be known as the doctrine of unconstitutional delegation of legislative authority: When authorized Executive reduction or augmentation is allowed to go too far, it usurps the nondelegable function of Congress and violates the separation of powers.

It is this doctrine, and not the Presentment Clause, that was discussed in the *Field* opinion, and it is this doctrine, and not the Presentment Clause, that is the issue presented by the statute before us here. That is why the

Court is correct to distinguish prior authorizations of Executive cancellation, such as the one involved in *Field*, on the ground that they were contingent upon an Executive finding of fact, and on the ground that they related to the field of foreign affairs, an area where the President has a special "degree of discretion and freedom." These distinctions have nothing to do with whether the details of Art. I, § 7 have been complied with, but everything to do with whether the authorizations went too far by transferring to the Executive a degree of political, lawmaking power that our traditions demand be retained by the Legislative Branch.

I turn, then, to the crux of the matter: whether Congress's authorizing the President to cancel an item of spending gives him a power that our history and traditions show must reside exclusively in the Legislative Branch. *** Insofar as the degree of political, "lawmaking" power conferred upon the Executive is concerned, there is not a dime's worth of difference between Congress's authorizing the President to cancel a spending item, and Congress's authorizing money to be spent on a particular item at the President's discretion. And the latter has been done since the Founding of the Nation. From 1789–1791, the First Congress made lump-sum appropriations for the entire Government—"sum[s] not exceeding" specified amounts for broad purposes. From a very early date Congress also made permissive individual appropriations, leaving the decision whether to spend the money to the President's unfettered discretion. *** The constitutionality of such appropriations has never seriously been questioned. *** Certain Presidents have claimed Executive authority to withhold appropriated funds even absent an express conferral of discretion to do so. In 1876, for example, President Grant reported to Congress that he would not spend money appropriated for certain harbor and river improvements *** President Franklin D. Roosevelt impounded funds appropriated for a flood control reservoir and levee in Oklahoma. President Truman ordered the impoundment of hundreds of millions of dollars that had been appropriated for military aircraft. President Nixon, the Mahatma Ghandi of all impounders, asserted at a press conference in 1973 that his "constitutional right" to impound appropriated funds was "absolutely clear." ***

The short of the matter is this: Had the Line Item Veto Act authorized the President to "decline to spend" any item of spending contained in the Balanced Budget Act of 1997, there is not the slightest doubt that authorization would have been constitutional. What the Line Item Veto Act does instead—authorizing the President to "cancel" an item of spending—is technically different. But the technical difference does not relate to the technicalities of the Presentment Clause, which have been fully complied with; and the doctrine of unconstitutional delegation, which is at issue here, is preeminently not a doctrine of technicalities. The title of the Line Item Veto Act, which was perhaps designed to simplify for public comprehension, or perhaps merely to comply with the terms of a campaign pledge, has succeeded in faking out the Supreme Court. The President's action it authorizes in fact is not a line-item veto and thus does not offend Art. I, § 7; and insofar as the substance of that action is concerned, it is no different from what Congress has permitted the President to do since the formation of the Union. ***

Notes

1.   **Congress' Options.** Is there any way Congress can respond effectively to this decision? (a) Consider the option of a constitutional amendment. Other than the difficulty of passage, how might you word such an amendment if you favored giving the President line-item veto authority? (b) Is there any way to accomplish the same goal through legislation? Consider the feasibility and desirability of Congress defining "to cancel" as meaning "to decline to spend or enforce." (c) Could Congress overcome the Court's decision through legislation establishing more explicit standards the President could use in declining to spend or in canceling a tax benefit? (d) Why not simply separately enroll each provision of an omnibus spending or tax bill?

2.   **Significance of the Line Item Veto Power.** Given how minor the provisions were that President Clinton "vetoed," are you skeptical that anything significant would ever be accomplished through a "line item veto"? Some political analysts think the real significance of the President's power might be that he would never have to use it, except in symbolic situations.

3.   **Problem.** On March 8, 1995, President Clinton issued Executive Order No. 12,954, which declared that it was the policy of the United States in procuring goods and services to cease contracting with companies that permanently replaced lawfully striking workers. In *Chamber of Commerce v. Reich*, 74 F.3d 1322 (D.C. Cir. 1996), the Circuit Court of Appeals held that this order was preempted by the National Labor Relations Act, which, nearly fifty years earlier, had been interpreted by the Supreme Court as allowing companies permanently to replace lawful strikers.   Most government contractor companies are also subject to the National Labor Relations Act. The preemption rationale of the Court of Appeals was developed by analogy from the doctrine of the preemptive supremacy of federal law over state law, which you will study in Chapter V. You are an advisor to President Clinton. Should he appeal this loss to the Supreme Court?

4.   **Presidential Orders.** Was President Lincoln's Emancipation Proclamation legislative? Are all Executive Orders legislative?

b. Foreign Affairs

Is the separation of powers between the President and Congress different when "foreign affairs" are involved? What is the Court's role in such cases? The next three cases help to answer these questions.

UNITED STATES v. CURTISS–WRIGHT
299 U.S. 304 (1936)

MR. JUSTICE SUTHERLAND delivered the opinion of the Court.

On January 27, 1936, an indictment was returned in the court below, the first count of which charges that appellees, *** conspired to sell in the United States certain arms of war, namely, fifteen machine guns, to Bolivia, a country then engaged in armed conflict in the Chaco, in violation of the Joint

Resolution of Congress approved May 28, 1934, and the provisions of a proclamation issued on the same day by the President of the United States pursuant to authority conferred by section 1 of the resolution. *** The Joint Resolution [states]:

Resolved by the Senate and House of Representatives of the United States of America in Congress assembled, That if the President finds that the prohibition of the sale of arms and munitions of war in the United States to those countries now engaged in armed conflict in the Chaco may contribute to the reestablishment of peace between those countries, and *** he makes proclamation to that effect, it shall be unlawful to sell *** any arms or munitions of war in any place in the United States to the countries now engaged in that armed conflict, or to any person, company, or association acting in the interest of either country, until otherwise ordered by the President or by Congress. ***

Whether, if the Joint Resolution had related solely to internal affairs, it would be open to the challenge that it constituted an unlawful delegation of legislative power to the Executive, we find it unnecessary to determine. The whole aim of the resolution is to affect a situation entirely external to the United States, and falling within the category of foreign affairs. The determination which we are called to make, therefore, is whether the Joint Resolution, as applied to that situation, is vulnerable to attack under the rule that forbids a delegation of the lawmaking power. In other words, assuming (but not deciding) that the challenged delegation, if it were confined to internal affairs, would be invalid, may it nevertheless be sustained on the ground that its exclusive aim is to afford a remedy for a hurtful condition within foreign territory?

It will contribute to the elucidation of the question if we first consider the differences between the powers of the federal government in respect of foreign or external affairs and those in respect of domestic or internal affairs. That there are differences between them, and that these differences are fundamental, may not be doubted.

The two classes of powers are different, both in respect of their origin and their nature. The broad statement that the federal government can exercise no powers except those specifically enumerated in the Constitution, and such implied powers as are necessary and proper to carry into effect the enumerated powers, is categorically true only in respect of our internal affairs. In that field, the primary purpose of the Constitution was to carve from the general mass of legislative powers then possessed by the states such portions as it was thought desirable to vest in the federal government, leaving those not included in the enumeration still in the states. That this doctrine applies only to powers which the states had is self-evident. And since the states severally never possessed international powers, such powers could not have been carved from the mass of state powers but obviously were transmitted to the United States from some other source. ***

As a result of the separation from Great Britain by the colonies, acting as a unit, the powers of external sovereignty passed from the Crown not to the colonies severally, but to the colonies in their collective and corporate capacity as the United States of America. *** Rulers come and go; governments end and forms of government change; but sovereignty survives. A political society cannot endure without a supreme will somewhere. Sovereignty is never held in suspense. When, therefore, the external sovereignty of Great Britain in respect of the colonies ceased, it immediately passed to the Union. *** It results that the investment of the federal government with the powers of external sovereignty did not depend upon the affirmative grants of the Constitution. The powers to declare and wage war, to conclude peace, to make treaties, to maintain diplomatic relations with other sovereignties, if they had never been mentioned in the Constitution, would have vested in the federal government as necessary concomitants of nationality. *** In this vast external realm, with its important, complicated, delicate and manifold problems, the President alone has the power to speak or listen as a representative of the nation. He makes treaties with the advice and consent of the Senate; but he alone negotiates. Into the field of negotiation the Senate cannot intrude; and Congress itself is powerless to invade it. As Marshall said in his great argument of March 7, 1800, in the House of Representatives, 'The President is the sole organ of the nation in its external relations, and its sole representative with foreign nations.' ***

[W]e are here dealing not alone with an authority vested in the President by an exertion of legislative power, but with such an authority plus the very delicate, plenary and exclusive power of the President as the sole organ of the federal government in the field of international relations—a power which does not require as a basis for its exercise an act of Congress, but which, of course, like every other governmental power, must be exercised in subordination to the applicable provisions of the Constitution. It is quite apparent that if, in the maintenance of our international relations, embarrassment—perhaps serious embarrassment—is to be avoided and success for our aims achieved, congressional legislation which is to be made effective through negotiation and inquiry within the international field must often accord to the President a degree of discretion and freedom from statutory restriction which would not be admissible were domestic affairs alone involved. Moreover, he, not Congress, has the better opportunity of knowing the conditions which prevail in foreign countries, and especially is this true in time of war. He has his confidential sources of information. He has his agents in the form of diplomatic, consular and other officials. Secrecy in respect of information gathered by them may be highly necessary, and the premature disclosure of it productive of harmful results. ***

MR. JUSTICE MCREYNOLDS does not agree. *** MR. JUSTICE STONE took no part in the consideration or decision of this case.

Notes

1. **Implied Presidential Powers.** Could this case have been decided without reference to the Constitution? Doesn't the Court's starting point seem diametrically opposite that of *Youngstown* and other cases involving constitutional allocation of domestic affairs powers? Were the broad pronouncements about Presidential power necessary to the decision? As an

interesting aside, Justice Department lawyers representing the President have been known to refer to the case informally as "*Curtiss-Wright*, so I'm right."

2.   **Preconstitutional Powers.**   Why does the Court say the President is "the sole organ of the federal government in the field of international relations"?   Is the text clear on this?   Is historical practice clear?   Are you comfortable with the Court's assessment of preconstitutional powers?

3.   **Functionalism.**   What preconceptions about the type of foreign policies the United States should have are implicit in the Court's analysis?

DAMES & MOORE v. REGAN
453 U.S. 654 (1981)

JUSTICE REHNQUIST delivered the opinion of the Court.

*** On November 4, 1979, the American Embassy in Tehran was seized and our diplomatic personnel were captured and held hostage. In response to that crisis, President Carter, acting pursuant to the International Emergency Economic Powers Act (hereinafter IEEPA), declared a national emergency on November 14, 1979, and blocked the removal or transfer of "all property and interests in property of the Government of Iran, its instrumentalities and controlled entities and the Central Bank of Iran which are or become subject to the jurisdiction of the United States. *** " On November 15, 1979, the Treasury Department's Office of Foreign Assets Control issued a regulation providing that "[u]nless licensed or authorized *** any attachment, judgment, decree, lien, execution, garnishment, or other judicial process is null and void with respect to any property in which on or since [November 14, 1979,] there existed an interest of Iran." The regulations also made clear that any licenses or authorizations granted could be "amended, modified, or revoked at any time." ***

On December 19, 1979, petitioner Dames & Moore filed suit *** against the Government of Iran, the Atomic Energy Organization of Iran, and a number of Iranian banks. In its complaint, petitioner alleged that its wholly owned subsidiary, Dames & Moore International, S. R. L., was a party to a written contract with the Atomic Energy Organization, and that the subsidiary's entire interest in the contract had been assigned to petitioner. Under the contract, the subsidiary was to conduct site studies for a proposed nuclear power plant in Iran. As provided in the terms of the contract, the Atomic Energy Organization terminated the agreement for its own convenience on June 30, 1979. Petitioner contended, however, that it was owed $3,436,694.30 plus interest for services performed under the contract prior to the date of termination. The District Court issued orders of attachment *** and the property of certain Iranian banks was then attached to secure any judgment that might be entered against them.

On January 20, 1981, the Americans held hostage were released by Iran pursuant to an [Executive] Agreement entered into the day before ***. The Agreement stated that "[i]t is the purpose of [the United States and Iran] *** to terminate all litigation as between the Government of each party and the nationals of the other, and to bring about the settlement and termination of all such claims through binding arbitration." In furtherance of this goal, the

Agreement called for the establishment of an Iran–United States Claims Tribunal which would arbitrate any claims not settled within six months. Awards of the Claims Tribunal are to be "final and binding" and "enforceable *** in the courts of any nation in accordance with its laws." Under the Agreement, the United States is obligated "to terminate all legal proceedings in United States courts involving claims of United States persons and institutions against Iran and its state enterprises, to nullify all attachments and judgments obtained therein, to prohibit all further litigation based on such claims, and to bring about the termination of such claims through binding arbitration." In addition, the United States must "act to bring about the transfer" by July 19, 1981, of all Iranian assets held in this country by American banks. One billion dollars of these assets will be deposited in a security account in the Bank of England, to the account of the Algerian Central Bank, and used to satisfy awards rendered against Iran by the Claims Tribunal.

On January 19, 1981, President Carter issued a series of Executive Orders implementing the terms of the agreement. *** On February 24, 1981, President Reagan issued an Executive Order in which he "ratified" the January 19th Executive Orders. Moreover, he "suspended" all "claims which may be presented to the *** Tribunal" and provided that such claims "shall have no legal effect in any action now pending in any court of the United States." The suspension of any particular claim terminates if the Claims Tribunal determines that it has no jurisdiction over that claim; claims are discharged for all purposes when the Claims Tribunal either awards some recovery and that amount is paid, or determines that no recovery is due. ***

The parties and the lower courts, confronted with the instant questions, have all agreed that much relevant analysis is contained in *Youngstown Sheet & Tube Co. v. Sawyer*, 343 U.S. 579 (1952). *** Although we have in the past found and do today find JUSTICE JACKSON's classification of executive actions into three general categories analytically useful, we should be mindful of JUSTICE HOLMES' admonition *** that "[t]he great ordinances of the Constitution do not establish and divide fields of black and white." JUSTICE JACKSON himself recognized that his three categories represented "a somewhat over-simplified grouping," and it is doubtless the case that executive action in any particular instance falls, not neatly in one of three pigeonholes, but rather at some point along a spectrum running from explicit congressional authorization to explicit congressional prohibition. This is particularly true as respects cases such as the one before us, involving responses to international crises the nature of which Congress can hardly have been expected to anticipate in any detail. ***

The Government *** principally relied on [this statutory language]: " *** [T]he President may, under such regulations as he may prescribe, by means of instructions, licenses, or otherwise, investigate, regulate, direct and compel, nullify, void, prevent or prohibit, any acquisition, holding, withholding, use, transfer, withdrawal, transportation, importation or exportation of, or dealing in, or exercising any right, power, or privilege with respect to, or transactions involving, any property in which any foreign country or a national thereof has any interest; by any person, or with respect to any property, subject to the jurisdiction of the United States."

The Government contends that the acts of "nullifying" the attachments and ordering the "transfer" of the frozen assets are specifically authorized by the plain language of the above statute. *** Because the President's action in nullifying the attachments and ordering the transfer of the assets was taken pursuant to specific congressional authorization, it is "supported by the strongest of presumptions and the widest latitude of judicial interpretation, and the burden of persuasion would rest heavily upon any who might attack it." *Youngstown* (JACKSON, J., concurring). Under the circumstances of this case, we cannot say that petitioner has sustained that heavy burden. A contrary ruling would mean that the Federal Government as a whole lacked the power exercised by the President, and that we are not prepared to say.

Although we have concluded that the IEEPA constitutes specific congressional authorization to the President to nullify the attachments and order the transfer of Iranian assets, there remains the question of the President's authority to suspend claims pending in American courts. Such claims have, of course, an existence apart from the attachments which accompanied them. In terminating these claims through Executive Order No. 12294 the President purported to act under authority of both the IEEPA and 22 U.S.C. § 1732, the so-called "Hostage Act." *** [We conclude] that neither the IEEPA nor the Hostage Act constitutes specific authorization of the President's action suspending claims[.] [H]owever, [this] is not to say that these statutory provisions are entirely irrelevant to the question of the validity of the President's action. We think both statutes highly relevant in the looser sense of indicating congressional acceptance of a broad scope for executive action in circumstances such as those presented in this case. *** [T]he IEEPA delegates broad authority to the President to act in times of national emergency with respect to property of a foreign country. The Hostage Act similarly indicates congressional willingness that the President have broad discretion when responding to the hostile acts of foreign sovereigns. ***

[W]e cannot ignore the general tenor of Congress' legislation in this area in trying to determine whether the President is acting alone or at least with the acceptance of Congress. As we have noted, Congress cannot anticipate and legislate with regard to every possible action the President may find it necessary to take or every possible situation in which he might act. Such failure of Congress specifically to delegate authority does not, "especially *** in the areas of foreign policy and national security," imply "congressional disapproval" of action taken by the Executive. On the contrary, the enactment of legislation closely related to the question of the President's authority in a particular case which evinces legislative intent to accord the President broad discretion may be considered to "invite" "measures on independent presidential responsibility," *Youngstown* (JACKSON, J., concurring). At least this is so where there is no contrary indication of legislative intent and when, as here, there is a history of congressional acquiescence in conduct of the sort engaged in by the President. It is to that history which we now turn.

Not infrequently in affairs between nations, outstanding claims by nationals of one country against the government of another country are "sources of friction" between the two sovereigns. To resolve these difficulties, nations have often entered into agreements settling the claims of their respective nationals. *** Crucial to our decision today is the conclusion that Congress has implicitly approved the practice of claim settlement by executive agreement. This is best demonstrated by Congress' enactment of the International Claims Settlement Act of 1949[.] *** Over the years Congress has frequently amended the International Claims Settlement Act to provide for particular problems arising out of settlement agreements, thus demonstrating Congress' continuing acceptance of the President's claim settlement authority. ***

In light of all of the foregoing—the inferences to be drawn from the character of the legislation Congress has enacted in the area, such as the IEEPA and the Hostage Act, and from the history of acquiescence in executive claims settlement—we conclude that the President was authorized to suspend pending claims. As JUSTICE FRANKFURTER pointed out in *Youngstown*, 343 U.S., at 610–611, "a systematic, unbroken, executive practice, long pursued to the knowledge of the Congress and never before questioned *** may be treated as a gloss on 'Executive Power' vested in the President by s 1 of Art. II." Past practice does not, by itself, create power, but "long-continued practice, known to and acquiesced in by Congress, would raise a presumption that the [action] had been [taken] in pursuance of its consent. *** " Such practice is present here and such a presumption is also appropriate. In light of the fact that Congress may be considered to have consented to the President's action in suspending claims, we cannot say that action exceeded the President's powers.

Our conclusion is buttressed by the fact that the means chosen by the President to settle the claims of American nationals provided an alternative forum, the Claims Tribunal, which is capable of providing meaningful relief. *** Just as importantly, Congress has not disapproved of the action taken here. Though Congress has held hearings on the Iranian Agreement itself, Congress has not enacted legislation, or even passed a resolution, indicating its displeasure with the Agreement. Quite the contrary, the relevant Senate Committee has stated that the establishment of the Tribunal is "of vital importance to the United States." We are thus clearly not confronted with a situation in which Congress has in some way resisted the exercise of Presidential authority.

Finally, we re-emphasize the narrowness of our decision. We do not decide that the President possesses plenary power to settle claims, even as against foreign governmental entities. *** But where, as here, the settlement of claims has been determined to be a necessary incident to the resolution of a major foreign policy dispute between our country and another, and where, as here, we can conclude that Congress acquiesced in the President's action, we are not prepared to say that the President lacks the power to settle such claims. ***

Notes

1.   **Political Necessity.**   The Court's decision has been criticized as pure politics (a "political decision politically made") and for its shoddy methodology ("crisis atmosphere *** Court should have demanded more specific legislative approval for the president's far-reaching measures").   Do you agree?

2.   **Comparisons.**

(a) Does *Dames & Moore* reject JUSTICE BLACK's methodology in *Youngstown*?   Is there anything in the Constitution's text that gives the President inherent foreign affairs (but not domestic affairs) powers?

(b) Do you agree that *Dames & Moore*, "[By] finding legislative 'approval' when Congress had given none, *** inverted the *Steel Seizure* holding—which construed statutory nonapproval of the president's act to mean legislative disapproval—[and] condoned legislative inactivity at a time that demanded interbranch dialogue and bipartisan consensus"? Harold Koh, THE NATIONAL SECURITY CONSTITUTION: SHARING POWER AFTER THE IRAN–CONTRA AFFAIR, 139–140 (1990).

(c) Why did the Court characterize President Truman's seizure of the steel mills as "domestic" and President Carter's Executive Agreement establishing the Iran–United States Claims Tribunal as "foreign affairs"?   Is the line between the two capable of principled judicial delineation?

(d) How did President Carter manage to avoid going to the Senate for its "Advice and Consent" under Article II, § 2, cl. 2 concerning the Claims Tribunal Agreement?

MEDELLÍN v. TEXAS
552 U.S. 491 (2008)

CHIEF JUSTICE ROBERTS delivered the opinion of the Court.

The International Court of Justice (ICJ), *** established pursuant to the United Nations Charter to adjudicate disputes between member states *** [in the *Avena* decision] held that, based on violations of the Vienna Convention, 51 named Mexican nationals were entitled to review and reconsideration of their state-court convictions and sentences in the United States. This was so regardless of any ***failure to comply with generally applicable state rules governing challenges to criminal convictions.

In *Sanchez-Llamas v. Oregon,* 548 U.S. 331 (2006) *** we held that, contrary to the ICJ's determination, the Vienna Convention did not preclude the application of state default rules. After [the ICJ] decision, President George W. Bush determined *** that the United States would "discharge its international obligations" *** "by having State courts give effect to the decision." *** Relying on the ICJ's decision and the President's Memorandum, Medellín filed an application for a writ of habeas corpus in state court. *** We granted certiorari to decide two questions. *First,* is the ICJ's judgment *** directly enforceable as domestic law in a state court in the

United States? [This portion of the opinion concluded that: "Nothing in the text, background, negotiating and drafting history, or practice among signatory nations suggests that the President or Senate intended the improbable result of giving the judgments of an international tribunal a higher status than that enjoyed by many of our most fundamental constitutional protections."] *Second,* does the President's Memorandum independently require the States to provide review and reconsideration of the claims of the 51 Mexican nationals named in *Avena* without regard to state procedural default rules? *****

In this case, the President seeks to vindicate United States interests in ensuring the reciprocal observance of the Vienna Convention, protecting relations with foreign governments, and demonstrating commitment to the role of international law. These interests are plainly compelling ***** [but] do not allow us to set aside first principles. The President's authority to act, as with the exercise of any governmental power, "must stem either from an act of Congress or from the Constitution itself." *Youngstown; Dames & Moore v. Regan.* ***** The United States maintains that ***** because the relevant treaties "create an obligation to comply with *Avena,*" they "*implicitly* give the President authority to implement that treaty-based obligation." As a result, the President's Memorandum is well grounded in the first category of the *Youngstown* framework.

We disagree. The President has an array of political and diplomatic means available to enforce international obligations, but unilaterally converting a non-self-executing treaty into a self-executing one is not among them. The responsibility for transforming an international obligation arising from a non-self-executing treaty into domestic law falls to Congress. ***** The requirement that Congress, rather than the President, implement a non-self-executing treaty derives from the text of the Constitution, which divides the treaty-making power between the President and the Senate. The Constitution vests the President with the authority to "make" a treaty. Art. II, § 2. If the Executive determines that a treaty should have domestic effect of its own force, that determination may be implemented "in mak[ing]" the treaty, by ensuring that it contains language plainly providing for domestic enforceability. ***** Once a treaty is ratified without provisions clearly according it domestic effect, however, whether the treaty will ever have such effect is governed by the fundamental constitutional principle that "'[t]he power to make the necessary laws is in Congress; the power to execute in the President.'" ***** [T]he terms of a non-self-executing treaty can become domestic law only in the same way as any other law-through passage of legislation by both Houses of Congress, combined with either the President's signature or a congressional override of a Presidential veto. Indeed, "the President's power to see that the laws are faithfully executed refutes the idea that he is to be a lawmaker." *Youngstown.*

A non-self-executing treaty, by definition, is one that was ratified with the understanding that it is not to have domestic effect of its own force. ***** We therefore conclude, given the absence of congressional legislation, that the non-self-executing treaties at issue here did not "express[ly] or implied[ly]" vest the President with the unilateral authority to make them self-executing. Accordingly, the President's Memorandum does not fall within the first category of the *Youngstown* framework.

Indeed, *** the non-self-executing character of the relevant treaties not only refutes the notion that the ratifying parties vested the President with the authority to unilaterally make treaty obligations binding on domestic courts, but also implicitly prohibits him from doing so. When the President asserts the power to "enforce" a non-self-executing treaty by unilaterally creating domestic law, he acts in conflict with the implicit understanding of the ratifying Senate. His assertion of authority, insofar as it is based on the pertinent non-self-executing treaties, is therefore within Justice Jackson's third category, not the first or even the second. ***

The United States nonetheless maintains that the President's Memorandum should be given effect as domestic law because "this case involves a valid Presidential action in the context of Congressional 'acquiescence'." *** [E]ven if we were persuaded that congressional acquiescence could support the President's asserted authority to create domestic law pursuant to a non-self-executing treaty, such acquiescence does not exist here. ***

We [now] turn to the United States' claim that-independent of the United States' treaty obligations-the Memorandum is a valid exercise of the President's foreign affairs authority to resolve claims disputes with foreign nations. The United States relies on a series of cases in which this Court has upheld the authority of the President to settle foreign claims pursuant to an executive agreement. In these cases this Court has explained that, if pervasive enough, a history of congressional acquiescence can be treated as a "gloss on 'Executive Power' vested in the President by § 1 of Art. II." *Dames & Moore.*

This argument is of a different nature than the one rejected above. Rather than relying on the United States' treaty obligations, the President relies on an independent source of authority in ordering Texas to put aside its procedural bar to successive habeas petitions. Nevertheless, we find that our claims-settlement cases do not support the authority that the President asserts in this case.

The claims-settlement cases involve a narrow set of circumstances: the making of executive agreements to settle civil claims between American citizens and foreign governments or foreign nationals. They are based on the view that "a systematic, unbroken, executive practice, long pursued to the knowledge of the Congress and never before questioned," can "raise a presumption that the [action] had been [taken] in pursuance of its consent." *Dames & Moore.* *** The President's Memorandum is not supported by a "particularly longstanding practice" of congressional acquiescence, but rather is what the United States itself has described as "unprecedented action," Indeed, the Government has not identified a single instance in which the President has attempted (or Congress has acquiesced in) a Presidential directive issued to state courts, much less one that reaches deep into the heart of the State's police powers and compels state courts to reopen final criminal judgments and set aside neutrally applicable state laws. The Executive's narrow and strictly limited authority to settle international claims disputes pursuant to an executive agreement cannot stretch so far as to support the current Presidential Memorandum.

Medellín argues that the President's Memorandum is a valid exercise of his "Take Care" power. *** This authority allows the President to execute the laws, not make them. *** [T]he *Avena* judgment is not domestic law; accordingly, the President cannot rely on his Take Care powers here. ***

JUSTICE STEVENS, concurring in the judgment.

*** When the honor of the Nation is balanced against the modest cost of compliance, Texas would do well to recognize that more is at stake than whether judgments of the ICJ, and the principled admonitions of the President of the United States, trump state procedural rules in the absence of implementing legislation. ***

JUSTICE BREYER, with whom JUSTICE SOUTER and JUSTICE GINSBURG join, dissenting.

*** The President here seeks to implement treaty provisions in which the United States agrees that the ICJ judgment is binding with respect to the *Avena* parties. Consequently, his actions draw upon his constitutional authority in the area of foreign affairs. In this case, his exercise of that power falls within that middle range of Presidential authority where Congress has neither specifically authorized nor specifically forbidden the Presidential action in question. See *Youngstown Sheet & Tube Co. v. Sawyer* (Jackson, J., concurring). At the same time, if the President were to have the authority he asserts here, it would require setting aside a state procedural law.

It is difficult to believe that in the exercise of his Article II powers pursuant to a ratified treaty, the President can *never* take action that would result in setting aside state law. Suppose that the President believes it necessary that he implement a treaty provision requiring a prisoner exchange involving someone in state custody in order to avoid a proven military threat. Or suppose he believes it necessary to secure a foreign consul's treaty-based rights to move freely or to contact an arrested foreign national. Does the Constitution require the President in each and every such instance to obtain a special statute authorizing his action? On the other hand, the Constitution must impose significant restrictions upon the President's ability, by invoking Article II treaty-implementation authority, to circumvent ordinary legislative processes and to pre-empt state law as he does so.

Previously this Court has said little about this question. It has held that the President has a fair amount of authority to make and to implement executive agreements, at least in respect to international claims settlement, and that this authority can require contrary state law to be set aside. It has made clear that principles of foreign sovereign immunity trump state law and that the Executive, operating without explicit legislative authority, can assert those principles in state court. It has also made clear that the Executive has inherent power to bring a lawsuit "to carry out treaty obligations." But it has reserved judgment as to "the scope of the President's power to preempt state law pursuant to authority delegated by ... a ratified treaty"-a fact that helps to explain the majority's inability to find support in precedent for its own conclusions.

Given the Court's comparative lack of expertise in foreign affairs; given the importance of the Nation's foreign relations; given the difficulty of finding the proper constitutional balance among state and federal, executive and legislative, powers in such matters; and given the likely future importance of this Court's efforts to do so, I would very much hesitate before concluding that the Constitution implicitly sets forth broad prohibitions (or permissions) in this area. *** The majority's two holdings *** unnecessarily complicate the President's foreign affairs task *** The holdings also encumber Congress with a task (postratification legislation) that, in respect to many decisions of international tribunals, it may not want and which it may find difficult to execute. *** These institutional considerations make it difficult to reconcile the majority's holdings with the workable Constitution that the Founders envisaged. ***

Notes

1. **Presidential Power and Justiciability.** Judicial intervention to prevent the President from enforcing the treaty may arguably lead to "potentiality of embarrassment for multifarious announcements by various departments on one question." Does this make it a political question under *Baker v. Carr*?

2. **Federalism and International Obligations**. One reason the Constitution replaced the Articles of Confederation was to allow the federal government supremacy in negotiating and enforcing treaty obligations with other nations. Does it make sense to allow individual states to take actions inconsistent with international obligations? What other precept of the Constitution do the Justices rely on to uphold Texas' right to try these defendants?

ZIVOTOFSKY v. KERRY
135 S. Ct. 2076 (2015)

JUSTICE KENNEDY delivered the opinion of the Court.

*** Jerusalem's political standing has long been, and remains, one of the most sensitive issues in American foreign policy. *** [I]n contrast to a consistent policy of formal recognition of Israel, neither President Truman nor any later United States President has issued an official statement or declaration acknowledging any country's sovereignty over Jerusalem. Instead, the Executive Branch has maintained that "'the status of Jerusalem should be decided not unilaterally but in consultation with all concerned.'" *** The President's position on Jerusalem is reflected in State Department policy regarding passports and consular reports of birth abroad. Understanding that passports will be construed as reflections of American policy, the State Department's Foreign Affairs Manual instructs its employees, in general, to record the place of birth on a passport as the "country [having] present sovereignty over the actual area of birth." ***

Because the United States does not recognize any country as having sovereignty over Jerusalem, the FAM instructs employees to record the place of birth for citizens born there as "Jerusalem."

In 2002, Congress passed *** the Foreign Relations Authorization Act. Section 214 of the Act is titled "United States Policy with Respect to Jerusalem as the Capital of Israel." The subsection that lies at the heart of this case, §214(d), addresses passports. That subsection seeks to override the FAM by allowing citizens born in Jerusalem to list their place of birth as "Israel." When he signed the Act into law, President George W. Bush issued a statement declaring his position that §214 would, "if construed as mandatory rather than advisory, impermissibly interfere with the President's constitutional authority to formulate the position of the United States, speak for the Nation in international affairs, and determine the terms on which recognition is given to foreign states." ***

In December 2002, Zivotofsky's mother visited the American Embassy in Tel Aviv to request both a passport and a consular report of birth abroad for her son. *** She asked that his place of birth be listed as "'Jerusalem, Israel.'" *** The Embassy clerks explained that, pursuant to State Department policy, the passport would list only "Jerusalem." *** Zivotofsky's parents *** brought suit on his behalf. *** [The lower courts] dismissed his case, reasoning that it presented a nonjusticiable political question *** This Court *** vacated the judgment, [held the question is not reserved for the political branches,] and remanded the case. *** On remand the Court of Appeals held the statute unconstitutional. ***

In considering claims of Presidential power this Court refers to Justice Jackson's familiar tripartite framework from *Youngstown Sheet & Tube Co.* v. *Sawyer* (concurring opinion). *** [W]hen "the President takes measures incompatible with the expressed or implied will of Congress . . . he can rely only upon his own constitutional powers minus any constitutional powers of Congress over the matter." *** To succeed in this third category, the President's asserted power must be both "exclusive" and "conclusive" on the issue. *** [T]he Secretary contends that §214(d) infringes on the President's exclusive recognition power by "requiring the President to contradict his recognition position regarding Jerusalem in official communications with foreign sovereigns." *** In so doing the Secretary acknowledges the President's power is "at its lowest ebb." *Youngstown.* *** To determine whether the President possesses the exclusive power of recognition the Court examines the Constitution's text and structure, as well as precedent and history bearing on the question.

Recognition is a "formal acknowledgement" that a particular "entity possesses the qualifications for statehood" or "that a particular regime is the effective government of a state." *** Recognition is often effected by an express "written or oral declaration" *** It may also be implied— for example, by concluding a bilateral treaty or by sending or receiving diplomatic agents. *** Legal consequences follow formal recognition. *** Recognition at international law is a precondition of regular diplomatic relations. *** Recognition is thus "useful, even necessary," to the existence of a state.

Despite the importance of the recognition power in foreign relations, the Constitution does not use the term "recognition," either in Article II or elsewhere. The Secretary asserts that the President exercises the recognition power based on the Reception Clause, which directs that the President "shall receive Ambassadors and other public Ministers." Art. II, §3. As Zivotofsky notes, the Reception Clause received little attention at the Constitutional Convention. *** At the time of the founding, however, prominent international scholars suggested that receiving an ambassador was tantamount to recognizing the sovereignty of the sending state. *** It is a logical and proper inference, then, that a Clause directing the President alone to receive ambassadors would be understood to acknowledge his power to recognize other nations. This in fact occurred early in the Nation's history when President Washington recognized the French Revolutionary Government by receiving its ambassador. *** The inference that the President exercises the recognition power is further supported by his additional Article II powers. It is for the President, "by and with the Advice and Consent of the Senate," to "make Treaties, provided two thirds of the Senators present concur." Art. II, §2, cl. 2. In addition, "he shall nominate, and by and with the Advice and Consent of the Senate, shall appoint Ambassadors" as well as "other public Ministers and Consuls."

As a matter of constitutional structure, these additional powers give the President control over recognition decisions. *** Congress, by contrast, has no constitutional power that would enable it to initiate diplomatic relations with a foreign nation. ***

The text and structure of the Constitution grant the President the power to recognize foreign nations and governments. The question then becomes whether that power is exclusive. The various ways in which the President may unilaterally effect recognition—and the lack of any similar power vested in Congress—suggest that it is. So, too, do functional considerations. *** Recognition is a topic on which the Nation must "'speak . . . with one voice.'" *American Ins. Assn.* v. *Garamendi*, 539 U. S. 396, 424 (2003). That voice must be the President's. Between the two political branches, only the Executive has the characteristic of unity at all times. And with unity comes the ability to exercise, to a greater degree, "[d]ecision, activity, secrecy, and dispatch." The Federalist No. 70. The President is capable, in ways Congress is not, of engaging [in diplomacy] that may lead to a decision on recognition [and] [in taking] unequivocal action necessary to recognize other states at international law. *** These qualities explain why the Framers listed the traditional avenues of recognition *** as among the President's Article II powers.

As described in more detail below, the President since the founding has exercised this unilateral power to recognize new states—and the Court has endorsed the practice. *** It remains true, of course, that many decisions affecting foreign relations require congressional action. Congress may "regulate Commerce with foreign Nations," [and, among other things,] "establish an uniform Rule of Naturalization." *** Under basic separation-of-powers principles, it is for the Congress to enact the laws, including "all Laws which shall be necessary and proper for carrying into Execution" the powers of the Federal Government. In foreign affairs, as in the domestic realm, the Constitution "enjoins upon its branches separateness but interdependence, autonomy but reciprocity." *Youngstown*. Although the President alone effects the formal act of recognition, *** [f]ormal recognition may seem a hollow act *** [without] action by the Senate or the whole Congress. In practice, then, the President's recognition determination is just one part of a political process that may require Congress to make laws. *** The formal act of recognition is an executive power that Congress may not qualify.

A clear rule that the formal power to recognize a foreign government subsists in the President therefore serves a necessary purpose in diplomatic relations. All this, of course, underscores that Congress has an important role in other aspects of foreign policy, and the President may be bound by any number of laws Congress enacts. In this way ambition counters ambition, ensuring that the democratic will of the people is observed and respected in foreign affairs as in the domestic realm. See The Federalist No. 51.

No single precedent resolves the question whether the President has exclusive recognition authority and, if so, how far that power extends. *** In the end, however, a fair reading of the cases shows that the President's role in the recognition process is both central and exclusive. *** The Secretary now urges the Court to define the executive power over foreign relations in even broader terms. He contends that under the Court's precedent [in *Curtiss-Wright*] the President has "exclusive authority to conduct diplomatic relations," along with "the bulk of foreign-affairs powers." *** This Court declines to acknowledge that unbounded power. ***

In a world that is ever more compressed and interdependent, it is essential the congressional role in foreign affairs be understood and respected. For it is Congress that makes laws, and in countless ways its laws will and should shape the Nation's course. The Executive is not free from the ordinary controls and checks of Congress merely because foreign affairs are at issue. See, *e.g.*, *Medellín* v. *Texas*; *Youngstown*; *** cf. *Dames & Moore* v. *Regan*. It is not for the President alone to determine the whole content of the Nation's foreign policy.

That said, judicial precedent and historical practice teach that it is for the President alone to make the specific decision of what foreign power he will recognize as legitimate ***. Congress cannot require him to contradict his own statement regarding a determination of formal recognition. *** In separation-of-powers cases this Court has often "put significant weight upon historical practice." *Noel Canning*. Here, history is not all on one side, but on balance it provides strong support for the conclusion that the recognition power is the President's alone. ***

From the first Administration forward, the President has claimed unilateral authority to recognize foreign sovereigns. For the most part, Congress has acquiesced in the Executive's exercise of the recognition power. *** This history confirms the Court's conclusion in the instant case that the power to recognize or decline to recognize a foreign state and its territorial bounds resides in the President alone. *** [Indeed], over the last 100 years, there has been scarcely any debate over the President's power to recognize foreign states.

As the power to recognize foreign states resides in the President alone, the question becomes whether §214(d) infringes on the Executive's consistent decision to withhold recognition with respect to Jerusalem. *** Section 214(d) requires *** the President, through the Secretary, to identify citizens born in Jerusalem who so request as being born in Israel. *** In this way, §214(d) "directly contradicts" the "carefully calibrated and longstanding Executive branch policy of neutrality toward Jerusalem." *** If the power over recognition is to mean anything, it must mean that the President not only makes the initial, formal recognition determination but also that he may maintain that determination in his and his agent's statements. *** [I]f Congress could alter the President's statements on matters of recognition or force him to contradict them, Congress in effect would exercise the recognition power. *** Although the statement required by §214(d) would not itself constitute a formal act of recognition, it is a mandate that the Executive contradict his prior recognition determination in an official document issued by the Secretary of State. *** As a result, it is unconstitutional.

The flaw in §214(d) is further underscored by the undoubted fact that the purpose of the statute was to infringe on the recognition power—a power the Court now holds is the sole prerogative of the President. *** From the face of §214, from the legislative history, and from its reception, it is clear that Congress wanted to express its displeasure with the President's policy by, among other things, commanding the Executive to contradict his own, earlier stated position on Jerusalem. This Congress may not do.

It is true, as Zivotofsky notes, that Congress has substantial authority over passports. *** The Court does not question the power of Congress to enact passport legislation of wide scope. *** The problem with §214(d), however, lies in how Congress exercised its authority over passports. It was an improper act for Congress to "aggrandiz[e] its power at the expense of another branch" by requiring the President to contradict an earlier recognition determination in an official document issued by the Executive Branch. *** To allow Congress to control the President's communication in the context of a formal recognition determination is to allow Congress to exercise that exclusive power itself. As a result, the statute is unconstitutional.

In holding §214(d) invalid the Court does not question the substantial powers of Congress over foreign affairs in general or passports in particular. This case is confined solely to the exclusive power of the President to control recognition determinations, including formal statements by the Executive Branch acknowledging the legitimacy of a state or government and its territorial bounds. Congress cannot command the President to contradict an earlier recognition determination in the issuance of passports. ***

JUSTICE BREYER, concurring [on the ground that the case poses a political question].

JUSTICE THOMAS, concurring in the judgment in part and dissenting in part.

Our Constitution allocates the powers of the Federal Government over foreign affairs in two ways. First, it expressly identifies certain foreign affairs powers and vests them in particular branches, either individually or jointly. Second, it vests the residual foreign affairs powers of the Federal Government—*i.e.,* those not specifically enumerated in the Constitution—in the President by way of Article II's Vesting Clause.

Rather than adhere to the Constitution's division of powers, the Court relies on a distortion of the President's recognition power to hold both of these parts of §214(d) unconstitutional. Because I cannot join this faulty analysis, I concur only in the portion of the Court's judgment holding §214(d) unconstitutional as applied to passports. *** The President is not constitutionally compelled to implement §214(d) as it applies to passports because passport regulation falls squarely within his residual foreign affairs power and Zivotofsky has identified no source of congressional power to require the President to list Israel as the place of birth for a citizen born in Jerusalem on that citizen's passport. *** [The] legislation is constitutionally permissible only insofar as it is promulgated pursuant to one of Congress' enumerated powers. I must therefore address whether Congress had constitutional authority to enact §214(d)'s regulation of passports.

The Constitution contains no Passport Clause, nor does it explicitly vest Congress with "plenary authority over passports." *** [T]he Necessary and Proper Clause gives Congress no authority here. *** The constitutional allocation of powers "does not depend on the views of individual Presidents, nor on whether the encroached upon branch approves the encroachment." *Free Enterprise Fund* v. *Public Company Accounting Oversight Bd.*, 561 U. S. 477, 497 (2010).

Because the President has residual foreign affairs authority to regulate passports and because there appears to be no congressional power that justifies §214(d)'s application to passports, Zivotofsky's challenge to the Executive's designation of his place of birth on his passport must fail. *** [N]o act of recognition is implicated here. ***

CHIEF JUSTICE ROBERTS, with whom JUSTICE ALITO joins, dissenting.

Today's decision is a first: Never before has this Court accepted a President's direct defiance of an Act of Congress in the field of foreign affairs. *** The expansive language in *Curtiss-Wright* casting the President as the "sole organ" of the Nation in foreign affairs certainly has attraction for members of the Executive Branch. *** But our precedents have never accepted such a sweeping understanding of executive power. *** Just a few Terms ago, this Court rejected the President's argument that a broad foreign relations power allowed him to override a state court decision that contradicted U. S. international law obligations. *Medellín.* *** [T]he majority strains to reach the question based on the mere possibility that observers overseas might misperceive the significance of the birthplace designation at issue in this case. And in the process, the Court takes the perilous step—for the first time in our history—of allowing the President to defy an Act of Congress in the field of foreign affairs.

JUSTICE SCALIA, with whom THE CHIEF JUSTICE and JUSTICE ALITO join, dissenting.

*** The Constitution contemplates that the political branches will make policy about the territorial claims of foreign nations the same way they make policy about other international matters: The President will exercise his powers on the basis of his views, Congress its powers on the basis of its views. That is just what has happened here. *** In the end, the Court's decision does not rest on text or history or precedent. It instead comes down to "functional considerations"—principally the Court's perception that the Nation "must speak with one voice" about the status of Jerusalem. The vices of this mode of analysis go beyond mere lack of footing in the Constitution. Functionalism of the sort the Court practices today will *systematically* favor the unitary President over the plural Congress in disputes involving foreign affairs. *** It is certain that, in the long run, [this approach] will erode the structure of separated powers that the People established for the protection of their liberty.

It turns the Constitution upside-down to suggest that in areas of shared authority, it is the executive policy that preempts the law, rather than the other way around. Congress *may* make laws necessary and proper for carrying into execution the President's powers, but the President *must* "take Care" that Congress's legislation "be faithfully executed." *** Justice Jackson was right to think that a President who "takes measures incompatible with the expressed or implied will of Congress" may "rely only upon his own constitutional powers *minus any constitutional powers of Congress over the matter.*" *Youngstown Sheet & Tube Co.* v. *Sawyer.* *** Under the Constitution [the Founders] approved, Congress may require Zivotofsky's passport and birth report to record his birthplace as Israel, even if that requirement clashes with the President's preference for neutrality about the status of Jerusalem.

Notes

1. "History is the version of past events that people have decided to agree upon." Each opinion, with the exception of JUSTICE BREYER'S, makes ample use of history: constitutional history, legislative history, and, in portions of JUSTICE THOMAS' opinion not excerpted above, English history. However, despite using similar (and, sometimes, the same) documents, the opinions differ on both the constitutionality of the statute at issue and the legitimacy of Presidential action. Which opinion persuades you? Does the historical evidence support the President's action or does lack of textual evidence support Congress?

2. Political Questions. Recall the earlier materials on the nonjusticiability of political questions. In the 2012 term, the Supreme Court held in *Zivotofsky v. Clinton*, 132 S. Ct. 1421 (2012), that the political question doctrine did not bar judicial resolution of Zivotofsky's claim. Do you think that was the proper decision? Does the Constitution commit the issue to the coordinate political departments? Does that create a "lack of judicially discoverable and manageable standards" necessary to resolve the issue? The Court notes that this issue is marked with political strife. Indeed, this strife – both international and national in nature – seems to influence the Court's to empower the Executive branch to decide the issue.

3. New Battle Lines. Alan Morrison, a law professor and author of an amicus brief supporting the Zivotofsky family, wrote the following shortly after the opinion was issued: "Although *Curtiss-Wright* has been largely neutered, the world of implied executive powers in foreign affairs and perhaps elsewhere is very much with us, in both their concurrent and exclusive varieties. President Obama may well decide to fight Congress on matters such as an arms agreement with Iran and his authority to negotiate trade agreements, even without exercising his constitutional veto. *** On the other side, Congress might decide to up the ante by *** using the power of the purse, especially as part of a bill that the president must sign to keep the government from shutting down." What do you make of *Zivotofsky*? Did the Court draw new "battle lines"? Or is this simply more of the same?

2. EXECUTIVE PRIVILEGES AND IMMUNITIES

Powers enable the President to engage in particular tasks; privileges and immunities shield the President from inquiries concerning whether particular actions taken were lawful or not. In the Presidential Powers cases above, the Supreme Court, at least arguably, was a neutral referee between the President and Congress. Is this true when the Court evaluates presidential claims that he may not be reached by judicial processes?

Pres. does not have absolute executive privilege, but does have some privilege

UNITED STATES v. NIXON
418 U.S. 683 (1974)

MR. CHIEF JUSTICE BURGER delivered the opinion of the Court.

This litigation presents for review the denial of a motion, filed in the District Court on behalf of the President of the United States, in the case of *United States v. Mitchell et al.*, to quash a third-party subpoena duces tecum *** The subpoena directed the President to produce certain tape recordings and documents relating to his conversations with aides and advisers. ***

On March 1, 1974, a grand jury *** returned an indictment charging seven named individuals[3] with various offenses, including conspiracy to defraud the United States and to obstruct justice. Although he was not designated as such in the indictment, the grand jury named the President, among others, as an unindicted coconspirator. On April 18, 1974, upon motion of the Special Prosecutor, a subpoena duces tecum was issued *** to the President by the United States District Court. The subpoena required the production, in advance of the September 9 trial date, of certain tapes,

---

[3] The seven defendants were John N. Mitchell, H. R. Haldeman, John D. Ehrlichman, Charles W. Colson, Robert C. Mardian, Kenneth W. Parkinson, and Gordon Strachan. Each had occupied either a position of responsibility on the White House staff or the Committee for the Re-election of the President. Colson entered a guilty plea on another charge and is no longer a defendant.

memoranda, papers, transcripts or other writings relating to certain precisely identified meetings between the President and others. On April 30, the President publicly released edited transcripts of 43 conversations; portions of 20 conversations subject to subpoena in the present case were included. On May 1, 1974, the President's counsel, filed a 'special appearance' and a motion to quash the subpoena ***. This motion was accompanied by a formal claim of privilege. ***

[T]he President's counsel argued that the court lacked jurisdiction to issue the subpoena because the matter was an intra-branch dispute between a subordinate and superior officer of the Executive Branch and hence not subject to judicial resolution. *** [T]he Attorney General has delegated the authority to represent the United States in these particular matters to a Special Prosecutor with unique authority and tenure. The regulation gives the Special Prosecutor explicit power to contest the invocation of executive privilege in the process of seeking evidence deemed relevant to the performance of these specially delegated duties. *** [I]t is theoretically possible for the Attorney General to amend or revoke the regulation defining the Special Prosecutor's authority. But he has not done so. So long as this regulation remains in force the Executive Branch is bound by it, and indeed the United States as the sovereign composed of the three branches is bound to respect and to enforce it. Moreover, *** with the authorization of the President, the Acting Attorney General provided in the regulation that the Special Prosecutor was not to be removed without the 'consensus' of eight designated leaders of Congress. *** In light of the uniqueness of the setting in which the conflict arises, the fact that both parties are officers of the Executive Branch cannot be viewed as a barrier to justiciability. It would be inconsistent with the applicable law and regulation, and the unique facts of this case to conclude other than that the Special Prosecutor has standing to bring this action and that a justiciable controversy is presented for decision.

*** [W]e turn to the claim that the subpoena should be quashed because it demands 'confidential conversations between a President and his close advisors that it would be inconsistent with the public interest to produce.' The first contention is a broad claim that the separation of powers doctrine precludes judicial review of a President's claim of privilege. The second contention is that if he does not prevail on the claim of absolute privilege, the court should hold as a matter of constitutional law that the privilege prevails over the subpoena duces tecum.

In the performance of assigned constitutional duties, each branch of the Government must initially interpret the Constitution, and the interpretation of its powers by any branch is due great respect from the others. The President's counsel reads the Constitution as providing an absolute privilege of confidentiality for all Presidential communications. Many decisions of this Court, however, have unequivocally reaffirmed the holding of *Marbury v. Madison* that '(i)t is emphatically the province and duty of the judicial department to say what the law is.'

No holding of the Court has defined the scope of judicial power specifically relating to the enforcement of a subpoena for confidential

Presidential communications for use in a criminal prosecution, but other exercises of power by the Executive Branch and the Legislative Branch have been found invalid as in conflict with the Constitution. *** Our system of government 'requires that federal courts on occasion interpret the Constitution in a manner at variance with the construction given the document by another branch.' Notwithstanding the deference each branch must accord the others, the 'judicial Power of the United States' vested in the federal courts by Art. III, § 1, of the Constitution can no more be shared with the Executive Branch than the Chief Executive, for example, can share with the Judiciary the veto power, or the Congress share with the Judiciary the power to override a Presidential veto. Any other conclusion would be contrary to the basic concept of separation of powers and the checks and balances that flow from the scheme of a tripartite government. The Federalist, No. 47. We therefore reaffirm that it is the province and duty of this Court 'to say what the law is' with respect to the claim of privilege presented in this case.

In support of his claim of absolute privilege, the President's counsel urges *** the valid need for protection of communications between high Government officials and those who advise and assist them in the performance of their manifold duties; the importance of this confidentiality is too plain to require further discussion. *** [T]he privilege can be said to derive from the supremacy of each branch within its own assigned area of constitutional duties. Certain powers and privileges flow from the nature of enumerated powers; the protection of the confidentiality of Presidential communications has similar constitutional underpinnings.

The second ground asserted by the President's counsel in support of the claim of absolute privilege rests on the doctrine of separation of powers. Here it is argued that the independence of the Executive Branch within its own sphere insulates a President from a judicial subpoena in an ongoing criminal prosecution, and thereby protects confidential Presidential communications.

However, neither the doctrine of separation of powers, nor the need for confidentiality of high-level communications, without more, can sustain an absolute, unqualified Presidential privilege of immunity from judicial process under all circumstances. The President's need for complete candor and objectivity from advisers calls for great deference from the courts. However, when the privilege depends solely on the broad, undifferentiated claim of public interest in the confidentiality of such conversations, a confrontation with other values arises. Absent a claim of need to protect military, diplomatic, or sensitive national security secrets, we find it difficult to accept the argument that even the very important interest in confidentiality of Presidential communications is significantly diminished by production of such material for in camera inspection with all the protection that a district court will be obliged to provide.

The impediment that an absolute, unqualified privilege would place in the way of the primary constitutional duty of the Judicial Branch to do justice in criminal prosecutions would plainly conflict with the function of the courts under Art. III. In designing the structure of our Government and dividing and allocating the sovereign power among three co-equal branches, the

Framers of the Constitution sought to provide a comprehensive system, but the separate powers were not intended to operate with absolute independence. ***

The expectation of a President to the confidentiality of his conversations and correspondence, like the claim of confidentiality of judicial deliberations, for example, has all the values to which we accord deference for the privacy of all citizens and, added to those values, is the necessity for protection of the public interest in candid, objective, and even blunt or harsh opinions in Presidential decisionmaking. *** The privilege is fundamental to the operation of Government *** [b]ut this presumptive privilege must be considered in light of our historic commitment to the rule of law. *** We have elected to employ an adversary system of criminal justice in which the parties contest all issues before a court of law. The need to develop all relevant facts in the adversary system is both fundamental and comprehensive *** To ensure that justice is done, it is imperative to the function of courts that compulsory process be available for the production of evidence needed either by the prosecution or by the defense. *** [T]the public *** has a right to every man's evidence,' except for those persons protected by a constitutional, common-law, or statutory privilege. The [evidentiary] privileges referred to by the Court are designed to protect weighty and legitimate competing interests. Thus, the Fifth Amendment to the Constitution provides that no man 'shall be compelled in any criminal case to be a witness against himself.' And, generally, an attorney or a priest may not be required to disclose what has been revealed in professional confidence.

due process requires evidence, no matter what the situation is

III–2. "Coming Down to the Tape" Lepelley© *The Christian Science Monitor.*

These and other interests are recognized in law by privileges against forced disclosure, established in the Constitution, by statute, or at common law. Whatever their origins, these exceptions to the demand for every man's evidence are not lightly created nor expansively construed, for they are in derogation of the search for truth.

In this case the President challenges a subpoena served on him as a third party requiring the production of materials for use in a criminal prosecution; he does so on the claim that he has a privilege against disclosure of confidential communications. He does not place his claim of privilege on the ground they are military or diplomatic secrets. As to these areas of Art. II duties the courts have traditionally shown the utmost deference to Presidential responsibilities. *** No case of the Court, however, has extended this high degree of deference to a President's generalized interest in confidentiality. Nowhere in the Constitution, as we have noted earlier, is there any explicit reference to a privilege of confidentiality, yet to the extent this interest relates to the effective discharge of a President's powers, it is constitutionally based.

The right to the production of all evidence at a criminal trial similarly has constitutional dimensions. The Sixth Amendment explicitly confers upon every defendant in a criminal trial the right 'to be confronted with the witnesses against him' and 'to have compulsory process for obtaining witnesses in his favor. Moreover, the Fifth Amendment also guarantees that no person shall be deprived of liberty without due process of law. It is the manifest duty of the courts to vindicate those guarantees, and to accomplish that it is essential that all relevant and admissible evidence be produced.

In this case we must weigh the importance of the general privilege of confidentiality of Presidential communications in performance of the President's responsibilities against the inroads of such a privilege on the fair administration of criminal justice. The interest in preserving confidentiality is weighty indeed and entitled to great respect. However, we cannot conclude that advisers will be moved to temper the candor of their remarks by the infrequent occasions of disclosure because of the possibility that such conversations will be called for in the context of a criminal prosecution.

On the other hand, the allowance of the privilege to withhold evidence that is demonstrably relevant in a criminal trial would cut deeply into the guarantee of due process of law and gravely impair the basic function of the courts. A President's acknowledged need for confidentiality in the communications of his office is general in nature, whereas the constitutional need for production of relevant evidence in a criminal proceeding is specific and central to the fair adjudication of a particular criminal case in the administration of justice. Without access to specific facts a criminal prosecution may be totally frustrated. The President's broad interest in confidentiality of communications will not be vitiated by disclosure of a limited number of conversations preliminarily shown to have some bearing on the pending criminal cases. ***

If a President concludes that compliance with a subpoena would be injurious to the public interest he may *** invoke a claim of privilege on the return of the subpoena. *** Here the District Court treated the material as presumptively privileged, proceeded to find that the Special Prosecutor had made a sufficient showing to rebut the presumption, and ordered an in camera examination of the subpoenaed material. *** We now turn to the important question of the District Court's responsibilities in conducting the in camera examination of Presidential materials or communications delivered under the compulsion of the subpoena duces tecum.

*** Statements that meet the test of admissibility and relevance must be isolated; all other material must be excised. *** It is elementary that in camera inspection of evidence is always a procedure calling for scrupulous protection against any release or publication of material not found by the court, at that stage, probably admissible in evidence and relevant to the issues of the trial for which it is sought. *** [T]he District Court has a very heavy responsibility to see to it that Presidential conversations, which are either not relevant or not admissible, are accorded that high degree of respect due the President of the United States. MR. CHIEF JUSTICE MARSHALL, sitting as a trial judge in the *Burr* case, was extraordinarily careful to point out that '(i)n no case of this kind would a court be required to proceed against the president as against an ordinary individual.' Marshall's statement cannot be read to mean in any sense that a President is above the law, but relates to the singularly unique role under Art. II of a President's communications and activities, related to the performance of duties under that Article. Moreover, a President's communications and activities encompass a vastly wider range of sensitive material than would be true of any 'ordinary individual.' It is therefore necessary in the public interest to afford Presidential confidentiality the greatest protection consistent with the fair administration of justice. *** We have no doubt that the District Judge will at all times accord to Presidential records that high degree of deference suggested in *United States v. Burr*, and will discharge his responsibility to see to it that until released to the Special Prosecutor no in camera material is revealed to anyone. This burden applies with even greater force to excised material; once the decision is made to excise, the material is restored to its privileged status and should be returned under seal to its lawful custodian. ***

MR. JUSTICE REHNQUIST took no part in the consideration or decision of this case.

Notes

1. **Political Question.** Was the issue posed a "political question" as that term is used consistent in *Marbury*? In *Baker v. Carr*?

2. **Judicial Trial and Congressional Impeachment.** At the time this case was pending, the House was considering three Articles of Impeachment against President Nixon: Article I concerned obstruction of justice; Article II dealt with violating citizens' rights through misuse of the IRS, FBI, and CIA; and Article III involved failure to respond to congressional subpoenas. Within five days after the Court's decision in *United States v. Nixon*, the House Judiciary Committee

adopted each of the three Articles of Impeachment; within seven days, President Nixon decided to make transcripts of the Watergate tapes available. Three days after that, President Nixon resigned. The House, presumably thinking the issue moot, dropped further impeachment proceedings. Should the Court have deferred to the impeachment process? If Nixon had been impeached, rather than resigning, would the issue of whether the President committed "high Crimes and Misdemeanors" have been judicially reviewable?

3. **Constitutional Theory of Immunity and Privilege.**

(a) Legislative immunity is provided in the "Speech or Debate" Clause of Art. I, § 6, cl. 1 (House and Senate members "shall not be questioned in any other Place"). Why didn't the Court find that, absent a comparable provision, the President has no executive privilege? Ironically, was the decision that the President was entitled to some privileged communications a victory?

(b) Even if their communications enjoy only a qualified privilege, Presidents enjoy absolute immunity from civil suits based on performance of official functions. *See Clinton v. Jones*, infra. If Presidential privileges and immunities are a function of separation of powers principles, do they extend to presidential aides? *See Harlow v. Fitzgerald*, 457 U.S. 800 (1982) (privilege is the President's, but Presidential aides have qualified immunity).

(c) Was it predictable that the Court would balance the "generalized" interests of the President adversely when faced by the "specific" needs of the criminal justice system? Is this simply institutional myopia by the judiciary? Some commentators have speculated that the balance might have been different if the counterweight to immunity had been an investigation by Congress.

(d) If you had represented Nixon, would an argument that the tapes contained materials affecting national security interests have been helpful? What should the judiciary do in the face of such a claim?

4. **Followup.** President Nixon lost yet another Supreme Court case when the Court held in *Nixon v. Administrator of General Services*, 433 U.S. 425 (1977), that a statute directing the Administrator to take custody of Nixon's presidential papers and tape recordings, sort them for archival purposes, and return only those personal in nature did not violate separation of powers principles. The Court noted that Presidents Ford and Carter supported the statute and that the materials remained in the Executive Branch.

CLINTON v. JONES
520 U.S. 681 (1997)

JUSTICE STEVENS delivered the opinion of the Court.

This case raises a constitutional and a prudential question concerning the Office of the President of the United States. Respondent, a private citizen, seeks to recover damages from the current occupant of that office based on actions allegedly taken before his term began. ***

Petitioner, William Jefferson Clinton, was elected to the Presidency in 1992, and re-elected in 1996. His term of office expires on January 20, 2001. In 1991 he was the Governor of the State of Arkansas. Respondent, Paula

issue - can a Pres. be sued in a civil claim?

Corbin Jones, is a resident of California. In 1991 she lived in Arkansas, and was an employee of the Arkansas Industrial Development Commission. *** As the case comes to us, we are required to assume the truth of the detailed—but as yet untested—factual allegations in the complaint. *** She alleges that [Governor Clinton] made "abhorrent" sexual advances that she vehemently rejected ***. [I]t is perfectly clear that the alleged misconduct of petitioner was unrelated to any of his official duties as President of the United States and, indeed, occurred before he was elected to that office. ***

Only three sitting Presidents have been defendants in civil litigation involving their actions prior to taking office. Complaints against Theodore Roosevelt and Harry Truman had been dismissed before they took office ***. Two companion cases arising out of an automobile accident were filed against John F. Kennedy in 1960 during the Presidential campaign. After taking office, he unsuccessfully argued that his status as Commander in Chief gave him a right to a stay under the Soldiers' and Sailors' Civil Relief Act of 1940. The motion for a stay was denied by the District Court, and the matter was settled out of court. Thus, none of those cases sheds any light on the constitutional issue before us.

The principal rationale for affording certain public servants immunity from suits for money damages arising out of their official acts is inapplicable to unofficial conduct. In cases involving prosecutors, legislators, and judges we have repeatedly explained that the immunity serves the public interest in enabling such officials to perform their designated functions effectively without fear that a particular decision may give rise to personal liability. *** That rationale provided the principal basis for our holding [in *Nixon v. Fitzgerald*, 457 U.S. 731 (1982)] that a former President of the United States was "entitled to absolute immunity from damages liability predicated on his official acts." Our central concern was to avoid rendering the President "unduly cautious in the discharge of his official duties."[19] *** But we have never suggested that the President, or any other official, has an immunity that extends beyond the scope of any action taken in an official capacity.

Moreover, when defining the scope of an immunity for acts clearly taken within an official capacity, we have applied a functional approach. *** Hence, for example, a judge's absolute immunity does not extend to actions performed in a purely administrative capacity. *** Petitioner's effort to construct an immunity from suit for unofficial acts grounded purely in the identity of his office is unsupported by precedent.

taking a functional approach

We are also unpersuaded by the evidence from the historical record to which petitioner has called our attention. *** Respondent, in turn, has called our attention to conflicting historical evidence. Speaking in favor of the Constitution's adoption at the Pennsylvania Convention, James Wilson—who

_____

[19] Petitioner draws our attention to dicta in *Fitzgerald* which he suggests are helpful to his cause. *** In context, however, it is clear that our dominant concern was with the diversion of the President's attention during the decisionmaking process caused by needless worry as to the possibility of damages actions stemming from any particular official decision. Moreover, *Fitzgerald* did not present the issue raised in this case because that decision involved claims against a former President.

DC gave stay citing abuse of discretion

had participated in the Philadelphia Convention at which the document was drafted—explained that, although the President "is placed [on] high," "not a single privilege is annexed to his character; far from being above the laws, he is amenable to them in his private character as a citizen, and in his public character by impeachment." This description is consistent with both the doctrine of presidential immunity as set forth in *Fitzgerald*, and rejection of the immunity claim in this case. With respect to acts taken in his "public character"—that is official acts—the President may be disciplined principally by impeachment, not by private lawsuits for damages. But he is otherwise subject to the laws for his purely private acts. ***

Petitioner's strongest argument supporting his immunity claim is based on the text and structure of the Constitution. He does not contend that the occupant of the Office of the President is "above the law," in the sense that his conduct is entirely immune from judicial scrutiny. The President argues merely for a postponement of the judicial proceedings that will determine whether he violated any law. His argument is grounded in the character of the office that was created by Article II of the Constitution, and relies on separation of powers principles that have structured our constitutional arrangement since the founding.

As a starting premise, petitioner contends that he occupies a unique office with powers and responsibilities so vast and important that the public interest demands that he devote his undivided time and attention to his public duties. *** We have no dispute with the initial premise of the argument. Former presidents, from George Washington to George Bush, have consistently endorsed petitioner's characterization of the office. *** It does not follow, however, that separation of powers principles would be violated by allowing this action to proceed. ***

Of course the lines between the powers of the three branches are not always neatly defined. But in this case there is no suggestion that the Federal Judiciary is being asked to perform any function that might in some way be described as "executive." Respondent is merely asking the courts to exercise their core Article III jurisdiction to decide cases and controversies. Whatever the outcome of this case, there is no possibility that the decision will curtail the scope of the official powers of the Executive Branch. The litigation of questions that relate entirely to the unofficial conduct of the individual who happens to be the President poses no perceptible risk of misallocation of either judicial power or executive power.

Rather than arguing that the decision of the case will produce either an aggrandizement of judicial power or a narrowing of executive power, petitioner contends that—as a by-product of an otherwise traditional exercise of judicial power—burdens will be placed on the President that will hamper the performance of his official duties. *** Petitioner's predictive judgment finds little support in either history or the relatively narrow compass of the issues raised in this particular case. *** If the past is any indicator, it seems unlikely that a deluge of such litigation will ever engulf the Presidency. As for the case at hand, if properly managed by the District Court, it appears to us highly unlikely to occupy any substantial amount of petitioner's time.

DC considered if you can be Pres. effectively if you are being sued all the time?

Of greater significance, petitioner errs by presuming that interactions between the Judicial Branch and the Executive, even quite burdensome interactions, necessarily rise to the level of constitutionally forbidden impairment of the Executive's ability to perform its constitutionally mandated functions. *** The fact that a federal court's exercise of its traditional Article III jurisdiction may significantly burden the time and attention of the Chief Executive is not sufficient to establish a violation of the Constitution. Two long-settled propositions, first announced by CHIEF JUSTICE MARSHALL, support that conclusion.

First, we have long held that when the President takes official action, the Court has the authority to determine whether he has acted within the law. *** Second, it is also settled that the President is subject to judicial process in appropriate circumstances. *** We unequivocally and emphatically endorsed Marshall's position when we held that President Nixon was obligated to comply with a subpoena commanding him to produce certain tape recordings of his conversations with his aides. *United States v. Nixon*. As we explained, "neither the doctrine of separation of powers, nor the need for confidentiality of high-level communications, without more, can sustain an absolute, unqualified Presidential privilege of immunity from judicial process under all circumstances."[39]

Sitting Presidents have responded to court orders to provide testimony and other information with sufficient frequency that such interactions between the Judicial and Executive Branches can scarcely be thought a novelty. President Monroe responded to written interrogatories, *** President Nixon—as noted above—produced tapes in response to a subpoena duces tecum, *** President Ford complied with an order to give a deposition in a criminal trial, *** and President Clinton has twice given videotaped testimony in criminal proceedings ***. Moreover, sitting Presidents have also voluntarily complied with judicial requests for testimony. President Grant gave a lengthy deposition in a criminal case *** and President Carter similarly gave videotaped testimony for use at a criminal trial ***.

In sum, "[i]t is settled law that the separation-of-powers doctrine does not bar every exercise of jurisdiction over the President of the United States." *Fitzgerald*. If the Judiciary may severely burden the Executive Branch by reviewing the legality of the President's official conduct, and if it may direct appropriate process to the President himself, it must follow that the federal courts have power to determine the legality of his unofficial conduct. The burden on the President's time and energy that is a mere by-product of such review surely cannot be considered as onerous as the direct burden imposed by judicial review and the occasional invalidation of his official actions. We therefore hold that the doctrine of separation of powers does not require federal courts to stay all private actions against the President until he leaves office. ***

---

[39] Of course, it does not follow that a court may "'proceed against the president as against an ordinary individual,'"*United States v. Nixon*. Special caution is appropriate if the materials or testimony sought by the court relate to a President's official activities ***.

[W]e turn to the question whether the District Court's decision to stay the trial until after petitioner leaves office was an abuse of discretion. *** [W]e are persuaded that it was an abuse of discretion ***. Such a lengthy and categorical stay takes no account whatever of the respondent's interest in bringing the case to trial. *** [D]elaying trial would increase the danger of prejudice resulting from the loss of evidence, including the inability of witnesses to recall specific facts, or the possible death of a party.

The decision to postpone the trial was, furthermore, premature. The proponent of a stay bears the burden of establishing its need. *** [T]here is nothing in the record to enable a judge to assess the potential harm that may ensue from scheduling the trial promptly after discovery is concluded. ***

We add a final comment on two matters ***: the risk that our decision will generate a large volume of politically motivated harassing and frivolous litigation, and the danger that national security concerns might prevent the President from explaining a legitimate need for a continuance.

We are not persuaded that either of these risks is serious. Most frivolous and vexatious litigation is terminated at the pleading stage or on summary judgment, with little if any personal involvement by the defendant. Moreover, the availability of sanctions provides a significant deterrent to litigation directed at the President in his unofficial capacity for purposes of political gain or harassment. History indicates that the likelihood that a significant number of such cases will be filed is remote. Although scheduling problems may arise, there is no reason to assume that the District Courts will be either unable to accommodate the President's needs or unfaithful to the tradition— especially in matters involving national security—of giving "the utmost deference to Presidential responsibilities." Several Presidents, including petitioner, have given testimony without jeopardizing the Nation's security. In short, we have confidence in the ability of our federal judges to deal with both of these concerns.

If Congress deems it appropriate to afford the President stronger protection, it may respond with appropriate legislation. ***

JUSTICE BREYER, concurring in the judgment.

I agree with the majority that the Constitution does not automatically grant the President an immunity from civil lawsuits based upon his private conduct. Nor does the "doctrine of separation of powers *** require federal courts to stay" virtually "all private actions against the President until he leaves office." *** In my view, however, once the President sets forth and explains a conflict between judicial proceeding and public duties, the matter changes. At that point, the Constitution permits a judge to schedule a trial in an ordinary civil damages action (where postponement normally is possible without overwhelming damage to a plaintiff) only within the constraints of a constitutional principle—a principle that forbids a federal judge in such a case to interfere with the President's discharge of his public duties. *** [A] sitting President is unusually busy, *** his activities have an unusually important impact upon the lives of others, and *** his conduct embodies an authority bestowed by the entire American electorate. *** [U]nlike Congress, which is regularly out of session, U.S. Const., Art. I, §§ 4, 5, 7, the President never adjourns.

More importantly, these constitutional objectives explain why a President, though able to delegate duties to others, cannot delegate ultimate responsibility or the active obligation to supervise that goes with it. And the related constitutional equivalence between President, Congress, and the Judiciary, means that judicial scheduling orders in a private civil case must not only take reasonable account of, say, a particularly busy schedule, or a job on which others critically depend, or an underlying electoral mandate. They must also reflect the fact that interference with a President's ability to carry out his public responsibilities is constitutionally equivalent to interference with the ability of the entirety of Congress, or the Judicial Branch, to carry out their public obligations. ***

The majority points to the fact that private plaintiffs have brought civil damage lawsuits against a sitting President only three times in our Nation's history; and it relies upon the threat of sanctions to discourage, and "the court's discretion" to manage, such actions so that "interference with the President's duties would not occur." I am less sanguine. Since 1960, when the last such suit was filed, the number of civil lawsuits filed annually in Federal District Courts has increased from under 60,000 to about 240,000 ***. And this Court has now made clear that such lawsuits may proceed against a sitting President. *** Should the majority's optimism turn out to be misplaced, then, in my view, courts will have to develop administrative rules applicable to such cases (including postponement rules of the sort at issue in this case) in order to implement the basic constitutional directive. *** I believe that ordinary case-management principles are unlikely to prove sufficient to deal with private civil lawsuits for damages unless supplemented with a constitutionally based requirement that district courts schedule proceedings so as to avoid significant interference with the President's ongoing discharge of his official responsibilities. *** Yet, I agree with the majority that there is no automatic temporary immunity and that the President should have to provide the District Court with a reasoned explanation of why the immunity is needed; and I also agree that, in the absence of that explanation, the court's postponement of the trial date was premature. For those reasons, I concur in the result.

Notes

1.   **Fallout.** Did the Supreme Court fail to understand the ramifications of its decision in *Clinton v. Jones*? Do you recall the role this decision played in President Clinton's being impeached by the House and tried by the Senate?

2.   **Other Privileges?** Are the President's conversations with the First Spouse privileged? Consider whether Secret Service agents who guard the President should be immune from a subpoena by Paula Jones' lawyers requiring them to appear for depositions concerning extramarital sexual activity by the President during his time in the White House. What arguments would you make on both sides of this issue? Would your answer change if the subpoena came from the Office of Independent Counsel? If it came from a House committee considering

the possibility of impeaching the President? If the request concerned not alleged sexual activities but alleged diversion of government money for personal use?

3.   **Independent Counsels.** Can you think of any alternative to independent counsels to control wrongdoing in the Executive Branch? Should independent counsels be appointed to deal with alleged wrongdoing by Members of Congress? Federal judges? Revisit these questions after reading *Morrison v. Olson*, *infra*.

4.   **Executive Privilege and Civil Discovery.** In *Cheney v. U.S. Dist Ct.*, 542 U.S. 367 (2004), the district court allowed discovery to find out whether a federal statute requiring disclosure of contacts with lobbyists applied to an energy policy task force headed by Vice-President Cheney. The Supreme Court reversed on separation of powers grounds, distinguishing *Nixon* as follows:

> [T]he narrow subpoena orders in *United States v. Nixon* stand on an altogether different footing from the overly broad discovery requests approved by the District Court in this case. *** In contrast to *Nixon*'s subpoena orders that "precisely identified" and "specific[ally] ... enumerated" the relevant materials, the discovery requests here *** ask for everything under the sky: *** *Nixon* does not leave [the courts] the sole option of inviting the Executive Branch to invoke executive privilege while remaining otherwise powerless to modify a party's overly broad discovery requests. Executive privilege is an extraordinary assertion of power "not to be lightly invoked." Once executive privilege is asserted, coequal branches of the Government are set on a collision course. The Judiciary is forced into the difficult task of balancing the need for information in a judicial proceeding and the Executive's Article II prerogatives. This inquiry places courts in the awkward position of evaluating the Executive's claims of confidentiality and autonomy, and pushes to the fore difficult questions of separation of powers and checks and balances. These "occasion[s] for constitutional confrontation between the two branches" should be avoided whenever possible. *United States v. Nixon* *** As this case implicates the separation of powers, the Court of Appeals must *** ask *** whether the District Court's actions constituted an unwarranted impairment of another branch in the performance of its constitutional duties.

C. LEGISLATIVE AUTHORITY

Until the New Deal era, it was generally assumed that Congress could not delegate lawmaking functions other than by establishing an "intelligible principle" by which others administering the law would thereafter be guided. The two cases which most exemplify this approach are *Panama Refining Co. v. Ryan*, 293 U.S. 388 (1935) (statute authorizing the President to prohibit interstate transportation of "hot oil" unconstitutionally delegated legislative powers since it provided no standards for the President to follow) and *A.L.A. Schechter Poultry Corp. v. United States*, 295 U.S. 495 (1935) (statute prohibiting "unfair competition" under "rules of competition deemed fair for each industry by representative members of that industry" unconstitutionally delegated legislative power). There are references to this doctrine and its inapplicability in the domestic context in *Curtiss-Wright*, supra.

Schechter marks the last time the Supreme Court invalidated a legislative delegation of authority. It has since *Schechter* approved statutes commanding agencies to act "in the public interest," to outlaw "unreasonable risks," and so forth. Occasionally, various members of the Court have said that the possibility of unconstitutional delegation was a reason for construing a statute more narrowly, but the nondelegation doctrine has not been revived. See *Loving v. United States*, 517 U.S. 748 (1996), upholding a delegation that courts-martial "may, under such limitations as the President [as Commander-in-Chief] may prescribe, adjudge any punishment *** including the penalty of death."

In *Whitman v. American Trucking Associations, Inc.*, 531 U.S. 457 (2001), the Supreme Court rejected the argument that § 109(b)(1) of the Clean Air Act (instructing the EPA to set "ambient air quality standards" that allow for "an adequate margin of safety *** requisite to protect the public health") unconstitutionally delegated legislative power to the Environmental Protection Agency. JUSTICE SCALIA explained for the majority:

> *** [W]hen Congress confers decisionmaking authority upon agencies Congress must "lay down by legislative act an intelligible principle to which the person or body authorized to [act] is directed to conform." We have never suggested that an agency can cure an unlawful delegation of legislative power by adopting in its discretion a limiting construction of the statute. *** [T]he text of § 109(b)(1) of the CAA at a minimum requires that "[f]or a discrete set of pollutants and based on published air quality criteria that reflect the latest scientific knowledge, [the] EPA must establish uniform national standards at a level that is requisite to protect public health from the adverse effects of the pollutant in the ambient air." Requisite, in turn, "mean[s] sufficient, but not more than necessary." *** "[A] certain degree of discretion, and thus of lawmaking, inheres in most executive or judicial action." Section 109(b)(1) of the CAA, which to repeat we interpret as requiring the EPA to set air quality standards at the level that is "requisite"–that is, not lower or higher than is necessary–to protect the public health with an adequate margin of safety, fits comfortably within the scope of discretion permitted by our precedent. ***

If the Court were to revive the nondelegation doctrine, Congress would either have to leave more private activity unregulated or work much harder to specify more precise standards to cover the same territory as one broad standard. Less obviously, a consequence of the demise of the nondelegation doctrine has been Congress' search for ways to control the President and agencies to whom broad authority is delegated.

The following opinions, concerning whether Congress has overreached its boundaries vis-a-vis the President, seem methodologically inconsistent.

Some are highly formalistic exercises in definitions of constitutional terms; others seem more functional, focusing on whether Congress is intruding into the Executive branch's functions. Dissatisfaction with the Court's body of work in these cases has led some to suggest that the Court ought to simply stay out of the business of serving as referee for the two political branches and focus on individual rights matters. As you read the following cases, consider whether you agree with this assessment.

INS v. CHADHA
462 U.S. 919 (1983)

CHIEF JUSTICE BURGER delivered the opinion of the Court.

*** Chadha is an East Indian who was born in Kenya and holds a British passport. He was lawfully admitted to the United States in 1966 on a nonimmigrant student visa. His visa expired on June 30, 1972. On October 11, 1973, the District Director of the Immigration and Naturalization Service [INS] ordered Chadha to show cause why he should not be deported for having "remained in the United States for a longer time than permitted." [At] a deportation hearing *** before an immigration judge, *** Chadha conceded that he was deportable for overstaying his visa and the hearing was adjourned to enable him to file an application for suspension of deportation under [the Immigration and Nationality Act]. *** On the basis of evidence adduced at the hearing, affidavits submitted with the application, and the results of a character investigation conducted by the INS, the immigration judge ordered that Chadha's deportation be suspended. The immigration judge found that Chadha met the requirements of [an exception provided for in the Act]: he had resided continuously in the United States for over seven years, was of good moral character, and would suffer "extreme hardship" if deported. *** [T]he immigration judge suspended Chadha's deportation and a report of the suspension was transmitted to Congress. [The Attorney General recommended Chadha's deportation be suspended as provided for under the Act.] Once the recommendation for suspension of Chadha's deportation was conveyed to Congress, Congress had the power under § 244(c)(2) *** to veto the Attorney General's determination that Chadha should not be deported.

On December 12, 1975, Representative Eilberg, Chairman of the Judiciary Subcommittee on Immigration, Citizenship, and International Law, introduced a resolution opposing "the granting of permanent residence in the United States to [six] aliens," including Chadha. The resolution was referred to the House Committee on the Judiciary. On December 16, 1975, the resolution was discharged from further consideration by the House Committee on the Judiciary and submitted to the House of Representatives for a vote. *** The resolution was passed without debate or recorded vote. Since the House action was pursuant to § 244(c)(2), the resolution was not treated as an Article I legislative act; it was not submitted to the Senate or presented to the President for his action.

After the House veto of the Attorney General's decision to allow Chadha to remain in the United States, the immigration judge reopened the deportation proceedings to implement the House order deporting Chadha.

Chadha moved to terminate the proceedings on the ground that § 244(c)(2) is unconstitutional. The immigration judge held that he had no authority to rule on the constitutional validity of § 244(c)(2) [and] the Board of Immigration Appeals *** held that it had "no power to declare unconstitutional an act of Congress" and Chadha's appeal was dismissed.

Pursuant to § 106(a) of the Act Chadha filed a petition for review of the deportation order in the United States Court of Appeals for the Ninth Circuit. *** [The Court determined that it had jurisdiction, that Chadha had standing, that the veto provision was severable for from the remainder of the Act, and that the issue was not a political question.] *** We turn now to the question whether action of one House of Congress under § 244(c)(2) violates strictures of the Constitution. ***

[T]he fact that a given law or procedure is efficient, convenient, and useful in facilitating functions of government, standing alone, will not save it if it is contrary to the Constitution. Convenience and efficiency are not the primary objectives—or the hallmarks—of democratic government and our inquiry is sharpened rather than blunted by the fact that Congressional veto provisions are appearing with increasing frequency in statutes which delegate authority to executive and independent agencies: "Since 1932, when the first veto provision was enacted into law, 295 congressional veto-type procedures have been inserted in 196 different statutes as follows: from 1932 to 1939, five statutes were affected; from 1940–49, nineteen statutes; between 1950–59, thirty-four statutes; and from 1960–69, forty-nine. From the year 1970 through 1975, at least one hundred sixty-three such provisions were included in eighty-nine laws." *** [T]he one-House veto [may be] a useful "political invention," and we need not challenge that assertion. *** But policy arguments supporting even useful "political inventions" are subject to the demands of the Constitution which defines powers and, with respect to this subject, sets out just how those powers are to be exercised.

Explicit and unambiguous provisions of the Constitution prescribe and define the respective functions of the Congress and of the Executive in the legislative process. Art. I provides: "All legislative Powers herein granted shall be vested in a Congress of the United States, which shall consist of a Senate and a House of Representatives." "Every Bill which shall have passed the House of Representatives and the Senate, shall, before it becomes a Law, be presented to the President of the United States; *** " [and] "Every Order, Resolution, or Vote to which the Concurrence of the Senate and House of Representatives may be necessary (except on a question of Adjournment) shall be presented to the President of the United States; and before the Same shall take Effect, shall be approved by him, or being disapproved by him, shall be repassed by two thirds of the Senate and House of Representatives, according to the Rules and Limitations prescribed in the Case of a Bill."

These provisions of Art. I are integral parts of the constitutional design for the separation of powers. *** The very structure of the articles delegating and separating powers under Arts. I, II, and III exemplify the concept of separation of powers and we now turn to Art I. The records of the Constitutional Convention reveal that the requirement that all legislation be presented to the President before becoming law was uniformly accepted by the Framers. Presentment to the President and the Presidential veto were considered so imperative that the draftsmen took special pains to assure that these requirements could not be circumvented.

The decision to provide the President with a limited and qualified power to nullify proposed legislation by veto was based on the profound conviction of the Framers that the powers conferred on Congress were the powers to be most carefully circumscribed. *** The bicameral requirement of Art. I, §§ 1, 7 was of scarcely less concern to the Framers than was the Presidential veto and indeed the two concepts are interdependent. *** [T]he prescription for legislative action in Art. I, §§ 1, 7 represents the Framers' decision that the legislative power of the Federal government be exercised in accord with a single, finely wrought and exhaustively considered, procedure. *** [W]hen, as here, one House of Congress purports to act, it is presumptively acting within its assigned sphere. Beginning with this presumption, we must nevertheless establish that the challenged action under § 244(c)(2) is of the kind to which the procedural requirements of Art. I, § 7 apply. Not every action taken by either House is subject to the bicameralism and presentment requirements of Art. I. Whether actions taken by either House are, in law and fact, an exercise of legislative power depends not on their form but upon "whether they contain matter which is properly to be regarded as legislative in its character and effect."

Examination of the action taken here by one House pursuant to § 244(c)(2) reveals that it was essentially legislative in purpose and effect. In purporting to exercise power defined in Art. I, § 8, cl. 4 to "establish an uniform Rule of Naturalization," the House took action that had the purpose and effect of altering the legal rights, duties and relations of persons, including the Attorney General, Executive Branch officials and Chadha, all outside the legislative branch. The one-House veto operated in this case to overrule the Attorney General and mandate Chadha's deportation; absent the House action, Chadha would remain in the United States. Congress has acted and its action has altered Chadha's status.

The legislative character of the one-House veto in this case is confirmed by the character of the Congressional action it supplants. Neither the House of Representatives nor the Senate contends that, absent the veto provision in § 244(c)(2), either of them, or both of them acting together, could effectively require the Attorney General to deport an alien once the Attorney General, in the exercise of legislatively delegated authority, had determined the alien should remain in the United States. Without the challenged provision in § 244(c)(2), this could have been achieved, if at all, only by legislation requiring deportation. ***

The nature of the decision implemented by the one-House veto in this case further manifests its legislative character. After long experience with the clumsy, time consuming private bill procedure, Congress made a deliberate choice to delegate to the Executive Branch, and specifically to the Attorney General, the authority to allow deportable aliens to remain in this country in certain specified circumstances. It is not disputed that this choice to delegate authority is precisely the kind of decision that can be implemented only in accordance with the procedures set out in Art. I. Disagreement with the Attorney General's decision on Chadha's deportation—that is, Congress' decision to deport Chadha—no less than Congress' original choice to delegate to the Attorney General the authority to make that decision, involves determinations of policy that Congress can implement in only one way; bicameral passage followed by presentment to the President. Congress must abide by its delegation of authority until that delegation is legislatively altered or revoked.

Finally, we see that when the Framers intended to authorize either House of Congress to act alone and outside of its prescribed bicameral legislative role, they narrowly and precisely defined the procedure for such action. There are but four provisions in the Constitution, explicit and unambiguous, by which one House may act alone with the unreviewable force of law, not subject to the President's veto:

(a) The House of Representatives alone was given the power to initiate impeachments. Art. I, § 2, cl. 6;

(b) The Senate alone was given the power to conduct trials following impeachment on charges initiated by the House and to convict following trial. Art. I, § 3, cl. 6;

(c) The Senate alone was given final unreviewable power to approve or to disapprove presidential appointments. Art. II, § 2, cl. 2;

(d) The Senate alone was given unreviewable power to ratify treaties negotiated by the President. Art. II, § 2, cl. 2.

Clearly, when the Draftsmen sought to confer special powers on one House, independent of the other House, or of the President, they did so in explicit, unambiguous terms. ***21 The bicameral requirement, the Presentment Clauses, the President's veto, and Congress' power to override a veto were intended to erect enduring checks on each Branch and to protect the people from the improvident exercise of power by mandating certain

---

21 JUSTICE POWELL's position is that the one-House veto in this case is a judicial act and therefore unconstitutional as beyond the authority vested in Congress by the Constitution. We agree that there is a sense in which one-House action pursuant to s 244(c)(2) has a judicial cast, since it purports to "review" Executive action. *** To be sure, it is normally up to the courts to decide whether an agency has complied with its statutory mandate. But the attempted analogy between judicial action and the one-House veto is less than perfect. Federal courts do not enjoy a roving mandate to correct alleged excesses of administrative agencies; we are limited by Art. III to hearing cases and controversies and no justiciable case or controversy was presented by the Attorney General's decision to allow Chadha to remain in this country. We are aware of no decision *** where a federal court has reviewed a decision of the Attorney General suspending deportation of an alien pursuant to the standards set out in § 244(a)(1). This is not surprising, given that no party to such action has either the motivation or the right to appeal from it. As JUSTICE WHITE correctly notes, "the courts have not been given the authority to review whether an alien should be given permanent status; review is limited to whether the Attorney General has properly applied the statutory standards for" denying a request for suspension of deportation. Thus, JUSTICE POWELL's statement that the one-House veto in this case is "clearly adjudicatory," simply is not supported by his accompanying assertion that the House has "assumed a function ordinarily entrusted to the federal courts."

prescribed steps. To preserve those checks, and maintain the separation of powers, the carefully defined limits on the power of each Branch must not be eroded. To accomplish what has been attempted by one House of Congress in this case requires action in conformity with the express procedures of the Constitution's prescription for legislative action: passage by a majority of both Houses and presentment to the President.[22] *** We hold that the Congressional veto provision in § 244(c)(2) is severable from the Act and that it is unconstitutional. ***

JUSTICE POWELL, concurring in the judgment.

*** The Constitution does not establish three branches with precisely defined boundaries. *** On its face, the House's action appears clearly adjudicatory. *** Even if the House did not make a de novo determination, but simply reviewed the Immigration and Naturalization Service's findings, it still assumed a function ordinarily entrusted to the federal courts. *** The impropriety of the House's assumption of this function is confirmed by the fact that its action raises the very danger the Framers sought to avoid—the exercise of unchecked power. In deciding whether Chadha deserves to be deported, Congress is not subject to any internal constraints that prevent it from arbitrarily depriving him of the right to remain in this country. Unlike the judiciary or an administrative agency, Congress is not bound by established substantive rules. Nor is it subject to the procedural safeguards, such as the right to counsel and a hearing before an impartial tribunal, that are present when a court or an agency adjudicates individual rights. The only effective constraint on Congress' power is political, but Congress is most accountable politically when it prescribes rules of general applicability. When it decides rights of specific persons, those rights are subject to "the tyranny of a shifting majority." *** I would not reach the broader question whether legislative vetoes are invalid under the Presentment Clauses.

JUSTICE WHITE, dissenting.

Today the Court not only invalidates § 244(c)(2) of the Immigration and Nationality Act, but also sounds the death knell for nearly 200 other statutory provisions in which Congress has reserved a "legislative veto." For this reason, the Court's decision is of surpassing importance. And it is for this reason that the Court would have been well-advised to decide the case, if possible, on the narrower grounds of separation of powers, leaving for full consideration the constitutionality of other congressional review statutes operating on such varied matters as war powers and agency rulemaking, some of which concern the independent regulatory agencies.

The prominence of the legislative veto mechanism in our contemporary political system and its importance to Congress can hardly be overstated. It has become a central means by which Congress secures the accountability of

---

[22] Neither can we accept the suggestion that the one-House veto provision in § 244(c)(2) either removes or modifies the bicameralism and presentation requirements for the enactment of future legislation affecting aliens. *** The legislative steps outlined in Art. I are not empty formalities; they were designed to assure that both Houses of Congress and the President participate in the exercise of lawmaking authority.

executive and independent agencies. Without the legislative veto, Congress is faced with a Hobson's choice: either to refrain from delegating the necessary authority, leaving itself with a hopeless task of writing laws with the requisite specificity to cover endless special circumstances across the entire policy landscape, or in the alternative, to abdicate its law-making function to the executive branch and independent agencies. To choose the former leaves major national problems unresolved; to opt for the latter risks unaccountable policymaking by those not elected to fill that role. Accordingly, over the past five decades, the legislative veto has been placed in nearly 200 statutes. The device is known in every field of governmental concern: reorganization, budgets, foreign affairs, war powers, and regulation of trade, safety, energy, the environment and the economy. *** It is an important if not indispensable political invention that allows the President and Congress to resolve major constitutional and policy differences, assures the accountability of independent regulatory agencies, and preserves Congress' control over lawmaking. ***

The history of the legislative veto *** makes clear that it has not been a sword with which Congress has struck out to aggrandize itself at the expense of the other branches—the concerns of Madison and Hamilton. Rather, the veto has been a means of defense, a reservation of ultimate authority necessary if Congress is to fulfill its designated role under Article I as the nation's lawmaker. While the President has often objected to particular legislative vetoes, generally those left in the hands of congressional committees, the Executive has more often agreed to legislative review as the price for a broad delegation of authority. *** [T]hat could be precisely why Congress thought it essential to retain a check on the exercise of delegated authority. ***

The Constitution does not directly authorize or prohibit the legislative veto. Thus, our task should be to determine whether the legislative veto is consistent with the purposes of Art. I and the principles of Separation of Powers which are reflected in that Article and throughout the Constitution. *** Only within the last half century has the complexity and size of the Federal Government's responsibilities grown so greatly that the Congress must rely on the legislative veto as the most effective if not the only means to insure their role as the nation's lawmakers. But the wisdom of the Framers was to anticipate that the nation would grow and new problems of governance would require different solutions. ***

If Congress may delegate lawmaking power to independent and executive agencies, it is most difficult to understand Article I as forbidding Congress from also reserving a check on legislative power for itself. Absent the veto, the agencies receiving delegations of legislative or quasi-legislative power may issue regulations having the force of law without bicameral approval and without the President's signature. It is thus not apparent why the reservation of a veto over the exercise of that legislative power must be subject to a more exacting test. In both cases, it is enough that the initial statutory authorizations comply with the Article I requirements. ***

The legislative veto provision does not "prevent the Executive Branch from accomplishing its constitutionally assigned functions." First, it is clear that the Executive Branch has no "constitutionally assigned" function of suspending the deportation of aliens. "'Over no conceivable subject is the legislative power of Congress more complete than it is over' the admission of aliens." *** Moreover, the Court believes that the legislative veto we consider today is best characterized as an exercise of legislative or quasi-legislative authority. Under this characterization, the practice does not, even on the surface, constitute an infringement of executive or judicial prerogative. The Attorney General's suspension of deportation is equivalent to a proposal for legislation. The nature of the Attorney General's role as recommendatory is not altered because § 244 provides for congressional action through disapproval rather than by ratification. In comparison to private bills, which must be initiated in the Congress and which allow a Presidential veto to be overriden by a two-thirds majority in both Houses of Congress, § 244 augments rather than reduces the executive branch's authority. ***

Nor does § 244 infringe on the judicial power, as JUSTICE POWELL would hold. *** Congressional action does not substitute for judicial review of the Attorney General's decisions. ***

I do not suggest that all legislative vetoes are necessarily consistent with separation of powers principles. A legislative check on an inherently executive function, for example that of initiating prosecutions, poses an entirely different question. But the legislative veto device here—and in many other settings—is far from an instance of legislative tyranny over the Executive. It is a necessary check on the unavoidably expanding power of the agencies, both executive and independent, as they engage in exercising authority delegated by Congress. *** Today's decision strikes down in one fell swoop provisions in more laws enacted by Congress than the Court has cumulatively invalidated in its history. I fear it will now be more difficult "to insure that the fundamental policy decisions in our society will be made not by an appointed official but by the body immediately responsible to the people." I must dissent.

Notes

1. **Theory.** Consider the extent to which constitutional text provides guidance in *Chadha.* Do legislative vetoes involve legislative encroachment on the executive branch, on the judicial branch, or both? Should the President be deemed to have waived objections to such encroachment when he (or a predecessor) signs into law a bill containing a legislative veto?

2. **Scope and Effect of *Chadha*.** Does this case invalidate all legislative vetoes? Only "one-house" vetoes? Only committee-driven vetoes? Only "adjudicatory" vetoes? There are many legislative vetoes on the books today that have not been challenged. Can you think of any reasons why not?

3. **Questions.** What impact would *Chadha* have on (a) congressional oversight processes where legislation is not forthcoming, or even contemplated, but Congress wants to deter executive action by increasing the visibility of disfavored decisions, (b) requirements that rules be submitted to Congress before they

become final to allow Congress to legislate, and (c) automatic "sunset" legislation whereby agencies disappear if not reauthorized by new legislation?

BOWSHER v. SYNAR
478 U.S. 714 (1986)

CHIEF JUSTICE BURGER delivered the opinion of the Court.

The question presented by these appeals is whether the assignment by Congress to the Comptroller General of the United States of certain functions under the Balanced Budget and Emergency Deficit Control Act of 1985 [the "Gramm-Rudman-Hollings Act"] violates the doctrine of separation of powers. *** The purpose of the Act is to eliminate the federal budget deficit. To that end, the Act sets a "maximum deficit amount" for federal spending for each of fiscal years 1986 through 1991. The size of that maximum deficit amount progressively reduces to zero in fiscal year 1991. If in any fiscal year the federal budget deficit exceeds the maximum deficit amount by more than a specified sum, the Act requires across-the-board cuts in federal spending to reach the targeted deficit level, with half of the cuts made to defense programs and the other half made to nondefense programs.

These "automatic" reductions are accomplished through a rather complicated procedure. *** Each year, the Directors of the Office of Management and Budget (OMB) and the Congressional Budget Office (CBO) independently estimate the amount of the federal budget deficit for the upcoming fiscal year. If that deficit exceeds the maximum targeted deficit amount for that fiscal year by more than a specified amount, the Directors of OMB and CBO independently calculate, on a program-by-program basis, the budget reductions necessary to ensure that the deficit does not exceed the maximum deficit amount. The Act then requires the Directors to report jointly their deficit estimates and budget reduction calculations to the Comptroller General.

The Comptroller General, after reviewing the Directors' reports, then reports his conclusions to the President. The President in turn must issue a "sequestration" order mandating the spending reductions specified by the Comptroller General. There follows a period during which Congress may by legislation reduce spending to obviate, in whole or in part, the need for the sequestration order. If such reductions are not enacted, the sequestration order becomes effective and the spending reductions included in that order are made.

Anticipating constitutional challenge to these procedures, the Act also contains a "fallback" deficit reduction process to take effect "[i]n the event that any of the reporting procedures described in section 251 are invalidated." Under these provisions, the report prepared by the Directors of OMB and the CBO is submitted directly to a specially created Temporary Joint Committee on Deficit Reduction, which must report in five days to both Houses a joint resolution setting forth the content of the Directors' report. Congress then must vote on the resolution under special rules, which render amendments out of order. If the resolution is passed and signed by the President, it then serves as the basis for a Presidential sequestration order.

Within hours of the President's signing of the Act, Congressman Synar, who had voted against the Act, filed a complaint seeking declaratory relief that the Act was unconstitutional. ***

The Constitution does not contemplate an active role for Congress in the supervision of officers charged with the execution of the laws it enacts. The President appoints "Officers of the United States" with the "Advice and Consent of the Senate. *** " Art. II, § 2. Once the appointment has been made and confirmed, however, the Constitution explicitly provides for removal of Officers of the United States by Congress only upon impeachment by the House of Representatives and conviction by the Senate. ***

This Court first directly addressed this issue in *Myers v. United States*, 272 U.S. 52 (1926). At issue in *Myers* was a statute providing that certain postmasters could be removed only "by and with the advice and consent of the Senate." The President removed one such Postmaster without Senate approval, and a lawsuit ensued. CHIEF JUSTICE TAFT, writing for the Court, declared the statute unconstitutional on the ground that for Congress to "draw to itself, or to either branch of it, the power to remove or the right to participate in the exercise of that power *** would be *** to infringe the constitutional principle of the separation of governmental powers."

A decade later, in *Humphrey's Executor v. United States*, 295 U.S. 602 (1935), relied upon heavily by appellants, a Federal Trade Commissioner who had been removed by the President sought backpay. *Humphrey's Executor* involved an issue not presented either in the *Myers* case or in this case—i.e., the power of Congress to limit the President's powers of removal of a Federal Trade Commissioner. The relevant statute permitted removal "by the President," but only "for inefficiency, neglect of duty, or malfeasance in office." *** [T]he Court upheld the statute, holding that "illimitable power of removal is not possessed by the President [with respect to Federal Trade Commissioners]." The Court distinguished *Myers*, reaffirming its holding that congressional participation in the removal of executive officers is unconstitutional. *** In light of these precedents, we conclude that Congress cannot reserve for itself the power of removal of an officer charged with the execution of the laws except by impeachment. To permit the execution of the laws to be vested in an officer answerable only to Congress would, in practical terms, reserve in Congress control over the execution of the laws. The structure of the Constitution does not permit Congress to execute the laws; it follows that Congress cannot grant to an officer under its control what it does not possess. ***

Appellants urge that the Comptroller General performs his duties independently and is not subservient to Congress. *** [T]his contention does not bear close scrutiny. *** The [Budget and Accounting Act of 1921] permits removal [of the Comptroller General] for "inefficiency," "neglect of duty," or "malfeasance." These terms are very broad and, as interpreted by Congress, could sustain removal of a Comptroller General for any number of actual or perceived transgressions of the legislative will. The Constitutional Convention chose to permit impeachment of executive officers only for "Treason, Bribery, or other high Crimes and Misdemeanors." It rejected language that would have permitted impeachment for "maladministration," with Madison arguing that "[s]o vague a term will be equivalent to a tenure during pleasure of the Senate." ***

[Further, it] is clear that Congress has consistently viewed the Comptroller General as an officer of the Legislative Branch. *** Over the years, the Comptrollers General have also viewed themselves as part of the Legislative Branch. *** Against this background, we see no escape from the conclusion that, because Congress has retained removal authority over the Comptroller General, he may not be entrusted with executive powers. The remaining question is whether the Comptroller General has been assigned such powers in the Balanced Budget and Emergency Deficit Control Act of 1985. ***

Appellants suggest that the duties assigned to the Comptroller General in the Act are essentially ministerial and mechanical so that their performance does not constitute "execution of the law" in a meaningful sense. On the contrary, we view these functions as plainly entailing execution of the law in constitutional terms. Interpreting a law enacted by Congress to implement the legislative mandate is the very essence of "execution" of the law. *** He must also interpret the provisions of the Act to determine precisely what budgetary calculations are required. Decisions of that kind are typically made by officers charged with executing a statute. *** Indeed, the Comptroller General commands the President himself to carry out, without the slightest variation (with exceptions not relevant to the constitutional issues presented), the directive of the Comptroller General as to the budget reductions. ***

Congress of course initially determined the content of the Balanced Budget and Emergency Deficit Control Act; and undoubtedly the content of the Act determines the nature of the executive duty. However, as *Chadha* makes clear, once Congress makes its choice in enacting legislation, its participation ends. Congress can thereafter control the execution of its enactment only indirectly—by passing new legislation. By placing the responsibility for execution of the Balanced Budget and Emergency Deficit Control Act in the hands of an officer who is subject to removal only by itself, Congress in effect has retained control over the execution of the Act and has intruded into the executive function. ***

JUSTICE STEVENS, with whom JUSTICE MARSHALL joins, concurring in the judgment.

*** I disagree with the Court, however, on the reasons why the Constitution prohibits the Comptroller General from exercising the powers assigned to him by § 251(b) and § 251(c)(2) of the Act. It is not the dormant, carefully circumscribed congressional removal power that represents the primary constitutional evil. Nor do I agree with the conclusion of both the majority and the dissent that the analysis depends on a labeling of the functions assigned to the Comptroller General as "executive powers." Rather, I am convinced that the Comptroller General must be characterized as an agent of Congress because of his longstanding statutory responsibilities; that the powers assigned to him under the Gramm–Rudman–Hollings Act require him to make policy that will bind the Nation; and that, when Congress, or a component or an agent of Congress, seeks to make policy that will bind the Nation, it must follow the procedures mandated by Article I of the Constitution—through passage by both Houses and presentment to the President. In short, Congress may not exercise its fundamental power to formulate national policy by delegating that power to one of its two Houses, to a legislative committee, or to an individual agent of the Congress such as the Speaker of the House of Representatives, the Sergeant at Arms of the Senate, or the Director of the Congressional Budget Office. That principle, I believe, is applicable to the Comptroller General. ***

The Gramm–Rudman–Hollings Act assigns to the Comptroller General the duty to make policy decisions that have the force of law. *** In short, even though it is well settled that Congress may delegate legislative power to independent agencies or to the Executive, and thereby divest itself of a portion of its lawmaking power, when it elects to exercise such power itself, it may not authorize a lesser representative of the Legislative Branch to act on its behalf. It is for this reason that I believe § 251(b) and § 251(c)(2) of the Act are unconstitutional. ***

JUSTICE WHITE, dissenting.

The Court, acting in the name of separation of powers, takes upon itself to strike down the Gramm–Rudman–Hollings Act, one of the most novel and far-reaching legislative responses to a national crisis since the New Deal. *** The Court's ["distressingly formalistic"] decision rests on a feature of the legislative scheme that is of minimal practical significance and that presents no substantial threat to the basic scheme of separation of powers. *** [W]ith the advent and triumph of the administrative state and the accompanying multiplication of the tasks undertaken by the Federal Government, the Court has been virtually compelled to recognize that Congress may reasonably deem it "necessary and proper" to vest some among the broad new array of governmental functions in officers who are free from the partisanship that may be expected of agents wholly dependent upon the President.

The Court's recognition of the legitimacy of legislation vesting "executive" authority in officers independent of the President does not imply derogation of the President's own constitutional authority *** Determining the level of spending by the Federal Government is not by nature a function central either to the exercise of the President's enumerated powers or to his general duty to ensure execution of the laws; rather, appropriating funds is a peculiarly legislative function. ***

[T]he question remains whether, as the Court concludes, the fact that the officer to whom Congress has delegated the authority to implement the Act is removable by a joint resolution of Congress should require invalidation of the Act. *** I have no quarrel with the proposition that the powers exercised by the Comptroller under the Act may be characterized as "executive" in that they involve the interpretation and carrying out of the Act's mandate. I can also accept the general proposition that although Congress has considerable authority in designating the officers who are to execute legislation the constitutional scheme of separated powers does prevent Congress from reserving an executive role for itself or for its "agents." I cannot accept, however, that the exercise of authority by an officer removable for cause by a joint resolution of Congress is analogous to the impermissible execution of the law by Congress itself, nor would I hold that the congressional role in the removal process renders the Comptroller an "agent" of the Congress, incapable of receiving "executive" power. ***

The deficiencies in the Court's reasoning are apparent. First, the Court baldly mischaracterizes the removal provision when it suggests that it allows Congress to remove the Comptroller for "executing the laws in any fashion found to be unsatisfactory"; in fact, Congress may remove the Comptroller only for one or more of five specified reasons, which "although not so narrow as to deny Congress any leeway, circumscribe Congress' power to some extent by providing a basis for judicial review of congressional removal." Second, and more to the point, the Court overlooks or deliberately ignores the decisive difference between the congressional removal provision and the legislative veto struck down in *Chadha*: under the Budget and Accounting Act, Congress may remove the Comptroller only through a joint resolution, which by definition must be passed by both Houses and signed by the President. In other words, a removal of the Comptroller under the statute satisfies the requirements of bicameralism and presentment laid down in *Chadha*. ***

That such action may represent a more or less successful attempt by Congress to "control" the actions of an officer of the United States surely does not in itself indicate that it is unconstitutional, for no one would dispute that Congress has the power to "control" administration through legislation imposing duties or substantive restraints on executive officers, through legislation increasing or decreasing the funds made available to such officers, or through legislation actually abolishing a particular office. *** The practical result of the removal provision is not to render the Comptroller unduly dependent upon or subservient to Congress, but to render him one of the most independent officers in the entire federal establishment. *** The majority's *** conclusion rests on the rigid dogma that, outside of the impeachment process, any "direct congressional role in the removal of officers charged with the execution of the laws *** is inconsistent with separation of powers." Reliance on such an unyielding principle to strike down a statute posing no real danger of aggrandizement of congressional power is extremely misguided and insensitive to our constitutional role. *** [T]he role of this Court should be limited to determining whether the Act so alters the balance of authority among the branches of government as to pose a genuine threat to the basic division between the lawmaking power and the power to execute the law. ***

Notes

1.   **Background Cases.** *Bowsher* discusses two cases, *Myers* and *Humphrey's Executor*, which involve congressional limits on the President's removal of

officials. In *Myers*, a majority of the Court found congressional limits on the President's removal of a postmaster unconstitutional, stating variously that removal was an executive act, that the President (not his subordinates) has a duty to "take Care" to enforce the law, and that Article II vests all executive power in the President. The dissenters (including JUSTICE HOLMES) thought that because Congress had created the office, it could "prescribe a term of life to it free from any interference." In *Humphrey's Executor*, along with *Wiener v. United States*, 357 U.S. 349 (1958), the Court concluded that Congress could limit the President's removal of members of regulatory agencies. In *Humphrey's Executor*, the Court said the Federal Trade Commission, since it was created to effectuate Congressional policies, was not "in any proper sense" "an arm or an eye of the executive." *Wiener* held that the War Claims Commission's adjudicatory nature implied a limit on the President's removal power. Another pre-*Bowsher* case, *Buckley v. Valeo*, 424 U.S. 1 (1976), held that (a) Congress could appoint members of the Federal Election Commission to the extent that their duties were "essentially of an investigative and informative nature" because Congress could delegate such tasks to its own committees, but (b) Congress could not vest rulemaking and adjudicatory powers in a commission that has any members appointed by Congress. Consider the following questions about these cases:

(a) What does the Constitution say about appointment and removal of officers of the United States?

(b) Are these cases consistent or inconsistent?

(c) Do they authorize a "headless fourth branch" of government not subject to control by either the President or Congress?

(d) Are these cases simply reflective of necessity in the modern administrative state?

(e) Is there a difference between Congress controlling agencies and Congress limiting the President's control of agencies?

2. **Case Comparison.** Compare the Court's analytical approaches in *Chadha* and *Bowsher*. The former holds Congress to formal processes when it legislates; the latter says the defect was that Congress was not legislating, but executing. Are these approaches consistent? Which do you think is preferable (and why)?

3. **Paradox?** If the Comptroller General's actions are executive, why isn't the "fall-back" provision, under which Congress would enact the budget cuts, also executive and therefore unconstitutional?

4. **Questions on "Framework" Statutes.** While many commentators call statutes like Gramm–Rudman–Hollings "quasi-constitutional" statutes, that term is confusing: such statutes can be repealed or amended by a majority vote in both houses of Congress and the President's signature, just like any other legislation.

(a) Is there any constitutional problem with Congress passing a statute tying its hands for the future, such as by requiring a 3/5ths or 2/3rds vote to engage in deficit spending, raise taxes, etc.?

(b) Is there a constitutional problem with the Senate's cloture rule, requiring a supermajority (3/5) vote to cut off debate on a measure favored by the majority of Senators?

(c)   If a statute could demand a balanced budget, why would so many members of Congress favor a balanced budget Constitutional Amendment? Sunstein et. al. argue in their casebook (at page 455) that: "To the extent that the amendment forces this generation to restrict borrowing, it is unnecessary because Congress can accomplish this goal by ordinary legislative processes. To the extent that it attempts to bind future generations, it is illegitimate because these generations have no role in the ratification process." Do you agree?

5.   **Problem.** Congress passes domestic legislation giving the Department of Labor authority to make "all appropriate rules and regulations to effectuate the policy of the Labor Act." Shortly thereafter, to meet budget reduction goals, the President issues an Executive Order requiring all agency rules to be prescreened by the President's Office of Management and Budget (OMB). OMB prescreens the Department of Labor's regulations, finds that they would create a "significant impact on federal spending," and refuses to release the regulations. Is OMB's action constitutional?

MORRISON v. OLSON
487 U.S. 654 (1988).

CHIEF JUSTICE REHNQUIST delivered the opinion of the Court.

This case presents us with a challenge to the independent counsel provisions of the Ethics in Government Act of 1978. We hold today that these provisions of the Act do not violate the Appointments Clause of the Constitution, Art. II, § 2, cl. 2, or the limitations of Article III, nor do they impermissibly interfere with the President's authority under Article II in violation of the constitutional principle of separation of powers.

Briefly stated, Title VI of the Ethics in Government Act allows for the appointment of an "independent counsel" to investigate and, if appropriate, prosecute certain high-ranking Government officials for violations of federal criminal laws. The Act requires the Attorney General, upon receipt of information that he determines is "sufficient to constitute grounds to investigate whether any person [covered by the Act] may have violated any Federal criminal law," to conduct a preliminary investigation of the matter. When the Attorney General has completed this investigation, or 90 days has elapsed, he is required to report to a special court (the Special Division) created by the Act "for the purpose of appointing independent counsels." If the Attorney General determines that "there are no reasonable grounds to believe that further investigation is warranted," then he must notify the Special Division of this result. In such a case, "the division of the court shall have no power to appoint an independent counsel." If, however, the Attorney General has determined that there are "reasonable grounds to believe that further investigation or prosecution is warranted," then he "shall apply to the division of the court for the appointment of an independent counsel." The Attorney General's application to the court "shall contain sufficient information to assist the [court] in selecting an independent counsel and in defining that independent counsel's prosecutorial jurisdiction." Upon receiving this application, the Special Division "shall appoint an appropriate independent counsel and shall define that independent counsel's prosecutorial jurisdiction." ***

Two statutory provisions govern the length of an independent counsel's tenure in office. The first defines the procedure for removing an independent counsel. Section 596(a)(1) provides: "An independent counsel appointed under this chapter may be removed from office, other than by impeachment and conviction, only by the personal action of the Attorney General and only for good cause, physical disability, mental incapacity, or any other condition that substantially impairs the performance of such independent counsel's duties." If an independent counsel is removed pursuant to this section, the Attorney General is required to submit a report to both the Special Division and the Judiciary Committees of the Senate and the House "specifying the facts found and the ultimate grounds for such removal." Under the current version of the Act, an independent counsel can obtain judicial review of the Attorney General's action by filing a civil action ***. Members of the Special Division "may not hear or determine any such civil action or any appeal of a decision in any such civil action." The reviewing court is authorized to grant reinstatement or "other appropriate relief."

The other provision governing the tenure of the independent counsel defines the procedures for "terminating" the counsel's office. Under § 596(b)(1), the office of an independent counsel terminates when he or she notifies the Attorney General that he or she has completed or substantially completed any investigations or prosecutions undertaken pursuant to the Act. In addition, the Special Division *** may terminate the office of an independent counsel at any time if it finds that "the investigation of all matters within the prosecutorial jurisdiction of such independent counsel *** have been completed or so substantially completed that it would be appropriate for the Department of Justice to complete such investigations and prosecutions." ***

The Appointments Clause of Article II reads as follows:

> [The President] shall nominate, and by and with the Advice and Consent of the Senate, shall appoint Ambassadors, other public Ministers and Consuls, Judges of the Supreme Court, and all other Officers of the United States, whose Appointments are not herein otherwise provided for, and which shall be established by Law: but the Congress may by Law vest the Appointment of such inferior Officers, as they think proper, in the President alone, in the Courts of Law, or in the Heads of Departments.

The parties do not dispute that "[t]he Constitution for purposes of appointment *** divides all its officers into two classes." As we stated in *Buckley v. Valeo*, 424 U.S. 1, 132 (1976): "[P]rincipal officers are selected by the President with the advice and consent of the Senate. Inferior officers Congress may allow to be appointed by the President alone, by the heads of departments, or by the Judiciary." The initial question is, accordingly, whether appellant is an "inferior" or a "principal" officer. If she is the latter, as the Court of Appeals concluded, then the Act is in violation of the Appointments Clause.

The line between "inferior" and "principal" officers is one that is far from clear, and the Framers provided little guidance into where it should be drawn. *** We need not attempt here to decide exactly where the line falls *** because in our view appellant clearly falls on the "inferior officer" side of that line. Several factors lead to this conclusion.

First, appellant is subject to removal by a higher Executive Branch official. Although appellant may not be "subordinate" to the Attorney General (and the President) insofar as she possesses a degree of independent discretion to exercise the powers delegated to her under the Act, the fact that she can be removed by the Attorney General indicates that she is to some degree "inferior" in rank and authority. Second, appellant is empowered by the Act to perform only certain, limited duties. *** Third, appellant's office is limited in jurisdiction. *** Finally, appellant's office is limited in tenure [as] an independent counsel is appointed essentially to accomplish a single task, and when that task is over the office is terminated, either by the counsel herself or by action of the Special Division. ***

This does not, however, end our inquiry under the Appointments Clause. Appellees argue that even if appellant is an "inferior" officer the Clause does not empower Congress to place the power to appoint such an officer outside the Executive Branch. They contend that the Clause does not contemplate congressional authorization of "interbranch appointments," in which an officer of one branch is appointed by officers of another branch. *** On its face, the language of this "excepting clause" admits of no limitation on interbranch appointments. Indeed, the inclusion of "as they think proper" seems clearly to give Congress significant discretion to determine whether it is "proper" to vest the appointment of, for example, executive officials in the "courts of Law." ***

We do not mean to say that Congress' power to provide for interbranch appointments of "inferior officers" is unlimited. In addition to separation-of-powers concerns, which would arise if such provisions for appointment had the potential to impair the constitutional functions assigned to one of the branches, *** Congress' decision to vest the appointment power in the courts would be improper if there was some "incongruity" between the functions normally performed by the courts and the performance of their duty to appoint. In this case, however, we do not think it impermissible for Congress to vest the power to appoint independent counsel in a specially created federal court. [There is no] inherent incongruity about a court having the power to appoint prosecutorial officers.[13] *** Congress, of course, was concerned when it created the office of independent counsel with the conflicts

---

[13] Indeed, in light of judicial experience with prosecutors in criminal cases, it could be said that courts are especially well qualified to appoint prosecutors. This is not a case in which judges are given power to appoint an officer in an area in which they have no special knowledge or expertise, as in, for example, a statute authorizing the courts to appoint officials in the Department of Agriculture or the Federal Energy Regulatory Commission.

of interest that could arise in situations when the Executive Branch is called upon to investigate its own high-ranking officers. If it were to remove the appointing authority from the Executive Branch, the most logical place to put it was in the Judicial Branch. In the light of the Act's provision making the judges of the Special Division ineligible to participate in any matters relating to an independent counsel they have appointed we do not think that appointment of the independent counsel by the court runs afoul of the constitutional limitation on "incongruous" interbranch appointments.

Appellees next contend that the powers vested in the Special Division by the Act conflict with Article III of the Constitution.

Leaving aside for the moment the Division's power to terminate an independent counsel, we do not think that Article III absolutely prevents Congress from vesting *** miscellaneous powers in the Special Division pursuant to the Act. As we observed above, one purpose of the broad prohibition upon the courts' exercise of "executive or administrative duties of a nonjudicial nature" is to maintain the separation between the Judiciary and the other branches of the Federal Government by ensuring that judges do not encroach upon executive or legislative authority or undertake tasks that are more properly accomplished by those branches. In this case, the miscellaneous powers described above do not impermissibly trespass upon the authority of the Executive Branch. Some of these allegedly "supervisory" powers conferred on the court are passive *** Other provisions of the Act do require the court to exercise some judgment and discretion, but the powers granted by these provisions are themselves essentially ministerial. The Act simply does not give the Division the power to "supervise" the independent counsel in the exercise of his or her investigative or prosecutorial authority.

We are more doubtful about the Special Division's power to terminate the office of the independent counsel *** Nonetheless, we do not, as did the Court of Appeals, view this provision as a significant judicial encroachment upon executive power or upon the prosecutorial discretion of the independent counsel.

Nor do we believe, as appellees contend, that the Special Division's exercise of the various powers specifically granted to it under the Act poses any threat to the "impartial and independent federal adjudication of claims within the judicial power of the United States." We reach this conclusion for two reasons. First, the Act as it currently stands gives the Special Division itself no power to review any of the actions of the independent counsel or any of the actions of the Attorney General with regard to the counsel. Accordingly, there is no risk of partisan or biased adjudication of claims regarding the independent counsel by that court. Second, the Act prevents members of the Special Division from participating in "any judicial proceeding concerning a matter which involves such independent counsel while such independent counsel is serving in that office or which involves the exercise of such independent counsel's official duties, regardless of whether such independent counsel is still serving in that office." We think both the special court and its judges are sufficiently isolated by these statutory provisions from the review of the activities of the independent counsel so as to avoid any taint of the independence of the Judiciary such as would render the Act invalid under Article III. ***

We now turn to consider whether the Act is invalid under the constitutional principle of separation of powers. Two related issues must be addressed: The first is whether the provision of the Act restricting the Attorney General's power to remove the independent counsel to only those instances in which he can show "good cause," taken by itself, impermissibly interferes with the President's exercise of his constitutionally appointed functions. The second is whether, taken as a whole, the Act violates the separation of powers by reducing the President's ability to control the prosecutorial powers wielded by the independent counsel. ***

We held in *Bowsher* that "Congress cannot reserve for itself the power of removal of an officer charged with the execution of the laws except by impeachment." A primary antecedent for this ruling was our 1926 decision in *Myers v. United States*, 272 U.S. 52 (1926). *** Unlike both *Bowsher* and *Myers*, this case does not involve an attempt by Congress itself to gain a role in the removal of executive officials other than its established powers of impeachment and conviction. The Act instead puts the removal power squarely in the hands of the Executive Branch; an independent counsel may be removed from office, "only by the personal action of the Attorney General, and only for good cause." There is no requirement of congressional approval of the Attorney General's removal decision, though the decision is subject to judicial review. In our view, the removal provisions of the Act make this case more analogous to *Humphrey's Executor v. United States*, 295 U.S. 602 (1935), and *Wiener v. United States*, 357 U.S. 349 (1958), than to *Myers* or *Bowsher*.

Appellees contend that *Humphrey's Executor* and *Wiener* are distinguishable from this case because they did not involve officials who performed a "core executive function." *** We undoubtedly did rely on the terms "quasi-legislative" and "quasi-judicial" to distinguish the officials involved in *Humphrey's Executor* and *Wiener* from those in *Myers*, but *** whether the Constitution allows Congress to impose a "good cause"-type restriction on the President's power to remove an official cannot be made to turn on whether or not that official is classified as "purely executive." The analysis contained in our removal cases is designed *** to ensure that Congress does not interfere with the President's exercise of the "executive power" and his constitutionally appointed duty to "take care that the laws be faithfully executed" under Article II.

Considering for the moment the "good cause" removal provision in isolation from the other parts of the Act at issue in this case, we cannot say that the imposition of a "good cause" standard for removal by itself unduly trammels on executive authority. *** Although the counsel exercises no small amount of discretion and judgment in deciding how to carry out his or her duties under the Act, we simply do not see how the President's need to control the exercise of that discretion is so central to the functioning of the Executive Branch as to require as a matter of constitutional law that the counsel be terminable at will by the President.

Nor do we think that the "good cause" removal provision at issue here impermissibly burdens the President's power to control or supervise the independent counsel, as an executive official, in the execution of his or her duties under the Act. This is not a case in which the power to remove an executive official has been completely stripped from the President, thus providing no means for the President to ensure the "faithful execution" of the laws. Rather, because the independent counsel may be terminated for "good cause," the Executive, through the Attorney General, retains ample authority to assure that the counsel is competently performing his or her statutory responsibilities in a manner that comports with the provisions of the Act. ***

The final question to be addressed is whether the Act, taken as a whole, violates the principle of separation of powers by unduly interfering with the role of the Executive Branch. [W]e have never held that the Constitution requires that the three branches of Government "operate with absolute independence." *United States v. Nixon*, 418 U.S., at 707.

We observe first that this case does not involve an attempt by Congress to increase its own powers at the expense of the Executive Branch. *** Similarly, we do not think that the Act works any judicial usurpation of properly executive functions. *** [T]he power to appoint inferior officers such as independent counsel is not in itself an "executive" function in the constitutional sense, at least when Congress has exercised its power to vest the appointment of an inferior office in the "courts of Law." *** [T]he Special Division has no power to appoint an independent counsel sua sponte; it may only do so upon the specific request of the Attorney General ***

Finally, we do not think that the Act "impermissibly undermine[s]" the powers of the Executive Branch, or "disrupts the proper balance between the coordinate branches [by] prevent[ing] the Executive Branch from accomplishing its constitutionally assigned functions" ***. It is undeniable that the Act reduces the amount of control or supervision that the Attorney General and, through him, the President exercises over the investigation and prosecution of a certain class of alleged criminal activity. The Attorney General is not allowed to appoint the individual of his choice; he does not determine the counsel's jurisdiction; and his power to remove a counsel is limited. Nonetheless, the Act does give the Attorney General several means of supervising or controlling the prosecutorial powers that may be wielded by an independent counsel. *** In sum, we conclude today that it does not violate the Appointments Clause for Congress to vest the appointment of independent counsel in the Special Division; that the powers exercised by the Special Division under the Act do not violate Article III; and that the Act does not violate the separation-of-powers principle by impermissibly interfering with the functions of the Executive Branch. ***

JUSTICE KENNEDY took no part in the consideration or decision of this case.

JUSTICE SCALIA, dissenting.

*** If to describe this case is not to decide it, the concept of a government of separate and coordinate powers no longer has meaning. The Court devotes most of its attention to such relatively technical details as the Appointments Clause and the removal power, addressing briefly and only at the end of its opinion the separation of powers. *** I think that has it backwards. Our opinions are full of the recognition that it is the principle of separation of powers *** which gives comprehensible content to the Appointments Clause, and determines the appropriate scope of the removal power. ***

Article II, § 1, cl. 1, of the Constitution provides: "The executive Power shall be vested in a President of the United States." *** [T]his does not mean some of the executive power, but all of the executive power. It seems to me, therefore, that the [statute violates] fundamental separation-of-powers principles if the following two questions are answered affirmatively: (1) Is the conduct of a criminal prosecution (and of an investigation to decide whether to prosecute) the exercise of purely executive power? (2) Does the statute deprive the President of the United States of exclusive control over the exercise of that power? Surprising to say, the Court appears to concede an affirmative answer to both questions, but seeks to avoid the inevitable conclusion that since the statute vests some purely executive power in a person who is not the President of the United States it is void. ***

The utter incompatibility of the Court's approach with our constitutional traditions can be made more clear, perhaps, by applying it to the powers of the other two branches. Is it conceivable that if Congress passed a statute depriving itself of less than full and entire control over some insignificant area of legislation, we would inquire whether the matter was "so central to the functioning of the Legislative Branch" as really to require complete control, or whether the statute gives Congress "sufficient control over the surrogate legislator to ensure that Congress is able to perform its constitutionally assigned duties"? Of course we would have none of that. Once we determined that a purely legislative power was at issue we would require it to be exercised, wholly and entirely, by Congress. Or to bring the point closer to home, consider a statute giving to non-Article III judges just a tiny bit of purely judicial power in a relatively insignificant field, with substantial control, though not total control, in the courts—perhaps "clear error" review, which would be a fair judicial equivalent of the Attorney General's "for cause" removal power here. Is there any doubt that we would not pause to inquire whether the matter was "so central to the functioning of the Judicial Branch" as really to require complete control, or whether we retained "sufficient control over the matters to be decided that we are able to perform our constitutionally assigned duties"? *** We should say here that the President's constitutionally assigned duties include complete control over investigation and prosecution of violations of the law, and that the inexorable command of Article II is clear and definite: the executive power must be vested in the President of the United States.

Is it unthinkable that the President should have such exclusive power, even when alleged crimes by him or his close associates are at issue? No more so than that Congress should have the exclusive power of legislation, even when what is at issue is its own exemption from the burdens of certain laws. No more so than that this Court should have the exclusive power to pronounce the final decision on justiciable cases and controversies, even those pertaining to the constitutionality of a statute reducing the salaries of the Justices. A system of separate and coordinate powers necessarily involves an acceptance of exclusive power that can theoretically be abused.

The Court has, nonetheless, replaced the clear constitutional prescription that the executive power belongs to the President with a "balancing test." What are the standards to determine how the balance is to be struck, that is, how much removal of Presidential power is too much? *** Besides weakening the Presidency by reducing the zeal of his staff, it must also be obvious that the institution of the independent counsel enfeebles him more directly in his constant confrontations with Congress, by eroding his public support. Nothing is so politically effective as the ability to charge that one's opponent and his associates are not merely wrongheaded, naive, ineffective, but, in all probability, "crooks." And nothing so effectively gives an appearance of validity to such charges as a Justice Department investigation and, even better, prosecution. The present statute provides ample means for that sort of attack, assuring that massive and lengthy investigations will occur, not merely when the Justice Department in the application of its usual standards believes they are called for, but whenever it cannot be said that there are "no reasonable grounds to believe" they are called for. ***

III–3. "Independent Counsel Act." AUTH © 1998 The Philadelphia Inquirer. Reprinted with permission of UNIVERSAL PRESS SYNDICATE. All rights reserved.

[T]he Court does not attempt to "decide exactly" what establishes the line between principal and "inferior" officers, but is confident that, whatever the line may be, appellant "clearly falls on the 'inferior officer' side" of it. The Court gives three reasons: First, she "is subject to removal by a higher Executive Branch official," namely, the Attorney General. Second, she is "empowered by the Act to perform only certain, limited duties." Third, her office is "limited in jurisdiction" and "limited in tenure."

The first of these lends no support to the view that appellant is an inferior officer. Appellant is removable only for "good cause" or physical or mental incapacity. By contrast, most (if not all) principal officers in the Executive Branch may be removed by the President at will. *** The second reason offered by the Court—that appellant performs only certain, limited duties—may be relevant to whether she is an inferior officer, but it mischaracterizes the extent of her powers. As the Court states: "Admittedly, the Act delegates to appellant [the] 'full power and independent authority to exercise all investigative and prosecutorial functions and powers of the Department of Justice.'" Moreover, [the Special Prosecutor has] a power not even the Attorney General possesses: to "contes[t] in court *** any claim of privilege or attempt to withhold evidence on grounds of national security." *** [U]nlike most high-ranking Executive Branch officials, she continues to serve until she (or the Special Division) decides that her work is substantially completed. *** As to the scope of her jurisdiction, there can be no doubt that is small (though far from unimportant). But within it she exercises more than the full power of the Attorney General. ***

I think it preferable to look to the text of the Constitution and the division of power that it establishes. These demonstrate, I think, that the independent counsel is not an inferior officer because she is not subordinate to any officer in the Executive Branch (indeed, not even to the President). Dictionaries in use at the time of the Constitutional Convention gave the word "inferior" two meanings which it still bears today: (1) "[l]ower in place, *** station, *** rank of life, *** value or excellency," and (2) "[s]ubordinate." In a document dealing with the structure *** of a government, one would naturally expect the word to bear the latter meaning—indeed, in such a context it would be unpardonably careless to use the word unless a relation of subordination was intended ***

There is, of course, no provision in the Constitution stating who may remove executive officers, except the provisions for removal by impeachment. Before the present decision it was established, however, (1) that the President's power to remove principal officers who exercise purely executive powers could not be restricted, *see Myers v. United States*, 272 U.S. 52, 127 (1926), and (2) that his power to remove inferior officers who exercise purely executive powers, and whose appointment Congress had removed from the usual procedure of Presidential appointment with Senate consent, could be restricted, at least where the appointment had been made by an officer of the Executive Branch, *United States v. Perkins*, 116 U.S. 483, 485 (1886). ***

Since our 1935 decision in *Humphrey's Executor v. United States*, which was considered by many at the time the product of an activist, anti-New Deal Court bent on reducing the power of President Franklin Roosevelt—it has been established that the line of permissible restriction upon removal of principal officers lies at the point at which the powers exercised by those officers are no longer purely executive. *** *Humphrey's Executor* at least had the decency formally to observe the constitutional principle that the

President had to be the repository of all executive power, which, as *Myers* carefully explained, necessarily means that he must be able to discharge those who do not perform executive functions according to his liking. By contrast, "our present considered view" is simply that any executive officer's removal can be restricted, so long as the President remains "able to accomplish his constitutional role." There are now no lines. If the removal of a prosecutor, the virtual embodiment of the power to "take care that the laws be faithfully executed," can be restricted, what officer's removal cannot? This is an open invitation for Congress to experiment. What about a special Assistant Secretary of State, with responsibility for one very narrow area of foreign policy, who would not only have to be confirmed by the Senate but could also be removed only pursuant to certain carefully designed restrictions? Could this possibly render the President "[un]able to accomplish his constitutional role"? Or a special Assistant Secretary of Defense for Procurement? The possibilities are endless, and the Court does not understand what the separation of powers, what "[a]mbition *** counteract[ing] ambition," Federalist No. 51 (Madison), is all about, if it does not expect Congress to try them. As far as I can discern from the Court's opinion, it is now open season upon the President's removal power for all executive officers, with not even the superficially principled restriction of *Humphrey's Executor* as cover. The Court essentially says to the President: "Trust us. We will make sure that you are able to accomplish your constitutional role." I think the Constitution gives the President—and the people—more protection than that.

Notes

1.   **Comparisons and Policies.**   Can you reconcile *Bowsher* and *Morrison*? Does *Morrison* permit Congress to create pockets of federal governmental authority (what JUSTICE SCALIA calls "mini-Executives") not subject to control by any official elected by the people? Is it true that special prosecutors have nothing to do with Congress reducing the power of the President?

2.   **Role of the Courts.**   Are you comfortable with the role played by the judiciary in the appointment of special prosecutors? Don't special prosecutors ultimately answer to the courts, who oversee any criminal actions which the prosecutor may initiate? It is interesting to compare the Supreme Court's early refusal to give an advisory opinion to President Washington with the Court's blessing of the collateral duty given to judges in *Morrison*. See also *Mistretta v. United States*, 488 U.S. 361 (1989), in which the Court upheld the constitutionality of the United States Sentencing Commission, "an independent commission located in the judicial branch" whose role is to create mandatory sentencing guidelines specifying narrow ranges of permissible sentences for various crimes in order to reduce the variation in sentences given by different judges. The seven members of the Sentencing Commission are appointed by the President; three of them must be federal judges. The Court held that "the participation of federal judges on the Sentencing Commission does not threaten, either in fact or in appearance, the impartiality of the judicial branch" because "sentencing will continue to be performed exclusively by the judicial branch." The Court said, of presidential appointment and removal power, that federal judges would not likely be influenced to "comport their actions to the wishes of the

President for the purpose of receiving an appointment" and that removal from the commission was a "negligible threat" since removal would still leave the judge with a lifetime appointment. In a scathing dissent, JUSTICE SCALIA argued that *Mistretta* "is not about commingling, but *** about the creation of a new branch altogether, a sort of junior-varsity Congress." With whom do you agree?

3. **Problem.** The United States owns Washington National Airport and Dulles International Airport. The 1987 Federal Airports Act provides for the lease of these airports to an Authority established by the State of Virginia and the District of Columbia. As a condition of the lease, the Airports Act establishes a Board of Review empowered to disapprove of Authority decisions, including budgets, adoption of regulations, and appointment of the Authority's President. The Airports Act states that the five members of this Board of Review serve "in their individual capacities as representatives of users of the airports." They are appointed by the Authority from lists of Congressmen and Senators "currently serving on" specified congressional committees responsible for formulating national aviation policies. The Airports Act says nothing about removal of members of the Board of Review. The Airports Act also provides that invalidation of the provisions concerning the Board of Review will make the lease to the Authority "null and void." Were the lease voided, major expansions of both airports contemplated by the Authority would be delayed. Citizens for the Abatement of Aircraft Noise ("Citizens") has filed suit on behalf of individuals who claim they would face increased noise and pollution from the expansion of the airports. The suit alleges that the Airports Act provisions outlined above are unconstitutional. Discuss whether the Airports Act is constitutional. After you have independently outlined your thoughts on this problem, you might look at *Metropolitan Washington Airports Authority v. Citizens for the Abatement of Aircraft Noise*, 501 U.S. 252 (1991). As a review exercise, you might also consider whether Citizens' suit is justiciable.

4. **Executive Searches of Congressional Offices**. On May 20, 2006, the FBI executed a search warrant on the offices of Congressman William J. Jefferson in the Rayburn House Office Building. This action raised immediate objections by congressional leaders, a threat to resign by the Attorney General if the President revoked authorization to execute the search warrant, and an agreement by all parties for the President to seal and sequester the materials seized for a period of time to allow the Attorney General and House of Representatives to engage in good faith discussion to resolve the issues and "if it should prove necessary after exhaustion of such discussion, through appropriate proceedings in the courts of the United States." Did this search, though authorized by a federal judge, violate separation of powers principles embodied in the Speech or Debate Clause (Art.1, § 6, cl. 1)? *See United States v. Jefferson*, 546 F.3d 300 (4th Cir. 2008) (protections of Speech or Debate Clause did not compel grand jury's indictment to be further reviewed for consideration of privileged legislative activities).

FREE ENTERPRISE FUND v. PCAOB
561 U. S. 477 (2010)

CHIEF JUSTICE ROBERTS delivered the opinion of the Court.

*** [May] the President be restricted in his ability to remove a principal officer, who is in turn restricted in his ability to remove an inferior officer, even though that inferior officer determines the policy and enforces the laws of the United States? *** After a series of celebrated accounting debacles, Congress enacted the Sarbanes-Oxley Act of 2002 (or Act). Among other measures, the Act introduced tighter regulation of the accounting industry under a new Public Company Accounting Oversight Board. The Board is composed of five members, appointed to staggered 5-year terms by the Securities and Exchange Commission. *** The Act places the Board under the SEC's oversight, particularly with respect to the issuance of rules or the imposition of sanctions ***. But the *** Commission cannot remove Board members at will, but only "for good cause shown," "in accordance with" certain procedures. ***

We hold that the dual for-cause limitations on the removal of Board members contravene the Constitution's separation of powers. The Constitution provides that "the executive Power shall be vested in a President of the United States of America." As Madison stated on the floor of the First Congress, "if any power whatsoever is in its nature Executive, it is the power of appointing, overseeing, and controlling those who execute the laws." *** Without a layer of insulation between the Commission and the Board, the Commission could remove a Board member at any time, and therefore would be fully responsible for what the Board does. The President could then hold the Commission to account for its supervision of the Board, to the same extent that he may hold the Commission to account for everything else it does.

A second level of tenure protection changes the nature of the President's review. Now the Commission cannot remove a Board member at will. The President therefore cannot hold the Commission fully accountable for the Board's conduct, to the same extent that he may hold the Commission accountable for everything else that it does. The Commissioners are not responsible for the Board's actions. They are only responsible for their own determination of whether the Act's rigorous good-cause standard is met. And even if the President disagrees with their determination, he is powerless to intervene—unless that determination is so unreasonable as to constitute "inefficiency, neglect of duty, or malfeasance in office."

This novel structure does not merely add to the Board's independence, but transforms it. Neither the President, nor anyone directly responsible to him, nor even an officer whose conduct he may review only for good cause, has full control over the Board. The President is stripped of the power our precedents have preserved, and his ability to execute the laws—by holding his subordinates accountable for their conduct—is impaired.

That arrangement is contrary to Article II's vesting of the executive power in the President. Without the ability to oversee the Board, or to attribute the Board's failings to those whom he can oversee, the President is no longer the judge of the Board's conduct. He is not the one who decides whether Board members are abusing their offices or neglecting their duties. He can neither ensure that the laws are faithfully executed, nor be held responsible for a Board member's breach of faith. This violates the basic principle that the President "cannot delegate ultimate responsibility or the active obligation to supervise that goes with it," because Article II "makes a single President responsible for the actions of the Executive Branch."

Indeed, if allowed to stand, this dispersion of responsibility could be multiplied. If Congress can shelter the bureaucracy behind two layers of good-cause tenure, why not a third? *** By granting the Board executive power without the Executive's oversight, this Act subverts the President's ability to ensure that the laws are faithfully executed—as well as the public's ability to pass judgment on his efforts. The Act's restrictions are incompatible with the Constitution's separation of powers.

Respondents and the dissent resist this conclusion, portraying the Board as "the kind of practical accommodation between the Legislature and the Executive that should be permitted in a 'workable government.'" *** No one doubts Congress's power to create a vast and varied federal bureaucracy. But where, in all this, is the role for oversight by an elected President? *** [T]he dissent dismisses the importance of removal as a tool of supervision, concluding that the President's "power to get something done" more often depends on "who controls the agency's budget requests and funding, the relationships between one agency or department and another, . . . purely political factors (including Congress' ability to assert influence)," and indeed whether particular unelected officials support or "resist" the President's policies. The Framers did not rest our liberties on such bureaucratic minutiae. ***

In fact, the multilevel protection that the dissent endorses "provides a blueprint for extensive expansion of the legislative power." *** Congress has plenary control over the salary, duties, and even existence of executive offices. Only Presidential oversight can counter its influence. *** In its pursuit of a "workable government," Congress cannot reduce the Chief Magistrate to a cajoler-in-chief. ***

Alternatively, respondents portray the Act's limitations on removal as irrelevant, because *** the Commission wields "at-will removal power over Board functions if not Board members." *** Broad power over Board functions is not equivalent to the power to remove Board members. The Commission may, for example, approve the Board's budget, issue binding regulations, relieve the Board of authority, amend Board sanctions, or enforce Board rules on its own. But altering the budget or powers of an agency as a whole is a problematic way to control an inferior officer. *** Nor do the employees referenced by the dissent enjoy the same significant and unusual protections from Presidential oversight as members of the Board. *** Nothing in our opinion, therefore, should be read to cast doubt on the use of what is colloquially known as the civil service system within independent agencies.[10]

---

[10]For similar reasons, our holding also does not address that subset of independent agency employees who serve as administrative law judges. Whether administrative law judges are necessarily "Officers of the United States" is disputed. And unlike members of the Board, many administrative law judges of course perform adjudicative rather than enforcement or policymaking functions, or possess purely recommendatory powers. The Government below refused to identify either "civil service tenure-protected employees in independent agencies" or administrative law judges as "precedent for the PCAOB."

Finally, *** we see little analogy between our Nation's armed services and the Public Company Accounting Oversight Board. Military officers are broadly subject to Presidential control through the chain of command and through the President's powers as Commander in Chief. *** Here, by contrast, the President has no authority to initiate a Board member's removal for cause.

Petitioners raise three more challenges to the Board under the Appointments Clause. None has merit. First, petitioners argue that Board members are principal officers requiring Presidential appointment with the Senate's advice and consent. We held in *Edmond [v. United States*, 20 U.S. 651 (1997), that "whether one is an 'inferior' officer depends on whether he has a superior," and that "'inferior officers' are officers whose work is directed and supervised at some level" by other officers appointed by the President with the Senate's consent. *** [U]nder *Edmond* the Board members are inferior officers *** [Second] Because the Commission is a freestanding component of the Executive Branch, not subordinate to or contained within any other such component, it constitutes a "Department" for the purposes of the Appointments Clause. *** [Third, petitioners] argue that the full Commission cannot constitutionally appoint Board members, because only the Chairman of the Commission is the Commission's "Head." *** [W]e see no reason why a multimember body may not be the "Head" of a "Department" that it governs. The Appointments Clause necessarily contemplates collective appointments by the "Courts of Law," and each House of Congress, too, appoints its officers collectively. ***

JUSTICE BREYER, with whom JUSTICE STEVENS, JUSTICE GINSBURG, and JUSTICE SOTOMAYOR join, dissenting.

*** [W]ith the exception of the general "vesting" and "take care" language, the Constitution is completely "silent with respect to the power of removal from office." *** [A] functional approach permits Congress and the President the flexibility needed to adapt statutory law to changing circumstances. *** If the President seeks to regulate through impartial adjudication, then insulation of the adjudicator from removal at will can help him achieve that goal. And to free a technical decisionmaker from the fear of removal without cause can similarly help create legitimacy with respect to that official's regulatory actions by helping to insulate his technical decisions from nontechnical political pressure. *** Thus, here, as in similar cases, we should decide the constitutional question in light of the provision's practical functioning in context. And our decision should take account of the Judiciary's comparative lack of institutional expertise.

To what extent then is the Act's "for cause" provision likely, as a practical matter, to limit the President's exercise of executive authority? *** [S]o long as the President is legitimately foreclosed from removing the Commissioners except for cause (as the majority assumes), nullifying the Commission's power to remove Board members only for cause will not resolve the problem the Court has identified: The President will still be "powerless to intervene" by removing the Board members if the Commission reasonably decides not to do so.

In other words, the Court fails to show why two layers of "for cause" protection—Layer One insulating the Commissioners from the President, and Layer Two insulating the Board from the Commissioners—impose any more serious limitation upon the President's powers than one layer. *** Congress and the President had good reason for enacting the challenged "for cause" provision. First and foremost, the Board adjudicates cases. *** Moreover, *** the Accounting Board members supervise, and are themselves, technical professional experts. ***

Even if the "for cause" provision before us does not itself significantly interfere with the President's authority or aggrandize Congress' power, is it nonetheless necessary to adopt a bright-line rule forbidding the provision lest, through a series of such provisions, each itself upheld as reasonable, Congress might undercut the President's central constitutional role? The answer to this question is that no such need has been shown. Moreover, insofar as the Court seeks to create such a rule, it fails. *** [E]ven if I assume that the majority categorically excludes the competitive service from the scope of its new rule, (leaving this question open), the exclusion would be insufficient. This is because the Court's "double for-cause" rule applies to appointees who are "inferior officers." And who are they? Courts and scholars have struggled for more than a century to define the constitutional term "inferior officers," without much success. ***

Notes

1. **Formalism and Functionalism.** The majority and dissent differ over whether the Board performs adjudicative and technical functions and the dissent says the Act does not give the Commission power to start, stop, or alter Board investigations. Do these disagreements matter?

2. **Breadth of the Ruling.** Do you share the dissent's concern that this decision may lessen the job security of millions of federal civil servants, removable only "for cause" through processes within executive branch units?

3. **Cooperative Federalism.** Numerous state regulatory regimes operate in the shadow of federal law in which states enforce regulatory regimes that meet or exceed federal minimum standards. The President may terminate federal funding and may exert other controls over these quasi-federal-quasi-state laws, but he cannot remove state officers who enforce these laws. Does this violate separation of powers principles? See Professor Ronald Krotoszynski, "Cooperative Federalism, the New Formalism, and the Separation of Powers Revisited: Free Enterprise Fund and the Problem of Presidential Oversight of State-Government Officer Enforcing Federal Law," 2012 DUKE LAW J. 1601.

NLRB v. NOEL CANNING
134 S. Ct. 2250 (2014)

JUSTICE BREYER delivered the opinion of the Court.

Ordinarily the President must obtain "the Advice and Consent of the Senate" before appointing an "Office[r] of the United States." But the Recess Appointments Clause *** gives the President alone the power "to fill up all Vacancies that may happen during the Recess of the Senate, by granting

Commissions which shall expire at the End of their next Session." We here consider three questions about the application of this Clause.

The first concerns the scope of the words "recess of the Senate." Does that phrase refer only to an inter-session recess (*i.e.,* a break between formal sessions of Congress), or does it also include an intra-session recess, such as a summer recess in the midst of a session? *** The second question concerns the scope of the words "vacancies that may happen." Does that phrase refer only to vacancies that first come into existence during a recess, or does it also include vacancies that arise prior to a recess but continue to exist during the recess? *** The third question concerns calculation of the length of a "recess." The President made the appointments here at issue on January 4, 2012. At that time the Senate was in recess pursuant to a December 17, 2011, resolution providing for a series of brief recesses punctuated by *"pro forma* session[s]," with "no business ... transacted," every Tuesday and Friday through January 20, 2012. In calculating the length of a recess are we to ignore the *pro forma* sessions, thereby treating the series of brief recesses as a single, month-long recess? ***

The National Labor Relations Board (NLRB) found *** Noel Canning had unlawfully refused to reduce to writing and execute a collective-bargaining agreement with a labor union. *** [Canning argued that because] three of the five Board members had been invalidly appointed, *** [the Board lacked] the three lawfully appointed members necessary for it to act. ***

Before turning to the specific questions presented, we shall mention two background considerations that we find relevant to all three. First, *the Recess Appointments Clause sets forth a subsidiary, not a primary, method for appointing officers of the United States.* *** [It] reflects the tension between, on the one hand, the President's continuous need for "the assistance of subordinates," and, on the other, the Senate's practice, particularly during the Republic's early years, of meeting for a single brief session each year. We seek to interpret the Clause as granting the President the power to make appointments during a recess but not offering the President the authority routinely to avoid the need for Senate confirmation. Second, *in interpreting the Clause, we put significant weight upon historical practice.* ***

The first question concerns the scope of the phrase *"the recess* of the Senate." The Constitution provides for congressional elections every two years. And the 2–year life of each elected Congress typically consists of two formal 1–year sessions, each separated from the next by an "inter-session recess." *** The Senate and the House also take breaks in the midst of a session. *** We recognize that the word "the" in *"the* recess" might suggest that the phrase refers to the single break separating formal sessions of Congress. That is because the word "the" frequently (but not always) indicates "a particular thing." But the word can also refer "to a term used generically or universally." The Constitution, for example, directs the Senate to choose a President *pro tempore* "in *the* Absence of the Vice–President." *** Reading "the" generically in this way, there is no linguistic problem applying the Clause's phrase to both kinds of recess. And, in fact, the phrase "the recess" was used to refer to intra-session recesses at the time of the founding.

The constitutional text is thus ambiguous. And we believe the Clause's purpose demands the broader interpretation*** so that the President can ensure the continued functioning of the Federal Government when the Senate is away. ***

History also offers strong support for the broad interpretation. *** In all, between the founding and the Great Depression, Congress took substantial intra-session breaks (other than holiday breaks) in four years: 1867, 1868, 1921, and 1929. And in each of those years the President made intra-session recess appointments. Since 1929, and particularly since the end of World War II, Congress has shortened its inter-session breaks as it has taken longer and more frequent intra-session breaks; Presidents have correspondingly made more intra-session recess appointments. *** Not surprisingly, the publicly available opinions of Presidential legal advisers that we have found are nearly unanimous in determining that the Clause authorizes these appointments. *** What about the Senate? *** [T]o the extent that the Senate or a Senate committee has expressed a view, that view has favored a functional definition of "recess," and a functional definition encompasses intra-session recesses. ***

The second question concerns the scope of the phrase "vacancies *that may happen* during the recess of the Senate." *** We concede that the most natural meaning of "happens" as applied to a "vacancy" (at least to a modern ear) is that the vacancy "happens" when it initially occurs. But that is not the only possible way to use the word. *** We can still understand this earlier use of "happen" if we think of it used together with another word that, like "vacancy," can refer to a continuing state, say, a financial crisis. A statute that gives the President authority to act in respect to "any financial crisis that may happen during his term" can easily be interpreted to include crises that arise before, and continue during, that term. *** We consequently go on to consider the Clause's purpose and historical practice.

The Clause's purpose *** is to permit the President to obtain the assistance of subordinate officers when the Senate, due to its recess, cannot confirm them. *** At the same time, we recognize one important purpose-related consideration that argues in the opposite direction. A broad interpretation might permit a President to avoid Senate confirmations as a matter of course. *** He might simply wait for a recess and then provide all potential nominees with recess appointments. *** The *** President has consistently and frequently interpreted the Recess Appointments Clause to apply to vacancies that initially occur before, but continue to exist during, a recess of the Senate. The Senate as a body has not countered this practice for nearly three-quarters of a century, perhaps longer. *** And we are reluctant to upset this traditional practice *** [T]he phrase "all vacancies" includes vacancies that come into existence while the Senate is in session.

The third question concerns the calculation of the length of the Senate's "recess." *** The Solicitor General argues that we must treat the *pro forma* sessions as periods of recess. *** In our view, however, the *pro forma* sessions count as sessions, not as periods of recess. *** [T]he Senate is in session when it says it is, provided that, under its own rules, it retains the capacity to transact Senate business. The Senate met that standard here. *** First, the Senate said it was in session. *** Second, the Senate's rules make clear that *** despite its resolution that it would conduct no business, the Senate retained the power to conduct business. *** Could the Senate "receive communications from the President"? It could. *** Was the Senate's Chamber "empty"? It was not. *** Did Senators "owe [a] duty of attendance"? They did. *** [W]e conclude that the Recess Appointments Clause does not give the President the constitutional authority to make the[se] appointments ***

JUSTICE SCALIA, with whom THE CHIEF JUSTICE, JUSTICE THOMAS, and JUSTICE ALITO join, concurring in the judgment.

*** To prevent the President's recess-appointment power from nullifying the Senate's role in the appointment process, the Constitution cabins that power in two significant ways. First, it may be exercised only in "the Recess of the Senate," that is, the intermission between two formal legislative sessions. Second, it may be used to fill only those vacancies that "happen during the Recess," that is, offices that become vacant during that intermission. Both conditions are clear from the Constitution's text and structure, and both were well understood at the founding. *** The Court's decision transforms the recess-appointment power from a tool carefully designed to fill a narrow and specific need into a weapon to be wielded by future Presidents against future Senates. *** I would hold that "the Recess" is the gap between sessions and that the appointments at issue here are invalid because they undisputedly were made *during* the Senate's session. *** The *** majority's assertion that the Clause's "purpose" of "ensur[ing] the continued functioning of the Federal Government" *** disregards another self-evident purpose of the Clause: to preserve the Senate's role in the appointment process—which the founding generation regarded as a critical protection against despotism *** Today's decision seriously undercuts *that* purpose. ***

And what about breaks longer than three days? *** The majority must hope that the *in terrorem* effect of its "presumptively too short" pronouncement will deter future Presidents from making any recess appointments during 4–to–9–day breaks and thus save us from the absurd spectacle of unelected judges evaluating (after an evidentiary hearing?) *** As for breaks of 10 or more days: We are presumably to infer that such breaks do not trigger any "presumpt[ion]" against recess appointments, but does that mean the President has an utterly free hand? Or can litigants seek invalidation of an appointment made during a 10–day break by pointing to an absence of "unusual" or "urgent" circumstances necessitating an immediate appointment, albeit without the aid of a "presumpt[ion]" in their favor? Or, to put the question as it will present itself to lawyers in the Executive Branch: Can the President make an appointment during a 10–day break simply to overcome "political opposition in the Senate" despite the absence of any "national catastrophe," even though it "go[es] without saying" that he cannot do so during a 9–day break? Who knows? The majority does not say, and neither does the Constitution. ***

The historical practice of the political branches is, of course, irrelevant when the Constitution is clear. But even if the Constitution were thought ambiguous on this point, history does not support the majority's interpretation. *** Intra-session recess appointments were virtually unheard of for the first 130 years of the Republic, were deemed unconstitutional by the first Attorney General to address them, were not openly defended by the Executive until 1921, were not made in significant numbers until after World War II, and have been repeatedly criticized as unconstitutional by Senators of both parties. *** The majority's methodology thus all but guarantees the continuing aggrandizement of the Executive Branch.

The second question presented is whether vacancies that "happen during the Recess of the Senate," which the President is empowered to fill with recess appointments, are (a) vacancies that *arise* during the recess, or (b) all vacancies that *exist* during the recess, regardless of when they arose. *** What the majority needs to sustain its judgment is an ambiguous text and a clear historical practice. What it has is a clear text and an at-best-ambiguous historical practice. *** The majority replaces the Constitution's text with a new set of judge-made rules to govern recess appointments. Henceforth, the Senate can avoid triggering the President's now-vast recess-appointment power by the odd contrivance of never adjourning for more than three days without holding a *pro forma* session at which it is understood that no business will be conducted. How this new regime will work in practice remains to be seen. *** In any event, the limitation upon the President's appointment power is there not for the benefit of the Senate, but for the protection of the people; it should not be dependent on Senate action for its existence.

The real tragedy of today's decision is *** the damage done to our separation-of-powers jurisprudence more generally. *** The Court's embrace of the adverse-possession theory of executive power (a characterization the majority resists but does not refute) will be cited in diverse contexts, including those presently unimagined, and will have the effect of aggrandizing the Presidency beyond its constitutional bounds and undermining respect for the separation of powers. ***

Notes

1. Interpretive Approaches. To what extent are the opinions in this case formalist? To what extent are they functional? How does history play into each opinion? What does the Court's lack of consistent methodology in separation of powers cases mean for lawyers advising clients?

2. Political Reactions? If you were the President, would you be licking your wounds from a 9-0 loss or be pleased with the outcome? What would your reaction be if you were Majority Leader of the Senate?

3. The Court. Does this decision damage the Court's separation-of-powers jurisprudence?

D. CONGRESS, PRESIDENT, COURT, AND WAR

A critical arena for operation of separation of powers principles concerns the allocation of authority for conducting war. There are numerous provisions scattered throughout the Constitution relating to making and waging war. However, what is war and what is peace may be problematic in a world of "cold war," "proxy wars," and conflicts involving non-state terrorist organizations. The Constitution does not explicitly adopt a different governing framework for war or other national emergencies, so it is questionable whether, when, and how national security should affect separation of power issues as well as the content of civil liberties, from free speech restrictions to jury trial availability to the application of equal protection guarantees.

The framers divided responsibility for making war between the political branches in order to deter the nation from lurching into war unwisely. The Constitution gives Congress the power to "declare" war, a word substituted for "make" in an earlier draft of the document. As for making war, the President is named as Commander-in-Chief, but the reach of his authority in this capacity is not explicit. Congress has the power of the purse in war as well as in peace and is provided the authority to make rules governing the army and the navy. Congress is required to protect the states from invasion, may respond to state calls for assistance in dealing with domestic violence, and may call forth the militia "to execute the Laws of the Union, suppress Insurrections, and repel Invasions." See Art. IV, § 4; Art. I, §8, cl 15.

The following case shows deep divisions over the Constitution's allocation of "war" power.

THE PRIZE CASES
67 U.S. 635 (1862)

MR. JUSTICE GRIER.

*** Had the President a right to institute a blockade of ports in possession of persons in armed rebellion against the Government, on the principles of international law ***? Was the property of persons domiciled or residing within those States a proper subject of capture on the sea as 'enemies' property?' *** [A] blockade *de facto* actually existed, and was formally declared and notified by the President on the 27th and 30th of April, 1861 *** The parties belligerent in a public war are independent nations. But it is not necessary to constitute war, that both parties should be acknowledged as independent nations or sovereign States. A war may exist where one of the belligerents claims sovereign rights as against the other. *** A civil war is never solemnly declared; it becomes such by *** the number, power, and organization of the persons who originate and carry it on. *** *They* claim to be in arms to establish their liberty and independence, in order to become a sovereign State, while the sovereign party treats them as insurgents and rebels who owe allegiance, and who should be punished with death for their treason. ***

By the Constitution, Congress alone has the power to declare a national or foreign war. It cannot declare war against a State, or any number of States, by virtue of any clause in the Constitution. The Constitution confers on the President the whole Executive power. He is bound to take care that the laws be faithfully executed. He is Commander-in-chief of the Army and Navy of the United States, and of the militia of the several States when called into the actual service of the United States. He has no power to initiate or declare a war either against a foreign nation or a domestic State. But by the Acts of Congress of February 28th, 1795, and 3d of March, 1807, he is authorized to called out the militia and use the military and naval forces of the United States in case of invasion by foreign nations, and to suppress insurrection against the government of a State or of the United States.

If a war be made by invasion of a foreign nation, the President is not only authorized but bound to resist force by force. He does not initiate the war, but is bound to accept the challenge without waiting for any special legislative authority. And whether the hostile party be a foreign invader, or States organized in rebellion, it is none the less a war, although the declaration of it be 'unilateral.' *** The President was bound to meet it in the shape it presented itself, without waiting for Congress to baptize it with a name; and no name given to it by him or them could change the fact. ***

Whether the President in fulfilling his duties, as Commander-in-chief, in suppressing an insurrection, has met with such armed hostile resistance, and a civil war of such alarming proportions as will compel him to accord to them the character of belligerents, is a question to be decided *by him*, and this Court must be governed by the decisions and acts of the political department of the Government to which this power was entrusted. *** The proclamation of blockade is itself official and conclusive evidence to the Court that a state of war existed which demanded and authorized a recourse to such a measure, under the circumstances peculiar to the case. ***

If it were necessary to the technical existence of a war, that it should have a legislative sanction, we find it in almost every act passed at the extraordinary session of the Legislature of 1861, which was wholly employed in enacting laws to enable the Government to prosecute the war with vigor and efficiency. *** The objection made to this act of ratification, that it is *ex post facto*, and therefore unconstitutional and void, might possibly have some weight on the trial of an indictment in a criminal Court. But precedents from that source cannot be received as authoritative in a tribunal administering public and international law. *** [T]he President had a right, *jure belli*, to institute a blockade of ports in possession of the States in rebellion, which neutrals are bound to regard.

We come now to the consideration of the second question. What is included in the term *'enemies' property?'* *** The appellants contend that the term 'enemy' is properly applicable to those only who are subjects or citizens of a foreign State at war with our own. *** They insist, moreover, that *** the acts of the usurping government cannot legally sever the bond of their allegiance; they have, therefore, a co-relative right to claim the protection of the government for their persons and property, and to be treated as loyal citizens, till legally convicted of having renounced their allegiance and made war against the Government by treasonably resisting its laws. ***

This argument rests on the assumption of two propositions, each of which is without foundation on the established law of nations. It assumes that where a civil war exists, the party belligerent claiming to be sovereign, cannot, for some unknown reason, exercise the rights of belligerents, although the revolutionary party may. Being sovereign, he can exercise only sovereign rights over the other party. The insurgent may be killed on the battle-field or by the executioner; his property on land may be confiscated under the municipal law; but the commerce on the ocean, which supplies the rebels with means to support the war, cannot be made the subject of capture under the laws of war, because it is *unconstitutional!!!'* *** [T]he belligerent party who claims to be sovereign, may exercise both belligerent and sovereign rights. ***

All persons residing within this territory whose property may be used to increase the revenues of the hostile power are, in this contest, liable to be treated as enemies, though not foreigners. They *** are none the less enemies because they are traitors. *** Whether property be liable to capture as 'enemies' property' does not in any manner depend on the personal allegiance of the owner. 'It is the illegal traffic that stamps it as 'enemies' property.' It is of no consequence whether it belongs to an ally or a citizen. *** The produce of the soil of the hostile territory, as well as other property engaged in the commerce of the hostile power, as the source of its wealth and strength, are always regarded as legitimate prize, without regard to the domicil of the owner, and much more so if he reside and trade within their territory. ***

MR. JUSTICE NELSON, dissenting.

*** All the property of the people of the two countries on land or sea are subject to capture and confiscation by the adverse party as enemies' property, *** all treaties between the belligerent parties are annulled, The ports of the respective countries may be blockaded, and letters of marque and reprisal granted as rights of war, and the law of prizes as defined by the law of nations comes into full and complete operation, resulting from maritime captures, *jure belli*. War also effects a change in the mutual relations of all States or countries *** though they take no part in the contest, but remain neutral. *** [T]he same code which has annexed to the existence of a war all these disturbing consequences has declared that the right of making war belongs exclusively to the supreme or sovereign power of the State. *** By our constitution this power is lodged in Congress. ***

[I]f a civil war existed between that portion of the people in organized insurrection to overthrow this Government at the time this vessel and cargo were seized, and if she was guilty of a violation of the blockade, she would be lawful prize of war. But before this insurrection against the established Government can be dealt with on the footing of a civil war, within the meaning of the law of nations and the Constitution *** it must be recognized or declared by the war-making power of the Government. *** There is no difference in this respect between a civil or a public war. *** [W]e are asked, what would become of the peace and integrity of the Union in case of an insurrection at home or invasion from abroad if this power could not be exercised by the President in the recess of Congress, and until that body could be assembled?

The framers of the Constitution fully comprehended this question, and provided for the contingency. *** The Constitution declares that Congress shall have power 'to provide for calling forth the militia to execute the laws of the Union, suppress insurrections, and repel invasions.' Another clause, 'that the President shall be Commander-in-chief of the Army and Navy of the United States, and of the militia of the several States when called into the actual service of United States;' and, again, 'He shall take care that the laws shall be faithfully executed.' *** [A]mple provision has been made under the Constitution and laws against any sudden and unexpected disturbance of the public peace from insurrection at home or invasion from abroad. *** It is the exercise of a power under the municipal laws of the country and not under the law of nations *** until the assembling of Congress, who can, if it be deemed necessary, bring into operation the war power ***

It has been argued that the authority conferred on the President by the Act of 1795 invests him with the war power. But the obvious answer is, that it proceeds from a different clause in the Constitution and which is given for different purposes and objects, namely, to execute the laws and preserve the public order and tranquillity of the country in a time of peace by preventing or suppressing any public disorder or disturbance by foreign or domestic enemies. Certainly, if there is any force in this argument, then we are in a state of war with all the rights of war, and all the penal consequences attending it every time this power is exercised by calling out a military force to execute the laws or to suppress insurrection or rebellion; for the nature of the power cannot depend upon the numbers called out. If so, what numbers will constitute war and what numbers will not? It has also been argued that this power of the President from necessity should be construed as vesting him with the war power, or the Republic might greatly suffer or be in danger from the attacks of the hostile party before the assembling to Congress. But we have seen that the whole military and naval force are in his hands under the municipal laws of the country. He can meet the adversary upon land and water with all the forces of the Government. The truth is, this idea of the existence of any necessity for clothing the President with the war power, under the Act of 1795, is simply a monstrous exaggeration; for, besides having the command of the whole of the army and navy, Congress can be assembled within any thirty days, if the safety of the country requires that the war power shall be brought into operation.

The Acts of 1795 and 1805 did not, and could not under the Constitution, confer on the President the power of declaring war against a State of this Union, or of deciding that war existed, and upon that ground authorize the capture and confiscation of the property of every citizen of the State whenever it was found on the waters. *** Congress alone can determine whether war exists or should be declared; and until they have acted, no citizen of the State can be punished in his person or property, unless he has committed some offence against a law of Congress passed before the act was committed, which made it a crime, and defined the punishment. The penalty of confiscation for the acts of others with which he had no concern cannot lawfully be inflicted. *** So the war carried on by the President against the insurrectionary districts in the Southern States *** was a personal war against those in rebellion *** until Congress assembled and acted upon this state of things. [Until then,} the only enemy recognized by the Government was the persons engaged in the rebellion, all others were peaceful citizens, entitled to all the privileges of citizens under the Constitution. Certainly it cannot rightfully be said that the President has the power to convert a loyal citizen into a belligerent enemy or confiscate his property as enemy's property. *** [Consequently] the President had no power to set on foot a blockade under the law of nations, and that the capture of the vessel and cargo in this case, and in all cases before us in which the capture occurred before the 13th of July, 1861, for breach of blockade, or as enemies' property, are illegal and void, and that the decrees of condemnation should be reversed and the vessel and cargo restored.

MR. CHIEF JUSTICE TANEY, MR. JUSTICE CATRON and MR. JUSTICE CLIFFORD, concurred in the dissenting opinion of MR. JUSTICE NELSON.

Notes

1. **Supreme Court Role**. The role of the Supreme Court in connetion with war is not specified in the Constitution. Yet *The Prize Cases* show the Court deciding whether there was a legally cognizable war to which important consequences would attach (forfeiture or taking of assets which, but for war, would have required return or compensation). *Boumediene* provided access to habeas hearings for military detainees at Guantanamo Bay. What do these two cases have in common that might justify judicial resolutions of questions of war?

2. **Civil Liberties in War and Peace**. Article I, §9, cl. 2 empowers Congress to suspend the "privilege of the Writ of Habeas Corpus *** when in Cases of Rebellion and Invasion the public Safety may require it." The Third Amendment protects owners from having to quarter soldiers in peacetime, but allows mandated quartering "in a manner prescribed by law" in wartime. The Fifth Amendment excepts "cases arising in the land or naval forces, or in the Militia, when in actual service in time of War or public danger" from Grand Jury presentment or indictment. Other constitutional rights and liberties are not explicitly changed during times of war. Should they change?

3. **Emergency as a Trump to Constitutional Rights?** Does the outcome of *The Prize Cases* turn on the fact of extensive hostilities (a de facto war)? Unlike many modern constitutions, the United States Constitution contains no emergency provision allowing for suspension of civil liberties. Should one nevertheless be implied? In a famous response to critics of his suspension of habeas corpus (later ratified by Congress), President Lincoln defended himself by saying: "Are all the laws, but one [habeas corpus], to go unexecuted, and the government itself go to pieces, lest that one be violated?"

4. **Nuance, Timing, and Civil Liberties**. After the Civil War ended, the Supreme Court in *Ex Parte Milligan*, 71 U.S. 2 (1866) rejected Lincoln's use of military tribunals to convict citizens detained during the Civil War, saying that

the Constitution applies "equally in war and in peace. *** No doctrine [allows for suspension of the Constitution] during any of the great exigencies of government. Such a doctrine leads directly to anarchy or despotism." Expressing a position somewhere between these poles, CHIEF JUSTICE REHNQUIST wrote, "the laws will not be silent in time of war, but they will speak with a somewhat different voice." William Rehnquist, ALL THE LAWS BUT ONE: CIVIL LIBERTIES IN WARTIME (1998).

*****

A number of World War II decisions affirmed a broad scope to Executive power, including *Korematsu*, infra Chapter IX. None is more striking, however, than the following opinion:

<h1 style="text-align:center">EX PARTE QUIRIN</h1>
317 U.S. 1 (1942)

MR. CHIEF JUSTICE STONE delivered the opinion of the Court.

*** The question for decision is whether the detention of petitioners *** for trial by Military Commission *** is in conformity to the laws and Constitution of the United States. *** [W]e directed that petitioners' applications be set down for full oral argument at a special term of this Court, convened on July 29, 1942. *** On July 31, 1942, *** this Court *** denied petitioners' *** leave to file petitions for habeas corpus. ***

All the petitioners were born in Germany; all have lived in the United States. All returned to Germany between 1933 and 1941. All except petitioner Haupt are admittedly citizens of the German Reich, with which the United States is at war. Haupt came to this country with his parents when he was five years old; it is contended that he became a citizen of the United States by virtue of the naturalization of his parents during his minority and that he has not since lost his citizenship. *** After the declaration of war between the United States and the German Reich, petitioners received training at a sabotage school near Berlin, Germany, where they were instructed in the use of explosives and in methods of secret writing. [Thereafter petitioners boarded two German submarines that crossed the Atlantic to Long Island, New York and Ponte Vedra Beach, Florida, landing at night on June 13 and June 17, 1942] *** carrying with them a supply of explosives, fuses and incendiary and timing devices. While landing they wore German Marine Infantry uniforms or parts of uniforms. Immediately after landing they buried their uniforms and the other articles mentioned and proceeded in civilian dress. *** All were taken into custody in New York or Chicago by agents of the Federal Bureau of Investigation. ***

The President, as President and Commander in Chief of the Army and Navy, by Order of July 2, 1942, appointed a Military Commission and directed it to try petitioners for offenses against the law of war and the Articles of War, and prescribed regulations for the procedure on the trial and for review of the record of the trial and of any judgment or sentence of the Commission. On the same day, by Proclamation, the President declared that 'all persons who are subjects, citizens or residents of any nation at war with the United States or who give obedience to or act under the direction of any such nation, and who during time of war enter or attempt to enter the United

States *** through coastal or boundary defenses, and are charged with committing or attempting or preparing to commit sabotage, espionage, hostile or warlike acts, or violations of the law of war, shall be subject to the law of war and to the jurisdiction of military tribunals'. *** [They] were denied access to the courts. *** On July 3, 1942 [charges were filed alleging violation of the law of war, Article 81 of the Articles of War (giving intelligence to the enemy), Article 82 (spying), and conspiracy to commit these offenses]. The Commission met on July 8, 1942, and proceeded with the trial, which continued in progress while the causes were pending in this Court. On July 27th, *** all the evidence for the prosecution and the defense had been taken by the Commission and the case had been closed except for arguments of counsel. ***

Petitioners' main contention is that the President is without any statutory or constitutional authority to order the petitioners to be tried by military tribunal for offenses with which they are charged; that in consequence they are entitled to be tried in the civil courts with the safeguards, including trial by jury, which the Fifth and Sixth Amendments guarantee to all persons charged in such courts with criminal offenses [and that the President's Order conflicts with certain of the Articles of War]. The Government challenges each of these propositions *** [and] also insists that petitioners must be denied access to the courts, both because they are enemy aliens or have entered our territory as enemy belligerents, and because the President's Proclamation undertakes in terms to deny such access to the class of persons defined by the Proclamation ***. But *** neither the Proclamation nor the fact that they are enemy aliens forecloses consideration by the courts of petitioners' contentions that the Constitution and laws of the United States constitutionally enacted forbid their trial by military commission. *** [W]e have resolved those questions by our conclusion that the Commission has jurisdiction to try the charge preferred against petitioners. ***

We are not here concerned with any question of the guilt or innocence of petitioners. Constitutional safeguards for the protection of all who are charged with offenses are not to be disregarded in order to inflict merited punishment on some who are guilty. But the detention and trial of petitioners—ordered by the President in the declared exercise of his powers as Commander in Chief of the Army in time of war and of grave public danger—are not to be set aside by the courts without the clear conviction that they are in conflict with the Constitution or laws of Congress constitutionally enacted.

Congress and the President, like the courts, possess no power not derived from the Constitution. But one of the objects of the Constitution, as declared by its preamble, is to 'provide for the common defence.' *** The Constitution thus invests the President as Commander in Chief with the power to wage war which Congress has declared, and to carry into effect all laws passed by Congress for the conduct of war and for the government and regulation of the Armed Forces, and all laws defining and punishing offences against the law of nations, including those which pertain to the conduct of war.

By the Articles of War, Congress has provided rules for the government of the Army. It has provided for the trial and punishment, by courts-martial, of violations of the Articles by members of the armed forces and by specified classes of persons associated or serving with the Army. But the Articles also recognize the 'military commission' appointed by military command as an appropriate tribunal for the trial and punishment of offenses against the law of war not ordinarily tried by court martial. Articles 38 and 46 authorize the President, with certain limitations, to prescribe the procedure for military commissions. Articles 81 and 82 authorize trial, either by court martial or military commission, of those charged with relieving, harboring or corresponding with the enemy and those charged with spying. And Article 15 declares that 'the provisions of these articles conferring jurisdiction upon courts-martial shall not be construed as depriving military commissions *** or other military tribunals of concurrent jurisdiction in respect of offenders or offenses that by statute or by the law of war may be triable by such military commissions *** or other military tribunals'. Article 2 includes among those persons subject to military law the personnel of our own military establishment. But this, as Article 12 provides, does not exclude from that class 'any other person who by the law of war is subject to trial by military tribunals' and who under Article 12 may be tried by court martial or under Article 15 by military commission.

Similarly the Espionage Act of 1917, which authorizes trial in the district courts of certain offenses that tend to interfere with the prosecution of war, provides that nothing contained in the act 'shall be deemed to limit the jurisdiction of the general courts-martial, military commissions, or naval courts-martial'.

From the very beginning of its history this Court has recognized and applied the law of war as including that part of the law of nations which prescribes, for the conduct of war, the status, rights and duties of enemy nations as well as of enemy individuals. By the Articles of War, and especially Article 15, Congress has explicitly provided, so far as it may constitutionally do so, that military tribunals shall have jurisdiction to try offenders or offenses against the law of war in appropriate cases. Congress, in addition to making rules for the government of our Armed Forces, has thus exercised its authority to define and punish offenses against the law of nations by sanctioning, within constitutional limitations, the jurisdiction of military commissions to try persons for offenses which, according to the rules and precepts of the law of nations, and more particularly the law of war, are cognizable by such tribunals. And the President, as Commander in Chief, by his Proclamation in time of war his invoked that law. By his Order creating the present Commission he has undertaken to exercise the authority conferred upon him by Congress, and also such authority as the Constitution itself gives the Commander in Chief, to direct the performance of those functions which may constitutionally be performed by the military arm of the nation in time of war.

An important incident to the conduct of war is the adoption of measures by the military command not only to repel and defeat the enemy, but to seize and subject to disciplinary measures those enemies who in their attempt to thwart or impede our military effort have violated the law of war. It is unnecessary for present purposes to determine to what extent the President as Commander in Chief has constitutional power to create military commissions without the support of Congressional legislation. For here Congress has authorized trial of offenses against the law of war before such commissions. We are concerned only with the question whether it is within the constitutional power of the national government to place petitioners upon trial before a military commission for the offenses with which they are charged. We must therefore first inquire whether any of the acts charged is an offense against the law of war cognizable before a military tribunal, and if so whether the Constitution prohibits the trial. We may assume that there are acts regarded in other countries, or by some writers on international law, as offenses against the law of war which would not be triable by military tribunal here, either because they are not recognized by our courts as violations of the law of war or because they are of that class of offenses constitutionally triable only by a jury. It was upon such grounds that the Court denied the right to proceed by military tribunal in *Ex parte Milligan*. But as we shall show, these petitioners were charged with an offense against the law of war which the Constitution does not require to be tried by jury. ***

But petitioners insist that even if the offenses with which they are charged are offenses against the law of war, their trial is subject to the requirement of the Fifth Amendment that no person shall be held to answer for a capital or otherwise infamous crime unless on a presentment or indictment of a grand jury, and that such trials by Article III, § 2, and the Sixth Amendment must be by jury in a civil court. *** Presentment by a grand jury and trial by a jury of the vicinage where the crime was committed were at the time of the adoption of the Constitution familiar parts of the machinery for criminal trials in the civil courts. But they were procedures unknown to military tribunals, which are not courts in the sense of the Judiciary Article, and which in the natural course of events are usually called upon to function under conditions precluding resort to such procedures. *** [W]e must conclude that § 2 of Article III and the Fifth and Sixth Amendments cannot be taken to have extended the right to demand a jury to trials by military commission, or to have required that offenses against the law of war not triable by jury at common law be tried only in the civil courts.

The fact that 'cases arising in the land or naval forces' are excepted from the operation of the Amendments does not militate against this conclusion. *** We may assume, without deciding, that a trial prosecuted before a military commission created by military authority is not one 'arising in the land *** forces', when the accused is not a member of or associated with those forces. But even so, the exception cannot be taken to affect those trials before military commissions which are neither within the exception nor within the provisions of Article III, § 2, whose guaranty the Amendments did not enlarge. No exception is necessary to exclude from the operation of these provisions cases never deemed to be within their terms. An express exception from Article III, § 2, and from the Fifth and Sixth Amendments, of trials of petty offenses and of criminal contempts has not been found necessary in order to preserve the traditional practice of trying those offenses without a jury. It is no more so in order to continue the practice of trying, before military tribunals without a jury, offenses committed by enemy belligerents against the law of war. *** We conclude that the Fifth and Sixth Amendments did not restrict whatever authority was conferred by the Constitution to try offenses against the law of war by military commission, and that petitioners, charged with such an offense not required to be tried by jury at common law, were lawfully placed on trial by the Commission ***

We have no occasion now to define with meticulous care the ultimate boundaries of the jurisdiction of military tribunals to try persons according to the law of war. It is enough that petitioners here, upon the conceded facts, were plainly within those boundaries, and were held in good faith for trial by military commission, charged with being enemies who, with the purpose of destroying war materials and utilities, entered or after entry remained in our territory without uniform--an offense against the law of war. We hold only that those particular acts constitute an offense against the law of war which the Constitution authorizes to be tried by military commission. ***

Notes

1.   **Questioning *Quirin*.** The *Quirin* appeal was extraordinary. The Supreme Court heard argument two days after the military commission evidence was closed and before counsel's final arguments. The decision was issued two days later and the written opinion followed three months thereafter on October 29, 1942. Meanwhile, six of the defendants had been executed. Is anything wrong with this picture? *See* Louis Fisher, *Military Tribunals: The Quirin Precedent*, Congressional Research Service Report to Congress (March 26, 2002).

2.   **Distinguishing *Milligan*.** *Quirin* distinguished a Civil War era case, *Ex parte Milligan*, 71 U.S. 2 (1866), in which the Court held that an Ohio civilian accused of aiding the enemy was not subject to court-martial jurisdiction because he could have been tried in a civilian court. Was the Court correct to place no emphasis on the availability of civilian courts to try the *Quirin* defendants?

*****

The Korean War provided the backdrop for the *Youngstown* decision, which opened this chapter, but the Court did not see the decision as involving presidential Commander-in-Chief powers. During the late 1960s and early 1970s, America's involvement in military operations in Vietnam became increasingly unpopular. This disenchantment led President Lyndon B. Johnson not to seek reelection in 1968. Congress subsequently passed the War Powers Resolution, 50 U.S.C.A. §§ 1541-1547, to control future executive military action by requiring the President to report to Congress, and if Congress did not approve the use of troops, to withdraw them. Johnson's successor, Richard M. Nixon, vetoed the resolution on the basis that it unconstitutionally intruded on the President's Article II powers. Congress overrode the veto. The requirements of the War Powers Resolution were never tested in court. One might fashion an academic position that such reporting intrudes on the President's constitutional sphere of powers, but in practice it has been easy for the President to comply with the notification provisions while controlling the depth and details of the notice provided. No judicial decision has ever construed the War Powers Resolution.

Which of the following provisions of the War Powers Resolution, if any, intrude on the President's powers? Section 1541 says in part "The constitutional powers of the President as Commander-in-Chief to introduce United States Armed Forces into hostilities, or into situations where imminent involvement in hostilities is clearly indicated by the circumstances, are exercised only pursuant to (1) a declaration of war, (2) specific statutory authorization, or (3) a national emergency created by attack upon the United States***." The President must report to Congress any use of troops and, if Congress does not authorize continuation of forces, the President "shall terminate" the use of military force. § 1544(b). A "concurrent resolution" of both houses of Congress is also sufficient to require removal of troops. § 1544(c). Despite these provisions, however, another provision says that nothing in the War Powers Resolution "is intended to alter the constitutional authority of the Congress or of the President, or the provisions of existing treaties." § 1547(d)(1). What other constitutional tools does Congress have to control war by the President? Now that you know a bit about the provisions of the War Powers Resolution, can you surmise why there are no Supreme Court decisions construing it?

*****

The post-9/11 "War on Terror" has provided a lodestar of separation of powers issues. The George W. Bush Administration pressed hard with a "unitary President" theory based on the "Vesting Clause," Article II, § 1, cl. 1 ["The executive Power shall be vested in a President of the United States of America."] This clause, argued the Administration, meant that execution of the War on Terror fell exclusively to the President. Congress passed the Authorization to Use Military Force (AUMF), which authorized the President to "use all necessary and appropriate force against those nations, organizations, or persons he determines planned, authorized committed, or aided the terrorist attacks." Congress also appropriated money to fund military operations in Afghanistan and later Iraq.

President Bush, on November 13, 2001, issued a comprehensive military order governing "Detention, Treatment, and Trial of Certain Non-Citizens in the War Against Terrorism." From this order flowed designation of various persons as "enemy combatants," establishment of the Guantanamo Bay detention facility to house alien enemy combatants, and creation of military commissions to try alien "unlawful enemy combatants." As the War on Terror played out during the Bush Administration, the courts became a central player in assessing various claims that the executive branch violated the Constitution.

Boumediene v. Bush, which you read in Chapter II, culminated a lengthy struggle between the President, Congress, and the Supreme Court over application of habeas corpus to detainees at Guantanamo Bay. As you know, the Court in *Boumediene* held that section 7(a) violated the Suspension Clause of Article I. That is not the end of the story, however. The Court has since *Boumediene* refused to grant cert in any Guantanamo detainee case denying habeas relief, no detainee has been released through a habeas proceeding, procedural rules fashioned by the DC Circuit make prevailing on a habeas claim very difficult, and relief does not include release into the United States (see notes following *Boumediene* in Chapter II).

Moreover, the Executive has many options for dealing with war situations overseas, and the courts tend to defer to the political branches more in "war" than otherwise. Language from a decision issued the same day as *Boumediene* makes the point well. In *Munaf v. Geren*, 553 U.S. 694 (2008) the Court unanimously assumed jurisdiction over the habeas petitions of two American citizens held in Iraq by American forces. It then denied the petitioners' request to be released from military detention:

> The habeas petitioners argue that the writ should be granted *** because they are innocent civilians who have been unlawfully detained by the United States in violation of the Due Process Clause. *** [H]abeas is not appropriate in these cases. *** [W]hat petitioners are really after is a court order requiring the United States to shelter them from the sovereign government seeking to have them answer for alleged crimes committed within that sovereign's borders. *** [T]he Constitution allows the Executive to transfer American citizens to foreign authorities for criminal prosecution *** for engaging in serious hostile acts against an ally in *** "an active theater of combat." ***

> Our constitutional framework "requires that the judiciary be as scrupulous not to interfere with legitimate Army matters as the Army must be scrupulous not to intervene in judicial matters." Those who commit crimes within a sovereign's territory may be transferred to that sovereign's government for prosecution *** Petitioners contend that these general principles are trumped in their cases because their transfer to Iraqi custody is likely to result in torture. *** Such allegations are of course a matter of serious concern, but in the present context that concern is to be addressed by the political branches, not the judiciary. *** Even with respect to claims that detainees would be denied constitutional rights if transferred, we have recognized that it is for the political branches, not the judiciary, to assess practices in foreign countries and to determine national policy in light of those assessments. *** Petitioners here allege only the possibility of mistreatment in a prison facility; this is not a more extreme case in which the Executive has determined that a detainee is likely to be tortured but decides to transfer him anyway. *** The Judiciary is not suited to second-guess such determinations-determinations that would require federal courts to pass judgment on foreign justice systems and undermine the Government's ability to speak with one voice in this area. ***

When post-9/11 military operations in Afghanistan produced captives, the captives were moved to Guantanamo Bay. In Iraq, and in Afghanistan after the initial operations there, those captured were not sent to

Guantanamo. Why might the Bush Administration have altered its detention policy? If habeas can be dodged so easily by the Executive, of what value is it?

Presidents in war may detain individuals as "enemy combatants" until the end of hostilities. Who is an enemy combatant? An individual captured on a battlefield with a weapon wearing a uniform of a nation at war with the United States, as in World War I and World War II, are the easy cases. But suppose an individual in the United States is thought by the authorities to be planning terrorist activities. He wears no uniform, carries no weapon, and is a citizen of a nation with whom the United States has amicable relations. If arrested, the person would have a variety of constitutional protections. Could such a person instead be designated as an enemy combatant and militarily detained? See *Padilla v. Hanft*, 423 F.3d 386 (4th Cir. 2005) (US citizen previously associated with hostile forces in Afghanistan and arrested by civilian law enforcement authorities at O'Hare Airport could be designated an enemy combatant).

IV

CONGRESS' ARTICLE I POWERS AND THEIR LIMITS

"This government is acknowledged by all, to be one of enumerated powers. The principle, that it can exercise only the powers granted to it, *** is now universally admitted. But the question respecting the extent of the powers actually granted, is perpetually arising, and will probably continue to arise, so long as our system shall exist. In discussing these questions, the conflicting powers of the general and state governments must be brought into view, and the supremacy of their respective laws, when they are in opposition, must be settled. *** [T]he government of the Union, though limited in its powers, is supreme within its sphere of action."

—CHIEF JUSTICE MARSHALL
McCulloch v. Maryland (1819)

The starting point to understanding the powers of Congress is the Constitution's text: "All legislative Powers herein granted shall be vested in a Congress of the United States, which shall consist of a Senate and House of Representatives." Art. I, § 1. The legislative powers given Congress fit, for the most part, into seventeen separate categories listed in Article I, § 8. REREAD this section. Another important power is provided in § 5 of the Fourteenth Amendment, which is the subject of Chapter X.

Part A of this chapter examines the breadth accorded the Article I powers of Congress; it contains the classic interpretation given the "necessary and proper" clause. Part B assesses Congress' power "[t]o regulate Commerce with foreign Nations, and among the several States, and with the Indian Tribes." This focus on the commerce power is appropriate: the power to regulate interstate commerce, if read broadly enough, moots the need for any other power. Part C outlines other Article I powers of Congress, concentrating on (a) taxing and spending powers and (b) treaty and war powers. Finally, Part D considers limits that federalism concerns, expressed in the Tenth and Eleventh Amendments, impose on the Article I powers of Congress.

A. BASIC FRAMEWORK OF CONGRESS' POWERS: THE NECESSARY AND PROPER CLAUSE

After enumerating seventeen specific powers of Congress, Article I, § 8 provides that Congress has the power "[t]o make all Laws which shall be necessary and proper for carrying into Execution the foregoing Powers, and

197

all other Powers vested by this Constitution in the Government of the United States, or in any Department or Officer thereof." The following early Supreme Court opinion gives a broad reading to this phrase, thus expanding federal power and limiting state power.

A bit of historical context is useful here. The charter of the First Bank of the United States, created in 1790, lapsed in 1811. Alexander Hamilton had been a strong supporter of that bank, Thomas Jefferson a strong opponent. Each grounded his position on the Constitution. The First Bank was not subjected to definitive constitutional scrutiny, but when the Second Bank of the United States was created in 1815, many states opposed the bank and some, including Maryland, sought to tax it. By this time, Jefferson supported the Bank as a tool for controlling financial turmoil after the War of 1812.

McCULLOCH v. MARYLAND
17 U.S. (4 Wheat.) 316 (1819)

*** [Congress passed in 1816] "an act to incorporate the subscribers to the Bank of the United States;" and *** the general assembly of Maryland [passed in February 1818] "an act to impose a tax on all banks, or branches thereof, in the state of Maryland, not chartered by the legislature," *** [T]he Bank of the United States did establish a branch, or an office of discount and deposit, in the city of Baltimore, in the state of Maryland, which has, from that time, until the first day of May 1818, ever since transacted and carried on business as a bank *** James William McCulloch [was] the cashier of the said branch, [and] that the said president, directors and company of the Bank of the United States [have not] paid *** $15,000 to ***the state of Maryland, [as required by state law].

MARSHALL, CH. J. delivered the opinion of the court.

*** The first question made in the cause is—has congress power to incorporate a bank? *** The power now contested was exercised by the first congress elected under the present constitution. The bill for incorporating the Bank of the United States did not steal upon an unsuspecting legislature, and pass unobserved. Its principle was completely understood, and was opposed with equal zeal and ability. *** It would require no ordinary share of intrepidity, to assert that a measure adopted under these circumstances, was a bold and plain usurpation, to which the constitution gave no countenance. *** In discussing this question, the counsel for the state of Maryland have deemed it of some importance, in the construction of the constitution, to consider that instrument, not as emanating from the people, but as the act of sovereign and independent states. The powers of the general government, it has been said, are delegated by the states, who alone are truly sovereign; and must be exercised in subordination to the states, who alone possess supreme dominion.

It would be difficult to sustain this proposition. The convention which framed the constitution was indeed elected by the state legislatures. But the instrument, when it came from their hands, was a mere proposal, without obligation, or pretensions to it. It was reported to the then existing congress of the United States, with a request that it might "be submitted to a convention of delegates, chosen in each state by the people thereof, under the recommendation of its legislature, for their assent and ratification." This mode of proceeding was adopted; and by the convention, by congress, and by the state legislatures, the instrument was submitted to the people. *** It is true, they assembled in their several states—and where else should they have assembled? ***

From these conventions, the constitution derives its whole authority. *** The assent of the states, in their sovereign capacity, is implied, in calling a convention, and thus submitting that instrument to the people. But the people were at perfect liberty to accept or reject it; and their act was final. It required not the affirmance, and could not be negatived, by the state governments. *** [T]he government of the Union, then (whatever may be the influence of this fact on the case), is, emphatically and truly, a government of the people. In form, and in substance, it emanates from them. Its powers are granted by them, and are to be exercised directly on them, and for their benefit.

gov. by the people of states, not the states themselves

This government is acknowledged by all, to be one of enumerated powers. The principle, that it can exercise only the powers granted to it, would seem too apparent, to have required to be enforced by all those arguments, which its enlightened friends, while it was depending before the people, found it necessary to urge; that principle is now universally admitted. But the question respecting the extent of the powers actually granted, is perpetually arising, and will probably continue to arise, so long as our system shall exist. In discussing these questions, the conflicting powers of the general and state governments must be brought into view, and the supremacy of their respective laws, when they are in opposition, must be settled.

If any one proposition could command the universal assent of mankind, we might expect it would be this—that the government of the Union, though limited in its powers, is supreme within its sphere of action. *** The nation, on those subjects on which it can act, must necessarily bind its component parts. But this question is not left to mere reason: the people have, in express terms, decided it, by saying, "this constitution, and the laws of the United States, which shall be made in pursuance thereof," "shall be the supreme law of the land," and by requiring that the members of the state legislatures, and the officers of the executive and judicial departments of the states, shall take the oath of fidelity to it. The government of the United States, then, though limited in its powers, is supreme; and its laws, when made in pursuance of the constitution, form the supreme law of the land, "anything in the constitution or laws of any state to the contrary notwithstanding."

2

Among the enumerated powers, we do not find that of establishing a bank or creating a corporation. But there is no phrase in the instrument which, like the articles of confederation, excludes incidental or implied powers; and which requires that everything granted shall be expressly and minutely described. Even the 10th amendment, which was framed for the purpose of quieting the excessive jealousies which had been excited, omits the word "expressly," and declares only, that the powers "not delegated to the United

States, nor prohibited to the states, are reserved to the states or to the people;" thus leaving the question, whether the particular power which may become the subject of contest, has been delegated to the one government, or prohibited to the other, to depend on a fair construction of the whole instrument. The men who drew and adopted this amendment had experienced the embarrassments resulting from the insertion of this word in the articles of confederation, and probably omitted it, to avoid those embarrassments. A constitution, to contain an accurate detail of all the subdivisions of which its great powers will admit, and of all the means by which they may be carried into execution, would partake of the prolixity of a legal code, and could scarcely be embraced by the human mind. It would, probably, never be understood by the public. Its nature, therefore, requires, that only its great outlines should be marked, its important objects designated, and the minor ingredients which compose those objects, be deduced from the nature of the objects themselves. That this idea was entertained by the framers of the American constitution, is not only to be inferred from the nature of the instrument, but from the language. Why else were some of the limitations, found in the 9th section of the 1st article, introduced? It is also, in some degree, warranted, by their having omitted to use any restrictive term which might prevent its receiving a fair and just interpretation. In considering this question, then, we must never forget that it is a constitution we are expounding.

Although, among the enumerated powers of government, we do not find the word "bank" or "incorporation," we find the great powers, to lay and collect taxes; to borrow money; to regulate commerce; to declare and conduct a war; and to raise and support armies and navies. The sword and the purse, all the external relations, and no inconsiderable portion of the industry of the nation, are intrusted to its government. It can never be pretended, that these vast powers draw after them others of inferior importance, merely because they are inferior. Such an idea can never be advanced. But it may with great reason be contended, that a government, intrusted with such ample powers, on the due execution of which the happiness and prosperity of the nation so vitally depends, must also be intrusted with ample means for their execution. *** The exigencies of the nation may require, that the treasure raised in the north should be transported to the south, that raised in the east, conveyed to the west, or that this order should be reversed. Is that construction of the constitution to be preferred, which would render these operations difficult, hazardous and expensive? Can we adopt that construction (unless the words imperiously require it), which would impute to the framers of that instrument, when granting these powers for the public good, the intention of impeding their exercise, by withholding a choice of means?

It is not denied, that the powers given to the government imply the ordinary means of execution. That, for example, of raising revenue, and applying it to national purposes, is admitted to imply the power of conveying money from place to place, as the exigencies of the nation may require, and of employing the usual means of conveyance ***.

But the constitution of the United States has not left the right of congress to employ the necessary means, for the execution of the powers conferred on the government, to general reasoning. To its enumeration of powers is added, that of making "all laws which shall be necessary and proper, for carrying into execution the foregoing powers, and all other powers vested by this constitution, in the government of the United States, or in any department thereof." The counsel for the state of Maryland have urged various arguments, to prove that this clause, though, in terms, a grant of power, is not so, in effect; but is really restrictive of the general right, which might otherwise be implied, of selecting means for executing the enumerated powers.

[handwritten margin note: Maryland args that enumerated powers should only be used when necessary]

[T]he argument on which most reliance is placed, is drawn from that peculiar language of this clause. Congress is not empowered by it to make all laws, which may have relation to the powers conferred on the government, but such only as may be "necessary and proper" for carrying them into execution. The word "necessary" is considered as controlling the whole sentence, and as limiting the right to pass laws for the execution of the granted powers, to such as are indispensable, and without which the power would be nugatory. That it excludes the choice of means, and leaves to congress, in each case, that only which is most direct and simple.

Is it true, that this is the sense in which the word "necessary" is always used? *** We think it does not. *** [W]e find that it frequently imports no more than that one thing is convenient, or useful, or essential to another. To employ the means necessary to an end, is generally understood as employing any means calculated to produce the end, and not as being confined to those single means, without which the end would be entirely unattainable. Such is the character of human language, that no word conveys to the mind, in all situations, one single definite idea; and nothing is more common than to use words in a figurative sense. *** It is essential to just construction, that many words which import something excessive, should be understood in a more mitigated sense—in that sense which common usage justifies. The word "necessary" is of this description. *** A thing may be necessary, very necessary, absolutely or indispensably necessary. To no mind would the same idea be conveyed by these several phrases. The comment on the word is well illustrated by the passage cited at the bar, from the 10th section of the 1st article of the constitution. It is, we think, impossible to compare the sentence which prohibits a state from laying 'imposts, or duties on imports or exports, except what may be absolutely necessary for executing its inspection laws,' with that which authorizes congress "to make all laws which shall be necessary and proper for carrying into execution" the powers of the general government, without feeling a conviction, that the convention understood itself to change materially the meaning of the word "necessary," by prefixing the word "absolutely." This word, then, like others, is used in various senses; and, in its construction, the subject, the context, the intention of the person using them, are all to be taken into view.

[handwritten margin note: N+P clause empowers gov. to carry out any means necessary to accomplish, not just the necessary ones]

[handwritten margin note: Congress did not limit the language by adding absolutely like in Art 1. §10]

Let this be done in the case under consideration. The subject is the execution of those great powers on which the welfare of a nation essentially depends. It must have been the intention of those who gave these powers, to insure, so far as human prudence could insure, their beneficial execution. This could not be done, by confiding the choice of means to such narrow limits as not to leave it in the power of congress to adopt any which might be appropriate, and which were conducive to the end. This provision is made in a constitution, intended to endure for ages to come, and consequently, to be adapted to the various crises of human affairs. To have prescribed the means by which government should, in all future time, execute its powers, would have been to change, entirely, the character of the instrument, and give it the properties of a legal code. ***

So, with respect to the whole penal code of the United States: whence arises the power to punish, in cases not prescribed by the constitution? All admit, that the government may, legitimately, punish any violation of its laws; and yet, this is not among the enumerated powers of congress. The right to enforce the observance of law, by punishing its infraction, might be denied, with the more plausibility, because it is expressly given in some cases.

Congress is empowered "to provide for the punishment of counterfeiting the securities and current coin of the United States," and "to define and punish piracies and felonies committed on the high seas, and offences against the law of nations." The several powers of congress may exist, in a very imperfect state, to be sure, but they may exist and be carried into execution, although no punishment should be inflicted, in cases where the right to punish is not expressly given.

Take, for example, the power "to establish post-offices and post-roads." This power is executed, by the single act of making the establishment. But, from this has been inferred the power and duty of carrying the mail along the post-road, from one post-office to another. And from this implied power, has again been inferred the right to punish those who steal letters from the post-office, or rob the mail. It may be said, with some plausibility, that the right to carry the mail, and to punish those who rob it, is not indispensably necessary to the establishment of a post-office and post-road. This right is indeed essential to the beneficial exercise of the power, but not indispensably necessary to its existence. So of the punishment of the crimes of stealing or falsifying a record or process of a court of the United States, or of perjury in such court. To punish these offences, is certainly conducive to the due administration of justice. But courts may exist, and may decide the causes brought before them, though such crimes escape punishment.

In ascertaining the sense in which the word "necessary" is used in this clause of the constitution, we may derive some aid from that with which it is associated. Congress shall have power "to make all laws which shall be necessary and proper to carry into execution" the powers of the government. If the word "necessary" was used in that strict and rigorous sense for which the counsel for the state of Maryland contend, it would be an extraordinary departure from the usual course of the human mind, as exhibited in composition, to add a word, the only possible effect of which is, to qualify that strict and rigorous meaning; to present to the mind the idea of some choice of means of legislation, not strained and compressed within the narrow limits for which gentlemen contend.

But the argument which most conclusively demonstrates the error of the construction contended for by the counsel for the state of Maryland, is founded on the intention of the convention, as manifested in the whole clause. To waste time and argument in proving that, without it, congress might carry its powers into execution, would be not much less idle, than to hold a lighted taper to the sun. As little can it be required to prove, that in the absence of this clause, congress would have some choice of means. That it might employ those which, in its judgment, would most advantageously effect the object to be accomplished. That any means adapted to the end, any means which tended directly to the execution of the constitutional powers of the government, were in themselves constitutional. This clause, as construed by the state of Maryland, would abridge, and almost annihilate, this useful and necessary right of the legislature to select its means. That this could not be intended, is, we should think, had it not been already controverted, too apparent for controversy.

[margin: MA interp. of N + P clause would leave the gov. ineffective to carry out its goals.]

We think so for the following reasons: 1st. The clause is placed among the powers of congress, not among the limitations on those powers. 2d. Its terms purport to enlarge, not to diminish the powers vested in the government. It purports to be an additional power, not a restriction on those already granted. No reason has been, or can be assigned, for thus concealing an intention to narrow the discretion of the national legislature, under words which purport to enlarge it. ***

[margin: reasons why]

We admit, as all must admit, that the powers of the government are limited, and that its limits are not to be transcended. But we think the sound construction of the constitution must allow to the national legislature that discretion, with respect to the means by which the powers it confers are to be carried into execution, which will enable that body to perform the high duties assigned to it, in the manner most beneficial to the people. Let the end be legitimate, let it be within the scope of the constitution, and all means which are appropriate, which are plainly adapted to that end, which are not prohibited, but consist with the letter and spirit of the constitution, are constitutional ***.

[margin: holding (rational basis review)]

If a corporation may be employed, indiscriminately with other means, to carry into execution the powers of the government, no particular reason can be assigned for excluding the use of a bank, if required for its fiscal operations. To use one, must be within the discretion of congress, if it be an appropriate mode of executing the powers of government. That it is a convenient, a useful, and essential instrument in the prosecution of its fiscal operations, is not now a subject of controversy. All those who have been concerned in the administration of our finances, have concurred in representing its importance and necessity; and so strongly have they been felt, that statesmen of the first class, whose previous opinions against it had been confirmed by every circumstance which can fix the human judgment, have yielded those opinions to the exigencies of the nation. Under the confederation, congress, justifying the measure by its necessity, transcended, perhaps, its powers, to obtain the advantage of a bank; and our own legislation attests the universal conviction of the utility of this measure. The time has passed away, when it can be necessary to enter into any discussion, in order to prove the importance of this instrument, as a means to effect the legitimate objects of the government.

But were its necessity less apparent, none can deny its being an appropriate measure; and if it is, the degree of its necessity, as has been very justly observed, is to be discussed in another place. Should congress, in the execution of its powers, adopt measures which are prohibited by the constitution; or should congress, under the pretext of executing its powers, pass laws for the accomplishment of objects not intrusted to the government; it would become the painful duty of this tribunal, should a case requiring such a decision come before it, to say, that such an act was not the law of the land. But where the law is not prohibited, and is really calculated to effect any of the objects intrusted to the government, to undertake here to inquire into the degree of its necessity, would be to pass the line which circumscribes the judicial department, and to tread on legislative ground. This court disclaims all pretensions to such a power.

After this declaration, it can scarcely be necessary to say, that the existence of state banks can have no possible influence on the question. No trace is to be found in the constitution, of an intention to create a dependence of the government of the Union on those of the states, for the execution of the great powers assigned to it. Its means are adequate to its ends; and on those means alone was it expected to rely for the accomplishment of its ends. To impose on it the necessity of resorting to means which it cannot control, which another government may furnish or withhold, would render its course precarious, the result of its measures uncertain, and create a dependence on other governments, which might disappoint its most important designs, and is incompatible with the language of the constitution. ***

It being the opinion of the court, that the act incorporating the bank is constitutional; and that the power of establishing a branch in the state of Maryland might be properly exercised by the bank itself, we proceed to inquire—

2. Whether the state of Maryland may, without violating the constitution, tax that branch? That the power of taxation is one of vital importance; that it is retained by the states; that it is not abridged by the grant of a similar power to the government of the Union; that it is to be concurrently exercised by the two governments—are truths which have never been denied. But such is the paramount character of the constitution, that its capacity to withdraw any subject from the action of even this power, is admitted. The states are expressly forbidden to lay any duties on imports or exports, except what may be absolutely necessary for executing their inspection laws. If the obligation of this prohibition must be conceded—if it may restrain a state from the exercise of its taxing power on imports and exports—the same paramount character would seem to restrain, as it certainly may restrain, a state from such other exercise of this power, as is in its nature incompatible with, and repugnant to, the constitutional laws of the Union. A law, absolutely

repugnant to another, as entirely repeals that other as if express terms of repeal were used.

On this ground, the counsel for the bank place its claim to be exempted from the power of a state to tax its operations. There is no express provision for the case, but the claim has been sustained on a principle which so entirely pervades the constitution, is so intermixed with the materials which compose it, so interwoven with its web, so blended with its texture, as to be incapable of being separated from it, without rending it into shreds. This great principle is, that the constitution and the laws made in pursuance thereof are supreme; that they control the constitution and laws of the respective states, and cannot be controlled by them. From this, which may be almost termed an axiom, other propositions are deduced as corollaries, on the truth or error of which, and on their application to this case, the cause has been supposed to depend. These are, 1st. That a power to create implies a power to preserve: 2d. That a power to destroy, if wielded by a different hand, is hostile to, and incompatible with these powers to create and to preserve: 3d. That where this repugnancy exists, that authority which is supreme must control, not yield to that over which it is supreme. ***

That the power of taxing it by the states may be exercised so as to destroy it, is too obvious to be denied. But taxation is said to be an absolute power, which acknowledges no other limits than those expressly prescribed in the constitution, and like sovereign power of every other description, is intrusted to the discretion of those who use it. But the very terms of this argument admit, that the sovereignty of the state, in the article of taxation itself, is subordinate to, and may be controlled by the constitution of the United States. How far it has been controlled by that instrument, must be a question of construction. In making this construction, no principle, not declared, can be admissible, which would defeat the legitimate operations of a supreme government. It is of the very essence of supremacy, to remove all obstacles to its action within its own sphere, and so to modify every power vested in subordinate governments, as to exempt its own operations from their own influence. This effect need not be stated in terms. It is so involved in the declaration of supremacy, so necessarily implied in it, that the expression of it could not make it more certain. We must, therefore, keep it in view, while construing the constitution.

The argument on the part of the state of Maryland, is, not that the states may directly resist a law of congress, but that they may exercise their acknowledged powers upon it, and that the constitution leaves them this right, in the confidence that they will not abuse it. *** The only security against the abuse of this power, is found in the structure of the government itself. In imposing a tax, the legislature acts upon its constituents. This is, in general, a sufficient security against erroneous and oppressive taxation.

The people of a state, therefore, give to their government a right of taxing themselves and their property, and as the exigencies of government cannot be limited, they prescribe no limits to the exercise of this right, resting confidently on the interest of the legislator, and on the influence of the constituent over their representative, to guard them against its abuse. But the means employed by the government of the Union have no such security, nor is the right of a state to tax them sustained by the same theory. Those means are not given by the people of a particular state, not given by the constituents of the legislature, which claim the right to tax them, but by the people of all the states. They are given by all, for the benefit of all—and upon theory, should be subjected to that government only which belongs to all.

It may be objected to this definition, that the power of taxation is not confined to the people and property of a state. It may be exercised upon every object brought within its jurisdiction. This is true. But to what source do we trace this right? It is obvious, that it is an incident of sovereignty, and is co-extensive with that to which it is an incident. All subjects over which the sovereign power of a state extends, are objects of taxation; but those over which it does not extend, are, upon the soundest principles, exempt from taxation. This proposition may almost be pronounced self-evident.

state is limited to taxing only those within its jurisdiction

The sovereignty of a state extends to everything which exists by its own authority, or is introduced by its permission; but does it extend to those means which are employed by congress to carry into execution powers conferred on that body by the people of the United States? We think it demonstrable, that it does not. Those powers are not given by the people of a single state. They are given by the people of the United States, to a government whose laws, made in pursuance of the constitution, are declared to be supreme. Consequently, the people of a single state cannot confer a sovereignty which will extend over them.

US law is supreme over any state law

We find, then, on just theory, a total failure of this original right to tax the means employed by the government of the Union, for the execution of its powers. The right never existed, and the question whether it has been surrendered, cannot arise.

But, waiving this theory for the present, let us resume the inquiry, whether this power can be exercised by the respective states, consistently with a fair construction of the constitution? *** Would the people of any one state trust those of another with a power to control the most insignificant operations of their state government? We know they would not. Why, then, should we suppose, that the people of any one state should be willing to trust those of another with a power to control the operations of a government to which they have confided their most important and most valuable interests? In the legislature of the Union alone, are all represented. The legislature of the Union alone, therefore, can be trusted by the people with the power of controlling measures which concern all ***.

If states should not have power over one another, then they should not have power over the fed. gov.

If we apply the principle for which the state of Maryland contends, to the constitution, generally, we shall find it capable of changing totally the character of that instrument. We shall find it capable of arresting all the measures of the government, and of prostrating it at the foot of the states. The American people have declared their constitution and the laws made in pursuance thereof, to be supreme; but this principle would transfer the supremacy, in fact, to the states. If the states may tax one instrument, employed by the government in the execution of its powers, they may tax any and every other instrument. They may tax the mail; they may tax the mint; *founders didn't intend for states to be able to tax everything on top of fed. taxes.* they may tax patent-rights; they may tax the papers of the custom-house; they may tax judicial process; they may tax all the means employed by the government, to an excess which would defeat all the ends of government. This was not intended by the American people. They did not design to make their government dependent on the states.

It has also been insisted, that, as the power of taxation in the general and state governments is acknowledged to be concurrent, every argument which would sustain the right of the general government to tax banks chartered by the states, will equally sustain the right of the states to tax banks chartered by the general government. But the two cases are not on the same reason. The people of all the states have created the general government, and have conferred upon it the general power of taxation. The people of all the states, and the states themselves, are represented in congress, and, by their representatives, exercise this power. When they tax the chartered institutions of the states, they tax their constituents; and these taxes must be uniform. But when a state taxes the operations of the government of the United States, it acts upon institutions created, not by their own constituents, but by people over whom they claim no control. It acts upon the measures of a government created by others as well as themselves, for the benefit of others in common with themselves. The difference is that which always exists, and always must exist, between the action of the whole on a part, and the action of a part on the whole—between the laws of a government declared to be supreme, and those of a government which, when in opposition to those laws, is not supreme.

But if the full application of this argument could be admitted, it might bring into question the right of congress to tax the state banks, and could not prove the rights of the states to tax the Bank of the United States. *** We are unanimously of opinion, that the law passed by the legislature of Maryland, imposing a tax on the Bank of the United States, is unconstitutional and void.***

Notes

1.   **Structure.** *McCulloch v. Maryland* is often referred to as an opinion based on a "structural" approach to constitutional interpretation. Identify components of the opinion that support this view of the case.

2.   **Logic and Limits.**

(a) Does CHIEF JUSTICE MARSHALL's opinion support the notion that Congress has implied powers?

(b) President Thomas Jefferson said that "the constitution allows only the means which are *necessary*, not merely 'convenient,' for effectuating the enumerated powers *** [Otherwise, the 'necessary and proper clause'] would swallow up all the delegated powers, and reduce the whole to one power." Do you agree or disagree with Jefferson?

(c) Do you agree or disagree with Virginia CHIEF JUSTICE SPENCER ROANE's argument that "[t]here is no earthly difference between an *unlimited* grant of power, and a grant limited to its terms, but accompanied with *unlimited* means of carrying it into execution"?

(d) What do you think of Marshall's mention of means-ends relationships and the Court's power to invalidate laws enacted "under the pretext" of exercising granted powers?

3. **Aphorisms.**

   • Marshall's phrase "it is a *constitution* we are expounding" has proven powerful. What does this phrase mean to you? What bearing should it have on judicial decision making?

   • Is Marshall's phrase "the power to tax involves the power to destroy" grounded in the Constitution?

4. **Policy.** Are the policy issues different concerning the two parts of the opinion, or are they really two sides to the same coin? Subsequent commentators have placed great emphasis on what they call the "representation-reinforcement" role played by the Court. Reread what Marshall says concerning the fact that Maryland is harming people not represented in its legislature and whether this is sufficient reason for the Supreme Court, rather than Congress, to protect unrepresented out-of-staters. Was the second part of the Court's opinion needed to preserve federal power?

5. **Federalism and Decentralization.** What is the distinction between a federal system and a governmental system that is merely decentralized?

6. **Intergovernmental Tax Immunity.** Prior to 1938, the intergovernmental tax immunity doctrine was broadly interpreted to prohibit federal and state governments from taxing the salaries of persons employed by other sovereign entities. Since then, however, the Court has held that the doctrine should be construed more narrowly. For example, in *Jefferson County, Ala. v. Acker*, 527 U.S. 423 (1999), an Alabama county imposed an occupational tax (as opposed to an income tax) on a group of professions pursuant to the Federal Public Salary Tax Act. Two federal judges claimed that the tax on their salaries interfered with the operation of the federal judiciary and violated the intergovernmental tax immunity doctrine. In upholding the constitutionality of the County's ordinance, the Court reaffirmed that a State's taxation of federal employees' salaries is permissible if the tax was not directly imposed on one sovereign entity by another and was not discriminatory.

UNITED STATES v. COMSTOCK
560 U.S. 126 (2010)

JUSTICE BREYER delivered the opinion of the Court.

   *** The federal statute before us allows a district court to order the civil commitment of an individual who is currently "in the custody of the [Federal] Bureau of Prisons," if that individual (1) has previously "engaged or attempted to engage in sexually violent conduct or child molestation," (2) currently "suffers from a serious mental illness, abnormality, or disorder," and (3) "as a result of" that mental illness, abnormality, or disorder is "sexually dangerous to others," in that "he would have serious difficulty in refraining from sexually violent conduct or child molestation if released." ***

If the Government proves its claims by "clear and convincing evidence," the court will order the prisoner's continued commitment in "the custody of the Attorney General," who must "make all reasonable efforts to cause" the State where that person was tried, or the State where he is domiciled, to "assume responsibility for his custody, care, and treatment." *** But if, "notwithstanding such efforts, neither such State will assume such responsibility," then "the Attorney General shall place the person for treatment in a suitable [federal] facility." Confinement in the federal facility will last until either (1) the person's mental condition improves to the point where he is no longer dangerous (with or without appropriate ongoing treatment), in which case he will be released; or (2) a State assumes responsibility for his custody, care, and treatment, in which case he will be transferred to the custody of that State. *** [T]he Government claimed that the respondent was about to be released from federal prison, that he had engaged in sexually violent conduct or child molestation in the past, and that he suffered from a mental illness that made him sexually dangerous to others. ***

The question presented is whether the Necessary and Proper Clause, Art. I, § 8, cl. 18, grants Congress authority sufficient to enact the statute before us. In resolving that question, we assume, but we do not decide, that other provisions of the Constitution -- such as the Due Process Clause -- do not prohibit civil commitment in these circumstances. *** [W]e conclude that the Constitution grants Congress legislative power sufficient to enact § 4248. We base this conclusion on five considerations, taken together.

First, the Necessary and Proper Clause grants Congress broad authority to enact federal legislation. [*McCulloch v. Maryland*] *** Thus, the Constitution, which nowhere speaks explicitly about the creation of federal crimes beyond those related to "counterfeiting," "treason," or "Piracies and Felonies committed on the high Seas" or "against the Law of Nations," nonetheless grants Congress broad authority to create such crimes. *** Neither Congress' power to criminalize conduct, nor its power to imprison individuals who engage in that conduct, nor its power to enact laws governing prisons and prisoners, is explicitly mentioned in the Constitution. But Congress nonetheless possesses broad authority to do each of those things in the course of "carrying into Execution" the enumerated powers "vested by" the "Constitution in the Government of the United States," authority granted by the Necessary and Proper Clause.

Second, the civil-commitment statute before us constitutes a modest addition to a set of federal prison-related mental-health statutes that have existed for many decades. *** Here, Congress has long been involved in the delivery of mental health care to federal prisoners, and has long provided for their civil commitment. *** [This statute] differs from earlier statutes in that it focuses directly upon persons who, due to a mental illness, are sexually dangerous. *** [I]t is a modest addition to a longstanding federal statutory framework, which has been in place since 1855.

Third, Congress reasonably extended its longstanding civil-commitment system to cover mentally ill and sexually dangerous persons who are already in federal custody, even if doing so detains them beyond the termination of their criminal sentence. For one thing, the Federal Government is the custodian of its prisoners. As federal custodian, it has the constitutional power to act in order to protect nearby (and other) communities from the danger federal prisoners may pose. *** Congress could have reasonably concluded that federal inmates who suffer from a mental illness that causes them to "have serious difficulty in refraining from sexually violent conduct," would pose an especially high danger to the public if released. And Congress could also have reasonably concluded *** that a reasonable number of such individuals would likely *not* be detained by the States if released from federal custody, in part because the Federal Government itself severed their claim to "legal residence in any State" by incarcerating them in remote federal prisons. ***

Fourth, the statute properly accounts for state interests. *** [It requires *accommodation* of state interests: The Attorney General must inform the State in which the federal prisoner "is domiciled or was tried" that he is detaining someone with respect to whom those States may wish to assert their authority, and he must encourage those States to assume custody of the individual. He must also immediately "release" that person "to the appropriate official of" either State "if such State will assume such responsibility." And either State has the right, at any time, to assert its authority over the individual, which will prompt the individual's immediate transfer to State custody. ***

Fifth, the links between § 4248 and an enumerated Article I power are not too attenuated. Neither is the statutory provision too sweeping in its scope. Invoking the cautionary instruction that we may not "pile inference upon inference" in order to sustain congressional action under Article I, respondents argue that, when legislating pursuant to the Necessary and Proper Clause, Congress' authority can be no more than one step removed from a specifically enumerated power. But this argument is irreconcilable with our precedents. *** Neither we nor the dissent can point to a single specific enumerated power "that justifies a criminal defendant's arrest or conviction." *** And the same enumerated power that justifies the creation of a federal criminal statute, and that justifies the additional implied federal powers that the dissent considers legitimate, justifies civil commitment under § 4248 as well. ***

We take these five considerations together. They include: (1) the breadth of the Necessary and Proper Clause, (2) the long history of federal involvement in this arena, (3) the sound reasons for the statute's enactment in light of the Government's custodial interest in safeguarding the public from dangers posed by those in federal custody, (4) the statute's accommodation of state interests, and (5) the statute's narrow scope. *** [T]he statute is a "necessary and proper" means of exercising the federal authority that permits Congress to create federal criminal laws, to punish their violation, to imprison violators, to provide appropriately for those imprisoned, and to maintain the security of those who are not imprisoned but who may be affected by the federal imprisonment of others. ***

JUSTICE KENNEDY with whom JUSTICE ALITO joins, concurring in the judgment.

*** This separate writing serves two purposes. The first is to withhold assent from certain statements and propositions of the Court's opinion. The second is to caution that the Constitution does require the invalidation of congressional attempts to extend federal powers in some instances. *** The terms "rationally related" and "rational basis" must be employed with care, particularly if either is to be used as a stand-alone test. *** [The] precedents require a tangible link to commerce, not a mere conceivable rational relation. *** The rational basis referred to in the Commerce Clause context is a demonstrated link in fact, based on empirical demonstration. While undoubtedly deferential, this may well be different from the rational-basis test. ***

A separate concern stems from the Court's *** inference that restrictions flowing from the federal system are of no import when defining the limits of the National Government's power, as it proceeds by first asking whether the power is within the National Government's reach, and if so it discards federalism concerns entirely. *** The federal program in question applies only to those in federal custody and thus involves little intrusion upon the ordinary processes and powers of the States. *** [T]his is a discrete and narrow exercise of authority over a small class of persons already subject to the federal power. Importantly, § 4248(d) requires the Attorney General to release any civil detainee "to the appropriate official of the State in which the person is domiciled or was tried if such State will assume responsibility for his custody, care, and treatment," providing a strong assurance that the proffered reason for the legislation's necessity is not a mere artifice. ***

JUSTICE ALITO, concurring in the judgment.

*** I entirely agree with the dissent that "the Necessary and Proper Clause empowers Congress to enact only those laws that [execute]the enumerated powers that support the federal criminal statutes under which the affected prisoners were convicted. *** [Is it] also necessary and proper for Congress to protect the public from dangers created by the federal criminal justice and prison systems[?] In my view, the answer to that question is "yes" *** [so] there is a substantial link to Congress' constitutional powers. ***

JUSTICE THOMAS, with whom JUSTICE SCALIA joins, dissenting.

*** [T]he Necessary and Proper Clause is not an independent fount of congressional authority, but rather "a *caveat* that Congress possesses all the means necessary to carry out the specifically granted 'foregoing' powers of § 8 'and all other Powers vested by this Constitution.'" *** The Government identifies no specific enumerated power or powers as a constitutional predicate for § 4248, and none are readily discernable. Indeed, not even the Commerce Clause -- the enumerated power this Court has interpreted most expansively -- can justify federal civil detention of sex offenders. *** To be sure, protecting society from violent sexual offenders is certainly an important end. Sexual abuse is a despicable act with untold consequences for the victim personally and society generally. But the Constitution does not vest in Congress the authority to protect society from every bad act that might befall it. *** The Court perfunctorily genuflects to *McCulloch*'s framework for assessing authority, and to the principle of dual sovereignty it helps to maintain, then promptly abandons both in favor of a novel five-factor test supporting its conclusion that § 4248 is a "'necessary and proper'" adjunct to a jumble of *unenumerated* "authorities." The Court's newly minted test cannot be reconciled with the Clause's plain text or with two centuries of our precedents interpreting it. It also raises more questions than it answers. *** At a minimum, this shift from the two-step *McCulloch* framework to this five-consideration approach warrants an explanation as to why *McCulloch* is no longer good enough and which of the five considerations will bear the most weight in future cases, assuming some number less than five suffices. (Or, if not, why all five are required.) *** Not long ago, this Court described the Necessary and Proper Clause as "the last, best hope of those who defend ultra vires congressional action." Regrettably, today's opinion breathes new life into that Clause, and *** comes perilously close to transforming the Necessary and Proper Clause into a basis for the federal police power that "we *always* have rejected." ***

Notes

1. **Theory.** *McCulloch* states that a statute is valid under the Necessary and Proper Clause if it is, in Congress' view, "plainly adapted" to the end it seeks to achieve. Does *Comstock* change that standard to a judicially administered five-factor test?

2. **History.** JUSTICE BREYER states that § 4248 is a modest addition to a longstanding federal statutory framework. Has the statutory framework been in place since 1855? 1948? Does it matter? Is the addition truly modest?

3. **Enumerated Powers.** The majority suggests that the power to enforce civil rights is one of Congress's enumerated powers. Where does Congress derive the power to enforce civil rights? *See Heart of Atlanta* and *Morrison*, infra; *see also* Chapter X.

B. THE COMMERCE CLAUSE POWER

Commercial interests were a driving force behind adoption of the Constitution. Barriers to trade among the states hindered the economic growth of the United States, and the Articles of Confederation did not provide sufficient powers for the central government to eliminate these barriers. In addition to specific disabilities placed by the Constitution on the States concerning tariffs and trade, Congress was given the power to regulate commerce so that national commercial interests might prevail over what the Federalists called local protectionist "factions." The classic exposition of the reach of this power is contained in CHIEF JUSTICE MARSHALL's opinion in *Gibbons v. Ogden*, set forth below in Section 1.

As the nation grew during the nineteenth and early part of the twentieth centuries, Congress generally regulated commerce lightly. When Congress did exercise its power, the Court sometimes attempted, with a notable lack of success, to cabin Congress' power to "direct" but not "indirect" regulation of commerce. With the advent of the Great Depression and Franklin Roosevelt's presidency, the Federal laissez-faire approach to commerce was challenged as insufficient to guarantee the well being of the American people. Roosevelt's appointees led the Court in allowing Congress wide latitude to regulate commerce. Section 2 presents some highlights of the Supreme Court's expansive New Deal and Post–New Deal approach to Congress' powers under the Commerce Clause.

You might conclude at the end of section 2 that there are no judicially enforceable limits to the Commerce Power, so the other powers of Congress in Article I, § 8 are superfluous. But you would be mistaken. Section 3 explores the extent to which the Supreme Court has recently established internal limits to the Commerce Power. Correlatively, the other Article I powers explored in Part B have become more important.

1.   CLASSICAL VIEW OF THE COMMERCE POWER

GIBBONS v. OGDEN
22 U.S. (9 Wheat.) 1 (1824).

*** Aaron Ogden filed [suit in New York state court] against Thomas Gibbons, setting forth the several acts of the Legislature thereof, enacted for the purpose of securing to Robert R. Livingston and Robert Fulton, the exclusive navigation of all the waters within the jurisdiction of that State, with boats moved by fire or steam, for a term of years which has not yet expired ***. The bill stated an assignment from Livingston and Fulton to one John R. Livingston, and from him to the complainant, Ogden, of the right to navigate the waters between Elizabethtown, and other places in New Jersey, and the city of New York; and that Gibbons, the defendant below, was in possession of two steam boats, called the Stoudinger and the Bellona, which were actually employed in running between New York and Elizabethtown, in violation of the exclusive privilege conferred on the complainant, and praying an injunction to restrain the said Gibbons from using the said boats, or any other propelled by fire or steam, in navigating the waters within the territory of New York. *** Gibbons [answered] that the boats employed by him were duly enrolled and licensed, to be employed in carrying on the coasting trade, under the [1793] act of Congress entitled, "An act for enrolling and licensing ships and vessels to be employed in the coasting trade and fisheries, and for regulating the same." And the defendant insisted on his right, in virtue of such licenses, to navigate the waters between Elizabethtown and the city of New York, the said acts of the Legislature of the State of New York to the contrary notwithstanding. ***

MR. CHIEF JUSTICE MARSHALL delivered the opinion of the Court ***

The appellant contends that *** the laws which purport to give the exclusive privilege it sustains, are repugnant to *** that clause in the constitution which authorizes Congress to regulate commerce. *** [R]eference has been made to the political situation of these States, anterior to its formation. It has been said, that they were sovereign, were completely independent, and were connected with each other only by a league. This is true. But, when these allied sovereigns converted their league into a government, *** the whole character in which the States appear, underwent a change, the extent of which must be determined by a fair consideration of the instrument by which that change was effected.

[The constitution] contains an enumeration of powers expressly granted by the people to their government. It has been said, that these powers ought to be construed strictly. But why ought they to be so construed? Is there one sentence in the constitution which gives countenance to this rule? *** If, from the imperfection of human language, there should be serious doubts respecting the extent of any given power, it is a well settled rule, that the objects for which it was given, especially when those objects are expressed in the instrument itself, should have great influence in the construction. We know of no reason for excluding this rule from the present case.

The words [of the constitution] are, "Congress shall have power to regulate commerce with foreign nations, and among the several States, and with the Indian tribes."

The subject to be regulated is commerce; and our constitution being, as was aptly said at the bar, one of enumeration, and not of definition, to ascertain the extent of the power, it becomes necessary to settle the meaning of the word. The counsel for the appellee would limit it to traffic, to buying and selling, or the interchange of commodities, and do not admit that it comprehends navigation. This would restrict a general term, applicable to many objects, to one of its significations. Commerce, undoubtedly, is traffic, but it is something more: it is intercourse. It describes the commercial intercourse between nations, and parts of nations, in all its branches, and is regulated by prescribing rules for carrying on that intercourse. The mind can scarcely conceive a system for regulating commerce between nations, which shall exclude all laws concerning navigation, which shall be silent on the admission of the vessels of the one nation into the ports of the other, and be confined to prescribing rules for the conduct of individuals, in the actual employment of buying and selling, or of barter.

If commerce does not include navigation, the government of the Union has no direct power over that subject, and can make no law prescribing what shall constitute American vessels, or requiring that they shall be navigated by American seamen. Yet this power has been exercised from the commencement of the government, has been exercised with the consent of all, and has been understood by all to be a commercial regulation. All America understands, and has uniformly understood, the word "commerce," to comprehend navigation. It was so understood, and must have been so understood, when the constitution was framed. The power over commerce, including navigation, was one of the primary objects for which the people of America adopted their government, and must have been contemplated in forming it. The convention must have used the word in that sense, because all have understood it in that sense; and the attempt to restrict it comes too late ***. The word used in the constitution, then, comprehends, and has been always understood to comprehend, navigation within its meaning; and a power to regulate navigation, is as expressly granted, as if that term had been added to the word "commerce."

To what commerce does this power extend? The constitution informs us, to commerce "with foreign nations, and among the several States, and with the Indian tribes." *** [T]hese words comprehend every species of commercial intercourse between the United States and foreign nations. *** The subject to which the power is next applied, is to commerce "among the several States." The word "among" means intermingled with. A thing which is among others, is intermingled with them. Commerce among the States, cannot stop at the external boundary line of each State, but may be introduced into the interior.

It is not intended to say that these words comprehend that commerce, which is completely internal, which is carried on between man and man in a State, or between different parts of the same State, and which does not extend to or affect other States. Such a power would be inconvenient, and is certainly unnecessary.

Comprehensive as the word "among" is, it may very properly be restricted to that commerce which concerns more States than one. The phrase is not one which would probably have been selected to indicate the completely interior traffic of a State, because it is not an apt phrase for that purpose; and the enumeration of the particular classes of commerce, to which the power was to be extended, would not have been made, had the intention been to extend the power to every description. *** The genius and character of the whole government seem to be, that its action is to be applied to all the external concerns of the nation, and to those internal concerns which affect the States generally; but not to those which are completely within a particular State, which do not affect other States, and with which it is not necessary to interfere, for the purpose of executing some of the general powers of the government. The completely internal commerce of a State, then, may be considered as reserved for the State itself.

But, in regulating commerce with foreign nations, the power of Congress does not stop at the jurisdictional lines of the several States. It would be a very useless power, if it could not pass those lines. The commerce of the United States with foreign nations, is that of the whole United States. Every district has a right to participate in it. The deep streams which penetrate our country in every direction, pass through the interior of almost every State in the Union, and furnish the means of exercising this right. If Congress has the power to regulate it, that power must be exercised whenever the subject exists. If it exists within the States, if a foreign voyage may commence or terminate at a port within a State, then the power of Congress may be exercised within a State.

This principle is, if possible, still more clear, when applied to commerce "among the several States." They either join each other, in which case they are separated by a mathematical line, or they are remote from each other, in which case other States lie between them. What is commerce "among" them; and how is it to be conducted? Can a trading expedition between two adjoining States, commence and terminate outside of each? And if the trading intercourse be between two States remote from each other, must it not commence in one, terminate in the other, and probably pass through a third? Commerce among the States must, of necessity, be commerce with the States. In the regulation of trade with the Indian tribes, the action of the law, especially when the constitution was made, was chiefly within a State. The power of Congress, then, whatever it may be, must be exercised within the territorial jurisdiction of the several States. The sense of the nation on this subject, is unequivocally manifested by the provisions made in the laws for transporting goods, by land, between Baltimore and Providence, between New York and Philadelphia, and between Philadelphia and Baltimore.

We are now arrived at the inquiry—What is this power?

It is the power to regulate; that is, to prescribe the rule by which commerce is to be governed. This power, like all others vested in Congress, is complete in itself, may be exercised to its utmost extent, and acknowledges no limitations, other than are prescribed in the constitution. These are expressed in plain terms, and do not affect the questions which arise in this case, or which have been discussed at the bar. If, as has always been understood, the sovereignty of Congress, though limited to specified objects, is plenary as to those objects, the power over commerce with foreign nations, and among the several States, is vested in Congress as absolutely as it would be in a single government ***. The wisdom and the discretion of Congress, their identity with the people, and the influence which their constituents possess at elections, are, in this, as in many other instances, as that, for example, of declaring war, the sole restraints on which they have relied, to secure them from its abuse. They are the restraints on which the people must often rely solely, in all representative governments.

The power of Congress, then, comprehends navigation, within the limits of every State in the Union; so far as that navigation may be, in any manner, connected with "commerce with foreign nations, or among the several States, or with the Indian tribes." It may, of consequence, pass the jurisdictional line of New York, and act upon the very waters to which the prohibition now under consideration applies.

But it has been urged [that] the States may severally exercise the same power, within their respective jurisdictions. *** [T]he grant of the power to lay and collect taxes is, like the power to regulate commerce, made in general terms, and has never been understood to interfere with the exercise of the same power by the State; and hence has been drawn an argument which has been applied to the question under consideration. But the two grants are not, it is conceived, similar in their terms or their nature. Although many of the powers formerly exercised by the States, are transferred to the government of the Union, yet the State governments remain, and constitute a most important part of our system. The power of taxation is indispensable to their existence, and is a power which, in its own nature, is capable of residing in, and being exercised by, different authorities at the same time. *** Taxation is the simple operation of taking small portions from a perpetually accumulating mass, susceptible of almost infinite division *** In imposing taxes for State purposes, they are not doing what Congress is empowered to do. Congress is not empowered to tax for those purposes which are within the exclusive province of the States. When, then, each government exercises the power of taxation, neither is exercising the power of the other. But, when a State proceeds to regulate commerce with foreign nations, or among the several States, it is exercising the very power that is granted to Congress, and is doing the very thing which Congress is authorized to do. There is no analogy, then, between the power of taxation and the power of regulating commerce ***.

The sole question is, can a State regulate commerce with foreign nations and among the States, while Congress is regulating it?

The counsel for the respondent answer this question in the affirmative, and rely very much on the restrictions in the 10th section, as supporting their opinion. They say, very truly, that limitations of a power, furnish a strong argument in favour of the existence of that power, and that the section which prohibits the States from laying duties on imports or exports, proves that this power might have been exercised, had it not been expressly forbidden; and, consequently, that any other commercial regulation, not expressly forbidden, to which the original power of the State was competent, may still be made. That this restriction shows the opinion of the Convention, that a State might impose duties on exports and imports, if not expressly forbidden, will be conceded; but that it follows as a consequence, from this concession, that a State may regulate commerce with foreign nations and among the States, cannot be admitted ***.

[I]nspection laws are said to be regulations of commerce, and are certainly recognised in the constitution, as being passed in the exercise of a power remaining with the States. That inspection laws may have a remote and considerable influence on commerce, will not be denied; but that a power to regulate commerce is the source from which the right to pass them is derived, cannot be admitted. The object of inspection laws, is to improve the quality of articles produced by the labour of a country; to fit them for exportation; or, it may be, for domestic use. They act upon the subject before it becomes an article of foreign commerce, or of commerce among the States, and prepare it for that purpose. They form a portion of that immense mass of legislation, which embraces every thing within the territory of a State, not surrendered to the general government: all which can be most advantageously exercised by the States themselves. Inspection laws, quarantine laws, health laws of every description, as well as laws for regulating the internal commerce of a State, and those which respect turnpike roads, ferries, &c., are component parts of this mass.

No direct general power over these objects is granted to Congress; and, consequently, they remain subject to State legislation. If the legislative power of the Union can reach them, it must be for national purposes; it must be where the power is expressly given for a special purpose, or is clearly incidental to some power which is expressly given. It is obvious, that the government of the Union, in the exercise of its express powers, that, for example, of regulating commerce with foreign nations and among the States, may use means that may also be employed by a State, in the exercise of its acknowledged powers; that, for example, of regulating commerce within the State. If Congress license vessels to sail from one port to another, in the same State, the act is supposed to be, necessarily, incidental to the power expressly granted to Congress, and implies no claim of a direct power to regulate the purely internal commerce of a State, or to act directly on its system of police. So, if a State, in passing laws on subjects acknowledged to be within its control, and with a view to those subjects, shall adopt a measure of the same character with one which Congress may adopt, it does not derive its authority from the particular power which has been granted, but from some other, which remains with the State, and may be executed by the same means. ***

In pursuing this inquiry at the bar, it has been said, that the constitution does not confer the right of intercourse between State and State. That right derives its source from those laws whose authority is acknowledged by civilized man throughout the world. This is true. The constitution found it an existing right, and gave to Congress the power to regulate it. In the exercise of this power, Congress has passed "an act for enrolling or licensing ships or vessels to be employed in the coasting trade and fisheries, and for regulating the same." *** This act demonstrates the opinion of Congress, that steam boats may be enrolled and licensed, in common with vessels using sails. They are, of course, entitled to the same privileges, and can no more be restrained from navigating waters, and entering ports which are free to such vessels, than if they were wafted on their voyage by the winds, instead of being propelled by the agency of fire. The one element may be as legitimately used as the other, for every commercial purpose authorized by the laws of the Union; and the act of a State inhibiting the use of either to any vessel having a license under the act of Congress, comes, we think, in direct collision with that act. ***

Powerful and ingenious minds, taking, as postulates, that the powers expressly granted to the government of the Union, are to be contracted by construction, into the narrowest possible compass, and that the original powers of the States are retained, if any possible construction will retain them, may, by a course of well digested, but refined and metaphysical reasoning, founded on these premises, explain away the constitution of our country, and leave it, a magnificent structure, indeed, to look at, but totally unfit for use. ***

MR. JUSTICE JOHNSON. [concurring]

*** It is impossible, with the views which I entertain of the principle on which the commercial privileges of the people of the United States, among themselves, rests, to concur in the view which this Court takes of the effect of the coasting license in this cause. *** And I cannot overcome the conviction, that if the licensing act was repealed to-morrow, the rights of the appellant to a reversal of the decision complained of, would be as strong as it is under this license. *** [I]f this instrument had been called an exemption instead of a license, it would have given a better idea of its character. ***

It has been contended, that the grants of power to the United States over any subject, do not, necessarily, paralyze the arm of the States, or deprive them of the capacity to act on the same subject. *** The practice of our government certainly has been, on many subjects, to occupy so much only of the field opened to them, as they think the public interests require. *** But the license furnishes a full answer to this objection; for, although one grant of power over commerce, should not be deemed a total relinquishment of power over the subject, but amounting only to a power to assume, still the power of the States must be at an end, so far as the United States have, by their legislative act, taken the subject under their immediate superintendence. So far as relates to the commerce coastwise, the act under which this license is granted, contains a full expression of Congress on this subject.

But the principal objections to these opinions arise, 1st. From the unavoidable action of some of the municipal powers of the States, upon commercial subjects [and] 2d. From passages in the constitution, which are supposed to imply a concurrent power in the States in regulating commerce.

It is no objection to the existence of distinct, substantive powers, that in their application, they bear upon the same subject. The same bale of goods, the same cask of provisions, or the same ship, that may be the subject of commercial regulation, may also be the vehicle of disease. And the health laws that require them to be stopped and ventilated, are no more intended as regulations on commerce, than the laws which permit their importation, are intended to innoculate the community with disease. Their different purposes mark the distinction between the powers brought into action, and while frankly exercised, they can produce no serious collision. As to laws affecting ferries, turnpike roads, and other subjects of the same class, so far from meriting the epithet of commercial regulations, they are, in fact, commercial facilities, for which, by the consent of mankind, a compensation is paid, upon the same principle that the whole commercial world submit to pay light money to the Danes. Inspection laws are of a more equivocal nature, and it is obvious, that the constitution has viewed that subject with much solicitude. But so far from sustaining an inference in favour of the power of the States over commerce, I cannot but think that the guarded provisions of the 10th section, on this subject, furnish a strong argument against that inference. It was obvious, that inspection laws must combine municipal with commercial regulations; and, while the power over the subject is yielded to the States, for obvious reasons, an absolute control is given over State legislation on the subject, as far as that legislation may be exercised, so as to affect the commerce of the country. The inferences, to be correctly drawn, from this whole article, appear to me to be altogether in favour of the exclusive grants to Congress of power over commerce, and the reverse of that which the appellee contends for.

This section contains the positive restrictions imposed by the constitution upon State power. The first clause of it, specifies those powers which the states are precluded from exercising, even though the Congress were to permit them. The second, those which the States may exercise with the consent of Congress. And here the sedulous attention to the subject of State exclusion from commercial power, is strongly marked. Not satisfied with the express grant to the United States of the power over commerce, this clause negatives the exercise of that power to the States, as to the only two objects which could ever tempt them to assume the exercise of that power, to wit, the collection of a revenue from imposts and duties on imports and exports; or from a tonnage duty. As to imposts on imports or exports, such a revenue might have been aimed at directly, by express legislation, or indirectly, in the form of inspection laws; and it became necessary to guard against both. Hence, first, the consent of Congress to such imposts or duties, is made necessary; and as to inspection laws, it is limited to the minimum of expenses. Then, the money so raised shall be paid into the treasury of the United States, or may be sued for, since it is declared to be for their use. And lastly, all such laws may be modified, or repealed, by an act of Congress. It is impossible for a right to be more guarded.

It would be in vain to deny the possibility of a clashing and collision between the measures of the two governments. The line cannot be drawn with sufficient distinctness between the municipal powers of the one, and the commercial powers of the other. In some points they meet and blend so as scarcely to admit of separation. Hitherto the only remedy has been applied which the case admits of, that of a frank and candid co-operation for the general good. Witness the laws of Congress requiring its officers to respect the inspection laws of the States, and to aid in enforcing their health laws; that which surrenders to the States the superintendence of pilotage, and the many laws passed to permit a tonnage duty to be levied for the use of their ports. Other instances could be cited, abundantly to prove that collision must be sought to be produced; and when it does arise, the question must be decided how far the powers of Congress are adequate to put it down. Wherever the powers of the respective governments are frankly exercised, with a distinct view to the ends of such powers, they may act upon the same object, or use the same means and yet the powers be kept perfectly distinct. A resort to the same means, therefore, is no argument to prove the identity of their respective powers. ***

Notes

1.   **Linguistic Limits.** Consider the Court's attempt to parse the language of the Commerce Clause.

> • *Commerce.* How does CHIEF JUSTICE MARSHALL define this term and relate it to navigation? To state inspection laws?

> • *Among the Several States.* How does Marshall view commerce that is "completely internal" and does not affect other states?

> • *Regulate.* Why are inspection laws a problem for Marshall in defining regulation?

2.   **Concurrence.** Compare and contrast JUSTICE JOHNSON's concurrence with CHIEF JUSTICE MARSHALL's opinion for the Court.

3.   **Judicial Competence.** Is the Court or Congress in the better position to determine whether a particular statutory provision regulates commerce among the several states?

2. THE COMMERCE CLAUSE AFTER THE NEW DEAL

WICKARD v. FILBURN
317 U.S. 111 (1942)

MR. JUSTICE JACKSON delivered the opinion of the Court.

[Filburn] *** sought to enjoin enforcement against himself of the marketing penalty imposed *** upon that part of his 1941 wheat crop which was available for marketing in excess of the marketing quota established for his farm. He also sought a declaratory judgment that the wheat marketing quota provisions of the Act as amended and applicable to him were unconstitutional because not sustainable under the Commerce Clause *** [Filburn] for many years past has owned and operated a small farm in Montgomery County, Ohio, maintaining a herd of dairy cattle, selling milk, raising poultry, and selling poultry and eggs. It has been his practice to raise a small acreage of winter wheat, sown in the Fall and harvested in the following July; to sell a portion of the crop; to feed part to poultry and livestock on the farm, some of which is sold; to use some in making flour for home consumption; and to keep the rest for the following seeding. The intended disposition of the crop here involved has not been expressly stated.

*** [T]here were established for [Filburn's]1941 crop a wheat acreage allotment of 11.1 acres and a normal yield of 20.1 bushels of wheat an acre. He was given notice of such allotment in July of 1940 before the Fall planting of his 1941 crop of wheat, and again in July of 1941, before it was harvested. *basis for the violation fee* He sowed, however, 23 acres, and harvested from his 11.9 acres of excess acreage 239 bushels, which under the terms of the Act as amended on May 26, 1941, constituted farm marketing excess, subject to a penalty of 49 cents a bushel, or $117.11 in all. The appellee has not paid the penalty and he has not postponed or avoided it by storing the excess under regulations of the Secretary of Agriculture, or by delivering it up to the Secretary. ***

The general scheme of the Agricultural Adjustment Act of 1938 as related to wheat is to control the volume moving in interstate and foreign commerce in order to avoid surpluses and shortages and the consequent abnormally low or high wheat prices and obstructions to commerce. Within prescribed limits and by prescribed standards the Secretary of Agriculture is directed to ascertain and proclaim each year a national acreage allotment for the next crop of wheat, which is then apportioned to the states and their counties, and is eventually broken up into allotments for individual farms. Loans and payments to wheat farmers are authorized in stated circumstances.

The Act provides further that whenever it appears that the total supply of wheat as of the beginning of any marketing year, beginning July 1, will *Sec of Ag creates quota, but farmers can vote on it.* exceed a normal year's domestic consumption and export by more than 35 per cent, the Secretary shall so proclaim not later than May 15 prior to the beginning of such marketing year; and that during the marketing year a compulsory national marketing quota shall be in effect with respect to the marketing of wheat. Between the issuance of the proclamation and June 10, the Secretary must, however, conduct a referendum of farmers who will be subject to the quota to determine whether they favor or oppose it; and if more than one-third of the farmers voting in the referendum do oppose, the Secretary must prior to the effective date of the quota by proclamation suspend its operation. *** [T]he referendum of wheat growers was held on May 31, 1941. *** 81 per cent of those voting favored the marketing quota, with 19 per cent opposed.

Quota passed

*** It is urged that under the Commerce Clause of the Constitution, Article I, s 8, clause 3, Congress does not possess the power it has in this instance sought to exercise. The question would merit little consideration since our decision in *United States v. Darby*, 312 U.S. 100, sustaining the federal power to regulate production of goods for commerce except for the fact that this Act extends federal regulation to production not intended in any part for commerce but wholly for consumption on the farm. *** [M]arketing quotas not only embrace all that may be sold without penalty but also what may be consumed on the premises. Wheat produced on excess acreage is designated as "available for marketing" as so defined and the penalty is imposed thereon. Penalties do not depend upon whether any part of the wheat either within or without the quota is sold or intended to be sold. The sum of this is that the Federal Government fixes a quota including all that the farmer may harvest for sale or for his own farm needs, and declares that wheat produced on excess acreage may neither be disposed of nor used except upon payment of the penalty or except it is stored as required by the Act or delivered to the Secretary of Agriculture.

F argues that commerce clause does not apply because wheat was to be consumed on his farm only

Ct. says quota was meant to cover both.

Appellee says that this is a regulation of production and consumption of wheat. Such activities are, he urges, beyond the reach of Congressional power under the Commerce Clause, since they are local in character, and their effects upon interstate commerce are at most "indirect." *** [Q]uestions of the power of Congress are not to be decided by reference to any formula which would give controlling force to nomenclature such as "production" and "indirect" and foreclose consideration of the actual effects of the activity in question upon interstate commerce. At the beginning CHIEF JUSTICE MARSHALL described the Federal commerce power with a breadth never yet exceeded. *Gibbons v. Ogden.* He made emphatic the embracing and penetrating nature of this power by warning that effective restraints on its exercise must proceed from political rather than from judicial processes. *** [T]he effects of many kinds of intrastate activity upon interstate commerce were such as to make them a proper subject of federal regulation. In some cases sustaining the exercise of federal power over intrastate matters the term "direct" was used for the purpose of stating, rather than of reaching, a result; in others it was treated as synonymous with "substantial" or "material;" and in others it was not used at all. Of late its use has been abandoned in cases dealing with questions of federal power under the Commerce Clause. ***

F args that wheat was only meant to stay in the state and any effect on the market would be indirect.

The Court's recognition of the relevance of the economic effects in the application of the Commerce Clause *** has made the mechanical application of legal formulas no longer feasible. Once an economic measure of the reach of the power granted to Congress in the Commerce Clause is accepted, questions of federal power cannot be decided simply by finding the activity in question to be "production" nor can consideration of its economic effects be foreclosed by calling them "indirect." *** Whether the subject of the regulation in question was "production," "consumption," or "marketing" is, therefore, not material for purposes of deciding the question of federal power before us. That an activity is of local character may help in a doubtful case to determine whether Congress intended to reach it. The same consideration might help in determining whether in the absence of Congressional action it would be permissible for the state to exert its power on the subject matter, even though in so doing it to some degree affected interstate commerce. But even if appellee's activity be local and though it may not be regarded as commerce, it may still, whatever its nature, be reached by Congress if it exerts a substantial economic effect on interstate commerce and this irrespective of whether such effect is what might at some earlier time have been defined as "direct" or "indirect."

[margin note: Doesn't matter what the activity is, if it can affect interstate commerce than it is in the reach of Congress]

The parties have stipulated a summary of the economics of the wheat industry. Commerce among the states in wheat is large and important. Although wheat is raised in every state but one, production in most states is not equal to consumption. *** The wheat industry has been a problem industry for some years. Largely as a result of increased foreign production and import restrictions, annual exports of wheat and flour from the United States during the ten-year period ending in 1940 averaged less than 10 per cent of total production, while during the 1920's they averaged more than 25 per cent. The decline in the export trade has left a large surplus in production which in connection with an abnormally large supply of wheat and other grains in recent years caused congestion in a number of markets; tied up railroad cars; and caused elevators in some instances to turn away grains, and railroads to institute embargoes to prevent further congestion. *** In the absence of regulation the price of wheat in the United States would be much affected by world conditions. During 1941 producers who cooperated with the Agricultural Adjustment program received an average price on the farm of about $1.16 a bushel as compared with the world market price of 40 cents a bushel.

[margin note: general problem with the wheat industry (background)]

*** The effect of consumption of homegrown wheat on interstate commerce is due to the fact that it constitutes the most variable factor in the disappearance of the wheat crop. Consumption on the farm where grown appears to vary in an amount greater than 20 per cent of average production. The total amount of wheat consumed as food varies but relatively little, and use as seed is relatively constant.

The maintenance by government regulation of a price for wheat undoubtedly can be accomplished as effectively by sustaining or increasing the demand as by limiting the supply. The effect of the statute before us is to restrict the amount which may be produced for market and the extent as well to which one may forestall resort to the market by producing to meet his own needs. That appellee's own contribution to the demand for wheat may be trivial by itself is not enough to remove him from the scope of federal regulation where, as here, his contribution, taken together with that of many others similarly situated, is far from trivial.

[margin note: F's actions may not have a big effect, but combined with others like him, the overall effect may be large.]

*** [A] factor of such volume and variability as home-consumed wheat [will] have a substantial influence on price and market conditions. This may arise because being in marketable condition such wheat overhangs the market and if induced by rising prices tends to flow into the market and check price increases. But if we assume that it is never marketed, it supplies a need of the man who grew it which would otherwise be reflected by purchases in the open market. Home-grown wheat in this sense competes with wheat in commerce. The stimulation of commerce is a use of the regulatory function quite as definitely as prohibitions or restrictions thereon. This record leaves us in no doubt that Congress may properly have considered that wheat consumed on the farm where grown if wholly outside the scheme of regulation would have a substantial effect in defeating and obstructing its purpose to stimulate trade therein at increased prices.

It is said, however, that this Act, forcing some farmers into the market to buy what they could provide for themselves, is an unfair promotion of the markets and prices of specializing wheat growers. It is of the essence of regulation that it lays a restraining hand on the self-interest of the regulated and that advantages from the regulation commonly fall to others. ***

Notes

1. **History.** *Wickard* was decided more than a hundred years after *Gibbons*. Between the two decisions, the Civil War led to a redefinition of the power of the states relative to the federal government; the Great Depression led to an expanded appreciation of economic interdependence; and technological progress greatly expanded both the modes and matters of commerce. Is the Court still looking at the same Commerce Clause in the more recent case?

2. **Limits?** In *NLRB v. Jones & Laughlin Steel Corp.*, 301 U.S. 1 (1937), the Court considered whether the National Labor Relations Act exceeded the commerce power. The Court found that the NLRA was an attempt to "reach only what might be deemed to burden or obstruct [interstate] commerce." The Court stated that, whether the statute exceeded Congress' power should be looked at with respect to particular applications; the Court then proceeded to document the huge steel company's many involvements with interstate commerce and found that the statute could properly be applied to the company under the authority of the Commerce Clause. The outcome of *Wickard* would surely have been different if this approach had been used. Does the Court's approach in *Wickard* signal that the Court has abandoned all efforts to distinguish interstate from local commerce?

3. **Statutory Construction.** What do you think JUSTICE JACKSON meant when he said: "That an activity is of local character may help in a doubtful case to determine whether Congress intended to reach it"? What is a "doubtful case"? In *United States v. Bass,* 404 U.S. 336 (1971), the Court upheld a statute which said that any person convicted of a felony who "receives, possesses or transports in commerce or affecting commerce [any] firearm" shall be fined or imprisoned by interpreting it to have an implied interstate component.

HEART OF ATLANTA MOTEL v. UNITED STATES
379 U.S. 241 (1964).

MR. JUSTICE CLARK delivered the opinion of the Court

This is a declaratory judgment action attacking the constitutionality of Title II of the Civil Rights Act of 1964. *** Appellant owns and operates the Heart of Atlanta Motel which has 216 rooms available to transient guests [and] is readily accessible to interstate highways 75 and 85 and state highways 23 and 41. Appellant solicits patronage from outside the State of Georgia through various national advertising media, including magazines of national circulation; it maintains over 50 billboards and highway signs within the State, soliciting patronage for the motel; it accepts convention trade from outside Georgia and approximately 75% of its registered guests are from out of State. Prior to passage of the Act the motel had followed a practice of refusing to rent rooms to Negroes, and it alleged that it intended to continue to do so. In an effort to perpetuate that policy this suit was filed.

P wanted to continue to refuse lodging to African Americans

*** [O]n June 19, 1963, the late President Kennedy called for civil rights legislation *** "to enforce the provisions of the fourteenth and fifteenth amendments, to regulate commerce among the several States, and to make laws necessary and proper to execute the powers conferred upon it by the Constitution." *** The Act as finally adopted was most comprehensive, undertaking to prevent through peaceful and voluntary settlement discrimination in voting, as well as in places of accommodation and public facilities, federally secured programs and in employment. Since Title II is the only portion under attack here, we confine our consideration to those public accommodation provisions.

CRA deals directly with places of accommodation (title II)

This Title is divided into seven sections beginning with § 201(a) which provides that: "All persons shall be entitled to the full and equal enjoyment of the goods, services, facilities, privileges, advantages, and accommodations of any place of public accommodation, as defined in this section, without discrimination or segregation on the ground of race, color, religion, or national origin." There are listed in § 201(b) four classes of business establishments, each of which "serves the public" and "is a place of public accommodation" within the meaning of § 201(a) "if its operations affect commerce, or if discrimination or segregation by it is supported by State action." The covered establishments are: "(1) any inn, hotel, motel, or other establishment which provides lodging to transient guests, other than an establishment located within a building which contains not more than five rooms for rent or hire and which is actually occupied by the proprietor of such establishment as his residence *** [and others not at issue]." Section 201(c) defines the phrase "affect commerce" as applied to the above establishments. It first declares that "any inn, hotel, motel, or other establishment which provides lodging to transient guests" affects commerce per se.

looking at the text of the CRA to show that P applies

IV–1. Heart of Atlanta. Atlanta Braves Program.

*** It is admitted that the operation of the motel brings it within the provisions of § 201(a) of the Act and that appellant refused to provide lodging for transient Negroes because of their race or color and that it intends to continue that policy unless restrained.

The sole question posed is, therefore, the constitutionality of the Civil Rights Act of 1964 as applied to these facts. The legislative history of the Act indicates that Congress based the Act on § 5 and the Equal Protection Clause of the Fourteenth Amendment as well as its power to regulate interstate commerce ***

how Congress justified the CRA when pushing for it to be passed

In light of our ground for decision, it might be well at the outset to discuss the *Civil Rights Cases*, which declared provisions of the Civil Rights Act of 1875 unconstitutional. We think that decision inapposite, and without precedential value in determining the constitutionality of the present Act. Unlike Title II of the present legislation, the 1875 Act broadly proscribed discrimination in "inns, public conveyances on land or water, theaters, and other places of public amusement," without limiting the categories of affected businesses to those impinging upon interstate commerce. In contrast, the applicability of Title II is carefully limited to enterprises having a direct and substantial relation to the interstate flow of goods and people, except where state action is involved. Further, the fact that certain kinds of businesses may not in 1875 have been sufficiently involved in interstate commerce to warrant bringing them within the ambit of the commerce power is not necessarily dispositive of the same question today. Our populace had not reached its present mobility, nor were facilities, goods and services circulating as readily in interstate commerce as they are today. Although the principles which we apply today are those first formulated by CHIEF JUSTICE MARSHALL in *Gibbons v. Ogden*, 9 Wheat. 1 (1824), the conditions of transportation and commerce have changed dramatically, and we must apply those principles to the present state of commerce. *** We, therefore, conclude that the *Civil Rights Cases* have no relevance to the basis of decision here where the Act explicitly relies upon the commerce power, and where the record is filled with testimony of obstructions and restraints resulting from the discriminations found to be existing. We now pass to that phase of the case.

Commerce has changed a lot since 1875 and legis. history shows that the CRA was intended to protect discrim. in commerce

While the Act as adopted carried no congressional findings the record of its passage through each house is replete with evidence of the burdens that discrimination by race or color places upon interstate commerce. *** These exclusionary practices were found to be nationwide *** This testimony indicated a qualitative as well as quantitative effect on interstate travel by Negroes. The former was the obvious impairment of the Negro traveler's pleasure and convenience that resulted when he continually was uncertain of finding lodging. As for the latter, there was evidence that this uncertainty stemming from racial discrimination had the effect of discouraging travel on the part of a substantial portion of the Negro community. *** We shall not burden this opinion with further details since the voluminous testimony presents overwhelming evidence that discrimination by hotels and motels impedes interstate travel.

The power of Congress to deal with these obstructions depends on the meaning of the Commerce Clause. *** In short, the determinative test of the exercise of power by the Congress under the Commerce Clause is simply whether the activity sought to be regulated is "Commerce which concerns more States than one" and has a real and substantial relation to the national interest. *** The same interest in protecting interstate commerce which led Congress to deal with segregation in interstate carriers and the white-slave traffic has prompted it to extend the exercise of its power to gambling, *Lottery Case (Champion v. Ames)*, 188 U.S. 321 (1903); to criminal enterprises, *Brooks v. United States*, 267 U.S. 432 (1925); to deceptive practices in the sale of products, *Federal Trade Comm. v. Mandel Bros., Inc.*, 359 U.S. 385 (1959); to fraudulent security transactions, *Securities & Exchange Comm. v. Ralston Purina Co.*, 346 U.S. 119 (1953); to misbranding of drugs, *Weeks v. United States*, 245 U.S. 618 (1918); to wages and hours, *United States v. Darby*, 312 U.S. 100 (1941); to members of labor unions, *National Labor Relations Board v. Jones & Laughlin Steel Corp.*, 301 U.S. 1, (1937); to crop control, *Wickard v. Filburn*; to discrimination against shippers, *United States v. Baltimore & Ohio R. Co.*, 333 U.S. 169 (1948); to the protection of small business from injurious price cutting, *Moore v. Mead's Fine Bread Co.*, 348 U.S. 115 (1954); to resale price maintenance, *Hudson Distributors, Inc. v. Eli Lilly & Co.*, 377

basis for exercising the commerce clause

history of using commerce clause to address moral wrongs (examples)

U.S. 386 (1964); to professional football, *Radovich v. National Football League*, 352 U.S. 445 (1957); and to racial discrimination by owners and managers of terminal restaurants, *Boynton v. Com. of Virginia*, 364 U.S. 454 (1960).

Like the ex.'s above, title II was created to address a moral wrong

That Congress was legislating against moral wrongs in many of these areas rendered its enactments no less valid. In framing Title II of this Act Congress was also dealing with what it considered a moral problem. But that fact does not detract from the overwhelming evidence of the disruptive effect that racial discrimination has had on commercial intercourse. It was this burden which empowered Congress to enact appropriate legislation, and, given this basis for the exercise of its power, Congress was not restricted by the fact that the particular obstruction to interstate commerce with which it was dealing was also deemed a moral and social wrong.

It is said that the operation of the motel here is of a purely local character. *** [T]he power of Congress to promote interstate commerce also includes the power to regulate the local incidents thereof, including local activities in both the States of origin and destination, which might have a substantial and harmful effect upon that commerce. ***

Nor does the Act deprive appellant of liberty or property under the Fifth Amendment. The commerce power invoked here by the Congress is a specific and plenary one authorized by the Constitution itself. The only questions are: (1) whether Congress had a rational basis for finding that racial discrimination by motels affected commerce, and (2) if it had such a basis, whether the means it selected to eliminate that evil are reasonable and appropriate. If they are, appellant has no "right" to select its guests as it sees fit, free from governmental regulation. *** It is doubtful if in the long run appellant will suffer economic loss as a result of the Act. *** But whether this be true or not is of no consequence since this Court has specifically held that the fact that a "member of the class which is regulated may suffer economic losses not shared by others *** has never been a barrier" to such legislation. *** We, therefore, conclude that the action of the Congress in the adoption of the Act as applied here to a motel which concededly serves interstate travelers is within the power granted it by the Commerce Clause of the Constitution, as interpreted by this Court for 140 years. *** How obstructions in commerce may be removed—what means are to be employed—is within the sound and exclusive discretion of the Congress. It is subject only to one caveat—that the means chosen by it must be reasonably adapted to the end permitted by the Constitution. We cannot say that its choice here was not so adapted. The Constitution requires no more.

Notes

1. **Commerce in People?** Is the interstate movement of people commerce? Heart of Atlanta's counsel argued that the Fourteenth Amendment did not prohibit "racial discrimination by an individual," that "the framers *** intended to cover commerce as commerce is known in business fields," that the Court had previously held that "People engage in commerce ***. But people themselves are not commerce." Does the Court answer these arguments?

2.   **Commerce or Other Power?**   Congress premised the Civil Rights Act of 1964 on the Commerce Clause.   Was the proximity of the motel to I–75/85 a necessary component of the Court's decision?   If you had been a member of Congress in 1964, would *Wickard* reassure you that the Civil Rights Act was within the scope of your constitutional authority?   What do you think of the argument that the activity affecting commerce is discrimination?   Would § 5 of the Fourteenth Amendment be a better (or additional) basis for the Civil Rights Act of 1964?   Could the Court turn to § 5 if it found the Commerce Clause insufficient, even though Congress did not rest its legislation on the Fourteenth Amendment?

3.   *Wickard + Heart of Atlanta.*   In *Katzenbach v. McClung*, 379 U.S. 294 (1964), a companion case to *Heart of Atlanta*, the Court considered the constitutionality of applying the same statute to Ollie's Barbecue, a family restaurant in Birmingham, Alabama.   Ollie's seated 220 (whites only), was located 11-miles from an interstate highway, and its customers were almost exclusively local.   The court upheld application of Title II of the Civil Rights Act, noting that the restaurant had purchased about $150,000 worth of food, 46% from a local supplier who had in turn received it from out of state.   The Court said that "viewed in isolation, the volume of food purchased by Ollie's Barbecue from sources supplied from out of state was insignificant when compared with the total foodstuffs moving in commerce."   Nonetheless, citing *Wickard* and extensive Congressional findings on depressed per capita spending by African Americans, the Court upheld Congress' "conclusive presumption that restaurants meeting the criteria set out in the Act 'affect commerce.'"

3. MODERN LIMITS TO THE COMMERCE CLAUSE POWER

UNITED STATES v. LOPEZ
514 U.S. 549 (1995)

CHIEF JUSTICE REHNQUIST delivered the opinion of the Court.

In the Gun–Free School Zones Act of 1990, Congress made it a federal offense "for any individual knowingly to possess a firearm at a place that the individual knows, or has reasonable cause to believe, is a school zone." 18 U.S.C. § 922(q)(1)(A). The Act neither regulates a commercial activity nor contains a requirement that the possession be connected in any way to interstate commerce. We hold that the Act exceeds the authority of Congress "[t]o regulate Commerce *** among the several States. *** "

On March 10, 1992, respondent, who was then a 12th-grade student, arrived at Edison High School in San Antonio, Texas, carrying a concealed .38 caliber handgun and five bullets. Acting upon an anonymous tip, school authorities confronted respondent, who admitted that he was carrying the weapon. He was arrested and charged under Texas law with firearm possession on school premises. The next day, the state charges were dismissed after federal agents charged respondent by complaint with violating the Gun–Free School Zones Act of 1990.[8] ***

We start with first principles. The Constitution creates a Federal Government of enumerated powers. *** For nearly a century thereafter, the Court's Commerce Clause decisions dealt but rarely with the extent of Congress' power, and almost entirely with the Commerce Clause as a limit on state legislation that discriminated against interstate commerce. *** In 1887, Congress enacted the Interstate Commerce Act and in 1890, Congress enacted the Sherman Antitrust Act. These laws ushered in a new era of federal regulation under the commerce power. When cases involving these laws first reached this Court, we imported from our negative Commerce Clause cases the approach that Congress could not regulate activities such as "production," "manufacturing," and "mining." Simultaneously, however, the Court held that, where the interstate and intrastate aspects of commerce were so mingled together that full regulation of interstate commerce required incidental regulation of intrastate commerce, the Commerce Clause authorized such regulation.

In *A.L.A. Schechter Poultry Corp. v. United States*, 295 U.S. 495 (1935), the Court struck down regulations that fixed the hours and wages of individuals employed by an intrastate business because the activity being regulated related to interstate commerce only indirectly. In doing so, the Court characterized the distinction between direct and indirect effects of intrastate transactions upon interstate commerce as "a fundamental one, essential to the maintenance of our constitutional system." Activities that affected interstate commerce directly were within Congress' power; activities that affected interstate commerce indirectly were beyond Congress' reach. The justification for this formal distinction was rooted in the fear that otherwise "there would be virtually no limit to the federal power and for all practical purposes we should have a completely centralized government."

Two years later, in the watershed case of *NLRB v. Jones & Laughlin Steel Corp.*, 301 U.S. 1 (1937), the Court upheld the National Labor Relations Act against a Commerce Clause challenge, and in the process, departed from the distinction between "direct" and "indirect" effects on interstate commerce. *** In *United States v. Darby*, 312 U.S. 100 (1941), the Court upheld the Fair Labor Standards Act, stating: "The power of Congress over interstate commerce is not confined to the regulation of commerce among the states. It extends to those activities intrastate which so affect interstate commerce or the exercise of the power of Congress over it as to make regulation of them appropriate means to the attainment of a legitimate end, the exercise of the granted power of Congress to regulate interstate commerce."

Jones & Laughlin Steel, *Darby*, and *Wickard* ushered in an era of Commerce Clause jurisprudence that greatly expanded the previously defined authority of Congress under that Clause. In part, this was a

---

[8] The term "school zone" is defined as "in, or on the grounds of, a public, parochial or private school" or "within a distance of 1,000 feet from the grounds of a public, parochial or private school." § 921(a)(25).

recognition of the great changes that had occurred in the way business was *wider view* carried on in this country. Enterprises that had once been local or at most *b/c US industry* regional in nature had become national in scope. But the doctrinal change *was becoming* also reflected a view that earlier Commerce Clause cases artificially had *more intertwined* constrained the authority of Congress to regulate interstate commerce.

But even these modern-era precedents which have expanded congressional power under the Commerce Clause confirm that this power is *but, the Ct. has* subject to outer limits. In *Jones & Laughlin Steel*, the Court warned that the *in fact set* scope of the interstate commerce power "must be considered in the light of *limits to CC* our dual system of government and may not be extended so as to embrace effects upon interstate commerce so indirect and remote that to embrace them, in view of our complex society, would effectually obliterate the distinction between what is national and what is local and create a completely centralized government." *** Consistent with this structure, we have identified three broad categories of activity that Congress may regulate under its commerce power. First, Congress may regulate the use of the *3 categories* channels of interstate commerce. See, e.g., *Darby, Heart of Atlanta Motel*. *of activity* Second, Congress is empowered to regulate and protect the instrumentalities *that can be* of interstate commerce, or persons or things in interstate commerce, even *regulated* though the threat may come only from intrastate activities. *** Finally, *under the CC* Congress' commerce authority includes the power to regulate those activities having a substantial relation to interstate commerce, i.e., those activities that substantially affect interstate commerce.

Within this final category, admittedly, our case law has not been clear *Needs to be* whether an activity must "affect" or "substantially affect" interstate *substantial* commerce in order to be within Congress' power to regulate it under the Commerce Clause. We conclude, consistent with the great weight of our case *3rd category* law, that the proper test requires an analysis of whether the regulated activity "substantially affects" interstate commerce.

We now turn to consider the power of Congress, in the light of this framework, to enact § 922(q). *** § 922(q) is not a regulation of the use of the *first two* channels of interstate commerce, nor is it an attempt to prohibit the *categories* interstate transportation of a commodity through the channels of commerce; *have no mention* nor can § 922(q) be justified as a regulation by which Congress has sought to *in the act.* protect an instrumentality of interstate commerce or a thing in interstate commerce. Thus, if § 922(q) is to be sustained, it must be under the third *3rd applies* category as a regulation of an activity that substantially affects interstate commerce. ***

Section 922(q) is a criminal statute that by its terms has nothing to do with "commerce" or any sort of economic enterprise, however broadly one might define those terms. Section 922(q) is not an essential part of a larger *Fails to meet* regulation of economic activity, in which the regulatory scheme could be *3rd category b/c* undercut unless the intrastate activity were regulated. It cannot, therefore, *it has no* be sustained under our cases upholding regulations of activities that arise out *connection to* of or are connected with a commercial transaction, which viewed in the *any commerce* aggregate, substantially affects interstate commerce. ***

Second, § 922(q) contains no jurisdictional element which would ensure, through case-by-case inquiry, that the firearm possession in question affects interstate commerce. For example, in *United States v. Bass*, 404 U.S. 336 (1971), the Court interpreted [a statute] which made it a crime for a felon to "receiv[e], posses[s], or transpor[t] in commerce or affecting commerce *** any firearm." The Court interpreted the possession component of [this statute] to require an additional nexus to interstate commerce both because the statute was ambiguous and because "unless Congress conveys its purpose clearly, it will not be deemed to have significantly changed the federal-state balance." The *Bass* Court set aside the conviction because although the Government had demonstrated that Bass had possessed a firearm, it had failed "to show the requisite nexus with interstate commerce." ***

Although as part of our independent evaluation of constitutionality under the Commerce Clause we of course consider legislative findings, and indeed even congressional committee findings, regarding effect on interstate commerce, the Government concedes that "[n]either the statute nor its legislative history contain[s] express congressional findings regarding the effects upon interstate commerce of gun possession in a school zone." We agree with the Government that Congress normally is not required to make formal findings as to the substantial burdens that an activity has on interstate commerce. But to the extent that congressional findings would enable us to evaluate the legislative judgment that the activity in question substantially affected interstate commerce, even though no such substantial effect was visible to the naked eye, they are lacking here. ***

The Government's essential contention, *in fine*, is that we may determine here that § 922(q) is valid because possession of a firearm in a local school zone does indeed substantially affect interstate commerce. The Government argues that possession of a firearm in a school zone may result in violent crime and that violent crime can be expected to affect the functioning of the national economy in two ways. First, the costs of violent crime are substantial, and, through the mechanism of insurance, those costs are spread throughout the population. Second, violent crime reduces the willingness of individuals to travel to areas within the country that are perceived to be unsafe. The Government also argues that the presence of guns in schools poses a substantial threat to the educational process by threatening the learning environment. A handicapped educational process, in turn, will result in a less productive citizenry. That, in turn, would have an adverse effect on the Nation's economic well-being. As a result, the Government argues that Congress could rationally have concluded that § 922(q) substantially affects interstate commerce.

We pause to consider the implications of the Government's arguments. The Government admits, under its "costs of crime" reasoning, that Congress could regulate not only all violent crime, but all activities that might lead to violent crime, regardless of how tenuously they relate to interstate commerce. Similarly, under the Government's "national productivity" reasoning, Congress could regulate any activity that it found was related to the economic productivity of individual citizens: family law (including marriage, divorce, and child custody), for example. *** [I]f we were to accept the Government's arguments, we are hard-pressed to posit any activity by an individual that Congress is without power to regulate. ***

Admittedly, a determination whether an intrastate activity is commercial or noncommercial may in some cases result in legal uncertainty. *** The Constitution mandates this uncertainty by withholding from Congress a plenary police power that would authorize enactment of every type of legislation. *** [However,] the question of congressional power under the Commerce Clause "is necessarily one of degree."

[margin note: Congress has the power to fix gaps in its own legis. outside of arguing CC]

These are not precise formulations, and in the nature of things they cannot be. But we think they point the way to a correct decision of this case. The possession of a gun in a local school zone is in no sense an economic activity that might, through repetition elsewhere, substantially affect any sort of interstate commerce. Respondent was a local student at a local school; there is no indication that he had recently moved in interstate commerce, and there is no requirement that his possession of the firearm have any concrete tie to interstate commerce.

To uphold the Government's contentions here, we would have to pile inference upon inference in a manner that would bid fair to convert congressional authority under the Commerce Clause to a general police power of the sort retained by the States. Admittedly, some of our prior cases have taken long steps down that road, giving great deference to congressional action. The broad language in these opinions has suggested the possibility of additional expansion, but we decline here to proceed any further. ***

[margin note: Ct. chose not to broaden congressional power]

JUSTICE KENNEDY, with whom JUSTICE O'CONNOR joins, concurring.

*** The theory that two governments accord more liberty than one requires for its realization two distinct and discernable lines of political accountability: one between the citizens and the Federal Government; the second between the citizens and the States. If, as Madison expected, the Federal and State Governments are to control each other, see The Federalist No. 51, and hold each other in check by competing for the affections of the people, see The Federalist No. 46, those citizens must have some means of knowing which of the two governments to hold accountable for the failure to perform a particular function. "Federalism serves to assign political responsibility, not to obscure it." Were the Federal Government to take over the regulation of entire areas of traditional state concern, areas having nothing to do with the regulation of commercial activities, the boundaries between the spheres of federal and state authority would blur and political responsibility would become illusory. The resultant inability to hold either branch of the government answerable to the citizens is more dangerous even than devolving too much authority to the remote central power. ***

[margin note: P arg is at odds with the founders vision of two govs.]

The statute before us upsets the federal balance to a degree that renders it an unconstitutional assertion of the commerce power, and our intervention is required. *** [U]nlike the earlier cases to come before the Court here neither the actors nor their conduct have a commercial character, and neither the purposes nor the design of the statute have an evident commercial nexus.

[margin note: gives too much power to fed gov.]

The statute makes the simple possession of a gun within 1,000 feet of the grounds of the school a criminal offense. *** The tendency of this statute to displace state regulation in areas of traditional state concern is evident from its territorial operation. There are over 100,000 elementary and secondary schools in the United States. Each of these now has an invisible federal zone extending 1,000 feet beyond the (often irregular) boundaries of the school property. *** [T]hroughout these areas, school officials would find their own programs for the prohibition of guns in danger of displacement by the federal authority unless the State chooses to enact a parallel rule. ***

JUSTICE THOMAS, concurring.

*** I write separately to observe that our case law has drifted far from the original understanding of the Commerce Clause. *** We have said that Congress may regulate not only "Commerce *** among the several states," but also anything that has a "substantial effect" on such commerce. This test, if taken to its logical extreme, would give Congress a "police power" over all aspects of American life. *** At an appropriate juncture, I think we must modify our Commerce Clause jurisprudence. Today, it is easy enough to say that the Clause certainly does not empower Congress to ban gun possession within 1,000 feet of a school.

JUSTICE STEVENS, dissenting.

*** Guns are both articles of commerce and articles that can be used to restrain commerce. Their possession is the consequence, either directly or indirectly, of commercial activity. In my judgment, Congress' power to regulate commerce in firearms includes the power to prohibit possession of guns at any location because of their potentially harmful use; it necessarily follows that Congress may also prohibit their possession in particular markets. ***

JUSTICE SOUTER, dissenting.

*** The question for the courts, as all agree, is not whether as a predicate to legislation Congress in fact found that a particular activity substantially affects interstate commerce. The legislation implies such a finding, and there is no reason to entertain claims that Congress acted ultra vires intentionally. Nor is the question whether Congress was correct in so finding. The only question is whether the legislative judgment is within the realm of reason. *** But review for congressional wisdom would just be the old judicial pretension discredited and abandoned in 1937, and review for deliberateness would be as patently unconstitutional as an Act of Congress mandating long opinions from this Court. Such a legislative process requirement would function merely as an excuse for covert review of the merits of legislation under standards never expressed and more or less arbitrarily applied. *** [T]he rationality standard of review would be a thing of the past. ***

JUSTICE BREYER, with whom JUSTICE STEVENS, JUSTICE SOUTER, and JUSTICE GINSBURG join, dissenting.

*** I apply three basic principles of Commerce Clause interpretation. First, the power to "regulate Commerce *** among the several States," encompasses the power to regulate local activities insofar as they significantly affect interstate commerce. I use the word "significant" because the word "substantial" implies a somewhat narrower power than recent precedent suggests. But, to speak of "substantial effect" rather than "significant effect" would make no difference in this case.

① Substantial

Second, in determining whether a local activity will likely have a significant effect upon interstate commerce, a court must consider, not the effect of an individual act (a single instance of gun possession), but rather the cumulative effect of all similar instances (i.e., the effect of all guns possessed in or near schools). See, e.g., *Wickard*.

② Aggregate

Third, the Constitution requires us to judge the connection between a regulated activity and interstate commerce, not directly, but at one remove. Courts must give Congress a degree of leeway in determining the existence of a significant factual connection between the regulated activity and interstate commerce—both because the Constitution delegates the commerce power directly to Congress and because the determination requires an empirical judgment of a kind that a legislature is more likely than a court to make with accuracy. The traditional words "rational basis" capture this leeway. ***

③ Rational Basis

Congress could also have found, given the effect of education upon interstate and foreign commerce, that gun-related violence in and around schools is a commercial, as well as a human, problem. [Further,] Congress could have found that gun-related violence near the classroom poses a serious economic threat (1) to consequently inadequately educated workers who must endure low paying jobs, and (2) to communities and businesses that might (in today's "information society") otherwise gain, from a well-educated work force, an important commercial advantage of a kind that location near a railhead or harbor provided in the past. ***

Guns at school do affect commerce

To hold this statute constitutional is not to "obliterate" the "distinction of what is national and what is local," nor is it to hold that the Commerce Clause permits the Federal Government to "regulate any activity that it found was related to the economic productivity of individual citizens," to regulate "marriage, divorce, and child custody," or to regulate any and all aspects of education. For one thing, this statute is aimed at curbing a particularly acute threat to the educational process—the possession (and use) of life-threatening firearms in, or near, the classroom. The empirical evidence *** unmistakably documents the special way in which guns and education are incompatible. ***

Ct. would not go too far because the act is about a particular issue.

The majority's holding *** creates three serious legal problems. First, the majority's holding runs contrary to modern Supreme Court cases that have upheld congressional actions despite connections to interstate or foreign commerce that are less significant than the effect of school violence. *** The second legal problem the Court creates comes from its apparent belief that it can reconcile its holding with earlier cases by making a critical distinction between "commercial" and noncommercial "transaction[s]." That is to say, the Court believes the Constitution would distinguish between two local activities, each of which has an identical effect upon interstate commerce, if

3 problems created:
① contrary to precedent overall
② contrary to precedent b/c it distinguished commercial from non-comm.
③ creates legal uncertainty.

one, but not the other, is "commercial" in nature. *** The third legal problem created by the Court's holding is that it threatens legal uncertainty in an area of law that, until this case, seemed reasonably well settled. *** In sum, to find this legislation within the scope of the Commerce Clause would *** interpret the Clause as this Court has traditionally interpreted it *** [and] simply recognize that Congress had a "rational basis" for finding a significant connection between guns in or near schools and (through their effect on education) the interstate and foreign commerce they threaten. ***

Notes

1.   **Significance.** Commentators are divided as to whether *Lopez* represents a "constitutional moment" like the Civil War or the New Deal in the relationship between the federal government and the states. Do you think the Court has overruled *Wickard* and/or *Heart of Atlanta*?

2.   **Ambiguities in *Lopez*.**

• Is the lack of congressional findings critical? If Congress had made more extensive interstate commerce findings, could the Court look behind them?

• How important is it that criminal law and education are "traditional areas" for exercise of state powers? How should courts decide what areas are traditionally state matters and which are not?

• Is it relevant that the statute involved regulated guns?

• How important is it that the statute at issue blurred "discernible lines of political accountability"?

• Is it important that the activity involved was noncommercial? How should the courts distinguish that which is commercial from that which is noncommercial?

3.   **Policy.** Has the Court forgotten its historically developed understanding that it is not a particularly effective institution for considering whether or not commerce has been substantially affected? Is it fearful of leaving Congress' power unchecked?

UNITED STATES v. MORRISON
529 U.S. 598 (2000)

CHIEF JUSTICE REHNQUIST delivered the opinion of the Court.

In these cases we consider the constitutionality of 42 U.S.C. § 13981, which provides a federal civil remedy for the victims of gender-motivated violence. *** Petitioner Christy Brzonkala enrolled at Virginia Polytechnic Institute (Virginia Tech) in the fall of 1994. In September of that year, Brzonkala met respondents Antonio Morrison and James Crawford, who were both students at Virginia Tech and members of its varsity football team. Brzonkala alleges that, within 30 minutes of meeting Morrison and Crawford, they assaulted and repeatedly raped her. *** Brzonkala alleges that this attack caused her to become severely emotionally disturbed and depressed. She sought assistance from a university psychiatrist, who prescribed antidepressant medication. Shortly after the rape Brzonkala stopped attending classes and withdrew from the university. *** In December 1995, Brzonkala sued Morrison, Crawford, and Virginia Tech [alleging] that Morrison's and Crawford's attack violated § 13981 ***. Morrison and Crawford moved to dismiss this complaint on the grounds that *** § 13981's civil remedy is unconstitutional. ***

Section 13981 was part of the Violence Against Women Act of 1994. It states that "[a]ll persons within the United States shall have the right to be free from crimes of violence motivated by gender." To enforce that right, *[civil rights provision]* subsection (c) declares [that "a person *** who commits a crime of violence motivated by gender *** shall be liable to the party injured"]. Section 13981 defines a "crim[e] of violence motivated by gender" as "a crime of violence committed because of gender or on the basis of gender, and due, at least in part, to an animus based on the victim's gender." ***

Congress explicitly identified the sources of federal authority on which it relied in enacting § 13981. It said that a "federal civil rights cause of action" *[power Congress cited to when enacting the legislation]* is established "[p]ursuant to the affirmative power of Congress *** under section 5 of the Fourteenth Amendment to the Constitution, as well as under section 8 of Article I of the Constitution." We address Congress' authority to enact this remedy under each of these constitutional provisions in turn.

Due respect for the decisions of a coordinate branch of Government demands that we invalidate a congressional enactment only upon a plain showing that Congress has exceeded its constitutional bounds. *See United States v. Lopez.* *** As we discussed at length in *Lopez*, our interpretation of *[Looks to Lopez to set the framework for their analysis]* the Commerce Clause has changed as our Nation has developed. *** *Lopez* emphasized, however, that even under our modern, expansive interpretation of the Commerce Clause, Congress' regulatory authority is not without effective bounds. *** Since *Lopez* most recently canvassed and clarified our case law governing [the power to regulate those activities having a substantial relation to interstate commerce], it provides the proper framework for conducting the required analysis of § 13981. In *Lopez*, *** [s]everal significant considerations contributed to our decision.

First, we observed that [it] was "a criminal statute that by its terms has nothing to do with 'commerce' or any sort of economic enterprise, however broadly one might define those terms." *** The second consideration that we found important *** was that the statute contained "no express jurisdictional element which might limit its reach to a discrete set of firearm possessions that additionally have an explicit connection with or effect on interstate *[Breakdown of Lopez analysis]* commerce." *** Third, we noted that neither [the statute] "nor its legislative history contain[s] express congressional findings regarding the effects upon interstate commerce of gun possession in a school zone." While "Congress normally is not required to make formal findings *** the existence of such *[what to look to:]* findings may "enable us to evaluate the legislative judgment that the activity in question substantially affect[s] interstate commerce, even though no such substantial effect [is] visible to the naked eye." Finally, our decision in *Lopez* rested in part on the fact that the link between gun possession and a substantial effect on interstate commerce was attenuated. ***

*[① plain text relating to commerce
② stated jurisdictional text
③ legislative history
④ connection between issue and commerce]*

④
no connection
to commerce

②
no mention that
this was intended
to be covered

③ CH is mentioned
gender violence,
but it is not
enough

P's arg. - evidence
of relation to
interstate commerce

Same concern as
in Lopez - Congress
would be able to
regulate all crime
under the cc

With these principles underlying our Commerce Clause jurisprudence as reference points, the proper resolution of the present cases is clear. Gender-motivated crimes of violence are not, in any sense of the phrase, economic activity. While we need not adopt a categorical rule against aggregating the effects of any noneconomic activity in order to decide these cases, thus far in our Nation's history our cases have upheld Commerce Clause regulation of intrastate activity only where that activity is economic in nature. *** [Moreover,] § 13981 contains no jurisdictional element establishing that the federal cause of action is in pursuance of Congress' power to regulate interstate commerce. ***

In contrast with the lack of congressional findings that we faced in *Lopez*, § 13981 is supported by numerous findings regarding the serious impact that gender-motivated violence has on victims and their families. But the existence of congressional findings is not sufficient, by itself, to sustain the constitutionality of Commerce Clause legislation. As we stated in *Lopez*, "'[S]imply because Congress may conclude that a particular activity substantially affects interstate commerce does not necessarily make it so.'" Rather, "'[w]hether particular operations affect interstate commerce sufficiently to come under the constitutional power of Congress to regulate them is ultimately a judicial rather than a legislative question, and can be settled finally only by this Court.'"

In these cases, Congress' findings are substantially weakened by the fact that they rely so heavily on a method of reasoning that we have already rejected as unworkable if we are to maintain the Constitution's enumeration of powers. Congress found that gender-motivated violence affects interstate commerce

by deterring potential victims from traveling interstate, from engaging in employment in interstate business, and from transacting with business, and in places involved in interstate commerce; *** by diminishing national productivity, increasing medical and other costs, and decreasing the supply of and the demand for interstate products.

Given these findings and petitioners' arguments, the concern that we expressed in *Lopez* that Congress might use the Commerce Clause to completely obliterate the Constitution's distinction between national and local authority seems well founded. The reasoning that petitioners advance seeks to follow the but-for causal chain from the initial occurrence of violent crime (the suppression of which has always been the prime object of the States' police power) to every attenuated effect upon interstate commerce. If accepted, petitioners' reasoning would allow Congress to regulate any crime as long as the nationwide, aggregated impact of that crime has substantial effects on employment, production, transit, or consumption. Indeed, if Congress may regulate gender-motivated violence, it would be able to regulate murder or any other type of violence since gender-motivated violence, as a subset of all violent crime, is certain to have lesser economic impacts than the larger class of which it is a part.

Petitioners' reasoning, moreover, will not limit Congress to regulating violence but may, as we suggested in *Lopez*, be applied equally as well to family law and other areas of traditional state regulation since the aggregate effect of marriage, divorce, and childrearing on the national economy is undoubtedly significant. ***

would go too far – too much of a stretch

We accordingly reject the argument that Congress may regulate noneconomic, violent criminal conduct based solely on that conduct's aggregate effect on interstate commerce. The Constitution requires a distinction between what is truly national and what is truly local. *** If the allegations here are true, no civilized system of justice could fail to provide her a remedy for the conduct of respondent Morrison. But under our federal system that remedy must be provided by the Commonwealth of Virginia, and not by the United States. ***

violent harm has no econ. effect to interstate commerce

take the issue to state court.

JUSTICE THOMAS, concurring.

*** I write separately only to express my view that the very notion of a "substantial effects" test under the Commerce Clause is inconsistent with the original understanding of Congress' powers and with this Court's early Commerce Clause cases. By continuing to apply this rootless and malleable standard, however circumscribed, the Court has encouraged the Federal Government to persist in its view that the Commerce Clause has virtually no limits. Until this Court replaces its existing Commerce Clause jurisprudence with a standard more consistent with the original understanding, we will continue to see Congress appropriating state police powers under the guise of regulating commerce.

agree, but ct. needs to get rid of the substantial affects test.

JUSTICE SOUTER, with whom JUSTICE STEVENS, JUSTICE GINSBURG, and JUSTICE BREYER join, dissenting.

*** One obvious difference from *United States v. Lopez*, 514 U.S. 549 (1995), is the mountain of data assembled by Congress, here showing the effects of violence against women on interstate commerce. *** Congress thereby explicitly stated the predicate for the exercise of its Commerce Clause power. *** The Act would have passed muster at any time between *Wickard* in 1942 and *Lopez* in 1995, a period in which the law enjoyed a stable understanding that congressional power under the Commerce Clause, complemented by the authority of the Necessary and Proper Clause, extended to all activity that, when aggregated, has a substantial effect on interstate commerce. *** The premise that the enumeration of powers implies that other powers are withheld is sound; the conclusion that some particular categories of subject matter are therefore presumptively beyond the reach of the commerce power is, however, a non sequitur. *** My disagreement with the majority is not, however, confined to logic, for history has shown that categorical exclusions have proven as unworkable in practice as they are unsupportable in theory.

there is enough data to easily support a substantial affect

Obviously, it would not be inconsistent with the text of the Commerce Clause itself to declare "noncommercial" primary activity beyond or presumptively beyond the scope of the commerce power. *** If we now ask why the formalistic economic/noneconomic distinction might matter today, after its rejection in *Wickard*, the answer is not that the majority fails to see causal connections in an integrated economic world. *** Just as the old formalism had value in the service of an economic conception, the new one is useful in serving a conception of federalism. *** The defect, in essence, is the majority's rejection of the Founders' considered judgment that politics, not judicial review, should mediate between state and national interests as the strength and legislative jurisdiction of the National Government inevitably increased through the expected growth of the national economy. *** The federalism of some earlier time is no more adequate to account for those facts today than the theory of laissez-faire was able to govern the national economy 70 years ago.

JUSTICE BREYER, with whom JUSTICE STEVENS joins, and with whom JUSTICE SOUTER and JUSTICE GINSBURG join *** dissenting.

*** Consider the problems. The "economic/noneconomic" distinction is not easy to apply. Does the local street corner mugger engage in "economic" activity or "noneconomic" activity when he mugs for money? Would evidence that desire for economic domination underlies many brutal crimes against women save the present statute? *** The Court itself would permit Congress to aggregate, hence regulate, "noneconomic" activity taking place at economic establishments. And it would permit Congress to regulate where that regulation is "an essential part of a larger regulation of economic activity, in which the regulatory scheme could be undercut unless the intrastate activity were regulated." Given the former exception, can Congress simply rewrite the present law and limit its application to restaurants, hotels, perhaps universities, and other places of public accommodation? Given the latter exception, can Congress save the present law by including it, or much of it, in a broader "Safe Transport" or "Workplace Safety" act?

More important, why should we give critical constitutional importance to the economic, or noneconomic, nature of an interstate-commerce-affecting cause? If chemical emanations through indirect environmental change cause identical, severe commercial harm outside a State, why should it matter whether local factories or home fireplaces release them? *** The language [of the Commerce Clause] says nothing about either the local nature, or the economic nature, of an interstate-commerce-affecting cause. ***

Most important, the Court's complex rules seem unlikely to help secure the very object that they seek, namely, the protection of "areas of traditional state regulation" from federal intrusion. The Court's rules, even if broadly interpreted, are underinclusive. The local pickpocket is no less a traditional subject of state regulation than is the local gender-motivated assault. Regardless, the Court reaffirms, as it should, Congress' well-established and frequently exercised power to enact laws that satisfy a commerce-related jurisdictional prerequisite—for example, that some item relevant to the federally regulated activity has at some time crossed a state line. *** Complex Commerce Clause rules creating fine distinctions that achieve only random results do little to further the important federalist interests that called them into being. ***

I would also note that Congress, when it enacted the statute, followed procedures that help to protect the federalism values at stake. It provided *Act at hand was approved by almost all the states* adequate notice to the States of its intent to legislate in an "are[a] of traditional state regulation." And in response, attorneys general in the overwhelming majority of States (38) supported congressional legislation, *** [T]he law before us seems to represent an instance, not of state/federal conflict, but of state/federal efforts to cooperate in order to help solve a mutually acknowledged national problem. ***

Notes

1. **Reviewing *Lopez*.** Which of the rationales in *Lopez* have prevailed?

2. **Judicial Myopia?** "In focusing narrowly on one target of the legislation—for example, on the gun-toting student and the alleged rapist—rather than on the intended beneficiaries, the ills triggering legislative action, or the ripple effects of regulatory intervention, *Lopez* and *Morrison* *** suggest a preference for a vantage point that diminishes the commercial connection." Robert A. Schapiro & William W. Buzbee, *Unidimensional Federalism: Power and Perspective in Commerce Clause Adjudication*, 88 CORNELL L. REV. 1199 (2003). Do you agree that the Court should broaden its perspective? If so, what role would the courts play in assessing whether Congress acted within the Commerce Clause power?

3. **Prescient dissent?** Review Justice Breyer's dissent about how Congress might avoid the reach of *Lopez* and *Morrison*. Then read the next case.

GONZALES v. RAICH
545 U.S. 1 (2005)

JUSTICE STEVENS delivered the opinion of the Court.

California is one of at least nine States that authorize the use of marijuana for medicinal purposes. *** California residents *** brought this action *** seeking injunctive and declaratory relief prohibiting the enforcement of the federal Controlled Substances Act (CSA), to the extent it prevents them from possessing, obtaining, or manufacturing cannabis for their personal medical use. *** Like the farmer in *Wickard*, respondents are cultivating, for home consumption, a fungible commodity for which there is an established, albeit illegal, interstate market. Just as the Agricultural Adjustment Act was designed to control the volume [of wheat] *** and consequently control the market price, a primary purpose of the CSA is to control the supply and demand of controlled substances in both lawful and unlawful drug markets. *** Congress had a rational basis for concluding that leaving home-consumed marijuana outside federal control would similarly affect price and market conditions.

More concretely, one concern prompting inclusion of wheat grown for home consumption in the 1938 Act was that rising market prices could draw such wheat into the interstate market, resulting in lower market prices. The *how the affect is similar to Wickard* parallel concern making it appropriate to include marijuana grown for home consumption in the CSA is the likelihood that the high demand in the interstate market will draw such marijuana into that market. *** In both cases, the regulation is squarely within Congress' commerce power because production of the commodity meant for home consumption, be it wheat or marijuana, has a substantial effect on supply and demand in the national market for that commodity.

Nonetheless, respondents suggest that *Wickard* differs from this case in three respects: (1) the Agricultural Adjustment Act, unlike the CSA, exempted small farming operations; (2) *Wickard* involved a 'quintessential economic activity'-- a commercial farm--whereas respondents do not sell marijuana; and (3) the *Wickard* record made it clear that the aggregate production of wheat for use on farms had a significant impact on market prices. Those differences, though factually accurate, do not diminish the precedential force of this Court's reasoning.

R arg.

The fact that Wickard's own impact on the market was 'trivial by itself ' was not a sufficient reason for removing him from the scope of federal regulation. *** Moreover, even though Wickard was indeed a commercial farmer, the activity he was engaged in--the cultivation of wheat for home consumption--was not treated by the Court as part of his commercial farming operation. And while it is true that the record in the *Wickard* case itself established the causal connection between the production for local use and the national market, we have before us findings by Congress to the same effect. *** Congress did not make a specific finding that the intrastate cultivation and possession of marijuana for medical purposes based on the recommendation of a physician would substantially affect the larger interstate marijuana market [but] *** the absence of particularized findings does not call into question Congress' authority to legislate. *** Congress had a rational basis for believing that failure to regulate the intrastate manufacture and possession of marijuana would leave a gaping hole in the CSA. ***

Congress used the rational basis test when enacting

[R]espondents rely heavily on *** *Lopez* and *Morrison*. *** [T]he CSA, *** was a lengthy and detailed statute creating a comprehensive framework for regulating the production, distribution, and possession of five classes of 'controlled substances.' *** Unlike those at issue in *Lopez* and *Morrison*, the activities regulated by the CSA are quintessentially economic. *** Because the CSA is a statute that directly regulates economic, commercial activity, our opinion in *Morrison* casts no doubt on its constitutionality. *** The congressional judgment that an exemption for such a significant segment of the total market would undermine the orderly enforcement of the entire regulatory scheme is entitled to a strong presumption of validity. *** [L]imiting the activity to marijuana possession and cultivation 'in accordance with state law' cannot serve to place respondents' activities beyond congressional reach. *** Just as state acquiescence to federal regulation cannot expand the bounds of the Commerce Clause, so too state action cannot circumscribe Congress' plenary commerce power.[38] ***

marijuana is an economic commodity unlike the issues in Lopez and Morrison

can't exclude marijuana

Fed gov. commerce power over state power

---

[38] *** JUSTICE THOMAS' *** rationale seemingly would require Congress to cede its constitutional power to regulate commerce whenever a State opts to exercise its 'traditional police powers to define the criminal law and to protect the health, safety, and welfare of their citizens.'.

Indeed, that the California exemptions will have a significant impact on both the supply and demand sides of the market for marijuana is not just 'plausible' as the principal dissent concedes, it is readily apparent. The exemption for physicians provides them with an economic incentive to grant their patients permission to use the drug. *** The exemption for cultivation by patients and caregivers can only increase the supply of marijuana in the California market.[41] The likelihood that all such production will promptly terminate when patients recover or will precisely match the patients' medical needs during their convalescence seems remote; whereas the danger that excesses will satisfy some of the admittedly enormous demand for recreational use seems obvious. Moreover, that the national and international narcotics trade has thrived in the face of vigorous criminal enforcement efforts suggests that no small number of unscrupulous people will make use of the California exemptions to serve their commercial ends whenever it is feasible to do so. *** Congress could have rationally concluded that the aggregate impact on the national market of all the transactions exempted from federal supervision is unquestionably substantial. ***

JUSTICE SCALIA, concurring in the judgment.

*** Congress's regulatory authority over intrastate activities that are not themselves part of interstate commerce (including activities that have a substantial effect on interstate commerce) derives from the Necessary and Proper Clause. *** Where necessary to make a regulation of interstate commerce effective, Congress may regulate even those intrastate activities that do not themselves substantially affect interstate commerce. *** Congress may regulate even noneconomic local activity if that regulation is a necessary part of a more general regulation of interstate commerce. The relevant question is simply whether the means chosen are 'reasonably adapted' to the attainment of a legitimate end under the commerce power. *** At bottom, respondents' state-sovereignty argument reduces to the contention that federal regulation of the activities permitted by California's Compassionate Use Act is not sufficiently necessary to be 'necessary and proper' to Congress's regulation of the interstate market. ***

JUSTICE O'CONNOR, with whom THE CHIEF JUSTICE and JUSTICE THOMAS join *** dissenting.

*** Today the Court *** announces a rule that gives Congress a perverse incentive to legislate broadly pursuant to the Commerce Clause--nestling questionable assertions of its authority into comprehensive regulatory schemes--rather than with precision. *** If the Court is right, then *Lopez*

---

[41] The state policy allows patients to possess up to eight ounces of dried marijuana, and to cultivate up to 6 mature or 12 immature plants. However, the quantity limitations serve only as a floor *** and cities and counties are given *carte blanche* to establish more generous limits. Indeed, several cities and counties have done just that. For example, patients residing in the cities of Oakland and Santa Cruz and in the counties of Sonoma and Tehama are permitted to possess up to 3 pounds of processed marijuana. Putting that quantity in perspective, 3 pounds of marijuana yields roughly 3,000 joints or cigarettes. And the street price for that amount can range anywhere from $900 to $24,000.

stands for nothing more than a drafting guide: Congress should have described the relevant crime as 'transfer or possession of a firearm anywhere in the nation'--thus including commercial and noncommercial activity, and clearly encompassing some activity with assuredly substantial effect on interstate commerce. Had it done so, the majority hints, we would have sustained its authority to regulate possession of firearms in school zones. Furthermore, today's decision suggests we would readily sustain a congressional decision to attach the regulation of intrastate activity to a pre-existing comprehensive (or even not-so-comprehensive) scheme. If so, the Court invites increased federal regulation of local activity even if, as it suggests, Congress would not enact a *new* interstate scheme exclusively for the sake of reaching intrastate activity. ***

In *Lopez* and *Morrison*, we suggested that economic activity usually relates directly to commercial activity. *** Everyone agrees that the marijuana at issue in this case was never in the stream of commerce, and neither were the supplies for growing it. *** *Lopez* makes clear that possession is not itself commercial activity. And respondents have not come into possession by means of any commercial transaction; they have simply grown, in their own homes, marijuana for their own use, without acquiring, buying, selling, or bartering a thing of value.

Even assuming that economic activity is at issue in this case, the Government has made no showing in fact that the possession and use of homegrown marijuana for medical purposes, in California or elsewhere, has a substantial effect on interstate commerce *** [or] is necessary to an interstate regulatory scheme. ***

JUSTICE THOMAS, dissenting.

*** If the Federal Government can regulate growing a half-dozen cannabis plants for personal consumption (not because it is interstate commerce, but because it is inextricably bound up with interstate commerce), then Congress' Article I powers--as expanded by the Necessary and Proper Clause--have no meaningful limits. *** The majority's decision is further proof that the 'substantial effects' test is a 'rootless and malleable standard' at odds with the constitutional design. *** By defining the class at a high level of generality (as the intrastate manufacture and possession of marijuana), the majority overlooks that individuals authorized by state law to manufacture and possess medical marijuana exert no demonstrable effect on the interstate drug market. ***

The substantial effects test is easily manipulated for another reason. This Court has never held that Congress can regulate noneconomic activity that substantially affects interstate commerce. *Morrison*; *Lopez*. *** If the majority is to be taken seriously, the Federal Government may now regulate quilting bees, clothes drives, and potluck suppers throughout the 50 States. *** Congress is authorized to regulate 'Commerce,' and respondents' conduct does not qualify under any definition of that term. The majority's opinion only illustrates the steady drift away from the text of the Commerce Clause. There is an inexorable expansion from ' 'commerce,' ' to 'commercial' and 'economic' activity, and finally to all 'production, distribution, and consumption' of goods or services for which there is an 'established ... interstate market'. Federal power expands, but never contracts, with each new locution. *****

Notes

1.   **States Rights**. Did JUSTICE SCALIA forget which side he was on in the states rights/federal authority fight?

2.   **Pragmatism**. Would a contrary decision have rendered the federal drug laws unenforceable because of easy access to prescription marijuana? Conversely, how can medical marijuana outlets persist today in California after *Raich*?

3.   **Comprehensive Regulation**. Is JUSTICE O'CONNOR correct that Congress from now on need only include unconstitutional provisions in broader regulatory schemes to avoid commerce clause challenges? Is *Raich* the death-knell of *Lopez* and *Morrison*?

NFIB v. SEBELIUS
132 S. Ct. 2566 (2012)

ROBERTS, C. J., announced the judgment of the Court and delivered the opinion of the Court with respect to [the commerce clause issue] *****

Today we resolve constitutional challenges to [a] provision of the Patient Protection and Affordable Care Act of 2010 which requires individuals to purchase a health insurance policy providing a minimum level of coverage. ***** Many individuals will receive the required coverage through their employer, or from a government program such as Medicaid or Medicare. But for individuals who are not exempt and do not receive health insurance through a third party, the means of satisfying the requirement is to purchase insurance from a private company. ***** [T]hose who do not comply with the mandate must make a "[s]hared responsibility payment" to the Federal Government. *****

[handwritten: individual mandate]

[T]he Government argues that Congress had the power to enact the mandate under the Commerce Clause. ***** According to the Government, the health care market is characterized by a significant cost-shifting problem. Everyone will eventually need health care at a time and to an extent they cannot predict, but if they do not have insurance, they often will not be able to pay for it. Because state and federal laws nonetheless require hospitals to provide a certain degree of care to individuals without regard to their ability to pay, hospitals end up receiving compensation for only a portion of the services they provide. To recoup the losses, hospitals pass on the cost to insurers through higher rates, and insurers, in turn, pass on the cost to policyholders in the form of higher premiums. Congress estimated that the cost of uncompensated care raises family health insurance premiums, on average, by over $1,000 per year. ***** By requiring that individuals purchase health insurance, the mandate prevents cost-shifting by those who would otherwise go without it. In addition, the mandate forces into the insurance risk pool more healthy individuals, whose premiums on average will be higher than their health care expenses. *****

[handwritten: Congress enacted ACA to combat negative econ. effects]

The Constitution grants Congress the power to "*regulate* Commerce." The power to *regulate* commerce presupposes the existence of commercial activity to be regulated. If the power to "regulate" something included the power to create it, many of the provisions in the Constitution would be superfluous. For example, the Constitution gives Congress the power to "coin Money," in addition to the power to "regulate the Value thereof." And it gives Congress the power to "raise and support Armies" and to "provide and maintain a Navy," in addition to the power to "make Rules for the Government and Regulation of the land and naval Forces." If the power to regulate the armed forces or the value of money included the power to bring the subject of the regulation into existence, the specific grant of such powers would have been unnecessary. The language of the Constitution reflects the natural understanding that the power to regulate assumes there is already something to be regulated. *** As expansive as our cases construing the scope of the commerce power have been, they all have one thing in common: They uniformly describe the power as reaching "activity." It is nearly impossible to avoid the word when quoting them.

Constitutional Power to regulate existing activities

The individual mandate *** does not regulate existing commercial activity. It instead compels individuals to *become* active in commerce by purchasing a product, on the ground that their failure to do so affects interstate commerce. Construing the Commerce Clause to permit Congress to regulate individuals precisely *because* they are doing nothing would open a new and potentially vast domain to congressional authority. Every day individuals do not do an infinite number of things. In some cases they decide not to do something; in others they simply fail to do it. Allowing Congress to justify federal regulation by pointing to the effect of inaction on commerce would bring countless decisions an individual could *potentially* make within the scope of federal regulation, and—under the Government's theory— empower Congress to make those decisions for him. *** The farmer in *Wickard* was at least actively engaged in the production of wheat, and the Government could regulate that activity because of its effect on commerce. *** [T]he Government's logic would justify a mandatory purchase to solve almost any problem. To consider a different example in the health care market, many Americans do not eat a balanced diet. That group makes up a larger percentage of the total population than those without health insurance. The failure of that group to have a healthy diet increases health care costs, to a greater extent than the failure of the uninsured to purchase insurance. Those increased costs are borne in part by other Americans who must pay more, just as the uninsured shift costs to the insured. Congress addressed the insurance problem by ordering everyone to buy insurance. Under the Government's theory, Congress could address the diet problem by ordering everyone to buy vegetables. ***

Individual mandate is not an existing market

Would give Congress too much power

That is not the country the Framers of our Constitution envisioned. *** Accepting the Government's theory would give Congress the same license to regulate what we do not do, fundamentally changing the relation between the citizen and the Federal Government. *** [T]he distinction between doing something and doing nothing would not have been lost on the Framers, who were "practical statesmen," not metaphysical philosophers. *** The Framers

Not in line with the views of the founders

gave Congress the power to *regulate* commerce, not to *compel* it, and for over 200 years both our decisions and Congress's actions have reflected this understanding. There is no reason to depart from that understanding now.

The Government *** argues that because sickness and injury are unpredictable but unavoidable, "the uninsured as a class are active in the market for health care, which they regularly seek and obtain" *** but that concept has no constitutional significance. An individual who bought a car two years ago and may buy another in the future is not "active in the car market" in any pertinent sense. The phrase "active in the market" cannot obscure the fact that most of those regulated by the individual mandate are not currently engaged in any commercial activity involving health care, and that fact is fatal to the Government's effort to "regulate the uninsured as a class." *** The proposition that Congress may dictate the conduct of an individual today because of prophesied future activity finds no support in our precedent. *** Each one of our cases *** involved preexisting economic activity. See, *e.g., Wickard* (producing wheat); *Raich* (growing marijuana).

Everyone will likely participate in the markets for food, clothing, transportation, shelter, or energy; that does not authorize Congress to direct them to purchase particular products in those or other markets today. *** Any police power to regulate individuals as such, as opposed to their activities, remains vested in the States. ***

The Government next contends that Congress has the power under the Necessary and Proper Clause to enact the individual mandate because the mandate is an "integral part of a comprehensive scheme of economic regulation"—the guaranteed-issue and community-rating insurance reforms. *** [T]he individual mandate cannot be sustained under the Necessary and Proper Clause as an essential component of the insurance reforms. Each of our prior cases upholding laws under that Clause involved exercises of authority derivative of, and in service to, a granted power. *** The individual mandate, by contrast, vests Congress with the extraordinary ability to create the necessary predicate to the exercise of an enumerated power. *** Even if the individual mandate is "necessary" to the Act's insurance reforms, such an expansion of federal power is not a "proper" means for making those reforms effective. ***

JUSTICE GINSBURG, with whom JUSTICE SOTOMAYOR joins, and with whom JUSTICE BREYER and JUSTICE KAGAN join *** dissenting in part.

*** [A]ssuming, for the moment, that Congress lacks authority under the Commerce Clause to "compel individuals not engaged in commerce to purchase an unwanted product," such a limitation would be inapplicable here. Everyone will, at some point, consume health-care products and services. *** [Moreover,] Congress has no way of separating those uninsured individuals who will need emergency medical care today (surely their consumption of medical care is sufficiently imminent) from those who will not need medical services for years to come. *** Second, it is Congress' role, not the Court's, to delineate the boundaries of the market the Legislature seeks to regulate. *** Congress could reasonably have viewed the market from a long-term perspective, encompassing all transactions virtually certain to

occur over the next decade, not just those occurring here and now. ***
[Third,] [o]ur decisions thus acknowledge Congress' authority, under the
Commerce Clause, to direct the conduct of an individual today (the farmer in
Wickard, stopped from growing excess wheat; the plaintiff in *Raich,* ordered
to cease cultivating marijuana) because of a prophesied future transaction
(the eventual sale of that wheat or marijuana in the interstate market).
Congress' actions are even more rational in this case, where the future
activity (the consumption of medical care) is certain to occur, the sole
uncertainty being the time the activity will take place. *** Upholding the
minimum coverage provision on the ground that all are participants or will
be participants in the health-care market would therefore carry no
implication that Congress may justify under the Commerce Clause a
mandate to buy other products and services.

Nor is it accurate to say that the minimum coverage provision "compel[s]
individuals ... to purchase an unwanted product," or "suite of products". If
unwanted today, medical service secured by insurance may be desperately
needed tomorrow. In requiring individuals to obtain insurance, Congress is
therefore not mandating the purchase of a discrete, unwanted product.
Rather, Congress is merely defining the terms on which individuals pay for
an interstate good they consume: Persons subject to the mandate must now
pay for medical care in advance (instead of at the point of service) and
through insurance (instead of out of pocket). ***

*** [Nothing separates] the power to regulate from the power to bring the
subject of the regulation into existence. *** Requiring individuals to obtain
insurance unquestionably regulates the interstate health-insurance and
health-care markets, both of them in existence well before the enactment of
the ACA. Thus, the "something to be regulated" was surely there when
Congress created the minimum coverage provision. [6]

Nor does our case law toe the activity versus inactivity line. In *Wickard,*
for example, we upheld the penalty imposed on a farmer who grew too much
wheat, even though the regulation had the effect of compelling farmers to
purchase wheat in the open market. *** It is not hard to show the difficulty
courts (and Congress) would encounter in distinguishing statutes that
regulate "activity" from those that regulate "inactivity." *** Did the statute
there at issue [in *Wickard*] target activity (the growing of too much wheat) or
inactivity (the farmer's failure to purchase wheat in the marketplace)? If
anything, the Court's analysis suggested the latter. *** Underlying [the] view
that the Commerce Clause must be confined to the regulation of active
participants in a commercial market is a fear that the commerce power would
otherwise know no limits. *** This concern is unfounded.

First, [the Court] could certainly uphold the individual mandate without
giving Congress *carte blanche* to enact any and all purchase mandates. ***

---

[6] *** The power to "regulate the Value" of the national currency presumably includes the power
to increase the currency's worth—*i.e.,* to create value where none previously existed. And if the
power to "[r]egulat[e] ... the land and naval Forces" presupposes "there is already [in existence]
something to be regulated," *i.e.,* an Army and a Navy, does Congress lack authority to create an
Air Force?

Congress would remain unable to regulate noneconomic conduct that has only an attenuated effect on interstate commerce and is traditionally left to state law [as in *Lopez* and *Morrison*]. *** Consider the chain of inferences the Court would have to accept to conclude that a vegetable-purchase mandate was likely to have a substantial effect on the health-care costs borne by lithe Americans. The Court would have to believe that individuals forced to buy vegetables would then eat them (instead of throwing or giving them away), would prepare the vegetables in a healthy way (steamed or raw, not deep-fried), would cut back on unhealthy foods, and would not allow other factors (such as lack of exercise or little sleep) to trump the improved diet.[9]   Such "pil[ing of] inference upon inference" is just what the Court refused to do in *Lopez* and *Morrison*.

[handwritten margin note: analogizing to cases to show that people will use health insurance]

Other provisions of the Constitution also check congressional overreaching. A mandate to purchase a particular product would be unconstitutional if, for example, the edict impermissibly abridged the freedom of speech, interfered with the free exercise of religion, or infringed on a liberty interest protected by the Due Process Clause. *** Supplementing these legal restraints is a formidable check on congressional power: the democratic process. *** Despite their possession of unquestioned authority to impose mandates, state governments have rarely done so. *** While an insurance-purchase mandate may be novel, *** the Court has declined to override legislation because of its novelty, and for good reason. ***

[handwritten margin note: Individual mandate would only overreach if it violated the Const. No state challenged]

Asserting that the Necessary and Proper Clause does not authorize the minimum coverage provision, THE CHIEF JUSTICE focuses on the word "proper", [citing] only two cases in which this Court concluded that a federal statute impermissibly transgressed the Constitution's boundary between state and federal authority. The statutes at issue in both cases, however, compelled *state officials* to act on the Federal Government's behalf. "[Federal] laws conscripting state officers," the Court reasoned, "violate state sovereignty and are thus not in accord with the Constitution." *Printz*; *New York*. The minimum coverage provision, in contrast, acts "directly upon individuals, without employing the States as intermediaries." The provision is thus entirely consistent with the Constitution's design.

[handwritten margin note: Not improper b/c it doesn't violate state sovereignty]

Lacking case law support [the Court] nevertheless declares the minimum coverage provision not "proper" because it is less "narrow in scope" than other laws this Court has upheld under the Necessary and Proper Clause [ironically relying on] cases in which this Court has *affirmed* Congress' "broad authority to enact federal legislation" under the Necessary and Proper Clause. *Comstock*. *** [10]

---

[9] The failure to purchase vegetables in *** [the] hypothetical, then, is *not* what leads to higher health-care costs for others; rather, it is the failure of individuals to maintain a healthy diet, and the resulting obesity, that creates the cost-shifting problem. Requiring individuals to purchase vegetables is thus several steps removed from solving the problem. The failure to obtain health insurance, by contrast, is the *immediate cause* of the cost-shifting Congress sought to address through the ACA. Requiring individuals to obtain insurance attacks the source of the problem directly, in a single step.

[10] Congress regularly and uncontroversially requires individuals who are "doing nothing," to take action. Examples include federal requirements to report for jury duty; to register for selective

How is a judge to decide, when ruling on the constitutionality of a federal statute, whether Congress employed an "independent power," or merely a "derivative" one? Whether the power used is "substantive," or just "incidental"? *** It is more than exaggeration to suggest that the minimum coverage provision improperly intrudes on "essential attributes of state sovereignty." *** As evidenced by Medicare, Medicaid, the Employee Retirement Income Security Act of 1974 (ERISA), and the Health Insurance Portability and Accountability Act of 1996 (HIPAA), the Federal Government plays a lead role in the health-care sector, both as a direct payer and as a regulator. Second, and perhaps most important, the minimum coverage provision, along with other provisions of the ACA, addresses the very sort of interstate problem that made the commerce power essential in our federal system. *** Far from trampling on States' sovereignty, the ACA attempts a federal solution for the very reason that the States, acting separately, cannot meet the need. Notably, the ACA serves the general welfare of the people of the United States while retaining a prominent role for the States. ***

Joint Opinion of JUSTICE SCALIA, JUSTICE KENNEDY, JUSTICE THOMAS, and JUSTICE ALITO (concurring on the Commerce Clause issue).

*** If [The Individual Mandate] "regulates" anything, it is the *failure* to maintain minimum essential coverage. *** But that failure—that abstention from commerce—is not "Commerce." *** Ultimately the dissent is driven to saying that there is really no difference between action and inaction, a proposition that has never recommended itself, neither to the law nor to common sense. To say, for example, that the inaction here consists of activity in "the self-insurance market," seems to us wordplay. By parity of reasoning the failure to buy a car can be called participation in the non-private-car-transportation market. Commerce becomes everything.

The *** individual mandate threatens our constitutional order" *** because it gives such an expansive meaning to the Commerce Clause that *all* private conduct (including failure to act) becomes subject to federal control, effectively destroying the Constitution's division of governmental powers. *** The Constitution *** enumerates not federally soluble *problems,* but federally available *powers.* The Federal Government can address whatever problems it wants but can bring to their solution only those powers that the Constitution confers, among which is the power to regulate commerce. *** Article I contains no whatever-it-takes-to-solve-a-national-problem power. ***

JUSTICE THOMAS, dissenting.

*** The Government's unprecedented claim *** that it may regulate *** *inactivity* that substantially affects interstate commerce is [inconsistent with the original understanding of Congress' powers].

---

service; to purchase firearms and gear in anticipation of service in the Militia; to turn *gold* currency over to the Federal Government in exchange for paper currency, and to file a tax return.

Notes

1. **The Activity/Inactivity Distinction**. Is this distinction unworkable or nothing novel? Can the "activity/inactivity" test be inferred from prior commerce clause case law?

2. **The Health Care Mandate and Civil Liberties**. All justices express concern over a boundless commerce clause power, but some think health care is different from cars, broccoli, etc. Who has the better of this argument? Do the Bill of Rights and political process suffice to protect against Congress overreaching?

3. **Formalists and Functionalists**. Some Justices are functionalist and others formalist about the commerce clause powers. Are the same Justices formalist and functionalist about separation of powers in Chapter III?

4. **Ramifications**. Professor Pamela Karlen argued (NEW YORK TIMES, 6/30/2012): "[T]he federal government can forbid landlords to reject a tenant based on his race or religion; prohibit development on fragile wetlands; finance the Medicare program for the elderly; require public schools to give girls an equal opportunity to play sports; collect revenue to pay for the National Institutes of Health and the national parks; encourage energy conservation by taxing gas guzzlers; prohibit discriminatory voter ID laws; and vindicate the right of state government employees to take unpaid leave to care for sick relatives. The conservative legal movement has already attacked many of these provisions, and the Roberts court has been steadily supplying it with ammunition to do so." Is *NFIB v. Sebelius* likely to work major change in the commerce clause power?

5. **Problems.** Consider whether the following would be within Congress' commerce clause power after *Lopez*, *Morrison*, and *NFIB*:

   • A federal law forbidding construction that would eliminate small ponds used by migrating birds.

   • A federal law punishing parents who fail to pay past due support obligations with respect to a child who resides in another state.

   • A federal law prohibiting any person from possessing a firearm who has previously been convicted of any crime involving domestic violence.

   • A federal law criminalizing destruction of "real or personal property used in interstate commerce *** or in any activity affecting commerce," including arson of a private residence. *See Jones v. United States*, 529 U.S. 848 (2000).

   • A federal law prohibiting the use or threat of force or physical obstruction against a person seeking to obtain or provide reproductive health services, including abortions.

C. OTHER ARTICLE I POWERS

1. TAXING POWER

Remember CHIEF JUSTICE MARSHALL's aphorism that "the power to tax is the power to destroy?" Consider the dramatic growth in the federal government that has occurred since 1913 when the Sixteenth Amendment gave the federal government the ability to tax incomes directly. Today, federal income taxes approximate $1 trillion, a significant portion of the nation's gross national product.

After the Sixteenth Amendment, what limits, if any, are there to federal taxation? In 1922, the Court held an excise tax imposed on profits of mines and factories that used child labor unconstitutional on the ground that this was a penalty, not a tax. *Bailey v. Drexel Furniture Co.*, 259 U.S. 20 (1922). Subsequently, however, the Court has repeatedly upheld "regulatory" taxes on firearms, narcotics, etc., refusing to inquire into Congress' motive in enacting a tax. The following excerpts from the Supreme Court Affordable Care Act decision offer further insight into the reach of the taxing power.

NFIB v. SEBELIUS
132 S. Ct. 2566 (2012)

ROBERTS, C. J., *** delivered the opinion of the Court [on whether the individual mandate of the Affordable Care Act was within the taxing power]

§8 , c I

*** Congress may also "lay and collect Taxes, Duties, Imposts and Excises, to pay the Debts and provide for the common Defence and general Welfare of the United States." *** This grant gives the Federal Government considerable influence even in areas where it cannot directly regulate. The Federal Government may enact a tax on an activity that it cannot authorize, forbid, or otherwise control. *** The reach of the Federal Government's enumerated powers is broader still because the Constitution authorizes Congress to "make all Laws which shall be necessary and proper for carrying into Execution the foregoing Powers." ***

penalty = % of income payable to the IRS - w/ some exceptions

Beginning in 2014, those who do not comply with the mandate must make a "[s]hared responsibility payment" to the Federal Government. That payment, which the Act describes as a "penalty," is calculated as a percentage of household income, subject to a floor based on a specified dollar amount and a ceiling based on the average annual premium the individual would have to pay for qualifying private health insurance. *** The Act provides that the penalty will be paid to the Internal Revenue Service with an individual's taxes, and "shall be assessed and collected in the same manner" as tax penalties, such as the penalty for claiming too large an income tax refund. The Act, however, bars the IRS from using several of its normal enforcement tools, such as criminal prosecutions and levies. And some individuals who are subject to the mandate are nonetheless exempt from the penalty—for example, those with income below a certain threshold and members of Indian tribes. ***

Different from CC argument.

The Government's tax power argument asks us to view the statute differently than we did in considering its commerce power theory. In making its Commerce Clause argument, the Government defended the mandate as a regulation requiring individuals to purchase health insurance. The Government does not claim that the taxing power allows Congress to issue such a command. Instead, the Government asks us to read the mandate not as ordering individuals to buy insurance, but rather as imposing a tax on those who do not buy that product. *** Under the mandate, if an individual does not maintain health insurance, the only consequence is that he must make an additional payment to the IRS when he pays his taxes. That, according to the Government, means the mandate can be regarded as establishing a condition—not owning health insurance—that triggers a tax—the required payment to the IRS. Under that theory, the mandate is not a legal command to buy insurance. Rather, it makes going without insurance just another thing the Government taxes, like buying gasoline or earning income. And if the mandate is in effect just a tax hike on certain taxpayers who do not have health insurance, it may be within Congress's constitutional power to tax. ***

Gov args that it is not commanding anything, just taxing another area

The exaction the Affordable Care Act imposes on those without health insurance looks like a tax in many respects. *** It does not apply to individuals who do not pay federal income taxes because their household income is less than the filing threshold in the Internal Revenue Code, or taxpayers who do owe the payment, its amount is determined by such familiar factors as taxable income, number of dependents, and joint filing status. The requirement to pay is found in the Internal Revenue Code and enforced by the IRS, which *** must assess and collect it "in the same manner as taxes." This process yields the essential feature of any tax: it produces at least some revenue for the Government. ***

Individual mandate looks like other fed. taxes

It is of course true that the Act describes the payment as a "penalty," not a "tax." But [that label] does not determine whether the payment may be viewed as an exercise of Congress's taxing power. *** Our cases confirm this functional approach. For example, in *Drexel Furniture,* 259 U.S. at 36-37, we focused on three practical characteristics of the so-called tax on employing child laborers that convinced us the "tax" was actually a penalty. First, the tax imposed an exceedingly heavy burden—10 percent of a company's net income—on those who employed children, no matter how small their infraction. Second, it imposed that exaction only on those who knowingly employed underage laborers. Such scienter requirements are typical of punitive statutes, because Congress often wishes to punish only those who intentionally break the law. Third, this "tax" was enforced in part by the Department of Labor, an agency responsible for punishing violations of labor laws, not collecting revenue.

tax v. penalty

three characteristics applied to Drexel

The same analysis here suggests that the shared responsibility payment may for constitutional purposes be considered a tax, not a penalty: First, for most Americans the amount due will be far less than the price of insurance, and, by statute, it can never be more. *** Second, the individual mandate contains no scienter requirement. Third, the payment is collected solely by the IRS through the normal means of taxation—except that the Service is *not* allowed to use those means most suggestive of a punitive sanction, such as criminal prosecution. The reasons the Court in *Drexel Furniture* held that what was called a "tax" there was a penalty support the conclusion that what is called a "penalty" here may be viewed as a tax.[9]

applied to individual mandate

---

[9] We do not suggest that any exaction lacking a scienter requirement and enforced by the IRS is within the taxing power. Congress could not, for example, expand its authority to impose criminal fines by creating strict liability offenses enforced by the IRS rather than the FBI. But the fact the exaction here is paid like a tax, to the agency that collects taxes—rather than, for

Scienter = knowledge of wrongdoing

None of this is to say that the payment is not intended to affect individual conduct. Although the payment will raise considerable revenue, it is plainly designed to expand health insurance coverage. But taxes that seek to influence conduct are nothing new. *** Indeed, "[e]very tax is in some measure regulatory. To some extent it interposes an economic impediment to the activity taxed as compared with others not taxed." That § 5000A seeks to shape decisions about whether to buy health insurance does not mean that it cannot be a valid exercise of the taxing power.

In distinguishing penalties from taxes, this Court has explained that "if the concept of penalty means anything, it means punishment for an unlawful act or omission." While the individual mandate clearly aims to induce the purchase of health insurance, it need not be read to declare that failing to do so is unlawful. Neither the Act nor any other law attaches negative legal consequences to not buying health insurance, beyond requiring a payment to the IRS. *** Indeed, it is estimated that four million people each year will choose to pay the IRS rather than buy insurance. We would expect Congress to be troubled by that prospect if such conduct were unlawful. That Congress apparently regards such extensive failure to comply with the mandate as tolerable suggests that Congress did not think it was creating four million outlaws. It suggests instead that the shared responsibility payment merely imposes a tax citizens may lawfully choose to pay in lieu of buying health insurance.

The plaintiffs contend that Congress's choice of language—stating that individuals "shall" obtain insurance or pay a "penalty"—requires reading § 5000A as punishing unlawful conduct, even if that interpretation would render the law unconstitutional. We have rejected a similar argument before. In *New York v. United States* we examined a statute providing that " '[e]ach State shall be responsible for providing ... for the disposal of ... low-level radioactive waste.' "A State that shipped its waste to another State was exposed to surcharges by the receiving State, a portion of which would be paid over to the Federal Government. And a State that did not adhere to the statutory scheme faced "[p]enalties for failure to comply," including increases in the surcharge. *** [W]e interpreted the statute to impose only "a series of incentives" for the State to take responsibility for its waste. We then sustained the charge paid to the Federal Government as an exercise of the taxing power. ***

Even if the taxing power enables Congress to impose a tax on not obtaining health insurance, any tax must still comply with other requirements in the Constitution. Plaintiffs argue that the shared responsibility payment does not do so, citing Article I, § 9, clause 4. That clause provides: "No Capitation, or other direct, Tax shall be laid, unless in Proportion to the Census or Enumeration herein before directed to be taken." This requirement means that any "direct Tax" must be apportioned so that each State pays in proportion to its population. According to the plaintiffs, if the individual mandate imposes a tax, it is a direct tax, and it is

example, exacted by Department of Labor inspectors after ferreting out willful malfeasance—suggests that this exaction may be viewed as a tax.

unconstitutional because Congress made no effort to apportion it among the States.

Even when the Direct Tax Clause was written it was unclear what else, other than a capitation (also known as a "head tax" or a "poll tax"), might be a direct tax. Soon after the framing, Congress passed a tax on ownership of carriages, over James Madison's objection that it was an unapportioned direct tax. This Court upheld the tax, in part reasoning that apportioning such a tax would make little sense, because it would have required taxing carriage owners at dramatically different rates depending on how many carriages were in their home State. The Court *** suggested that only two forms of taxation were direct: capitations and land taxes. *** A tax on going without health insurance does not fall within any recognized category of direct tax. It is not a capitation. Capitations are taxes paid by every person, "without regard to property, profession, or *any other circumstance.*" The whole point of the shared responsibility payment is that it is triggered by specific circumstances—earning a certain amount of income but not obtaining health insurance. The payment is also plainly not a tax on the ownership of land or personal property. The shared responsibility payment is thus not a direct tax that must be apportioned among the several States.

There may, however, be a more fundamental objection to a tax on those who lack health insurance. Even if only a tax, the payment under § 5000A(b) remains a burden that the Federal Government imposes for an omission, not an act. *** Three considerations allay this concern. First, and most importantly, it is abundantly clear the Constitution does not guarantee that individuals may avoid taxation through inactivity. A capitation, after all, is a tax that everyone must pay simply for existing, and capitations are expressly contemplated by the Constitution. *** Second, Congress's ability to use its taxing power to influence conduct is not without limits. A few of our cases policed these limits aggressively, invalidating punitive exactions obviously designed to regulate behavior otherwise regarded at the time as beyond federal authority. *** [W]e need not here decide the precise point at which an exaction becomes so punitive that the taxing power does not authorize it. *** Third, although the breadth of Congress's power to tax is greater than its power to regulate commerce, the taxing power does not give Congress the same degree of control over individual behavior. Once we recognize that Congress may regulate a particular decision under the Commerce Clause, *** [a]n individual who disobeys may be subjected to criminal sanctions. *** By contrast, Congress's authority under the taxing power is limited to requiring an individual to pay money into the Federal Treasury, no more. ***

JUSTICE SCALIA, JUSTICE KENNEDY, JUSTICE THOMAS, and JUSTICE ALITO, dissenting.

*** The provision challenged under the Constitution is either a penalty or else a tax. *** Our cases establish a clear line between a tax and a penalty: "[A] tax is an enforced contribution to provide for the support of government; a penalty ... is an exaction imposed by statute as punishment for an unlawful act." In a few cases, this Court has held that a "tax" imposed upon private conduct was so onerous as to be in effect a penalty. But we have never held—

taxes can be penalties, but penalties cannot be taxes

never—that a penalty imposed for violation of the law was so trivial as to be in effect a tax. We have never held that *any* exaction imposed for violation of the law is an exercise of Congress' taxing power—even when the statute *calls* it a tax, much less when (as here) the statute repeatedly calls it a penalty. When an act "adopt[s] the criteria of wrongdoing" and then imposes a monetary penalty as the "principal consequence on those who transgress its standard," it creates a regulatory penalty, not a tax.

penalty is the result of a violation of the law

So the question is, quite simply, whether the exaction here is imposed for violation of the law. It unquestionably is. The minimum-coverage provision is *** entitled "*Requirement* to maintain minimum essential coverage." It commands that every "applicable individual *shall* ... ensure that the individual ... is covered under minimum essential coverage." And the immediately following provision states that, "[i]f ... an applicable individual ... fails to meet the *requirement* of subsection (a) ... there is hereby imposed ... a *penalty*." And several of Congress' legislative "findings" *** confirm that it sets forth a legal requirement and constitutes the assertion of regulatory power, not mere taxing power. ***

Quite separately, the fact that Congress (in its own words) "imposed ... a penalty," for failure to buy insurance is alone sufficient to render that failure unlawful. *** [S]ome are exempt from the tax who are not exempt from the mandate—a distinction that would make no sense if the mandate were not a mandate ***

Against the mountain of evidence that the minimum coverage requirement is what the statute calls it—a requirement—and that the penalty for its violation is what the statute calls it—a penalty—the Government brings forward the flimsiest of indications to the contrary. It notes that "[t]he minimum coverage provision amends the Internal Revenue Code *** and that "[t]he [Internal Revenue Service (IRS)] will assess and collect the penalty in the same manner as assessable penalties under the Internal Revenue Code." The manner of collection could perhaps suggest a tax if IRS penalty-collection were unheard-of or rare. It is not. In *Reorganized CF & I Fabricators of Utah, Inc.,* 518 U.S. 213, we held that an exaction not only *enforced* by the Commissioner of Internal Revenue but even *called* a "tax" was in fact a penalty. *** Moreover, while the penalty is assessed and collected by the IRS, § 5000A is administered both by that agency and by the Department of Health and Human Services (and also the Secretary of Veteran Affairs), which is responsible for defining its substantive scope—a feature that would be quite extraordinary for taxes.

case law supporting it as a penalty

The Government points out that "[t]he amount of the penalty will be calculated as a percentage of household income for federal income tax purposes, subject to a floor and [a] ca[p]," and that individuals who earn so little money that they "are not required to file income tax returns for the taxable year are not subject to the penalty" (though they are, as we discussed earlier, subject to the mandate). But varying a penalty according to ability to pay is an utterly familiar practice.

The last of the feeble arguments in favor of petitioners that we will address is the contention that what this statute repeatedly calls a penalty is in fact a tax because it contains no scienter requirement. The *presence* of such a requirement suggests a penalty—though one can imagine a tax imposed only on willful action; but the *absence* of such a requirement does not suggest a tax. Penalties for absolute-liability offenses are commonplace. *** And the nail in the coffin is that the mandate and penalty are located in Title I of the Act, its operative core, rather than where a tax would be found—in Title IX, containing the Act's "Revenue Provisions." *** Congress imposed a regulatory penalty, not a tax.

[handwritten margin note: tax is in the wrong place of the act.]

For all these reasons, to say that the Individual Mandate merely imposes a tax is not to interpret the statute but to rewrite it. *** We have no doubt that Congress knew precisely what it was doing when it rejected an earlier version of this legislation that imposed a tax instead of a requirement-with-penalty. Imposing a tax through judicial legislation inverts the constitutional scheme, and places the power to tax in the branch of government least accountable to the citizenry.

Finally, we must observe that rewriting § 5000A as a tax in order to sustain its constitutionality would force us to confront a difficult constitutional question: whether this is a direct tax that must be apportioned among the States according to their population. Art. I, § 9, cl. 4. Perhaps it is not (we have no need to address the point); but the meaning of the Direct Tax Clause is famously unclear, and its application here is a question of first impression that deserves more thoughtful consideration than the lick-and-a-promise accorded by the Government and its supporters. *** The Court's disposition, invented and atextual as it is, does not even have the merit of avoiding constitutional difficulties. It creates them. ***

Notes

1. **Penalty or Tax?** When the Court restricted federal commerce power in the 1920's and 1930's, it distinguished between taxes to raise revenue and penalties to regulate behavior. Yet many federal exactions have done both. CHIEF JUSTICE ROBERTS finds the following facts persuasive: 1) the money collected is at a moderate level 2) the money is collected by the IRS and 3) there is no scienter requirement. Are you persuaded? If Congress raises the tax to more than the cost of insurance, does the tax become a penalty?

2. **Taxing Economic Inactivity.** CHIEF JUSTICE ROBERTS rejected the individual mandate under the Commerce Clause: not buying insurance was not commerce to regulate. Yet, under the taxing power, he says "going without insurance [is] just another thing the Government taxes, like buying gasoline or earning income." Is the Chief Justice inconsistent? Might naming something a "tax" implicitly limit Congress's power since taxes are unpopular?

3. **Dictum?** Reversing the order of the commerce clause and taxing issues would have made the commerce clause discussion unnecessary. Is it dictum?

2. SPENDING POWER

The Spending Power gives Congress leverage over states: particular things must be done or the state is denied federal money. The next two cases consider this power.

SOUTH DAKOTA v. DOLE
483 U.S. 203 (1987)

CHIEF JUSTICE REHNQUIST delivered the opinion of the Court.

P arg

Petitioner South Dakota permits persons 19 years of age or older to purchase beer containing up to 3.2% alcohol. In 1984 Congress enacted [legislation] which directs the Secretary of Transportation to withhold a percentage of federal highway funds otherwise allocable from States "in which the purchase or public possession *** of any alcoholic beverage by a person who is less than twenty-one years of age is lawful." The State [argues] that § 158 [of the Act] violates the constitutional limitations on congressional exercise of the spending power and violates the Twenty-first Amendment to the United States Constitution. ***

P argues that it violates § 2 of 21st Amendment

↓

Gov. response

In this Court, the parties direct most of their efforts to defining the proper scope of the Twenty-first Amendment. Relying on our statement in *California Retail Liquor Dealers Assn. v. Midcal Aluminum, Inc.*, 445 U.S. 97 (1980), that the "Twenty-first Amendment grants the States virtually complete control over whether to permit importation or sale of liquor and how to structure the liquor distribution system," South Dakota asserts that the setting of minimum drinking ages is clearly within the "core powers" reserved to the States under § 2 of the Amendment.[1] [The Act], petitioner claims, usurps that core power. The Secretary in response asserts that the Twenty-first Amendment is simply not implicated by § 158; the plain language of § 2 confirms the States' broad power to impose restrictions on the sale and distribution of alcoholic beverages but does not confer on them any power to permit sales that Congress seeks to prohibit. That Amendment, under this reasoning, would not prevent Congress from affirmatively enacting a national minimum drinking age more restrictive than that provided by the various state laws; and it would follow *a fortiori* that the indirect inducement involved here is compatible with the Twenty-first Amendment.

Ruled in favor of Fed. gov. (congress)

[W]e need not decide in this case whether that Amendment would prohibit an attempt by Congress to legislate directly a national minimum drinking age. Here, Congress has acted indirectly under its spending power to encourage uniformity in the States' drinking ages. As we explain below, we find this legislative effort within constitutional bounds even if Congress may not regulate drinking ages directly.

within Congress' power to make certain funding conditional

↓

The Constitution empowers Congress to "lay and collect Taxes, Duties, Imposts, and Excises, to pay the Debts and provide for the common Defence and general Welfare of the United States." Incident to this power, Congress may attach conditions on the receipt of federal funds, and has repeatedly employed the power "to further broad policy objectives by conditioning receipt of federal moneys upon compliance by the recipient with federal statutory and administrative directives." The breadth of this power was made clear in *United States v. Butler*, 297 U.S. 1 (1936), where the Court, resolving a

---

[1] Section 2 of the Twenty-first Amendment provides: "The transportation or importation into any State, Territory, or possession of the United States for delivery or use therein of intoxicating liquors, in violation of the laws thereof, is hereby prohibited."

longstanding debate over the scope of the Spending Clause, determined that "the power of Congress to authorize expenditure of public moneys for public purposes is not limited by the direct grants of legislative power found in the Constitution." Thus, objectives not thought to be within Article I's "enumerated legislative fields," may nevertheless be attained through the use of the spending power and the conditional grant of federal funds.

The spending power is of course not unlimited but is instead subject to several general restrictions articulated in our cases. The first of these limitations is derived from the language of the Constitution itself: the exercise of the spending power must be in pursuit of "the general welfare." In considering whether a particular expenditure is intended to serve general public purposes, courts should defer substantially to the judgment of Congress. Second, we have required that if Congress desires to condition the States' receipt of federal funds, it "must do so unambiguously ***, enabl[ing] the States to exercise their choice knowingly, cognizant of the consequences of their participation." Third, our cases have suggested (without significant elaboration) that conditions on federal grants might be illegitimate if they are unrelated "to the federal interest in particular national projects or programs." Finally, we have noted that other constitutional provisions may provide an independent bar to the conditional grant of federal funds.

South Dakota does not seriously claim that [the Act] is inconsistent with any of the first three restrictions mentioned above. *** Congress found that the differing drinking ages in the States created particular incentives for young persons to combine their desire to drink with their ability to drive, and that this interstate problem required a national solution. The means it chose to address this dangerous situation were reasonably calculated to advance the general welfare. The conditions upon which States receive the funds, moreover, could not be more clearly stated by Congress. And the State itself, rather than challenging the germaneness of the condition to federal purposes, admits that it "has never contended that the congressional action was *** unrelated to a national concern in the absence of the Twenty-first Amendment." Indeed, the condition imposed by Congress is directly related to one of the main purposes for which highway funds are expended—safe interstate travel. ***

The remaining question about the validity of § 158—and the basic point of disagreement between the parties—is whether the Twenty-first Amendment constitutes an "independent constitutional bar" to the conditional grant of federal funds. Petitioner, relying on its view that the Twenty-first Amendment prohibits direct regulation of drinking ages by Congress, asserts that "Congress may not use the spending power to regulate that which it is prohibited from regulating directly under the Twenty-first Amendment." But our cases show that this "independent constitutional bar" limitation on the spending power is not of the kind petitioner suggests. *** We have also held that a perceived Tenth Amendment limitation on congressional regulation of state affairs did not concomitantly limit the range of conditions legitimately placed on federal grants. ***

[handwritten margin note: It is not allowing states to do what they are not empowered to do but rather allowing states to engage in unconstitutional activity]

[T]he "independent constitutional bar" limitation on the spending power is not, as petitioner suggests, a prohibition on the indirect achievement of objectives which Congress is not empowered to achieve directly. Instead, we think that the language in our earlier opinions stands for the unexceptionable proposition that the power may not be used to induce the States to engage in activities that would themselves be unconstitutional. Thus, for example, a grant of federal funds conditioned on invidiously discriminatory state action or the infliction of cruel and unusual punishment would be an illegitimate exercise of the Congress' broad spending power. But no such claim can be or is made here. ***

[handwritten margin note: not compulsive b/c it was only a small % of funds]

Our decisions have recognized that in some circumstances the financial inducement offered by Congress might be so coercive as to pass the point at which "pressure turns into compulsion." Here, however, Congress has directed only that a State desiring to establish a minimum drinking age lower than 21 lose a relatively small percentage of certain federal highway funds. Petitioner contends that the coercive nature of this program is evident from the degree of success it has achieved. We cannot conclude, however, that a conditional grant of federal money of this sort is unconstitutional simply by reason of its success in achieving the congressional objective.

When we consider, for a moment, that all South Dakota would lose if she adheres to her chosen course as to a suitable minimum drinking age is 5% of the funds otherwise obtainable under specified highway grant programs, the argument as to coercion is shown to be more rhetoric than fact. *** Here Congress has offered relatively mild encouragement to the States to enact higher minimum drinking ages than they would otherwise choose. But the enactment of such laws remains the prerogative of the States not merely in theory but in fact. Even if Congress might lack the power to impose a national minimum drinking age directly, we conclude that encouragement to state action *** is a valid use of the spending power. ***

JUSTICE O'CONNOR, dissenting.

*** My disagreement with the Court is relatively narrow on the spending power issue: it is a disagreement about the application of a principle rather than a disagreement on the principle itself. *** [T]he Court's application of the requirement that the condition imposed be reasonably related to the purpose for which the funds are expended is cursory and unconvincing. *** In my view, establishment of a minimum drinking age of 21 is not sufficiently related to interstate highway construction to justify so conditioning funds appropriated for that purpose. *** The Court reasons that Congress wishes that the roads it builds may be used safely, that drunken drivers threaten highway safety, and that young people are more likely to drive while under the influence of alcohol under existing law than would be the case if there were a uniform national drinking age of 21. *** [I]f the purpose of § 158 is to deter drunken driving, it is far too over and under-inclusive. It is over-inclusive because it stops teenagers from drinking even when they are not about to drive on interstate highways. It is under-inclusive because teenagers pose only a small part of the drunken driving problem in this Nation.

[handwritten margin note: Not related]

When Congress appropriates money to build a highway, it is entitled to insist that the highway be a safe one. But it is not entitled to insist as a condition of the use of highway funds that the State impose or change regulations in other areas of the State's social and economic life because of an attenuated or tangential relationship to highway use or safety. Indeed, if the rule were otherwise, the Congress could effectively regulate almost any area of a State's social, political, or economic life on the theory that use of the interstate transportation system is somehow enhanced. If, for example, the United States were to condition highway moneys upon moving the state capital, I suppose it might argue that interstate transportation is facilitated by locating local governments in places easily accessible to interstate highways—or, conversely, that highways might become overburdened if they had to carry traffic to and from the state capital. *** There is a clear place at which the Court can draw the line between permissible and impermissible conditions on federal grants. *** The appropriate inquiry is whether the spending requirement or prohibition is a condition on a grant or whether it is regulation. The difference turns on whether the requirement specifies in some way how the money should be spent, so that Congress' intent in making the grant will be effectuated. Congress has no power under the Spending Clause to impose requirements on a grant that go beyond specifying how the money should be spent. A requirement that is not such a specification is not a condition, but a regulation. *** [A] condition that a State will raise its drinking age to 21 cannot fairly be said to be reasonably related to the expenditure of funds for highway construction. The only possible connection, highway safety, has nothing to do with how the funds Congress has appropriated are expended. *** [R]egulation of the age of the purchasers of liquor, just as the regulation of the price at which liquor may be sold, falls squarely within the scope of those powers reserved to the States by the Twenty-first Amendment. ***

gives Congress too much power

Notes

1. **Background.** *Dole* mentions a fifth factor: funding where inducement becomes coercive. How can giving money to the states become coercive? Is the only downside to a state not having the money? See the next case, infra.

2. **Analysis of *Dole*.** How well do you think *Dole* deals with the scope of the Spending Power? How does JUSTICE REHNQUIST define the outer limits to this power? Do you agree or disagree with JUSTICE O'CONNOR's dissent?

3. **Question.** Consider whether Congress could condition the receipt of any federal funds by a school district on prohibition of guns (or drugs) within 1000 feet of any school within the district. What if Congress conditioned a state's receipt of all federal funds on the same "no guns (or drugs) near schools" rule?

4. **Problem.** Consider how you might use the spending power post-*Dole* to accomplish the goals of the regulations hypothesized in the problems at the end of the commerce clause portion of this chapter.

5. **Conditional Spending and Social Policy.** Cultural liberals might see conditional spending as a tool for progressive nationwide changes, a way to circumvent the Rehnquist Court's restricted readings of Congress' powers. Two

scholars suggest this is short-sighted and that the following conservative conditional spending schemes would be permissible under *Dole*: "(1) Congress conditions grants for state law enforcement on a state's enactment of right-to-carry laws and on enactment, and enforcement, of the death penalty; (2) Congress conditions Head Start funds on a state's prohibiting affirmative action even by private educational institutions; and (3) Congress conditions a package of funds designed to promote child welfare (perhaps in health and education) on a state's prohibiting homosexual couples from adopting." Lynn A. Baker & Mitchell N. Berman, *Getting off the Dole: Why the Court Should Abandon its Spending Doctrine, and How a Too-Clever Congress Could Provoke It to Do So*, 78 INDIANA L. J. 459, 482-83 (2003).

6. **Will the *Dole* Test Last?** If Congress uses conditional spending when it could not legislate, will the Court abandon or alter the *Dole* test to reestablish a federalist balance? JUSTICE KENNEDY, joined by CHIEF JUSTICE REHNQUIST, JUSTICE SCALIA and JUSTICE THOMAS said that "[T]he Spending Clause power, if wielded without concern for the federal balance, has the potential to obliterate distinctions between national and local spheres of interest and power by permitting the Federal Government to set policy in the most sensitive areas of traditional state concerns, areas which would otherwise be out of reach." *Davis v. Monroe County Bd. of Educ.*, 526 U.S. 629, 654-55 (1999). Consider what the Court might do with a challenge to the Religious Land Use and Institutionalized Persons Act of 2000 (RLIUPA). Programs receiving federal financial assistance under RLIUPA may not "impose a substantial burden on the religious exercise" of an institutionalized person "even if the burden results from a rule of general applicability" and government must use the "least restrictive means" to meet a compelling interest when imposing such a general rule.

NFIB v. SEBELIUS
132 S. Ct. 2566 (2012)

ROBERTS, C. J., announced the judgment of the Court ***

[margin note: expanding Medicaid]

Today we resolve constitutional challenges to *** the Medicaid expansion, which gives funds to the States on the condition that they provide specified health care to all citizens whose income falls below a certain threshold. *** Enacted in 1965, Medicaid offers federal funding to States to assist pregnant women, children, needy families, the blind, the elderly, and the disabled in obtaining medical care. In order to receive that funding, States must comply with federal criteria governing matters such as who receives care and what services are provided at what cost. By 1982 every State had chosen to participate in Medicaid. Federal funds received through the Medicaid program have become a substantial part of state budgets, now constituting over 10 percent of most States' total revenue.

The Affordable Care Act expands the scope of the Medicaid program and increases the number of individuals the States must cover. *** The Act increases federal funding to cover the States' costs in expanding Medicaid coverage, although States will bear a portion of the costs on their own. If a State does not comply with the Act's new coverage requirements, it may lose not only the federal funding for those requirements, but all of its federal Medicaid funds. *** The States *** contend that the Medicaid expansion

[margin note: State arg.]

exceeds Congress's authority under the Spending Clause. They claim that

Congress is coercing the States to adopt the changes it wants by threatening to withhold all of a State's Medicaid grants, unless the State accepts the new expanded funding and complies with the conditions that come with it. This, they argue, violates the basic principle that the "Federal Government may not compel the States to enact or administer a federal regulatory program." *New York* [*v. United States*, 505 U.S. 144, 188 (1992), infra section D].

[margin: coercion]

There is no doubt that the Act dramatically increases state obligations under Medicaid. *** On average States cover only those unemployed parents who make less than 37 percent of the federal poverty level, and only those employed parents who make less than 63 percent of the poverty line. The Medicaid provisions of the Affordable Care Act, in contrast, require States to expand their Medicaid programs by 2014 to cover *all* individuals under the age of 65 with incomes below 133 percent of the federal poverty line. The Act also establishes a new "[e]ssential health benefits" package, which States must provide to all new Medicaid recipients—a level sufficient to satisfy a recipient's obligations under the individual mandate. The Affordable Care Act provides that the Federal Government will pay 100 percent of the costs of covering these newly eligible individuals through 2016. In the following years, the federal payment level gradually decreases, to a minimum of 90 percent. In light of the expansion in coverage mandated by the Act, the Federal Government estimates that its Medicaid spending will increase by approximately $100 billion per year, nearly 40 percent above current levels.

[margin: detail of expansion]

[margin: decrease of Fed. funding despite having to cover more]

The Spending Clause grants Congress the power "to pay the Debts and provide for the ... general Welfare of the United States." *** Congress may use its spending power to create incentives for States to act in accordance with federal policies. But when "pressure turns into compulsion," the legislation runs contrary to our system of federalism. "[T]he Constitution simply does not give Congress the authority to require the States to regulate." That is true whether Congress directly commands a State to regulate or indirectly coerces a State to adopt a federal regulatory system as its own.

[margin: 88, c I]

[margin: okay so long as it is not compulsion of regulation]

Permitting the Federal Government to force the States to implement a federal program would threaten the political accountability key to our federal system. *** Spending Clause programs do not pose this danger when a State has a legitimate choice whether to accept the federal conditions in exchange for federal funds. In such a situation, state officials can fairly be held politically accountable for choosing to accept or refuse the federal offer. But when the State has no choice, the Federal Government can achieve its objectives without accountability ***. Indeed, this danger is heightened when Congress acts under the Spending Clause, because Congress can use that power to implement federal policy it could not impose directly under its enumerated powers. *** Congress may attach appropriate conditions to federal taxing and spending programs to preserve its control over the use of federal funds. In the typical case we look to the States to defend their prerogatives by adopting "the simple expedient of not yielding" to federal blandishments when they do not want to embrace the federal policies as their own. The States are separate and independent sovereigns. Sometimes they have to act like it.

[margin: state has a choice]

[margin: states need to argue against congressional overreach]

The States, however, argue that the Medicaid expansion is far from the typical case. They object that Congress has "crossed the line distinguishing encouragement from coercion," in the way it has structured the funding: Instead of simply refusing to grant the new funds to States that will not accept the new conditions, Congress has also threatened to withhold those States' existing Medicaid funds. The States claim that this threat serves no purpose other than to force unwilling States to sign up for the dramatic expansion in health care coverage effected by the Act.

Given the nature of the threat and the programs at issue here, we must agree. We have upheld Congress's authority to condition the receipt of funds on the States' complying with restrictions on the use of those funds, because that is the means by which Congress ensures that the funds are spent according to its view of the "general Welfare." Conditions that do not here govern the use of the funds, however, cannot be justified on that basis. When, for example, such conditions take the form of threats to terminate other significant independent grants, the conditions are properly viewed as a means of pressuring the States to accept policy changes.

In *South Dakota v. Dole,* we *** found that the inducement was not impermissibly coercive, because Congress was offering only "relatively mild encouragement to the States." *** In this case, the financial "inducement" Congress has chosen is much more than "relatively mild encouragement"—it is a gun to the head. *** A State that opts out of the Affordable Care Act's expansion in health care coverage thus stands to lose not merely "a relatively small percentage" of its existing Medicaid funding, but *all* of it. Medicaid spending accounts for over 20 percent of the average State's total budget, with federal funds covering 50 to 83 percent of those costs. The Federal Government estimates that it will pay out approximately $3.3 trillion between 2010 and 2019 in order to cover the costs of *pre*-expansion Medicaid. In addition, the States have developed intricate statutory and administrative regimes over the course of many decades to implement their objectives under existing Medicaid. *** The threatened loss of over 10 percent of a State's overall budget, in contrast, is economic dragooning that leaves the States with no real option but to acquiesce in the Medicaid expansion. *** The Medicaid expansion *** accomplishes a shift in kind, not merely degree. *** Under the Affordable Care Act, Medicaid is *** no longer a program to care for the neediest among us, but rather an element of a comprehensive national plan to provide universal health insurance coverage. *** A State could hardly anticipate that Congress's reservation of the right to "alter" or "amend" the Medicaid program included the power to transform it so dramatically. *** We have no need to fix a line either [for] this statute is surely beyond it. Congress may not simply "conscript state [agencies] into the national bureaucratic army," and that is what it is attempting to do with the Medicaid expansion.

JUSTICE GINSBURG, with whom JUSTICE SOTOMAYOR joins *** dissenting.

*** I would also hold that the Spending Clause permits the Medicaid expansion exactly as Congress enacted it. *** A ritualistic requirement that Congress repeal and reenact spending legislation in order to enlarge the population served by a federally funded program would advance no

---

Handwritten margin notes:

states argue that there is unequal bargaining power and it leaves them w/ no real choice

↓

Ct. agrees

goes far beyond the level of encouragement in Dole.

would complicate existing, intricate state regulations

*

constitutional principle and would scarcely serve the interests of federalism. To the contrary, such a requirement would rigidify Congress' efforts to empower States by partnering with them in the implementation of federal programs. ***

Medicaid, as amended by the ACA, *** is a single program with a constant aim—to enable poor persons to receive basic health care when they need it. Given past expansions, plus express statutory warning that Congress may change the requirements participating States must meet, there can be no tenable claim that the ACA fails for lack of notice. Moreover, States have no entitlement to receive any Medicaid funds; they enjoy only the opportunity to accept funds on Congress' terms. *** The Federal Government, therefore, is not *** threatening States with the loss of "existing" funds from one spending program in order to induce them to opt into another program. Congress is simply requiring States to do what States have long been required to do to receive Medicaid funding: comply with the conditions Congress prescribes for participation. ***

The alternative to conditional federal spending, it bears emphasis, is not state autonomy but state marginalization. In 1965, Congress elected to nationalize health coverage for seniors through Medicare. It could similarly have established Medicaid as an exclusively federal program. *** Absent from the nationalized model, of course, is the state-level policy discretion and experimentation that is Medicaid's hallmark; undoubtedly the interests of federalism are better served when States retain a meaningful role in the implementation of a program of such importance. ***

Yes, there are federalism-based limits on the use of Congress' conditional spending power. *** The Court in *Dole* mentioned, but did not adopt, a further limitation, one hypothetically raised a half-century earlier: In "some circumstances," Congress might be prohibited from offering a "financial inducement ... so coercive as to pass the point at which 'pressure turns into compulsion.' Prior to today's decision, however, the Court has never ruled that the terms of any grant crossed the indistinct line between temptation and coercion. *** The ACA *** relates solely to the federally funded Medicaid program; if States choose not to comply, Congress has not threatened to withhold funds earmarked for any other program. Nor does the ACA use Medicaid funding to induce States to take action Congress itself could not undertake. The Federal Government undoubtedly could operate its own health-care program for poor persons, just as it operates Medicare for seniors' health care. ***

When future Spending Clause challenges arrive, as they likely will in the wake of today's decision, how will litigants and judges assess whether "a State has a legitimate choice whether to accept the federal conditions in exchange for federal funds"? Are courts to measure the number of dollars the Federal Government might withhold for noncompliance? The portion of the State's budget at stake? And which State's—or States'—budget is determinative: the lead plaintiff, all challenging States (26 in this case, many with quite different fiscal situations), or some national median? Does it matter that Florida, unlike most States, imposes no state income tax, and therefore might be able to replace foregone federal funds with new state revenue? Or that the coercion state officials in fact fear is punishment at the ballot box for turning down a politically popular federal grant?

The coercion inquiry, therefore, appears to involve political judgments that defy judicial calculation. ***

At bottom, my colleagues' position is that the States' reliance on federal funds limits Congress' authority to alter its spending programs. This gets things backwards: Congress, not the States, is tasked with spending federal money in service of the general welfare. And each successive Congress is empowered to appropriate funds as it sees fit. When the 110th Congress reached a conclusion about Medicaid funds that differed from its predecessors' view, it abridged no State's right to "existing," or "pre-existing," funds. For, in fact, there are no such funds. There is only money States *anticipate* receiving from future Congresses. ***

JUSTICE SCALIA, JUSTICE KENNEDY, JUSTICE THOMAS, and JUSTICE ALITO [concurring with CHIEF JUSTICE ROBERTS on this issue]

*** Coercing States to accept conditions risks the destruction of the "unique role of the States in our system." *** When a heavy federal tax is levied to support a federal program that offers large grants to the States, States may, as a practical matter, be unable to refuse to participate in the federal program and to substitute a state alternative. Even if a State believes that the federal program is ineffective and inefficient, withdrawal would likely force the State to impose a huge tax increase on its residents, and this new state tax would come on top of the federal taxes already paid by residents to support subsidies to participating States.

Acceptance of the Federal Government's interpretation of the anticoercion rule would permit Congress to dictate policy in areas traditionally governed primarily at the state or local level. Suppose, for example, that Congress enacted legislation offering each State a grant equal to the State's entire annual expenditures for primary and secondary education. Suppose also that this funding came with conditions governing such things as school curriculum, the hiring and tenure of teachers, the drawing of school districts, the length and hours of the school day, the school calendar, a dress code for students, and rules for student discipline. *As a matter of law,* a State could turn down that offer, but if it did so, its residents would not only be required to pay the federal taxes needed to support this expensive new program, but they would also be forced to pay an equivalent amount in state taxes. And if the State gave in to the federal law, the State and its subdivisions would surrender their traditional authority in the field of education. Asked at oral argument whether such a law would be allowed under the spending power, the Solicitor General responded that it would.

Whether federal spending legislation crosses the line from enticement to coercion is often difficult to determine, and courts should not conclude that legislation is unconstitutional on this ground unless the coercive nature of an offer is unmistakably clear. In this case, however, there can be no doubt. In structuring the ACA, Congress unambiguously signaled its belief that every

State would have no real choice but to go along with the Medicaid Expansion. If the anticoercion rule does not apply in this case, then there is no such rule. ***

What the statistics suggest is confirmed by the goal and structure of the ACA. In crafting the ACA, Congress clearly expressed its informed view that no State could possibly refuse the offer that the ACA extends. *** The Federal Government does not dispute the inference that Congress anticipated 100% state participation, but it argues that this assumption was based on the fact that ACA's offer was an "exceedingly generous" gift. *** Congress could have made just the *new* funding provided under the ACA contingent on acceptance of the terms of the Medicaid Expansion. Congress took such an approach in some earlier amendments to Medicaid, separating new coverage requirements and funding from the rest of the program so that only new funding was conditioned on new eligibility extensions. *** [T]he offer of the Medicaid Expansion was one that Congress understood no State could refuse. The Medicaid Expansion therefore exceeds Congress' spending power and cannot be implemented. ***

Notes

1. **A Muscular Coercion Test?** It is unclear how far *NFIB v. Sebelius'* newly muscled coercion test will go. The factors making the ACA's Medicaid expansion unconstitutional include (1) significant change in the program, (2) state reliance on settled expectations, and (3) overall amount states could lose. Would courts uphold a congressional threat to shut off all highway funds to states that do not adopt stringent vehicle pollution controls? Where else might NFIB apply?

2. **A Gun to the Head?** The Court takes a *contractual* view of cooperative federalism: there must be "real choice" for an agreement between the federal government and state sovereigns. The difficulty is distinguishing between ordinary financial persuasion and improper compulsion. Is the financial inducement here equivalent to "a gun to the head?" Or does Medicaid expansion leave the states a difficult but constitutionally permissible choice? Does *NFIB* revise *McCulloch's* aphorism "the power to tax is the power to destroy" to "the power to spend is the power to destroy"? Are the two related?

3. **Severability.** Congress stated in the Act that if any portion were ruled unconstitutional, the rest would remain. CHIEF JUSTICE ROBERTS agreed with the four "liberals" on this issue. The dissenters took a more functionalist approach (inconsistently?) as follows:

> When an unconstitutional provision is *** part of a more comprehensive statute, the question arises as to the validity of the remaining provisions. *** [T]wo inquiries—whether the remaining provisions will operate as Congress designed them, and whether Congress would have enacted the remaining provisions standing alone—often are interrelated. *** There are, however, occasions in which the severability standard's first inquiry (statutory functionality) is not a proxy for the second inquiry (whether the Legislature intended the remaining provisions to stand alone). *** Absent the invalid portions, the other major provisions could impose enormous risks of unexpected burdens on patients, the health-care community, and the federal budget. That consequence would be in

absolute conflict with the ACA's design of "shared responsibility," and would pose a threat to the Nation that Congress did not intend. *** To sever the statute in that manner "would be to make a new law, not to enforce an old one." *** [T]he judgment on the Medicaid Expansion issue ushers in new federalism concerns and places an unaccustomed strain upon the Union. Those States that decline the Medicaid Expansion must subsidize, by the federal tax dollars taken from their citizens, vast grants to the States that accept the Medicaid Expansion. If that destabilizing political dynamic, *** is to be introduced at all, it should be by Congress, not by the Judiciary. *** [W]e would find the Act invalid in its entirety.

Critics claim the joint dissent's effort to invalidate the entire Act amounts to "an astonishing act of judicial activism," but the dissenters say the majority has arrogantly rewritten the statute. Who has the better of the argument?

3. TREATY POWER

Where is the "treaty power," an original power granted the United States under the Constitution? See Articles II and VI. Does this make a difference in how that power is analyzed? The leading case on the treaty power, *Missouri v. Holland*, 252 U.S. 416 (1920), said: "Acts of Congress are the supreme law of the land only when made in pursuance of the Constitution, while treaties are declared to be so when made under the authority of the United States." While JUSTICE HOLMES noted that the treaty involved "does not contravene any prohibitory words to be found in the Constitution," the opinion seems to assume that treaties may violate federalism principles and perhaps constitutional rights of American citizens.

In the early 1950s, a proposed constitutional amendment (the Bricker Amendment) provided (1) "a provision of a treaty which conflicts with the Constitution shall be of no force or effect," and (2) "a treaty shall become effective as internal law [only] through legislation valid in the absence of a treaty." This amendment did not become part of the Constitution, but the Supreme Court, in *Reid v. Covert*, 354 U.S. 1 (1957), said nothing in the Supremacy Clause "intimates that treaties and laws enacted pursuant to them do not have to comply with the provisions of the Constitution."

Congress and the President possess several tools to limit the domestic effects of treaties. The first, as CHIEF JUSTICE (formerly President) TAFT noted is to pass legislation: "A treaty may repeal a statute and a statute may repeal a treaty." The second is that the President and Congress can control application of treaties domestically by expressing reservations to particular treaties. Professor Johan D. van der Vyver, in "Religious Fundamentalism and Human Rights," J. INT. AFF. (1996) at pp. 34–35, says United States reservations to treaties mean: "The United States shall abide by the principles enunciated in the concerned conventions and covenants in so far as it would make no difference to the country's municipal law."

The following case examines the reach of the treaty power, albeit in dictum:

BOND v. UNITED STATES
134 S. Ct. 2077 (2014)

CHIEF JUSTICE ROBERTS delivered the opinion of the Court.

*** To fulfill the United States' obligations under the [Chemical Weapons] Convention, Congress enacted the Chemical Weapons Convention Implementation Act of 1998 *** [which] forbids any person knowingly "to develop, produce, otherwise acquire, transfer directly or indirectly, receive, stockpile, retain, own, possess, or use, or threaten to use, any chemical weapon." *** Petitioner Carol Anne Bond is a microbiologist ***. In 2006, Bond's closest friend, Myrlinda Haynes, announced that she was pregnant. When Bond discovered that her husband was the child's father, she sought revenge against Haynes. Bond stole a quantity of [two chemicals] toxic to humans *** [and] hoped that Haynes would touch the chemicals and develop an uncomfortable rash. *** The chemicals that Bond used are easy to see, and Haynes was able to avoid them all but once. *** Federal prosecutors *** charged her with two counts of possessing and using a chemical weapon ***. Bond moved to dismiss *** on the ground that [the statute] exceeded Congress's enumerated powers and invaded powers reserved to the States by the Tenth Amendment. *** The Government frequently defends federal criminal legislation on the ground that the legislation is authorized pursuant to Congress's power to regulate interstate commerce. In this case, however, *** the Government *** disavowed that argument ***. As a result, in this Court the parties have devoted significant effort to arguing whether [the statute] as applied to Bond's offense, is a necessary and proper means of executing the National Government's power to make treaties. ***

Notwithstanding this debate, it is "a well-established principle governing the prudent exercise of this Court's jurisdiction that normally the Court will not decide a constitutional question if there is some [statutory] ground upon which to dispose of the case." ***

To begin, as a matter of natural meaning, an educated user of English would not describe Bond's crime as involving a "chemical weapon." *** When used in the manner here, the chemicals in this case are not of the sort that an ordinary person would associate with instruments of chemical warfare *** More to the point, the use of something as a "weapon" typically connotes "[a]n instrument of offensive or defensive combat" *** [N]o speaker in natural parlance would describe Bond's feud-driven act of spreading irritating chemicals on Haynes's door knob and mailbox as "combat." Nor do the other circumstances of Bond's offense—an act of revenge born of romantic jealousy, meant to cause discomfort, that produced nothing more than a minor thumb burn—suggest that a chemical weapon was deployed in Norristown, Pennsylvania. *** It is also clear that the laws of the Commonwealth of Pennsylvania (and every other State) are sufficient to prosecute Bond. *** Our disagreement with our colleagues reduces to whether [the statute] is "utterly clear." We think it is not, given that the definition of "chemical weapon" in a particular case can reach beyond any normal notion of such a weapon, that the context from which the statute arose demonstrates a much more limited prohibition was intended, and that the most sweeping reading of the statute would fundamentally upset the Constitution's balance between national and local power. ***

JUSTICE SCALIA, with whom JUSTICE THOMAS [and] JUSTICE ALITO [join] concurring in the judgment.

*** As sweeping and unsettling as the Chemical Weapons Convention Implementation Act of 1998 may be, it is clear beyond doubt that it covers what Bond did; and we have no authority to amend it. *** A "chemical weapon" is "[a] toxic chemical and its precursors, except where intended for a purpose not prohibited under this chapter as long as the type and quantity is consistent with such a purpose." A "toxic chemical" is "any chemical which through its chemical action on life processes can cause death, temporary incapacitation or permanent harm to humans or animals. The term includes all such chemicals, regardless of their origin or of their method of production, and regardless of whether they are produced in facilities, in munitions or elsewhere." A "purpose not prohibited" is "[a]ny peaceful purpose related to an industrial, agricultural, research, medical, or pharmaceutical activity or other activity." *** Bond possessed and used "chemical[s] which through [their] chemical action on life processes can cause death, temporary incapacitation or permanent harm." Thus, she possessed "toxic chemicals." And, because they were not possessed or used only for a "purpose not prohibited," they were "chemical weapons." Ergo, Bond violated the Act. End of statutory analysis, I would have thought.

The Court does not think the interpretive exercise so simple. But that is only because its result-driven antitextualism befogs what is evident. *** No one should have to ponder the totality of the circumstances in order to determine whether his conduct is a felony. Yet that is what the Court will now require of all future handlers of harmful toxins—that is to say, all of us. Thanks to the Court's revisions, the Act, which before was merely broad, is now broad and unintelligible. ***

Since the Act is clear, the *real* question this case presents is whether the Act is constitutional as applied to petitioner. An unreasoned and citation-less sentence from our opinion in *Missouri v. Holland,* 252 U.S. 416 (1920), purported to furnish the answer: "If the treaty is valid"—and no one argues that the Convention is not— "there can be no dispute about the validity of the statute under Article I, § 8, as a necessary and proper means to execute the powers of the Government." *** Congress has the power "[t]o make all Laws which shall be necessary and proper for carrying into Execution the foregoing Powers and all other Powers vested by this Constitution in the Government of the United States, or in any Department or Officer thereof." One such "other Powe[r]" appears in Article II, § 2, cl. 2: "[The President] shall have Power, by and with the Advice and Consent of the Senate, to make Treaties, provided two thirds of the Senators present concur." Read together, the two Clauses empower Congress to pass laws "necessary and proper for carrying into Execution ... [the] Power ... to make Treaties."

It is obvious what the Clauses, read together, do *not* say. They do not authorize Congress to enact laws for carrying into execution "Treaties," even treaties that do not execute themselves, such as the Chemical Weapons Convention. Surely it makes sense, the Government contends, that Congress would have the power to carry out the obligations to which the President and the Senate have committed the Nation. The power to "carry into Execution" the "Power ... to make Treaties," it insists, *has to* mean the power to execute the treaties themselves.

That argument, which makes no pretense of resting on text, unsurprisingly misconstrues it. Start with the phrase "to make Treaties." A treaty is a contract with a foreign nation *made,* the Constitution states, by the President with the concurrence of "two thirds of the Senators present." That is true of self-executing and non-self-executing treaties alike; the Constitution does not distinguish between the two. So, because the President and the Senate can enter into a non-self-executing compact with a foreign nation but can never by themselves (without the House) give that compact domestic effect through legislation, the power of the President and the Senate "to make" a Treaty cannot possibly mean to "enter into a compact with a foreign nation and then give that compact domestic legal effect." *** Upon the President's agreement and the Senate's ratification, a treaty—no matter what kind—has been *made* and is not susceptible of any more making.

How might Congress have helped "carr[y]" the power to make the treaty—here, the Chemical Weapons Convention—"into Execution"? In any number of ways. It could have appropriated money for hiring treaty negotiators, empowered the Department of State to appoint those negotiators, formed a commission to study the benefits and risks of entering into the agreement, or paid for a bevy of spies to monitor the treaty-related deliberations of other potential signatories. The Necessary and Proper Clause interacts similarly with other Article II powers: "[W]ith respect to the executive branch, the Clause would allow Congress to institute an agency to help the President wisely employ his pardoning power.... Most important, the Clause allows Congress to establish officers to assist the President in exercising his 'executive Power.'

But a power to help the President *make* treaties is not a power to *implement* treaties already made. Once a treaty has been made, Congress's power to do what is "necessary and proper" to assist the making of treaties drops out of the picture. To legislate compliance with the United States' treaty obligations, Congress must rely upon its independent (though quite robust) Article I, § 8, powers.

"[T]he Constitutio[n] confer[s] upon Congress ... not all governmental powers, but only discrete, enumerated ones." *** But in *Holland,* the proponents of unlimited congressional power found a loophole: "By negotiating a treaty and obtaining the requisite consent of the Senate, the President ... may endow Congress with a source of legislative authority independent of the powers enumerated in Article I." Though *Holland* 's change to the Constitution's text appears minor (the power to carry into execution the *power to make treaties* becomes the power to carry into execution *treaties*), the change to its structure is seismic.

To see why vast expansion of congressional power is not just a remote possibility, consider two features of the modern practice of treaty making. In our Nation's early history, and extending through the time when *Holland* was written, treaties were typically bilateral, and addressed only a small range of topics relating to the obligations of each state to the other, and to citizens of the other—military neutrality, for example, or military alliance, or guarantee of most-favored-nation trade treatment. But beginning in the last half of the last century, many treaties were "detailed multilateral instruments negotiated and drafted at international conferences," and they sought to regulate states' treatment of their own citizens, or even "the activities of individuals and private entities." "[O]ften vague and open-ended," such treaties "touch on almost every aspect of domestic civil, political, and cultural life."

Consider also that, at least according to some scholars, the Treaty Clause comes with no implied subject-matter limitations. On this view, "[t]he Tenth Amendment ... does not limit the power to make treaties or other agreements," and the treaty power can be used to regulate matters of strictly domestic concern.

If that is true, then the possibilities of what the Federal Government may accomplish, with the right treaty in hand, are endless and hardly farfetched. It could begin, as some scholars have suggested, with abrogation of this Court's constitutional rulings. For example, the holding that a statute prohibiting the carrying of firearms near schools went beyond Congress's enumerated powers, could be reversed by negotiating a treaty with Latvia providing that neither sovereign would permit the carrying of guns near schools. Similarly, Congress could reenact the invalidated part of the Violence Against Women Act of 1994 that provided a civil remedy for victims of gender-motivated violence, just so long as there were a treaty on point— and some authors think there already is.

But reversing some of this Court's decisions is the least of the problem. Imagine the United States' entry into an Antipolygamy Convention, which called for—and Congress enacted—legislation providing that, when a spouse of a man with more than one wife dies intestate, the surviving husband may inherit no part of the estate. Constitutional? *** [G]iven the Antipolygamy Convention, *Holland* would uphold it. Or imagine that, to execute a treaty, Congress enacted a statute prohibiting state inheritance taxes on real property. Constitutional? Of course not. *** As these examples show, *Holland* places Congress only one treaty away from acquiring a general police power.

The Necessary and Proper Clause cannot bear such weight. *** No law that flattens the principle of state sovereignty, whether or not "necessary," can be said to be "proper." *** We would not give the Government's support of the *Holland* principle the time of day were we confronted with "treaty-implementing" legislation that abrogated the freedom of speech or some other constitutionally protected individual right. ***

The Government raises a functionalist objection: If the Constitution does not limit a *self-executing treaty* to the subject matter delineated in Article I, §

8, then it makes no sense to impose that limitation upon a statute implementing a *non-self-executing treaty*. The premise of the objection (that the power to make self-executing treaties is limitless) is, to say the least, arguable. But even if it is correct, refusing to extend that proposition to non-self-executing treaties makes a great deal of sense. Suppose, for example, that the self-aggrandizing Federal Government wishes to take over the law of intestacy. If the President and the Senate find in some foreign state a ready accomplice, they have two options. First, they can enter into a treaty with "stipulations" specific enough that they "require no legislation to make them operative," which would mean in this example something like a comprehensive probate code. But for that to succeed, the President and a supermajority of the Senate would need to reach agreement on all the details—which, when once embodied in the treaty, could not be altered or superseded by ordinary legislation. The second option—far the better one—is for Congress to gain lasting and flexible control over the law of intestacy by means of a non-self-executing treaty. "[Implementing] legislation is as much subject to modification and repeal by Congress as legislation upon any other subject." And to make such a treaty, the President and Senate would need to agree only that they desire power over the law of intestacy. ***

We have here a supposedly "narrow" opinion which, in order to be "narrow," sets forth interpretive principles never before imagined that will bedevil our jurisprudence (and proliferate litigation) for years to come. The immediate product of these interpretive novelties is a statute that should be the envy of every lawmaker bent on trapping the unwary with vague and uncertain criminal prohibitions. All this to leave in place an ill-considered *ipse dixit* that enables the fundamental constitutional principle of limited federal powers to be set aside by the President and Senate's exercise of the treaty power. We should not have shirked our duty and distorted the law to preserve that assertion; we should have welcomed and eagerly grasped the opportunity—nay, the obligation—to consider and repudiate it.

JUSTICE THOMAS, with whom JUSTICE SCALIA [and] JUSTICE ALITO [join] concurring in the judgment.

*** I write separately to suggest that the Treaty Power is itself a limited federal power. *** [T]o interpret the Treaty Power as extending to every conceivable domestic subject matter—even matters without any nexus to foreign relations—would destroy the basic constitutional distinction between domestic and foreign powers. *** And a treaty-based police power would pose an even greater threat when exercised through a self-executing treaty because it would circumvent the role of the House of Representatives in the legislative process.

I doubt the Treaty Power creates such a gaping loophole in our constitutional structure. *** Today, it is enough to highlight some of the structural and historical evidence suggesting that the Treaty Power can be used to arrange intercourse with other nations, but not to regulate purely domestic affairs. *** The Treaty Power was not drafted on a blank slate. *** Preconstitutional practice *** reflects the use of the treaty-making power only for matters of international intercourse; that practice provides no support for using treaties to regulate purely domestic affairs. *** [E]vidence from the ratification campaign suggests that the Treaty Power was limited and, in particular, confined to matters of intercourse with other nations. *** Whatever its other defects, *Missouri v. Holland* is consistent with that view. *** The Court observed that the treaty at issue addressed *migratory* birds that were "only transitorily within the State and ha[d] no permanent habitat therein." ***

JUSTICE ALITO, concurring in the judgment.

*** The control of true chemical weapons *** is a matter of great international concern, and therefore the heart of the Convention clearly represents a valid exercise of the treaty power. But insofar as the Convention may be read to obligate the United States to enact domestic legislation criminalizing conduct of the sort at issue in this case, which typically is the sort of conduct regulated by the States, the Convention exceeds the scope of the treaty power *** cannot be regarded as necessary and proper to carry into execution the treaty power, and accordingly it lies outside Congress' reach unless supported by some other power enumerated in the Constitution. ***

Notes

1.   **Statutory Construction.** Does the majority unfairly construe the statute to avoid the constitutional question? Would the majority, if necessary, reach the same result in construing the treaty power as the concurrences?

2.   **Executive Overreach?** Why did the government prosecute Bond for "possessing and using a chemical weapon?" Is its prosecutorial authority justifiable under the Commerce Clause?

3.   **Treaty Power.** The North American Free Trade Agreement (NAFTA) was negotiated by President Clinton, passed by majorities of both houses of Congress, and signed by the President. NAFTA was not ratified by 2/3rds of the Senate. Did it need to be? What additional information concerning NAFTA would help answer this question? Is the "Commerce with foreign Nations" clause relevant? Can the President terminate a treaty, or must the Senate ratify termination?

4.   **Choice of Powers.** What Article I powers might Congress rely upon (if any) to accomplish the following, and how might it exercise such powers?

- Punishing hate crimes based on victim race or sexual orientation.

- Barring execution of pregnant women.

- Encouraging state and local school voucher programs.

- Prohibiting homosexual marriages.

- Outlawing bungee-jumping.

D. FEDERALISM LIMITS ON ARTICLE I POWERS

Assuming Congress has a substantive power justifying regulation in a particular area, are there any federalism bars to its exercise of power vis-à-vis the states? Even if a law is within Congress' powers, is it unconstitutional if it intrudes too much on state authority? If so, when is intrusion on state authority excessive?

The materials in this section consider the extent to which Congress can regulate the States using its extensive, if not limitless, Commerce Clause powers. Section 1 examines attempts by Congress to regulate a state, command a state to engage in regulation, or command state officials to assist in executing federal laws without violating the Tenth Amendment. Section 2 assesses the role of the Eleventh Amendment and, more broadly, state sovereign immunity in insulating states from suits authorized by Congress.

1. THE TENTH AMENDMENT AND REGULATION OF THE STATES

GARCIA v. SAN ANTONIO METROPOLITAN TRANSIT AUTHORITY
469 U.S. 528 (1985)

JUSTICE BLACKMUN delivered the opinion of the Court.

We revisit in these cases an issue raised in *National League of Cities v. Usery*, 426 U.S. 833 (1976). In that litigation, this Court, by a sharply divided vote, ruled that the Commerce Clause does not empower Congress to enforce the minimum-wage and overtime provisions of the Fair Labor Standards Act (FLSA) against the States "in areas of traditional governmental functions." Although *National League of Cities* supplied some examples of "traditional governmental functions," it did not offer a general explanation of how a "traditional" function is to be distinguished from a "nontraditional" one. Since then, federal and state courts have struggled with the task, thus imposed, of identifying a traditional function for purposes of state immunity under the Commerce Clause.

In the present cases, a Federal District Court concluded that municipal ownership and operation of a mass-transit system is a traditional governmental function and thus, under *National League of Cities*, is exempt from the obligations imposed by the FLSA. *** Our examination of this "function" standard applied in these and other cases over the last eight years now persuades us that the attempt to draw the boundaries of state regulatory immunity in terms of "traditional governmental function" is not only unworkable but is also inconsistent with established principles of federalism and, indeed, with those very federalism principles on which *National League of Cities* purported to rest. That case, accordingly, is overruled. ***

Appellees have not argued that SAMTA is immune from regulation under the FLSA on the ground that it is a local transit system engaged in intrastate commercial activity. *** Were SAMTA a privately owned and operated enterprise, it could not credibly argue that Congress exceeded the bounds of its Commerce Clause powers in prescribing minimum wages and overtime rates for SAMTA's employees. Any constitutional exemption from the requirements of the FLSA therefore must rest on SAMTA's status as a governmental entity rather than on the "local" nature of its operations. ***

[U]nder *National League of Cities*, four conditions must be satisfied before a state activity may be deemed immune from a particular federal regulation under the Commerce Clause. First, it is said that the federal statute at issue must regulate "the 'States as States.'" Second, the statute must "address matters that are indisputably 'attribute[s]' of state sovereignty.'" Third, state compliance with the federal obligation must "directly impair [the States'] ability 'to structure integral operations in areas of traditional governmental functions.'" "Finally, the relation of state and federal interests must not be such that 'the nature of the federal interest *** justifies state submission.'"

The controversy in the present cases has focused on the third requirement—that the challenged federal statute trench on "traditional governmental functions." *** We find it difficult, if not impossible, to identify an organizing principle that places each of the cases in the first group on one side of a line and each of the cases in the second group on the other side. The constitutional distinction between licensing drivers and regulating traffic, for example, or between operating a highway authority and operating a mental health facility, is elusive at best. *** The most obvious defect of a historical approach to state immunity is that it prevents a court from accommodating changes in the historical functions of States, changes that have resulted in a number of once-private functions like education being assumed by the States and their subdivisions. At the same time, the only apparent virtue of a rigorous historical standard, namely, its promise of a reasonably objective measure for state immunity, is illusory. Reliance on history as an organizing principle results in line-drawing of the most arbitrary sort; the genesis of state governmental functions stretches over a historical continuum from before the Revolution to the present, and courts would have to decide by fiat precisely how longstanding a pattern of state involvement had to be for federal regulatory authority to be defeated.

A nonhistorical standard for selecting immune governmental functions is likely to be just as unworkable as is a historical standard. The goal of identifying "uniquely" governmental functions, for example, has been rejected by the Court [in] part because the notion of a "uniquely" governmental function is unmanageable. ***

We believe, however, that there is a more fundamental problem at work here, a problem that explains why the Court was never able to provide a basis for the governmental/proprietary distinction in the intergovernmental tax-immunity cases and why an attempt to draw similar distinctions with respect to federal regulatory authority under *National League of Cities* is unlikely to succeed regardless of how the distinctions are phrased. The problem is that neither the governmental/proprietary distinction nor any other that purports to separate out important governmental functions can be faithful to the role of federalism in a democratic society. The essence of our federal system is that within the realm of authority left open to them under the Constitution, the States must be equally free to engage in any activity that their citizens choose for the common weal, no matter how unorthodox or unnecessary anyone else—including the judiciary—deems state involvement to be. Any rule of state immunity that looks to the "traditional," "integral," or "necessary" nature of governmental functions inevitably invites an unelected federal judiciary to make decisions about which state policies it favors and which ones it dislikes. ***

We therefore now reject, as unsound in principle and unworkable in practice, a rule of state immunity from federal regulation that turns on a judicial appraisal of whether a particular governmental function is "integral" or "traditional." *** We accordingly return to the underlying issue that confronted this Court in *National League of Cities*—the manner in which the Constitution insulates States from the reach of Congress' power under the Commerce Clause.

The central theme of *National League of Cities* was that the States occupy a special position in our constitutional system and that the scope of Congress' authority under the Commerce Clause must reflect that position. Of course, the Commerce Clause by its specific language does not provide any special limitation on Congress' actions with respect to the States. It is equally true, however, that the text of the Constitution provides the beginning rather than the final answer to every inquiry into questions of federalism, for "[b]ehind the words of the constitutional provisions are postulates which limit and control." *National League of Cities* reflected the general conviction that the Constitution precludes "the National Government [from] devour[ing] the essentials of state sovereignty." In order to be faithful to the underlying federal premises of the Constitution, courts must look for the "postulates which limit and control."

What has proved problematic is not the perception that the Constitution's federal structure imposes limitations on the Commerce Clause, but rather the nature and content of those limitations. *** The States unquestionably do "retai[n] a significant measure of sovereign authority." They do so, however, only to the extent that the Constitution has not divested them of their original powers and transferred those powers to the Federal Government. ***

As a result, to say that the Constitution assumes the continued role of the States is to say little about the nature of that role. Only recently, this Court recognized that the purpose of the constitutional immunity recognized in *National League of Cities* is not to preserve "a sacred province of state autonomy." With rare exceptions, like the guarantee, in Article IV, § 3, of state territorial integrity, the Constitution does not carve out express elements of state sovereignty that Congress may not employ its delegated powers to displace. The power of the Federal Government is a "power to be respected" as well, and the fact that the States remain sovereign as to all powers not vested in Congress or denied them by the Constitution offers no guidance about where the frontier between state and federal power lies. ***

When we look for the States' "residuary and inviolable sovereignty," in the shape of the constitutional scheme rather than in predetermined notions of sovereign power, a different measure of state sovereignty emerges. Apart from the limitation on federal authority inherent in the delegated nature of Congress' Article I powers, the principal means chosen by the Framers to ensure the role of the States in the federal system lies in the structure of the Federal Government itself. It is no novelty to observe that the composition of the Federal Government was designed in large part to protect the States from overreaching by Congress.

[The extent to which the structure of the Federal Government itself was relied on to insulate the interests of the States is evident in the views of the Framers. *** In short, the Framers chose to rely on a federal system in which special restraints on federal power over the States inhered principally in the workings of the National Government itself, rather than in discrete limitations on the objects of federal authority. State sovereign interests, then, are more properly protected by procedural safeguards inherent in the structure of the federal system than by judicially created limitations on federal power.

The effectiveness of the federal political process in preserving the States' interests is apparent even today in the course of federal legislation. On the one hand, the States have been able to direct a substantial proportion of federal revenues into their own treasuries in the form of general and program-specific grants in aid. The federal role in assisting state and local governments is a longstanding one. *** Moreover, at the same time that the States have exercised their influence to obtain federal support, they have been able to exempt themselves from a wide variety of obligations imposed by Congress under the Commerce Clause. *** The fact that some federal statutes such as the FLSA extend general obligations to the States cannot obscure the extent to which the political position of the States in the federal system has served to minimize the burdens that the States bear under the Commerce Clause.

We realize that changes in the structure of the Federal Government have taken place since 1789, not the least of which has been the substitution of popular election of Senators by the adoption of the Seventeenth Amendment in 1913, and that these changes may work to alter the influence of the States in the federal political process. Nonetheless, against this background, we are convinced that the fundamental limitation that the constitutional scheme imposes on the Commerce Clause to protect the "States as States" is one of process rather than one of result. Any substantive restraint on the exercise of Commerce Clause powers must find its justification in the procedural nature of this basic limitation, and it must be tailored to compensate for possible failings in the national political process rather than to dictate a "sacred province of state autonomy."

Insofar as the present cases are concerned, then, we need go no further than to state that we perceive nothing in the overtime and minimum-wage requirements of the FLSA, as applied to SAMTA, that is destructive of state sovereignty or violative of any constitutional provision. SAMTA faces nothing more than the same minimum-wage and overtime obligations that hundreds of thousands of other employers, public as well as private, have to meet. *** These cases do not require us to identify or define what affirmative limits the constitutional structure might impose on federal action affecting the States under the Commerce Clause. ***

JUSTICE POWELL, with whom THE CHIEF JUSTICE, JUSTICE REHNQUIST, and JUSTICE O'CONNOR join, dissenting.

*** [T]oday's decision effectively reduces the Tenth Amendment to meaningless rhetoric when Congress acts pursuant to the Commerce Clause. *** The Court apparently thinks that the State's success at obtaining federal funds for various projects and exemptions from the obligations of some federal statutes is indicative of the effectiveness of the federal political process in preserving the States' interests. *** But such political success is not relevant to the question whether the political processes are the proper means of enforcing constitutional limitations. The fact that Congress generally does not transgress constitutional limits on its power to reach state activities does not make judicial review any less necessary to rectify the cases in which it does do so. The States' role in our system of government is a matter of constitutional law, not of legislative grace. ˄ ˄ ˄

More troubling than the logical infirmities in the Court's reasoning is the result of its holding, i.e., that federal political officials, invoking the Commerce Clause, are the sole judges of the limits of their own power. *** Much of the initial opposition to the Constitution was rooted in the fear that the National Government would be too powerful and eventually would eliminate the States as viable political entities. *** This history, which the Court simply ignores, documents the integral role of the Tenth Amendment in our constitutional theory. It exposes as well, I believe, the fundamental character of the Court's error today. Far from being "unsound in principle," judicial enforcement of the Tenth Amendment is essential to maintaining the federal system so carefully designed by the Framers and adopted in the Constitution. ***

In *National League of Cities*, we spoke of fire prevention, police protection, sanitation, and public health as "typical of [the services] performed by state and local governments in discharging their dual functions of administering the public law and furnishing public services." Not only are these activities remote from any normal concept of interstate commerce, they are also activities that epitomize the concerns of local, democratic self-government. In emphasizing the need to protect traditional governmental functions, we identified the kinds of activities engaged in by state and local governments that affect the everyday lives of citizens. These are services that people are in a position to understand and evaluate, and in a democracy, have the right to oversee. We recognized that *** the States and local governments are better able than the National Government to perform them.

The Court maintains that the standard approved in *National League of Cities* "disserves principles of democratic self-goverance." In reaching this conclusion, the Court looks myopically only to persons elected to positions in the Federal Government. It disregards entirely the far more effective role of democratic self-government at the state and local levels. *** The administration and enforcement of federal laws and regulations necessarily are largely in the hands of staff and civil service employees. These employees may have little or no knowledge of the States and localities that will be affected by the statutes and regulations for which they are responsible. *** [M]embers of the immense federal bureaucracy are not elected, know less about the services traditionally rendered by States and localities, and are inevitably less responsive to recipients of such services, than are state legislatures, city councils, boards of supervisors, and state and local commissions, boards, and agencies. It is at these state and local levels—not in Washington as the Court so mistakenly thinks—that "democratic self-government" is best exemplified.

The question presented in these cases is whether the extension of the FLSA to the wages and hours of employees of a city-owned transit system unconstitutionally impinges on fundamental state sovereignty. The Court's sweeping holding does far more than simply answer this question in the negative. In overruling *National League of Cities*, today's opinion apparently authorizes federal control, under the auspices of the Commerce Clause, over the terms and conditions of employment of all state and local employees. ***

The Court emphasizes that municipal operation of an intra-city mass transit system is relatively new in the life of our country. It nevertheless is a classic example of the type of service traditionally provided by local government. It is local by definition. It is indistinguishable in principle from the traditional services of providing and maintaining streets, public lighting, traffic control, water, and sewerage systems. *** State and local officials of course must be intimately familiar with these services and sensitive to their quality as well as cost. Such officials also know that their constituents and the press respond to the adequacy, fair distribution, and cost of these services. It is this kind of state and local control and accountability that the Framers understood would insure the vitality and preservation of the federal system that the Constitution explicitly requires. ***

JUSTICE REHNQUIST, dissenting. [omitted]

JUSTICE O'CONNOR, with whom JUSTICE POWELL and JUSTICE REHNQUIST join, dissenting.

*** Due to the emergence of an integrated and industrialized national economy, this Court has been required to examine and review a breathtaking expansion of the powers of Congress. In doing so the Court correctly perceived that the Framers of our Constitution intended Congress to have sufficient power to address national problems. But the Framers were not single-minded. The Constitution is animated by an array of intentions. Just as surely as the Framers envisioned a National Government capable of solving national problems, they also envisioned a republic whose vitality was assured by the diffusion of power not only among the branches of the Federal Government, but also between the Federal Government and the States. In the 18th century these intentions did not conflict because technology had not yet converted every local problem into a national one. A conflict has now emerged, and the Court today retreats rather than reconcile the Constitution's dual concerns for federalism and an effective commerce power. *** [A]ll that stands between the remaining essentials of state sovereignty and Congress is the latter's underdeveloped capacity for self-restraint. ***

NEW YORK v. UNITED STATES
505 U.S. 144 (1992).

JUSTICE O'CONNOR delivered the opinion of the Court.

This case implicates one of our Nation's newest problems of public policy and perhaps our oldest question of constitutional law. *** In this case, we address the constitutionality of three provisions of the Low–Level Radioactive Waste Policy Amendments Act of 1985. *** We conclude that while Congress has substantial power under the Constitution to encourage the States to provide for the disposal of the radioactive waste generated within their borders, the Constitution does not confer upon Congress the ability simply to compel the States to do so. ***

Faced with the possibility that the Nation would be left with no disposal sites for low level radioactive waste, Congress responded by enacting the Low-Level Radioactive Waste Policy Act. Relying largely on a report submitted by the National Governors' Association, Congress declared a federal policy of holding each State "responsible for providing for the availability of capacity either within or outside the State for the disposal of low-level radioactive waste generated within its borders." *** The 1980 Act authorized States to enter into regional compacts that, once ratified by Congress, would have the authority beginning in 1986 to restrict the use of their disposal facilities to waste generated within member States.

By 1985, only three approved regional compacts had operational disposal facilities ***. Congress once again took up the issue of waste disposal. *** The 1985 Act was again based largely on a proposal submitted by the National Governors' Association. In broad outline, the Act embodies a compromise among the sited and unsited States. The sited States agreed to extend for seven years the period in which they would accept low level radioactive waste from other States. In exchange, the unsited States agreed to end their reliance on the sited States by 1992. ***

The Act provides three types of incentives to encourage the States to comply with their statutory obligation to provide for the disposal of waste generated within their borders.

1. Monetary incentives. One quarter of the surcharges collected by the sited States must be transferred to an escrow account held by the Secretary of Energy. The Secretary then makes payments from this account to each State that has *** ratified legislation either joining a regional compact or indicating an intent to develop a disposal facility within the State. ***

2. Access incentives. The second type of incentive involves the denial of access to disposal sites. States that fail to meet the July 1986 deadline may be charged twice the ordinary surcharge for the remainder of 1986 and may be denied access to disposal facilities thereafter. ***

3. The take title provision. The third type of incentive is the most severe. The Act provides: "If a State (or, where applicable, a compact region) in which low-level radioactive waste is generated is unable to provide for the disposal

of all such waste generated within such State or compact region by January 1, 1996, each State in which such waste is generated *** shall take title to the waste, be obligated to take possession of the waste, and shall be liable for all damages directly or indirectly incurred by such generator or owner as a consequence of the failure of the State to take possession of the waste." ***

New York, a State whose residents generate a relatively large share of the Nation's low level radioactive waste, did not join a regional compact. Instead, the State complied with the Act's requirements by enacting legislation providing for the siting and financing of a disposal facility in New York. *** [P]etitioners claim only that the Act is inconsistent with the Tenth Amendment and the Guarantee Clause. *** [T]he task of ascertaining the constitutional line between federal and state power has given rise to many of the Court's most difficult and celebrated cases. At least as far back as *Martin v. Hunter's Lessee* (1816), the Court has resolved questions "of great importance and delicacy" in determining whether particular sovereign powers have been granted by the Constitution to the Federal Government or have been retained by the States.

These questions can be viewed in either of two ways. In some cases the Court has inquired whether an Act of Congress is authorized by one of the powers delegated to Congress in Article I of the Constitution. In other cases the Court has sought to determine whether an Act of Congress invades the province of state sovereignty reserved by the Tenth Amendment. *See, e.g., Garcia v. San Antonio Metropolitan Transit Authority*, 469 U.S. 528 (1985). In a case like this one, involving the division of authority between federal and state governments, the two inquiries are mirror images of each other. If a power is delegated to Congress in the Constitution, the Tenth Amendment expressly disclaims any reservation of that power to the States; if a power is an attribute of state sovereignty reserved by the Tenth Amendment, it is necessarily a power the Constitution has not conferred on Congress. ***

Congress exercises its conferred powers subject to the limitations contained in the Constitution. Thus, for example, under the Commerce Clause Congress may regulate publishers engaged in interstate commerce, but Congress is constrained in the exercise of that power by the First Amendment. The Tenth Amendment likewise restrains the power of Congress, but this limit is not derived from the text of the Tenth Amendment itself, which is essentially a tautology. Instead, the Tenth Amendment confirms that the power of the Federal Government is subject to limits that may, in a given instance, reserve power to the States. The Tenth Amendment thus directs us to determine whether an incident of state sovereignty is protected by a limitation on an Article I power.

The benefits of this federal structure have been extensively catalogued elsewhere, but they need not concern us here. Our task would be the same even if one could prove that federalism secured no advantages to anyone. It consists not of devising our preferred system of government, but of understanding and applying the framework set forth in the Constitution. ***

This framework has been sufficiently flexible over the past two centuries to allow for enormous changes in the nature of government. *** Petitioners do not contend that Congress lacks the power to regulate the disposal of low level radioactive waste. *** Petitioners likewise do not dispute that under the Supremacy Clause Congress could, if it wished, pre-empt state radioactive waste regulation. Petitioners contend only that the Tenth Amendment limits the power of Congress to regulate in the way it has chosen. Most of our recent cases interpreting the Tenth Amendment have concerned the authority of Congress to subject state governments to generally applicable laws. *** This case presents no occasion to apply or revisit the holdings of any of these cases, as this is not a case in which Congress has subjected a State to the same legislation applicable to private parties. This case instead concerns the circumstances under which Congress may use the States as implements of regulation; that is, whether Congress may direct or otherwise motivate the States to regulate in a particular field or a particular way.

As an initial matter, Congress may not simply "commandee[r] the legislative processes of the States by directly compelling them to enact and enforce a federal regulatory program." *** While Congress has substantial powers to govern the Nation directly, including in areas of intimate concern to the States, the Constitution has never been understood to confer upon Congress the ability to require the States to govern according to Congress' instructions. *** Indeed, the question whether the Constitution should permit Congress to employ state governments as regulatory agencies was a topic of lively debate among the Framers. Under the Articles of Confederation, Congress lacked the authority in most respects to govern the people directly. *** Alexander Hamilton observed: "The great and radical vice in the construction of the existing Confederation is in the principle of LEGISLATION for STATES or GOVERNMENTS, in their CORPORATE or COLLECTIVE CAPACITIES, and as contra-distinguished from the INDIVIDUALS of whom they consist." The Federalist No. 15.

In the end, the [Constitutional] Convention opted for a Constitution in which Congress would exercise its legislative authority directly over individuals rather than over States. This choice was made clear to the subsequent state ratifying conventions. Oliver Ellsworth, a member of the Connecticut delegation in Philadelphia, explained the distinction to his State's convention: "This Constitution does not attempt to coerce sovereign bodies, states, in their political capacity. *** In providing for a stronger central government, therefore, the Framers explicitly chose a Constitution that confers upon Congress the power to regulate individuals, not States. We have always understood that even where Congress has the authority under the Constitution to pass laws requiring or prohibiting certain acts, it lacks the power directly to compel the States to require or prohibit those acts. The allocation of power contained in the Commerce Clause, for example, authorizes Congress to regulate interstate commerce directly; it does not authorize Congress to regulate state governments' regulation of interstate commerce.

This is not to say that Congress lacks the ability to encourage a State to regulate in a particular way, or that Congress may not hold out incentives to the States as a method of influencing a State's policy choices. Our cases have identified a variety of methods, short of outright coercion, by which Congress may urge a State to adopt a legislative program consistent with federal interests. Two of these methods are of particular relevance here.

First, under Congress' spending power, "Congress may attach conditions on the receipt of federal funds." *South Dakota v. Dole.* ** Second, where Congress has the authority to regulate private activity under the Commerce Clause, we have recognized Congress' power to offer States the choice of regulating that activity according to federal standards or having state law pre-empted by federal regulation. ***

By contrast, where the Federal Government compels States to regulate, the accountability of both state and federal officials is diminished. If the citizens of New York, for example, do not consider that making provision for the disposal of radioactive waste is in their best interest, they may elect state officials who share their view. That view can always be preempted under the Supremacy Clause if it is contrary to the national view, but in such a case it is the Federal Government that makes the decision in full view of the public, and it will be federal officials that suffer the consequences if the decision turns out to be detrimental or unpopular. But where the Federal Government directs the States to regulate, it may be state officials who will bear the brunt of public disapproval, while the federal officials who devised the regulatory program may remain insulated from the electoral ramifications of their decision. ***

[The Court then turned to the challenged incentives, upholding the first two.] *** The take title provision is of a different character. This third so-called "incentive" offers States, as an alternative to regulating pursuant to Congress' direction, the option of taking title to and possession of the low level radioactive waste generated within their borders and becoming liable for all damages waste generators suffer as a result of the States' failure to do so promptly. In this provision, Congress has crossed the line distinguishing encouragement from coercion.

The take title provision offers state governments a "choice" of either accepting ownership of waste or regulating according to the instructions of Congress. On one hand, the Constitution would not permit Congress simply to transfer radioactive waste from generators to state governments. Such a forced transfer, standing alone, would in principle be no different than a congressionally compelled subsidy from state governments to radioactive waste producers. The same is true of the provision requiring the States to become liable for the generators' damages. Standing alone, this provision would be indistinguishable from an Act of Congress directing the States to assume the liabilities of certain state residents. Either type of federal action would "commandeer" state governments into the service of federal regulatory purposes, and would for this reason be inconsistent with the Constitution's division of authority between federal and state governments. On the other hand, the second alternative held out to state governments—regulating pursuant to Congress' direction—would, standing alone, present a simple command to state governments to implement legislation enacted by Congress. As we have seen, the Constitution does not empower Congress to subject state governments to this type of instruction.

Because an instruction to state governments to take title to waste, standing alone, would be beyond the authority of Congress, and because a direct order to regulate, standing alone, would also be beyond the authority of Congress, it follows that Congress lacks the power to offer the States a choice between the two. *** A choice between two unconstitutionally coercive regulatory techniques is no choice at all. Either way, "the Act commandeers the legislative processes of the States by directly compelling them to enact and enforce a federal regulatory program," an outcome that has never been understood to lie within the authority conferred upon Congress by the Constitution.

Respondents emphasize the latitude given to the States to implement Congress' plan. *** This line of reasoning, however, only underscores the critical alternative a State lacks: A State may not decline to administer the federal program. No matter which path the State chooses, it must follow the direction of Congress.

The take title provision appears to be unique. *** Whether one views the take title provision as lying outside Congress' enumerated powers, or as infringing upon the core of state sovereignty reserved by the Tenth Amendment, the provision is inconsistent with the federal structure of our Government established by the Constitution. ***

The United States proposes three alternative views of the constitutional line separating state and federal authority. *** First, the United States argues that the Constitution's prohibition of congressional directives to state governments can be overcome where the federal interest is sufficiently important to justify state submission. *** But whether or not a particularly strong federal interest enables Congress to bring state governments within the orbit of generally applicable federal regulation, no Member of the Court has ever suggested that such a federal interest would enable Congress to command a state government to enact state regulation. No matter how powerful the federal interest involved, the Constitution simply does not give Congress the authority to require the States to regulate. The Constitution instead gives Congress the authority to regulate matters directly and to pre-empt contrary state regulation. Where a federal interest is sufficiently strong to cause Congress to legislate, it must do so directly; it may not conscript state governments as its agents.

Second, the United States argues that the Constitution does, in some circumstances, permit federal directives to state governments. *** These cases involve no more than an application of the Supremacy Clause's provision that federal law "shall be the supreme Law of the Land," enforceable in every State. More to the point, all involve congressional regulation of individuals, not congressional requirements that States regulate. Federal statutes enforceable in state courts do, in a sense, direct state judges to enforce them, but this sort of federal "direction" of state judges is mandated by the text of the Supremacy Clause. No comparable constitutional provision authorizes Congress to command state legislatures to legislate. ***

Third, the United States argues that the Constitution envisions a role for Congress as an arbiter of interstate disputes. *** While the Framers no doubt endowed Congress with the power to regulate interstate commerce in order to avoid further instances of the interstate trade disputes that were common under the Articles of Confederation, the Framers did not intend that Congress should exercise that power through the mechanism of mandating state regulation. The Constitution established Congress as "a superintending authority over the reciprocal trade" among the States, The Federalist No. 42, by empowering Congress to regulate that trade directly, not by authorizing Congress to issue trade-related orders to state governments. As Madison and Hamilton explained, "a sovereignty over sovereigns, a government over governments, a legislation for communities, as contradistinguished from individuals, as it is a solecism in theory, so in practice it is subversive of the order and ends of civil polity."

The sited state respondents focus their attention on the process by which the Act was formulated. *** How can a federal statute be found an unconstitutional infringement of state sovereignty when state officials consented to the statute's enactment? *** Where Congress exceeds its authority relative to the States, therefore, the departure from the constitutional plan cannot be ratified by the "consent" of state officials. *** The interests of public officials may not coincide with the Constitution's intergovernmental allocation of authority. ***

States are not mere political subdivisions of the United States. State governments are neither regional offices nor administrative agencies of the Federal Government. *** Whatever the outer limits of that sovereignty may be, one thing is clear: The Federal Government may not compel the States to enact or administer a federal regulatory program. The Constitution permits both the Federal Government and the States to enact legislation regarding the disposal of low level radioactive waste. The Constitution enables the Federal Government to pre-empt state regulation contrary to federal interests, and it permits the Federal Government to hold out incentives to the States as a means of encouraging them to adopt suggested regulatory schemes. It does not, however, authorize Congress simply to direct the States to provide for the disposal of the radioactive waste generated within their borders. ***

JUSTICE WHITE, with whom JUSTICE BLACKMUN and JUSTICE STEVENS join, dissenting in part [as to the "take title" holding].

My disagreement with the Court's analysis begins at the basic descriptive level of how the legislation at issue in this case came to be enacted ***. The Low–Level Radioactive Waste Policy Act of 1980, and its amendatory 1985 Act, resulted from the efforts of state leaders to achieve a state-based set of remedies to the waste problem. They sought not federal pre-emption or intervention, but rather congressional sanction of interstate compromises they had reached. *** [T]he 1985 Act was very much the product of cooperative federalism, in which the States bargained among themselves to achieve compromises for Congress to sanction. *** [T]hese statutes are best understood as the products of collective state action, rather than as impositions placed on States by the Federal Government. ***

[S]een as a term of an agreement entered into between the several States, this measure proves to be less constitutionally odious than the Court opines. First, the practical effect of New York's position is that because it is unwilling to honor its obligations to provide in-state storage facilities for its low-level radioactive waste, other States with such plants must accept New York's waste, whether they wish to or not. Otherwise, the many economically and socially beneficial producers of such waste in the State would have to cease their operations. The Court's refusal to force New York to accept responsibility for its own problem inevitably means that some other State's sovereignty will be impinged by it being forced, for public health reasons, to accept New York's low-level radioactive waste. ***

The Court announces that it has no occasion to revisit such decisions as *Garcia v. San Antonio Metropolitan Transit Authority*, because "this is not a case in which Congress has subjected a State to the same legislation applicable to private parties." *** The Court's distinction between a federal statute's regulation of States and private parties for general purposes, as opposed to a regulation solely on the activities of States, is unsupported by our recent Tenth Amendment cases. *** Moreover, the Court makes no effort to explain why this purported distinction should affect the analysis of Congress' power under general principles of federalism and the Tenth Amendment. *** An incursion on state sovereignty hardly seems more constitutionally acceptable if the federal statute that "commands" specific action also applies to private parties. ***

The ultimate irony of the decision today is that in its formalistically rigid obeisance to "federalism," the Court gives Congress fewer incentives to defer to the wishes of state officials in achieving local solutions to local problems. This legislation was a classic example of Congress acting as arbiter among the States in their attempts to accept responsibility for managing a problem of grave import. The States urged the National Legislature not to impose from Washington a solution to the country's low-level radioactive waste management problems. Instead, they sought a reasonable level of local and regional autonomy consistent with Art. I, § 10, cl. 3, of the Constitution. By invalidating the measure designed to ensure compliance for recalcitrant States, such as New York, the Court upsets the delicate compromise achieved among the States and forces Congress to erect several additional formalistic hurdles to clear before achieving exactly the same objective. ***

JUSTICE STEVENS, concurring in part and dissenting in part.

Under the Articles of Confederation, the Federal Government had the power to issue commands to the States. See Arts. VIII, IX. Because that indirect exercise of federal power proved ineffective, the Framers of the

Constitution empowered the Federal Government to exercise legislative authority directly over individuals within the States, even though that direct authority constituted a greater intrusion on state sovereignty. Nothing in that history suggests that the Federal Government may not also impose its will upon the several States as it did under the Articles. The Constitution enhanced, rather than diminished, the power of the Federal Government. *** [T]he Federal Government directs state governments in many realms. The Government regulates state-operated railroads, state school systems, state prisons, state elections, and a host of other state functions. Similarly, there can be no doubt that, in time of war, Congress could either draft soldiers itself or command the States to supply their quotas of troops. I see no reason why Congress may not also command the States to enforce federal water and air quality standards or federal standards for the disposition of low-level radioactive wastes. ***

PRINTZ v. UNITED STATES
521 U.S. 898 (1997)

JUSTICE SCALIA delivered the opinion of the Court.

The question presented in these cases is whether certain interim provisions of the Brady Handgun Violence Prevention Act, commanding state and local law enforcement officers to conduct background checks on prospective handgun purchasers and to perform certain related tasks, violate the Constitution.

The Gun Control Act of 1968 (GCA) establishes a detailed federal scheme governing the distribution of firearms. It prohibits firearms dealers from transferring handguns to any person under 21, not resident in the dealer's State, or prohibited by state or local law from purchasing or possessing firearms. It also forbids possession of a firearm by, and transfer of a firearm to, convicted felons, fugitives from justice, unlawful users of controlled substances, persons adjudicated as mentally defective or committed to mental institutions, aliens unlawfully present in the United States, persons dishonorably discharged from the Armed Forces, persons who have renounced their citizenship, and persons who have been subjected to certain restraining orders or been convicted of a misdemeanor offense involving domestic violence.

In 1993, Congress amended the GCA by enacting the Brady Act. The Act requires the Attorney General to establish a national instant background check system by November 30, 1998 and immediately puts in place certain interim provisions until that system becomes operative. Under the interim provisions, a firearms dealer who proposes to transfer a handgun must first: (1) receive from the transferee a statement (the Brady Form), containing the name, address and date of birth of the proposed transferee along with a sworn statement that the transferee is not among any of the classes of prohibited purchasers; (2) verify the identity of the transferee by examining an identification document; and (3) provide the "chief law enforcement officer" (CLEO) of the transferee's residence with notice of the contents (and a copy) of the Brady Form. With some exceptions, the dealer must then wait five business days before consummating the sale, unless the CLEO earlier notifies the dealer that he has no reason to believe the transfer would be illegal.

The Brady Act creates two significant alternatives to the foregoing scheme. A dealer may sell a handgun immediately if the purchaser possesses a state handgun permit issued after a background check, or if state law provides for an instant background check. In States that have not rendered one of these alternatives applicable to all gun purchasers, CLEOs are required to perform certain duties. When a CLEO receives the required notice of a proposed transfer from the firearms dealer, the CLEO must "make a reasonable effort to ascertain within 5 business days whether receipt or possession would be in violation of the law, including research in whatever State and local recordkeeping systems are available and in a national system designated by the Attorney General." The Act does not require the CLEO to take any particular action if he determines that a pending transaction would be unlawful; he may notify the firearms dealer to that effect, but is not required to do so. If, however, the CLEO notifies a gun dealer that a prospective purchaser is ineligible to receive a handgun, he must, upon request, provide the would-be purchaser with a written statement of the reasons for that determination. Moreover, if the CLEO does not discover any basis for objecting to the sale, he must destroy any records in his possession relating to the transfer, including his copy of the Brady Form. Under a separate provision of the GCA, any person who "knowingly violates [the section of the GCA amended by the Brady Act] shall be fined under this title, imprisoned for no more than 1 year, or both."

Petitioners Jay Printz and Richard Mack, the CLEOs for Ravalli County, Montana, and Graham County, Arizona, respectively, filed separate actions challenging the constitutionality of the Brady Act's interim provisions. ***

[T]he Brady Act purports to direct state law enforcement officers to participate, albeit only temporarily, in the administration of a federally enacted regulatory scheme. *** Petitioners contend that compelled enlistment of state executive officers for the administration of federal programs is, until very recent years at least, unprecedented. *** The only early federal law the Government has brought to our attention that imposed duties on state executive officers is the Extradition Act of 1793, which required the "executive authority" of a State to cause the arrest and delivery of a fugitive from justice upon the request of the executive authority of the State from which the fugitive had fled. That was in direct implementation, however, of the Extradition Clause of the Constitution itself, see Art. IV, § 2.

Not only do the enactments of the early Congresses, as far as we are aware, contain no evidence of an assumption that the Federal Government may command the States' executive power in the absence of a particularized constitutional authorization, they contain some indication of precisely the opposite assumption. On September 23, 1789—the day before its proposal of the Bill of Rights—the First Congress *** "recommended to the legislatures of the several States to pass laws, making it expressly the duty of the keepers of their [jails], to receive and safe keep therein all prisoners committed under the authority of the United States," and offered to pay 50 cents per month for each prisoner. Moreover, when Georgia refused to comply with the request, Congress's only reaction was a law authorizing the marshal in any State that failed to comply *** to rent a temporary jail until provision for a permanent one could be made. *** [T]here is not only an absence of executive-commandeering statutes in the early Congresses, but there is an absence of them in our later history as well, at least until very recent years. *** Compare *INS v. Chadha*, 462 U.S. 919 (1983), in which the legislative veto, though enshrined in perhaps hundreds of federal statutes, most of which were enacted in the 1970's and the earliest of which was enacted in 1932, was nonetheless held unconstitutional.

The constitutional practice we have examined above tends to negate the existence of the congressional power asserted here, but is not conclusive. We turn next to consideration of the structure of the Constitution, to see if we can discern among its "essential postulate[s]" a principle that controls the present cases.

It is incontestible that the Constitution established a system of "dual sovereignty." *** The Framers' experience under the Articles of Confederation had persuaded them that using the States as the instruments of federal governance was both ineffectual and provocative of federal-state conflict. *** "The Framers explicitly chose a Constitution that confers upon Congress the power to regulate individuals, not States." *** The power of the Federal Government would be augmented immeasurably if it were able to impress into its service—and at no cost to itself—the police officers of the 50 States. ***

The Constitution does not leave to speculation who is to administer the laws enacted by Congress; the President, it says, "shall take Care that the Laws be faithfully executed," personally and through officers whom he appoints (save for such inferior officers as Congress may authorize to be appointed by the "Courts of Law" or by "the Heads of Departments" who are themselves presidential appointees), Art. II, § 2. The Brady Act effectively transfers this responsibility to thousands of CLEOs in the 50 States, who are left to implement the program without meaningful Presidential control (if indeed meaningful Presidential control is possible without the power to appoint and remove). The insistence of the Framers upon unity in the Federal Executive—to insure both vigor and accountability—is well known. That unity would be shattered, and the power of the President would be subject to reduction, if Congress could act as effectively without the President as with him, by simply requiring state officers to execute its laws.

The dissent of course resorts to the last, best hope of those who defend ultra vires congressional action, the Necessary and Proper Clause. *** What destroys the dissent's Necessary and Proper Clause argument, however, is not the Tenth Amendment but the Necessary and Proper Clause itself. When a "La[w] *** for carrying into Execution" the Commerce Clause violates the principle of state sovereignty reflected in the various constitutional provisions we mentioned earlier, it is not a "La[w] *** proper for carrying into

Execution the Commerce Clause," and is thus, in the words of The Federalist, "merely [an] ac[t] of usurpation" which "deserve[s] to be treated as such." ***

The Government contends that *New York* is distinguishable on the following ground: unlike the "take title" provisions invalidated there, the background-check provision of the Brady Act does not require state legislative or executive officials to make policy, but instead issues a final directive to state CLEOs. *** The Government's distinction between "making" law and merely "enforcing" it, between "policymaking" and mere "implementation," is an interesting one. It is perhaps not meant to be the same as, but it is surely reminiscent of, the line that separates proper congressional conferral of Executive power from unconstitutional delegation of legislative authority for federal separation-of-powers purposes. *** Executive action that has utterly no policymaking component is rare, particularly at an executive level as high as a jurisdiction's chief law-enforcement officer. Is it really true that there is no policymaking involved in deciding, for example, what "reasonable efforts" shall be expended to conduct a background check? It may well satisfy the Act for a CLEO to direct that (a) no background checks will be conducted that divert personnel time from pending felony investigations, and (b) no background check will be permitted to consume more than one-half hour of an officer's time. *** Is this decision whether to devote maximum "reasonable efforts" or minimum "reasonable efforts" not preeminently a matter of policy? It is quite impossible, in short, to draw the Government's proposed line at "no policymaking," and we would have to fall back upon a line of "not too much policymaking." ***

Even assuming, moreover, that the Brady Act leaves no "policymaking" discretion with the States, we fail to see how that improves rather than worsens the intrusion upon state sovereignty. *** It is no more compatible with this independence and autonomy that their officers be "dragooned" into administering federal law, than it would be compatible with the independence and autonomy of the United States that its officers be impressed into service for the execution of state laws. ***

The Government also maintains that requiring state officers to perform discrete, ministerial tasks specified by Congress does not violate the principle of *New York* because it does not diminish the accountability of state or federal officials. This argument fails even on its own terms. By forcing state governments to absorb the financial burden of implementing a federal regulatory program, Members of Congress can take credit for "solving" problems without having to ask their constituents to pay for the solutions with higher federal taxes. And even when the States are not forced to absorb the costs of implementing a federal program, they are still put in the position of taking the blame for its burdensomeness and for its defects. Under the present law, for example, it will be the CLEO and not some federal official who stands between the gun purchaser and immediate possession of his gun. And it will likely be the CLEO, not some federal official, who will be blamed for any error (even one in the designated federal database) that causes a purchaser to be mistakenly rejected.

The dissent makes no attempt to defend the Government's basis for distinguishing *New York*, but instead advances what seems to us an even more implausible theory. *** While the Brady Act is directed to "individuals," it is directed to them in their official capacities as state officers; it controls their actions, not as private citizens, but as the agents of the State. *** To say that the Federal Government cannot control the State, but can control all of its officers, is to say nothing of significance.[15] ***

Finally, the Government puts forward a cluster of arguments that can be grouped under the heading: "The Brady Act serves very important purposes, is most efficiently administered by CLEOs during the interim period, and places a minimal and only temporary burden upon state officers." *** Assuming all the mentioned factors were true, *** [i]t is the very principle of separate state sovereignty that such a law offends, and no comparative assessment of the various interests can overcome that fundamental defect. *** The Federal Government may neither issue directives requiring the States to address particular problems, nor command the States' officers, or those of their political subdivisions, to administer or enforce a federal regulatory program. *** [N]o case-by-case weighing of the burdens or benefits is necessary. ***

JUSTICE STEVENS, with whom JUSTICE SOUTER, JUSTICE GINSBURG, and JUSTICE BREYER join, dissenting.

When Congress exercises the powers delegated to it by the Constitution, it may impose affirmative obligations on executive and judicial officers of state and local governments as well as ordinary citizens. *** The question is whether Congress, acting on behalf of the people of the entire Nation, may require local law enforcement officers to perform certain duties during the interim needed for the development of a federal gun control program. It is remarkably similar to the question, heavily debated by the Framers of the Constitution, whether the Congress could require state agents to collect federal taxes. ***

Indeed, since the ultimate issue is one of power, we must consider its implications in times of national emergency. Matters such as the enlistment of air raid wardens, the administration of a military draft, the mass inoculation of children to forestall an epidemic, or perhaps the threat of an international terrorist, may require a national response before federal personnel can be made available to respond. If the Constitution empowers Congress and the President to make an appropriate response, is there anything in the Tenth Amendment, "in historical understanding and practice, in the structure of the Constitution, [or] in the jurisprudence of this Court," that forbids the enlistment of state officers to make that response effective? More narrowly, what basis is there in any of those sources for concluding that

---

[15] Contrary to the dissent's suggestion, the distinction in our Eleventh Amendment jurisprudence between States and municipalities is of no relevance here. We long ago made clear that the distinction is peculiar to the question of whether a governmental entity is entitled to Eleventh Amendment sovereign immunity; we have refused to apply it to the question of whether a governmental entity is protected by the Constitution's guarantees of federalism, including the Tenth Amendment.

it is the Members of this Court, rather than the elected representatives of the people, who should determine whether the Constitution contains the unwritten rule that the Court announces today? *** There is not a clause, sentence, or paragraph in the entire text of the Constitution of the United States that supports the proposition that a local police officer can ignore a command contained in a statute enacted by Congress pursuant to an express delegation of power enumerated in Article I.

Under the Articles of Confederation the National Government had the power to issue commands to the several sovereign states, but it had no authority to govern individuals directly. *** That method of governing proved to be unacceptable, not because it demeaned the sovereign character of the several States, but rather because it was cumbersome and inefficient. *** Perversely, the majority's rule seems more likely to damage than to preserve the safeguards against tyranny provided by the existence of vital state governments. By limiting the ability of the Federal Government to enlist state officials in the implementation of its programs, the Court creates incentives for the National Government to aggrandize itself. In the name of State's rights, the majority would have the Federal Government create vast national bureaucracies to implement its policies. ***

The provision of the Brady Act that crosses the Court's newly defined constitutional threshold is more comparable to a statute requiring local police officers to report the identity of missing children to the Crime Control Center of the Department of Justice than to an offensive federal command to a sovereign state. If Congress believes that such a statute will benefit the people of the Nation, and serve the interests of cooperative federalism better than an enlarged federal bureaucracy, we should respect both its policy judgment and its appraisal of its constitutional power. ***

JUSTICE BREYER, with whom JUSTICE STEVENS joins, dissenting.

*** [T]he United States is not the only nation that seeks to reconcile the practical need for a central authority with the democratic virtues of more local control. At least some other countries, facing the same basic problem, have found that local control is better maintained through application of a principle that is the direct opposite of the principle the majority derives from the silence of our Constitution. The federal systems of Switzerland, Germany, and the European Union, for example, all provide that constituent states, not federal bureaucracies, will themselves implement many of the laws, rules, regulations, or decrees enacted by the central "federal" body. *** Of course, we are interpreting our own Constitution, not those of other nations, and there may be relevant political and structural differences between their systems and our own. But their experience may nonetheless cast an empirical light on the consequences of different solutions to a common legal problem— in this case the problem of reconciling central authority with the need to preserve the liberty-enhancing autonomy of a smaller constituent governmental entity. ***

Notes

1.   **Overruling?** JUSTICE BLACKMUN's switch of sides between 1976 and 1985 explains *Garcia*'s overruling of *National League of Cities*. The addition of Reagan appointees Scalia (1986) and Kennedy (1988) as well as Bush appointees Souter (1990) and Thomas (1991) may be viewed as critical to the outcome of *New York* and *Printz*. But these cases do not explicitly overrule *Garcia*. Can you reconcile these cases?

2.   **Judicial "Commandeering."** The Court attempts to distinguish "commandeering" the states in the context of "requirements that the States regulate" (unconstitutional under *New York*) or execute the laws (unconstitutional under *Printz*) from the "well established power of Congress to pass laws enforceable in state courts" (not unconstitutional under *Hunter v. Martin's Lessee*). Is this distinction justified by the text of the Constitution?

3.   **Limits to "Commandeering."** The distinction between imposing a federal rule and commandeering the states is critical. In *Reno v. Condon*, 528 U.S. 141 (2000), the Court unanimously upheld the 1994 Driver's Privacy Protection Act, which restricts disclosure by state motor vehicle departments and private parties of "personal information about any individual" contained in motor vehicle records. The Court held that the states, as owners of databases, were properly regulated under Congress' Commerce Clause powers; the statute commandeered neither legislative nor executive components of state governments.

4.   **Federalism and Social Policy**. "Mormons moved from Illinois to Utah, while African-Americans migrated from the Jim Crow South. Rail travel and, later, automobiles and airplanes enabled residents of conservative states to escape constraints on divorce and remarriage. *** [W]omen from states with restrictive abortion laws sought reproductive autonomy in more sympathetic jurisdictions. Today, the lesbian who finds herself in Utah, like the gun lover who lives in Washington, D.C., and the gambler in Pennsylvania, need only cross a state border to be free of constraining rules. There are liberties that come only with the variations in local norms made possible by federalism." Seth F. Kreimer, *Federalism and Freedom*, 574 ANNALS AM. ACAD. POL. & SCI. 66, 72 (2001).

5.   **Four New Words?** Former JUSTICE STEVENS suggested in October 2012 that Article VI be amended to read: "The *** Laws of the United States ***shall be the supreme Law of the Land; and the Judges <u>and other public officials</u> in every state shall be bound thereby ***." What would be the effects of this amendment?

2. THE ELEVENTH AMENDMENT AND STATE SOVEREIGN IMMUNITY

The cases that follow deal with the sovereign immunity of the States from suit brought under federal law. The Eleventh Amendment states that "The Judicial power of the United States shall not be construed to extend to any suit in law or equity, commenced or prosecuted against one of the United States by Citizens of another State, or by Citizens or Subjects of any Foreign State." However, the Supreme Court's reading of the Constitutional design concerning the immunity of States from suit is far from straightforward. The Eleventh Amendment, despite is language, serves more as a limit on Congress' power than the power of the Court.

A brief historical introduction is appropriate. The Eleventh Amendment responded to a 1793 Supreme Court decision, *Chisholm v. Georgia*, which allowed a diversity suit by a nonresident of Georgia against the State of Georgia to proceed in federal court. The plaintiff, a citizen of South Carolina, claimed Georgia owed him a debt incurred during the Revolutionary War. The Supreme Court held Article III allowed this suit. The following description of what happened next, taken from *Alden v. Maine*, is instructive:

> The Court's decision "fell upon the country with a profound shock." *** The States, in particular, responded with outrage to the decision. The Massachusetts Legislature, for example, denounced the decision as "repugnant to the first principles of a federal government," and called upon the State's Senators and Representatives to take all necessary steps to "remove any clause or article of the Constitution, which can be construed to imply or justify a decision, that, a State is compellable to answer in any suit by an individual or individuals in any Court of the United States." Georgia's response was more intemperate: Its House of Representatives passed a bill providing that anyone attempting to enforce the Chisholm decision would be "'guilty of felony and shall suffer death, without benefit of clergy, by being hanged.'"

> An initial proposal to amend the Constitution was introduced in the House of Representatives the day after *Chisholm* was announced; the proposal adopted as the Eleventh Amendment was introduced in the Senate promptly following an intervening recess. *** Each House spent but a single day discussing the Amendment, and the vote in each House was close to unanimous. All attempts to weaken the Amendment were defeated. *** Simply put, "The Constitution never would have been ratified if the States and their courts were to be stripped of their sovereign authority except as expressly provided by the Constitution itself." *** [S]overeign immunity derives not from the Eleventh Amendment but from the structure of the original Constitution itself. "

With this historical perspective, we now turn to three modern cases exploring the contours of the Eleventh Amendment and sovereign immunity.

SEMINOLE TRIBE OF FLORIDA v. FLORIDA
517 U.S. 44 (1996)

CHIEF JUSTICE REHNQUIST delivered the opinion of the Court.

The Indian Gaming Regulatory Act provides that an Indian tribe may conduct certain gaming activities only in conformance with a valid compact between the tribe and the State in which the gaming activities are located. The Act, passed by Congress under the Indian Commerce Clause, U.S. Const., Art. I, § 8, cl. 3, imposes upon the States a duty to negotiate in good faith with an Indian tribe toward the formation of a compact, and authorizes a tribe to bring suit in federal court against a State in order to compel performance of that duty. We hold that notwithstanding Congress' clear intent to abrogate the States' sovereign immunity, the Indian Commerce Clause does not grant Congress that power, and therefore cannot grant jurisdiction over a State that does not consent to be sued. ***

Congress passed the Indian Gaming Regulatory Act in 1988 in order to provide a statutory basis for the operation and regulation of gaming by Indian tribes. *** The Act provides that class III gaming [slot machines, casino games, banking card games, dog racing, and lotteries] is lawful only where it is: (1) authorized by an ordinance or resolution that (a) is adopted by the governing body of the Indian tribe, (b) satisfies certain statutorily prescribed requirements, and (c) is approved by the National Indian Gaming Commission; (2) located in a State that permits such gaming for any purpose by any person, organization, or entity; and (3) "conducted in conformance with a Tribal–State compact entered into by the Indian tribe and the State under paragraph (3) that is in effect." *** "Any Indian tribe having jurisdiction over the Indian lands upon which a class III gaming activity is being conducted, or is to be conducted, shall request the State in which such lands are located to enter into negotiations for the purpose of entering into a Tribal–State compact governing the conduct of gaming activities. Upon receiving such a request, the State shall negotiate with the Indian tribe in good faith to enter into such a compact."

The State's obligation to "negotiate with the Indian tribe in good faith," is made judicially enforceable. *** In September 1991, the Seminole Tribe of Indians, petitioner, sued the State of Florida and its Governor, Lawton Chiles, [alleging] that respondents had "refused to enter into any negotiation for inclusion of [certain gaming activities] in a tribal-state compact," thereby violating the "requirement of good faith negotiation" ***

Although the text of the [Eleventh] Amendment would appear to restrict only the Article III diversity jurisdiction of the federal courts, "we have understood the Eleventh Amendment to stand not so much for what it says, but for the presupposition *** which it confirms." *Blatchford v. Native Village of Noatak*, 501 U.S. 775 (1991). That presupposition has two parts: first, that each State is a sovereign entity in our federal system; and second, that "[i]t is inherent in the nature of 'face right' directions sovereignty not to be amenable to the suit of an individual without its consent." For over a century we have reaffirmed that federal jurisdiction over suits against unconsenting States "was not contemplated by the Constitution when establishing the judicial power of the United States."

Here, petitioner has sued the State of Florida and it is undisputed that Florida has not consented to the suit. *** Petitioner argues that Congress through the Act abrogated the States' immunity from suit. In order to determine whether Congress has abrogated the States' sovereign immunity, we ask two questions: first, whether Congress has "unequivocally expresse[d] its intent to abrogate the immunity," and second, whether Congress has acted "pursuant to a valid exercise of power." *** Here, *** Congress has in the Act provided an "unmistakably clear" statement of its intent to abrogate. *** [The Act refers] to the "State" in a context that makes it clear that the State is the defendant to the suit brought by an Indian tribe. *** Previously, *** we have found authority to abrogate under only two provisions of the Constitution. In *Fitzpatrick*, we recognized that the Fourteenth Amendment, by expanding federal power at the expense of state autonomy, had fundamentally altered the balance of state and federal power struck by the Constitution. *** We held that through the Fourteenth Amendment, federal power extended to intrude upon the province of the Eleventh Amendment and therefore that § 5 of the Fourteenth Amendment allowed Congress to abrogate the immunity from suit guaranteed by that Amendment.

In only one other case has congressional abrogation of the States' Eleventh Amendment immunity been upheld. In *Pennsylvania v. Union Gas Co.*, 491 U.S 1 (1989), a plurality of the Court found that the Interstate Commerce Clause, granted Congress the power to abrogate state sovereign immunity, stating that the power to regulate interstate commerce would be "incomplete without the authority to render States liable in damages." *** Following the rationale of the *Union Gas* plurality, our inquiry is limited to determining whether the Indian Commerce Clause, like the Interstate Commerce Clause, is a grant of authority to the Federal Government at the expense of the States. The answer to that question is obvious. If anything, the Indian Commerce Clause accomplishes a greater transfer of power from the States to the Federal Government than does the Interstate Commerce Clause. *** We agree *** that the plurality opinion in *Union Gas* allows no principled distinction in favor of the States to be drawn between the Indian Commerce Clause and the Interstate Commerce Clause. *** Generally, the principle of *stare decisis* *** counsel strongly against reconsideration of our precedent. Nevertheless, we always have treated *stare decisis* as a "principle of policy," and not as an "inexorable command." Our willingness to reconsider our earlier decisions has been "particularly true in constitutional cases, because in such cases 'correction through legislative action is practically impossible.'"

The Court in *Union Gas* reached a result without an expressed rationale agreed upon by a majority of the Court. *** Since it was issued, *Union Gas* has created confusion among the lower courts that have sought to understand and apply the deeply fractured decision. *** As the dissent in *Union Gas* recognized, the plurality's conclusion—that Congress could under Article I expand the scope of the federal courts' jurisdiction under Article III— "contradict[ed] our unvarying approach to Article III as setting forth the exclusive catalog of permissible federal court jurisdiction." *** Reconsidering the decision in *Union Gas*, we conclude that none of the policies underlying *stare decisis* require our continuing adherence to its holding. *** Finally, both the result in *Union Gas* and the plurality's rationale depart from our established understanding of the Eleventh Amendment and undermine the accepted function of Article III. We feel bound to conclude that *Union Gas* was wrongly decided and that it should be, and now is, overruled. ***

In overruling *Union Gas* today, we reconfirm that the background principle of state sovereign immunity embodied in the Eleventh Amendment is not so ephemeral as to dissipate when the subject of the suit is an area, like the regulation of Indian commerce, that is under the exclusive control of the Federal Government. Even when the Constitution vests in Congress complete law-making authority over a particular area, the Eleventh Amendment prevents congressional authorization of suits by private parties against unconsenting States. The Eleventh Amendment restricts the judicial power under Article III, and Article I cannot be used to circumvent the constitutional limitations placed upon federal jurisdiction. Petitioner's suit against the State of Florida must be dismissed for a lack of jurisdiction. ***

JUSTICE STEVENS, dissenting.

This case is about power—the power of the Congress of the United States to create a private federal cause of action against a State, or its Governor, for the violation of a federal right. *** The majority's opinion does not simply preclude Congress from establishing the rather curious statutory scheme under which Indian tribes may seek the aid of a federal court to secure a State's good faith negotiations over gaming regulations. Rather, it prevents Congress from providing a federal forum for a broad range of actions against States, from those sounding in copyright and patent law, to those concerning bankruptcy, environmental law, and the regulation of our vast national economy. *** There is a special irony in the fact that the error committed by the *Chisholm* majority was its decision that this Court, rather than Congress, should define the scope of the sovereign immunity defense. That, of course, is precisely the same error the Court commits today. ***

JUSTICE SOUTER, with whom JUSTICE GINSBURG and JUSTICE BREYER join, dissenting.

In holding the State of Florida immune to suit under the Indian Gaming Regulatory Act, the Court today holds for the first time since the founding of the Republic that Congress has no authority to subject a State to the jurisdiction of a federal court at the behest of an individual asserting a federal right. *** It is useful to separate three questions: (1) whether the States enjoyed sovereign immunity if sued in their own courts in the period prior to ratification of the National Constitution; (2) if so, whether after ratification the States were entitled to claim some such immunity when sued in a federal court exercising jurisdiction either because the suit was between a State and a non-state litigant who was not its citizen, or because the issue in the case raised a federal question; and (3) whether any state sovereign immunity recognized in federal court may be abrogated by Congress.

The answer to the first question is not clear, although some of the Framers assumed that States did enjoy immunity in their own courts. The second question was not debated at the time of ratification; there was no unanimity, but in due course the Court in *Chisholm v. Georgia*, 2 Dall. 419 (1793) answered that a state defendant enjoyed no such immunity. As to federal question jurisdiction, state sovereign immunity seems not to have been debated prior to ratification, the silence probably showing a general understanding at the time that the States would have no immunity in such cases. *** The Court's answer today to the third question is [at] odds with the Founders' view that common law *** was always subject to legislative amendment. In ignoring the reasons for this pervasive understanding at the time of the ratification, and in holding that a nontextual common-law rule limits a clear grant of congressional power under Article I, the Court follows a course that has brought it to grief before in our history, and promises to do so again.

The doctrine of sovereign immunity comprises two distinct rules, which are not always separately recognized. The one rule holds that the King or the Crown, as the font of law, is not bound by the law's provisions; the other provides that the King or Crown, as the font of justice, is not subject to suit in its own courts. The one rule limits the reach of substantive law; the other, the jurisdiction of the courts. *** The Eleventh Amendment, of course, repudiated *Chisholm* and clearly divested federal courts of some jurisdiction as to cases against state parties ***. There are two plausible readings of this provision's text. Under the first, it simply repeals the Citizen–State Diversity Clauses of Article III for all cases in which the State appears as a defendant. Under the second, it strips the federal courts of jurisdiction in any case in which a state defendant is sued by a citizen not its own, even if jurisdiction might otherwise rest on the existence of a federal question in the suit.

The history and structure of the Eleventh Amendment convincingly show that it reaches only to suits subject to federal jurisdiction exclusively under the Citizen–State Diversity Clauses. *** [R]eading the Eleventh Amendment solely as a limit on citizen-state diversity jurisdiction has the virtue of coherence with this Court's practice, with the views of John Marshall, with the history of the Amendment's drafting, and with its allusive language. Today's majority does not appear to disagree, at least insofar as the constitutional text is concerned; the Court concedes, after all, that "the text of the Amendment would appear to restrict only the Article III diversity jurisdiction of the federal courts." ***

Notes

1. *Seminole Tribe* **and the Eleventh Amendment.** Now that you have read both the case and the amendment carefully, consider these questions.

(a) Does the Eleventh Amendment have any effect on a suit by a citizen of Florida against the State of Florida in the Federal District Court for the Northern District of Florida?

(b) Is the Seminole Tribe a citizen of Florida? Of any state? Does this matter?

(c) Can plaintiffs circumvent the Eleventh Amendment by filing suit against state officials rather than the State itself? Why didn't the plaintiffs merely restyle their complaint in *Seminole Tribe* to name the Governor as defendant?

(d) Does the Eleventh Amendment bar suit against a city or county in federal court?

(e) Couldn't the tribe simply have filed suit in state court against the State of Florida to avoid Eleventh Amendment problems?

(f) What does the Eleventh Amendment have to do with sovereign immunity? Do you see any reason to be skeptical of "sovereign immunity," a concept developed in Europe before the American Revolution, in light of our Constitution and its values?

(g) If the Court had not barred the suit and the Seminole Tribe had proceeded to judgment, what judicial relief could be granted? Would this make any judgment an advisory opinion?

(h) Can you construct an argument for Florida based on the Tenth Amendment?

2.   **Problems.**
(a) Mary Doe, who attends Western State University, sues the University for failure to provide equal athletic programs and facilities for women in accordance with the requirements of Title IX of the Civil Rights Act of 1964. What factors would you consider in advising her whether she is foreclosed from suit in federal court under *Seminole Tribe*?

(b) Metrodata, Inc. developed and patented computer software subsequently used by Eastern State without obtaining a license from Metrodata. Metrodata asks you whether it can get around the Eleventh Amendment and sue the state in federal court. Advise Metrodata.

3.   **State Waiver of Immunity.**   If a State voluntarily removes a suit from state court to federal court, does the State waive its Eleventh Amendment immunity? In *Lapides v. Board of Regents of University System of Georgia*, 535 U.S. 613 (2002), JUSTICE BREYER wrote for a unanimous court:

> It would seem anomalous and inconsistent for a State both (1) to invoke federal jurisdiction *** contending that the 'Judicial power of the United States' extends to the case at hand, and (2) to claim Eleventh Amendment immunity *** denying that the 'Judicial power of the United States' extends to the case at hand. *** [W]here a State *voluntarily* becomes a party to a cause and submits its rights for judicial determination, it will be bound thereby and cannot escape the result of its own voluntary act by invoking the prohibitions of the Eleventh Amendment.

4.   **Exception to Eleventh Amendment Immunity**. In *Verizon Maryland v. Public Service Commission of Maryland*, 535 U.S. 635 (2002), the Court allowed a claim for prospective injunctive and declaratory relief against a state commission based on its violation of the Constitution, citing *Ex Parte Young*, 209 U.S. 123 (1908).

ALDEN v. MAINE
527 U.S. 706 (1999)

JUSTICE KENNEDY delivered the opinion of the Court.

In 1992, petitioners, a group of probation officers, *** alleged [in a state court suit that] the State had violated the overtime provisions of the Fair Labor Standards Act of 1938 (FLSA), and sought compensation and liquidated damages. *** We hold that the powers delegated to Congress under Article I of the United States Constitution do not include the power to subject nonconsenting States to private suits for damages in state courts. ***

We have *** sometimes referred to the States' immunity from suit as "Eleventh Amendment immunity." The phrase is convenient shorthand but something of a misnomer, for the sovereign immunity of the States neither derives from nor is limited by the terms of the Eleventh Amendment. Rather, *** the States' immunity from suit is a fundamental aspect of the sovereignty which the States enjoyed before the ratification of the Constitution, and which they retain today (either literally or by virtue of their admission into the Union upon an equal footing with the other States) except as altered by the plan of the Convention or certain constitutional Amendments.   *** Although the American people had rejected other aspects of English political theory, the doctrine that a sovereign could not be sued without its consent was universal in the States when the Constitution was drafted and ratified. [For example, Alexander Hamilton in The Federalist No. 81 wrote:]

> It is inherent in the nature of sovereignty not to be amenable to the suit of an individual without its consent. *** To what purpose would it be to authorize suits against States for the debts they owe? How could recoveries be enforced? It is evident that it could not be done without waging war against the contracting State; and to ascribe to the federal courts, by mere implication, and in destruction of the preexisting right of the State governments, a power which would involve such a consequence, would be altogether forced and unwarrantable. ***

In this case we must determine whether Congress has the power, under Article I, to subject nonconsenting States to private suits in their own courts. As the foregoing discussion makes clear, the fact that the Eleventh Amendment by its terms limits only "the Judicial power of the United States" does not resolve the question. *** While the constitutional principle of sovereign immunity does pose a bar to federal jurisdiction over suits against nonconsenting States, *** "there is also the postulate that States of the Union, still possessing attributes of sovereignty, shall be immune from suits, without their consent, save where there has been 'a surrender of this immunity in the plan of the convention.'" *** This separate and distinct structural principle is not directly related to the scope of the judicial power established by Article III, but inheres in the system of federalism established by the Constitution. *** When a State asserts its immunity to suit, the question is not the primacy of federal law but the implementation of the law in a manner consistent with the constitutional sovereignty of the States. ***

Petitioners contend that because the ratification debates and the events surrounding the adoption of the Eleventh Amendment focused on the States' immunity from suit in federal courts, the historical record gives no instruction as to the founding generation's intent to preserve the States' immunity from suit in their own courts. We believe, however, that the founders' silence is best explained by the simple fact that no one, not even the Constitution's most ardent opponents, suggested the document might strip the States of the immunity. *** The point of the argument was that federal jurisdiction under Article III would circumvent the States' immunity from suit in their own courts. The argument would have made little sense if the States were understood to have relinquished the immunity in all events.

The response the Constitution's advocates gave to the argument is also telling. Relying on custom and practice—and, in particular, on the States' immunity from suit in their own courts—they contended that no individual could sue a sovereign without its consent. It is true the point was directed toward the power of the Federal Judiciary, for that was the only question at issue. The logic of the argument, however, applies with even greater force in the context of a suit prosecuted against a sovereign in its own courts, for in this setting, more than any other, sovereign immunity was long established and unquestioned. *** The concerns voiced at the ratifying conventions, the furor raised by *Chisholm*, and the speed and unanimity with which the Amendment was adopted, moreover, underscore the jealous care with which the founding generation sought to preserve the sovereign immunity of the States. To read this history as permitting the inference that the Constitution stripped the States of immunity in their own courts and allowed Congress to subject them to suit there would turn on its head the concern of the founding generation—that Article III might be used to circumvent state-court immunity. ***

Our historical analysis is supported by early congressional practice, which provides "contemporaneous and weighty evidence of the Constitution's meaning." *** The provisions of the FLSA at issue here, *** are among the first statutory enactments purporting in express terms to subject nonconsenting States to private suits. ***

Our final consideration is whether a congressional power to subject nonconsenting States to private suits in their own courts is consistent with the structure of the Constitution. *** Private suits against nonconsenting States *** present "the indignity of subjecting a State to the coercive process of judicial tribunals at the instance of private parties," regardless of the forum. Not only must a State defend or default but also it must face the prospect of being thrust, by federal fiat and against its will, into the disfavored status of a debtor, subject to the power of private citizens to levy on its treasury or perhaps even government buildings or property which the State administers on the public's behalf.

In some ways, of course, a congressional power to authorize private suits against nonconsenting States in their own courts would be even more offensive to state sovereignty than a power to authorize the suits in a federal forum. *** Such plenary federal control of state governmental processes denigrates the separate sovereignty of the States.

It is unquestioned that the Federal Government retains its own immunity from suit not only in state tribunals but also in its own courts. In light of our constitutional system recognizing the essential sovereignty of the States, we are reluctant to conclude that the States are not entitled to a reciprocal privilege.

Underlying constitutional form are considerations of great substance. Private suits against nonconsenting States—especially suits for money damages—may threaten the financial integrity of the States. *** A congressional power to strip the States of their immunity from private suits in their own courts would [also compromise] the autonomy, the decisionmaking ability, and the sovereign capacity of the States. ***

The asserted authority would blur not only the distinct responsibilities of the State and National Governments but also the separate duties of the judicial and political branches of the state governments, displacing "state decisions that 'go to the heart of representative government.'" ***

The constitutional privilege of a State to assert its sovereign immunity in its own courts does not confer upon the State a concomitant right to disregard the Constitution or valid federal law. The States and their officers are bound by obligations imposed by the Constitution and by federal statutes that comport with the constitutional design. We are unwilling to assume the States will refuse to honor the Constitution or obey the binding laws of the United States. ***

[C]ertain limits are implicit in the constitutional principle of state sovereign immunity. The first of these limits is that sovereign immunity bars suits only in the absence of consent. *** Nor, subject to constitutional limitations, does the Federal Government lack the authority or means to seek the States' voluntary consent to private suits. Cf. *South Dakota v. Dole.* The States have consented, moreover, to some suits pursuant to the plan of the Convention or to subsequent constitutional amendments. In ratifying the Constitution, the States consented to suits brought by other States or by the Federal Government ***. A suit which is commenced and prosecuted against a State in the name of the United States by those who are entrusted with the constitutional duty to "take Care that the Laws be faithfully executed," U.S. Const., Art. II, § 3, differs in kind from the suit of an individual *** Suits brought by the United States itself require the exercise of political responsibility for each suit prosecuted against a State, a control which is absent from a broad delegation to private persons to sue nonconsenting States.

We have held also that in adopting the Fourteenth Amendment, the people required the States to surrender a portion of the sovereignty that had been preserved to them by the original Constitution, so that Congress may authorize private suits against nonconsenting States pursuant to its § 5 enforcement power. *Fitzpatrick v. Bitzer,* 427 U.S. 445 (1976). *** The second important limit to the principle of sovereign immunity is that it bars suits against States but not lesser entities. *** Nor does sovereign immunity bar all suits against state officers. Some suits against state officers are barred by the rule that sovereign immunity is not limited to suits which name the State as a party if the suits are, in fact, against the State ***. The rule, however, does not bar certain actions against state officers for injunctive or declaratory relief. *** Even a suit for money damages may be prosecuted against a state officer in his individual capacity for unconstitutional or wrongful conduct fairly attributable to the officer himself, so long as the relief is sought not from the state treasury but from the officer personally. ***

JUSTICE SOUTER, with whom JUSTICE STEVENS, JUSTICE GINSBURG, and JUSTICE BREYER join, dissenting.

*** The [Court's] conception is not one of common law so much as of natural law, a universally applicable proposition discoverable by reason. *** The State of Maine is not sovereign with respect to the national objective of the FLSA. It is not the authority that promulgated the FLSA, on which the right of action in this case depends. That authority is the United States acting through the Congress, whose legislative power under Article I of the Constitution to extend FLSA coverage to state employees has already been decided, see *Garcia*, and is not contested here. *** It is symptomatic of the weakness of the structural notion proffered by the Court that it seeks to buttress the argument by relying on "the dignity and respect afforded a State, which the immunity is designed to protect," and by invoking the many demands on a State's fisc. *** The Court apparently believes that because state courts have not historically entertained Commerce Clause-based federal-law claims against the States, such an innovation carries a presumption of unconstitutionality. *** But [*Garcia*] settled that federal legislation enacted under the Commerce Clause may bind the States without having to satisfy a test of undue incursion into state sovereignty. *** *Garcia* remains good law, its reasoning has not been repudiated, and it has not been challenged here.

The FLSA has not, however, fared as well in practice as it has in theory. The Court in *Seminole Tribe* created a significant impediment to the statute's practical application by rendering its damages provisions unenforceable against the States by private suit in federal court. Today's decision blocking private actions in state courts makes the barrier to individual enforcement a total one. *** [T]he allusion to enforcement of private rights by the National Government is probably not much more than whimsy. *** [T]here is no reason today to suspect that enforcement by the Secretary of Labor alone would likely prove adequate to assure compliance with this federal law in the multifarious circumstances of some 4.7 million employees of the 50 States of the Union. *** [T]he Court abandons a principle nearly as inveterate, and much closer to the hearts of the Framers: that where there is a right, there must be a remedy. ***

Notes

1.   **Judicial Reasoning.** Do you find the majority's or the dissent's view of sovereign immunity more compelling? Why?

2.   ***Alden* and *Garcia*.** If you had been in the dissent in *Garcia*, would you have found this case an appropriate vehicle for overruling *Garcia*? Why didn't the Court overrule *Garcia*?

3.   ***Alden* and the Powers to Tax and Spend.** Can't Congress simply use its 16th Amendment power to enhance federal power while reducing the resources available to the states? Can Congress engage in spending conditioned upon the states waiving their sovereign immunity?

4.   **Amendment.** Consider whether you would support either of the following proposed constitutional amendments:

(a) "The Eleventh Amendment is hereby repealed."

(b) "No State shall interpose sovereign immunity as a defense in any action brought in state or federal court when that action is premised upon a federal statute or a treaty of the United States."

FEDERAL MARITIME COMMISSION v. SOUTH CAROLINA STATE PORTS AUTHORITY
535 U.S. 743 (2002)

JUSTICE THOMAS delivered the opinion of the Court.

This case presents the question whether state sovereign immunity precludes petitioner Federal Maritime Commission (FMC or Commission) from adjudicating a private party's complaint that a state-run port has violated the Shipping Act of 1984. *** On five occasions, South Carolina Maritime Services, Inc. (Maritime Services), asked respondent South Carolina State Ports Authority (SCSPA) for permission to berth a cruise ship, the M/V *Tropic Sea,* at the SCSPA's port facilities in Charleston, South Carolina. *** The SCSPA repeatedly denied Maritime Services' requests, contending that it had an established policy of denying berths in the Port of Charleston to vessels whose primary purpose was gambling. As a result, Maritime Services filed a complaint with the FMC, contending that the SCSPA's refusal to provide berthing space to the M/V *Tropic Sea* violated the Shipping Act. *** Maritime Services' complaint was referred to an administrative law judge (ALJ). The SCSPA *** filed a motion to dismiss, asserting *** that the SCSPA, as an arm of the State of South Carolina, was "entitled to Eleventh Amendment immunity" from Maritime Services' suit. The SCSPA argued that "the Constitution prohibits Congress from passing a statute authorizing Maritime Services to file [this] Complaint before the Commission and, thereby, sue the State of South Carolina for damages and injunctive relief." ***

We now consider whether the sovereign immunity enjoyed by States as part of our constitutional framework applies to adjudications conducted by the FMC. *** For purposes of this case, we will assume, *arguendo,* that in adjudicating complaints filed by private parties under the Shipping Act, the FMC does not exercise the judicial power of the United States. ***

"[L]ook[ing] first to evidence of the original understanding of the Constitution," *Alden v. Maine*, as well as early congressional practice, we find a relatively barren historical record, from which the parties draw radically different conclusions. *** The Framers, who envisioned a limited Federal Government, could not have anticipated the vast growth of the administrative state. Because formalized administrative adjudications were all but unheard of in the late 18th century and early 19th century, the dearth of specific evidence indicating whether the Framers believed that the States' sovereign immunity would apply in such proceedings is unsurprising.

This Court, however, has applied a presumption–first explicitly stated in *Hans* v. *Louisiana*–that the Constitution was not intended to "rais[e] up" any proceedings against the States that were "anomalous and unheard of when the Constitution was adopted." We therefore attribute great significance to the fact that States were not subject to private suits in administrative adjudications at the time of the founding or for many years thereafter. *** To decide whether the *Hans* presumption applies here, however, we must examine FMC adjudications to determine whether they are the type of proceedings from which the Framers would have thought the States possessed immunity when they agreed to enter the Union.

In another case asking whether an immunity present in the judicial context also applied to administrative adjudications, this Court considered whether ALJs share the same absolute immunity from suit as do Article III judges. See *Butz* v. *Economou*, 438 U.S. 478 (1978). Examining in that case the duties performed by an ALJ, this Court observed:

> There can be little doubt that the role of the modern federal hearing examiner or administrative law judge *** is 'functionally comparable' to that of a judge. *** He may issue subpoenas, rule on proffers of evidence, regulate the course of the hearing, and make or recommend decisions. More importantly, the process of agency adjudication is currently structured so as to assure that the hearing examiner exercises his independent judgment ***

Turning to FMC adjudications specifically, neither the Commission nor the United States disputes the Court of Appeals' characterization below that such a proceeding "walks, talks, and squawks very much like a lawsuit." Nor do they deny that the similarities identified in *Butz* between administrative adjudications and trial court proceedings are present here. *** Simply put, if the Framers thought it an impermissible affront to a State's dignity to be required to answer the complaints of private parties in federal courts, we cannot imagine that they would have found it acceptable to compel a State to do exactly the same thing before the administrative tribunal of an agency, such as the FMC. Cf. *Alden*. ***

The United States first contends that sovereign immunity should not apply to FMC adjudications because the Commission's orders are not self-executing. *** The United States next suggests that sovereign immunity should not apply to FMC proceedings because they do not present the same threat to the financial integrity of States as do private judicial suits. *** [The Court rejected both arguments.]

Two final arguments raised by the FMC and the United States remain to be addressed. *** The FMC maintains that sovereign immunity should not bar the Commission from adjudicating Maritime Services' complaint because "[t]he constitutional necessity of uniformity in the regulation of maritime commerce limits the States' sovereignty with respect to the Federal Government's authority to regulate that commerce." *** *Seminole Tribe* precludes us from creating a new "maritime commerce" exception to state sovereign immunity. *** Finally, the United States maintains that even if sovereign immunity were to bar the FMC from adjudicating a private party's complaint against a state-run port for purposes of issuing a reparation order, the FMC should not be precluded from considering a private party's request for other forms of relief, such as a cease-and-desist order. *** [W]e explained in *Seminole Tribe* that "the relief sought by a plaintiff suing a State is irrelevant to the question whether the suit is barred by the Eleventh Amendment." *** Although the Framers likely did not envision the intrusion on state sovereignty at issue in today's case, we are nonetheless confident that it is contrary to their constitutional design ***.

JUSTICE BREYER, with whom JUSTICE STEVENS, JUSTICE SOUTER, and JUSTICE GINSBURG join, dissenting.

*** Federal administrative agencies do not exercise the "[j]udicial power of the United States." *** [The Court] has never said that the words "[j]udicial power of the United States" mean "the executive power of the United States." Nor should it. *** A private citizen, believing that a State has violated federal law, seeks a determination by an Executive Branch agency that he is right; the agency will make that determination through use of its own adjudicatory agency processes; and, if the State fails to comply, the Federal Government may bring an action against the State in federal court to enforce the federal law. ***

The Court argues that the basic purpose of "sovereign immunity" doctrine—namely preservation of a State's "dignity"–requires application of that doctrine here. *** Only the Federal Government, acting through the Commission or the Attorney General, has the authority to compel the State to act *** and, in deciding whether to do so, the Federal Government will exercise appropriate political responsibility. *** The statutes clearly provide the State with full judicial review [which] cannot "affront" the State's "dignity, for it takes place in a court proceeding in which the Commission, not the private party, will oppose the State." *** The Court's decision may undermine enforcement against state employers of many laws designed to protect worker health and safety. And it may inhibit the development of federal fair, rapid, and efficient, informal nonjudicial responses to complaints, for example, of improper medical care (involving state hospitals). ***

Notes

1. **Flip-flopping Formalists?** Have the traditionally conservative and formalist justices in the majority abandoned textualism, history, and strict constructionist principles in this case?

2. **Particular Procedures.** If an ALJ or other decision-maker for a federal agency operates under procedures that depart significantly from the procedures used by courts, is sovereign immunity available to a State defendant in such a proceeding? How closely would such procedures need to mirror court procedures?

3. **Trials and Deportation Proceedings**. The public and the press have a right to attend civil trials. Deportation proceedings resemble civil trials. Is there a comparable right to attend deportation proceedings, or may the Attorney General close proceedings that he believes relate to terrorism without having a case-by-case hearing on that issue? Compare *Detroit Free Press v. Ashcroft*, 303

F. 3d 681 (6th Cir. 2002) with *North Jersey Media Group v. Ashcroft*, 308 F. 3d 198 (3rd Cir. 2002).

4. **Federalism, In Rem and In Personam.** In *Tennessee Student Assistance Corp. v. Hood*, 541 U.S. 440 (2004), the Court relied on the distinction between in rem and in personam jurisdiction to hold that the Eleventh Amendment does not prevent debts owed to a state from being discharged in a bankruptcy proceeding. Writing for the Court, CHIEF JUSTICE REHNQUIST said: "No matter how difficult Congress has decided to make the discharge of student loan debt, the bankruptcy court's jurisdiction is premised on the res, not on the persona; that States were granted the presumptive benefit of nondischargeability does not alter the court's underlying authority. A debtor does not seek monetary damages or any affirmative relief from a State by seeking to discharge a debt; nor does he subject an unwilling State to a coercive judicial process. He seeks only a discharge of his debts." In dissent, JUSTICES SCALIA and THOMAS argued: "Although the Court ignores *Federal Maritime Comm'n* altogether, its reasoning applies to this case. The similarities between adversary proceedings in bankruptcy and federal civil litigation are striking. *** [A]lthough the adversary proceeding in this case does not require the State to "defend itself" against petitioner in the ordinary sense, the effect is the same, whether done by adversary proceeding or by motion, and whether the proceeding is *in personam* or *in rem.*"

5. **Problem.** In *Jinks v. Richland County*, 538 U.S. 456 (2003), the Court unanimously upheld a federal statute providing that, when certain claims are dismissed from federal court, state statutes of limitations are tolled to allow the claims to be refiled in state court. JUSTICE SCALIA said the statute was "necessary and proper" to Congress' Art. I power "[t]o constitute Tribunals inferior to the supreme Court" and facilitated fair exercise of "[t]he judicial Power of the United States." The Court rejected the argument that *Printz* precluded federal regulation of state court procedures because statutes of limitation are substantive, not procedural; it also rejected the county's Eleventh Amendment argument because only states receive that immunity. Would a federal statute be constitutional that required jury trials in state court civil cases that, if tried in federal courts, would be tried before juries because of the Seventh Amendment?

V.

FEDERALISM'S LIMITS ON
THE STATES

———————

Federalism was our Nation's own discovery. The Framers split the atom of sovereignty. It was the genius of their idea that our citizens would have two political capacities, one state and one federal, each protected from incursion by the other. The resulting Constitution created a legal system unprecedented in form and design, establishing two orders of government, each with its own direct relationship, its own privity, its own set of mutual rights and obligations to the people who sustain it and are governed by it.

— JUSTICE KENNEDY, concurring in
U.S. Term Limits v. Thornton

There is considerable controversy concerning where federalism positions the boundary lines between federal and state spheres of authority. Whether Congress possesses certain powers—an aspect of this controversy—was considered in the previous chapter. Just as "our federalism" imposes limits on the federal government, it imposes limits on the states.

This chapter looks at three constitutional restrictions on state power based on federalism considerations. Part A examines the original Constitution's explicit limits on the States with a special focus on the Contracts Clause. Part B considers what protection the Constitution provides federal institutions from state alteration. Part C concerns the effect of federal preemption of state law through operation of the Supremacy Clause of Article VI.

A. ARTICLE I LIMITATIONS ON THE STATES

Reread Article I, section 10. These three paragraphs impose a number of limits on the states. The prohibitions on coining money and emitting bills of credit have the effect of giving the federal government exclusive authority under its section 8 powers concerning these subjects. The restriction that keeps the States from entering into treaties, alliances, and confederations, has the effect of making the treaty power exclusive to the President (with advice and consent of the Senate). Several prohibitions, including the quite arcane denial of State authority to issue letters of marque and reprisal, keep the States from interfering with matters of war jointly entrusted under the Constitution to Congress and the President. Finally, there are prohibitions on the States that mirror restrictions placed on Congress under Article I, section 9 (no bills of attainder, ex post facto laws, or titles of nobility).

One explicit limitation on the authority of the States that is not mirrored by restrictions on Congress is the provision that "No State shall *** pass [any] Law impairing the Obligation of Contracts." In *Fletcher v. Peck*, 10 U.S. (6 Cranch) 87 (1810), and the *Dartmouth College Case*, 17 U.S. (4 Wheat.) 518 (1819), the Marshall Court used this clause to invalidate Georgia's rescission of land grants and a New Hampshire law changing the provisions of Dartmouth's state charter. The Marshall Court also used this clause to limit state regulation of business corporations. The Taney Court (1836–64) retreated from these cases, however, most notably in *Charles River Bridge v. Warren Bridge*, 36 U.S. (11 Pet.) 420 (1837), in which it permitted Massachusetts to adopt new policies that abrogated a public charter to a ferry company. So let us see how much of a limit the Contracts Clause places on the broad police powers of the States.

HOME BUILDING & LOAN ASS'N v. BLAISDELL
290 U.S. 398 (1934)

MR. CHIEF JUSTICE HUGHES delivered the opinion of the Court.

Appellant contests the validity of *** the Minnesota Mortgage Moratorium Law, as being repugnant to the contract clause *** The act provides that, during the emergency declared to exist, relief may be had through authorized judicial proceedings with respect to foreclosures of mortgages, and execution sales, of real estate; that sales may be postponed and periods of redemption may be extended. *** The act is to remain in effect only during the continuance of the emergency and in no event beyond May 1, 1935. *** We are here concerned with the provisions *** authorizing the district court of the county to extend the period of redemption from foreclosure sales 'for such additional time as the court may deem just and equitable,' subject to the above-described limitation. *** [The Blaisdell] petition stated that they owned a lot in Minneapolis which they had mortgaged to appellant; that the mortgage contained a valid power of sale by advertisement, and that by reason of their default the mortgage had been foreclosed and sold to appellant on May 2, 1932, for $3,700.98; that appellant was the holder of the sheriff's certificate of sale; that, because of the economic depression, appellees had been unable to obtain a new loan or to redeem, and that, unless the period of redemption were extended, the property would be irretrievably lost; and that the reasonable value of the property greatly exceeded the amount due on the mortgage, including all liens, costs, and expenses. *** The state court upheld the statute as an emergency measure. Although conceding that the obligations of the mortgage contract were impaired, the court decided that what it thus described as an impairment was, notwithstanding the contract cause of the Federal Constitution, within the police power of the state *** The court said:

"In addition to the weight to be given the determination of the Legislature that an economic emergency exists which demands relief, the court must take notice of other considerations. *** It is common knowledge that in the last few years land values have shrunk enormously. Loans made a few years ago upon the basis of the then going values cannot possibly be replaced on the basis of present values. We all know that when this law was enacted the large financial companies, which had made it their business to invest in mortgages, had ceased to do so. No bank would directly or indirectly loan on real estate mortgages. Life insurance companies, large investors in such mortgages, had even declared a moratorium as to the loan provisions of their policy contracts. The President had closed banks temporarily. The Congress, in addition to many extraordinary measures looking to the relief of the economic emergency, had passed an act to supply funds whereby mortgagors may be able within a reasonable time to refinance their mortgages or redeem from sales where the redemption has not expired. With this knowledge the court cannot well hold that the Legislature had no basis in fact for the conclusion that an economic emergency existed which called for the exercise of the police power to grant relief."

Justice Olsen of the state court, in a concurring opinion, added the following:

'The present nation wide and worldwide business and financial crisis has the same results as if it were caused by flood, earthquake, or disturbance in nature. It has deprived millions of persons in this nation of their employment and means of earning a living for themselves and their families; it has destroyed the value of and the income from all property on which thousands of people depended for a living; it actually has resulted in the loss of their homes by a number of our people, and threatens to result in the loss of their homes by many other people in this state; it has resulted in such widespread want and suffering among our people that private, state, and municipal agencies are unable to adequately relieve the want and suffering, and Congress has found it necessary to step in and attempt to remedy the situation by federal aid. ***"

*** The statute does not impair the integrity of the mortgage indebtedness. The obligation for interest remains. The statute does not affect the validity of the sale or the right of a mortgagee-purchaser to title in fee, or his right to obtain a deficiency judgment, if the mortgagor fails to redeem within the prescribed period. Aside from the extension of time, the other conditions of redemption are unaltered. While the mortgagor remains in possession, he must pay the rental value as that value has been determined, upon notice and hearing, by the court. The rental value so paid is devoted to the carrying of the property by the application of the required payments to taxes, insurance, and interest on the mortgage indebtedness. While the mortgagee-purchaser is debarred from actual possession, he has, so far as rental value is concerned, the equivalent of possession during the extended period. ***

Emergency does not create power. Emergency does not increase granted power or remove or diminish the restrictions imposed upon power granted or reserved. The Constitution was adopted in a period of grave emergency. Its grants of power to the federal government and its limitations of the power of the States were determined in the light of emergency, and they are not altered by emergency. *** While emergency does not create power, emergency may furnish the occasion for the exercise of power. *** The constitutional question presented in the light of an emergency is whether the power possessed embraces the particular exercise of it in response to particular conditions. *** Thus, emergency would not permit a state to have more than two Senators in the Congress, or permit the election of President by a general popular vote without regard to the number of electors to which the States are respectively entitled, or permit the States to 'coin money' ***. But, where constitutional grants and limitations of power are set forth in general clauses, which afford a broad outline, the process of construction is essential to fill in the details. That is true of the contract clause. ***

The widespread distress following the revolutionary period and the plight of debtors had called forth in the States an ignoble array of legislative schemes for the defeat of creditors and the invasion of contractual obligations. Legislative interferences had been so numerous and extreme that the confidence essential to prosperous trade had been undermined and the utter destruction of credit was threatened. 'The sober people of America' were convinced that some 'thorough reform' was needed which would 'inspire a general prudence and industry, and give a regular course to the business of society.' The Federalist, No. 44. *** The occasion and general purpose of the contract clause are summed up in the terse statement of Chief Justice Marshall ***: 'The power of changing the relative situation of debtor and creditor, of interfering with contracts, a power which comes home to every man, touches the interest of all, and controls the conduct of every individual in those things which he supposes to be proper for his own exclusive management, had been used to such an excess by the state legislatures, as to break in upon the ordinary intercourse of society, and destroy all confidence between man and man. *** To guard against the continuance of the evil *** was one of the important benefits expected from a reform of the government.'

But full recognition of the occasion and general purpose of the clause does not suffice to fix its precise scope. Nor does an examination of the details of prior legislation in the States yield criteria which can be considered controlling. To ascertain the scope of the constitutional prohibition, we examine the course of judicial decisions in its application. *** The inescapable problems of construction have been: What is a contract? What are the obligations of contracts? What constitutes impairment of these obligations? What residuum of power is there still in the States, in relation to the operation of contracts, to protect the vital interests of the community? Questions of this character, 'of no small nicety and intricacy, have vexed the legislative halls, as well as the judicial tribunals, with an uncounted variety and frequency of litigation and speculation.'

The obligation of a contract is the law which binds the parties to perform their agreement. * * * The ideas of validity and remedy are inseparable, and both are parts of the obligation, which is guaranteed by the Constitution against invasion. But this broad language cannot be taken without qualification. *** Not only is the constitutional provision qualified by the measure of control which the state retains over remedial processes, but the state also continues to possess authority to safeguard the vital interests of its people. *** The policy of protecting contracts against impairment presupposes the maintenance of a government by virtue of which contractual relations are worth while, a government which retains adequate authority to secure the peace and good order of society. ***

While the charters of private corporations constitute contracts, a grant of exclusive privilege is not to be implied as against the state. And all contracts are subject to the right of eminent domain. The reservation of this necessary authority of the state is deemed to be a part of the contract. *** The Legislature cannot 'bargain away the public health or the public morals.' *** The states retain adequate power to protect the public health against the maintenance of nuisances despite insistence upon existing contracts. ***

Undoubtedly, whatever is reserved of state power must be consistent with the fair intent of the constitutional limitation of that power. *** It cannot be maintained that the constitutional prohibition should be so construed as to prevent limited and temporary interpositions with respect to the enforcement of contracts if made necessary by a great public calamity such as fire, flood, or earthquake. The reservation of state power appropriate to such extraordinary conditions may be deemed to be as much a part of all contracts as is the reservation of state power to protect the public interest in the other situations to which we have referred. And, if state power exists to give temporary relief from the enforcement of contracts in the presence of disasters due to physical causes such as fire, flood, or earthquake, that power cannot be said to be nonexistent when the urgent public need demanding such relief is produced by other and economic causes. ***

It is no answer to say that this public need was not apprehended a century ago, or to insist that what the provision of the Constitution meant to the vision of that day it must mean to the vision of our time. If by the statement that what the Constitution meant at the time of its adoption it means to-day, it is intended to say that the great clauses of the Constitution must be confined to the interpretation which the framers, with the conditions and outlook of their time, would have placed upon them, the statement carries its own refutation. It was to guard against such a narrow conception that Chief Justice Marshall uttered the memorable warning: 'We must never forget, that it is a constitution we are expounding'; 'a constitution intended to endure for ages to come, and, consequently, to be adapted to the various crises of human affairs.' ***'

[W]e conclude: An emergency existed in Minnesota which furnished a proper occasion for the exercise of the reserved power of the state to protect the vital interests of the community. *** The conditions upon which the period of redemption is extended do not appear to be unreasonable. *** Also important is the fact that mortgagees *** are predominantly corporations, such as insurance companies, banks, and investment and mortgage companies. These, and such individual mortgagees as are small investors, are not seeking homes or the opportunity to engage in farming. Their chief concern is the reasonable protection of their investment security. *** The Legislature was entitled to deal with the general or typical situation. The relief afforded by the statute has regard to the interest of mortgagees as well as to the interest of mortgagors. The legislation seeks to prevent the impending ruin of both by a considerate measure of relief. ***

The legislation is temporary in operation. It is limited to the exigency which called it forth. *** We are of the opinion that the Minnesota statute as here applied does not violate the contract clause of the Federal Constitution. Whether the legislation is wise or unwise as a matter of policy is a question with which we are not concerned. ***

MR. JUSTICE SUTHERLAND, dissenting.

Few questions of greater moment than that just decided have been submitted for judicial inquiry during this generation. *** The effect of the Minnesota legislation, though serious enough in itself, is of trivial significance compared with the far more serious and dangerous inroads upon the limitations of the Constitution which are almost certain to ensue as a consequence naturally following any step beyond the boundaries fixed by that instrument. ***

The present exigency is nothing new. From the beginning of our existence as a nation, periods of depression, of industrial failure, of financial distress, of unpaid and unpayable indebtedness, have alternated with years of plenty. The vital lesson that expenditure beyond income begets poverty, that public or private extravagance, financed by promises to pay, either must end in complete or partial repudiation or the promises be fulfilled by self-denial and painful effort, though constantly taught by bitter experience, seems never to be learned; and the attempt by legislative devices to shift the misfortune of the debtor to the shoulders of the creditor without coming into conflict with the contract impairment clause has been persistent and oft-repeated.

The defense of the Minnesota law is made upon grounds which were discountenanced by the makers of the Constitution and have many times been rejected by this Court. *** With due regard for the processes of logical thinking, it legitimately cannot be urged that conditions which produced the rule may now be invoked to destroy it.

The lower court, and counsel *** here, frankly admitted that the statute does constitute a material impairment of the contract, but contended that such legislation is brought within the state power by the present emergency. If I understand the opinion just delivered, this court is not wholly in accord with that view. *** I can only interpret what is said on that subject as meaning that, while an emergency does not diminish a restriction upon power, it furnishes an occasion for diminishing it; and this, as it seems to me, is merely to say the same thing by the use of another set of words, with the effect of affirming that which has just been denied.

It is quite true that an emergency may supply the occasion for the exercise of power, dependent upon the nature of the power and the intent of the Constitution with respect thereto. The emergency of war furnishes an occasion for the exercise of certain of the war powers. This the Constitution contemplates, since they cannot be exercised upon any other occasion. The existence of another kind of emergency authorizes the United States to protect each of the states of the Union against domestic violence. But we are here dealing, not with a power granted by the Federal Constitution, but with the state police power, which exists in its own right. Hence the question is, not whether an emergency furnishes the occasion for the exercise of that state power, but whether an emergency furnishes an occasion for the relaxation of the restrictions upon the power imposed by the contract impairment clause; and the difficulty is that the contract impairment clause forbids state action under any circumstances, if it have the effect of impairing the obligation of contracts. That clause restricts every state power in the particular specified, no matter what may be the occasion. ***

The Minnesota statute either impairs the obligation of contracts or it does not. *** If it does, the emergency no more furnishes a proper occasion for its exercise than if the emergency were nonexistent. ***

The contract [at issue here] is to repay a loan within a fixed time, with the express condition that upon failure the property given as security shall be sold, and that, in the absence of a timely redemption, title shall be vested absolutely in the purchaser. This contract was lawful when made; and it has never been anything else. What the Legislature has done is to pass a statute which does not have the effect of frustrating the contract by rendering its performance unlawful, but one which, at the election of one of the parties, postpones for a time the effective enforcement of the contractual obligation, notwithstanding the obligation, under the exact terms of the contract, remains lawful and possible of performance after the passage of the statute as it was before. *** The statute *** is not merely a modification of the remedy; it effects a material and injurious change in the obligation. *** The phrase 'obligation of a contract' in the constitutional sense imports a legal duty to perform the specified obligation of that contract, not to substitute and perform, against the will of one of the parties, a different, albeit equally valuable, obligation. And a state, under the contract impairment clause, has no more power to accomplish such a substitution than has one of the parties to the contract against the will of the other. *** [W]hatever tends to postpone or retard the enforcement of a contract, to that extent weakens the obligation.' *** [W]hether the legislation under review is wise or unwise is a matter with which we have nothing to do. *** [

MR. JUSTICE V DEVANTER, MR. JUSTICE MCREYNOLDS, and MR. JUSTICE BUTLER concur in this opinion.

Notes

1. **Modern Relevance of *Blaisdell*.** Responding to the economic recession of 2008-2009, several states enacted 90-day moratoriums on home foreclosures, required homeowners to pay rent during the extension period, made *Blaisdell-*

like findings of emergency, and enacted only temporary relief. *Blaisdell* has been criticized but never overruled. Does this recent recession rise to the level of the emergency created by the Great Depression? Consider, for instance, that the unemployment level in 1933 was 25% (versus less than 10% through mid-2009).

2. **Construction.** The majority finds wiggle room in the language of the Contracts Clause (No State shall *** pass any *** Law impairing the Obligation of Contracts), suggesting that the clause "is not to be read with literal exactness like a mathematical formula." The dissent sees a strict provision which "forbids state action under any circumstances, if it have the effect of impairing the obligation of contracts." Which view is better supported by the language? There is no mention of an exception for times of emergency. But what does "obligation" encompass? Is time the same kind of "obligation" as money? What was bargained for in the contract? After all, under the legislation, the defaulting homeowner is still obligated to pay all debts and interest owed to the bank.

3. **Other Cases.** After *Blaisdell*, the Contracts Clause was believed dead until the late 1970s, when two cases, *United States Trust Co. v. New Jersey*, 431 U.S. 1 (1977) and *Allied Structural Steel Co. v. Spannaus*, 438 U.S. 234 (1978), struck down state statutes abrogating contractual commitments in circumstances where the public justifications were far weaker than in *Blaisdell*. More recent cases, however, seem to give more deference to state laws which abrogate contractual expectations. *See, e.g., Energy Reserves Group, Inc. v. Kansas Power & Light Co.*, 459 U.S. 400 (1983) (upholding abrogation of natural gas contracts where the state was not a beneficiary of a law concerning a "highly regulated industry" to avoid "unforeseen windfall profits").

4. **Federal Ramifications**. The Contracts Clause applies to the states but not to the United States. Consider whether the principles of the clause restrict the federal government through the provisions of the Fifth Amendment (due process and takings clauses). Economic due process is considered in Chapter VIII.

B. PROTECTION OF FEDERAL INSTITUTIONS

U.S. TERM LIMITS v. THORNTON
514 U.S. 779 (1995)

JUSTICE STEVENS delivered the opinion of the Court.

The Constitution sets forth qualifications for membership in the Congress of the United States. Article I, § 2, cl. 2, which applies to the House of Representatives, provides: "No Person shall be a Representative who shall not have attained to the Age of twenty-five Years, and been seven Years a Citizen of the United States, and who shall not, when elected, be an Inhabitant of that State in which he shall be chosen." Article I, § 3, cl. 3, which applies to the Senate, similarly provides: "No Person shall be a Senator who shall not have attained to the Age of thirty Years, and been nine Years a Citizen of the United States, and who shall not, when elected, be an Inhabitant of that State for which he shall be chosen."

Today's cases present a challenge to an amendment to the Arkansas State Constitution that prohibits the name of an otherwise-eligible candidate for Congress from appearing on the general election ballot if that candidate has already served three terms in the House of Representatives or two terms in the Senate. *** Such a state-imposed restriction is contrary to the "fundamental principle of our representative democracy," embodied in the Constitution, that "the people should choose whom they please to govern them." *Powell v. McCormack*, 395 U.S. 486, 547 (1969) (internal quotation marks omitted). Allowing individual States to adopt their own qualifications for congressional service would be inconsistent with the Framers' vision of a uniform National Legislature representing the people of the United States. If the qualifications set forth in the text of the Constitution are to be changed, that text must be amended.

At the general election on November 3, 1992, the voters of Arkansas adopted Amendment 73 to their State Constitution. Proposed as a "Term Limitation Amendment," its preamble stated: "The people of Arkansas find and declare that elected officials who remain in office too long become preoccupied with reelection and ignore their duties as representatives of the people. Entrenched incumbency has reduced voter participation and has led to an electoral system that is less free, less competitive, and less representative than the system established by the Founding Fathers. Therefore, the people of Arkansas, exercising their reserved powers, herein limit the terms of the elected officials." ***

[T]he constitutionality of Amendment 73 depends critically on the resolution of two distinct issues. The first is whether the Constitution forbids States from adding to or altering the qualifications specifically enumerated in the Constitution. The second is, if the Constitution does so forbid, whether the fact that Amendment 73 is formulated as a ballot access restriction rather than as an outright disqualification is of constitutional significance. ***

Twenty-six years ago, in *Powell v. McCormack*, 395 U.S. 486 (1969), we reviewed the history and text of the Qualifications Clauses in a case involving an attempted exclusion of a duly elected Member of Congress. The principal issue was whether the power granted to each House in Art. I, § 5, to judge the "Qualifications of its own Members" includes the power to impose qualifications other than those set forth in the text of the Constitution. *** [W]e held that it does not. *** We *** conclude now, as we did in *Powell*, that history shows that, with respect to Congress, the Framers intended the Constitution to establish fixed qualifications.

In *Powell*, of course, we did not rely solely on an analysis of the historical evidence, but instead complemented that analysis with "an examination of the basic principles of our democratic system" *** 'that the people should choose whom they please to govern them.'" *** First, we emphasized the egalitarian concept that the opportunity to be elected was open to all. *** Second, we recognized the critical postulate that sovereignty is vested in the people, and that sovereignty confers on the people the right to choose freely their representatives to the National Government. ***

Our reaffirmation of *Powell* does not necessarily resolve the specific questions presented in these cases. For petitioners argue that whatever the constitutionality of additional qualifications for membership imposed by Congress, the historical and textual materials discussed in *Powell* do not support the conclusion that the Constitution prohibits additional qualifications imposed by States. In the absence of such a constitutional prohibition, petitioners argue, the Tenth Amendment and the principle of reserved powers require that States be allowed to add such qualifications. ***

Petitioners argue that the Constitution contains no express prohibition against state-added qualifications, and that Amendment 73 is therefore an appropriate exercise of a State's reserved power to place additional restrictions on the choices that its own voters may make. We disagree for two independent reasons. First, we conclude that the power to add qualifications is not within the "original powers" of the States, and thus is not reserved to the States by the Tenth Amendment. Second, even if States possessed some original power in this area, *** the Framers intended the Constitution to be the exclusive source of qualifications for members of Congress, and that the Framers thereby "divested" States of any power to add qualifications. ***

Even if we believed that States possessed as part of their original powers some control over congressional qualifications, the text and structure of the Constitution, the relevant historical materials, and, most importantly, the "basic principles of our democratic system" all demonstrate that the Qualifications Clauses were intended to preclude the States from exercising any such power and to fix as exclusive the qualifications in the Constitution. *** The Framers feared that the diverse interests of the States would undermine the National Legislature, and thus they adopted provisions intended to minimize the possibility of state interference with federal elections. *** Indeed, one of the more anomalous consequences of petitioners' argument is that it accepts federal supremacy over the procedural aspects of determining the times, places, and manner of elections while allowing the states carte blanche with respect to the substantive qualifications for membership in Congress. *** In our view, it is inconceivable that the Framers would provide a specific constitutional provision to ensure that federal elections would be held while at the same time allowing States to render those elections meaningless by simply ensuring that no candidate could be qualified for office. *** The Constitution's provision for each House to be the judge of its own qualifications *** provides further evidence that the Framers believed that the primary source of those qualifications would be federal law.

We also find compelling the complete absence in the ratification debates of any assertion that States had the power to add qualifications. In those debates, the question whether to require term limits, or "rotation," was a major source of controversy. The draft of the Constitution that was submitted for ratification contained no provision for rotation. In arguments that echo in the preamble to Arkansas' Amendment 73, opponents of ratification condemned the absence of a rotation requirement, noting that "there is no doubt that senators will hold their office perpetually; and in this situation, they must of necessity lose their dependence, and their attachments to the people." Even proponents of ratification expressed concern about the "abandonment in every instance of the necessity of rotation in office." At several ratification conventions, participants proposed amendments that would have required rotation.

The Federalists' responses to those criticisms and proposals addressed the merits of the issue, arguing that rotation was incompatible with the people's right to choose. *** [Additionally,] Congress' subsequent experience with state-imposed qualifications provides further evidence of the general consensus on the lack of state power in this area. *** [T]he *Powell* Court recognized that an egalitarian ideal—that election to the National Legislature should be open to all people of merit—provided a critical foundation for the Constitutional structure. ***

Similarly, we believe that state-imposed qualifications, as much as congressionally imposed qualifications, would undermine the second critical idea recognized in *Powell*: that an aspect of sovereignty is the right of the people to vote for whom they wish. Again, the source of the qualification is of little moment in assessing the qualification's restrictive impact.

Finally, state-imposed restrictions, unlike the congressionally imposed restrictions at issue in *Powell*, violate a third idea central to this basic principle: that the right to choose representatives belongs not to the States, but to the people. *** Consistent with these views, the constitutional structure provides for a uniform salary to be paid from the national treasury, allows the States but a limited role in federal elections, and maintains strict checks on state interference with the federal election process. The Constitution also provides that the qualifications of the representatives of each State will be judged by the representatives of the entire Nation. The Constitution thus creates a uniform national body representing the interests of a single people.

Permitting individual States to formulate diverse qualifications for their representatives would result in a patchwork of state qualifications, undermining the uniformity and the national character that the Framers envisioned and sought to ensure. Such a patchwork would also sever the direct link that the Framers found so critical between the National Government and the people of the United States.

Petitioners attempt to overcome this formidable array of evidence against the States' power to impose qualifications by arguing that the practice of the States immediately after the adoption of the Constitution demonstrates their understanding that they possessed such power. One may properly question the extent to which the States' own practice is a reliable indicator of the contours of restrictions that the Constitution imposed on States, especially when no court has ever upheld a state-imposed qualification of any sort. But petitioners' argument is unpersuasive even on its own terms. *** At the time of the Convention, States widely supported term limits in at least some circumstances. The Articles of Confederation contained a provision for term limits.[36] As we have noted, some members of the Convention had sought to impose term limits for Members of Congress. In addition, many States imposed term limits on state officers, four placed limits on delegates to the Continental Congress, and several States voiced support for term limits for Members of Congress.[40] Despite this widespread support, no State sought to impose any term limits on its own federal representatives. Thus, a proper assessment of contemporaneous state practice provides further persuasive evidence of a general understanding that the qualifications in the Constitution were unalterable by the States. ***

Petitioners argue that, even if States may not add qualifications, Amendment 73 is constitutional because it is not such a qualification, and because Amendment 73 is a permissible exercise of state power to regulate the "Times, Places and Manner of Holding Elections." *** In our view, an amendment with the avowed purpose and obvious effect of evading the requirements of the Qualifications Clauses by handicapping a class of candidates cannot stand. To argue otherwise is to suggest that the Framers spent significant time and energy in debating and crafting Clauses that could be easily evaded. More importantly, allowing States to evade the Qualifications Clauses by "dress[ing] eligibility to stand for Congress in ballot access clothing" trivializes the basic principles of our democracy that underlie those Clauses.

Petitioners make the related argument that Amendment 73 merely regulates the "Manner" of elections, and that the Amendment is therefore a permissible exercise of state power under Article I, § 4, cl. 1 (the Elections Clause) to regulate the "Times, Places and Manner" of elections. We cannot agree.

A necessary consequence of petitioners' argument is that Congress itself would have the power to "make or alter" a measure such as Amendment 73. That the Framers would have approved of such a result is unfathomable. As our decision in *Powell* and our discussion above make clear, the Framers were particularly concerned that a grant to Congress of the authority to set its own qualifications would lead inevitably to congressional self-aggrandizement and the upsetting of the delicate constitutional balance. *** The Framers intended the Elections Clause to grant States authority to create procedural regulations, not to provide States with license to exclude classes of candidates from federal office. ***

The merits of term limits, or "rotation," have been the subject of debate since the formation of our Constitution, when the Framers unanimously rejected a proposal to add such limits to the Constitution. The cogent arguments on both sides of the question that were articulated during the process of ratification largely retain their force today. Over half the States have adopted measures that impose such limits on some offices either directly

---

[36] *** ("[N]o person shall be capable of being a delegate for more than three years in any term of six years").

[40] [During the ratification debates] at least three states proposed some form of constitutional amendment supporting term limits for Members of Congress.

or indirectly, and the Nation as a whole, notably by constitutional amendment, has imposed a limit on the number of terms that the President may serve.[49] ***

We are, however, firmly convinced that allowing the several States to adopt term limits for congressional service would effect a fundamental change in the constitutional framework. Any such change must come not by legislation adopted either by Congress or by an individual State, but rather—as have other important changes in the electoral process[50]—through the Amendment procedures set forth in Article V. The Framers decided that the qualifications for service in the Congress of the United States be fixed in the Constitution and be uniform throughout the Nation. That decision reflects the Framers' understanding that Members of Congress are chosen by separate constituencies, but that they become, when elected, servants of the people of the United States. They are not merely delegates appointed by separate, sovereign States; they occupy offices that are integral and essential components of a single National Government. ***

JUSTICE KENNEDY, concurring.

*** Federalism was our Nation's own discovery. The Framers split the atom of sovereignty. It was the genius of their idea that our citizens would have two political capacities, one state and one federal, each protected from incursion by the other. The resulting Constitution created a legal system unprecedented in form and design, establishing two orders of government, each with its own direct relationship, its own privity, its own set of mutual rights and obligations to the people who sustain it and are governed by it. ***

A distinctive character of the National Government, the mark of its legitimacy, is that it owes its existence to the act of the whole people who created it. *** It might be objected that because the States ratified the Constitution, the people can delegate power only through the States or by acting in their capacities as citizens of particular States. But in *McCulloch v. Maryland*, the Court set forth its authoritative rejection of this idea:

> " *** [The Constitution] was submitted to the people. *** It is true, they assembled in their several States—and where else should they have assembled? *** But the measures they adopt do not, on that account, cease to be the measures of the people themselves, or become the measures of the state governments."

The political identity of the entire people of the Union is reinforced by the proposition, which I take to be beyond dispute, that, though limited as to its objects, the National Government is, and must be, controlled by the people without collateral interference by the States. *McCulloch* affirmed this proposition as well, when the Court rejected the suggestion that States could interfere with federal powers. *** That the States may not invade the sphere

---

[49] See U.S. Const., Amdt. 22 (1951) (limiting Presidents to two 4–year terms).

[50] See, e.g., Amdt. 17 (1913) (direct elections of Senators); Amdt. 19 (1920) (extending suffrage to women); Amdt. 22 (1951) (Presidential term limits); Amdt. 24 (1964) (prohibition against poll taxes); Amdt. 26 (1971) (lowering age of voter eligibility to 18).

of federal sovereignty is as incontestable, in my view, as the corollary proposition that the Federal Government must be held within the boundaries of its own power when it intrudes upon matters reserved to the States. See *United States v. Lopez*, 514 U.S. 549 (1995). *** There can be no doubt, if we are to respect the republican origins of the Nation and preserve its federal character, that there exists a federal right of citizenship, a relationship between the people of the Nation and their National Government, with which the States may not interfere. Because the Arkansas enactment intrudes upon this federal domain, it exceeds the boundaries of the Constitution.

JUSTICE THOMAS, with whom THE CHIEF JUSTICE, JUSTICE O'CONNOR, and JUSTICE SCALIA join, dissenting.

It is ironic that the Court bases today's decision on the right of the people to "choose whom they please to govern them." Under our Constitution, there is only one State whose people have the right to "choose whom they please" to represent Arkansas in Congress. The Court holds, however, that neither the elected legislature of that State nor the people themselves (acting by ballot initiative) may prescribe any qualifications for those representatives. The majority therefore defends the right of the people of Arkansas to "choose whom they please to govern them" by invalidating a provision that won nearly 60% of the votes cast in a direct election and that carried every congressional district in the State. *** The ultimate source of the Constitution's authority is the consent of the people of each individual State, not the consent of the undifferentiated people of the Nation as a whole.

When they adopted the Federal Constitution, of course, the people of each State surrendered some of their authority to the United States (and hence to entities accountable to the people of other States as well as to themselves). *** Because the people of the several States are the only true source of power, however, the Federal Government enjoys no authority beyond what the Constitution confers: the Federal Government's powers are limited and enumerated. *** In each State, the remainder of the people's powers*** are either delegated to the state government or retained by the people. *** The Federal Government and the States thus face different default rules: where the Constitution is silent about the exercise of a particular power—that is, where the Constitution does not speak either expressly or by necessary implication—the Federal Government lacks that power and the States enjoy it. ***

To be sure, when the Tenth Amendment uses the phrase "the people," it does not specify whether it is referring to the people of each State or the people of the Nation as a whole. But the latter interpretation would make the Amendment pointless: there would have been no reason to provide that where the Constitution is silent about whether a particular power resides at the state level, it might or might not do so. In addition, it would make no sense to speak of powers as being reserved to the undifferentiated people of the Nation as a whole, because the Constitution does not contemplate that those people will either exercise power or delegate it. The Constitution simply does not recognize any mechanism for action by the undifferentiated people of the Nation. Thus, the amendment provision of Article V calls for amendments to be ratified not by a convention of the national people, but by conventions of the people in each State or by the state legislatures elected by those people. Likewise, the Constitution calls for Members of Congress to be chosen State by State, rather than in nationwide elections. Even the selection of the President—surely the most national of national figures—is accomplished by an electoral college made up of delegates chosen by the various States, and candidates can lose a Presidential election despite winning a majority of the votes cast in the Nation as a whole. ***

The majority's essential logic is that the state governments could not "reserve" any powers that they did not control at the time the Constitution was drafted. But it was not the state governments that were doing the reserving. The Constitution derives its authority instead from the consent of the people of the States. *** The majority is therefore quite wrong to conclude that the people of the States cannot authorize their state governments to exercise any powers that were unknown to the States when the Federal Constitution was drafted. Indeed, the majority's position frustrates the apparent purpose of the Amendment's final phrase. The Amendment does not pre-empt any limitations on state power found in the state constitutions, as it might have done if it simply had said that the powers not delegated to the Federal Government are reserved to the States. But the Amendment also does not prevent the people of the States from amending their state constitutions to remove limitations that were in effect when the Federal Constitution and the Bill of Rights were ratified. *** As for the fact that a State has no reserved power to establish qualifications for the office of President, it surely need not follow that a State has no reserved power to establish qualifications for the Members of Congress who represent the people of that State. ***

[JUSTICE THOMAS indicates the "Qualifications Clauses are merely recitations of minimum eligibility requirements that the Framers thought essential for every Member of Congress to meet." He suggests that they restrict state power only in that "they prevent the States from abolishing all eligibility," argues that "the Framers' decision to withhold this power from Congress do not prove that the Framers also deprived the people of the States of their reserved authority to set eligibility requirements," and concludes that "the historical evidence refutes any notion that the Qualifications Clauses were generally understood to be exclusive."]

The majority appears to believe that restrictions on eligibility for office are inherently undemocratic. But the Qualifications Clauses themselves prove that the Framers did not share this view; eligibility requirements to which the people of the States consent are perfectly consistent with the Framers' scheme. *** The majority never explains why giving effect to the people's decision would violate the "democratic principles" that undergird the Constitution. ***

[T]he detail with which the majority recites the historical evidence set forth in *Powell v. McCormack*, 395 U.S. 486, 489 (1969), should not obscure the fact that this evidence has no bearing on the question now before the Court. *** If anything, the solidity of the evidence supporting *Powell*'s view that Congress lacks the power to supplement the constitutional disqualifications merely highlights the weakness of the majority's evidence that the States and the people of the States also lack this power. ***

It is radical enough for the majority to hold that the Constitution implicitly precludes the people of the States from prescribing any eligibility requirements for the congressional candidates who seek their votes. This holding, after all, does not stop with negating the term limits that many States have seen fit to impose on their Senators and Representatives. Today's decision also means that no State may disqualify congressional candidates whom a court has found to be mentally incompetent, who are currently in prison, or who have past vote-fraud convictions. Likewise, after today's decision, the people of each State must leave open the possibility that they will trust someone with their vote in Congress even though they do not trust him with a vote in the election for Congress. ***

I do not mean to suggest that States have unbridled power to handicap particular classes of candidates ***. But laws that allegedly have the purpose and effect of handicapping a particular class of candidates traditionally are reviewed under the First and Fourteenth Amendments rather than the Qualifications Clauses. Term-limit measures have tended to survive such review without difficulty. ***

Notes

1. **Two Preliminary Exercises.**

    (a) If you had been an Arkansas voter presented with the opportunity to vote for or against this term limits initiative, how would you have voted and why? Make a list of the factors on both sides of the question that you would consider.

    (b) Outline the positions of the majority and dissenting opinions on (1) the meaning of the textual language, (2) historical evidence concerning the intent of the Framers, (3) use of precedent, and (4) first principles. After contemplation, consider whether you find the majority or the dissent to be more persuasive and be prepared to articulate why.

2. **History.** As you can tell, historians may have differing views on the issue before the Court. Should the Supreme Court provide definitive historical analysis, especially when few (if any) members of the Court are trained historians? Do you think the answer to the historical question would have come out differently if the issue had been exclusion of a convicted felon from congressional service?

3. **Alternatives.**

    • What alternatives do you see to historical analysis when the text is indeterminate? Would you find a Supreme Court decision more (or less) satisfying which argued that "current democratic principles within our federal system now demand" uniformity of qualifications for Senators and Representatives, even if that was not required two centuries ago?

    • Should the Supreme Court have considered that its decision is unlikely to be reversed since the virtually exclusive mode of amending the Constitution to date has been through the process of a 2/3 majority vote in the Senate and House, whose members are unlikely to support term limits? What potential would there be for amendment if the decision had gone 5–4 the other way?

4. **Principles and Term Limits?** ASSOCIATE JUSTICE BREYER, in *Judicial Review: A Practicing Judge's Perspective*, 78 TEX. L. REV. 761, 769 (2000), wrote that in *U.S. Term Limits*:

> The ordinary 'nonsubjective' factors [language, history, purpose, and structure] *** were close to equipoise. The more one sees the Constitution as providing a stable democratic government over time, the more one sees a state term limits requirement as making a major change (with unforeseeable but certainly important institutional consequences) ***. The more one sees in the Constitution's division of powers an insistence upon the continued influence, power, and authority of the individual states, the more one would likely believe that the Constitution, without amendment, permits a state to impose the additional requirements. *** I find it difficult to characterize the resulting conclusion as unusually 'political' or particularly 'ideological' or even highly 'subjective,' as those terms are normally used. Rather, differences in outcome reflect somewhat different views of the same constitutional framework ***.

Do you agree with JUSTICE BREYER that this fundamental choice is not political, ideological, or subjective?

5. **Elections Clause Analysis.** In rejecting the argument that the amendment regulated the manner of elections, *Term Limits* said: "The Framers intended the Elections Clause to grant States the authority to create procedural regulations, not to provide States with license to exclude classes of candidates from federal office." After *Term Limits*, those who sought to advance the cause of term limits couched their arguments in terms of Elections Clause procedures. An amendment to Article VIII of the Missouri State Constitution required those elected as U.S. Representatives and Senators from Missouri to use their powers to bring about passage of an amendment to the federal constitution that would "limit service in the U.S. Congress to three terms in the House of Representatives and two terms in the Senate." *Cook v. Gralike*, 531 U.S. 510 (2001), held this amendment unconstitutional:

> *** Three provisions in Article VIII combine to advance its purpose. Section 17 prescribes that the statement "DISREGARDED VOTERS' INSTRUCTION ON TERM LIMITS" be printed on all primary and general ballots adjacent to the name of a Senator or Representative who fails to take any one of eight legislative acts in support of the proposed amendment. Section 18 provides that the statement "DECLINED TO PLEDGE TO SUPPORT TERM LIMITS" be printed on all primary and general election ballots next to the name of every nonincumbent congressional candidate who refuses to take a "Term Limit" pledge that commits the candidate, if elected, to performing the legislative acts enumerated in § 17. And § 19 directs the Missouri Secretary of State to determine and declare, *** whether either statement should be printed alongside the name of each candidate for Congress. *** Article VIII is not a procedural

regulation. It does not regulate the time of elections; it does not regulate the place of elections; nor, we believe, does it regulate the manner of elections. *** Rather, Article VIII is plainly designed to favor candidates who are willing to support the particular form of a term limits amendment set forth in its text and to disfavor those who either oppose term limits entirely or would prefer a different proposal. *** In describing the two labels, the courts below have employed terms such as "pejorative," "negative," "derogatory," "intentionally intimidating," "particularly harmful," "politically damaging," "a serious sanction," "a penalty," and "official denunciation." *** Thus, far from regulating the procedural mechanisms of elections, Article VIII attempts to "dictate electoral outcomes." ***

6. **Political Questions and the Elections Clause.** Consider the six *Baker v. Carr* political question factors. Doesn't the text of the Elections Clause commit resolution of disputes regarding the exercise of state power under the clause to Congress? If it is not clear whether an action by a state is procedural or substantive, does this indicate a lack of judicially discoverable and manageable standards? Is the Supreme Court in a better position than Congress to discern what works a substantive change in the congressional electoral process? What does this indicate about the respect Congress receives as a coequal, coordinate branch of the federal government? *U.S. Term Limits* could have allowed Congress to revise Arkansas' action by statute, so long as Congress did not substantively change the electoral process in contravention of the Qualifications Clauses. Instead, the Court held that the states had no power to add to the qualifications; the Court rather than Congress defined federalism's limits on the states.

C. FEDERAL PREEMPTION OF STATE LAW

Federal and state powers overlap extensively. Such overlap guarantees that there will be conflicts between the laws of the two sovereigns. The doctrine for resolving such conflicts—preemption—stems from Article VI, cl. 2 of the Constitution:

> This Constitution, and the Laws of the United States which shall be made in Pursuance thereof; and all Treaties made, or which shall be made, under the Authority of the United States, shall be the supreme Law of the Land; and the Judges in every State shall be bound thereby, any Thing in the Constitution or Laws of any State to the Contrary notwithstanding.

An analogous clause of the Articles of Confederation, Article XIII, reads: "Every State shall abide by the determinations of the United States in Congress assembled, on all questions which by this confederation are submitted to them."

The Constitution's Supremacy Clause is stronger than its counterpart in the Articles of Confederation. First, it clearly requires state courts to implement the priority of the laws passed by Congress "pursuant to" the powers surveyed in Chapter IV. Arguably, implementing legislation was required from the state legislatures under Article XIII. Second, it establishes the rule that federal law trumps state law, just as the rule "later in time, first in priority" governs the relationship between two statutes passed by the same sovereign's legislature. Third, as discussed in Chapter II, the ultimate arbiter of such conflicts is the United States Supreme Court. No such institution existed under the Articles.

The Supreme Court has decided hundreds of preemption cases, a fact that has led some commentators to deem preemption the most active field of constitutional law. Commentators also have observed that preemption is a "muddle," "chaos," an "awful mess," and "confused," largely because the *extent* to which federal law ought to prevail in our federal system remains ambiguous. Yet this casebook devotes only two cases to this topic, and some professors who use the book will not assign either of them.

Why such a cursory treatment of such an important subject? First, preemption is often covered as a substantive component of other law school courses. Second, preemption cases generally involve extensive construction of both federal and state law; the constitutional framework within which such decisions are made is secondary.

The following cases raise basic constitutional framework issues about the scope of preemption relatively directly. They also demonstrate deep disagreements, not predictably grounded in specific visions of federalism.

GEIER v. AMERICAN HONDA MOTOR COMPANY
529 U.S. 861 (2000)

JUSTICE BREYER delivered the opinion of the Court.

This case focuses on the 1984 version of a Federal Motor Vehicle Safety Standard promulgated by the Department of Transportation under the authority of the National Traffic and Motor Vehicle Safety Act of 1966. The standard, FMVSS 208, required auto manufacturers to equip some but not all of their 1987 vehicles with passive restraints [airbags]. We ask whether the Act pre-empts a state common-law tort action in which the plaintiff claims that the defendant auto manufacturer, who was in compliance with the standard, should nonetheless have equipped a 1987 automobile with airbags. [Alexis Geier, while driving a 1987 Honda Accord equipped with manual shoulder and lap belts which Geier had buckled, collided with a tree and was seriously injured. Geier sued in tort, claiming American Honda had designed the car negligently and defectively by not providing a driver's side airbag.] *** The basic question, then, is whether a common-law "no airbag" action like the one before us actually conflicts with FMVSS 208. We hold that it does.

In petitioners' and the dissent's view, FMVSS 208 sets a minimum airbag standard. As far as FMVSS 208 is concerned, the more airbags, and the sooner, the better. But that was not the Secretary's view. DOT's comments, which accompanied the promulgation of FMVSS 208, make clear that the standard deliberately provided the manufacturer with a range of choices among different passive restraint devices. Those choices would bring about a mix of different devices introduced gradually over time; and FMVSS 208 would thereby lower costs, overcome technical safety problems, encourage technological development, and win widespread consumer acceptance—all of which would promote FMVSS 208's safety objectives. *** DOT's own contemporaneous explanation of FMVSS 208 makes clear that the 1984 version of FMVSS 208 reflected the following significant considerations. First, buckled up seatbelts are a vital ingredient of automobile safety. Second, despite the enormous and unnecessary risks that a passenger runs by not buckling up manual lap and shoulder belts, more than 80% of front seat passengers would leave their manual seatbelts unbuckled. Third, airbags could make up for the dangers caused by unbuckled manual belts, but they could not make up for them entirely. Fourth, passive restraint systems had their own disadvantages, for example, the dangers associated with, intrusiveness of, and corresponding public dislike for, nondetachable automatic belts. Fifth, airbags brought with them their own special risks to safety, such as the risk of danger to out-of-position occupants (usually children) in small cars. Sixth, airbags were expected to be significantly more expensive than other passive restraint devices, raising the average cost of a vehicle price $320 for full frontal airbags over the cost of a car with manual lap and shoulder seatbelts (and potentially much more if production volumes were low). And the agency worried that the high replacement cost—estimated to be $800—could lead car owners to refuse to replace them after deployment. Seventh, the public, for reasons of cost, fear, or physical intrusiveness, might resist installation or use of any of the then-available passive restraint devices—a particular concern with respect to airbags.

FMVSS 208 *** deliberately sought variety—a mix of several different passive restraint systems. *** The 1984 FMVSS 208 standard also deliberately sought a gradual phase-in of passive restraints. ***

In effect, petitioners' tort action depends upon its claim that manufacturers had a duty to install an airbag when they manufactured the 1987 Honda Accord. Such a state law—i.e., a rule of state tort law imposing such a duty—by its terms would have required manufacturers of all similar cars to install airbags rather than other passive restraint systems, such as automatic belts or passive interiors. It thereby would have presented an obstacle to the variety and mix of devices that the federal regulation sought. It would have required all manufacturers to have installed airbags in respect to the entire District-of-Columbia-related portion of their 1987 new car fleet, even though FMVSS 208 at that time required only that 10% of a manufacturer's nationwide fleet be equipped with any passive restraint device at all. It thereby also would have stood as an obstacle to the gradual passive restraint phase-in that the federal regulation deliberately imposed. In addition, it could have made less likely the adoption of a state mandatory buckle-up law. Because the rule of law for which petitioners contend would have stood "as an obstacle to the accomplishment and execution of" the important means-related federal objectives that we have just discussed, it is pre-empted. *** [W]e do not "put the burden" of proving pre-emption on petitioners. We simply find unpersuasive their arguments attempting to undermine the Government's demonstration of actual conflict. ***

The dissent would require a formal agency statement of pre-emptive intent as a prerequisite to concluding that a conflict exists. It relies on cases, or portions thereof, that did not involve conflict pre-emption. And conflict pre-emption is different in that it turns on the identification of "actual conflict," and not on an express statement of pre-emptive intent. *** [T]hough the Court has looked for a specific statement of pre-emptive intent where it is claimed that the mere "volume and complexity" of agency regulations demonstrate an implicit intent to displace all state law in a particular area— so-called "field pre-emption"—the Court has never before required a specific, formal agency statement identifying conflict in order to conclude that such a conflict in fact exists. Indeed, one can assume that Congress or an agency ordinarily would not intend to permit a significant conflict. *** To insist on a specific expression of agency intent to pre-empt, made after notice-and-comment rulemaking, would be in certain cases to tolerate conflicts that an agency, and therefore Congress, is most unlikely to have intended. ***

Nor do we agree with the dissent that the agency's views, as presented here, lack coherence. *** It is possible that some special design-related circumstance concerning a particular kind of car might require airbags, rather than automatic belts, and that a suit seeking to impose that requirement could escape pre-emption—say, because it would affect so few cars that its rule of law would not create a legal "obstacle" to 208's mixed-fleet, gradual objective. But that is not what petitioners claimed. They have argued generally that, to be safe, a car must have an airbag. *** FMVSS 208 sought a gradually developing mix of alternative passive restraint devices for safety-related reasons. The rule of state tort law for which petitioners argue would stand as an "obstacle" to the accomplishment of that objective. And the statute foresees the application of ordinary principles of pre-emption in cases of actual conflict. Hence, the tort action is pre-empted. ***

JUSTICE STEVENS, with whom JUSTICE SOUTER, JUSTICE THOMAS, and JUSTICE GINSBURG join, dissenting.

*** "This is a case about federalism," that is, about respect for "the constitutional role of the States as sovereign entities." It raises important questions concerning the way in which the Federal Government may exercise its undoubted power to oust state courts of their traditional jurisdiction over common-law tort actions. The rule the Court enforces today was not enacted by Congress and is not to be found in the text of any Executive Order or regulation. *** Perhaps such a rule would be a wise component of a legislative reform of our tort system. *** It is, however, quite clear to me that Congress neither enacted any such rule itself nor authorized the Secretary of Transportation to do so. It is equally clear to me that the objectives that the Secretary intended to achieve through the adoption of Federal Motor Vehicle Safety Standard 208 would not be frustrated one whit by allowing state courts to determine whether in 1987 the life-saving advantages of airbags had become sufficiently obvious that their omission might constitute a design defect in some new cars. Finally, I submit that the Court is quite wrong to characterize its rejection of the presumption against pre-emption, and its reliance on history and regulatory commentary rather than either statutory or regulatory text, as "ordinary experience-proved principles of conflict pre-emption." ***

Standard 208 covers "[o]ccupant crash protection." Its purpose "is to reduce the number of deaths of vehicle occupants, and the severity of injuries, by specifying vehicle crashworthiness requirements *** [and] equipment requirements for active and passive restraint systems." *** [T]here is no mention, either in the text of the final standard or in the accompanying comments, of the possibility that the risk of potential tort liability would provide an incentive for manufacturers to install airbags. Nor is there any other specific evidence of an intent to preclude common-law tort actions. ***

Honda has not crossed the high threshold established by our decisions regarding pre-emption of state laws that allegedly frustrate federal purposes: it has not demonstrated that allowing a common-law no-airbag claim to go forward would impose an obligation on manufacturers that directly and irreconcilably contradicts any primary objective that the Secretary set forth with clarity in Standard 208. Furthermore, it is important to note that the text of Standard 208 *** does not contain any expression of an intent to displace state law. ***

Our presumption against pre-emption is rooted in the concept of federalism. *** The signal virtues of this presumption are its placement of the power of pre-emption squarely in the hands of Congress, which is far more suited than the Judiciary to strike the appropriate state/federal balance (particularly in areas of traditional state regulation), and its requirement that Congress speak clearly when exercising that power. *** [T]he presumption serves as a limiting principle that prevents federal judges from running amok with our potentially boundless (and perhaps inadequately considered) doctrine of implied conflict pre-emption based on frustration of purposes—i.e., that state law is pre-empted if it "stands as an obstacle to the accomplishment and execution of the full purposes and objectives of Congress."

While the presumption is important in assessing the pre-emptive reach of federal statutes, it becomes crucial when the pre-emptive effect of an administrative regulation is at issue. Unlike Congress, administrative agencies are clearly not designed to represent the interests of States, yet with relative ease they can promulgate comprehensive and detailed regulations that have broad pre-emption ramifications for state law. *** Honda has not overcome the presumption in this case. Neither Standard 208 nor its accompanying commentary includes the slightest specific indication of an intent to pre-empt common-law no-airbag suits. *** I cannot agree with the Court's unprecedented use of inferences from regulatory history and commentary as a basis for implied pre-emption. ***

Notes

1. **Judicial Inconsistency?** The Justices line up differently in preemption and federalism cases. One could, as some commentators have suggested, see this as an example of judicial inconsistency. Another way of viewing the difference is this: while the federalism cases involve application of general principles, the

preemption cases are strongly grounded in facts and statutory language. Do these factors indicate less likelihood of judicial ideology?

2.   **Federalism and Presumptions.** Do you agree that federalism requires a presumption against preemption? If so, what should it take to overcome that presumption? Should the presumption be different depending on the nature of the federal lawmaker and its mode of communication (Congress' text, congressional intent, agency regulations, or agency interpretations of regulations)? If Congress' intent should be clear, what evidence shows clear intent? Should there be a presumption of preemption when foreign affairs are involved? See the next case.

3.   **Commandeering and Commands.** Is federal commandeering more threatening to state autonomy than preempting state acts? Is preemption more threatening than requiring states to adopt specific regulations or submit to a federal regulatory scheme? More threatening than cutting off federal funds if the state doesn't do what Congress wants?

AMERICAN INS. ASSOC. v. GARAMENDI
539 U.S. 396 (2003)

JUSTICE SOUTER delivered the opinion of the Court.

California's Holocaust Victim Insurance Relief Act of 1999 (HVIRA or Act) requires any insurer doing business in that State to disclose information about all policies sold in Europe between 1920 and 1945 by the company itself or any one "related" to it. The issue here is whether HVIRA interferes with the National Government's conduct of foreign relations. ***

The Nazi Government of Germany engaged not only in genocide and enslavement but theft of Jewish assets, including the value of insurance policies, and in particular policies of life insurance, a form of savings held by many Jews in Europe before the Second World War. *** These confiscations and frustrations of claims fell within the subject of reparations, which became a principal object of Allied diplomacy soon after the war. *** Ensuing negotiations at the national level produced the German Foundation Agreement, signed by President Clinton and German Chancellor Schroeder in July 2000, in which Germany agreed to enact legislation establishing a foundation funded with 10 billion deutsch marks contributed equally by the German Government and German companies, to be used to compensate all those "who suffered at the hands of German companies during the National Socialist era."

The willingness of the Germans to create a voluntary compensation fund was conditioned on some expectation of security from lawsuits in United States courts, and after extended dickering President Clinton put his weight behind two specific measures toward that end. First, the Government agreed that whenever a German company was sued on a Holocaust-era claim in an American court, the Government of the United States would submit a statement that "it would be in the foreign policy interests of the United States for the Foundation to be the exclusive forum and remedy for the resolution of all asserted claims against German companies arising from their involvement in the National Socialist era and World War II." *** On top of that undertaking, the Government promised to use its "best efforts, in a manner it considers appropriate," to get state and local governments to respect the foundation as the exclusive mechanism.

As for insurance claims specifically, both countries agreed that the German Foundation would work with the International Commission on Holocaust Era Insurance Claims (ICHEIC), a voluntary organization formed in 1998 ***. The job of the ICHEIC *** includes negotiation with European insurers to provide information about unpaid insurance policies issued to Holocaust victims and settlement of claims brought under them. ***

While these international efforts were underway, California's Department of Insurance began its own enquiry into the issue of unpaid claims under Nazi-era insurance policies, prompting state legislation designed to force payment by defaulting insurers. *** The section of the [1998] bill codified as HVIRA, at issue here, requires "[a]ny insurer currently doing business in the state" to disclose the details of "life, property, liability, health, annuities, dowry, educational, or casualty insurance policies" issued "to persons in Europe, which were in effect between 1920 and 1945." *** The mandatory penalty for default is suspension of the company's license to do business in the State, and there are misdemeanor criminal sanctions for falsehood in certain required representations about whether and to whom the proceeds of each policy have been distributed. ***

After HVIRA was enacted, administrative subpoenas were issued against several subsidiaries of European insurance companies participating in the ICHEIC. Immediately, in November 1999, Deputy Secretary Eizenstat wrote to the insurance commissioner of California that although HVIRA "reflects a genuine commitment to justice for Holocaust victims and their families, it has the unfortunate effect of damaging the one effective means now at hand to process quickly and completely unpaid insurance claims from the Holocaust period [ICHEIC]." *** The same day, Deputy Secretary Eizenstat also wrote to California's Governor making the same points ***. These expressions of the National Government's concern proved to be of no consequence, for the state commissioner announced *** he would enforce HVIRA to its fullest, requiring the affected insurers to make the disclosures, leave the State voluntarily, or lose their licenses. ***

The principal argument for preemption made by petitioners and the United States as *amicus curiae* is that HVIRA interferes with foreign policy of the Executive Branch *** [O]ur cases have recognized that the President has authority to make "executive agreements" with other countries, requiring no ratification by the Senate or approval by Congress, this power having been exercised since the early years of the Republic. *** Given the fact that the practice goes back over 200 years to the first Presidential administration, and has received congressional acquiescence throughout its history, the conclusion "[t]hat the President's control of foreign relations includes the settlement of claims is indisputable."

The executive agreements at issue here do differ in one respect from those just mentioned insofar as they address claims associated with formerly belligerent states, but against corporations, not the foreign governments. But the distinction does not matter. *** While a sharp line between public and private acts works for many purposes in the domestic law, insisting on the same line in defining the legitimate scope of the Executive's international negotiations would hamstring the President in settling international controversies.

Generally, then, valid executive agreements are fit to preempt state law, just as treaties are, and if the agreements here had expressly preempted laws like HVIRA, the issue would be straightforward. But petitioners and the United States as *amicus curiae* both have to acknowledge that the agreements include no preemption clause, and so leave their claim of preemption to rest on asserted interference with the foreign policy those agreements embody. Reliance is placed on our decision in *Zschernig v. Miller,* 389 U.S. 429 (1968).

Zschernig dealt with an Oregon probate statute prohibiting inheritance by a nonresident alien, absent showings that the foreign heir would take the property "without confiscation" by his home country and that American citizens would enjoy reciprocal rights of inheritance there. *** [I]t was clear that the Oregon law in practice had invited "minute inquiries concerning the actual administration of foreign law," and so was providing occasions for state judges to disparage certain foreign regimes, employing the language of the anti-Communism prevalent here at the height of the Cold War. Although the Solicitor General, speaking for the State Department, denied that the state statute "unduly interfere[d] with the United States' conduct of foreign relations," the Court was not deterred from exercising its own judgment to invalidate the law as an "intrusion by the State into the field of foreign affairs which the Constitution entrusts to the President and the Congress."

The *Zschernig* majority relied on statements in a number of previous cases open to the reading that state action with more than incidental effect on foreign affairs is preempted, even absent any affirmative federal activity in the subject area of the state law, and hence without any showing of conflict. *** It is a fair question whether respect for the executive foreign relations power requires a categorical choice between the contrasting theories of field and conflict preemption evident in the *Zschernig* opinions, but the question requires no answer here. *** [W]e think petitioners and the Government have demonstrated a sufficiently clear conflict to require finding preemption here.

To begin with, resolving Holocaust-era insurance claims that may be held by residents of this country is a matter well within the Executive's responsibility for foreign affairs. Since claims remaining in the aftermath of hostilities may be "sources of friction" acting as an "impediment to resumption of friendly relations" between the countries involved, there is a "longstanding practice" of the national Executive to settle them in discharging its responsibility to maintain the Nation's relationships with other countries. *Dames & Moore.* *** Vindicating victims injured by acts and omissions of enemy corporations in wartime is thus within the traditional subject matter of foreign policy in which national, not state, interests are overriding, and which the National Government has addressed.

The exercise of the federal executive authority means that state law must give way where, as here, there is evidence of clear conflict between the policies adopted by the two. *** As for insurance claims in particular, the national position, expressed unmistakably in the executive agreements signed by the President with Germany and Austria, has been to encourage European insurers to work with the ICHEIC to develop acceptable claim procedures, including procedures governing disclosure of policy information. *** The approach taken serves to resolve the several competing matters of national concern apparent in the German Foundation Agreement: the national interest in maintaining amicable relationships with current European allies; survivors' interests in a "fair and prompt" but nonadversarial resolution of their claims so as to "bring some measure of justice *** in their lifetimes"; and the companies' interest in securing "legal peace" when they settle claims in this fashion. As a way for dealing with insurance claims, moreover, the voluntary scheme protects the companies' ability to abide by their own countries' domestic privacy laws limiting disclosure of policy information.

California has taken a different tack of providing regulatory sanctions to compel disclosure and payment, supplemented by a new cause of action for Holocaust survivors if the other sanctions should fail. HVIRA's economic compulsion to make public disclosure, of far more information about far more policies than ICHEIC rules require, employs "a different, state system of economic pressure," and in doing so undercuts the President's diplomatic discretion and the choice he has made exercising it. *** The law thus "compromise[s] the very capacity of the President to speak for the Nation with one voice in dealing with other governments" to resolve claims against European companies arising out of World War II.[14] ***

HVIRA threatens to frustrate the operation of the particular mechanism the President has chosen. *** California's indiscriminate disclosure provisions place a handicap on the ICHEIC's effectiveness (and raise a further irritant to the European allies) by undercutting European privacy protections. *** The express federal policy and the clear conflict raised by the state statute are alone enough to require state law to yield. If any doubt about the clarity of the conflict remained, however, it would have to be resolved in the National Government's favor, given the weakness of the State's interest, against the backdrop of traditional state legislative subject matter, in regulating disclosure of European Holocaust-era insurance policies in the manner of HVIRA. ***

The basic fact is that California seeks to use an iron fist where the President has consistently chosen kid gloves. *** The question relevant to preemption in this case is conflict, and the evidence here is "more than

---

[14] It is true that the President in this case is acting without express congressional authority, and thus does not have the "plenitude of Executive authority" that "controll[ed] the issue of preemption" in *Crosby*. But in *Crosby* we were careful to note that the President possesses considerable independent constitutional authority to act on behalf of the United States on international issues, and conflict with the exercise of that authority is a comparably good reason to find preemption of state law.

sufficient to demonstrate that the state Act stands in the way of [the President's] diplomatic objectives." *Crosby*. *** [I]t is worth noting that Congress has done nothing to express disapproval of the President's policy. Legislation along the lines of HVIRA has been introduced in Congress repeatedly, but none of the bills has come close to making it into law. *** Given the President's independent authority "in the areas of foreign policy and national security, *** congressional silence is not to be equated with congressional disapproval." ***

JUSTICE GINSBURG, with whom JUSTICE STEVENS, JUSTICE SCALIA, and JUSTICE THOMAS join, dissenting.

*** [N]o executive agreement or other formal expression of foreign policy disapproves state disclosure laws like the HVIRA. Absent a clear statement aimed at disclosure requirements by the "one voice" to which courts properly defer in matters of foreign affairs, I would leave intact California's enactment. *** Despite the absence of express preemption, the Court holds that the HVIRA interferes with foreign policy objectives implicit in the executive agreements. I would not venture down that path.

The Court's analysis draws substantially on *Zschernig v. Miller*, 389 U.S. 429 (1968). *** We have not relied on *Zschernig* since it was decided, and I would not resurrect that decision here. The notion of "dormant foreign affairs preemption" with which *Zschernig* is associated resonates most audibly when a state action "reflect[s] a state policy critical of foreign governments and involve[s] 'sitting in judgment' on them." The HVIRA entails no such state action or policy. It takes no position on any contemporary foreign government and requires no assessment of any existing foreign regime. It is directed solely at private insurers doing business in California, and it requires them solely to disclose information in their or their affiliates' possession or control. I would not extend *Zschernig* into this dissimilar domain.[14] ***

If it is uncertain whether insurance *litigation* may continue given the executive agreements on which the Court relies, it should be abundantly clear that those agreements leave *disclosure* laws like the HVIRA untouched. *** To fill the agreements' silences, the Court points to statements by individual members of the Executive Branch. But we have never premised foreign affairs preemption on statements of that order. We should not do so here lest we place the considerable power of foreign affairs preemption in the hands of individual sub-Cabinet members of the Executive Branch. *** As I see it, courts step out of their proper role when they rely on no legislative or even executive text, but only on inference and implication, to preempt state laws on foreign affairs grounds. ***

---

[14] The Court also places considerable weight on *Crosby*. *** *Crosby* was a statutory preemption case. The state law there at issue posed "an obstacle to the accomplishment of Congress's full objectives under the [relevant] federal Act." That statutory decision provides little support for preempting a state law by inferring preclusive foreign policy objectives from precatory language in executive agreements.

Notes

1.   **Foreign and Domestic Preemption**. Is the Court's preemption analysis consistent with the analysis in *Geier v. American Honda*, or is preemption broader when foreign affairs interests are opposed to state interests instead of federal domestic interests?

2.   **Dormant Foreign Commerce Clause**. Is this case about preemption at all? Or does it concern a judicial exercise of power rather than a Presidential exercise of power? The cases in the following section should help you answer these questions.

3.   **Whose Sovereignty?** In *Arizona v. United States*, 132 S. Ct. 2492 (2012), the Court struck down portions of an Arizona statute making failure to comply with federal alien-registration requirements illegal, making it a misdemeanor for an unauthorized alien to work in the State, authorizing officers to arrest without a warrant a person "the officer has probable cause to believe ... has committed any public offense that makes the person removable from the United States," and providing that "officers who conduct a stop, detention, or arrest *must* in some circumstances make efforts to verify the person's immigration status with the Federal Government." The Court stressed the broad Federal power over immigration, the "pervasiveness of federal regulation," and the potential for additional state penalties to frustrate federal policies. It invalidated the statute except for the portion that permitted state officials to detain aliens while awaiting verification of immigration status from federal authorities. JUSTICE SCALIA's partial dissent stressed the decision's effects on state sovereignty:

> Today's opinion *** deprives States of what most would consider the defining characteristic of sovereignty: the power to exclude from the sovereign's territory people who have no right to be there. *** The mere existence of federal action in the immigration area *** cannot be regarded as such a prohibition. *** We are talking about a federal law going to the *core* of state sovereignty: the power to exclude. *** The State has the sovereign power to protect its borders more rigorously if it wishes, absent any valid federal prohibition. The Executive's policy choice of lax federal enforcement does not constitute such a prohibition."

Would the States have entered into the Union if the Constitution prohibited laws like Arizona's? Should this matter? How should preemption operate when an issue is vital both nationally and locally? Is immigration on equal ground with direct foreign relations for preemption purposes? Compare *AIA v. Garamendi*.

VI

JUDICIAL PROTECTION OF INTERSTATE COMMERCE

[To] the extent that we have gone beyond guarding against rank discrimination against citizens of other States—which is regulated not by the Commerce Clause but by the Privileges and Immunities Clause—the Court for over a century has engaged in an enterprise that it has been unable to justify by textual support or even coherent nontextual theory, that it was almost certainly not intended to undertake, and that it has not undertaken very well ***. There is no conceivable reason why congressional inaction under the Commerce Clause should be deemed to have the same preemptive effect elsewhere accorded only to congressional action. There, as elsewhere, Congress' silence is just that—silence.

—JUSTICE SCALIA in
*Tyler Pipe Industries v. Washington
State Department of Revenue,*
483 U.S. 232 (1987).

This chapter continues the theme of the previous one: constitutional limits on state power. Although this chapter focuses on commerce as did Chapter IV, the cases in this chapter involve situations in which Congress has **not** exercised legislative power pursuant to the Commerce Clause. In these cases, nevertheless, the Supreme Court considers invalidation of state regulations on the ground that they are inconsistent with the **policies behind** the constitutional allocation of power to Congress to regulate interstate commerce. The chapter also considers a related matter: whether state commerce-related actions violate the Article IV guarantee that "the Citizens of each State shall be entitled to all Privileges and Immunities of Citizens in the several States."

Typically, these cases have both economic and political components. The economic component involves whether a state or local law discriminates against or has an adverse effect on interstate commercial transactions, reducing efficiency in the delivery of goods and services. The political component deals with whether the citizens of a state are seeking to impose burdens on those not part of the state's polity or to confer benefits on the state's citizens at the expense of outsiders. Often these components are intertwined, but it is sometimes useful to evaluate the economic and political factors separately.

Another common characteristic of these cases is their contingent nature as constitutional law: Congress can reverse Supreme Court decisions in this area by passing legislation validating a state burden on commerce invalidated by the Court. See *Prudential Ins. Co. v. Benjamin*, 328 U.S. 408 (1946) (state tax on the insurance business "which in its silence might be held to be invalid as discriminatory" allowed by the federal McCarran Act). Conversely, as you saw in Chapter IV and V, Congress can statutorily override otherwise constitutional state laws when it chooses to regulate nationally using its commerce clause power.

Section A reviews the origins of the Court's active role in protecting interstate commerce in the absence of federal statutory law. Section B examines the doctrinal frameworks that have developed for evaluating explicitly discriminatory state legislation and neutral state laws having negative effects on interstate commerce. Section C looks at the market participant exception to the Court's dormant commerce clause jurisprudence. Finally, Section D explores a related constitutional provision, the privileges and immunities clause of Article IV.

As you read these materials, assess when, in your view, the Court *should* step in to invalidate state law that interferes with interstate commerce.

A. ORIGINS OF THE DORMANT COMMERCE CLAUSE

WILLSON v. THE BLACK BIRD
CREEK MARSH COMPANY
27 U.S. (2 Pet.) 245 (1829)

*** The Black Bird Creek Marsh Company [was] empowered to make and construct a good and sufficient dam across said creek ***. [T]he company proceeded to erect and place in the creek a dam, by which the navigation of the creek was obstructed ***. The defendants being the owners of a sloop called the Sally, regularly licensed and enrolled according to the navigation laws of the United States, broke and injured the dam so erected by the company; and thereupon an action of trespass *** was instituted against them ***.

MR. CHIEF JUSTICE MARSHALL delivered the opinion of the Court.

*** [The appeal] denies the state's capacity to authorize the construction of a dam across a navigable stream, in which the tide ebbs and flows; and in which there was, and of right ought to have been, a certain common and public way in the nature of a highway. This plea draws nothing into question but the validity of the act; and the judgment of the [Delaware] court must have been in favor of its validity. Its consistency with, or repugnancy to the constitution of the United States, necessarily arises upon these pleadings, and must have been determined [in the action below]. This Court has repeatedly decided in favor of its jurisdiction in such a case. *Martin v. Hunter's Lessee* [and other cases] are expressly in point. They establish, as far as precedents can establish any thing, that it is not necessary to state in terms on the record, that the constitution or a law of the United States was drawn in question. It is sufficient to bring the case within the provisions of the 25th section of the judicial act, if the record shows, that the constitution or a law or a treaty of the United States must have been misconstrued, or the decision could not be made. Or, as in this case, that the constitutionality of a state law was questioned, and the decision has been in favor of the party claiming under such law.

The jurisdiction of the Court being established, the more doubtful question is to be considered, whether the act incorporating the Black Bird Creek Marsh Company is repugnant to the constitution, so far as it authorizes a dam across the creek. The plea states the creek to be navigable, in the nature of a highway, through which the tide ebbs and flows.

The act of assembly by which the plaintiffs were authorized to construct their dam, shows plainly that this is one of those many creeks, passing through a deep level marsh adjoining the Delaware, up which the tide flows for some distance. The value of the property on its banks must be enhanced by excluding the water from the marsh, and the health of the inhabitants probably improved. Measures calculated to produce these objects, provided they do not come into collision with the powers of the general government, are undoubtedly within those which are reserved to the states. But the measure authorized by this act stops a navigable creek, and must be supposed to abridge the rights of those who have been accustomed to use it. But this abridgment, unless it comes in conflict with the constitution or a law of the United States, is an affair between the government of Delaware and its citizens, of which this Court can take no cognizance.

The counsel for the plaintiffs in error insist that it comes in conflict with the power of the United States "to regulate commerce with foreign nations and among the several states."

If congress had passed any act which bore upon the case; any act in execution of the power to regulate commerce, the object of which was to control state legislation over those small navigable creeks into which the tide flows, and which abound throughout the lower country of the middle and southern states; we should feel not much difficulty in saying that a state law coming in conflict with such act would be void. But congress has passed no such act. The repugnancy of the law of Delaware to the constitution is placed entirely on its repugnancy to the power to regulate commerce with foreign nations and among the several states; a power which has not been so exercised as to affect the question.

We do not think that the act empowering the Black Bird Creek Marsh Company to place a dam across the creek, can, under all the circumstances of the case, be considered as repugnant to the power to regulate commerce in its dormant state, or as being in conflict with any law passed on the subject. ***

Notes

1. **Language.** The Commerce Clause speaks only to Congress' power, not to the Court's power. How do the federal courts even have jurisdiction if Congress

has not enacted legislation arguably in conflict with Delaware's authorization of a dam?

2.   **Precedent.** Isn't there such a federal law—the licensing act which controlled the outcome of *Gibbons v. Ogden*, supra Ch. IV? Shouldn't *Gibbons* control this case? If not, what is different?

3.   **The *Willson* Reasoning and Dormant Commerce Clause Policy.**

     •   Why did the Court stress Delaware's police power to enhance property values and the health of its people? Isn't it true that, whatever Delaware's purpose, the effect of the dam was to block a navigable waterway? Do you think the Court would have decided the case differently if the Hudson River (rather than Black Bird Creek) had been dammed?

     •   Do you think the Court would have viewed this case differently if the owners of the sloop Sally had sued to enjoin construction rather than asserting a Commerce Clause defense to a trespass action for damaging the dam?

     •   Should it be relevant that the dam's benefits inured exclusively (so far as we know) to Delaware residents? That the disadvantages of the dam fell equally on Delaware and non-Delaware sloop owners?

B. DISCRIMINATION AGAINST AND BURDENS ON COMMERCE

PHILADELPHIA v. NEW JERSEY
437 U.S. 617 (1978)

MR. JUSTICE STEWART delivered the opinion of the Court.

     *** The statutory provision in question *** provides: "No person shall bring into this State any solid or liquid waste which originated or was collected outside the territorial limits of the State, except garbage to be fed to swine in the State of New Jersey, until the commissioner [of the State Department of Environmental Protection] shall determine that such action can be permitted without endangering the public health, safety and welfare and has promulgated regulations permitting and regulating the treatment and disposal of such waste in this State." *** [T]he Commissioner promulgated regulations permitting four categories of waste to enter the State. Apart from these narrow exceptions, however, New Jersey closed its borders to all waste from other States.

     Immediately affected by these developments were the operators of private landfills in New Jersey, and several cities in other States that had agreements with these operators for waste disposal. They brought suit against New Jersey *** attacking the statute and regulations on [preemption and other constitutional] grounds. *** The New Jersey Supreme Court *** found that [the Act] advanced vital health and environmental objectives with no economic discrimination against, and with little burden upon, interstate commerce, and that the law was therefore permissible under the Commerce Clause of the Constitution. The court also found no congressional intent to pre-empt. *** We agree with the New Jersey court that the state law has not been pre-empted by federal legislation. The dispositive question, therefore, is whether the law is constitutionally permissible in light of the Commerce Clause of the Constitution.

Before it addressed the merits of the appellants' claim, the New Jersey Supreme Court questioned whether the interstate movement of those wastes banned by ch. 363 is "commerce" at all within the meaning of the Commerce Clause. Any doubts on that score should be laid to rest at the outset. *** All objects of interstate trade merit Commerce Clause protection; none is excluded by definition at the outset. *** Hence, we reject the state court's suggestion that the banning of "valueless" out-of-state wastes *** implicates no constitutional protection. Just as Congress has power to regulate the interstate movement of these wastes, States are not free from constitutional scrutiny when they restrict that movement.

Although the Constitution gives Congress the power to regulate commerce among the States, many subjects of potential federal regulation under that power inevitably escape congressional attention "because of their local character and their number and diversity." In the absence of federal legislation, these subjects are open to control by the States so long as they act within the restraints imposed by the Commerce Clause itself. The bounds of these restraints appear nowhere in the words of the Commerce Clause, but have emerged gradually in the decisions of this Court giving effect to its basic purpose. That broad purpose was well expressed by MR. JUSTICE JACKSON in his opinion for the Court in *H. P. Hood & Sons, Inc. v. Du Mond*, 336 U.S. 525, 537–538: "This principle that our economic unit is the Nation, which alone has the gamut of powers necessary to control of the economy, including the vital power of erecting customs barriers against foreign competition, has as its corollary that the states are not separable economic units. *** [W]hat is ultimate is the principle that one state in its dealings with another may not place itself in a position of economic isolation."

The opinions of the Court through the years have reflected an alertness to the evils of "economic isolation" and protectionism, while at the same time recognizing that incidental burdens on interstate commerce may be unavoidable when a State legislates to safeguard the health and safety of its people. Thus, where simple economic protectionism is effected by state legislation, a virtually per se rule of invalidity has been erected. The clearest example of such legislation is a law that overtly blocks the flow of interstate commerce at a State's borders. But where other legislative objectives are credibly advanced and there is no patent discrimination against interstate trade, the Court has adopted a much more flexible approach, the general contours of which were outlined in *Pike v. Bruce Church, Inc.*, 397 U.S. 137, 142:

> Where the statute regulates evenhandedly to effectuate a legitimate local public interest, and its effects on interstate commerce are only incidental, it will be upheld unless the burden imposed on such commerce is clearly excessive in relation to the putative local benefits. *** If a legitimate local purpose is found, then the question becomes one of degree. And the extent of the

burden that will be tolerated will of course depend on the nature of the local interest involved, and on whether it could be promoted as well with a lesser impact on interstate activities.

The crucial inquiry, therefore, must be directed to determining whether ch. 363 is basically a protectionist measure, or whether it can fairly be viewed as a law directed to legitimate local concerns, with effects upon interstate commerce that are only incidental.

The purpose of ch. 363 is set out in the statute itself as follows:

> The Legislature finds and determines that *** the volume of solid and liquid waste continues to rapidly increase, that the treatment and disposal of these wastes continues to pose an even greater threat to the quality of the environment of New Jersey, that the available and appropriate land fill sites within the State are being diminished, that the environment continues to be threatened by the treatment and disposal of waste which originated or was collected outside the State, and that the public health, safety and welfare require that the treatment and disposal within this State of all wastes generated outside of the State be prohibited.

The New Jersey Supreme Court accepted this statement of the state legislature's purpose. The state court additionally found that New Jersey's existing landfill sites will be exhausted within a few years; that to go on using these sites or to develop new ones will take a heavy environmental toll, both from pollution and from loss of scarce open lands; that new techniques to divert waste from landfills to other methods of disposal and resource recovery processes are under development, but that these changes will require time; and finally, that "the extension of the lifespan of existing landfills, resulting from the exclusion of out-of-state waste, may be of crucial importance in preventing further virgin wetlands or other undeveloped lands from being devoted to landfill purposes." Based on these findings, the court concluded that ch. 363 was designed to protect, not the State's economy, but its environment, and that its substantial benefits outweigh its "slight" burden on interstate commerce.

The appellants strenuously contend that ch. 363, "while outwardly cloaked 'in the currently fashionable garb of environmental protection,' *** is actually no more than a legislative effort to suppress competition and stabilize the cost of solid waste disposal for New Jersey residents ***." They cite passages of legislative history suggesting that the problem addressed by ch. 363 is primarily financial: Stemming the flow of out-of-state waste into certain landfill sites will extend their lives, thus delaying the day when New Jersey cities must transport their waste to more distant and expensive sites.

The appellees, on the other hand, deny that ch. 363 was motivated by financial concerns or economic protectionism. In the words of their brief, "[n]o New Jersey commercial interests stand to gain advantage over competitors from outside the state as a result of the ban on dumping out-of-state waste." Noting that New Jersey landfill operators are among the plaintiffs, the appellee's brief argues that "[t]he complaint is not that New Jersey has forged an economic preference for its own commercial interests, but rather that it has denied a small group of its entrepreneurs an economic opportunity to traffic in waste in order to protect the health, safety and welfare of the citizenry at large."

This dispute about ultimate legislative purpose need not be resolved, because its resolution would not be relevant to the constitutional issue to be decided in this case. *** [T]he evil of protectionism can reside in legislative means as well as legislative ends. Thus, it does not matter whether the ultimate aim of ch. 363 is to reduce the waste disposal costs of New Jersey residents or to save remaining open lands from pollution, for we assume New Jersey has every right to protect its residents' pocketbooks as well as their environment. And it may be assumed as well that New Jersey may pursue those ends by slowing the flow of all waste into the State's remaining landfills, even though interstate commerce may incidentally be affected. But whatever New Jersey's ultimate purpose, it may not be accomplished by discriminating against articles of commerce coming from outside the State unless there is some reason, apart from their origin, to treat them differently. Both on its face and in its plain effect, ch. 363 violates this principle of nondiscrimination.

The Court has consistently found parochial legislation of this kind to be constitutionally invalid, whether the ultimate aim of the legislation was to assure a steady supply of milk by erecting barriers to allegedly ruinous outside competition, or to create jobs by keeping industry within the State, or to preserve the State's financial resources from depletion by fencing out indigent immigrants. In each of these cases, a presumably legitimate goal was sought to be achieved by the illegitimate means of isolating the State from the national economy.

Also relevant here are the Court's decisions holding that a State may not accord its own inhabitants a preferred right of access over consumers in other States to natural resources located within its borders. These cases stand for the basic principle that a "State is without power to prevent privately owned articles of trade from being shipped and sold in interstate commerce on the ground that they are required to satisfy local demands or because they are needed by the people of the State."

The New Jersey law at issue in this case falls squarely within the area that the Commerce Clause puts off limits to state regulation. On its face, it imposes on out-of-state commercial interests the full burden of conserving the State's remaining landfill space. It is true that in our previous cases the scarce natural resource was itself the article of commerce, whereas here the scarce resource and the article of commerce are distinct. But that difference is without consequence. In both instances, the State has overtly moved to slow or freeze the flow of commerce for protectionist reasons. It does not matter that the State has shut the article of commerce inside the State in one case and outside the State in the other. What is crucial is the attempt by one State to isolate itself from a problem common to many by erecting a barrier against the movement of interstate trade.

The appellees argue that not all laws which facially discriminate against out-of-state commerce are forbidden protectionist regulations. In particular, they point to quarantine laws, which this Court has repeatedly upheld even though they appear to single out interstate commerce for special treatment. *** It is true that certain quarantine laws have not been considered forbidden protectionist measures, even though they were directed against out-of-state commerce. But those quarantine laws banned the importation of articles such as diseased livestock that required destruction as soon as possible because their very movement risked contagion and other evils. Those laws thus did not discriminate against interstate commerce as such, but simply prevented traffic in noxious articles, whatever their origin.

The New Jersey statute is not such a quarantine law. There has been no claim here that the very movement of waste into or through New Jersey endangers health, or that waste must be disposed of as soon and as close to its point of generation as possible. The harms caused by waste are said to arise after its disposal in landfill sites, and at that point, as New Jersey concedes, there is no basis to distinguish out-of-state waste from domestic waste. If one is inherently harmful, so is the other. Yet New Jersey has banned the former while leaving its landfill sites open to the latter. The New Jersey law blocks the importation of waste in an obvious effort to saddle those outside the State with the entire burden of slowing the flow of refuse into New Jersey's remaining landfill sites. That legislative effort is clearly impermissible under the Commerce Clause of the Constitution.

Today, cities in Pennsylvania and New York find it expedient or necessary to send their waste into New Jersey for disposal, and New Jersey claims the right to close its borders to such traffic. Tomorrow, cities in New Jersey may find it expedient or necessary to send their waste into Pennsylvania or New York for disposal, and those States might then claim the right to close their borders. The Commerce Clause will protect New Jersey in the future, just as it protects her neighbors now, from efforts by one State to isolate itself in the stream of interstate commerce from a problem shared by all. ***

MR. JUSTICE REHNQUIST, with whom THE CHIEF JUSTICE joins, dissenting.

A growing problem in our Nation is the sanitary treatment and disposal of solid waste. For many years, solid waste was incinerated. Because of the significant environmental problems attendant on incineration, however, this method of solid waste disposal has declined in use in many localities, including New Jersey. "Sanitary" landfills have replaced incineration as the principal method of disposing of solid waste. *** New Jersey legislatively recognized the unfortunate fact that landfills also present extremely serious health and safety problems. *** The health and safety hazards associated with landfills present appellees with a currently unsolvable dilemma. Other, hopefully safer, methods of disposing of solid wastes are still in the development stage and cannot presently be used. But appellees obviously cannot completely stop the tide of solid waste that its citizens will produce in the interim. For the moment, therefore, appellees must continue to use sanitary landfills to dispose of New Jersey's own solid waste despite the critical environmental problems thereby created.

The question presented in this case is whether New Jersey must also continue to receive and dispose of solid waste from neighboring States, even though these will inexorably increase the health problems discussed above. The Court answers this question in the affirmative. New Jersey must either prohibit all landfill operations, leaving itself to cast about for a presently nonexistent solution to the serious problem of disposing of the waste generated within its own borders, or it must accept waste from every portion of the United States, thereby multiplying the health and safety problems which would result if it dealt only with such wastes generated within the State. Because past precedents establish that the Commerce Clause does not present appellees with such a Hobson's choice, I dissent. ***

In my opinion, [quarantine] cases are dispositive of the present one. Under them, New Jersey may require germ-infected rags or diseased meat to be disposed of as best as possible within the State, but at the same time prohibit the importation of such items for disposal at the facilities that are set up within New Jersey for disposal of such material generated within the State. The physical fact of life that New Jersey must somehow dispose of its own noxious items does not mean that it must serve as a depository for those of every other State. Similarly, New Jersey should be free under our past precedents to prohibit the importation of solid waste because of the health and safety problems that such waste poses to its citizens. The fact that New Jersey continues to, and indeed must continue to, dispose of its own solid waste does not mean that New Jersey may not prohibit the importation of even more solid waste into the State. I simply see no way to distinguish solid waste, on the record of this case, from germ-infected rags, diseased meat, and other noxious items.

The Court's effort to distinguish these prior cases is unconvincing. *** I think it far from clear that the State's law has as limited a focus as the Court imputes to it: Solid waste which is a health hazard when it reaches its destination may in all likelihood be an equally great health hazard in transit.

Even if the Court is correct in its characterization of New Jersey's concerns, I do not see why a State may ban the importation of items whose movement risks contagion, but cannot ban the importation of items which, although they may be transported into the State without undue hazard, will then simply pile up in an ever increasing danger to the public's health and safety. The Commerce Clause was not drawn with a view to having the validity of state laws turn on such pointless distinctions.

Second, the Court implies that the challenged laws must be invalidated because New Jersey has left its landfills open to domestic waste. But, as the Court notes, this Court has repeatedly upheld quarantine laws "even though they appear to single out interstate commerce for special treatment." The fact that New Jersey has left its landfill sites open for domestic waste does not, of course, mean that solid waste is not innately harmful. Nor does it mean that New Jersey prohibits importation of solid waste for reasons other than the health and safety of its population. New Jersey must out of sheer necessity treat and dispose of its solid waste in some fashion, just as it must treat New Jersey cattle suffering from hoof-and-mouth disease. It does not follow that New Jersey must *** accept solid waste or diseased cattle from outside its borders and thereby exacerbate its problems. ***

Notes

1.   **Benefits and Burdens Analysis.** What is the commerce in *Philadelphia*? Who gains the benefits and who bears the burdens of the New Jersey statute (consider out-of-state waste producers, out-of-state landfill operators, in-state waste producers, and in-state landfill operators)? Note that it may be difficult to determine whether the locality's overall economic benefits exceed its overall costs.

2.   **Facial Discrimination.** Does the Court really care about the aggregate benefits and burdens when there is facial discrimination against outsiders? Maybe the Court has simply established a default rule: discriminatory legislation is normally (per se?) unconstitutional unless and until Congress acts to permit such discrimination. On the other hand, there are a few cases in which the Court has found compelling local justifications sufficient to validate even facially discriminatory local statutes. *See Maine v. Taylor*, 477 U.S. 131 (1986) (prohibition on import of live baitfish permissible to protect local species when there is no way to inspect imported baitfish for harmful parasites).

3.   **Discriminatory Taxation.** State taxes that discriminate against foreign or out-of-state firms, like discriminatory regulations, frequently violate the Commerce Clause.   What should the Court do with facially different but potentially offsetting taxes between local and out-of-state entities? *South Central Bell Telephone Co. v. Alabama*, 526 U.S. 160 (1999), concerned an Alabama statute that required all foreign and out-of-state companies to pay a franchise tax equal to 0.3% of the value of the actual amount of capital employed in the State. In-state firms, however, were required to pay a franchise tax equal to 1% of the par value of the firm's stock. Local firms thus were taxed at a nominally higher rate, but had considerable flexibility to set their own levels of tax liability by setting the par value much lower than the market value of their stock. The Court determined that the statute was facially discriminatory in light of the different tax standards set for out-of-state and in-state firms.   It then noted that a "discriminatory tax cannot be upheld as 'compensatory' unless the State proves that the special burden that the franchise tax imposes upon foreign corporations is 'roughly *** approximate' to the special burden on domestic corporations, and that the taxes are similar enough 'in substance' to serve as 'mutually exclusive' proxies for one another." Alabama did not prove that its taxes met this standard.

GRANHOLM v. HEALD
544 U.S. 460 (2005)

JUSTICE KENNEDY delivered the opinion of the Court.

These consolidated cases present challenges to state laws regulating the sale of wine from out-of-state wineries to consumers in Michigan and New York. The *** object and effect of the laws are the same: to allow in-state wineries to sell wine directly to consumers in that State but to prohibit out-of-state wineries from doing so, or, at the least, to make direct sales impractical from an economic standpoint. It is evident that the object and design of the Michigan and New York statutes is to grant in-state wineries a competitive advantage over wineries located beyond the States' borders. *** The current patchwork of laws--with some States banning direct shipments altogether, others doing so only for out-of-state wines, and still others requiring reciprocity--is essentially the product of an ongoing, low-level trade war. Allowing States to discriminate against out-of-state wine "invite[s] a multiplication of preferential trade areas destructive of the very purpose of the Commerce Clause." ***

Before 1919, the temperance movement fought to curb the sale of alcoholic beverages one State at a time. *** In a series of cases before ratification of the Eighteenth Amendment the Court, relying on the Commerce Clause, invalidated a number of state liquor regulations. *** [Under the federal 1913 Webb-Kenyon Act] States were now empowered to forbid shipments of alcohol to consumers for personal use, provided that the States treated in-state and out-of-state liquor on the same terms. *** The ratification of the Eighteenth Amendment in 1919 provided a brief respite from the legal battles over the validity of state liquor regulations. With the ratification of the Twenty-first Amendment 14 years later, however, nationwide Prohibition came to an end. Section 1 of the Twenty-first Amendment repealed the Eighteenth Amendment. Section 2 of the Twenty-first Amendment is at issue here.

Michigan and New York say the provision grants to the States the authority to discriminate against out-of-state goods. The history we have recited does not support this position. *** "The wording of § 2 of the Twenty-first Amendment closely follows the Webb-Kenyon and Wilson Acts, expressing the framers' clear intention of constitutionalizing the Commerce Clause framework established under those statutes." The aim of the Twenty-first Amendment was to allow States to maintain an effective and uniform system for controlling liquor by regulating its transportation, importation, and use. The Amendment did not give States the authority to pass nonuniform laws in order to discriminate against out-of-state goods, a privilege they had not enjoyed at any earlier time.

Our more recent cases, furthermore, confirm that the Twenty-first Amendment does not supersede other provisions of the Constitution and, in particular, does not displace the rule that States may not give a discriminatory preference to their own producers. *** First, the Court has held that state laws that violate other provisions of the Constitution are not saved by the Twenty-first Amendment. The Court has applied this rule in the context of the First Amendment, the Establishment Clause, the Equal Protection Clause, the Due Process Clause, and the Import-Export Clause. Second, the Court has held that § 2 does not abrogate Congress' Commerce Clause powers with regard to liquor. *** Finally, and most relevant to the issue at hand, the Court has held that state regulation of alcohol is limited by the nondiscrimination principle of the Commerce Clause. *** State policies are protected under the Twenty-first Amendment when they treat liquor produced out of state the same as its domestic equivalent. The instant cases, in contrast, involve straightforward attempts to discriminate in favor of local producers. The discrimination is contrary to the Commerce Clause and is not saved by the Twenty-first Amendment. ***

The States offer two primary justifications for restricting direct shipments from out-of-state wineries: keeping alcohol out of the hands of minors and facilitating tax collection. *** The States provide little evidence that the purchase of wine over the Internet by minors is a problem. Indeed, there is some evidence to the contrary. A recent study by the staff of the FTC found that the 26 States currently allowing direct shipments report no problems with minors' increased access to wine. *** Even were we to credit the States' largely unsupported claim that direct shipping of wine increases the risk of underage drinking, this would not justify regulations limiting only out-of-state direct shipments. As the wineries point out, minors are just as likely to order wine from in-state producers as from out-of-state ones. *** In addition, the States can take less restrictive steps to minimize the risk that minors will order wine by mail. For example, the Model Direct Shipping Bill developed by the National Conference of State Legislatures requires an adult signature on delivery and a label so instructing on each package.

The States' tax-collection justification is also insufficient. Increased direct shipping, whether originating in state or out of state, brings with it the potential for tax evasion. *** New York could protect itself against lost tax revenue by requiring a permit as a condition of direct shipping. This is the approach taken by New York for in-state wineries. The State offers no reason to believe the system would prove ineffective for out-of-state wineries. Licensees could be required to submit regular sales reports and to remit taxes. Indeed, various States use this approach for taxing direct interstate wine shipments, and report no problems with tax collection. *** The States have not shown that tax evasion from out-of-state wineries poses such a unique threat that it justifies their discriminatory regimes.

Michigan and New York offer a handful of other rationales, such as facilitating orderly market conditions, protecting public health and safety, and ensuring regulatory accountability. These objectives can also be achieved through the alternative of an evenhanded licensing requirement. *** In summary, the States provide little concrete evidence for the sweeping assertion that they cannot police direct shipments by out-of-state wineries. Our Commerce Clause cases demand more than mere speculation to support discrimination against out-of-state goods. The "burden is on the State to show that the *discrimination* is demonstrably justified." *** Without demonstrating the need for discrimination, New York and Michigan have enacted regulations that disadvantage out-of-state wine producers. Under our Commerce Clause jurisprudence, these regulations cannot stand.

JUSTICE STEVENS, with whom JUSTICE O'CONNOR joins, dissenting.

*** The New York and Michigan laws challenged in these cases would be patently invalid under well settled dormant Commerce Clause principles if they regulated sales of an ordinary article of commerce rather than wine. But ever since the adoption of the Eighteenth Amendment and the Twenty-first

Amendment, our Constitution has placed commerce in alcoholic beverages in a special category. Section 2 of the Twenty-first Amendment expressly provides that "[t]he transportation or importation into any State, Territory, or possession of the United States for delivery or use therein of intoxicating liquors, in violation of the laws thereof, is hereby prohibited." *** Today's decision may represent sound economic policy and may be consistent with the policy choices of the contemporaries of Adam Smith who drafted our original Constitution; it is not, however, consistent with the policy choices made by those who amended our Constitution in 1919 and 1933. *** Because the New York and Michigan laws regulate the "transportation or importation" of "intoxicating liquors" for "delivery or use therein," they are exempt from dormant Commerce Clause scrutiny. ***

JUSTICE THOMAS, with whom THE CHIEF JUSTICE, JUSTICE STEVENS, and JUSTICE O'CONNOR join, dissenting

A century ago, this Court repeatedly invalidated, as inconsistent with the negative Commerce Clause, state liquor legislation that prevented out-of-state businesses from shipping liquor directly to a State's residents. The Webb-Kenyon Act and the Twenty-first Amendment cut off this intrusive review, as their text and history make clear and as this Court's early cases on the Twenty-first Amendment recognized. The Court today seizes back this power, based primarily on a historical argument that this Court decisively rejected long ago. Because I would follow ***the language of both the statute that Congress enacted and the Amendment that the Nation ratified, rather than the Court's questionable reading of history and the "negative implications" of the Commerce Clause, I respectfully dissent. *** The Twenty-first Amendment did not impliedly repeal the Commerce Clause, but that does not justify narrowing of the Twenty-first Amendment to its "core concerns." *** Given the uniformity of our early case law supporting even discriminatory state laws regulating imports into States, then, Michigan's and New York's laws easily pass muster under this Court's cases. *** [T]he Court does this Nation no service by ignoring the textual commands of the Constitution and Acts of Congress. The Twenty-first Amendment and the Webb-Kenyon Act displaced the negative Commerce Clause as applied to regulation of liquor imports into a State. ***

Notes

1.　**Policy and Reality**. Free-market economists and wine drinkers celebrated *Granholm*, but direct internet sales of wine to consumers today is only 1% of total wine sales while internet sales are 12% of retail sales otherwise. Why didn't *Granholm* end the "low-level trade wars" deplored by the Court?

2.　**Statutory Sources for Constitutional Interpretation**.　The Court examines a statute preceding the 21st Amendment to conclude that state control over liquor does not include the ability to discriminate against out-of-state wine vendors.　Is statutory exegesis an appropriate tool for interpreting the Constitution?

3.　**The Last Ratified Rule**. In earlier chapters, the 11th Amendment trumped Congress' Article I powers, and the 14th Amendment modified the reach of the

11th Amendment. Why, then, doesn't the 21st Amendment override dormant commerce doctrine?

KASSEL v. CONSOLIDATED FREIGHTWAYS
450 U.S. 662 (1981)

JUSTICE POWELL announced the judgment of the Court and delivered an opinion, in which JUSTICE WHITE, JUSTICE BLACKMUN, and JUSTICE STEVENS joined.

The question is whether an Iowa statute that prohibits the use of certain large trucks within the State unconstitutionally burdens interstate commerce.

Appellee Consolidated Freightways Corporation of Delaware (Consolidated) is one of the largest common carriers in the country. *** Consolidated mainly uses two kinds of trucks. One consists of a three-axle tractor pulling a 40–foot two-axle trailer. This unit, commonly called a single, or "semi," is 55 feet in length overall. Such trucks have long been used on the Nation's highways. Consolidated also uses a two-axle tractor pulling a single-axle trailer which, in turn, pulls a single-axle dolly and a second single-axle trailer. This combination, known as a double, or twin, is 65 feet long overall. Many trucking companies, including Consolidated, increasingly prefer to use doubles to ship certain kinds of commodities. Doubles have larger capacities, and the trailers can be detached and routed separately if necessary. Consolidated would like to use 65–foot doubles on many of its trips through Iowa.

The State of Iowa, however, by statute restricts the length of vehicles that may use its highways. Unlike all other States in the West and Midwest, Iowa generally prohibits the use of 65–foot doubles within its borders. Instead, most truck combinations are restricted to 55 feet in length. Doubles, mobile homes, trucks carrying vehicles such as tractors and other farm equipment, and singles hauling livestock are permitted to be as long as 60 feet. Notwithstanding these restrictions, Iowa's statute permits cities abutting the state line by local ordinance to adopt the length limitations of the adjoining State. Where a city has exercised this option, otherwise oversized trucks are permitted within the city limits and in nearby commercial zones.[6]

Iowa also provides for two other relevant exemptions. An Iowa truck manufacturer may obtain a permit to ship trucks that are as large as 70 feet. Permits also are available to move oversized mobile homes, provided that the

---

[6] The Iowa Legislature in 1974 passed House Bill 671, which would have permitted 65–foot doubles. But Iowa Governor Ray vetoed the bill, noting that it "would benefit only a few Iowa-based companies while providing a great advantage for out-of-state trucking firms and competitors at the expense of our Iowa citizens." Governor's Veto Message of March 2, 1974 ***. The "border-cities exemption" was passed by the General Assembly and signed by the Governor shortly thereafter. ***

unit is to be moved from a point within Iowa or delivered for an Iowa resident.[7]

Because of Iowa's statutory scheme, Consolidated cannot use its 65–foot doubles to move commodities through the State. Instead, the company must do one of four things: (i) use 55–foot singles; (ii) use 60–foot doubles; (iii) detach the trailers of a 65–foot double and shuttle each through the State separately; or (iv) divert 65–foot doubles around Iowa. *** Iowa defended the law as a reasonable safety measure enacted pursuant to its police power. The State asserted that 65–foot doubles are more dangerous than 55–foot singles and, in any event, that the law promotes safety and reduces road wear within the State by diverting much truck traffic to other States.

In a 14–day trial, both sides adduced evidence on safety, and on the burden on interstate commerce imposed by Iowa's law. On the question of safety, the District Court found that the "evidence clearly establishes that the twin is as safe as the semi." *** In light of these findings, the District Court applied the standard we enunciated in *Raymond Motor Transportation, Inc. v. Rice*, 434 U.S. 429 (1978), and concluded that the state law impermissibly burdened interstate commerce:

> "[T]he balance here must be struck in favor of the federal interests. The *total effect* of the law as a safety measure in reducing accidents and casualties is so slight and problematical that it does not outweigh the national interest in keeping interstate commerce free from interferences that seriously impede it."

*** The Commerce Clause does not, of course, invalidate all state restrictions on commerce. *** Those who would challenge such bona fide safety regulations must overcome a "strong presumption of validity." *** Regulations designed for that salutary purpose nevertheless may further the purpose so marginally, and interfere with commerce so substantially, as to be invalid under the Commerce Clause. ***Applying these general principles, we conclude that the Iowa truck-length limitations unconstitutionally burden interstate commerce.

In *Raymond Motor Transportation, Inc. v. Rice*, the Court held that a Wisconsin statute that precluded the use of 65–foot doubles violated the Commerce Clause. This case is *Raymond* revisited. Here, as in *Raymond*, the State failed to present any persuasive evidence that 65–foot doubles are less safe than 55–foot singles. Moreover, Iowa's law is now out of step with the laws of all other Midwestern and Western States. Iowa thus substantially burdens the interstate flow of goods by truck. In the absence of congressional action to set uniform standards, some burdens associated with state safety regulations must be tolerated. But where, as here, the State's safety interest

---

[7] The parochial restrictions in the mobile home provision were enacted after Governor Ray vetoed a bill that would have permitted the interstate shipment of all mobile homes through Iowa. Governor Ray commented, in his veto message: "This bill *** would make Iowa a bridge state as these oversized units are moved into Iowa after being manufactured in another state and sold in a third. None of this activity would be of particular economic benefit to Iowa."

has been found to be illusory, and its regulations impair significantly the federal interest in efficient and safe interstate transportation, the state law cannot be harmonized with the Commerce Clause.[12]

Iowa made a more serious effort to support the safety rationale of its law than did Wisconsin in *Raymond,* but its effort was no more persuasive. *** The trial focused on a comparison of the performance of the two kinds of trucks in various safety categories. The evidence showed, and the District Court found, that the 65–foot double was at least the equal of the 55–foot single in the ability to brake, turn, and maneuver. The double, because of its axle placement, produces less splash and spray in wet weather. And, because of its articulation in the middle, the double is less susceptible to dangerous "off-tracking," to wind.

None of these findings is seriously disputed by Iowa. Indeed, the State points to only three ways in which the 55–foot single is even arguably superior: singles take less time to be passed and to clear intersections; they may back up for longer distances; and they are somewhat less likely to jackknife.

The first two of these characteristics are of limited relevance on modern interstate highways. As the District Court found, the negligible difference in the time required to pass, and to cross intersections, is insignificant on 4–lane divided highways because passing does not require crossing into oncoming traffic lanes, and interstates have few, if any, intersections. The concern over backing capability also is insignificant because it seldom is necessary to back up on an interstate. In any event, no evidence suggested any difference in backing capability between the 60–foot doubles that Iowa permits and the 65–foot doubles that it bans. Similarly, although doubles tend to jackknife somewhat more than singles, 65–foot doubles actually are less likely to jackknife than 60–foot doubles. Statistical studies supported the view that 65–foot doubles are at least as safe overall as 55–foot singles and 60–foot doubles. ***[16]

Consolidated, meanwhile, demonstrated that Iowa's law substantially burdens interstate commerce. Trucking companies that wish to continue to use 65–foot doubles must route them around Iowa or detach the trailers of the doubles and ship them through separately. Alternatively, trucking companies must use the smaller 55–foot singles or 60–foot doubles permitted under Iowa law. Each of these options engenders inefficiency and added expense. The record shows that Iowa's law added about $12.6 million each year to the costs of trucking companies. Consolidated alone incurred about $2 million per year in increased costs.

---

[12] It is highly relevant that here, as in *Raymond*, the state statute contains exemptions that weaken the deference traditionally accorded to a state safety regulation.

[16] In suggesting that Iowa's law actually promotes safety, the dissenting opinion ignores the findings of the courts below and relies on largely discredited statistical evidence. The dissent implies that a statistical study identified doubles as more dangerous than singles. At trial, however, the author of that study—Iowa's own statistician—conceded that his calculations were statistically biased, and therefore "not very meaningful." ***

In addition to increasing the costs of the trucking companies (and, indirectly, of the service to consumers), Iowa's law may aggravate, rather than ameliorate, the problem of highway accidents. *** Either more small trucks must be used to carry the same quantity of goods through Iowa, or the same number of larger trucks must drive longer distances to bypass Iowa. *** Other things being equal, accidents are proportional to distance traveled. Thus, if 65–foot doubles are as safe as 55–foot singles, Iowa's law tends to increase the number of accidents, and to shift the incidence of them from Iowa to other States.[18] Perhaps recognizing the weakness of the evidence supporting its safety argument, and the substantial burden on commerce that its regulations create, Iowa urges the Court simply to "defer" to the safety judgment of the State. It argues that the length of trucks is generally, although perhaps imprecisely, related to safety. The task of drawing a line is one that Iowa contends should be left to its legislature.

The Court normally does accord "special deference" to state highway safety regulations. *Raymond.* This traditional deference "derives in part from the assumption that where such regulations do not discriminate on their face against interstate commerce, their burden usually falls on local economic interests as well as other States' economic interests, thus insuring that a State's own political processes will serve as a check against unduly burdensome regulations." Less deference to the legislative judgment is due, however, where the local regulation bears disproportionately on out-of-state residents and businesses. Such a disproportionate burden is apparent here. Iowa's scheme, although generally banning large doubles from the State, nevertheless has several exemptions that secure to Iowans many of the benefits of large trucks while shunting to neighboring States many of the costs associated with their use.

At the time of trial there were two particularly significant exemptions. First, singles hauling livestock or farm vehicles were permitted to be as long as 60 feet. *** Second, cities abutting other States were permitted to enact local ordinances adopting the larger length limitation of the neighboring State. This exemption offered the benefits of longer trucks to individuals and businesses in important border cities without burdening Iowa's highways with interstate through traffic.

The origin of the "border cities exemption" also suggests that Iowa's statute may not have been designed to ban dangerous trucks, but rather to discourage interstate truck traffic. In 1974, the legislature passed a bill that would have permitted 65–foot doubles in the State. Governor Ray vetoed the bill. He said:

> "I find sympathy with those who are doing business in our
> state and whose enterprises could gain from increased cargo

---

[18] The District Court *** noted that Iowa's law causes "more accidents, more injuries, more fatalities and more fuel consumption." Appellant Kassel conceded as much at trial. Kassel explained, however, that most of these additional accidents occur in States other than Iowa because truck traffic is deflected around the State. He noted: "Our primary concern is the citizens of Iowa and our own highway system we operate in this state."

carrying ability by trucks. However, with this bill, the Legislature has pursued a course that would benefit only a few Iowa-based companies while providing a great advantage for out-of-state trucking firms and competitors at the expense of our Iowa citizens."

After the veto, the "border cities exemption" was immediately enacted and signed by the Governor.

It is thus far from clear that Iowa was motivated primarily by a judgment that 65–foot doubles are less safe than 55–foot singles. Rather, Iowa seems to have hoped to limit the use of its highways by deflecting some through traffic. *** Because Iowa has imposed this burden without any significant countervailing safety interest, its statute violates the Commerce Clause. ***

JUSTICE BRENNAN, with whom JUSTICE MARSHALL joins, concurring in the judgment.

*** For me, analysis of Commerce Clause challenges to state regulations must take into account three principles: (1) The courts are not empowered to second-guess the empirical judgments of lawmakers concerning the utility of legislation. (2) The burdens imposed on commerce must be balanced against the local benefits actually sought to be achieved by the State's lawmakers, and not against those suggested after the fact by counsel. (3) Protectionist legislation is unconstitutional under the Commerce Clause, even if the burdens and benefits are related to safety rather than economics. ***

In considering a Commerce Clause challenge to a state regulation, the judicial task is to balance the burden imposed on commerce against the local benefits sought to be achieved by the State's *lawmakers*. In determining those benefits, a court should focus ultimately on the regulatory purposes identified by the lawmakers and on the evidence before or available to them that might have supported their judgment. *** It is not the function of the court to decide whether in fact the regulation promotes its intended purpose, so long as an examination of the evidence before or available to the lawmaker indicates that the regulation is not wholly irrational in light of its purposes.[9]

My Brothers POWELL and REHNQUIST make the mistake of disregarding the intention of Iowa's lawmakers and assuming that resolution of the case must hinge upon the argument offered by Iowa's attorneys: that 65–foot doubles are more dangerous than shorter trucks. They then canvass the factual record and findings of the courts below and reach opposite conclusions as to whether the evidence adequately supports that empirical judgment. *** Iowa's actual rationale for maintaining the regulation had nothing to do with these purported differences. Rather, Iowa sought to discourage interstate truck traffic on Iowa's highways. Thus, the safety advantages and

---

[9] Moreover, I would emphasize that in the field of safety—and perhaps in other fields where the decisions of state lawmakers are deserving of a heightened degree of deference—the role of the courts is not to balance asserted burdens against intended benefits as it is in other fields. In the field of safety, once the court has established that the intended safety benefit is not illusory, insubstantial, or nonexistent, it must defer to the State's lawmakers on the appropriate balance to be struck against other interests. ***.

disadvantages of the types and lengths of trucks involved in this case are irrelevant to the decision. *** Though my Brother POWELL recognizes that the State's actual purpose in maintaining the truck-length regulation was "to limit the use of its highways by deflecting some through traffic," he fails to recognize that this purpose, being protectionist in nature, is impermissible under the Commerce Clause. The Governor admitted that he blocked legislative efforts to raise the length of trucks because the change "would benefit only a few Iowa-based companies while providing a great advantage for out-of-state trucking firms and competitors at the expense of our Iowa citizens." ***

Iowa may not shunt off its fair share of the burden of maintaining interstate truck routes, nor may it create increased hazards on the highways of neighboring States in order to decrease the hazards on Iowa highways. Such an attempt has all the hallmarks of the "simple *** protectionism" this Court has condemned in the economic area. *** Here, the decision of Iowa's lawmakers to promote Iowa's safety and other interests at the direct expense of the safety and other interests of neighboring States merits no such deference. *** As JUSTICE CARDOZO has written, the Commerce Clause "was framed upon the theory that the peoples of the several states must sink or swim together, and that in the long run prosperity and salvation are in union and not division." ***

JUSTICE REHNQUIST, with whom THE CHIEF JUSTICE and JUSTICE STEWART join, dissenting.

*** Although the plurality opinion and the opinion concurring in the judgment strike down Iowa's law by different routes, I believe the analysis in both opinions oversteps our "limited authority to review state legislation under the commerce clause" and seriously intrudes upon the fundamental right of the States to pass laws to secure the safety of their citizens. *** Iowa's action in limiting the length of trucks which may travel on its highways is in no sense unusual. Every State in the Union regulates the length of vehicles permitted to use the public roads. Nor is Iowa a renegade in having length limits which operate to exclude the 65–foot doubles favored by Consolidated. These trucks are prohibited in other areas of the country as well, some 17 States and the District of Columbia, including all of New England and most of the Southeast. *** A determination that a state law is a rational safety measure does not end the Commerce Clause inquiry. A "sensitive consideration" of the safety purpose in relation to the burden on commerce is required. When engaging in such a consideration the Court does not directly compare safety benefits to commerce costs and strike down the legislation if the latter can be said in some vague sense to "outweigh" the former. Such an approach would *** arrogate to this Court functions of forming public policy, functions which, in the absence of congressional action, were left by the Framers of the Constitution to state legislatures. *** [H]ere, the question involves the difficult comparison of financial losses and "the loss of lives and limbs of workers and people using the highways." *** 4

The purpose of the "sensitive consideration" referred to above is rather to determine if the asserted safety justification, although rational, is merely a pretext for discrimination against interstate commerce. *** Iowa defends its statute as a highway safety regulation. There can be no doubt that the challenged statute is a valid highway safety regulation and thus entitled to the strongest presumption of validity against Commerce Clause challenges. *** There can also be no question that the particular limit chosen by Iowa— 60 feet—is rationally related to Iowa's safety objective. Most truck limits are between 55 and 65 feet and Iowa's choice is thus well within the widely accepted range.

Iowa adduced evidence supporting the relation between vehicle length and highway safety. The evidence indicated that longer vehicles take greater time to be passed, *** [l]onger trucks are more likely to clog intersections *** longer vehicles pose greater problems at the scene of an accident *** [and] doubles are more likely than singles to jackknife or upset. *** In sum, there was sufficient evidence presented at trial to support the legislative determination that length is related to safety, and nothing in Consolidated's evidence undermines this conclusion. ***

The question, however, is whether the Iowa Legislature has acted rationally in regulating vehicle lengths and whether the safety benefits from this regulation are more than slight or problematical. ***8 It is emphatically not our task to balance any incremental safety benefits from prohibiting 65– foot doubles as opposed to 60–foot doubles against the burden on interstate commerce. Lines drawn for safety purposes will rarely pass muster if the question is whether a slight increment can be permitted without sacrificing safety. *** The particular line chosen by Iowa—60 feet—is relevant only to the question whether the limit is a rational one. *** Under our constitutional scheme, *** only one legislative body can pre-empt the rational policy determination of the Iowa Legislature and that is Congress. Forcing Iowa to

---

4 It should not escape notice that a majority of the Court goes on record today as agreeing that courts in Commerce Clause cases do not sit to weigh safety benefits against burdens on commerce when the safety benefits are not illusory. Even the plurality gives lipservice to this principle. I do not agree with my Brother BRENNAN, however, that only those safety benefits somehow articulated by the legislature as the motivation for the challenged statute can be considered in supporting the state law.

8 The opinion of my Brother BRENNAN concurring in the judgment mischaracterizes this dissent when it states that I assume "resolution of the case must hinge upon the argument offered by Iowa's attorneys: that 65–foot doubles are more dangerous than shorter trucks." I assume nothing of the sort. *** As I read this Court's opinions, the State must simply prove, aided by a "strong presumption of validity," that the safety benefits of its law are not illusory. I review the evidence presented at trial simply to demonstrate that Iowa made such a showing in this case, not because the validity of Iowa's law depends on its proving by a preponderance of the evidence that the excluded trucks are unsafe. As I thought was made clear, it is my view that Iowa must simply show a relation between vehicle length limits and safety, and that the benefits from its length limit are not illusory. Iowa's arguments on passing time, intersection obstruction, and problems at the scene of accidents have validity beyond a comparison of the 65–and 60–foot trucks. In sum, I fully agree with JUSTICE BRENNAN that the validity of Iowa's length limit does not turn on whether 65–foot trucks are less safe than 60–foot trucks.

yield to the policy choices of neighboring States perverts the primary purpose of the Commerce Clause, that of vesting power to regulate interstate commerce in Congress, where all the States are represented. ***

My Brother BRENNAN argues that the Court should consider only the purpose the Iowa legislators actually sought to achieve by the length limit, and not the purposes advanced by Iowa's lawyers in defense of the statute. *** The problems with a view such as that advanced in the opinion concurring in the judgment are apparent. To name just a few, it assumes that individual legislators are motivated by one discernible "actual" purpose, and ignores the fact that different legislators may vote for a single piece of legislation for widely different reasons. *** Both the plurality and the concurrence attach great significance to the Governor's veto of a bill passed by the Iowa Legislature permitting 65–foot doubles. Whatever views one may have about the significance of legislative motives, it must be emphasized that the law which the Court strikes down today was not passed to achieve the protectionist goals the plurality and the concurrence ascribe to the Governor. Iowa's 60–foot length limit was established in 1963, at a time when very few States permitted 65–foot doubles. Striking down legislation on the basis of asserted legislative motives is dubious enough, but the plurality and concurrence strike down the legislation involved in this case because of asserted impermissible motives for not enacting other legislation, motives which could not possibly have been present when the legislation under challenge here was considered and passed. Such action is, so far as I am aware, unprecedented ***

Whenever a State enacts more stringent safety measures than its neighbors, in an area which affects commerce, the safety law will have the incidental effect of deflecting interstate commerce to the neighboring States. Indeed, the safety and protectionist motives cannot be separated: The whole purpose of safety regulation of vehicles is to protect the State from unsafe vehicles. *** The true problem with today's decision is that it gives no guidance whatsoever to these States as to whether their laws are valid or how to defend them. For that matter, the decision gives no guidance to Consolidated or other trucking firms either. Perhaps, after all is said and done, the Court today neither says nor does very much at all. We know only that Iowa's law is invalid and that the jurisprudence of the "negative side" of the Commerce Clause remains hopelessly confused.

Notes

1. **Background.** Does the analysis proceed any differently because Iowa's statute was facially neutral? Consider for a moment a facially neutral state statute that has an adverse effect only on out-of-state companies, benefits some local businesses, and may adversely affect in-state consumers. Should the Court use the Dormant Commerce Clause power to invalidate the statute? *See, e.g., Exxon Corp. v. Governor of Maryland*, 437 U.S. 117 (1978) (upholding by an 8–1 margin a statute providing that a producer or refiner of petroleum products could not operate a retail service station in the state; the statute had been enacted

following a gasoline shortage in which refiners provided gasoline products to stations they owned in preference to stations owned by independent operators).

2. *Kassel* **Analysis.**

• What is the effect of the statutory exceptions to Iowa's 55-foot maximum length rule? Are there nondiscriminatory explanations for these exceptions?

• What do you think of JUSTICE BRENNAN's point that Iowa must bear its "fair share" of safety problems in the region?

• Do you think that courts are more or less institutionally capable than state legislatures and Congress in assessing burdens on interstate commerce?

• Is the Court's balancing a purely economic calculus or does it have a political dimension also?

3. **Judicial Activism.** The most fundamental question about this case is why the Court should do anything about such state statutes. Is there cost-exporting or benefits-reserving activity similar to that involved in *Philadelphia* (which included a facially discriminatory statute)? Or is there merely a redistributive effect of the statutes, both among commercial players within the state and commercial players outside the state? Is the Court seeking to discourage the states from drafting facially neutral statutes that accomplish most of what the states could do with facially discriminatory statutes? Can the Court deal with such issues better or worse than Congress?

4. **Burdening Commerce.** Does the Constitution express a preference for free trade over nondiscriminatory but regulated interstate commerce?

5. **The Surface Transportation Act.** In 1982, Congress imposed an excise tax on fuel and eliminated state restrictions on double-long trucks on interstate highways. A 1984 amendment allowed the Secretary of Transportation, on safety grounds, to exclude "doubles" from portions of the interstate system. It also allowed, with the Governor's consent, opening portions of the state's noninterstate highways to "doubles." What, if any, bearing does this legislation have on your thinking about the Court's decision in *Kassel*?

6. **Internet Commerce.** Could a state ban internet "spam" to residents of the state? How would such legislation fare under a benefits/burdens analysis?

C. THE MARKET PARTICIPANT EXCEPTION

SOUTH-CENTRAL TIMBER DEV. v. WUNNICKE
467 U.S. 82 (1984)

JUSTICE WHITE announced the judgment of the Court and delivered the opinion of the Court ***.

We granted certiorari in this case to review a decision of the Court of Appeals for the Ninth Circuit that held that Alaska's requirement that timber taken from state lands be processed within the State prior to export was "implicitly authorized" by Congress and therefore does not violate the Commerce Clause. We hold that it was not authorized and reverse the judgment of the Court of Appeals.

In September 1980, the Alaska Department of Natural Resources published a notice that it would sell approximately 49 million board-feet of timber in the area of Icy Cape, Alaska, on October 23, 1980. The notice of sale, the prospectus, and the proposed contract for the sale all provided, pursuant to [Alaska law], that "[p]rimary manufacture within the State of Alaska will be required as a special provision of the contract." Under the primary-manufacture requirement, the successful bidder must partially process the timber prior to shipping it outside of the State. *** The stated purpose of the requirement is to "protect existing industries, provide for the establishment of new industries, derive revenue from all timber resources, and manage the State's forests on a sustained yield basis." When it imposes the requirement, the State charges a significantly lower price for the timber than it otherwise would.

Petitioner, South–Central Timber Development, Inc., is an Alaska corporation engaged in the business of purchasing standing timber, logging the timber, and shipping the logs into foreign commerce, almost exclusively to Japan. It does not operate a mill in Alaska and customarily sells unprocessed logs. *** We must first decide whether the court was correct in concluding that Congress has authorized the challenged requirement. If Congress has not, we must respond to respondents' submission that we should affirm the judgment on two grounds not reached by the Court of Appeals: (1) whether in the absence of congressional approval Alaska's requirement is permissible because Alaska is acting as a market participant, rather than as a market regulator; and (2), if not, whether the local-processing requirement is forbidden by the Commerce Clause. [JUSTICE WHITE found no approval, since Congressional consent was not "unmistakably clear."]

We now turn to the issues left unresolved by the Court of Appeals. The first of these issues is whether Alaska's restrictions on export of unprocessed timber from state-owned lands are exempt from Commerce Clause scrutiny under the "market-participant doctrine."

Our cases make clear that if a State is acting as a market participant, rather than as a market regulator, the dormant Commerce Clause places no limitation on its activities. *See White v. Massachusetts Council of Construction Employers, Inc.*, 460 U.S., at 206–208 (1983); *Reeves, Inc. v. Stake*, 447 U.S. 429, 436–437 (1980); *Hughes v. Alexandria Scrap Corp.*, 426 U.S. 794, 810 (1976). The precise contours of the market-participant doctrine have yet to be established, however, the doctrine having been applied in only three cases of this Court to date.

The first of the cases, *Hughes v. Alexandria Scrap Corp.*, supra, involved a Maryland program designed to reduce the number of junked automobiles in the State. A "bounty" was established on Maryland-licensed junk cars, and the State imposed more stringent documentation requirements on out-of-state scrap processors than on in-state ones. The Court rejected a Commerce Clause attack on the program, although it noted that under traditional Commerce Clause analysis the program might well be invalid because it had the effect of reducing the flow of goods in interstate commerce. The Court concluded that Maryland's action was not "the kind of action with which the Commerce Clause is concerned" because "[n]othing in the purposes animating the Commerce Clause prohibits a State, in the absence of congressional action, from participating in the market and exercising the right to favor its own citizens over others."

In *Reeves, Inc. v. Stake*, the Court upheld a South Dakota policy of restricting the sale of cement from a state-owned plant to state residents, declaring that "[t]he basic distinction drawn in *Alexandria Scrap* between States as market participants and States as market regulators makes good sense and sound law." The Court relied upon "'the long recognized right of trader or manufacturer, engaged in an entirely private business, freely to exercise his own independent discretion as to parties with whom he will deal.'" In essence, the Court recognized the principle that the Commerce Clause places no limitations on a State's refusal to deal with particular parties when it is participating in the interstate market in goods.

The most recent of this Court's cases developing the market-participant doctrine is *White v. Massachusetts Council of Construction Employers, Inc.*, in which the Court sustained against a Commerce Clause challenge an executive order of the Mayor of Boston that required all construction projects funded in whole or in part by city funds or city-administered funds to be performed by a work force of at least 50% city residents. The Court rejected the argument that the city was not entitled to the protection of the doctrine because the order had the effect of regulating employment contracts between public contractors and their employees. Recognizing that "there are some limits on a state or local government's ability to impose restrictions that reach beyond the immediate parties with which the government transacts business," the Court found it unnecessary to define those limits because "[e]veryone affected by the order [was], in a substantial if informal sense, 'working for the city.'" The fact that the employees were "working for the city" was "crucial" to the market-participant analysis in *White*.

The State of Alaska contends that its primary-manufacture requirement fits squarely within the market-participant doctrine, arguing that "Alaska's entry into the market may be viewed as precisely the same type of subsidy to local interests that the Court found unobjectionable in *Alexandria Scrap*." However, when Maryland became involved in the scrap market it was as a purchaser of scrap; Alaska, on the other hand, participates in the timber market, but imposes conditions downstream in the timber-processing market. Alaska is not merely subsidizing local timber processing in an amount "roughly equal to the difference between the price the timber would fetch in the absence of such a requirement and the amount the state actually receives." If the State directly subsidized the timber-processing industry by such an amount, the purchaser would retain the option of taking advantage of the subsidy by processing timber in the State or forgoing the benefits of the subsidy and exporting unprocessed timber. Under the Alaska requirement, however, the choice is made for him: if he buys timber from the State he is not free to take the timber out of state prior to processing.

The State also would have us find *Reeves* controlling. It states that "*Reeves* made it clear that the Commerce Clause imposes no limitation on Alaska's power to choose the terms on which it will sell its timber." Such an unrestrained reading of *Reeves* is unwarranted. Although the Court in *Reeves* did strongly endorse the right of a State to deal with whomever it chooses when it participates in the market, it did not—and did not purport to—sanction the imposition of any terms that the State might desire. For example, the Court expressly noted in *Reeves* that "Commerce Clause scrutiny may well be more rigorous when a restraint on foreign commerce is alleged," that a natural resource "like coal, timber, wild game, or minerals," was not involved, but instead the cement was "the end product of a complex process whereby a costly physical plant and human labor act on raw materials," and that South Dakota did not bar resale of South Dakota cement to out-of-state purchasers. In this case, all three of the elements that were not present in *Reeves*—foreign commerce, a natural resource, and restrictions on resale—are present.

Finally, Alaska argues that since the Court in *White* upheld a requirement that reached beyond "the boundary of formal privity of contract," then, a fortiori, the primary-manufacture requirement is permissible, because the State is not regulating contracts for resale of timber or regulating the buying and selling of timber, but is instead "a seller of timber, pure and simple." Yet it is clear that the State is more than merely a seller of timber. In the commercial context, the seller usually has no say over, and no interest in, how the product is to be used after sale; in this case, however, payment for the timber does not end the obligations of the purchaser, for, despite the fact that the purchaser has taken delivery of the timber and has paid for it, he cannot do with it as he pleases. Instead, he is obligated to deal with a stranger to the contract after completion of the sale.

That privity of contract is not always the outer boundary of permissible state activity does not necessarily mean that the Commerce Clause has no application within the boundary of formal privity. The market-participant doctrine permits a State to influence "a discrete, identifiable class of economic activity in which [it] is a major participant." *White*. Contrary to the State's contention, the doctrine is not carte blanche to impose any conditions that the State has the economic power to dictate, and does not validate any requirement merely because the State imposes it upon someone with whom it is in contractual privity.

The limit of the market-participant doctrine must be that it allows a State to impose burdens on commerce within the market in which it is a participant, but allows it to go no further. The State may not impose conditions, whether by statute, regulation, or contract, that have a substantial regulatory effect outside of that particular market. Unless the "market" is relatively narrowly defined, the doctrine has the potential of swallowing up the rule that States may not impose substantial burdens on interstate commerce even if they act with the permissible state purpose of fostering local industry.

At the heart of the dispute in this case is disagreement over the definition of the market. Alaska contends that it is participating in the processed timber market, although it acknowledges that it participates in no way in the actual processing. South–Central argues, on the other hand, that although the State may be a participant in the timber market, it is using its leverage in that market to exert a regulatory effect in the processing market, in which it is not a participant. We agree with the latter position.

There are sound reasons for distinguishing between a State's preferring its own residents in the initial disposition of goods when it is a market participant and a State's attachment of restrictions on dispositions subsequent to the goods coming to rest in private hands. First, simply as a matter of intuition a state market participant has a greater interest as a "private trader" in the immediate transaction than it has in what its purchaser does with the goods after the State no longer has an interest in them. The common law recognized such a notion in the doctrine of restraints on alienation. Similarly, the antitrust laws place limits on vertical restraints. It is no defense in an action charging vertical trade restraints that the same end could be achieved through vertical integration; if it were, there would be virtually no antitrust scrutiny of vertical arrangements. We reject the contention that a State's action as a market regulator may be upheld against a Commerce Clause challenge on the ground that the State could achieve the same end as a market participant. We therefore find it unimportant for present purposes that the State could support its processing industry by selling only to Alaska processors, by vertical integration, or by direct subsidy.

Second, downstream restrictions have a greater regulatory effect than do limitations on the immediate transaction. Instead of merely choosing its own trading partners, the State is attempting to govern the private, separate economic relationships of its trading partners; that is, it restricts the post-purchase activity of the purchaser, rather than merely the purchasing activity. In contrast to the situation in *White*, this restriction on private economic activity takes place after the completion of the parties' direct commercial obligations, rather than during the course of an ongoing commercial relationship in which the city retained a continuing proprietary interest in the subject of the contract. In sum, the State may not avail itself of the market-participant doctrine to immunize its downstream regulation of the timber-processing market in which it is not a participant.

Finally, the State argues that even if we find that Congress did not authorize the processing restriction, and even if we conclude that its actions do not qualify for the market-participant exception, the restriction does not substantially burden interstate or foreign commerce under ordinary Commerce Clause principles. We need not labor long over that contention. *** Because of the protectionist nature of Alaska's local-processing requirement and the burden on commerce resulting therefrom, we conclude that it falls within the rule of virtual per se invalidity of laws that "bloc[k] the flow of interstate commerce at a State's borders." *City of Philadelphia v. New Jersey*, 437 U.S. 617, 624 (1978).

We are buttressed in our conclusion that the restriction is invalid by the fact that foreign commerce is burdened by the restriction. It is a well-accepted rule that state restrictions burdening foreign commerce are subjected to a more rigorous and searching scrutiny. It is crucial to the efficient execution of the Nation's foreign policy that "the Federal Government *** speak with one voice when regulating commercial relations with foreign governments." In light of the substantial attention given by Congress to the subject of export restrictions on unprocessed timber, it would be peculiarly inappropriate to permit state regulation of the subject. ***

JUSTICE MARSHALL took no part in the decision of this case.

JUSTICE BRENNAN, concurring. [omitted]

JUSTICE POWELL, with whom THE CHIEF JUSTICE joins, concurring in part and concurring in the judgment. [omitted]

JUSTICE REHNQUIST, with whom JUSTICE O'CONNOR joins, dissenting.

In my view, the line of distinction drawn in the plurality opinion between the State as market participant and the State as market regulator is both artificial and unconvincing. The plurality draws this line "simply as a matter of intuition," but then seeks to bolster its intuition through a series of remarks more appropriate to antitrust law than to the Commerce Clause.[1]

Perhaps the State's actions do raise antitrust problems. But what the plurality overlooks is that the antitrust laws apply to a State only when it is acting as a market participant. When the State acts as a market regulator, it is immune from antitrust scrutiny. Of course, the line of distinction in cases under the Commerce Clause need not necessarily parallel the line drawn in antitrust law. But the plurality can hardly justify placing Alaska in the market-regulator category, in this Commerce Clause case, by relying on antitrust cases that are relevant only if the State is a market participant.

The contractual term at issue here no more transforms Alaska's sale of timber into "regulation" of the processing industry than the resident-hiring preference imposed by the city of Boston in *White v. Massachusetts Council of Construction Employers, Inc.*, 460 U.S. 204 (1983), constituted regulation of the construction industry. Alaska is merely paying the buyer of the timber indirectly, by means of a reduced price, to hire Alaska residents to process the timber. Under existing precedent, the State could accomplish that same result in any number of ways. For example, the State could choose to sell its timber only to those companies that maintain active primary-processing plants in Alaska. [*Reeves, Inc. v. Stake*] Or the State could directly subsidize the primary-processing industry within the State. [*Hughes v. Alexandria*

---

[1] The plurality does offer one other reason for its demarcation of the boundary between these two concepts. "[D]ownstream restrictions have a greater regulatory effect than do limitations on the immediate transaction. Instead of merely choosing its own trading partners, the State is attempting to govern the private, separate economic relationships of its trading partners; that in it restricts the post-purchase activity of the purchaser, rather than merely the purchasing activity." But, of course, this is not a "reason" at all, but merely a restatement of the conclusion. The line between participation and regulation is what we are trying to determine. To invoke that very distinction in support of the line drawn is merely to fall back again on intuition.

Scrap Corp.] The State could even pay to have the logs processed and then enter the market only to sell processed logs. It seems to me unduly formalistic to conclude that the one path chosen by the State as best suited to promote its concerns is the path forbidden it by the Commerce Clause. ***

Notes

1. **Downstream Regulation.** Do you find the Court's exception to the market participant exception convincing?

2. **Natural Resources.** Why didn't the Court simply decide that Alaska could not hoard a natural resource like timber? Should a State be permitted more latitude to manufacture goods than to "hoard" natural resources for the benefit of its own citizens? In *Reeves*, the Court found that "[c]ement is not a natural resource, like coal, timber, wild game or minerals." Does it trouble you that the Court might have reached a different result if it had looked at cement's components (such as limestone and sand)?

3. **Regulation vs. Participation.** "The line between state market participation and state market regulation is a fuzzy one that has perplexed courts and commentators alike." *Big Country Foods, Inc. v. Board of Educ.,* 952 F.2d 1173 (9th Cir. 1992). In *Alexandria Scrap,* the state did not go into the auto wrecking business or the scrap processing business. How, then, was the state a market participant at all? What is the test for whether the state is regulating or is a market participant?

4. **Questions on the Scope of the Market Participation Exception.**

    • There is no indication that the framers of the Commerce Clause distinguished between the state as a regulator and the state as market participant. Adam Smith, whose work preceded the American Revolution, discussed extensively the evils of mercantilism, including state bounties that distorted free markets. Should this matter?

    • Some of the impetus for the market participant doctrine comes from analogizing the state to "just another private party." Given the State's power to tax as well as its other coercive powers, isn't this a flawed analogy?

    • Is this case a return to the governmental/proprietary distinction rejected by the Court in the "active" Commerce Clause context in *Garcia*? Why does this distinction only apply in Dormant Commerce Clause cases?

5. **Definition of "Market".** If a state owns and operates a farmer's market and assigns inferior sales locations to nonresident sellers, is it acting as a regulator or a market participant? Does the answer turn on whether the market involves selling/leasing space or selling produce? *Smith v. Department of Agric.,* 630 F.2d 1081 (5th Cir.1980), cert. denied, 452 U.S. 910 (1981).

UNITED HAULERS v. ONEIDA-HERKIMER SOLID WASTE MANAGEMENT AUTHORITY
550 U.S. 330 (2007)

CHIEF JUSTICE ROBERTS delivered the opinion of the Court, except as to Part II-D.

"Flow control" ordinances require trash haulers to deliver solid waste to a particular waste processing facility. *** In this case, we face flow control ordinances quite similar to the one invalidated in *Carbone* [v. *Town of Clarkstown,* 511 U.S. 383 (1994)]. The only salient difference is that the laws at issue here require haulers to bring waste to facilities owned and operated by a state-created public benefit corporation.   We find this difference constitutionally significant. Disposing of trash has been a traditional government activity for years, and laws that favor the government in such areas-but treat every private business, whether in-state or out-of-state, exactly the same-do not discriminate against interstate commerce for purposes of the Commerce Clause. Applying the Commerce Clause test reserved for regulations that do not discriminate against interstate commerce, we uphold these ordinances because any incidental burden they may have on interstate commerce does not outweigh the benefits they confer on the citizens of Oneida and Herkimer Counties. ***

In 1989, the Authority and the Counties entered into a Solid Waste Management Agreement, under which the Authority agreed to manage all solid waste within the Counties.   Private haulers would remain free to pick up citizens' trash from the curb, but the Authority would take over the job of processing the trash, sorting it, and sending it off for disposal. *** [T]he Authority agreed to purchase and develop facilities for the processing and disposal of solid waste and recyclables generated in the Counties. *** If the Authority's operating costs and debt service were not recouped through tipping fees and other charges, the agreement provided that the Counties would make up the difference. *** To avoid being stuck with the bill for facilities that citizens voted for but then chose not to use, the Counties enacted "flow control" ordinances requiring that all solid waste generated within the Counties be delivered to the Authority's processing sites. Private haulers must obtain a permit from the Authority to collect waste in the Counties. ***

II

*** [T]he haulers argue vigorously that the Counties' ordinances discriminate against interstate commerce under *Carbone*.   In *Carbone*, the town of Clarkstown, New York, hired a private contractor to build a waste transfer station.   According to the terms of the deal, the contractor would operate the facility for five years, charging an above-market tipping fee of $81 per ton; after five years, the town would buy the facility for one dollar.   The town guaranteed that the facility would receive a certain volume of trash per year.   To make good on its promise, Clarkstown passed a flow control ordinance requiring that all nonhazardous solid waste within the town be deposited at the transfer facility.

This Court struck down the ordinance, holding that it discriminated against interstate commerce by "hoard[ing] solid waste, and the demand to get rid of it, for the benefit of the preferred processing facility." *** The flow control ordinances in this case benefit a clearly public facility, while treating all private companies exactly the same.   *** Compelling reasons justify treating these laws differently from laws favoring particular private businesses over their competitors. *** Unlike private enterprise, government is vested with the responsibility of protecting the health, safety, and welfare of its citizens.   These important responsibilities set state and local government apart from a typical private business.

Given these differences, it does not make sense to regard laws favoring local government and laws favoring private industry with equal skepticism. As our local processing cases demonstrate, when a law favors in-state business over out-of-state competition, rigorous scrutiny is appropriate because the law is often the product of "simple economic protectionism." Laws favoring local government, by contrast, may be directed toward any number of legitimate goals unrelated to protectionism. Here the flow control ordinances enable the Counties to pursue particular policies with respect to the handling and treatment of waste generated in the Counties, while allocating the costs of those policies on citizens and businesses according to the volume of waste they generate.

The contrary approach of treating public and private entities the same under the dormant Commerce Clause would lead to unprecedented and unbounded interference by the courts with state and local government. The dormant Commerce Clause is not a roving license for federal courts to decide what activities are appropriate for state and local government to undertake, and what activities must be the province of private market competition. In this case, the citizens of Oneida and Herkimer Counties have chosen the government to provide waste management services, with a limited role for the private sector in arranging for transport of waste from the curb to the public facilities. The citizens could have left the entire matter for the private sector, in which case any regulation they undertook could not discriminate against interstate commerce. But it was also open to them to vest responsibility for the matter with their government, and to adopt flow control ordinances to support the government effort. ***

We should be particularly hesitant to interfere with the Counties' efforts under the guise of the Commerce Clause because "[w]aste disposal is both typically and traditionally a local government function." *** The policy of the State of New York favors "displac[ing] competition with regulation or monopoly control" in this area. We may or may not agree with that approach, but nothing in the Commerce Clause vests the responsibility for that policy judgment with the Federal Judiciary.

Finally, it bears mentioning that the most palpable harm imposed by the ordinances-more expensive trash removal-is likely to fall upon the very people who voted for the laws. Our dormant Commerce Clause cases often find discrimination when a State shifts the costs of regulation to other States, because when "the burden of state regulation falls on interests outside the state, it is unlikely to be alleviated by the operation of those political restraints normally exerted when interests within the state are affected." Here, the citizens and businesses of the Counties bear the costs of the ordinances. There is no reason to step in and hand local businesses a victory they could not obtain through the political process.

We hold that the Counties' flow control ordinances, which treat in-state private business interests exactly the same as out-of-state ones, do not "discriminate against interstate commerce" for purposes of the dormant Commerce Clause.

[JUSTICES ROBERTS, SOUTER, GINSBURG, AND BREYER]

The Counties' flow control ordinances are properly analyzed under the test *** reserved for laws "directed to legitimate local concerns, with effects upon interstate commerce that are only incidental." Under [this] test, we will uphold a nondiscriminatory statute like this one "unless the burden imposed on [interstate] commerce is clearly excessive in relation to the putative local benefits." After years of discovery, both the Magistrate Judge and the District Court could not detect *any* disparate impact on out-of-state as opposed to in-state businesses. *** We find it unnecessary to decide whether the ordinances impose any incidental burden on interstate commerce because any arguable burden does not exceed the public benefits of the ordinances.

The ordinances give the Counties a convenient and effective way to finance their integrated package of waste-disposal services. *** At the same time, the ordinances are more than financing tools. They increase recycling in at least two ways, conferring significant health and environmental benefits upon the citizens of the Counties. First, they create enhanced incentives for recycling and proper disposal of other kinds of waste. *** Second, by requiring all waste to be deposited at Authority facilities, the Counties have markedly increased their ability to enforce recycling laws. *** For these reasons, any arguable burden the ordinances impose on interstate commerce does not exceed their public benefits.

* * *

The Counties' ordinances are exercises of the police power in an effort to address waste disposal, a typical and traditional concern of local government. The haulers nevertheless ask us to hold that laws favoring public entities while treating all private businesses the same are subject to an almost *per se* rule of invalidity, because of asserted discrimination. *** [They invite us] to rigorously scrutinize economic legislation passed under the auspices of the police power. There was a time when this Court presumed to make such binding judgments for society, under the guise of interpreting the Due Process Clause. See *Lochner v. New York* (1905). We should not seek to reclaim that ground for judicial supremacy under the banner of the dormant Commerce Clause. ***

JUSTICE SCALIA, concurring in part.

*** I have been willing to enforce on *stare decisis* grounds a "negative" self-executing Commerce Clause in two situations: "(1) against a state law that facially discriminates against interstate commerce, and (2) against a state law that is indistinguishable from a type of law previously held unconstitutional by the Court." As today's opinion makes clear, the flow-control law at issue in this case meets neither condition. It benefits a *public entity* performing a traditional local-government function and treats *all private entities* precisely the same way. *** None of this Court's cases concludes that public entities and private entities are similarly situated for Commerce Clause purposes. *** I am unable to join Part II-D *** Generally speaking, the balancing of various values is left to Congress-which is precisely what the Commerce Clause (the *real* Commerce Clause) envisions.

JUSTICE THOMAS, concurring in the judgment.

*** Although I joined [*Carbone*], I no longer believe it was correctly decided. *** Because this Court has no policy role in regulating interstate commerce, I would discard the Court's negative Commerce Clause jurisprudence. *** [N]one of the cases the Court cites explains how the absence or presence of discrimination is relevant to deciding whether the ordinances are constitutionally permissible, and at least one case affirmatively admits that the nondiscrimination rule has no basis in the Constitution. *Philadelphia v. New Jersey* ("The bounds of these restraints appear nowhere in the words of the Commerce Clause, but have emerged gradually in the decisions of this Court giving effect to its basic purpose"). Thus cloaked in the "purpose" of the Commerce Clause, the rule against discrimination that the Court applies to decide this case exists untethered from the written Constitution. The rule instead depends upon the policy preferences of a majority of this Court. ***

Many of the [Court's] cases (and today's majority and dissent) rest on the erroneous assumption that the Court must choose between economic protectionism and the free market. But the Constitution vests that fundamentally legislative choice in Congress. To the extent that Congress does not exercise its authority to make that choice, the Constitution does not limit the States' power to regulate commerce. ***

Despite its acceptance of negative Commerce Clause jurisprudence, the Court expresses concern about "unprecedented and unbounded interference by the courts with state and local government." *** I agree that the Commerce Clause is not a "roving license" and that the Court should not deliver to businesses victories that they failed to obtain through the political process. I differ with the Court because I believe its powerful rhetoric is completely undermined by the doctrine it applies.

In this regard, the Court's analogy to *Lochner v. New York*, 198 U.S. 45 (1905), suggests that the Court should reject the negative Commerce Clause, rather than tweak it. *** Rather, it further propagates the error by narrowing the negative Commerce Clause for policy reasons-reasons that later majorities of this Court may find to be entirely illegitimate. ***

JUSTICE ALITO, with whom JUSTICE STEVENS and JUSTICE KENNEDY join, dissenting.

*** The fact that the flow control laws at issue discriminate in favor of a government-owned enterprise does not meaningfully distinguish this case from *Carbone*. The preferred facility in *Carbone* was, to be sure, nominally owned by a private contractor who had built the facility on the town's behalf, but it would be misleading to describe the facility as private. In exchange for the contractor's promise to build the facility for the town free of charge and then to sell it to the town five years later for $1, the town guaranteed that, during the first five years of the facility's existence, the contractor would receive "a minimum waste flow of 120,000 tons per year" and that the contractor could charge an above-market tipping fee. If the facility "received less than 120,000 tons in a year, the town [would] make up the tipping fee deficit." To prevent residents, businesses, and trash haulers from taking their waste elsewhere in pursuit of lower tipping fees (leaving the town responsible for covering any shortfall in the contractor's guaranteed revenue stream), the town enacted an ordinance "requir[ing] all nonhazardous solid waste within the town to be deposited at" the preferred facility.

This Court observed that "[t]he object of this arrangement was to amortize the cost of the transfer station: The town would finance *its new facility* with the income generated by the tipping fees." "In other words," the Court explained, "the flow control ordinance [wa]s a financing measure," for what everyone-including the Court-regarded as *the town's* new transfer station.

The only real difference between the facility at issue in *Carbone* and its counterpart in this case is that title to the former had not yet formally passed to the municipality. *** In any event, we have never treated discriminatory legislation with greater deference simply because the entity favored by that legislation was a government-owned enterprise. *** Nor has this Court ever suggested that discriminatory legislation favoring a state-owned enterprise is entitled to favorable treatment.   To be sure, state-owned entities are accorded special status under the market-participant doctrine.   But that doctrine is not applicable here. *** Respondents are doing exactly what the market-participant doctrine says they cannot: While acting as market participants by operating a fee-for-service business enterprise in an area in which there is an established interstate market, respondents are also regulating that market in a discriminatory manner and claiming that their special governmental status somehow insulates them from a dormant Commerce Clause challenge.

Respondents insist that the market-participant doctrine has no application here because they are not asserting a defense under the market-participant doctrine, but that argument misses the point. Regardless of whether respondents can assert a defense under the market-participant doctrine, this Court's cases make clear that States cannot discriminate against interstate commerce unless they are acting solely as market participants. Today, however, the Court suggests, contrary to its prior holdings, that States can discriminate in favor of in-state interests while acting both as a market participant *and* as a market regulator.

Despite precedent condemning discrimination in favor of government-owned enterprises, the Court attempts to develop a logical justification for the rule it creates today. That justification rests on three principal assertions. First, the Court insists that it simply "does not make sense to regard laws favoring local government and laws favoring private industry with equal skepticism," because the latter are "often the product of 'simple economic protectionism,' " while the former "may be directed toward any number of legitimate goals unrelated to protectionism". Second, the Court reasons that deference to legislation discriminating in favor of a municipal landfill is especially appropriate considering that "'[w]aste disposal is both typically and traditionally a local government function.'" Third, the Court suggests that respondents' flow-control laws are not discriminatory because they "treat in-state private business interests exactly the same as out-of-state ones." I find each of these arguments unpersuasive.

I see no basis for the Court's assumption that discrimination in favor of an in-state facility owned by the government is likely to serve "legitimate goals unrelated to protectionism." *** By the same token, discrimination in favor of an in-state, privately owned facility may serve legitimate ends, such as the promotion of public health and safety. *** Proper analysis under the dormant Commerce Clause involves more than an inquiry into whether the challenged Act is in some sense "directed toward ... legitimate goals unrelated to protectionism"; equally important are the means by which those goals are realized. If the chosen means take the form of a statute that discriminates against interstate commerce-"'either on its face or in practical effect'"-then "the burden falls on [the enacting government] to demonstrate both that the statute 'serves a legitimate local purpose,' and that this purpose could not be served as well by available nondiscriminatory means." *** [T]he laws at issue in this case serve legitimate goals, [but] offend the dormant Commerce Clause because those goals could be attained effectively through nondiscriminatory means. ***

The Court next suggests that deference to legislation discriminating in favor of a municipal landfill is especially appropriate considering that "'[w]aste disposal is both typically and traditionally a local government function.'" I disagree on two grounds. First, this Court has previously recognized that any standard "that turns on a judicial appraisal of whether a particular governmental function is 'integral' or 'traditional'" is "'unsound in principle and unworkable in practice.'" *** See *Garcia* (overruling *National League of Cities*); *New York v. United States* (overruling *South Carolina v. United States*). Thus, to the extent today's holding rests on a distinction between "traditional" governmental functions and their nontraditional counterparts, it cannot be reconciled with prior precedent. Second, although many municipalities in this country have long assumed responsibility for disposing of local garbage, most of the garbage produced in this country is still managed by the private sector. *** In that respect, the Court is simply mistaken in concluding that waste disposal is "typically" a local government function. [Third,] especially considering the Court's recognition that "'any notion of discrimination assumes a comparison of substantially similar entities,'" a "traditional" municipal landfill is for present purposes entirely different from a monopolistic landfill supported by the kind of discriminatory legislation at issue in this case and in *Carbone*. While the former may be rooted in history and tradition, the latter has been deemed unconstitutional until today. It is therefore far from clear that the laws at issue here can fairly be described as serving a function "typically and traditionally" performed by local governments.

Equally unpersuasive is the Court's suggestion that the flow-control laws do not discriminate against interstate commerce because they "treat in-state private business interests exactly the same as out-of-state ones." Again, the critical issue is whether the challenged legislation discriminates against interstate commerce. If it does, then regardless of whether those harmed by it reside entirely outside the State in question, the law is subject to strict scrutiny. Indeed, this Court has long recognized that "'a burden imposed by a State upon interstate commerce is not to be sustained simply because the statute imposing it applies alike to the people of all the States, including the people of the State enacting such statute.'" It therefore makes no difference that the flow-control laws at issue here apply to in-state and out-of-state businesses alike. ***

Notes

1. **State Run Businesses.** Has the Court broadened the market participant exception to dormant commerce clause analysis in a way that is inconsistent with *Wunnicke's* "no downstream restrictions" approach? Should the "market participant" be restated as a "state-run businesses" exception?

2. **The Thomas Position.** As you read later cases in the casebook, consider whether Thomas' new position is compelled by (or at least more consistent with) other federalism positions he has taken.

3. **"Discrimination."** Has the Court narrowed the notion of discrimination by excluding private trash facilities as not "similarly situated" to the public facility favored?

4. **Taxing and Subsidizing.** The Court in *West Lynn Creamery, Inc. v. Healy*, 512 U.S. 186 (1994), used Dormant Commerce Clause analysis to invalidate a Massachusetts program in which a nondiscriminatory tax levied on all milk dealers (in-state and out-of-state) was coupled with a subsidy to local milk producers. A concurrence by JUSTICES SCALIA and THOMAS said it would have been permissible for the State to "subsidize its domestic industry so long as it does so from nondiscriminatory taxes that go into the State's general revenue fund." CHIEF JUSTICE REHNQUIST and JUSTICE BLACKMUN dissented. One academic has distinguished regulation from spending programs because the latter are "less coercive," "less hostile to other states [and the notion of union]," "positively beneficial [and] would not exist [if not local]," "expensive [and therefore] less likely to proliferate than measures like tariffs," and "less likely to produce resentment and retaliation." Regan, "The Supreme Court and State Protectionism: Making Sense of the Dormant Commerce Clause," 84 MICH. L. REV. 1091 (1986). Are you convinced?

5. **Tax-exempt Bonds.** Forty-three states tax out-of-state bonds by exempting the interest paid on their own bonds but not those issued by other states from their taxes. Does this preferential treatment violate the dormant commerce clause? In *Davis v. Kentucky*, 553 U.S. 328 (2008), the Court held that "*United Haulers* provides a firm basis for reversal. Just like the ordinances upheld there, Kentucky's tax exemption favors a traditional government function without any differential treatment favoring local entities over substantially similar out-of-state interests." Because the government of Kentucky was acting in its official capacity, Kentucky was acting as a market participant, even though the tax rates for bond interest were different for in state and out-of-state purchasers.

D. STATE PRIVILEGES AND IMMUNITIES

Art. IV, § 2, cl. 2 pronounces that "The Citizens of each State shall be entitled to all Privileges and Immunities of Citizens in the several States." Its origin is Art. IV of the Articles of Confederation. See App. A, p. 826. What are these Privileges and Immunities? An early case, *Paul v. Virginia*, 75 U.S. (8 Wall.) 168, 180 (1869), said:

> It was undoubtedly the object of this clause *** to place the citizens of each State on the same footing with citizens of other States, so far as the advantages resulting from citizenship in those States are concerned. It relieves them from the disabilities of alienage in other States; it inhibits discriminating legislation against them by other States; it gives them the right of free ingress into other States, and egress from them; it insures to them in other States the same freedom possessed by the citizens of those States in the acquisition and enjoyment of property and in the pursuit of happiness; and it secures to them in other States the equal protection of their laws. *** [W]ithout some provision of the kind *** the Republic would have constituted little more than a league of States.

The clause extends only to rights "fundamental to the promotion of interstate harmony." *S. Ct. of N.H. v. Piper*, 470 U.S. 274 (1985). This raises the question where to draw the line between fundamental and lesser matters. One fundamental privilege and immunity is employment, covered in the next case. An example of a lesser one is a recreational hunting license. *Baldwin v. Fish and Game Comm. of Montana*, 436 U.S. 371 (1978).

Even if there is a fundamental privilege or immunity, as in the next case, a state may discriminate if it has strong enough reasons. "[N]o one would suggest that the Privileges and Immunities Clause requires a State to open its polls to a person who declines to assert that the state is the only one where he claims a right to vote." *Baldwin*. As you read the next case, compare and contrast how this clause, which promotes interstate harmony, differs from the Dormant Commerce Clause in furthering that goal.

UNITED BUILDING AND CONSTRUCTION TRADES COUNCIL v. CITY OF CAMDEN
465 U.S. 208 (1984).

JUSTICE REHNQUIST delivered the opinion of the Court.

A municipal ordinance of the city of Camden, New Jersey requires that at least 40% of the employees of contractors and subcontractors working on city construction projects be Camden residents. Appellant, the United Building and Construction Trades Council of Camden and Vicinity (the Council), challenges that ordinance as a violation of the Privileges and Immunities Clause, Article IV, § 2, of the United States Constitution. *** [We first address the argument *** that the Clause does not even apply to a municipal ordinance such as this. Two separate contentions are advanced in support of this position: first, that the Clause only applies to laws passed by a State and, second, that the Clause only applies to laws that discriminate on the basis of state citizenship.

The first argument can be quickly rejected. The fact that the ordinance in question is a municipal, rather than a state, law does not somehow place it outside the scope of the Privileges and Immunities Clause. First of all, one cannot easily distinguish municipal from state action in this case: the municipal ordinance would not have gone into effect without express approval by the State Treasurer.

More fundamentally, a municipality is merely a political subdivision of the State from which its authority derives. It is as true of the Privileges and Immunities Clause as of the Equal Protection Clause that what would be unconstitutional if done directly by the State can no more readily be accomplished by a city deriving its authority from the State. Thus, even if the ordinance had been adopted solely by Camden, and not pursuant to a state program or with state approval, the hiring preference would still have to comport with the Privileges and Immunities Clause.

The second argument merits more consideration. *** The Clause is phrased in terms of state citizenship and was designed "to place the citizens of each State upon the same footing with citizens of other States, so far as the advantages resulting from citizenship in those States are concerned." *Paul v. Virginia*, 8 Wall. 168, 180 (1869).

> The primary purpose of this clause, like the clauses between which it is located—those relating to full faith and credit and to interstate extradition of fugitives from justice—was to help fuse into one Nation a collection of independent, sovereign States. It was designed to insure to a citizen of State A who ventures into State B the same privileges which the citizens of State B enjoy. For protection of such equality the citizen of State A was not to be restricted to the uncertain remedies afforded by diplomatic processes and official retaliation.

Toomer v. Witsell, 334 U.S. 385, 395 (1948). Municipal residency classifications, it is argued, simply do not give rise to the same concerns.

We cannot accept this argument. *** A person who is not residing in a given State is ipso facto not residing in a city within that State. Thus, whether the exercise of a privilege is conditioned on state residency or on municipal residency he will just as surely be excluded.

Given the Camden ordinance, an out-of-state citizen who ventures into New Jersey will not enjoy the same privileges as the New Jersey citizen residing in Camden. It is true that New Jersey citizens not residing in Camden will be affected by the ordinance as well as out-of-state citizens. And it is true that the disadvantaged New Jersey residents have no claim under the Privileges and Immunities Clause. *The Slaughter–House Cases*, 16 Wall. 36, 77 (1872). But New Jersey residents at least have a chance to remedy at the polls any discrimination against them. Out-of-state citizens have no similar opportunity and they must "not be restricted to the uncertain remedies afforded by diplomatic processes and official retaliation."[9] We conclude that Camden's ordinance is not immune from constitutional review at the behest of out-of-state residents merely because some in-state residents are similarly disadvantaged.

Application of the Privileges and Immunities Clause to a particular instance of discrimination against out-of-state residents entails a two-step inquiry. As an initial matter, the court must decide whether the ordinance burdens one of those privileges and immunities protected by the Clause. Not all forms of discrimination against citizens of other States are constitutionally suspect. *** As a threshold matter, then, we must determine whether an out-of-state resident's interest in employment on public works contracts in another State is sufficiently "fundamental" to the promotion of interstate harmony so as to "fall within the purview of the Privileges and Immunities Clause."

Certainly, the pursuit of a common calling is one of the most fundamental of those privileges protected by the Clause. *** Public employment, however, is qualitatively different from employment in the private sector; it is a subspecies of the broader opportunity to pursue a common calling. We have held that there is no fundamental right to government employment for purposes of the Equal Protection Clause. *Massachusetts v. Murgia*, 427 U.S. 307, 313 (1976) (per curiam). And in *White* [discussed in *Wunnicke*, above], we held that for purposes of the Commerce Clause everyone employed on a city public works project is, "in a substantial if informal sense, 'working for the city.'"

It can certainly be argued that for purposes of the Privileges and Immunities Clause everyone affected by the Camden ordinance is also "working for the city" and, therefore, has no grounds for complaint when the city favors its own residents. But we decline to transfer mechanically into this context an analysis fashioned to fit the Commerce Clause. Our decision

---

[9] The dissent suggests that New Jersey citizens not residing in Camden will adequately protect the interests of out-of-state residents and that the scope of the Privileges and Immunities Clause should be measured in light of this political reality. What the dissent fails to appreciate is that the Camden ordinance at issue in this case was adopted pursuant to a comprehensive, state-wide program applicable in all New Jersey cities. The Camden resident-preference ordinance has already received state sanction and approval, and every New Jersey city is free to adopt a similar protectionist measure. Some have already done so. Thus, it is hard to see how New Jersey residents living outside Camden will protect the interests of out-of-state citizens.

More fundamentally, the dissent's proposed blanket exemption for all classifications that are less than state-wide would provide States with a simple means for evading the strictures of the Privileges and Immunities Clause. Suppose, for example, that California wanted to guarantee that all employees of contractors and subcontractors working on construction projects funded in whole or in part by state funds are state residents. Under the dissent's analysis, the California legislature need merely divide the State in half, providing one resident-hiring preference for Northern Californians on all such projects taking place in Northern California, and one for Southern Californians on all projects taking place in Southern California. State residents generally would benefit from the law at the expense of out-of-state residents; yet, the law would be immune from scrutiny under the Clause simply because it was not phrased in terms of state citizenship or residency. Such a formalistic construction would effectively write the Clause out of the Constitution.

in *White* turned on a distinction between the city acting as a market participant and the city acting as a market regulator. The question whether employees of contractors and subcontractors on public works projects were or were not, in some sense, working for the city was crucial to that analysis. The question had to be answered in order to chart the boundaries of the distinction. But the distinction between market participant and market regulator relied upon in *White* to dispose of the Commerce Clause challenge is not dispositive in this context. The two Clauses have different aims and set different standards for state conduct.

The Commerce Clause acts as an implied restraint upon state regulatory powers. Such powers must give way before the superior authority of Congress to legislate on (or leave unregulated) matters involving interstate commerce. When the State acts solely as a market participant, no conflict between state regulation and federal regulatory authority can arise. The Privileges and Immunities Clause, on the other hand, imposes a direct restraint on state action in the interests of interstate harmony. This concern with comity cuts across the market regulator-market participant distinction that is crucial under the Commerce Clause. It is discrimination against out-of-state residents on matters of fundamental concern which triggers the Clause, not regulation affecting interstate commerce. Thus, the fact that Camden is merely setting conditions on its expenditures for goods and services in the marketplace does not preclude the possibility that those conditions violate the Privileges and Immunities Clause.

In *Hicklin v. Orbeck*, 437 U.S. 518 (1978), we struck down as a violation of the Privileges and Immunities Clause an "Alaska Hire" statute containing a resident hiring preference for all employment related to the development of the State's oil and gas resources. Alaska argued in that case "that because the oil and gas that are the subject of Alaska Hire are owned by the State, this ownership, of itself, is sufficient justification for the Act's discrimination against nonresidents, and takes the Act totally without the scope of the Privileges and Immunities Clause." We concluded, however, that the State's interest in controlling those things it claims to own is not absolute. *** Much the same analysis, we think, is appropriate to a city's efforts to bias private employment decisions in favor of its residents on construction projects funded with public monies. The fact that Camden is expending its own funds or funds it administers in accordance with the terms of a grant is certainly a factor—perhaps the crucial factor—to be considered in evaluating whether the statute's discrimination violates the Privileges and Immunities Clause. But it does not remove the Camden ordinance completely from the purview of the Clause.

In sum, Camden may, without fear of violating the Commerce Clause, pressure private employers engaged in public works projects funded in whole or in part by the city to hire city residents. But that same exercise of power to bias the employment decisions of private contractors and subcontractors against out-of-state residents may be called to account under the Privileges and Immunities Clause. A determination of whether a privilege is "fundamental" for purposes of that Clause does not depend on whether the employees of private contractors and subcontractors engaged in public works projects can or cannot be said to be "working for the city." The opportunity to seek employment with such private employers is "sufficiently basic to the livelihood of the Nation" as to fall within the purview of the Privileges and Immunities Clause even though the contractors and subcontractors are themselves engaged in projects funded in whole or part by the city.

The conclusion that Camden's ordinance discriminates against a protected privilege does not, of course, end the inquiry. *** It does not preclude discrimination against citizens of other States where there is a "substantial reason" for the difference in treatment. "[T]he inquiry in each case must be concerned with whether such reasons do exist and whether the degree of discrimination bears a close relation to them." As part of any justification offered for the discriminatory law, nonresidents must somehow be shown to "constitute a peculiar source of the evil at which the statute is aimed."

The city of Camden contends that its ordinance is necessary to counteract grave economic and social ills. Spiralling unemployment, a sharp decline in population, and a dramatic reduction in the number of businesses located in the city have eroded property values and depleted the city's tax base. The resident hiring preference is designed, the city contends, to increase the number of employed persons living in Camden and to arrest the "middle class flight" currently plaguing the city. The city also argues that all non-Camden residents employed on city public works projects, whether they reside in New Jersey or Pennsylvania, constitute a "source of the evil at which the statute is aimed." That is, they "live off" Camden without "living in" Camden. Camden contends that the scope of the discrimination practiced in the ordinance, with its municipal residency requirement, is carefully tailored to alleviate this evil without unreasonably harming nonresidents, who still have access to 60% of the available positions.

Every inquiry under the Privileges and Immunities Clause "must *** be conducted with due regard for the principle that the states should have considerable leeway in analyzing local evils and in prescribing appropriate cures." This caution is particularly appropriate when a government body is merely setting conditions on the expenditure of funds it controls. The Alaska Hire statute at issue in *Hicklin v. Orbeck* swept within its strictures not only contractors and subcontractors dealing directly with the State's oil and gas; it also covered suppliers who provided goods and services to those contractors and subcontractors. We invalidated the Act as "an attempt to force virtually all businesses that benefit in some way from the economic ripple effect of Alaska's decision to develop its oil and gas resources to bias their employment practices in favor of the State's residents." No similar "ripple effect" appears to infect the Camden ordinance. It is limited in scope to employees working directly on city public works projects.

Nonetheless, we find it impossible to evaluate Camden's justification on the record as it now stands. No trial has ever been held in the case. No findings of fact have been made. *** We, therefore, deem it wise to remand the case to the New Jersey Supreme Court ***

JUSTICE BLACKMUN, dissenting.

For over a century the underlying meaning of the Privileges and Immunities Clause of the Constitution's Article IV has been regarded as settled: at least absent some substantial, non-invidious justification, a State may not discriminate between its own residents and residents of other States on the basis of state citizenship. *** [T]he Privileges and Immunities Clause was not intended to apply to the kind of municipal discrimination presented by this case. *** By the time the Constitution was adopted, most state legislatures had assumed the power to grant and alter municipal charters and the power to legislate with respect to municipal affairs. *** As a result, the Framers had every reason to believe that intrastate discrimination based on municipal residence could and would be dealt with by the States themselves in those instances where it persisted.

In light of the historical context in which the Privileges and Immunities Clause was adopted, it hardly is surprising that none of this Court's intervening decisions has suggested that the Clause applies to discrimination on the basis of municipal residence. *** [T]he Court *** reaffirmed this principle only two Terms ago in *Zobel v. Williams*, 457 U.S. 55 (1982). In *Zobel*, the Court held that an Alaska statute which allocated state treasury refunds to state residents on the basis of the length of their residence violated the Equal Protection Clause. The Court declined, however, to hold that the statute violated the Privileges and Immunities Clause. It observed that the statute "does not simply make distinctions between native-born Alaskans and those who migrate to Alaska from other States;" instead, it "also discriminates among long-time residents and even native-born residents." *** The Court recognizes, as it must, that the Privileges and Immunities Clause does not afford state residents any protection against their own State's laws. When this settled rule is combined with the Court's newly-fashioned rule concerning municipal discrimination, however, it has the perverse effect of vesting non-New Jersey residents with constitutional privileges that are not enjoyed by most New Jersey residents themselves. *** [T]he Privileges and Immunities Clause does not give nonresidents "higher and greater privileges than are enjoyed by the citizens of the state itself." ***

Finally, the Court fails to attend to the functional considerations that underlie the Privileges and Immunities Clause. *** [D]iscrimination on the basis of municipal residence *** penalizes persons within the State's political community as well as those without. The Court itself points out that while New Jersey citizens who reside outside Camden are not protected by the Privileges and Immunities Clause, they may resort to the State's political processes to protect themselves. What the Court fails to appreciate is that this avenue of relief for New Jersey residents works to protect residents of other States as well; disadvantaged state residents who turn to the state legislature to displace ordinances like Camden's further the interests of nonresidents as well as their own. ***

Notes

1.   **Different Provisions.**   Are you troubled that different provisions of the Constitution yield different results in *White* and *Camden*? Is this any different from saying that whipping of all prisoners constitutes cruel and unusual punishment but not a violation of the equal protection clause? Perhaps confusion arises because discrimination against out-of-staters is at the heart of both the Dormant Commerce Clause and the Privileges and Immunities Clause. However, aliens and corporations cannot invoke the Privileges and Immunities Clause. Moreover, the Dormant Commerce Clause deals with goods and services while the Privileges and Immunities Clause focuses on people.

2.   **Remand of *Camden*.**   As an advocate, what would you seek to present to the court on remand?

3.   **Question.**   Would the flow control ordinance in *United Haulers* survive an Article IV Privileges and Immunities claim?

4.   **Problem.**   Many states charge higher state university tuition for nonresidents than for residents. Do such differential tuition charges violate the Commerce Clause? The Privileges and Immunities Clause?

5.   **Full Faith & Credit**. Like dormant commerce and privileges and immunities doctrine, Art. IV, Sec. 1 ("Full Faith and Credit shall be given in each State to the [1] public Acts, [2] Records, and [3] judicial Proceedings of every other State. ***") facilitates interstate harmony ("horizontal federalism"). The Court treats public acts (state statutes) as having no effect in other states, but gives judgments of other states great deference. See *Baker v. General Motors*, 522 U.S. 222 (1997) ("The *** Clause does not compel 'a state to substitute the statues of other states for its own statutes [on] which it is competent to legislate.' Regarding judgments, however, the full faith and credit obligation is exacting. A final judgment in one state, if rendered by a court with [subject matter and personal jurisdiction], qualifies for recognition throughout the land.") Records certify a state's acts, but another state need not accept acts certified that violate its public policy.

McBURNEY v. YOUNG
133 S. Ct. 1709 (2013)

JUSTICE ALITO delivered the opinion of the Court.

In this case, we must decide whether the Virginia Freedom of Information Act, violates either the Privileges and Immunities Clause of Article IV of the Constitution or the dormant Commerce Clause. The Virginia Freedom of Information Act (FOIA), provides that "all public records shall be open to inspection and copying by any citizens of the Commonwealth," but it grants no such right to non-Virginians. Petitioners, *** citizens of other States, unsuccessfully sought information ***

Under the Privileges and Immunities Clause, "[t]he Citizens of each State [are] entitled to all Privileges and Immunities of Citizens in the several States." We have said that "[t]he object of the Privileges and Immunities Clause is to 'strongly ... constitute the citizens of the United States [as] one people,' by 'plac[ing] the citizens of each State upon the same footing with citizens of other States, so far as the advantages resulting from citizenship in those States are concerned.' " This does not mean, we have cautioned, that "state citizenship or residency may never be used by a State to distinguish among persons." "Nor must a State always apply all its laws or all its services equally to anyone, resident or nonresident, who may request it so to do." Rather, we have long held that the Privileges and Immunities Clause protects only those privileges and immunities that are "fundamental."

Petitioners allege that Virginia's citizens-only FOIA provision violates four different "fundamental" privileges or immunities: the opportunity to pursue a common calling, the ability to own and transfer property, access to the Virginia courts, and access to public information. The first three items on that list, however, are not abridged by the Virginia FOIA, and the fourth—framed broadly—is not protected by the Privileges and Immunities Clause.

[handwritten margin note: 4 P/I VA. may be violating]

Hurlbert *** obtain[s] property records from state and local governments on behalf of clients. He is correct that the Privileges and Immunities Clause protects the right of citizens to "ply their trade, practice their occupation, or pursue a common calling." But the Virginia FOIA does not abridge Hurlbert's ability to engage in a common calling in the sense prohibited by the Privileges and Immunities Clause. Rather, the Court has struck laws down as violating the privilege of pursuing a common calling only when those laws were enacted for the protectionist purpose of burdening out-of-state citizens. *** By its own terms, Virginia's FOIA was enacted to "ensur[e] the people of the Commonwealth ready access to public records in the custody of a public body or its officers and employees, and free entry to meetings of public bodies wherein the business of the people is being conducted." *** In addition, the provision limiting the use of the state FOIA to Virginia citizens recognizes that Virginia taxpayers foot the bill for the fixed costs underlying recordkeeping in the Commonwealth. The challenged provision of the state FOIA does not violate the Privileges and Immunities Clause simply because it has the incidental effect of preventing citizens of other States from making a profit by trading on information contained in state records. While the Clause forbids a State from intentionally giving its own citizens a competitive advantage in business or employment, the Clause does not require that a State tailor its every action to avoid any incidental effect on out-of-state tradesmen.

Hurlbert next alleges that the challenged provision of the Virginia FOIA abridges the right to own and transfer property in the Commonwealth. Like the right to pursue a common calling, the right to "take, hold and dispose of property, either real or personal," has long been seen as one of the privileges of citizenship. Thus, if a State prevented out-of-state citizens from accessing records—like title documents and mortgage records—that are necessary to the transfer of property, the State might well run afoul of the Privileges and Immunities Clause. Virginia, however, does not prevent citizens of other States from obtaining such documents. ***

A similar flaw undermines Hurlbert's claim that Virginia violates the Privileges and Immunities Clause by preventing citizens of other States from accessing real estate tax assessment records. It is true that those records, while available to Virginia citizens under the state FOIA, are not required by statute to be made available to noncitizens. But in fact Virginia and its subdivisions generally make even these less essential records readily available to all. These records are considered nonconfidential under Virginia law and, accordingly, they may be posted online. Henrico County, from which Hurlbert sought real estate tax assessments, follows this practice, as does almost every other county in the Commonwealth. Requiring noncitizens to conduct a few minutes of Internet research in lieu of using a relatively cumbersome state FOIA process cannot be said to impose any significant burden on noncitizens' ability to own or transfer property in Virginia.

McBurney alleges that Virginia's citizens-only FOIA provision impermissibly burdens his "access to public proceedings." McBurney is correct that the Privileges and Immunities Clause "secures citizens of one State the right to resort to the courts of another, equally with the citizens of the latter State." But petitioners do not suggest that the Virginia FOIA slams the courthouse door on noncitizens; rather, the most they claim is that the law creates "[a]n information asymmetry between adversaries based solely on state citizenship."

The Privileges and Immunities Clause does not require States to erase any distinction between citizens and non-citizens that might conceivably give state citizens some detectable litigation advantage. Rather, the Court has made clear that "the constitutional requirement is satisfied if the non-resident is given access to the courts of the State upon terms which in themselves are reasonable and adequate for the enforcing of any rights he may have, even though they may not be technically and precisely the same in extent as those accorded to resident citizens."

The challenged provision of the Virginia FOIA clearly does not deprive noncitizens of "reasonable and adequate" access to the Commonwealth's courts. Virginia's rules of civil procedure provide for both discovery, and subpoenas *duces tecum*. *** Moreover, Virginia law gives citizens and noncitizens alike access to judicial records. And if Virginia has in its possession information about any person, whether a citizen of the Commonwealth or of another State, that person has the right under the Government Data Collection and Dissemination Practices Act to inspect that information. *** When his FOIA request was denied, McBurney was told that he should request the materials he sought pursuant to the Government Data Collection and Dissemination Practices Act. Upon placing a request under that Act, he ultimately received much of what he sought. Accordingly, Virginia's citizens-only FOIA provision does not impermissibly burden noncitizens' ability to access the Commonwealth's courts.

Finally, we reject petitioners' sweeping claim that the challenged provision of the Virginia FOIA violates the Privileges and Immunities Clause because it denies them the right to access public information on equal terms with citizens of the Commonwealth. *** [T]here is no constitutional right to obtain all the information provided by FOIA laws. *** No such right was recognized at common law. Most founding-era English cases provided that only those persons who had a personal interest in non-judicial records were permitted to access them. *** Nor is such a sweeping right "basic to the maintenance or well-being of the Union." FOIA laws are of relatively recent vintage. ***

In addition to his Privileges and Immunities Clause claim, Hurlbert contends that Virginia's citizens-only FOIA provision violates the dormant Commerce Clause. *** Virginia's FOIA law neither "regulates" nor "burdens" interstate commerce; rather, it merely provides a service to local citizens *** Virginia neither prohibits access to an interstate market nor imposes burdensome regulation on that market. Rather, it merely creates and provides to its own citizens copies—which would not otherwise exist—of state records. *** Because it does not pose the question of the constitutionality of a state law that interferes with an interstate market through prohibition or burdensome regulations, this case is not governed by the dormant Commerce Clause. *** Insofar as there is a "market" for public documents in Virginia, it is a market for a product that the Commonwealth has created and of which the Commonwealth is the sole manufacturer. We have held that a State does not violate the dormant Commerce Clause when, having created a market through a state program, it "limits benefits generated by [that] state program to those who fund the state treasury and whom the State was created to serve." *** Virginia's citizens-only FOIA provision does not violate the dormant Commerce Clause. ***

JUSTICE THOMAS, concurring.

*** "The negative Commerce Clause has no basis in the text of the Constitution, makes little sense, and has proved virtually unworkable in application, and, consequently, cannot serve as a basis for striking down a state statute." ***

Notes

1. List of Privileges and Immunities. What privileges and immunities does this case alert you to beyond those listed in *Camden*?

2. What Privileges and Immunities are 'Fundamental"? Petitioners claim "the opportunity to pursue a common calling, the ability to own and transfer property, access to the Virginia courts, and access to public information" are fundamental. What are the Court's reasons for rejecting each of these claims?

3. Balancing. What role does the availability of another source of information play in Privileges and Immunities analysis?

4. Dormant and Active Commerce Clauses. Why does this claim fail? Does the inaccessibility of records to the plaintiffs "substantially affect interstate commerce," the test in the active commerce clause area (see Chapter IV)? How does the dormant commerce clause test for "commerce" differ from the active commerce clause test? Was there discrimination against the plaintiffs?

VII

RECONSTRUCTION OF FEDERAL-STATE RELATIONS

The remainder of this book explores how the Supreme Court has interpreted the Fourteenth Amendment. The text of § 1 reads as follows:

> All persons born or naturalized in the United States, and subject to the jurisdiction thereof, are citizens of the United States and of the State wherein they reside. No State shall make or enforce any law which shall abridge the privileges or immunities of citizens of the United States; nor shall any State deprive any person of life, liberty, or property, without due process of law; nor deny to any person within its jurisdiction the equal protection of the laws.

At the risk of gross oversimplification, three themes dominate the remainder of this book:

- First, precisely how much did the Fourteenth Amendment restructure the relationship between the United States and the individual states covered earlier in this book?
- Second—and more centrally—how has the Court interpreted the Fourteenth Amendment's grand but vague guarantees of privileges or immunities, due process, and equal protection? These phrases are a lynchpin for the Court's work as expositor of individual rights rather than as umpire over structural boundaries between governmental units.
- Third, what is Congress' role in implementing the principles of due process and equal protection set forth in section 1 of the Fourteenth Amendment. What falls within Congress' power to "enforce" the Fourteenth Amendment?

This chapter begins, in Part A, with the most reviled opinion in the history of the United States Supreme Court, *Dred Scott v. Sandford*. *Dred Scott* highlights the legal regime the Thirteenth, Fourteenth, and Fifteenth Amendments changed. It also raises issues of judicial interpretation of the Constitution, the potential for evil as well as good from the work of the Court, and the relationship between the Court and the larger society. Part B examines state action, a concept central to the operation of the Fourteenth Amendment. Finally, Part C considers an early interpretation of the Privileges or Immunities clause of the Fourteenth Amendment that largely gutted this clause and a recent decision that may (or may not) foreshadow its revival.

A. ORIGINS OF THE RECONSTRUCTION AMENDMENTS

Antislavery forces before the Civil War argued that slavery was unconstitutional, despite clauses in the Constitution that prohibited Congress from abolishing the slave trade until 1808, apportioned representatives on the whole number of free persons plus "three fifths of all other persons," and required states to "[deliver] up Person[s] held to Service or Labour in one State." For example, abolitionist William Lloyd Garrison in 1831 told the Philadelphia Convention of the Free People of Color that "The Constitution *** knows nothing of white or black men *** those State Laws which disenfranchise and degrade you are unconstitutional[.] *** [I]f they fall upon the Constitution, they will be dashed to pieces. I say it is your duty to carry this question up to the Supreme Court of the United States, and have it settled forever[.] *** [G]et yourself acknowledged, by that august tribunal, as citizens of the United States ***." Frederick Douglass in an 1852 speech argued that "the constitution is a glorious liberty document. Read its preamble, consider its purposes. Is slavery among them? *** [I]f the Constitution were intended to be, by its framers and adopters, a slave-holding instrument, why [can] neither *slavery, slaveholding,* nor *slave **** anywhere be found in it[?]"

During the first half of the 19th century, the North and South (other than abolitionists) were reconciled to the former remaining "free" and the latter "slave." The problem lay in the territories: neither side wanted the other to obtain control over the slavery issue in Congress through admission of disproportionate numbers of free or slave states as the country rapidly expanded westward. Congress believed it had the power (Art. IV, § 3, cl. 2) to prohibit or protect slavery in the territories, and exercised that power several times, most famously in the Northwest Ordinance of 1789 and the Missouri Compromise of 1820.

The Supreme Court, however, stalled further political compromise of the slavery issue when it decided, in the following case, that the Missouri Compromise was unconstitutional and that a slave taken to a free state by his master was not a citizen of the United States. As you read this case, pay particular attention to the components of citizenship, the relationship between citizenship and legal rights, and the extent to which control over these matters is entrusted to the states and to the federal government.

DRED SCOTT v. SANDFORD
60 U.S. (19 How.) 393 (1856)

MR. CHIEF JUSTICE TANEY delivered the opinion of the court.

*** Can a negro, whose ancestors were imported into this country, and sold as slaves, become a member of the political community formed and brought into existence by the Constitution of the United States, and as such become entitled to all the rights, and privileges, and immunities, guarantied by that instrument to the citizen? One of which rights is the privilege of suing in a court of the United States in the cases specified in the Constitution. *** [Scott suing in fed. court.]

The situation of this population was altogether unlike that of the Indian race. The latter, it is true, formed no part of the colonial communities, and never amalgamated with them in social connections or in government. But although they were uncivilized, they were yet a free and independent people, associated together in nations or tribes, and governed by their own laws. *** [T]hey may, without doubt, like the subjects of any other foreign Government, be naturalized by the authority of Congress, and become citizens of a State, and of the United States; and if an individual should leave his nation or tribe, and take up his abode among the white population, he would be entitled to all the rights and privileges which would belong to an emigrant from any other foreign people. ***

The words "people of the United States" and "citizens" *** describe the political body who*** form the sovereignty, and who hold the power and conduct the Government through their representatives. *** [Can descendants of slaves] compose a portion of this people, and [be] constituent members of this sovereignty? We think they are not, and that they are not included, and were not intended to be included, under the word "citizens" in the Constitution, and can therefore claim none of the rights and privileges which that instrument provides for and secures to citizens of the United States. On the contrary, they were at that time considered as a subordinate and inferior class of beings, who had been subjugated by the dominant race, and, whether emancipated or not, yet remained subject to their authority, and had no rights or privileges but such as those who held the power and the Government might choose to grant them.

It is not the province of the court to decide upon the justice or injustice, the policy or impolicy, of these laws. *** The duty of the court is, to interpret the instrument *** according to its true intent and meaning when it was adopted. *** [W]e must not confound the rights of citizenship which a State may confer within its own limits, and the rights of citizenship as a member of the Union. It does not by any means follow, because he has all the rights and privileges of a citizen of a State, that he must be a citizen of the United States. *** Each State may still confer them upon an alien, or any one it thinks proper, or upon any class or description of persons; yet he would not be a citizen in the sense in which that word is used in the Constitution of the United States, nor entitled to sue as such in one of its courts, nor to the privileges and immunities of a citizen in the other States. The rights which he would acquire would be restricted to the State which gave them. The Constitution has conferred on Congress the right to establish an uniform rule of naturalization ***. Consequently, no State, since the adoption of the Constitution, can by naturalizing an alien invest him with the rights and privileges secured to a citizen of a State under the Federal Government. ***

The question then arises, whether the provisions of the Constitution, in relation to the personal rights and privileges to which the citizen of a State should be entitled, embraced the negro African race, at that time in this country, or who might afterwards be imported, who had then or should afterwards be made free in any State; and to put it in the power of a single State to make him a citizen of the United States, and endue him with the full rights of citizenship in every other State without their consent? Does the Constitution of the United States act upon him whenever he shall be made free under the laws of a State, and raised there to the rank of a citizen, and immediately clothe him with all the privileges of a citizen in every other State, and in its own courts? *** [Scott] could not be a citizen of the State of Missouri, within the meaning of the Constitution of the United States, and, consequently, was not entitled to sue in its courts. ***

[T]he legislation and histories of the times, and the language used in the Declaration of Independence, show, that neither the class of persons who had been imported as slaves, nor their descendants, whether they had become free or not, were then acknowledged as a part of the people, nor intended to be included in the general words used in that memorable instrument. *** They had for more than a century before been regarded as beings of an inferior order, and altogether unfit to associate with the white race, either in social or political relations; and so far inferior, that they had no rights which the white man was bound to respect; and that the negro might justly and lawfully be reduced to slavery for his benefit. He was bought and sold, and treated as an ordinary article of merchandise and traffic, whenever a profit could be made by it. *** The language of the Declaration of Independence is equally conclusive: *** "We hold these truths to be self-evident: that all men are created equal; that they are endowed by their Creator with certain unalienable rights; that among them is life, liberty, and the pursuit of happiness; that to secure these rights, Governments are instituted, deriving their just powers from the consent of the governed."

The general words above quoted would seem to embrace the whole human family, and if they were used in a similar instrument at this day would be so understood. But it is too clear for dispute, that the enslaved African race were not intended to be included, and formed no part of the people who framed and adopted this declaration; for if the language, as understood in that day, would embrace them, the conduct of the distinguished men who framed the Declaration of Independence would have been utterly and flagrantly inconsistent with the principles they asserted; and instead of the sympathy of mankind, to which they so confidently appealed, they would have deserved and received universal rebuke and reprobation.

Yet the men who framed this declaration *** knew that it would not in any part of the civilized world be supposed to embrace the negro race, which, by common consent, had been excluded from civilized Governments and the family of nations, and doomed to slavery. They spoke and acted according to the then established doctrines and principles, and in the ordinary language of the day, and no one misunderstood them. The unhappy black race were separated from the white by indelible marks, and laws long before established, and were never thought of or spoken of except as property, and when the claims of the owner or the profit of the trader were supposed to need protection.

This state of public opinion had undergone no change when the Constitution was adopted, as is equally evident from its provisions and language. *** [T]wo clauses in the Constitution *** point directly and specifically to the negro race as a separate class of persons, and show clearly that they were not regarded as a portion of the people or citizens of the Government then formed. One of these clauses reserves to each of the thirteen States the right to import slaves until the year 1808, if it thinks proper. *** And by the other provision the States pledge themselves to each other to maintain the right of property of the master, by delivering up to him any slave who may have escaped from his service, and be found within their respective territories. *** [T]hese two clauses were not intended to confer on them or their posterity the blessings of liberty, or any of the personal rights so carefully provided for the citizen. ***

The legislation of the States *** shows, in a manner not to be mistaken, the inferior and subject condition of that race ***. More especially, it cannot be believed that the large slaveholding States regarded them as included in the word citizens, or would have consented to a Constitution which might compel them to receive them in that character from another State. For if they were so received, and entitled to the privileges and immunities of citizens, it would exempt them from the operation of the special laws and from the police regulations which they considered to be necessary for their own safety. ***

[W]hen [the founders] gave to the citizens of each State the privileges and immunities of citizens in the several States, they at the same time took from the several States the power of naturalization, and confined that power exclusively to the Federal Government. *** [T]hey could never have left with the States a much more important power—that is, the power of transforming into citizens a numerous class of persons, who in that character would be much more dangerous to the peace and safety of a large portion of the Union, than the few foreigners one of the States might improperly naturalize. *** And no law of a State, therefore, passed since the Constitution was adopted, can give any right of citizenship outside of its own territory.

A clause similar to the one in the Constitution, in relation to the rights and immunities of citizens of one State in the other States, was contained in the Articles of Confederation. But there is a difference of language, which is worthy of note. The provision in the Articles of Confederation was, "that the *free inhabitants* of each of the States, paupers, vagabonds, and fugitives from justice, excepted, should be entitled to all the privileges and immunities of free citizens in the several States." *** [T]he comprehensive word inhabitant, which might be construed to include an emancipated slave, is omitted; and the privilege is confined to citizens of the State. ***

To all this mass of proof we have still to add, that Congress has repeatedly legislated upon the same construction of the Constitution that we have given. Three laws *** will be abundantly sufficient to show this. *** The first of these acts is the naturalization law [of 1790], which *** confines the right of becoming citizens *"to aliens being free white persons."* *** [The first militia law, passed in 1792] directs that every "free able-bodied white male citizen" shall be enrolled in the militia. *** The third act *** provides: "That *** it shall not be lawful to employ, on board of any public or private vessels of the United States, any person or persons except citizens of the United

States, *or* persons of color, natives of the United States." *** Persons of color, in the judgment of Congress, were not included in the word citizens. ***

But it is said that a person may be a citizen, and entitled to that character, although he does not possess all the rights which may belong to other citizens; as, for example, the right to vote, or to hold particular offices; and that yet, when he goes into another State, he is entitled to be recognized there as a citizen, although the State may measure his rights by the rights which it allows to persons of a like character or class resident in the State, and refuse to him the full rights of citizenship. *** Women and minors, who form a part of the political family, cannot vote; and when a property qualification is required to vote or hold a particular office, those who have not the necessary qualification cannot vote or hold the office, yet they are citizens.

[handwritten margin note: acknowledges there are classes of citizens who do not have full rights]

So, too, a person may be entitled to vote by the law of the State, who is not a citizen even of the State itself. *** And the State may give the right to free negroes and mulattoes, but that does not make them citizens of the State, and still less of the United States. *** Dred Scott was not a citizen of Missouri within the meaning of the Constitution of the United States, and not entitled as such to sue in its courts. *** [B]ut if that plea is regarded as waived, or out of the case upon any other ground, [we proceed to the merits of Dred Scott's claim to freedom under federal law]. ***

[handwritten margin note: states can give people rights but not citizenship]

The act of Congress, upon which the plaintiff relies, declares that slavery and involuntary servitude, except as a punishment for crime, shall be forever prohibited in all that part of the territory ceded by France, under the name of Louisiana ***. [Was] Congress authorized to pass this law under any of the powers granted to it by the Constitution [?] *** The counsel for the plaintiff has laid much stress upon that article in the Constitution which confers on Congress the power 'to dispose of and make all needful rules and regulations respecting the territory or other property belonging to the United States;' but, in the judgment of the court, that provision has no bearing on the present controversy. *** The power is given in relation only to the territory of the United States—that is, to a territory then in existence, and then known or claimed as the territory of the United States. ***

As Scott was a slave when taken into the State of Illinois by his owner, and was there held as such***depended on the laws of Missouri, and not of Illinois. *** Scott and his family upon their return were not free, but were, by the laws of Missouri, the property of the defendant; and the Circuit Court of the United States had no jurisdiction, when, by the laws of the State, the plaintiff was a slave, and not a citizen. ***

MR. JUSTICE DANIEL concurring.

*** For who, it may be asked, is a citizen? *** The institution of slavery, as it exists and has existed from the period of its introduction into the United States, though more humane and mitigated in character than was the same institution, either under the republic or the empire of Rome, bears, both in its tenure and in the simplicity incident to the mode of its exercise, a closer resemblance to Roman slavery than it does to the condition of *villanage*, as it

[handwritten margin note: historical consideration of slavery to support that slaves are not citizens]

formerly existed in England. *** [W]ith regard to slavery amongst the Romans, it is by no means true that emancipation, either during the republic or the empire, conferred, by the act itself, or implied, the *status* or the rights of citizenship. ***

MR. JUSTICE MCLEAN dissenting.

*** Being born under our Constitution and laws, no naturalization is required, as one of foreign birth, to make him a citizen. The most general and appropriate definition of the term citizen is "a freeman." Being a freeman, and having his domicil in a State different from that of the defendant, he is a citizen within the act of Congress, and the courts of the Union are open to him. *** Several of the States have admitted persons of color to the right of suffrage, and in this view have recognized them as citizens; and this has been done in the slave as well as the free States. ***

[U]nder the commercial power, Congress had a right to regulate the slave trade among the several States; but the court held that Congress had no power to interfere with slavery as it exists in the States, or to regulate what is called the slave trade among them. If this trade were subject to the commercial power, it would follow that Congress could abolish or establish slavery in every State of the Union. *** But if we are to turn our attention to the dark ages of the world, why confine our view to colored slavery? On the same principles, white men were made slaves. All slavery has its origin in power, and is against right. ***

It would be singular, if in 1804 Congress had power to prohibit the introduction of slaves in Orleans Territory from any other part of the Union, under the penalty of freedom to the slave, if the same power, embodied in the Missouri compromise, could not be exercised in 1820. But this law of Congress, which prohibits slavery north of Missouri and of thirty-six degrees thirty minutes, is declared to have been null and void by my brethren. And this opinion is founded mainly, as I understand, on the distinction drawn between the ordinance of 1787 and the Missouri compromise line. *** If Congress may establish a Territorial Government in the exercise of its discretion, it is a clear principle that a court cannot control that discretion. *** I do not see on what ground the act is held to be void. It did not purport to forfeit property, or take it for public purposes. It only prohibited slavery; in doing which, it followed the ordinance of 1787. ***

Does the master carry with him the law of the State from which he removes into the Territory? *** In this case, a majority of the court have said that a slave may be taken by his master into a Territory of the United States, the same as a horse, or any other kind of property. *** The question of jurisdiction, being before the court, was decided by them authoritatively, but nothing beyond that question. A slave is not a mere chattel. He bears the impress of his Maker, and is amenable to the laws of God and man; and he is destined to an endless existence. *** The Supreme Court of Missouri refused to notice the act of Congress or the Constitution of Illinois, under which Dred Scott, his wife and children, claimed that they are entitled to freedom. *** If a State court may do this, on a question involving the liberty of a human being, what protection do the laws afford? ***

MR. JUSTICE CURTIS dissenting.

*** Citizens of the United States at the time of the adoption of the Constitution can have been no other than citizens of the United States under the Confederation. *** [I]n some of the original thirteen States, free colored persons, before and at the time of the formation of the Constitution, were citizens of those States.

The fourth of the fundamental articles of the Confederation was as follows: "The free inhabitants of each of these States, paupers, vagabonds, and fugitives from justice, excepted, shall be entitled to all the privileges and immunities of free citizens in the several States." *** [F]ree persons of color were citizens of some of the several States, [with] the consequence, that this fourth article of the Confederation would have the effect to confer on such persons the privileges and immunities of general citizenship. *** Did the Constitution of the United States deprive them or their descendants of citizenship? *** [M]y opinion is, that, under the Constitution of the United States, every free person born on the soil of a State, who is a citizen of that State by force of its Constitution or laws, is also a citizen of the United States. ***

[handwritten margin note: B/c freed slaves were citizens under the AoC, they are considered as free people under the Const]

Among the powers expressly granted to Congress is "the power to establish a uniform rule of naturalization." *** [T]he only power expressly granted to Congress to legislate concerning citizenship, is confined to the removal of the disabilities of foreign birth. *** Among the powers unquestionably possessed by the several States, was that of determining what persons should and what persons should not be citizens. *** "The citizens of each State shall be entitled to all the privileges and immunities of citizens of the several States." Nowhere else in the Constitution is there anything concerning a general citizenship; but here, privileges and immunities to be enjoyed throughout the United States, under and by force of the national compact, are granted and secured. In selecting those who are to enjoy these national rights of citizenship, how are they described? As citizens of each State. It is to them these national rights are secured. ***

[handwritten margin note: Const. doesn't address general mode of citizenship]

It has been often asserted that the Constitution was made exclusively by and for the white race*** [I]t is not true *** One [state] may confine the right of suffrage to white male citizens; another may extend it to colored persons and females; one may allow all persons above a prescribed age to convey property and transact business; another may exclude married women. But whether native-born women, or persons under age, or under guardianship because insane or spendthrifts, be excluded from voting or holding office, or allowed to do so, I apprehend no one will deny that they are citizens of the United States. *** It has been suggested, that in adopting it into the Constitution, the words "free inhabitants" were changed for the word "citizens." An *** attention to the substance of this article of the Confederation, will show that the words "free inhabitants," as then used, were synonymous with citizens. ***

[handwritten margin note: Const. is for all citizens, not just white]

Masters have no control over citizenship

It may be further objected, that if free colored persons may be citizens of the United States, it depends only on the will of a master whether he will emancipate his slave, and thereby make him a citizen. Not so. The master is subject to the will of the State. ***

State law going against fed. due process

Looking at the power of Congress over the Territories ***, what positive prohibition exists in the Constitution, which restrained Congress from enacting a law in 1820 to prohibit slavery north of thirty-six degrees thirty minutes north latitude? The only one suggested is that clause in the fifth article of the amendments of the Constitution which declares that no person shall be deprived of his life, liberty, or property, without due process of law. *** Slavery, being contrary to natural right, is created only by municipal law. *** The Constitution refers to slaves as "persons held to service in one State, under the laws thereof." Nothing can more clearly describe a status created by municipal law. *** [U]nder the power to regulate commerce, Congress could prohibit the importation of slaves; and the exercise of the power was restrained till 1808. A citizen of the United States owns slaves in Cuba, and brings them to the United States, where they are set free by the legislation of Congress. Does this legislation deprive him of his property without due process of law? If so, what becomes of the laws prohibiting the slave trade? If not, how can similar regulation respecting a Territory violate the fifth amendment of the Constitution? ***

Notes

1.   **Critique of *Dred Scott*.** What was wrong about the decision as a matter of constitutional theory (as opposed to theories of fundamental human rights and morality)? Could the Court have reached a different result with a textual, as opposed to an original intent, approach? Was the Court wrong to ignore the language of the Declaration of Independence ("All men are created equal *** ") in assessing original intent? Would structural interpretation have been of use to the Court in reaching a contrary decision? Should the Court have envisioned the Constitution as growing and changing to embody societal aspirations? Should the Court have held that slavery violated the natural law right of human freedom?

2.   **Limits of the Court's Power.** Quite erroneously, the Court thought its decision would take the slavery issue "out of politics." Instead, it inflamed preexisting passions. It encouraged the southern states to assert the power to leave the Union and convinced the abolitionists that only superior force could undo the injustice of the Court's interpretation of the Constitution. William Lloyd Garrison publicly burned a copy of the Constitution following the *Dred Scott* decision, calling the Constitution a "compact with the devil," a judgment perhaps confirmed by this proposed Thirteenth Amendment, which passed both houses of the Republican Congress less than a week before Lincoln's inauguration in a Congress lacking representation from the Deep South:

> *No amendment shall be made to the Constitution which will authorize or give to Congress the power to abolish or interfere, within any State, with the domestic institutions thereof, including that of persons held to labor or service by the laws of said state.*

The rest–Lincoln's election, the Civil War, Reconstruction, and Jim Crow–is history.

3. **Reversing *Dred Scott*.** Three constitutional amendments were passed to overturn various aspects of this one decision. The Thirteenth Amendment (1865) abolished slavery. But this manumission did not give former slaves the benefits of being citizens. The first sentence of the Fourteenth Amendment (1868) established a national rule of citizenship for those born (like the former slaves) in the United States. This sentence gave the freed slaves, among other things, the right of citizens to sue in federal court. The second sentence of the Fourteenth Amendment guaranteed "privileges or immunities of citizens of the United States," and that states could not deprive "any person" of "due process of law" and "equal protection of the laws." The Fifteenth Amendment (1870) prohibited the United States and the states from denying the right to vote "on account of race, color, or previous condition of servitude."

4. **Beyond Reversal.** Most of the remainder of this book examines judicial interpretation of the second sentence of the Fourteenth Amendment. Three further amendments addressed other situations alluded to in this case: the Nineteenth Amendment (1920) ended the era where females could be citizens but denied the right to vote; the Twenty–Fourth Amendment (1964) abolished poll taxes used covertly to deny African–Americans the right to vote on an equal basis with white citizens; and the Twenty–Sixth Amendment (1971) set a uniform age of 18 at which citizens were guaranteed the right to vote.

B. STATE ACTION AND THE FOURTEENTH AMENDMENT

THE CIVIL RIGHTS CASES
109 U.S. 3 (1883)

BRADLEY, J.

*** [T]he primary and important question in all the cases is the constitutionality of th[is] law ***: "That all persons within the jurisdiction of the United States shall be entitled to the full and equal enjoyment of the accommodations, advantages, facilities, and privileges of inns, public conveyances on land or water, theaters, and other places of public amusement; subject only to the conditions and limitations established by law, and applicable alike to citizens of every race and color, regardless of any previous condition of servitude [and that violations shall be remedied by civil suits by the "person aggrieved" and criminal sanctions.]"

Has congress constitutional power to make such a law? Of course, no one will contend that the power to pass it was contained in the constitution before the adoption of the last three amendments. *** [In t]he first section of the fourteenth amendment *** it is state action of a particular character that is prohibited. Individual invasion of individual rights is not the subject-matter of the amendment. It has a deeper and broader scope. It nullifies and makes void all state legislation, and state action of every kind, which impairs the privileges and immunities of citizens of the United States, or which injures them in life, liberty, or property without due process of law, or which denies to any of them the equal protection of the laws. *** [T]he last section of the amendment invests congress with power to enforce it by appropriate legislation. To enforce what? To enforce the prohibition. To adopt appropriate legislation for correcting the effects of such prohibited state law and state acts, and thus to render them effectually null, void, and innocuous. This is the legislative power conferred upon congress, and this is the whole of it. It does not invest congress with power to legislate upon subjects which are within the domain of state legislation; but to provide modes of relief against state legislation, or state action, of the kind referred to. ***

An apt illustration of this distinction may be found in some of the provisions of the original constitution. Take the subject of contracts, for example. The constitution prohibited the states from passing any law impairing the obligation of contracts. This did not give to congress power to provide laws for the general enforcement of contracts; nor power to invest the courts of the United States with jurisdiction over contracts, so as to enable parties to sue upon them in those courts. It did, however, give the power to provide remedies by which the impairment of contracts by state legislation might be counteracted and corrected; and this power was exercised. *** Some obnoxious state law passed, or that might be passed, is necessary to be assumed in order to lay the foundation of any federal remedy in the case, and for the very sufficient reason that the constitutional prohibition is against state laws impairing the obligation of contracts.

And so in the present case, until some state law has been passed, or some state action through its officers or agents has been taken, adverse to the rights of citizens sought to be protected by the fourteenth amendment, no legislation of the United States under said amendment, nor any proceeding under such legislation, can be called into activity, for the prohibitions of the amendment are against state laws and acts done under state authority. *** An inspection of the law shows that it makes no reference whatever to any supposed or apprehended violation of the fourteenth amendment on the part of the states. *** If this legislation is appropriate for enforcing the prohibitions of the amendment, it is difficult to see where it is to stop. Why may not congress, with equal show of authority, enact a code of laws for the enforcement and vindication of all rights of life, liberty, and property? *** [This law] is repugnant to the tenth amendment of the constitution ***.

[C]ivil rights, such as are guaranteed by the constitution against state aggression, cannot be impaired by the wrongful acts of individuals, unsupported by state authority in the shape of laws, customs, or judicial or executive proceedings. The wrongful act of an individual, unsupported by any such authority, is simply a private wrong, or a crime of that individual; an invasion of the rights of the injured party, it is true, whether they affect his person, his property, or his reputation; but if not sanctioned in some way by the state, or not done under state authority, his rights remain in full force, and may presumably be vindicated by resort to the laws of the state for redress. An individual cannot deprive a man of his right to vote, to hold property, to buy and to sell, to sue in the courts, or to be a witness or a juror; he may, by force or fraud, interfere with the enjoyment of the right in a particular case; he may commit an assault against the person, or commit murder, or use ruffian violence at the polls, or slander the good name of a fellow-citizen; but unless protected in these wrongful acts by some shield of state law or state authority, he cannot destroy or injure the right; he will only render himself amenable to satisfaction or punishment; and amenable therefor to the laws of the state where the wrongful acts are committed. Hence, in all those cases where the constitution seeks to protect the rights of the citizen against discriminative and unjust laws of the state by prohibiting such laws, it is not individual offenses, but abrogation and denial of rights, which it denounces, and for which it clothes the congress with power to provide a remedy. This abrogation and denial of rights, for which the states alone were or could be responsible, was the great seminal and fundamental wrong which was intended to be remedied. And the remedy to be provided must necessarily be predicated upon that wrong. It must assume that in the cases provided for, the evil or wrong actually committed rests upon some state law or state authority for its excuse and perpetration.

Of course, these remarks do not apply to those cases in which congress is clothed with direct and plenary powers of legislation over the whole subject, accompanied with an express or implied denial of such power to the states, as in the regulation of commerce with foreign nations, among the several states, and with the Indian tribes, the coining of money, the establishment of post-offices and post-roads, the declaring of war, etc. ***

[T]he law in question cannot be sustained by any grant of legislative power made to congress by the fourteenth amendment. That amendment prohibits the states from denying to any person the equal protection of the laws, and declares that congress shall have power to enforce, by appropriate legislation, the provisions of the amendment. The law in question, without any reference to adverse state legislation on the subject, declares that all persons shall be entitled to equal accommodation and privileges of inns, public conveyances, and places of public amusement, and imposes a penalty upon any individual who shall deny to any citizen such equal accommodations and privileges. This is not corrective legislation; it is primary and direct; it takes immediate and absolute possession of the subject of the right of admission to inns, public conveyances, and places of amusement. It supersedes and displaces state legislation on the same subject, or only allows it permissive force. It ignores such legislation, and assumes that the matter is one that belongs to the domain of national regulation. Whether it would not have been a more effective protection of the rights of citizens to have clothed congress with plenary power over the whole subject, is not now the question. What we have to decide is, whether such plenary power has been conferred upon congress by the fourteenth amendment, and, in our judgment, it has not. ***

But the power of congress to adopt direct and primary, as distinguished from corrective, legislation on the subject in hand, is sought, in the second place, from the thirteenth amendment, which abolishes slavery. *** It is true that slavery cannot exist without law any more than property in lands and goods can exist without law, and therefore the thirteenth amendment may be

regarded as nullifying all state laws which establish or uphold slavery. ***
[I]t is assumed that the power vested in congress to enforce the article by
appropriate legislation, clothes congress with power to pass all laws
necessary and proper for abolishing all badges and incidents of slavery in the
United States; and upon this assumption it is claimed that this is sufficient
authority for declaring by law that all persons shall have equal
accommodations and privileges in all inns, public conveyances, and places of
public amusement; the argument being that the denial of such equal
accommodations and privileges is in itself a subjection to a species of
servitude within the meaning of the amendment. ***

But is there any similarity between such servitudes and a denial by the
owner of an inn, a public conveyance, or a theater, of its accommodations and
privileges to an individual, even though the denial be founded on the race or
color of that individual? Where does any slavery or servitude, or badge of
either, arise from such an act of denial? Whether it might not be a denial of a
right which, if sanctioned by the state law, would be obnoxious to the
prohibitions of the fourteenth amendment, is another question. But what has
it to do with the question of slavery? It may be that by the black code, (as it
was called,) in the times when slavery prevailed, the proprietors of inns and
public conveyances were forbidden to receive persons of the African race,
because it might assist slaves to escape from the control of their masters.
This was merely a means of preventing such escapes, and was no part of the
servitude itself. ***

We must not forget that the province and scope of the thirteenth and
fourteenth amendments are different: the former simply abolished slavery
***. The only question under the present head, therefore, is, whether the
refusal to any persons of the accommodations of an inn, or a public
conveyance, or a place of public amusement, by an individual, and without
any sanction or support from any state law or regulation, does inflict upon
such persons any manner of servitude, or form of slavery, as those terms are
understood in this country? *** It would be running the slavery argument
into the ground to make it apply to every act of discrimination which a person
may see fit to make as to the guests he will entertain, or as to the people he
will take into his coach or cab or car, or admit to his concert or theater, or
deal with in other matters of intercourse or business. Innkeepers and public
carriers, by the laws of all the states, so far as we are aware, are bound, to
the extent of their facilities, to furnish proper accommodation to all
unobjectionable persons who in good faith apply for them. If the laws
themselves make any unjust discrimination, amenable to the prohibitions of
the fourteenth amendment, congress has full power to afford a remedy under
that amendment and in accordance with it.

When a man has emerged from slavery, and by the aid of beneficent
legislation has shaken off the inseparable concomitants of that state, there
must be some stage in the progress of his elevation when he takes the rank of
a mere citizen, and ceases to be the special favorite of the laws, and when his
rights as a citizen, or a man, are to be protected in the ordinary modes by
which other men's rights are protected. There were thousands of free colored

people in this country before the abolition of slavery, enjoying all the essential rights of life, liberty, and property the same as white citizens; yet no one, at that time, thought that it was any invasion of their personal status as freemen because they were not admitted to all the privileges enjoyed by white citizens, or because they were subjected to discriminations in the enjoyment of accommodations in inns, public conveyances, and places of amusement. Mere discriminations on account of race or color were not regarded as badges of slavery. ***

HARLAN, J., dissenting.

The opinion in these cases proceeds, as it seems to me, upon grounds entirely too narrow and artificial. ***

The thirteenth amendment, my brethren concede, did something more than to prohibit slavery as an institution, resting upon distinctions of race, and upheld by positive law. *** That there are burdens and disabilities which constitute badges of slavery and servitude, and that the express power delegated to congress to enforce, by appropriate legislation, the thirteenth amendment, may be exerted by legislation of a direct and primary character, for the eradication, not simply of the institution, but of its badges and incidents, are propositions which ought to be deemed indisputable. *** I do not contend that the thirteenth amendment invests congress with authority, by legislation, to regulate the entire body of the civil rights which citizens enjoy, or may enjoy, in the several states. But I do hold that since slavery, as the court has repeatedly declared, was the moving or principal cause of the adoption of that amendment, and since that institution rested wholly upon the inferiority, as a race, of those held in bondage, their freedom necessarily involved immunity from, and protection against, all discrimination against them, because of their race, in respect of such civil rights as belong to freemen of other races. ***

It remains now to inquire what are the legal rights of colored persons in respect of the accommodations, privileges, and facilities of public conveyances, inns, and places of public amusement. *** I am of opinion that such discrimination is a badge of servitude, the imposition of which congress may prevent under its power, through appropriate legislation, to enforce the thirteenth amendment; and consequently, without reference to its enlarged power under the fourteenth amendment, the act of March 1, 1875, is not, in my judgment, repugnant to the constitution.

It remains now to consider these cases with reference to the power congress has possessed since the adoption of the fourteenth amendment. *** [T]he court refers to the clause of the constitution forbidding the passage by a state of any law impairing the obligation of contracts. The clause does not, I submit, furnish a proper illustration of the scope and effect of the fifth section of the fourteenth amendment. No express power is given congress to enforce, by primary direct legislation, the prohibition upon state laws impairing the obligation of contracts. ***

[The § 1] prohibition upon a state is not a *power* in *congress* or *in the national government*. It is simply a denial of power to the state [enforceable by suit in federal court to invalidate any such law]. *** The fourteenth amendment presents the first instance in our history of the investiture of congress with affirmative power, by legislation, to enforce an express prohibition upon the states. ***

The assumption that this amendment consists wholly of prohibitions upon state laws and state proceedings in hostility to its provisions, is unauthorized by its language. *** The citizenship thus acquired by that race, in virtue of an affirmative grant by the nation, may be protected, not alone by the judicial branch of the government, but by congressional legislation of a primary direct character; this, because the power of congress is not restricted to the enforcement of prohibitions upon state laws or state action. It is, in terms distinct and positive, to enforce 'the provisions of this article' of amendment ***.

What are the privileges and immunities to which, by that clause of the constitution, they became entitled? *** [W]hat was secured to colored citizens of the United States—as between them and their respective states—by the grant to them of state citizenship? With what rights, privileges, or immunities did this grant from the nation invest them? There is one, if there be no others—exemption from race discrimination in respect of any civil right belonging to citizens of the white race in the same state. That, surely, is their constitutional privilege when within the jurisdiction of other states. And such must be their constitutional right, in their own state, unless the recent amendments be "splendid baubles," thrown out to delude those who deserved fair and generous treatment at the hands of the nation. Citizenship in this country necessarily imports equality of civil rights among citizens of every race in the same state. It is fundamental in American citizenship that, in respect of such rights, there shall be no discrimination by the state, or its officers, or by individuals, or corporations exercising public functions or authority, against any citizen because of his race or previous condition of servitude. ***

If, then, exemption from discrimination in respect of civil rights is a new constitutional right, secured by the grant of state citizenship to colored citizens of the United States, why may not the nation, by means of its own legislation of a primary direct character, guard, protect, and enforce that right? *** This court has always given a broad and liberal construction to the constitution, so as to enable congress, by legislation, to enforce rights secured by that instrument. *** *McCulloch v. Maryland.* ***

It is said that any interpretation of the fourteenth amendment different from that adopted by the court, would authorize congress to enact a municipal code for all the states, covering every matter affecting the life, liberty, and property of the citizens of the several states. Not so. *** The rights and immunities of persons recognized in the prohibitive clauses of the amendments were always under the protection, primarily, of the states, while rights created by or derived from the United States have always been, and, in the nature of things, should always be, primarily, under the protection of the general government. Exemption from race discrimination in respect of the civil rights which are fundamental in citizenship in a republican government, is, as we have seen, a new constitutional right, created by the nation, with express power in congress, by legislation, to enforce the constitutional provision from which it is derived. *** In every material sense applicable to the practical enforcement of the fourteenth amendment, railroad corporations, keepers of inns, and managers of places of public amusement are agents of the state, because amenable, in respect of their public duties and functions, to public regulation. It seems to me that *** a denial by these instrumentalities of the state to the citizen, because of his race, of that equality of civil rights secured to him by law, is a denial by the state within the meaning of the fourteenth amendment. If it be not, then that race is left, in respect of the civil rights under discussion, practically at the mercy of corporations and individuals wielding power under public authority.

*** What I affirm is that no state, nor the officers of any state, nor any corporation or individual wielding power under state authority for the public benefit or the public convenience, can, consistently either with the freedom established by the fundamental law, or with that equality of civil rights which now belongs to every citizen, discriminate against freemen or citizens, in their civil rights, because of their race, or because they once labored under disabilities imposed upon them as a race. *** The right, for instance, of a colored citizen to use the accommodations of a public highway upon the same terms as are permitted to white citizens is no more a social right than his right, under the law, to use the public streets of a city, or a town, or a turnpike road, or a public market, or a post-office, or his right to sit in a public building with others, of whatever race, for the purpose of hearing the political questions of the day discussed. Scarcely a day passes without our seeing in this court-room citizens of the white and black races sitting side by side watching the progress of our business. ***

The court, in its opinion, reserves the question whether congress, in the exercise of its power to regulate commerce among the several states, might or might not pass a law regulating rights in public conveyances passing from one state to another. *** I suggest that it may become a pertinent inquiry whether congress may, in the exertion of its power to regulate commerce among the states, enforce among passengers on public conveyances equality of right without regard to race, color, or previous condition of servitude ***.

My brethren say that when a man has emerged from slavery, and by the aid of beneficient legislation has shaken off the inseparable concomitants of that state, there must be some stage in the progress of his elevation when he takes the rank of a mere citizen, and ceases to be the special favorite of the laws, and when his rights as a citizen, or a man, are to be protected in the ordinary modes by which other men's rights are protected. It is, I submit, scarcely just to say that the colored race has been the special favorite of the laws. *** To-day it is the colored race which is denied, by corporations and individuals wielding public authority, rights fundamental in their freedom and citizenship. At some future time it may be some other race that will fall under the ban. ***

Notes

1.   **Holdings.** List the holdings of the case. For each, consider whether you think the majority or the dissent has the better of the argument and why.

2.   **Original Intent.** Suppose the framers of the 13th and 14th Amendments thought they were authorized to pass the law invalidated in *The Civil Rights Cases*, a fair assumption since the same legislators who passed the law also approved these amendments.   Neither the majority nor the dissent lays significant emphasis on this argument. Would you?

3.   **Ramifications.** Consider the immediate effects of this decision on the development of race relations in this country.   Why didn't Congress simply reenact the invalidated statute using the Commerce Clause powers discussed by the dissent? Why didn't the decision at least have the effect of nullifying the Jim Crow laws which relegated blacks to the back of public buses, to separate railroad cars, and to segregated classrooms for so many decades? *See Plessy v. Ferguson* and *Brown v. Board of Education*, infra Chapter IX.

4.   **The *Civil Rights Cases* Today.** The *Civil Rights Cases* have been distinguished but not overruled. Here are excerpts from the majority and dissent in *United States v. Morrison*, supra Chapter III, assessing whether the Violence Against Women Act could be supported by Congress' § 5 power:

> Shortly after the Fourteenth Amendment was adopted, we decided two cases interpreting the Amendment's provisions, *United States v. Harris*, 106 U.S. 629 (1883), and the *Civil Rights Cases*, 109 U.S. 3 (1883). In *Harris*, the Court considered a challenge to § 2 of the Civil Rights Act of 1871. That section sought to punish "private persons" for "conspiring to deprive any one of the equal protection of the laws enacted by the State." We concluded that this law exceeded Congress' § 5 power because the law was "directed exclusively against the action of private persons, without reference to the laws of the State, or their administration by her officers." *** [I]n the *Civil Rights Cases* *** we held that the public accommodation provisions of the Civil Rights Act of 1875, which applied to purely private conduct, were beyond the scope of the § 5 enforcement power. *** The force of the doctrine of stare decisis behind these decisions stems not only from the length of time they have been on the books, but also from the insight attributable to the Members of the Court at that time *** [who] had intimate knowledge and familiarity with the events surrounding the adoption of the Fourteenth Amendment. *** [This VAWA §] is not aimed at proscribing discrimination by officials which the Fourteenth Amendment might not itself proscribe; it is directed not at any State or state actor, but at individuals who have committed criminal acts motivated by gender bias. *** Congress' power under § 5 does not extend to the enactment of § 13981. ***

> JUSTICE BREYER, dissenting, opined:

> But why can Congress not provide a remedy against private actors? Those private actors, of course, did not themselves violate the Constitution. But this Court has held that Congress at least sometimes can enact remedial "[l]egislation *** [that] prohibits

conduct which is not itself unconstitutional." The statutory remedy does not in any sense purport to "determine what constitutes a constitutional violation." It intrudes little upon either States or private parties. It may lead state actors to improve their own remedial systems, primarily through example. It restricts private actors only by imposing liability for private conduct that is, in the main, already forbidden by state law.

How might Congress restrict § 13981 to make it constitutional? Could the section be premised on protecting the citizenship of women (see the first sentence of §1)? On the scope of the §5 power generally, see Chapter X.

5. **Scope of the Thirteenth Amendment Enforcement Power.** The Thirteenth Amendment abolishes "slavery or involuntary servitude," whether engaged in by the state or private individuals, and gives Congress "power to enforce this article by appropriate legislation." The Thirteenth Amendment has been read to permit Congress to eliminate "badges of slavery" through statutes barring private race discrimination, *Jones v. Alfred H. Mayer Co.*, 392 U.S. 409 (1968), but not sex discrimination. *Runyon v. McCrary*, 427 U.S. 160 (1976). Could Congress forbid State Bar Associations from requiring lawyers to do pro bono work? Is such unpaid work akin to slavery?

SHELLEY v. KRAEMER
334 U.S. 1 (1948).

MR. CHIEF JUSTICE VINSON delivered the opinion of the Court.

These cases present for our consideration questions relating to the validity of court enforcement of private agreements, generally described as restrictive covenants, which have as their purpose the exclusion of persons of designated race or color from the ownership or occupancy of real property. ***

On August 11, 1945, pursuant to a contract of sale, petitioners Shelley, who are Negroes, for valuable consideration received from one Fitzgerald a warranty deed to the parcel in question. The trial court found that petitioners had no actual knowledge of the restrictive agreement at the time of the purchase.

On October 9, 1945, respondents, as owners of other property subject to the terms of the restrictive covenant, brought suit in Circuit Court of the city of St. Louis praying that petitioners Shelley be restrained from taking possession of the property and that judgment be entered divesting title out of petitioners Shelley and revesting title in the immediate grantor or in such other person as the court should direct. ***

Whether the equal protection clause of the Fourteenth Amendment inhibits judicial enforcement by state courts of restrictive covenants based on race or color is a question which this Court has not heretofore been called upon to consider. *** [The Missouri] covenant declares that no part of the affected property shall be "occupied by any person not of the Caucasian race, it being intended hereby to restrict the use of said property *** against the occupancy as owners or tenants of any portion of said property for resident or other purpose by people of the Negro or Mongolian Race." Not only does the restriction seek to proscribe use and occupancy of the affected properties by members of the excluded class, but as construed by the Missouri courts, the agreement requires that title of any person who uses his property in violation of the restriction shall be divested. ***

It cannot be doubted that among the civil rights intended to be protected from discriminatory state action by the Fourteenth Amendment are the rights to acquire, enjoy, own and dispose of property. Equality in the enjoyment of property rights was regarded by the framers of that Amendment as an essential pre-condition to the realization of other basic civil rights and liberties which the Amendment was intended to guarantee. Thus, [42 U.S.C. § 1982], derived from § 1 of the Civil Rights Act of 1866 which was enacted by Congress while the Fourteenth Amendment was also under consideration, provides:

> "All citizens of the United States shall have the same right, in every State and Territory, as is enjoyed by white citizens thereof to inherit, purchase, lease, sell, hold, and convey real and personal property."

It is likewise clear that restrictions on the right of occupancy of the sort sought to be created by the private agreements in these cases could not be squared with the requirements of the Fourteenth Amendment if imposed by state statute or local ordinance. We do not understand respondents to urge the contrary. *** But the present cases do not involve action by state legislatures or city councils. Here the particular patterns of discrimination and the areas in which the restrictions are to operate, are determined, in the first instance, by the terms of agreements among private individuals. Participation of the State consists in the enforcement of the restrictions so defined. ***

Since the decision of this Court in the *Civil Rights Cases,* the principle has become firmly embedded in our constitutional law that the action inhibited by the first section of the Fourteenth Amendment is only such action as may fairly be said to be that of the States. That Amendment erects no shield against merely private conduct, however discriminatory or wrongful.

We conclude, therefore, that the restrictive agreements standing alone cannot be regarded as a violation of any rights guaranteed to petitioners by the Fourteenth Amendment. *** But here there was more. These are cases in which the purposes of the agreements were secured only by judicial enforcement by state courts of the restrictive terms of the agreements. The respondents urge that judicial enforcement of private agreements does not amount to state action; or, in any event, the participation of the State is so attenuated in character as not to amount to state action within the meaning of the Fourteenth Amendment. ***

That the action of state courts and of judicial officers in their official capacities is to be regarded as action of the State within the meaning of the Fourteenth Amendment, is a proposition which has long been established by decisions of this Court. *** One of the earliest applications of the prohibitions contained in the Fourteenth Amendment to action of state judicial officials occurred in cases in which Negroes had been excluded from jury service in criminal prosecutions by reason of their race or color. These cases demonstrate, also, the early recognition by this Court that state action in violation of the Amendment's provisions is equally repugnant to the constitutional commands whether directed by state statute or taken by a judicial official in the absence of statute. Thus, in *Strauder v. West Virginia*, 100 U.S. 303 (1880), this Court declared invalid a state statute restricting jury service to white persons as amounting to a denial of the equal protection of the laws to the colored defendant in that case. *** *Ex parte Virginia*, [100 U.S. 339 (1880)], held that a similar discrimination imposed by the action of a state judge denied rights protected by the Amendment, despite the fact that the language of the state statute relating to jury service contained no such restrictions.

The action of state courts in imposing penalties or depriving parties of other substantive rights without providing adequate notice and opportunity to defend, has, of course, long been regarded as a denial of the due process of law guaranteed by the Fourteenth Amendment.

In numerous cases, this Court has reversed criminal convictions in state courts for failure of those courts to provide the essential ingredients of a fair hearing. *** But the examples of state judicial action which have been held by this Court to violate the Amendment's commands are not restricted to situations in which the judicial proceedings were found in some manner to be procedurally unfair. ***

We have no doubt that there has been state action in these cases in the full and complete sense of the phrase. The undisputed facts disclose that petitioners were willing purchasers of properties upon which they desired to establish homes. The owners of the properties were willing sellers; and contracts of sale were accordingly consummated. It is clear that but for the active intervention of the state courts, supported by the full panoply of state power, petitioners would have been free to occupy the properties in question without restraint. *** The difference between judicial enforcement and nonenforcement of the restrictive covenants is the difference to petitioners between being denied rights of property available to other members of the community and being accorded full enjoyment of those rights on an equal footing. ***

Respondents urge, however, that since the state courts stand ready to enforce restrictive covenants excluding white persons from the ownership or occupancy of property covered by such agreements, enforcement of covenants excluding colored persons may not be deemed a denial of equal protection of the laws to the colored persons who are thereby affected. This contention does not bear scrutiny. The parties have directed our attention to no case in which a court, state or federal, has been called upon to enforce a covenant excluding members of the white majority from ownership or occupancy of real property on grounds of race or color. But there are more fundamental considerations. The rights created by the first section of the Fourteenth Amendment are, by its terms, guaranteed to the individual. The rights established are personal rights. It is, therefore, no answer to these petitioners to say that the courts may also be induced to deny white persons rights of ownership and occupancy on grounds of race or color. Equal protection of the laws is not achieved through indiscriminate imposition of inequalities. ***

The historical context in which the Fourteenth Amendment became a part of the Constitution should not be forgotten. Whatever else the framers sought to achieve, it is clear that the matter of primary concern was the establishment of equality in the enjoyment of basic civil and political rights and the preservation of those rights from discriminatory action on the part of the States based on considerations of race or color. *** [W]e find it unnecessary to consider whether petitioners have also been deprived of property without due process of law or denied privileges and immunities of citizens of the United States. ***

Notes

1.   **The Problem with *Shelley*.**   The covenant the beneficiaries sought to enforce in *Shelley* was private. What is not "neutral" about the Court's role if it simply enforces bargains, whatever they might be? Do the courts serve as enforcers of all private bargains? Is the problem that the bargain violates public policy? But isn't the public policy embodied in the Equal Protection Clause limited to race discrimination by the state? In short, if applied in other contexts, *Shelley* would eliminate the public/private distinction central to the *Civil Rights Cases*. As one author notes: "Courts enforce agreements that limit a party's ability to speak publicly in various respects, despite the fact that statutory limitations on the identical speech would be unconstitutional. Similarly, courts regularly have enforced testamentary provisions that condition inheritance on a child's marrying within a particular faith, despite the fact that the Establishment Clause precludes states from enacting the identical provision." Mark D. Rosen, "Was Shelley v. Kraemer Incorrectly Decided? Some New Answers," 94 CAL L. REV. 451 (2007)

2.   **Narrowing *Shelley*.**   Consider whether a private homeowner can exclude someone from her home on the basis of race without violating the Constitution. Before you answer "yes, because there is no state action," consider the homeowner's options: personal physical removal, which would not involve the state, and calling the police to evict the person. But if the police are called in to help with the removal, doesn't that involve state action under *Shelley*? Several possibilities for narrowing *Shelley* which might solve this hypothetical have been suggested: (1) since the common law of property disfavored restraints on alienation, the case merely applies that doctrine to a racial restraint on alienation; and (2) the land mass involved in *Shelley* was large (*see Marsh v. Alabama*, discussed infra), and the covenants therefore operated like zoning. Neither of these is very satisfactory, in part because neither is mentioned in the case. Another solution suggested is to say that the state is not doing anything *extraordinary* to encourage or ratify racial discrimination in the hypothetical, while it is "using its coercive power to allow persons tangential to the transaction (the complaining neighbors in *Shelley*) for racially discriminatory reasons to prevent a transaction between a willing, nondiscriminatory buyer and seller." Farber, Eskridge and Frickey, CONSTITUTIONAL LAW: THEMES FOR THE

CONSTITUTION'S THIRD CENTURY (2d Ed. West 1998), at p. 195. Is this a satisfactory explanation?

3.   **A Thirteenth Amendment Rationale?** The Court's rationale implies that racially restrictive covenants are legal, even if judicial enforcement is not. However, federal statutory law in effect since the late nineteenth century has provided all citizens the same rights as white citizens "to inherit, purchase, lease, sell, hold and convey real and personal property" and the same right as white citizens "to make and enforce contracts." Are these statutes outside Congress' power to "enforce" the 14th Amendment? The 13th Amendment? Could it be argued that the restrictive covenants in *Shelley* were "badges of slavery" in light of these statutes (or even without these statutes)?

EDMONSON v. LEESVILLE CONCRETE COMPANY
500 U.S. 614 (1991)

JUSTICE KENNEDY delivered the opinion of the Court.

We must decide in the case before us whether a private litigant in a civil case may use peremptory challenges to exclude jurors on account of their race. *** Thaddeus Donald Edmonson, a construction worker *** sued Leesville Concrete Company for negligence *** During *voir dire*, Leesville used two of its three peremptory challenges authorized by statute to remove black persons from the prospective jury. Citing our decision in *Batson v. Kentucky*, 476 U.S. 79 (1986), Edmonson, who is himself black, requested that the District Court require Leesville to articulate a race-neutral explanation for striking the two jurors. *** As empaneled, the jury included 11 white persons and 1 black person. ***

In *Powers v. Ohio*, 499 U.S. 400 (1991), we held that a criminal defendant, regardless of his or her race, may object to a prosecutor's race-based exclusion of persons from the petit jury. *** *Powers* relied upon over a century of jurisprudence dedicated to the elimination of race prejudice within the jury selection process. See, e.g., *Batson*, supra; *Strauder v. West Virginia*, 100 U.S. 303 (1880). While these decisions were for the most part directed at discrimination by a prosecutor or other government officials in the context of criminal proceedings, we have not intimated that race discrimination is permissible in civil proceedings. Indeed, discrimination on the basis of race in selecting a jury in a civil proceeding harms the excluded juror no less than discrimination in a criminal trial. In either case, race is the sole reason for denying the excluded venire person the honor and privilege of participating in our system of justice.

That an act violates the Constitution when committed by a government official, however, does not answer the question whether the same act offends constitutional guarantees if committed by a private litigant or his attorney. *** Racial discrimination, though invidious in all contexts, violates the Constitution only when it may be attributed to state action. *Moose Lodge No. 107 v. Irvis*, 407 U.S. 163 (1972). Thus, the legality of the exclusion at issue here turns on the extent to which a litigant in a civil case may be subject to the Constitution's restrictions.

The Constitution structures the National Government, confines its actions, and, in regard to certain individual liberties and other specified matters, confines the actions of the States. With a few exceptions, such as the provisions of the Thirteenth Amendment, constitutional guarantees of individual liberty and equal protection do not apply to the actions of private entities. This fundamental limitation on the scope of constitutional guarantees "preserves an area of individual freedom by limiting the reach of federal law" and "avoids imposing on the State, its agencies or officials, responsibility for conduct for which they cannot fairly be blamed." *Lugar v. Edmondson Oil Co.*, 457 U.S. 922 (1982). ***

To implement these principles, courts must consider from time to time where the governmental sphere ends and the private sphere begins. Although the conduct of private parties lies beyond the Constitution's scope in most instances, governmental authority may dominate an activity to such an extent that its participants must be deemed to act with the authority of the government and, as a result, be subject to constitutional constraints. This is the jurisprudence of state action, which explores the "essential dichotomy" between the private sphere and the public sphere, with all its attendant constitutional obligations.

We begin our discussion within the framework for state-action analysis set forth in *Lugar*. There we considered the state-action question in the context of a due process challenge to a State's procedure allowing private parties to obtain prejudgment attachments. We asked first whether the claimed constitutional deprivation resulted from the exercise of a right or privilege having its source in state authority; and second, whether the private party charged with the deprivation could be described in all fairness as a state actor.

There can be no question that the first part of the *Lugar* inquiry is satisfied here. By their very nature, peremptory challenges have no significance outside a court of law. Their sole purpose is to permit litigants to assist the government in the selection of an impartial trier of fact. *** Legislative authorizations, as well as limitations, for the use of peremptory challenges date as far back as the founding of the Republic; and the common-law origins of peremptories predate that. *** In the case before us, the challenges were exercised under a federal statute. *** Without this authorization, granted by an Act of Congress itself, Leesville would not have been able to engage in the alleged discriminatory acts.

Given that the statutory authorization for the challenges exercised in this case is clear, the remainder of our state-action analysis centers around the second part of the *Lugar* test, whether a private litigant in all fairness must be deemed a government actor in the use of peremptory challenges. *** Our precedents establish that, in determining whether a particular action or course of conduct is governmental in character, it is relevant to examine the following: the extent to which the actor relies on governmental assistance and benefits, see *Burton v. Wilmington Parking Authority*, 365 U.S. 715 (1961); whether the actor is performing a traditional governmental function, see *Marsh v. Alabama*, 326 U.S. 501 (1946); and whether the injury caused is aggravated in a unique way by the incidents of governmental authority, see *Shelley v. Kraemer*, 334 U.S. 1 (1948). Based on our application of these three principles to the circumstances here, we hold that the exercise of peremptory challenges by the defendant in the District Court was pursuant to a course of state action.

Although private use of state-sanctioned private remedies or procedures does not rise, by itself, to the level of state action, our cases have found state action when private parties make extensive use of state procedures with "the overt, significant assistance of state officials". It cannot be disputed that, without the overt, significant participation of the government, the peremptory challenge system, as well as the jury trial system of which it is a part, simply could not exist. *** By enforcing a discriminatory peremptory challenge, the court "has not only made itself a party to the [biased act], but has elected to place its power, property and prestige behind the [alleged] discrimination." *Burton v. Wilmington Parking Authority*, 365 U.S., at 725. In so doing, the government has "create[d] the legal framework governing the [challenged] conduct," *National Collegiate Athletic Assn.*, 488 U.S., at 192, and in a significant way has involved itself with invidious discrimination.

In determining Leesville's state-actor status, we next consider whether the action in question involves the performance of a traditional function of the government. A traditional function of government is evident here. The peremptory challenge is used in selecting an entity that is a quintessential governmental body, having no attributes of a private actor. The jury exercises the power of the court and of the government that confers the court's jurisdiction. ***

We find respondent's reliance on *Polk County v. Dodson*, 454 U.S. 312 (1981), unavailing. In that case, we held that a public defender is not a state actor in his general representation of a criminal defendant, even though he may be in his performance of other official duties. *** "[A] defense lawyer is not, and by the nature of his function cannot be, the servant of an administrative superior. Held to the same standards of competence and integrity as a private lawyer, a public defender works under canons of professional responsibility that mandate his exercise of independent judgment on behalf of the client."

In the ordinary context of civil litigation in which the government is not a party, an adversarial relation does not exist between the government and a private litigant. In the jury-selection process, the government and private litigants work for the same end. Just as a government employee was deemed a private actor because of his purpose and functions in *Dodson*, so here a private entity becomes a government actor for the limited purpose of using peremptories during jury selection. The selection of jurors represents a unique governmental function delegated to private litigants by the government and attributable to the government for purposes of invoking constitutional protections against discrimination by reason of race.

Our decision in *West v. Atkins*, 487 U.S. 42 (1988), provides a further illustration. We held there that a private physician who contracted with a state prison to attend to the inmates' medical needs was a state actor. He was not on a regular state payroll, but we held his "function[s] within the state system, not the precise terms of his employment, [determined] whether his actions can fairly be attributed to the State." ***

In the case before us, the parties do not act pursuant to any contractual relation with the government. Here, as in most civil cases, the initial decision whether to sue at all, the selection of counsel, and any number of ensuing tactical choices in the course of discovery and trial may be without the requisite governmental character to be deemed state action. That cannot be said of the exercise of peremptory challenges, however; when private litigants participate in the selection of jurors, they serve an important function within the government and act with its substantial assistance. If peremptory challenges based on race were permitted, persons could be required by summons to be put at risk of open and public discrimination as a condition of their participation in the justice system. The injury to excluded jurors would be the direct result of governmental delegation and participation.

Finally, we note that the injury caused by the discrimination is made more severe because the government permits it to occur within the courthouse itself. Few places are a more real expression of the constitutional authority of the government than a courtroom, where the law itself unfolds. Within the courtroom, the government invokes its laws to determine the rights of those who stand before it. In full view of the public, litigants press their cases, witnesses give testimony, juries render verdicts, and judges act with the utmost care to ensure that justice is done.

Race discrimination within the courtroom raises serious questions as to the fairness of the proceedings conducted there. Racial bias mars the integrity of the judicial system and prevents the idea of democratic government from becoming a reality. In the many times we have addressed the problem of racial bias in our system of justice, we have not "questioned the premise that racial discrimination in the qualification or selection of jurors offends the dignity of persons and the integrity of the courts." To permit racial exclusion in this official forum compounds the racial insult inherent in judging a citizen by the color of his or her skin. ***

JUSTICE O'CONNOR, with whom THE CHIEF JUSTICE and JUSTICE SCALIA join, dissenting.

The Court concludes that the action of a private attorney exercising a peremptory challenge is attributable to the government and therefore may compose a constitutional violation. This conclusion is based on little more than that the challenge occurs in the course of a trial. Not everything that happens in a courtroom is state action. A trial, particularly a civil trial is by design largely a stage on which private parties may act; it is a forum through which they can resolve their disputes in a peaceful and ordered manner. The government erects the platform; it does not thereby become responsible for all that occurs upon it. As much as we would like to eliminate completely from the courtroom the specter of racial discrimination, the Constitution does not sweep that broadly. Because I believe that a peremptory strike by a private litigant is fundamentally a matter of private choice and not state action, I dissent.

In order to establish a constitutional violation, Edmonson must first demonstrate that Leesville's use of a peremptory challenge can fairly be attributed to the government. Unfortunately, our cases deciding when private action might be deemed that of the state have not been a model of consistency. Perhaps this is because the state action determination is so closely tied to the "framework of the peculiar facts or circumstances present." *See Burton v. Wilmington Parking Authority*. Whatever the reason, and despite the confusion, a coherent principle has emerged. We have stated the rule in various ways, but at base, "constitutional standards are invoked only when it can be said that the [government] is responsible for the specific conduct of which the plaintiff complains." Constitutional "liability attaches only to those wrongdoors 'who carry a badge of authority of [the government] and represent it in some capacity.'"

The Court concludes that this standard is met in the present case. It rests this conclusion primarily on two empirical assertions. First, that private parties use peremptory challenges with the "overt, significant participation of the government." Second, that the use of a peremptory challenge by a private party "involves the performance of a traditional function of the government." Neither of these assertions is correct. *** It is the nature of a peremptory that its exercise is left wholly within the discretion of the litigant. *** In both criminal and civil trials, the peremptory challenge is a mechanism for the exercise of private choice in the pursuit of fairness. The peremptory is, by design, an enclave of private action in a government-managed proceeding. ***

The entirety of the government's actual participation in the peremptory process boils down to a single fact: "When a lawyer exercises a peremptory challenge, the judge advises the juror he or she has been excused." This is not significant participation. *** [T]he judge does not "encourage" the use of a peremptory challenge at all. The decision to strike a juror is entirely up to the litigant, and the reasons for doing so are of no consequence to the judge. ***

The alleged state action here is a far cry from that which the Court found, for example, in *Shelley v. Kraemer*, 334 U.S. 1 (1948). In that case, state courts were called upon to enforce racially restrictive covenants against sellers of real property who did not wish to discriminate. *** There is another important distinction between *Shelley* and this case. The state courts in *Shelley* used coercive force to impose conformance on parties who did not wish to discriminate. "Enforcement" of peremptory challenges, on the other hand, does not compel anyone to discriminate; the discrimination is wholly a matter of private choice. ***

The Court relies also on *Burton v. Wilmington Parking Authority*, 365 U.S. 715 (1961). But the decision in that case depended on the perceived symbiotic relationship between a restaurant and the state parking authority from whom it leased space in a public building. The State had "so far insinuated itself into a position of interdependence with" the restaurant that it had to be "recognized as a joint participant in the challenged activity."

Among the "peculiar facts [and] circumstances" leading to that conclusion was that the State stood to profit from the restaurant's discrimination. *** Whatever the continuing vitality of *Burton* beyond its facts, see *Jackson v. Metropolitan Edison Co.*, 419 U.S. 345 (1974), it does not support the Court's conclusion here.

Jackson is a more appropriate analogy to this case. Metropolitan Edison terminated Jackson's electrical service under authority granted it by the State, pursuant to a procedure approved by the state utility commission. Nonetheless, we held that Jackson could not challenge the termination procedure on due process grounds. The termination was not state action because the State had done nothing to encourage the particular termination practice: "*** *Respondent's exercise of the choice allowed by state law where the initiative comes from it and not from the State, does not make its action in doing so 'state action' for purposes of the Fourteenth Amendment.*" *** That the government allows this choice and that the judge approves it, does not turn this private decision into state action. ***

The Court errs also when it concludes that the exercise of a peremptory challenge is a traditional government function. *** Peremptory challenges are not a traditional government function; the "tradition" is one of unguided private choice. ***

None of this should be news, as this case is fairly well controlled by *Polk County v. Dodson*, 454 U.S. 312 (1981). We there held that a public defender, employed by the State, does not act under color of state law when representing a defendant in a criminal trial.* *** This is because a lawyer, when representing a private client, cannot at the same time represent the government. *** The Court does not challenge the rule of *Dodson*, yet concludes that private attorneys performing this adversarial function are state actors. Where is the distinction? *** Attorneys in an adversarial relation to the state are not state actors, but that does not mean that attorneys who are not in such a relation are state actors. *** *** If *Dodson* stands for anything, it is that the actions of a lawyer in a courtroom do not become those of the government by virtue of their location. This is true even if those actions are based on race.

Racism is a terrible thing. *** But not every opprobrious and inequitable act is a constitutional violation. *** The Government is not responsible for a peremptory challenge by a private litigant. ***

JUSTICE SCALIA, dissenting.

*** The concrete benefits of the Court's newly discovered constitutional rule are problematic. It will not necessarily be a net help rather than hindrance to minority litigants in obtaining racially diverse juries. In

---

* *Dodson* was a case brought under 42 U.S.C. § 1983, the statutory mechanism for many constitutional claims. The issue in that case, therefore, was whether the public defender had acted "under color of state law." In *Lugar v. Edmondson Oil Co.*, 457 U.S. 922, 929 (1982), the Court held that the statutory requirement of action "under color of state law" is identical to the "state action" requirement for other constitutional claims.

criminal cases, *Batson v. Kentucky* already prevents the prosecution from using race-based strikes. The effect of today's decision (which logically must apply to criminal prosecutions) will be to prevent the defendant from doing so—so that the minority defendant can no longer seek to prevent an all-white jury, or to seat as many jurors of his own race as possible. To be sure, it is ordinarily more difficult to prove race-based strikes of white jurors, but defense counsel can generally be relied upon to do what we say the Constitution requires. So in criminal cases, today's decision represents a net loss to the minority litigant. In civil cases that is probably not true—but it does not represent an unqualified gain either. Both sides have peremptory challenges, and they are sometimes used to assure rather than to prevent a racially diverse jury.

The concrete costs of today's decision, on the other hand, are not at all doubtful; and they are enormous. We have now added to the duties of already-submerged state and federal trial courts the obligation to assure that race is not included among the other factors (sex, age, religion, political views, economic status) used by private parties in exercising their peremptory challenges. That responsibility would be burden enough if it were not to be discharged through the adversary process; but of course it is. When combined with our decision this Term in *Powers v. Ohio*, 499 U.S. 400 (1991), which held that the party objecting to an allegedly race-based peremptory challenge need not be of the same race as the challenged juror, today's decision means that both sides, in all civil jury cases, no matter what their race (and indeed, even if they are artificial entities such as corporations), may lodge racial-challenge objections and, after those objections have been considered and denied, appeal the denials—with the consequence, if they are successful, of having the judgments against them overturned. Thus, yet another complexity is added to an increasingly Byzantine system of justice that devotes more and more of its energy to sideshows and less and less to the merits of the case. *** Alternatively, of course, the States and Congress may simply abolish peremptory challenges, which would cause justice to suffer in a different fashion.

Although today's decision neither follows the law nor produces desirable concrete results, it certainly has great symbolic value. *** The price of the demonstration is, alas, high, and much of it will be paid by the minority litigants who use our courts. ***

Notes

1. **State Involvement in Private Conduct.** As JUSTICE O'CONNOR's dissent discusses, *Burton* involved a private coffee shop's refusal to serve black customers prior to the Civil Rights Act of 1964. The coffee shop was located in a parking complex owned by a state agency which had the power to require the restaurant to adopt rules governing admission to the shop. The Court found sufficient state action. Is this because (as in *Shelley* and *Edmonson*) the case involves race discrimination? More recent cases have generally been reluctant to find state action from even significant state economic support of private entities. *See Jackson v. Metropolitan Edison,* described by JUSTICE O'CONNOR. *See Rendell–*

Baker v. Kohn, 457 U.S. 830 (1982) (although 90–99% of school's budget comes from the state and its operations were closely regulated, no First Amendment protection for employees fired for voicing opinions concerning school policies).

2.   **Public Functions.**   In *Marsh v. Alabama*, 326 U.S. 501 (1946), Gulf Shipbuilding Corporation, a private company, owned the town of Chickasaw, Alabama. When a Jehovah's Witness sought to distribute religious literature on a sidewalk of the town, she was arrested for trespass. Her defense was that the First Amendment protected her distribution of literature on the sidewalk. In rejecting the state's response that she had no first Amendment rights on private property, the Court said "Ownership does not always mean absolute dominion," that the corporation had opened up its property "for use by the public in general," and that "there is no more reason for depriving [residents of company-owned towns] of the liberties guaranteed by the First and fourteenth Amendments than there is for curtailing these freedoms with respect to any other citizen." The Court pointed out that the State had "permitt[ed] a corporation to govern a community of citizens" and that such governance could not be free of constitutional rights. Should the holding of *Marsh* be extended to a remote sugar plantation which has no stores or other town amenities but which is so remote from any town that workers have to be driven there on weekends? To a large shopping center in a city? What exactly are public functions? In another context, remember the Court's reluctance to answer this question (*Garcia v. SAMTA*)?

3. Peremptory Challenges in Operation. In *Snyder v. Louisiana*, 552 U.S. 472 (2008), the Court overturned the prosecution's peremptory challenge of potential jurors, including an African-American college student-teacher, Jeffrey Brooks. The prosecutor gave two reasons for the challenge: (1) Brooks was "nervous" during *voir dire* and (2) Brooks's worry about missing class might mean he would "want to go home quickly, come back with guilty of a lesser verdict." The trial judge allowed the peremptory challenge, but without addressing the prosecution's two reasons (to which the defense had objected). As to the first, the Court said: "It is possible that the judge did not have any impression one way or the other concerning Mr. Brooks' demeanor." As for the second, the Court found that the "quick resolution" scenario was "highly speculative." The trial was short, the judge had agreed to Brooks being on the jury, and a white prospective juror had not been challenged despite having more compelling conflicts than Brooks. JUSTICES THOMAS and SCALIA dissented, saying trial judges had not previously been required to articulate their reasons in resolving peremptory challenges.

4.   **Leadership Organizations.**   If a private entity produced many leaders in government, politics, and civic affairs, could its actions be deemed state action? In the First Amendment case of *Roberts v. United States Jaycees*, 468 U.S. 609 (1984), the Court was faced with the Jaycees' refusal to admit women to the organization as full-fledged members. Those challenging the practice couched their complaint in terms of statutory rights provided under the state law of Minnesota. The Jaycees countered that the application of the statute violated their First Amendment rights to Freedom of Association. Could the petitioner have claimed that the denial of membership constituted a violation of the Equal Protection Clause? Two of the *Roberts* justices (CHIEF JUSTICE BURGER and JUSTICE BLACKMUN) recused themselves from consideration of the case because of affiliation with the Jaycees.

5.   "Entwinement." In *Brentwood Academy v. Tennessee Secondary School Athletic Association*, 531 U.S. 288 (2001), the TSSAA had penalized Brentwood Academy for its use of "undue influence" in recruiting football players. The Court considered whether the TSSAA had engaged in regulatory state action which would have entitled Brentwood to due process according to the Fourteenth Amendment. The TSSAA is a private, voluntary organization, neither created nor funded by the state. Nevertheless, the Court held that the association had engaged in state action, because of the "pervasive entwinement of public institutions and public officials in its compositions and workings." At the time, 84% of the association's member schools were Tennessee Public Schools, and the association's voting board was composed entirely of public school officials. In his dissenting opinion, JUSTICE THOMAS argued that "entwinement" had not been defined by the majority, and was not a recognized standard for applying Fourteenth Amendment Due Process principles. Should a presumption of state action apply to any organization whose membership consists mostly of state employees? When a state employee labor union member is expelled by the union, is that member automatically entitled to due process rights?

DESHANEY v. WINNEBAGO COUNTY DEPARTMENT OF SOCIAL SERVICES
489 U.S. 189 (1989)

CHIEF JUSTICE REHNQUIST delivered the opinion of the Court.

Petitioner is a boy who was beaten and permanently injured by his father, with whom he lived. Respondents are social workers and other local officials who received complaints that petitioner was being abused by his father and had reason to believe that this was the case, but nonetheless did not act to remove petitioner from his father's custody. Petitioner sued respondents claiming that their failure to act deprived him of his liberty in violation of the Due Process Clause of the Fourteenth Amendment to the United States Constitution. We hold that it did not.

The facts of this case are undeniably tragic. Petitioner Joshua DeShaney was born in 1979. In 1980, a Wyoming court granted his parents a divorce and awarded custody of Joshua to his father, Randy DeShaney. The father shortly thereafter moved to Neenah, a city located in Winnebago County, Wisconsin, taking the infant Joshua with him. There he entered into a second marriage, which also ended in divorce.

The Winnebago County authorities first learned that Joshua DeShaney might be a victim of child abuse in January 1982, when his father's second wife complained to the police, at the time of their divorce, that he had previously "hit the boy causing marks and [was] a prime case for child abuse." The Winnebago County Department of Social Services (DSS) interviewed the father, but he denied the accusations, and DSS did not pursue them further. In January 1983, Joshua was admitted to a local hospital with multiple bruises and abrasions. The examining physician suspected child abuse and notified DSS, which immediately obtained an order from a Wisconsin juvenile court placing Joshua in the temporary custody of the hospital. Three days later, the county convened an ad hoc

"Child Protection Team"—consisting of a pediatrician, a psychologist, a police detective, the county's lawyer, several DSS caseworkers, and various hospital personnel—to consider Joshua's situation. At this meeting, the Team decided that there was insufficient evidence of child abuse to retain Joshua in the custody of the court. The Team did, however, decide to recommend several measures to protect Joshua, including enrolling him in a preschool program, providing his father with certain counselling services, and encouraging his father's girlfriend to move out of the home. Randy DeShaney entered into a voluntary agreement with DSS in which he promised to cooperate with them in accomplishing these goals.

Based on the recommendation of the Child Protection Team, the juvenile court dismissed the child protection case and returned Joshua to the custody of his father. A month later, emergency room personnel called the DSS caseworker handling Joshua's case to report that he had once again been treated for suspicious injuries. The caseworker concluded that there was no basis for action. For the next six months, the caseworker made monthly visits to the DeShaney home, during which she observed a number of suspicious injuries on Joshua's head; she also noticed that he had not been enrolled in school, and that the girlfriend had not moved out. The caseworker dutifully recorded these incidents in her files, along with her continuing suspicions that someone in the DeShaney household was physically abusing Joshua, but she did nothing more. In November 1983, the emergency room notified DSS that Joshua had been treated once again for injuries that they believed to be caused by child abuse. On the caseworker's next two visits to the DeShaney home, she was told that Joshua was too ill to see her. Still DSS took no action.

In March 1984, Randy DeShaney beat 4–year-old Joshua so severely that he fell into a life-threatening coma. Emergency brain surgery revealed a series of hemorrhages caused by traumatic injuries to the head inflicted over a long period of time. Joshua did not die, but he suffered brain damage so severe that he is expected to spend the rest of his life confined to an institution for the profoundly retarded. Randy DeShaney was subsequently tried and convicted of child abuse.

Joshua and his mother brought this action under 42 U.S.C. § 1983 in the United States District Court for the Eastern District of Wisconsin against respondents Winnebago County, DSS, and various individual employees of DSS. The complaint alleged that respondents had deprived Joshua of his liberty without due process of law, in violation of his rights under the Fourteenth Amendment, by failing to intervene to protect him against a risk of violence at his father's hands of which they knew or should have known. The District Court granted summary judgment for respondents.

*** Petitioners contend that the State deprived Joshua of his liberty interest in "free[dom] from *** unjustified intrusions on personal security," by failing to provide him with adequate protection against his father's violence. The claim is one invoking the substantive rather than the procedural component of the Due Process Clause; petitioners do not claim that the State denied Joshua protection without according him appropriate procedural safeguards, but that it was categorically obligated to protect him in these circumstances.

But nothing in the language of the Due Process Clause itself requires the State to protect the life, liberty, and property of its citizens against invasion by private actors. The Clause is phrased as a limitation on the State's power to act, not as a guarantee of certain minimal levels of safety and security. It forbids the State itself to deprive individuals of life, liberty, or property without "due process of law," but its language cannot fairly be extended to impose an affirmative obligation on the State to ensure that those interests do not come to harm through other means. Nor does history support such an expansive reading of the constitutional text. ***

Consistent with these principles, our cases have recognized that the Due Process Clauses generally confer no affirmative right to governmental aid, even where such aid may be necessary to secure life, liberty, or property interests of which the government itself may not deprive the individual. *** As we said in *Harris v. McRae*, 448 U.S. 297 (1980): "Although the liberty protected by the Due Process Clause affords protection against unwarranted *government* interference ***, it does not confer an entitlement to such [governmental aid] as may be necessary to realize all the advantages of that freedom." If the Due Process Clause does not require the State to provide its citizens with particular protective services, it follows that the State cannot be held liable under the Clause for injuries that could have been averted had it chosen to provide them. As a general matter, then, we conclude that a State's failure to protect an individual against private violence simply does not constitute a violation of the Due Process Clause.

Petitioners contend, however, that even if the Due Process Clause imposes no affirmative obligation on the State to provide the general public with adequate protective services, such a duty may arise out of certain "special relationships" created or assumed by the State with respect to particular individuals. Petitioners argue that such a "special relationship" existed here because the State knew that Joshua faced a special danger of abuse at his father's hands, and specifically proclaimed, by word and by deed, its intention to protect him against that danger. Having actually undertaken to protect Joshua from this danger—which petitioners concede the State played no part in creating—the State acquired an affirmative "duty," enforceable through the Due Process Clause, to do so in a reasonably competent fashion. Its failure to discharge that duty, so the argument goes, was an abuse of governmental power that so "shocks the conscience" as to constitute a substantive due process violation.

We reject this argument. It is true that in certain limited circumstances the Constitution imposes upon the State affirmative duties of care and protection with respect to particular individuals. *** But these cases afford petitioners no help. Taken together, they stand only for the proposition that when the State takes a person into its custody and holds him there against his will, the Constitution imposes upon it a corresponding duty to assume some responsibility for his safety and general well-being. The rationale for this principle is simple enough: when the State by the affirmative exercise of its power so restrains an individual's liberty that it renders him unable to care for himself, and at the same time fails to provide for his basic human needs—e.g., food, clothing, shelter, medical care, and reasonable safety—it transgresses the substantive limits on state action set by the Eighth Amendment and the Due Process Clause. The affirmative duty to protect arises not from the State's knowledge of the individual's predicament or from its expressions of intent to help him, but from the limitation which it has imposed on his freedom to act on his own behalf. In the substantive due process analysis, it is the State's affirmative act of restraining the individual's freedom to act on his own behalf—through incarceration, institutionalization, or other similar restraint of personal liberty—which is the "deprivation of liberty" triggering the protections of the Due Process Clause, not its failure to act to protect his liberty interests against harms inflicted by other means. ***

It may well be that, by voluntarily undertaking to protect Joshua against a danger it concededly played no part in creating, the State acquired a duty under state tort law to provide him with adequate protection against that danger. *** But the claim here is based on the Due Process Clause of the Fourteenth Amendment, which, as we have said many times, does not transform every tort committed by a state actor into a constitutional violation. ***

Judges and lawyers, like other humans, are moved by natural sympathy in a case like this to find a way for Joshua and his mother to receive adequate compensation for the grievous harm inflicted upon them. But before yielding to that impulse, it is well to remember once again that the harm was inflicted not by the State of Wisconsin, but by Joshua's father. The most that can be said of the state functionaries in this case is that they stood by and did nothing when suspicious circumstances dictated a more active role for them. In defense of them it must also be said that had they moved too soon to take custody of the son away from the father, they would likely have been met with charges of improperly intruding into the parent-child relationship, charges based on the same Due Process Clause that forms the basis for the present charge of failure to provide adequate protection.

JUSTICE BRENNAN, with whom JUSTICE MARSHALL and JUSTICE BLACKMUN join, dissenting.

*** It may well be, as the Court decides, that the Due Process Clause as construed by our prior cases creates no general right to basic governmental services. That, however, is not the question presented here *** In a constitutional setting that distinguishes sharply between action and inaction, one's characterization of the misconduct alleged *** may effectively decide the case. *** The Court's baseline is the absence of positive rights in the Constitution and a concomitant suspicion of any claim that seems to depend on such rights. From this perspective, the DeShaneys' claim is first and foremost about inaction (the failure, here, of respondents to take steps to protect Joshua), and only tangentially about action (the establishment of a state program specifically designed to help children like Joshua). And from this perspective, holding these Wisconsin officials liable—where the only difference between this case and one involving a general claim to protective services is Wisconsin's establishment and operation of a program to protect children—would seem to punish an effort that we should seek to promote.

I would begin from the opposite direction. I would focus first on the action that Wisconsin *has* taken with respect to Joshua and children like him, rather than on the actions that the State failed to take. *** Wisconsin has established a child-welfare system specifically designed to help children like Joshua. Wisconsin law places upon the local departments of social services such as respondent (DSS or Department) a duty to investigate reported instances of child abuse. *** Even when it is the sheriff's office or police department that receives a report of suspected child abuse, that report is referred to local social services departments for action; the only exception to this occurs when the reporter fears for the child's *immediate* safety. In this way, Wisconsin law invites indeed, directs—citizens and other governmental entities to depend on local departments of social services such as respondent to protect children from abuse. ***

In these circumstances, a private citizen, or even a person working in a government agency other than DSS, would doubtless feel that her job was done as soon as she had reported her suspicions of child abuse to DSS. Through its child-welfare program, in other words, the State of Wisconsin has relieved ordinary citizens and governmental bodies other than the Department of any sense of obligation to do anything more than report their suspicions of child abuse to DSS. If DSS ignores or dismisses these suspicions, no one will step in to fill the gap. Wisconsin's child-protection program thus effectively confined Joshua DeShaney within the walls of Randy DeShaney's violent home until such time as DSS took action to remove him. Conceivably, then, children like Joshua are made worse off by the existence of this program when the persons and entities charged with carrying it out fail to do their jobs.

It simply belies reality, therefore, to contend that the State "stood by and did nothing" with respect to Joshua. Through its child-protection program, the State actively intervened in Joshua's life and, by virtue of this intervention, acquired ever more certain knowledge that Joshua was in grave danger. *** It will be meager comfort to Joshua and his mother to know that, if the State had "selectively den[ied] its protective services" to them because they were "disfavored minorities," their § 1983 suit might have stood on sturdier ground. Because of the posture of this case, we do not know why respondents did not take steps to protect Joshua; the Court, however, tells us that their reason is irrelevant so long as their inaction was not the product of invidious discrimination. Presumably, then, if respondents decided not to help Joshua because his name began with a "J," or because he was born in the spring, or because they did not care enough about him even to formulate an intent to discriminate against him based on an arbitrary reason, respondents would not be liable to the DeShaneys because they were not the ones who dealt the blows that destroyed Joshua's life. *** Today's opinion construes the Due Process Clause to permit a State to displace private sources of protection and then, at the critical moment, to shrug its shoulders and turn away from the harm that it has promised to try to prevent. Because I cannot agree that our Constitution is indifferent to such indifference, I respectfully dissent.

JUSTICE BLACKMUN, dissenting.

Today, the Court purports to be the dispassionate oracle of the law, unmoved by "natural sympathy." But, in this pretense, the Court itself retreats into a sterile formalism which prevents it from recognizing either the facts of the case before it or the legal norms that should apply to those facts. *** Like the antebellum judges who denied relief to fugitive slaves, the Court today claims that its decision, however harsh, is compelled by existing legal doctrine. *** I would adopt a "sympathetic" reading, one which comports with dictates of fundamental justice and recognizes that compassion need not be exiled from the province of judging.

Poor Joshua! Victim of repeated attacks by an irresponsible, bullying, cowardly, and intemperate father, and abandoned by respondents who placed him in a dangerous predicament and who knew or learned what was going on, and yet did essentially nothing except, as the Court revealingly observes, "dutifully recorded these incidents in [their] files." It is a sad commentary upon American life, and constitutional principles—so full of late of patriotic fervor and proud proclamations about "liberty and justice for all"—that this child, Joshua DeShaney, now is assigned to live out the remainder of his life profoundly retarded. Joshua and his mother, as petitioners here, deserve—but now are denied by this Court—the opportunity to have the facts of their case considered in the light of the constitutional protection that 42 U.S.C. § 1983 is meant to provide.

Notes

1. ***DeShaney* Baseline for State Inaction.**   One difference between the majority and the dissent is that the dissent assumes the State has a basic obligation to ensure citizen safety.   More narrowly, when the State establishes systems for dealing with violence on which the citizenry relies, the dissent says it should be required to do its job with a minimum level of competence.   Did the Department of Social Services act minimally competently?   What would have been the likely upshot of *DeShaney* had the plaintiff prevailed?

2.   **A Thirteenth Amendment Approach to *DeShaney*?**   In *A Thirteenth Amendment Response to DeShaney*, 105 HARV. L. REV. 1359 (1992), Professors Amar and Widawsky suggest that the case should have been argued on the theory that Joshua had been subjected to "involuntary servitude," which they define as the "unconstrained power" of one person over another.   They argue that the Thirteenth Amendment prohibition applies to children, that it applies even in situations where the "master" is not seeking financial profit, and that "[u]nder the Thirteenth Amendment, a State has an obligation only in cases of slavery and involuntary servitude rather than in every case of interpersonal violence" to provide adequate assistance.   Do you find this argument convincing?   Would the Court likely find it so?

3.   **Problem: State Action and Sovereign Immunity**. Plaintiff wants to sue a company and the state for copyright infringement under a federal law protecting copyright holders. The core of her factual allegation is that the company, with the knowledge and cooperation of state officials, under contract to and for the benefit of the state, used her copyrighted computer program without permission and without paying royalties. What problems do you see with her suit? Consider, at a minimum (1) whether sovereign immunity would bar suing the state in federal or state court, and (2) whether the company can piggyback on that defense by arguing it should be considered a state actor.

C. FEDERAL PRIVILEGES OR IMMUNITIES

Historian Edwin Corwin observed that "Unique among constitutional provisions, the privileges and immunities clause of the Fourteenth Amendment enjoys the distinction of having been rendered a 'practical nullity' by a single decision of the Supreme Court within five years after its ratification." The decision that accomplished this nullification has not been overruled but a more recent case in this section *may* signal that the Court is moving toward reopening the door it closed over a century ago.

SLAUGHTER-HOUSE CASES
83 U.S. (16 Wall.) 36 (1873)

MR. JUSTICE MILLER *** delivered the opinion of the court.

*** The statute *** [here] assailed as unconstitutional was passed March 8th, 1869, and is entitled "An act to protect the health of the city of New Orleans, to locate the stock-landings and slaughter-houses, and to incorporate the Crescent City Live–Stock Landing and Slaughter–House Company." *** It declares that the company *** shall have the sole and exclusive privilege of conducting and carrying on the live-stock landing and slaughter-house business within the limits and privilege granted by the act, and that all such animals shall be landed at the stock-landings and slaughtered at the slaughter-houses of the company, and nowhere else. Penalties are enacted for infractions of this provision, and prices fixed for the maximum charges of the company for each steamboat and for each animal landed. *** [The statute] makes it the duty of the company to permit any person to slaughter animals in their slaughter-houses under a heavy penalty for each refusal. Another section fixes a limit to the charges to be made by the company for each animal so slaughtered in their building, and another provides for an inspection of all animals intended to be so slaughtered, by an officer appointed by the governor of the State for that purpose. ***

This statute is denounced not only as creating a monopoly and conferring odious and exclusive privileges upon a small number of persons at the expense of the great body of the community of New Orleans, but it is asserted that it deprives a large and meritorious class of citizens—the whole of the butchers of the city—of the right to exercise their trade, the business to which they have been trained and on which they depend for the support of themselves and their families, and that the unrestricted exercise of the business of butchering is necessary to the daily subsistence of the population of the city. ***

The [police] power here exercised by the legislature of Louisiana is, in its essential nature, one which has been, up to the present period in the constitutional history of this country, always conceded to belong to the States. *** The regulation of the place and manner of conducting the slaughtering of animals, and the business of butchering within a city, and the inspection of the animals to be killed for meat, and of the meat afterwards, are among the most necessary and frequent exercises of this power. It is not, therefore, needed that we should seek for a comprehensive definition, but rather look for the proper source of its exercise. ***

The proposition is, therefore, reduced to these terms: Can any exclusive privileges be granted to any of its citizens, or to a corporation, by the legislature of a State? *** The plaintiffs in error accepting this issue, allege that the statute is a violation of the Constitution of the United States in these several particulars: *** That it abridges the privileges and immunities of citizens of the United States ***

[I]n the light of *** events, almost too recent to be called history, but which are familiar to us all; and on the most casual examination of the language of these amendments, no one can fail to be impressed with the one pervading purpose found in them all, lying at the foundation of each, and without which none of them would have been even suggested; we mean the freedom of the slave race, the security and firm establishment of that freedom, and the protection of the newly-made freeman and citizen from the oppressions of those who had formerly exercised unlimited dominion over him. It is true that only the fifteenth amendment, in terms, mentions the negro by speaking of his color and his slavery. But it is just as true that each of the other articles was addressed to the grievances of that race, and designed to remedy them as the fifteenth.

We do not say that no one else but the negro can share in this protection. *** But what we do say, and what we wish to be understood is, that in any fair and just construction of any section or phrase of these amendments, it is necessary to look to the purpose which we have said was the pervading spirit of them all, the evil which they were designed to remedy, and the process of continued addition to the Constitution, until that purpose was supposed to be accomplished, as far as constitutional law can accomplish it.

The first section of the fourteenth article, to which our attention is more specially invited, opens with a definition of citizenship—not only citizenship of the United States, but citizenship of the States. *** [T]o establish a clear and comprehensive definition of citizenship which should declare what should constitute citizenship of the United States, and also citizenship of a State, the first clause of the first section was framed.

"All persons born or naturalized in the United States, and subject to the jurisdiction thereof, are citizens of the United States and of the State wherein they reside." *** [The clause] declares that persons may be citizens of the

United States without regard to their citizenship of a particular State, and it overturns the *Dred Scott* decision by making all persons born within the United States and subject to its jurisdiction citizens of the United States.

*** [Here] the distinction between citizenship of the United States and citizenship of a State is clearly recognized and established. Not only may a man be a citizen of the United States without being a citizen of a State, but an important element is necessary to convert the former into the latter. He must reside within the State to make him a citizen of it, but it is only necessary that he should be born or naturalized in the United States to be a citizen of the Union. It is quite clear, then, that there is a citizenship of the United States, and a citizenship of a State, which are distinct from each other, and which depend upon different characteristics or circumstances in the individual.

We think this distinction *** speaks only of privileges and immunities of citizens of the United States, and does not speak of those of citizens of the several States. The argument, however, in favor of the plaintiffs rests wholly on the assumption that the citizenship is the same, and the privileges and immunities guaranteed by the clause are the same.

The language is, "No State shall make or enforce any law which shall abridge the privileges or immunities of citizens of the United States." It is a little remarkable, if this clause was intended as a protection to the citizen of a State against the legislative power of his own State, that the word citizen of the State should be left out when it is so carefully used, and used in contradistinction to citizens of the United States, in the very sentence which precedes it. It is too clear for argument that the change in phraseology was adopted understandingly and with a purpose.

Of the privileges and immunities of the citizen of the United States, and of the privileges and immunities of the citizen of the State, and what they respectively are, we will presently consider; but we wish to state here that it is only the former which are placed by this clause under the protection of the Federal Constitution, and that the latter, whatever they may be, are not intended to have any additional protection by this paragraph of the amendment.

If, then, there is a difference between the privileges and immunities belonging to a citizen of the United States as such, and those belonging to the citizen of the State as such the latter must rest for their security and protection where they have heretofore rested [in Article IV, §2]; for they are not embraced by this paragraph of the amendment. ***

There can be but little question that the purpose of both these provisions is the same, and that the privileges and immunities intended are the same in each. *** The first and the leading case on the subject is that of *Corfield v. Coryell*, decided by MR. JUSTICE WASHINGTON in the Circuit Court for the District of Pennsylvania in 1823.

"The inquiry *** is, what are the privileges and immunities of citizens of the several States? We feel no hesitation in confining these expressions to those privileges and immunities which are fundamental; which belong of right to the citizens of all free governments, and which have at all times been enjoyed by citizens of the several States which compose this Union, from the time of their becoming free, independent, and sovereign. What these fundamental principles are, it would be more tedious than difficult to enumerate. They may all, however, be comprehended under the following general heads: protection by the government, with the right to acquire and possess property of every kind, and to pursue and obtain happiness and safety, subject, nevertheless, to such restraints as the government may prescribe for the general good of the whole." ***

The constitutional provision there alluded to did not create those rights, which it called privileges and immunities of citizens of the States. It threw around them in that clause no security for the citizen of the State in which they were claimed or exercised. Nor did it profess to control the power of the State governments over the rights of its own citizens. Its sole purpose was to declare to the several States, that whatever those rights, as you grant or establish them to your own citizens, or as you limit or qualify, or impose restrictions on their exercise, the same, neither more nor less, shall be the measure of the rights of citizens of other States within your jurisdiction. ***

[U]p to the adoption of the recent amendments, no claim or pretence was set up that those rights depended on the Federal government for their existence or protection ***. Was it the purpose of the fourteenth amendment, by the simple declaration that no State should make or enforce any law which shall abridge the privileges and immunities of citizens of the United States, to transfer the security and protection of all the civil rights which we have mentioned, from the States to the Federal government? And where it is declared that Congress shall have the power to enforce that article, was it intended to bring within the power of Congress the entire domain of civil rights heretofore belonging exclusively to the States?

All this and more must follow *** [S]uch a construction *** would constitute this court a perpetual censor upon all legislation of the States, on the civil rights of their own citizens, with authority to nullify such as it did not approve as consistent with those rights, as they existed at the time of the adoption of this amendment. The argument we admit is not always the most conclusive which is drawn from the consequences urged against the adoption of a particular construction of an instrument. But when, as in the case before us, these consequences are so serious, so far-reaching and pervading, so great a departure from the structure and spirit of our institutions; when the effect is to fetter and degrade the State governments by subjecting them to the control of Congress, in the exercise of powers heretofore universally conceded to them of the most ordinary and fundamental character; when in fact it radically changes the whole theory of the relations of the State and Federal governments to each other and of both these governments to the people; the argument has a force that is irresistible, in the absence of language which expresses such a purpose too clearly to admit of doubt.

We are convinced that no such results were intended by the Congress which proposed these amendments, nor by the legislatures of the States which ratified them. *** But lest it should be said that no such privileges and immunities are to be found if those we have been considering are excluded, we venture to suggest some which own their existence to the Federal government, its National character, its Constitution, or its laws.

One of these is well described in the case of *Crandall v. Nevada.* [73 U.S. 35 (1867).] It is said to be the right of the citizen of this great country, protected by implied guarantees of its Constitution, 'to come to the seat of government to assert any claim he may have upon that government, to transact any business he may have with it, to seek its protection, to share its offices, to engage in administering its functions. He has the right of free access to its seaports, through which all operations of foreign commerce are conducted, to the subtreasuries, land offices, and courts of justice in the several States.' *** Another privilege of a citizen of the United States is to demand the care and protection of the Federal government over his life, liberty, and property when on the high seas or within the jurisdiction of a foreign government. Of this there can be no doubt, nor that the right depends upon his character as a citizen of the United States. The right to peaceably assemble and petition for redress of grievances, the privilege of the writ of habeas corpus, are rights of the citizen guaranteed by the Federal Constitution. The right to use the navigable waters of the United States, however they may penetrate the territory of the several States, all rights secured to our citizens by treaties with foreign nations, are dependent upon citizenship of the United States, and not citizenship of a State. One of these privileges is conferred by the very article under consideration. It is that a citizen of the United States can, of his own volition, become a citizen of any State of the Union by a bona fide residence therein, with the same rights as other citizens of that State. To these may be added the rights secured by the thirteenth and fifteenth articles of amendment, and by the other clause of the fourteenth, next to be considered. *** [The Court also rejected claims under the Thirteenth and other parts of the Fourteenth Amendment.]

MR. JUSTICE FIELD, dissenting:

*** The amendment does not attempt to confer any new privileges or immunities upon citizens, or to enumerate or define those already existing. It assumes that there are such privileges and immunities which belong of right to citizens as such, and ordains that they shall not be abridged by State legislation. If this inhibition has no reference to privileges and immunities of this character, but only refers, as held by the majority of the court in their opinion, to such privileges and immunities as were before its adoption specially designated in the Constitution or necessarily implied as belonging to citizens of the United States, it was a vain and idle enactment, which accomplished nothing, and most unnecessarily excited Congress and the people on its passage. With privileges and immunities thus designated or implied no State could ever have interfered by its laws, and no new constitutional provision was required to inhibit such interference. The supremacy of the Constitution and the laws of the United States always controlled any State legislation of that character. But if the amendment refers to the natural and inalienable rights which belong to all citizens, the inhibition has a profound significance and consequence.

What, then, are the privileges and immunities which are secured against abridgment by State legislation? *** In *Corfield v. Coryell*, MR. JUSTICE WASHINGTON said he had "no hesitation in confining these expressions to those privileges and immunities which were, in their nature, fundamental; which belong of right to citizens of all free governments, and which have at all times been enjoyed by the citizens of the several States which compose the Union, from the time of their becoming free, independent, and sovereign." *** This appears to me to be a sound construction of the clause in question. The privileges and immunities designated are *those which of right belong to the citizens of all free governments*. Clearly among these must be placed the right to pursue a lawful employment in a lawful manner, without other restraint than such as equally affects all persons. ***

What [Article IV, § 2] did for the protection of the citizens of one State against hostile and discriminating legislation of other States, the fourteenth amendment does for the protection of every citizen of the United States against hostile and discriminating legislation against him in favor of others, whether they reside in the same or in different States. If under the fourth article of the Constitution equality of privileges and immunities is secured between citizens of different States, under the fourteenth amendment the same equality is secured between citizens of the United States.

It will not be pretended that under the fourth article of the Constitution any State could create a monopoly in any known trade or manufacture in favor of her own citizens, or any portion of them, which would exclude an equal participation *** by citizens of other States. She could not confer, for example, upon any of her citizens the sole right to manufacture shoes, or boots, or silk, or the sole right to sell those articles in the State so as to exclude non-resident citizens from engaging in a similar manufacture or sale. *** Now, what [Article IV, § 2] does for the protection of citizens of one State against the creation of monopolies in favor of citizens of other States, the fourteenth amendment does for the protection of every citizen of the United States against the creation of any monopoly whatever. The privileges and immunities of citizens of the United States, of every one of them, is secured against abridgment in any form by any State. The fourteenth amendment places them under the guardianship of the National authority. All monopolies in any known trade or manufacture are an invasion of these privileges, for they encroach upon the liberty of citizens to acquire property and pursue happiness. *** [T[he CHIEF JUSTICE, MR. JUSTICE SWAYNE, and MR. JUSTICE BRADLEY ***concur with me in this dissenting opinion.

MR. JUSTICE BRADLEY, also dissenting:

*** The right of a State to regulate the conduct of its citizens is undoubtedly a very broad and extensive one, and not to be lightly restricted. But there are certain fundamental rights which this right of regulation cannot infringe. *** I speak now of the rights of citizens of any free government. *** [C]itizenship means something. It has certain privileges and immunities attached to it which the government*** cannot take away or impair. It may do so temporarily by force, but it cannot do so by right. And these privileges and immunities attach as well to citizenship of the United States as to citizenship of the States. ***

[The] right to choose one's calling is an essential part of that liberty which it is the object of government to protect; and a calling, when chosen, is a man's property and right. *** The keeping of a slaughter-house is part of, and incidental to, the trade of a butcher—one of the ordinary occupations of human life. To compel a butcher, or rather all the butchers of a large city and an extensive district, to slaughter their cattle in another person's slaughter-house and pay him a toll therefor, is such a restriction upon the trade as materially to interfere with its prosecution. It is onerous, unreasonable, arbitrary, and unjust. It has none of the qualities of a police regulation. If it were really a police regulation, it would undoubtedly be within the power of the legislature. That portion of the act which requires all slaughter-houses to be located below the city, and to be subject to inspection, &c., is clearly a police regulation. That portion which allows no one but the favored company to build, own, or have slaughter-houses is not a police regulation, and has not the faintest semblance of one. It is one of those arbitrary and unjust laws made in the interest of a few scheming individuals, by which some of the Southern States have, within the past few years, been so deplorably oppressed and impoverished. It seems to me strange that it can be viewed in any other light. ***

[G]reat fears are expressed that this construction of the amendment will lead to enactments by Congress interfering with the internal affairs of the States *** In my judgment no such practical inconveniences would arise. *** As the privileges and immunities protected are only those fundamental ones which belong to every citizen, they would soon become so far defined as to cause but a slight accumulation of business in the Federal courts. ***

Notes

1. **Some "Irrelevant" History.** What did the drafters and ratifiers of the Fourteenth Amendment intend to accomplish through the Privileges or Immunities Clause? Granting to the former slaves the same rights that white citizens had enjoyed was a paramount consideration. But what were these rights? Consider the following possibilities:

> (a) Many historians have argued that the clause was intended to constitutionalize, and thus insulate from congressional reversal, the Civil Rights Act of 1866, which guaranteed "all persons born in the United States the same rights as white citizens to make and enforce contracts, to sue, be parties, and give evidence, to inherit, purchase, lease, sell, hold, and convey real and personal property, and to full and equal benefit of all laws and proceedings for the security of person and property *** and shall be subject to like punishment, pains, and penalties, and to none other." *The Slaughter-House Cases* read the Privileges or Immunities Clause much more narrowly

than this statute even though, on its face, the Clause might easily have been read more broadly than the statute.

(b) The clause could have been read as elevating to national status all the rights which might previously have been given to any citizen under any state law. Do you see any problem with such an interpretation?

(c) Should the clause be read to accord with the views of its chief sponsor in Congress, Representative Bingham, who said: "the privileges and immunities of citizens of the United States [are] chiefly defined in the first eight amendments to the Constitution"? Cong. Globe, 42d Cong., 1st Sess., app. 85 (1871). Should we be concerned that Representative Bingham's view seems anomalous in light of the fact that the similarly-phrased Privileges and Immunities Clause of Article IV preceded the Bill of Rights? Does this concern fade if we view the Bill of Rights as merely expressive of generally understood natural law rights? But then there would have been no need for a written Bill of Rights, would there?

(d) Assuming a rough congruence between the Article IV Privileges and Immunities Clause and the Fourteenth Amendment Privileges or Immunities Clause would not help to clarify the clause much. Remember the vagueness of the former clause from the *City of Camden* case?

(e) The Privileges or Immunities Clause stated only vague aspirations. Perhaps Representative Bingham was a sloppy draftsman, perhaps he and other astute politicians thought vagueness made ratification more likely, or perhaps the clause was deliberately left to be filled out by the judiciary over time.

(f) One exploration of the clause's history concludes that it "ensures that all the citizens of every state shall be entitled to the privileges and immunities of state citizenship, thereby mandating equality of rights." John Harrison, "Reconstructing the Privileges or Immunities Clause," 101 YALE L.J. 1385 (1992). So read, would the clause support the existence of any nationwide privileges and immunities of all United States citizens (either trivial ones, as *The Slaughter–House Cases* held, or substantial ones, considered earlier in this note)?

2.	**Ironies of the *Slaughter–House Cases*.**

•	The plaintiffs were white, not black.

•	The plaintiffs were asserting business rights, not personal rights.

•	The plaintiffs did not pursue a Dormant Commerce Clause theory.

•	The Court undid (or at least delayed) the transformation of the Constitution by the post-Civil War amendments.

3.	**The "Dead Hand" of the *Slaughter-House Cases*.** The untimely death of the substantive rights which might have been articulated as "Privileges or Immunities" has been a driving force in the twentieth century for expansive interpretation of two other clauses of Section 1 of the Fourteenth Amendment: the Due Process Clause and the Equal Protection Clause. As you read the following case, and again after you read Chapters VIII and IX of these materials, consider whether the Privileges or Immunities Clause might provide a different (and perhaps more straightforward) source of some or all the substantive due process rights the Court has created over the past century.

SAENZ v. ROE
526 U.S. 489 (1999)

JUSTICE STEVENS delivered the opinion of the Court.

In 1992, California enacted a statute limiting the maximum welfare benefits available to newly arrived residents. The scheme limits the amount payable to a family that has resided in the State for less than 12 months to the amount payable by the State of the family's prior residence. *** [T]hree California residents who were eligible for AFDC benefits filed an action *** challenging the constitutionality of the durational residency requirement in § 11450.03. Each plaintiff alleged that she had recently moved to California to live with relatives in order to escape abusive family circumstances. ^^^

III

The word "travel" is not found in the text of the Constitution. Yet the "constitutional right to travel from one State to another" is firmly embedded in our jurisprudence. Indeed, as JUSTICE STEWART reminded us in *Shapiro v. Thompson,* 394 U.S. 618 (1969), the right is so important that it is "assertable against private interference as well as governmental action *** a virtually unconditional personal right, guaranteed by the Constitution to us all." (concurring opinion).

In *Shapiro,* we reviewed the constitutionality of three statutory provisions that denied welfare assistance to residents of Connecticut, the District of Columbia, and Pennsylvania, who had resided within those respective jurisdictions less than one year immediately preceding their applications for assistance. Without pausing to identify the specific source of the right, we began by noting that the Court had long "recognized that the nature of our Federal Union and our constitutional concepts of personal liberty unite to require that all citizens be free to travel throughout the length and breadth of our land uninhibited by statutes, rules, or regulations which unreasonably burden or restrict this movement." We squarely held that it was "constitutionally impermissible" for a State to enact durational residency requirements for the purpose of inhibiting the migration by needy persons into the State. We further held that a classification that had the effect of imposing a penalty on the exercise of the right to travel violated the Equal Protection Clause "unless shown to be necessary to promote a compelling governmental interest," and that no such showing had been made.

In this case California argues that § 11450.03 was not enacted for the impermissible purpose of inhibiting migration by needy persons and that, unlike the legislation reviewed in *Shapiro,* it does not penalize the right to travel because new arrivals are not ineligible for benefits during their first year of residence. California submits that, instead of being subjected to the strictest scrutiny, the statute should be upheld if it is supported by a rational basis and that the State's legitimate interest in saving over $10 million a year satisfies that test. *** [The United States] has advanced the novel argument that the enactment of PRWORA allows the States to adopt a "specialized choice-of-law-type provision" that "should be subject to an intermediate level of constitutional review," merely requiring that durational residency requirements be "substantially related to an important governmental objective." The debate about the appropriate standard of review, together with the potential relevance of the federal statute, persuades us that it will be useful to focus on the source of the constitutional right on which respondents rely.

IV

The "right to travel" discussed in our cases embraces at least three different components. It protects the right of a citizen of one State to enter and to leave another State, the right to be treated as a welcome visitor rather than an unfriendly alien when temporarily present in the second State, and, for those travelers who elect to become permanent residents, the right to be treated like other citizens of that State.

It was the right to go from one place to another, including the right to cross state borders while en route, that was vindicated in *Edwards v. California,* 314 U.S. 160 (1941), which invalidated a state law that impeded the free interstate passage of the indigent. We reaffirmed that right in *United States v. Guest,* 383 U.S. 745 (1966), which afforded protection to the "'right to travel freely to and from the State of Georgia and to use highway facilities and other instrumentalities of interstate commerce within the State of Georgia.'" Given that § 11450.03 imposed no obstacle to respondents' entry into California, we think the State is correct when it argues that the statute does not directly impair the exercise of the right to free interstate movement. For the purposes of this case, therefore, we need not identify the source of that particular right in the text of the Constitution. The right of "free ingress and regress to and from" neighboring States, which was expressly mentioned in the text of the Articles of Confederation, may simply have been "conceived from the beginning to be a necessary concomitant of the stronger Union the Constitution created."

The second component of the right to travel is, however, expressly protected by the *** first sentence of Article IV, § 2, [which] provides:

> The Citizens of each State shall be entitled to all Privileges and Immunities of Citizens in the several States.

Thus, by virtue of a person's state citizenship, a citizen of one State who travels in other States, intending to return home at the end of his journey, is entitled to enjoy the "Privileges and Immunities of Citizens in the several States" that he visits.[14] *** It provides important protections for nonresidents who enter a State whether to obtain employment, to procure medical services, or even to engage in commercial shrimp fishing. Those protections are not "absolute," but the Clause "does bar discrimination against citizens of other States where there is no substantial reason for the discrimination beyond the

---

[14] *Corfield v. Coryell,* 6 F. Cas. 546 (C.C.E.D.Pa.1823) (WASHINGTON, J., on circuit) ("fundamental" rights protected by the privileges and immunities clause include "the right of a citizen of one state to pass through, or to reside in any other state").

mere fact that they are citizens of other states." There may be a substantial reason for requiring the nonresident to pay more than the resident for a hunting license, or to enroll in the state university, but our cases have not identified any acceptable reason for qualifying the protection afforded by the Clause for "the 'citizen of State A who ventures into State B' to settle there and establish a home." *Zobel*, 457 U.S. at 74 (O'CONNOR, J., concurring in judgment). Permissible justifications for discrimination between residents and nonresidents are simply inapplicable to a nonresident's exercise of the right to move into another State and become a resident of that State.

What is at issue in this case, then, is this third aspect of the right to travel—the right of the newly arrived citizen to the same privileges and immunities enjoyed by other citizens of the same State. That right is protected not only by the new arrival's status as a state citizen, but also by her status as a citizen of the United States.[15] ***

Despite fundamentally differing views concerning the coverage of the Privileges or Immunities Clause of the Fourteenth Amendment, *** it has always been common ground that this Clause protects the third component of the right to travel. Writing for the majority in the *Slaughter-House Cases*, JUSTICE MILLER explained that one of the privileges conferred by this Clause "is that a citizen of the United States can, of his own volition, become a citizen of any State of the Union by a bona fide residence therein, with the same rights as other citizens of that State." JUSTICE BRADLEY, in dissent, used even stronger language to make the same point:

> The states have not now, if they ever had, any power to restrict their citizenship to any classes or persons. A citizen of the United States has a perfect constitutional right to go to and reside in any State he chooses, and to claim citizenship therein, and an equality of rights with every other citizen; and the whole power of the nation is pledged to sustain him in that right. He is not bound to cringe to any superior, or to pray for any act of grace, as a means of enjoying all the rights and privileges enjoyed by other citizens.

That newly arrived citizens "have two political capacities, one state and one federal," adds special force to their claim that they have the same rights as others who share their citizenship. ***

V

Because this case involves discrimination against citizens who have completed their interstate travel, the State's argument that its welfare

---

[15] The Framers of the Fourteenth Amendment modeled this Clause upon the "Privileges and Immunities" Clause found in Article IV. Cong. Globe, 39th Cong., 1st Sess., 1033–1034 (1866) (statement of Rep. Bingham). In *Dred Scott v. Sandford,* 60 U.S. 393 (1857), this Court had limited the protection of Article IV to rights under state law and concluded that free blacks could not claim citizenship. The Fourteenth Amendment overruled this decision. The Amendment's Privileges and Immunities Clause and Citizenship Clause guaranteed the rights of newly freed black citizens by ensuring that they could claim the state citizenship of any State in which they resided and by precluding that State from abridging their rights of national citizenship.

scheme affects the right to travel only "incidentally" is beside the point. *** [S]ince the right to travel embraces the citizen's right to be treated equally in her new State of residence, the discriminatory classification is itself a penalty.

It is undisputed that respondents and the members of the class that they represent are citizens of California and that their need for welfare benefits is unrelated to the length of time that they have resided in California. *** Moreover, because whatever benefits they receive will be consumed while they remain in California, there is no danger that recognition of their claim will encourage citizens of other States to establish residency for just long enough to acquire some readily portable benefit, such as a divorce or a college education, that will be enjoyed after they return to their original domicile.

The classifications challenged in this case—and there are many—are defined entirely by (a) the period of residency in California and (b) the location of the prior residences of the disfavored class members. The favored class of beneficiaries includes all eligible California citizens who have resided there for at least one year, plus those new arrivals who last resided in another country or in a State that provides benefits at least as generous as California's. *** To justify § 11450.03, California must therefore explain not only why it is sound fiscal policy to discriminate against those who have been citizens for less than a year, but also why it is permissible to apply such a variety of rules within that class.

These classifications may not be justified by a purpose to deter welfare applicants from migrating to California for three reasons. First, although it is reasonable to assume that some persons may be motivated to move for the purpose of obtaining higher benefits, the empirical evidence reviewed by the District Judge, which takes into account the high cost of living in California, indicates that the number of such persons is quite small—surely not large enough to justify a burden on those who had no such motive. Second, California has represented to the Court that the legislation was not enacted for any such reason. Third, even if it were, as we squarely held in *Shapiro v. Thompson,* 394 U.S. 618 (1969), such a purpose would be unequivocally impermissible.

Disavowing any desire to fence out the indigent, California has instead advanced an entirely fiscal justification ***. The question is not whether such saving is a legitimate purpose but whether the State may accomplish that end by the discriminatory means it has chosen. An evenhanded, across-the-board reduction of about 72 cents per month for every beneficiary would produce the same result. But *** the Citizenship Clause of the Fourteenth Amendment expressly equates citizenship with residence: "That Clause does not provide for, and does not allow for, degrees of citizenship based on length of residence." *Zobel.* It is equally clear that the Clause does not tolerate a hierarchy of 45 subclasses of similarly situated citizens based on the location of their prior residence. Thus § 11450.03 is doubly vulnerable: Neither the duration of respondents' California residence, nor the identity of their prior States of residence, has any relevance to their need for benefits. Nor do those factors bear any relationship to the State's interest in making an equitable allocation of the funds to be distributed among its needy citizens. *** In short, the State's legitimate interest in saving money provides no justification for its decision to discriminate among equally eligible citizens.

VI

The question that remains is whether congressional approval of durational residency requirements in the 1996 amendment to the Social Security Act somehow resuscitates the constitutionality of § 11450.03. That question is readily answered, for we have consistently held that Congress may not authorize the States to violate the Fourteenth Amendment. Moreover, the protection afforded to the citizen by the Citizenship Clause of that Amendment is a limitation on the powers of the National Government as well as the States. *** Citizens of the United States, whether rich or poor, have the right to choose to be citizens "of the State wherein they reside." U.S. Const., Amdt. 14, § 1. The States, however, do not have any right to select their citizens. The Fourteenth Amendment, like the Constitution itself, was, as JUSTICE CARDOZO put it, "framed upon the theory that the peoples of the several states must sink or swim together, and that in the long run prosperity and salvation are in union and not division." *Baldwin v. G. A. F. Seelig, Inc.,* 294 U.S. 511, 523 (1935). ***

CHIEF JUSTICE REHNQUIST, with whom JUSTICE THOMAS joins, dissenting.

The Court today breathes new life into the previously dormant Privileges or Immunities Clause of the Fourteenth Amendment. *** It uses this Clause to strike down what I believe is a reasonable measure falling under the head of a "good-faith residency requirement." ***

I cannot see how the right to become a citizen of another State is a necessary "component" of the right to travel, or why the Court tries to marry these separate and distinct rights. A person is no longer "traveling" in any sense of the word when he finishes his journey to a State which he plans to make his home. Indeed, under the Court's logic, the protections of the Privileges or Immunities Clause recognized in this case come into play only when an individual stops traveling with the intent to remain and become a citizen of a new State. The right to travel and the right to become a citizen are distinct, their relationship is not reciprocal, and one is not a "component" of the other. ***

Under [the Court's] new analytical framework, a State, outside certain ill-defined circumstances, cannot classify its citizens by the length of their residence in the State without offending the Privileges or Immunities Clause of the Fourteenth Amendment. The Court thus departs from *Shapiro* and its progeny, and, while paying lipservice to the right to travel, the Court does little to explain how the right to travel is involved at all. *** [T]his case is only about respondents' right to immediately enjoy all the privileges of being a California citizen in relation to that State's ability to test the good-faith assertion of this right. The Court has thus come full circle by effectively disavowing the analysis of *Shapiro*, segregating the right to travel and the rights secured by Article IV from the right to become a citizen under the

Privileges or Immunities Clause, and then testing the residence requirement here against this latter right. ***

In unearthing from its tomb the right to become a state citizen and to be treated equally in the new State of residence, however, the Court ignores a State's need to assure that only persons who establish a bona fide residence receive the benefits provided to current residents of the State. *** If States can require individuals to reside in-state for a year before exercising the right to educational benefits, the right to terminate a marriage, or the right to vote in primary elections that all other state citizens enjoy, then States may surely do the same for welfare benefits. *** The Court tries to distinguish education and divorce benefits by contending that the welfare payment here will be consumed in California, while a college education or a divorce produces benefits that are "portable" and can be enjoyed after individuals return to their original domicile. But this "you can't take it with you" distinction is more apparent than real, and offers little guidance to lower courts who must apply this rationale in the future. Welfare payments *** will no doubt be spent in California, but the benefits from receiving this income and having the opportunity to become employed or employable will stick with the welfare recipients if they stay in California or go back to their true domiciles. Similarly, tuition subsidies are "consumed" in-state but the recipient takes the benefits of a college education with him wherever he goes. A welfare subsidy is thus as much an investment in human capital as is a tuition subsidy, and their attendant benefits are just as "portable." *** [T]he Court *** requires lower courts to plumb the policies animating certain benefits like welfare to define their "essence" and hence their "portability." *** I therefore believe that the durational residence requirement challenged here is a permissible exercise of the State's power to "assur[e] that services provided for its residents are enjoyed only by residents." *** Finally, Congress' express approval *** of durational residence requirements for welfare recipients like the one established by California [shows] California has reasonably exercised it through an objective, narrowly tailored residence requirement. ***

JUSTICE THOMAS, with whom the CHIEF JUSTICE joins, dissenting.

*** [T]he Court all but read the Privileges or Immunities Clause out of the Constitution in the *Slaughter-House Cases*, 83 U.S. 36 (1873). *** Unlike the majority, I would look to history to ascertain the original meaning of the Clause.[10] At least in American law, the phrase (or its close approximation) appears to stem from the 1606 Charter of Virginia, *** Years later, as tensions between England and the American Colonies increased, the colonists adopted resolutions reasserting their entitlement to the privileges or immunities of English citizenship. *** [A]t the time of the founding, the terms "privileges" and "immunities" (and their counterparts) were understood to refer to those fundamental rights and liberties specifically enjoyed by English citizens, and more broadly, by all persons. Presumably members of

---

[10] Legal scholars agree on little beyond the conclusion that the Clause does not mean what the Court said it meant in 1873.

the Second Continental Congress so understood these terms when they employed them in the Articles of Confederation, which guaranteed that "the free inhabitants of each of these States, paupers, vagabonds and fugitives from justice excepted, shall be entitled to all privileges and immunities of free citizens in the several States." Art. IV. The Constitution, which superceded the Articles of Confederation, similarly guarantees that "[t]he Citizens of each State shall be entitled to all Privileges and Immunities of Citizens in the several States." Art. IV, § 2, cl. 1.

JUSTICE BUSHROD WASHINGTON's landmark opinion in *Corfield v. Coryell* reflects this historical understanding. In *Corfield*, a citizen of Pennsylvania challenged a New Jersey law that prohibited any person who was not an "actual inhabitant and resident" of New Jersey from harvesting oysters from New Jersey waters. JUSTICE WASHINGTON, sitting as Circuit Justice, rejected the argument that the New Jersey law violated Article IV's Privileges and Immunities Clause. He reasoned, "we cannot accede to the proposition *** that, under this provision of the constitution, the citizens of the several states are permitted to participate in all the rights which belong exclusively to the citizens of any other particular state, merely upon the ground that they are enjoyed by those citizens." Instead, WASHINGTON concluded:

> "We feel no hesitation in confining these expressions to those privileges and immunities which are, in their nature, fundamental; which belong, of right, to the citizens of all free governments; and which have, at all times, been enjoyed by the citizens of the several states which compose this Union, from the time of their becoming free, independent, and sovereign. What these fundamental principles are, it would perhaps be more tedious than difficult to enumerate. They may, however, be all comprehended under the following general heads: Protection by the government; the enjoyment of life and liberty, with the right to acquire and possess property of every kind, and to pursue and obtain happiness and safety; subject nevertheless to such restraints as the government may justly prescribe for the general good of the whole. The right of a citizen of one state to pass through, or to reside in any other state, for purposes of trade, agriculture, professional pursuits, or otherwise; to claim the benefit of the writ of habeas corpus; to institute and maintain actions of any kind in the courts of the state; *** and an exemption from higher taxes or impositions than are paid by the other citizens of the state; *** the elective franchise, as regulated and established by the laws or constitution of the state in which it is to be exercised. These, and many others which might be mentioned, are, strictly speaking, privileges and immunities."

WASHINGTON rejected the proposition that the Privileges and Immunities Clause guaranteed equal access to all public benefits (such as the right to harvest oysters in public waters) that a State chooses to make available. Instead, he endorsed the colonial-era conception of the terms "privileges" and "immunities," concluding that Article IV encompassed only *fundamental* rights that belong to all citizens of the United States.

JUSTICE WASHINGTON's opinion in *Corfield* indisputably influenced the Members of Congress who enacted the Fourteenth Amendment. *** Accordingly, the majority's conclusion—that a State violates the Privileges or Immunities Clause when it "discriminates" against citizens who have been domiciled in the State for less than a year in the distribution of welfare benefit appears contrary to the original understanding and is dubious at best. *** Because I believe that the demise of the Privileges or Immunities Clause has contributed in no small part to the current disarray of our Fourteenth Amendment jurisprudence, I would be open to reevaluating its meaning in an appropriate case. Before invoking the Clause, however, we should endeavor to understand what the framers of the Fourteenth Amendment thought that it meant. We should also consider whether the Clause should displace, rather than augment, portions of our equal protection and substantive due process jurisprudence. The majority's failure to consider these important questions raises the specter that the Privileges or Immunities Clause will become yet another convenient tool for inventing new rights, limited solely by the "predilections of those who happen at the time to be Members of this Court." *Moore v. East Cleveland*, 431 U.S. 494 (1977). ***

Notes

1.   **Significance.** Try writing a one paragraph opinion affirming or reversing based on *Shapiro v. Thompson*. Why didn't the Court do this? The fact that it revisited a clause that had been "dead" for over 100 years may signify that the Court is moving toward reviving the Privileges or Immunities clause of the Fourteenth Amendment. Make sure you understand the points made in JUSTICE THOMAS' dissent, which are not addressed by the majority.

2.   **Portability.** If you study the law of your State (rather than the federal and generic state law covered in this course) in your law school, how portable is your education? If a State premises health care benefits on durational residency, would that be constitutional after *Saenz*? Isn't your restored health portable? Many states once required durational residency for candidates sitting for the state bar exam. Such requirements were struck down based on *Shapiro*. If reinstituted now, could a state argue that its bar membership is not portable under *Saenz*?

3.   **Two Clauses.** Review the materials concerning Article IV Privileges and Immunities and compare them with the scope of the Fourteenth Amendment Privileges or Immunities Clause.

4.   **Other Privileges and Immunities.** What privileges and immunities can you think of which this case might foreshadow? Reconsider this question after you have read the Substantive Due Process materials in the next chapter.

VIII

DUE PROCESS, PROCEDURAL AND SUBSTANTIVE

Due process has not been reduced to any formula; its content cannot be determined by reference to any code. The best that can be said is that through the course of this Court's decisions it has represented the balance which our Nation, built upon postulates of respect for the liberty of the individual, has struck between that liberty and the demands of organized society. *** A decision of this Court which radically departs from it could not long survive, while a decision which builds on what has survived is likely to be sound. No formula could serve as a substitute, in this area, for judgment and restraint.

—JUSTICE HARLAN, dissenting in
Poe v. Ullmann (1961)

A. PROCEDURAL DUE PROCESS

The more straightforward meaning of "due process" is procedural. In the criminal law field, there are elaborate procedures, many required by the Constitution, that federal, state, and local authorities must observe before they can convict and imprison a person. Criminal procedures, however, are left to other courses and will not be examined here.

The following cases involve governmental procedures challenged as inadequate when someone is deprived of "life, liberty or property." As the cases show, it is essential to understand (1) when there is a constitutionally protected deprivation of "life, liberty or property" and (2) what process is due when there is such a deprivation. The cases presented here concern three matters that affect millions of people: government employment, government benefits, and immigration processes.

1. PROPERTY AND LIBERTY DEPRIVATION

With approximately 20% of the civilian workforce employed by federal, state, and local governments, dismissal of an employee is likely to be met with arguments that the employee's statutory or constitutional rights were violated. We have already looked at the constitutionality of federal substantive law protecting state and local employees (*Garcia*), and restrictions on suits against state governments (*Seminole Tribe* and *Alden*). Does the Constitution, unaided by federal legislation, protect the "property" rights of such employees in continued employment? The next case involves the due process clause of the Fourteenth Amendment, but the issues would be the same under the due process clause of the Fifth Amendment.

Two background cases mentioned in the opinion may be worth preliminary mention. The Court in *Board of Regents v. Roth*, 408 U.S. 564 (1972), said that "property interests protected by procedural due process extend well beyond actual ownership of real estate, chattels, or money" and that more than a "unilateral expectation" of continued employment was needed to constitute a property interest. The Court held that nonrenewal of a one-year contract to teach at a state university did not require any explanation because there was no reasonable expectation of continued employment. *Perry v. Sindermann*, 408 U.S. 593 (1972), decided the same day, involved a tenth-year employee who had worked under a succession of one-year contracts and was told that his contract would not be renewed. The Court said that this employee was entitled to attempt to prove that he had "de facto tenure," and that such an implied contract would be a property interest under the Fourteenth Amendment.

CLEVELAND BOARD OF EDUCATION
v. LOUDERMILL
470 U.S. 532 (1985)

JUSTICE WHITE delivered the opinion of the Court.

In these cases we consider what pretermination process must be accorded a public employee who can be discharged only for cause.

In 1979 the Cleveland Board of Education hired respondent James Loudermill as a security guard. On his job application, Loudermill stated that he had never been convicted of a felony. Eleven months later, as part of a routine examination of his employment records, the Board discovered that in fact Loudermill had been convicted of grand larceny in 1968. By letter dated November 3, 1980, the Board's Business Manager informed Loudermill that he had been dismissed because of his dishonesty in filling out the employment application. Loudermill was not afforded an opportunity to respond to the charge of dishonesty or to challenge his dismissal. On November 13, the Board adopted a resolution officially approving the discharge.

Under Ohio law, Loudermill was a "classified civil servant." Such employees can be terminated only for cause, and may obtain administrative review if discharged. Pursuant to this provision, Loudermill filed an appeal with the Cleveland Civil Service Commission on November 12. On July 20, 1981, the full Commission heard argument and orally announced that it would uphold the dismissal.

Respondents' federal constitutional claim depends on [his] having had a property right in continued employment. If [he] did, the State could not deprive [him] of this property without due process. *Board of Regents v. Roth*, 408 U.S. 564 (1972).

Property interests are not created by the Constitution, "they are created and their dimensions are defined by existing rules or understandings that stem from an independent source such as state law ***." *Roth*, at 577. The Ohio statute plainly creates such an interest. Respondents were "classified civil service employees," entitled to retain their positions "during good behavior and efficient service," who could not be dismissed "except *** for *** misfeasance, malfeasance, or nonfeasance in office." The statute plainly supports the conclusion, reached by both lower courts, that respondents possessed property rights in continued employment. Indeed, this question does not seem to have been disputed below.

The *** Board argues, however, that the property right is defined by, and conditioned on, the legislature's choice of procedures for its deprivation. The Board stresses that in addition to specifying the grounds for termination, the statute sets out procedures by which termination may take place. The procedures were adhered to in these cases. According to petitioner, "[t]o require additional procedures would in effect expand the scope of the property interest itself."

This argument, which was accepted by the District Court, has its genesis in the plurality opinion in *Arnett v. Kennedy*, 416 U.S. 134 (1974). *Arnett* involved a challenge by a former federal employee to the procedures by which he was dismissed. The plurality reasoned that where the legislation conferring the substantive right also sets out the procedural mechanism for enforcing that right, the two cannot be separated:

> The employee's statutorily defined right is not a guarantee against removal without cause in the abstract, but such a guarantee as enforced by the procedures which Congress has designated for the determination of cause. *** " [W]here the grant of a substantive right is inextricably intertwined with the limitations on the procedures which are to be employed in determining that right, a litigant in the position of appellee must take the bitter with the sweet.

This view garnered three votes in *Arnett*, but was specifically rejected by the other six Justices. Since then, this theory has at times seemed to gather some additional support. More recently, however, the Court has clearly rejected it. In *Vitek v. Jones*, 445 U.S. 480, 491 (1980), we pointed out that "minimum [procedural] requirements [are] a matter of federal law, they are not diminished by the fact that the State may have specified its own procedures that it may deem adequate for determining the preconditions to adverse official action." ***

In light of [recent cases], it is settled that the "bitter with the sweet" approach misconceives the constitutional guarantee. If a clearer holding is needed, we provide it today. The point is straightforward: the Due Process Clause provides that certain substantive rights—life, liberty, and property—cannot be deprived except pursuant to constitutionally adequate procedures. The categories of substance and procedure are distinct. Were the rule otherwise, the Clause would be reduced to a mere tautology. "Property" cannot be defined by the procedures provided for its deprivation any more than can life or liberty. The right to due process "is conferred, not by legislative grace, but by constitutional guarantee. While the legislature may elect not to confer a property interest in [public] employment, it may not constitutionally authorize the deprivation of such an interest, once conferred, without appropriate procedural safeguards." *Arnett v. Kennedy* ***.

We conclude that all the process that is due is provided by a pretermination opportunity to respond, coupled with post-termination administrative procedures as provided by the Ohio statute. Because respondents allege in their complaints that they had no chance to respond, the District Court erred in dismissing for failure to state a claim. ***

Opinions by JUSTICE MARSHALL, JUSTICE BRENNAN, and JUSTICE POWELL are omitted.

JUSTICE REHNQUIST, dissenting.

In *Arnett v. Kennedy*, six Members of this Court agreed that a public employee could be dismissed for misconduct without a full hearing prior to termination. A plurality of Justices agreed that the employee was entitled to exactly what Congress gave him, and no more. THE CHIEF JUSTICE [BURGER], JUSTICE STEWART, and I said:

> Here appellee did have a statutory expectancy that he not be removed other than for 'such cause as will promote the efficiency of [the] service.' But the very section of the statute which granted him that right, a right which had previously existed only by virtue of administrative regulation, expressly provided also for the procedure by which 'cause' was to be determined, and expressly omitted the procedural guarantees which appellee insists are mandated by the Constitution. Only by bifurcating the very sentence of the Act of Congress which conferred upon appellee the right not to be removed save for cause could it be said that he had an expectancy of that substantive right without the procedural limitations which Congress attached to it. *** Where the focus of legislation was thus strongly on the procedural mechanism for enforcing the substantive right which was simultaneously conferred, we decline to conclude that the substantive right may be viewed wholly apart from the procedure provided for its enforcement. The employee's statutorily defined right is not a guarantee against removal without cause in the abstract, but such a guarantee as enforced by the procedures which Congress has designated for the determination of cause.

In [this case], the relevant Ohio statute provides in its first paragraph that "[t]he tenure of every officer or employee in the classified service of the state *** shall be during good behavior and efficient service ***." The very next paragraph of this section of the Ohio Revised Code provides that in the event of suspension of more than three days or removal the appointing authority shall furnish the employee with the stated reasons for his removal. The next paragraph provides that within 10 days following the receipt of such a statement, the employee may appeal in writing to the State Personnel Board of Review or the Commission, such appeal shall be heard within 30 days from the time of its filing, and the Board may affirm, disaffirm, or modify the judgment of the appointing authority.

Thus in one legislative breath Ohio has conferred upon civil service employees such as respondents in these cases a limited form of tenure during good behavior, and prescribed the procedures by which that tenure may be terminated. Here, as in Arnett, "[t]he employee's statutorily defined right is not a guarantee against removal without cause in the abstract, but such a guarantee as enforced by the procedures which [the Ohio Legislature] has designated for the determination of cause." *** We ought to recognize the totality of the State's definition of the property right in question, and not merely seize upon one of several paragraphs in a unitary statute to proclaim that in that paragraph the State has inexorably conferred upon a civil service employee something which it is powerless under the United States Constitution to qualify in the next paragraph of the statute. *** [T]he Fourteenth Amendment *** does not support the conclusion that Ohio's effort to confer a limited form of tenure upon respondents resulted in the creation of a "property right" in their employment.

Notes

1. **Context of Notice and Hearing.** The Constitution says nothing specific about notice and hearing requirements to congressional lawmaking or presidential actions. *See Bi–Metallic Investment Co. v. State Board of Equalization*, 239 U.S. 441 (1915) (legislative bodies need not provide notice and opportunity to be heard, both because representative processes legitimize decisions and because such due process is impracticable in legislative contexts). Administrative proceedings, not contemplated under the original constitutional framework, provide the context for virtually all the Supreme Court's procedural due process cases. In essence, the Court has established more relaxed and flexible procedural requirements for agency adjudications than for civil trials. Why should agencies be able to decide cases adversely affecting individuals without the full panoply of protections given in court proceedings? Consider that there may be two very different benefits to procedural requirements in adjudications: (1) more accurate factual determinations and (2) enhanced dignity for the affected individuals. Are jury trials, counsel, and the like not mandated by the Court because the traditional trial procedures may not be the only or even the best way to afford these benefits? Trial processes are costly and the Court's hybrid processes may be much cheaper than full trials. Why are there relatively few procedural due process cases concerning property interests adjudicated in civil litigation or liberty restrictions following criminal conviction?

2. **"Property" and "Liberty" Definitions.** You have a right to a hearing if and only if you have an entitlement, a Court-approved "property" or "liberty" interest. Property seems to encompass benefits you are receiving, but not benefits for which you would like to qualify (see discussion in *Loudermill*). In short, the government has total discretion as to whether to create a benefit which will become property to the recipient, but is constrained concerning the procedures available to protect the entitlement it has created. Liberty interests, not the

focus of the procedural due process cases in these materials, include certain "grievous losses" to the individual but not other losses which seem almost equally serious. *See Ingraham v. Wright*, 430 U.S. 651 (1977) (paddling of student implicates a liberty interest). Compare *Owen v. City of Independence*, 445 U.S. 622 (1980) (right to reputation when combined with at-will employment is liberty interest) with *Paul v. Davis*, 424 U.S. 693 (1976) (reputation alone of one accused of being a shoplifter is not a liberty interest) and with *Board of Regents of State Colleges v. Roth*, 408 U.S. 564 (1972) (untenured assistant professor who is at-will employee has no liberty or property interest in continued employment).

3. **A Conundrum.** Why should a "for cause" provision in a statute, ordinance, or rule create a property interest, while the procedural restrictions in the same statute, ordinance, or rule are ignored? Don't the procedures in fact define the worth of the substantive entitlement? Is it possible that people don't read the procedures (like fine print in a boilerplate contract)? Does the Constitution distinguish "life, liberty, and property" from "due process"? Would failure to let the courts decide how much process is due "end judicial enforcement of the due process clause [because any legislature] that wishes to limit procedural rights need only make the limitation part of the definition of the underlying substantive right"? Douglas Laycock, *Due Process and Separation of Powers: The Effort to Make the Due Process Clauses Nonjusticiable*, 60 TEX. L. REV. 875 (1982).

4. **Is Police Protection a Property Right?** Over a period of several hours Jessica Gonzales implored the police to arrest her violent and estranged husband, who had taken their children from her front yard to an amusement park. The husband killed the children, fired a gun at a police station, and was shot dead by the police. *Castle Rock v. Gonzales*, 545 U.S. 748 (2005), held that, although Ms. Gonzales had a court-issued protective order against the husband that had clearly been violated, she had no "property interest" in police protection, even though the order said that the police "shall" arrest or issue a warrant for arrest of the husband upon violation of the order. The Court said a right to police protection "would not *** resemble any traditional conception of property" and that the language of the order should be read in light of "a well-established tradition of police discretion." In the absence of a property interest, Ms. Gonzales was owed no <u>procedural</u> due process by the police who had largely ignored her calls. Dissenting JUSTICES STEVENS and GINSBURG found this approach inconsistent with "the wave of domestic violence statutes that provides the crucial context for understanding Colorado's law" and this order. Compare *Castle Rock* to *DeShaney*, supra Ch. VII, which found no <u>substantive</u> constitutional duty when social services officials did not protect a child from a brutal beating by his father.

2. PROCESS DUE

MATHEWS v. ELDRIDGE
424 U.S. 319 (1976).

MR. JUSTICE POWELL delivered the opinion of the Court.

The issue in this case is whether the Due Process Clause of the Fifth Amendment requires that prior to the termination of Social Security disability benefit payments the recipient be afforded an opportunity for an evidentiary hearing. *** Respondent Eldridge was first awarded benefits in June 1968. In March 1972, he received a questionnaire from the state agency charged with monitoring his medical condition. Eldridge completed the questionnaire, indicating that his condition had not improved and identifying the medical sources, including physicians, from whom he had received treatment recently. The state agency then obtained reports from his physician and a psychiatric consultant. After considering these reports and other information in his file the agency informed Eldridge by letter that it had made a tentative determination that his disability had ceased in May 1972. The letter included a statement of reasons for the proposed termination of benefits, and advised Eldridge that he might request reasonable time in which to obtain and submit additional information pertaining to his condition.

[margin note: Cut off his disability check despite his condition]

In his written response, Eldridge disputed one characterization of his medical condition and indicated that the agency already had enough evidence to establish his disability. The state agency then made its final determination that he had ceased to be disabled in May 1972. *** [T]he Social Security Administration (SSA) *** notified Eldridge in July that his benefits would terminate after that month [and] advised him of his right to seek reconsideration by the state agency of this initial determination within six months. Instead of requesting reconsideration Eldridge commenced this action challenging the constitutional validity of the administrative procedures established by the Secretary of Health, Education, and Welfare for assessing whether there exists a continuing disability. ***

[margin note: SSA offered to let him seek consideration]

[margin note: E sued instead]

Procedural due process imposes constraints on governmental decisions which deprive individuals of "liberty" or "property" interests within the meaning of the Due Process Clause of the Fifth or Fourteenth Amendment. The Secretary does not contend that procedural due process is inapplicable to terminations of Social Security disability benefits. *** Rather, the Secretary contends that the existing administrative procedures *** provide all the process that is constitutionally due before a recipient can be deprived of that interest.

[margin note: SSA argues that they have internal procedures that ensure due process]

This Court consistently has held that some form of hearing is required before an individual is finally deprived of a property interest. *** The fundamental requirement of due process is the opportunity to be heard "at a meaningful time and in a meaningful manner." Eldridge agrees that the review procedures available to a claimant before the initial determination of ineligibility becomes final would be adequate if disability benefits were not terminated until after the evidentiary hearing stage of the administrative process. The dispute centers upon what process is due prior to the initial termination of benefits, pending review.

In recent years this Court increasingly has had occasion to consider the extent to which due process requires an evidentiary hearing prior to the deprivation of some type of property interest even if such a hearing is provided thereafter. In only one case, *Goldberg v. Kelly*, 397 U.S. 254 (1970), has the Court held that a hearing closely approximating a judicial trial is

[margin note: only one case supporting E]

necessary. In other cases requiring some type of pretermination hearing as a matter of constitutional right the Court has spoken sparingly about the requisite procedures. *** "(D)ue process is flexible and calls for such procedural protections as the particular situation demands." Accordingly, resolution of the issue whether the administrative procedures provided here are constitutionally sufficient requires analysis of the governmental and private interests that are affected. More precisely, our prior decisions indicate that identification of the specific dictates of due process generally requires consideration of three distinct factors: First, the private interest that will be affected by the official action; second, the risk of an erroneous deprivation of such interest through the procedures used, and the probable value, if any, of additional or substitute procedural safeguards; and finally, the Government's interest, including the function involved and the fiscal and administrative burdens that the additional or substitute procedural requirement would entail. ***

In order to establish initial and continued entitlement to disability benefits a worker must demonstrate that he is unable "to engage in any substantial gainful activity by reason of any medically determinable physical or mental impairment ***." To satisfy this test the worker bears a continuing burden of showing, by means of "medically acceptable clinical and laboratory diagnostic techniques," that he has a physical or mental impairment of such severity that "he is not only unable to do his previous work but cannot *** engage in any other kind of substantial gainful work which exists in the national economy." *** The continuing-eligibility investigation is made by a state agency acting through a "team" consisting of a physician and a nonmedical person trained in disability evaluation. The agency periodically communicates with the disabled worker, usually by mail in which case he is sent a detailed questionnaire or by telephone, and requests information concerning his present condition, including current medical restrictions and sources of treatment, and any additional information that he considers relevant to his continued entitlement to benefits.

Information regarding the recipient's current condition is also obtained from his sources of medical treatment. If there is a conflict between the information provided by the beneficiary and that obtained from medical sources such as his physician, or between two sources of treatment, the agency may arrange for an examination by an independent consulting physician. Whenever the agency's tentative assessment of the beneficiary's condition differs from his own assessment, the beneficiary is informed that benefits may be terminated, provided a summary of the evidence upon which the proposed determination to terminate is based, and afforded an opportunity to review the medical reports and other evidence in his case file. He also may respond in writing and submit additional evidence.

The state agency then makes its final determination, which is reviewed by an examiner in the SSA Bureau of Disability Insurance. *** Upon acceptance by the SSA, benefits are terminated effective two months after the month in which medical recovery is found to have occurred.

If the recipient seeks reconsideration by the state agency and the determination is adverse, the SSA reviews the reconsideration determination and notifies the recipient of the decision. He then has a right to an evidentiary hearing before an SSA administrative law judge. The hearing is nonadversary and the SSA is not represented by counsel. As at all prior and subsequent stages of the administrative process, however, the claimant may be represented by counsel or other spokesmen. If this hearing results in an adverse decision, the claimant is entitled to request discretionary review by the SSA Appeals Council and finally may obtain judicial review.

Should it be determined at any point after termination of benefits, that the claimant's disability extended beyond the date of cessation initially established, the worker is entitled to retroactive payments. If, on the other hand, a beneficiary receives any payments to which he is later determined not to be entitled, the statute authorizes the Secretary to attempt to recoup these funds in specified circumstances.

SSA procedure ↑

Despite the elaborate character of the administrative procedures provided by the Secretary, the courts below held them to be constitutionally inadequate, concluding that due process requires an evidentiary hearing prior to termination. In light of the private and governmental interests at stake here and the nature of the existing procedures, we think this was error.

Cts have held that the practice wasn't enough

Ct. disagrees

Since a recipient whose benefits are terminated is awarded full retroactive relief if he ultimately prevails, his sole interest is in the uninterrupted receipt of this source of income pending final administrative decision on his claim. His potential injury is thus similar in nature to that of the welfare recipient in *Goldberg* v. *Kelly*, 397 U.S. 254 (1970).

Retroactive relief puts them back where they were

Only in *Goldberg* has the Court held that due process requires an evidentiary hearing prior to a temporary deprivation. It was emphasized there that welfare assistance is given to persons on the very margin of subsistence. *** Eligibility for disability benefits, in contrast, is not based upon financial need. Indeed, it is wholly unrelated to the worker's income or support from many other sources, such as earnings of other family members, workmen's compensation awards, tort claims awards, savings, private insurance, public or private pensions, veterans' benefits, food stamps, public assistance, or the "many other important programs, both public and private, which contain provisions for disability payments affecting a substantial portion of the work force ***."

Diff from Goldberg b/c not about food and basic requirements to live.

As *Goldberg* illustrates, the degree of potential deprivation that may be created by a particular decision is a factor to be considered in assessing the validity of any administrative decisionmaking process. The potential deprivation here is generally likely to be less than in *Goldberg*, although the degree of difference can be overstated. *** [T]o remain eligible for benefits a recipient must be "unable to engage in substantial gainful activity." Thus, in contrast to the discharged federal employee in *Arnett*, there is little possibility that the terminated recipient will be able to find even temporary employment to ameliorate the interim loss. [Moreover,] "the possible length of wrongful deprivation of *** benefits (also) is an important factor in assessing the impact of official action on the private interests." The Secretary concedes that the delay between a request for a hearing before an administrative law judge and a decision on the claim is currently between 10 and 11 months. Since a terminated recipient must first obtain a reconsideration decision as a prerequisite to invoking his right to an evidentiary hearing, the delay between the actual cutoff of benefits and final decision after a hearing exceeds one year.

In view of the torpidity of this administrative review process, and the typically modest resources of the family unit of the physically disabled worker, the hardship imposed upon the erroneously terminated disability recipient may be significant. Still, the disabled worker's need is likely to be less than that of a welfare recipient. In addition to the possibility of access to private resources, other forms of government assistance will become available where the termination of disability benefits places a worker or his family below the subsistence level. In view of these potential sources of temporary income, there is less reason here than in *Goldberg* to depart from the ordinary principle, established by our decisions, that something less than an evidentiary hearing is sufficient prior to adverse administrative action.

An additional factor to be considered here is the fairness and reliability of the existing pretermination procedures, and the probable value, if any, of additional procedural safeguards. Central to the evaluation of any administrative process is the nature of the relevant inquiry. In order to remain eligible for benefits the disabled worker must demonstrate by means of "medically acceptable clinical and laboratory diagnostic techniques," that he is unable "to engage in any substantial gainful activity by reason of any medically determinable physical or mental impairment ***." In short, a medical assessment of the worker's physical or mental condition is required. This is a more sharply focused and easily documented decision than the typical determination of welfare entitlement. In the latter case, a wide variety of information may be deemed relevant, and issues of witness credibility and veracity often are critical to the decisionmaking process. *Goldberg* noted that in such circumstances "written submissions are a wholly unsatisfactory basis for decision."

By contrast, the decision whether to discontinue disability benefits will turn, in most cases, upon "routine, standard, and unbiased medical reports by physician specialists," concerning a subject whom they have personally examined. *** To be sure, credibility and veracity may be a factor in the ultimate disability assessment in some cases. But procedural due process rules are shaped by the risk of error inherent in the truthfinding process as applied to the generality of cases, not the rare exceptions. The potential value of an evidentiary hearing, or even oral presentation to the decisionmaker, is substantially less in this context than in *Goldberg*.

The decision in *Goldberg* also was based on the Court's conclusion that written submissions were an inadequate substitute for oral presentation because they did not provide an effective means for the recipient to communicate his case to the decisionmaker. Written submissions were viewed as an unrealistic option, for most recipients lacked the "educational attainment necessary to write effectively" and could not afford professional assistance. In addition, such submissions would not provide the "flexibility of oral presentations" or "permit the recipient to mold his argument to the issues the decision maker appears to regard as important." In the context of the disability-benefits-entitlement assessment the administrative procedures under review here fully answer these objections. ***

Case against written submissions

A further safeguard against mistake is the policy of allowing the disability recipient's representative full access to all information relied upon by the state agency. In addition, prior to the cutoff of benefits the agency informs the recipient of its tentative assessment, the reasons therefor, and provides a summary of the evidence that it considers most relevant. Opportunity is then afforded the recipient to submit additional evidence or arguments, enabling him to challenge directly the accuracy of information in his file as well as the correctness of the agency's tentative conclusions. These procedures, again as contrasted with those before the Court in *Goldberg*, enable the recipient to "mold" his argument to respond to the precise issues which the decisionmaker regards as crucial.

Despite these carefully structured procedures, amici point to the significant reversal rate for appealed cases as clear evidence that the current process is inadequate. Depending upon the base selected and the line of analysis followed, the relevant reversal rates urged by the contending parties vary from a high of 58.6% for appealed reconsideration decisions to an overall reversal rate of only 3.3%. Bare statistics rarely provide a satisfactory measure of the fairness of a decisionmaking process. Their adequacy is especially suspect here since the administrative review system is operated on an open-file basis. A recipient may always submit new evidence, and such submissions may result in additional medical examinations. Such fresh examinations were held in approximately 30% to 40% of the appealed cases, in fiscal 1973, either at the reconsideration or evidentiary hearing stage of the administrative process. In this context, the value of reversal rate statistics as one means of evaluating the adequacy of the pretermination process is diminished. ***

Reversal rates are inconsistent

In striking the appropriate due process balance the final factor to be assessed is the public interest. This includes the administrative burden and other societal costs that would be associated with requiring, as a matter of constitutional right, an evidentiary hearing upon demand in all cases prior to the termination of disability benefits. The most visible burden would be the incremental cost resulting from the increased number of hearings and the expense of providing benefits to ineligible recipients pending decision. No one can predict the extent of the increase, but the fact that full benefits would continue until after such hearings would assure the exhaustion in most cases of this attractive option. *** [E]xperience with the constitutionalizing of government procedures suggests that the ultimate additional cost in terms of money and administrative burden would not be insubstantial.

Financial burden of having to pay for people who may not be eligible

Financial cost alone is not a controlling weight in determining whether due process requires a particular procedural safeguard prior to some administrative decision. But the Government's interest, and hence that of the public, in conserving scarce fiscal and administrative resources is a factor that must be weighed. At some point the benefit of an additional safeguard to the individual affected by the administrative action and to society in terms of increased assurance that the action is just, may be outweighed by the cost. Significantly, the cost of protecting those whom the preliminary administrative process has identified as likely to be found undeserving may in the end come out of the pockets of the deserving since resources available for any particular program of social welfare are not unlimited.

But more is implicated in cases of this type than ad hoc weighing of fiscal and administrative burdens against the interests of a particular category of claimants. The ultimate balance involves a determination as to when, under our constitutional system, judicial-type procedures must be imposed upon administrative action to assure fairness. *** The judicial model of an evidentiary hearing is neither a required, nor even the most effective, method of decisionmaking in all circumstances. The essence of due process is the requirement that "a person in jeopardy of serious loss (be given) notice of the case against him and opportunity to meet it." All that is necessary is that the procedures be tailored, in light of the decision to be made, to "the capacities and circumstances of those who are to be heard," *Goldberg* at 268–269, to insure that they are given a meaningful opportunity to present their case. In assessing what process is due in this case, substantial weight must be given to the good-faith judgments of the individuals charged by Congress with the administration of social welfare programs that the procedures they have provided assure fair consideration of the entitlement claims of individuals. *** [A]n evidentiary hearing is not required prior to the termination of disability benefits ***

MR. JUSTICE STEVENS took no part in the consideration or decision of this case.

MR. JUSTICE BRENNAN, with whom MR. JUSTICE MARSHALL concurs, dissenting.

*** [P]rior to termination of benefits, Eldridge must be afforded an evidentiary hearing of the type required for welfare beneficiaries *** . *See Goldberg v. Kelly.* I would add that the Court's consideration that a discontinuance of disability benefits may cause the recipient to suffer only a limited deprivation is no argument. It is speculative. Moreover, the very legislative determination to provide disability benefits, without any prerequisite determination of need in fact, presumes a need by the recipient which is not this Court's function to denigrate. Indeed, in the present case, it is indicated that because disability benefits were terminated there was a foreclosure upon the Eldridge home and the family's furniture was repossessed, forcing Eldridge, his wife, and their children to sleep in one bed. Finally, it is also no argument that a worker, who has been placed in the untenable position of having been denied disability benefits, may still seek other forms of public assistance.

Notes

1. **Utilitarian Balancing or "How Much Process is Due?"**

• *Mathews* is the classic statement of the Court's three-part balancing test and therefore you should commit its components—degree of potential deprivation, fairness of procedure and value of additional safeguards, and the public interest—to memory.

• Note that the *Mathews* balancing is NOT a balancing of the costs and benefits of the substantive regulations themselves, but only of the procedures connected with terminating the benefit conferred by the regulations.

• Does the Court ignore the "dignitary value" of full procedures before adverse things are done to individuals by government?

• Aren't the three things balanced by the Court incommensurable? That is, how does one weigh individual hardship versus social costs?

• Is the Court evenhanded in balancing the factors, or does it put its finger on the scales by calling individual hardships "speculative" and accepting at face value "obscure suggestions of necessity" by the government?

• How does one know what extra processes will be productive in arriving at "the truth"? For example, is it really true that a technical medical determination rather than subjective impressions and credibility are at the heart of termination of disability benefits?

2. **Balancing in the Employment Termination Context.** In a portion of *Loudermill* not reproduced above, the Court held that Loudermill was not entitled to a full adversary hearing prior to termination of his employment, but that some "opportunity to respond prior to termination" was necessary. The Court balanced the competing interests of "the private interests in retaining employment, the governmental interest in the expeditious removal of unsatisfactory employees and the avoidance of administrative burdens, and the risk of erroneous termination." It found that all that was required was "notice and an opportunity to respond [to the reasons given for termination]" where Loudermill was accorded a "full post-termination hearing." JUSTICES MARSHALL and BRENNAN dissented, the former on the ground that a nine-month delay after wage termination until the full hearing might be "devastating" to the employee, the latter on the ground that there should be a remand to examine the issue of "overlong delay."

3. **Policy.** There is substantial debate concerning the wisdom of the procedural due process revolution inaugurated by *Goldberg v. Kelly*. JUSTICE BRENNAN once said that this case was the decision of which he was most proud. Critics argue that *Goldberg*'s due process revolution has in fact hurt the poor, in effect transferring money from programs for the poor to middle-class government officials who administer the procedural aspects of programs for the poor. If you were a welfare recipient, how much would you be willing to pay for notice and a full due process hearing prior to termination of benefits? If you were running a school, would you rather have more freedom to implement what you believed were educationally-desirable programs or more money with your discretion

limited by due process considerations? Is any of this policy debate relevant to the decisions you have read in this unit?

4.   **Problems.**

(a) State law makes discharge for age, disability and other reasons unlawful and provides that where a claim is filed, the state agency must begin a proceeding within 120 days to consider the claim. The agency inadvertently scheduled the proceeding on the 125th day, and state courts held that the agency was without jurisdiction to hear the matter at this time. Consider the claimant's procedural due process claim. *Logan v. Zimmerman Brush Co.*, 455 U.S. 422 (1982).

(b) Suppose a state university decides to dismiss a student for cheating on an examination. How would you apply procedural due process to this situation? Would your analysis differ if the university proposed to dismiss the student for not maintaining the required grade-point average? What if the proposed dismissal was for drunken and disorderly conduct and sexually harassing advances at a fraternity party?

(c) Assume that the President and Congress agree to a package of welfare reforms that limit a recipient to two years of benefits in a lifetime. No process is provided prior to termination; once a person receives a 24th monthly check, a letter is issued saying "That's it for you. Get a job." Does the new welfare package violate procedural due process requirements?

HAMDI v. RUMSFELD
542 U.S. 507 (2004)

JUSTICE O'CONNOR announced the judgment of the Court and delivered an opinion, in which THE CHIEF JUSTICE, JUSTICE KENNEDY, and JUSTICE BREYER join.

At this difficult time in our Nation's history, we are called upon to consider the legality of the Government's detention of a United States citizen on United States soil as an "enemy combatant" and to address the process that is constitutionally owed to one who seeks to challenge his classification as such. *** We hold that although Congress authorized the detention of combatants in the narrow circumstances alleged here, due process demands that a citizen held in the United States as an enemy combatant be given a meaningful opportunity to contest the factual basis for that detention before a neutral decisionmaker. *** This case arises out of the detention of a man whom the Government alleges took up arms with the Taliban during this conflict. His name is Yaser Esam Hamdi. Born an American citizen in Louisiana in 1980, Hamdi moved with his family to Saudi Arabia as a child. By 2001, the parties agree, he resided in Afghanistan. At some point that year, he was seized by members of the Northern Alliance, a coalition of military groups opposed to the Taliban government, and eventually was turned over to the United States military. The Government asserts that it initially detained and interrogated Hamdi in Afghanistan before transferring him to the United States Naval Base in Guantanamo Bay in January 2002. In April 2002, upon learning that Hamdi is an American citizen, authorities transferred him to a naval brig in Norfolk, Virginia, where he remained until a recent transfer to a brig in Charleston, South Carolina. ***

[A] declaration from one Michael Mobbs (hereinafter "Mobbs Declaration"), who identified himself as Special Advisor to the Under Secretary of Defense for Policy *** set[s] forth what remains the sole evidentiary support that the Government has provided to the courts for Hamdi's detention. The declaration states that Hamdi "traveled to Afghanistan" in July or August 2001, and that he thereafter "affiliated with a Taliban military unit and received weapons training." It asserts that Hamdi "remained with his Taliban unit following the attacks of September 11" and that, during the time when Northern Alliance forces were "engaged in battle with the Taliban," "Hamdi's Taliban unit surrendered" to those forces, after which he "surrender[ed] his Kalishnikov assault rifle" to them. The Mobbs Declaration also states that, because al Qaeda and the Taliban "were and are hostile forces engaged in armed conflict with the armed forces of the United States," "individuals associated with" those groups "were and continue to be enemy combatants." Mobbs states that Hamdi was labeled an enemy combatant "[b]ased upon his interviews and in light of his association with the Taliban." According to the declaration, a series of "U.S. military screening team[s]" determined that Hamdi met "the criteria for enemy combatants," and "a subsequent interview of Hamdi has confirmed that he surrendered and gave his firearm to Northern Alliance forces, which supports his classification as an enemy combatant." ***

The threshold question before us is whether the Executive has the authority to detain citizens who qualify as "enemy combatants." *** The Government maintains that no explicit congressional authorization is required, because the Executive possesses plenary authority to detain pursuant to Article II of the Constitution. We do not reach the question whether Article II provides such authority, however, because we agree with the Government's alternative position, that Congress has in fact authorized Hamdi's detention, through the AUMF [Authorization for Use of Military Force]. *** Hamdi objects, nevertheless, that Congress has not authorized the *indefinite* detention to which he is now subject. *** We take Hamdi's objection to be not to the lack of certainty regarding the date on which the conflict will end, but to the substantial prospect of perpetual detention. *** Certainly, we agree that indefinite detention for the purpose of interrogation is not authorized. *** [But] [i]f the record establishes that United States troops are still involved in active combat in Afghanistan, those detentions are part of the exercise of "necessary and appropriate force," and therefore are authorized by the AUMF. ***

Even in cases in which the detention of enemy combatants is legally authorized, there remains the question of what process is constitutionally due to a citizen who disputes his enemy-combatant status. Hamdi argues that he is owed a meaningful and timely hearing and that "extra-judicial detention [that] begins and ends with the submission of an affidavit based on third-hand hearsay" does not comport with the Fifth and Fourteenth Amendments. The Government counters that any more process than was provided below would be both unworkable and "constitutionally intolerable." Our resolution of this dispute requires a careful examination both of the writ of habeas corpus, which Hamdi now seeks to employ as a mechanism of judicial review, and of the Due Process Clause, which informs the procedural contours of that mechanism in this instance.

*** Congress envisioned that habeas petitioners would have some opportunity to present and rebut facts and that courts in cases like this retain some ability to vary the ways in which they do so as mandated by due process. The Government *** asks us to hold that *** the presentation of the Mobbs Declaration to the habeas court completed the required factual development. *** Under the Government's most extreme rendition of this argument, "[r]espect for separation of powers and the limited institutional capabilities of courts in matters of military decision-making in connection with an ongoing conflict" ought to eliminate entirely any individual process, restricting the courts to investigating only whether legal authorization exists for the broader detention scheme. At most, the Government argues, courts should review its determination that a citizen is an enemy combatant under a very deferential "some evidence" standard. Under this review, a court would assume the accuracy of the Government's articulated basis for Hamdi's detention, as set forth in the Mobbs Declaration, and assess only whether that articulated basis was a legitimate one.

In response, Hamdi emphasizes that this Court consistently has recognized that an individual challenging his detention may not be held at the will of the Executive without recourse to some proceeding before a neutral tribunal to determine whether the Executive's asserted justifications for that detention have basis in fact and warrant in law. *** The ordinary mechanism that we use for balancing such serious competing interests, and for determining the procedures that are necessary to ensure that a citizen is not "deprived of life, liberty, or property, without due process of law," is the test that we articulated in *Mathews v. Eldridge,* 424 U.S. 319 (1976). *Mathews* dictates that the process due in any given instance is determined by weighing "the private interest that will be affected by the official action" against the Government's asserted interest, "including the function involved" and the burdens the Government would face in providing greater process. ***

[S]ubstantial interests lie on both sides of the scale in this case. Hamdi's "private interest ... affected by the official action," is the most elemental of liberty interests—the interest in being free from physical detention by one's own government. *** Nor is the weight on this side of the *Mathews* scale offset by the circumstances of war or the accusation of treasonous behavior, for "[i]t is clear that commitment for *any* purpose constitutes a significant deprivation of liberty that requires due process protection," and at this stage in the *Mathews* calculus, we consider the interest of the *erroneously* detained individual. *** [T]he risk of erroneous deprivation of a citizen's liberty in the absence of sufficient process here is very real. Moreover, as critical as the Government's interest may be in detaining those who actually pose an immediate threat to the national security of the United States during ongoing international conflict, history and common sense teach us that an unchecked system of detention carries the potential to become a means for oppression and abuse of others who do not present that sort of threat. ***

On the other side of the scale are the weighty and sensitive governmental interests in ensuring that those who have in fact fought with the enemy during a war do not return to battle against the United States. As discussed above, the law of war and the realities of combat may render such detentions both necessary and appropriate, and our due process analysis need not blink at those realities. *** The Government also argues [that] *** military officers who are engaged in the serious work of waging battle would be unnecessarily and dangerously distracted by litigation half a world away, and discovery into military operations would both intrude on the sensitive secrets of national defense and result in a futile search for evidence buried under the rubble of war. To the extent that these burdens are triggered by heightened procedures, they are properly taken into account in our due process analysis.

Striking the proper constitutional balance here is of great importance to the Nation during this period of ongoing combat. *** We therefore hold that a citizen-detainee seeking to challenge his classification as an enemy combatant must receive notice of the factual basis for his classification, and a fair opportunity to rebut the Government's factual assertions before a neutral decisionmaker. *** At the same time, the exigencies of the circumstances may demand that, aside from these core elements, enemy combatant proceedings may be tailored to alleviate their uncommon potential to burden the Executive at a time of ongoing military conflict. Hearsay, for example, may need to be accepted as the most reliable available evidence from the Government in such a proceeding. Likewise, the Constitution would not be offended by a presumption in favor of the Government's evidence, so long as that presumption remained a rebuttable one and fair opportunity for rebuttal were provided. *** A burden-shifting scheme of this sort would meet the goal of ensuring that the errant tourist, embedded journalist, or local aid worker has a chance to prove military error while giving due regard to the Executive once it has put forth meaningful support for its conclusion that the detainee is in fact an enemy combatant. ***

We think it unlikely that this basic process will have the dire impact on the central functions of warmaking that the Government forecasts. The parties agree that initial captures on the battlefield need not receive the process we have discussed here; that process is due only when the determination is made to *continue* to hold those who have been seized. *** This focus meddles little, if at all, in the strategy or conduct of war ***

[T]he proposed "some evidence" standard is inadequate. Any process in which the Executive's factual assertions go wholly unchallenged or are simply presumed correct without any opportunity for the alleged combatant to demonstrate otherwise falls constitutionally short. *** This standard therefore is ill suited to the situation in which a habeas petitioner has received no prior proceedings before any tribunal and had no prior opportunity to rebut the Executive's factual assertions before a neutral decisionmaker. *** Aside from unspecified "screening" processes, and military interrogations in which the Government suggests Hamdi could have contested his classification, Hamdi has received no process. ***

There remains the possibility that the standards we have articulated could be met by an appropriately authorized and properly constituted military tribunal. *** [H]owever, a court that receives a petition for a writ of habeas corpus from an alleged enemy combatant must itself ensure that the minimum requirements of due process are achieved. Both courts below recognized as much, focusing their energies on the question of whether Hamdi was due an opportunity to rebut the Government's case against him. The Government, too, proceeded on this assumption, presenting its affidavit and then seeking that it be evaluated under a deferential standard of review based on burdens that it alleged would accompany any greater process. As we have discussed, a habeas court in a case such as this may accept affidavit evidence like that contained in the Mobbs Declaration, so long as it also permits the alleged combatant to present his own factual case to rebut the Government's return. *** He unquestionably has the right to access to counsel in connection with the proceedings on remand.

JUSTICE SOUTER, with whom JUSTICE GINSBURG joins, concurring in part, dissenting in part, and concurring in the judgment.

*** Hamdi has been locked up for over two years. *** I would not reach any questions of what process he may be due in litigating disputed issues in a proceeding under the habeas statute or prior to the habeas enquiry itself. *** [T]he terms of the plurality's remand will allow Hamdi to offer evidence that he is not an enemy combatant, and he should at the least have the benefit of that opportunity. *** I do not mean to imply agreement that the Government could claim an evidentiary presumption casting the burden of rebuttal on Hamdi, or that an opportunity to litigate before a military tribunal might obviate or truncate enquiry by a court on habeas. ***

JUSTICE SCALIA, with whom JUSTICE STEVENS joins, dissenting.

*** Where the Government accuses a citizen of waging war against it, our constitutional tradition has been to prosecute him in federal court for treason or some other crime. *** The relevant question, then, is whether there is a different, special procedure for imprisonment of a citizen accused of wrongdoing *by aiding the enemy in wartime.* *** Citizens aiding the enemy have been treated as traitors subject to the criminal process. ***

There are times when military exigency renders resort to the traditional criminal process impracticable. *** Our Federal Constitution contains a provision explicitly permitting suspension, but limiting the situations in which it may be invoked *** The proposition that the Executive lacks indefinite wartime detention authority over citizens is consistent with the Founders' general mistrust of military power permanently at the Executive's disposal. *** A view of the Constitution that gives the Executive authority to use military force rather than the force of law against citizens on American soil flies in the face of the mistrust that engendered these provisions.*** It follows from what I have said that Hamdi is entitled to a habeas decree requiring his release unless (1) criminal proceedings are promptly brought, or (2) Congress has suspended the writ of habeas corpus. ***

The plurality finds justification for Hamdi's imprisonment in the Authorization for Use of Military Force *** This is not remotely a congressional suspension of the writ, and no one claims that it is. ***

It should not be thought, however, that the plurality's evisceration of the Suspension Clause augments, principally, the power of Congress. As usual, the major effect of its constitutional improvisation is to increase the power of the Court. Having found a congressional authorization for detention of citizens where none clearly exists; and having discarded the categorical procedural protection of the Suspension Clause; the plurality then proceeds, under the guise of the Due Process Clause, to prescribe what procedural protections *it* thinks appropriate. ***

There is a certain harmony of approach in the plurality's making up for Congress's failure to invoke the Suspension Clause and its making up for the Executive's failure to apply what it says are needed procedures—an approach that reflects what might be called a Mr. Fix-it Mentality. The plurality seems to view it as its mission to Make Everything Come Out Right, rather than merely to decree the consequences, as far as individual rights are concerned, of the other two branches' actions and omissions. Has the Legislature failed to suspend the writ in the current dire emergency? Well, we will remedy that failure by prescribing the reasonable conditions that a suspension should have included. And has the Executive failed to live up to those reasonable conditions? Well, we will ourselves make that failure good, so that this dangerous fellow (if he is dangerous) need not be set free. The problem with this approach is not only that it steps out of the courts' modest and limited role in a democratic society; but that by repeatedly doing what it thinks the political branches ought to do it encourages their lassitude and saps the vitality of government by the people. *** If civil rights are to be curtailed during wartime, it must be done openly and democratically, as the Constitution requires, rather than by silent erosion through an opinion of this Court. ***

JUSTICE THOMAS, dissenting.

The Executive Branch, acting pursuant to the powers vested in the President by the Constitution and with explicit congressional approval, has determined that Yaser Hamdi is an enemy combatant and should be detained. This detention falls squarely within the Federal Government's war powers, and we lack the expertise and capacity to second-guess that decision. As such, petitioners' habeas challenge should fail, and there is no reason to remand the case. *** I acknowledge that the question whether Hamdi's executive detention is lawful is a question properly resolved by the Judicial Branch, though the question comes to the Court with the strongest presumptions in favor of the Government. *** [T]he question whether Hamdi is actually an enemy combatant is "of a kind for which the Judiciary has neither aptitude, facilities nor responsibility and which has long been held to belong in the domain of political power not subject to judicial intrusion or inquiry." *** In this context, due process requires nothing more than a good-faith executive determination. *** I therefore believe that this is no occasion to balance the competing interests, as the plurality unconvincingly attempts to do.

Although I do not agree with the plurality that the balancing approach of *Mathews v. Eldridge,* 424 U.S. 319 (1976), is the appropriate analytical tool with which to analyze this case,[5] I cannot help but explain that the plurality misapplies its chosen framework, one that if applied correctly would probably lead to the result I have reached. *** At issue here is the far more significant interest of the security of the Nation. The Government seeks to further that interest by detaining an enemy soldier not only to prevent him from rejoining the ongoing fight. Rather, as the Government explains, detention can serve to gather critical intelligence regarding the intentions and capabilities of our adversaries, a function that the Government avers has become all the more important in the war on terrorism.

Additional process, the Government explains, will destroy the intelligence gathering function. *** Ultimately, the plurality's dismissive treatment of the Government's asserted interests arises from its apparent belief that enemy-combatant determinations are not part of "the actual prosecution of a war," or one of the "central functions of war making." This seems wrong: Taking *and holding* enemy combatants is a quintessential aspect of the prosecution of war. Moreover, this highlights serious difficulties in applying the plurality's balancing approach here. First, in the war context, we know neither the strength of the Government's interests nor the costs of imposing additional process. Second, it is at least difficult to explain why the result should be different for other military operations that the plurality would ostensibly recognize as "central functions of war making." *** Because a decision to bomb a particular target might extinguish *life* interests, the plurality's analysis seems to require notice to potential targets. ***

Notes

1.   ***Mathews* Balancing.** Is *Mathews* balancing appropriate in cases of military detention? Does the plurality properly apply *Mathews*?

2.   **Citizen, Noncitizen.** Do the due process rights granted Hamdi apply to aliens? Note the language of both the Fifth and Fourteenth Amendments, which refer to "persons," not just citizens. Do aliens overseas have rights to due process under the U.S Constitution? What if Hamdi, a citizen, had continued to be held overseas in Afghanistan or at Guantanamo Bay? Review *Boumediene* (Chapter II) and *Munaf* (Chapter III).

3.   **Enemy Combatant?** One arrested domestically is normally entitled to a bail hearing and a speedy trial, neither of which Hamdi received. Hamdi was captured in Afghanistan, allegedly with a rifle and aligned with Taliban forces. Another U.S. citizen, allegedly an al Qaeda saboteur, was arrested deplaning at O'Hare airport in Chicago and then was transferred to military detention. At oral argument, the Solicitor General was asked whether, if this person was an enemy combatant, could the authorities shoot him as he got off the plane. What do you

---

[5] Evidently, neither do the parties, who do not cite *Mathews* even once.

think? Should the government be allowed to hold the alleged saboteur, originally arrested, in military detention? Would it matter if the person had been trained by al Qaeda and fought against U.S. forces before flying to the U.S.?

B. SUBSTANTIVE DUE PROCESS

In the late 19th century, the Supreme Court first recognized that the Due Process Clause of the Fourteenth Amendment has a non-procedural component that protects economic interests. That era of the Court's work, often called the *Lochner* era of substantive due process, was eventually abandoned. *Lochner*, its demise, and the Court's current use of substantive due process in economic areas, are discussed in section 1 below. The Court's broader protection of personal or noneconomic rights is covered in section 2. Before commencing these two separate enterprises, however, it is worthwhile taking a look at one early case in which the economic and the personal strands of substantive due process are fused rather than separated.

PIERCE v. SOCIETY OF THE SISTERS
268 U.S. 510 (1925)

Mr. Justice McREYNOLDS delivered the opinion of the Court.

*** [Oregon's Compulsory Education Act of 1922] requires every parent, guardian, or other person having control or charge or custody of a child between 8 and 16 years to send him 'to a public school for the period of time a public school shall be held during the current year' in the district where the child resides; and failure so to do is declared a misdemeanor. There are exemptions-not specially important here-for children who are not normal, or who have completed the eighth grade, or whose parents or private teachers reside at considerable distances from any public school, or who hold special permits from the county superintendent. The manifest purpose is to compel general attendance at public schools by normal children, between 8 and 16, who have not completed the eighth grade. ***

Appellee the Society of Sisters is an Oregon corporation, organized in 1880, with power to care for orphans, educate and instruct the youth, establish and maintain academies or schools, and acquire necessary real and personal property. *** In its primary schools many children *** are taught the subjects usually pursued in Oregon public schools during the first eight years. Systematic religious instruction and moral training according to the tenets of the Roman Catholic Church are also regularly provided. *** The business is remunerative *** -and *** requires long time contracts with teachers and parents. The Compulsory Education Act of 1922 has already caused the withdrawal from its schools of children who would otherwise continue, and their income has steadily declined. The appellants, public officers, have proclaimed their purpose strictly to enforce the statute. ***

No question is raised concerning the power of the state reasonably to regulate all schools, to inspect, supervise and examine them, their teachers and pupils; to require that all children of proper age attend some school, that teachers shall be of good moral character and patriotic disposition, that certain studies plainly essential to good citizenship must be taught, and that nothing be taught which is manifestly inimical to the public welfare.

The inevitable practical result of enforcing the act under consideration would be destruction of appellees' primary schools, and perhaps all other private primary schools for normal children within the state of Oregon. Appellees are engaged in a kind of undertaking not inherently harmful, but long regarded as useful and meritorious. Certainly there is nothing in the present records to indicate that they have failed to discharge their obligations to patrons, students, or the state. And there are no peculiar circumstances or present emergencies which demand extraordinary measures relative to primary education. *** [T]he Act of 1922 unreasonably interferes with the liberty of parents and guardians to direct the upbringing and education of children under their control. *** [R]ights guaranteed by the Constitution may not be abridged by legislation which has no reasonable relation to some purpose within the competency of the state. The fundamental theory of liberty upon which all governments in this Union repose excludes any general power of the state to standardize its children by forcing them to accept instruction from public teachers only. The child is not the mere creature of the state; those who nurture him and direct his destiny have the right, coupled with the high duty, to recognize and prepare him for additional obligations.

Appellees' *** business and property *** are threatened with destruction through the unwarranted compulsion which appellants are exercising over present and prospective patrons of their schools. And this court has gone very far to protect against loss threatened by such action. *** Generally *** no person in any business has such an interest in possible customers as to enable him to restrain exercise of proper power of the state upon the ground that he will be deprived of patronage. But the injunctions here sought are not against the exercise of any proper power. Appellees asked protection against arbitrary, unreasonable, and unlawful interference with their patrons and the consequent destruction of their business and property. *** [The Oregon statute violates due process, and thus is voided.]

Notes

1. **Regulation and Reasonableness.** Why does the Court find Oregon's regulation to be "arbitrary, unreasonable, and unlawful?" What is the relation between the liberty of the school as a business and the "liberty of parents and guardians"? What role do children's rights play in the Court's opinion?

2. **Inequality?** The Court alludes to the legitimacy of "the power of the state reasonably to regulate all schools". Is there an equal protection problem with Oregon's regulation? Does the regulation apply unequally to children? Their parents? The Society of Sisters? We will look at such issues systematically in Chapter IX.

1. ECONOMIC RIGHTS

LOCHNER v. NEW YORK

198 U.S. 45 (1905)

MR. JUSTICE PECKHAM *** delivered the opinion of the Court:

[The petitioner had been indicted under the following New York statute, *[NY law]* and claimed it violated the Due Process clause:

No employee shall be required or permitted to work in a biscuit, bread, or cake bakery or confectionery establishment more than sixty hours in any one week, or more than ten hours in any one day, unless for the purpose of making a shorter work day on the last day of the week; nor more hours in any one week than will make an average of ten hours per day for the number of days during such week in which such employee shall work.]

[bakers cannot work more than 10 hours a day]

*** The statute necessarily interferes with the right of contract between the employer and employees, concerning the number of hours in which the latter may labor in the bakery of the employer. The general right to make a contract in relation to his business is part of the liberty of the individual protected by the 14th Amendment of the Federal Constitution. *Allgeyer v. Louisiana*, 165 U.S. 578. Under that provision no state can deprive any person of life, liberty, or property without due process of law. The right to purchase or to sell labor is part of the liberty protected by this amendment, unless there are circumstances which exclude the right. There are, however, certain powers, existing in the sovereignty of each state in the Union, somewhat vaguely termed police powers, the exact description and limitation of which have not been attempted by the courts. Those powers, broadly stated, and without, at present, any attempt at a more specific limitation, relate to the safety, health, morals, and general welfare of the public. Both property and liberty are held on such reasonable conditions as may be imposed by the governing power of the state in the exercise of those powers, and with such conditions the 14th Amendment was not designed to interfere. *Mugler v. Kansas*, 123 U. S. 623.

[14th A protects the right to purchase or sell labor]

[however, gov. does police that right to protect the pp.]

The state, therefore, has power to prevent the individual from making certain kinds of contracts, and in regard to them the Federal Constitution offers no protection. If the contract be one which the state, in the legitimate exercise of its police power, has the right to prohibit, it is not prevented from prohibiting it by the 14th Amendment. Contracts in violation of a statute, either of the Federal or state government, or a contract to let one's property for immoral purposes, or to do any other unlawful act, could obtain no protection from the Federal Constitution, as coming under the liberty of person or of free contract. ***

[not protected if at odds w/ state or fed. law.]

This court has recognized the existence and upheld the exercise of the police powers of the states in many cases which might fairly be considered as border ones, and it has, in the course of its determination of questions regarding the asserted invalidity of such statutes, on the ground of their violation of the rights secured by the Federal Constitution, been guided by rules of a very liberal nature, the application of which has resulted, in numerous instances, in upholding the validity of state statutes thus assailed. Among the later cases where the state law has been upheld by this court is that of *Holden v. Hardy.* A provision in the act of the legislature of Utah was there under consideration, the act limiting the employment of workmen in all underground mines or workings, to eight hours per day, 'except in cases of emergency, where life or property is in imminent danger.' *** The act was held to be a valid exercise of the police powers of the state. *** It was held that the kind of employment, mining, smelting, etc., and the character of the employees in such kinds of labor, were such as to make it reasonable and proper for the state to interfere to prevent the employees from being constrained by the rules laid down by the proprietors in regard to labor. [However, there] is nothing in *Holden v. Hardy* which covers the case now before us. ***

It must, of course, be conceded that there is a limit to the valid exercise of the police power by the state. There is no dispute concerning this general proposition. *** In every case that comes before this court, therefore, where legislation of this character is concerned, and where the protection of the Federal Constitution is sought, the question necessarily arises: Is this a fair, reasonable, and appropriate exercise of the police power of the state, or is it an unreasonable, unnecessary, and arbitrary interference with the right of the individual to his personal liberty, or to enter into those contracts in relation to labor which may seem to him appropriate or necessary for the support of himself and his family?

[margin note:] Question asked to determine the legitimacy of a police power.

This is not a question of substituting the judgment of the court for that of the legislature. If the act be within the power of the state it is valid, although the judgment of the court might be totally opposed to the enactment of such a law. But the question would still remain: Is it within the police power of the state? ***

The question whether this act is valid as a labor law, pure and simple, may be dismissed in a few words. There is no reasonable ground for interfering with the liberty of person or the right of free contract, by determining the hours of labor, in the occupation of a baker. There is no contention that bakers as a class are not equal in intelligence and capacity to men in other trades or manual occupations, or that they are not able to assert their rights and care for themselves without the protecting arm of the state, interfering with their independence of judgment and of action. They are in no sense wards of the state. Viewed in the light of a purely labor law, with no reference whatever to the question of health, we think that a law like the one before us involves neither the safety, the morals, nor the welfare, of the public, and that the interest of the public is not in the slightest degree affected by such an act. The law must be upheld, if at all, as a law pertaining to the health of the individual engaged in the occupation of a baker. It does not affect any other portion of the public than those who are engaged in that occupation. Clean and wholesome bread does not depend upon whether the baker works but ten hours per day or only sixty hours a week. The limitation

[margin note:] law is not within the police power of NY

of the hours of labor does not come within the police power on that ground. ***

VIII–1. Joseph Lochner's Bakery. Photograph by Dante Tranquille for the Utica Observer–Dispatch, ca. 1930.

The mere assertion that the subject relates, though but in a remote degree, to the public health, does not necessarily render the enactment valid. The act must have a more direct relation, *** before an act can be held to be valid which interferes with the general right of an individual to be free in his person and in his power to contract in relation to his own labor. ***

[handwritten margin note: Does not relate enough to public health]

We think the limit of the police power has been reached and passed in this case. There is, in our judgment, no reasonable foundation for holding this to be necessary or appropriate as a health law to safeguard the public health, or the health of the individuals who are following the trade of a baker. If this statute be valid, and if, therefore, a proper case is made out in which to deny the right of an individual, sui juris, as employer or employee, to make contracts for the labor of the latter under the protection of the provisions of the Federal Constitution, there would seem to be no length to which legislation of this nature might not go. ***

[handwritten margin note: Goes too far and would give the state too much power]

We think that there can be no fair doubt that the trade of a baker, in and of itself, is not an unhealthy one to that degree which would authorize the legislature to interfere with the right to labor, and with the right of free contract on the part of the individual, either as employer or employee. In looking through statistics regarding all trades and occupations, it may be true that the trade of a baker does not appear to be as healthy as some other

Although bakers may be commonly unhealthy, they are far more healthy than other areas

trades, and is also vastly more healthy than still others. To the common understanding the trade of a baker has never been regarded as an unhealthy one. *** There must be more than the mere fact of the possible existence of some small amount of unhealthiness to warrant legislative interference with liberty. It is unfortunately true that labor, even in any department, may possibly carry with it the seeds of unhealthiness. But are we all, on that account, at the mercy of legislative majorities? *** No trade, no occupation, no mode of earning one's living, could escape this all-pervading power, and the acts of the legislature in limiting the hours of labor in all employments would be valid, although such limitation might seriously cripple the ability of the laborer to support himself and his family. ***

It is also urged, pursuing the same line of argument, that it is to the interest of the state that its population should be strong and robust, and therefore any legislation which may be said to tend to make people healthy must be valid as health laws, enacted under the police power. If this be a valid argument and a justification for this kind of legislation, it follows that the protection of the Federal Constitution from undue interference with liberty of person and freedom of contract is visionary, wherever the law is sought to be justified as a valid exercise of the police power. Scarcely any law but might find shelter under such assumptions, and conduct, properly so called, as well as contract, would come under the restrictive sway of the legislature. Not only the hours of employees, but the hours of employers, could be regulated, and doctors, lawyers, scientists, all professional men, as well as athletes and artisans, could be forbidden to fatigue their brains and bodies by prolonged hours of exercise, lest the fighting strength of the state be impaired. *** [Such a law] is not, within any fair meaning of the term, a health law, but is an illegal interference with the rights of individuals, both employers and employees, to make contracts regarding labor upon such terms as they may think best, or which they may agree upon with the other parties to such contracts. Statutes of the nature of that under review, limiting the hours in which grown and intelligent men may labor to earn their living, are mere meddlesome interferences with the rights of the individual, and they are not saved from condemnation by the claim that they are passed in the exercise of the police power and upon the subject of the health of the individual whose rights are interfered with, unless there be some fair ground, reasonable in and of itself, to say that there is material danger to the public health, or to the health of the employees, if the hours of labor are not curtailed. *** All that [the State] could properly do has been done by it with

State should stick with just maintaining standards

regard to the conduct of bakeries, as provided for in the other sections of the act, [which] provide for the inspection of the premises where the bakery is carried on, with regard to furnishing proper wash rooms and waterclosets, *** with regard to providing proper drainage, plumbing, and painting, *** and for other things of that nature. ***

NY also argued that bakers were cleaner when working less

It was further urged *** that restricting the hours of labor in the case of bakers was valid because it tended to cleanliness on the part of the workers, as a man was more apt to be cleanly when not overworked, and if cleanly then his "output" was also more likely to be so ***. In our judgment it is not possible in fact to discover the connection between the number of hours a baker may work in the bakery and the healthful quality of the bread made by the workman. *** When assertions such as [these are made], it gives rise to at least a suspicion that there was some other motive dominating the legislature than the purpose to subserve the public health or welfare. *** Under such circumstances the freedom of master and employee to contract with each other in relation to their employment, and in defining the same, cannot be prohibited or interfered with, without violating the Federal Constitution. ***

MR. JUSTICE HOLMES dissenting:

*** This case is decided upon an economic theory which a large part of the country does not entertain. If it were a question whether I agreed with that theory, I should desire to study it further and long before making up my mind. But I do not conceive that to be my duty, because I strongly believe that my agreement or disagreement has nothing to do with the right of a majority to embody their opinions in law. It is settled by various decisions of this court that state constitutions and state laws may regulate life in many ways which we as legislators might think as injudicious, or if you like as tyrannical, as this, and which, equally with this, interfere with the liberty to contract. Sunday laws and usury laws are ancient examples. A more modern one is the prohibition of lotteries. The liberty of the citizen to do as he likes so long as he does not interfere with the liberty of others to do the same, which has been a shibboleth for some well-known writers, is interfered with by school laws, by the Post Office, by every state or municipal institution which takes his money for purposes thought desirable, whether he likes it or not. The 14th Amendment does not enact Mr. Herbert Spencer's Social Statics. The other day we sustained the Massachusetts vaccination law. *Jacobson v. Massachusetts*, 197 U.S. 11. United States and State statutes and decisions cutting down the liberty to contract by way of combination are familiar to this court. *** The decision sustaining an eight-hour law for miners is still recent. *Holden v. Hardy.* Some of these laws embody convictions or prejudices which judges are likely to share. Some may not. But a Constitution is not intended to embody a particular economic theory, whether of paternalism and the organic relation of the citizen to the state or of laissez faire. It is made for people of fundamentally differing views, and the accident of our finding certain opinions natural and familiar, or novel, and even shocking, ought not to conclude our judgment upon the question whether statutes embodying them conflict with the Constitution of the United States.

Due Process clause does not protect capitalism

General propositions do not decide concrete cases. The decision will depend on a judgment or intuition more subtle than any articulate major premise. But I think that the proposition just stated, if it is accepted, will carry us far toward the end. Every opinion tends to become a law. I think that the word "liberty," in the 14th Amendment, is perverted when it is held to prevent the natural outcome of a dominant opinion, unless it can be said that a rational and fair man necessarily would admit that the statute proposed would infringe fundamental principles as they have been understood by the traditions of our people and our law. It does not need research to show that no such sweeping condemnation can be passed upon the statute before us. A reasonable man might think it a proper measure on the score of health. Men whom I certainly could not pronounce unreasonable would uphold it as a first instalment of a general regulation of the hours of work. ***

MR. JUSTICE HARLAN (with whom MR. JUSTICE WHITE and MR. JUSTICE DAY concurred) dissenting:

*** It is plain that this statute was enacted in order to protect the physical well-being of those who work in bakery and confectionery establishments. It may be that the statute had its origin, in part, in the belief that employers and employees in such establishments were not upon an equal footing, and that the necessities of the latter often compelled them to submit to such exactions as unduly taxed their strength. Be this as it may, the statute must be taken as expressing the belief of the people of New York that, as a general rule, and in the case of the average man, labor in excess of sixty hours during a week in such establishments may endanger the health of those who thus labor. Whether or not this be wise legislation it is not the province of the court to inquire. *** [I]n determining the question of power to interfere with liberty of contract, the court may inquire whether the means devised by the state are germane to an end which may be lawfully accomplished and have a real or substantial relation to the protection of health, as involved in the daily work of the persons, male and female, engaged in bakery and confectionery establishments. ***

> Professor Hirt in his treatise on the "Diseases of the Workers" has said:

> "The labor of the bakers is among the hardest and most laborious imaginable, because it has to be performed under conditions injurious to the health of those engaged in it. It is hard, very hard, work, not only because it requires a great deal of physical exertion in an overheated workshop and during unreasonably long hours, but more so because of the erratic demands of the public, compelling the baker to perform the greater part of his work at night, thus depriving him of an opportunity to enjoy the necessary rest and sleep,—a fact which is highly injurious to his health."

Another writer says:

> "The constant inhaling of flour dust causes inflammation of the lungs and of the bronchial tubes. The eyes also suffer through this dust, which is responsible for the many cases of running eyes among the bakers. The long hours of toil to which all bakers are subjected produce rheumatism, cramps, and swollen legs. The intense heat in the workshops induces the workers to resort to cooling drinks, which, together with their habit of exposing the greater part of their bodies to the change in the atmosphere, is another source of a number of diseases of various organs."

*** We judicially know that the question of the number of hours during which a workman should continuously labor has been, for a long period, and is yet, a subject of serious consideration among civilized peoples, and by those having special knowledge of the laws of health. *** We cannot say that the state has acted without reason, nor ought we to proceed upon the theory that its action is a mere sham. *** [T]he health and safety of the people of a state are primarily for the state to guard and protect. ***

WEST COAST HOTEL CO. v. PARRISH
300 U.S. 379 (1937)

MR. CHIEF JUSTICE HUGHES delivered the opinion of the Court.

This case presents the question of the constitutional validity of the minimum wage law of the state of Washington. *** The appellant conducts a hotel. The appellee Elsie Parrish was employed as a chambermaid and (with her husband) brought this suit to recover the difference between the wages paid her and the minimum wage fixed pursuant to the state law.

Paid less then state min. wage

The appellant relies upon the decision of this Court in *Adkins v. Children's Hospital*, 261 U.S. 525, which held invalid the District of Columbia Minimum Wage Act which was attacked under the due process clause of the Fifth Amendment. On the argument at bar, counsel for the appellees attempted to distinguish the *Adkins* Case upon the ground that the appellee was employed in a hotel and that the business of an innkeeper was affected with a public interest. That effort at distinction is obviously futile, as it appears that in one of the cases ruled by the *Adkins* opinion the employee was a woman employed as an elevator operator in a hotel. ***

The Supreme Court of Washington has upheld the minimum wage statute of that state. It has decided that the statute is a reasonable exercise of the police power of the state. *** The state court has refused to regard the decision in the *Adkins* Case as determinative and has pointed to our decisions both before and since that case as justifying its position. We are of the opinion that this ruling of the state court demands on our part a re-examination of the *Adkins* Case***

The principle which must control our decision is not in doubt. The constitutional provision invoked is the due process clause of the Fourteenth Amendment governing the states, as the due process clause invoked in the *Adkins* Case governed Congress. In each case the violation alleged by those attacking minimum wage regulation for women is deprivation of freedom of contract. What is this freedom? The Constitution does not speak of freedom of contract. It speaks of liberty and prohibits the deprivation of liberty without due process of law. In prohibiting that deprivation, the Constitution does not recognize an absolute and uncontrollable liberty. Liberty in each of its phases has its history and connotation. But the liberty safeguarded is liberty in a social organization which requires the protection of law against the evils which menace the health, safety, morals, and welfare of the people. Liberty under the Constitution is thus necessarily subject to the restraints of due process, and regulation which is reasonable in relation to its subject and is adopted in the interests of the community is due process. ***

Right to contract is not fundamental

This power under the Constitution to restrict freedom of contract has had many illustrations. That it may be exercised in the public interest with respect to contracts between employer and employee is undeniable. *** In dealing with the relation of employer and employed, the Legislature has necessarily a wide field of discretion in order that there may be suitable protection of health and safety, and that peace and good order may be promoted through regulations designed to insure wholesome conditions of work and freedom from oppression. ***

The minimum wage to be paid under the Washington statute is fixed after full consideration by representatives of employers, employees, and the public. It may be assumed that the minimum wage is fixed in consideration of the services that are performed in the particular occupations under normal conditions. Provision is made for special licenses at less wages in the case of women who are incapable of full service. The statement of MR. JUSTICE HOLMES in the *Adkins* Case is pertinent: "This statute does not compel anybody to pay anything. It simply forbids employment at rates below those fixed as the minimum requirement of health and right living. It is safe to assume that women will not be employed at even the lowest wages allowed unless they earn them, or unless the employer's business can sustain the burden. In short the law in its character and operation is like hundreds of so-called police laws that have been up-held." ***

We think that the view thus expressed [is] sound and that the decision in the *Adkins* Case was a departure from the true application of the principles governing the regulation by the state of the relation of employer and employed. Those principles have been reinforced by our subsequent decisions. *** What can be closer to the public interest than the health of women and their protection from unscrupulous and overreaching employers? And if the protection of women is a legitimate end of the exercise of state power, how can it be said that the requirement of the payment of a minimum wage fairly fixed in order to meet the very necessities of existence is not an admissible means to that end? The Legislature of the state was clearly entitled to consider the situation of women in employment, the fact that they are in the class receiving the least pay, that their bargaining power is relatively weak, and that they are the ready victims of those who would take advantage of their necessitous circumstances. The Legislature was entitled to adopt measures to reduce the evils of the "sweating system," the exploiting of workers at wages so low as to be insufficient to meet the bare cost of living, thus making their very helplessness the occasion of a most injurious competition. The Legislature had the right to consider that its minimum wage requirements would be an important aid in carrying out its policy of protection. The adoption of similar requirements by many states evidences a deep-seated conviction both as to the presence of the evil and as to the means adapted to check it. Legislative response to that conviction cannot be regarded as arbitrary or capricious and that is all we have to decide. Even if the wisdom of the policy be regarded as debatable and its effects uncertain, still the Legislature is entitled to its judgment.

There is an additional and compelling consideration which recent economic experience has brought into a strong light. The exploitation of a class of workers who are in an unequal position with respect to bargaining power and are thus relatively defenseless against the denial of a living wage is not only detrimental to their health and well being, but casts a direct burden for their support upon the community. What these workers lose in wages the taxpayers are called upon to pay. The bare cost of living must be met. We may take judicial notice of the unparalleled demands for relief which arose during the recent period of depression and still continue to an alarming extent despite the degree of economic recovery which has been achieved. ***
The argument that the legislation in question constitutes an arbitrary discrimination, because it does not extend to men, is unavailing. This Court has frequently held that the legislative authority, acting within its proper field, is not bound to extend its regulation to all cases which it might possibly reach. The Legislature "is free to recognize degrees of harm and it may confine its restrictions to those classes of cases where the need is deemed to be clearest." If "the law presumably hits the evil where it is most felt, it is not to be overthrown because there are other instances to which it might have been applied." There is no 'doctrinaire requirement' that the legislation should be couched in all embracing terms. *** *Adkins v. Children's Hospital*, should be, and it is, overruled. ***

MR. JUSTICE SUTHERLAND, MR. JUSTICE VAN DEVANTER, MR. JUSTICE MCREYNOLDS, and MR. JUSTICE BUTLER, [dissenting].

*** [The statutes challenged here fix] minimum wages for adult women. Adult men and their employers are left free to bargain as they please; and it is a significant and an important fact that all state statutes to which our attention has been called are of like character. The common-law rules restricting the power of women to make contracts have, under our system, long since practically disappeared. Women today stand upon a legal and political equality with men. There is no longer any reason why they should be put in different classes in respect of their legal right to make contracts; nor should they be denied, in effect, the right to compete with men for work paying lower wages which men may be willing to accept. And it is an arbitrary exercise of the legislative power to do so. *** Since the contractual rights of men and women are the same, does the legislation here involved, by restricting only the rights of women to make contracts as to wages, create an arbitrary discrimination? We think it does. Difference of sex affords no reasonable ground for making a restriction applicable to the wage contracts of all working women from which like contracts of all working men are left free. Certainly a suggestion that the bargaining ability of the average woman is not equal to that of the average man would lack substance. The ability to make a fair bargain, as every one knows, does not depend upon sex. If *** such legislation in respect of men was properly omitted on the ground that it would be unconstitutional, the same conclusion of unconstitutionality is inescapable in respect of similar legislative restraint in the case of women. ***

Notes

1. **Critique of *Lochner*.**

   • The Constitution says nothing about theories of economics.

   • The state had legitimate justifications for regulation.

   • There is no "private" sphere of worker-management "liberty."

   • The Court took as a given an inappropriate common law "baseline."

2. **Defense of *Lochner*.**

   • The decision was good policy, at least for consumers of baked goods.

   • The statute was not a health measure at all, nor the result of bargaining inequality; it was rent-seeking by big unions and large employers.

   • There was more Constitutional text (if you include the Contracts and Takings Clauses) than with other substantive due process interpretations.

3. **Modern Economic Substantive Due Process**. Does the following case indicate a revival of economic substantive due process? Do other parts of the constitutional scheme underlie the application of due process here?

STATE FARM v. CAMPBELL
538 U.S. 408 (2003)

JUSTICE KENNEDY delivered the opinion of the Court.

We address once again the measure of punishment, by means of punitive damages, a State may impose upon a defendant in a civil case. The question is whether, in the circumstances we shall recount, an award of $145 million in punitive damages, where full compensatory damages are $1 million, is excessive and in violation of the Due Process Clause of the Fourteenth Amendment to the Constitution of the United States.

In 1981, Curtis Campbell (Campbell) was driving with his wife, Inez Preece Campbell, in Cache County, Utah. He decided to pass six vans traveling ahead of them on a two-lane highway. Todd Ospital was driving a small car approaching from the opposite direction. To avoid a head-on collision with Campbell, who by then was driving on the wrong side of the highway and toward oncoming traffic, Ospital swerved onto the shoulder, lost control of his automobile, and collided with a vehicle driven by Robert G. Slusher. Ospital was killed, and Slusher was rendered permanently disabled. The Campbells escaped unscathed.

In the ensuing wrongful death and tort action, *** "a consensus was reached early on by the investigators and witnesses that Mr. Campbell's unsafe pass had indeed caused the crash." Campbell's insurance company, petitioner State Farm Mutual Automobile Insurance Company (State Farm), nonetheless decided to contest liability and declined offers *** to settle the claims for the policy limit of $50,000 ($25,000 per claimant). State Farm also ignored the advice of one of its own investigators and took the case to trial, assuring the Campbells that "their assets were safe, that they had no liability for the accident, that [State Farm] would represent their interests, and that they did not need to procure separate counsel." To the contrary, a jury determined that Campbell was 100 percent at fault, and a judgment was returned for $185,849, far more than the amount offered in settlement.

At first State Farm refused to cover the $135,849 in excess liability. *** In 1989, the Utah Supreme Court denied Campbell's appeal in the wrongful death and tort actions. State Farm then paid the entire judgment, including the amounts in excess of the policy limits. The Campbells nonetheless filed a complaint against State Farm alleging bad faith, fraud, and intentional infliction of emotional distress. *** [At trial] the jury determined that State Farm's decision not to settle was unreasonable because there was a substantial likelihood of an excess verdict.

Before the second phase of the action against State Farm we decided *BMW of North America, Inc. v. Gore,* 517 U.S. 559 (1996), and refused to sustain a $2 million punitive damages award which accompanied a verdict of only $4,000 in compensatory damages. *** The jury awarded the Campbells $2.6 million in compensatory damages [later reduced to $1 million] and $145 million in punitive damages. *** [I]n our judicial system compensatory and punitive damages, although usually awarded at the same time by the same decisionmaker, serve different purposes. Compensatory damages "are intended to redress the concrete loss that the plaintiff has suffered by reason of the defendant's wrongful conduct." By contrast, punitive damages serve a broader function; they are aimed at deterrence and retribution.

While States possess discretion over the imposition of punitive damages, it is well established that there are procedural and substantive constitutional limitations on these awards. The Due Process Clause of the Fourteenth Amendment prohibits the imposition of grossly excessive or arbitrary punishments on a tortfeasor. *** To the extent an award is grossly excessive, it furthers no legitimate purpose and constitutes an arbitrary deprivation of property. *** "[T]he most important indicium of the reasonableness of a punitive damages award is the degree of reprehensibility of the defendant's conduct. *** [W]e must acknowledge that State Farm's handling of the claims against the Campbells merits no praise. *** While we do not suggest there was error in awarding punitive damages based upon State Farm's conduct toward the Campbells, a more modest punishment for this reprehensible conduct could have satisfied the State's legitimate objectives, and the Utah courts should have gone no further.

This case, instead, was used as a platform to expose, and punish, the perceived deficiencies of State Farm's operations throughout the country. The Utah Supreme Court's opinion makes explicit that State Farm was being condemned for its nationwide policies rather than for the conduct direct toward the Campbells. This was, as well, an explicit rationale of the trial court's decision in approving the award ***. The Campbells contend that State Farm has only itself to blame for the reliance upon dissimilar and out-of-state conduct evidence. The record does not support this contention. From their opening statements onward the Campbells framed this case as a chance to rebuke State Farm for its nationwide activities. *** A State cannot punish a defendant for conduct that may have been lawful where it occurred. Nor, as a general rule, does a State have a legitimate concern in imposing punitive damages to punish a defendant for unlawful acts committed outside of the State's jurisdiction. Any proper adjudication of conduct that occurred outside Utah to other persons would require their inclusion, and, to those parties, the Utah courts, in the usual case, would need to apply the laws of their relevant jurisdiction.

Here, the Campbells do not dispute that much of the out- of-state conduct was lawful where it occurred. They argue, however, that such evidence was not the primary basis for the punitive damages award and was relevant to the extent it demonstrated, in a general sense, State Farm's motive against its insured. This argument misses the mark. Lawful out-of-state conduct may be probative when it demonstrates the deliberateness and culpability of the defendant's action in the State where it is tortious, but that conduct must have a nexus to the specific harm suffered by the plaintiff. A jury must be instructed, furthermore, that it may not use evidence of out-of-state conduct to punish a defendant for action that was lawful in the jurisdiction where it occurred. A basic principle of federalism is that each State may make its own reasoned judgment about what conduct is permitted or proscribed within its borders, and each State alone can determine what measure of punishment, if any, to impose on a defendant who acts within its jurisdiction.

For a more fundamental reason, however, the Utah courts erred in relying upon this and other evidence: The courts awarded punitive damages to punish and deter conduct that bore no relation to the Campbells' harm. A defendant's dissimilar acts, independent from the acts upon which liability was premised, may not serve as the basis for punitive damages. A defendant should be punished for the conduct that harmed the plaintiff, not for being an unsavory individual or business. Due process does not permit courts, in the calculation of punitive damages, to adjudicate the merits of other parties' hypothetical claims against a defendant under the guise of the reprehensibility analysis, but we have no doubt the Utah Supreme Court did that here. Punishment on these bases creates the possibility of multiple punitive damages awards for the same conduct; for in the usual case nonparties are not bound by the judgment some other plaintiff obtains. ***

[W]e have been reluctant to identify concrete constitutional limits on the ratio between harm, or potential harm, to the plaintiff and the punitive damages award. We decline again to impose a bright-line ratio which a punitive damages award cannot exceed. Our jurisprudence and the principles it has now established demonstrate, however, that, in practice, few awards exceeding a single-digit ratio between punitive and compensatory damages, to a significant degree, will satisfy due process. In [earlier cases,] in upholding a punitive damages award, we concluded that an award of more than four times the amount of compensatory damages might be close to the line of constitutional impropriety. *** The Court further referenced a long legislative history, dating back over 700 years and going forward to today, providing for sanctions of double, treble, or quadruple damages to deter and punish. While these ratios are not binding, they are instructive. They demonstrate what should be obvious: Single-digit multipliers are more likely to comport with due process, while still achieving the State's goals of deterrence and retribution, than awards with ratios in range of 500 to 1, or, in this case, of 145 to 1.

Nonetheless, because there are no rigid benchmarks that a punitive damages award may not surpass, ratios greater than those we have previously upheld may comport with due process where "a particularly egregious act has resulted in only a small amount of economic damages." The converse is also true, however. When compensatory damages are substantial, then a lesser ratio, perhaps only equal to compensatory damages, can reach the outermost limit of the due process guarantee. The precise award in any case, of course, must be based upon the facts and circumstances of the defendant's conduct and the harm to the plaintiff.

In sum, courts must ensure that the measure of punishment is both reasonable and proportionate to the amount of harm to the plaintiff and to the general damages recovered. In the context of this case, we have no doubt that there is a presumption against an award that has a 145-to-1 ratio. The compensatory award in this case was substantial; the Campbells were awarded $1 million for a year and a half of emotional distress. This was complete compensation. The harm arose from a transaction in the economic realm, not from some physical assault or trauma; there were no physical injuries; and State Farm paid the excess verdict before the complaint was filed, so the Campbells suffered only minor economic injuries for the 18-month period in which State Farm refused to resolve the claim against them. The compensatory damages for the injury suffered here, moreover, likely were based on a component which was duplicated in the punitive award. Much of the distress was caused by the outrage and humiliation the Campbells suffered at the actions of their insurer; and it is a major role of punitive damages to condemn such conduct. Compensatory damages, however, already contain this punitive element.

The Utah Supreme Court sought to justify the massive award by pointing to State Farm's purported failure to report a prior $100 million punitive damages award in Texas to its corporate headquarters; the fact that State Farm's policies have affected numerous Utah consumers; the fact that State Farm will only be punished in one out of every 50,000 cases as a matter of statistical probability; and State Farm's enormous wealth. Since the Supreme Court of Utah discussed the Texas award when applying the ratio guidepost, we discuss it here. The Texas award, however, should have been analyzed in the context of the reprehensibility guidepost only. The failure of the company to report the Texas award is out-of-state conduct that, if the conduct were similar, might have had some bearing on the degree of reprehensibility, subject to the limitations we have described. Here, it was dissimilar, and of such marginal relevance that it should have been accorded little or no weight. The award was rendered in a first-party lawsuit; no judgment was entered in the case; and it was later settled for a fraction of the verdict. With respect to the Utah Supreme Court's second justification, the Campbells' inability to direct us to testimony demonstrating harm to the people of Utah (other than those directly involved in this case) indicates that the adverse effect on the State's general population was in fact minor.

The remaining premises for the Utah Supreme Court's decision bear no relation to the award's reasonableness or proportionality to the harm. They are, rather, arguments that seek to defend a departure from well-established constraints on punitive damages. While States enjoy considerable discretion in deducing when punitive damages are warranted, each award must comport with the principles set forth in *Gore*. Here the argument that State Farm will be punished in only the rare case, coupled with reference to its assets (which, of course, are what other insured parties in Utah and other States must rely upon for payment of claims) had little to do with the actual harm sustained by the Campbells. The wealth of a defendant cannot justify an otherwise unconstitutional punitive damages award. The principles set forth in *Gore* must be implemented with care, to ensure both reasonableness and proportionality.

The third guidepost in *Gore* is the disparity between the punitive damages award and the "civil penalties authorized or imposed in comparable cases." *** Great care must be taken to avoid use of the civil process to assess criminal penalties that can be imposed only after the heightened protections of a criminal trial have been observed, including, of course, its higher standards of proof. Punitive damages are not a substitute for the criminal process ***. The most relevant civil sanction under Utah state law for the wrong done to the Campbells appears to be a $10,000 fine for an act of fraud, an amount dwarfed by the $145 million punitive damages award. The Supreme Court of Utah speculated about the loss of State Farm's business license, the disgorgement of profits, and possible imprisonment, but here again its references were to the broad fraudulent scheme drawn from evidence of out-of-state and dissimilar conduct. This analysis was insufficient to justify the award. *** The punitive award of $145 million, therefore, was neither reasonable nor proportionate to the wrong committed, and it was an irrational and arbitrary deprivation of the property of the defendant. The proper calculation of punitive damages under the principles we have discussed should be resolved, in the first instance, by the Utah courts. ***

JUSTICE SCALIA, dissenting.

*** [T]he Due Process Clause provides no substantive protections against "excessive" or "'unreasonable'" awards of punitive damages. ***

JUSTICE THOMAS, dissenting.

*** [T]he Constitution does not constrain the size of punitive damages awards. ***

JUSTICE GINSBURG, dissenting.

*** The large size of the award upheld by the Utah Supreme Court in this case indicates why damage-capping legislation may be altogether fitting and proper. Neither the amount of the award nor the trial record, however, justifies this Court's substitution of its judgment for that of Utah's competent decisionmakers. *** State Farm's "policies and practices," the trial evidence thus bore out, were "responsible for the injuries suffered by the Campbells," and the means used to implement those policies could be found "callous, clandestine, fraudulent, and dishonest." The Utah Supreme Court, relying on the trial court's record-based recitations, understandably characterized State Farm's behavior as "egregious and malicious." ***

What is infirm about the Campbells' theory that their experience with State Farm exemplifies and reflects an overarching underpayment scheme, one that caused "repeated misconduct of the sort that injured them"? The Court's silence on that score is revealing: Once one recognizes that the Campbells did show "conduct by State Farm similar to that which harmed them," it becomes impossible to shrink the reprehensibility analysis to this sole case, or to maintain, at odds with the determination of the trial court, that "the adverse effect on the State's general population was in fact minor."

Evidence of out-of-state conduct, the Court acknowledges, may be probative [even if the conduct is lawful in the state where it occurred] when it demonstrates the deliberateness and culpability of the defendant's action in the State where it is tortuous *** Viewed in this light, there surely was "a nexus" between much of the "other acts" evidence and "the specific harm suffered by [the Campbells]."

When the Court first ventured to override state-court punitive damages awards, it did so moderately. The Court recalled that "[i]n our federal system, States necessarily have considerable flexibility in determining the level of punitive damages that they will allow in different classes of cases and in any particular case." Today's decision exhibits no such respect and restraint. No longer content to accord state-court judgments "a strong presumption of validity," the Court announces that "few awards exceeding a single-digit ratio between punitive and compensatory damages, to a significant degree, will satisfy due process." Moreover, the Court adds, when compensatory damages are substantial, doubling those damages "can reach the outermost limit of the due process guarantee." In a legislative scheme or a state high court's design to cap punitive damages, the handiwork in setting single-digit and 1-to-1 benchmarks could hardly be questioned; in a judicial decree imposed on the States by this Court under the banner of substantive due process, the numerical controls today's decision installs seem to me boldly out of order. ***

Notes

1. **Horizontal Federalism**. This case protects states from overreaching by their neighbors. That, as we have seen earlier in this book, is often a matter of Dormant Commerce Clause concern or the Article IV Privileges and Immunities Clause. Consider whether these other approaches would work in *State Farm*.

2. **Dormant Commerce Clause**. Is the Court using Due Process Clause analysis like Dormant Commerce Clause analysis in Chapter VI to restrict states from exporting economic consequences outside their borders? Consider this language: "[A] State [does not] have a legitimate concern in imposing punitive damages to punish a defendant for unlawful acts committed outside of the State's

jurisdiction. Any proper adjudication of conduct that occurred outside Utah to other persons would require their inclusion, and, to those parties, the Utah courts, in the usual case, would need to apply the laws of their relevant jurisdiction." Should discrimination or burdens on commerce analysis have been argued here?

3.   **Federal Legislation**. Does the Court's decision point to the need for a Congressional solution to tort liability issues?

4.   **The Substance and Process of Punitive Damages**. In *Philip Morris USA v. Williams*, 549 U.S. 346, (2007), a jury found that Williams' death was caused by smoking induced by Philip Morris' advertising. It awarded compensatory damages of about $821,000 along with $79.5 million in punitive damages. The case seemed similar to *Campbell*, but the Court decided it on procedural grounds, dodging whether the award was grossly excessive. The Court explained: "How can we know whether a jury, in taking account of harm caused others under the rubric of reprehensibility, also seeks to *punish* the defendant for having caused injury to others? Our answer is that state courts cannot authorize procedures that create an unreasonable and unnecessary risk of any such confusion occurring." JUSTICE THOMAS said that "It matters not that the Court styles today's holding as 'procedural' because the 'procedural' rule is simply a confusing implementation of the substantive due process regime this Court has created for punitive damages." JUSTICES GINSBURG, SCALIA and THOMAS further dissented, saying; "[C]onduct that risks harm to many is likely more reprehensible than conduct that risks harm to only a few." *Philip Morris* may provide a way for the Court to avoid bright-line rules concerning the relationship between actual damages and punitive damages.

5.   **Maritime Law, Federal Law, and more Due Process Limits?** In *Exxon v. Baker*, 554 U.S. 471 (2008), the Supreme Court held that a jury award of $5 billion dollars for a massive oil tanker spill in Alaska should be reduced to $507.5 million, an amount equal to the compensatory damages awarded. The Court said the ratio between compensatory and punitive damages was "a central feature in our due process analysis." It then cited studies showing that "the compensatory award exceeds the punitive award in most cases" and concluded that "given the need to protect against the possibility (and the disruptive cost to the legal system) of awards that are unpredictable and unnecessary, either for deterrence or for measured retribution, we consider that a 1:1 ratio *** is a fair upper limit in such maritime cases." JUSTICE GINSBURG, concurring in part and dissenting in part, noted: "[T]he Court's lawmaking prompts many questions. *** What ratio will the Court set for defendants who acted maliciously or in pursuit of financial gain? Should the magnitude of the risk increase the ratio and, if so, by how much? *** [I]s the Court holding only that 1:1 is the maritime-law ceiling, or is it also signaling that any ratio higher than 1:1 will be held to exceed "the constitutional outer limit"? On next opportunity, will the Court rule, definitively, that 1:1 is the ceiling due process requires in all of the States, and for all federal claims?"

6. **The Takings Clause.** The final clause of the Fifth Amendment provides: "nor shall private property be taken for public use, without just compensation." Generally, American law schools cover the Takings Clause in Property rather than Constitutional Law. Despite this, a few words about this clause are appropriate. Its most obvious application is to government condemnation of real estate for roads and other public projects. *Loretto v. Teleprompter*, 458 U.S. 419

(1982) established the bright-line rule that a permanent physical occupation is always a taking – even something as small as a cable line attached to a building. The clause has also been applied where governmental activity, from flooding connected with damming rivers to noise associated with a public airport, renders private real estate unusable or virtually unusable. More complex issues are raised when governmental regulation reduces the value of individual or business properties. Compare *Pennsylvania Coal v. Mahon*, 260 U.S. 393 (1922) (regulation making coal mining completely uneconomical violates Takings Clause) with *Keystone Bituminous Coal Association v. DeBenedictis*, 480 U.S. 470 (1987) (regulation does not violate clause absent findings that coal holdings were worthless). The Court has recognized that "Government hardly could go on if to some extent values incident to property could not be diminished without paying for every such change *** [therefore] government may execute laws or programs that adversely affect recognized economic values." *Penn Central Transportation Co. v. City of New York*, 438 U.S. 104 (1978). However, even in a regulatory context, it has sometimes required the state to compensate property owners for loss of "all beneficial uses" unless the state can "identify background principles of nuisance and property law that prohibit the uses he now intends in the circumstances in which the property is presently found." *Lucas v. South Carolina Coastal Council*, 505 U.S. 1003 (1992). To date, the Supreme Court has not addressed what compensation, if any, would be required if a regulation partially takes a person's property nor has it considered how damages should be measured in regulatory takings cases. In *Kelo v. City of New London*, 545 U.S. 469 (2005), the Court held that, although government cannot take a person's property for private use, a city development plan that included commercial, recreational, and residential elements designed to revitalize the city's ailing economy was a "public use."

7. **The Contracts Clause.** One clause that explicitly protects economic liberty or property interests is Article I, § 10, cl. 1: "No State shall [pass any Law] impairing the Obligation of Contracts." Because this clause is a restriction on States, it is considered in Chapter V.

2. "INCORPORATED" PERSONAL RIGHTS

While strongly repudiating economic substantive due process, the Court has taken a very different course in interpreting what "personal rights" are protected by the Due Process Clause of the Fourteenth Amendment. This introductory note will examine how this clause has come to protect virtually all the personal rights enumerated in the first eight amendments to the Constitution. It will also touch on how the Due Process Clause of the Fifth Amendment, applicable to the federal government, has come to encompass an equal protection component. The remainder of the chapter will focus on personal rights other than those explicitly applicable against either the state or federal government that have come to be protected through judicial interpretation.

Both the Fifth and Fourteenth Amendments require "due process of law." The former provision was adopted to ensure that the federal government did not dispense with basic protections of rights with origins going back to the English Magna Carta of 1215. The latter added a similarly worded limitation applicable to the states. The textual parallelism appears to end here, however. The Fifth Amendment does not contain any reference to the "equal protection of the laws" and the Fourteenth Amendment does not say anything about matters contained in the Bill of Rights (freedom of speech, freedom of religion, the right to bear arms, cruel and unusual punishment, jury trials, double jeopardy, self-incrimination, etc.). During the end of the 19th century and the first half of the 20th century, the Supreme Court struggled over the meaning of these textual differences between constitutional rights asserted against the United States and its agents and those asserted against the states and their agents.

James Madison, who introduced the Bill of Rights in Congress, initially proposed that some of the protections adopted in the Bill of Rights be applied also to the states. *See* Appendix B. In making these proposals, Madison was of course aware that most states had their own bills of rights, and that the wording and content of these protections varied somewhat from state to state. Thus, Madison would have established certain minimum standards or a "floor" below which a state could not go in denying certain citizen rights. But Madison's views did not prevail, and the Bill of Rights as adopted made no mention of application to the states. The Ninth Amendment reserved "certain rights" not enumerated to "the people" without specifying whether these rights would apply against the federal government, the states, or both. Further, the Tenth Amendment reserved the "powers not delegated to the United States" to "the States respectively, or to the people."

Thus, it should come as no shock to you that, prior to adoption of the Fourteenth Amendment, the Supreme Court held the Bill of Rights inapplicable to the states. *Barron v. Mayor and City Council of Baltimore*, 32 U.S. (7 Pet.) 243 (1833). Less forthright is the course by which the Bill of Rights has been held by the Court to apply, for the most part, to the states. The easiest route for this to happen would have been for the Court to hold that the "privileges or immunities" of the Fourteenth Amendment established the Bill of Rights guarantees as a minimum floor of United States citizens' rights. But, as we have seen, that route was foreclosed by the *Slaughter-House Cases*.

The *Slaughter-House Cases* were far less definitive in restricting the reach of the Due Process Clause of the Fourteenth Amendment. JUSTICE MILLER's famous opinion had concluded that the Due Process Clause of the Fourteenth Amendment was limited to procedural due process. In the late 1800s, however, several justices were appointed to the Supreme Court who saw the Due Process Clause in economic terms. *See Lochner*, supra. Within a few years, the Court would state that if a law "purporting to have been enacted to protect the public health, the public morals, or the public safety, has no real or substantial relations to those objects, or is a palpable invasion of rights secured by the fundamental law, it is the duty of the courts to so adjudge, and thereby give effect to the Constitution." *Mugler v. Kansas*, 123 U.S. 623 (1887). Beginning with *Chicago, Burlington & Quincy Railroad v. Chicago*, 166 U.S. 226 (1897), the Court began incorporating the various Bill of Rights provisions into the Due Process Clause of the Fourteenth

Amendment. This case held that the Takings Clause of the Fifth Amendment applied to state takings of property.

The full expansion of the Due Process Clause of the Fourteenth Amendment to accommodate the Bill of Rights protections came during the middle third of the twentieth century. In *Palko v. Connecticut*, 302 U.S. 319 (1937), JUSTICE CARDOZO wrote what has become the leading case concerning whether the Bill of Rights applies to the States through the Due Process Clause of the Fourteenth Amendment. Cardozo rejected the notion that all the Bill of Rights provisions were incorporated, whether substantive (like free speech) or procedural (like grand jury indictment). He first summarized a significant number of the Court's apparently inconsistent decisions, including cases which had guaranteed against free speech infringement by the states but had rejected the need for states to commence criminal prosecutions by grand jury indictment. Then Cardozo wrote that only those portions of the Bill of Rights "implicit in the concept of ordered liberty," those matters "so rooted in the traditions and conscience of our people as to be ranked as fundamental" were part of the "due process" limiting state power. The problem, of course, is in deciding what specific matters fit these general descriptions without resorting to concepts of natural law (see the discussion of *Calder v. Bull*, Ch. II). In *Palko*, the state retried a defendant because the first trial court had erroneously excluded evidence and misinstructed the jury on the difference between first and second-degree murder; the defendant claimed this was double jeopardy. How would you decide the issue in *Palko*? Although opaque, Cardozo's definition of fundamental rights (i.e. those "*implicit in the concept of ordered liberty*," and "*so rooted in the traditions and conscience of our people as to be ranked as fundamental*") has lasted since it was written in 1937 and is used by today's Court in determining what constitutes a fundamental right. *See Washington v. Glucksberg*, 521 U.S. 702 (1997), infra Ch. VIII.

Another leading case, *Adamson v. California*, 332 U.S. 46 (1947), concerned whether the Fifth Amendment's privilege against self-incrimination, applicable in federal court, applied in state court. *Adamson* contains a spirited exchange between JUSTICE FELIX FRANKFURTER (an erudite former Harvard Law School teacher appointed by FDR) and JUSTICE HUGO BLACK (a populist former Alabama Senator also appointed by FDR). JUSTICE FRANKFURTER reaffirmed the *Palko* approach, saying that 42 of the 43 Supreme Court Justices who had looked at the scope of the Fourteenth Amendment's Due Process Clause agreed with that approach. Only one "eccentric exception," wrote Frankfurter, "indicated a belief that the Fourteenth Amendment was a shorthand summary of the first eight Amendments." JUSTICE BLACK, in response, derided "the 'natural law' theory of the Constitution" which "degrade[s] the constitutional safeguards of the Bill of Rights" and "simultaneously appropriate[s] for this Court a broad power which we are not authorized by the Constitution to exercise." In the long run, JUSTICE BLACK prevailed. The only provisions of the first eight amendments not "selectively incorporated" are the Third Amendment, the Fifth Amendment requirement of grand jury indictment, and the Seventh Amendment right to jury trial in civil cases. Many of these developments are reviewed in *Duncan v. Louisiana*, 391 U.S. 145 (1968), in which the Court rephrased the inquiry as whether "given this kind of system a particular procedure is fundamental—whether, that is, a procedure is necessary to an Anglo–American regime of ordered liberty."

JUSTICE THOMAS' concurrence in *Zelman v. Simmons-Harris*, 536 U.S. 639 (2002), which upheld Cleveland's school voucher program, suggests a different approach to at least some selective incorporations of the Bill of Rights.

*** The Establishment Clause originally protected States, and by extension their citizens, from the imposition of an established religion by the Federal Government. Whether and how this Clause should constrain state action under the Fourteenth Amendment is a more difficult question. *** When rights are incorporated against the States through the Fourteenth Amendment they should advance, not constrain, individual liberty.

Consequently, in the context of the Establishment Clause, it may well be that state action should be evaluated on different terms than similar action by the Federal Government. *** Thus, while the Federal Government may "make no law respecting an establishment of religion," the States may pass laws that include or touch on religious matters so long as these laws do not impede free exercise rights or any other individual religious liberty interest. By considering the particular religious liberty right alleged to be invaded by a State, federal courts can strike a proper balance between the demands of the Fourteenth Amendment on the one hand and the federalism prerogatives of States on the other. ***

Faced with a severe educational crisis, the State of Ohio enacted wide-ranging educational reform that allows voluntary participation of private and religious schools in educating poor urban children otherwise condemned to failing public schools. The program does not force any individual to submit to religious indoctrination or education. It simply gives parents a greater choice as to where and in what manner to educate their children. This is a choice that those with greater means have routinely exercised. *** [S]chool choice programs that involve religious schools appear unconstitutional only to those who would twist the Fourteenth Amendment against itself by expansively incorporating the Establishment Clause. Converting the Fourteenth Amendment from a guarantee of opportunity to an obstacle against education reform distorts our constitutional values and disserves those in the greatest need.

There is even less textual support for applying the equal protection clause of the Fourteenth Amendment to constrain the federal government than there is for incorporating the Bill of Rights into the Fourteenth Amendment to constrain state governments. Yet that is precisely what has happened. The equal protection component of the Fourteenth Amendment has been "reverse incorporated" into the Due Process Clause of the Fifth Amendment. The seminal case, *Bolling v. Sharpe*, 347 U.S. 497 (1954), held that segregation of schools in the District of Columbia violated the "equal protection component" of the Due Process Clause of the Fifth Amendment.

McDONALD v. CHICAGO
561 U. S. 742 (2010)

JUSTICE ALITO announced the judgment of the Court and delivered the opinion of the Court with respect to Parts I, II–A, II–B, II–D, III–A, and III–B, in which THE CHIEF JUSTICE, JUSTICE SCALIA, JUSTICE KENNEDY, and JUSTICE THOMAS join, and an opinion with respect to Parts II–C, IV, and V, in which THE CHIEF JUSTICE, JUSTICE SCALIA, and JUSTICE KENNEDY join.

Two years ago, in *District of Columbia* v. *Heller*, we held that the Second Amendment protects the right to keep and bear arms for the purpose of self-defense, and we struck down a District of Columbia law that banned the possession of handguns in the home. The city of Chicago (City) and the village of Oak Park, a Chicago suburb, have laws that are similar to the District of Columbia's, but Chicago and Oak Park argue that their laws are constitutional because the Second Amendment has no application to the States. *** Petitioners' primary submission is that this right is among the "privileges or immunities of citizens of the United States" and that the narrow interpretation of the Privileges or Immunities Clause adopted in the *Slaughter-House Cases*, should now be rejected. As a secondary argument, petitioners contend that the Fourteenth Amendment's Due Process Clause "incorporates" the Second Amendment right.

II. C

[Plurality only; JUSTICE THOMAS does not join this section]

*** We see no need to reconsider [the *Slaughter-House Cases*]. For many decades, the question of the rights protected by the Fourteenth Amendment against state infringement has been analyzed under the Due Process Clause *** and not under the Privileges or Immunities Clause. ***

D

In the late 19th century, the Court began to consider whether the Due Process Clause prohibits the States from infringing rights set out in the Bill of Rights. *** Five features of the approach taken during the ensuing era should be noted.

First, the Court viewed the due process question as entirely separate from the question whether a right was a privilege or immunity of national citizenship. Second, *** the only rights protected against state infringement by the Due Process Clause were those rights "of such a nature that they are included in the conception of due process of law." *** While it was "possible that some of the personal rights safeguarded by the first eight Amendments against National action [might] also be safeguarded against state action," the

Court stated, this was "not because those rights are enumerated in the first eight Amendments." *** Third, in some cases decided during this era the Court "can be seen as having asked, when inquiring into whether some particular procedural safeguard was required of a State, if a civilized system could be imagined that would not accord the particular protection. *** Fourth, the Court during this era was not hesitant to hold that a right set out in the Bill of Rights failed to meet the test for inclusion within the protection of the Due Process Clause. The Court found that some such rights qualified. Finally, even when a right set out in the Bill of Rights was held to fall within the conception of due process, the protection or remedies afforded against state infringement sometimes differed from the protection or remedies provided against abridgment by the Federal Government. ***

An alternative theory regarding the relationship between the Bill of Rights and §1 of the Fourteenth Amendment was championed by JUSTICE BLACK. This theory held that §1 of the Fourteenth Amendment totally incorporated all of the provisions of the Bill of Rights. *** While JUSTICE BLACK's theory was never adopted, the Court eventually moved in that direction by initiating what has been called a process of "selective incorporation," *i.e.*, the Court began to hold that the Due Process Clause fully incorporates particular rights contained in the first eight Amendments. *** The Court made it clear that the governing standard is not whether *any* "civilized system [can] be imagined that would not accord the particular protection." Instead, the Court inquired whether a particular Bill of Rights guarantee is fundamental to *our* scheme of ordered liberty and system of justice. *** The Court eventually incorporated almost all of the provisions of the Bill of Rights. *** Finally, the Court *** decisively held that incorporated Bill of Rights protections "are all to be enforced against the States under the Fourteenth Amendment according to the same standards that protect those personal rights against federal encroachment." ***

III

With this framework in mind, we now turn directly to the question whether the Second Amendment right to keep and bear arms is incorporated in the concept of due process. In answering that question, *** we must decide whether the right to keep and bear arms is fundamental to *our* scheme of ordered liberty *** or as we have said in a related context, whether this right is "deeply rooted in this Nation's history and tradition." *** *Heller* makes it clear that this right is "deeply rooted in this Nation's history and tradition." *** The right to keep and bear arms was considered no less fundamental by those who drafted and ratified the Bill of Rights. *** [T]hose who were fearful that the new Federal Government would infringe traditional rights such as the right to keep and bear arms insisted on the adoption of the Bill of Rights as a condition for ratification of the Constitution. *** This is surely powerful evidence that the right was regarded as fundamental in the sense relevant here. ***

By the 1850's, the perceived threat that had prompted the inclusion of the Second Amendment in the Bill of Rights—the fear that the National Government would disarm the universal militia—had largely faded as a popular concern, but the right to keep and bear arms was highly valued for purposes of self-defense. *** In debating the Fourteenth Amendment, the 39th Congress referred to the right to keep and bear arms as a fundamental right deserving of protection. *** In sum, it is clear that the Framers and ratifiers of the Fourteenth Amendment counted the right to keep and bear arms among those fundamental rights necessary to our system of ordered liberty.

Despite all this evidence, municipal respondents contend that Congress, in the years immediately following the Civil War, merely sought to outlaw "discriminatory measures taken against freedmen, which it addressed by adopting a non-discrimination principle" and that even an outright ban on the possession of firearms was regarded as acceptable, "so long as it was not done in a discriminatory manner." *** This argument is implausible.

First, while §1 of the Fourteenth Amendment contains "an antidiscrimination rule," namely, the Equal Protection Clause, municipal respondents can hardly mean that §1 does no more than prohibit discrimination. If that were so, then the First Amendment, as applied to the States, would not prohibit nondiscriminatory abridgments of the rights to freedom of speech or freedom of religion; the Fourth Amendment, as applied to the States, would not prohibit all unreasonable searches and seizures but only discriminatory searches and seizures—and so on. *** Second, municipal respondents' argument ignores the clear terms of the Freedmen's Bureau Act of 1866, which acknowledged the existence of the right to bear arms. *** Third, if the 39th Congress had outlawed only those laws that discriminate on the basis of race or previous condition of servitude, African Americans in the South would likely have remained vulnerable to attack by many of their worst abusers: the state militia and state peace officers. *** Fourth, municipal respondents' purely antidiscrimination theory of the Fourteenth Amendment disregards the plight of whites in the South who opposed the Black Codes. *** Fifth, the 39th Congress' response to proposals to disband and disarm the Southern militias is instructive. Despite recognizing and deploring the abuses of these militias, the 39th Congress balked at a proposal to disarm them. Disarmament, it was argued, would violate the members' right to bear arms, and it was ultimately decided to disband the militias but not to disarm their members. It cannot be doubted that the right to bear arms was regarded as a substantive guarantee, not a prohibition that could be ignored so long as the States legislated in an evenhanded manner.

IV

[Plurality only— JUSTICE THOMAS does not join this section]

*** Municipal respondents' main argument is nothing less than a plea to disregard 50 years of incorporation precedent and return (presumably for this case only) to a bygone era. *** Municipal respondents maintain that the Second Amendment differs from all of the other provisions of the Bill of Rights because it concerns the right to possess a deadly implement and thus has implications for public safety. And they note that there is intense disagreement on the question whether the private possession of guns in the home increases or decreases gun deaths and injuries. The right to keep and bear arms, however, is not the only constitutional right that has controversial public safety implications. All of the constitutional provisions that impose restrictions on law enforcement and on the prosecution of crimes fall into the same category. *** Municipal respondents cite no case in which we have refrained from holding that a provision of the Bill of Rights is binding on the States on the ground that the right at issue has disputed public safety implications.

We likewise reject municipal respondents' argument that we should depart from our established incorporation methodology on the ground that making the Second Amendment binding on the States and their subdivisions is inconsistent with principles of federalism and will stifle experimentation. *** Under our precedents, if a Bill of Rights guarantee is fundamental from an American perspective, then, unless *stare decisis* counsels otherwise, that guarantee is fully binding on the States and thus *limits* (but by no means eliminates) their ability to devise solutions to social problems that suit local needs and values. ***

As evidence that the Fourteenth Amendment has not historically been understood to restrict the authority of the States to regulate firearms, municipal respondents *** cite a variety of state and local firearms laws that courts have upheld. But what is most striking about their research is the paucity of precedent sustaining bans comparable to those at issue here and in *Heller*. ***

Municipal respondents argue, finally, that the right to keep and bear arms is unique among the rights set out in the first eight Amendments "because the reason for codifying the Second Amendment (to protect the militia) differs from the purpose (primarily, to use firearms to engage in self-defense) that is claimed to make the right implicit in the concept of ordered liberty." *** [T]his contention repackages one of the chief arguments that we rejected in *Heller*, *i.e.*, that the scope of the Second Amendment right is defined by the immediate threat that led to the inclusion of that right in the Bill of Rights. *** As we put it, self-defense was "the *central component* of the right itself."

V

[Plurality only–JUSTICE THOMAS does not join this section]

*** [N]othing written since *Heller* persuades us to reopen the question there decided. *** First, we have never held that a provision of the Bill of Rights applies to the States only if there is a "popular consensus" that the right is fundamental, and we see no basis for such a rule. *** Second, petitioners and many others who live in high-crime areas dispute the proposition that the Second Amendment right does not protect minorities and those lacking political clout. *** [[It] protects the rights of minorities and other residents of high-crime areas whose needs are not being met by elected public officials. Third, *** incorporation of the Second Amendment right will to some extent limit the legislative freedom of the States, but this is always true when a Bill of Rights provision is incorporated. *** Finally, JUSTICE BREYER is incorrect that incorporation will require judges to assess the costs and benefits of firearms restrictions and thus to make difficult empirical judgments in an area in which they lack expertise. ***

JUSTICE SCALIA, concurring [omitted]

JUSTICE THOMAS, concurring in part and concurring in the judgment.

*** I cannot agree that [the Second Amendment] is enforceable against the States through a clause that speaks only to "process." Instead, the right to keep and bear arms is a privilege of American citizenship that applies to the States through the Fourteenth Amendment's Privileges or Immunities Clause. *** [E]vidence] plainly shows that the ratifying public understood the Privileges or Immunities Clause to protect constitutionally enumerated rights, including the right to keep and bear arms. ***

The next question is whether the Privileges or Immunities Clause merely prohibits States from discriminating among citizens if they recognize the Second Amendment's right to keep and bear arms, or whether the Clause requires States to recognize the right. *** I must explain why this Clause in particular protects against more than just state discrimination, and in fact establishes a minimum baseline of rights for all American citizens. *** The Privileges or Immunities Clause opens with the command that *"No State shall* abridge the privileges or immunities of citizens of the United States." *** [T]he fact that the Privileges or Immunities Clause uses the command "[n]o State shall"–which Article IV, § 2 does not–strongly suggests that the former imposes a greater restriction on state power than the latter.

This interpretation is strengthened when one considers that the Privileges or Immunities Clause uses the verb "abridge," rather than "discriminate," to describe the limit it imposes on state authority. The Webster's dictionary in use at the time of Reconstruction defines the word "abridge" to mean "[t]o deprive; to cut off; ... as, to *abridge* one of his rights." The Clause is thus best understood to impose a limitation on state power to infringe upon pre-existing substantive rights. *** The argument that the Privileges or Immunities Clause prohibits no more than discrimination often is followed by a claim that public discussion of the Clause, and of § 1 generally, was not extensive. *** [H]istory confirms what the text of the Privileges or Immunities Clause most naturally suggests: Consistent with its command that "[n]o State shall ... abridge" the rights of United States citizens, the Clause establishes a minimum baseline of federal rights, and the constitutional right to keep and bear arms plainly was among them.

My conclusion is contrary to this Court's precedents [but] *** I agree with the Court that the Second Amendment is fully applicable to the States. I do so because the right to keep and bear arms is guaranteed by the Fourteenth Amendment as a privilege of American citizenship.

JUSTICE STEVENS, dissenting [omitted]

JUSTICE BREYER, with whom JUSTICE GINSBURG and JUSTICE SOTOMAYOR join, dissenting.

*** Unlike other forms of substantive liberty, the carrying of arms for that purpose often puts others' lives at risk. *** I can find nothing in the

Second Amendment's text, history, or underlying rationale that could warrant characterizing it as "fundamental" insofar as it seeks to protect the keeping and bearing of arms for private self-defense purposes. Nor can I find any justification for interpreting the Constitution as transferring ultimate regulatory authority over the private uses of firearms from democratically elected legislatures to courts or from the States to the Federal Government. I therefore conclude that the Fourteenth Amendment does not "incorporate" the Second Amendment's right "to keep and bear Arms." *** [T]o incorporate the private self-defense right, the majority must show that the right is, *e.g.*, "fundamental to the American scheme of justice." *** And this it fails to do.

The majority here, like that in *Heller,* relies almost exclusively upon history to make the necessary showing. *** [However,] our society has historically made mistakes—for example, when considering certain 18th- and 19th-century property rights to be fundamental. And in the incorporation context, as elsewhere, history often is unclear about the answers. *** I thus think it proper, above all where history provides no clear answer, to look to other factors in considering whether a right is sufficiently "fundamental" to remove it from the political process in every State. I would include among those factors the nature of the right; any contemporary disagreement about whether the right is fundamental; the extent to which incorporation will further other, perhaps more basic, constitutional aims; and the extent to which incorporation will advance or hinder the Constitution's structural aims, including its division of powers among different governmental institutions (and the people as well). Is incorporation needed, for example, to further the Constitution's effort to ensure that the government treats each individual with equal respect? Will it help maintain the democratic form of government that the Constitution foresees? In a word, will incorporation prove consistent, or inconsistent, with the Constitution's efforts to create governmental institutions well suited to the carrying out of its constitutional promises? ***

Further, there is no popular consensus that the private self-defense right described in *Heller* is fundamental. *** Moreover, there is no reason here to believe that incorporation of the private self-defense right will further any other or broader constitutional objective. We are aware of no argument that gun-control regulations target or are passed with the purpose of targeting "discrete and insular minorities." Nor will incorporation help to assure equal respect for individuals. *** Unlike the protections offered by many of these same Amendments, it does not involve matters as to which judges possess a comparative expertise, by virtue of their close familiarity with the justice system and its operation. And, unlike the Fifth Amendment's insistence on just compensation, it does not involve a matter where a majority might unfairly seize for itself property belonging to a minority.

Finally, incorporation of the right *will* work a significant disruption in the constitutional allocation of decisionmaking authority, thereby interfering with the Constitution's ability to further its objectives. *First* *** the incorporation of the right recognized in *Heller* would amount to a significant incursion on a traditional and important area of state concern ***

Second, determining the constitutionality of a particular state gun law requires finding answers to complex empirically based questions of a kind that legislatures are better able than courts to make. *** *Third,* the ability of States to reflect local preferences and conditions—both key virtues of federalism—here has particular importance. *** For example, in 2008, the murder rate was 40 times higher in New Orleans than it was in Lincoln, Nebraska. *** *Fourth,* although incorporation of any right removes decisions from the democratic process, the incorporation of this particular right does so without strong offsetting justification. *** [W]hy, in a Nation whose Constitution foresees democratic decisionmaking, is it so *fundamental* a matter as to require taking that power from the people? What is it here that the people did not know? What is it that a judge knows better? *** Where the incorporation of other rights has been at issue, *some* of these problems have arisen. But in this instance *all* these problems are present, *all* at the same time, and *all* are likely to be present in most, perhaps nearly all, of the cases in which the constitutionality of a gun regulation is at issue. At the same time, the important factors that favor incorporation in other instances— *e.g.,* the protection of broader constitutional objectives—are not present here. ***

Thus, the specific question [is] whether there is a consensus that *so substantial* a private self-defense right as the one described in *Heller* applies to the States. *** [A] historical record that is so ambiguous cannot itself provide an adequate basis for incorporating a private right of self-defense and applying it against the States. ***

Notes

1. **Consequences for State Law.** *McDonald* holds that states must recognize the right of the people to bear arms. This only affects eight states directly, however, since forty-two states recognized the right to bear arms. For the larger group of states, the case would be significant only if the federal right were read more broadly than the state right.

2. **Regulation of Firearms.** The Court does not extend its explanation of what firearm regulations are "reasonable" beyond the discussion in *Heller.* Most analysts therefore predict substantial litigation over the content of the right recognized in these two cases.

3. **Voting Paradox.** The outcome of the case is 5-4 for McDonald because five justices thought the Fourteenth Amendment makes the Second Amendment applicable to the states. On the issue of whether there is incorporation through the Due Process Clause of the Fourteenth Amendment, the case was 5-4 against incorporation (the dissenters plus JUSTICE THOMAS). Does this set of outcomes have any ramifications for *McDonald* as a precedent?

4. **Due Process Incorporation Theory.** Try to articulate exactly what divides the plurality from the dissenters in terms of how fundamental a right must be to be incorporated and precisely what is incorporated of the federal right involved. Who has the better of the argument and why?

3. PERSONAL RIGHTS: BEYOND INCORPORATED RIGHTS

The cases below go one step beyond those discussed above: they involve application of rights mentioned neither in the Bill of Rights nor in the Fourteenth Amendment.

a. *Origins of Unenumerated Personal Rights*

BUCK v. BELL
274 U. S. 200 (1927)

MR. JUSTICE HOLMES delivered the opinion of the Court.

*** The case comes here upon the contention that the statute authorizing the judgment is void under the Fourteenth Amendment as denying to the plaintiff in error due process of law and the equal protection of the laws.

Carrie Buck is a feeble-minded white woman who was committed to the State Colony above mentioned in due form. She is the daughter of a feeble-minded mother in the same institution, and the mother of an illegitimate feeble-minded child. She was eighteen years old at the time of the trial of her case in the Circuit Court in the latter part of 1924. An Act of Virginia approved March 20, 1924 (Laws 1924, c. 394) recites that the health of the patient and the welfare of society may be promoted in certain cases by the sterilization of mental defectives, under careful safeguard, etc.; that the sterilization may be effected in males by vasectomy and in females by salpingectomy, without serious pain or substantial danger to life; that the Commonwealth is supporting in various institutions many defective persons who if now discharged would become a menace but if incapable of procreating might be discharged with safety and become self-supporting with benefit to themselves and to society; and that experience has shown that heredity plays an important part in the transmission of insanity, imbecility, etc. The statute then enacts that whenever the superintendent of certain institutions including the abovenamed State Colony shall be of opinion that it is for the best interest of the patients and of society that an inmate under his care should be sexually sterilized, he may have the operation performed upon any patient afflicted with hereditary forms of insanity, imbecility, etc., on complying with the very careful provisions by which the act protects the patients from possible abuse.

*** There can be no doubt that so far as procedure is concerned the rights of the patient are most carefully considered, and as every step in this case was taken in scrupulous compliance with the statute and after months of observation, there is no doubt that in that respect the plaintiff in error has had due process at law.

The attack is not upon the procedure but upon the substantive law. It seems to be contended that in no circumstances could such an order be justified. It certainly is contended that the order cannot be justified upon the existing grounds. The judgment finds the facts that have been recited and that Carrie Buck 'is the probable potential parent of socially inadequate offspring, likewise afflicted, that she may be sexually sterilized without detriment to her general health and that her welfare and that of society will be promoted by her sterilization,' and thereupon makes the order. In view of the general declarations of the Legislature and the specific findings of the Court obviously we cannot say as matter of law that the grounds do not exist, and if they exist they justify the result. We have seen more than once that the public welfare may call upon the best citizens for their lives. It would be strange if it could not call upon those who already sap the strength of the State for these lesser sacrifices, often not felt to be such by those concerned, in order to prevent our being swamped with incompetence. It is better for all the world, if instead of waiting to execute degenerate offspring for crime, or to let them starve for their imbecility, society can prevent those who are manifestly unfit from continuing their kind. The principle that sustains compulsory vaccination is broad enough to cover cutting the Fallopian tubes. Three generations of imbeciles are enough.

But, it is said, however it might be if this reasoning were applied generally, it fails when it is confined to the small number who are in the institutions named and is not applied to the multitudes outside. It is the usual last resort of constitutional arguments to point out shortcomings of this sort. But the answer is that the law does all that is needed when it does all that it can, indicates a policy, applies it to all within the lines, and seeks to bring within the lines all similarly situated so far and so fast as its means allow. Of course so far as the operations enable those who otherwise must be kept confined to be returned to the world, and thus open the asylum to others, the equality aimed at will be more nearly reached. ***

Notes

1. **Substantive Due Process**. This opinion was written during an era when substantive due process was recognized by the Court, yet the Court did not recognize a substantive due process right to reproduce. Why not? Was it because the science of the day supported the result? After you have read the cases in the remainder of this chapter, consider whether *Buck v. Bell* would be decided the same way today.

2. **Other Theories**. Note how procedural due process was fully met. What process do you think would be required under the modern *Mathews v. Eldridge* formula? Do you agree with what JUSTICE HOLMES, the most respected member of the Court at the time, had to say about Carrie Buck's equal protection argument ("the usual last resort of constitutional arguments")?

3. **Parental Liberty**. In *Meyer v. Nebraska*, 262 U.S. 390 (1923), the Court held that the Due Process Clause includes the right of parents to "establish a home and bring up children" and "to control the education of their own." Two years later, in *Pierce v. Society of Sisters*, 268 U.S. 510 (1925), supra, it held that the "liberty of parents and guardians" includes the right "to direct the upbringing and education of children under their control." What distinguishes the rights in *Meyer* and *Pierce* from the absence of a due process right in *Buck*?

[handwritten margin note: fundamental right is the right of married people to use contraception]

GRISWOLD v. CONNECTICUT
381 U.S. 479 (1965)

MR. JUSTICE DOUGLAS delivered the opinion of the Court.

Appellant Griswold is Executive Director of the Planned Parenthood League of Connecticut. Appellant Buxton is a licensed physician and a professor at the Yale Medical School who served as Medical Director for the League at its Center in New Haven—a center open and operating from November 1 to November 10, 1961, when appellants were arrested.

They gave information, instruction, and medical advice to married persons as to the means of preventing conception. They examined the wife and prescribed the best contraceptive device or material for her use. Fees were usually charged, although some couples were serviced free.

[handwritten margin note: Challenging the constitutionality of statutes preventing the prescribing or assisting in contraceptives]

The statutes whose constitutionality is involved in this appeal *** provide: "Any person who uses any drug, medicinal article or instrument for the purpose of preventing conception shall be fined not less than fifty dollars or imprisoned not less than sixty days nor more than one year or be both fined and imprisoned." [and] "Any person who assists, abets, counsels, causes, hires or commands another to commit any offense may be prosecuted and punished as if he were the principal offender."

[handwritten margin note: arg'd it violated 14th Amendment]

The appellants were found guilty as accessories and fined $100 each, against the claim that the accessory statute as so applied violated the Fourteenth Amendment. *** Coming to the merits, we *** do not sit as a super-legislature to determine the wisdom, need, and propriety of laws that touch economic problems, business affairs, or social conditions. This law, however, operates directly on an intimate relation of husband and wife and their physician's role in one aspect of that relation.

The association of people is not mentioned in the Constitution nor in the Bill of Rights. The right to educate a child in a school of the parents' choice—whether public or private or parochial—is also not mentioned. Nor is the right to study any particular subject or any foreign language. Yet the First Amendment has been construed to include certain of those rights. *** [The] State may not, consistently with the spirit of the First Amendment, contract the spectrum of available knowledge. The right of freedom of speech and press includes not only the right to utter or to print, but the right to *[handwritten margin note: 1A contains a certain right to privacy]* distribute, the right to receive, the right to read, and freedom of inquiry, freedom of thought, and freedom to teach. Without those peripheral rights the specific rights would be less secure. *** In other words, the First Amendment has a penumbra where privacy is protected from governmental intrusion. In like context, we have protected forms of "association" that are not political in the customary sense but pertain to the social, legal, and economic benefit of the members. ***

[Specific] guarantees in the Bill of Rights have penumbras, formed by emanations from those guarantees that help give them life and substance. Various guarantees create zones of privacy. The right of association contained in the penumbra of the First Amendment is one, as we have seen. The Third

Amendment in its prohibition against the quartering of soldiers "in any house" in time of peace without the consent of the owner is another facet of that privacy. The Fourth Amendment explicitly affirms the "right of the people to be secure in their persons, houses, papers, and effects, against unreasonable searches and seizures." The Fifth Amendment in its Self–Incrimination Clause enables the citizen to create a zone of privacy which government may not force him to surrender to his detriment. The Ninth Amendment provides: "The enumeration in the Constitution, of certain rights, shall not be construed to deny or disparage others retained by the people."

The Fourth and Fifth Amendments were described in *Boyd v. United States*, 116 U.S. 616, 630, as protection against all governmental invasions "of the sanctity of a man's home and the privacies of life." We recently referred in *Mapp v. Ohio*, 367 U.S. 643, 656, to the Fourth Amendment as creating a "right to privacy, no less important than any other right carefully and particularly reserved to the people." ***

The present case, then, concerns a relationship lying within the zone of privacy created by several fundamental constitutional guarantees. And it concerns a law which, in forbidding the use of contraceptives rather than regulating their manufacture or sale, seeks to achieve its goals by means having a maximum destructive impact upon that relationship. Such a law cannot stand in light of the familiar principle, so often applied by this Court, that a "governmental purpose to control or prevent activities constitutionally subject to state regulation may not be achieved by means which sweep unnecessarily broadly and thereby invade the area of protected freedoms." *NAACP v. Alabama*. Would we allow the police to search the sacred precincts of marital bedrooms for telltale signs of the use of contraceptives? The very idea is repulsive to the notions of privacy surrounding the marriage relationship.

We deal with a right of privacy older than the Bill of Rights—older than our political parties, older than our school system. Marriage is a coming together for better or for worse, hopefully enduring, and intimate to the degree of being sacred. It is an association that promotes a way of life, not causes; a harmony in living, not political faiths; a bilateral loyalty, not commercial or social projects. Yet it is an association for as noble a purpose as any involved in our prior decisions.

MR. JUSTICE GOLDBERG, whom THE CHIEF JUSTICE and MR. JUSTICE BRENNAN join, concurring.

*** This Court, in a series of decisions, has held that the Fourteenth Amendment absorbs and applies to the States those specifics of the first eight amendments which express fundamental personal rights. The language and history of the Ninth Amendment reveal that the Framers of the Constitution believed that there are additional fundamental rights, protected from governmental infringement, which exist alongside those fundamental rights specifically mentioned in the first eight constitutional amendments. *** The Ninth Amendment reads, "The enumeration in the Constitution, of certain *can't be used to deny other Const. rights. i.e. privacy*

rights, shall not be construed to deny or disparage others retained by the people." The Amendment *** was proffered to quiet expressed fears that a bill of specifically enumerated rights could not be sufficiently broad to cover all essential rights and that the specific mention of certain rights would be interpreted as a denial that others were protected. *** While this Court has had little occasion to interpret the Ninth Amendment, "(i)t cannot be presumed that any clause in the constitution is intended to be without effect." *Marbury v. Madison*, 1 Cranch 137, 174. In interpreting the Constitution, "real effect should be given to all the words it uses." *** To hold that a right so basic and fundamental and so deep-rooted in our society as the right of privacy in marriage may be infringed because that right is not guaranteed in so many words by the first eight amendments to the Constitution is to ignore the Ninth Amendment and to give it no effect whatsoever. *** The logic of the dissents would sanction federal or state legislation that seems to me even more plainly unconstitutional than the statute before us. Surely the Government, absent a showing of a compelling subordinating state interest, could not decree that all husbands and wives must be sterilized after two children have been born to them. Yet by their reasoning such an invasion of marital privacy would not be subject to constitutional challenge because, while it might be "silly," no provision of the Constitution specifically prevents the Government from curtailing the marital right to bear children and raise a family. *** In sum, I believe that the right of privacy in the marital relation is fundamental and basic—a personal right "retained by the people" within the meaning of the Ninth Amendment. Connecticut cannot constitutionally abridge this fundamental right, which is protected by the Fourteenth Amendment from infringement by the States. ***

9A protects 4A and right to privacy

MR. JUSTICE HARLAN, concurring in the judgment.

*** In my view, the proper constitutional inquiry in this case is whether this Connecticut statute infringes the Due Process Clause of the Fourteenth Amendment because the enactment violates basic values "implicit in the concept of ordered liberty," *Palko v. State of Connecticut*, 302 U.S. 319, 325(1961). *** [What follows is an edited version of JUSTICE HARLAN's dissent in *Poe v. Ullman*, in which the Court declined to reach the merits of the constitutionality of the same Connecticut statute.]

*** Due process has not been reduced to any formula; its content cannot be determined by reference to any code. The best that can be said is that through the course of this Court's decisions it has represented the balance which our Nation, built upon postulates of respect for the liberty of the individual, has struck between that liberty and the demands of organized society. *** A decision of this Court which radically departs from it could not long survive, while a decision which builds on what has survived is likely to be sound. No formula could serve as a substitute, in this area, for judgment and restraint. *** Appellants contend that the Connecticut statute deprives them, as it unquestionably does, of a substantial measure of liberty in carrying on the most intimate of all personal relationships, and that it does so arbitrarily and without any rational, justifying purpose. The State, on the other hand, asserts that it is acting to protect the moral welfare of its

statutes deny 14A rights

citizenry, both directly, in that it considers the practice of contraception immoral in itself, and instrumentally, in that the availability of contraceptive materials tends to minimize "the disastrous consequence of dissolute action," that is fornication and adultery.

It is argued by appellants that the judgment, implicit in this statute—that the use of contraceptives by married couples is immoral—is an irrational one, that in effect it subjects them in a very important matter to the arbitrary whim of the legislature, and that it does so for no good purpose. *** Yet the very inclusion of the category of morality among state concerns indicates that society is not limited in its objects only to the physical well-being of the community, but has traditionally concerned itself with the moral soundness of its people as well. Indeed to attempt a line between public behavior and that which is purely consensual or solitary would be to withdraw from community concern a range of subjects with which every society in civilized times has found it necessary to deal. The laws regarding marriage which provide both when the sexual powers may be used and the legal and societal context in which children are born and brought up, as well as laws forbidding adultery, fornication and homosexual practices which express the negative of the proposition, confining sexuality to lawful marriage, form a pattern so deeply pressed into the substance of our social life that any Constitutional doctrine in this area must build upon that basis.

tried to prevent non-procreative sex

It is in this area of sexual morality, which contains many proscriptions of consensual behavior having little or no direct impact on others, that the State of Connecticut has expressed its moral judgment that all use of contraceptives is improper. Appellants cite an impressive list of authorities who, from a great variety of points of view, commend the considered use of contraceptives by married couples. What they do not emphasize is that not too long ago the current of opinion was very probably quite the opposite, and that even today the issue is not free of controversy. Certainly, Connecticut's judgment is no more demonstrably correct or incorrect than are the varieties of judgment, expressed in law, on marriage and divorce, on adult consensual homosexuality, abortion, and sterilization, or euthanasia and suicide. If we had a case before us which required us to decide simply, and in abstraction, whether the moral judgment implicit in the application of the present statute to married couples was a sound one, the very controversial nature of these questions would, I think, require us to hesitate long before concluding that the Constitution precluded Connecticut from choosing as it has among these various views.

Ct. made the statutes based on a moral belief

P showed that many couples disagree

But, as might be expected, we are not presented simply with this moral judgment to be passed on as an abstract proposition. *** Precisely what is involved here is this: the State is asserting the right to enforce its moral judgment by intruding upon the most intimate details of the marital relation with the full power of the criminal law. *** The statute must pass a more rigorous Constitutional test than that going merely to the plausibility of its underlying rationale. This enactment involves what, by common understanding throughout the English-speaking world, must be granted to be a most fundamental aspect of "liberty," the privacy of the home in its most

Morality isn't the issue, it is a state using morality to curb a Consti. right to privacy

first time strict scrutiny is mentioned in SDP

basic sense, and it is this which requires that the statute be subjected to "strict scrutiny." *** Of this whole "private realm of family life" it is difficult to imagine what is more private or more intimate than a husband and wife's marital relations. ***

Of course, *** the family *** is not beyond regulation," and it would be an absurdity to suggest either that offenses may not be committed in the bosom of the family or that the home can be made a sanctuary for crime. The right of privacy most manifestly is not an absolute. Thus, I would not suggest that adultery, homosexuality, fornication and incest are immune from criminal enquiry, however privately practiced. *** Adultery, homosexuality and the like are sexual intimacies which the State forbids altogether, but the intimacy of husband and wife is necessarily an essential and accepted feature of the institution of marriage, an institution which the State not only must allow, but which always and in every age it has fostered and protected. It is one thing when the State exerts its power either to forbid extra-marital

Right to privacy applies to legal issues of marriage and sexuality

sexuality altogether, or to say who may marry, but it is quite another when, having acknowledged a marriage and the intimacies inherent in it, it undertakes to regulate by means of the criminal law the details of that intimacy.

In sum, even though the State has determined that the use of contraceptives is as iniquitous as any act of extra-marital sexual immorality, the intrusion of the whole machinery of the criminal law into the very heart of marital privacy, requiring husband and wife to render account before a criminal tribunal of their uses of that intimacy, is surely a very different thing indeed from punishing those who establish intimacies which the law has always forbidden and which can have no claim to social protection. *** Since, as it appears to me, the statute marks an abridgment of important fundamental liberties protected by the Fourteenth Amendment, it will not do to urge in justification of that abridgment simply that the statute is rationally related to the effectuation of a proper state purpose. A closer scrutiny and stronger justification than that are required. *** [C]onclusive, in my view, is the utter novelty of this enactment. Although the Federal Government and many States have at one time or other had on their books statutes forbidding or regulating the distribution of contraceptives, none, so far as I can find, has made the use of contraceptives a crime. Indeed, a diligent search has revealed that no nation, including several which quite evidently share Connecticut's moral policy, has seen fit to effectuate that policy by the means presented here. ***

MR. JUSTICE WHITE, concurring in the judgment.

In my view this Connecticut law as applied to married couples deprives them of "liberty" without due process of law, as that concept is used in the Fourteenth Amendment. *** Suffice it to say that this is not the first time this Court has had occasion to articulate that the liberty entitled to protection under the Fourteenth Amendment includes the right "to marry, establish a home and bring up children," [*Meyer v. Nebraska*] and "the liberty ***to direct the upbringing and education of children," [*Pierce v. Society of Sisters*] and that these are among the "basic civil rights of man." [*Skinner v.*

Oklahoma]. These decisions affirm that there is a "realm of family life which the state cannot enter" without substantial justification. Surely the right invoked in this case, to be free of regulation of the intimacies of the marriage relationship, "come(s) to this Court with a momentum for respect lacking when appeal is made to liberties which derive merely from shifting economic arrangements." ***

[T]he State claims but one justification for its anti-use statute. There is no serious contention that Connecticut thinks the use of artificial or external methods of contraception immoral or unwise in itself, or that the anti-use statute is founded upon any policy of promoting population expansion. Rather, the statute is said to serve the State's policy against all forms of promiscuous or illicit sexual relationships, be they premarital or extramarital, concededly a permissible and legitimate legislative goal. *** In these circumstances one is rather hard pressed to explain how the ban on use by married persons in any way prevents use of such devices by persons engaging in illicit sexual relations and thereby contributes to the State's policy against such relationships. *** Perhaps the theory is that the flat ban on use prevents married people from possessing contraceptives and without the ready availability of such devices for use in the marital relationship, there will be no or less temptation to use them in extramarital ones. *** At most the broad ban is of marginal utility to the declared objective. A statute limiting its prohibition on use to persons engaging in the prohibited relationship would serve the end posited by Connecticut in the same way, and with the same effectiveness, or ineffectiveness, as the broad anti-use statute under attack in this case. ***

MR. JUSTICE BLACK, with whom MR. JUSTICE STEWART joins, dissenting.

this is not our job and it is up to the legislature

*** The Court talks about a constitutional "right of privacy" as though there is some constitutional provision or provisions forbidding any law ever to be passed which might abridge the "privacy" of individuals. But there is not. *** One of the most effective ways of diluting or expanding a constitutionally guaranteed right is to substitute for the crucial word or words of a constitutional guarantee another word or words, more or less flexible and more or less restricted in meaning. This fact is well illustrated by the use of the term "right of privacy" as a comprehensive substitute for the Fourth Amendment's guarantee against "unreasonable searches and seizures." "Privacy" is a broad, abstract and ambiguous concept which can easily be shrunken in meaning but which can also, on the other hand, easily be interpreted as a constitutional ban against many things other than searches and seizures. I have expressed the view many times that First Amendment freedoms, for example, have suffered from a failure of the courts to stick to the simple language of the First Amendment in construing it, instead of invoking multitudes of words substituted for those the Framers used. For these reasons I get nowhere in this case by talk about a constitutional "right or privacy" as an emanation from one or more constitutional provisions. I like my privacy as well as the next one, but I am nevertheless compelled to admit that government has a right to invade it unless prohibited by some specific constitutional provision.

*** I think that if properly construed neither the Due Process Clause nor the Ninth Amendment, nor both together, could under any circumstances be a proper basis for invalidating the Connecticut law. I discuss the due process and Ninth Amendment arguments together because on analysis they turn out to be the same thing—merely using different words to claim for this Court and the federal judiciary power to invalidate any legislative act which the judges find irrational, unreasonable or offensive. *** I realize that many good and able men have eloquently spoken and written, sometimes in rhapsodical strains, about the duty of this Court to keep the Constitution in tune with the times. The idea is that the Constitution must be changed from time to time and that this Court is charged with a duty to make those changes. For myself, I must with all deference reject that philosophy. The Constitution makers knew the need for change and provided for it. Amendments suggested by the people's elected representatives can be submitted to the people or their selected agents for ratification. *** And so, I cannot rely on the Due Process Clause or the Ninth Amendment or any mysterious and uncertain natural law concept as a reason for striking down this state law. The Due Process Clause with an "arbitrary and capricious" or "shocking to the conscience" formula was liberally used by this Court to strike down economic legislation in the early decades of this century, threatening, many people thought, the tranquility and stability of the Nation. That formula, based on subjective considerations of "natural justice," is no less dangerous when used to enforce this Court's views about personal rights than those about economic rights. *** Connecticut's law as applied here is not forbidden by any provision of the Federal Constitution as that Constitution was written ***

MR. JUSTICE STEWART, whom MR. JUSTICE BLACK joins, dissenting.

Since 1879 Connecticut has had on its books a law which forbids the use of contraceptives by anyone. I think this is an uncommonly silly law. But we are not asked in this case to say whether we think this law is unwise, or even asinine. We are asked to hold that it violates the United States Constitution. And that I cannot do.

In the course of its opinion the Court refers to no less than six Amendments to the Constitution: the First, the Third, the Fourth, the Fifth, the Ninth, and the Fourteenth. But the Court does not say which of these Amendments, if any, it thinks is infringed by this Connecticut law.

We are told that the Due Process Clause of the Fourteenth Amendment is not, as such, the "guide" in this case. With that much I agree. There is no claim that this law, duly enacted by the Connecticut Legislature, is unconstitutionally vague. There is no claim that the appellants were denied any of the elements of procedural due process at their trial, so as to make their convictions constitutionally invalid. And, as the Court says, the day has long passed since the Due Process Clause was regarded as a proper instrument for determining "the wisdom, need, and propriety" of state laws. *** What provision of the Constitution, then, does make this state law invalid? The Court says it is the right of privacy "created by several fundamental constitutional guarantees." With all deference, I can find no such general right of privacy in the Bill of Rights, in any other part of the Constitution, or in any case ever before decided by this Court.

At the oral argument in this case we were told that the Connecticut law does not "conform to current community standards." But it is not the function of this Court to decide cases on the basis of community standards. We are here to decide cases "agreeably to the Constitution and laws of the United States." *** If, as I should surely hope, the law before us does not reflect the standards of the people of Connecticut, the people of Connecticut can freely exercise their true Ninth and Tenth Amendment rights to persuade their elected representatives to repeal it. That is the constitutional way to take this law off the books.

Notes

1. **Methodology.** Summarize the approaches of each opinion. Consider the strengths and weaknesses of each. Which do you like best? Why?

2. **Unmarried People.**

    (a) If the plaintiffs in *Griswold* had been single (or doctors asserting the right to provide contraceptive advice and devices to unmarried people), would the case come out differently? See *Eisenstadt v. Baird*, 405 U.S. 438 (1972), which decided on equal protection grounds that a law prohibiting the sale of contraceptives to unmarried individuals was unconstitutional.

    (b) In *Eisenstadt*, the Court said: "It is true that in *Griswold* the right of privacy in question inhered in the marital relationship. Yet the marital couple is not an independent entity with a mind and a heart of its own, but an association of two individuals each with a separate intellectual and emotional makeup. If the right of privacy means anything, it is the right of the individual, married or single, to be free from unwarranted government intrusion into matters so fundamentally affecting a person as the decision whether to bear or beget a child." *[handwritten: equal protection clause]*

    (c) Do you agree with Judge Posner of the Seventh Circuit that *Eisenstadt* means that "unmarried persons have a right to engage in sexual intercourse"?

3. **Access to Contraceptives.** Would a state law that says nothing about use of contraceptives but prohibits any person other than a licensed physician from distributing contraceptives violate due process? *See Carey v. Population Services*, 431 U.S. 678 (1977).

4. **Privacy Theory.** There are two main branches of privacy theory. The first is a negative theory, originally formulated as "the right to be let alone." Brandeis and Warren, *The Right to Privacy*, 4 HARV. L. REV. 193 (1890). The second is a more positive theory, concerned not so much with legal intrusion but with the law's role in forming "the totality of a person's life." Rubenfeld, *The Right to Privacy*, 102 HARV. L. REV. 737 (1989). Which theory produced *Griswold*?

5. **Alternatives.** Since the consequences of lack of birth control fall more heavily on those who get pregnant than those who do not, should Connecticut's statute be viewed as gender discriminatory? If only poor people have trouble receiving birth control information and supplies, should this be considered an

equal protection issue? Since the Roman Catholic Church was the primary source of continued support for the Connecticut statute, should the statute (whose secular purposes were minimal) be found unconstitutional under the First Amendment? The first two questions can be analyzed with the tools you will obtain in Chapter IX; the last one, alas, is for First Amendment courses.

b. Abortion

ROE v. WADE
410 U.S. 113 (1973)

MR. JUSTICE BLACKMUN delivered the opinion of the Court.

statute only allows abortions to save the life of the mother

*** The Texas statutes *** make it a crime to "procure an abortion," as therein defined, or to attempt one, except with respect to "an abortion procured or attempted by medical advice for the purpose of saving the life of the mother." Similar statutes are in existence in a majority of the States.

Jane Roe, a single woman who was residing in Dallas County, Texas, instituted this federal action in March 1970 against the District Attorney of the county. She sought a declaratory judgment that the Texas criminal abortion statutes were unconstitutional on their face*** Roe alleged that she was unmarried and pregnant; that she wished to terminate her pregnancy by an abortion "performed by a competent, licensed physician, under safe, clinical conditions"; that she was unable to get a "legal" abortion in Texas because her life did not appear to be threatened by the continuation of her pregnancy; and that she could not afford to travel to another jurisdiction in order to secure a legal abortion under safe conditions. She claimed that the Texas statutes were unconstitutionally vague and that they abridged her right of personal privacy, protected by the First, Fourth, Fifth, Ninth, and Fourteenth Amendments. *** Roe purported to sue "on behalf of herself and all other women" similarly situated. ***

Right to privacy

The principal thrust of appellant's attack on the Texas statutes is that they improperly invade a right, said to be possessed by the pregnant woman, to choose to terminate her pregnancy. Appellant would discover this right in the concept of personal "liberty" embodied in the Fourteenth Amendment's Due Process Clause; or in personal marital, familial, and sexual privacy said to be protected by the Bill of Rights or its penumbras, see Griswold v. Connecticut, 381 U.S. 479 (1965); or among those rights reserved to the people by the Ninth Amendment, Griswold v. Connecticut, 381 U.S., at 486 (GOLDBERG, J., concurring). Before addressing this claim, we feel it desirable briefly to survey, in several aspects, the history of abortion, for such insight as that history may afford us, and then to examine the state purposes and interests behind the criminal abortion laws.

Roe argued 14A and 9A, citing to Griswold

walking through the history of abortion

It perhaps is not generally appreciated that the restrictive criminal abortion laws in effect in a majority of States today are of relatively recent vintage. Those laws, generally proscribing abortion or its attempt at any time during pregnancy except when necessary to preserve the pregnant woman's life, are not of ancient or even of common-law origin. Instead, they derive from statutory changes effected, for the most part, in the latter half of the

19th century. *** By the end of the 1950's a large majority of the jurisdictions banned abortion, however and whenever performed, unless done to save or preserve the life of the mother.

It is thus apparent that at common law, at the time of the adoption of our Constitution, and throughout the major portion of the 19th century, abortion was viewed with less disfavor than under most American statutes currently in effect. Phrasing it another way, a woman enjoyed a substantially broader right to terminate a pregnancy than she does in most States today. ***

Three reasons have been advanced to explain historically the enactment of criminal abortion laws in the 19th century and to justify their continued existence.

It has been argued occasionally that these laws were the product of a Victorian social concern to discourage illicit sexual conduct. Texas, however, does not advance this justification in the present case, and it appears that no court or commentator has taken the argument seriously. *** A second reason is concerned with abortion as a medical procedure. When most criminal abortion laws were first enacted, the procedure was a hazardous one. *** Modern medical techniques have altered this situation. *** Mortality rates for women undergoing early abortions, where the procedure is legal, appear to be as low as or lower than the rates for normal childbirth. Consequently, any interest of the State in protecting the woman from an inherently hazardous procedure, except when it would be equally dangerous for her to forgo it, has largely disappeared. Of course, important state interests in the areas of health and medical standards do remain. The State has a legitimate interest in seeing to it that abortion, like any other medical procedure, is performed under circumstances that insure maximum safety for the patient *** [and] the State retains a definite interest in protecting the woman's own health and safety when an abortion is proposed at a late stage of pregnancy. *** The third reason is the State's interest *** in protecting prenatal life. Some of the argument for this justification rests on the theory that a new human life is present from the moment of conception. *** [However, in] assessing the State's interest, recognition may be given to the less rigid claim that as long as at least potential life is involved, the State may assert interests beyond the protection of the pregnant woman alone. ***

The Constitution does not explicitly mention any right of privacy. *** [However,] the Court has recognized that a right of personal privacy, or a guarantee of certain areas or zones of privacy, does exist under the Constitution. In varying contexts, the Court or individual Justices have, indeed, found at least the roots of that right in the First Amendment, in the Fourth and Fifth Amendments, in the penumbras of the Bill of Rights, [*Griswold*], in the Ninth Amendment, or in the concept of liberty guaranteed by the first section of the Fourteenth Amendment, *see Meyer v. Nebraska*. These decisions make it clear that only personal rights that can be deemed "fundamental" or "implicit in the concept of ordered liberty," are included in this guarantee of personal privacy. They also make it clear that the right has some extension to activities relating to marriage, *Loving v. Virginia*, 388 U.S. 1, 12 (1967); procreation, *Skinner v. Oklahoma*, 316 U.S. 535, 541–542 (1942);

contraception, *Eisenstadt v. Baird*, 405 U.S., at 453–454 (1972); family relationships, *Prince v. Massachusetts*, 321 U.S. 158, 166 (1944); and child rearing and education, *Pierce v. Society of Sisters*, 268 U.S. 510 (1925), *Meyer v. Nebraska*, 262 U.S. 390 (1923).

Right to privacy applies to pregnancy and the right to terminate

too many risks not to

This right of privacy, whether it be founded in the Fourteenth Amendment's concept of personal liberty and restrictions upon state action, as we feel it is, or [in] the Ninth Amendment's reservation of rights to the people, is broad enough to encompass a woman's decision whether or not to terminate her pregnancy. The detriment that the State would impose upon the pregnant woman by denying this choice altogether is apparent. Specific and direct harm medically diagnosable even in early pregnancy may be involved. Maternity, or additional offspring, may force upon the woman a distressful life and future. Psychological harm may be imminent. Mental and physical health may be taxed by child care. There is also the distress, for all concerned, associated with the unwanted child, and there is the problem of bringing a child into a family already unable, psychologically and otherwise, to care for it. In other cases, as in this one, the additional difficulties and continuing stigma of unwed motherhood may be involved. All these are factors the woman and her responsible physician necessarily will consider in consultation.

Roe arg'd that women have the right to terminate at any time

Right to terminate exists but can be limited by State interests

On the basis of elements such as these, appellant [argues] that the woman's right is absolute and that she is entitled to terminate her pregnancy at whatever time, in whatever way, and for whatever reason she alone chooses. With this we do not agree. *** The Court's decisions recognizing a right of privacy also acknowledge that some state regulation in areas protected by that right is appropriate. As noted above, a State may properly assert important interests in safeguarding health, in maintaining medical standards, and in protecting potential life. *** We, therefore, conclude that the right of personal privacy includes the abortion decision, but that this right is not unqualified and must be considered against important state interests in regulation. *** Where certain "fundamental rights" are involved, the Court has held that regulation limiting these rights may be justified only by a "compelling state interest," and that legislative enactments must be narrowly drawn to express only the legitimate state interests at stake. ***

Wade argues that the fetus has 14th rights

but no case law was available

The appellee [argues] that the fetus is a "person" within the language and meaning of the Fourteenth Amendment. *** If this suggestion of personhood is established, the appellant's case, of course, collapses, for the fetus' right to life would then be guaranteed specifically by the Amendment. The appellant conceded as much on reargument. On the other hand, the appellee conceded on reargument that no case could be cited that holds that a fetus is a person within the meaning of the Fourteenth Amendment.

The Constitution does not define "person" in so many words. Section 1 of the Fourteenth Amendment contains three references to "person." The first, in defining "citizens," speaks of "persons born or naturalized in the United States." The word also appears both in the Due Process Clause and in the Equal Protection Clause. "Person" is used in other places in the Constitution: in the listing of qualifications for Representatives and Senators, Art, I, § 2, cl.

2, and § 3, cl. 3; in the Apportionment Clause, Art. I, § 2, cl. 3; in the Migration and Importation provision, Art. I, § 9, cl. 1; in the Emolument Clause, Art, I, § 9, cl. 8; in the Electors provisions, Art. II, § 1, cl. 2, and the superseded cl. 3; in the provision outlining qualifications for the office of President, Art. II, § 1, cl. 5; in the Extradition provisions, Art. IV, § 2, cl. 2, and the superseded Fugitive Slave Clause 3; and in the Fifth, Twelfth, and Twenty-second Amendments, as well as in §§ 2 and 3 of the Fourteenth Amendment. But in nearly all these instances, the use of the word is such that it has application only postnatally. None indicates, with any assurance, that it has any possible prenatal application.[54]

[handwritten margin note: looks to const. text but all references to people are postnatal]

All this, together with our observation *** that throughout the major portion of the 19th century prevailing legal abortion practices were far freer than they are today, persuades us that the word "person," as used in the Fourteenth Amendment, does not include the unborn. *** This conclusion, however, does not of itself fully answer the contentions raised by Texas, and we pass on to other considerations.

[handwritten margin note: unborn people are not protected by the const.]

The pregnant woman cannot be isolated in her privacy. She carries an embryo and, later, a fetus, if one accepts the medical definitions of the developing young in the human uterus. The situation therefore is inherently different from marital intimacy, or bedroom possession of obscene material, or marriage, or procreation, or education, with which *Eisenstadt* and *Griswold, Stanley, Loving, Skinner* and *Pierce* and *Meyer* were respectively concerned. As we have intimated above, it is reasonable and appropriate for a State to decide that at some point in time another interest, that of health of the mother or that of potential human life, becomes significantly involved. The woman's privacy is no longer sole and any right of privacy she possesses must be measured accordingly.

[handwritten margin note: Diff. from pure marraige privacy and at one point becomes a state issue]

Texas urges that, apart from the Fourteenth Amendment, life begins at conception and is present throughout pregnancy, and that, therefore, the State has a compelling interest in protecting that life from and after conception. We need not resolve the difficult question of when life begins. *** In areas other than criminal abortion, the law has been reluctant to endorse any theory that life, as we recognize it, begins before live birth or to accord legal rights to the unborn except in narrowly defined situations and except when the rights are contingent upon live birth. *** In view of all this, we do not agree that, by adopting one theory of life, Texas may override the rights of the pregnant woman that are at stake. We repeat, however, that the State does have an important and legitimate interest in preserving and protecting the health of the pregnant woman, *** and that it has still another important and legitimate interest in protecting the potentiality of human life. These

[handwritten margin note: Wade argues that life begins at conception]

[handwritten margin note: Ct. takes no stance on when life begins but acknowledges that states have an interest in protecting women + fetuses]

---

[54] When Texas urges that a fetus is entitled to Fourteenth Amendment protection as a person, it faces a dilemma. Neither in Texas nor in any other State are all abortions prohibited. Despite broad proscription, an exception always exists. The exception [in Texas] for an abortion procured or attempted by medical advice for the purpose of saving the life of the mother, is typical. But if the fetus is a person who is not to be deprived of life without due process of law, and if the mother's condition is the sole determinant, does not the Texas exception appear to be out of line with the Amendment's command?

interests are separate and distinct. Each grows in substantiality as the woman approaches term and, at a point during pregnancy, each becomes "compelling."

With respect to the State's important and legitimate interest in the health of the mother, the "compelling" point, in the light of present medical knowledge, is at approximately the end of the first trimester. This is so because of the now-established medical fact that until the end of the first trimester mortality in abortion may be less than mortality in normal childbirth. It follows that, from and after this point, a State may regulate the abortion procedure to the extent that the regulation reasonably relates to the preservation and protection of maternal health. Examples of permissible state regulation in this area are requirements as to the qualifications of the person who is to perform the abortion; as to the licensure of that person; as to the facility in which the procedure is to be performed, that is, whether it must be a hospital or may be a clinic or some other place of less-than-hospital status; as to the licensing of the facility; and the like.

1st trimester is a threshold

This means, on the other hand, that, for the period of pregnancy prior to this "compelling" point, the attending physician, in consultation with his patient, is free to determine, without regulation by the State, that, in his medical judgment, the patient's pregnancy should be terminated. If that decision is reached, the judgment may be effectuated by an abortion free of interference by the State.

Abortion is legal during the first trimester

With respect to the State's important and legitimate interest in potential life, the "compelling" point is at viability. This is so because the fetus then presumably has the capability of meaningful life outside the mother's womb. State regulation protective of fetal life after viability thus has both logical and biological justifications. If the State is interested in protecting fetal life after viability, it may go so far as to proscribe abortion during that period, except when it is necessary to preserve the life or health of the mother.

because a baby can't live outside the womb until that point.

Measured against these standards, [the Texas statute], in restricting legal abortions to those "procured or attempted by medical advice for the purpose of saving the life of the mother," sweeps too broadly. The statute makes no distinction between abortions performed early in pregnancy and those performed later, and it limits to a single reason, "saving" the mother's life, the legal justification for the procedure. The statute, therefore, cannot survive the constitutional attack made upon it here.

Statute is unconst because it is a blanket ban on abortion

To summarize and to repeat:

1. A state criminal abortion statute of the current Texas type, that excepts from criminality only a life-saving procedure on behalf of the mother, without regard to pregnancy stage and without recognition of the other interests involved, is violative of the Due Process Clause of the Fourteenth Amendment.

(a) For the stage prior to approximately the end of the first trimester, the abortion decision and its effectuation must be left to the medical judgment of the pregnant woman's attending physician.

(b) For the stage subsequent to approximately the end of the first trimester, the State, in promoting its interest in the health of the mother, may, if it chooses, regulate the abortion procedure in ways that are reasonably related to maternal health.

state can regulate after first trimester

(c) For the stage subsequent to viability, the State in promoting its interest in the potentiality of human life may, if it chooses, regulate, and even proscribe, abortion except where it is necessary, in appropriate medical judgment, for the preservation of the life or health of the mother. ***

MR. JUSTICE STEWART, concurring.

*** The Constitution nowhere mentions a specific right of personal choice in matters of marriage and family life, but the "liberty" protected by the Due Process Clause of the Fourteenth Amendment covers more than those freedoms explicitly named in the Bill of Rights. *** As recently as last Term, in *Eisenstadt v. Baird*, 405 U.S. 438, 453, we recognized "the right of the individual, married or single, to be free from unwarranted governmental intrusion into matters so fundamentally affecting a person as the decision whether to bear or beget a child." That right necessarily includes the right of a woman to decide whether or not to terminate her pregnancy.

The asserted state interests are protection of the health and safety of the pregnant woman, and protection of the potential future human life within her. These are legitimate objectives, amply sufficient to permit a State to regulate abortions as it does other surgical procedures, and perhaps sufficient to permit a State to regulate abortions more stringently or even to prohibit them in the late stages of pregnancy. But such legislation is not before us, and I think the Court today has thoroughly demonstrated that these state interests cannot constitutionally support the broad abridgment of personal liberty worked by the existing Texas law. ***

[Concurrences of MR. JUSTICE BURGER and MR. JUSTICE DOUGLAS omitted]

MR. JUSTICE REHNQUIST, dissenting.

*** I have difficulty in concluding, as the Court does, that the right of "privacy" is involved in this case. Texas, by the statute here challenged, bars the performance of a medical abortion by a licensed physician on a plaintiff such as Roe. A transaction resulting in an operation such as this is not "private" in the ordinary usage of that word. Nor is the "privacy" that the Court finds here even a distant relative of the freedom from searches and seizures protected by the Fourth Amendment to the Constitution, which the Court has referred to as embodying a right to privacy.

If the Court means by the term "privacy" no more than that the claim of a person to be free from unwanted state regulation of consensual transactions may be a form of "liberty" protected by the Fourteenth Amendment, there is no doubt that similar claims have been upheld in our earlier decisions on the basis of that liberty. I agree *** that the "liberty," against deprivation of which without due process the Fourteenth Amendment protects, embraces more than the rights found in the Bill of Rights. But that liberty is not

Abortion is not a matter of privacy

Rational Basis

guaranteed absolutely against deprivation, only against deprivation without due process of law. The test traditionally applied in the area of social and economic legislation is whether or not a law such as that challenged has a rational relation to a valid state objective. *Williamson v. Lee Optical Co.*, 348 U.S. 483, 491 (1955). The Due Process Clause of the Fourteenth Amendment undoubtedly does place a limit, albeit a broad one, on legislative power to enact laws such as this. If the Texas statute were to prohibit an abortion even where the mother's life is in jeopardy, I have little doubt that such a statute would lack a rational relation to a valid state objective under the test stated in *Williamson*. But the Court's sweeping invalidation of any restrictions on abortion during the first trimester is impossible to justify under that standard, and the conscious weighing of competing factors that the Court's opinion apparently substitutes for the established test is far more appropriate to a legislative judgment than to a judicial one.

Should have applied it

The Court eschews the history of the Fourteenth Amendment in its reliance on the "compelling state interest" test. *** But the Court adds a new wrinkle to this test by transposing it from the legal considerations associated with the Equal Protection Clause of the Fourteenth Amendment to this case arising under the Due Process Clause of the Fourteenth Amendment. Unless I misapprehend the consequences of this transplanting of the "compelling state interest test," the Court's opinion will accomplish the seemingly impossible feat of leaving this area of the law more confused than it found it. *** As in *Lochner* and similar cases applying substantive due process standards to economic and social welfare legislation, the adoption of the compelling state interest standard will inevitably require this Court to examine the legislative policies and pass on the wisdom of these policies in the very process of deciding whether a particular state interest put forward may or may not be 'compelling.' The decision here to break pregnancy into three distinct terms and to outline the permissible restrictions the State may impose in each one, for example, partakes more of judicial legislation than it does of a determination of the intent of the drafters of the Fourteenth Amendment. ***

Says that the majority was legislating

To reach its result, the Court necessarily has had to find within the Scope of the Fourteenth Amendment a right that was apparently completely unknown to the drafters of the Amendment. *** By the time of the adoption of the Fourteenth Amendment in 1868, there were at least 36 laws enacted by state or territorial legislatures limiting abortion. ***

Even if one were to agree that the case that the Court decides were here, and that the enunciation of the substantive constitutional law in the Court's opinion were proper, the actual disposition of the case by the Court is still difficult to justify. The Texas statute is struck down in toto, even though the Court apparently concedes that at later periods of pregnancy Texas might impose these selfsame statutory limitations on abortion. My understanding of past practice is that a statute found to be invalid as applied to a particular plaintiff, but not unconstitutional as a whole, is not simply 'struck down' but is, instead, declared unconstitutional as applied to the fact situation before the Court. ***

Could have just said it was wrong in the case at hand

PLANNED PARENTHOOD v. CASEY

505 U.S. 833 (1992).

JUSTICE O'CONNOR, JUSTICE KENNEDY, and JUSTICE SOUTER announced the judgment of the Court and delivered the opinion of the Court with respect to Parts I, II, III, V–A, V–C, and VI, an opinion with respect to Part V-E, in which JUSTICE STEVENS joins, and an opinion with respect to Parts IV, V-B, and V–D.

I

Liberty finds no refuge in a jurisprudence of doubt. Yet 19 years after our holding that the Constitution protects a woman's right to terminate her pregnancy in its early stages, *Roe v. Wade*, 410 U.S. 113 (1973), that definition of liberty is still questioned. Joining the respondents as amicus curiae, the United States, as it has done in five other cases in the last decade, again asks us to overrule *Roe*.

At issue in these cases are five provisions of the Pennsylvania Abortion Control Act of 1982 *** The Act requires that a woman seeking an abortion give her informed consent prior to the abortion procedure, and specifies that she be provided with certain information at least 24 hours before the abortion is performed. For a minor to obtain an abortion, the Act requires the informed consent of one of her parents, but provides for a judicial bypass option if the minor does not wish to or cannot obtain a parent's consent. Another provision of the Act requires that, unless certain exceptions apply, a married woman seeking an abortion must sign a statement indicating that she has notified her husband of her intended abortion. The Act exempts compliance with these three requirements in the event of a "medical emergency." In addition to the above provisions regulating the performance of abortions, the Act imposes certain reporting requirements on facilities that provide abortion services. *** After considering the fundamental constitutional questions resolved by *Roe*, principles of institutional integrity, and the rule of stare decisis, we are led to conclude this: the essential holding of *Roe v. Wade* should be retained and once again reaffirmed.

*** *Roe*'s essential holding, the holding we reaffirm, has three parts. First is a recognition of the right of the woman to choose to have an abortion before viability and to obtain it without undue interference from the State. Before viability, the State's interests are not strong enough to support a prohibition of abortion or the imposition of a substantial obstacle to the woman's effective right to elect the procedure. Second is a confirmation of the State's power to restrict abortions after fetal viability, if the law contains exceptions for pregnancies which endanger the woman's life or health. And third is the principle that the State has legitimate interests from the outset of the pregnancy in protecting the health of the woman and the life of the fetus that may become a child. These principles do not contradict one another; and we adhere to each.

II

Constitutional protection of the woman's decision to terminate her pregnancy derives from the Due Process Clause of the Fourteenth Amendment. *** It is tempting *** to suppose that the Due Process Clause protects only those practices, defined at the most specific level, that were protected against government interference by other rules of law when the Fourteenth Amendment was ratified. But such a view would be inconsistent with our law. It is a promise of the Constitution that there is a realm of personal liberty which the government may not enter. We have vindicated this principle before. Marriage is mentioned nowhere in the Bill of Rights and interracial marriage was illegal in most States in the 19th century, but the Court was no doubt correct in finding it to be an aspect of liberty protected against state interference by the substantive component of the Due Process Clause in *Loving v. Virginia*, 388 U.S. 1, 12 (1967). *** Neither the Bill of Rights nor the specific practices of States at the time of the adoption of the Fourteenth Amendment marks the outer limits of the substantive sphere of liberty which the Fourteenth Amendment protects. *See* U.S. Const., Amdt. 9.

*** Though abortion is conduct, it does not follow that the State is entitled to proscribe it in all instances. That is because the liberty of the woman is at stake in a sense unique to the human condition and so unique to the law. The mother who carries a child to full term is subject to anxieties, to physical constraints, to pain that only she must bear. That these sacrifices have from the beginning of the human race been endured by woman with a pride that ennobles her in the eyes of others and gives to the infant a bond of love cannot alone be grounds for the State to insist she make the sacrifice. Her suffering is too intimate and personal for the State to insist, without more, upon its own vision of the woman's role, however dominant that vision has been in the course of our history and our culture. The destiny of the woman must be shaped to a large extent on her own conception of her spiritual imperatives and her place in society. ***

IV.

*** [T]he basic decision in *Roe* was based on a constitutional analysis which we cannot now repudiate. The woman's liberty is not so unlimited, however, that from the outset the State cannot show its concern for the life of the unborn, and at a later point in fetal development the State's interest in life has sufficient force so that the right of the woman to terminate the pregnancy can be restricted. *** We conclude the line should be drawn at viability, so that before that time the woman has a right to choose to terminate her pregnancy. We adhere to this principle for two reasons. First, as we have said, is the doctrine of stare decisis. *** The second reason is that the concept of viability, as we noted in *Roe*, is the time at which there is a realistic possibility of maintaining and nourishing a life outside the womb, so that the independent existence of the second life can in reason and all fairness be the object of state protection that now overrides the rights of the woman. *** *Roe v. Wade* speaks with clarity in establishing not only the woman's liberty but also the State's "important and legitimate interest in potential life." ***

Roe established a trimester framework to govern abortion regulations. *** We reject the trimester framework, which we do not consider to be part of the essential holding of *Roe*. *** The trimester framework suffers from these basic flaws: in its formulation it misconceives the nature of the pregnant woman's interest; and in practice it undervalues the State's interest in potential life, as recognized in *Roe*. ***

Numerous forms of state regulation might have the incidental effect of increasing the cost or decreasing the availability of medical care, whether for abortion or any other medical procedure. The fact that a law which serves a valid purpose, one not designed to strike at the right itself, has the incidental effect of making it more difficult or more expensive to procure an abortion cannot be enough to invalidate it. Only where state regulation imposes an undue burden on a woman's ability to make this decision does the power of the State reach into the heart of the liberty protected by the Due Process Clause. *** Not all governmental intrusion is of necessity unwarranted; and that brings us to the other basic flaw in the trimester framework: even in *Roe*'s terms, in practice it undervalues the State's interest in the potential life within the woman. *** Not all burdens on the right to decide whether to terminate a pregnancy will be undue. In our view, the undue burden standard is the appropriate means of reconciling the State's interest with the woman's constitutionally protected liberty.

A finding of an undue burden is a shorthand for the conclusion that a state regulation has the purpose or effect of placing a substantial obstacle in the path of a woman seeking an abortion of a nonviable fetus. A statute with this purpose is invalid because the means chosen by the State to further the interest in potential life must be calculated to inform the woman's free choice, not hinder it. And a statute which, while furthering the interest in potential life or some other valid state interest, has the effect of placing a substantial obstacle in the path of a woman's choice cannot be considered a permissible means of serving its legitimate ends. *** Understood another way, we answer the question, left open in previous opinions discussing the undue burden formulation, whether a law designed to further the State's interest in fetal life which imposes an undue burden on the woman's decision before fetal viability could be constitutional. The answer is no *** [but] regulations which do no more than create a structural mechanism by which the State, or the parent or guardian of a minor, may express profound respect for the life of the unborn are permitted, if they are not a substantial obstacle to the woman's exercise of the right to choose. Unless it has that effect on her right of choice, a state measure designed to persuade her to choose childbirth over abortion will be upheld if reasonably related to that goal. Regulations designed to foster the health of a woman seeking an abortion are valid if they do not constitute an undue burden.

*** We give this summary:

(a) To protect the central right recognized by *Roe v. Wade* while at the same time accommodating the State's profound interest in potential life, we will employ the undue burden analysis as explained in this opinion. ***

(b) We reject the rigid trimester framework of *Roe v. Wade*. ***

(c) As with any medical procedure, the State may enact regulations to further the health or safety of a woman seeking an abortion. Unnecessary health regulations that have the purpose or effect of presenting a substantial obstacle to a woman seeking an abortion impose an undue burden on the right.

(d) Our adoption of the undue burden analysis does not disturb the central holding of *Roe v. Wade*, and we reaffirm that holding. *** [A] state may not prohibit any woman from making the ultimate decision to terminate her pregnancy before viability.

(e) We also reaffirm *Roe*'s holding that "subsequent to viability, the State in promoting its interest in the potentiality of human life may, if it chooses, regulate, and even proscribe, abortion except where it is necessary, in appropriate medical judgment, for the preservation of the life or health of the mother."

These principles control our assessment of the Pennsylvania statute, and we now turn to the issue of the validity of its challenged provisions.

V

*** We now consider the separate statutory sections at issue.

A. Because it is central to the operation of various other requirements, we begin with the statute's definition of medical emergency. Under the statute, a medical emergency is "[t]hat condition which, on the basis of the physician's good faith clinical judgment, so complicates the medical condition of a pregnant woman as to necessitate the immediate abortion of her pregnancy to avert her death or for which a delay will create serious risk of substantial and irreversible impairment of a major bodily function." *** The District Court found that there were three serious conditions which would not be covered by the statute: preeclampsia, inevitable abortion, and premature ruptured membrane. Yet, as the Court of Appeals observed, it is undisputed that under some circumstances each of these conditions could lead to an illness with substantial and irreversible consequences. While the definition could be interpreted in an unconstitutional manner, the Court of Appeals construed the phrase "serious risk" to include those circumstances. *** [A]s construed by the Court of Appeals, the medical emergency definition imposes no undue burden on a woman's abortion right.

B. We next consider the informed consent requirement. Except in a medical emergency, the statute requires that at least 24 hours before performing an abortion a physician inform the woman of the nature of the procedure, the health risks of the abortion and of childbirth, and the "probable gestational age of the unborn child." The physician or a qualified nonphysician must inform the woman of the availability of printed materials published by the State describing the fetus and providing information about medical assistance for childbirth, information about child support from the father, and a list of agencies which provide adoption and other services as alternatives to abortion. An abortion may not be performed unless the woman certifies in writing that she has been informed of the availability of these printed materials and has been provided them if she chooses to view them. *** In attempting to ensure that a woman apprehend the full consequences of her decision, the State furthers the legitimate purpose of reducing the risk that a woman may elect an abortion, only to discover later, with devastating psychological consequences, that her decision was not fully informed. If the information the State requires to be made available to the woman is truthful and not misleading, the requirement may be permissible.

We also see no reason why the State may not require doctors to inform a woman seeking an abortion of the availability of materials relating to the consequences to the fetus, even when those consequences have no direct relation to her health. *** Since there is no evidence on this record that requiring a doctor to give the information as provided by the statute would amount in practical terms to a substantial obstacle to a woman seeking an abortion, we conclude that it is not an undue burden. ***

Our analysis of Pennsylvania's 24–hour waiting period *** under the undue burden standard requires us to reconsider the premise behind the decision in *Akron I* invalidating a parallel requirement. *** The idea that important decisions will be more informed and deliberate if they follow some period of reflection does not strike us as unreasonable, particularly where the statute directs that important information become part of the background of the decision. ***

Whether the mandatory 24–hour waiting period is nonetheless invalid because in practice it is a substantial obstacle to a woman's choice to terminate her pregnancy is a closer question. The *** District Court found that for those women who have the fewest financial resources, those who must travel long distances, and those who have difficulty explaining their whereabouts to husbands, employers, or others, the 24–hour waiting period will be "particularly burdensome."

These findings are troubling in some respects, but they do not demonstrate that the waiting period constitutes an undue burden. *** A particular burden is not of necessity a substantial obstacle. *** We are left with the argument that the various aspects of the informed consent requirement are unconstitutional because they place barriers in the way of abortion on demand. Even the broadest reading of *Roe*, however, has not suggested that there is a constitutional right to abortion on demand. Rather, the right protected by *Roe* is a right to decide to terminate a pregnancy free of undue interference by the State. *** The informed consent requirement is not an undue burden on that right.

C. Section 3209 of Pennsylvania's abortion law provides, except in cases of medical emergency, that no physician shall perform an abortion on a married woman without receiving a signed statement from the woman that she has notified her spouse that she is about to undergo an abortion. The woman has the option of providing an alternative signed statement certifying that her husband is not the man who impregnated her; that her husband could not be located; that the pregnancy is the result of spousal sexual assault which she has reported; or that the woman believes that notifying her husband will cause him or someone else to inflict bodily injury upon her. A physician who performs an abortion on a married woman without receiving the appropriate signed statement will have his or her license revoked, and is liable to the husband for damages.

The District Court *** made detailed findings *** which suggested that women in a physically abusive relationship are unlikely to take the exceptions to the notification requirement. *** These findings are supported by studies of domestic violence. *** Other studies fill in the rest of this troubling picture. Physical violence is only the most visible form of abuse. Psychological abuse, particularly forced social and economic isolation of women, is also common. *** If anything in this field is certain, it is that [millions of] victims of spousal sexual assault are extremely reluctant to report the abuse to the government; hence, a great many spousal rape victims will not be exempt from the notification requirement imposed by § 3209.

Respondents attempt to avoid the conclusion that § 3209 is invalid by pointing out that it imposes almost no burden at all for the vast majority of women seeking abortions. *** The analysis does not end with the one percent of women upon whom the statute operates; it begins there. *** The proper focus of constitutional inquiry is the group for whom the law is a restriction, not the group for whom the law is irrelevant. *** It is an undue burden, and therefore invalid.

This conclusion is in no way inconsistent with our decisions upholding parental notification or consent requirements. Those enactments, and our judgment that they are constitutional, are based on the quite reasonable assumption that minors will benefit from consultation with their parents and that children will often not realize that their parents have their best interests at heart. We cannot adopt a parallel assumption about adult women. ***

The husband's interest in the life of the child his wife is carrying does not permit the State to empower him with this troubling degree of authority over his wife. *** If a husband's interest in the potential life of the child outweighs a wife's liberty, the State could require a married woman to notify her husband before she uses a postfertilization contraceptive. Perhaps next in line would be a statute requiring pregnant married women to notify their husbands before engaging in conduct causing risks to the fetus. After all, if the husband's interest in the fetus' safety is a sufficient predicate for state regulation, the State could reasonably conclude that pregnant wives should notify their husbands before drinking alcohol or smoking. *** A State may not give to a man the kind of dominion over his wife that parents exercise over their children. ***

D. We next consider the parental consent provision. Except in a medical emergency, an unemancipated young woman under 18 may not obtain an abortion unless she and one of her parents (or guardian) provides informed consent as defined above. If neither a parent nor a guardian provides consent, a court may authorize the performance of an abortion upon a determination that the young woman is mature and capable of giving informed consent and has in fact given her informed consent, or that an abortion would be in her best interests. *** The only argument made by petitioners respecting this provision and to which our prior decisions do not speak is the contention that the parental consent requirement is invalid because it requires informed parental consent. For the most part, petitioners' argument is a reprise of their argument with respect to the informed consent requirement in general, and we reject it for the reasons given above. Indeed, some of the provisions regarding informed consent have particular force with respect to minors: the waiting period, for example, may provide the parent or parents of a pregnant young woman the opportunity to consult with her in private, and to discuss the consequences of her decision in the context of the values and moral or religious principles of their family.

E. Under the recordkeeping and reporting requirements of the statute, every facility which performs abortions is required to file a report stating its name and address as well as the name and address of any related entity, such as a controlling or subsidiary organization. In the case of state-funded institutions, the information becomes public. *** In *Danforth*, 428 U.S., at 80, we held that recordkeeping and reporting provisions "that are reasonably directed to the preservation of maternal health and that properly respect a patient's confidentiality and privacy are permissible." We think that under this standard, all the provisions at issue here, except that relating to spousal notice, are constitutional. Although they do not relate to the State's interest in informing the woman's choice, they do relate to health. *** At most they might increase the cost of some abortions by a slight amount. While at some point increased cost could become a substantial obstacle, there is no such showing on the record before us. ***

JUSTICE STEVENS, concurring in part and dissenting in part.

*** In my opinion, a correct application of the "undue burden" standard leads to the [following] conclusion concerning the constitutionality of these requirements. A state-imposed burden on the exercise of a constitutional right is measured both by its effects and by its character: A burden may be "undue" either because the burden is too severe or because it lacks a legitimate, rational justification. *** The 24–hour delay requirement fails both parts of this test. *** The counseling provisions are similarly infirm. *** This information is of little decisional value in most cases, because 90% of all abortions are performed during the first trimester when fetal age has less relevance than when the fetus nears viability. ***

JUSTICE BLACKMUN, concurring in part, concurring in the judgment in part, and dissenting in part. [JUSTICE BLACKMUN reiterated his belief in the correctness of *Roe v. Wade*. He dissented from substituting the undue burden test for strict scrutiny.]

CHIEF JUSTICE REHNQUIST, with whom JUSTICE WHITE, JUSTICE SCALIA, and JUSTICE THOMAS join, concurring in the judgment in part and dissenting in part.

The joint opinion, following its newly minted variation on stare decisis, retains the outer shell of *Roe v. Wade*, but beats a wholesale retreat from the substance of that case. We believe that *Roe* was wrongly decided, and that it can and should be overruled consistently with our traditional approach to stare decisis in constitutional cases. *** Unlike marriage, procreation, and contraception, abortion "involves the purposeful termination of a potential life." *** Nor do the historical traditions of the American people support the view that the right to terminate one's pregnancy is "fundamental." ***

JUSTICE SCALIA, with whom CHIEF JUSTICE REHNQUIST, JUSTICE WHITE, and JUSTICE THOMAS join, concurring in the judgment in part and dissenting in part.

*** A State's choice between two positions on which reasonable people can disagree is constitutional even when (as is often the case) it intrudes upon a "liberty" in the absolute sense. *** That is, quite simply, the issue in these cases: not whether the power of a woman to abort her unborn child is a "liberty" in the absolute sense; or even whether it is a liberty of great importance to many women. Of course it is both. The issue is whether it is a liberty protected by the Constitution of the United States. I am sure it is not. I reach that conclusion *** for the same reason I reach the conclusion that bigamy is not constitutionally protected—because of two simple facts: (1) the Constitution says absolutely nothing about it, and (2) the longstanding traditions of American society have permitted it to be legally proscribed. *** The emptiness of the "reasoned judgment" that produced *Roe* is displayed in plain view by the fact that, after more than 19 years of effort by some of the brightest (and most determined) legal minds in the country, after more than 10 cases upholding abortion rights in this Court, and after dozens upon dozens of amicus briefs submitted in these and other cases, the best the Court can do to explain how it is that the word "liberty" must be thought to include the right to destroy human fetuses is to rattle off a collection of adjectives that simply decorate a value judgment and conceal a political choice. *** Not only did *Roe* not, as the Court suggests, resolve the deeply divisive issue of abortion; it did more than anything else to nourish it, by elevating it to the national level where it is infinitely more difficult to resolve. *** *Roe*'s mandate for abortion on demand destroyed the compromises of the past, rendered compromise impossible for the future, and required the entire issue to be resolved uniformly, at the national level. ***

There comes vividly to mind a portrait by Emanuel Leutze that hangs in the Harvard Law School: Roger Brooke Taney, painted in 1859, the 82d year of his life, the 24th of his Chief Justiceship, the second after his opinion in *Dred Scott*. He is all in black, sitting in a shadowed red armchair, left hand resting upon a pad of paper in his lap, right hand hanging limply, almost lifelessly, beside the inner arm of the chair. He sits facing the viewer and staring straight out. There seems to be on his face, and in his deep-set eyes, an expression of profound sadness and disillusionment. Perhaps he always looked that way, even when dwelling upon the happiest of thoughts. But those of us who know how the lustre of his great Chief Justiceship came to be eclipsed by *Dred Scott* cannot help believing that he had that case—its already apparent consequences for the Court and its soon-to-be-played-out consequences for the Nation—burning on his mind. I expect that two years earlier he, too, had thought himself "call[ing] the contending sides of national controversy to end their national division by accepting a common mandate rooted in the Constitution."

It is no more realistic for us in this litigation, than it was for him in that, to think that an issue of the sort they both involved—an issue involving life and death, freedom and subjugation—can be "speedily and finally settled" by the Supreme Court ***. Quite to the contrary, by foreclosing all democratic outlet for the deep passions this issue arouses, by banishing the issue from the political forum that gives all participants, even the losers, the satisfaction of a fair hearing and an honest fight, by continuing the imposition of a rigid national rule instead of allowing for regional differences, the Court merely prolongs and intensifies the anguish. ***

Notes

1. **Criticisms of *Roe*.** Scholars were very critical of *Griswold's* methodology but the case led to no popular protests or legislative reactions in Connecticut or elsewhere. *Roe*, conversely, has fueled a political firestorm for over twenty-five years. Consider the following commonly-articulated views of why *Roe* has been so controversial, and decide whether or not you agree:

• In *Roe*, the Court acted like a legislature rather than a court.

• *Roe* is the *Dred Scott* of the Court's work in the 20th Century.

• *Roe* ended the possibility of political compromise on abortion rather than initiating a dialogue on the topic.

• *Roe* shifted the debate over abortion from the States, where it might be resolved, to the nation, where it is far harder to resolve.

• *Roe* is merely *Lochner* in liberal garb.

• The Court's decision "reads like a set of hospital rules" which will be "destroyed with new statistics" concerning medical advances.

2. **Defenses of *Roe*.** Do you agree or disagree with the following?

• *Roe* involves a stronger case for privacy than *Griswold:* the woman's interest in controlling her own body and her bodily integrity.

• *Roe* is essential to the lives and well-being of millions of women. It needs no further justification.

• The result in *Roe* was correct, but it should have been decided on gender-discrimination grounds.

• The outcome in *Roe* is strongly supported by First Amendment freedom of religion considerations.

3. **Other Perspectives on *Roe*.**

• Does it matter whether we phrase the right in *Roe* as one of "abortion" or "control over reproduction"?

• "Is the pregnant woman being required to confer a benefit on the fetus, or is she being prevented from harming it? This depends on whether the baseline is a world in which women control their pregnancies, or one in which pregnancies proceed to term." Farber, Eskridge, and Frickey, CONSTITUTIONAL LAW: THEMES FOR THE CONSTITUTION'S THIRD CENTURY, pp. 512–13 (West 1993).

• The right to obtain an abortion "does not free women, it frees male sexual aggression. The availability of abortion [removes] the one remaining legitimized reason that women have had for refusing sex besides the headache." MacKinnon, *Roe v. Wade: A Study in Male Ideology*, in ABORTION: MORAL AND LEGAL PERSPECTIVES 45, 49–51 (J. Garfield ed. 1985).

• Consider a hypothetical situation in which your circulatory system is involuntarily hooked up to a concert violinist who will die if detached from you in less than nine months. Are you morally justified in detaching the violinist? Can government compel you not to do so, under penalty of imprisonment? How, if at all, does this hypothetical differ from the situation of a woman carrying a fetus? *See* Thomson, *A Defense of Abortion*, 1 PHIL. & PUB. AFF. 47 (1971).

4.   *Roe* **and** *Casey.* How much of *Roe* survives and how much is discarded in *Casey*? What problems, if any, does the "undue burden" framework resolve? What new problems, if any, does it create? Do you find the Joint Opinion's selective use of stare decisis troubling or appropriate? Should the Court be more reluctant to correct big errors than small ones? Is it right to say that *Lochner* and *Plessy* primarily involved factual errors?

5.   *Casey.*

• Many people's views on abortion are determined by whether they consider the fetus a "person." Consider whether the state can regulate abortion even if the fetus is not a person within the meaning of the Constitution. If you are pro-choice, are you barred from recognizing the fetus as potential life? If you are pro-life, are there any circumstances where you might find abortion justifiable? Why isn't the State's interest in protection of fetal life compelling enough at every stage of pregnancy to permit regulation, even to the point of prohibition?

• The Joint Opinion approaches the meaning of "liberty" as an exercise in common law analogical thinking. JUSTICE SCALIA's dissent argues that "liberty" should only be protected when it is an outgrowth of deductive logic. Which is the correct approach? Does this component of *Casey* remind you of Frankfurter and Black's argument in *Adamson*?

• Consider the Court's analysis of Pennsylvania's spousal notification, parental consent, and waiting period provisions. Construct variations on each that would at least arguably lead to different results than those of the Court. What does this exercise tell you about the definitiveness of the Court's decision?

GONZALES v. CARHART
550 U.S.124 (2007)

JUSTICE KENNEDY delivered the opinion of the Court.

These cases require us to consider the validity of the Partial-Birth Abortion Ban Act of 2003 (Act), a federal statute regulating abortion procedures. *** In 2003, after this Court's decision in *Stenberg,* Congress passed the Act at issue here. *** The Act punishes "knowingly perform[ing]" a "partial-birth abortion." *** First, the person performing the abortion must "vaginally deliver a living fetus." The Act does not restrict an abortion procedure involving the delivery of an expired fetus. The Act, furthermore, is inapplicable to abortions that do not involve vaginal delivery (for instance, hysterotomy or hysterectomy). The Act does apply both previability and postviability because *** a fetus is a living organism while within the womb, whether or not it is viable outside *** Second, the Act's definition of partial-birth abortion requires the fetus to be delivered "until, in the case of a head-first presentation, the entire fetal head is outside the body of the mother, or, in the case of breech presentation, any part of the fetal trunk past the navel is outside the body of the mother." ***[I]f an abortion procedure does not involve the delivery of a living fetus to one of these "anatomical 'landmarks'" *** the prohibitions of the Act do not apply. Third, to fall within the Act, a doctor must perform an "overt act, other than completion of delivery, that kills the partially delivered living fetus." For purposes of criminal liability, the overt act causing the fetus' death must be separate from delivery. And the overt act must occur after the delivery to an anatomical landmark. *** Fourth, the Act contains scienter requirements concerning all the actions involved in the prohibited abortion. To begin with, the physician must have "deliberately and intentionally" delivered the fetus to one of the Act's anatomical landmarks. If a living fetus is delivered past the critical point by accident or inadvertence, the Act is inapplicable. In addition, the fetus must have been delivered "for the purpose of performing an overt act that the [doctor] knows will kill [it]." ***

We next determine whether the Act imposes an undue burden, as a facial matter, because its restrictions on second-trimester abortions are too broad. *** The Act prohibits intact D & E [Dilation and extraction of a mostly intact fetus]; *** it does not prohibit the D & E [Dilation and evacuation] procedure in which the fetus is removed in parts. *** The statute in *Stenberg* prohibited "'deliberately and intentionally delivering into the vagina a living unborn child, or a substantial portion thereof, for the purpose of performing a procedure that the person performing such procedure knows will kill the unborn child and does kill the unborn child.' *** Congress, it is apparent, responded to these concerns because the Act departs in material ways from the statute in *Stenberg*. It adopts the phrase "delivers a living fetus," instead of "'delivering *** a living unborn child, or a substantial portion thereof.'" The Act's language, unlike the statute in *Stenberg,* expresses the usual meaning of "deliver" when used in connection with "fetus," namely, extraction of an entire fetus rather than removal of fetal pieces. ***

The identification of specific anatomical landmarks to which the fetus must be partially delivered also differentiates the Act from the statute at issue in *Stenberg*. The Court in *Stenberg* interpreted "'substantial portion'" of the fetus to include an arm or a leg. The Act's anatomical landmarks, by contrast, clarify that the removal of a small portion of the fetus is not prohibited. The landmarks also require the fetus to be delivered so that it is partially "outside the body of the mother." To come within the ambit of the Nebraska statute, on the other hand, a substantial portion of the fetus only had to be delivered into the vagina; no part of the fetus had to be outside the body of the mother before a doctor could face criminal sanctions.

By adding an overt act requirement Congress sought further to meet the Court's objections to the state statute considered in *Stenberg*. *** The fatal overt act must occur after delivery to an anatomical landmark, and it must be something "other than [the] completion of delivery." This distinction matters because, unlike intact D & E, standard D & E does not involve a delivery followed by a fatal act. *** In *Stenberg* the Court found the statute covered D & E. Here, by contrast, interpreting the Act so that it does not prohibit standard D & E is the most reasonable reading and understanding of its terms. ***

The evidence also supports a legislative determination that an intact delivery is almost always a conscious choice rather than a happenstance. *** [T]hose doctors who intend to perform a D & E that would involve delivery of a living fetus to one of the Act's anatomical landmarks must adjust their conduct to the law by not attempting to deliver the fetus to either of those points. Respondents have not shown that requiring doctors to intend dismemberment before delivery to an anatomical landmark will prohibit the vast majority of D & E abortions. ***

*** The question is whether the Act, measured by its text in this facial attack, imposes a substantial obstacle to late-term, but previability, abortions. The Act does not on its face impose a substantial obstacle, and we reject this further facial challenge to its validity. *** The Act proscribes a method of abortion in which a fetus is killed just inches before completion of the birth process. *** The Act expresses respect for the dignity of human life.

Congress was concerned, furthermore, with the effects on the medical community and on its reputation caused by the practice of partial-birth abortion. *** Where it has a rational basis to act, and it does not impose an undue burden, the State may use its regulatory power to bar certain procedures and substitute others, all in furtherance of its legitimate interests in regulating the medical profession in order to promote respect for life, including life of the unborn.

The Act's ban on abortions that involve partial delivery of a living fetus furthers the Government's objectives. No one would dispute that, for many, D & E is a procedure itself laden with the power to devalue human life. Congress could nonetheless conclude that the type of abortion proscribed by the Act requires specific regulation because it implicates additional ethical and moral concerns that justify a special prohibition. Congress determined that the abortion methods it proscribed had a "disturbing similarity to the killing of a newborn infant," and thus it was concerned with "draw[ing] a bright line that clearly distinguishes abortion and infanticide." ***

Respect for human life finds an ultimate expression in the bond of love the mother has for her child. *** Whether to have an abortion requires a difficult and painful moral decision. While we find no reliable data to measure the phenomenon, it seems unexceptionable to conclude some women come to regret their choice to abort the infant life they once created and sustained. Severe depression and loss of esteem can follow. *** The State has an interest in ensuring so grave a choice is well informed. It is self-evident that a mother who comes to regret her choice to abort must struggle with grief more anguished and sorrow more profound when she learns, only after the event, what she once did not know: that she allowed a doctor to pierce the skull and vacuum the fast-developing brain of her unborn child, a child assuming the human form.

It is a reasonable inference that a necessary effect of the regulation and the knowledge it conveys will be to encourage some women to carry the infant to full term, thus reducing the absolute number of late-term abortions. The medical profession, furthermore, may find different and less shocking methods to abort the fetus in the second trimester, thereby accommodating legislative demand. ***

It is objected that the standard D & E is in some respects as brutal, if not more, than the intact D & E, so that the legislation accomplishes little. *** Partial-birth abortion, as defined by the Act, differs from a standard D & E because the former occurs when the fetus is partially outside the mother to the point of one of the Act's anatomical landmarks. It was reasonable for Congress to think that partial-birth abortion, more than standard D & E, "undermines the public's perception of the appropriate role of a physician during the delivery process, and perverts a process during which life is brought into the world." ***

The Act's furtherance of legitimate government interests bears upon, but does not resolve, the next question: whether the Act has the effect of imposing an unconstitutional burden on the abortion right because it does not allow use of the barred procedure where "'necessary, in appropriate medical judgment, for [the] preservation of the ... health of the mother.'" The prohibition in the Act would be unconstitutional, under precedents we here assume to be controlling, if it "subject[ed] [women] to significant health risks." *** [W]hether the Act creates significant health risks for women has been a contested factual question. The evidence presented in the trial courts and before Congress demonstrates both sides have medical support for their position. *** The medical uncertainty over whether the Act's prohibition creates significant health risks provides a sufficient basis to conclude in this facial attack that the Act does not impose an undue burden.

The conclusion that the Act does not impose an undue burden is supported by other considerations. Alternatives are available to the prohibited procedure. ***

In reaching the conclusion the Act does not require a health exception we reject certain arguments made by the parties on both sides of these cases. *** Although we review congressional factfinding under a deferential standard, we do not in the circumstances here place dispositive weight on Congress' findings. The Court retains an independent constitutional duty to review factual findings where constitutional rights are at stake. *** [S]ome recitations in the Act are factually incorrect. Whether or not accurate at the time, some of the important findings have been superseded. *** Uncritical deference to Congress' factual findings in these cases is inappropriate. *** The Act is not invalid on its face where there is uncertainty over whether the barred procedure is ever necessary to preserve a woman's health, given the availability of other abortion procedures that are considered to be safe alternatives. *** The Act is open to a proper as-applied challenge in a discrete case. *** Respondents have not demonstrated that the Act, as a facial matter, is void for vagueness, or that it imposes an undue burden on a woman's right to abortion based on its overbreadth or lack of a health exception.

JUSTICE THOMAS, with whom JUSTICE SCALIA joins, concurring.

*** [T]he Court's abortion jurisprudence, including *Casey* and *Roe v. Wade,* has no basis in the Constitution. *** [W]hether the Act constitutes a permissible exercise of Congress' power under the Commerce Clause is not before the Court. ***

JUSTICE GINSBURG, with whom JUSTICE STEVENS, JUSTICE SOUTER, and JUSTICE BREYER join, dissenting.

*** Today's decision *** refuses to take *Casey* and *Stenberg* seriously. It tolerates, indeed applauds, federal intervention to ban nationwide a procedure found necessary and proper in certain cases by the American College of Obstetricians and Gynecologists (ACOG). It blurs the line, firmly drawn in *Casey,* between previability and postviability abortions. And, for the first time since *Roe,* the Court blesses a prohibition with no exception safeguarding a woman's health. *** Retreating from prior rulings that abortion restrictions cannot be imposed absent an exception safeguarding a woman's health, the Court upholds an Act that surely would not survive under the close scrutiny that previously attended state-decreed limitations on a woman's reproductive choices. ***

The congressional findings on which the Partial-Birth Abortion Ban Act rests do not withstand inspection, as the lower courts have determined and this Court is obliged to concede. *** In contrast to Congress, the District Courts made findings after full trials at which all parties had the opportunity to present their best evidence. *** The law saves not a single fetus from destruction, for it targets only a *method* of performing abortion. And surely the statute was not designed to protect the lives or health of pregnant women. *** The Court emphasizes that the Act does not proscribe the nonintact D & E procedure. But why not, one might ask. Nonintact D & E could equally be characterized as "brutal," involving as it does "tear[ing] [a fetus] apart" and "ripp[ing] off" its limbs. "[T]he notion that either of these two equally gruesome procedures ... is more akin to infanticide than the other, or that the State furthers any legitimate interest by banning one but not the other, is simply irrational." ***

[T]he Court invokes an antiabortion shibboleth for which it concededly has no reliable evidence: Women who have abortions come to regret their choices, and consequently suffer from "[s]evere depression and loss of esteem."[7] Because of women's fragile emotional state and because of the "bond of love the mother has for her child," the Court worries, doctors may withhold information about the nature of the intact D & E procedure. The solution the Court approves, then, is *not* to require doctors to inform women, accurately and adequately, of the different procedures and their attendant risks. Instead, the Court deprives women of the right to make an autonomous choice, even at the expense of their safety.[9]

This way of thinking reflects ancient notions about women's place in the family and under the Constitution--ideas that have long since been discredited. ***

In cases on a "woman's liberty to determine whether to [continue] her pregnancy," this Court has identified viability as a critical consideration. *** Instead of drawing the line at viability, the Court refers to Congress' purpose to differentiate "abortion and infanticide" based not on whether a fetus can survive outside the womb, but on where a fetus is anatomically located when a particular medical procedure is performed. ***

The Court further confuses our jurisprudence when it declares that "facial attacks" are not permissible in "these circumstances," *i.e.,* where medical uncertainty exists. This holding is perplexing given that, in materially identical circumstances we held that a statute lacking a health exception was unconstitutional on its face.

Without attempting to distinguish *Stenberg* and earlier decisions, the majority asserts that the Act survives review because respondents have not shown that the ban on intact D & E would be unconstitutional "in a large fraction of relevant cases." But *Casey* makes clear that, in determining whether any restriction poses an undue burden on a "large fraction" of women, the relevant class is *not* "all women," nor "all pregnant women," nor even all women "seeking abortions." Rather, a provision restricting access to abortion, "must be judged by reference to those [women] for whom it is an actual rather than an irrelevant restriction." *** The very purpose of a health *exception* is to protect women in *exceptional* cases.

If there is anything at all redemptive to be said of today's opinion, it is that the Court is not willing to foreclose entirely *** "a proper as-applied challenge in a discrete case." But the Court offers no clue on what a "proper" lawsuit might look like. *** In candor, the Act, and the Court's defense of it, cannot be understood as anything other than an effort to chip away at a right declared again and again by this Court--and with increasing comprehension of its centrality to women's lives. ***

---

[7] The Court is surely correct that, for most women, abortion is a painfully difficult decision. But "neither the weight of the scientific evidence to date nor the observable reality of 33 years of legal abortion in the United States comports with the idea that having an abortion is any more dangerous to a woman's long-term mental health than delivering and parenting a child that she did not intend to have ... ."

[9] Eliminating or reducing women's reproductive choices is manifestly *not* a means of protecting them. When safe abortion procedures cease to be an option, many women seek other means to end unwanted or coerced pregnancies.

Notes

1. **Distinguishing *Stenberg*.** The Court distinguishes rather than overrules *Stenberg v. Carhart* (2000). Are the distinctions convincing or has the Court simply changed its (collective) mind with the departure of JUSTICE O'CONNOR and the arrival of JUSTICE ALITO? Do you agree with commentators who say that the Court "effectively overruled the 'undue burden' test for facial challenges to abortion-restriction statutes"? Is the procedure outlawed limited in ways that doctors, law enforcement officers, and lower courts can understand?

2. **Health Exception.** The majority opinion in *Stenberg* said: "[T]he governing standard requires an exception where it is necessary, in appropriate medical judgment for the preservation of the life or health of the mother. *** '[N]ecessary' *** cannot refer to an absolute necessity or to absolute proof." In *Gonzales*, the majority said: "Considerations of marginal safety, including the balance of risks, are within the legislative competence. *** [I]f some procedures have different risks than others, it does not follow that the State is altogether barred from imposing reasonable regulations. *** The law does not require a health exception unless there is a *need* for such an exception." Can these statements be reconciled?

3. **Facial Challenges Theory.** In *United States v. Salerno*, 481 U.S. 739 (1987), the Court upheld provisions of The Bail Reform Act of 1984 (Act), allowing federal courts to detain arrestees pending trial if the Government shows that no release conditions "will reasonably assure *** the safety of any other person and the community." The challengers of the statute argued that the statute was facially unconstitutional under the Due Process Clause. Rejecting this challenge, the Court said:

> The fact that the Bail Reform Act might operate unconstitutionally under some conceivable set of circumstances is insufficient to render it wholly invalid, since we have not recognized an 'overbreadth' doctrine outside the limited context of the First Amendment. *** To sustain [the procedures of the Bail Reform Act] against such a challenge, we need only find them 'adequate to authorize the pretrial detention of at least some [persons] charged with crimes,' whether or not they might be insufficient in some particular circumstances. We think they pass that test.

After *Stenberg*, it was argued that the *Salerno* approach to facial unconstitutionality was no longer valid, because the Court found the Nebraska law facially unconstitutional even though some applications might prove constitutionally permissible. More recently, in *Ayotte v. Planned Parenthood of Northern New England*, 546 U.S. 320 (2006), the court unanimously found some parts of the state law requiring parental notification before a minor can receive an abortion to be invalid for not having the proper safeguards concerning maternal health. Contrary to *Stenberg*, however, the Court did not strike down the entire law. JUSTICE O'CONNOR noted for a unanimous Court: "We prefer *** to enjoin only the unconstitutional applications of a statute while leaving other applications in force, or to sever its problematic portions while leaving the remainder intact. *** After finding an application or portion of a statute unconstitutional, we must next ask: Would the legislature have preferred what is left of its statute to no statute at all?" Does *Ayotte* raise questions concerning the remedy in *Stenberg*? Is it consistent with the Court's approach in *Gonzales*?

4.   **Facial Challenge Applications**. In *Casey*, the husband notification provision was ruled facially unconstitutional even though only 1% of women seeking abortions do not notify their husbands. For that 1%, notification would pose an undue burden on the right to obtain an abortion, said the Court. Conversely, the *Gonzales* majority said that a health exception was not necessary in a large number of cases in which a doctor might recommend the intact D & E procedure. The dissenters focused on those cases in which there would be a health issue if another procedure were used and said there would be a substantial burden on abortion in those cases. How significant is it that there seems to be a majority view that the statute is open to an as-applied challenge?

5.   **Women's Equality**. Compare JUSTICE KENNEDY'S statements about women and abortion ("Respect for human life finds an ultimate expression in the bond of love the mother has for her child *** [S]ome women come to regret their choice to abort the infant life they once created and sustained. Severe depression and loss of esteem can follow.") with those of JUSTICE GINSBURG ("[T]he Court deprives women of the right to make an autonomous choice, even at the expense of their safety. This way of thinking reflects ancient notions about women's place in the family and under the Constitution--ideas that have long since been discredited. *** [L]egal challenges to undue restrictions on abortion procedures do not seek to vindicate some generalized notion of privacy; rather, they center on a woman's autonomy to determine her life's course, and thus to enjoy equal citizenship stature.")

6.   **Ramifications**. Are *Roe* and *Casey* endangered precedents? Will the opinion encourage states to consider other regulations limiting abortion, such as informed consent laws? Of what significance is it that the majority of Americans are neither totally pro-life nor totally pro-choice? A Pew Forum poll in 2005 found that 63% of all Americans (and of American women) would like to limit abortion's availability and that 40% (42% of women) would ban abortion except to save the life of the mother or in rape or incest cases. Only 11% of men and 8% of women, the poll found, would ban abortion altogether.

WHOLE WOMAN'S HEALTH v. HELLERSTEDT
136 S.Ct. 2292 (2016)

JUSTICE BREYER delivered the opinion of the Court.

In [*Casey*] a plurality of the Court concluded that there "exists" an "undue burden" on a woman's right to decide to have an abortion, and consequently a provision of law is constitutionally invalid, if the "purpose or effect" of the provision "is to place a substantial obstacle in the path of a woman seeking an abortion before the fetus attains viability." The plurality added that "[u]nnecessary health regulations that have the purpose or effect of presenting a substantial obstacle to a woman seeking an abortion impose an undue burden on the right."

We must here decide whether two provisions of Texas' House Bill 2 violate the Federal Constitution as interpreted in *Casey*. The first provision, which we shall call the "admitting-privileges requirement," says that "[a] physician performing or inducing an abortion ... must, on the date the abortion is performed or induced, have active admitting privileges at a hospital that ... is located not further than 30 miles from the location at which the abortion is performed or induced." *** The second provision, which we shall call the "surgical-center requirement," says that "the minimum standards for an abortion facility must be equivalent to the minimum standards adopted under [the Texas Health and Safety Code section] for ambulatory surgical centers." ***

ⓘ   Undue Burden—Admitting–Privileges Requirement

*** Before the enactment of H.B. 2, doctors who provided abortions were required to "have admitting privileges or have a working arrangement with a physician(s) who has admitting privileges at a local hospital in order to ensure the necessary back up for medical complications." The new law changed this requirement by requiring that a "physician performing or inducing an abortion ... must, on the date the abortion is performed or induced, have active admitting privileges at a hospital that ... is located not further than 30 miles from the location at which the abortion is performed or induced." *** The purpose of the admitting-privileges requirement is to help ensure that women have easy access to a hospital should complications arise during an abortion procedure. But the District Court found that *** "[t]he great weight of evidence demonstrates that, before the act's passage, abortion in Texas was extremely safe with particularly low rates of serious complications and virtually no deaths occurring on account of the procedure." Thus, there was no significant health-related problem that the new law helped to cure.

The evidence upon which the court based this conclusion included *** at least five peer-reviewed studies on abortion complications in the first trimester, showing that the highest rate of major complications—including those complications requiring hospital admission—was less than one-quarter of 1%. *** Figures in three peer-reviewed studies showing that the highest complication rate found for the much rarer second trimester abortion was less than one-half of 1% (0.45% or about 1 out of about 200). *** Expert testimony [showed] that complications rarely require hospital admission, much less immediate transfer to a hospital from an outpatient clinic [and] most of these complications occur in the days after the abortion, not on the spot. *** Some experts added that, if a patient needs a hospital in the day or week following her abortion, she will likely seek medical attention at the hospital nearest her home. *** We have found nothing in Texas' record evidence that shows *** the new law advanced Texas' legitimate interest in protecting women's health.

We add that, when directly asked at oral argument whether Texas knew of a single instance in which the new requirement would have helped even one woman obtain better treatment, Texas admitted that there was no evidence in the record of such a case. *** At the same time, the record evidence indicates that the admitting-privileges requirement places a "substantial obstacle in the path of a woman's choice." The District Court found, as of the time the admitting-privileges requirement began to be enforced, the number of facilities providing abortions dropped in half, from about 40 to about 20. Eight abortion clinics closed in the months leading up to the requirement's effective date. Eleven more closed on the day the admitting-privileges requirement took effect.

Other evidence helps to explain why the new requirement led to the closure of clinics. *** In a word, doctors would be unable to maintain admitting privileges or obtain those privileges for the future, because the fact that abortions are so safe meant that providers were unlikely to have any patients to admit. *** The admitting-privileges requirement does not serve any relevant credentialing function.

Dr's couldn't get privileges b/c they couldn't bring in any new patients

In our view, the record contains sufficient evidence that the admitting-privileges requirement led to the closure of half of Texas' clinics, or thereabouts. Those closures meant fewer doctors, longer waiting times, and increased crowding. Record evidence also supports the finding that after the admitting-privileges provision went into effect, the "number of women of reproductive age living in a county ... more than 150 miles from a provider increased from approximately 86,000 to 400,000 ... and the number of women living in a county more than 200 miles from a provider from approximately 10,000 to 290,000." We recognize that increased driving distances do not always constitute an "undue burden." But here, those increases are but one additional burden, which, when taken together with others that the closings brought about, and when viewed in light of the virtual absence of any health benefit, lead us to conclude that the record adequately supports the District Court's "undue burden" conclusion.

had a negative effect on the industry

Placed a burden on potential patients

The dissent's only argument why these clinic closures *** may not have imposed an undue burden is this: Although "H. B. 2 caused the closure of some clinics," other clinics may have closed for other reasons (so we should not "actually count" the burdens resulting from those closures against H.B. 2). But petitioners satisfied their burden to present evidence of causation by presenting direct testimony as well as plausible inferences to be drawn from the timing of the clinic closures. ***

Undue Burden—Surgical–Center Requirement

The second challenged provision of Texas' new law sets forth the surgical-center requirement. Prior to enactment of the new requirement, Texas law required abortion facilities to meet a host of health and safety requirements. Under those pre-existing laws, facilities were subject to annual reporting and recordkeeping requirements; a quality assurance program; personnel policies and staffing requirements; physical and environmental requirements; infection control standards; disclosure requirements; patient-rights standards; and medical- and clinical-services standards, including anesthesia standards. These requirements are policed by random and announced inspections, at least annually, as well as administrative penalties, injunctions, civil penalties, and criminal penalties for certain violations.

Clinics were already subject to strict standards by TX

H.B. 2 added the requirement that an "abortion facility" meet the "minimum standards ... for ambulatory surgical centers" under Texas law. The surgical-center regulations include, among other things, detailed specifications relating to the size of the nursing staff, building dimensions, and other building requirements. The nursing staff must comprise at least "an adequate number of [registered nurses] on duty to meet the following minimum staff requirements: director of the department (or designee), and supervisory and staff personnel for each service area to assure the immediate availability of [a registered nurse] for emergency care or for any patient when needed," as well as "a second individual on duty on the premises who is trained and currently certified in basic cardiac life support until all patients have been discharged from the facility" for facilities that provide moderate sedation, such as most abortion facilities. Facilities must include a full surgical suite with an operating room that has "a clear floor area of at least 240 square feet" in which "[t]he minimum clear dimension between built-in cabinets, counters, and shelves shall be 14 feet." There must be a preoperative patient holding room and a postoperative recovery suite. The former "shall be provided and arranged in a one-way traffic pattern so that patients entering from outside the surgical suite can change, gown, and move directly into the restricted corridor of the surgical suite," and the latter "shall be arranged to provide a one-way traffic pattern from the restricted surgical corridor to the postoperative recovery suite, and then to the extended observation rooms or discharge". Surgical centers must meet numerous other spatial requirements, including specific corridor widths. Surgical centers must also have an advanced heating, ventilation, and air conditioning system, and must satisfy particular piping system and plumbing requirements. Dozens of other sections list additional requirements that apply to surgical centers.

There is considerable evidence in the record supporting the District Court's findings indicating that the statutory provision requiring all abortion facilities to meet all surgical-center standards does not benefit patients and is not necessary. *** [T]he surgical-center provision imposes "a requirement that simply is not based on differences" between abortion and other surgical procedures "that are reasonably related to" preserving women's health, the asserted "purpos[e] of the Act in which it is found."

Moreover, many surgical-center requirements are inappropriate as applied to surgical abortions. Requiring scrub facilities; maintaining a one-way traffic pattern through the facility; having ceiling, wall, and floor finishes; separating soiled utility and sterilization rooms; and regulating air pressure, filtration, and humidity control can help reduce infection where doctors conduct procedures that penetrate the skin. But abortions typically involve either the administration of medicines or procedures performed through the natural opening of the birth canal, which is itself not sterile. Nor do provisions designed to safeguard heavily sedated patients (unable to help themselves) during fire emergencies provide any help to abortion patients, as abortion facilities do not use general anesthesia or deep sedation. Further, since the few instances in which serious complications do arise following an abortion almost always require hospitalization, not treatment at a surgical center, surgical-center standards will not help in those instances either.*** [T]he surgical-center requirement is not necessary.

At the same time, the record provides adequate evidentiary support ***
that the surgical-center requirement places a substantial obstacle in the path
of women seeking an abortion. The parties stipulated that the requirement
would further reduce the number of abortion facilities available to seven or
eight facilities, located in Houston, Austin, San Antonio, and Dallas/Fort
Worth. In the District Court's view, the proposition that these "seven or eight
providers could meet the demand of the entire State stretches credulity." ***
For another thing, common sense suggests that, more often than not, a
physical facility that satisfies a certain physical demand will not be able to
meet five times that demand without expanding or otherwise incurring
significant costs. *** The dissent takes issue with this general, intuitive point
by arguing that many places operate below capacity and that in any event,
facilities could simply hire additional providers. We disagree that, according
to common sense, medical facilities, well known for their wait times, operate
below capacity as a general matter. And the fact that so many facilities were
forced to close by the admitting-privileges requirement means that hiring
more physicians would not be quite as simple as the dissent suggests. ***
[R]equiring seven or eight clinics to serve five times their usual number of
patients does indeed represent an undue burden on abortion access. ***

More fundamentally, in the face of no threat to women's health, Texas
seeks to force women to travel long distances to get abortions in crammed-to-
capacity superfacilities. Patients seeking these services are less likely to get
the kind of individualized attention, serious conversation, and emotional
support that doctors at less taxed facilities may have offered. Healthcare
facilities and medical professionals are not fungible commodities. Surgical
centers attempting to accommodate sudden, vastly increased demand, may
find that quality of care declines. Another commonsense inference that the
District Court made is that these effects would be harmful to, not supportive
of, women's health.

Finally, the District Court found that the costs that a currently licensed
abortion facility would have to incur to meet the surgical-center requirements
were considerable, ranging from $1 million per facility (for facilities with
adequate space) to $3 million per facility (where additional land must be
purchased). This evidence supports the conclusion that more surgical centers
will not soon fill the gap when licensed facilities are forced to close. *** [T]he
surgical-center requirement, like the admitting-privileges requirement,
provides few, if any, health benefits for women, poses a substantial obstacle
to women seeking abortions, and constitutes an "undue burden" on their
constitutional right to do so. ***

JUSTICE GINSBURG, concurring.

The Texas law called H.B. 2 inevitably will reduce the number of clinics
and doctors allowed to provide abortion services. Texas argues that H.B. 2's
restrictions are constitutional because they protect the health of women who
experience complications from abortions. In truth, "complications from an
abortion are both rare and rarely dangerous." Many medical procedures,
including childbirth, are far more dangerous to patients, yet are not subject

to ambulatory-surgical-center or hospital admitting-privileges requirements. Given those realities, it is beyond rational belief that H.B. 2 could genuinely protect the health of women, and certain that the law "would simply make it more difficult for them to obtain abortions." When a State severely limits access to safe and legal procedures, women in desperate circumstances may resort to unlicensed rogue practitioners *** at great risk to their health and safety. So long as this Court adheres to *Roe v. Wade* and *Casey*, *** laws like H.B. 2 that "do little or nothing for health, but rather strew impediments to abortion," cannot survive judicial inspection.

JUSTICE THOMAS, dissenting.

Today the Court strikes down two state statutory provisions in all of their applications, at the behest of abortion clinics and doctors. That decision exemplifies the Court's troubling tendency "to bend the rules when any effort to limit abortion, or even to speak in opposition to abortion, is at issue." *** This case also underscores the Court's increasingly common practice of invoking a given level of scrutiny—here, the abortion-specific undue burden standard—while applying a different standard of review entirely. Whatever scrutiny the majority applies to Texas' law, it bears little resemblance to the undue-burden test *** Even taking *Casey* as the baseline, however, the majority radically rewrites the undue-burden test in three ways. First, today's decision requires courts to "consider the burdens a law imposes on abortion access together with the benefits those laws confer." Second, today's opinion tells the courts that, when the law's justifications are medically uncertain, they need not defer to the legislature, and must instead assess medical justifications for abortion restrictions by scrutinizing the record themselves. Finally, even if a law imposes no "substantial obstacle" to women's access to abortions, the law now must have more than a "reasonabl[e] relat[ion] to ... a legitimate state interest." These precepts *** transform the undue-burden test to something much more akin to strict scrutiny. *** Today's opinion *** will surely mystify lower courts for years to come. *** [T]he majority's undue-burden balancing approach risks ruling out even minor, previously valid infringements on access to abortion. Moreover, by second-guessing medical evidence and making its own assessments of "quality of care" issues, the majority reappoints this Court as "the country's ex officio medical board with powers to disapprove medical and operative practices and standards throughout the United States."). And the majority seriously burdens States, which must guess at how much more compelling their interests must be to pass muster ***.

The majority's furtive reconfiguration of the standard of scrutiny applicable to abortion restrictions also points to a deeper problem. The undue-burden standard is just one variant of the Court's tiers-of-scrutiny approach to constitutional adjudication. And the label the Court affixes to its level of scrutiny in assessing whether the government can restrict a given right—be it "rational basis," intermediate, strict, or something else—is increasingly a meaningless formalism. As the Court applies whatever standard it likes to any given case, nothing but empty words separates our constitutional decisions from judicial fiat.

Though the tiers of scrutiny have become a ubiquitous feature of constitutional law, they are of recent vintage. Only in the 1960's did the Court begin in earnest to speak of "strict scrutiny" versus reviewing legislation for mere rationality, and to develop the contours of these tests. In short order, the Court adopted strict scrutiny as the standard for reviewing everything from race-based classifications under the Equal Protection Clause to restrictions on constitutionally protected speech. *Roe v. Wade* then applied strict scrutiny to a purportedly "fundamental" substantive due process right for the first time. Then the tiers of scrutiny proliferated into ever more gradations. *Casey's* undue-burden test added yet another right-specific test on the spectrum between rational-basis and strict-scrutiny review.

The illegitimacy of using "made-up tests" to "displace longstanding national traditions as the primary determinant of what the Constitution means" has long been apparent. The Constitution does not prescribe tiers of scrutiny. ***

But the problem now goes beyond that. If our recent cases illustrate anything, it is how easily the Court tinkers with levels of scrutiny to achieve its desired result. This Term, it is easier for a State to survive strict scrutiny despite discriminating on the basis of race in college admissions than it is for the same State to regulate how abortion doctors and clinics operate under the putatively less stringent undue-burden test. All the State apparently needs to show to survive strict scrutiny is a list of aspirational educational goals (such as the "cultivat[ion of] a set of leaders with legitimacy in the eyes of the citizenry") and a "reasoned, principled explanation" for why it is pursuing them—then this Court defers. Yet the same State gets no deference under the undue-burden test, despite producing evidence that abortion safety, one rationale for Texas' law, is medically debated. Likewise, it is now easier for the government to restrict judicial candidates' campaign speech than for the Government to define marriage—even though the former is subject to strict scrutiny and the latter was supposedly subject to some form of rational-basis review.

[handwritten margin note: Abortion is held to a different level of scrutiny]

These more recent decisions reflect the Court's tendency to relax purportedly higher standards of review for less-preferred rights. *** Meanwhile, the Court selectively applies rational-basis review—under which the question is supposed to be whether "any state of facts reasonably may be conceived to justify" the law. *** The Court should abandon the pretense that anything other than policy preferences underlies its balancing of constitutional rights and interests in any given case.

It is tempting to identify the Court's invention of a constitutional right to abortion in *Roe v. Wade*, as the tipping point that transformed third-party standing doctrine and the tiers of scrutiny into an unworkable morass of special exceptions and arbitrary applications. But those roots run deeper, to the very notion that some constitutional rights demand preferential treatment. During the *Lochner* era, the Court considered the right to contract and other economic liberties to be fundamental requirements of due process of law. The Court in 1937 repudiated *Lochner 's* foundations. But the Court then created a new taxonomy of preferred rights.

In 1938, seven Justices heard a constitutional challenge to a federal ban on shipping adulterated milk in interstate commerce. Without economic substantive due process, the ban clearly invaded no constitutional right. See *United States v. Carolene Products Co.* Within Justice Stone's opinion for the Court, however, was a footnote that just three other Justices joined—the famous *Carolene Products* Footnote 4. The footnote's first paragraph suggested that the presumption of constitutionality that ordinarily attaches to legislation might be "narrower ... when legislation appears on its face to be within a specific prohibition of the Constitution." Its second paragraph appeared to question "whether legislation which restricts those political processes, which can ordinarily be expected to bring about repeal of undesirable legislation, is to be subjected to more exacting judicial scrutiny under the general prohibitions of the [14th] Amendment than are most other types of legislation." And its third and most familiar paragraph raised the question "whether prejudice against discrete and insular minorities may be a special condition, which tends seriously to curtail the operation of those political processes ordinarily to be relied upon to protect minorities, and which may call for a correspondingly more searching judicial inquiry."

Though the footnote was pure dicta, the Court seized upon it to justify its special treatment of certain personal liberties like the First Amendment and the right against discrimination on the basis of race—but also rights not enumerated in the Constitution. As the Court identified which rights deserved special protection, it developed the tiers of scrutiny as part of its equal protection (and, later, due process) jurisprudence as a way to demand extra justifications for encroachments on these rights. And, having created a new category of fundamental rights, the Court loosened the reins to recognize even putative rights like abortion, which hardly implicate "discrete and insular minorities." ***

Eighty years on, the Court has come full circle. The Court has simultaneously transformed judicially created rights like the right to abortion into preferred constitutional rights, while disfavoring many of the rights actually enumerated in the Constitution. But our Constitution renounces the notion that some constitutional rights are more equal than others. A plaintiff either possesses the constitutional right he is asserting, or not—and if not, the judiciary has no business creating ad hoc exceptions so that others can assert rights that seem especially important to vindicate. A law either infringes a constitutional right, or not; there is no room for the judiciary to invent tolerable degrees of encroachment. Unless the Court abides by one set of rules to adjudicate constitutional rights, it will continue reducing constitutional law to policy-driven value judgments until the last shreds of its legitimacy disappear. *** The majority's embrace of a jurisprudence of rights-specific exceptions and balancing tests is "a regrettable concession of defeat—an acknowledgement that we have passed the point where 'law,' properly speaking, has any further application." ***

JUSTICE ALITO, with whom THE CHIEF JUSTICE and JUSTICE THOMAS join, dissenting. [OMITTED]

Notes

1.   **Facts and Law.** To what extent is this decision based on facts (District Court findings) rather than law? If primarily factual, why don't the dissenters just say "narrow factual decision" and move on? Does the decision likely resolve other abortion clinic restrictions states might make, even ones differing from those imposed by Texas?

2.   **Malleability of Tests.** Is Justice Thomas correct in his assertion that the Court has played fast and loose with application of levels of scrutiny that sound different but are applied to comport with policy preferences of judges? He makes this complaint in the context of a substantive due process case, where "levels of scrutiny" have been less fully theorized and brightly divided than in the equal protection context. When you have read Chapter IX, infra, return to this part of his dissent and see if you agree or disagree with his assessment as applied to the cases in that chapter.

3.   **Question.** Does it violate substantive due process for the State to impose criminal punishment for harm to the fetus on a woman who uses illegal drugs during her pregnancy?

c. Family

MOORE v. CITY OF EAST CLEVELAND, OHIO
431 U.S. 494 (1977)

MR. JUSTICE POWELL announced the judgment of the Court, and delivered an opinion in which MR. JUSTICE BRENNAN, MR. JUSTICE MARSHALL, and MR. JUSTICE BLACKMUN joined.

East Cleveland's housing ordinance, like many throughout the country, limits occupancy of a dwelling unit to members of a single family. But the ordinance contains an unusual and complicated definitional section that recognizes as a "family" only a few categories of related individuals. Because her family, living together in her home, fits none of those categories, appellant stands convicted of a criminal offense. The question in this case is whether the ordinance violates the Due Process Clause of the Fourteenth Amendment.

Appellant, Mrs. Inez Moore, lives in her East Cleveland home together with her son, Dale Moore Sr., and her two grandsons, Dale, Jr., and John Moore, Jr. The two boys are first cousins rather than brothers; we are told that John came to live with his grandmother and with the elder and younger Dale Moores after his mother's death.

In early 1973, Mrs. Moore received a notice of violation from the city, stating that John was an "illegal occupant" and directing her to comply with the ordinance. When she failed to remove him from her home, the city filed a criminal charge. Mrs. Moore moved to dismiss, claiming that the ordinance was constitutionally invalid on its face. Her motion was overruled, and upon conviction she was sentenced to five days in jail and a $25 fine.

The city argues that our decision in *Village of Belle Terre v. Boraas*, 416 U.S. 1 (1974), requires us to sustain the ordinance attacked here. Belle Terre, like East Cleveland, imposed limits on the types of groups that could occupy a single dwelling unit. Applying the constitutional standard announced in this Court's leading land-use case, *Euclid v. Ambler Realty Co.*, 272 U.S. 365 (1926), we sustained the Belle Terre ordinance on the ground that it bore a rational relationship to permissible state objectives. *Euclid* held that land-use regulations violate the Due Process Clause if they are "clearly arbitrary and unreasonable, having no substantial relation to the public health, safety, morals, or general welfare." Later cases have emphasized that the general welfare is not to be narrowly understood; it embraces a broad range of governmental purposes. But our cases have not departed from the requirement that the government's chosen means must rationally further some legitimate state purpose.

But one overriding factor sets this case apart from *Belle Terre*. The ordinance there affected only unrelated individuals. It expressly allowed all who were related by "blood, adoption, or marriage" to live together, and in sustaining the ordinance we were careful to note that it promoted "family needs" and "family values." East Cleveland, in contrast, has chosen to regulate the occupancy of its housing by slicing deeply into the family itself. This is no mere incidental result of the ordinance. On its face it selects certain categories of relatives who may live together and declares that others may not. In particular, it makes a crime of a grandmother's choice to live with her grandson in circumstances like those presented here.

When a city undertakes such intrusive regulation of the family, *** the usual judicial deference to the legislature is inappropriate. "This Court has long recognized that freedom of personal choice in matters of marriage and family life is one of the liberties protected by the Due Process Clause of the Fourteenth Amendment." A host of cases *** have consistently acknowledged a "private realm of family life which the state cannot enter." *** Of course, the family is not beyond regulation. But when the government intrudes on choices concerning family living arrangements, this Court must examine carefully the importance of the governmental interests advanced and the extent to which they are served by the challenged regulation.

When thus examined, this ordinance cannot survive. The city seeks to justify it as a means of preventing overcrowding, minimizing traffic and parking congestion, and avoiding an undue financial burden on East Cleveland's school system. Although these are legitimate goals, the ordinance before us serves them marginally, at best. For example, the ordinance permits any family consisting only of husband, wife, and unmarried children to live together, even if the family contains a half dozen licensed drivers, each with his or her own car. At the same time it forbids an adult brother and sister to share a household, even if both faithfully use public transportation. The ordinance would permit a grandmother to live with a single dependent son and children, even if his school-age children number a dozen, yet it forces Mrs. Moore to find another dwelling for her grandson John, simply because of the presence of his uncle and cousin in the same household. ***

Substantive due process has at times been a treacherous field for this Court. There are risks when the judicial branch gives enhanced protection to certain substantive liberties without the guidance of the more specific provisions of the Bill of Rights. As the history of the *Lochner* era demonstrates, there is reason for concern lest the only limits to such judicial intervention become the predilections of those who happen at the time to be Members of this Court. That history counsels caution and restraint. But it does not counsel abandonment, nor does it require what the city urges here: cutting off any protection of family rights at the first convenient, if arbitrary boundary the boundary of the nuclear family. *** Our decisions establish that the Constitution protects the sanctity of the family precisely because the institution of the family is deeply rooted in this Nation's history and tradition. It is through the family that we inculcate and pass down many of our most cherished values, moral and cultural.

Ours is by no means a tradition limited to respect for the bonds uniting the members of the nuclear family. The tradition of uncles, aunts, cousins, and especially grandparents sharing a household along with parents and children has roots equally venerable and equally deserving of constitutional recognition. *** Whether or not such a household is established because of personal tragedy, the choice of relatives in this degree of kinship to live together may not lightly be denied by the State. ***

MR. JUSTICE BRENNAN, with whom MR. JUSTICE MARSHALL joins, concurring.

*** [Z]oning power is not a license for local communities to enact senseless and arbitrary restrictions which cut deeply into private areas of protected family life. *** I write only to underscore the cultural myopia of the arbitrary boundary drawn by the East Cleveland ordinance in the light of the tradition of the American home that has been a feature of our society since our beginning as a Nation the "tradition" in the plurality's words, "of uncles, aunts, cousins, and especially grandparents sharing a household along with parents and children ***." The line drawn by this ordinance displays a depressing insensitivity toward the economic and emotional needs of a very large part of our society. ***

MR. JUSTICE STEVENS, concurring in the judgment.

*** Long before the original States adopted the Constitution, the common law protected an owner's right to decide how best to use his own property. This basic right has always been limited by the law of nuisance which proscribes uses that impair the enjoyment of other property in the vicinity. But the question whether an individual owner's use could be further limited by a municipality's comprehensive zoning plan was not finally decided until this century. *** East Cleveland's unprecedented ordinance constitutes a taking of property without due process and without just compensation. ***

MR. JUSTICE STEWART, with whom MR. JUSTICE REHNQUIST joins, dissenting.

*** In my view, the appellant's claim that the ordinance in question invades constitutionally protected rights of association and privacy is in large part answered by the *Belle Terre* decision. *** To be sure, the ordinance involved in *Belle Terre* did not prevent blood relatives from occupying the same dwelling, and the Court's decision in that case does not, therefore, foreclose the appellant's arguments based specifically on the ties of kinship present in this case. Nonetheless, I would hold *** that the existence of those ties does not elevate either the appellant's claim of associational freedom or her claim of privacy to a level invoking constitutional protection.

To suggest that the biological fact of common ancestry necessarily gives related persons constitutional rights of association superior to those of unrelated persons is to misunderstand the nature of the associational freedoms that the Constitution has been understood to protect. The "association" in this case is not for any purpose relating to the promotion of speech, assembly, the press, or religion. And wherever the outer boundaries of constitutional protection of freedom of association may eventually turn out to be, they surely do not extend to those who assert no interest other than the gratification, convenience, and economy of sharing the same residence.

The appellant is considerably closer to the constitutional mark in asserting that the East Cleveland ordinance intrudes upon "the private realm of family life which the state cannot enter." *** Although the appellant's desire to share a single-dwelling unit also involves "private family life" in a sense, *** the ordinance about which the appellant complains did not impede her choice to have or not to have children, and it did not dictate to her how her own children were to be nurtured and reared. The ordinance clearly does not prevent parents from living together or living with their unemancipated offspring. *** Viewed in the light of these principles, I do not think East Cleveland's definition of "family" offends the Constitution. The city has undisputed power to ordain single-family residential occupancy. And that power plainly carries with it the power to say what a "family" is. ***

MR. JUSTICE WHITE, dissenting.

*** [The] Court should be extremely reluctant to breathe still further substantive content into the Due Process Clause so as to strike down legislation adopted by a State or city to promote its welfare. Whenever the Judiciary does so, it unavoidably pre-empts for itself another part of the governance of the country without express constitutional authority. *** [Tthe threshold question in any due process attack on legislation, whether the challenge is procedural or substantive, is whether there is a deprivation of life, liberty, or property. *** [Previous] cases at most assert that only fundamental liberties will be given substantive protection; and they may be understood as merely identifying certain fundamental interests that the Court has deemed deserving of a heightened degree of protection under the Due Process Clause. *** There are various "liberties," *** which require that infringing legislation be given closer judicial scrutiny, not only with respect to existence of a purpose and the means employed, but also with respect to the importance of the purpose itself relative to the invaded interest. Some interest would appear almost impregnable to invasion, such as the freedoms of speech, press, and religion, and the freedom from cruel and unusual punishments. *** Under our cases, the Due Process Clause extends substantial protection to various phases of family life, but none requires that the claim made here be sustained. I cannot believe that the interest in residing with more than one set of grandchildren is one that calls for any kind of heightened protection under the Due Process Clause. ***

Notes

1. **Limits to *Moore*.**

(a) Is this case distinguishable from *Belle Terre*? Compare the definitions of family in the two statutes.

(b) If this distinction holds, it is because there is some tradition defining the reach of constitutional rights to some particular conception of family. Isn't the Court likely to be torn between the precise tradition (e.g. nuclear family) and the broader tradition (biologically related individuals) in many cases?

(c) Can a city, after these two cases, prohibit biologically unrelated individuals who "feel like a family" or "significant others" from living together?

(d) What, if any, ramifications do you see in these cases for "adult communities" which exclude children (defined as anyone under 21) from living there for more than two weeks in any 52–week period?

2. ***Moore* and Class.** Would your views of this case change if, as Professor Burt shows, the case involved an effort by a mainly black middle-class neighborhood to define itself as different from mainly black lower-class surrounding neighborhoods? Consider whether you agree with the comment that "The Court in *Moore* myopically saw the case as a dispute between 'a family' and 'the state' rather than as a dispute among citizens about the meaning of 'family.'" Burt, *The Constitution of the Family*, 1979 SUP. CT. REV. 329, 391.

3. **Family and Marriage Traditions.** Does the substantive due process protection of the family reach to a family which includes adopted children? Illegitimate children? Remote cousins, aunts and uncles? Likewise, does the protection of marriage extend to homosexual marriage? Multiple marriages (polygamy)? Incestuous marriages? Marriages which, for physical reasons, cannot be consummated? Perhaps the most fascinating case dealing with such issues is *Reynolds v. United States*, 98 U.S. 145 (1878), in which a Mormon convicted of violating an antibigamy statute countered that his conviction violated his free exercise of religion. The Court unanimously rejected his claim. While the First Amendment issue is not within the scope of this book, what the Court said about marriage may have ramifications today on some of the above questions:

> [T]here never has been a time in any State of the Union when polygamy has not been an offense against society, cognizable by the civil courts and punishable with more or less severity. *** [It] is within the legitimate scope of the power of every civil government to determine whether polygamy or monogamy shall be the law of social life under its dominion.

4. **Specificity of Traditions**. In *Michael H. v. Gerald D.*, 491 U.S. 110 (1989), the Court considered whether preclusion of visitation rights by the genetic father of a child under a California statute providing that a child born to a married

woman living with her husband is conclusively presumed to be a child of the marriage was constitutional. JUSTICE SCALIA's plurality opinion upheld the statute on the ground that the interest asserted by the father was not "an interest traditionally protected by our society." In a footnote responding to JUSTICE BRENNAN's suggestion that "parenthood is an interest that historically has received our attention and protection," JUSTICE SCALIA argued this formulation of the tradition was too broad, and that the Court should look to "the most specific level at which a relevant tradition protecting, or denying protection to, the asserted right can be identified" and that the "more specific tradition" "unqualifiedly denies protection to [the natural father of a child adulterously conceived]." JUSTICE BRENNAN responded that "many a decision would have reached a different result" under the "narrowest tradition" and that "We are not an assimilative, homogeneous society, but a facilitative, pluralistic one *** it is absurd to assume that we can agree on the content of ['family' and 'parenthood'] and destructive to pretend that we do." With whom do you agree and why?

5. **Questions.**

    (a) Does an unwed father have a constitutional right to custody of his illegitimate children when the mother dies? Does that right survive a state statute that denies him the right to veto the adoption of his illegitimate children by the mother's husband? Compare *Stanley v. Illinois*, 405 U.S. 645 (1972), with *Quilloin v. Walcott*, 434 U.S. 246 (1978).

    (b) Is a prison rule that inmates may not marry anyone unless the warden concludes there are compelling reasons for marriage constitutional? Pregnancy and birth of a child outside marriage are the only such reasons accepted to date. *See Turner v. Safley*, 482 U.S. 78 (1987).

TROXEL v. GRANVILLE
530 U.S. 57 (2000)

JUSTICE O'CONNOR announced the judgment of the court and delivered an opinion, in which THE CHIEF JUSTICE, JUSTICE GINSBURG, and JUSTICE BREYER join.

Section 26.10.160(3) of the Revised Code of Washington permits "[a]ny person" to petition a superior court for visitation rights "at any time," and authorizes that court to grant such visitation rights whenever "visitation may serve the best interest of the child." *** Tommie Granville and Brad Troxel shared a relationship that ended in June 1991. The two never married, but they had two daughters, Isabelle and Natalie. Jenifer and Gary Troxel are Brad's parents, and thus the paternal grandparents of Isabelle and Natalie. After Tommie and Brad separated in 1991, Brad lived with his parents and regularly brought his daughters to his parents' home for weekend visitation. Brad committed suicide in May 1993. Although the Troxels at first continued to see Isabelle and Natalie on a regular basis after their son's death, Tommie Granville informed the Troxels in October 1993 that she wished to limit their visitation with her daughters to one short visit per month.

In December 1993, the Troxels commenced the present action by filing, in the Washington Superior Court for Skagit County, a petition to obtain visitation rights with Isabelle and Natalie. *** At trial, the Troxels requested two weekends of overnight visitation per month and two weeks of visitation each summer. Granville did not oppose visitation altogether, but instead asked the court to order one day of visitation per month with no overnight stay. In 1995, the Superior Court issued an oral ruling and entered a visitation decree ordering visitation one weekend per month, one week during the summer, and four hours on both of the petitioning grandparents' birthdays. Granville appealed, during which time she married Kelly Wynn. *** Granville's husband formally adopted Isabelle and Natalie.

The demographic changes of the past century make it difficult to speak of an average American family. *** In 1996, children living with only one parent accounted for 28 percent of all children under age 18 in the United States. Understandably, in these single-parent households, persons outside the nuclear family are called upon with increasing frequency to assist in the everyday tasks of child rearing. In many cases, grandparents play an important role. For example, in 1998, approximately 4 million children—or 5.6 percent of all children under age 18—lived in the household of their grandparents.

The nationwide enactment of nonparental visitation statutes is assuredly due, in some part, to the States' recognition of these changing realities of the American family. Because grandparents and other relatives undertake duties of a parental nature in many households, States have sought to ensure the welfare of the children therein by protecting the relationships those children form with such third parties. The States' nonparental visitation statutes are further supported by a recognition, which varies from State to State, that children should have the opportunity to benefit from relationships with statutorily specified persons—for example, their grandparents. The extension of statutory rights in this area to persons other than a child's parents, however, comes with an obvious cost. For example, the State's recognition of an independent third-party interest in a child can place a substantial burden on the traditional parent-child relationship. *** In this case, *** we are asked to decide whether § 26.10.160(3), as applied to Tommie Granville and her family, violates the Federal Constitution. ***

The liberty interest at issue in this case—the interest of parents in the care, custody, and control of their children—is perhaps the oldest of the fundamental liberty interests recognized by this Court. More than 75 years ago, in *Meyer v. Nebraska*, 262 U.S. 390 (1923), we held that the "liberty" protected by the Due Process Clause includes the right of parents to "establish a home and bring up children" and "to control the education of their own." Two years later, in *Pierce v. Society of Sisters*, 268 U.S. 510 (1925), we again held that the "liberty of parents and guardians" includes the right "to direct the upbringing and education of children under their control." *** We returned to the subject in *Prince v. Massachusetts*, 321 U.S. 158 (1944), and again confirmed that there is a constitutional dimension to the right of parents to direct the upbringing of their children. ***

In subsequent cases also, we have recognized the fundamental right of parents to make decisions concerning the care, custody, and control of their children. *** In light of this extensive precedent, it cannot now be doubted that the Due Process Clause of the Fourteenth Amendment protects the fundamental right of parents to make decisions concerning the care, custody, and control of their children.

Section 26.10.160(3), as applied to Granville and her family in this case, unconstitutionally infringes on that fundamental parental right. The Washington nonparental visitation statute is breathtakingly broad. According to the statute's text, "[a]ny person may petition the court for visitation rights at any time," and the court may grant such visitation rights whenever "visitation may serve the best interest of the child." That language effectively permits any third party seeking visitation to subject any decision by a parent concerning visitation of the parent's children to state-court review. Once the visitation petition has been filed in court and the matter is placed before a judge, a parent's decision that visitation would not be in the child's best interest is accorded no deference. Section 26.10.160(3) contains no requirement that a court accord the parent's decision any presumption of validity or any weight whatsoever. Instead, the Washington statute places the best-interest determination solely in the hands of the judge. Should the judge disagree with the parent's estimation of the child's best interests, the judge's view necessarily prevails. Thus, in practical effect, in the State of Washington a court can disregard and overturn any decision by a fit custodial parent concerning visitation whenever a third party affected by the decision files a visitation petition, based solely on the judge's determination of the child's best interests. The Washington Supreme Court had the opportunity to give § 26.10.160(3) a narrower reading, but it declined to do so.

Turning to the facts of this case, the record reveals that the Superior Court's order was based on precisely the type of mere disagreement we have just described and nothing more. The Superior Court's order was not founded on any special factors that might justify the State's interference with Granville's fundamental right to make decisions concerning the rearing of her two daughters. To be sure, this case involves a visitation petition filed by grandparents soon after the death of their son—the father of Isabelle and Natalie—but the combination of several factors here compels our conclusion that § 26.10.160(3), as applied, exceeded the bounds of the Due Process Clause.

First, the Troxels did not allege, and no court has found, that Granville was an unfit parent. That aspect of the case is important, for there is a presumption that fit parents act in the best interests of their children. *** The judge's comments suggest that he presumed the grandparents' request should be granted unless the children would be "impact[ed] adversely." In effect, the judge placed on Granville, the fit custodial parent, the burden of disproving that visitation would be in the best interest of her daughters. The judge reiterated moments later: "I think [visitation with the Troxels] would be in the best interest of the children and I haven't been shown it is not in [the] best interest of the children."

The decisional framework employed by the Superior Court directly contravened the traditional presumption that a fit parent will act in the best interest of his or her child. In that respect, the court's presumption failed to provide any protection for Granville's fundamental constitutional right to make decisions concerning the rearing of her own daughters. *** [I]f a fit parent's decision of the kind at issue here becomes subject to judicial review, the court must accord at least some special weight to the parent's own determination.

Finally, we note that there is no allegation that Granville ever sought to cut off visitation entirely. Rather, the present dispute originated when Granville informed the Troxels that she would prefer to restrict their visitation with Isabelle and Natalie to one short visit per month and special holidays. *** Significantly, many other States expressly provide by statute that courts may not award visitation unless a parent has denied (or unreasonably denied) visitation to the concerned third party. *** [T]he combination of these factors demonstrates that the visitation order in this case was an unconstitutional infringement on Granville's fundamental right to make decisions concerning the care, custody, and control of her two daughters. The Washington Superior Court *** made only two formal findings in support of its visitation order. First, the Troxels "are part of a large, central, loving family, all located in this area, and the [Troxels] can provide opportunities for the children in the areas of cousins and music." Second, "[t]he children would be benefitted from spending quality time with the [Troxels], provided that that time is balanced with time with the childrens' [sic] nuclear family." These slender findings, in combination with the court's announced presumption in favor of grandparent visitation and its failure to accord significant weight to Granville's already having offered meaningful visitation to the Troxels, show that this case involves nothing more than a simple disagreement between the Washington Superior Court and Granville concerning her children's best interests. *** [T]he Due Process Clause does not permit a State to infringe on the fundamental right of parents to make childrearing decisions simply because a state judge believes a "better" decision could be made. Neither the Washington nonparental visitation statute generally—which places no limits on either the persons who may petition for visitation or the circumstances in which such a petition may be granted—nor the Superior Court in this specific case required anything more. Accordingly, we hold that § 26.10.160(3), as applied in this case, is unconstitutional.

Because we rest our decision on the sweeping breadth of § 26.10.160(3) and the application of that broad, unlimited power in this case, we do not consider *** whether the Due Process Clause requires all nonparental visitation statutes to include a showing of harm or potential harm to the child as a condition precedent to granting visitation. We do not, and need not, define today the precise scope of the parental due process right in the visitation context. *** Because much state-court adjudication in this context occurs on a case-by-case basis, we would be hesitant to hold that specific nonparental visitation statutes violate the Due Process Clause as a per se matter. ***

JUSTICE THOMAS, concurring in the judgment.

I write separately to note that neither party has argued that our substantive due process cases were wrongly decided and that the original understanding of the Due Process Clause precludes judicial enforcement of unenumerated rights under that constitutional provision. As a result, I express no view on the merits of this matter *** I would apply strict scrutiny to infringements of fundamental rights. Here, the State of Washington lacks even a legitimate governmental interest—to say nothing of a compelling one—in second-guessing a fit parent's decision regarding visitation with third parties. On this basis, I would affirm the judgment below.

JUSTICE STEVENS, dissenting.

*** In my view, the State Supreme Court erred in its federal constitutional analysis because neither the provision granting "any person" the right to petition the court for visitation, nor the absence of a provision requiring a "threshold *** finding of harm to the child," provides a sufficient basis for holding that the statute is invalid in all its applications. *** Under the Washington statute, there are plainly any number of cases—indeed, one suspects, the most common to arise—in which the "person" among "any" seeking visitation is a once-custodial caregiver, an intimate relation, or even a genetic parent. Even the Court would seem to agree that in many circumstances, it would be constitutionally permissible for a court to award some visitation of a child to a parent or previous caregiver in cases of parental separation or divorce, cases of disputed custody, cases involving temporary foster care or guardianship, and so forth. As the statute plainly sweeps in a great deal of the permissible, the State Supreme Court majority incorrectly concluded that a statute authorizing "any person" to file a petition seeking visitation privileges would invariably run afoul of the Fourteenth Amendment.

The second key aspect of the Washington Supreme Court's holding—that the Federal Constitution requires a showing of actual or potential "harm" to the child before a court may order visitation continued over a parent's objections—finds no support in this Court's case law. *** [W]e have never held that the parent's liberty interest in this relationship is so inflexible as to establish a rigid constitutional shield, protecting every arbitrary parental decision from any challenge absent a threshold finding of harm. *** A parent's rights with respect to her child have *** never been regarded as absolute, but rather are limited by the existence of an actual, developed relationship with a child, and are tied to the presence or absence of some embodiment of family. ***

While this Court has not yet had occasion to elucidate the nature of a child's liberty interests in preserving established familial or family-like bonds, it seems to me extremely likely that, to the extent parents and families have fundamental liberty interests in preserving such intimate relationships, so, too, do children have these interests, and so, too, must their interests be balanced in the equation. At a minimum, our prior cases recognizing that children are, generally speaking, constitutionally protected actors require that this Court reject any suggestion that when it comes to parental rights, children are so much chattel.

*** The almost infinite variety of family relationships that pervade our ever-changing society strongly counsel against the creation by this Court of a constitutional rule that treats a biological parent's liberty interest in the care and supervision of her child as an isolated right that may be exercised arbitrarily. It is indisputably the business of the States, rather than a federal court employing a national standard, to assess in the first instance the relative importance of the conflicting interests that give rise to disputes such as this. *** [T]he Washington law merely gives an individual—with whom a child may have an established relationship—the procedural right to ask the State to act as arbiter, through the entirely well-known best-interests standard, between the parent's protected interests and the child's. ***

JUSTICE SCALIA, dissenting.

In my view, a right of parents to direct the upbringing of their children is among the "unalienable Rights" with which the Declaration of Independence proclaims "all Men *** are endowed by their Creator." And in my view that right is also among the "othe[r] [rights] retained by the people" which the Ninth Amendment says the Constitution's enumeration of rights "shall not be construed to deny or disparage." The Declaration of Independence, however, is not a legal prescription conferring powers upon the courts; and the Constitution's refusal to "deny or disparage" other rights is far removed from affirming any one of them, and even farther removed from authorizing judges to identify what they might be, and to enforce the judges' list against laws duly enacted by the people. Consequently, while I would think it entirely compatible with the commitment to representative democracy set forth in the founding documents to argue, in legislative chambers or in electoral campaigns, that the state has no power to interfere with parents' authority over the rearing of their children, I do not believe that the power which the Constitution confers upon me as a judge entitles me to deny legal effect to laws that (in my view) infringe upon what is (in my view) that unenumerated right.

Only three holdings of this Court rest in whole or in part upon a substantive constitutional right of parents to direct the upbringing of their children—two of them from an era rich in substantive due process holdings that have since been repudiated. See *Meyer v. Nebraska*, 262 U.S. 390 (1923); *Pierce v. Society of Sisters*, 268 U.S. 510 (1925); *Wisconsin v. Yoder*, 406 U.S. 205 (1972). The sheer diversity of today's opinions persuades me that the theory of unenumerated parental rights underlying these three cases has small claim to stare decisis protection. *** While I would not now overrule those earlier cases (that has not been urged), neither would I extend the theory upon which they rested to this new context. *** I think it obvious *** that we will be ushering in a new regime of judicially prescribed, and federally prescribed, family law. I have no reason to believe that federal judges will be better at this than state legislatures; and state legislatures have the great advantages of doing harm in a more circumscribed area, of being able to correct their mistakes in a flash, and of being removable by the people. ***

JUSTICE KENNEDY, dissenting.

*** My principal concern is that the holding seems to proceed from the assumption that the parent or parents who resist visitation have always been the child's primary caregivers and that the third parties who seek visitation have no legitimate and established relationship with the child. That idea, in turn, appears influenced by the concept that the conventional nuclear family ought to establish the visitation standard for every domestic relations case. As we all know, this is simply not the structure or prevailing condition in many households. See, *e.g., Moore v. East Cleveland*, 431 U.S. 494 (1977). ***

Cases are sure to arise—perhaps a substantial number of cases—in which a third party, by acting in a caregiving role over a significant period of time, has developed a relationship with a child which is not necessarily subject to absolute parental veto. See *Michael H. v. Gerald D.*, 491 U.S. 110 (1989) (putative natural father not entitled to rebut state law presumption that child born in a marriage is a child of the marriage); *Quilloin v. Walcott*, 434 U.S. 246 (1978) (best interests standard sufficient in adoption proceeding to protect interests of natural father who had not legitimated the child) ***. In the design and elaboration of their visitation laws, States may be entitled to consider that certain relationships are such that to avoid the risk of harm, a best interests standard can be employed by their domestic relations courts in some circumstances. ***

Many States limit the identity of permissible petitioners by restricting visitation petitions to grandparents, or by requiring petitioners to show a substantial relationship with a child, or both. The statutes vary in other respects—for instance, some permit visitation petitions when there has been a change in circumstances such as divorce or death of a parent, and some apply a presumption that parental decisions should control. Georgia's is the sole State Legislature to have adopted a general harm to the child standard, and it did so only after the Georgia Supreme Court held the State's prior visitation statute invalid under the Federal and Georgia Constitutions. *** I would be hard pressed to conclude the right to be free of such review in all cases is itself "implicit in the concept of ordered liberty." *** We must keep in mind that family courts in the 50 States confront these factual variations each day, and are best situated to consider the unpredictable, yet inevitable, issues that arise. ***

Notes

1. **Circumventing *Troxel*?** Was the Court criticizing only the Washington law, or all laws that provide for grandparent visitations? Can you suggest how the State could rewrite its statute to pass muster under the due process clause?

2. **Mothers and Fathers.** If the children's father (rather than mother) had been raising the children, would that make a difference to the Court's analysis?

3. **Biology Versus Caregiving.** Would the decision be different if the children are being raised by someone who adopted them? What if the adoptive parent now has a same-sex partner?

4. **Parents v. Children**. In *Pierce*, the children are only mentioned indirectly. Do parental rights trump child liberty? Suppose a teenager acknowledges having a homosexual orientation. Shocked, the parents consult a "reparative therapist" who promises (for a fee) to restore the teenager to a"normal heterosexual orientation." The techniques used by the therapist involve electric shocks and psychotropic drugs. Do the parents have a right to order reparative therapy against the wishes of the minor?

d. Homosexuality

LAWRENCE v. TEXAS
539 U.S. 558 (2003)

JUSTICE KENNEDY delivered the opinion of the Court.

Liberty protects the person from unwarranted government intrusions into a dwelling or other private places. *** Liberty presumes an autonomy of self that includes freedom of thought, belief, expression, and certain intimate conduct. *** The question before the Court is the validity of a Texas statute making it a crime for two persons of the same sex to engage in certain intimate sexual conduct. *** The two petitioners were arrested, held in custody over night, and charged and convicted ***. The complaints described their crime as "deviate sexual intercourse, namely anal sex, with a member of the same sex (man)." *** Tex. Penal Code Ann. § 21.06(a) (2003) *** provides: "A person commits an offense if he engages in deviate sexual intercourse with another individual of the same sex." The statute defines "[d]eviate sexual intercourse" as follows:

"(A) any contact between any part of the genitals of one person and the mouth or anus of another person; or
"(B) the penetration of the genitals or the anus of another person with an object."

The petitioners *** challenged the statute as a violation of the Equal Protection Clause of the Fourteenth Amendment *** The petitioners were adults at the time of the alleged offense. Their conduct was in private and consensual.

We conclude the case should be resolved by determining whether the petitioners were free as adults to engage in the private conduct in the exercise of their liberty under the Due Process Clause of the Fourteenth Amendment to the Constitution. For this inquiry we deem it necessary to reconsider the Court's holding in *Bowers*. *** The facts in *Bowers* had some similarities to the instant case. A police officer *** observed Hardwick, in his own bedroom, engaging in intimate sexual conduct with another adult male. The conduct was in violation of a Georgia statute making it a criminal offense to engage in sodomy. One difference between the two cases is that the Georgia statute prohibited the conduct whether or not the participants were of the same sex, while the Texas statute, as we have seen, applies only to participants of the same sex. *** The Court sustained the Georgia law. *** Four Justices dissented.

The Court began its substantive discussion in *Bowers* as follows: "The issue presented is whether the Federal Constitution confers a fundamental right upon homosexuals to engage in sodomy and hence invalidates the laws of the many States that still make such conduct illegal and have done so for a very long time." That statement, we now conclude, discloses the Court's own failure to appreciate the extent of the liberty at stake. To say that the issue in *Bowers* was simply the right to engage in certain sexual conduct demeans the claim the individual put forward, just as it would demean a married couple were it to be said marriage is simply about the right to have sexual intercourse. The laws involved in *Bowers* and here are, to be sure, statutes that purport to do no more than prohibit a particular sexual act. Their penalties and purposes, though, have more far-reaching consequences, touching upon the most private human conduct, sexual behavior, and in the most private of places, the home. The statutes do seek to control a personal relationship that, whether or not entitled to formal recognition in the law, is within the liberty of persons to choose without being punished as criminals. *** When sexuality finds overt expression in intimate conduct with another person, the conduct can be but one element in a personal bond that is more enduring. The liberty protected by the Constitution allows homosexual persons the right to make this choice.

Having misapprehended the claim of liberty there presented to it, and thus stating the claim to be whether there is a fundamental right to engage in consensual sodomy, the *Bowers* Court said: "Proscriptions against that conduct have ancient roots." *** [T]he following considerations counsel against adopting the definitive conclusions upon which *Bowers* placed such reliance.

*** [T]here is no longstanding history in this country of laws directed at homosexual conduct as a distinct matter. *** [A]ccording to some scholars the concept of the homosexual as a distinct category of person did not emerge until the late 19th century. Thus early American sodomy laws were not directed at homosexuals as such but instead sought to prohibit nonprocreative sexual activity more generally. *** [F]ar from possessing "ancient roots," *Bowers*, American laws targeting same-sex couples did not develop until the last third of the 20th century. *** It was not until the 1970's that any State singled out same-sex relations for criminal prosecution, and only nine States have done so. *** Over the course of the last decades, States with same-sex prohibitions have moved toward abolishing them. ***

It must be acknowledged, of course, that the Court in *Bowers* was making the broader point that for centuries there have been powerful voices to condemn homosexual conduct as immoral. *** In all events we think that our laws and traditions in the past half century are of most relevance here. These references show an emerging awareness that liberty gives substantial protection to adult persons in deciding how to conduct their private lives in matters pertaining to sex. "[H]istory and tradition are the starting point but not in all cases the ending point of the substantive due process inquiry." *County of Sacramento v. Lewis*, 523 U. S. 833, 857 (1998) (KENNEDY, J., concurring).

This emerging recognition should have been apparent when *Bowers* was decided. In 1955 the American Law Institute promulgated the Model Penal Code and made clear that it did not recommend or provide for "criminal penalties for consensual sexual relations conducted in private." *** In *Bowers* the Court referred to the fact that before 1961 all 50 States had outlawed sodomy, and that at the time of the Court's decision 24 States and the District of Columbia had sodomy laws [but] other authorities point[ed] in an opposite direction. A committee advising the British Parliament recommended in 1957 repeal of laws punishing homosexual conduct. Parliament enacted the substance of those recommendations 10 years later. *** [A]lmost five years before *Bowers* was decided the European Court of Human Rights *** held that the laws proscribing the conduct were invalid under the European Convention on Human Rights. *Dudgeon v. United Kingdom*, 45 Eur. Ct. H. R. (1981). Authoritative in all countries that are members of the Council of Europe (21 nations then, 45 nations now), the decision is at odds with the premise in *Bowers* that the claim put forward was insubstantial in our Western civilization.

In our own constitutional system the deficiencies in *Bowers* became even more apparent in the years following its announcement. The 25 States with laws prohibiting the relevant conduct referenced in the *Bowers* decision are reduced now to 13, of which 4 enforce their laws only against homosexual conduct. In those States where sodomy is still proscribed, *** there is a pattern of nonenforcement with respect to consenting adults acting in private. *** Two principal cases decided after *Bowers* cast its holding into even more doubt. In *Planned Parenthood*, the Court reaffirmed the substantive force of the liberty protected by the Due Process Clause. *** *Bowers* would deny them this right.

The second post-*Bowers* case of principal relevance is *Romer v. Evans*, 517 U. S. 620 (1996). There the Court struck down class-based legislation directed at homosexuals as a violation of the Equal Protection Clause. *Romer* invalidated an amendment to Colorado's constitution which named as a solitary class persons who were homosexuals, lesbians, or bisexual either by "orientation, conduct, practices or relationships," and deprived them of protection under state antidiscrimination laws. *** Were we to hold the statute invalid under the Equal Protection Clause some might question whether a prohibition would be valid if drawn differently, say, to prohibit the conduct both between same-sex and different-sex participants.

Equality of treatment and the due process right to demand respect for conduct protected by the substantive guarantee of liberty are linked in important respects, and a decision on the latter point advances both interests. If protected conduct is made criminal and the law which does so remains unexamined for its substantive validity, its stigma might remain even if it were not enforceable as drawn for equal protection reasons. When homosexual conduct is made criminal by the law of the State, that declaration in and of itself is an invitation to subject homosexual persons to discrimination both in the public and in the private spheres. The central holding of *Bowers* has been brought in question by this case, and it should be addressed. Its continuance as precedent demeans the lives of homosexual persons.

The stigma this criminal statute imposes, moreover, is not trivial. *** The petitioners will bear on their record the history of their criminal convictions. *** Furthermore, the Texas criminal conviction carries with it the other collateral consequences always following a conviction *** In the United States criticism of *Bowers* has been substantial and continuing, disapproving of its reasoning in all respects, not just as to its historical assumptions. The courts of five different States have declined to follow it in interpreting provisions in their own state constitutions parallel to the Due Process Clause of the Fourteenth Amendment ***.

The rationale of *Bowers* does not withstand careful analysis. In his dissenting opinion in *Bowers* JUSTICE STEVENS came to these conclusions:

> Our prior cases make two propositions abundantly clear. First, the fact that the governing majority in a State has traditionally viewed a particular practice as immoral is not a sufficient reason for upholding a law prohibiting the practice; neither history nor tradition could save a law prohibiting miscegenation from constitutional attack. Second, individual decisions by married persons, concerning the intimacies of their physical relationship, even when not intended to produce offspring, are a form of 'liberty' protected by the Due Process Clause of the Fourteenth Amendment. Moreover, this protection extends to intimate choices by unmarried as well as married persons.

*** *Bowers* was not correct when it was decided, and it is not correct today. It ought not to remain binding precedent. *Bowers v. Hardwick* should be and now is overruled.

The present case does not involve minors. It does not involve persons who might be injured or coerced or who are situated in relationships where consent might not easily be refused. It does not involve public conduct or prostitution. It does not involve whether the government must give formal recognition to any relationship that homosexual persons seek to enter. The case does involve two adults who, with full and mutual consent from each other, engaged in sexual practices common to a homosexual lifestyle. The petitioners are entitled to respect for their private lives. The State cannot demean their existence or control their destiny by making their private sexual conduct a crime. *** "It is a promise of the Constitution that there is a realm of personal liberty which the government may not enter." The Texas statute furthers no legitimate state interest which can justify its intrusion into the personal and private life of the individual. ***

JUSTICE O'CONNOR, concurring in the judgment.

The Court today overrules *Bowers v. Hardwick,* 478 U. S. 186 (1986). *** Rather than relying on the substantive component of the Fourteenth Amendment's Due Process Clause, as the Court does, I base my conclusion on the Fourteenth Amendment's Equal Protection Clause. *** When a law exhibits *** a desire to harm a politically unpopular group, we have applied a more searching form of rational basis review to strike down such laws under the Equal Protection Clause. *** The statute at issue here makes sodomy a crime only if a person "engages in deviate sexual intercourse with another individual of the same sex." Sodomy between opposite-sex partners, however, is not a crime in Texas. That is, Texas treats the same conduct differently based solely on the participants. Those harmed by this law are people who have a same-sex sexual orientation *** Texas' sodomy law brands all homosexuals as criminals, thereby making it more difficult for homosexuals to be treated in the same manner as everyone else. *** Texas attempts to justify its law, and the effects of the law, by arguing that the statute satisfies rational basis review because it furthers the legitimate governmental interest of the promotion of morality. ***

This case raises a different issue than *Bowers:* whether, under the Equal Protection Clause, moral disapproval is a legitimate state interest to justify by itself a statute that bans homosexual sodomy, but not heterosexual sodomy. It is not. Moral disapproval of this group, like a bare desire to harm the group, is an interest that is insufficient to satisfy rational basis review under the Equal Protection Clause. *** Texas argues, however, that the sodomy law does not discriminate against homosexual persons. Instead, the State maintains that the law discriminates only against homosexual conduct. While it is true that the law applies only to conduct, the conduct targeted by this law is conduct that is closely correlated with being homosexual. Under such circumstances, Texas' sodomy law is targeted at more than conduct. It is instead directed toward gay persons as a class. *** When a State makes homosexual conduct criminal, and not "deviate sexual intercourse" committed by persons of different sexes, "that declaration in and of itself is an invitation to subject homosexual persons to discrimination both in the public and in the private spheres." ***

Whether a sodomy law that is neutral both in effect and application, would violate the substantive component of the Due Process Clause is an issue that need not be decided today. *** Texas cannot assert any legitimate state interest here, such as national security or preserving the traditional institution of marriage. Unlike the moral disapproval of same-sex relations–the asserted state interest in this case–other reasons exist to promote the institution of marriage beyond mere moral disapproval of an excluded group. ***

JUSTICE SCALIA, with whom THE CHIEF JUSTICE and JUSTICE THOMAS join, dissenting.

*** Though there is discussion of "fundamental proposition[s]," and "fundamental decisions," nowhere does the Court's opinion declare that homosexual sodomy is a "fundamental right" under the Due Process Clause; nor does it subject the Texas law to the standard of review that would be appropriate (strict scrutiny) if homosexual sodomy *were* a "fundamental right." Thus, while overruling the *outcome* of *Bowers,* the Court leaves strangely untouched its central legal conclusion: "[R]espondent would have us announce *** a fundamental right to engage in homosexual sodomy. This we are quite unwilling to do."   Instead the Court simply describes petitioners' conduct as "an exercise of their liberty"–which it undoubtedly is–and proceeds to apply an unheard-of form of rational-basis review that will have far-reaching implications beyond this case.

I begin with the Court's surprising readiness to reconsider a decision rendered a mere 17 years ago in *Bowers v. Hardwick*. *** State laws against bigamy, same-sex marriage, adult incest, prostitution, masturbation, adultery, fornication, bestiality, and obscenity are *** sustainable only in light of *Bowers'* validation of laws based on moral choices. Every single one of these laws is called into question by today's decision; the Court makes no effort to cabin the scope of its decision to exclude them from its holding. The impossibility of distinguishing homosexuality from other traditional "morals" offenses is precisely why *Bowers* rejected the rational-basis challenge. *** Having decided that it need not adhere to *stare decisis*, the Court still must establish that *Bowers* was wrongly decided and that the Texas statute, as applied to petitioners, is unconstitutional.

Texas Penal Code Ann. § 21.06(a) (2003) undoubtedly imposes constraints on liberty. So do laws prohibiting prostitution, recreational use of heroin, and, for that matter, working more than 60 hours per week in a bakery. But there is no right to "liberty" under the Due Process Clause, though today's opinion repeatedly makes that claim *** Our opinions applying the doctrine known as "substantive due process" hold that the Due Process Clause prohibits States from infringing *fundamental* liberty interests, unless the infringement is narrowly tailored to serve a compelling state interest. *Washington v. Glucksberg*, 521 U. S., at 721. We have held repeatedly, in cases the Court today does not overrule, that *only* fundamental rights qualify for this so-called "heightened scrutiny" protection–that is, rights which are "'deeply rooted in this Nation's history and tradition.'" *** All other liberty interests may be abridged or abrogated pursuant to a validly enacted state law if that law is rationally related to a legitimate state interest. ***

Bowers' conclusion that homosexual sodomy is not a fundamental right "deeply rooted in this Nation's history and tradition" is utterly unassailable. *** States continue to prosecute all sorts of crimes by adults "in matters pertaining to sex": prostitution, adult incest, adultery, obscenity, and child pornography.   Sodomy laws, too, have been enforced "in the past half century," in which there have been 134 reported cases involving prosecutions for consensual, adult, homosexual sodomy. In relying, for evidence of an "emerging recognition," upon the American Law Institute's 1955 recommendation not to criminalize "'consensual sexual relations conducted in private,'" the Court ignores the fact that this recommendation was "a point of resistance in most of the states that considered adopting the Model Penal Code."

In any event, an "emerging awareness" is by definition not "deeply rooted in this Nation's history and tradition[s]," as we have said "fundamental right" status requires.   Constitutional entitlements do not spring into existence because some States choose to lessen or eliminate criminal sanctions on certain behavior. Much less do they spring into existence, as the Court seems to believe, because *foreign nations* decriminalize conduct. *** "[T]his Court *** should not impose foreign moods, fads, or fashions on Americans."

I turn now to the ground on which the Court squarely rests its holding: the contention that there is no rational basis for the law here under attack. *** The Texas statute undeniably seeks to further the belief of its citizens that certain forms of sexual behavior are "immoral and unacceptable"–the same interest furthered by criminal laws against fornication, bigamy, adultery, adult incest, bestiality, and obscenity. *Bowers* held that this *was* a legitimate state interest. *** If, as the Court asserts, the promotion of majoritarian sexual morality is not even a *legitimate* state interest, none of the above-mentioned laws can survive rational-basis review.

Finally, I turn to petitioners' equal-protection challenge, which no Member of the Court save JUSTICE O'CONNOR, embraces: On its face § 21.06(a) applies equally to all persons. Men and women, heterosexuals and homosexuals, are all subject to its prohibition of deviate sexual intercourse with someone of the same sex. To be sure, § 21.06 does distinguish between the sexes insofar as concerns the partner with whom the sexual acts are performed: men can violate the law only with other men, and women only with other women. But this cannot itself be a denial of equal protection, since it is precisely the same distinction regarding partner that is drawn in state laws prohibiting marriage with someone of the same sex while permitting marriage with someone of the opposite sex.

The objection is made, however, that the antimiscegenation laws invalidated in *Loving v. Virginia*, 388 U. S. 1, 8 (1967), similarly were applicable to whites and blacks alike, and only distinguished between the races insofar as the *partner* was concerned. In *Loving*, however, we correctly applied heightened scrutiny, rather than the usual rational-basis review, because the Virginia statute was "designed to maintain White Supremacy." *** No purpose to discriminate against men or women as a class can be gleaned from the Texas law, so rational- basis review applies. That review is readily satisfied here by the same rational basis that satisfied it in *Bowers*– society's belief that certain forms of sexual behavior are "immoral and unacceptable." *** A law against public nudity targets "the conduct that is closely correlated with being a nudist," and hence "is targeted at more than conduct"; it is "directed toward nudists as a class." But be that as it may. Even if the Texas law *does* deny equal protection to "homosexuals as a class," that denial *still* does not need to be justified by anything more than a rational basis, which our cases show is satisfied by the enforcement of traditional notions of sexual morality. ***

Today's opinion is the product of a Court, which is the product of a law-profession culture, that has largely signed on to the so-called homosexual agenda, by which I mean the agenda promoted by some homosexual activists directed at eliminating the moral opprobrium that has traditionally attached to homosexual conduct. *** [T]he Court has taken sides in the culture war, departing from its role of assuring, as neutral observer, that the democratic rules of engagement are observed. ***

Let me be clear that I have nothing against homosexuals, or any other group, promoting their agenda through normal democratic means. Social perceptions of sexual and other morality change over time, and every group has the right to persuade its fellow citizens that its view of such matters is the best. That homosexuals have achieved some success in that enterprise is attested to by the fact that Texas is one of the few remaining States that criminalize private, consensual homosexual acts. But persuading one's fellow citizens is one thing, and imposing one's views in absence of democratic majority will is something else. I would no more *require* a State to criminalize homosexual acts—or, for that matter, display *any* moral disapprobation of them—than I would *forbid* it to do so.

One of the benefits of leaving regulation of this matter to the people rather than to the courts is that the people, unlike judges, need not carry things to their logical conclusion. *** Today's opinion dismantles the structure of constitutional law that has permitted a distinction to be made between heterosexual and homosexual unions, insofar as formal recognition in marriage is concerned. If moral disapproval of homosexual conduct is "no legitimate state interest" for purposes of proscribing that conduct, *** what justification could there possibly be for denying the benefits of marriage to homosexual couples exercising "[t]he liberty protected by the Constitution"? Surely not the encouragement of procreation, since the sterile and the elderly are allowed to marry. This case "does not involve" the issue of homosexual marriage only if one entertains the belief that principle and logic have nothing to do with the decisions of this Court. Many will hope that, as the Court comfortingly assures us, this is so. ***

JUSTICE THOMAS, dissenting.

*** I write separately to note that the law before the Court today "is *** uncommonly silly." If I were a member of the Texas Legislature, I would vote to repeal it. *** Notwithstanding this, *** I "can find [neither in the Bill of Rights nor any other part of the Constitution a] general right of privacy," or as the Court terms it today, the "liberty of the person both in its spatial and more transcendent dimensions."

Notes

1. **Overruling *Bowers*.** Do the Court's reasons justify overruling *Bowers*? Was JUSTICE O'CONNOR correct in avoiding overruling it? Was JUSTICE SCALIA correct in his assessment of the ramifications of the case?

2. **Neutral or Anti-homosexual?** Does the Texas statute discriminate against homosexuals? Compare the Georgia statute in *Bowers*: "A person commits the offense of sodomy when he performs or submits to any sexual act involving the sex organs of one person and the mouth or anus of another." Was Georgia's statute limited to homosexual sodomy? If not, how could the Court limit its inquiry to homosexual sodomy? Would a statute making sodomy between unmarried heterosexuals unlawful be unconstitutional?

3. **Ramifications.** The majority and dissents have very different views of the meaning of this case in other areas. Consider these:

a. **Marriage.** How does this decision affect the political and legal status of efforts to legalize marriage by homosexual couples?

b. **Adoption.** Many states do not allow same-sex couples to adopt children. Are these prohibitions unconstitutional?

4. **Practices of Other Nations.** To what extent did the Court rely upon European experience? Should it have also considered African, Mid-East, and Asian experience? What weight should each be given?

OBERGEFELL *v.* HODGES
135 S. Ct. 2584 (2015)

JUSTICE KENNEDY delivered the opinion of the Court.

The Constitution promises liberty to all within its reach, a liberty that includes certain specific rights that allow persons, within a lawful realm, to define and express their identity. The petitioners in these cases seek to find that liberty by marrying someone of the same sex and having their marriages deemed lawful on the same terms and conditions as marriages between persons of the opposite sex.

These cases come from *** States that define marriage as a union between one man and one woman. The petitioners are 14 same-sex couples and two men whose same-sex partners are deceased. *** The petitioners claim the respondents violate the Fourteenth Amendment by denying them the right to marry or to have their marriages, lawfully performed in another State, given full recognition. *** Before addressing the principles and precedents that govern these cases, it is appropriate to note the history of the subject now before the Court. *** Since the dawn of history, marriage has transformed strangers into relatives, binding families and societies together. *** It is fair and necessary to say these references were based on the understanding that marriage is a union between two persons of the opposite sex.

That history is the beginning of these cases. The respondents say it should be the end as well. To them, it would demean a timeless institution if the concept and lawful status of marriage were extended to two persons of the same sex. *** Far from seeking to devalue marriage, the petitioners seek it for themselves because of their respect—and need—for its privileges and responsibilities. And their immutable nature dictates that same-sex marriage is their only real path to this profound commitment. *** The history of marriage is one of both continuity and change. That institution—even as confined to opposite-sex relations—has evolved over time.

For example, marriage was once viewed as an arrangement by the couple's parents based on political, religious, and financial concerns; but by the time of the Nation's founding it was understood to be a voluntary contract between a man and a woman. *** As women gained legal, political, and property rights, and as society began to understand that women have their own equal dignity, the law of coverture was abandoned. *** These new insights have strengthened, not weakened, the institution of marriage.

Indeed, changed understandings of marriage are characteristic of a Nation where new dimensions of freedom become apparent to new generations, often through perspectives that begin in pleas or protests and then are considered in the political sphere and the judicial process.

This dynamic can be seen in the Nation's experiences with the rights of gays and lesbians. Until the mid-20th century, same-sex intimacy long had been condemned as immoral by the state itself in most Western nations, a belief often embodied in the criminal law. *** Only in more recent years have psychiatrists and others recognized that sexual orientation is both a normal expression of human sexuality and immutable. *** This Court first gave detailed consideration to the legal status of homosexuals in *Bowers* v. *Hardwick*. There it upheld the constitutionality of a Georgia law deemed to criminalize certain homosexual acts. Ten years later, in *Romer* v. *Evans*, the Court invalidated an amendment to Colorado's Constitution that sought to foreclose any branch or political subdivision of the State from protecting persons against discrimination based on sexual orientation. Then, in 2003, the Court overruled *Bowers*, holding that laws making same-sex intimacy a crime "demea[n] the lives of homosexual persons." *Lawrence* v. *Texas*. *** [I]n 1996, Congress passed the Defense of Marriage Act (DOMA), defining marriage for all federal-law purposes as "only a legal union between one man and one woman as husband and wife." *** Two Terms ago, in *United States* v. *Windsor*, this Court invalidated DOMA to the extent it barred the Federal Government from treating same-sex marriages as valid even when they were lawful in the State where they were licensed. *** [T]he States are now divided on the issue of same-sex marriage.

Under the Due Process Clause of the Fourteenth Amendment, no State shall "deprive any person of life, liberty, or property, without due process of law." *** The identification and protection of fundamental rights is an enduring part of the judicial duty to interpret the Constitution. That responsibility, however, "has not been reduced to any formula." *Poe* v. *Ullman* (HARLAN, J., dissenting). Rather, it requires courts to exercise reasoned judgment in identifying interests of the person so fundamental that the State must accord them its respect. *** History and tradition guide and discipline this inquiry but do not set its outer boundaries. That method respects our history and learns from it without allowing the past alone to rule the present. *** Applying these established tenets, the Court has long held the right to marry is protected by the Constitution. In *Loving* v. *Virginia*, which invalidated bans on interracial unions, a unanimous Court held marriage is "one of the vital personal rights essential to the orderly pursuit of happiness by free men." The Court reaffirmed that holding in *Zablocki* v. *Redhail*, which held the right to marry was burdened by a law prohibiting fathers who were behind on child support from marrying. *** Over time and in other contexts, the Court has reiterated that the right to marry is fundamental under the Due Process Clause. See, *e.g., Griswold*; *Skinner* v. *Oklahoma*; *Meyer* v. *Nebraska*.

It cannot be denied that this Court's cases describing the right to marry presumed a relationship involving opposite-sex partners. *** Still, there are other, more instructive precedents. This Court's cases have expressed constitutional principles of broader reach. In defining the right to marry these cases have identified essential attributes of that right based in history, tradition, and other constitutional liberties inherent in this intimate bond. See, *e.g., Lawrence; Zablocki; Loving; Griswold*. And in assessing whether the force and rationale of its cases apply to same-sex couples, the Court must respect the basic reasons why the right to marry has been long protected. See, *e.g., Eisenstadt; Poe* (HARLAN, J., dissenting).

This analysis compels the conclusion that same-sex couples may exercise the right to marry. The four principles and traditions to be discussed demonstrate that the reasons marriage is fundamental under the Constitution apply with equal force to same-sex couples.

A first premise of the Court's relevant precedents is that the right to personal choice regarding marriage is inherent in the concept of individual autonomy. *** There is dignity in the bond between two men or two women who seek to marry and in their autonomy to make such pro-found choices. *** A second principle in this Court's jurisprudence is that the right to marry is fundamental because it supports a two-person union unlike any other in its importance to the committed individuals. *** The right to marry thus dignifies couples who "wish to define themselves by their commitment to each other." *Windsor*. Marriage responds to the universal fear that a lonely person might call out only to find no one there. *** A third basis for protecting the right to marry is that it safeguards children and families and thus draws meaning from related rights of childrearing, procreation, and education. See *Pierce* v. *Society of Sisters; Meyer*. *** Without the recognition, stability, and predictability marriage offers, their children suffer the stigma of knowing their families are somehow lesser. *** The marriage laws at issue here thus harm and humiliate the children of same-sex couples. See *Windsor*. *** Fourth and finally, this Court's cases and the Nation's traditions make clear that marriage is a keystone of our social order. *** The limitation of marriage to opposite-sex couples may long have seemed natural and just, but its inconsistency with the central meaning of the fundamental right to marry is now manifest. *** With that knowledge must come the recognition that laws excluding same-sex couples from the marriage right impose stigma and injury of the kind prohibited by our basic charter.

Objecting that this does not reflect an appropriate framing of the issue, the respondents refer to *Washington* v. *Glucksberg*, which called for a "'careful description'" of fundamental rights. They assert the petitioners do not seek to exercise the right to marry but rather a new and nonexistent "right to same-sex marriage." *Glucksberg* did insist that liberty under the Due Process Clause must be defined in a most circumscribed manner, with central reference to specific historical practices. Yet while that approach may have been appropriate for the asserted right there involved (physician-assisted suicide), it is inconsistent with the approach this Court has used in discussing other fundamental rights, including marriage and intimacy. *Loving* did not ask about a "right to interracial marriage." *** Rather, each case inquired about the right to marry in its comprehensive sense, asking if there was a sufficient justification for excluding the relevant class from the right.

That principle applies here. If rights were defined by who exercised them in the past, then received practices could serve as their own continued justification and new groups could not invoke rights once denied. This Court has rejected that approach, both with respect to the right to marry and the rights of gays and lesbians. See *Loving*; *Lawrence*.

The right to marry is fundamental as a matter of history and tradition, but rights come not from ancient sources alone. They rise, too, from a better-informed understanding of how constitutional imperatives define a liberty that remains urgent in our own era. *** The right of same-sex couples to marry that is part of the liberty promised by the Fourteenth Amendment is derived, too, from that Amendment's guarantee of the equal protection of the laws. *** The Court's cases touching upon the right to marry reflect this dynamic. [See *Loving* (invalidating prohibition on interracial marriage under both Equal Protection Clause and Due Process Clause); *Zablocki* (same).] *** [T]he Court has recognized that new insights and societal understandings can reveal unjustified inequality within our most fundamental institutions that once passed unnoticed and unchallenged. *** Other cases confirm [the] relation between liberty and equality. *** In *Eisenstadt* v. *Baird*, the Court invoked both principles to invalidate a prohibition on the distribution of contraceptives to unmarried persons but not married persons. And in *Skinner* v. *Oklahoma*, the Court invalidated under both principles a law that allowed sterilization of habitual criminals. *Skinner.*

In *Lawrence* the Court acknowledged the interlocking nature of these constitutional safeguards in the context of the legal treatment of gays and lesbians. *** *Lawrence* therefore drew upon principles of liberty and equality to define and protect the rights of gays and lesbians, holding the State "cannot demean their existence or control their destiny by making their private sexual conduct a crime." *** It is now clear that the challenged laws burden the liberty of same-sex couples, and it must be further acknowledged that they abridge central precepts of equality. *** These considerations lead to the conclusion that the right to marry is a fundamental right inherent in the liberty of the person, and under the Due Process and Equal Protection Clauses of the Fourteenth Amendment couples of the same-sex may not be deprived of that right and that liberty. ***

Of course, the Constitution contemplates that democracy is the appropriate process for change, so long as that process does not abridge fundamental rights. *** The dynamic of our constitutional system is that individuals need not await legislative action before asserting a fundamental right. *** An individual can invoke a right to constitutional protection when he or she is harmed, even if the broader public disagrees and even if the legislature refuses to act. ***

Finally, it must be emphasized that religions, and those who adhere to religious doctrines, may continue to advocate with utmost, sincere conviction that, by divine precepts, same-sex marriage should not be condoned. The

First Amendment ensures that religious organizations and persons are given proper protection as they seek to teach the principles that are so fulfilling and so central to their lives and faiths, and to their own deep aspirations to continue the family structure they have long revered. ***

These cases also present the question whether the Constitution requires States to recognize same-sex marriages validly performed out of State. *** As counsel for the respondents acknowledged at argument, if States are required by the Constitution to issue marriage licenses to same-sex couples, the justifications for refusing to recognize those marriages performed else-where are undermined. *** [T]here is no lawful basis for a State to refuse to recognize a lawful same-sex marriage performed in another State on the ground of its same-sex character. *** As some of the petitioners in these cases demonstrate, marriage embodies a love that may endure even past death. *** They ask for equal dignity in the eyes of the law. The Constitution grants them that right. ***

CHIEF JUSTICE ROBERTS, with whom JUSTICE SCALIA and JUSTICE THOMAS join, dissenting.

Petitioners make strong arguments rooted in social policy and considerations of fairness. *** But this Court is not a legislature. Whether same -sex marriage is a good idea should be of no concern to us. Under the Constitution, judges have power to say what the law is, not what it should be. *** Although the policy arguments for extending marriage to same-sex couples may be compelling, the legal arguments for requiring such an extension are not. The fundamental right to marry does not include a right to make a State change its definition of marriage. And a State's decision to maintain the meaning of marriage that has persisted in every culture throughout human history can hardly be called irrational. In short, our Constitution does not enact any one theory of marriage. The people of a State are free to expand marriage to include same-sex couples, or to retain the historic definition. *** The need for restraint in administering the strong medicine of substantive due process is a lesson this Court has learned the hard way. *Dred Scott.* *** Our precedents have required that implied fundamental rights be "objectively, deeply rooted in this Nation's history and tradition," and "implicit in the concept of ordered liberty, such that neither liberty nor justice would exist if they were sacrificed." *Glucksberg.* [The Court's] aggressive application of substantive due process breaks sharply with decades of precedent and returns the Court to the unprincipled approach of *Lochner.* ***

[The] privacy cases provide no support for the majority's position, because petitioners do not seek privacy. Quite the opposite, they seek public recognition of their relationships, along with corresponding government benefits. Our cases have consistently refused to allow litigants to convert the shield provided by constitutional liberties into a sword to demand positive entitlements from the State. See *DeShaney* v. *Winnebago County Dept. of Social Servs.*; *San Antonio Independent School Dist.* v. *Rodriguez.* ***

In addition to their due process argument, petitioners contend that the Equal Protection Clause requires their States to license and recognize same-sex marriages. *** The central point seems to be that there is a "synergy between" the Equal Protection Clause and the Due Process Clause, and that some precedents relying on one Clause have also relied on the other. *** In any event, the marriage laws at issue here do not violate the Equal Protection Clause, because distinguishing between opposite-sex and same-sex couples is rationally related to the States' "legitimate state interest" in "preserving the traditional institution of marriage." ***

If you are among the many Americans—of whatever sexual orientation—who favor expanding same-sex marriage, by all means celebrate today's decision. Celebrate the achievement of a desired goal. Celebrate the opportunity for a new expression of commitment to a partner. Celebrate the availability of new benefits. But do not celebrate the Constitution. It had nothing to do with it. ***

JUSTICE SCALIA, with whom JUSTICE THOMAS joins, dissenting.

*** I write separately to call attention to this Court's threat to American democracy. *** [I]t is not of special importance to me what the law says about marriage. It is of overwhelming importance, however, who it is that rules me. Today's decree says that my Ruler, and the Ruler of 320 million Americans coast-to-coast, is a majority of the nine lawyers on the Supreme Court. *** This practice of constitutional revision by an unelected committee of nine, always accompanied (as it is today) by extravagant praise of liberty, robs the People of the most important liberty they asserted in the Declaration of Independence and won in the Revolution of 1776: the freedom to govern themselves. *** When the Fourteenth Amendment was ratified in 1868, every State limited marriage to one man and one woman, and no one doubted the constitutionality of doing so. That resolves these cases. *** We have no basis for striking down a practice that is not expressly prohibited by the Fourteenth Amendment's text, and that bears the endorsement of a long tradition of open, widespread, and unchallenged use dating back to the Amendment's ratification. Since there is no doubt whatever that the People never decided to prohibit the limitation of marriage to opposite-sex couples, the public debate over same-sex marriage must be allowed to continue. *** This [decision] is a naked judicial claim to legislative—indeed, *super*-legislative—power; a claim fundamentally at odds with our system of government. *** With each decision of ours that takes from the People a question properly left to them—with each decision that is unabashedly based not on law, but on the "reasoned judgment" of a bare majority of this Court—we move one step closer to being reminded of our impotence.

JUSTICE THOMAS, with whom JUSTICE SCALIA joins, dissenting.

The Court's decision today is at odds not only with the Constitution, but with the principles upon which our Nation was built. Since well before 1787, liberty has been understood as freedom from government action, not entitlement to government benefits. The Framers created our Constitution to preserve that understanding of liberty. Yet the majority invokes our

Constitution in the name of a "liberty" that the Framers would not have recognized, to the detriment of the liberty they sought to protect. Along the way, it rejects the idea—captured in our Declaration of Independence—that human dignity is innate and suggests instead that it comes from the Government. This distortion of our Constitution not only ignores the text, it inverts the relationship between the individual and the state in our Republic. ***

The majority's decision today will require States to issue marriage licenses to same-sex couples and to recognize same-sex marriages entered in other States largely based on a constitutional provision guaranteeing "due process" before a person is deprived of his "life, liberty, or property." I have elsewhere explained the dangerous fiction of treating the Due Process Clause as a font of substantive rights. *McDonald* v. *Chicago*. It distorts the constitutional text, which guarantees only whatever "process" is "due" before a person is deprived of life, liberty, and property. Worse, it invites judges to do exactly what the majority has done here—"roa[m] at large in the constitutional field guided only by their personal views" as to the fundamental rights protected by that document. *** Our Constitution—like the Declaration of Independence before it—was predicated on a simple truth: One's liberty, not to mention one's dignity, was something to be shielded from—not provided by—the State. Today's decision casts that truth aside. ***

JUSTICE ALITO, with whom JUSTICE SCALIA and JUSTICE THOMAS join, dissenting.

Until the federal courts intervened, the American people were engaged in a debate about whether their States should recognize same-sex marriage. *** The Constitution leaves that question to be decided by the people of each State. *** For today's majority, it does not matter that the right to same-sex marriage lacks deep roots or even that it is contrary to long-established tradition. The Justices in the majority claim the authority to confer constitutional protection upon that right simply because they believe that it is fundamental. *** [The Court's] understanding of marriage *** is not the traditional one. For millennia, marriage was inextricably linked to the one thing that only an opposite-sex couple can do: procreate. ***

Today's decision *** will also have other important consequences. *** Perhaps recognizing how its reasoning may be used [to vilify opposition], the majority attempts, toward the end of its opinion, to reassure those who oppose same-sex marriage that their rights of conscience will be protected. We will soon see whether this proves to be true. I assume that those who cling to old beliefs will be able to whisper their thoughts in the recesses of their homes, but if they repeat those views in public, they will risk being labeled as bigots and treated as such by governments, employers, and schools. *** If a bare majority of Justices can invent a new right and impose that right on the rest of the country, the only real limit on what future majorities will be able to do is their own sense of what those with political power and cultural influence are willing to tolerate. *** Most Americans—understandably—will cheer or lament today's decision because of their views on the issue of same-sex marriage. But all Americans, whatever their thinking on that issue, should worry about what the majority's claim of power portends.

Notes

1. A Definition of Marriage. The dissenting Justices argued that the marriage precedents cited by the Court did not involve the definition of marriage. Would the decision in *Loving* have been different if the Virginia statute *defined* marriage as an institution between a man and a woman of the same race instead of criminalizing intecial marriage?

2. Equal Protection, Due Process, and Synergy. The Court rested its holding primarily on due process grounds. JUSTICE KENNEDY noted a "synergy" between Due Process and Equal Protection, arguing that a violation of the former may abridge "central precepts of equality." JUSTICE THOMAS argued that equal protection was used to "shore up" the substantive due process analysis, weakened as it was by "an imaginary constitutional protection and revisionist view of our history and tradition." Which side persuades you?

3. Fundamental Rights. Commentators have criticized *Obergefell* for "inventing" a new, fundamental right to marriage. Equal Protection, the argument goes, would have reached the same result without cementing a new right. Why do you think the majority rested its decision on Due Process grounds? Do you think the majority created a new right?

4. Positive versus Negative Rights. JUSTICE THOMAS argues that liberty – as envisioned at the time of the founding-era – refered to "negative" liberty and not positive liberty, freedom "from" government interference rather than freedom "to" something. Thus, for Thomas, denial of same-sex marriage does not deprive one of "liberty" because there is no freedom "to" marriage, but only a freedom "from" government interference. Because the benefits that flow from a marriage are government entitlements, he opines that no deprivation has been worked. Do you find this persuasive? Can "liberty" encompass both positive-entitlements and negative-freedoms? Does this matter or is it all semantics?

5. Non-Monogomous Marriages. The dissent, in a passage omitted above, says the majority's references to "two" individuals in a marriage is makeweight and that the majority's logic commands recognition of polygamous and polyandrous marriages. Do you agree with the dissent on this point? Why or why not?

6. Consequences for Democracy. The dissent says the Court has usurped the right of "the People" to define marriage. Do you agree?

e. The Right to Die

whether Mo. violated Due Process by refusing to remove life support?

CRUZAN v. DIRECTOR, MISSOURI DEPARTMENT OF HEALTH
497 U.S. 261 (1990)

CHIEF JUSTICE REHNQUIST delivered the opinion of the Court.

*** On the night of January 11, 1983, Nancy Cruzan lost control of her car as she traveled down Elm Road in Jasper County, Missouri. The vehicle overturned, and Cruzan was discovered lying face down in a ditch without detectable respiratory or cardiac function. Paramedics were able to restore her breathing and heartbeat at the accident site, and she was transported to a hospital in an unconscious state. An attending neurosurgeon diagnosed her as having sustained probable cerebral contusions compounded by significant anoxia (lack of oxygen). The Missouri trial court in this case found that permanent brain damage generally results after 6 minutes in an anoxic state; it was estimated that Cruzan was deprived of oxygen from 12 to 14 minutes. She remained in a coma for approximately three weeks and then progressed to an unconscious state in which she was able to orally ingest some nutrition. In order to ease feeding and further the recovery, surgeons implanted a gastrostomy feeding and hydration tube in Cruzan with the consent of her then husband. Subsequent rehabilitative efforts proved unavailing. She now lies in a Missouri state hospital in what is commonly referred to as a persistent vegetative state: generally, a condition in which a person exhibits motor reflexes but evinces no indications of significant cognitive function. The State of Missouri is bearing the cost of her care.

After it had become apparent that Nancy Cruzan had virtually no chance of regaining her mental faculties, her parents asked hospital employees to terminate the artificial nutrition and hydration procedures. All agree that such a removal would cause her death. The employees refused to honor the request without court approval. *** We granted certiorari to consider the question whether Cruzan has a right under the United States Constitution which would require the hospital to withdraw life-sustaining treatment from her under these circumstances.

At common law, even the touching of one person by another without consent and without legal justification was a battery. *** This notion of bodily integrity has been embodied in the requirement that informed consent is generally required for medical treatment. *** The logical corollary of the doctrine of informed consent is that the patient generally possesses the right not to consent, that is, to refuse treatment. ***With the advance of medical technology capable of sustaining life well past the point where natural forces would have brought certain death in earlier times, cases involving the right to refuse life-sustaining treatment have burgeoned. *** This is the first case in which we have been squarely presented with the issue whether the United States Constitution grants what is in common parlance referred to as a "right to die." ***

The Fourteenth Amendment provides that no State shall "deprive any person of life, liberty, or property, without due process of law." The principle that a competent person has a constitutionally protected liberty interest in refusing unwanted medical treatment may be inferred from our prior decisions. In *Jacobson v. Massachusetts*, 197 U.S. 11, 24–30 (1905), for instance, the Court balanced an individual's liberty interest in declining an unwanted smallpox vaccine against the State's interest in preventing disease. *** Just this Term, *** we recognized that prisoners possess "a significant liberty interest in avoiding the unwanted administration of antipsychotic drugs under the Due Process Clause of the Fourteenth Amendment." *Washington v. Harper*, 494 U.S. 210, 221–222 (1990). ***

[handwritten margin note: Ct. has ruled in favor of allowing people to control their own bodies]

But determining that a person has a "liberty interest" under the Due Process Clause does not end the inquiry; "whether respondent's constitutional rights have been violated must be determined by balancing his liberty interests against the relevant state interests." Petitioners insist that under the general holdings of our cases, the forced administration of life-sustaining medical treatment, and even of artificially delivered food and water essential to life, would implicate a competent person's liberty interest. Although we think the logic of the cases discussed above would embrace such a liberty interest, the dramatic consequences involved in refusal of such treatment would inform the inquiry as to whether the deprivation of that interest is constitutionally permissible. But for purposes of this case, we assume that the United States Constitution would grant a competent person a constitutionally protected right to refuse lifesaving hydration and nutrition.

P args that an incompetent person should be treated the same

Petitioners go on to assert that an incompetent person should possess the same right in this respect as is possessed by a competent person. *** The difficulty with petitioners' claim is that in a sense it begs the question: An incompetent person is not able to make an informed and voluntary choice to exercise a hypothetical right to refuse treatment or any other right. Such a "right" must be exercised for her, if at all, by some sort of surrogate. Here, Missouri has in effect recognized that under certain circumstances a surrogate may act for the patient in electing to have hydration and nutrition withdrawn in such a way as to cause death, but it has established a procedural safeguard to assure that the action of the surrogate conforms as best it may to the wishes expressed by the patient while competent. Missouri requires that evidence of the incompetent's wishes as to the withdrawal of treatment be proved by clear and convincing evidence. The question, then, is whether the United States Constitution forbids the establishment of this procedural requirement by the State. We hold that it does not.

Mo. state action requiring evidence of wishes

Ct. says action is okay.

Mo. wants to protect human life

*** Missouri relies on its interest in the protection and preservation of human life, and there can be no gainsaying this interest. *** We believe Missouri may legitimately seek to safeguard the personal element of this choice through the imposition of heightened evidentiary requirements. *** Not all incompetent patients will have loved ones available to serve as surrogate decisionmakers. And even where family members are present, "[t]here will, of course, be some unfortunate situations in which family members will not act to protect a patient." A State is entitled to guard against potential abuses in such situations. Similarly, a State is entitled to consider that a judicial proceeding to make a determination regarding an incompetent's wishes may very well not be an adversarial one, with the added guarantee of accurate factfinding that the adversary process brings with it. Finally, we think a State may properly decline to make judgments about the "quality" of life that a particular individual may enjoy, and simply assert an unqualified interest in the preservation of human life to be weighed against the constitutionally protected interests of the individual.

Protecting the patient w/o a surrogate or from bad intentions

Puts aside quality of life to protect const. right to life

In our view, Missouri has permissibly sought to advance these interests through the adoption of a "clear and convincing" standard of proof to govern such proceedings. *** The Supreme Court of Missouri held that in this case the testimony adduced at trial did not amount to clear and convincing proof of the patient's desire to have hydration and nutrition withdrawn. *** The testimony adduced at trial consisted primarily of Nancy Cruzan's statements made to a housemate about a year before her accident that she would not want to live should she face life as a "vegetable," and other observations to the same effect. The observations did not deal in terms with withdrawal of medical treatment or of hydration and nutrition. We cannot say that the Supreme Court of Missouri committed constitutional error in reaching the conclusion that it did.

Petitioners alternatively contend that Missouri must accept the "substituted judgment" of close family members even in the absence of substantial proof that their views reflect the views of the patient. *** Here again petitioners would seek to turn a decision which allowed a State to rely on family decisionmaking into a constitutional requirement that the State recognize such decisionmaking. But constitutional law does not work that way.

No doubt is engendered by anything in this record but that Nancy Cruzan's mother and father are loving and caring parents. If the State were required by the United States Constitution to repose a right of "substituted judgment" with anyone, the Cruzans would surely qualify. But we do not think the Due Process Clause requires the State to repose judgment on these matters with anyone but the patient herself. ***

JUSTICE O'CONNOR, concurring.

*** [T]he Court does not today decide the issue whether a State must also give effect to the decisions of a surrogate decisionmaker. In my view, such a duty may well be constitutionally required to protect the patient's liberty interest in refusing medical treatment. Few individuals provide explicit oral or written instructions regarding their intent to refuse medical treatment should they become incompetent.

JUSTICE SCALIA, concurring.

The various opinions in this case portray quite clearly the difficult, indeed agonizing, questions that are presented by the constantly increasing power of science to keep the human body alive for longer than any reasonable person would want to inhabit it. The States have begun to grapple with these problems through legislation. I am concerned, from the tenor of today's opinions, that we are poised to confuse that enterprise as successfully as we have confused the enterprise of legislating concerning abortion—requiring it to be conducted against a background of federal constitutional imperatives that are unknown because they are being newly crafted from Term to Term. That would be a great misfortune.

While I agree with the Court's analysis today, and therefore join in its opinion, I would have preferred that we announce, clearly and promptly, that the federal courts have no business in this field; that American law has always accorded the State the power to prevent, by force if necessary, suicide—including suicide by refusing to take appropriate measures necessary to preserve one's life; that the point at which life becomes "worthless," and the point at which the means necessary to preserve it become "extraordinary" or "inappropriate," are neither set forth in the Constitution nor known to the nine Justices of this Court any better than they are known to nine people picked at random from the Kansas City telephone directory; and hence, that even when it is demonstrated by clear and convincing evidence that a patient no longer wishes certain measures to be taken to preserve his or her life, it is up to the citizens of Missouri to decide, through their elected representatives, whether that wish will be honored. *** Petitioners rely on three distinctions to separate Nancy Cruzan's case from ordinary suicide: (1) that she is permanently incapacitated and in pain; (2) that she would bring on her death not by any affirmative act but by merely declining treatment that provides nourishment; and (3) that preventing her from effectuating her presumed wish to die requires violation of her bodily integrity. None of these suffices. ***

out of the scope of due process   What I have said above is not meant to suggest that I would think it desirable, if we were sure that Nancy Cruzan wanted to die, to keep her alive by the means at issue here. I assert only that the Constitution has nothing to say about the subject. *** Are there, then, no reasonable and humane limits that ought not to be exceeded in requiring an individual to preserve his own life? There obviously are, but they are not set forth in the Due Process Clause. *** Our salvation is the Equal Protection Clause, which requires the democratic majority to accept for themselves and their loved ones what they impose on you and me. This Court need not, and has no authority to, inject itself into every field of human activity where irrationality and oppression may theoretically occur, and if it tries to do so it will destroy itself.

JUSTICE BRENNAN, with whom JUSTICE MARSHALL and JUSTICE BLACKMUN join, dissenting.

*** [F]reedom from unwanted medical attention is unquestionably among those principles "so rooted in the traditions and conscience of our people as to be ranked as fundamental." *** No material distinction can be drawn between the treatment to which Nancy Cruzan continues to be subject— artificial nutrition and hydration—and any other medical treatment. *** The only state interest asserted here is a general interest in the preservation of life. But the State has no legitimate general interest in someone's life, completely abstracted from the interest of the person living that life, that could outweigh the person's choice to avoid medical treatment. *** This is not to say that the State has no legitimate interests to assert here. As the majority recognizes, Missouri has a parens patriae interest in providing Nancy Cruzan, now incompetent, with as accurate as possible a determination of how she would exercise her rights under these circumstances. Second, if and when it is determined that Nancy Cruzan would want to continue treatment, the State may legitimately assert an interest in providing that treatment. But until Nancy's wishes have been determined, the only state interest that may be asserted is an interest in safe-guarding the accuracy of that determination.

Accuracy, therefore, must be our touchstone. Missouri may *[should protect life*
constitutionally impose only those procedural requirements that serve to *so much so that*
enhance the accuracy of a determination of Nancy Cruzan's wishes or are at *it is in line with*
least consistent with an accurate determination. The Missouri "safeguard" *the patient's*
that the Court upholds today does not meet that standard. *** Missouri's rule *wishes]*
of decision imposes a markedly asymmetrical evidentiary burden. Only
evidence of specific statements of treatment choice made by the patient when
competent is admissible to support a finding that the patient, now in a
persistent vegetative state, would wish to avoid further medical treatment.
Moreover, this evidence must be clear and convincing. No proof is required to
support a finding that the incompetent person would wish to continue
treatment. ***

Even more than its heightened evidentiary standard, the Missouri court's
categorical exclusion of relevant evidence dispenses with any semblance of
accurate factfinding. *** Too few people execute living wills or equivalently
formal directives for such an evidentiary rule to ensure adequately that the
wishes of incompetent persons will be honored. While it might be a wise
social policy to encourage people to furnish such instructions, no general
conclusion about a patient's choice can be drawn from the absence of
formalities. *** [T]he bodies and preferences and memories of the victims do
not escheat to the State; nor does our Constitution permit the State or any
other government to commandeer them. ***

JUSTICE STEVENS, dissenting.

*** To be constitutionally permissible, Missouri's intrusion upon ***
fundamental liberties must, at a minimum, bear a reasonable relationship to
a legitimate state end. Missouri asserts that its policy is related to a state
interest in the protection of life. In my view, however, it is an effort to define
life, rather than to protect it, that is the heart of Missouri's policy. Missouri
insists, without regard to Nancy Cruzan's own interests, upon equating her
life with the biological persistence of her bodily functions. *** If Nancy
Cruzan's life were defined by reference to her own interests, so that her life
expired when her biological existence ceased serving any of her own interests,
then her constitutionally protected interest in freedom from unwanted
treatment would not come into conflict with her constitutionally protected
interest in life. Conversely, if there were any evidence that Nancy Cruzan
herself defined life to encompass every form of biological persistence by a
human being, so that the continuation of treatment would serve Nancy's own
liberty, then once again there would be no conflict between life and liberty.
The opposition of life and liberty in this case *** the artificial consequence of
Missouri's effort, and this Court's willingness, to abstract Nancy Cruzan's life
from Nancy Cruzan's person. ***

The Cruzan family's continuing concern provides a concrete reminder
that Nancy Cruzan's interests did not disappear with her vitality or her
consciousness. However commendable may be the State's interest in human *[using Nancy to*
life, it cannot pursue that interest by appropriating Nancy Cruzan's life as a *serve their own*
symbol for its own purposes. *** A State that seeks to demonstrate its *purposes]*

commitment to life may do so by aiding those who are actively struggling for life and health. ***

VIII-8. By permission of Chip Bok and Creators Syndicate

WASHINGTON v. GLUCKSBERG
521 U.S. 702 (1997)

CHIEF JUSTICE REHNQUIST delivered the opinion of the Court.

The question presented in this case is whether Washington's prohibition against "caus[ing]" or "aid[ing]" a suicide offends the Fourteenth Amendment to the United States Constitution. We hold that it does not.

It has always been a crime to assist a suicide in the State of Washington. *** At the same time, Washington's Natural Death Act, enacted in 1979, states that the "withholding or withdrawal of life-sustaining treatment" at a patient's direction "shall not, for any purpose, constitute a suicide."[2]

Petitioners in this case are the State of Washington and its Attorney General. Respondents *** are physicians who practice in Washington. These doctors occasionally treat terminally ill, suffering patients, and declare that

---

[2] Under Washington's Natural Death Act, "adult persons have the fundamental right to control the decisions relating to the rendering of their own health care, including the decision to have life-sustaining treatment withheld or withdrawn in instances of a terminal condition or permanent unconscious condition." In Washington, "[a]ny adult person may execute a directive directing the withholding or withdrawal of life-sustaining treatment in a terminal condition or permanent unconscious condition," and a physician who, in accordance with such a directive, participates in the withholding or withdrawal of life-sustaining treatment is immune from civil, criminal, or professional liability.

they would assist these patients in ending their lives if not for Washington's assisted-suicide ban [which they contend is] on its face, unconstitutional.

The plaintiffs asserted "the existence of a liberty interest protected by the Fourteenth Amendment which extends to a personal choice by a mentally competent, terminally ill adult to commit physician-assisted suicide." *** We begin, as we do in all due-process cases, by examining our Nation's history, legal traditions, and practices. In almost every State—indeed, in almost every western democracy—it is a crime to assist a suicide. The States' assisted-suicide bans are *** expressions of the States' commitment to the protection and preservation of all human life. *** And the prohibitions against assisting suicide never contained exceptions for those who were near death. *** Though deeply rooted, the States' assisted-suicide bans have in recent years been reexamined and, generally, reaffirmed. ***

[handwritten: custom/history are against suicide]

The Washington statute at issue *** specifically stated that the "withholding or withdrawal of life-sustaining treatment *** shall not, for any purpose, constitute a suicide" and that "[n]othing in this chapter shall be construed to condone, authorize, or approve mercy killing." *** On the other hand, in 1994, voters in Oregon enacted, also through ballot initiative, that State's "Death With Dignity Act," which legalized physician-assisted suicide for competent, terminally ill adults. Since the Oregon vote, many proposals to legalize assisted-suicide have been and continue to be introduced in the States' legislatures, but none has been enacted. *** President Clinton signed the Federal Assisted Suicide Funding Restriction Act of 1997, which prohibits the use of federal funds in support of physician-assisted suicide.[16] Thus, the States are currently engaged in serious, thoughtful examinations of physician-assisted suicide and other similar issues. ***

[handwritten: some states are applying it.]

[handwritten: everyone except OR has banned it.]

Our established method of substantive-due-process analysis has two primary features: First, we have regularly observed that the Due Process Clause specially protects those fundamental rights and liberties which are, objectively, "deeply rooted in this Nation's history and tradition and 'implicit in the concept of ordered liberty,' such that 'neither liberty nor justice would exist if they were sacrificed,' *Palko v. Connecticut*, (1937). Second, we have required in substantive-due-process cases a 'careful description' of the asserted fundamental liberty interest." Our Nation's history, legal traditions, and practices thus provide the crucial "guideposts for responsible decisionmaking," that direct and restrain our exposition of the Due Process Clause. *** [T]he development of this Court's substantive-due-process jurisprudence *** has been a process whereby the outlines of the "liberty" specially protected by the Fourteenth Amendment—never fully clarified, to be sure, and perhaps not capable of being fully clarified—have at least been

[handwritten: two prongs of SDP]
[handwritten: ① fundamental right deeply rooted in history]
[handwritten: ② SDP]

---

[16] Other countries are embroiled in similar debates: The Supreme Court of Canada recently rejected a claim that the Canadian Charter of Rights and Freedoms establishes a fundamental right to assisted suicide; the British House of Lords Select Committee on Medical Ethics refused to recommend any change in Great Britain's assisted-suicide prohibition; New Zealand's Parliament rejected a proposed "Death With Dignity Bill" that would have legalized physician-assisted suicide in August 1995; and the Northern Territory of Australia legalized assisted suicide and voluntary euthanasia in. On the other hand, on May 20, 1997, Colombia's Constitutional Court legalized voluntary euthanasia for terminally ill people.

carefully refined by concrete examples involving fundamental rights found to be deeply rooted in our legal tradition. This approach tends to rein in the subjective elements that are necessarily present in due-process judicial review. In addition, by establishing a threshold requirement—that a challenged state action implicate a fundamental right—before requiring more than a reasonable relation to a legitimate state interest to justify the action, it avoids the need for complex balancing of competing interests in every case.

*** The question presented in this case, however, is whether the protections of the Due Process Clause include a right to commit suicide with another's assistance. With this "careful description" of respondents' claim in mind, we turn to *Casey* and *Cruzan*.

Respondents contend that in *Cruzan* we "acknowledged that competent, dying persons have the right to direct the removal of life-sustaining medical treatment and thus hasten death," and that "the constitutional principle behind recognizing the patient's liberty to direct the withdrawal of artificial life support applies at least as strongly to the choice to hasten impending death by consuming lethal medication." *** The right assumed in *Cruzan*, however, was not simply deduced from abstract concepts of personal autonomy. Given the common-law rule that forced medication was a battery, and the long legal tradition protecting the decision to refuse unwanted medical treatment, our assumption was entirely consistent with this Nation's history and constitutional traditions. The decision to commit suicide with the assistance of another may be just as personal and profound as the decision to refuse unwanted medical treatment, but it has never enjoyed similar legal protection. Indeed, the two acts are widely and reasonably regarded as quite distinct. ***

Respondents also rely on *Casey*. There, the Court's opinion concluded that "the essential holding of *Roe v. Wade* should be retained and once again reaffirmed." In reaching this conclusion, the opinion discussed in some detail this Court's substantive-due-process tradition of interpreting the Due Process Clause to protect certain fundamental rights and "personal decisions relating to marriage, procreation, contraception, family relationships, child rearing, and education," and noted that many of those rights and liberties "involv[e] the most intimate and personal choices a person may make in a lifetime." *** That many of the rights and liberties protected by the Due Process Clause sound in personal autonomy does not warrant the sweeping conclusion that any and all important, intimate, and personal decisions are so protected. *** *Casey* did not suggest otherwise.

The history of the law's treatment of assisted suicide in this country has been and continues to be one of the rejection of nearly all efforts to permit it. That being the case, our decisions lead us to conclude that the asserted "right" to assistance in committing suicide is not a fundamental liberty interest protected by the Due Process Clause. The Constitution also requires, however, that Washington's assisted-suicide ban be rationally related to legitimate government interests. This requirement is unquestionably met here.

First, Washington has an "unqualified interest in the preservation of human life." *Cruzan.* *** Those who attempt suicide—terminally ill or not— often suffer from depression or other mental disorders. Research indicates, however, that many people who request physician-assisted suicide withdraw that request if their depression and pain are treated. Thus, legal physician-assisted suicide could make it more difficult for the State to protect depressed or mentally ill persons, or those who are suffering from untreated pain, from suicidal impulses.

The State also has an interest in protecting the integrity and ethics of the medical profession. *** And physician-assisted suicide could, it is argued, undermine the trust that is essential to the doctor-patient relationship by blurring the time-honored line between healing and harming.

Next, the State has an interest in protecting vulnerable groups— including the poor, the elderly, and disabled persons—from abuse, neglect, and mistakes. ***

Finally, the State may fear that permitting assisted suicide will start it down the path to voluntary and perhaps even involuntary euthanasia. *** Washington's ban on assisting suicide prevents such erosion.

This concern is further supported by evidence about the practice of euthanasia in the Netherlands. The Dutch government's own study revealed that in 1990, there were 2,300 cases of voluntary euthanasia (defined as "the deliberate termination of another's life at his request"), 400 cases of assisted suicide, and more than 1,000 cases of euthanasia without an explicit request. In addition to these latter 1,000 cases, the study found an additional 4,941 cases where physicians administered lethal morphine overdoses without the patients' explicit consent. This study suggests that, despite the existence of various reporting procedures, euthanasia in the Netherlands has not been limited to competent, terminally ill adults who are enduring physical suffering, and that regulation of the practice may not have prevented abuses in cases involving vulnerable persons, including severely disabled neonates and elderly persons suffering from dementia. Washington, like most other States, reasonably ensures against this risk by banning, rather than regulating, assisting suicide.

We need not weigh exactly the relative strengths of these various interests. They are unquestionably important and legitimate, and Washington's ban on assisted suicide is at least reasonably related to their promotion and protection. *** Throughout the Nation, Americans are engaged in an earnest and profound debate about the morality, legality, and practicality of physician-assisted suicide. Our holding permits this debate to continue, as it should in a democratic society. ***

[JUSTICE O'CONNOR, joined by JUSTICE GINSBERG and JUSTICE BREYER, concurred that "there is no generalized right to commit suicide" and noted that there was no reason to move beyond the facial challenges to the Washington statute mounted by Petitioners. She reserved the question whether "a mentally competent person who is experiencing great suffering has a constitutionally cognizable interest in controlling the circumstances of his or her imminent death." JUSTICE STEVENS concurred but argued that a decision "upholding a general statutory prohibition of assisted suicide does not mean that every possible application of the statute would be valid."]

JUSTICE SOUTER, concurring in the judgment.

*** There can be no stronger claim to a physician's assistance than at the time when death is imminent, a moral judgment implied by the State's own recognition of the legitimacy of medical procedures necessarily hastening the moment of impending death. *** Whether that interest might in some circumstances, or at some time, be seen as "fundamental" to the degree entitled to prevail is not, however, a conclusion that I need draw here, for I am satisfied that the State's interests *** are sufficiently serious to defeat the present claim that its law is arbitrary or purposeless.

The State has put forward several interests to justify the Washington law as applied to physicians treating terminally ill patients, even those competent to make responsible choices: protecting life generally, discouraging suicide even if knowing and voluntary, and protecting terminally ill patients from involuntary suicide and euthanasia, both voluntary and nonvoluntary. *** [T]he third is dispositive for me. *** Leaving aside any difficulties in coming to a clear concept of imminent death, mistaken decisions may result from inadequate palliative care or a terminal prognosis that turns out to be error; coercion and abuse may stem from the large medical bills that family members cannot bear or unreimbursed hospitals decline to shoulder. *** The mere assertion that the terminally sick might be pressured into suicide decisions by close friends and family members would not alone be very telling. Of course that is possible, not only because the costs of care might be more than family members could bear but simply because they might naturally wish to see an end of suffering for someone they love. But one of the points of restricting any right of assistance to physicians, would be to condition the right on an exercise of judgment by someone qualified to assess the patient's responsible capacity and detect the influence of those outside the medical relationship.

The State, however, goes further, to argue that dependence on the vigilance of physicians will not be enough. First, the lines proposed here (particularly the requirement of a knowing and voluntary decision by the patient) would be more difficult to draw than the lines that have limited other recently recognized due process rights. *** Second, this difficulty could become the greater by combining with another fact within the realm of plausibility, that physicians simply would not be assiduous to preserve the line. ***

Respondents propose an answer to all this, the answer of state regulation with teeth. Legislation proposed in several States, for example, would authorize physician-assisted suicide but require two qualified physicians to confirm the patient's diagnosis, prognosis, and competence; and would mandate that the patient make repeated requests witnessed by at least two others over a specified time span; and would impose reporting requirements and criminal penalties for various acts of coercion. *** Respondents' proposals, as it turns out, sound much like the guidelines now in place in the Netherlands. *** The Court should accordingly stay its hand to allow reasonable legislative consideration. *** I acknowledge the legislative institutional competence as the better one to deal with that claim at this time.

Notes

1.   **Concurrences.** What do you make of the concurrences? What if a state, unlike Washington, did not permit physicians to administer potentially lethal doses of painkilling medications?

2.   ***Glucksburg, Bowers,* and *Lawrence.*** Does the *Glucksburg* Court return to the analytical framework of *Bowers*? Is this return suspect after *Lawrence*?

3.   **Executive Acts and Substantive Due Process.** What scrutiny should be applied in cases dealing with actions of individual executive officers as they perform their duties? *See County of Sacramento v. Lewis*, 523 U.S. 833 (1998) (the level of scrutiny applied to police officers' actions varies depending on whether the actions occurred during pursuit or while in a jail setting).

f. Substance, Procedure, and Methodology

The Supreme Court sometimes considers both substantive and procedural due process issues in the same case. See, e.g. *Buck v. Bell.* A Court skeptical of creating new substantive rights might be inclined to resolve such cases where possible on procedural due process grounds. Moreover, there may be internal disagreements about whether a particular case involves procedural or substantive due process. The next decision illustrates these substance/procedure issues.

DA'S OFFICE FOR THE THIRD JUDICIAL DIST. v. OSBORNE
557 U. S. 52 (2009)

CHIEF JUSTICE ROBERTS delivered the opinion of the Court.

DNA testing has an unparalleled ability both to exonerate the wrongly convicted and to identify the guilty. *** The Federal Government and the States have recognized this, and have developed special approaches to ensure that this evidentiary tool can be effectively incorporated into established criminal procedure-usually but not always through legislation. *** [T]he respondent, William Osborne, proposes a different approach: the recognition of a freestanding and far-reaching constitutional right of access to this new type of evidence. ***

This lawsuit arose out of a violent crime committed 16 years ago ***. On the evening of March 22, 1993, two men driving through Anchorage, Alaska, solicited sex from a female prostitute, K. G. She agreed to perform fellatio on both men for $100 and got in their car. *** When K. G. demanded payment in advance, the two men pulled out a gun and forced her to perform fellatio on the driver while the passenger penetrated her vaginally, using a blue condom she had brought. The passenger then ordered K. G. out of the car and told her to lie face-down in the snow. Fearing for her life, she refused, and the two men choked her and beat her with the gun. When K. G. tried to flee, the passenger beat her with a wooden axe handle and shot her in the head while she lay on the ground. They kicked some snow on top of her and left her for dead. *** K. G. did not die; the bullet had only grazed her head. Once the two men left, she found her way back to the road, and flagged down a passing car to take her home. Ultimately, she received medical care and spoke to the police. At the scene of the crime, the police recovered a spent shell casing, the axe handle, some of K. G.'s clothing stained with blood, and the blue condom. *** Six days later, two military police officers at Fort Richardson pulled over Dexter Jackson for flashing his headlights at another vehicle. In his car they discovered a gun (which matched the shell casing), as well as several items K. G. had been carrying the night of the attack. The car also matched the description K. G. had given to the police. Jackson admitted that he had been the driver during the rape and assault, and told the police that William Osborne had been his passenger. Other evidence also implicated Osborne. K. G. picked out his photograph (with some uncertainty) and at trial she identified Osborne as her attacker. Other witnesses testified that shortly before the crime, Osborne had called Jackson from an arcade, and then driven off with him. An axe handle similar to the one at the scene of the crime was found in Osborne's room on the military base where he lived. ***

While of course many criminal trials proceed without any forensic and scientific testing at all, there is no technology comparable to DNA testing for matching tissues when such evidence is at issue. *** At the same time, DNA testing alone does not always resolve a case. Where there is enough other incriminating evidence and an explanation for the DNA result, science alone cannot prove a prisoner innocent. The availability of technologies not available at trial cannot mean that every criminal conviction, or even every criminal conviction involving biological evidence, is suddenly in doubt. The dilemma is how to harness DNA's power to prove innocence without unnecessarily overthrowing the established system of criminal justice.

That task belongs primarily to the legislature. *** Alaska is one of a handful of States yet to enact legislation specifically addressing the issue of evidence requested for DNA testing. But that does not mean that such evidence is unavailable for those seeking to prove their innocence. Instead, Alaska courts are addressing how to apply existing laws for discovery and postconviction relief to this novel technology. The same is true with respect to other States that do not have DNA-specific statutes.

First, access to evidence is available under Alaska law for those who seek to subject it to newly available DNA testing that will prove them to be actually innocent. *** Osborne does have a liberty interest [but] does not have the same liberty interests as a free man. At trial, the defendant is presumed innocent *** "Once a defendant has been afforded a fair trial and convicted of the offense for which he was charged, the presumption of innocence disappears." *** We see nothing inadequate about the procedures Alaska has provided to vindicate its state right to postconviction relief in general, and nothing inadequate about how those procedures apply to those who seek access to DNA evidence. ***

The Court of Appeals below relied only on procedural due process, but Osborne seeks to defend the judgment on the basis of substantive due process as well. *** Osborne seeks access to state evidence so that he can apply new DNA-testing technology that might prove him innocent. There is no long history of such a right, and "[t]he mere novelty of such a claim is reason enough to doubt that 'substantive due process' sustains it."

And there are further reasons to doubt. The elected governments of the States are actively confronting the challenges DNA technology poses to our criminal justice systems and our traditional notions of finality, as well as the opportunities it affords. To suddenly constitutionalize this area would short-circuit what looks to be a prompt and considered legislative response. ***

Establishing a freestanding right to access DNA evidence for testing would force us to act as policymakers, and our substantive-due-process rulemaking authority would not only have to cover the right of access but a myriad of other issues. We would soon have to decide if there is a constitutional obligation to preserve forensic evidence that might later be tested. If so, for how long? Would it be different for different types of evidence? Would the State also have some obligation to gather such evidence in the first place? How much, and when? No doubt there would be a miscellany of other minor directives.

In this case, the evidence has already been gathered and preserved, but if we extend substantive due process to this area, these questions would be before us in short order, and it is hard to imagine what tools federal courts would use to answer them. At the end of the day, there is no reason to suppose that their answers to these questions would be any better than those of state courts and legislatures, and good reason to suspect the opposite. ***

JUSTICE ALITO, with whom JUSTICE KENNEDY joins, and with whom JUSTICE THOMAS joins [in part] concurring.

*** [Because] respondent did not exhaust his state remedies, [and] because a defendant who declines the opportunity to perform DNA testing at trial for tactical reasons has no constitutional right to perform such testing after conviction ***

JUSTICE STEVENS, with whom JUSTICE GINSBURG and JUSTICE BREYER join, and with whom JUSTICE SOUTER joins [in part], dissenting.

The State of Alaska possesses physical evidence that, if tested, will conclusively establish whether respondent William Osborne committed rape and attempted murder. If he did, justice has been served by his conviction and sentence. If not, Osborne has needlessly spent decades behind bars while the true culprit has not been brought to justice. The DNA test Osborne seeks is a simple one, its cost modest, and its results uniquely precise. Yet for reasons the State has been unable or unwilling to articulate, it refuses to allow Osborne to test the evidence at his own expense and to thereby ascertain the truth once and for all. *** Whether framed as a "substantive liberty interest ... protected through a procedural due process right" to have evidence made available for testing, or as a substantive due process right to be free of arbitrary government action, the result is the same: On the record now before us, Osborne has established his entitlement to test the State's evidence. ***

The majority *** offers two meager reasons for its decision. First, citing a general reluctance to "expand the concept of substantive due process, the Court observes that there is no long history of postconviction access to DNA evidence." *** The flaw is in the framing. Of course courts have not historically granted convicted persons access to physical evidence for [DNA] testing. But, as discussed above, courts have recognized a residual substantive interest in both physical liberty and in freedom from arbitrary government action. It is Osborne's interest in those well-established liberties that justifies the Court of Appeals' decision to grant him access to the State's evidence for purposes of previously unavailable DNA testing.

The majority also asserts that this Court's recognition of a limited federal right of access to DNA evidence would be ill advised because it would "short circuit what looks to be a prompt and considered legislative response" by the States and Federal Government to the issue of access to DNA evidence. *** On the record before us, there is no reason to deny access to the evidence and there are many reasons to provide it, not least of which is a fundamental concern in ensuring that justice has been done in this case. ***

JUSTICE SOUTER, dissenting.

*** Osborne's claim can be resolved by resort to the procedural due process requirement of an effective way to vindicate a liberty interest already recognized in state law. *** There is no denying that the Court is correct when it notes that a claim of right to DNA testing, post-trial at that, is a novel one, but that only reflects the relative novelty of testing DNA, and in any event is not a sufficient reason alone to reject the right asserted. Tradition is of course one serious consideration in judging whether a challenged rule or practice, or the failure to provide a new one, should be seen as violating the guarantee of substantive due process as being arbitrary *** [S]ociety finds reasons to modify some of its traditional practices, and the accumulation of new empirical knowledge can turn yesterday's reasonable range of the government's options into a due process anomaly over time. ***

Notes

1. **Due Process in Criminal Cases.** *Osborne* is the rare criminal appeal argued on general Due Process rather than specific Bill of Rights provisions. That is because post-conviction access to DNA technology unavailable at time of conviction does not fit the specific provisions.

2. **Freestanding Innocence Right?** Should a prisoner convicted at a fair trial have a freestanding right to be released from prison if he can prove he was actually innocent? The Court suggests "the threshold for any hypothetical freestanding innocence claim [is] 'extraordinarily high.'" *House v. Bell*, 547 U.S. 518 (2006). Why? Such a right pits two models of the criminal process against each other, the "due process" model which values individual rights of defendants and the "crime control model" which stresses criminal process as a tool for reducing crime in society.   Herbert Packer, THE LIMITS OF THE CRIMINAL

SANCTION (1968). *Osborne* focused on the "due process" right to DNA testing, but CHIEF JUSTICE ROBERTS expressed "crime control" concerns when he wrote: "The dilemma is how to harness DNA's power to prove innocence without unnecessarily overthrowing the established system of criminal justice." Would a freestanding right to post-conviction DNA really overthrow the system? What about the mountain of evidence linking Osborne to the crime (circumstantial evidence, witness testimony, and confession)? With a defendant convicted on thinner evidence, might the Court find a constitutional right to DNA testing?

3. **Jury Role in Criminal Trials**. As DNA testing becomes more accurate and available, tests may be better indicators of identity in particular cases than twelve jurors based decisions upon circumstantial or even eyewitness testimony. Where does this leave the jury? Can you imagine disposing of the jury altogether? See Julie A. Seaman, *Black Boxes*, 58 EMORY LAW JOURNAL 427, 434 (2008) ("If the fact-finding function of the jury were to (continue to) diminish over time due to scientific advances *** would trial by jury ultimately become an anachronism like the medieval trials by ordeal and by battle?").

4. **Methodology**. The *Osborne* Court uses numerous state statutes providing access to DNA evidence as evidence that there is no constitutional right. Is this consistent with how state statutes were used in *Griswold* and the abortion cases?

5. **Procedure or Substance—Immigration Cases.** Two cases, *Zadvydas v. Davis*, 533 U.S. 678 (2001) and *Demore v. Kim*, 538 U.S. 510 (2003) consider the liberty of aliens in deportation contexts. *Zadvydas*, before the September 11 attacks, held that a statute appearing to give detention discretion to the Attorney General implicitly was limited to "a period reasonably necessary to bring about that alien's removal from the United States." The Court alluded to a substantive due process problem: "whether, irrespective of the procedures used, the Constitution permits detention that is indefinite and potentially permanent." JUSTICES SCALIA and THOMAS dissented: "Whether a due process right is denied when removable aliens who are flight risks or dangers to the community are detained turns *** not on the substantive right to be free, but on whether there are adequate procedures to review their cases***." In *Demore*, after September 11, the Court distinguished *Zadvydas* because "the detention here [usually] lasts for less than the 90 days we considered presumptively valid in *Zadvydas*." JUSTICES SOUTER, STEVENS, AND GINSBURG in dissent said: "The substantive demands of due process necessarily go hand in hand with the procedural *** Kim's detention *** violates both components of due process." One important consideration in both cases is the level of abstraction at which the Court defines the liberty interest involved. *Zadvydas* defined the liberty interest at a high level of generality: The right to be free from indefinite civil detention.   JUSTICE SCALIA's dissent framed the right in specific terms: "a claimed right of release into this country by an individual who concededly has no right to be here." In *Demore*, the Court stressed the length of detention (usually short) and the strength of the government's interests (usually strong). Would an individual determination predict whether an alien will show up at a hearing?

6. **A Third Way? Structural, not Substantive, Due Process.** Nathan Chapman and Michael McConnell, "Due Process as Separation of Powers," 121 YALE L. J. 1672 (2012), say that due process, the "oldest phrase and the oldest idea in our Constitution" has, perversely, become "the most unrecognizable in modern interpretation." It is used to "subvert the separation of powers" and give

courts "a super-legislative power to change rather than enforce and interpret the law." The article's core conclusion is:

> Legislative acts violated due process not because they were unreasonable or in violation of higher law, but because they exercised judicial power or abrogated common law procedural protections. *** [D]ue process extended to acts of the legislature in two narrow ways: statutes that purported to empower the other branches to deprive persons of rights without adequate procedural guarantees were subject to judicial review, and acts by the legislature that deprived specific individuals of rights or property were subject to similar challenge, either in the legislative forum itself or in the course of subsequent judicial consideration.

In short, the Constitution rejected the British notion of Parliament's supremacy, but did not trade it for judicial platonic guardianship. Were the Supreme Court to adopt this view, how would the decisions in this chapter come out? Are there implications elsewhere to this theory (e.g. separation of powers, congressional delegation, judicial function)?

IX

EQUAL PROTECTION OF THE LAWS

No State shall make any distinction in civil rights and privileges among the naturalized citizens of the United States residing within its limits, or among persons born on its soil of parents permanently resident there, on account of race, color, or descent.

> —*National Anti–Slavery Standard*
> *Editorial Page Banner*
> July 22, 1865— March 31, 1866

As you study the materials in this chapter, consider how the Constitution would differ if the above language had been adopted. *Rice v. Cayetano*, 528 U.S. 495 (2000), a case in which voting had been limited to native Hawaiians, stated that race is a "prohibited classification." But that was a Fifteenth Amendment case based on this text: "The right of citizens of the United States to vote shall not be denied or abridged by the United States or any State on account of race, color, or previous condition of servitude." The Equal Protection Clause language ("No State shall *** deny to any person within its jurisdiction the equal protection of the laws") is both more general and more equivocal than that of the Fifteenth Amendment.

Hornbook Law. There is only one Equal Protection Clause. Nevertheless, the Supreme Court during the past half-century has adopted three "tiers" of equal protection analysis. The following is a useful simplification of the case law you will study:

(a) <u>Strict Scrutiny</u>. When dealing with a "suspect classification," such as race, or a "fundamental right," such as the right to vote, the Court has applied "strict scrutiny" to the governmental classification. Strict scrutiny means that, to sustain the classification, the government must prove it has a "compelling governmental interest" in the subject matter about which it has made the classification and that it has "narrowly tailored" its classification to fulfill that interest.

(b) <u>Middle Tier Scrutiny</u>. When the Court is dealing with gender classifications made by government, it has applied "middle tier" scrutiny, which requires at least an "important governmental interest" which is "closely related" to the government's classification.

(c) <u>Rational Basis Scrutiny</u>. "Rational basis" scrutiny, applied to all other governmental classifications, requires only that the classification be "rationally related" to some "legitimate governmental interest."

With three tiers of scrutiny, an obvious first problem is how to classify the classification at issue. If a legislative classification is deemed suspect, strict scrutiny is likely to be "fatal in fact" to the legislation. Conversely, if a legislative classification is not suspect, rational basis scrutiny will validate all but the most irrational legislation. Thus, a great deal would seem to turn on this first analytical step, though there is a substantial amount of discretion involved in application of these tiers. Remember Justice Thomas' dissent in *Whole Woman's Health v. Hellerstedt* in the last chapter?

Theory of Heightened Scrutiny. The theory behind heightened scrutiny is often said to come from footnote four of *United States v. Carolene Products*, 304 U.S. 144 (1938), in which the Court upheld the constitutionality of a federal statute prohibiting interstate shipment of "filled milk" (milk having vegetable oil substituted for butter fat). The footnote reads:

> There may be narrower scope for operation of the presumption of constitutionality when legislation appears on its face to be within a specific prohibition of the Constitution, such as those of the first ten amendments ***. It is unnecessary to consider now whether legislation which restricts those political processes which can ordinarily be expected to bring about repeal of undesirable legislation, is to be subjected to more exacting judicial scrutiny. *** Nor need we enquire whether similar considerations enter into the review of statutes directed at particular religious *** or national *** or racial minorities[;] whether prejudice against discrete and insular minorities may be a special condition, which tends seriously to curtail the operation of those political processes ordinarily to be relied upon to protect minorities, and which may call for a correspondingly more searching judicial inquiry. ***

As you read these materials, consider (as the Court did not in *Carolene Products*) when legislation (1) restricts ordinary political processes, (2) targets particular minorities, or (3) curtails processes that protect minorities. Do not, however, rely too heavily on this theory, for the courts often have not followed it.* Moreover, modern political theory is quite skeptical of many components of this footnote; majoritarian political processes have regularly produced legislation benefiting "discrete and insular" minorities.

---

* *See Hernandez v. Robles*, 855 N.E.2d 1 (N.Y. 2006), in which New York Court of Appeals Chief Judge Kaye in dissent chastised the majority for <u>not</u> applying this theory:

"[T]he Supreme Court has generally looked to three criteria in determining whether a group subject to legislative classification must be considered "suspect." First, the Court has considered whether the group has historically been subjected to purposeful discrimination. Homosexuals plainly have been ***. Second, the Court has considered whether the trait used to define the class is unrelated to the ability to perform and participate in society. *** Obviously, sexual orientation is irrelevant to one's ability to perform or contribute. Third, the Court has taken into account the group's relative political powerlessness."

Most of this chapter concerns robust uses of equal protection theory in which the Court uses strict or middle-tier scrutiny to carefully assess and often invalidate legislation or executive actions. To understand how few classifications may be challenged successfully under the clause, however, we need to first consider traditional—and very deferential—rational basis scrutiny.

A. TRADITIONAL RATIONAL BASIS REVIEW

Legislative and administrative bodies classify people and things all the time. The Internal Revenue Code, for example, draws innumerable distinctions that govern how much a person or a corporation owes in taxes. Moreover, these often seemingly arbitrary distinctions change from year to year. If the Supreme Court applied strict scrutiny or even middle-tier scrutiny to such distinctions, it would be very busy indeed. In fact, most distinctions drawn by governmental bodies and officials are examined not at all or only cursorily. The cases in this section purport to examine a variety of governmental distinctions under this less searching "rational basis" standard. What makes the cases interesting is that the Court sometimes seems to "bend" this permissive standard. When and how it does so merits careful study.

First, however, a brief overview of traditional rational basis equal protection analysis is appropriate. The verbal formulations the Court has used for rational basis or low-level equal protection review have varied from case to case. Some examples are: (1) "the classification must be reasonable, not arbitrary, and must rest upon some ground of difference having a fair and substantial relation to the object of the legislation"; (2) "rationally related to a legitimate state interest"; and (3) "the classification [must not rest] on grounds wholly irrelevant to the achievement of the State's objective". While these standards sound progressively more tolerant of state conduct bordering on the irrational, if not totally irrational, "general propositions do not decide concrete cases," as JUSTICE HOLMES observed aphoristically in his *Lochner* dissent. Philosophical theories of equality, while fascinating intellectually, do not do so either.

So we turn to concrete cases. One frequently cited example of traditional rational basis review is *Railway Express Agency, Inc. v. New York*. Let's look at this case more carefully:

RAILWAY EXPRESS AGENCY v. NEW YORK
336 U.S. 106 (1949)

MR. JUSTICE DOUGLAS delivered the opinion of the Court.

Section 124 of the Traffic Regulations of the City of New York *** provides: 'No person shall operate, or cause to be operated, in or upon any street an advertising vehicle; provided that nothing herein contained shall prevent the putting of business notices upon business delivery vehicles, so long as such vehicles are engaged in the usual business or regular work of the owner and not used merely or mainly for advertising.'

Appellant is engaged in a nation-wide express business. It operates about 1,900 trucks in New York City and sells the space on the exterior sides of these trucks for advertising. That advertising is for the most part unconnected with its own business.[2] It was convicted in the magistrates court and fined. *** The Court of Special Sessions concluded that advertising on vehicles using the streets of New York City constitutes a distraction to vehicle drivers and to pedestrians alike and therefore affects the safety of the public in the use of the streets. We do not sit to weigh evidence on the due process issue in order to determine whether the regulation is sound or appropriate; nor is it our function to pass judgment on its wisdom. We would be trespassing on one of the most intensely local and specialized of all municipal problems if we held that this regulation had no relation to the traffic problem of New York City. It is the judgment of the local authorities that it does have such a relation. And nothing has been advanced which shows that to be palpably false.

The question of equal protection of the laws is pressed more strenuously on us. It is pointed out that the regulation draws the line between advertisements of products sold by the owner of the truck and general advertisements. It is argued that unequal treatment on the basis of such a distinction is not justified by the aim and purpose of the regulation. It is said, for example, that one of appellant's trucks carrying the advertisement of a commercial house would not cause any greater distraction of pedestrians and vehicle drivers than if the commercial house carried the same advertisement on its own truck. Yet the regulation allows the latter to do what the former is forbidden from doing. It is therefore contended that the classification which the regulation makes has no relation to the traffic problem since a violation turns not on what kind of advertisements are carried on trucks but on whose trucks they are carried.

That, however, is a superficial way of analyzing the problem, even if we assume that it is premised on the correct construction of the regulation. The local authorities may well have concluded that those who advertised their own wares on their trucks do not present the same traffic problem in view of the nature or extent of the advertising which they use. It would take a degree of omniscience which we lack to say that such is not the case. If that judgment is correct, the advertising displays that are exempt have less incidence on traffic than those of appellants.

We cannot say that that judgment is not an allowable one. Yet if it is, the classification has relation to the purpose for which it is made and does not contain the kind of discrimination against which the Equal Protection Clause affords protection. It is by such practical considerations based on experience rather than by theoretical inconsistencies that the question of equal protection is to be answered. And the fact that New York City sees fit to eliminate from traffic this kind of distraction but does not touch what may be

---

[2] The advertisements for which appellant was convicted consisted of posters from three by seven feet to four by ten feet portaying Camel Cigarettes, Ringling Brothers and Barnum & Bailey Circus, and radio station WOR. Drivers of appellant's trucks carrying advertisements of Prince Albert Smoking Tobacco and U.S. Navy were also convicted.

even greater ones in a different category, such as the vivid displays on Times Square, is immaterial. It is no requirement of equal protection that all evils of the same genus be eradicated or none at all. ***

MR. JUSTICE JACKSON, concurring.

*** While claims of denial of equal protection are frequently asserted, they are rarely sustained. But the Court frequently uses the due process clause to strike down measures taken by municipalities to deal with activities in their streets and public places which the local authorities consider to create hazards, annoyances or discomforts to their inhabitants. And I have frequently dissented when I thought local power was improperly denied.

The burden should rest heavily upon one who would persuade us to use the due process clause to strike down a substantive law or ordinance. Even its provident use against municipal regulations frequently disables all government--state, municipal and federal--from dealing with the conduct in question because the requirement of due process is also applicable to State and Federal Governments. Invalidation of a statute or an ordinance on due process grounds leaves ungoverned and ungovernable conduct which many people find objectionable.

Invocation of the equal protection clause, on the other hand, does not disable any governmental body from dealing with the subject at hand. It merely means that the prohibition or regulation must have a broader impact. I regard it as a salutary doctrine that cities, states and the Federal Government must exercise their powers so as not to discriminate between their inhabitants except upon some reasonable differentiation fairly related to the object of regulation. This equality is not merely abstract justice. The framers of the Constitution knew, and we should not forget today, that there is no more effective practical guaranty against arbitrary and unreasonable government than to require that the principles of law which officials would impose upon a minority must be imposed generally. Conversely, nothing opens the door to arbitrary action so effectively as to allow those officials to pick and choose only a few to whom they will apply legislation and thus to escape the political retribution that might be visited upon them if larger numbers were affected. Courts can take no better measure to assure that laws will be just than to require that laws be equal in operation.

This case affords an illustration. Even casual observations from the sidewalks of New York will show that an ordinance which would forbid all advertising on vehicles would run into conflict with many interests, including some, if not all, of the great metropolitan newspapers, which use that advertising extensively. Their blandishment of the latest sensations is not less a cause of diverted attention and traffic hazard than the commonplace cigarette advertisement which this truck-owner is forbidden to display. But any regulation applicable to all such advertising would require much clearer justification in local conditions to enable its enactment than does some regulation applicable to a few. I do not mention this to criticize the motives of those who enacted this ordinance, but it dramatizes the point that we are much more likely to find arbitrariness in the regulation of the few than of the many. Hence, for my part, I am more receptive to attack on local ordinances for denial of equal protection than for denial of due process, while the Court has more often used the latter clause.

In this case, if the City of New York should assume that display of any advertising on vehicles tends and intends to distract the attention of persons using the highways and to increase the dangers of its traffic, I should think it fully within its constitutional powers to forbid it all. *** It is argued that, while this does not eliminate vehicular advertising, it does eliminate such advertising for hire and to this extent cuts down the hazard sought to be controlled.

That the difference between carrying on any business for hire and engaging in the same activity on one's own is a sufficient one to sustain some types of regulations of the one that is not applied to the other, is almost elementary. But it is usual to find such regulations applied to the very incidents wherein the two classes present different problems, such as in charges, liability and quality of service.

The difference, however, is invoked here to sustain a discrimination in a problem in which the two classes present identical dangers. The courts of New York have declared that the sole nature and purpose of the regulation before us is to reduce traffic hazards. There is not even a pretense here that the traffic hazard created by the advertising which is forbidden is in any manner or degree more hazardous than that which is permitted. It is urged with considerable force that this local regulation does not comply with the equal protection clause because it applies unequally upon classes whose differentiation is in no way relevant to the objects of the regulation.

As a matter of principle and in view of my attitude toward the equal protection clause, I do not think differences of treatment under law should be approved on classification because of differences unrelated to the legislative purpose. The equal protection clause ceases to assure either equality or protection if it is avoided by any conceivable difference that can be pointed out between those bound and those left free. This Court has often announced the principle that the differentiation must have an appropriate relation to the object of the legislation or ordinance. *** If that were the situation here, I should think we should reach a similar conclusion.

The question in my mind comes to this. Where individuals contribute to an evil or danger in the same way and to the same degree, may those who do so for hire be prohibited, while those who do so for their own commercial ends but not for hire be allowed to continue? I think the answer has to be that the hireling may be put in a class by himself and may be dealt with differently than those who act on their own. But this is not merely because such a discrimination will enable the lawmaker to diminish the evil. That might be done by many classifications, which I should think wholly unsustainable. It is rather because there is a real difference between doing in self-interest and doing for hire, so that it is one thing to tolerate action from those who act on their own and it is another thing to permit the same action to be promoted for a price.

Certainly the presence of absence of hire has been the hook by which much highway regulations has been supported. Rights usual to passengers may be denied to the nonpaying guest in an automobile to limit vexatious litigation. A state may require security against injuries from one using the highways for hire that it does not exact from others because, as Mr. Justice Sutherland put it, 'The streets belong to the public and are primarily for the use of the public in the ordinary way. Their use for the purposes of gain is special and extraordinary, and, generally at least, may be prohibited or conditioned as the Legislature deems proper.' *** However, it is otherwise if the discriminations within the regulated class are based on arbitrary differences as to commodities carried having no relation to the object of the regulation.

Of course, this appellant did not hold itself out to carry or display everybody's advertising, and its rental of space on the sides of its trucks was only incidental to the main business which brought its trucks into the streets. But it is not difficult to see that, in a day of extravagant advertising more or less subsidized by tax deduction, the rental of truck space could become an obnoxious enterprise. While I do not think highly of this type of regulation, that is not my business, and in view of the control I would concede to cities to protect citizens in quiet and orderly use for their proper purposes of the highways and public places, I think the judgment below must be affirmed.

Notes

1. **Rationality.** Is the classification rational? Under what theory of rationality? How carefully does the court examine whether the classification is rational?

2. **Justice Jackson.** What does his concurrence add to your understanding of rational basis scrutiny?

3. **Another Example.** *Williamson v. Lee Optical of Okla., Inc.*, 348 U.S. 483 (1955) upheld a statute making it unlawful for anyone who was not a licensed optometrist or opthalmologist to fit, duplicate, or replace lenses without a prescription from an opthalmologist or optometrist. Opticians, as a practical matter, were precluded by the state from engaging in such tasks. To add insult to injury, the statute exempted sellers of ready-to-wear glasses. The Court assumed health factors justified favoring optometrists over opticians, even though the law was blatantly interest-group driven. JUSTICE DOUGLAS, zealous champion of individual rights in other areas, opined:

> The problem of legislative classification is a perennial one, admitting of no doctrinaire definition. Evils in the same field may be of different dimensions and proportions, requiring different remedies. Or so the legislature may think. Or the reform may take one step at a time ***. We cannot say that the point has been reached here. For all this record shows, the ready-to-wear branch of this business may not loom large in Oklahoma or may present problems or regulation distinct from the other branch.

4. **Rational Basis and Taxation**. In *Fitzgerald v. Racing Ass'n of Central Iowa*, 539 U.S. 103 (2003), the Court unanimously upheld the imposition of a 36% tax on slot machines at racetracks and a 20% tax on slot machines on riverboats on the ground that the different tax rates might be supported by a "plausible policy reason." The following case explores whether there is some irreducible minimum rationality that even tax legislation must possess.

ARMOUR v. INDIANAPOLIS
132 S. Ct. 2073 (2012)

JUSTICE BREYER delivered the opinion of the Court.

For many years, an Indiana statute, the "Barrett Law," authorized Indiana's cities to impose upon benefited lot owners the cost of sewer improvement projects [known as Brisbane/Manning Project assessment fees]. The Law also permitted those lot owners to pay either immediately in the form of a lump sum or over time in installments. In 2005, the city of Indianapolis (City) adopted a new assessment and payment method, the "STEP" plan, and it forgave any Barrett Law installments that lot owners had not yet paid. *** The upshot was that those who still owed Barrett Law assessments would not have to make further payments but those who had already paid their assessments would not receive refunds.

In February 2006, the 38 homeowners who had paid the full Brisbane/Manning Project assessment asked the City for a partial refund (in an amount equal to the smallest forgiven Brisbane/Manning installment debt, apparently $8,062). The City denied the request in part because "[r]efunding payments made in your project area, or any portion of the payments, would establish a precedent of unfair and inequitable treatment to all other property owners who have also paid Barrett Law assessments ... and while [the November 1, 2005, cutoff date] might seem arbitrary to you, it is essential for the City to establish this date and move forward with the new funding approach." *** [These homeowners claim] the City's refusal to provide them with refunds at the same time that the City forgave the outstanding Project debts of other Brisbane/Manning homeowners violated the Federal Constitution's Equal Protection Clause. ***

Indianapolis' classification involves neither a "fundamental right" nor a "suspect" classification. *** Hence, this case falls directly within the scope of our precedents holding such a law constitutionally valid if "there is a plausible policy reason for the classification, the legislative facts on which the classification is apparently based rationally may have been considered to be true by the governmental decisionmaker, and the relationship of the classification to its goal is not so attenuated as to render the distinction arbitrary or irrational." And it falls within the scope of our precedents holding that there is such a plausible reason if "there is any reasonably conceivable state of facts that could provide a rational basis for the classification." *** Further, because the classification is presumed constitutional, the 'burden is on the one attacking the legislative arrangement to negative every conceivable basis which might support it.' " *** Ordinarily, administrative considerations can justify a tax-related distinction. And the City's decision to stop collecting outstanding Barrett Law debts finds rational support in related administrative concerns.

The City had decided to switch to the STEP system. After that change, to continue Barrett Law unpaid-debt collection could have proved complex and expensive. *** *** [Also,] the rationality of the distinction draws support from the fact that the line that the City drew—distinguishing past payments from future obligations—is a line well known to the law. Sometimes such a line takes the form of an amnesty program, involving, say, mortgage payments, taxes, or parking tickets. This kind of line is consistent with the distinction that the law often makes between actions previously taken and those yet to come. ***

The Indiana Supreme Court wrote that the City's classification was "rationally related" in part "to its legitimate interests *in reducing its administrative costs.*" The record of the City's proceedings is consistent with that determination. ***

Petitioners go on to propose various other forgiveness systems that would have included refunds for at least some of those who had already paid in full. *** [E]ven if petitioners have found a superior system, the Constitution does not require the City to draw the perfect line nor even to draw a line superior to some other line it might have drawn. It requires only that the line actually drawn be a rational line. *** [W]e believe that the line the City drew here is rational.

Petitioners further argue that administrative considerations alone should not justify a tax distinction, lest a city arbitrarily allocate taxes among a few citizens while forgiving many similarly situated citizens on the ground that it is cheaper and easier to collect taxes from a few people than from many. Petitioners are right that administrative considerations could not justify such an unfair system. But that is not because administrative considerations can *never* justify tax differences (any more than they can *always* do so). The question is whether reducing those expenses, in the particular circumstances, provides a rational basis justifying the tax difference in question.

In this case, "in the light of the facts made known or generally assumed," it is reasonable to believe that to graft a refund system onto the City's forgiveness decision could have (for example) imposed an administrative burden of both collecting and paying out small sums (say, $25 per month) for years. As we have said, it is rational for the City to draw a line that avoids that burden. Petitioners, who are the ones "attacking the legislative arrangement," have the burden of showing that the circumstances are otherwise, *i.e.,* that the administrative burden is too insubstantial to justify the classification. That they have not done. ***

[Petitioners next refer to] *Allegheny Pittsburgh Coal Co. v. Commission of Webster Cty,* 488 U.S. 336 (1989). The Court there took into account a state constitution and related laws that required equal valuation of equally valuable property. It considered the constitutionality of a county tax assessor's practice (over a period of many years) of determining property values as of the time of the property's last sale; that practice meant highly unequal valuations for two identical properties that were sold years or decades apart. The Court first found that the assessor's practice was not rationally related to the county's avowed purpose of assessing properties equally at true current value because of the intentional systemic discrepancies the practice created. The Court then noted that, in light of the state constitution and related laws requiring equal valuation, there could be no other rational basis for the practice. *** *Allegheny,* however, involved a clear state law requirement clearly and dramatically violated. Indeed, we have described *Allegheny* as "the rare case where the facts precluded" any alternative reading of state law and thus any alternative rational basis. Here, the City followed state law by apportioning the cost of its Barrett Law projects equally. State law says nothing about forgiveness, how to design a forgiveness program, or whether or when rational distinctions in doing so are permitted. To adopt petitioners' view would risk transforming ordinary violations of ordinary state tax law into violations of the Federal Constitution. * * *

CHIEF JUSTICE ROBERTS, with whom JUSTICE SCALIA and JUSTICE ALITO join, dissenting.

*** In *Allegheny Pittsburgh,* we held that a county failed to comport with equal protection requirements when it assessed property taxes primarily on the basis of purchase price, with no appropriate adjustments over time. The result was that new property owners were assessed at "roughly 8 to 35 times" the rate of those who had owned their property longer. We found such a "gross disparit[y]" in tax levels could not be justified in a state system that demanded that "taxation ... be equal and uniform." The case affirmed the common sense proposition that the Equal Protection Clause is violated by state action that deprives a citizen of even "rough equality in tax treatment," when state law itself specifically provides that all the affected taxpayers are in the same category for tax purposes.

In this case, *** [p]etitioners paid between 10 and 30 times as much for their sewer hook-ups as their neighbors. *** And what did the City believe was sufficient to justify a system that would effectively charge petitioners *30 times more* than their neighbors for the *same* service—when state law promised equal treatment? Two things: the desire to avoid administrative hassle and the "fiscal[ ] challeng[e]" of giving back money it wanted to keep. I cannot agree that those reasons pass constitutional muster, even under rational basis review. *** Indiana's tax scheme explicitly provides that costs will "be primarily apportioned *equally* among all abutting lands or lots." *** The Equal Protection Clause does not provide that no State shall "deny to any person within its jurisdiction the equal protection of the laws, unless it's too much of a bother."

Even if the Court were inclined to decide that administrative burdens alone may sometimes justify grossly disparate treatment of members of the same class, this would hardly be the case to do that. *** To the extent a ruling for petitioners would require issuing refunds to others who overpaid under the Barrett Law, I think the city workers are up to the task. The City has in fact already produced records showing exactly how much each lump-sum payer overpaid in *every* active Barrett Law Project—to the penny. What the city employees would need to do, therefore, is cut the checks and mail them out. *** The Court compares the City's decision to forgive the installment balances to *** amnesty programs that currently abound. This analogy is misplaced: Amnesty programs are designed to entice those who are unlikely ever to pay their debts to come forward and pay at least a portion of what they owe. It is not administrative convenience alone that justifies such schemes. In a sense, these schemes help remedy payment inequities by prompting those who would pay nothing to pay at least some of their fair share. The same cannot be said of the City's system. ***

The Court reminds us that *Allegheny Pittsburgh* is a "rare case." It is and should be; we give great leeway to taxing authorities in this area, for good and sufficient reasons. But every generation or so a case comes along when this Court needs to say enough is enough, if the Equal Protection Clause is to retain any force in this context. *Allegheny Pittsburgh* was such a case; so is this one. ***

Notes

1. **Interpreting State Law**. The majority believed the Barrett Law only required equal apportionment of the project costs at the outset of a project, not when it is cancelled. The dissent reads state law to require equal apportionment of costs regardless of later developments. Why should the Supreme Court interpret an ambiguous state statue?

2. **Preemption of Local Action**. The majority says that because Indiana law "involves nothing about forgiveness," equality is not as "clearly and dramatically violated" as in *Allegheny*. Does state law preempt local action only when state law specifically targets that particular action?

3. **Inequality and Taxes**. Is the right to "roughly equal" taxation when mandated by state statue a fundamental right? Are the dissenters seeking to revisit, under the Equal Protection Clause, economic substantive due process? Note the dissent's view that "every generation or so a case comes along when this Court needs to say enough is enough, if the Equal Protection Clause is to retain any force in this context."

4. **Rational Basis and *Carolene Products* Theory**. As you read the following case, consider whether it is consistent with the theory at the beginning of this chapter.

NEW YORK CITY TRANSIT AUTHORITY v. BEAZER
440 U.S. 568 (1979)

MR. JUSTICE STEVENS delivered the opinion of the Court.

The New York City Transit Authority refuses to employ persons who use methadone. The District Court found that this policy violates the Equal Protection Clause of the Fourteenth Amendment. *** The Court of Appeals affirmed ***. The departure by those courts from the procedure normally followed in addressing statutory and constitutional questions in the same case, as well as concern that the merits of these important questions had been decided erroneously, led us to grant certiorari. We now reverse.

The Transit Authority (TA) operates the subway system and certain bus lines in New York City. It employs about 47,000 persons, of whom many—perhaps most—are employed in positions that involve danger to themselves or to the public. *** TA enforces a general policy against employing persons who use narcotic drugs. The policy is reflected in *** TA's Rules and Regulations. *** [Methadone is considered by TA to be a narcotic, and though the Rules allow for an exception by the medical director of TA, no] written permission has ever been given by TA's medical director for the employment of a person using methadone. *** Methadone has been used legitimately in at least three ways—as a pain killer, in "detoxification units" of hospitals as an immediate means of taking addicts off of heroin, and in long-range "methadone maintenance programs" as part of an intended cure for heroin addiction. In such programs the methadone is taken orally in regular doses for a prolonged period. As so administered, it does not produce euphoria or any pleasurable effects associated with heroin; on the contrary, it prevents users from experiencing those effects when they inject heroin, and also alleviates the severe and prolonged discomfort otherwise associated with an addict's discontinuance of the use of heroin.

About 40,000 persons receive methadone maintenance treatment in New York City, of whom about 26,000 participate in the five major public or semipublic programs, and 14,000 are involved in about 25 private programs. The sole purpose of all these programs is to treat the addiction of persons who have been using heroin for at least two years.

The evidence indicates that methadone is an effective cure for the physical aspects of heroin addiction. But the District Court also found "that many persons attempting to overcome heroin addiction have psychological or life-style problems which reach beyond what can be cured by the physical taking of doses of methadone." *** [Further,] evidence relied upon by the District Court reveals that even among participants with more than 12 months' tenure in methadone maintenance programs, the incidence of drug and alcohol abuse may often approach and even exceed 25%. ***

This litigation was brought by the four respondents as a class action on behalf of all persons who have been, or would in the future be, subject to discharge or rejection as employees of TA by reason of participation in a methadone maintenance program. ***

The trial record contains extensive evidence concerning the success of methadone maintenance programs, the employability of persons taking methadone, and the ability of prospective employers to detect drug abuse or other undesirable characteristics of methadone users. In general, the District Court concluded that there are substantial numbers of methadone users who are just as employable as other members of the general population and that normal personnel-screening procedures—at least if augmented by some method of obtaining information from the staffs of methadone programs—would enable TA to identify the unqualified applicants on an individual basis.

On the other hand, the District Court recognized that at least one-third of the persons receiving methadone treatment—and probably a good many more—would unquestionably be classified as unemployable.

After extensively reviewing the evidence, the District Court briefly stated its conclusion that TA's methadone policy is unconstitutional. The conclusion rested on the legal proposition that a public entity "cannot bar persons from employment on the basis of criteria which have no rational relation to the demands of the jobs to be performed." Because it is clear that substantial numbers of methadone users are capable of performing many of the jobs at TA, the court held that the Constitution will not tolerate a blanket exclusion of all users from all jobs.

The District Court enjoined TA from denying employment to any person solely because of participation in a methadone maintenance program. Recognizing, however, the special responsibility for public safety borne by certain TA employees and the correlation between longevity in a methadone maintenance program and performance capability, the injunction authorized TA to exclude methadone users from specific categories of safety-sensitive positions and also to condition eligibility on satisfactory performance in a methadone program for at least a year. In other words, the court held that TA could lawfully adopt general rules excluding all methadone users from some jobs and a large number of methadone users from all jobs. ***

At its simplest, the District Court's conclusion was that TA's rule is broader than necessary to exclude those methadone users who are not actually qualified to work for TA. We may assume not only that this conclusion is correct but also that it is probably unwise for a large employer like TA to rely on a general rule instead of individualized consideration of every job applicant. But these assumptions concern matters of personnel policy that do not implicate the principle safeguarded by the Equal Protection Clause. As the District Court recognized, the special classification created by TA's rule serves the general objectives of safety and efficiency. Moreover, the exclusionary line challenged by respondents "is not one which is directed 'against' any individual or category of persons, but rather it represents a policy choice *** made by that branch of Government vested with the power to make such choices." *Marshall v. United States*, 414 U.S. 417, 428. Because it does not circumscribe a class of persons characterized by some unpopular trait or affiliation, it does not create or reflect any special likelihood of bias on the part of the ruling majority. Under these circumstances, it is of no constitutional significance that the degree of rationality is not as great with respect to certain ill-defined subparts of the classification as it is with respect to the classification as a whole. ***

MR. JUSTICE POWELL, concurring in part and dissenting in part. [omitted]

MR. JUSTICE BRENNAN, dissenting. [omitted]

MR. JUSTICE WHITE, with whom MR. JUSTICE MARSHALL joins, dissenting.

*** The question before us is the rationality of placing successfully maintained or recently cured persons in the same category as those just attempting to escape heroin addiction or who have failed to escape it, rather than in with the general population. The asserted justification for the challenged classification is the objective of a capable and reliable work force, and thus the characteristic in question is employability. "Employability," in this regard, does not mean that any particular applicant, much less every member of a given group of applicants, will turn out to be a model worker. Nor does it mean that no such applicant will ever become or be discovered to be a malingerer, thief, alcoholic, or even heroin addict. All employers take such risks. Employability, as the District Court used it in reference to successfully maintained methadone users, means only that the employer is no more likely to find a member of that group to be an unsatisfactory employee than he would an employee chosen from the general population.

Petitioners had every opportunity, but presented nothing to negative the employability of successfully maintained methadone users as distinguished from those who were unsuccessful. *** That 20% to 30% are unsuccessful after one year in a methadone program tells us nothing about the employability of the successful group, and it is the latter category of applicants that the District Court and the Court of Appeals held to be unconstitutionally burdened by the blanket rule disqualifying them from employment. *** Of course, the District Court's order permitting total exclusion of all methadone users maintained for less than one year, whether successfully or not, would still exclude some employables and would to this extent be overinclusive. "Overinclusiveness" as to the primary objective of employability is accepted for less successful methadone users because it fulfills a secondary purpose and thus is not "overinclusive" at all. Although many of those who have not been successfully maintained for a year are employable, as a class they, unlike the protected group, are not as employable as the general population. Thus, even assuming the bad risks could be identified, serving the end of employability would require unusual efforts to determine those more likely to revert. But that legitimate secondary goal is not fulfilled by excluding the protected class: The District Court found that the fact of successful participation for one year could be discovered through petitioners' normal screening process without additional effort and, I repeat, that those who meet that criterion are no more likely than the average applicant to turn out to be poor employees. Accordingly, the rule's classification of successfully maintained persons as dispositively different from the general population is left without any justification and, with its irrationality and invidiousness thus uncovered, must fall before the Equal Protection Clause. ***

Finally, even were the District Court wrong, and even were successfully maintained persons marginally less employable than the average applicant, the blanket exclusion of only these people, when but a few are actually unemployable and when many other groups have varying numbers of unemployable members, is arbitrary and unconstitutional. Many persons now suffer from or may again suffer from some handicap related to employability. But petitioners have singled out respondents—unlike ex-offenders, former alcoholics and mental patients, diabetics, epileptics, and those currently using tranquilizers, for example—for sacrifice to this at best ethereal and likely nonexistent risk of increased unemployability. Such an arbitrary assignment of burdens among classes that are similarly situated with respect to the proffered objectives is the type of invidious choice forbidden by the Equal Protection Clause.

Notes

1.   **Rational Basis and Employment.**   *Beazer* is essentially a traditional rational basis equal protection case. But aren't drug users a "discrete and insular minority," to use the *Carolene Products* language? The Court assumes that the city's rule that it will not hire people who use methodone is "broader than necessary" and perhaps even "unwise" compared with "individualized consideration of every job applicant." Still, the Court says this is a permissible "policy choice" by the city which "does not circumscribe a class of persons characterized by some unpopular trait or affiliation." The Court dismisses the dissenters' concerns, that methodone-maintained former drug addicts are inappropriately lumped with those who are recovering or who have failed treatment, as "of no constitutional significance." Do you agree?

2.   **Prima Facie Case and Defenses.** Is *Beazer* explicable on the ground that the plaintiffs' evidence simply was too weak to make out a prima facie case? Were the city's responses to this evidence so straightforward as to be intuitively obvious?

3.   **Contextual Factors.**   What if the city was supportive of methadone treatment programs for drug addiction and conscious of the cost of welfare payments to drug addicts? What if New York required those in publicly funded methodone maintenance programs to seek jobs? Would New York be viewed as irrational for sending contradictory messages to recovering addicts in different programs? Does the nature of the jobs at issue make a difference?

4.   **Hybrid Review.** The final section of this chapter examines cases in which the Court speaks in terms of rational basis review, but arguably does not apply it in the traditional ways set forth above in *Beazer*. These cases will be considered after we study the Court's more active equal protection review in race, gender, and other areas.

B. RACE AND THE EQUAL PROTECTION CLAUSE

1. SEPARATE AND UNEQUAL

The next two cases, which discuss the meaning of "equal" when state law requires "separate but equal" treatment of racial groups, provide an excellent opportunity to reconsider interpretive issues discussed earlier in this course. What roles do text, original understanding, precedent, and public policy play in Supreme Court decisions?

PLESSY v. FERGUSON
163 U.S. 537 (1896)

[An 1890 Louisiana statute required railroad companies to provide "separate but equal" accommodations for whites and "colored races." Plessy, a United States citizen who resided in Louisiana, had seven-eighths Caucasian and one-eighth African blood. On June 7, 1892, he bought a first-class ticket

[handwritten: LA state law requiring sep. but equal accommodations]

on the East Louisiana Railway and took a vacant seat in a coach designated for white passengers. Plessy was required by the conductor to move to a coach for non-white passengers. When he refused to move, Plessy was (with the aid of a police officer) ejected from the coach, imprisoned, and charged with violating state law.]

MR. JUSTICE BROWN *** delivered the opinion of the court.

*** By the fourteenth amendment, all persons born or naturalized in the United States, and subject to the jurisdiction thereof, are made citizens of the United States and of the state wherein they reside; and the states are forbidden from making or enforcing any law which shall abridge the privileges or immunities of citizens of the United States, or shall deprive any person of life, liberty, or property without due process of law, or deny to any person within their jurisdiction the equal protection of the laws. ***

The object of the amendment was undoubtedly to enforce the absolute equality of the two races before the law, but, in the nature of things, it could not have been intended to abolish distinctions based upon color, or to enforce social, as distinguished from political, equality, or a commingling of the two races upon terms unsatisfactory to either. Laws permitting, and even requiring, their separation, in places where they are liable to be brought into contact, do not necessarily imply the inferiority of either race to the other, and have been generally, if not universally, recognized as within the competency of the state legislatures in the exercise of their police power. The most common instance of this is connected with the establishment of separate schools for white and colored children, which have been held to be a valid exercise of the legislative power even by courts of states where the political rights of the colored race have been longest and most earnestly enforced.

*** [I]t is *** suggested by the learned counsel for the plaintiff in error that the same argument that will justify the state legislature in requiring railways to provide separate accommodations for the two races will also authorize them to require separate cars to be provided for people whose hair is of a certain color, or who are aliens, or who belong to certain nationalities, or to enact laws requiring colored people to walk upon one side of the street, and white people upon the other, or requiring white men's houses to be painted white, and colored men's black, or their vehicles or business signs to be of different colors, upon the theory that one side of the street is as good as the other, or that a house or vehicle of one color is as good as one of another color. The reply to all this is that every exercise of the police power must be reasonable, and extend only to such laws as are enacted in good faith for the promotion of the public good, and not for the annoyance or oppression of a particular class. ***

So far, then, as a conflict with the fourteenth amendment is concerned, the case reduces itself to the question whether the statute of Louisiana is a reasonable regulation, and with respect to this there must necessarily be a large discretion on the part of the legislature. In determining the question of reasonableness, it is at liberty to act with reference to the established usages, customs, and traditions of the people, and with a view to the promotion of their comfort, and the preservation of the public peace and good order. Gauged by this standard, we cannot say that a law which authorizes or even requires the separation of the two races in public conveyances is unreasonable, or more obnoxious to the fourteenth amendment than the acts of congress requiring separate schools for colored children in the District of Columbia, the constitutionality of which does not seem to have been questioned, or the corresponding acts of state legislatures.

ct. says history and custom show that the reg. is reasonable

We consider the underlying fallacy of the plaintiff's argument to consist in the assumption that the enforced separation of the two races stamps the colored race with a badge of inferiority. If this be so, it is not by reason of anything found in the act, but solely because the colored race chooses to put that construction upon it. The argument necessarily assumes that if, as has been more than once the case, and is not unlikely to be so again, the colored race should become the dominant power in the state legislature, and should enact a law in precisely similar terms, it would thereby relegate the white race to an inferior position. We imagine that the white race, at least, would not acquiesce in this assumption. The argument also assumes that social prejudices may be overcome by legislation, and that equal rights cannot be secured to the negro except by an enforced commingling of the two races. We cannot accept this proposition. If the two races are to meet upon terms of social equality, it must be the result of natural affinities, a mutual appreciation of each other's merits, and a voluntary consent of individuals. *** Legislation is powerless to eradicate racial instincts, or to abolish distinctions based upon physical differences, and the attempt to do so can only result in accentuating the difficulties of the present situation. If the civil and political rights of both races be equal, one cannot be inferior to the other civilly or politically. If one race be inferior to the other socially, the constitution of the United States cannot put them upon the same plane. ***

P args. that minorities feel inferior

ct. says they only feel inferior b/c they choose to

legis. cannot fix prejudices

b/c all races are equal, no one can be inferior

MR. JUSTICE HARLAN dissenting.

*** In respect of civil rights, common to all citizens, the constitution of the United States does not, I think, permit any public authority to know the race of those entitled to be protected in the enjoyment of such rights. Every true man has pride of race, and under appropriate circumstances, when the rights of others, his equals before the law, are not to be affected, it is his privilege to express such pride and to take such action based upon it as to him seems proper. But I deny that any legislative body or judicial tribunal may have regard to the race of citizens when the civil rights of those citizens are involved. ***

It was said in argument that the statute of Louisiana does not discriminate against either race, but prescribes a rule applicable alike to white and colored citizens. But this argument does not meet the difficulty. Every one knows that the statute in question had its origin in the purpose, not so much to exclude white persons from railroad cars occupied by blacks, as to exclude colored people from coaches occupied by or assigned to white persons. Railroad corporations of Louisiana did not make discrimination among whites in the matter of accommodation for travelers. The thing to accomplish was, under the guise of giving equal accommodation for whites

purpose of the law was to discriminate

and blacks, to compel the latter to keep to themselves while traveling in railroad passenger coaches. No one would be so wanting in candor as to assert the contrary. The fundamental objection, therefore, to the statute, is that it interferes with the personal freedom of citizens. 'Personal liberty,' it has been well said, 'consists in the power of locomotion, of changing situation, or removing one's person to whatsoever places one's own inclination may direct, without imprisonment or restraint, unless by due course of law.' If a white man and a black man choose to occupy the same public conveyance on a public highway, it is their right to do so; and no government, proceeding alone on grounds of race, can prevent it without infringing the personal liberty of each.

It is one thing for railroad carriers to furnish, or to be required by law to furnish, equal accommodations for all whom they are under a legal duty to carry. It is quite another thing for government to forbid citizens of the white and black races from traveling in the same public conveyance, and to punish officers of railroad companies for permitting persons of the two races to occupy the same passenger coach. If a state can prescribe, as a rule of civil conduct, that whites and blacks shall not travel as passengers in the same railroad coach, why may it not so regulate the use of the streets of its cities and towns as to compel white citizens to keep on one side of a street, and black citizens to keep on the other? Why may it not, upon like grounds, punish whites and blacks who ride together in street cars or in open vehicles on a public road or street? Why may it not require sheriffs to assign whites to one side of a court room, and blacks to the other? And why may it not also prohibit the commingling of the two races in the galleries of legislative halls or in public assemblages convened for the consideration of the political questions of the day? Further, if this statute of Louisiana is consistent with the personal liberty of citizens, why may not the state require the separation in railroad coaches of native and naturalized citizens of the United States, or of Protestants and Roman Catholics?

The answer given at the argument to these questions was that regulations of the kind they suggest would be unreasonable, and could not, therefore, stand before the law. Is it meant that the determination of questions of legislative power depends upon the inquiry whether the statute whose validity is questioned is, in the judgment of the courts, a reasonable one, taking all the circumstances into consideration? A statute may be unreasonable merely because a sound public policy forbade its enactment. But I do not understand that the courts have anything to do with the policy or expediency of legislation. A statute may be valid, and yet, upon grounds of public policy, may well be characterized as unreasonable. ***

The white race deems itself to be the dominant race in this country. And so it is, in prestige, in achievements, in education, in wealth, and in power. So, I doubt not, it will continue to be for all time, if it remains true to its great heritage, and holds fast to the principles of constitutional liberty. But in view of the constitution, in the eye of the law, there is in this country no superior, dominant, ruling class of citizens. There is no caste here. Our constitution is color-blind, and neither knows nor tolerates classes among citizens. In respect of civil rights, all citizens are equal before the law. The humblest is the peer of the most powerful. The law regards man as man, and takes no account of his surroundings or of his color when his civil rights as guaranteed by the supreme law of the land are involved. ***

In my opinion, the judgment this day rendered will, in time, prove to be quite as pernicious as the decision made by this tribunal in the *Dred Scott* Case. *** [It] seems that we have yet, in some of the states, a dominant race—a superior class of citizens—which assumes to regulate the enjoyment of civil rights, common to all citizens, upon the basis of race. The present decision *** will not only stimulate aggressions, more or less brutal and irritating, upon the admitted rights of colored citizens, but will encourage the belief that it is possible, by means of state enactments, to defeat the beneficent purposes which the people of the United States had in view when they adopted the recent amendments of the constitution, by one of which the blacks of this country were made citizens of the United States and of the states in which they respectively reside, and whose privileges and immunities, as citizens, the states are forbidden to abridge. Sixty millions of whites are in no danger from the presence here of eight millions of blacks. The destinies of the two races, in this country, are indissolubly linked together, and the interests of both require that the common government of all shall not permit the seeds of race hate to be planted under the sanction of law. What can more certainly arouse race hate, what more certainly create and perpetuate a feeling of distrust between these races, than state enactments which, in fact, proceed on the ground that colored citizens are so inferior and degraded that they cannot be allowed to sit in public coaches occupied by white citizens? That, as all will admit, is the real meaning of such legislation as was enacted in Louisiana. *** [The Louisiana statute] is inconsistent with the personal liberty of citizens, white and black, in that state, and hostile to both the spirit and letter of the constitution of the United States. ***

[handwritten margin note: history will look back on this decision poorly]

[handwritten margin note: everyone knows LA passed the law b/c they thought AA's were inferior]

Notes

1.   **Judicial Discretion.**   The *Plessy* Court had a social vision of appropriate race relations.   The Court retained discretion to permit governmental practices matching that vision, while discarding those that did not match that vision. JUSTICE HARLAN's famous dissent is not only a call for racial equality, but for a Constitution not subject to change with judicial and societal whims.   Do you think the Court should retain discretion on racial matters?

2.   **Trains to Education.**   *Plessy* involved trains, not education, but in *Cumming v. Board of Education of Richmond County*, 175 U.S. 528 (1899), the Court both upheld segregation in public education and leniently applied its requirement of equal facilities (the only black high school in Richmond County, Georgia was closed).   JUSTICE HARLAN, seemingly inconsistently, wrote an opinion that said education was "a matter belonging to the respective states."

3.   **Road to *Brown*.**   The NAACP, formed in 1909 in conjunction with the hundredth anniversary of Lincoln's birth, submitted its first Supreme Court brief amicus curiae in 1915.   This brief successfully urged the Supreme Court to use

the Fifteenth Amendment to overturn an Oklahoma law which required a literacy test for all voters other than those entitled to vote prior to 1866 or descendants of those entitled to vote before 1866. Under the leadership of Howard Law Center Dean Charles Hamilton Houston, the NAACP repeatedly attacked Jim Crow (separate but equal) laws using the theory that separate facilities were in fact not equal. Despite some notable wins, the strategy seemed endless; it had to be carried out fact by fact and facility by facility. Yet the NAACP adhered to the strategy because it thought there was no hope of obtaining a reversal of the basic "separate but equal" holding of *Plessy*.[*]

In 1938, Houston returned to private practice and leadership of the NAACP passed to 30 year-old Thurgood Marshall. During the 1940's, Marshall began working toward a frontal assault on *Plessy*. At first, the Court took a narrower course, holding in cases like *Sweatt v. Painter*, 339 U.S. 629 (1950), that separate was not in fact equal (separate Texas law schools would not provide the same professional opportunities even if facilities were equal). In 1952, the Court granted certiorari in four cases in which it was argued that segregated schools were unconstitutional. The Court was divided, however, and reargument was requested at the end of the 1952–53 term on the issue of the "original intent" of the Equal Protection Clause. During the course of the summer, CHIEF JUSTICE VINSON died and was replaced by Eisenhower appointee Earl Warren, who provided the leadership to pull the Court together for a unanimous opinion overruling *Plessy*. JUSTICE FELIX FRANKFURTER, who had favored overruling the "separate but equal" doctrine, thought such a dramatic move should be unanimous to put the full weight of the Court's authority behind the change. Frankfurter told a former law clerk that the change of Chief Justices was "the first indication I have ever had that there is a God."

BROWN v. BOARD OF EDUCATION
347 U.S. 483 (1954)

MR. CHIEF JUSTICE WARREN delivered the opinion of the Court.

*** [M]inors of the Negro race, through their legal representatives, seek the aid of the courts in obtaining admission to the public schools of their community on a nonsegregated basis. In each instance, they have been denied admission to schools attended by white children under laws requiring

---

[*] *Plessy* was enforced by the courts for over half a century. Typical is *Carr v. Corning*, 182 F.2d 14 (D.C.Cir. 1950):

> We do not believe that the makers of the *** Fourteenth Amendment in 1866 meant to foreclose legislative treatment of the problem [of segregation] in this country. *** [T]he social and economic interrelationship of two races living together is a legislative problem, as yet not solved ***. We must remember that on this particular point we are interpreting a constitution *** ['Our question is merely whether the Federal Constitution prohibited segregation.'] *** [T]he actions of Congress [concerning the Fourteenth Amendment and Civil Rights Acts of 1866 and 1875], the discussion in the Civil Rights Cases, and the fact that in 1862, 1864, 1866, and 1874 Congress *** enacted legislation which specifically provided for separation of the races in the schools of the District of Columbia, conclusively support our view of the Amendment and its effect. [The court cites 12 Supreme Court and 16 lower court cases for the proposition that 'the races may be separated.'] [C]onstitutional invalidity does not arise from the mere fact of separation but may arise from an inequality of treatment.

or permitting segregation according to race. This segregation was alleged to deprive the plaintiffs of the equal protection of the laws under the Fourteenth Amendment. *** The plaintiffs contend that segregated public schools are not "equal" and cannot be made "equal," and that hence they are deprived of the equal protection of the laws. *** Argument was heard in the 1952 Term, and reargument was heard this Term on certain questions propounded by the Court.

≠

Reargument was largely devoted to the circumstances surrounding the adoption of the Fourteenth Amendment in 1868. It covered exhaustively consideration of the Amendment in Congress, ratification by the states, then existing practices in racial segregation, and the views of proponents and opponents of the Amendment. This discussion and our own investigation convince us that, although these sources cast some light, it is not enough to resolve the problem with which we are faced. At best, they are inconclusive. *** What others in Congress and the state legislatures had in mind cannot be determined with any degree of certainty.

14A is unclear on segregation

An additional reason for the inconclusive nature of the Amendment's history, with respect to segregated schools, is the status of public education at that time. In the South, the movement toward free common schools, supported by general taxation, had not yet taken hold. Education of white children was largely in the hands of private groups. Education of Negroes was almost nonexistent, and practically all of the race were illiterate. In fact, any education of Negroes was forbidden by law in some states. Today, in contrast, many Negroes have achieved outstanding success in the arts and sciences as well as in the business and professional world. It is true that public school education at the time of the Amendment had advanced further in the North, but the effect of the Amendment on Northern States was generally ignored in the congressional debates. Even in the North, the conditions of public education did not approximate those existing today. The curriculum was usually rudimentary; ungraded schools were common in rural areas; the school term was but three months a year in many states; and compulsory school attendance was virtually unknown. As a consequence, it is not surprising that there should be so little in the history of the Fourteenth Amendment relating to its intended effect on public education. ***

Public schools did not exist at the time of the 14A

society has changed

14A makes no mention of public schools

In approaching this problem, we cannot turn the clock back to 1868 when the Amendment was adopted, or even to 1896 when *Plessy v. Ferguson* was written. We must consider public education in the light of its full development and its present place in American life throughout the Nation. Only in this way can it be determined if segregation in public schools deprives these plaintiffs of the equal protection of the laws.

Today, education is perhaps the most important function of state and local governments. Compulsory school attendance laws and the great expenditures for education both demonstrate our recognition of the importance of education to our democratic society. It is required in the performance of our most basic public responsibilities, even service in the armed forces. It is the very foundation of good citizenship. Today it is a principal instrument in awakening the child to cultural values, in preparing

importance of education in society

him for later professional training, and in helping him to adjust normally to his environment. In these days, it is doubtful that any child may reasonably be expected to succeed in life if he is denied the opportunity of an education. Such an opportunity, where the state has undertaken to provide it, is a right which must be made available to all on equal terms.

Ct. looks to tangible harm of segregation

We come then to the question presented: Does segregation of children in public schools solely on the basis of race, even though the physical facilities and other "tangible" factors may be equal, deprive the children of the minority group of equal educational opportunities? We believe that it does. In *Sweatt v. Painter*, 339 U.S. 629, in finding that a segregated law school for Negroes could not provide them equal educational opportunities, this Court relied in large part on "those qualities which are incapable of objective measurement but which make for greatness in a law school." In *McLaurin v. Oklahoma State Regents*, 339 U.S. 637, the Court, in requiring that a Negro admitted to a white graduate school be treated like all other students, again resorted to intangible considerations: " *** his ability to study, to engage in discussions and exchange views with other students, and, in general, to learn his profession." Such considerations apply with added force to children in grade and high schools. To separate them from others of similar age and

IX–1. "I've Decided I Want My Seat Back" by Bill Mauldin. Reprinted with special permission from the Chicago Sun–Times, Inc. © 2000.

qualifications solely because of their race generates a feeling of inferiority as *[handwritten: psychological effects]* to their status in the community that may affect their hearts and minds in a way unlikely ever to be undone. The effect of this separation on their educational opportunities was well stated by a finding in the Kansas case by a court which nevertheless felt compelled to rule against the Negro plaintiffs:

> "Segregation of white and colored children in public schools has a detrimental effect upon the colored children. The impact is greater when it has the sanction of the law; for the policy of separating the races is usually interpreted as denoting the inferiority of the negro group. A sense of inferiority affects the motivation of a child to learn. Segregation with the sanction of law, therefore, has a tendency to (retard) the educational and mental development of Negro children and to deprive them of some of the benefits they would receive in a racial(ly) integrated school system."

Whatever may have been the extent of psychological knowledge at the time of *Plessy v. Ferguson*, this finding is amply supported by modern authority. Any language in *Plessy v. Ferguson* contrary to this finding is rejected.

We conclude that in the field of public education the doctrine of "separate but equal" has no place. Separate educational facilities are inherently *[handwritten: gets rid of separate but equal.]* unequal. Therefore, we hold that the plaintiffs and others similarly situated for whom the actions have been brought are, by reason of the segregation complained of, deprived of the equal protection of the laws guaranteed by the Fourteenth Amendment. ***

Notes

1. **Rationale of *Brown*.** While there is virtually no dissent to the correctness of *Brown* as a matter of constitutional interpretation, there is substantial criticism of the Court's approach. Rather than returning to the language and original intent of the Fourteenth Amendment, the Court relied heavily on social science research and testimony presented to the lower courts, much of which was methodologically weak. Moreover, the Court's focus on how segregation "generates a feeling of inferiority" among blacks did not address the broader issue: how segregation disserved blacks and whites alike by dividing the citizenry into two racial groups with minimal opportunities for interchange and understanding between them.

2. **Education to Trains.** Technically, the Court's decision dealt only with state-sponsored educational segregation; soon thereafter, however, the Court proceeded to grant certiorari on numerous cases involving other components of Jim Crow laws in the South and to summarily reverse or affirm decisions of the lower courts, citing *Brown*. Should the Court have articulated why it was extending *Brown*?

3. **Remedies.** The Court held over for the following term the issue of the appropriate remedy for segregation. When it issued its decision in *Brown II*, it ambiguously required desegregation with "all deliberate speed." This was not

very speedy in a South committed to a strategy of "massive resistance" to desegregation. Despite heroic efforts by the Fifth Circuit Court of Appeals (spanning the South from Texas to Georgia and Florida) to enforce *Brown*, it was not until the political branches of the government put their resources behind desegregation following the Civil Rights Act of 1964 that substantial changes in levels of segregation began to occur in southern public schools. Should one conclude that the Court was the catalyst for desegregation or that it was really powerless to act without the assistance of the rest of the Federal Government?

4. **Other Issues Related to *Brown*.**

(a) Desegregation or Integration? In *Swann v. Charlotte–Mecklenburg Board of Education*, 402 U.S. 1 (1971), the Court said the "nature of the [constitutional] violation determines the scope of the remedy." It noted that, in light of the history of state-enforced segregation, it would apply "a presumption against schools that are substantially disproportionate in their racial composition." The Court upheld "sometimes drastic" remedies including pairing and clustering of schools, creation of noncontiguous school zones, and bussing of students to nonneighborhood schools. The Court did note that, at some point, when the school officials had achieved "full compliance" in creating a "unitary" school district, "further intervention by a district court should not be necessary."

(b) De Facto Segregation. In *Keyes v. School District No. 1, Denver, Colo.*, 413 U.S. 189 (1973), the State had never mandated segregation but the Denver School Board had gerrymandered the Park Hill section of the city to avoid racial integration. The Court permitted a Denver-wide remedy for this violation. Conversely, in *Milliken v. Bradley*, 418 U.S. 717 (1974), the Court held that federal courts lacked the power to impose interdistrict remedies for school segregation absent an interdistrict violation or interdistrict effects. The remedy was limited to the Detroit School System despite the involvement of the State of Michigan and state agencies in the segregation of Detroit schools. Recently, in *Missouri v. Jenkins*, 515 U.S. 70 (1995), the Court stressed that *intra*district violations should not lead to *inter*district remedies (here, attempts to attract white students into a core school system which was predominantly black). JUSTICE THOMAS' concurrence blasted the willingness of the courts "to assume that anything that is predominantly black must be inferior." He then pointed out "two threads" of dysfunctional Supreme Court jurisprudence: (1) its theory of "unspecified psychological harm" to blacks from segregation based on "questionable social science research" and "an assumption of black inferiority" and (2) its willingness to give "virtually unlimited equitable powers" to the courts, "trampl[ing] on principles of federalism and the separation of powers," letting courts "pursue other agendas unrelated to the narrow purpose of precisely remedying a constitutional harm." Four Justices dissented, complaining that the Court had retreated from the "redress the harms" component of earlier decisions.

(c) Ending Judicial Oversight. *Freeman v. Pitts*, 503 U.S. 467 (1992), held that courts can "relinquish supervision and control of school districts in incremental stages, before full compliance has been achieved in every area of school operations." In the Court's opinion, racial imbalance in the DeKalb County, Georgia school system was the result not of segregation but of "demographic factors not traceable to the initial violation." The dissent argued for continuing judicial oversight due to lack of a "proper unitary status record" including examination of test scores to see if the school system had "cured a deficiency in student achievement to the extent practicable."

2. INVIDIOUS RACE DISCRIMINATION

Outside the "separate but equal" context, how does the Equal Protection Clause deal with race discrimination? Are racial distinctions made by government always unconstitutional? Or are some racial distinctions permissible when the government's reasons for the distinction are strong or remedial? Does the prohibition apply even when the race discrimination does not fit the "black-white paradigm" stemming from slavery of African–Americans? When the discriminating entity is the federal government rather than state or local government? When all races are identically affected by a state-drawn racial line? When a statute is facially neutral but has a disproportionate effect on one race? These questions are addressed by the cases in the following sections.

a. Strict Scrutiny for Invidious Race Discrimination

STRAUDER v. WEST VIRGINIA
100 U.S. (10 Otto) 303 (1879)

MR. JUSTICE STRONG delivered the opinion of the court.

The plaintiff in error, a colored man, was indicted for murder in the Circuit Court of Ohio County, in West Virginia, on the 20th of October, 1874, and upon trial was convicted and sentenced. *** [I]t is now, in substance, averred that at the trial in the State court the defendant (now plaintiff in error) was denied rights to which he was entitled under the Constitution and laws of the United States. *** [Plaintiff argued that, by] virtue of the laws of the State of West Virginia no colored man was eligible to be a member of the grand jury or to serve on a petit jury in the State; that white men are so eligible, and that by reason of his being a colored man and having been a slave, he had reason to believe, and did believe, he could not have the full and equal benefit of all laws and proceedings in the State of West Virginia for the security of his person as is enjoyed by white citizens, and that he had less chance of enforcing in the courts of the State his rights on the prosecution, as a citizen of the United States, and that the probabilities of a denial of them to him as such citizen on every trial which might take place on the indictment in the courts of the State were much more enhanced than if he was a white man. *** [The question] is not whether a colored man, when an indictment has been preferred against him, has a right to a grand or a petit jury composed in whole or in part of persons of his own race or color, but it is whether, in the composition or selection of jurors by whom he is to be indicted or tried, all persons of his race or color may be excluded by law, solely because of their race or color, so that by no possibility can any colored man sit upon the jury. ***

[The Fourteenth Amendment] is one of a series of constitutional provisions having a common purpose; namely, securing to a race recently emancipated, a race that through many generations had been held in slavery, all the civil rights that the superior race enjoy. The true spirit and meaning of the amendments, as we said in the *Slaughter-House Cases*, cannot be understood without keeping in view the history of the times when they were adopted, and the general objects they plainly sought to accomplish. At the time when they were incorporated into the Constitution, it required little knowledge of human nature to anticipate that those who had long been regarded as an inferior and subject race would, when suddenly raised to the rank of citizenship, be looked upon with jealousy and positive dislike, and that State laws might be enacted or enforced to perpetuate the distinctions that had before existed. Discriminations against them had been habitual. It was well known that in some States laws making such discriminations then existed, and others might well be expected. The colored race, as a race, was abject and ignorant, and in that condition was unfitted to command the respect of those who had superior intelligence. Their training had left them mere children, and as such they needed the protection which a wise government extends to those who are unable to protect themselves. They especially needed protection against unfriendly action in the States where they were resident. It was in view of these considerations the Fourteenth Amendment was framed and adopted. It was designed to assure to the colored race the enjoyment of all the civil rights that under the law are enjoyed by white persons, and to give to that race the protection of the general government, in that enjoyment, whenever it should be denied by the States. It not only gave citizenship and the privileges of citizenship to persons of color, but it denied to any State the power to withhold from them the equal protection of the laws, and authorized Congress to enforce its provisions by appropriate legislation. ***

What is this but declaring that the law in the States shall be the same for the black as for the white; that all persons, whether colored or white, shall stand equal before the laws of the States, and, in regard to the colored race, for whose protection the amendment was primarily designed, that no discrimination shall be made against them by law because of their color? The words of the amendment, it is true, are prohibitory, but they contain a necessary implication of a positive immunity, or right, most valuable to the colored race—the right to exemption from unfriendly legislation against them distinctively as colored—exemption from legal discriminations, implying inferiority in civil society, lessening the security of their enjoyment of the rights which others enjoy, and discriminations which are steps towards reducing them to the condition of a subject race.

That the West Virginia statute respecting juries—the statute that controlled the selection of the grand and petit jury in the case of the plaintiff in error—is such a discrimination ought not to be doubted. *** The very fact that colored people are singled out and expressly denied by a statute all right to participate in the administration of the law, as jurors, because of their color, though they are citizens, and may be in other respects fully qualified, is practically a brand upon them, affixed by the law, an assertion of their inferiority, and a stimulant to that race prejudice which is an impediment to securing to individuals of the race that equal justice which the law aims to secure to all others. *** It is well known that prejudices often exist against particular classes in the community, which sway the judgment of jurors, and which, therefore, operate in some cases to deny to persons of those classes the full enjoyment of that protection which others enjoy. ***

In view of these considerations, it is hard to see why the statute of West Virginia should not be regarded as discriminating against a colored man when he is put upon trial for an alleged criminal offense against the State. It is not easy to comprehend how it can be said that while every white man is entitled to a trial by a jury selected from persons of his own race or color, or, rather, selected without discrimination against his color, and a negro is not, the latter is equally protected by the law with the former. *** We do not say that within the limits from which it is not excluded by the amendment a State may not prescribe the qualifications of its jurors, and in so doing make discriminations. It may confine the selection to males, to freeholders, to citizens, to persons within certain ages, or to persons having educational qualifications. We do not believe the Fourteenth Amendment was ever intended to prohibit this. Looking at its history, it is clear it had no such purpose. Its aim was against discrimination because of race or color. ***

YICK WO v. HOPKINS
118 U.S. 356 (1886)

MATTHEWS, J.

*** [T]he supreme court of California *** considered these ordinances ["It [*laundries in SF must be built with brick or stone*] shall be unlawful, from and after the passage of this order, for any person or persons to establish, maintain, or carry on a laundry, within the corporate limits of the city and county of San Francisco, without having first obtained the consent of the board of supervisors, except the same be located in a building constructed either of brick or stone,"] as vesting in the board of supervisors a not unusual discretion in granting or withholding their assent to the use of wooden buildings as laundries, to be exercised in reference to the circumstances of each case, with a view to the protection of the public against the dangers of fire. We are not able to concur in that interpretation of the power conferred upon the supervisors. There is nothing in the ordinances which points to such a regulation of the business of keeping and conducting laundries. They seem intended to confer, and actually to confer, not a discretion to be exercised upon a consideration of the circumstances of each case, but a naked and arbitrary power to give or withhold consent, not only as to places, but as to persons; so that, if an applicant for such consent, being in every way a competent and qualified person, and having complied with every reasonable condition demanded by any public interest, should, failing to obtain the requisite consent of the supervisors to the prosecution of his business, apply for redress by the judicial process of mandamus to require the supervisors to consider and act upon his case, it would be a sufficient answer for them to say that the law had conferred upon them authority to withhold their assent, without reason and without responsibility. The power given to them is not confided to their discretion in the legal sense of that term, but is granted to their mere will. It is purely arbitrary, and acknowledges neither guidance nor restraint. ***

Directed at Chinese

protected by 14A

The rights of the petitioners, as affected by the proceedings of which they complain, are not less because they are aliens and subjects of the emperor of China. *** The fourteenth amendment to the constitution is not confined to the protection of citizens. It says: "Nor shall any state deprive any person of life, liberty, or property without due process of law; nor deny to any person within its jurisdiction the equal protection of the laws." These provisions are universal in their application *** and the equal protection of the laws is a pledge of the protection of equal laws. ***

Ordinance has a direct effect on a specific class of people

a law that is facially equal can be unjust

In the present cases, we are not obliged to reason from the probable to the actual, and pass upon the validity of the ordinances complained of, as tried merely by the opportunities which their terms afford, of unequal and unjust discrimination in their administration; for the cases present the ordinances in actual operation, and the facts shown establish an administration directed so exclusively against a particular class of persons as to warrant and require the conclusion that, whatever may have been the intent of the ordinances as adopted, they are applied by the public authorities charged with their administration, and thus representing the state itself, with a mind so unequal and oppressive as to amount to a practical denial by the state of that equal protection of the laws which is secured to the petitioners, as to all other persons, by the broad and benign provisions of the fourteenth amendment to the constitution of the United States. Though the law itself be fair on its face, and impartial in appearance, yet, if it is applied and administered by public authority with an evil eye and an unequal hand, so as practically to make unjust and illegal discriminations between persons in similar circumstances, material to their rights, the denial of equal justice is still within the prohibition of the constitution. ***

directly affect Chinese as compared to others

The present cases, as shown by the facts disclosed in the record, are within this class. It appears that both petitioners have complied with every requisite deemed by the law, or by the public officers charged with its administration, necessary for the protection of neighboring property from fire, or as a precaution against injury to the public health. No reason whatever, except the will of the supervisors, is assigned why they should not be permitted to carry on, in the accustomed manner, their harmless and useful occupation, on which they depend for a livelihood; and while this consent of the supervisors is withheld from them, and from 200 others who have also petitioned, all of whom happen to be Chinese subjects, 80 others, not Chinese subjects, are permitted to carry on the same business under similar conditions. The fact of this discrimination is admitted. No reason for it is shown, and the conclusion cannot be resisted that no reason for it exists except hostility to the race and nationality to which the petitioners belong, and which, in the eye of the law, is not justified. The discrimination is therefore illegal, and the public administration which enforces it is a denial of the equal protection of the laws, and a violation of the fourteenth amendment of the constitution. ***

KOREMATSU v. UNITED STATES
323 U.S. 214 (1944).

MR. JUSTICE BLACK delivered the opinion of the Court.

*** [An] Act of Congress of March 21, 1942 *** provides that " *** whoever shall enter, remain in, leave, or commit any act in any military area or military zone prescribed, under the authority of an Executive order of the President, *** by any military commander designated by the Secretary of War, contrary to *** the order of *** any such military commander, shall *** be guilty of a misdemeanor and upon conviction shall be liable to a fine of not to exceed $5,000 or to imprisonment for not more than one year, or both, for each offense."

Exclusion Order No. 34 *** was one of a number of military orders and proclamations, all of which were substantially based upon Executive Order No. 9066 ***. That order, issued after we were at war with Japan, declared *in order to* that "the successful prosecution of the war requires every possible protection *deter espionage* against espionage and against sabotage to national-defense material, *and sabotage* national-defense premises, and national-defense utilities ***." [Persons of Japanese descent, whether they were United States citizens, were forced to leave their homes and move to Relocation Centers. Petitioner "knowingly and willfully violated" the order.]

One of the series of orders and proclamations, a curfew order, which like the exclusion order here was promulgated pursuant to Executive Order 9066, subjected all persons of Japanese ancestry in prescribed West Coast military *curfew* areas to remain in their residences from 8 p.m. to 6 a.m. [That order's constitutionality was upheld by the Court in a companion case, *Hirabayashi v. United States*, 320 U.S. 81 (1943).]

It should be noted, to begin with, that all legal restrictions which curtail the civil rights of a single racial group are immediately suspect. That is not to say that all such restrictions are unconstitutional. It is to say that courts must subject them to the most rigid scrutiny. Pressing public necessity may sometimes justify the existence of such restrictions; racial antagonism never can. ***

In the light of the principles we announced in the *Hirabayashi* case, we are unable to conclude that it was beyond the war power of Congress and the Executive to exclude those of Japanese ancestry from the West Coast war area at the time they did. True, exclusion from the area in which one's home is located is a far greater deprivation than constant confinement to the home from 8 p.m. to 6 a.m. Nothing short of apprehension by the proper military authorities of the gravest imminent danger to the public safety can constitutionally justify either. But exclusion from a threatened area, no less than curfew, has a definite and close relationship to the prevention of espionage and sabotage. The military authorities, charged with the primary responsibility of defending our shores, concluded that curfew provided inadequate protection and ordered exclusion. *** Here, as in the *Hirabayashi* case,

*** [W]e cannot reject as unfounded the judgment of the military authorities and of Congress that there were disloyal members of that population, whose number and strength could not be precisely and quickly ascertained. We cannot say that the war-making branches of the Government did not have ground for believing that in a critical hour such persons could not readily be isolated and separately dealt with, and constituted a menace to the national defense and safety, which demanded that prompt and adequate measures be taken to guard against it.

reason for the curfew

Like curfew, exclusion of those of Japanese origin was deemed necessary because of the presence of an unascertained number of disloyal members of the group, most of whom we have no doubt were loyal to this country. It was because we could not reject the finding of the military authorities that it was impossible to bring about an immediate segregation of the disloyal from the loyal that we sustained the validity of the curfew order as applying to the whole group. In the instant case, temporary exclusion of the entire group was rested by the military on the same ground. The judgment that exclusion of the whole group was for the same reason a military imperative answers the contention that the exclusion was in the nature of group punishment based on antagonism to those of Japanese origin. That there were members of the group who retained loyalties to Japan has been confirmed by investigations made subsequent to the exclusion. Approximately five thousand American citizens of Japanese ancestry refused to swear unqualified allegiance to the United States and to renounce allegiance to the Japanese Emperor, and several thousand evacuees requested repatriation to Japan.

too many unknown out of the overall pop.

We uphold the exclusion order as of the time it was made and when the petitioner violated it. In doing so, we are not unmindful of the hardships imposed by it upon a large group of American citizens. But hardships are part of war, and war is an aggregation of hardships. All citizens alike, both in and out of uniform, feel the impact of war in greater or lesser measure. Citizenship has its responsibilities as well as its privileges, and in time of war the burden is always heavier. Compulsory exclusion of large groups of citizens from their homes, except under circumstances of direst emergency and peril, is inconsistent with our basic governmental institutions. But when under conditions of modern warfare our shores are threatened by hostile forces, the power to protect must be commensurate with the threatened danger. ***

We do not agree with the action, but it needs to be done

It is said that we are dealing here with the case of imprisonment of a citizen in a concentration camp solely because of his ancestry, without evidence or inquiry concerning his loyalty and good disposition towards the United States. Our task would be simple, our duty clear, were this a case involving the imprisonment of a loyal citizen in a concentration camp because of racial prejudice. Regardless of the true nature of the assembly and relocation centers—and we deem it unjustifiable to call them concentration camps with all the ugly connotations that term implies—we are dealing specifically with nothing but an exclusion order. To cast this case into outlines of racial prejudice, without reference to the real military dangers

differentiating from concentration camps

which were presented, merely confuses the issue. Korematsu was not excluded from the Military Area because of hostility to him or his race. He was excluded because we are at war with the Japanese Empire, because the properly constituted military authorities feared an invasion of our West Coast and felt constrained to take proper security measures, because they decided that the military urgency of the situation demanded that all citizens of Japanese ancestry be segregated from the West Coast temporarily, and finally, because Congress, reposing its confidence in this time of war in our military leaders—as inevitably it must—determined that they should have the power to do just this. There was evidence of disloyalty on the part of some, the military authorities considered that the need for action was great, and time was short. We cannot—by availing ourselves of the calm perspective of hindsight—now say that at that time these actions were unjustified.

[handwritten marginalia: justified by the nature of the war and its risks]

IX–2. Barrack homes at Manzanar relocation camp. Photograph by Dorothea Lange, volume 78 Section C WRA no. 838, *War Relocation Authority Photographs of Japanese–American Evacuation and Resettlement*, BANC PIC 1967.014—PIC, The Bancroft Library, University of California, Berkeley.

MR. JUSTICE FRANKFURTER, concurring and MR. JUSTICE ROBERTS, dissenting. [both omitted]

MR. JUSTICE MURPHY, dissenting.

This exclusion of "all persons of Japanese ancestry, both alien and non-alien," from the Pacific Coast area on a plea of military necessity in the absence of martial law ought not to be approved. Such exclusion goes over

RBT?

"the very brink of constitutional power" and falls into the ugly abyss of racism.

It was right to listen to military leaders in a time of war

In dealing with matters relating to the prosecution and progress of a war, we must accord great respect and consideration to the judgments of the military authorities who are on the scene and who have full knowledge of the military facts. The scope of their discretion must, as a matter of necessity and common sense, be wide. And their judgments ought not to be overruled lightly by those whose training and duties ill-equip them to deal intelligently with matters so vital to the physical security of the nation.

however, military orders over civilian matters must be reasonable

At the same time, however, it is essential that there be definite limits to military discretion, especially where martial law has not been declared. Individuals must not be left impoverished of their constitutional rights on a plea of military necessity that has neither substance nor support. Thus, like other claims conflicting with the asserted constitutional rights of the individual, the military claim must subject itself to the judicial process of having its reasonableness determined and its conflicts with other interests reconciled. ***

This action was not reasonable

It must be conceded that the military and naval situation in the spring of 1942 was such as to generate a very real fear of invasion of the Pacific Coast, accompanied by fears of sabotage and espionage in that area. The military command was therefore justified in adopting all reasonable means necessary to combat these dangers. *** But the exclusion, either temporarily or permanently, of all persons with Japanese blood in their veins has no such reasonable relation. And that relation is lacking because the exclusion order necessarily must rely for its reasonableness upon the assumption that all persons of Japanese ancestry may have a dangerous tendency to commit sabotage and espionage and to aid our Japanese enemy in other ways. It is difficult to believe that reason, logic or experience could be marshalled in support of such an assumption. ***

Military action was based off racist social views

The main reasons relied upon by those responsible for the forced evacuation, therefore, do not prove a reasonable relation between the group characteristics of Japanese Americans and the dangers of invasion, sabotage and espionage. The reasons appear, instead, to be largely an accumulation of much of the misinformation, half-truths and insinuations that for years have been directed against Japanese Americans by people with racial and economic prejudices—the same people who have been among the foremost advocates of the evacuation. A military judgment based upon such racial and sociological considerations is not entitled to the great weight ordinarily given the judgments based upon strictly military considerations. Especially is this so when every charge relative to race, religion, culture, geographical location, and legal and economic status has been substantially discredited by independent studies made by experts in these matters. ***

No one denies, of course, that there were some disloyal persons of Japanese descent on the Pacific Coast who did all in their power to aid their ancestral land. Similar disloyal activities have been engaged in by many persons of German, Italian and even more pioneer stock in our country. But to infer that examples of individual disloyalty prove group disloyalty and justify discriminatory action against the entire group is to deny that under our system of law individual guilt is the sole basis for deprivation of rights. ***

[margin note: can't discrim. against an entire group]

MR. JUSTICE JACKSON, dissenting.

*** It would be impracticable and dangerous idealism to expect or insist that each specific military command in an area of probable operations will conform to conventional tests of constitutionality. When an area is so beset that it must be put under military control at all, the paramount consideration is that its measures be successful, rather than legal. *** But if we cannot confine military expedients by the Constitution, neither would I distort the Constitution to approve all that the military may deem expedient. This is what the Court appears to be doing, whether consciously or not. *** The limitation under which courts always will labor in examining the necessity for a military order are illustrated by this case. How does the Court know that these orders have a reasonable basis in necessity? No evidence whatever on that subject has been taken by this or any other court. ***

[margin note: Military actions should be constitutional]

Much is said of the danger to liberty from the Army program for deporting and detaining these citizens of Japanese extraction. But a judicial construction of the due process clause that will sustain this order is a far more subtle blow to liberty than the promulgation of the order itself. A military order, however unconstitutional, is not apt to last longer than the military emergency. Even during that period a succeeding commander may revoke it all. But once a judicial opinion rationalizes such an order to show that it conforms to the Constitution, or rather rationalizes the Constitution to show that the Constitution sanctions such an order, the Court for all time has validated the principle of racial discrimination in criminal procedure and of transplanting American citizens. The principle then lies about like a loaded weapon ready for the hand of any authority that can bring forward a plausible claim of an urgent need. Every repetition imbeds that principle more deeply in our law and thinking and expands it to new purposes. ***

[margin note: Military commands are temporary ↓ sustaining the order would make this a permanent option]

I should hold that a civil court cannot be made to enforce an order which violates constitutional limitations even if it is a reasonable exercise of military authority. The courts can exercise only the judicial power, can apply only law, and must abide by the Constitution, or they cease to be civil courts and become instruments of military policy. ***

Notes

1.   **What is "Race"?** The Fourteenth Amendment's origins in the enslavement of African Americans makes it pretty clear why *Strauder* is a race case. Why are *Yick Wo* and *Korematsu*, which involved Asian immigrant groups, treated as race cases rather than "national origin" cases? CHIEF JUSTICE WARREN's opinion in *Hernandez v. Texas*, 347 U.S. 475 (1954), holds that the state can't exclude persons of Mexican descent from juries, but avoids calling the discrimination "racial" or using the strict scrutiny model. The Court said that "the Fourteenth Amendment is not directed solely against discrimination due to a 'two-class

theory'—that is, based upon differences between 'white' and Negro. *** The petitioner's initial burden in substantiating his charge of group discrimination was to prove that persons of Mexican descent constitute a separate class in Jackson County, distinct from 'whites.'" What do you make of this last comment? Consider further whether a statute discriminating against Native American Indians would be subject to strict scrutiny under the Equal Protection Clause. *See Morton v. Mancari*, 417 U.S. 535 (1974) (hiring preferences for Indians "does not constitute 'racial discrimination' ***. Here, where the preference is reasonable and rationally designed to further Indian self-government, we cannot say that Congress' classification violates due process."). Is there special constitutional treatment of Native American Indians that makes them different (for constitutional purposes) from other racial groups? Are religious groups (e.g. Jews or Muslims) racial for equal protection purposes? *See Shaare Tefila Congregation v. Cobb*, 481 U.S. 615 (1987), and *Saint Francis College v. Al–Khazraji*, 481 U.S. 604 (1987) (yes; authors of 1866 and 1870 civil rights acts believed them to be distinct races; "Congress intended to protect from discrimination identifiable classes of persons who are subjected to intentional discrimination solely because of their ancestry or ethnic characteristics *** whether or not it would be characterized as racial in terms of modern scientific theory.").

2. **Questions about *Strauder*, *Yick Wo*, and *Korematsu*.**

    (a) *Strauder*. Is it fair to say that the Court finds a per se violation of the Fourteenth Amendment? What is the violation and how does Strauder get standing to litigate that violation? Would the historical approach of this case have provided an alternative rationale for *Brown*?

    (b) *Yick Wo*. Is there an argument that the ordinance is unconstitutional on its face from a clause in the Constitution other than the Equal Protection Clause? Would the remedy differ if the case had been decided under the other clause? Is there any problem with the Court inferring invidious motives to laws like this one? How do you prove such a motive if you are Yick Wo's lawyer?

    (c) *Korematsu*. Do you agree with the *Korematsu* majority or dissenters? Do the dissenters disagree as a matter of principle or application? Would this case have been a good precedent for the Court (or advocates) to cite in *Brown*?

3. **Theory.** Do these cases stand for the principle that race should not be taken into account by government? Do they speak to the question whether and to what extent the state may seek to rectify past discrimination (or "racial subordination")?

4. **Federal Equal Protection.** Despite "reverse incorporation," applying the Equal Protection component of the Fourteenth Amendment to the federal government through the Fifth Amendment's due process guarantee, *Korematsu* may be an application of the Court's observation that, "Not only does the language of the two amendments differ, but more importantly, there may be overriding national interests which justify federal legislation that would be unacceptable for an individual state [unless the federal law is only applicable to DC or another limited territory]." *Hampton v. Mow Sun Wong*, 426 U.S. 88 (1976).

5. **Immigration.** Despite *Yick Wo's* invocation of equal protection for persons, not just citizens, immigration may be an exception to normal equal protection principles on the basis that "the power of Congress over the admission of aliens to this country is absolute." *See The Chinese Exclusion Case*, 130 U.S. 581 (1889) (resident aliens returning from overseas visits could be excluded based on race) and *Fong Yue Ting v. United States*, 149 U.S. 698 (1893) (resident aliens may be deported if Congress concluded their race was undesirable). These decisions have been followed by the lower courts in recent years. *See Achacoso–Sanchez v. INS*, 779 F.2d 1260 (7th Cir. 1985) ("Congress has the power to make distinctions on account of race" in immigration context). Recent academic commentary argues that these cases should be overruled.

6. **Legislative Apportionment.** Is race discrimination more permissible when legislative districts are drawn which take account of race as well as other demographic and geographic factors? *See Miller v. Johnson*, 515 U.S. 900 (1995) (plaintiff in redistricting case must show "race was the predominant factor" by proving "the legislature subordinated traditional race-neutral districting principles"); *Bush v. Vera*, 517 U.S. 952 (1996) ("redistricting legislation that is so extremely irregular on its face that it rationally can be viewed only as an effort to segregate the races for purposes of voting" states an Equal Protection claim); and *Hunt v. Cromartie*, 526 U.S. 541 (1999) (political gerrymandering is permissible; "high correlation between race and party preference" does not suffice, without more, to demonstrate impermissible racial districting).

7. **Role of the Courts.** *Korematsu*, like *Dred Scott*, *Plessy*, and *Lochner*, is generally viewed as a low point of the Supreme Court's interpretation of the Constitution. Like *Ex parte McCardle* and *Ex parte Quirin*, supra, it may demonstrate the Court's reluctance to overrule the unified efforts of both the President and Congress on *constitutional* grounds during wartime. But the Court has been less reluctant to rule against military actions during war on *nonconstitutional* grounds. *Ex parte Endo*, 323 U.S. 283 (1944), announced the same day as *Korematsu*, illustrates the point. *Endo* unanimously invalidated the internment of Japanese-Americans as unsupported by the statute and order (held constitutional in *Korematsu*) that excluded them from the West Coast. Why would *Korematsu* be remembered so vividly and *Endo* forgotten almost entirely? *See* Patrick O. Gudridge, *Remember Endo?* 116 HARV. L. REV. 1933 (2003).

b. What Makes a Law Racially Discriminatory?

It is one thing to say that strict scrutiny applies when government discriminates against people because they are of African, Chinese, or Japanese racial origin, as in *Strauder*, *Yick Wo*, and *Korematsu*. Would the same scrutiny apply if a restriction were placed on all races, not solely a disfavored racial group? What if a neutral government rule has a disparate impact or effect on a racial group that has traditionally been disadvantaged by government actions? What if a governmental decision-making process is changed in a way that makes it more difficult for racial or other groups? The following cases have one theme: what makes a law racially discriminatory?

LOVING v. VIRGINIA
388 U.S. 1 (1967)

MR. CHIEF JUSTICE WARREN delivered the opinion of the Court.

This case presents a constitutional question never addressed by this Court: whether a statutory scheme adopted by the State of Virginia to prevent marriages between persons solely on the basis of racial classifications violates the Equal Protection and Due Process Clauses of the Fourteenth Amendment. For reasons which seem to us to reflect the central meaning of those constitutional commands, we conclude that these statutes cannot stand consistently with the Fourteenth Amendment.

In June 1958, two residents of Virginia, Mildred Jeter, a Negro woman, and Richard Loving, a white man, were married in the District of Columbia pursuant to its laws. Shortly after their marriage, the Lovings returned to Virginia and *** a grand jury issued an indictment charging the Lovings with violating Virginia's ban on interracial marriages. On January 6, 1959, the Lovings pleaded guilty to the charge and were sentenced to one year in jail; however, the trial judge suspended the sentence for a period of 25 years on the condition that the Lovings leave the State and not return to Virginia together for 25 years. He stated in an opinion that: "Almighty God created the races white, black, yellow, malay and red, and he placed them on separate continents. And but for the interference with his arrangement there would be no cause for such marriages. The fact that he separated the races shows that he did not intend for the races to mix."

After their convictions, the Lovings took up residence in the District of Columbia. On *** October 28, 1964, the Lovings instituted a class action in the United States District Court for the Eastern District of Virginia requesting that a three-judge court be convened to declare the Virginia antimiscegenation statutes unconstitutional and to enjoin state officials from enforcing their convictions. *** [The] three-judge District Court continued the case to allow the Lovings to present their constitutional claims to the highest state court.

The Supreme Court of Appeals [of Virginia] upheld the constitutionality of the antimiscegenation statutes and *** affirmed the convictions. *** [The section of the Virginia Code,] which defines the penalty for miscegenation, provides:

> Punishment for marriage.—If any white person intermarry with a colored person, or any colored person intermarry with a white person, he shall be guilty of a felony and shall be punished by confinement in the penitentiary for not less than one nor more than five years. ***

Virginia is now one of 16 States which prohibit and punish marriages on the basis of racial classifications. Penalties for miscegenation arose as an incident to slavery and have been common in Virginia since the colonial period. The present statutory scheme dates from the adoption of the Racial Integrity Act of 1924, passed during the period of extreme nativism which followed the end of the First World War. The central features of this Act, and current Virginia law, are the absolute prohibition of a "white person" marrying other than another "white person," a prohibition against issuing marriage licenses until the issuing official is satisfied that the applicants' statements as to their race are correct, certificates of "racial composition" to be kept by both local and state registrars, and the carrying forward of earlier prohibitions against racial intermarriage.

white people can only marry other white people

*** While the state court is no doubt correct in asserting that marriage is a social relation subject to the State's police power, *Maynard v. Hill*, 125 U.S. 190 (1888), the State does not contend in its argument before this Court that its powers to regulate marriage are unlimited notwithstanding the commands of the Fourteenth Amendment. *** Instead, the State argues that the meaning of the Equal Protection Clause, as illuminated by the statements of the Framers, is only that state penal laws containing an interracial element as part of the definition of the offense must apply equally to whites and Negroes in the sense that members of each race are punished to the same degree. Thus, the State contends that, because its miscegenation statutes punish equally both the white and the Negro participants in an interracial marriage, these statutes, despite their reliance on racial classifications do not constitute an invidious discrimination based upon race. ***

states are limited in regulating marraige

VA arg'd that it was racial w/o being racist

Because we reject the notion that the mere "equal application" of a statute containing racial classifications is enough to remove the classifications from the Fourteenth Amendment's proscription of all invidious racial discriminations, we do not accept the State's contention that these statutes should be upheld if there is any possible basis for concluding that they serve a rational purpose. The mere fact of equal application does not mean that our analysis of these statutes should follow the approach we have taken in cases involving no racial discrimination where the Equal Protection Clause has been arrayed against a statute discriminating between the kinds of advertising which may be displayed on trucks in New York City, *Railway Express Agency, Inc. v. People of State of New York*, 336 U.S. 106 (1949), or an exemption in Ohio's ad valorem tax for merchandise owned by a non-resident in a storage warehouse, *Allied Stores of Ohio, Inc. v. Bowers*, 358 U.S. 522 (1959). In these cases, involving distinctions not drawn according to race, the Court has merely asked whether there is any rational foundation for the discriminations, and has deferred to the wisdom of the state legislatures. In the case at bar, however, we deal with statutes containing racial classifications, and the fact of equal application does not immunize the statute from the very heavy burden of justification which the Fourteenth Amendment has traditionally required of state statutes drawn according to race ***.

There can be no question but that Virginia's miscegenation statutes rest solely upon distinctions drawn according to race. The statutes proscribe generally accepted conduct if engaged in by members of different races. Over the years, this Court has consistently repudiated "(d)istinctions between citizens solely because of their ancestry" as being "odious to a free people

Statute was based on race

strict scrutiny

whose institutions are founded upon the doctrine of equality." *Hirabayashi v. United States*, 320 U.S. 81 (1943). At the very least, the Equal Protection Clause demands that racial classifications, especially suspect in criminal statutes, be subjected to the "most rigid scrutiny," *Korematsu v. United States*, 323 U.S. 214, 216 (1944), and, if they are ever to be upheld, they must be shown to be necessary to the accomplishment of some permissible state objective, independent of the racial discrimination which it was the object of the Fourteenth Amendment to eliminate. ***

No leg. interest (only to achieve white supremacy)

There is patently no legitimate overriding purpose independent of invidious racial discrimination which justifies this classification. The fact that Virginia prohibits only interracial marriages involving white persons demonstrates that the racial classifications must stand on their own justification, as measures designed to maintain White Supremacy.[11] We have consistently denied the constitutionality of measures which restrict the rights of citizens on account of race. There can be no doubt that restricting the freedom to marry solely because of racial classifications violates the central meaning of the Equal Protection Clause. ***

MR. JUSTICE STEWART, concurring.

I have previously expressed the belief that "it is simply not possible for a state law to be valid under our Constitution which makes the criminality of an act depend upon the race of the actor."

JOHNSON v. CALIFORNIA
543 U.S. 499 (2005)

JUSTICE O'CONNOR delivered the opinion of the Court.

The California Department of Corrections (CDC) has an unwritten policy of racially segregating prisoners in double cells in reception centers for up to 60 days each time they enter a new correctional facility. *** The CDC's asserted rationale for this practice is that it is necessary to prevent violence caused by racial gangs. It cites numerous incidents of racial violence in CDC facilities and identifies five major prison gangs in the State: Mexican Mafia, Nuestra Familia, Black Guerilla Family, Aryan Brotherhood, and Nazi Low Riders. The CDC also notes that prison-gang culture is violent and murderous. An associate warden testified that if race were not considered in making initial housing assignments, she is certain there would be racial conflict in the cells and in the yard. Other prison officials also expressed their belief that violence and conflict would result if prisoners were not segregated. The CDC claims that it must therefore segregate all inmates while it determines whether they pose a danger to others.

---

[11] Appellants point out that the State's concern in these statutes *** extends only to the integrity of the white race. While Virginia prohibits whites from marrying any nonwhite ([with] the exception for the descendants of Pocahontas), Negroes, Orientals, and any other racial class may intermarry without statutory interference. Appellants contend that this distinction renders [the] statutes arbitrary and unreasonable even assuming the constitutional validity of *** [a] purpose to preserve "racial integrity." We need not reach this contention because we find the racial classifications in these statutes repugnant to the Fourteenth Amendment, even assuming an even-handed state purpose to protect the "integrity" of all races.

With the exception of the double cells in reception areas, the rest of the state prison facilities--dining areas, yards, and cells--are fully integrated. After the initial 60-day period, prisoners are allowed to choose their own cellmates. The CDC usually grants inmate requests to be housed together, unless there are security reasons for denying them. ***

We have held that "*all* racial classifications [imposed by government] ... must be analyzed by a reviewing court under strict scrutiny." *** The CDC claims that its policy should be exempt from our categorical rule because it is "neutral"--that is, it "neither benefits nor burdens one group or individual more than any other group or individual." In other words, strict scrutiny should not apply because all prisoners are "equally" segregated. The CDC's argument ignores our repeated command that "racial classifications receive close scrutiny even when they may be said to burden or benefit the races equally." *** The need for strict scrutiny is no less important here, where prison officials cite racial violence as the reason for their policy. As we have recognized in the past, racial classifications "threaten to stigmatize individuals by reason of their membership in a racial group and to *incite racial hostility*." Indeed, by insisting that inmates be housed only with other inmates of the same race, it is possible that prison officials will breed further hostility among prisoners and reinforce racial and ethnic divisions. By perpetuating the notion that race matters most, racial segregation of inmates "may exacerbate the very patterns of [violence that it is] said to counteract."

*** Virtually all other States and the Federal Government manage their prison systems without reliance on racial segregation. *** As to transferees, in particular, whom the CDC has already evaluated at least once, it is not clear why more individualized determinations are not possible. ***

The CDC protests that strict scrutiny will handcuff prison administrators and render them unable to address legitimate problems of race-based violence in prisons. Not so. Strict scrutiny is not "strict in theory, but fatal in fact." Strict scrutiny does not preclude the ability of prison officials to address the compelling interest in prison safety. Prison administrators, however, will have to demonstrate that any race-based policies are narrowly tailored to that end. *** On remand, the CDC will have the burden of demonstrating that its policy is narrowly tailored with regard to new inmates as well as transferees. Prisons are dangerous places, and the special circumstances they present may justify racial classifications in some contexts. ***

JUSTICE GINSBURG, with whom JUSTICE SOUTER and JUSTICE BREYER join, concurring.

*** Disagreeing with the Court that "strict scrutiny" properly applies to any and all racial classifications, but agreeing that the stereotypical classification at hand warrants rigorous scrutiny, I join the Court's opinion.

JUSTICE STEVENS, dissenting [omitted].

JUSTICE THOMAS, with whom JUSTICE SCALIA joins, dissenting.

*** The Constitution has always demanded less within the prison walls. *** California oversees roughly 160,000 inmates, in prisons that have been a breeding ground for some of the most violent prison gangs in America--all of them organized along racial lines. In that atmosphere, California racially segregates a portion of its inmates, in a part of its prisons, for brief periods of up to 60 days, until the State can arrange permanent housing. *** California is concerned with their safety and saving their lives. *** [T]he CDC's policy passes constitutional muster, because it is reasonably related to legitimate penological interests. *** California has a history like no other. There are at least five major gangs in this country--the Aryan Brotherhood, the Black Guerrilla Family, the Mexican Mafia, La Nuestra Familia, and the Texas Syndicate--all of which originated in California's prisons. Unsurprisingly, then, California has the largest number of gang-related inmates of any correctional system in the country, including the Federal Government.

As their very names suggest, prison gangs like the Aryan Brotherhood and the Black Guerrilla Family organize themselves along racial lines, and these gangs perpetuate hate and violence. Interracial murders and assaults among inmates perpetrated by these gangs are common. And, again, that brutality is particularly severe in California's prisons. *** The CDC's policy is reasonably related to a legitimate penological interest; alternative means of exercising the restricted right remain open to inmates; racially integrating double cells might negatively impact prison inmates, staff, and administrators; and there are no obvious, easy alternatives to the CDC's policy. ***

Even under strict scrutiny analysis, "it is possible, even likely, that prison officials could show that the current policy meets the test." As Johnson concedes, all States have a compelling interest in maintaining order and internal security within their prisons. Thus the question on remand will be whether the CDC's policy is narrowly tailored to serve California's compelling interest. ***

WASHINGTON v. DAVIS
426 U.S. 229 (1976)

MR. JUSTICE WHITE delivered the opinion of the Court.

*** [Respondents argue] that the [District of Columbia Metropolitan Police] Department's recruiting procedures discriminated on the basis of race against black applicants by a series of practices including, but not limited to, a written personnel test which excluded a disproportionately high number of Negro applicants. *** [To] be accepted by the Department and to enter an intensive 17–week training program, the police recruit was required to satisfy certain physical and character standards, to be a high school graduate or its equivalent, and to receive a grade of at least 40 out of 80 on "Test 21," which is "an examination that is used generally throughout the federal service," which "was developed by the Civil Service Commission, not the Police Department," and which was "designed to test verbal ability, vocabulary, reading and comprehension." *** Respondents' evidence, the District Court said, warranted three conclusions: "(a) The number of black police officers, while substantial, is not proportionate to the population mix of the city. (b) A higher percentage of blacks fail the Test than whites. (c) The Test has not been validated to establish its reliability for measuring subsequent job performance." *** It was undisputed that the Department had systematically and affirmatively sought to enroll black officers many of whom passed the test but failed to report for duty. ***

[handwritten margin note: test has a negative effect on AAs]

The central purpose of the Equal Protection Clause of the Fourteenth Amendment is the prevention of official conduct discriminating on the basis of race. But our cases have not embraced the proposition that a law or other official act, without regard to whether it reflects a racially discriminatory purpose, is unconstitutional solely because it has a racially disproportionate impact.

[handwritten margin note: case deals w/ impact rather than purpose]

Almost 100 years ago, *Strauder v. West Virginia* established that the exclusion of Negroes from grand and petit juries in criminal proceedings violated the Equal Protection Clause, but the fact that a particular jury or a series of juries does not statistically reflect the racial composition of the community does not in itself make out an invidious discrimination forbidden by the Clause. *** The rule is the same in other contexts. *Wright v. Rockefeller*, 376 U.S. 52 (1964), upheld a New York congressional apportionment statute against claims that district lines had been racially gerrymandered. The challenged districts were made up predominantly of whites or of minority races, and their boundaries were irregularly drawn. The challengers did not prevail because they failed to prove that [the] statute "was the product of a state contrivance to segregate on the basis of race or place of origin." ***

[handwritten margin note: history of case law where laws may or may not have intentionally discriminated, but had that affect on a class]

The school desegregation cases have also adhered to the basic equal protection principle that the invidious quality of a law claimed to be racially discriminatory must ultimately be traced to a racially discriminatory purpose. That there are both predominantly black and predominantly white schools in a community is not alone violative of the Equal Protection Clause. The essential element of *de jure* segregation is "a current condition of segregation resulting from intentional state action." The Court has also recently rejected allegations of racial discrimination based solely on the statistically disproportionate racial impact of various provisions of the Social Security Act because "(t)he acceptance of appellants' constitutional theory would render suspect each difference in treatment among the grant classes, however lacking in racial motivation and however otherwise rational the treatment might be." *Jefferson v. Hackney*, 406 U.S. 535, 548 (1972).

This is not to say that the necessary discriminatory racial purpose must be express or appear on the face of the statute, or that a law's disproportionate impact is irrelevant in cases involving Constitution-based claims of racial discrimination. A statute, otherwise neutral on its face, must not be applied so as invidiously to discriminate on the basis of race. ***

Necessarily, an invidious discriminatory purpose may often be inferred from the totality of the relevant facts, including the fact, if it is true, that the law bears more heavily on one race than another. It is also not infrequently

[handwritten margin note: purpose can be assumed from the effects]

true that the discriminatory impact in the jury cases for example, the total or seriously disproportionate exclusion of Negroes from jury venires may for all practical purposes demonstrate unconstitutionality because in various circumstances the discrimination is very difficult to explain on nonracial grounds. Nevertheless, we have not held that a law, neutral on its face and serving ends otherwise within the power of government to pursue, is invalid under the Equal Protection Clause simply because it may affect a greater proportion of one race than of another. Disproportionate impact is not irrelevant, but it is not the sole touchstone of an invidious racial discrimination forbidden by the Constitution. Standing alone, it does not trigger the rule that racial classifications are to be subjected to the strictest scrutiny and are justifiable only by the weightiest of considerations.

*** [W]e have difficulty understanding how a law establishing a racially neutral qualification for employment is nevertheless racially discriminatory and denies "any person *** equal protection of the laws" simply because a greater proportion of Negroes fail to qualify than members of other racial or ethnic groups. Had respondents, along with all others who had failed [the test], whether white or black, brought an action claiming that [it] denied each of them equal protection of the laws as compared with those who had passed with high enough scores to qualify them as police recruits, it is most unlikely that their challenge would have been sustained. [The test], which is administered generally to prospective Government employees, concededly seeks to ascertain whether those who take it have acquired a particular level of verbal skill; and it is untenable that the Constitution prevents the Government from seeking modestly to upgrade the communicative abilities of its employees rather than to be satisfied with some lower level of competence, particularly where the job requires special ability to communicate orally and in writing. Respondents, as Negroes, could no more successfully claim that the test denied them equal protection than could white applicants who also failed. The conclusion would not be different in the face of proof that more Negroes than whites had been disqualified by [the test]. That other Negroes also failed to score well would, alone, not demonstrate that respondents individually were being denied equal protection of the laws by the application of an otherwise valid qualifying test being administered to prospective police recruits.

Nor on the facts of the case before us would the disproportionate impact of [the test] warrant the conclusion that it is a purposeful device to discriminate against Negroes and hence an infringement of the constitutional rights of respondents as well as other black applicants. As we have said, the test is neutral on its face and rationally may be said to serve a purpose the Government is constitutionally empowered to pursue. Even agreeing with the District Court that the differential racial effect of [the test] called for further inquiry, we think the District Court correctly held that the affirmative efforts of the Metropolitan Police Department to recruit black officers, the changing racial composition of the recruit classes and of the force in general, and the relationship of the test to the training program negated any inference that the Department discriminated on the basis of race or that "a police officer qualifies on the color of his skin rather than ability." ***

A rule that a statute designed to serve neutral ends is nevertheless invalid, absent compelling justification, if in practice it benefits or burdens one race more than another would be far-reaching and would raise serious questions about, and perhaps invalidate, a whole range of tax, welfare, public service, regulatory, and licensing statutes that may be more burdensome to the poor and to the average black than to the more affluent white. ***

MR. JUSTICE STEVENS, concurring.

*** The requirement of purposeful discrimination is a common thread running through the cases summarized in [the majority's opinion]. These cases include criminal convictions which were set aside because blacks were excluded from the grand jury, a reapportionment case in which political boundaries were obviously influenced to some extent by racial considerations, a school desegregation case, and a case involving the unequal administration of an ordinance purporting to prohibit the operation of laundries in frame buildings. Although it may be proper to use the same language to describe the constitutional claim in each of these contexts, the burden of proving a prima facie case may well involve differing evidentiary considerations. The extent of deference that one pays to the trial court's determination of the factual issue, and indeed, the extent to which one characterizes the intent issue as a question of fact or a question of law, will vary in different contexts.

Frequently the most probative evidence of intent will be objective evidence of what actually happened rather than evidence describing the subjective state of mind of the actor. For normally the actor is presumed to have intended the natural consequences of his deeds. This is particularly true in the case of governmental action which is frequently the product of compromise, of collective decisionmaking, and of mixed motivation. It is unrealistic, on the one hand, to require the victim of alleged discrimination to uncover the actual subjective intent of the decisionmaker or, conversely, to invalidate otherwise legitimate action simply because an improper motive affected the deliberation of a participant in the decisional process. A law conscripting clerics should not be invalidated because an atheist voted for it.

My point in making this observation is to suggest that the line between discriminatory purpose and discriminatory impact is not nearly as bright, and perhaps not quite as critical, as the reader of the Court's opinion might assume. I agree, of course, that a constitutional issue does not arise every time some disproportionate impact is shown. On the other hand, when the disproportion is dramatic, *** it really does not matter whether the standard is phrased in terms of purpose or effect. Therefore, although I accept the statement of the general rule in the Court's opinion, I am not yet prepared to indicate how that standard should be applied in the many cases which have formulated the governing standard in different language. ***

MR. JUSTICE BRENNAN, dissenting. [omitted]

Notes

1. **Alternative Theories in *Loving*.**

   (a) Does *Loving* involve a racial classification? While race is used to classify permissible and impermissible marriages, the statute affects individuals of various races; it is not directed at one race the way the legislation was in *Strauder* and *Korematsu*. How, if at all, should this affect the Court's equal protection analysis?

   (b) If "strict scrutiny" applies, does the State have a "compelling interest" in preventing interracial marriage? If *Loving* does not involve a racial classification, does the state have a "rational basis" for its ban on interracial marriage?

   (c) Does the Court's decision in *Loving* necessarily follow from the *Brown* decision? Consider the fact that segregation imposes a rule on both white and black school children. Consider also whether there is a difference between the education and the marriage contexts of the cases.

   (d) Should the Court have treated *Loving* as a due process case? There is some discussion of this issue by CHIEF JUSTICE WARREN in a part of the opinion not reproduced here: "These statutes also deprive the Lovings of liberty without due process of law ***. The freedom to marry has long been recognized as one of the vital personal rights essential to the orderly pursuit of happiness ***. To deny this fundamental freedom on so unsupportable a basis as the racial classification embodied in these statutes [violates due process] ***."

   (e) Should Mr. Loving (a white man) be able to raise all the arguments available to Mrs. Loving (a black woman)?

2. ***Johnson v. California* and *Loving*.** What does *Johnson* add to *Loving*, both concerning the applicability of strict scrutiny and to the narrow tailoring of justifications for a race-based category applying equally to all races?

3. ***Washington v. Davis*: Intent and Effects.**

   (a) Why doesn't the Court use *Brown* and *Loving* or even *Yick Wo* to support the proposition that racially neutral classifications adversely affecting blacks are subject to strict scrutiny?

   (b) How does a plaintiff prove discriminatory intent when the harm to her stems from a facially race-neutral statute?

   (c) Consider the extent to which you agree or disagree with the following reasons for not applying strict scrutiny to statutes having a disparate impact:

   > (1) Disparate impact may be both unintended and unavoidable. Statutes may be passed not because of the impact, but despite the impact. *See Personnel Administrator v. Feeney*, 442 U.S. 256 (1979) (upholding Massachusetts veterans' preference for civil service jobs despite adverse effect on females).

(2) Judicial voiding of statutes having a disparate impact would mire the Court in a flood of litigation. How much impact would trigger unconstitutionality?

(3) Voiding statutes that have a disparate impact would show too little deference to legislatures and majoritarian processes.

(d) Is *Washington v. Davis* simply an instance of legislatures having to make hard decisions concerning allocation of scarce resources? See JUSTICE MARSHALL's dissent in *Rogers v. Lodge*, 458 U.S. 613 (1982), in which he distinguishes Fifteenth Amendment voting rights cases as not involving allocation of scarce resources and argues that an effect standard should be applied.

(e) Is *Washington v. Davis* merely an application of *Carolene Products* footnote four? Do these cases fail to deal adequately with perpetuation of past discrimination?

4. **More on Intent and Effects.** What is required to show discriminatory intent and is the intent requirement applied the same way in different contexts (sex rather than race, group participation in politics rather than individual employment)? *Arlington Heights v. Metropolitan Housing Dev. Corp.*, 429 U.S. 252 (1977), rejected a challenge to a refusal to rezone from single to multi-family that might have had racial effects. The Court opined: "Rarely can it be said that a legislature or administrative body operating under a broad mandate made a decision motivated solely by a single concern, or even that a particular purpose was the 'dominant' or 'primary' one. *** Absent a pattern as stark as in *** *Yick Wo*, impact alone is not determinative." *Personnel Administrator of Mass. v. Feeney*, 442 U.S. 256 (1979), upheld an absolute veterans' preference for public employment even though 98.2% of all veterans were male. The Court held that the "distinction made [was] quite simply between veterans and nonveterans, not between men and women." To render the statute unconstitutional, the legislature must have acted "at least in part 'because of,' not merely 'in spite of,' its adverse effects" on females.

SCHUETTE v. COALITION TO DEFEND AFFIRMATIVE ACTION
134 S. Ct. 1623 (2014)

JUSTICE KENNEDY announced the judgment of the Court and delivered an opinion, in which THE CHIEF JUSTICE and JUSTICE ALITO join.

*** Under the terms of [a Michigan constitutional] amendment, race-based preferences cannot be part of the admissions process for state universities. *** [T]his case is not about *** the constitutionality, or the merits, of race-conscious admissions policies in higher education. *** The question here concerns *** whether, and in what manner, voters in the States may choose to prohibit the consideration of racial preferences in governmental decisions, in particular with respect to school admissions. *** In Michigan, the State Constitution invests independent boards of trustees with plenary authority over public universities, including admissions policies. Although the members of the boards are elected, some evidence in the record suggests they delegated authority over admissions policy to the faculty. But whether the boards or the faculty set the specific policy, Michigan's public universities did consider race as a factor in admissions decisions before 2006. ***

Though it has not been prominent in the arguments of the parties, this Court's decision in *Reitman v. Mulkey,* 387 U.S. 369 (1967), is a proper beginning point for discussing the controlling decisions. In *Mulkey,* voters amended the California Constitution to prohibit any state legislative interference with an owner's prerogative to decline to sell or rent residential property on any basis. *** [T[he complaining parties were barred, on account of race, from invoking the protection of California's statutes; and, as a result, they were unable to lease residential property. This Court concluded that the state constitutional provision was a denial of equal protection. *** The Court agreed that the amendment "expressly authorized and constitutionalized the private right to discriminate." The effect of the state constitutional amendment was to "significantly encourage and involve the State in private racial discriminations." In a dissent joined by three other Justices, Justice Harlan disagreed with the majority's holding. The dissent reasoned that California, by the action of its voters, simply wanted the State to remain neutral in this area, so that the State was not a party to discrimination. That dissenting voice did not prevail against the majority's conclusion that the state action in question encouraged discrimination, causing real and specific injury.

The next precedent of relevance, *Hunter v. Erickson,* 393 U.S. 385 (1969), is central to the arguments the respondents make in the instant case. In *Hunter,* the Court for the first time elaborated what the Court of Appeals here styled the "political process" doctrine. There, the Akron City Council found that the citizens of Akron consisted of "'people of different race[s], ... many of whom live in circumscribed and segregated areas, under sub-standard unhealthful, unsafe, unsanitary and overcrowded conditions, because of discrimination in the sale, lease, rental and financing of housing.' "To address the problem, Akron enacted a fair housing ordinance to prohibit that sort of discrimination. In response, voters amended the city charter to overturn the ordinance and to require that any additional antidiscrimination housing ordinance be approved by referendum. But most other ordinances "regulating the real property market" were not subject to those threshold requirements. The plaintiff, a black woman in Akron, Ohio, alleged that her real estate agent could not show her certain residences because the owners had specified they would not sell to black persons.

Central to the Court's reasoning in *Hunter* was that the charter amendment was enacted in circumstances where widespread racial discrimination in the sale and rental of housing led to segregated housing, forcing many to live in "'unhealthful, unsafe, unsanitary and overcrowded conditions.' *** The Court found that the city charter amendment, by singling out antidiscrimination ordinances, "places special burden on racial minorities within the governmental process," thus becoming as impermissible as any other government action taken with the invidious intent to injure a racial minority. Justice Harlan filed a concurrence. He argued the city charter amendment "has the clear purpose of making it more difficult for certain racial and religious minorities to achieve legislation that is in their interest." But without regard to the sentence just quoted, *Hunter* rests on the unremarkable principle that the State may not alter the procedures of government to target racial minorities. The facts in *Hunter* established that invidious discrimination would be the necessary result of the procedural restructuring. Thus, in *Mulkey* and *Hunter,* there was a demonstrated injury on the basis of race that, by reasons of state encouragement or participation, became more aggravated.

Seattle is the third case of principal relevance here. There, the school board adopted a mandatory busing program to alleviate racial isolation of minority students in local schools. Voters who opposed the school board's busing plan passed a state initiative that barred busing to desegregate. The Court first determined that, although "white as well as Negro children benefit from" diversity, the school board's plan "inures primarily to the benefit of the minority." The Court next found that "the practical effect" of the state initiative was to "remov[e] the authority to address a racial problem—and only a racial problem—from the existing decisionmaking body, in such a way as to burden minority interests" because advocates of busing "now must seek relief from the state legislature, or from the statewide electorate." The Court therefore found that the initiative had "explicitly us[ed] the racial nature of a decision to determine the decisionmaking process."

Seattle is best understood as a case in which the state action in question (the bar on busing enacted by the State's voters) had the serious risk, if not purpose, of causing specific injuries on account of race, just as had been the case in *Mulkey* and *Hunter*. Although there had been no judicial finding of *de jure* segregation with respect to Seattle's school district, it appears as though school segregation in the district in the 1940's and 1950's may have been the partial result of school board policies that "permitted white students to transfer out of black schools while restricting the transfer of black students into white schools." *** [T]he legitimacy and constitutionality of the remedy in question (busing for desegregation) was assumed, and *Seattle* must be understood on that basis. *Seattle* involved a state initiative that "was carefully tailored to interfere only with desegregative busing." The *Seattle* Court, accepting the validity of the school board's busing remedy as a predicate to its analysis of the constitutional question, found that the State's disapproval of the school board's busing remedy was an aggravation of the very racial injury in which the State itself was complicit.

The broad language used in *Seattle,* however, went well beyond the analysis needed to resolve the case. *** In essence, according to the broad reading of *Seattle,* any state action with a "racial focus" that makes it "more difficult for certain racial minorities than for other groups" to "achieve legislation that is in their interest" is subject to strict scrutiny. *** [T]hat reading must be rejected *** as unnecessary to the decision in *Seattle*; it has no support in precedent; and it raises serious constitutional concerns. *** It cannot be entertained as a serious proposition that all individuals of the same race think alike. Yet that proposition would be a necessary beginning point were the *Seattle* formulation to control *** Even assuming these initial steps could be taken in a manner consistent with a sound analytic and judicial framework, the court would next be required to determine the policy realms in which certain groups—groups defined by race—have a political interest. That undertaking, again without guidance from any accepted legal standards, would risk, in turn, the creation of incentives for those who support or oppose certain policies to cast the debate in terms of racial advantage or disadvantage. *** Those who seek to represent the interests of particular racial groups could attempt to advance those aims by demanding an equal protection ruling that any number of matters be foreclosed from voter review or participation. In a nation in which governmental policies are wide ranging, those who seek to limit voter participation might be tempted, were this Court to adopt the *Seattle* formulation, to urge that a group they choose to define by race or racial stereotypes are advantaged or disadvantaged by any number of laws or decisions. Tax policy, housing subsidies, wage regulations, and even the naming of public schools, highways, and monuments are just a few examples of what could become a list of subjects that some organizations could insist should be beyond the power of voters to decide, or beyond the power of a legislature to decide when enacting limits on the power of local authorities or other governmental entities to address certain subjects. Racial division would be validated, not discouraged, were the *Seattle* formulation ***to remain in force. ***

One response to these concerns may be that objections to the larger consequences of the *Seattle* formulation need not be confronted in this case, for here race was an undoubted subject of the ballot issue. But a number of problems raised by *Seattle,* such as racial definitions, still apply. *** Here there was no infliction of a specific injury of the kind at issue in *Mulkey* and *Hunter* and in the history of the Seattle schools. Here there is no precedent for extending these cases to restrict the right of Michigan voters to determine that race-based preferences granted by Michigan governmental entities should be ended. *** The instant case presents *** not how to address or prevent injury caused on account of race but whether voters may determine whether a policy of race-based preferences should be continued. ***

The freedom secured by the Constitution consists, in one of its essential dimensions, of the right of the individual not to be injured by the unlawful exercise of governmental power. *** [I]ndividual liberty has constitutional protection, and that liberty's full extent and meaning may remain yet to be discovered and affirmed. Yet freedom does not stop with individual rights. Our constitutional system embraces, too, the right of citizens to debate so they can learn and decide and then, through the political process, act in concert to try to shape the course of their own times and the course of a nation that must strive always to make freedom ever greater and more secure. Here Michigan voters acted in concert and statewide to seek consensus and adopt a policy on a difficult subject against a historical background of race in America that has been a source of tragedy and persisting injustice. That history demands that we continue to learn, to listen, and to remain open to new approaches if we are to aspire always to a constitutional order in which all persons are treated with fairness and equal dignity. Were the Court to rule that the question addressed by Michigan voters is too sensitive or complex to be within the grasp of the electorate; or that the policies at issue remain too delicate to be resolved save by university officials or faculties, acting at some remove from immediate public scrutiny and control; or that these matters are so arcane that the electorate's power must be limited because the people cannot prudently exercise that power even after a full debate, that holding would be an unprecedented restriction on the exercise of a fundamental right held not just by one person but by all in common. It is the right to speak and debate and learn and then, as a matter of political will, to act through a lawful electoral process.

The respondents in this case insist that a difficult question of public policy must be taken from the reach of the voters, and thus removed from the realm of public discussion, dialogue, and debate in an election campaign. Quite in addition to the serious First Amendment implications of that position with respect to any particular election, it is inconsistent with the underlying premises of a responsible, functioning democracy. One of those premises is that a democracy has the capacity—and the duty—to learn from its past mistakes; to discover and confront persisting biases; and by respectful, rational deliberation to rise above those flaws and injustices. That process is impeded, not advanced, by court decrees based on the proposition that the public cannot have the requisite repose to discuss certain issues. It is demeaning to the democratic process to presume that the voters are not capable of deciding an issue of this sensitivity on decent and rational grounds. The process of public discourse and political debate should not be foreclosed even if there is a risk that during a public campaign there will be those, on both sides, who seek to use racial division and discord to their own political advantage. An informed public can, and must, rise above this. The idea of democracy is that it can, and must, mature. Freedom embraces the right, indeed the duty, to engage in a rational, civic discourse in order to determine how best to form a consensus to shape the destiny of the Nation and its people. These First Amendment dynamics would be disserved if this Court were to say that the question here at issue is beyond the capacity of the voters to debate and then to determine.

These precepts are not inconsistent with the well-established principle that when hurt or injury is inflicted on racial minorities by the encouragement or command of laws or other state action, the Constitution requires redress by the courts. *** This case is not about how the debate about racial preferences should be resolved. It is about who may resolve it. There is no authority in the Constitution of the United States or in this Court's precedents for the Judiciary to set aside Michigan laws that commit this policy determination to the voters. ***

JUSTICE KAGAN took no part in the consideration or decision of this case.

CHIEF JUSTICE ROBERTS, concurring.

The dissent *** expound[s] its own policy preferences in favor of taking race into account in college admissions, while nonetheless concluding that it "do[es] not mean to suggest that the virtues of adopting race-sensitive admissions policies should inform the legal question before the Court." The dissent concedes that the governing boards of the State's various universities could have implemented a policy making it illegal to "discriminate against, or grant preferential treatment to," any individual on the basis of race. On the dissent's view, if the governing boards conclude that drawing racial distinctions in university admissions is undesirable or counterproductive, they are permissibly exercising their policymaking authority. But others who might reach the same conclusion are failing to take race seriously. *** To disagree with the dissent's views on the costs and benefits of racial preferences is not to "wish away, rather than confront" racial inequality. People can disagree in good faith on this issue, but it similarly does more harm than good to question the openness and candor of those on either side of the debate.

JUSTICE SCALIA, with whom JUSTICE THOMAS joins, concurring in the judgment.

It has come to this. Called upon to explore the jurisprudential twilight zone between two errant lines of precedent, we confront a frighteningly bizarre question: Does the Equal Protection Clause of the Fourteenth Amendment *forbid* what its text plainly *requires*? Needless to say (except that this case obliges us to say it), the question answers itself. "The Constitution proscribes government discrimination on the basis of race, and state-provided education is no exception." It is precisely this understanding—the correct understanding—of the federal Equal Protection Clause that the people of the State of Michigan have adopted for their own fundamental law. By adopting it, they did not simultaneously *offend* it. *** But the battleground for this case is not the constitutionality of race-based admissions—at least, not quite. Rather, it is the so-called political-process doctrine *** I agree with those parts of the plurality opinion that repudiate this doctrine. But I do not agree with its reinterpretation of *Seattle* and *Hunter,* which makes them stand in part for the cloudy and doctrinally anomalous proposition that whenever state action poses "the serious risk ... of causing specific injuries on account of race," it denies equal protection. I would instead reaffirm that the "ordinary principles of our law [and] of our democratic heritage" require "plaintiffs alleging equal protection violations" stemming from facially neutral acts to "prove intent and causation and not merely the existence of racial disparity." I would further hold that a law directing state actors to provide equal protection is (to say the least) facially neutral, and cannot violate the Constitution. *** Patently atextual, unadministrable, and contrary to our traditional equal-protection jurisprudence, *Hunter* and *Seattle* should be overruled. *** The Equal Protection Clause "cannot mean one thing when applied to one individual and something else when applied to a person of another color. If both are not accorded the same protection it is not equal."

The dissent trots out the old saw, derived from dictum in a footnote, that legislation motivated by "prejudice against discrete and insular minorities" merits "more exacting judicial scrutiny." I say derived from that dictum (expressed by the four-Justice majority of a seven-Justice Court) because the dictum itself merely said "*[n]or need we enquire* ... whether prejudice against discrete and insular minorities may be a special condition." The dissent does not argue, of course, that such "prejudice" produced [the Michigan proposal]. Nor does it explain why certain racial minorities in Michigan qualify as "insular," meaning that "other groups will not form coalitions with them—and, critically, not because of lack of common interests but because of 'prejudice.' "Nor does it even make the case that a group's "discreteness" and "insularity" are political *liabilities* rather than political *strengths*—a serious question that alone demonstrates the prudence of the *Carolene Products* dictumizers in leaving the "enquir[y]" for another day. As for the question whether "legislation which restricts those political processes which can ordinarily be expected to bring about repeal of undesirable legislation ... is to be subjected to more exacting judicial scrutiny," the *Carolene Products* Court found it "unnecessary to consider [that] now." If the dissent thinks that worth considering today, it should explain why the election of a university's governing board is a "political process which can ordinarily be expected to bring about repeal of undesirable legislation," but Michigan voters' ability to amend their Constitution is not. It seems to me quite the opposite. Amending the Constitution requires the approval of only "a majority of the electors voting on the question." By contrast, voting in a favorable board (each of which has eight members) at the three major public universities requires electing by majority vote at least 15 different candidates, several of whom would be running during different election cycles. So if Michigan voters, instead of amending their Constitution, had pursued the dissent's preferred path of electing board members promising to "abolish race-sensitive admissions policies," it would have been *harder,* not easier, for racial minorities favoring affirmative action to overturn that decision. But the more important point is that we should not design our jurisprudence to conform to dictum in a footnote in a four-Justice opinion.

Moving from the appalling to the absurd, I turn now to the second part of the *Hunter-Seattle* analysis—which is apparently no more administrable than the first. This part of the inquiry directs a court to determine whether the challenged act "place[s] effective decisionmaking authority over [the] racial issue at a different level of government." *** Taken to the limits of its logic, *Hunter-Seattle* is the gaping exception that nearly swallows the rule of structural state sovereignty. If indeed the Fourteenth Amendment forbids States to "place effective decisionmaking authority over" racial issues at "different level[s] of government," then it must be true that the Amendment's ratification in 1868 worked a partial ossification of each State's governing structure, rendering basically irrevocable the power of any subordinate state official who, the day *before* the Fourteenth Amendment's passage, happened to enjoy legislatively conferred authority over a "racial issue." *** *Seattle* 's logic would create affirmative-action safe havens wherever subordinate officials in public universities (1) traditionally have enjoyed "effective decisionmaking authority" over admissions policy but (2) have not yet used that authority to prohibit race-conscious admissions decisions. The mere existence of a subordinate's discretion over the matter would work a kind of reverse pre-emption. It is "a strange notion—alien to our system—that local governmental bodies can forever pre-empt the ability of a State—the sovereign power—to address a matter of compelling concern to the State." But that is precisely what the political-process doctrine contemplates. ***

I part ways with *Hunter, Seattle,* and (I think) the plurality for an additional reason: Each endorses a version of the proposition that a facially neutral law may deny equal protection solely because it has a disparate racial impact. Few equal-protection theories have been so squarely and soundly rejected. *** Since these formulations enable a determination of an equal-protection violation where there is no discriminatory intent, they are inconsistent with the long *Washington v. Davis* line of cases. *** In my view, any law expressly requiring state actors to afford all persons equal protection of the laws (such as Initiative 350 in *Seattle,* though not the charter amendment in *Hunter*) does not—*cannot*—deny "to any person ... equal protection of the laws," regardless of whatever evidence of seemingly foul purposes plaintiffs may cook up in the trial court.

As JUSTICE HARLAN observed over a century ago, "[o]ur Constitution is color-blind, and neither knows nor tolerates classes among citizens." The people of Michigan wish the same for their governing charter. It would be shameful for us to stand in their way.

JUSTICE BREYER, concurring in the judgment.

*** I agree with the plurality that the amendment is consistent with the Federal Equal Protection Clause. But I believe this for different reasons. First, we do not address the amendment insofar as it forbids the use of race-conscious admissions programs designed to remedy past exclusionary racial discrimination or the direct effects of that discrimination. *** Second, *** The Constitution allows local, state, and national communities to adopt narrowly tailored race-conscious programs designed to bring about greater inclusion and diversity. But the Constitution foresees the ballot box, not the courts, as the normal instrument for resolving differences and debates about the merits of these programs. *** Third, cases such as [*Hunter* and *Seattle*] reflect an important principle, namely, that an individual's ability to participate meaningfully in the political process should be independent of his race. *** In my view, however, *** the doctrine set forth in *Hunter* and *Seattle* does not easily fit this case. In those cases minorities had participated in the political process and they had won. The majority's subsequent reordering of the political process repealed the minority's successes and made it more difficult for the minority to succeed in the future. *** But one cannot as easily characterize the movement of the decisionmaking mechanism at issue here—from an administrative process to an electoral process—as diminishing the minority's ability to participate meaningfully in the *political* process. There is no prior electoral process in which the minority participated. For another thing, *** to apply *Hunter* and *Seattle* to the administrative process would, by tending to hinder change, risk discouraging experimentation, interfering with efforts to see when and how race-conscious policies work. Finally, the principle that underlies *Hunter* and *Seattle* runs up against a competing principle, discussed above. This competing principle favors decisionmaking though the democratic process. ***

JUSTICE SOTOMAYOR, with whom JUSTICE GINSBURG joins, dissenting.

We are fortunate to live in a democratic society. But without checks, democratically approved legislation can oppress minority groups. For that reason, our Constitution places limits on what a majority of the people may do. This case implicates one such limit: the guarantee of equal protection of the laws. Although that guarantee is traditionally understood to prohibit intentional discrimination under existing laws, equal protection does not end there. Another fundamental strand of our equal protection jurisprudence focuses on process, securing to all citizens the right to participate meaningfully and equally in self-government. That right is the bedrock of our democracy, for it preserves all other rights.

Yet to know the history of our Nation is to understand its long and lamentable record of stymieing the right of racial minorities to participate in the political process. At first, the majority acted with an open, invidious purpose. *** [Then] the majority [replaced] outright bans on voting with literacy tests, good character requirements, poll taxes, and gerrymandering. *** [Then] although it allowed the minority access to the political process, the majority changed the ground rules of the process so as to make it more difficult for the minority, and the minority alone, to obtain policies designed to foster racial integration. Although these political restructurings may not have been discriminatory in purpose, the Court reaffirmed the right of minority members of our society to participate meaningfully and equally in the political process.

This case involves this last chapter of discrimination: A majority of the Michigan electorate changed the basic rules of the political process in that State in a manner that uniquely disadvantaged racial minorities. Prior to the enactment of the constitutional initiative at issue here, all of the admissions policies of Michigan's public colleges and universities—including race-sensitive admissions policies—were in the hands of each institution's governing board. *** [T]he majority of Michigan voters changed the rules in the middle of the game, reconfiguring the existing political process in Michigan in a manner that burdened racial minorities. *** Our precedents do not permit political restructurings that create one process for racial minorities and a separate, less burdensome process for everyone else. ***

Hunter and *Seattle* vindicated a principle that is as elementary to our equal protection jurisprudence as it is essential: The majority may not suppress the minority's right to participate on equal terms in the political process. Under this doctrine, governmental action deprives minority groups of equal protection when it (1) has a racial focus, targeting a policy or program that "inures primarily to the benefit of the minority"; and (2) alters the political process in a manner that uniquely burdens racial minorities' ability to achieve their goals through that process. A faithful application of the doctrine resoundingly resolves this case in respondents' favor. *** And what now of the political-process doctrine? After the plurality's revision of *Hunter* and *Seattle,* it is unclear what is left. ***

The political-process doctrine also follows from the rest of our equal protection jurisprudence—in particular, our reapportionment and vote dilution cases. *** *Romer* involved a Colorado constitutional amendment that removed from the local political process an issue primarily affecting gay and lesbian citizens. *** Although the Court did not apply the political-process doctrine in *Romer,* the case resonates with the principles undergirding the political-process doctrine*** Rather than being able to appeal to municipalities for policy changes, the Court commented, the minority was forced to "enlis[t] the citizenry of Colorado to amend the State Constitution,"—just as in this case. ***

In my colleagues' view, examining the racial impact of legislation only perpetuates racial discrimination. This refusal to accept the stark reality that race matters is regrettable. *** The Constitution does not protect racial minorities from political defeat. But neither does it give the majority free rein to erect selective barriers against racial minorities. *** [Today's decision eviscerates an important strand of our equal protection jurisprudence. For members of historically marginalized groups, which rely on the federal courts to protect their constitutional rights, the decision can hardly bolster hope for a vision of democracy that preserves for all the right to participate meaningfully and equally in self-government. ***

Notes

1.   **Law.** Is the majority or dissent more consistent with the Equal Protection Clause? Is "political process equal protection" compatible with *Washington v. Davis*, which rejects disparate impact equal protection? Why shouldn't "mere repeal" of laws that benefit blacks be subject to strict scrutiny? Should strict scrutiny apply to a legislature's refusal to enact legislation benefiting blacks?

2.   **Distinguishing *Seattle* and *Crawford*.**   One casebook suggests that *Washington v. Davis* and *Crawford* are "ultimately inconsistent" with *Brown, Loving,* and *Seattle,* and that the two lines of authority can only be reconciled if the Justices "articulate and justify a substantive theory about the distribution of resources among groups in our society. *** [T]rying to think about *Seattle* and *Crawford* without a theory of distribution is like trying to think about the race problem without a theory of justice." Stone, Seidman, Sunstein, and Tushnett CONSTITUTIONAL LAW (Little, Brown & Co., 3d Ed. 1996) at p. 648. Do you agree? If so, have the Justices articulated such a substantive theory in *Schuette*?

3.   **Affirmative Action.** The next section considers the Supreme Court's race-based affirmative action decisions. The Court does not treat *Schuette* as an affirmative action case. As you read the following cases, ask yourself why not.

4. **Racial Data and Descriptions**. Is collection of data by race permissible? California's Racial Privacy Initiative (RPI), which did not pass, would have prohibited any public entity (including schools, employers, and law enforcement agencies) from collecting any data on the basis of race or ethnicity. Would the RPI, if successful, have violated the Equal Protection Clause? On a more individualized level, may a police bulletin describe a suspect as "Black male, 6' tall, wearing jeans and an Eminem t-shirt?"

3. AFFIRMATIVE ACTION

CITY OF RICHMOND v. J.A. CROSON COMPANY
488 U.S. 469 (1989)

JUSTICE O'CONNOR announced the judgment of the Court and delivered the opinion of the Court with respect to Parts I, III–B, and IV, an opinion with respect to Part II, in which THE CHIEF JUSTICE and JUSTICE WHITE join, and an opinion with respect to Parts III–A and V, in which THE CHIEF JUSTICE, JUSTICE WHITE, and JUSTICE KENNEDY join.

In this case, we confront once again the tension between the Fourteenth Amendment's guarantee of equal treatment to all citizens, and the use of race-based measures to ameliorate the effects of past discrimination on the opportunities enjoyed by members of minority groups in our society. In *Fullilove v. Klutznick*, 448 U.S. 448 (1980), we held that a congressional program requiring that 10% of certain federal construction grants be awarded to minority contractors did not violate the equal protection principles embodied in the Due Process Clause of the Fifth Amendment. ***

I

On April 11, 1983, the Richmond City Council adopted the Minority Business Utilization Plan (the Plan). The Plan required prime contractors to whom the city awarded construction contracts to subcontract at least 30% of the dollar amount of the contract to one or more Minority Business Enterprises (MBE's). *** The Plan defined an MBE as "[a] business at least fifty-one (51) percent of which is owned and controlled *** by minority group members." "Minority group members" were defined as "[c]itizens of the United States who are Blacks, Spanish-speaking, Orientals, Indians, Eskimos, or Aleuts." *** [City set-aside rules provided that] "[no] partial or complete waiver of the [30% set-aside] requirement shall be granted by the city other than in exceptional circumstances. To justify a waiver, it must be shown that every feasible attempt has been made to comply, and it must be demonstrated that sufficient, relevant, qualified Minority Business Enterprises *** are unavailable or unwilling to participate in the contract to enable meeting the 30% MBE goal." *** The Plan was adopted by the Richmond City Council after a public hearing. *** Proponents of the set-aside provision relied on a study which indicated that, while the general population of Richmond was 50% black, only 0.67% of the city's prime construction contracts had been awarded to minority businesses in the 5–year period from 1978 to 1983. It was also established that a variety of contractors' associations, whose representatives appeared in opposition to the ordinance, had virtually no minority businesses within their membership. *** There was no direct evidence of race discrimination on the part of the city in letting contracts or any evidence that the city's prime contractors had discriminated against minority-owned subcontractors. ***

II

*** Appellant and its supporting *amici* rely heavily on *Fullilove* for the proposition that a city council, like Congress, need not make specific findings of discrimination to engage in race-conscious relief. Thus, appellant argues "[i]t would be a perversion of federalism to hold that the federal government has a compelling interest in remedying the effects of racial discrimination in its own public works program, but a city government does not."

What appellant ignores is that Congress, unlike any State or political subdivision, has a specific constitutional mandate to enforce the dictates of the Fourteenth Amendment. The power to "enforce" may at times also include the power to define situations which Congress determines threaten principles of equality and to adopt prophylactic rules to deal with those situations. *See Katzenbach v. Morgan*, 384 U.S., at 651. The Civil War Amendments themselves worked a dramatic change in the balance between congressional and state power over matters of race. *** That Congress may identify and redress the effects of society-wide discrimination does not mean that, a fortiori, the States and their political subdivisions are free to decide that such remedies are appropriate. *** [H]owever, a state or local subdivision (if delegated the authority from the State) has the authority to eradicate the effects of private discrimination within its own legislative jurisdiction. *** [A]ny public entity *** has a compelling interest in assuring that public dollars *** do not serve to finance the evil of private prejudice.

[margin note: not all redress will be deemed appropriate]

[margin note: states have the authority to provide redress to hinder private prejudices]

III

A

*** The Richmond Plan denies certain citizens the opportunity to compete for a fixed percentage of public contracts based solely upon their race. To whatever racial group these citizens belong, their "personal rights" to be treated with equal dignity and respect are implicated by a rigid rule erecting race as the sole criterion in an aspect of public decisionmaking.

[margin note: plan is not constitutional]

Absent searching judicial inquiry into the justification for such race-based measures, there is simply no way of determining what classifications are "benign" or "remedial" and what classifications are in fact motivated by illegitimate notions of racial inferiority or simple racial politics. Indeed, the purpose of strict scrutiny is to "smoke out" illegitimate uses of race by assuring that the legislative body is pursuing a goal important enough to warrant use of a highly suspect tool. The test also ensures that the means chosen "fit" this compelling goal so closely that there is little or no possibility that the motive for the classification was illegitimate racial prejudice or stereotype.

Classifications based on race carry a danger of stigmatic harm. Unless they are strictly reserved for remedial settings, they may in fact promote notions of racial inferiority and lead to a politics of racial hostility. ***

Under the standard proposed by JUSTICE MARSHALL's dissent, "race-conscious classifications designed to further remedial goals" are forthwith subject to a relaxed standard of review. How the dissent arrives at the legal conclusion that a racial classification is "designed to further remedial goals," without first engaging in an examination of the factual basis for its enactment and the nexus between its scope and that factual basis, we are not told. However, once the "remedial" conclusion is reached, the dissent's standard is singularly deferential, and bears little resemblance to the close examination of legislative purpose we have engaged in when reviewing classifications based either on race or gender. The dissent's watered-down version of equal protection review effectively assures that race will always be relevant in American life ***.

Even were we to accept a reading of the guarantee of equal protection under which the level of scrutiny varies according to the ability of different groups to defend their interests in the representative process, heightened scrutiny would still be appropriate in the circumstances of this case [in which] blacks constitute approximately 50% of the population of the city of Richmond. Five of the nine seats on the city council are held by blacks. ***

strict scrutiny applied

B

*** [A] generalized assertion that there has been past discrimination in an entire industry provides no guidance for a legislative body to determine the precise scope of the injury it seeks to remedy. It "has no logical stopping point." "Relief" for such an ill-defined wrong could extend until the percentage of public contracts awarded to MBE's in Richmond mirrored the percentage of minorities in the population as a whole.

needs to be more specific

Appellant argues that it is attempting to remedy various forms of past discrimination that are alleged to be responsible for the small number of minority businesses in the local contracting industry. Among these the city cites the exclusion of blacks from skilled construction trade unions and training programs. This past discrimination has prevented them "from following the traditional path from laborer to entrepreneur." The city also lists a host of nonracial factors which would seem to face a member of any racial group attempting to establish a new business enterprise, such as deficiencies in working capital, inability to meet bonding requirements, unfamiliarity with bidding procedures, and disability caused by an inadequate track record.

While there is no doubt that the sorry history of both private and public discrimination in this country has contributed to a lack of opportunities for black entrepreneurs, this observation, standing alone, cannot justify a rigid racial quota in the awarding of public contracts in Richmond, Virginia. *** It is sheer speculation how many minority firms there would be in Richmond absent past societal discrimination ***. Defining these sorts of injuries as "identified discrimination" would give local governments license to create a patchwork of racial preferences based on statistical generalizations about any particular field of endeavor.

needs to be a factual basis for a specific need.

These defects are readily apparent in this case. The 30% quota cannot in any realistic sense be tied to any injury suffered by anyone. The District Court relied upon five predicate "facts" in reaching its conclusion that there was an adequate basis for the 30% quota: (1) the ordinance declares itself to

action needs t be tied to a specific injury.

DC's five reasons

be remedial; (2) several proponents of the measure stated their views that there had been past discrimination in the construction industry; (3) minority businesses received 0.67% of prime contracts from the city while minorities constituted 50% of the city's population; (4) there were very few minority contractors in local and state contractors' associations; and (5) in 1977, Congress made a determination that the effects of past discrimination had stifled minority participation in the construction industry nationally.

None of these "findings," singly or together, provide the city of Richmond with a "strong basis in evidence for its conclusion that remedial action was necessary." ***

The factfinding process of legislative bodies is generally entitled to a presumption of regularity and deferential review by the judiciary. But when a legislative body chooses to employ a suspect classification, it cannot rest upon a generalized assertion as to the classification's relevance to its goals. A governmental actor cannot render race a legitimate proxy for a particular condition merely by declaring that the condition exists. The history of racial classifications in this country suggests that blind judicial deference to legislative or executive pronouncements of necessity has no place in equal protection analysis.

Richmond did not show that the low % was based on discrimination

Reliance on the disparity between the number of prime contracts awarded to minority firms and the minority population of the city of Richmond is similarly misplaced. *** In this case, the city does not even know how many MBE's in the relevant market are qualified to undertake prime or subcontracting work in public construction projects. Nor does the city know what percentage of total city construction dollars minority firms now receive as subcontractors on prime contracts let by the city.

no concrete evidence

AA's may not be interested

To a large extent, the set-aside of subcontracting dollars seems to rest on the unsupported assumption that white prime contractors simply will not hire minority firms. *** The city and the District Court also relied on evidence that MBE membership in local contractors' associations was extremely low. Again, standing alone this evidence is not probative of any discrimination in the local construction industry. There are numerous explanations for this dearth of minority participation, including past societal discrimination in education and economic opportunities as well as both black and white career and entrepreneurial choices. Blacks may be disproportionately attracted to industries other than construction. ***

cannot compare facts to other jurisdictions

Finally, the city and the District Court relied on Congress' finding in connection with the set-aside approved in *Fullilove* that there had been nationwide discrimination in the construction industry. *** We have never approved the extrapolation of discrimination in one jurisdiction from the experience of another.

*** To accept Richmond's claim that past societal discrimination alone can serve as the basis for rigid racial preferences would be to open the door to competing claims for "remedial relief" for every disadvantaged group. The dream of a Nation of equal citizens in a society where race is irrelevant to personal opportunity and achievement would be lost in a mosaic of shifting preferences based on inherently unmeasurable claims of past wrongs. *** We think such a result would be contrary to both the letter and spirit of a constitutional provision whose central command is equality.

[handwritten: at odds w/ the purpose of equality]

The foregoing analysis applies only to the inclusion of blacks within the Richmond set-aside program. There is *absolutely no evidence* of past discrimination against Spanish-speaking, Oriental, Indian, Eskimo, or Aleut persons in any aspect of the Richmond construction industry. *** The random inclusion of racial groups that, as a practical matter, may never have suffered from discrimination in the construction industry in Richmond suggests that perhaps the city's purpose was not in fact to remedy past discrimination. *** [O]ne may legitimately ask why they are forced to share this "remedial relief" with an Aleut citizen who moves to Richmond tomorrow? The gross overinclusiveness of Richmond's racial preference strongly impugns the city's claim of remedial motivation.

[handwritten: no evidence that it harms AAs or other groups]

IV

As noted by the court below, it is almost impossible to assess whether the Richmond Plan is narrowly tailored to remedy prior discrimination since it is not linked to identified discrimination in any way. ***

First, there does not appear to have been any consideration of the use of race-neutral means to increase minority business participation in city contracting. *** Second, the 30% quota cannot be said to be narrowly tailored to any goal, except perhaps outright racial balancing. It rests upon the "completely unrealistic" assumption that minorities will choose a particular trade in lockstep proportion to their representation in the local population.

[handwritten: SS analysis]

Since the city must already consider bids and waivers on a case-by-case basis, it is difficult to see the need for a rigid numerical quota. *** [T]he congressional scheme upheld in *Fullilove* allowed for a waiver of the set-aside provision where an MBE's higher price was not attributable to the effects of past discrimination. *** Unlike the program upheld in *Fullilove*, the Richmond Plan's waiver system focuses solely on the availability of MBE's; there is no inquiry into whether or not the particular MBE seeking a racial preference has suffered from the effects of past discrimination by the city or prime contractors. *** [T]he city's only interest in maintaining a quota system rather than investigating the need for remedial action in particular cases would seem to be simple administrative convenience. *** [This] program is not narrowly tailored to remedy the effects of prior discrimination.

V

Nothing we say today precludes a state or local entity from taking action to rectify the effects of identified discrimination within its jurisdiction. *** Even in the absence of evidence of discrimination, the city has at its disposal a whole array of race-neutral devices to increase the accessibility of city contracting opportunities to small entrepreneurs of all races. *** In the case at hand, the city has not ascertained how many minority enterprises are present in the local construction market nor the level of their participation in city construction projects. The city points to no evidence that qualified minority contractors have been passed over for city contracts or subcontracts, either as a group or in any individual case. *** Proper findings *** define both the scope of the injury and the extent of the remedy necessary to cure its effects. Such findings also serve to assure all citizens that the deviation from the norm of equal treatment of all racial and ethnic groups is a temporary matter *** Because the city of Richmond has failed to identify the need for remedial action in the awarding of its public construction contracts, its treatment of its citizens on a racial basis violates the dictates of the Equal Protection Clause. ***

JUSTICE STEVENS, concurring in part and concurring in the judgment.

First, the city makes no claim that the public interest in the efficient performance of its construction contracts will be served by granting a preference to minority-business enterprises. *** Second, this litigation involves an attempt by a legislative body, rather than a court, to fashion a remedy for a past wrong. *** It is the judicial system, rather than the legislative process, that is best equipped to identify past wrongdoers and to fashion remedies that will create the conditions that presumably would have existed had no wrong been committed. *** Third, instead of engaging in a debate over the proper standard of review to apply in affirmative-action litigation, I believe it is more constructive to try to identify the characteristics of the advantaged and disadvantaged classes that may justify their disparate treatment. In this case that approach convinces me that *** the Richmond City Council has merely engaged in the type of stereotypical analysis that is a hallmark of violations of the Equal Protection Clause. ***

JUSTICE SCALIA, concurring in the judgment.

*** [S]trict scrutiny must be applied to all governmental classification by race, whether or not its asserted purpose is "remedial" or "benign." *** At least where state or local action is at issue, only a social emergency rising to the level of imminent danger to life and limb—for example, a prison race riot, requiring temporary segregation of inmates—can justify an exception to the principle embodied in the Fourteenth Amendment that "[o]ur Constitution is color-blind, and neither knows nor tolerates classes among citizens," *Plessy v. Ferguson*, (HARLAN, J., dissenting). *** In my view there is only one circumstance in which the States may act by race to "undo the effects of past discrimination": where that is necessary to eliminate their own maintenance of a system of unlawful racial classification. *** This distinction explains our school desegregation cases, in which we have made plain that States and localities sometimes have an obligation to adopt race-conscious remedies. ***

I agree with the Court's dictum that a fundamental distinction must be drawn between the effects of "societal" discrimination and the effects of "identified" discrimination, and that the situation would be different if Richmond's plan were "tailored" to identify those particular bidders who "suffered from the effects of past discrimination by the city or prime contractors." In my view, however, the reason that would make a difference is not, as the Court states, that it would justify race-conscious action but rather that it would enable race-neutral remediation. ***

It is plainly true that in our society blacks have suffered discrimination immeasurably greater than any directed at other racial groups. But those who believe that racial preferences can help to "even the score" display, and reinforce, a manner of thinking by race that was the source of the injustice and that will, if it endures within our society, be the source of more injustice still. The relevant proposition is not that it was blacks, or Jews, or Irish who were discriminated against, but that it was individual men and women, "created equal," who were discriminated against. And the relevant resolve is that that should never happen again. *** Since blacks have been disproportionately disadvantaged by racial discrimination, any race-neutral remedial program aimed at the disadvantaged as such will have a disproportionately beneficial impact on blacks. Only such a program, and not one that operates on the basis of race, is in accord with the letter and the spirit of our Constitution. ***

JUSTICE MARSHALL, with whom JUSTICE BRENNAN and JUSTICE BLACKMUN join, dissenting.

It is a welcome symbol of racial progress when the former capital of the Confederacy acts forthrightly to confront the effects of racial discrimination in its midst. In my view, nothing in the Constitution can be construed to prevent Richmond, Virginia, from allocating a portion of its contracting dollars for businesses owned or controlled by members of minority groups. *** In any event, the Richmond City Council *has* supported its determination that minorities have been wrongly excluded from local construction contracting. Its proof includes statistics showing that minority-owned businesses have received virtually no city contracting dollars and rarely if ever belonged to area trade associations; testimony by municipal officials that discrimination has been widespread in the local construction industry; and the same exhaustive and widely publicized federal studies relied on in *Fullilove*, studies which showed that pervasive discrimination in the Nation's tight-knit construction industry had operated to exclude minorities from public contracting. ***

More fundamentally, today's decision marks a deliberate and giant step backward in this Court's affirmative-action jurisprudence. *** The majority's unnecessary pronouncements will inevitably discourage or prevent governmental entities, particularly States and localities, from acting to rectify the scourge of past discrimination. ***

will have harmful effects

Richmond has two powerful interests in setting aside a portion of public contracting funds for minority-owned enterprises. The first is the city's interest in eradicating the effects of past racial discrimination. *** Richmond has a second compelling interest *** of preventing the city's own spending decisions from reinforcing and perpetuating the exclusionary effects of past discrimination. *** The city's local evidence confirmed that Richmond's construction industry did not deviate from this pernicious national pattern. The fact that just 0.67% of public construction expenditures over the previous five years had gone to minority-owned prime contractors, despite the city's racially mixed population, strongly suggests that construction contracting in the area was rife with "present economic inequities." *** The fact that area trade associations had virtually no minority members dramatized the extent of present inequities and suggested the lasting power of past discriminatory systems. ***

In my judgment, Richmond's set-aside plan also comports with the second prong of the equal protection inquiry, for it is substantially related to the interests it seeks to serve in remedying past discrimination and in ensuring that municipal contract procurement does not perpetuate that discrimination. The most striking aspect of the city's ordinance is the similarity it bears to the "appropriately limited" federal set-aside provision upheld in *Fullilove*. Like the federal provision, Richmond's is limited to five years in duration, and was not renewed when it came up for reconsideration in 1988. Like the federal provision, Richmond's contains a waiver provision freeing from its subcontracting requirements those nonminority firms that demonstrate that they cannot comply with its provisions. Like the federal provision, Richmond's has a minimal impact on innocent third parties. While the measure affects 30% of public contracting dollars, that translates to only 3% of overall Richmond area contracting.

Finally, like the federal provision, Richmond's does not interfere with any vested right of a contractor to a particular contract; instead it operates entirely prospectively. ***

The majority takes issue *** with two aspects of Richmond's tailoring *** First, the majority overlooks the fact that since 1975, Richmond has barred both discrimination by the city in awarding public contracts and discrimination by public contractors. The virtual absence of minority businesses from the city's contracting rolls, indicated by the fact that such businesses have received less than 1% of public contracting dollars, strongly suggests that this ban has not succeeded in redressing the impact of past discrimination or in preventing city contract procurement from reinforcing racial homogeneity. Second, the majority's suggestion that Richmond should have first undertaken such race-neutral measures as a program of city financing for small firms ignores the fact that such measures, while theoretically appealing, have been discredited by Congress as ineffectual in eradicating the effects of past discrimination in this very industry. ***

As for Richmond's 30% target, the majority *** ignores two important facts. First, the set-aside measure affects only 3% of overall city contracting; thus, any imprecision in tailoring has far less impact than the majority suggests. But more important, the majority ignores the fact that Richmond's 30% figure was patterned directly on the *Fullilove* precedent. Congress' 10% figure fell "roughly halfway between the present percentage of minority contractors and the percentage of minority group members in the Nation." The Richmond City Council's 30% figure similarly falls roughly halfway between the present percentage of Richmond-based minority contractors (almost zero) and the percentage of minorities in Richmond (50%). ***

Today, for the first time, a majority of this Court has adopted strict scrutiny as its standard of Equal Protection Clause review of race-conscious remedial measures. This is an unwelcome development. *** The majority's view that remedial measures undertaken by municipalities with black leadership must face a stiffer test of Equal Protection Clause scrutiny than remedial measures undertaken by municipalities with white leadership implies a lack of political maturity on the part of this Nation's elected minority officials that is totally unwarranted. Such insulting judgments have no place in constitutional jurisprudence.

Today's decision, finally, is particularly noteworthy for the daunting standard it imposes upon States and localities contemplating the use of race-conscious measures to eradicate the present effects of prior discrimination and prevent its perpetuation. The majority restricts the use of such measures to situations in which a State or locality can put forth "a prima facie case of a constitutional or statutory violation." *** The majority today sounds a full-scale retreat from the Court's longstanding solicitude to race-conscious remedial efforts "directed toward deliverance of the century-old promise of equality of economic opportunity." *Fullilove*, 448 U.S., at 463. The new and restrictive tests it applies scuttle one city's effort to surmount its discriminatory past, and imperil those of dozens more localities. *** The battle against pernicious racial discrimination or its effects is nowhere near won. I must dissent.

JUSTICE BLACKMUN, with whom JUSTICE BRENNAN joins, dissenting.

I never thought that I would live to see the day when the city of Richmond, Virginia, the cradle of the Old Confederacy, sought on its own, within a narrow confine, to lessen the stark impact of persistent discrimination. *** I am confident, however, that, given time, [the Court] one day again will do its best to fulfill the great promises of the Constitution's Preamble and of the guarantees embodied in the Bill of Rights—a fulfillment that would make this Nation very special.29

Notes

1.   **Pros and Cons of Race–Conscious Affirmative Action.** Make two lists, one of reasons for and one of reasons against race-conscious affirmative action by governmental entities. Which list do you find more compelling? Why? Do any of these reasons have anything to do with legal reasoning as opposed to policy choices? Is your choice based on empirical evidence, or is it intuitive?

2.   **Strict Scrutiny of Affirmative Action.** Think about how each of the following relates to whether strict scrutiny of racial affirmative action is appropriate:

   (a) Distrust of political processes where racial issues are involved.

   (b) Language of the Equal Protection Clause.

   (c) History and intent of the Equal Protection Clause.

   (d) Slavery, Jim Crow laws, and other racial subordination.

   (e) Concerns about "innocent victims."

   (f) Difficulties in distinguishing between invidious and benign racial classifications.

3. **Meaning of Strict Scrutiny.** It is clear now that strict scrutiny applies to race-conscious affirmative action programs, but it is unclear what proportion of such programs that standard will invalidate. Will judicial strict scrutiny here be "fatal in fact" or not? Consider both the ends and means issues posed by strict scrutiny in this context:

(a) *Ends.* The Court seems willing to accept that some "compelling governmental purposes" may exist for "benign" race discrimination. Past discrimination is an acceptable reason, if the discrimination is by the governmental unit or within that unit's jurisdiction, at least if the discrimination continues into the present. Why is the Court uncomfortable with the notion that "societal discrimination" can justify affirmative action responses by governments? Other candidates for compelling purposes are "diversity" and "role modeling." Is diversity more acceptable in some contexts, like education, than in others, like employment or contracting? And what is meant by "diversity"? "Role modeling" was rejected by the Court in the context of layoff of a white teacher to retain a black teacher. *Wygant v. Jackson Bd. of Ed.*, 476 U.S. 267 (1986). Would it be legal for a city to demand that a person hired to counsel delinquent teenagers in a predominantly-black neighborhood be black?

(b) *Means.* How specifically must the means and ends coincide? Why would Richmond define minorities to include Aleuts and other minorities, and what is it about such overinclusion that the Court finds objectionable? After *Croson*, must a city considering a set-aside for city contracting look separately at construction contracting and non-construction contracting? Must it look at plumbing versus roofing contracting?

4. **Exploring Race–Neutral Alternatives.** *Croson* requires exploration of race-neutral alternatives prior to adoption of race-conscious government programs. Would such alternatives be unconstitutional if adopted for the purpose of benefiting racial minorities? Would it be unlawful for a college to recognize all other forms of affirmative action (economics, geography, etc.) but not affirmative action based on societal race discrimination? In "gerrymandering" cases, where the lines drawn are not racial on their face, but purely geographic, the Court has held that "bizarre" lines "unexplainable on grounds other than race" are unconstitutional. The Court explained in *Miller v. Johnson*, 515 U.S. 900 (1995), that "[t]he distinction between being aware of racial motivations and being motivated by them may be difficult to make. *** [A] plaintiff must prove that the legislature subordinated traditional race-neutral districting principles, including but not limited to compactness, contiguity, respect for political subdivisions of communities defined by actual shared interests, to racial considerations."

5. ***Brown* and Affirmative Action.** Did the Court act in a race-neutral or race-conscious fashion in *Brown*? One commentator says, "The prohibition against discrimination established by *Brown* is not rooted in colorblindness at all. Instead, it is, like affirmative action, deeply race-conscious." Strauss, *The Myth of Colorblindness*, 1986 SUP. CT. REV. 99.

6. **Problem.** Advise a local governmental unit on how to establish a constitutionally permissible race-conscious set-aside program.

7. **Federal Race–Consciousness.** *Croson* concerned state and local set-aside programs. In *Adarand Constructors v. Pena*, 515 U.S. 200 (1995), a construction

company claimed that federal use of racial presumptions in providing incentives for government contractors to hire subcontractors controlled by "socially and economically disadvantaged individuals" violated the equal protection component of the Fifth Amendment Due Process Clause. The Court overruled *Metro Broadcasting,* 497 U.S. 547 (1990), which held "that 'benign' federal racial classifications need only satisfy intermediate scrutiny, even though *Croson* had recently concluded that such classifications enacted by a State must satisfy strict scrutiny." JUSTICE THOMAS concurred, saying "I believe that there is a 'moral [and] constitutional equivalence,' between laws designed to subjugate a race and those that distribute benefits on the basis of race in order to foster some current notion of equality." JUSTICE STEVENS and JUSTICE GINSBURG dissented saying:

> The Fourteenth Amendment directly empowers Congress at the same time it expressly limits the States. This is no accident. It represents our Nation's consensus, achieved after hard experience throughout our sorry history of race relations, that the Federal Government must be the primary defender of racial minorities against the States, some of which may be inclined to oppress such minorities. A rule of "congruence" that ignores a purposeful "incongruity" so fundamental to our system of government is unacceptable.

8. **Flip-flopping Justices?** Formalist arguments are aligned against extension of *Croson* to the federal sphere, just as they were when the Court "reverse-incorporated" equal protection into the due process clause of the Fifth Amendment in *Bolling v. Sharpe.* Consider the differences in text between the Fifth and Fourteenth Amendments ("due process" versus "equal protection"), the history of affirmative action following the Civil War (Federal Freedman's Bureau Acts, in which land, education, and other benefits were provided to former slaves), and Madisonian notions that the federal government would be less influenced by factional politics than state and local governments. It is unseemly for the federal government to take racial actions (invidious or benign) that the states cannot. But this is a results-oriented, political-regarding, non-originalist argument. How do you account for the fact that the Court's "conservatives" ignored these precepts and the Court's liberals embraced them?

GRUTTER v. BOLLINGER
539 U.S. 306 (2003)

JUSTICE O'CONNOR delivered the opinion of the Court.

This case requires us to decide whether the use of race as a factor in student admissions by the University of Michigan Law School (Law School) is unlawful. *** Seeking to "admit a group of students who individually and collectively are among the most capable," the Law School looks for individuals with "substantial promise for success in law school" and "a strong likelihood of succeeding in the practice of law and contributing in diverse ways to the well-being of others." More broadly, the Law School seeks "a mix of students with varying backgrounds and experiences who will respect and learn from each other." *** The [Law School's admissions] policy requires admissions officials to evaluate each applicant based on all the information available in the file, including *** an essay describing the ways in which the applicant will contribute to the life and diversity of the Law School. In reviewing an applicant's file, admissions officials must consider the applicant's undergraduate grade point average (GPA) and Law School Admissions Test (LSAT) score because they are important (if imperfect) predictors of academic success in law school. *** The policy makes clear, however, that even the highest possible score does not guarantee admission to the Law School. Nor does a low score automatically disqualify an applicant. *** So-called "'soft' variables" such as "the enthusiasm of recommenders, the quality of the undergraduate institution, the quality of the applicant's essay, and the areas and difficulty of undergraduate course selection" are all brought to bear in assessing an "applicant's likely contributions to the intellectual and social life of the institution."

The policy aspires to "achieve that diversity which has the potential to enrich everyone's education and thus make a law school class stronger than the sum of its parts." The policy does not restrict the types of diversity contributions eligible for "substantial weight" in the admissions process, but instead recognizes "many possible bases for diversity admissions." The policy does, however, reaffirm the Law School's longstanding commitment to "one particular type of diversity," that is, "racial and ethnic diversity with special reference to the inclusion of students from groups which have been historically discriminated against, like African-Americans, Hispanics and Native Americans, who without this commitment might not be represented in our student body in meaningful numbers." ***

[margin note: Michigan Law Policy goal]

Petitioner Barbara Grutter is a white Michigan resident who applied to the Law School in 1996 with a 3.8 grade point average and 161 LSAT score. The Law School initially placed petitioner on a waiting list, but subsequently rejected her application. *** Petitioner alleged that respondents discriminated against her on the basis of race in violation of the Fourteenth Amendment ***

We last addressed the use of race in public higher education over 25 years ago. In the landmark *Bakke* case, [438 U.S. 265 (1978),] we reviewed a racial set-aside program that reserved 16 out of 100 seats in a medical school class for members of certain minority groups. The decision produced six separate opinions, none of which commanded a majority of the Court. *** [T]oday we endorse JUSTICE POWELL's view that student body diversity is a compelling state interest that can justify the use of race in university admissions. *** The Law School's educational judgment that such diversity is essential to its educational mission is one to which we defer. *** Our conclusion that the Law School has a compelling interest in a diverse student body is informed by our view that attaining a diverse student body is at the heart of the Law School's proper institutional mission, and that "good faith" on the part of a university is "presumed" absent "a showing to the contrary."

[margin note: Ct. agrees diversity is a compelling school interest]

[margin note: will only disagree with action upon evidence of bad faith.]

As part of its goal of "assembling a class that is both exceptionally academically qualified and broadly diverse," the Law School seeks to "enroll a 'critical mass' of minority students." The Law School's interest is not simply "to assure within its student body some specified percentage of a particular group merely because of its race or ethnic origin." That would amount to outright racial balancing, which is patently unconstitutional. Rather, the

Law School's concept of critical mass is defined by reference to the educational benefits that diversity is designed to produce.

These benefits are substantial. *** [M]ajor American businesses have made clear that the skills needed in today's increasingly global marketplace can only be developed through exposure to widely diverse people, cultures, ideas, and viewpoints. What is more, high-ranking retired officers and civilian leaders of the United States military assert that, "[b]ased on [their] decades of experience," a "highly qualified, racially diverse officer corps *** is essential to the military's ability to fulfill its principle mission to provide national security [and] the military cannot achieve an officer corps that is *both* highly qualified *and* racially diverse unless the service academies and the ROTC used limited race-conscious recruiting and admissions policies." *** We have repeatedly acknowledged the overriding importance of preparing students for work and citizenship, describing education as pivotal to "sustaining our political and cultural heritage" with a fundamental role in maintaining the fabric of society. *** And, "[n]owhere is the importance of such openness more acute than in the context of higher education." *** Moreover, universities, and in particular, law schools, represent the training ground for a large number of our Nation's leaders. *** The pattern is even more striking when it comes to highly selective law schools. ***

In order to cultivate a set of leaders with legitimacy in the eyes of the citizenry, it is necessary that the path to leadership be visibly open to talented and qualified individuals of every race and ethnicity. *** The Law School has determined, based on its experience and expertise, that a "critical mass" of underrepresented minorities is necessary to further its compelling interest in securing the educational benefits of a diverse student body.

*** To be narrowly tailored, a race-conscious admissions program cannot use a quota system—it cannot "insulat[e] each category of applicants with certain desired qualifications from competition with all other applicants." Instead, a university may consider race or ethnicity only as a "'plus' in a particular applicant's file," without "insulat[ing] the individual from comparison with all other candidates for the available seats." *** The Law School's goal of attaining a critical mass of underrepresented minority students does not transform its program into a quota. *** [T]he number of underrepresented minority students who ultimately enroll in the Law School differs substantially from their representation in the applicant pool and varies considerably for each group from year to year.

That a race-conscious admissions program does not operate as a quota does not, by itself, satisfy the requirement of individualized consideration. *** Here, the Law School engages in a highly individualized, holistic review of each applicant's file, giving serious consideration to all the ways an applicant might contribute to a diverse educational environment. *** Unlike the program at issue in *Gratz v. Bollinger*, the Law School awards no mechanical, predetermined diversity "bonuses" based on race or ethnicity. See *Gratz* (distinguishing a race-conscious admissions program that automatically awards 20 points based on race from the Harvard plan, which considered race but "did not contemplate that any single characteristic automatically ensured a specific and identifiable contribution to a university's diversity"). *** We also find that *** the Law School's race-conscious admissions program adequately ensures that all factors that may contribute to student body diversity are meaningfully considered alongside race in admissions decisions. *** What is more, the Law School actually gives substantial weight to diversity factors besides race. ***

Petitioner and the United States argue that the Law School's plan is not narrowly tailored because race-neutral means exist to obtain the educational benefits of student body diversity that the Law School seeks. We disagree. Narrow tailoring does not require exhaustion of every conceivable race-neutral alternative. Nor does it require a university to choose between maintaining a reputation for excellence or fulfilling a commitment to provide educational opportunities to members of all racial groups. *** [I]n the context of its individualized inquiry into the possible diversity contributions of all applicants, the Law School's race-conscious admissions program does not unduly harm nonminority applicants. *** The Law School, too, concedes that all "race-conscious programs must have reasonable durational limits." *** It has been 25 years since JUSTICE POWELL first approved the use of race to further an interest in student body diversity in the context of public higher education. Since that time, the number of minority applicants with high grades and test scores has indeed increased. We expect that 25 years from now, the use of racial preferences will no longer be necessary to further the interest approved today. ***

JUSTICE GINSBURG, with whom JUSTICE BREYER joins, concurring.

*** From today's vantage point, one may hope, but not firmly forecast, that over the next generation's span, progress toward nondiscrimination and genuinely equal opportunity will make it safe to sunset affirmative action.

JUSTICE SCALIA, with whom JUSTICE THOMAS joins, concurring in part and dissenting in part.

*** The "educational benefit" that the University of Michigan seeks to achieve by racial discrimination consists, according to the Court, of "'cross-racial understanding,'" and "'better prepar[ation of] students for an increasingly diverse workforce and society,'" all of which is necessary not only for work, but also for good "citizenship". This is not, of course, an "educational benefit" on which students will be graded on their Law School transcript (Works and Plays Well with Others: B+) or tested by the bar examiners (Q: Describe in 500 words or less your cross-racial understanding). For it is a lesson of life rather than law *** If it is appropriate for the University of Michigan Law School to use racial discrimination for the purpose of putting together a "critical mass" that will convey generic lessons in socialization and good citizenship, surely it is no less appropriate—indeed, *particularly* appropriate—for the civil service system of the State of Michigan to do so. There, also, those exposed to "critical masses" of certain races will presumably become better Americans, better Michiganders, better civil servants. And surely private employers cannot be criticized—indeed, should be praised—if they also "teach" good citizenship to their adult employees through a patriotic, all-American system of racial discrimination in hiring. The nonminority individuals who are deprived of a legal education, a civil service job, or any job at all by reason of their skin color will surely understand.

*** [T]oday's *Grutter-Gratz* split double header seems perversely designed to prolong the controversy and the litigation. Some future lawsuits will presumably focus on whether the discriminatory scheme in question contains enough evaluation of the applicant "as an individual," and sufficiently avoids "separate admissions tracks" to fall under *Grutter* rather than *Gratz*. *** And still other suits may claim that the institution's racial preferences have gone below or above the mystical *Grutter*-approved "critical mass." Finally, litigation can be expected on behalf of minority groups intentionally short changed in the institution's composition of its generic minority "critical mass." ***

[handwritten: doesn't like the balancing test established]

JUSTICE THOMAS, with whom JUSTICE SCALIA joins ***, concurring in part and dissenting in part.

*** The Law School's argument, as facile as it is, can only be understood in one way: Classroom aesthetics yield educational benefits, racially discriminatory admissions policies are required to achieve the right racial mix, and therefore the policies are required to achieve the educational benefits. It is the *educational benefits* that are the end, or allegedly compelling state interest, not "diversity." *** Under the proper standard, there is no pressing public necessity in maintaining a public law school at all and, it follows, certainly not an elite law school. Likewise, marginal improvements in legal education do not qualify as a compelling state interest. *** Michigan has no compelling interest in having a law school at all, much less an *elite* one. *** The only cognizable state interests vindicated by operating a public law school are, therefore, the education of that State's citizens and the training of that State's lawyers. *** The Law School today, however, does precious little training of those attorneys who will serve the citizens of Michigan. ***

[handwritten: improving the educational quality at a public law school is not a state interest]

[T]he Court holds, implicitly and under the guise of narrow tailoring, that the Law School has a compelling state interest in doing what it wants to do. I cannot agree. First, under strict scrutiny, the Law School's assessment of the benefits of racial discrimination and devotion to the admissions status quo are not entitled to any sort of deference, grounded in the First Amendment or anywhere else. Second, even if its "academic selectivity" must be maintained at all costs along with racial discrimination, the Court ignores the fact that other top law schools have succeeded in meeting their aesthetic demands without racial discrimination. *** The Court relies heavily on social science evidence to justify its deference. The Court never acknowledges, however, the growing evidence that racial (and other sorts) of heterogeneity actually impairs learning among black students. *** Contained within today's majority opinion is the seed of a new constitutional justification for a concept I thought long and rightly rejected–racial segregation.

[handwritten: fails under strict scrutiny]

[handwritten: minorities actually do worse]

[handwritten: other schools do just fine w/o it.]

*** [M]uch has been made of the fact that elite institutions utilize a so-called "legacy" preference to give the children of alumni an advantage in admissions. ***The Equal Protection Clause does not, however, prohibit the use of unseemly legacy preferences or many other kinds of arbitrary admissions procedures. What the Equal Protection Clause does prohibit are classifications made on the basis of race. So while legacy preferences can stand under the Constitution, racial discrimination cannot.[10]   ***

takes issue with legacy policies being allowed to discriminate

The Law School tantalizes unprepared students with the promise of a University of Michigan degree and all of the opportunities that it offers. These overmatched students take the bait, only to find that they cannot succeed in the cauldron of competition. *** "These programs stamp minorities with a badge of inferiority and may cause them to develop dependencies or to adopt an attitude that they are 'entitled' to preferences." ***

no certainty they will ever do well

Under today's decision, it is still the case that racial discrimination that does not help a university to enroll an unspecified number, or "critical mass," of underrepresented minority students is unconstitutional. *** The majority does not and cannot rest its time limitation on any evidence that the gap in credentials between black and white students is shrinking or will be gone in that timeframe. In recent years there has been virtually no change, for example, in the proportion of law school applicants with LSAT scores of 165 and higher who are black. *** Indeed, the very existence of racial discrimination of the type practiced by the Law School may impede the narrowing of the LSAT testing gap. *** Whites *** aspiring to admission at the Law School have every incentive to improve their score to levels above that range. Blacks, on the other hand, are nearly guaranteed admission ***

disagree w/ majority that trends will change

CHIEF JUSTICE REHNQUIST, with whom JUSTICE SCALIA, JUSTICE KENNEDY, and JUSTICE THOMAS join, dissenting.

*** In practice, the Law School's program bears little or no relation to its asserted goal of achieving "critical mass." ***From 1995 through 2000, the Law School admitted between 1,130 and 1,310 students. Of those, between 13 and 19 were Native American, between 91 and 108 were African-Americans, and between 47 and 56 were Hispanic. If the Law School is admitting between 91 and 108 African-Americans in order to achieve "critical mass," thereby preventing African-American students from feeling "isolated or like spokespersons for their race," one would think that a number of the same order of magnitude would be necessary to accomplish the same purpose for Hispanics and Native Americans. *** *** Finally, I believe that the Law School's program fails strict scrutiny because it is devoid of any reasonably precise time limit on the Law School's use of race in admissions. *** The Court suggests a possible 25-year limitation [but] *** permit[s] the Law School's use of racial preferences on a seemingly permanent basis. ***

Needs to be more balanced and not help just AA=

needs a time limit.

---

[10] Were this Court to have the courage to forbid the use of racial discrimination in admissions, legacy preferences (and similar practices) might quickly become less popular–a possibility not lost, I am certain, on the elites (both individual and institutional) supporting the Law School in this case.

JUSTICE KENNEDY, dissenting.

*** It remains to point out how critical mass becomes inconsistent with individual consideration in some more specific aspects of the admissions process. *** There was little deviation among admitted minority students during the years from 1995 to 1998. The percentage of enrolled minorities fluctuated only by 0.3%, from 13.5% to 13.8%. *** The narrow fluctuation band raises an inference that the Law School subverted individual determination, and strict scrutiny requires the Law School to overcome the inference. ***

[handwritten margin note: policy has not changed school diverst trends]

Notes

1. ***Grutter's* Sibling.** The companion case to *Grutter*, *Gratz v. Bollinger*, 539 U.S. 244 (2003), held that the University of Michigan undergraduate admissions point-bonus system was unconstitutional. Here are a few central points made in the *Gratz* opinions:

> CHIEF JUSTICE REHNQUIST for the Court: *** Respondents contend that '[t]he volume of applications and the presentation of applicant information make it impractical for [LSA] to use the *** admissions system' upheld by the Court today in *Grutter*. But the fact that the implementation of a program capable of providing individualized consideration might present administrative challenges does not render constitutional an otherwise problematic system. *** [B]ecause the University's use of race in its current freshman admissions policy is not narrowly tailored to achieve respondents' asserted compelling interest in diversity, the admissions policy violates the Equal Protection Clause of the Fourteenth Amendment. ***

> JUSTICE O'CONNOR, concurring: *** Even the most outstanding national high school leader could never receive more than five points for his or her accomplishments—a mere quarter of the points automatically assigned to an underrepresented minority solely based on the fact of his or her race. *** [T]he selection index, by setting up automatic, predetermined point allocations for the soft variables, ensures that the diversity contributions of applicants cannot be individually assessed. This policy stands in sharp contrast to the law school's admissions plan ***

> JUSTICE SOUTER, with whom JUSTICE GINSBURG joins, dissenting: *** The record does not describe a system with a quota like the one struck down in *Bakke*, which 'insulate[d]' all nonminority candidates from competition from certain seats. *** The college simply does by a numbered scale what the law school accomplishes in its 'holistic review'; the distinction does not imply that applicants to the undergraduate college are denied individualized consideration or a fair chance to compete on the basis of all the various merits their applications may disclose. *** Equal protection cannot become an exercise in which the winners are the ones who hide the ball. ***

> JUSTICE GINSBURG, with whom JUSTICE SOUTER joins, dissenting: *** [A]s I see it, government decisionmakers may properly distinguish

between policies of exclusion and inclusion. *** Our jurisprudence ranks race a 'suspect' category, 'not because [race] is inevitably an impermissible classification, but because it is one which usually, to our national shame, has been drawn for the purpose of maintaining racial inequality.' *** To avoid conflict with the equal protection clause, a classification that denies a benefit, causes harm, or imposes a burden must not be based on race. In that sense, the Constitution is color blind. But the Constitution is color conscious to prevent discrimination being perpetuated and to undo the effects of past discrimination.' ***

2. **Litigation: Boom or Bust?** JUSTICE SCALIA predicts more litigation and describes what he believes are the fault lines. Do you agree? Consider what college and university admissions policies will read like after *Grutter*. Consider how these policies will be administered. How likely are you to prevail in a suit if you are a rejected white applicant and believe you would have been admitted had you been a minority?

3. **Other Academic Contexts.** How will *Grutter* affect scholarship programs that target minorities? Need-based scholarships mainly given to minority students? Will minority summer programs before college and law school remain viable? Will the deference to educators be as strong in these areas as in the admissions context?

4. **Non-academic Contexts.** How, if at all, will affirmative action programs in government employment and set-asides be affected? Will *Grutter* have any effect on private employers' affirmative action programs?

5. **Discrimination Among Minorities.** Will schools eliminate admissions processes that provide (either explicitly or implicitly) a larger plus for African-American candidates than Hispanic candidates? Can schools refuse to consider Asian-Americans as minorities entitled to any affirmative action plus?

PARENTS INVOLVED v. SEATTLE SCHOOL DIST. NO. 1
551 U.S. 701 (2007)

CHIEF JUSTICE ROBERTS announced the judgment of the Court, and delivered the opinion of the Court with respect to Parts I, II, III-A, and III-C, and an opinion with respect to Parts III-B and IV, in which JUSTICES SCALIA, THOMAS, and ALITO join.

*** The Seattle school district classifies children as white or nonwhite; the Jefferson County school district as black or "other." In Seattle, this racial classification is used to allocate slots in oversubscribed high schools. In Jefferson County, it is used to make certain elementary school assignments and to rule on transfer requests. In each case, the school district relies upon an individual student's race in assigning that student to a particular school, so that the racial balance at the school falls within a predetermined range based on the racial composition of the school district as a whole. *** Both cases present the same underlying legal question-whether a public school that had not operated legally segregated schools or has been found to be unitary may choose to classify students by race and rely upon that classification in making school assignments.

III

A

*** [W]hen the government distributes burdens or benefits on the basis of individual racial classifications, that action is reviewed under strict scrutiny. *** [O]ur prior cases, in evaluating the use of racial classifications in the school context, have recognized two interests that qualify as compelling. The first is the compelling interest of remedying the effects of past intentional discrimination. Yet the Seattle public schools have not shown that they were ever segregated by law, and were not subject to court-ordered desegregation decrees. The Jefferson County *** had remedied the constitutional wrong that allowed race-based assignments. Any continued use of race must be justified on some other basis.

The second government interest we have recognized as compelling for purposes of strict scrutiny is the interest in diversity in higher education upheld in *Grutter*. *** The diversity interest was not focused on race alone but encompassed "all factors that may contribute to student body diversity." *** In the present cases, by contrast, race is not considered as part of a broader effort to achieve "exposure to widely diverse people, cultures, ideas, and viewpoints"; race, for some students, is determinative standing alone. *** [Race] is not simply one factor weighed with others in reaching a decision, as in *Grutter*; it is *the* factor. ***

Even when it comes to race, the plans here employ only a limited notion of diversity, viewing race exclusively in white/nonwhite terms in Seattle and black/"other" terms in Jefferson County. *** [U]nder the Seattle plan, a school with 50 percent Asian-American students and 50 percent white students but no African-American, Native-American, or Latino students would qualify as balanced, while a school with 30 percent Asian-American, 25 percent African-American, 25 percent Latino, and 20 percent white students would not. It is hard to understand how a plan that could allow these results can be viewed as being concerned with achieving enrollment that is "'broadly diverse" ***

B

Perhaps recognizing that reliance on *Grutter* cannot sustain their plans, both school districts assert additional interests, distinct from the interest upheld in *Grutter*, to justify their race-based assignments. *** Seattle contends that its use of race helps to reduce racial concentration in schools and to ensure that racially concentrated housing patterns do not prevent nonwhite students from having access to the most desirable schools. Jefferson County has articulated a similar goal, phrasing its interest in terms of educating its students "in a racially integrated environment." ***

[Moreover,] it is clear that the racial classifications employed by the districts are not narrowly tailored to the goal of achieving the educational and social benefits asserted to flow from racial diversity. In design and operation, the plans are directed only to racial balance, pure and simple, an objective this Court has repeatedly condemned as illegitimate. ***

The districts offer no evidence that the level of racial diversity necessary to achieve the asserted educational benefits happens to coincide with the racial demographics of the respective school districts-or rather the white/nonwhite or black/"other" balance of the districts, since that is the only diversity addressed by the plans. *** [T]hey offer no definition of the interest that suggests it differs from racial balance. ***

C

The districts assert, as they must, that the way in which they have employed individual racial classifications is necessary to achieve their stated ends. The minimal effect these classifications have on student assignments, however, suggests that other means would be effective. Seattle's racial tiebreaker results, in the end, only in shifting a small number of students between schools. *** While we do not suggest that *greater* use of race would be preferable, the minimal impact of the districts' racial classifications on school enrollment casts doubt on the necessity of using racial classifications. In *Grutter*, the consideration of race was viewed as indispensable in more than tripling minority representation at the law school-from 4 to 14.5 percent. ***

IV

*** If the need for the racial classifications embraced by the school districts is unclear, even on the districts' own terms, the costs are undeniable. *** As the Court explained in *Rice* v. *Cayetano*, 528 U. S. 495, 517 (2000), "[o]ne of the principal reasons race is treated as a forbidden classification is that it demeans the dignity and worth of a person to be judged by ancestry instead of by his or her own merit and essential qualities."

*** In *Brown* v. *Board of Education*, 347 U. S. 483 (1954) (*Brown I*), we held that segregation deprived black children of equal educational opportunities regardless of whether school facilities and other tangible factors were equal, because government classification and separation on grounds of race themselves denoted inferiority. It was not the inequality of the facilities but the fact of legally separating children on the basis of race on which the Court relied to find a constitutional violation in 1954. The next Term, we accordingly stated that "full compliance" with *Brown I* required school districts "to achieve a system of determining admission to the public schools *on a nonracial basis*." *** What do the racial classifications do in these cases, if not determine admission to a public school on a racial basis? ***

JUSTICE THOMAS, concurring.

*** Contrary to the dissent's arguments, resegregation is not occurring in Seattle or Louisville; these school boards have no present interest in remedying past segregation; and these race-based student-assignment programs do not serve any compelling state interest. Accordingly, the plans are unconstitutional. *** Racial imbalance is not segregation, and the mere incantation of terms like resegregation and remediation cannot make up the difference. ***

Just as the school districts lack an interest in preventing resegregation, they also have no present interest in remedying past segregation. *** The dissent asserts that racially balanced schools improve educational outcomes for black children. In support, the dissent unquestioningly cites certain social science research to support propositions that are hotly disputed among social scientists. In reality, it is far from apparent that coerced racial mixing has any educational benefits, much less that integration is necessary to black achievement. *** Furthermore, it is unclear whether increased interracial contact improves racial attitudes and relations. ***

Most of the dissent's criticisms of today's result can be traced to its rejection of the color-blind Constitution. *** The dissent appears to pin its interpretation of the Equal Protection Clause to current societal practice and expectations, deference to local officials, likely practical consequences, and reliance on previous statements from this and other courts. *** [T]he dissent would constitutionalize today's faddish social theories ***. The Constitution is not that malleable. *** [I]f our history has taught us anything, it has taught us to beware of elites bearing racial theories. ***

JUSTICE KENNEDY, concurring in part and concurring in the judgment.

*** Diversity, depending on its meaning and definition, is a compelling educational goal a school district may pursue. *** [The plurality opinion is too dismissive of the legitimate interest government has in ensuring all people have equal opportunity regardless of their race. The plurality's postulate that "[t]he way to stop discrimination on the basis of race is to stop discriminating on the basis of race," is not sufficient to decide these cases. ***

School boards may pursue the goal of bringing together students of diverse backgrounds and races through other means, including strategic site selection of new schools; drawing attendance zones with general recognition of the demographics of neighborhoods; allocating resources for special programs; recruiting students and faculty in a targeted fashion; and tracking enrollments, performance, and other statistics by race. These mechanisms are race conscious but do not lead to different treatment based on a classification that tells each student he or she is to be defined by race, so it is unlikely any of them would demand strict scrutiny to be found permissible. *** Assigning to each student a personal designation according to a crude system of individual racial classifications is quite a different matter; and the legal analysis changes accordingly. ***

This Nation has a moral and ethical obligation to fulfill its historic commitment to creating an integrated society that ensures equal opportunity for all of its children. *** What the government is not permitted to do, absent a showing of necessity not made here, is to classify every student on the basis of race and to assign each of them to schools based on that classification. Crude measures of this sort threaten to reduce children to racial chits valued and traded according to one school' s supply and another' s demand. *** The decision today should not prevent school districts from continuing the important work of bringing together students of different racial, ethnic, and economic backgrounds. ***

JUSTICE STEVENS, dissenting.

*** There is a cruel irony in The Chief Justice's reliance on our decision in *Brown* v. *Board of Education*. *** The Chief Justice fails to note that it was only black schoolchildren who were so ordered; indeed, the history books do not tell stories of white children struggling to attend black schools. *** It is my firm conviction that no Member of the Court that I joined in 1975 would have agreed with today's decision.

JUSTICE BREYER, with whom JUSTICE STEVENS, JUSTICE SOUTER, and JUSTICE GINSBURG join, dissenting.

*** [T]he Equal Protection Clause permits local school boards to use race-conscious criteria to achieve positive race-related goals, even when the Constitution does not compel it. *** [T]he districts' plans reflect efforts to overcome a history of segregation, embody the results of broad experience and community consultation, seek to expand student choice while reducing the need for mandatory busing, and use race-conscious criteria in highly limited ways that diminish the use of race compared to preceding integration efforts. They do not seek to award a scarce commodity on the basis of merit, for they are not magnet schools; rather, by design and in practice, they offer substantially equivalent academic programs and electives. Although some parents or children prefer some schools over others, school popularity has varied significantly over the years. *** In a word, the school plans under review do not involve the kind of race-based harm that has led this Court, in other contexts, to find the use of race-conscious criteria unconstitutional. ***

*** The compelling interest at issue here, then, includes an effort to eradicate the remnants, not of general "societal discrimination," but of primary and secondary school segregation; it includes an effort to create school environments that provide better educational opportunities for all children; it includes an effort to help create citizens better prepared to know, to understand, and to work with people of all races and backgrounds, thereby furthering the kind of democratic government our Constitution foresees. If an educational interest that combines these three elements is not "compelling," what is? ***

I next ask whether the plans before us are "narrowly tailored" to achieve these "compelling" objectives. *** Several factors *** lead me to conclude that the boards' use of race-conscious criteria in these plans passes even the strictest "tailoring" test. First, the race-conscious criteria at issue only help set the outer bounds of *broad* ranges. *** Second, broad-range limits on voluntary school choice plans are less burdensome, and hence more narrowly tailored, than other race-conscious restrictions this Court has previously approved. *** Third, the manner in which the school boards developed these plans itself reflects "narrow tailoring." Each plan was devised to overcome a history of segregated public schools. Each plan embodies the results of local experience and community consultation. Each plan is the product of a process that has sought to enhance student choice, while diminishing the need for mandatory busing. And each plan's use of race-conscious elements is *diminished* compared to the use of race in preceding integration plans. ***

Nor could the school districts have accomplished their desired aims (*e.g.*, avoiding forced busing, countering white flight, maintaining racial diversity) by other means. *** [T]oday's opinion will require setting aside the laws of several States and many local communities. *** *[D]e facto* resegregation is on the rise. It is reasonable to conclude that such resegregation can create serious educational, social, and civic problems. *** Yet the plurality would deprive them of at least one tool that some districts now consider vital-the limited use of broad race-conscious student population ranges. ***

Finally, what of the hope and promise of *Brown?* For much of this Nation's history, the races remained divided. It was not long ago that people of different races drank from separate fountains, rode on separate buses, and studied in separate schools. In this Court's finest hour, *Brown* v. *Board of Education* challenged this history and helped to change it. For *Brown* held out a promise. It was a promise embodied in three Amendments designed to make citizens of slaves. It was the promise of true racial equality-not as a matter of fine words on paper, but as a matter of everyday life in the Nation's cities and schools. It was about the nature of a democracy that must work for all Americans. It sought one law, one Nation, one people, not simply as a matter of legal principle but in terms of how we actually live. *** Today, almost 50 years later, attitudes toward race in this Nation have changed dramatically. Many parents, white and black alike, want their children to attend schools with children of different races. Indeed, the very school districts that once spurned integration now strive for it. The long history of their efforts reveals the complexities and difficulties they have faced. And in light of those challenges, they have asked us not to take from their hands the instruments they have used to rid their schools of racial segregation, instruments that they believe are needed to overcome the problems of cities divided by race and poverty. *** The last half-century has witnessed great strides toward racial equality, but we have not yet realized the promise of *Brown.* ***

Notes

1. ***Brown* and *Parents Involved*.** Is *Parents Involved* the most important equal protection decision since *Brown?* Who has the better argument about the meaning of *Brown?*

2. **Affirmative Action**. Is the application of strict scrutiny in *Parents Involved* faithful to *Croson, Adarand, Grutter*, and *Gratz?*

3. **The Kennedy Concurrence—Compelling Interest**. JUSTICE KENNEDY's opinion is important because it has the narrowest rationale for why the Seattle and Louisville plans violated equal protection. He finds a compelling interest for public school districts "in increasing diversity, including *** avoiding racial isolation." What is "racial isolation" in the context of school demographics? Could we agree that if 90% of a school is one racial group, a school district should be able to reduce that racial isolation? Could a school try to reduce less dramatic disparities, say, reducing a 70%-30% disparity to 65%-35%? What if the minorities are not all one race? What role should the demographics of the district as a whole (or a multi-district area) play in framing what counts as "racial isolation?"

4.   **The Kennedy Concurrence—Narrow Tailoring.**   JUSTICE KENNEDY finds that the Seattle and Louisville plans are not narrowly tailored; neither district shows that "there is no other way to avoid racial isolation in the school districts" other than by "classifying individual students because of their race," perhaps causing them "hurt or anger of the type the Constitution prevents." He suggests that such student assignments might consider race, but only as "one component" along with other demographic factors. This sounds like the *Grutter-Gratz* split, but the context of an "open to all" public school district is quite different from highly selective admissions at the University of Michigan. Could school districts assign students to schools on the basis of race coupled with an assessment of whether students were academically gifted, athletically talented, or from under-represented socio-economic groups?

5.   **The Kennedy Dictum.** JUSTICE KENNEDY suggests more broadly that the following "mechanisms are race conscious but do not lead to different treatment ***so it is unlikely any of them would demand strict scrutiny": "strategic site selection of new schools; drawing attendance zones with general recognition of the demographics of neighborhoods; allocating resources for special programs; recruiting students and faculty in a targeted fashion; and tracking enrollments, performance, and other statistics by race." Do you agree that these mechanisms will not trigger strict scrutiny? Will Kennedy's dictum likely spur school boards and parents to discuss and implement new strategies?

6.   **Applying *Parents Involved*.** *Comfort v. Lynn School Dist.*, 418 F.3d 1 (1st Cir. 2005) (en banc) upheld a race-based student assignment plan. Here are the main differences in that plan and the *Parents Involved* plans: (1) Lynn's plan affects only students wishing to transfer from neighborhood schools and applies equally to all grades (1-12); (2) the schools in Lynn are uniform (no school is superior) with no unique programs (magnets); (3) all children have the right to attend their neighborhood schools; (4) no racial group is harmed, but some individuals may have transfer requests denied (because their race would not enhance the racial diversity at the school requested); (5) Lynn's plan is not underinclusive (Seattle only excludes students from over-subscribed schools); (6) Lynn has nothing like Seattle's African-American Academy; (7) students can (and do) change their racial self-designations; and (8) students in Lynn denied transfers on racial mix grounds can seek transfer for non race-related reasons. Is *Comfort* good law after *Parents Involved*?

7.   **Circumvention of *Parents Involved*?** Professor Michael Klarman (UVA Law School) was quoted by the NEW YORK TIMES three days after *Parents Involved* as follows: "Just as *Brown* produced massive resistance in the South and therefore had little impact on desegregation for a decade, this decision is going to be similarly inconsequential *** because there are so many opportunities for committed school boards to circumvent it." Professor Peter Schuck (Yale Law School) was quoted in the same article as saying: "[T]hey will look for proxies for race."   Do you agree with these professors?   What "opportunities *** to circumvent" or "proxies for race" would you try if you were a school board member committed to diversity or reducing racial isolation?

9.   **Federal and State Legislative Responses?** A number of analysts trace the success of desegregation to legislation (The Civil Rights Act of 1964) threatening to cut off federal funding to school districts that did not desegregate. Would it be constitutional for Congress to threaten funding cuts for school

districts that try to circumvent *Parents Involved*? Would it violate equal protection for state legislatures to bar school board race-consciousness? Could states or the federal government pass legislation supporting integration, such as facilitating student transfers out of urban poor-performing schools to suburban high-performing schools?

10. Higher Education Reprise. The Supreme Court twice reexamined affirmative action in higher education in a suit brought by a Caucasian applicant against the University of Texas. Both opinions were written by JUSTICE KENNEDY. In the first, *Fisher v. University of Texas at Austin*, 133 S. Ct. 2411 (2013), he wrote for the entire Court other than JUSTICE GINSBERG:

"Texas *** grants automatic admission to any public state college, including the University, to all students in the top 10% of their class at high school in Texas *** The University's revised admissions process, coupled with the operation of the Top Ten Percent Law, resulted in a more racially diverse environment at the University. *** The University *** concluded that [it] lacked a "critical mass" of minority students and that to remedy the deficiency it was necessary to give explicit consideration to race in the undergraduate admissions program. *** Race is not assigned an explicit numerical value, but *** is a meaningful factor. *** [A] university's "educational judgment that such diversity is essential to its educational mission is one to which we defer. *** [H]owever, there must still be a further judicial determination that the admissions process meets strict scrutiny in its implementation. The University must prove that the means chosen to attain diversity are narrowly tailored to that goal. On this point, the University receives no deference. *** Narrow tailoring *** involves careful judicial inquiry into whether a university could achieve sufficient diversity without using racial classifications. *** [S]trict scrutiny imposes on the university the ultimate burden of demonstrating, before turning to racial classification, that available, workable race-neutral alternatives do not suffice. *** [T]he Court of Appeals held petitioner could challenge only "whether [the University's] decision to reintroduce race as a factor in admissions was made in good faith" [and] would "presume the University acted in good faith" and place on petitioner the burden of rebutting that presumption. *** [This is] at odds with *Grutter*'s command *** Strict scrutiny must not be "strict in theory, but fatal in fact." But the opposite is also true. Strict scrutiny must not be strict in theory but feeble in fact."

The Court remanded, the Fifth Circuit upheld its earlier decision, and the Court rendered the following decision by a 5-3 majority in 2016 subsequent to JUSTICE SCALIA'S death.

FISHER v. UNIVERSITY OF TEXAS
136 S. Ct. 2198 (2016)

JUSTICE KENNEDY delivered the opinion of the Court.

*** *Fisher I* set forth three controlling principles relevant to assessing the constitutionality of a public university's affirmative-action program. First, *** "[s]trict scrutiny requires the university to demonstrate with clarity that its "purpose or interest is both constitutionally permissible and substantial, and that its use of the classification is necessary . . . to the accomplishment of its purpose." *** Second, *Fisher I* confirmed that 'the decision to pursue 'the educational benefits that flow from student body diversity' . . . is, in substantial measure, an academic judgment to which some, but not complete, judicial deference is proper.' *** Third, *Fisher I* clarified that no deference is owed when determining whether the use of race is narrowly tailored to achieve the university's permissible goals. *** Though '[n]arrow tailoring does not require exhaustion of every conceivable race-neutral alternative' or 'require a university to choose between maintaining a reputation for excellence [and] fulfilling a commitment to provide educational opportunities to members of all racial groups,' it does impose 'on the university the ultimate burden of demonstrating' that 'race-neutral alternatives' that are both 'available' and 'workable' 'do not suffice.' ***

The University's program is *sui generis*. Unlike other approaches to college admissions considered by this Court, it combines holistic review with a percentage plan. *** Because petitioner did not graduate in the top 10 percent of her high school class, she was categorically ineligible for more than three-fourths of the slots in the incoming freshman class. It seems quite plausible, then, to think that petitioner would have had a better chance of being admitted to the University if the school used race-conscious holistic review to select its entire incoming class, as was the case in *Grutter*. ***

Petitioner's acceptance of the Top Ten Percent Plan *** has led to a record that is almost devoid of information about the students who secured admission to the University through the Plan. *** If the University had no reason to think that it could deviate from the Top Ten Percent Plan, it similarly had no reason to keep extensive data on the Plan or the students admitted under it--particularly in the years before *Fisher I* clarified the stringency of the strict-scrutiny burden for a school that employs race-conscious review. Under the circumstances of this case, then, a remand would do nothing more than prolong a suit that has already persisted for eight years and cost the parties on both sides significant resources. *** [This] may limit its value for prospective guidance. *** The University's examination of the data it has acquired in the years since petitioner's application *** must proceed with full respect for the constraints imposed by the Equal Protection Clause. The type of data collected, and the manner in which it is considered, will have a significant bearing on how the University must shape its admissions policy to satisfy strict scrutiny in the years to come. ***

In seeking to reverse the judgment of the Court of Appeals, petitioner makes four arguments. First, she argues that the University has not articulated its compelling interest with sufficient clarity [and] must set forth more precisely the level of minority enrollment that would constitute a 'critical mass.' *** [A] university may institute a race-conscious admissions program as a means of obtaining 'the educational benefits that flow from student body diversity.' As this Court has said, enrolling a diverse student body 'promotes cross-racial understanding, helps to break down racial stereotypes, and enables students to better understand persons of different races.' Equally important, 'student body diversity promotes learning outcomes, and better prepares students for an increasingly diverse workforce and society.' *** [A]sserting an interest in the educational benefits of diversity writ large is insufficient. A university's goals cannot be elusory or amorphous--they must be sufficiently measurable to permit judicial scrutiny of the policies adopted to reach them.

The record reveals that in first setting forth its current admissions policy, the University articulated concrete and precise goals ***: the destruction of stereotypes, the 'promot[ion of] cross-racial understanding,' the preparation of a student body 'for an increasingly diverse workforce and society,' and the 'cultivat[ion of] a set of leaders with legitimacy in the eyes of the citizenry.' Later in the proposal, the University explains that it strives to provide an 'academic environment' that offers a 'robust exchange of ideas, exposure to differing cultures, preparation for the challenges of an increasingly diverse workforce, and acquisition of competencies required of future leaders.' All of these objectives, as a general matter, mirror the 'compelling interest' this Court has approved in its prior cases.

The University has provided in addition a 'reasoned, principled explanation' for its decision to pursue these goals. The University's 39-page proposal was written following a year-long study, which concluded that '[t]he use of race-neutral policies and programs ha[d] not been successful' in 'provid[ing] an educational setting that fosters cross-racial understanding, provid[ing] enlightened discussion and learning, [or] prepar[ing] students to function in an increasingly diverse workforce and society.' Further support for the University's conclusion can be found in the depositions and affidavits from various admissions officers, all of whom articulate the same, consistent 'reasoned, principled explanation.' Petitioner's contention that the University's goal was insufficiently concrete is rebutted by the record.

Second, petitioner argues that the University has no need to consider race because it had already 'achieved critical mass' by 2003 using the Top Ten Percent Plan and race-neutral holistic review. Petitioner is correct that a university bears a heavy burden in showing that it had not obtained the educational benefits of diversity before it turned to a race-conscious plan. *** Before changing its policy the University conducted 'months of study and deliberation, including retreats, interviews, [and] review of data,' and concluded that '[t]he use of race-neutral policies and programs ha[d] not been successful in achieving' sufficient racial diversity at the University. At no stage in this litigation has petitioner challenged the University's good faith in conducting its studies, and the Court properly declines to consider the extrarecord materials the dissent relies upon, many of which are tangential to this case at best and none of which the University has had a full opportunity to respond to. *** The record itself contains significant evidence, both statistical and anecdotal, in support of the University's position *** consistent stagnation in terms of the percentage of minority students enrolling at the University from 1996 to 2002 *** [and] evidence that minority students admitted *** experienced feelings of loneliness and isolation. *** 52 percent of undergraduate classes with at least five students had no African-American students enrolled in them, and 27 percent had only one African-American student. ***

Third, petitioner argues that considering race was not necessary because such consideration has had only a 'minimal impact' in advancing the [University's] compelling interest. Again, the record does not support this assertion. *** The fact that race consciousness played a role in only a small portion of admissions decisions should be a hallmark of narrow tailoring, not evidence of unconstitutionality.

Petitioner's final argument is that 'there are numerous other available race-neutral means of achieving' the University's compelling interest. A review of the record reveals, however, that, at the time of petitioner's application, none of her proposed alternatives was a workable means for the University to attain the benefits of diversity it sought. ***

In short, none of petitioner's suggested alternatives--nor other proposals considered or discussed in the course of this litigation--have been shown to be 'available' and 'workable' means through which the University could have met its educational goals, as it understood and defined them in 2008. The University has thus met its burden of showing that the admissions policy it used at the time it rejected petitioner's application was narrowly tailored. ***

A university is in large part defined by those intangible 'qualities which are incapable of objective measurement but which make for greatness.' Considerable deference is owed to a university in defining those intangible characteristics, like student body diversity, that are central to its identity and educational mission. But still, it remains an enduring challenge to our Nation's education system to reconcile the pursuit of diversity with the constitutional promise of equal treatment and dignity.

In striking this sensitive balance, public universities, like the States themselves, can serve as 'laboratories for experimentation.' The University of Texas at Austin has a special opportunity to learn and to teach. The University now has at its disposal valuable data about the manner in which different approaches to admissions may foster diversity or instead dilute it. The University must continue to use this data to scrutinize the fairness of its admissions program; to assess whether changing demographics have undermined the need for a race-conscious policy; and to identify the effects, both positive and negative, of the affirmative-action measures it deems necessary.

The Court's affirmance of the University's admissions policy today does not necessarily mean the University may rely on that same policy without refinement. It is the University's ongoing obligation to engage in constant deliberation and continued reflection regarding its admissions policies. ***

JUSTICE THOMAS, dissenting.

*** I write separately to reaffirm that 'a State's use of race in higher education admissions decisions is categorically prohibited by the Equal Protection Clause.' ***That constitutional imperative does not change in the face of a 'faddish theor[y]' that racial discrimination may produce 'educational benefits.' *** I would overrule *Grutter***.

JUSTICE ALITO, with whom THE CHIEF JUSTICE and JUSTICE THOMAS join, dissenting.

Something strange has happened since our prior decision in this case [*Fisher I*]. *** On remand, UT failed to do what our prior decision demanded. The University has still not identified with any degree of specificity the interests that its use of race and ethnicity is supposed to serve. *** [I]ts efforts have been shifting, unpersuasive, and, at times, less than candid. When it adopted its race-based plan, UT said that the plan was needed to promote classroom diversity. *** But UT *** presents no evidence that its admissions officers, in administering the 'holistic' component of its plan, make any effort to determine whether an African-American, Hispanic, or Asian-American student is likely to enroll in classes in which minority students are underrepresented. *** Nor has UT explained why the underrepresentation of Asian-American students in many classes justifies its plan, which discriminates *against* those students. *** UT has [also] claimed that its plan is needed to achieve a 'critical mass' of African-American and Hispanic students, but it has never explained what this term means. *** UT has also claimed at times that the race-based component of its plan is needed because the Top Ten Percent Plan admits *the wrong kind* of African-American and Hispanic students, namely, students from poor families who attend schools in which the student body is predominantly African-American or Hispanic. *** After making this argument in its first trip to this Court, UT apparently had second thoughts, and in the latest round of briefing UT has attempted to disavow ever having made the argument. But it did, and the argument turns affirmative action on its head. Affirmative-action programs were created to help *disadvantaged* students. ***

Although UT's primary argument is that it need not point to any interest more specific than 'the educational benefits of diversity,' it has *** identified four more specific goals: demographic parity, classroom diversity, intraracial diversity, and avoiding racial isolation. Neither UT nor the majority has demonstrated that any of these four goals provides a sufficient basis for satisfying strict scrutiny. And UT's arguments to the contrary depend on a series of invidious assumptions. *** UT's failure to provide any definition of the various racial and ethnic groups is also revealing. UT does not specify what it means to be 'African-American,' 'Hispanic,' 'Asian American,' 'Native American,' or 'White.' *** It instead relies on applicants to 'classify themselves.' This is an invitation for applicants to game the system.

Finally, it seems clear that the lack of classroom diversity is attributable in good part to factors other than the representation of the favored groups in the UT student population. *** Having designed an undergraduate program that virtually ensures a lack of classroom diversity, UT is poorly positioned to argue that this very result provides a justification for racial and ethnic discrimination, which the Constitution rarely allows. *** UT's purported interest in intraracial diversity, or 'diversity within diversity,' also falls short. At bottom, this argument relies on the unsupported assumption that there is something deficient or at least radically different about the African-American and Hispanic students admitted through the Top Ten Percent Plan. *** It is also far from clear that UT's assumptions about the socioeconomic status of minorities admitted through the Top Ten Percent Plan are even remotely accurate. *** [T]he minorities that UT characterizes as 'coming from depressed socioeconomic backgrounds,' generally come from households with education levels exceeding the norm in Texas *** [and] its minority students disproportionally come from families that are wealthier and better educated than the average Texas family. *** To the extent that intraracial diversity refers to something other than admitting privileged minorities and minorities with higher SAT scores, UT has failed to define that interest with any clarity. ***

UT also alleges--and the majority embraces--an interest in avoiding 'feelings of loneliness and isolation' among minority students. In support of this argument, they cite only demographic data and anecdotal statements by UT officials that some students (we are not told how many) feel 'isolated.' This vague interest cannot possibly satisfy strict scrutiny. ***

Even assuming UT is correct that, under *Grutter*, it need only cite a generic interest in the educational benefits of diversity, its plan still fails strict scrutiny because it is not narrowly tailored. *** Here, there is no evidence that race-blind, holistic review would not achieve UT's goals at least 'about as well' as UT's race-based policy. In addition, UT could have adopted other approaches to further its goals, such as intensifying its outreach efforts, uncapping the Top Ten Percent Law, or placing greater weight on socioeconomic factors. *** The majority purports to agree with much of the above analysis. *** Yet, somehow, the majority concludes that *petitioner* must lose as a result of UT's failure to provide evidence justifying its decision to employ racial discrimination. *** To the extent the record is inadequate, the responsibility lies with UT. ***

It is important to understand what is and what is not at stake in this case. *What is not at stake* is whether UT or any other university may adopt an admissions plan that results in a student body with a broad representation of students from all racial and ethnic groups. *** *What is at stake* is whether university administrators may justify systematic racial discrimination simply by asserting that such discrimination is necessary to achieve 'the educational benefits of diversity,' without explaining--much less proving--why the discrimination is needed or how the discriminatory plan is well crafted to serve its objectives. Even though UT has never provided any coherent explanation for its asserted need to discriminate on the basis of race, and even though UT's position relies on a series of unsupported and noxious racial assumptions, the majority concludes that UT has met its heavy burden. This conclusion is remarkable--and remarkably wrong. ***

Notes

1. **What About *Parents Involved*?** In *Parents Involved*, the Court said "the way to stop discrimination on the basis of race is to stop discriminating on the basis of race." Is *Fisher II* consistent with this rationale?

2. **Extending *Grutter*?** The University of Texas's plan goes further than *Grutter* by seeking to achieve diversity within different major fields of education and within classrooms, rather than within the incoming class a whole and supplements the top 10% program, which was designed to increase ethnic diversity. Has *Grutter* been extended?

3. **Alternatives to Race-Based Affirmative Action**. Is the top 10% program a form of (surreptitious} affirmative action? Is it subject to strict scrutiny? Would use of economic class (income) provide an alternative to racial affirmative action? If legacy preferences mainly go to whites, may public universities constitutionally eliminate them?

4. **Disparate Impact Versus Intentional Discrimination?** The Supreme Court decided *Ricci v. DeStefano*, 557 U.S. 557 (2009) on statutory grounds, avoiding a potential constitutional issue. JUSTICE SCALIA, concurring in an opinion not joined by any other Justice, wrote: "[The Court] merely postpones the evil day on which the Court will have to confront the question: Whether, or to what extent, are the disparate-impact provisions of Title VII of the Civil Rights Act of 1964 consistent with the Constitution's guarantee of equal protection? *** [I]f the Federal Government is prohibited from discriminating on the basis of race, then surely it is also prohibited from enacting laws mandating that third parties-*e.g.*, employers, whether private, State, or municipal-discriminate on the basis of race. *** [T]he war between disparate impact and equal protection will be waged sooner or later, and it behooves us to begin thinking about how-and on what terms-to make peace between them." JUSTICE GINSBURG, joined by JUSTICE STEVENS, JUSTICE SOUTER, and JUSTICE BREYER, said: "Respondents were no doubt conscious of race during their decisionmaking process, *** but this did not mean they had engaged in racially disparate treatment. *** New Haven's action, which gave no individual a preference, "was simply not analogous to a quota system or a minority set-aside where candidates, on the basis of their race, are not treated uniformly." *** This litigation does not involve affirmative action."

C. GENDER AND EQUAL PROTECTION

To what extent does the Constitution mandate governmental gender equality? The language of the original Constitution said nothing about women, but there are gender-specific references in several amendments. Section 2 of the Fourteenth Amendment repeals the 3/5 bargain concerning counting slaves for apportionment of the House of Representatives, but it explicitly notes that state representation will be tied to voting eligibility of the state's "male inhabitants." The right of women to vote in federal and state elections was not guaranteed until ratification of the Nineteenth Amendment in 1920.

Section 1 of the Fourteenth Amendment speaks of "equal protection of the laws" for all "persons," not just "male inhabitants," and the Supreme Court, in *Minor v. Happersett*, 88 U.S. (21 Wall.) 162 (1875), acknowledged that women are "persons" and "citizens," even though the right to vote was not then seen as a privilege of U.S. citizenship. In another case of similar vintage, *Bradwell v. Illinois*, 83 U.S. (16 Wall.) 130 (1873), the Court held that Illinois could refuse to license women to practice law. JUSTICE BRADLEY's concurring opinion contains this classic statement of the Court's attitude then toward gender discrimination:

> The natural and proper timidity and delicacy which belongs to the female sex evidently unfits it for many of the occupations of civil life. The constitution of the family organization, which is founded in the divine ordinance, as well as in the nature of things, indicates the domestic sphere as that which properly belongs to the domain and functions of womanhood. The harmony, not to say identity, of interests and views which belong or should belong to the family institution, is repugnant to the idea of a woman adopting a distinct and independent career from that of her husband. *** The paramount destiny and mission of woman are to fulfill the noble and benign offices of wife and mother. This is the law of the Creator. And the rules of civil society must be adapted to the general constitution of things, and cannot be based on exceptional cases.

Most of you will be glad *Bradwell* is not the law.

For many decades, rational basis scrutiny was used in evaluating the constitutionality of laws that used gender categories. See, for example, *Muller v. Oregon*, 208 U.S. 412 (1908) (upholding a statute prohibiting employment of women in factories more than ten hours a day). Then, during the 1960s and early 1970s, the Supreme Court began applying a more demanding explanation for gender differences in equal protection cases and came within one vote of applying strict scrutiny to invidious governmental discrimination against women. In 1972, Congress submitted to the states a proposed Equal Rights Amendment (ERA) for ratification. The ERA's operative language was: "Equality of rights under the law shall not be denied or abridged by the United States or by any State on account of sex."

The Court subsequently drew back from applying strict scrutiny to governmental gender distinctions and the ERA was not ratified by ¾ of the states. The following cases reveal the current state of equal protection gender jurisprudence.

CRAIG v. BOREN
429 U.S. 190 (1976)

MR. JUSTICE BRENNAN delivered the opinion of the Court.

discriminates against 18-21 y/o men

The interaction of two sections of an Oklahoma statute prohibits the sale of "nonintoxicating" 3.2% beer to males under the age of 21 and to females under the age of 18. The question to be decided is whether such a gender-based differential constitutes a denial to males 18–20 years of age of the equal protection of the laws in violation of the Fourteenth Amendment. *** [S]tatutory classifications that distinguish between males and females are "subject to scrutiny under the Equal Protection Clause." To withstand constitutional challenge, previous cases establish that classifications by gender must serve important governmental objectives and must be substantially related to achievement of those objectives. Thus, in [*Reed v. Reed*, 404 U.S. 71 (1971)], the objectives of "reducing the workload on probate courts" and "avoiding intrafamily controversy" were deemed of insufficient importance to sustain use of an overt gender criterion in the appointment of administrators of intestate decedents' estates. Decisions following *Reed* similarly have rejected administrative ease and convenience as sufficiently important objectives to justify gender-based classifications. ***

Reed v. Reed has also provided the underpinning for decisions that have invalidated statutes employing gender as an inaccurate proxy for other, more germane bases of classification. Hence, "archaic and overbroad" generalizations could not justify use of a gender line in determining eligibility for certain governmental entitlements. Similarly, increasingly outdated misconceptions concerning the role of females in the home rather than in the "marketplace and world of ideas" were rejected as loose-fitting characterizations incapable of supporting state statutory schemes that were premised upon their accuracy. *** We turn then to the question whether, under *Reed*, the difference between males and females with respect to the purchase of 3.2% beer warrants the differential in age drawn by the Oklahoma statute. We conclude that it does not.

The District Court recognized that *Reed v. Reed* was controlling. In applying the teachings of that case, the court found the requisite important governmental objective in the traffic-safety goal proffered by the Oklahoma Attorney General. It then concluded that the statistics introduced by the appellees established that the gender-based distinction was substantially related to achievement of that goal.

We accept for purposes of discussion the District Court's identification of the objective underlying [the statute] as the enhancement of traffic safety. Clearly, the protection of public health and safety represents an important function of state and local governments. However, appellees' statistics in our view cannot support the conclusion that the gender-based distinction closely serves to achieve that objective and therefore the distinction cannot under *Reed* withstand equal protection challenge.

The appellees introduced a variety of statistical surveys. *** Conceding that "the case is not free from doubt," the District Court nonetheless concluded that this statistical showing substantiated "a rational basis for the legislative judgment underlying the challenged classification." *** Even were this statistical evidence accepted as accurate, it nevertheless offers only a weak answer to the equal protection question presented here. The most focused and relevant of the statistical surveys, arrests of 18–20–year-olds for alcohol-related driving offenses, exemplifies the ultimate unpersuasiveness of this evidentiary record. Viewed in terms of the correlation between sex and the actual activity that Oklahoma seeks to regulate driving while under the influence of alcohol the statistics broadly establish that .18% of females and 2% of males in that age group were arrested for that offense. While such a disparity is not trivial in a statistical sense, it hardly can form the basis for employment of a gender line as a classifying device. Certainly if maleness is to serve as a proxy for drinking and driving, a correlation of 2% must be considered an unduly tenuous "fit."[12] Indeed, prior cases have consistently rejected the use of sex as a decisionmaking factor even though the statutes in question certainly rested on far more predictive empirical relationships than this.[13]

Moreover, the statistics exhibit a variety of other shortcomings that seriously impugn their value to equal protection analysis. Setting aside the obvious methodological problems,[14] the surveys do not adequately justify the salient features of Oklahoma's gender-based traffic-safety law. None purports to measure the use and dangerousness of 3.2% beer as opposed to alcohol generally, a detail that is of particular importance since, in light of its low alcohol level, Oklahoma apparently considers the 3.2% beverage to be "nonintoxicating." Moreover, many of the studies, while graphically documenting the unfortunate increase in driving while under the influence of alcohol, make no effort to relate their findings to age-sex differentials as involved here. Indeed, the only survey that explicitly centered its attention upon young drivers and their use of beer albeit apparently not of the diluted 3.2% variety reached results that hardly can be viewed as impressive in justifying either a gender or age classification.

There is no reason to belabor this line of analysis. It is unrealistic to expect either members of the judiciary or state officials to be well versed in the rigors of experimental or statistical technique. But this merely illustrates that proving broad sociological propositions by statistics is a dubious business, and one that inevitably is in tension with the normative philosophy that underlies the Equal Protection Clause. Suffice to say that the showing offered by the appellees does not satisfy us that sex represents a legitimate, accurate proxy for the regulation of drinking and driving. In fact, when it is further recognized that Oklahoma's statute prohibits only the selling of 3.2% beer to young males and not their drinking the beverage once acquired (even after purchase by their 18–20–year-old female companions), the relationship between gender and traffic safety becomes far too tenuous to satisfy *Reed*'s requirement that the gender-based difference be substantially related to achievement of the statutory objective.

---

[12] Obviously, arrest statistics do not embrace all individuals who drink and drive. But for purposes of analysis, this "underinclusiveness" must be discounted somewhat by the shortcomings inherent in this statistical sample, see n. 14. In any event, we decide this case in light of the evidence offered by Oklahoma and know of no way of extrapolating these arrest statistics to take into account the driving and drinking population at large, including those who avoided arrest.

[13] For example, we can conjecture that in *Reed*, Idaho's apparent premise that women lacked experience in formal business matters (particularly compared to men) would have proved to be accurate in substantially more than 2% of all cases. And in both *Frontiero* and *Wiesenfeld*, we expressly found appellees' empirical defense of mandatory dependency tests for men but not women to be unsatisfactory, even though we recognized that husbands are still far less likely to be dependent on their wives than vice versa.

[14] The very social stereotypes that find reflection in age-differential laws are likely substantially to distort the accuracy of these comparative statistics. Hence "reckless" young men who drink and drive are transformed into arrest statistics, whereas their female counterparts are chivalrously escorted home. ***

We hold, therefore, that under *Reed*, Oklahoma's 3.2% beer statute invidiously discriminates against males 18–20 years of age. *** We conclude that the gender-based differential contained in [the statute] constitutes a denial of the equal protection of the laws to males aged 18–20 and reverse the judgment of the District Court.

MR. JUSTICE POWELL, concurring.

*** I view this as a relatively easy case. No one questions the legitimacy or importance of the asserted governmental objective: the promotion of highway safety. The decision of the case turns on whether the state legislature, by the classification it has chosen, had adopted a means that bears a "'fair and substantial relation'" to this objective.

It seems to me that the statistics offered by appellees and relied upon by the District Court do tend generally to support the view that young men drive more, possibly are inclined to drink more, and for various reasons are involved in more accidents than young women. Even so, I am not persuaded that these facts and the inferences fairly drawn from them justify this classification based on a three-year age differential between the sexes, and especially one that it so easily circumvented as to be virtually meaningless. Putting it differently, this gender-based classification does not bear a fair and substantial relation to the object of the legislation.

MR. JUSTICE STEVENS, concurring.

*** The classification is not totally irrational. For the evidence does indicate that there are more males than females in this age bracket who drive and also more who drink. Nevertheless, there are several reasons why I regard the justification as unacceptable. It is difficult to believe that the statute was actually intended to cope with the problem of traffic safety, since it has only a minimal effect on access to a not very intoxicating beverage and does not prohibit its consumption. Moreover, the empirical data submitted by the State accentuate the unfairness of treating all 18–21–year-old males as inferior to their female counterparts. The legislation imposes a restraint on 100% of the males in the class allegedly because about 2% of them have probably violated one or more laws relating to the consumption of alcoholic beverages. It is unlikely that this law will have a significant deterrent effect either on that 2% or on the law-abiding 98%. But even assuming some such slight benefit, it does not seem to me that an insult to all of the young men of the State can be justified by visiting the sins of the 2% on the 98%.

Concurrences of MR. JUSTICE BLACKMUN and MR. JUSTICE STEWART and dissent of MR. CHIEF JUSTICE BURGER omitted.

MR. JUSTICE REHNQUIST, dissenting.

The Court's disposition of this case is objectionable on two grounds. First is its conclusion that men challenging a gender-based statute which treats them less favorably than women may invoke a more stringent standard of judicial review than pertains to most other types of classifications. Second is the Court's enunciation of this standard, without citation to any source, as being that "classifications by gender must serve important governmental objectives and must be substantially related to achievement of those objectives." The only redeeming feature of the Court's opinion, to my mind, is that it apparently signals a retreat by those who joined the plurality opinion in *Frontiero v. Richardson*, 411 U.S. 677 (1973), from their view that sex is a "suspect" classification for purposes of equal protection analysis. I think the Oklahoma statute challenged here need pass only the "rational basis" equal protection analysis ***, and I believe that it is constitutional under that analysis. ***

The Court does not discuss the nature of the right involved, and there is no reason to believe that it sees the purchase of 3.2% beer as implicating any important interest, let alone one that is "fundamental" in the constitutional sense of invoking strict scrutiny. Indeed, the Court's accurate observation that the statute affects the selling but not the drinking of 3.2% beer, further emphasizes the limited effect that it has on even those persons in the age group involved. There is, in sum, nothing about the statutory classification involved here to suggest that it affects an interest, or works against a group, which can claim under the Equal Protection Clause that it is entitled to special judicial protection. ***

The Court's conclusion that a law which treats males less favorably than females "must serve important governmental objectives and must be substantially related to achievement of those objectives" apparently comes out of thin air. The Equal Protection Clause contains no such language, and none of our previous cases adopt that standard. I would think we have had enough difficulty with the two standards of review which our cases have recognized—the norm of "rational basis," and the "compelling state interest" required where a "suspect classification" is involved—so as to counsel weightily against the insertion of still another "standard" between those two. How is this Court to divine what objectives are important? How is it to determine whether a particular law is "substantially" related to the achievement of such objective, rather than related in some other way to its achievement? Both of the phrases used are so diaphanous and elastic as to invite subjective judicial preferences or prejudices relating to particular types of legislation, masquerading as judgments whether such legislation is directed at "important" objectives or, whether the relationship to those objectives is "substantial" enough.

*** The Court "accept(s) for purposes of discussion" the District Court's finding that the purpose of the provisions in question was traffic safety, and proceeds to examine the statistical evidence in the record in order to decide if "the gender-based distinction closely serves to achieve that objective." *** One need not immerse oneself in the fine points of statistical analysis, however, in order to see the weaknesses in the Court's attempted denigration of the evidence at hand.

One survey of arrest statistics assembled in 1973 indicated that males in the 18–20 age group were arrested for "driving under the influence" almost 18 times as often as their female counterparts, and for "drunkenness" in a ratio of almost 10 to 1. Accepting, as the Court does, appellants' comparison of the total figures with 1973 Oklahoma census data, this survey indicates a

2% arrest rate among males in the age group, as compared to a .18% rate among females. *** The Court's criticism of the statistics relied on by the District Court conveys the impression that a legislature in enacting a new law is to be subjected to the judicial equivalent of a doctoral examination in statistics. Legislatures are not held to any rules of evidence such as those which may govern courts or other administrative bodies, and are entitled to draw factual conclusions on the basis of the determination of probable cause which an arrest by a police officer normally represents. In this situation, they could reasonably infer that the incidence of drunk driving is a good deal higher than the incidence of arrest.

And while *** such statistics may be distorted as a result of stereotyping, the legislature is not required to prove before a court that its statistics are perfect. In any event, if stereotypes are as pervasive as the Court suggests, they may in turn influence the conduct of the men and women in question, and cause the young men to conform to the wild and reckless image which is their stereotype. *** Quite apart from these alleged methodological deficiencies in the statistical evidence, the Court appears to hold that that evidence, on its face, fails to support the distinction drawn in the statute. The Court notes that only 2% of males (as against .18% of females) in the age group were arrested for drunk driving, and that this very low figure establishes "an unduly tenuous 'fit'" between maleness and drunk driving in the 18 to 20–year-old group. *** Notwithstanding the Court's critique of the statistical evidence, that evidence suggests clear differences between the drinking and driving habits of young men and women. Those differences are grounds enough for the State reasonably to conclude that young males pose by far the greater drunk-driving hazard, both in terms of sheer numbers and in terms of hazard on a per-driver basis. The gender-based difference in treatment in this case is therefore not irrational.

The Court's argument that a 2% correlation between maleness and drunk driving is constitutionally insufficient therefore does not pose an equal protection issue concerning discrimination between males and females. The clearest demonstration of this is the fact that the precise argument made by the Court would be equally applicable to a flat bar on such purchases by anyone, male or female, in the 18–20 age group; in fact it would apply a fortiori in that case given the even more "tenuous 'fit'" between drunk-driving arrests and femaleness. The statistics indicate that about 1% of the age group population as a whole is arrested. What the Court's argument is relevant to is not equal protection, but due process whether there are enough persons in the category who drive while drunk to justify a bar against purchases by all members of the group.

This is not a case where the classification can only be justified on grounds of administrative convenience. There being no apparent way to single out persons likely to drink and drive, it seems plain that the legislature was faced here with the not atypical legislative problem of legislating in terms of broad categories with regard to the purchase and consumption of alcohol. I trust, especially in light of the Twenty-first Amendment, that there would be no due process violation if no one in this age group were allowed to purchase

3.2% beer. Since males drink and drive at a higher rate than the age group as a whole, I fail to see how a statutory bar with regard only to them can create any due process problem. ***

UNITED STATES v. VIRGINIA
518 U.S. 515 (1996)
JUSTICE GINSBURG delivered the opinion of the Court.

Virginia's public institutions of higher learning include an incomparable military college, Virginia Military Institute (VMI). The United States maintains that the Constitution's equal protection guarantee precludes Virginia from reserving exclusively to men the unique educational opportunities VMI affords. We agree.

Founded in 1839, VMI is today the sole single-sex school among Virginia's 15 public institutions of higher learning. VMI's distinctive mission is to produce "citizen-soldiers," men prepared for leadership in civilian life and in military service. *** Assigning prime place to character development, VMI uses an "adversative method" modeled on English public schools and once characteristic of military instruction. VMI constantly endeavors to instill physical and mental discipline in its cadets and impart to them a strong moral code. The school's graduates leave VMI with heightened comprehension of their capacity to deal with duress and stress, and a large sense of accomplishment for completing the hazardous course.

VMI has notably succeeded in its mission to produce leaders; among its alumni are military generals, Members of Congress, and business executives. The school's alumni overwhelmingly perceive that their VMI training helped them to realize their personal goals. VMI's endowment reflects the loyalty of its graduates; VMI has the largest per-student endowment of all public undergraduate institutions in the Nation.

Neither the goal of producing citizen-soldiers nor VMI's implementing methodology is inherently unsuitable to women. And the school's impressive record in producing leaders has made admission desirable to some women. Nevertheless, Virginia has elected to preserve exclusively for men the advantages and opportunities a VMI education affords.

From its establishment in 1839 as one of the Nation's first state military colleges, VMI has remained financially supported by Virginia and "subject to the control of the [Virginia] General Assembly" *** [and] VMI today enrolls about 1,300 men as cadets.[2] Its academic offerings in the liberal arts, sciences, and engineering are also available at other public colleges and universities in Virginia. But VMI's mission is special. *** VMI produces its "citizen-soldiers" through "an adversative, or doubting, model of education" which features "[p]hysical rigor, mental stress, absolute equality of treatment, absence of privacy, minute regulation of behavior, and indoctrination in desirable values." *** VMI cadets live in spartan barracks

---

[2] Historically, most of Virginia's public colleges and universities were single-sex; by the mid–1970's, however, all except VMI had become coeducational. ***

where surveillance is constant and privacy nonexistent; they wear uniforms, eat together in the mess hall, and regularly participate in drills. *** VMI attracts some applicants because of its reputation as an extraordinarily challenging military school, and "because its alumni are exceptionally close to the school." *** "[W]omen have no opportunity anywhere to gain the benefits of [the system of education at VMI]."

In 1990, prompted by a complaint filed with the Attorney General by a female high-school student seeking admission to VMI, the United States sued the Commonwealth of Virginia and VMI, alleging that VMI's exclusively male admission policy violated the Equal Protection Clause of the Fourteenth Amendment. ***

In the two years preceding the lawsuit, the District Court noted, VMI had received inquiries from 347 women, but had responded to none of them. *** [It] was also established that "some women are capable of all of the individual activities required of VMI cadets." *** The cross-petitions in this case present two ultimate issues. First, does Virginia's exclusion of women from the educational opportunities provided by VMI—extraordinary opportunities for military training and civilian leadership development—deny to women "capable of all of the individual activities required of VMI cadets," the equal protection of the laws guaranteed by the Fourteenth Amendment? Second, if VMI's "unique" situation—as Virginia's sole single-sex public institution of higher education—offends the Constitution's equal protection principle, what is the remedial requirement?

We note, once again, the core instruction of this Court's pathmarking decisions in *J.E.B. v. Alabama ex rel. T. B.*, 511 U.S. 127, and *Mississippi Univ. for Women*, 458 U.S., at 724: Parties who seek to defend gender-based government action must demonstrate an "exceedingly persuasive justification" for that action. *** Without equating gender classifications, for all purposes, to classifications based on race or national origin,[6] the Court, in post-*Reed* decisions, has carefully inspected official action that closes a door or denies opportunity to women (or to men). To summarize the Court's current directions for cases of official classification based on gender: Focusing on the differential treatment or denial of opportunity for which relief is sought, the reviewing court must determine whether the proffered justification is "exceedingly persuasive." The burden of justification is demanding and it rests entirely on the State. The State must show "at least that the [challenged] classification serves 'important governmental objectives and that the discriminatory means employed' are 'substantially related to the achievement of those objectives.'" The justification must be genuine, not hypothesized or invented post hoc in response to litigation. And it must not rely on overbroad generalizations about the different talents, capacities, or preferences of males and females.

[handwritten margin note: Part of the doctrine of intermediate scrutiny, but not part of the test officially]

---

[6] The Court has thus far reserved most stringent judicial scrutiny for classifications based on race or national origin, but last Term observed that strict scrutiny of such classifications is not inevitably "fatal in fact." *Adarand Constructors, Inc. v. Pena.* ***

The heightened review standard our precedent establishes does not make sex a proscribed classification. Supposed "inherent differences" are no longer accepted as a ground for race or national origin classifications. *See Loving v. Virginia*, 388 U.S. 1 (1967). Physical differences between men and women, however, are enduring: "[T]he two sexes are not fungible; a community made up exclusively of one [sex] is different from a community composed of both." *Ballard v. United States*, 329 U.S. 187 (1946).

"Inherent differences" between men and women, we have come to appreciate, remain cause for celebration, but not for denigration of the members of either sex or for artificial constraints on an individual's opportunity. Sex classifications may be used to compensate women "for particular economic disabilities [they have] suffered," to "promot[e] equal employment opportunity," to advance full development of the talent and capacities of our Nation's people.[7] But such classifications may not be used, as they once were, to create or perpetuate the legal, social, and economic inferiority of women. ***

*** Virginia *** asserts two justifications in defense of VMI's exclusion of women. First, the Commonwealth contends, "single-sex education provides important educational benefits," and the option of single-sex education contributes to "diversity in educational approaches". Second, the Commonwealth argues, "the unique VMI method of character development and leadership training," the school's adversarial approach, would have to be modified were VMI to admit women. ***

Single-sex education affords pedagogical benefits to at least some students, Virginia emphasizes, and that reality is uncontested in this litigation. Similarly, it is not disputed that diversity among public educational institutions can serve the public good. But Virginia has not shown that VMI was established, or has been maintained, with a view to diversifying, by its categorical exclusion of women, educational opportunities within the State. In cases of this genre, our precedent instructs that "benign" justifications proffered in defense of categorical exclusions will not be accepted automatically; a tenable justification must describe actual state purposes, not rationalizations for actions in fact differently grounded. ***

Neither recent nor distant history bears out Virginia's alleged pursuit of diversity through single-sex educational options. In 1839, when the State established VMI, a range of educational opportunities for men and women was scarcely contemplated. Higher education at the time was considered dangerous for women; reflecting widely held views about women's proper

---

[7] Several amici have urged that diversity in educational opportunities is an altogether appropriate governmental pursuit and that single-sex schools can contribute importantly to such diversity. *** We do not question the State's prerogative evenhandedly to support diverse educational opportunities. We address specifically and only an educational opportunity *** uniquely available only at Virginia's premier military institute, the State's sole single-sex public university or college. Cf. *Mississippi Univ. for Women v. Hogan*, 458 U.S. 718 (1982) ("Mississippi maintains no other single-sex public university or college. Thus, we are not faced with the question of whether States can provide 'separate but equal' undergraduate institutions for males and females.").

place, the Nation's first universities and colleges—for example, Harvard in Massachusetts, William and Mary in Virginia—admitted only men. *** Virginia eventually provided for several women's seminaries and colleges. *** By the mid–1970's, all four schools had become coeducational. *** Virginia describes the current absence of public single-sex higher education for women as "an historical anomaly." But the historical record indicates action more deliberate than anomalous: First, protection of women against higher education; next, schools for women far from equal in resources and stature to schools for men; finally, conversion of the separate schools to coeducation. *** In sum, we find no persuasive evidence in this record that VMI's male-only admission policy "is in furtherance of a state policy of 'diversity.'" *** A purpose genuinely to advance an array of educational options *** is not served by VMI's historic and constant plan—a plan to "affor[d] a unique educational benefit only to males." However "liberally" this plan serves the State's sons, it makes no provision whatever for her daughters. That is not *equal* protection.

Virginia next argues that VMI's adversative method of training provides educational benefits that cannot be made available, unmodified, to women. *** Neither sex would be favored by the transformation, Virginia maintains: Men would be deprived of the unique opportunity currently available to them; women would not gain that opportunity because their participation would "eliminat[e] the very aspects of [the] program that distinguish [VMI] from *** other institutions of higher education in Virginia." *** It may be assumed, for purposes of this decision, that most women would not choose VMI's adversative method. *** The issue, however, is not whether "women—or men—should be forced to attend VMI"; rather, the question is whether the State can constitutionally deny to women who have the will and capacity, the training and attendant opportunities that VMI uniquely affords. The notion that admission of women would downgrade VMI's stature, destroy the adversative system and, with it, even the school, is a judgment hardly proved. *** Women's successful entry into the federal military academies, and their participation in the Nation's military forces, indicate that Virginia's fears for the future of VMI may not be solidly grounded. ***

The [State's] misunderstanding *** is apparent from VMI's mission: to produce "citizen-soldiers," individuals "'imbued with love of learning, confident in the functions and attitudes of leadership, possessing a high sense of public service, advocates of the American democracy and free enterprise system, and ready *** to defend their country in time of national peril.'"

Surely that goal is great enough to accommodate women, who today count as citizens in our American democracy equal in stature to men. Just as surely, the State's great goal is not substantially advanced by women's categorical exclusion, in total disregard of their individual merit, from the State's premier "citizen-soldier" corps.[16] Virginia, in sum, "has fallen far

---

[16] VMI has successfully managed another notable change. The school admitted its first African–American cadets in 1968. ***

short of establishing the 'exceedingly persuasive justification,'" that must be the solid base for any gender-defined classification.

In the second phase of the litigation, Virginia presented its remedial plan—maintain VMI as a male-only college and create VWIL [Virginia Women's Institute for Leadership at Mary Baldwin College] as a separate program for women. *** Virginia described VWIL as a "parallel program," and asserted that VWIL shares VMI's mission of producing "citizen-soldiers" and VMI's goals of providing "education, military training, mental and physical discipline, character *** and leadership development." If the VWIL program could not "eliminate the discriminatory effects of the past," could it at least "bar like discrimination in the future"? A comparison of the programs said to be "parallel" informs our answer. *** VWIL affords women no opportunity to experience the rigorous military training for which VMI is famed. *** [It] "deemphasize[s]" military education, and uses a "cooperative method" of education "which reinforces self-esteem[.]" ***

In myriad respects other than military training, VWIL does not qualify as VMI's equal. VWIL's student body, faculty, course offerings, and facilities hardly match VMI's. Nor can the VWIL graduate anticipate the benefits associated with VMI's 157–year history, the school's prestige, and its influential alumni network. *** The VWIL student does not graduate with the advantage of a VMI degree. Her diploma does not unite her with the legions of VMI "graduates [who] have distinguished themselves" in military and civilian life. "[VMI] alumni are exceptionally close to the school," and that closeness accounts, in part, for VMI's success in attracting applicants. A VWIL graduate cannot assume that the "network of business owners, corporations, VMI graduates and non-graduate employers *** interested in hiring VMI graduates," will be equally responsive to her search for employment. *** Virginia, in sum, while maintaining VMI for men only, has failed to provide any "comparable single-gender women's institution." *** Virginia's VWIL solution is reminiscent of the remedy Texas proposed 50 years ago, in response to a state trial court's 1946 ruling that, given the equal protection guarantee, African Americans could not be denied a legal education at a state facility. *See Sweatt v. Painter*, 339 U.S. 629 (1950). ***

A generation ago, "the authorities controlling Virginia higher education," despite long established tradition, agreed "to innovate and favorably entertain the [then] relatively new idea that there must be no discrimination by sex in offering educational opportunity." Commencing in 1970, Virginia opened to women "educational opportunities at the Charlottesville campus that [were] not afforded in other [state-operated] institutions." *** VMI, too, offers an educational opportunity no other Virginia institution provides, and the school's "prestige"—associated with its success in developing "citizen-soldiers"—is unequaled. *** Women seeking and fit for a VMI-quality education cannot be offered anything less, under the State's obligation to afford them genuinely equal protection.

A prime part of the history of our Constitution, historian Richard Morris recounted, is the story of the extension of constitutional rights and protections to people once ignored or excluded. VMI's story continued as our comprehension of "We the People" expanded. There is no reason to believe that the admission of women capable of all the activities required of VMI cadets would destroy the Institute rather than enhance its capacity to serve the "more perfect Union."

JUSTICE THOMAS took no part in the consideration or decision of the case.

CHIEF JUSTICE REHNQUIST, concurring in judgment.

*** Two decades ago in *Craig v. Boren*, 429 U.S. 190 (1976), we announced that "[t]o withstand constitutional challenge, *** classifications by gender must serve important governmental objectives and must be substantially related to achievement of those objectives." We have adhered to that standard of scrutiny ever since. While the majority adheres to this test today, it also says that the State must demonstrate an "'exceedingly persuasive justification'" to support a gender-based classification. It is unfortunate that the Court thereby introduces an element of uncertainty respecting the appropriate test. ***

*** [I]t is not the "exclusion of women" that violates the Equal Protection Clause, but the maintenance of an all-men school without providing any—much less a comparable—institution for women. Accordingly, the remedy should not necessarily require either the admission of women to VMI, or the creation of a VMI clone for women. An adequate remedy in my opinion might be a demonstration by Virginia that its interest in educating men in a single-sex environment is matched by its interest in educating women in a single-sex institution. *** It would be a sufficient remedy, I think, if the two institutions offered the same quality of education and were of the same overall calibre. ***

JUSTICE SCALIA, dissenting.

Today the Court shuts down an institution that has served the people of the Commonwealth of Virginia with pride and distinction for over a century and a half. To achieve that desired result, it rejects (contrary to our established practice) the factual findings of two courts below, sweeps aside the precedents of this Court, and ignores the history of our people. As to facts: it explicitly rejects the finding that there exist "gender-based developmental differences" supporting Virginia's restriction of the "adversative" method to only a men's institution, and the finding that the all-male composition of the Virginia Military Institute (VMI) is essential to that institution's character. As to precedent: it drastically revises our established standards for reviewing sex-based classifications. And as to history: it counts for nothing the long tradition, enduring down to the present, of men's military colleges supported by both States and the Federal Government. ***

I have no problem with a system of abstract tests such as rational-basis, intermediate, and strict scrutiny (though I think we can do better than applying strict scrutiny and intermediate scrutiny whenever we feel like it). *** But in my view the function of this Court is to *preserve* our society's values regarding (among other things) equal protection, not to revise them; to prevent backsliding from the degree of restriction the Constitution imposed upon democratic government, not to prescribe, on our own authority, progressively higher degrees. ***

Only the amorphous "exceedingly persuasive justification" phrase, and not the standard elaboration of intermediate scrutiny, can be made to yield this conclusion that VMI's single-sex composition is unconstitutional because there exist several women (or, one would have to conclude under the Court's reasoning, a single woman) willing and able to undertake VMI's program. Intermediate scrutiny has never required a least-restrictive-means analysis, but only a "substantial relation" between the classification and the state interests that it serves. *** There is simply no support in our cases for the notion that a sex-based classification is invalid unless it relates to characteristics that hold true in every instance.

Not content to execute a *de facto* abandonment of the intermediate scrutiny that has been our standard for sex-based classifications for some two decades, the Court purports to reserve the question whether, even in principle, a higher standard (i.e., strict scrutiny) should apply. *** Our task is to clarify the law—not to muddy the waters, and not to exact over-compliance by intimidation. The States and the Federal Government are entitled to know before they act the standard to which they will be held, rather than be compelled to guess about the outcome of Supreme Court peek-a-boo. *** The question to be answered, I repeat, is whether the exclusion of women from VMI is "substantially related to an important governmental objective."

It is beyond question that Virginia has an important state interest in providing effective college education for its citizens. That single-sex instruction is an approach substantially related to that interest should be evident enough from the long and continuing history in this country of men's and women's colleges. *** But besides its single-sex constitution, VMI is different from other colleges in another way. It employs a "distinctive educational method," sometimes referred to as the "adversative, or doubting, model of education." *** No one contends that this method is appropriate for all individuals; education is not a "one size fits all" business. Just as a State may wish to support junior colleges, vocational institutes, or a law school that emphasizes case practice instead of classroom study, so too a State's decision to maintain within its system one school that provides the adversative method is "substantially related" to its goal of good education. ***

There can be no serious dispute that, as the District Court found, single-sex education and a distinctive educational method "represent legitimate contributions to diversity in the Virginia higher education system." *** In these circumstances, Virginia's election to fund one public all-male institution and one on the adversative model—and to concentrate its resources in a single entity that serves both these interests in diversity—is substantially related to the State's important educational interests. ***

Under the constitutional principles announced and applied today, single-sex public education is unconstitutional. *** And the rationale of today's decision is sweeping: for sex-based classifications, a redefinition of intermediate scrutiny that makes it indistinguishable from strict scrutiny. Indeed, the Court indicates that if any program restricted to one sex is "uniqu[e]," it must be opened to members of the opposite sex "who have the will and capacity" to participate in it. I suggest that the single-sex program that will not be capable of being characterized as "unique" is not only unique but nonexistent.[8]

In any event, regardless of whether the Court's rationale leaves some small amount of room for lawyers to argue, it ensures that single-sex public education is functionally dead. The costs of litigating the constitutionality of a single-sex education program, and the risks of ultimately losing that litigation, are simply too high to be embraced by public officials. *** There are few extant single-sex public educational programs. The potential of today's decision for widespread disruption of existing institutions lies in its application to *private* single-sex education. *** The issue will be not whether government assistance turns private colleges into state actors, but whether the government itself would be violating the Constitution by providing state support to single-sex colleges. *** The only hope for state-assisted single-sex private schools is that the Court will not apply in the future the principles of law it has applied today. That is a substantial hope, I am happy and ashamed to say. ***

Notes

1.   **General.**   Is gender like race with respect to (1) the history of the Fourteenth Amendment, (2) the history of group repression or subordination, (3) the relative ability of women and minorities to win through majoritarian processes, and (4) other factors? Does your assessment of the similarities and differences explain the Court's use of "intermediate scrutiny"?

2.   **Questions about *Craig v. Boren.***

(a) In *Craig*, the Court announced the intermediate scrutiny standard which had been building for some time. Do you see this as ironic in light of the fact that women were, at least superficially, the beneficiaries of Oklahoma's law? Ironic in light of the fact that the law was so trivial?

(b) Do you think the Oklahoma law meets either rational basis or intermediate scrutiny standards? Why?

(c) How do stereotypes or social assumptions relate to the Oklahoma law and to an appropriate response by the Supreme Court to that law?

3.   **Questions about *United States v. Virginia.***   Has the standard of scrutiny changed from *Craig*? How important are facts versus theory in this case? Do you agree with JUSTICE SCALIA that virtually all single-gender schools and components of schools that are single gender are now illegal?

---

[8] In this regard, I note that the Court—which I concede is under no obligation to do so—provides no example of a program that would pass muster under its reasoning today: not even, for example, a football or wrestling program. On the Court's theory, any woman ready, willing, and physically able to participate in such a program would, as a constitutional matter, be entitled to do so.

4. **From Schools to Bathrooms.** Are single-sex restrooms in a government office building constitutionally permissible? For those who have observed or endured different length bathroom waiting, is "separate and unequal" alive and well despite the cases you have read? If so, how and why? Would pure strict scrutiny make a difference here? Would the ERA ("Equality of rights under the law shall not be denied or abridged by the United States or by any State on account of sex") affect the potty problem?

MICHAEL M. v. SUPERIOR COURT OF SONOMA COUNTY
450 U.S. 464 (1981)

JUSTICE REHNQUIST announced the judgment of the Court and delivered an opinion, in which THE CHIEF JUSTICE, JUSTICE STEWART, and JUSTICE POWELL joined.

The question presented in this case is whether California's "statutory rape" law violates the Equal Protection Clause of the Fourteenth Amendment. [The law] defines unlawful sexual intercourse as "an act of sexual intercourse accomplished with a female not the wife of the perpetrator, where the female is under the age of 18 years." The statute thus makes men alone criminally liable for the act of sexual intercourse.

In July 1978, a complaint was filed in the Municipal Court of Sonoma County, Cal., alleging that petitioner, then a 17 1/2-year-old male, had had unlawful sexual intercourse with a female under the age of 18, in violation of [the law]. *** Prior to trial, petitioner sought to set aside the information on both state and federal constitutional grounds, asserting that [the law] unlawfully discriminated on the basis of gender. ***

*** [A] legislature may not "make overbroad generalizations based on sex which are entirely unrelated to any differences between men and women or which demean the ability or social status of the affected class." *Parham v. Hughes*, 441 U.S. 347, 354 (1979) (plurality opinion of STEWART, J.). But because the Equal Protection Clause does not "demand that a statute necessarily apply equally to all persons" or require "'things which are different in fact *** to be treated in law as though they were the same,'" this Court has consistently upheld statutes where the gender classification is not invidious, but rather realistically reflects the fact that the sexes are not similarly situated in certain circumstances.

Applying those principles to this case, the fact that the California Legislature criminalized the act of illicit sexual intercourse with a minor female is a sure indication of its intent or purpose to discourage that conduct. Precisely why the legislature desired that result is of course somewhat less clear. *** [For] example, the individual legislators may have voted for the statute for a variety of reasons. Some legislators may have been concerned about preventing teenage pregnancies, others about protecting young females from physical injury or from the loss of "chastity," and still others about promoting various religious and moral attitudes towards premarital sex.

The justification for the statute offered by the State, and accepted by the Supreme Court of California, is that the legislature sought to prevent illegitimate teenage pregnancies. That finding, of course, is entitled to great deference. *** We are satisfied not only that the prevention of illegitimate pregnancy is at least one of the "purposes" of the statute, but also that the State has a strong interest in preventing such pregnancy. ***

We need not be medical doctors to discern that young men and young women are not similarly situated with respect to the problems and the risks of sexual intercourse. Only women may become pregnant, and they suffer disproportionately the profound physical, emotional and psychological consequences of sexual activity. The statute at issue here protects women from sexual intercourse at an age when those consequences are particularly severe.[7]

The question thus boils down to whether a State may attack the problem of sexual intercourse and teenage pregnancy directly by prohibiting a male from having sexual intercourse with a minor female. We hold that such a statute is sufficiently related to the State's objectives to pass constitutional muster.

Because virtually all of the significant harmful and inescapably identifiable consequences of teenage pregnancy fall on the young female, a legislature acts well within its authority when it elects to punish only the participant who, by nature, suffers few of the consequences of his conduct. It is hardly unreasonable for a legislature acting to protect minor females to exclude them from punishment. Moreover, the risk of pregnancy itself constitutes a substantial deterrence to young females. No similar natural sanctions deter males. A criminal sanction imposed solely on males thus serves to roughly "equalize" the deterrents on the sexes.

*** [We] cannot say that a gender-neutral statute would be as effective as the statute California has chosen to enact. The State persuasively contends that a gender-neutral statute would frustrate its interest in effective enforcement. Its view is that a female is surely less likely to report violations of the statute if she herself would be subject to criminal prosecution. In an area already fraught with prosecutorial difficulties, we decline to hold that the Equal Protection Clause requires a legislature to enact a statute so broad that it may well be incapable of enforcement.

We similarly reject petitioner's argument that [the law] is impermissibly overbroad because it makes unlawful sexual intercourse with prepubescent females, who are, by definition, incapable of becoming pregnant. Quite apart from the fact that the statute could well be justified on the grounds that very young females are particularly susceptible to physical injury from sexual intercourse, it is ludicrous to suggest that the Constitution requires the

---

[7] Although petitioner concedes that the State has a "compelling" interest in preventing teenage pregnancy, he contends that the "true" purpose of § 261.5 is to protect the virtue and chastity of young women. As such, the statute is unjustifiable because it rests on archaic stereotypes. What we have said above is enough to dispose of that contention. The question for us—and the only question under the Federal Constitution—is whether the legislation violates the Equal Protection Clause of the Fourteenth Amendment, not whether its supporters may have endorsed it for reasons no longer generally accepted. ***

California Legislature to limit the scope of its rape statute to older teenagers and exclude young girls.

There remains only petitioner's contention that the statute is unconstitutional as it is applied to him because he, like [his partner], was under 18 at the time of sexual intercourse. Petitioner argues that the statute is flawed because it presumes that as between two persons under 18, the male is the culpable aggressor. We find petitioner's contentions unpersuasive. Contrary to his assertions, the statute does not rest on the assumption that males are generally the aggressors. It is instead an attempt by a legislature to prevent illegitimate teenage pregnancy by providing an additional deterrent for men. The age of the man is irrelevant since young men are as capable as older men of inflicting the harm sought to be prevented. ***

JUSTICE STEWART, concurring. [omitted]

JUSTICE BLACKMUN, concurring in the judgment.

It is gratifying that the plurality recognizes that "[a]t the risk of stating the obvious, teenage pregnancies *** have increased dramatically over the last two decades" and "have significant social, medical, and economic consequences for both the mother and her child, and the State." *** I, however, cannot vote to strike down the California statutory rape law ***. For me, there is an important difference between this state action and a State's adamant and rigid refusal to face, or even to recognize, the "significant *** consequences"—to the woman—of a forced or unwanted conception. *** I think, too, that it is only fair, with respect to this particular petitioner, to point out that his partner, Sharon, appears not to have been an unwilling participant in at least the initial stages of the intimacies that took place the night of June 3, 1978. Petitioner's and Sharon's nonacquaintance with each other before the incident; their drinking; their withdrawal from the others of the group; their foreplay, in which she willingly participated and seems to have encouraged; and the closeness of their ages (a difference of only one year and 18 days) are factors that should make this case an unattractive one to prosecute at all, and especially to prosecute as a felony, rather than as a misdemeanor. But the State has chosen to prosecute in that manner, and the facts, I reluctantly conclude, may fit the crime.

JUSTICE BRENNAN, with whom JUSTICES WHITE and MARSHALL join, dissenting.

It is disturbing to find the Court so splintered on a case that presents such a straightforward issue: Whether the admittedly gender-based classification in [the statute] bears a sufficient relationship to the State's asserted goal of preventing teenage pregnancies to survive the "mid-level" constitutional scrutiny mandated by *Craig v. Boren*, 429 U.S. 190 (1976). ***

The State of California vigorously asserts that the "important governmental objective" to be served by [the statute] is the prevention of teenage pregnancy. It claims that its statute furthers this goal by deterring sexual activity by males—the class of persons it considers more responsible for causing those pregnancies.[4] But even assuming that prevention of teenage pregnancy is an important governmental objective and that it is in fact an objective of [the statute], California still has the burden of proving that there are fewer teenage pregnancies under its gender-based statutory rape law than there would be if the law were gender neutral. To meet this burden, the State must show that because its statutory rape law punishes only males, and not females, it more effectively deters minor females from having sexual intercourse.

The plurality assumes that a gender-neutral statute would be less effective than [the statute] in deterring sexual activity because a gender-neutral statute would create significant enforcement problems. *** However, a State's bare assertion that its gender-based statutory classification substantially furthers an important governmental interest is not enough to meet its burden of proof under *Craig v. Boren*. Rather, the State must produce evidence that will persuade the court that its assertion is true. *** [Even] assuming that a gender-neutral statute would be more difficult to enforce, the State has still not shown that those enforcement problems would make such a statute less effective than a gender-based statute in deterring minor females from engaging in sexual intercourse. Common sense, however, suggests that a gender-neutral statutory rape law is potentially a greater deterrent of sexual activity than a gender-based law, for the simple reason that a gender-neutral law subjects both men and women to criminal sanctions and thus arguably has a deterrent effect on twice as many potential violators. Even if fewer persons were prosecuted under the gender-neutral law, as the State suggests, it would still be true that twice as many persons would be subject to arrest. The State's failure to prove that a gender-neutral law would be a less effective deterrent than a gender-based law, like the State's failure to prove that a gender-neutral law would be difficult to enforce, should have led this Court to invalidate [the statute].

Until very recently, no California court or commentator had suggested that the purpose of California's statutory rape law was to protect young women from the risk of pregnancy. Indeed, the historical development of [the statute] demonstrates that the law was initially enacted on the premise that young women, in contrast to young men, were to be deemed legally incapable of consenting to an act of sexual intercourse. Because their chastity was considered particularly precious, those young women were felt to be uniquely in need of the State's protection. In contrast, young men were assumed to be capable of making such decisions for themselves; the law therefore did not offer them any special protection. ***

JUSTICE STEVENS, dissenting.

Local custom and belief—rather than statutory laws of venerable but doubtful ancestry—will determine the volume of sexual activity among

---

[4] In a remarkable display of sexual stereotyping, the California Supreme Court stated: "The Legislature is well within its power in imposing criminal sanctions against males, alone, because they are the only persons who may physiologically cause the result which the law properly seeks to avoid."

unmarried teenagers. The empirical evidence cited by the plurality demonstrates the futility of the notion that a statutory prohibition will significantly affect the volume of that activity or provide a meaningful solution to the problems created by it. Nevertheless, as a matter of constitutional power *** I would have no doubt about the validity of a state law prohibiting all unmarried teenagers from engaging in sexual intercourse. The societal interests in reducing the incidence of venereal disease and teenage pregnancy are sufficient, in my judgment, to justify a prohibition of conduct that increases the risk of those harms. ***

The fact that the Court did not immediately acknowledge that the capacity to become pregnant is what primarily differentiates the female from the male does not impeach the validity of the plurality's newly found wisdom. I think the plurality is quite correct in making the assumption that the joint act that this law seeks to prohibit creates a greater risk of harm for the female than for the male. But the plurality surely cannot believe that the risk of pregnancy confronted by the female—any more than the risk of venereal disease confronted by males as well as females—has provided an effective deterrent to voluntary female participation in the risk-creating conduct. Yet the plurality's decision seems to rest on the assumption that the California Legislature acted on the basis of that rather fanciful notion.

In my judgment, the fact that a class of persons is especially vulnerable to a risk that a statute is designed to avoid is a reason for making the statute applicable to that class. The argument that a special need for protection provides a rational explanation for an exemption is one I simply do not comprehend.[14]

In this case, the fact that a female confronts a greater risk of harm than a male is a reason for applying the prohibition to her—not a reason for granting her a license to use her own judgment on whether or not to assume the risk. Surely, if we examine the problem from the point of view of society's interest in preventing the risk-creating conduct from occurring at all, it is irrational to exempt 50% of the potential violators. And, if we view the government's interest as that of a parens patriae seeking to protect its subjects from harming themselves, the discrimination is actually perverse. Would a rational parent making rules for the conduct of twin children of opposite sex simultaneously forbid the son and authorize the daughter to engage in conduct that is especially harmful to the daughter? That is the effect of this statutory classification. ***

In my opinion, the only acceptable justification for a general rule requiring disparate treatment of the two participants in a joint act must be a legislative judgment that one is more guilty than the other. The risk-creating

---

[14] A hypothetical racial classification will illustrate my point. Assume that skin pigmentation provides some measure of protection against cancer caused by exposure to certain chemicals in the atmosphere and, therefore, that white employees confront a greater risk than black employees in certain industrial settings. Would it be rational to require black employees to wear protective clothing but to exempt whites from that requirement? It seems to me that the greater risk of harm to white workers would be a reason for including them in the requirement—not for granting them an exemption.

conduct that this statute is designed to prevent requires the participation of two persons—one male and one female. In many situations it is probably true that one is the aggressor and the other is either an unwilling, or at least a less willing, participant in the joint act. If a statute authorized punishment of only one participant and required the prosecutor to prove that that participant had been the aggressor, I assume that the discrimination would be valid. ***

The fact that the California Legislature has decided to apply its prohibition only to the male may reflect a legislative judgment that in the typical case the male is actually the more guilty party. Any such judgment must, in turn, assume that the decision to engage in the risk-creating conduct is always—or at least typically—a male decision. If that assumption is valid, the statutory classification should also be valid. But what is the support for the assumption? *** [T]he possibility that such a habitual attitude may reflect nothing more than an irrational prejudice makes it an insufficient justification for discriminatory treatment that is otherwise blatantly unfair. *** Nor do I find at all persuasive the suggestion that this discrimination is adequately justified by the desire to encourage females to inform against their male partners. Even if the concept of a wholesale informant's exemption were an acceptable enforcement device, what is the justification for defining the exempt class entirely by reference to sex rather than by reference to a more neutral criterion such as relative innocence? Indeed, if the exempt class is to be composed entirely of members of one sex, what is there to support the view that the statutory purpose will be better served by granting the informing license to females rather than to males? If a discarded male partner informs on a promiscuous female, a timely threat of prosecution might well prevent the precise harm the statute is intended to minimize.

Finally, even if my logic is faulty and there actually is some speculative basis for treating equally guilty males and females differently, I still believe that any such speculative justification would be outweighed by the paramount interest in evenhanded enforcement of the law. A rule that authorizes punishment of only one of two equally guilty wrongdoers violates the essence of the constitutional requirement that the sovereign must govern impartially.

NGUYEN v. INS
533 U.S. 53 (2001)

JUSTICE KENNEDY delivered the opinion of the Court.

*** 8 U.S.C. § 1409 governs the acquisition of United States citizenship by persons born to one United States citizen parent and one noncitizen parent when the parents are unmarried and the child is born outside of the United States or its possessions. The statute imposes different requirements for the child's acquisition of citizenship depending upon whether the citizen parent is the mother or the father. *** [Section] 1409(a)(4) requires one of three affirmative steps to be taken if the citizen parent is the father, but not if the citizen parent is the mother: legitimation; a declaration of paternity under oath by the father; or a court order of paternity. Congress' decision to impose requirements on unmarried fathers that differ from those on unmarried mothers is based on *** two important governmental objectives. *** The first governmental interest to be served is the importance of assuring that a biological parent-child relationship exists. In the case of the mother, the relation is verifiable from the birth itself. The mother's status is documented in most instances by the birth certificate or hospital records and the witnesses who attest to her having given birth. *** Section 1409(a)(4)'s provision of three options for a father seeking to establish paternity–legitimation, paternity oath, and court order of paternity–is designed to ensure an acceptable documentation of paternity.

Petitioners argue that the requirement *** that a father provide clear and convincing evidence of parentage, is sufficient to achieve the end of establishing paternity, given the sophistication of modern DNA tests. Section 1409(a)(1) does not actually mandate a DNA test, however. *** The requirement of § 1409(a)(4) represents a reasonable conclusion by the legislature that the satisfaction of one of several alternatives will suffice to establish the blood link between father and child required as a predicate to the child's acquisition of citizenship. Given the proof of motherhood that is inherent in birth itself, it is unremarkable that Congress did not require the same affirmative steps of mothers. ***

The second important governmental interest furthered in a substantial manner by § 1409(a)(4) is the determination to ensure that the child and the citizen parent have some demonstrated opportunity or potential to develop not just a relationship that is recognized, as a formal matter, by the law, but one that consists of the real, everyday ties that provide a connection between child and citizen parent and, in turn, the United States. In the case of a citizen mother and a child born overseas, the opportunity for a meaningful relationship between citizen parent and child inheres in the very event of birth *** Even if a father knows of the fact of conception, moreover, it does not follow that he will be present at the birth of the child. Thus, unlike the case of the mother, there is no assurance that the father and his biological child will ever meet. ***

Congress is well within its authority in refusing, absent proof of at least the opportunity for the development of a relationship between citizen parent and child, to commit this country to embracing a child as a citizen entitled as of birth to the full protection of the United States, to the absolute right to enter its borders, and to full participation in the political process. *** There is nothing irrational or improper in the recognition that at the moment of birth–a critical event in the statutory scheme and in the whole tradition of citizenship law–the mother's knowledge of the child and the fact of parenthood have been established in a way not guaranteed in the case of the unwed father. This is not a stereotype.

*** [T]he question remains whether the means Congress chose to further its objective–the imposition of certain additional requirements upon an unwed father–substantially relate to that end. Under this test, the means Congress adopted must be sustained. *** In this difficult context of conferring citizenship on vast numbers of persons, the means adopted by Congress are in substantial furtherance of important governmental objectives. The fit between the means and the important end is "exceedingly persuasive." *** In analyzing § 1409(a)(4), we are mindful that the obligation it imposes with respect to the acquisition of citizenship by the child of a citizen father is minimal. This circumstance shows that Congress has not erected inordinate and unnecessary hurdles to the conferral of citizenship on the children of citizen fathers in furthering its important objectives. Only the least onerous of the three options provided for in § 1409(a)(4) must be satisfied. *** The statute can be satisfied on the day of birth, or the next day, or for the next 18 years. In this case, the unfortunate, even tragic, circumstance is that Boulais did not pursue, or perhaps did not know of, these simple steps and alternatives. Any omission, however, does not nullify the statutory scheme.

Section 1409(a), moreover, is not the sole means by which the child of a citizen father can attain citizenship. An individual who fails to comply with § 1409(a), but who has substantial ties to the United States, can seek citizenship in his or her own right, rather than via reliance on ties to a citizen parent. ***

JUSTICE SCALIA, with whom JUSTICE THOMAS joins, concurring. [omitted]

JUSTICE O'CONNOR, with whom JUSTICE SOUTER, JUSTICE GINSBURG, and JUSTICE BREYER join, dissenting.

*** [T]he majority glosses over the crucial matter of the burden of justification. *** For example, the majority hypothesizes about the interests served by the statute and fails adequately to inquire into the actual purposes of § 1409(a)(4). The Court also does not always explain adequately the importance of the interests that it claims to be served by the provision. The majority also *** casually dismisses the relevance of available sex-neutral alternatives. And, contrary to the majority's conclusion, the fit between the means and ends of § 1409(a)(4) is far too attenuated for the provision to survive heightened scrutiny. ***[A]vailable sex-neutral alternatives would at least replicate, and could easily exceed, whatever fit there is between § 1409(a)(4)'s discriminatory means and the majority's asserted end. *** Congress could simply substitute for § 1409(a)(4) a requirement that the parent be present at birth or have knowledge of birth. Congress could at least allow proof of such presence or knowledge to be one way of demonstrating an opportunity for a relationship. *** There is no reason, other than stereotype, to say that fathers who are present at birth lack an opportunity for a relationship on similar terms. *** Congress could require some degree of regular contact between the child and the citizen parent over a period of time. *** We have repeatedly rejected efforts to justify sex-based classifications on the ground of administrative convenience. There is no reason to think that this is a case where administrative convenience concerns are so powerful that they would justify the sex-based discrimination, especially where the use of sex as a proxy is so ill fit to the purported ends as it is here. ***

The Court has also failed even to acknowledge the "volumes of history" to which "[t]oday's skeptical scrutiny of official action denying rights or opportunities based on sex responds." *** The 1940 Act had been proposed by the President, forwarding a report by a specially convened Committee of Advisors, including the Attorney General. The *** rationale for § 205, whose sex-based classification remains in effect today:

> [T]he Department of State has, at least since 1912, uniformly held that an illegitimate child born abroad of an American mother acquires at birth the nationality of the mother ***. This ruling is based *** on the ground that the mother in such case stands in the place of the father ***. [U]nder American law the mother has a right to custody and control of such child as against the putative father, and *is bound* to maintain it as its *natural guardian*. This rule seems to be in accord with the old Roman law and with the laws of Spain and France.

Section 1409(a)(4) is thus paradigmatic of a historic regime that left women with responsibility, and freed men from responsibility, for nonmarital children. ***

Notes

1.   **Question about *Michael M.*** Does the Court, in your opinion, adequately distinguish between real gender differences and sexist overgeneralizations? How important are California's justifications for the gender difference in the law? How closely does the law match these justifications?

2.   **Real, Not Hypothetical.** JUSTICE O' CONNOR in *Nguyen v. INS* calls attention to the reasons attributed to Congress for having enacted the gender-based classification and that this rationale was neither put forward by the INS nor contained in the statute's legislative history. If *United States v. Virginia* requires the legislative rationale for passage of a gender-based classification to be articulated at or before enactment, how can the majority of the Court speculate regarding Congress' reasons for passing the statute?

3.   **Flexibility.** Does *Nguyen* indicate that standards for assessing equal protection classifications (here, the middle-tier standard) are flexible, depending upon the factual circumstances in which the standard is being employed?

4.   **Other Suspect Classes.** There are a number of cases deciding whether aliens can be treated unequally to citizens (answer: sometimes yes, sometimes no, depending mainly on whether the federal government or a state government is making the distinction and the context of the distinction). Other cases hold that the law cannot treat illegitimate children differently from legitimate children.

D. FUNDAMENTAL INTERESTS
EQUAL PROTECTION

The preceding cases concern racial and gender classifications, often referred to as "suspect classes." Some of these cases involved fundamental interests as well as suspect classes. *See Strauder* (jury trial), *Korematsu* (detention), *Loving* (marriage), and *Michael M.* (criminal liability). We turn now to equal protection law that focuses on whether heightened scrutiny should be applied when a person's "fundamental interests" are involved rather than membership in a suspect class. Consider, as you read the cases, if fundamental interests are the same for equal protection and substantive due process purposes.

SKINNER v. STATE OF OKLAHOMA
316 U.S. 535 (1942)

MR. JUSTICE DOUGLAS delivered the opinion of the Court.

This case touches a sensitive and important area of human rights. Oklahoma deprives certain individuals of a right which is basic to the perpetuation of a race--the right to have offspring. *** The statute involved is Oklahoma's Habitual Criminal Sterilization Act. That Act defines an 'habitual criminal' as a person who, having been convicted two or more times for crimes 'amounting to felonies involving moral turpitude' either in an Oklahoma court or in a court of any other State, is thereafter convicted of such a felony in Oklahoma and is sentenced to a term of imprisonment in an Oklahoma penal institution. Machinery is provided for the institution by the Attorney General of a proceeding against such a person *** for a judgment that such person shall be rendered sexually sterile. Notice, an opportunity to be heard, and the right to a jury trial are provided. The issues triable in such a proceeding are narrow and confined. If the court or jury finds that the defendant is an 'habitual criminal' and that he 'may be rendered sexually sterile without detriment to his or her general health', then the court 'shall render judgment to the effect that said defendant be rendered sexually sterile' by the operation of vasectomy in case of a male and of salpingectomy in case of a female. Only one other provision of the Act is material here [a section] which provides that 'offenses arising out of the violation of the prohibitory laws, revenue acts, embezzlement, or political offenses, shall not come or be considered within the terms of this Act.'

Petitioner was convicted in 1926 of the crime of stealing chickens and was sentenced to the Oklahoma State Reformatory. In 1929 he was convicted of the crime of robbery with fire arms and was sentenced to the reformatory. In 1934 he was convicted again of robbery with firearms and was sentenced to the penitentiary. He was confined there in 1935 when the Act was passed. In 1936 the Attorney General instituted proceedings against him. Petitioner in his answer challenged the Act as unconstitutional by reason of the Fourteenth Amendment. A jury trial was had. The court instructed the jury that the crimes of which petitioner had been convicted were felonies involving moral turpitude and that the only question for the jury was whether the operation of vasectomy could be performed on petitioner without detriment to his general health. The jury found that it could be. A judgment directing that the operation of vasectomy be performed on petitioner was affirmed by the Supreme Court of Oklahoma by a five to four decision.

Several objections to the constitutionality of the Act have been pressed upon us. It is urged that the Act cannot be sustained as an exercise of the police power in view of the state of scientific authorities respecting inheritability of criminal traits. It is argued that due process is lacking because under this Act, unlike the act upheld in *Buck v. Bell*, the defendant is given no opportunity to be heard on the issue as to whether he is the probable potential parent of socially undesirable offspring. It is also suggested that the Act is penal in character and that the sterilization provided for is cruel and unusual punishment and violative of the Fourteenth Amendment. We pass those points without intimating an opinion on them, for there is a feature of the Act which clearly condemns it. That is its failure to meet the requirements of the equal protection clause of the Fourteenth Amendment.

We do not stop to point out all of the inequalities in this Act. A few examples will suffice. In Oklahoma grand larceny is a felony. Larceny is grand larceny when the property taken exceeds $20 in value. Embezzlement is punishable 'in the manner prescribed for feloniously stealing property of the value of that embezzled.' Hence he who embezzles property worth more than $20 is guilty of a felony. A clerk who appropriates over $20 from his employer's till and a stranger who steals the same amount are thus both guilty of felonies. If the latter repeats his act and is convicted three times, he may be sterilized. But the clerk is not subject to the pains and penalties of the Act no matter how large his embezzlements nor how frequent his convictions. A person who enters a chicken coop and steals chickens commits a felony; and he may be sterilized if he is thrice convicted. If, however, he is a bailee of the property and fraudulently appropriates it, he is an embezzler. Hence no matter how habitual his proclivities for embezzlement are and no matter how often his conviction, he may not be sterilized. Thus the nature of the two crimes is intrinsically the same and they are punishable in the same manner. ***

It was stated in *Buck v. Bell* that the claim that state legislation violates the equal protection clause of the Fourteenth Amendment is 'the usual last resort of constitutional arguments.' Under our constitutional system the States in determining the reach and scope of particular legislation need not provide 'abstract symmetry'. They may mark and set apart the classes and types of problems according to the needs and as dictated or suggested by experience. *** [T]he Constitution does not require things which are different in fact or opinion to be treated in law as though they were the same. Thus, if we had here only a question as to a State's classification of crimes, such as embezzlement or larceny, no substantial federal question would be raised. For a State is not constrained in the exercise of its police power to ignore experience which marks a class of offenders or a family of offenses for special treatment. Nor is it prevented by the equal protection clause from confining 'its restrictions to those classes of cases where the need is deemed to be clearest'. ***

But the instant legislation runs afoul of the equal protection clause, though we give Oklahoma that large deference which the rule of the foregoing cases requires. We are dealing here with legislation which involves one of the basic civil rights of man. Marriage and procreation are fundamental to the very existence and survival of the race. The power to sterilize, if exercised, may have subtle, farreaching and devastating effects. In evil or reckless hands it can cause races or types which are inimical to the dominant group to wither and disappear. There is no redemption for the individual whom the law touches. Any experiment which the State conducts is to his irreparable injury. He is forever deprived of a basic liberty. We mention these matters not to reexamine the scope of the police power of the States. We advert to them merely in emphasis of our view that strict scrutiny of the classification which a State makes in a sterilization law is essential, lest unwittingly or otherwise invidious discriminations are made against groups or types of individuals in violation of the constitutional guaranty of just and equal laws. The guaranty of 'equal protection of the laws is a pledge of the protection of equal laws.' *Yick Wo v. Hopkins.* When the law lays an unequal hand on those who have committed intrinsically the same quality of offense and sterilizes one and not the other, it has made as an invidious a discrimination as if it had selected a particular race or nationality for oppressive treatment. Sterilization of those who have thrice committed grand larceny with immunity for those who are embezzlers is a clear, pointed, unmistakable discrimination. Oklahoma makes no attempt to say that he who commits larceny by trespass or trick or fraud has biologically inheritable traits which he who commits embezzlement lacks. *** We have not the slightest basis for inferring that that line has any significance in eugenics nor that the inheritability of criminal traits follows the neat legal distinctions which the law has marked between those two offenses. In terms of fines and imprisonment the crimes of larceny and embezzlement rate the same under the Oklahoma code. Only when it comes to sterilization are the pains and penalties of the law different. *** In *Buck v. Bell*, the Virginia statute was upheld though it applied only to feebleminded persons in institutions of the State. But it was pointed out that 'so far as the operations enable those who otherwise must be kept confined to be returned to the world, and thus open the asylum to others, the equality aimed at will be more nearly reached.' Here there is no such saving feature. Embezzlers are forever free. Those who steal or take in other ways are not. If such a classification were permitted, the technical common law concept of a 'trespass' based on distinctions which are 'very largely dependent upon history for explanation' could readily become a rule of human genetics. ***

MR. CHIEF JUSTICE STONE concurring.

I concur in the result, but I am not persuaded that we are aided in reaching it by recourse to the equal protection clause.

If Oklahoma may resort generally to the sterilization of criminals on the assumption that their propensities are transmissible to future generations by inheritance, I seriously doubt that the equal protection clause requires it to apply the measure to all criminals in the first instance, or to none.

Moreover, if we must presume that the legislature knows--what science has been unable to ascertain--that the criminal tendencies of any class of habitual offenders are transmissible regardless of the varying mental characteristics of its individuals, I should suppose that we must likewise presume that the legislature, in its wisdom, knows that the criminal tendencies of some classes of offenders are more likely to be transmitted than those of others. And so I think the real question we have to consider is not one of equal protection, but whether the wholesale condemnation of a class to such an invasion of personal liberty, without opportunity to any individual to show that his is not the type of case which would justify resort to it, satisfies the demands of due process.

There are limits to the extent to which the presumption of constitutionality can be pressed, especially where the liberty of the person is concerned (*see United States v. Carolene Products*, 304 U.S. 144, 152, n.4.) and *** prudence would seem to demand for the protection of the individual from arbitrary action. Although petitioner here was given a hearing to ascertain whether sterilization would be detrimental to his health, he was given none to discover whether his criminal tendencies are of an inheritable type. Undoubtedly a state may, after appropriate inquiry, constitutionally interfere with the personal liberty of the individual to prevent the transmission by inheritance of his socially injurious tendencies. *Buck v. Bell*. But until now we have not been called upon to say that it may do so without giving him a hearing and opportunity to challenge the existence as to him of the only facts which could justify so drastic a measure.

Science has found and the law has recognized that there are certain types of mental deficiency associated with delinquency which are inheritable. But the State does not contend--nor can there be any pretense--that either common knowledge or experience, or scientific investigation, has given assurance that the criminal tendencies of any class of habitual offenders are universally or even generally inheritable. *** A law which condemns, without hearing, all the individuals of a class to so harsh a measure as the present because some or even many merit condemnation, is lacking in the first principles of due process. *** The state is called on to sacrifice no permissible end when it is required to reach its objective by a reasonable and just procedure adequate to safeguard rights of the individual which concededly the Constitution protects.

MR. JUSTICE JACKSON, concurring.

I join the CHIEF JUSTICE in holding that the hearings provided are too limited in the context of the present Act to afford due process of law. I also agree with the opinion of MR. JUSTICE DOUGLAS that the scheme of classification set forth in the Act denies equal protection of the law. I disagree with the opinion of each in so far as it rejects or minimizes the grounds taken by the other.

Perhaps to employ a broad and loose scheme of classification would be permissible if accompanied by the individual hearings indicated by the CHIEF JUSTICE. On the other hand, narrow classification with reference to the end to be accomplished by the Act might justify limiting individual hearings to the issue whether the individual belonged to a class so defined. Since this Act does not present these questions, I reserve judgment on them.

[T]he present plan to sterilize the individual in pursuit of a eugenic plan to eliminate from the race characteristics that are only vaguely identified and which in our present state of knowledge are uncertain as to transmissibility presents other constitutional questions of gravity. This Court has sustained such an experiment with respect to an imbecile, a person with definite and observable characteristics where the condition had persisted through three generations and afforded grounds for the belief that it was transmissible and would continue to manifest itself in generations to come. *Buck v. Bell*.

There are limits to the extent to which a legislatively represented majority may conduct biological experiments at the expense of the dignity and personality and natural powers of a minority--even those who have been guilty of what the majority define as crimes. But this Act falls down before reaching this problem. ***

Notes

1. ***Buck* and *Skinner*.** Consider why the Court was more receptive to Skinner's petition than to Carrie Buck's. Was the difference that Carrie Buck was viewed as an "imbecile" while Skinner was a "criminal"? Had changes in the Court, American society, and geopolitics occurred in the interim?

2. **A Tale of Two Justices.** JUSTICE OLIVER WENDELL HOLMES, JR., a veteran of the Civil War, was the most respected member of the Court in his day. When he wrote *Buck*, Holmes was in his final years on the Court. Sometimes referred to as "the Boston Brahmin," JUSTICE HOLMES was generally viewed as an intellectual snob. His line "three generations of imbeciles is enough" was as much a personal judgment as a reflection of social policy embedded in law. JUSTICE WILLIAM O. DOUGLAS, when he wrote *Skinner*, was a young man. Part of FDR's "Brain Trust," Douglas was a westerner who subsequently led the Securities and Exchange Commission in its infancy. He did not suffer fools (or even brilliant law clerks) gladly but was a champion of the environment and individual liberty.

3. **Imbeciles and Criminals.** Eugenics, the science of human perfectibility, was in its heyday when *Buck* was written. All manner of traits were thought to be inherited, including traits far beyond those we view as having genetic origins today. For example, some eugenicists viewed thriftiness and criminal tendencies as inherited rather than determined by environment and education. By the time *Skinner* was penned, skepticism had begun to undermine the broader claims of eugenicists. Interestingly, of the inmates in Oklahoma's McAllister Prison, which housed Skinner, only a small percentage had any parents or offspring with criminal histories. Skinner, a repeat chicken thief, likely stole out of desperation born of the Depression.

4. **Geopolitical Changes.** The rise of Adolf Hitler proved the undoing of the American eugenics movement. By 1942, the Nazis' vicious slaughter of Jewish and other populations in the name of creating a pure Aryan race was well known, providing context to this line in *Skinner*: "In evil or reckless hands [the power to sterilize] can cause races or types which are inimical to the dominant group to wither and disappear."

5. **Suspect Classes and Fundamental Rights.** While JUSTICE DOUGLAS talks of "races or types" and of "dominant groups," Skinner (a white male) was not a member of a "suspect class" in America during World War II. JUSTICE DOUGLAS' opinion turns on human rights, marriage and procreation, and reproductive matters "basic to the perpetuation of the race." However, when the Oklahoma legislature passed the law at issue in *Skinner*, it exempted "political offenses." Why? Legislators did not want activities for which they might be convicted to lead to sterilization. Thus, on one level, the case is about class—social and political elites versus lower class criminals—even if it is not about racial class.

ZABLOCKI v. REDHAIL
434 U.S. 374 (1978)

MR. JUSTICE MARSHALL delivered the opinion of the Court.

At issue in this case is the constitutionality of a Wisconsin statute which provides that [any Wisconsin resident having minor issue not in his custody and which he is under obligation to support by any court order or judgment] may not marry, within the State or elsewhere, without first obtaining a court order granting permission to marry. *** The statute specifies that court permission cannot be granted unless the marriage applicant submits proof of compliance with the support obligation and, in addition, demonstrates that the children covered by the support order "are not then and are not likely thereafter to become public charges." *** After being denied a marriage license because of his failure to comply with [the Act], appellee brought this class action challenging the statute as violative of the Equal Protection and Due Process Clauses of the Fourteenth Amendment ***.

Appellee Redhail is a Wisconsin resident who is unable to enter into a lawful marriage in Wisconsin or elsewhere so long as he maintains his Wisconsin residency. In January 1972, when appellee was a minor and a high school student, a paternity action was instituted against him in Milwaukee County Court, alleging that he was the father of a baby girl born out of wedlock on July 5, 1971. After he appeared and admitted that he was the child's father, the court entered an order on May 12, 1972, adjudging appellee the father and ordering him to pay $109 per month as support for the child until she reached 18 years of age. From May 1972 until August 1974, appellee was unemployed and indigent, and consequently was unable to make any support payments. On September 27, 1974, appellee filed an application for a marriage license with appellant Zablocki, the County Clerk of Milwaukee County, and a few days later the application was denied on the sole ground that appellee had not obtained a court order granting him permission to marry, as required by [the Act]. *** [I]t is stipulated that he would not have been able to satisfy either of the statutory prerequisites for an order granting permission to marry. ***

[*Loving v. Virginia* held that Virginia's antimiscegenation] laws arbitrarily deprived [citizens] of a fundamental liberty protected by the Due Process Clause, the freedom to marry. The Court's language on the latter point bears repeating: "The freedom to marry has long been recognized as one of the vital personal rights essential to the orderly pursuit of happiness by free men." "Marriage is one of the 'basic civil rights of man,' fundamental to our very existence and survival." *** More recent decisions have established that the right to marry is part of the fundamental "right of privacy" implicit in the Fourteenth Amendment's Due Process Clause. *** It is not surprising that the decision to marry has been placed on the same level of importance as decisions relating to procreation, childbirth, child rearing, and family relationships. As the facts of this case illustrate, it would make little sense to recognize a right of privacy with respect to other matters of family life and not with respect to the decision to enter the relationship that is the foundation of the family in our society. *** [If] appellee's right to procreate means anything at all, it must imply some right to enter the only relationship in which the State of Wisconsin allows sexual relations legally to take place.

By reaffirming the fundamental character of the right to marry, we do not mean to suggest that every state regulation which relates in any way to the incidents of or prerequisites for marriage must be subjected to rigorous scrutiny. To the contrary, reasonable regulations that do not significantly interfere with decisions to enter into the marital relationship may legitimately be imposed. The statutory classification at issue here, however, clearly does interfere directly and substantially with the right to marry.

Under the challenged statute, no Wisconsin resident in the affected class may marry in Wisconsin or elsewhere without a court order, and marriages contracted in violation of the statute are both void and punishable as criminal offenses. Some of those in the affected class, like appellee, will never be able to obtain the necessary court order, because they either lack the financial means to meet their support obligations or cannot prove that their children will not become public charges. These persons are absolutely prevented from getting married. Many others, able in theory to satisfy the statute's requirements, will be sufficiently burdened by having to do so that they will in effect be coerced into forgoing their right to marry. And even those who can be persuaded to meet the statute's requirements suffer a serious intrusion into their freedom of choice in an area in which we have held such freedom to be fundamental. ***

When a statutory classification significantly interferes with the exercise of a fundamental right, it cannot be upheld unless it is supported by sufficiently important state interests and is closely tailored to effectuate only those interests. Appellant asserts that two interests are served by the challenged statute: the permission-to-marry proceeding furnishes an opportunity to counsel the applicant as to the necessity of fulfilling his prior support obligations; and the welfare of the out-of-custody children is protected. We may accept for present purposes that these are legitimate and substantial interests, but, since the means selected by the State for achieving these interests unnecessarily impinge on the right to marry, the statute cannot be sustained.

*** With regard to safeguarding the welfare of the out-of-custody children, appellant's brief does not make clear the connection between the State's interest and the statute's requirements. At argument, appellant's counsel suggested that, since permission to marry cannot be granted unless the applicant shows that he has satisfied his court-determined support obligations to the prior children and that those children will not become public charges, the statute provides incentive for the applicant to make support payments to his children. This "collection device" rationale cannot justify the statute's broad infringement on the right to marry. First, with respect to individuals who are unable to meet the statutory requirements, the statute merely prevents the applicant from getting married, without delivering any money at all into the hands of the applicant's prior children. More importantly, regardless of the applicant's ability or willingness to meet the statutory requirements, the State already has numerous other means for exacting compliance with support obligations, means that are at least as effective as the instant statute's and yet do not impinge upon the right to marry. ***

The statutory classification created by [the Act] thus cannot be justified by the interests advanced in support of it.

MR. JUSTICE STEWART, concurring in the judgment.

*** To hold, as the Court does, that the Wisconsin statute violates the Equal Protection Clause seems to me to misconceive the meaning of that constitutional guarantee. *** The problem in this case is not one of discriminatory classifications, but of unwarranted encroachment upon a constitutionally protected freedom. I think that the Wisconsin statute is unconstitutional because it exceeds the bounds of permissible state regulation of marriage, and invades the sphere of liberty protected by the Due Process Clause of the Fourteenth Amendment. ***

The Constitution does not specifically mention freedom to marry, but it is settled that the "liberty" protected by the Due Process Clause of the Fourteenth Amendment embraces more than those freedoms expressly enumerated in the Bill of Rights. And the decisions of this Court have made clear that freedom of personal choice in matters of marriage and family life is one of the liberties so protected. *** The question is whether the state interests that support the abridgment can overcome the substantive protections of the Constitution.

The Wisconsin law makes permission to marry turn on the payment of money in support of one's children by a previous marriage or liaison. Those who cannot show both that they have kept up with their support obligations and that their children are not and will not become wards of the State are altogether prohibited from marrying. *** The Wisconsin law makes no allowance for the truly indigent. The State flatly denies a marriage license to anyone who cannot afford to fulfill his support obligations and keep his children from becoming wards of the State. We may assume that the State has legitimate interests in collecting delinquent support payments and in reducing its welfare load. We may also assume that, as applied to those who can afford to meet the statute's financial requirements but choose not to do so, the law advances the State's objectives in ways superior to other means available to the State. The fact remains that some people simply cannot afford to meet the statute's financial requirements. To deny these people permission to marry penalizes them for failing to do that which they cannot do. Insofar as it applies to indigents, the state law is an irrational means of achieving these objectives of the State. ***

MR. JUSTICE POWELL, concurring in the judgment.

*** The Court apparently would subject all state regulation which "directly and substantially" interferes with the decision to marry in a traditional family setting to "critical examination" or "compelling state interest" analysis. Presumably, "reasonable regulations that do not significantly interfere with decisions to enter into the marital relationship may legitimately be imposed." The Court does not present, however, any principled means for distinguishing between the two types of regulations. Since state regulation in this area typically takes the form of a prerequisite or barrier to marriage or divorce, the degree of "direct" interference with the decision to marry or to divorce is unlikely to provide either guidance for state legislatures or a basis for judicial oversight. ***

In my view, analysis must start from the recognition of domestic relations as "an area that has long been regarded as a virtually exclusive province of the States." *** State regulation has included bans on incest, bigamy, and homosexuality, as well as various preconditions to marriage, such as blood tests. Likewise, a showing of fault on the part of one of the partners traditionally has been a prerequisite to the dissolution of an unsuccessful union. A "compelling state purpose" inquiry would cast doubt on the network of restrictions that the States have fashioned to govern marriage and divorce.

State power over domestic relations is not without constitutional limits. The Due Process Clause requires a showing of justification "when the government intrudes on choices concerning family living arrangements" in a manner which is contrary to deeply rooted traditions. *** Furthermore, under the Equal Protection Clause the means chosen by the State in this case must bear "'a fair and substantial relation'" to the object of the legislation.

The Wisconsin measure in this case does not pass muster under either due process or equal protection standards. Appellant identifies three objectives which are supposedly furthered by the statute in question: (i) a counseling function; (ii) an incentive to satisfy outstanding support obligations; and (iii) a deterrent against incurring further obligations. The opinion of the Court amply demonstrates that the asserted counseling objective bears no relation to this statute. *** The so-called "collection device" rationale presents a somewhat more difficult question. I do not agree with the suggestion in the Court's opinion that a State may never condition the right to marry on satisfaction of existing support obligations simply because the State has alternative methods of compelling such payments. To the extent this restriction applies to persons who are able to make the required support payments but simply wish to shirk their moral and legal obligation, the Constitution interposes no bar to this additional collection mechanism. The vice inheres, not in the collection concept, but in the failure to make provision for those without the means to comply with child-support obligations. *** Because the State has not established a justification for this unprecedented foreclosure of marriage to many of its citizens solely because of their indigency, I concur in the judgment of the Court.

MR. JUSTICE STEVENS, concurring in the judgment.

*** A classification based on marital status is fundamentally different from a classification which determines who may lawfully enter into the marriage relationship. The individual's interest in making the marriage decision independently is sufficiently important to merit special constitutional protection. It is not, however, an interest which is constitutionally immune from evenhanded regulation. Thus, laws prohibiting marriage to a child, a close relative, or a person afflicted with venereal disease, are unchallenged even though they "interfere directly and substantially with the right to marry." This Wisconsin statute has a different character.

Under this statute, a person's economic status may determine his eligibility to enter into a lawful marriage. A noncustodial parent whose children are "public charges" may not marry even if he has met his court-ordered obligations. Thus, within the class of parents who have fulfilled their court-ordered obligations, the rich may marry and the poor may not. This type of statutory discrimination is, I believe, totally unprecedented, as well as inconsistent with our tradition of administering justice equally to the rich and to the poor. *** The statute prevents impoverished parents from marrying even though their intended spouses are economically independent. Presumably, the Wisconsin Legislature assumed (a) that only fathers would be affected by the legislation, and (b) that they would never marry employed women. The first assumption ignores the fact that fathers are sometimes awarded custody, and the second ignores the composition of today's work force. To the extent that the statute denies a hard-pressed parent any opportunity to prove that an intended marriage will ease rather than aggravate his financial straits, it not only rests on unreliable premises, but also defeats its own objectives.

In sum, the public-charge provision is either futile or perverse insofar as it applies to childless couples, couples who will have illegitimate children if they are forbidden to marry, couples whose economic status will be improved by marriage, and couples who are so poor that the marriage will have no impact on the welfare status of their children in any event. Even assuming that the right to marry may sometimes be denied on economic grounds, this clumsy and deliberate legislative discrimination between the rich and the poor is irrational in so many ways that it cannot withstand scrutiny under the Equal Protection Clause of the Fourteenth Amendment.

MR. JUSTICE REHNQUIST, dissenting.

*** I think that under the Equal Protection Clause the statute need pass only the "rational basis test." The statute so viewed is a permissible exercise of the State's power to regulate family life and to assure the support of minor children, despite its possible imprecision in the extreme cases envisioned in the concurring opinions. ***

Notes

1. **Theory behind *Zablocki*.** How does the fundamental right at issue in *Zablocki* compare to the right in *Skinner*? Would you say after reading *Zablocki* that any fundamental liberty interest in a "deeply rooted traditions" sense is also a fundamental interest for equal protection purposes? Do we need to be equally aware in the equal protection context of the level of generality involved in defining the right?

2.   **Comparisons of *Moore* and *Zablocki*.**   *Moore* was a substantive due process decision; *Zablocki* was decided on equal protection grounds. Which approach do you think preferable?   Do you agree that "[judicial] discovery of fundamental [values] outside the constitutional text [should] be grounded in the due process clause. [The] equality strand [should] not bear a substantive content"?   Lupu, *Untangling the Strands of the Fourteenth Amendment*, 77 MICH. L. REV. 981, 985 (1979).

3. **Marriage and Family.** *Moore* is often considered for the proposition that there is a fundamental right to family; *Zablocki* for the proposition that there is a fundamental right to marry.   Yet both may be contextually limited, the former to prohibited living arrangements, the latter to debt-based bars to marriage.   Should the Court invalidate an AFDC requirement that recipient families include within the family unit all children living within the household, including those receiving child support payments from noncustodial parents, with a consequent reduction of the family's benefit levels?   *See Bowen v. Gilliard*, 483 U.S. 587 (1987) ("That some families may decide to modify their living arrangements" because of the regulation is not an impermissible intrusion on family).   What should the Court do about a Social Security Act provision terminating benefits received by a disabled dependent child of a covered wage earner when the child marries an individual who is not independently entitled to benefits, even if the spouse is also disabled?   *See Califano v. Jobst*, 434 U.S. 47 (1977) (rule valid despite fact that "some persons who might otherwise have married were deterred by the rule or because some who did marry were burdened thereby").   What distinguishes these cases from *Moore* and *Zablocki*?

SAN ANTONIO INDEPENDENT SCHOOL DISTRICT v. RODRIGUEZ
411 U.S. 1 (1973)

MR. JUSTICE POWELL delivered the opinion of the Court.

*** Until recent times, Texas was a predominantly rural State and its population and property wealth were spread relatively evenly across the State. Sizable differences in the value of assessable property between local school districts became increasingly evident as the State became more industrialized and as rural-to-urban population shifts became more pronounced. The location of commercial and industrial property began to play a significant role in determining the amount of tax resources available to each school district. These growing disparities in population and taxable property between districts were responsible in part for increasingly notable differences in levels of local expenditure for education. *** [A Foundation Program was begun in 1949 to ameliorate the problem.] The Program calls for state and local contributions to a fund earmarked specifically for teacher salaries, operating expenses, and transportation costs. The State, supplying funds from its general revenues, finances approximately 80% of the Program, and the school districts are responsible—as a unit—for providing the remaining 20%. ***

The school district in which appellees reside, the Edgewood Independent School District, has been compared throughout this litigation with the Alamo Heights Independent School District. This comparison between the least and most affluent districts in the San Antonio area serves to illustrate the manner in which the dual system of finance operates and to indicate the extent to which substantial disparities exist despite the State's impressive progress in recent years. Edgewood is one of seven public school districts in the metropolitan area. The district is situated in the core-city sector of San Antonio in a residential neighborhood that has little commercial or industrial property. The residents are predominantly of Mexican–American descent *** [and] [t]he average assessed property value per pupil is $5,960—the lowest in the metropolitan area. *** At an equalized tax rate of $1.05 per $100 of assessed property—the highest in the metropolitan area—the district contributed $26 to the education of each child for the 1967—1968 school year. *** The Foundation Program contributed $222 per pupil for a state-local total of $248. ***

Alamo Heights is the most affluent school district in San Antonio. Its six schools, housing approximately 5,000 students, are situated in a residential community quite unlike the Edgewood District. The school population is predominantly "Anglo," having only 18% Mexican–Americans and less than 1% Negroes. The assessed property value per pupil exceeds $49,000, and *** [i]n 1967—1968 the local tax rate of $.85 per $100 of valuation yielded $333 per pupil over and above its contribution to the Foundation Program. Coupled with the $225 provided from that Program, the district was able to supply $558 per student. *** Alamo Heights, because of its relative wealth, was required to contribute out of its local property tax collections approximately $100 per pupil, or about 20% of its Foundation grant. Edgewood, on the other hand, paid only $8.46 per pupil, which is about 2.4% of its grant. It appears then that, at least as to these two districts, the Local Fund Assignment does reflect a rough approximation of the relative taxpaying potential of each.

*** The District Court held that the Texas system discriminates on the basis of wealth in the manner in which education is provided for its people. Finding that wealth is a "suspect" classification and that education is a "fundamental" interest, the District Court held that the Texas system could be sustained only if the State could show that it was premised upon some compelling state interest. *** [W]e find neither the suspect-classification nor the fundamental-interest analysis persuasive.

*** The individuals, or groups of individuals, who constituted the class discriminated against in our prior cases shared two distinguishing characteristics: because of their impecunity they were completely unable to pay for some desired benefit, and as a consequence, they sustained an absolute deprivation of a meaningful opportunity to enjoy that benefit. In *Griffin v. Illinois*, 351 U.S. 12 (1956), and its progeny, the Court invalidated state laws that prevented an indigent criminal defendant from acquiring a transcript, or an adequate substitute for a transcript, for use at several stages of the trial and appeal process. The payment requirements in each case were found to occasion de facto discrimination against those who, because of their indigency, were totally unable to pay for transcripts. And the Court in each case emphasized that no constitutional violation would have been shown if the State had provided some "adequate substitute" for a full stenographic transcript.

Likewise, in *Douglas v. California*, 372 U.S. 353 (1963), a decision establishing an indigent defendant's right to court-appointed counsel on direct appeal, the Court dealt only with defendants who could not pay for counsel from their own resources and who had no other way of gaining representation. *Douglas* provides no relief for those on whom the burdens of paying for a criminal defense are relatively speaking, great but not insurmountable. Nor does it deal with relative differences in the quality of counsel acquired by the less wealthy. *** Finally, in *Bullock v. Carter*, 405 U.S. 134 (1972), the Court invalidated the Texas filing-fee requirement for primary elections. Both of the relevant classifying facts found in the previous cases were present there. The size of the fee, often running into the thousands of dollars and, in at least one case, as high as $8,900, effectively barred all potential candidates who were unable to pay the required fee. As the system provided "no reasonable alternative means of access to the ballot", inability to pay occasioned an absolute denial of a position on the primary ballot.

*** [N]either of the two distinguishing characteristics of wealth classifications can be found here. First, in support of their charge that the system discriminates against the "poor," appellees have made no effort to demonstrate that it operates to the peculiar disadvantage of any class fairly definable as indigent, or as composed of persons whose incomes are beneath any designated poverty level. Indeed, there is reason to believe that the poorest families are not necessarily clustered in the poorest property districts. ***

Second *** lack of personal resources has not occasioned an absolute deprivation of the desired benefit. *** Apart from the unsettled and disputed question whether the quality of education may be determined by the amount of money expended for it, a sufficient answer to appellees' argument is that, at least where wealth is involved, the Equal Protection Clause does not require absolute equality or precisely equal advantages. ***

In *Brown v. Board of Education*, a unanimous Court recognized that "education is perhaps the most important function of state and local governments." *** Nothing this Court holds today in any way detracts from our historic dedication to public education. *** But the importance of a service performed by the State does not determine whether it must be regarded as fundamental for purposes of examination under the Equal Protection Clause. *** Thus, the key to discovering whether education is "fundamental" is not to be found in comparisons of the relative societal significance of education as opposed to subsistence or housing. Nor is it to be found by weighing whether education is as important as the right to travel. Rather, the answer lies in assessing whether there is a right to education explicitly or implicitly guaranteed by the Constitution.

Education, of course, is not among the rights afforded explicit protection under our Federal Constitution. Nor do we find any basis for saying it is implicitly so protected. *** It is appellees' contention, however, that education is *** a fundamental personal right because it is essential to the effective exercise of First Amendment freedoms and to intelligent utilization of the right to vote. *** A similar line of reasoning is pursued with respect to the right to vote.[78] Exercise of the franchise, it is contended, cannot be divorced from the educational foundation of the voter ***: a voter cannot cast his ballot intelligently unless his reading skills and thought processes have been adequately developed.

We need not dispute any of these propositions. The Court has long afforded zealous protection against unjustifiable governmental interference with the individual's rights to speak and to vote. Yet we have never presumed to possess either the ability or the authority to guarantee to the citizenry the most effective speech or the most informed electoral choice. That these may be desirable goals of a system of freedom of expression and of a representative form of government is not to be doubted. These are indeed goals to be pursued by a people whose thoughts and beliefs are freed from governmental interference. But they are not values to be implemented by judicial intrusion into otherwise legitimate state activities. *** [And] no charge fairly could be made that the system fails to provide each child with an opportunity to acquire the basic minimal skills necessary for the enjoyment of the rights of speech and of full participation in the political process.

Furthermore, the logical limitations on appellees' nexus theory are difficult to perceive. How, for instance, is education to be distinguished from the significant personal interests in the basics of decent food and shelter? Empirical examination might well buttress an assumption that the ill-fed, ill-clothed, and ill-housed are among the most ineffective participants in the political process, and that they derive the least enjoyment from the benefits of the First Amendment. ***

We need not rest our decision, however, solely on the inappropriateness of the strict-scrutiny test. A century of Supreme Court adjudication under the Equal Protection Clause affirmatively supports the application of the traditional standard of review, which requires only that the State's system be shown to bear some rational relationship to legitimate state purposes. *** No scheme of taxation, whether the tax is imposed on property, income, or purchases of goods and services, has yet been devised which is free of all discriminatory impact. In such a complex arena in which no perfect alternatives exist, the Court does well not to impose too rigorous a standard of scrutiny lest all local fiscal schemes become subjects of criticism under the Equal Protection Clause.

---

[78] Since the right to vote, per se, is not a constitutionally protected right, we assume that appellees' references to that right are simply shorthand references to the protected right, implicit in our constitutional system, to participate in state elections on an equal basis with other qualified voters whenever the State has adopted an elective process for determining who will represent any segment of the State's population.

In addition to matters of fiscal policy, this case also involves the most persistent and difficult questions of educational policy, another area in which this Court's lack of specialized knowledge and experience counsels against premature interference with the informed judgments made at the state and local levels. *** The Texas system of school finance, *** [w]hile assuring a basic education for every child in the State, [also] permits and encourages a large measure of participation in and control of each district's schools at the local level. *** [L]ocal control means *** the freedom to devote more money to the education of one's children. Equally important, however, is the opportunity it offers for participation in the decisionmaking process that determines how those local tax dollars will be spent. Each locality is free to tailor local programs to local needs. *** Only where state action impinges on the exercise of fundamental constitutional rights or liberties must it be found to have chosen the least restrictive alternative. ***

IX–3. "***One Nation***Indivisible***" by Herbert Block. © 1977 Herblock—from *Herblock On All Fronts* (New American Library, 1980).

The people of Texas may be justified in believing that other systems of school financing, which place more of the financial responsibility in the hands of the State, will result in a comparable lessening of desired local autonomy. *** In sum, to the extent that the Texas system of school financing results in unequal expenditures between children who happen to reside in different districts, we cannot say that such disparities are the product of a system that is so irrational as to be invidiously discriminatory. ***

MR. JUSTICE WHITE, with whom MR. JUSTICE DOUGLAS and MR. JUSTICE BRENNAN join, dissenting.

*** If the State aims at maximizing local initiative and local choice, by permitting school districts to resort to the real property tax if they choose to do so, it utterly fails in achieving its purpose in districts with property tax bases so low that there is little if any opportunity for interested parents, rich or poor, to augment school district revenues. Requiring the State to establish only that unequal treatment is in furtherance of a permissible goal, without also requiring the State to show that the means chosen to effectuate that goal are rationally related to its achievement, makes equal protection analysis no more than an empty gesture. In my view, the parents and children in Edgewood, and in like districts, suffer from an invidious discrimination violative of the Equal Protection Clause. ***

MR. JUSTICE MARSHALL, with whom MR. JUSTICE DOUGLAS concurs, dissenting.

*** [I cannot accept] that fundamental interests, which call for strict scrutiny of the challenged classification, encompass only established rights which we are somehow bound to recognize from the text of the Constitution itself. To be sure, some interests which the Court has deemed to be fundamental for purposes of equal protection analysis are themselves constitutionally protected rights. Thus, discrimination against the guaranteed right of freedom of speech has called for strict judicial scrutiny. Further, every citizen's right to travel interstate, although nowhere expressly mentioned in the Constitution, has long been recognized as implicit in the premises underlying that document ***. *Shapiro v. Thompson.* But it will not do to suggest that the "answer" to whether an interest is fundamental for purposes of equal protection analysis is always determined by whether that interest "is a right *** explicitly or implicitly guaranteed by the Constitution."[59]

I would like to know where the Constitution guarantees the right to procreate, *Skinner v. Oklahoma ex rel. Williamson,* or the right to vote in state elections, e.g., *Reynolds v. Sims,* or the right to an appeal from a criminal conviction, e.g., *Griffin v. Illinois.* These are instances in which, due to the importance of the interests at stake, the Court has displayed a strong concern with the existence of discriminatory state treatment. But the Court has never said or indicated that these are interests which independently enjoy fullblown constitutional protection. ***

The task in every case should be to determine the extent to which constitutionally guaranteed rights are dependent on interests not mentioned

---

[59] Indeed, the Court's theory would render the established concept of fundamental interests in the context of equal protection analysis superfluous, for the substantive constitutional right itself requires that this Court strictly scrutinize any asserted state interest for restricting or denying access to any particular guaranteed right.

in the Constitution. As the nexus between the specific constitutional guarantee and the nonconstitutional interest draws closer, the nonconstitutional interest becomes more fundamental and the degree of judicial scrutiny applied when the interest is infringed on a discriminatory basis must be adjusted accordingly. Thus, it cannot be denied that interests such as procreation, the exercise of the state franchise, and access to criminal appellate processes are not fully guaranteed to the citizen by our Constitution. But these interests have nonetheless been afforded special judicial consideration in the face of discrimination because they are, to some extent, interrelated with constitutional guarantees. ***

It is true that this Court has never deemed the provision of free public education to be required by the Constitution. *** Nevertheless, the fundamental importance of education is amply indicated by the prior decisions of this Court, by the unique status accorded public education by our society, and by the close relationship between education and some of our most basic constitutional values. *** It is this very sort of intimate relationship between a particular personal interest and specific constitutional guarantees that has heretofore caused the Court to attach special significance, for purposes of equal protection analysis, to individual interests such as procreation and the exercise of the state franchise.[74] ***

The State's interest in local educational control—which certainly includes questions of educational funding—has deep roots in the inherent benefits of community support for public education. *** [However,] on this record, it is apparent that the State's purported concern with local control is offered primarily as an excuse rather than as a justification for interdistrict inequality. *** If Texas had a system truly dedicated to local fiscal control, one would expect the quality of the educational opportunity provided in each district to vary with the decision of the voters in that district as to the level of sacrifice they wish to make for public education. In fact, the Texas scheme produces precisely the opposite result. Local school districts cannot choose to have the best education in the State by imposing the highest tax rate. Instead, the quality of the educational opportunity offered by any particular district is largely determined by the amount of taxable property located in the district—a factor over which local voters can exercise no control. ***

---

[74] I believe that the close nexus between education and our established constitutional values with respect to freedom of speech and participation in the political process makes this a different case from our prior decisions concerning discrimination affecting public welfare, *see, e.g., Dandridge v. Williams,* or housing, *see, e.g., Lindsey v. Normet.* There can be no question that, as the majority suggests, constitutional rights may be less meaningful for someone without enough to eat or without decent housing. But the crucial difference lies in the closeness of the relationship. Whatever the severity of the impact of insufficient food or inadequate housing on a person's life, they have never been considered to bear the same direct and immediate relationship to constitutional concerns for free speech and for our political processes as education has long been recognized to bear. Perhaps, the best evidence of this fact is the unique status which has been accorded public education as the single public service nearly unanimously guaranteed in the constitutions of our States. Education, in terms of constitutional values, is much more analogous in my judgment, to the right to vote in state elections than to public welfare or public housing. Indeed, it is not without significance that we have long recognized education as an essential step in providing the disadvantaged with the tools necessary to achieve economic self-sufficiency.

In my judgment, any substantial degree of scrutiny of the operation of the Texas financing scheme reveals that the State has selected means wholly inappropriate to secure its purported interest in assuring its school districts local fiscal control.[96] At the same time, appellees have pointed out a variety of alternative financing schemes which may serve the State's purported interest in local control as well as, if not better than, the present scheme without the current impairment of the educational opportunity of vast numbers of Texas schoolchildren. *** I believe that the wide disparities in taxable district property wealth inherent in the local property tax element of the Texas financing scheme render that scheme violative of the Equal Protection Clause. ***

PLYLER v. DOE
457 U.S. 202 (1982)

JUSTICE BRENNAN delivered the opinion of the Court.

The question presented by these cases is whether, consistent with the Equal Protection Clause of the Fourteenth Amendment, Texas may deny to undocumented school-age children the free public education that it provides to children who are citizens of the United States or legally admitted aliens. *** Aliens, even aliens whose presence in this country is unlawful, have long been recognized as "persons" guaranteed due process of law by the Fifth and Fourteenth Amendments. [*Yick Wo v. Hopkins*, 118 U.S. 356 (1886)]. *** The more difficult question is whether the Equal Protection Clause has been violated by the refusal of the State of Texas to reimburse local school boards for the education of children who cannot demonstrate that their presence within the United States is lawful, or by the imposition by those school boards of the burden of tuition on those children. It is to this question that we now turn.

*** A legislature must have substantial latitude to establish classifications that roughly approximate the nature of the problem perceived, that accommodate competing concerns both public and private, and that account for limitations on the practical ability of the State to remedy every ill. In applying the Equal Protection Clause to most forms of state action, we thus seek only the assurance that the classification at issue bears some fair relationship to a legitimate public purpose.

But we would not be faithful to our obligations under the Fourteenth Amendment if we applied so deferential a standard to every classification.

---

[96] My Brother WHITE, in concluding that the Texas financing scheme runs afoul of the Equal Protection Clause, likewise finds on analysis that the means chosen by Texas—local property taxation dependent upon local taxable wealth—is completely unsuited in its present form to the achievement of the asserted goal of providing local fiscal control. Although my Brother WHITE purports to reach this result by application of that lenient standard of mere rationality traditionally applied in the context of commercial interest, it seems to me that the care with which he scrutinizes the practical effectiveness of the present local property tax as a device for affording local fiscal control reflects the application of a more stringent standard of review, a standard which at the least is influenced by the constitutional significance of the process of public education.

The Equal Protection Clause was intended as a restriction on state legislative action inconsistent with elemental constitutional premises. Thus we have treated as presumptively invidious those classifications that disadvantage a "suspect class," or that impinge upon the exercise of a "fundamental right." With respect to such classifications, it is appropriate to enforce the mandate of equal protection by requiring the State to demonstrate that its classification has been precisely tailored to serve a compelling governmental interest. In addition, we have recognized that certain forms of legislative classification, while not facially invidious, nonetheless give rise to recurring constitutional difficulties; in these limited circumstances we have sought the assurance that the classification reflects a reasoned judgment consistent with the ideal of equal protection by inquiring whether it may fairly be viewed as furthering a substantial interest of the State. ***

Sheer incapability or lax enforcement of the laws barring entry into this country *** has resulted in the creation of a substantial "shadow population" of illegal migrants—numbering in the millions—within our borders. This situation raises the specter of a permanent caste of undocumented resident aliens, encouraged by some to remain here as a source of cheap labor, but nevertheless denied the benefits that our society makes available to citizens and lawful residents. The existence of such an underclass presents most difficult problems for a Nation that prides itself on adherence to principles of equality under law.[19]

The children who are plaintiffs in these cases are special members of this underclass. Persuasive arguments support the view that a State may withhold its beneficence from those whose very presence within the United States is the product of their own unlawful conduct. These arguments do not apply with the same force to classifications imposing disabilities on the minor *children* of such illegal entrants. *** It is thus difficult to conceive of a rational justification for penalizing these children for their presence within the United States. ***

Public education is not a "right" granted to individuals by the Constitution. *San Antonio Independent School Dist. v. Rodriguez*. But neither is it merely some governmental "benefit" indistinguishable from other forms of social welfare legislation. Both the importance of education in maintaining our basic institutions, and the lasting impact of its deprivation on the life of the child, mark the distinction. *** In sum, education has a fundamental role

---

[19] We reject the claim that "illegal aliens" are a "suspect class." No case in which we have attempted to define a suspect class, has addressed the status of persons unlawfully in our country. Unlike most of the classifications that we have recognized as suspect, entry into this class, by virtue of entry into this country, is the product of voluntary action. Indeed, entry into the class is itself a crime. In addition, it could hardly be suggested that undocumented status is a "constitutional irrelevancy." With respect to the actions of the Federal Government, alienage classifications may be intimately related to the conduct of foreign policy, to the federal prerogative to control access to the United States, and to the plenary federal power to determine who has sufficiently manifested his allegiance to become a citizen of the Nation. No State may independently exercise a like power. But if the Federal Government has by uniform rule prescribed what it believes to be appropriate standards for the treatment of an alien subclass, the States may, of course, follow the federal direction.

in maintaining the fabric of our society. We cannot ignore the significant social costs borne by our Nation when select groups are denied the means to absorb the values and skills upon which our social order rests.

In addition to the pivotal role of education in sustaining our political and cultural heritage, denial of education to some isolated group of children poses an affront to one of the goals of the Equal Protection Clause: the abolition of governmental barriers presenting unreasonable obstacles to advancement on the basis of individual merit. *** Illiteracy is an enduring disability. ***

These well-settled principles allow us to determine the proper level of deference to be afforded [the Act]. Undocumented aliens cannot be treated as a suspect class because their presence in this country in violation of federal law is not a "constitutional irrelevancy." Nor is education a fundamental right; a State need not justify by compelling necessity every variation in the manner in which education is provided to its population. But more is involved in these cases than the abstract question whether [the Act] discriminates against a suspect class, or whether education is a fundamental right. [The Act] imposes a lifetime hardship on a discrete class of children not accountable for their disabling status. *** In light of these countervailing costs, the discrimination contained in [the Act] can hardly be considered rational unless it furthers some substantial goal of the State.

It is the State's principal argument, and apparently the view of the dissenting Justices, that the undocumented status of these children *vel non* establishes a sufficient rational basis for denying them benefits that a State might choose to afford other residents. *** But we are unable to find in the congressional immigration scheme any statement of policy that might weigh significantly in arriving at an equal protection balance concerning the State's authority to deprive these children of an education.

The Constitution grants Congress the power to "establish an uniform Rule of Naturalization." Art. I., § 8, cl. 4. Drawing upon this power, upon its plenary authority with respect to foreign relations and international commerce, and upon the inherent power of a sovereign to close its borders, Congress has developed a complex scheme governing admission to our Nation and status within our borders. *** The State does not claim that the conservation of state educational resources was ever a congressional concern in restricting immigration. More importantly, the classification *** does not operate harmoniously within the federal program.

To be sure, like all persons who have entered the United States unlawfully, these children are subject to deportation. But there is no assurance that a child subject to deportation will ever be deported. *** [W]e perceive no national policy that supports the State in denying these children an elementary education. *** Apart from the asserted state prerogative to act against undocumented children solely on the basis of their undocumented status *** we discern three colorable state interests that might support [the Act].

First, appellants appear to suggest that the State may seek to protect itself from an influx of illegal immigrants. While a State might have an interest in mitigating the potentially harsh economic effects of sudden shifts in population, [the Act] hardly offers an effective method of dealing with an urgent demographic or economic problem. There is no evidence in the record suggesting that illegal entrants impose any significant burden on the State's economy. To the contrary, the available evidence suggests that illegal aliens underutilize public services, while contributing their labor to the local economy and tax money to the state fisc. ***

Second, while it is apparent that a State may "not *** reduce expenditures for education by barring [some arbitrarily chosen class of] children from its schools," appellants suggest that undocumented children are appropriately singled out for exclusion because of the special burdens they impose on the State's ability to provide high-quality public education. But the record in no way supports the claim that exclusion of undocumented children is likely to improve the overall quality of education in the State. *** [Further,] even if improvement in the quality of education were a likely result of barring some *number* of children from the schools of the State, the State must support its selection of *this* group as the appropriate target for exclusion. In terms of educational cost and need, however, undocumented children are "basically indistinguishable" from legally resident alien children.

Finally, appellants suggest that undocumented children are appropriately singled out because their unlawful presence within the United States renders them less likely than other children to remain within the boundaries of the State, and to put their education to productive social or political use within the State. Even assuming that such an interest is legitimate, it is an interest that is most difficult to quantify. The State has no assurance that any child, citizen or not, will employ the education provided by the State within the confines of the State's borders. In any event, the record is clear that many of the undocumented children disabled by this classification will remain in this country indefinitely, and that some will become lawful residents or citizens of the United States. It is difficult to understand precisely what the State hopes to achieve by promoting the creation and perpetuation of a subclass of illiterates within our boundaries, surely adding to the problems and costs of unemployment, welfare, and crime. It is thus clear that whatever savings might be achieved by denying these children an education, they are wholly insubstantial in light of the costs involved to these children, the State, and the Nation. ***

JUSTICE MARSHALL, concurring.

*** It continues to be my view that a class-based denial of public education is utterly incompatible with the Equal Protection Clause of the Fourteenth Amendment.

JUSTICE BLACKMUN, concurring.

*** I believe the Court's experience has demonstrated that the *Rodriguez* formulation does not settle every issue of "fundamental rights" arising under the Equal Protection Clause. *** To the contrary, *Rodriguez* implicitly acknowledged that certain interests, though not constitutionally guaranteed, must be accorded a special place in equal protection analysis. ***

In my view, when the State provides an education to some and denies it to others, it immediately and inevitably creates class distinctions of a type fundamentally inconsistent with those purposes *** of the Equal Protection Clause. Children denied an education are placed at a permanent and insurmountable competitive disadvantage, for an uneducated child is denied even the opportunity to achieve. And when those children are members of an identifiable group, that group—through the State's action—will have been converted into a discrete underclass. Other benefits provided by the State, such as housing and public assistance, are of course important; to an individual in immediate need, they may be more desirable than the right to be educated. But classifications involving the complete denial of education are in a sense unique, for they strike at the heart of equal protection values by involving the State in the creation of permanent class distinctions. In a sense, then, denial of an education is the analogue of denial of the right to vote: the former relegates the individual to second-class social status; the latter places him at a permanent political disadvantage. *** In such circumstances, the voting decisions suggest that the State must offer something more than a rational basis for its classification. ***

JUSTICE POWELL, concurring.

*** Although the analogy is not perfect, our holding today does find support in decisions of this Court with respect to the status of illegitimates. *** "[V]isiting *** condemnation on the head of an infant" for the misdeeds of the parents is illogical, unjust, and "contrary to the basic concept of our system that legal burdens should bear some relationship to individual responsibility or wrongdoing." *** The appellee children are innocent in this respect. *** A legislative classification that threatens the creation of an underclass of future citizens and residents cannot be reconciled with one of the fundamental purposes of the Fourteenth Amendment. In these unique circumstances, the Court properly may require that the State's interests be substantial and that the means bear a "fair and substantial relation" to these interests.[11] In my view, the State's denial of education to these children bears no substantial relation to any substantial state interest. ***

CHIEF JUSTICE BURGER, with whom JUSTICE WHITE, JUSTICE REHNQUIST, and JUSTICE O'CONNOR join, dissenting.

Were it our business to set the Nation's social policy, I would agree without hesitation that it is senseless for an enlightened society to deprive any children—including illegal aliens—of an elementary education. *** However, the Constitution does not constitute us as "Platonic Guardians" nor

---

[11] The CHIEF JUSTICE argues in his dissenting opinion that this heightened standard of review is inconsistent with the Court's decision in [*Rodriguez*]. But in *Rodriguez* no group of children was singled out by the State and then penalized because of their parents' status. Rather, funding for education varied across the State because of the tradition of local control. Nor, in that case, was any group of children totally deprived of all education as in these cases. If the resident children of illegal aliens were denied welfare assistance, made available by government to all other children who qualify, this also—in my opinion—would be an impermissible penalizing of children because of their parents' status.

does it vest in this Court the authority to strike down laws because they do not meet our standards of desirable social policy, "wisdom," or "common sense." We trespass on the assigned function of the political branches under our structure of limited and separated powers when we assume a policymaking role as the Court does today.

*** The Equal Protection Clause does not mandate identical treatment of different categories of persons. *** The dispositive issue in these cases, simply put, is whether, for purposes of allocating its finite resources, a state has a legitimate reason to differentiate between persons who are lawfully within the state and those who are unlawfully there. The distinction the State of Texas has drawn—based not only upon its own legitimate interests but on classifications established by the Federal Government in its immigration laws and policies—is not unconstitutional. *** [B]y patching together bits and pieces of what might be termed quasi-suspect-class and quasi-fundamental-rights analysis, the Court spins out a theory custom-tailored to the facts of these cases. In the end, we are told little more than that the level of scrutiny employed to strike down the Texas law applies only when illegal alien children are deprived of a public education. If ever a court was guilty of an unabashedly result-oriented approach, this case is a prime example.

The Court first suggests that these illegal alien children, although not a suspect class, are entitled to special solicitude under the Equal Protection Clause because they lack "control" over or "responsibility" for their unlawful entry into this country. Similarly, the Court appears to take the position that [the Act] is presumptively "irrational" because it has the effect of imposing "penalties" on "innocent" children. *** The Equal Protection Clause protects against arbitrary and irrational classifications, and against invidious discrimination stemming from prejudice and hostility; it is not an all-encompassing "equalizer" designed to eradicate every distinction for which persons are not "responsible." ***

The Court's analogy to cases involving discrimination against illegitimate children is grossly misleading. The State has not thrust any disabilities upon appellees due to their "status of birth." Rather, appellees' status is predicated upon the circumstances of their concededly illegal presence in this country. *** The second strand of the Court's analysis rests on the premise that, although public education is not a constitutionally guaranteed right, "neither is it merely some governmental 'benefit' indistinguishable from other forms of social welfare legislation." Whatever meaning or relevance this opaque observation might have in some other context, it simply has no bearing on the issues at hand. Indeed, it is never made clear what the Court's opinion means on this score. *** [I]t simply is not "irrational" for a state to conclude that it does not have the same responsibility to provide benefits for persons whose very presence in the state and this country is illegal as it does to provide for persons lawfully present. *** [T]he Federal Government has seen fit to exclude illegal aliens from numerous social welfare programs, such as the food stamp program, the old-age assistance, aid to families with dependent children, aid to the blind, aid to the permanently and totally disabled, and supplemental security income programs, the Medicare hospital insurance benefits program, and the Medicaid hospital insurance benefits for the aged and disabled program. *** [T]he fact that there are sound policy arguments against the Texas Legislature's choice does not render that choice an unconstitutional one. ***

Notes

1.   **Two Approaches in *Rodriguez*.** Note the difference between the majority's recognition of "fundamental interests" under the Equal Protection Clause as encompassing only rights "explicitly or implicitly guaranteed by the Constitution" versus JUSTICE MARSHALL's focus on the "extent to which constitutionally protected rights are dependent on interests not mentioned in the Constitution." The Court also reaffirmed the "tiers" approach to equal protection claims (once two tiers, now three) versus JUSTICE MARSHALL's "sliding scale" approach. After *Rodriguez*, does the importance of the right affect Equal Protection Clause analysis? Compare these approaches to developments under the Due Process Clause, which you studied earlier.

2.   **Pragmatic Considerations.** Had the Court decided that education was a fundamental right under the Equal Protection Clause, how would it assess what kind of education and how much education a person was constitutionally entitled to receive? Could it avoid such difficulties by simply saying "this one won't work" and "remanding" the problem to the state legislature?

3.   **State Law**. The Supreme Court of Texas, more than 15 years later, decided that Rodriguez was correct in his claim that the Texas school financing system violated the *state* constitution's "free and equal" education clause.

4.   **Comparing *Rodriguez* and *Plyler*.** Which case is the norm, and which is the special circumstance? Is *Plyler*'s combination of a semi-suspect class with a semi-fundamental right analogous to "middle tier" scrutiny in the gender cases?

5.   **Judging.** We tend to think that justices are relatively consistent, at least in cases that look very similar. JUSTICES POWELL and BLACKMUN, both of whom were with the majority in both cases, seem consistent in that *Plyler* involves total educational deprivation and a more narrowly defined class, children of illegal immigrants. What accounts for JUSTICE WHITE's dissents in both cases?

6.   **Problem Concerning Wealth.** Suppose a city has a golf course for which it charges a green fee of $2000 per year. A golfer who recently declared bankruptcy can't afford the fee. Does she have an equal protection right to use the course? *See Kadrmas v. Dickinson Public Schools*, 487 U.S. 450 (1988) (upholding school bus fees covering 11% of actual costs). What if the city prohibited anyone not having an annual income of $50,000 per year from using the golf course? What if the city said that only those with a net worth of over $1,000,000 could use the course?

7.   **Other Equal Protection Fundamental Rights.**

    (a) Reproduction. *Skinner v. Oklahoma*, 316 U.S. 535 (1942), said the "right to have offspring" was fundamental. The Court found it was a denial of equal protection for the state to treat theft (of chickens, incidentally) differently from embezzlement (a more upscale crime?), with the consequence that a repeat offender of the former kind was sterilized while a repeat offender of the second variety was not.

(b) <u>Voting</u>. Voting is sometimes viewed as a fundamental right, despite the fact that it has its own constitutional amendments (the 15th and the 19th). Representation-reinforcement notions play a role in these cases (see *McCulloch v. Maryland* from the early part of the course). While some of these cases are race cases, several of which are discussed in earlier notes, others involve denial or dilution of voting on other bases (e.g. party affiliation). *See Bush v. Gore*, infra.

(c) <u>Courts</u>. There are also cases involving what the Court describes as "access to the judicial process." Access to judicial processes is a right explicitly treated in the Constitution. Federal court jurisdiction is limited under Article III (see Chapter II), but state court access, in both criminal and civil cases, is broader.

(d) <u>Interstate Travel</u>. The issue of "travel" was reconceptualized in *Saenz v. Roe*, supra, leaving unclear whether it is "fundamental" for EP purposes.

8.   **Implied Rights Theory.**   Do you agree with JUSTICE MARSHALL that "the Court's theory would render the established concept of fundamental interests in the context of equal protection analysis superfluous, for the substantive constitutional right itself requires that this Court strictly scrutinize any asserted state interest for restricting or denying access to any particular guaranteed right"?

BUSH v. GORE
531 U.S. 98 (2000)

PER CURIAM.

On December 8, 2000, the Supreme Court of Florida ordered that the Circuit Court of Leon County tabulate by hand 9,000 ballots in Miami-Dade County. It also ordered the inclusion in the certified vote totals of 215 votes identified in Palm Beach County and 168 votes identified in Miami-Dade County for Vice President Albert Gore, Jr., and Senator Joseph Lieberman, Democratic Candidates for President and Vice President. The Supreme Court noted that petitioner, Governor George W. Bush asserted that the net gain for Vice President Gore in Palm Beach County was 176 votes, and directed the Circuit Court to resolve that dispute on remand. The court further held that relief would require manual recounts in all Florida counties where so-called "undervotes" had not been subject to manual tabulation. The court ordered all manual recounts to begin at once. Governor Bush and Richard Cheney, Republican Candidates for the Presidency and Vice Presidency, filed an emergency application for a stay of this mandate. *** The petition presents the following questions: whether the Florida Supreme Court established new standards for resolving Presidential election contests, thereby violating Art. II, § 1, cl. 2, of the United States Constitution and failing to comply with 3 U.S.C. § 5, and whether the use of standardless manual recounts violates the Equal Protection and Due Process Clauses. With respect to the equal protection question, we find a violation of the Equal Protection Clause.

The closeness of this election, and the multitude of legal challenges which have followed in its wake, have brought into sharp focus a common, if heretofore unnoticed, phenomenon. Nationwide statistics reveal that an estimated 2% of ballots cast do not register a vote for President for whatever reason, including deliberately choosing no candidate at all or some voter error, such as voting for two candidates or insufficiently marking a ballot. In certifying election results, the votes eligible for inclusion in the certification are the votes meeting the properly established legal requirements.

This case has shown that punch card balloting machines can produce an unfortunate number of ballots, which are not punched in a clean, complete way by the voter. After the current counting, it is likely legislative bodies nationwide will examine ways to improve the mechanisms and machinery for voting.

The individual citizen has no federal constitutional right to vote for electors for the President of the United States unless and until the state legislature chooses a statewide election as the means to implement its power to appoint members of the Electoral College. U.S. Const., Art. II, § 1. This is the source for the statement in *McPherson v. Blacker*, 146 U.S. 1, 35 (1892), that the State legislature's power to select the manner for appointing electors is plenary; it may, if it so chooses, select the electors itself, which indeed was the manner used by State legislatures in several States for many years after the Framing of our Constitution. History has now favored the voter, and in each of the several States the citizens themselves vote for Presidential electors. When the state legislature vests the right to vote for President in its people, the right to vote as the legislature has prescribed is fundamental; and one source of its fundamental nature lies in the equal weight accorded to each vote and the equal dignity owed to each voter. The State, of course, after granting the franchise in the special context of Article II, can take back the power to appoint electors.

The right to vote is protected in more than the initial allocation of the franchise. Equal protection applies as well to the manner of its exercise. Having once granted the right to vote on equal terms, the State may not, by later arbitrary and disparate treatment, value one person's vote over that of another. It must be remembered that "the right of suffrage can be denied by a debasement or dilution of the weight of the citizen's vote just as effectively as by wholly prohibiting the free exercise of the franchise." *Reynolds v. Sims*, 377 U.S. 533, 555 (1964).

There is no difference between the two sides of the present controversy on these basic propositions. Respondents say that the very purpose of vindicating the right to vote justifies the recount procedures now at issue. The question before us, however, is whether the recount procedures the Florida Supreme Court has adopted are consistent with its obligation to avoid arbitrary and disparate treatment of the members of its electorate.

Much of the controversy seems to revolve around ballot cards designed to be perforated by a stylus but which, either through error or deliberate omission, have not been perforated with sufficient precision for a machine to count them. In some cases a piece of the card–a chad–is hanging, say by two corners. In other cases there is no separation at all, just an indentation.

The Florida Supreme Court has ordered that the intent of the voter be discerned from such ballots. *** The recount mechanisms implemented in response to the decisions of the Florida Supreme Court do not satisfy the minimum requirement for nonarbitrary treatment of voters necessary to secure the fundamental right. Florida's basic command for the count of legally cast votes is to consider the "intent of the voter." This is unobjectionable as an abstract proposition and a starting principle. The problem inheres in the absence of specific standards to ensure its equal application. The formulation of uniform rules to determine intent based on these recurring circumstances is practicable and, we conclude, necessary. *** [T]he question is not whether to believe a witness but how to interpret the marks or holes or scratches on an inanimate object, a piece of cardboard or paper which, it is said, might not have registered as a vote during the machine count. The factfinder confronts a thing, not a person. The search for intent can be confined by specific rules designed to ensure uniform treatment.

The want of those rules here has led to unequal evaluation of ballots in various respects. See *Gore v. Harris*, 772 So.2d. 1243, at 1267 (2000) (WELLS, C.J., dissenting) ("Should a county canvassing board count or not count a 'dimpled chad' where the voter is able to successfully dislodge the chad in every other contest on that ballot? Here, the county canvassing boards disagree"). As seems to have been acknowledged at oral argument, the standards for accepting or rejecting contested ballots might vary not only from county to county but indeed within a single county from one recount team to another. ***

An early case in our one person, one vote jurisprudence arose when a State accorded arbitrary and disparate treatment to voters in its different counties. *Gray v. Sanders*, 372 U.S. 368 (1963). The Court found a constitutional violation. We relied on these principles in the context of the Presidential selection process in *Moore v. Ogilvie*, 394 U.S. 814 (1969), where we invalidated a county-based procedure that diluted the influence of citizens in larger counties in the nominating process. ***

The State Supreme Court ratified this uneven treatment. It mandated that the recount totals from two counties, Miami-Dade and Palm Beach, be included in the certified total. The court also appeared to hold *sub silentio* that the recount totals from Broward County *** were to be considered part of the new certified vote totals even though the county certification was not contested by Vice President Gore. Yet each of the counties used varying standards to determine what was a legal vote. *** In addition, the recounts in these three counties were not limited to so- called undervotes but extended to all of the ballots. The distinction has real consequences. A manual recount of all ballots identifies not only those ballots which show no vote but also those which contain more than one, the so-called overvotes. Neither category will be counted by the machine. This is not a trivial concern. At oral argument, respondents estimated there are as many as 110,000 overvotes statewide. As a result, the citizen whose ballot was not read by a machine because he failed to vote for a candidate in a way readable by a machine may still have his vote counted in a manual recount; on the other hand, the citizen who marks two candidates in a way discernable by the machine will not have the same opportunity to have his vote count, even if a manual examination of the ballot would reveal the requisite indicia of intent. Furthermore, the citizen who marks two candidates, only one of which is discernable by the machine, will have his vote counted even though it should have been read as an invalid ballot. The State Supreme Court's inclusion of vote counts based on these variant standards exemplifies concerns with the remedial processes that were under way. *** The press of time does not diminish the constitutional concern. A desire for speed is not a general excuse for ignoring equal protection guarantees.

In addition to these difficulties the actual process by which the votes were to be counted under the Florida Supreme Court's decision raises further concerns. That order did not specify who would recount the ballots. The county canvassing boards were forced to pull together ad hoc teams comprised of judges from various Circuits who had no previous training in handling and interpreting ballots. Furthermore, while others were permitted to observe, they were prohibited from objecting during the recount.

The recount process, in its features here described, is inconsistent with the minimum procedures necessary to protect the fundamental right of each voter in the special instance of a statewide recount under the authority of a single state judicial officer. Our consideration is limited to the present circumstances, for the problem of equal protection in election processes generally presents many complexities.

The question before the Court is not whether local entities, in the exercise of their expertise, may develop different systems for implementing elections. Instead, we are presented with a situation where a state court with the power to assure uniformity has ordered a statewide recount with minimal procedural safeguards. When a court orders a statewide remedy, there must be at least some assurance that the rudimentary requirements of equal treatment and fundamental fairness are satisfied.

Given the Court's assessment that the recount process underway was probably being conducted in an unconstitutional manner, the Court stayed the order directing the recount so it could hear this case and render an expedited decision. *** Upon due consideration of the difficulties identified to this point, it is obvious that the recount cannot be conducted in compliance with the requirements of equal protection and due process without substantial additional work. ***

The Supreme Court of Florida has said that the legislature intended the State's electors to "participat[e] fully in the federal electoral process," as provided in 3 U.S.C. § 5. That statute, in turn, requires that any controversy or contest that is designed to lead to a conclusive selection of electors be completed by December 12. That date is upon us, and there is no recount procedure in place under the State Supreme Court's order that comports with minimal constitutional standards. Because it is evident that any recount seeking to meet the December 12 date will be unconstitutional for the reasons we have discussed, we reverse the judgment of the Supreme Court of Florida ordering a recount to proceed.

Seven Justices of the Court agree that there are constitutional problems with the recount ordered by the Florida Supreme Court that demand a remedy. The only disagreement is as to the remedy. Because the Florida Supreme Court has said that the Florida Legislature intended to obtain the safe-harbor benefits of 3 U.S.C. § 5, JUSTICE BREYER's proposed remedy– remanding to the Florida Supreme Court for its ordering of a constitutionally proper contest until December 18-contemplates action in violation of the Florida election code, and hence could not be part of an "appropriate" order ***

CHIEF JUSTICE REHNQUIST, with whom JUSTICE SCALIA and JUSTICE THOMAS join, concurring.

*** We deal here not with an ordinary election, but with an election for the President of the United States. *** In most cases, comity and respect for federalism compel us to defer to the decisions of state courts on issues of state law. That practice reflects our understanding that the decisions of state courts are definitive pronouncements of the will of the States as sovereigns. *** But there are a few exceptional cases in which the Constitution imposes a duty or confers a power on a particular branch of a State's government. This is one of them. Article II, § 1, cl. 2, provides that "[e]ach State shall appoint, in such Manner as the *Legislature* thereof may direct," electors for President and Vice President. Thus, the text of the election law itself, and not just its interpretation by the courts of the States, takes on independent significance. *** [W]ith respect to a Presidential election, the court must be both mindful of the legislature's role under Article II in choosing the manner of appointing electors and deferential to those bodies expressly empowered by the legislature to carry out its constitutional mandate.

In order to determine whether a state court has infringed upon the legislature's authority, we necessarily must examine the law of the State as it existed prior to the action of the court. *** What we would do in the present case is precisely parallel: Hold that the Florida Supreme Court's interpretation of the Florida election laws impermissibly distorted them beyond what a fair reading required, in violation of Article II.

This inquiry does not imply a disrespect for state *courts* but rather a respect for the constitutionally prescribed role of state *legislatures*. To attach definitive weight to the pronouncement of a state court, when the very question at issue is whether the court has actually departed from the statutory meaning, would be to abdicate our responsibility to enforce the explicit requirements of Article II.

Acting pursuant to its constitutional grant of authority, the Florida Legislature has created a detailed, if not perfectly crafted, statutory scheme that provides for appointment of Presidential electors by direct election. *** The state legislature has also provided mechanisms both for protesting election returns and for contesting certified election results. *** In its latest opinion, however, the court empties certification of virtually all legal consequence during the contest, and in doing so departs from the provisions enacted by the Florida Legislature. *** Moreover, the court's interpretation of "legal vote," and hence its decision to order a contest-period recount, plainly departed from the legislative scheme. Florida statutory law cannot reasonably be thought to *require* the counting of improperly marked ballots. *** In precincts using punch-card ballots, voters are instructed to punch out the ballot cleanly:

"AFTER VOTING, CHECK YOUR BALLOT CARD TO BE SURE YOUR VOTING SELECTIONS ARE CLEARLY AND CLEANLY PUNCHED AND THERE ARE NO CHIPS LEFT HANGING ON THE BACK OF THE CARD.

No reasonable person would call it "an error in the vote tabulation," or a "rejection *** of legal votes,"[4] when electronic or electromechanical equipment performs precisely in the manner designed, and fails to count those ballots that are not marked in the manner that these voting instructions explicitly and prominently specify. ***

But as we indicated in our remand of the earlier case, in a Presidential election the clearly expressed intent of the legislature must prevail. And there is no basis for reading the Florida statutes as requiring the counting of improperly marked ballots, as an examination of the Florida Supreme Court's textual analysis shows. ***

The scope and nature of the remedy ordered by the Florida Supreme Court jeopardizes the "legislative wish" to take advantage of the safe harbor provided by 3 U.S.C. § 5. December 12, 2000, is the last date for a final determination of the Florida electors that will satisfy § 5. Yet in the late afternoon of December 8th–four days before this deadline–the Supreme Court of Florida ordered recounts of tens of thousands of so-called "undervotes" spread through 64 of the State's 67 counties. This was done in a search for elusive–perhaps delusive–certainty as to the exact count of 6 million votes. But no one claims that these ballots have not previously been tabulated; they were initially read by voting machines at the time of the election, and thereafter reread by virtue of Florida's automatic recount provision. No one claims there was any fraud in the election. The Supreme Court of Florida ordered this additional recount under the provision of the election code giving the circuit judge the authority to provide relief that is "appropriate under such circumstances."

Surely when the Florida Legislature empowered the courts of the State to grant "appropriate" relief, it must have meant relief that would have become final by the cut-off date of 3 U.S.C. § 5. *** [T]he entire recounting process could not possibly be completed by that date. *** Given all these factors ***

---

[4] It is inconceivable that what constitutes a vote that must be counted under the "error in the vote tabulation" language of the protest phase is different from what constitutes a vote that must be counted under the "legal votes" language of the contest phase.

the remedy prescribed by the Supreme Court of Florida cannot be deemed an "appropriate" one as of December 8. ***

JUSTICE STEVENS, with whom JUSTICE GINSBURG and JUSTICE BREYER join, dissenting.

The Constitution assigns to the States the primary responsibility for determining the manner of selecting the Presidential electors. See Art. II, § 1 cl. 2. *** The federal questions that ultimately emerged in this case are not substantial. Article II provides that "[e]ach *State* shall appoint, in such Manner as the Legislature *thereof* may direct, a Number of Electors." It does not create state legislatures out of whole cloth, but rather takes them as they come–as creatures born of, and constrained by, their state constitutions. Lest there be any doubt, we stated over 100 years ago in *McPherson v. Blacker,* 146 U.S. 1, 25 (1892), that "[w]hat is forbidden or required to be done by a State" in the Article II context "is forbidden or required of the legislative power under state constitutions as they exist." In the same vein, we also observed that "[t]he [State's] legislative power is the supreme authority except as limited by the constitution of the State."[1] The legislative power in Florida is subject to judicial review pursuant to Article V of the Florida Constitution, and nothing in Article II of the Federal Constitution frees the state legislature from the constraints in the state constitution that created it. Moreover, the Florida Legislature's own decision to employ a unitary code for all elections indicates that it intended the Florida Supreme Court to play the same role in Presidential elections that it has historically played in resolving electoral disputes. The Florida Supreme Court's exercise of appellate jurisdiction therefore was wholly consistent with, and indeed contemplated by, the grant of authority in Article II.

It hardly needs stating that Congress, pursuant to 3 U.S.C. § 5, did not impose any affirmative duties upon the States that their governmental branches could "violate." Rather, § 5 provides a safe harbor for States to select electors in contested elections "by judicial or other methods" established by laws prior to the election day. *** Neither § 5 nor Article II grants federal judges any special authority to substitute their views for those of the state judiciary on matters of state law.

Nor are petitioners correct in asserting that the failure of the Florida Supreme Court to specify in detail the precise manner in which the "intent of the voter," is to be determined rises to the level of a constitutional violation.[2] We found such a violation when individual votes within the same State were weighted unequally, see, *e.g., Reynolds v. Sims,* 377 U.S. 533, 568 (1964), but

---

[1] "Wherever the term 'legislature' is used in the Constitution it is necessary to consider the nature of the particular action in view." It is perfectly clear that the meaning of the words "Manner" and "Legislature" as used in Article II, § 1, parallels the usage in Article I, § 4, rather than the language in Article V. *U.S. Term Limits, Inc. v. Thornton,* 514 U.S. 779, 805 (1995). Article I, § 4, and Article II, § 1, both call upon legislatures to act in a lawmaking capacity whereas Article V simply calls on the legislative body to deliberate upon a binary decision.***

[2] The Florida statutory standard is consistent with the practice of the majority of States, which apply either an "intent of the voter" standard or an "impossible to determine the elector's choice" standard in ballot recounts. ***

we have never before called into question the substantive standard by which a State determines that a vote has been legally cast. And there is no reason to think that the guidance provided to the factfinders, specifically the various canvassing boards, by the "intent of the voter" standard is any less sufficient—or will lead to results any less uniform—than, for example, the "beyond a reasonable doubt" standard employed everyday by ordinary citizens in courtrooms across this country.

Admittedly, the use of differing substandards for determining voter intent in different counties employing similar voting systems may raise serious concerns. Those concerns are alleviated—if not eliminated—by the fact that a single impartial magistrate will ultimately adjudicate all objections arising from the recount process. *** Florida's decision to leave to each county the determination of what balloting system to employ—despite enormous differences in accuracy[4]—might run afoul of equal protection. So, too, might the similar decisions of the vast majority of state legislatures to delegate to local authorities certain decisions with respect to voting systems and ballot design.

Even assuming that aspects of the remedial scheme might ultimately be found to violate the Equal Protection Clause, I could not subscribe to the majority's disposition of the case. As the majority explicitly holds, once a state legislature determines to select electors through a popular vote, the right to have one's vote counted is of constitutional stature. As the majority further acknowledges, Florida law holds that all ballots that reveal the intent of the voter constitute valid votes. Recognizing these principles, the majority nonetheless orders the termination of the contest proceeding before all such votes have been tabulated. Under their own reasoning, the appropriate course of action would be to remand to allow more specific procedures for implementing the legislature's uniform general standard to be established. *** [T]he majority effectively orders the disenfranchisement of an unknown number of voters whose ballots reveal their intent—and are therefore legal votes under state law—but were for some reason rejected by ballot-counting machines. *** They do not prohibit a State from counting what the majority concedes to be legal votes until a bona fide winner is determined. ***

Finally, neither in this case, nor in its earlier opinion in *Palm Beach County Canvassing Bd. v. Harris,* 772 So.2d 1220 (2000), did the Florida Supreme Court make any substantive change in Florida electoral law. *** It did what courts do—it decided the case before it in light of the legislature's intent to leave no legally cast vote uncounted. In so doing, it relied on the sufficiency of the general "intent of the voter" standard articulated by the state legislature, coupled with a procedure for ultimate review by an impartial judge, to resolve the concern about disparate evaluations of

---

[4] The percentage of nonvotes in this election in counties using a punch-card system was 3.92%; in contrast, the rate of error under the more modern optical-scan systems was only 1.43%. Put in other terms, for every 10,000 votes cast, punch-card systems result in 250 more nonvotes than optical-scan systems. A total of 3,718,305 votes were cast under punch- card systems, and 2,353,811 votes were cast under optical-scan systems.

contested ballots. If we assume—as I do—that the members of that court and the judges who would have carried out its mandate are impartial, its decision does not even raise a colorable federal question.

What must underlie petitioners' entire federal assault on the Florida election procedures is an unstated lack of confidence in the impartiality and capacity of the state judges who would make the critical decisions if the vote count were to proceed. *** Although we may never know with complete certainty the identity of the winner of this year's Presidential election, the identity of the loser is perfectly clear. It is the Nation's confidence in the judge as an impartial guardian of the rule of law. ***

JUSTICE SOUTER, with whom JUSTICE BREYER joins and with whom JUSTICE STEVENS and JUSTICE GINSBURG join *** dissenting.

*** There are three issues: whether the State Supreme Court's interpretation of the statute providing for a contest of the state election results somehow violates 3 U.S.C. § 5; whether that court's construction of the state statutory provisions governing contests impermissibly changes a state law from what the State's legislature has provided, in violation of Article II, § 1, cl. 2, of the National Constitution; and whether the manner of interpreting markings on disputed ballots failing to cause machines to register votes for President (the undervote ballots) violates the equal protection or due process guaranteed by the Fourteenth Amendment. None of these issues is difficult to describe or to resolve. ***

It is only on the third issue before us that there is a meritorious argument for relief *** Petitioners have raised an equal protection claim (or, alternatively, a due process claim), in the charge that unjustifiably disparate standards are applied in different electoral jurisdictions to otherwise identical facts. It is true that the Equal Protection Clause does not forbid the use of a variety of voting mechanisms within a jurisdiction, even though different mechanisms will have different levels of effectiveness in recording voters' intentions; local variety can be justified by concerns about cost, the potential value of innovation, and so on. But evidence in the record here suggests that a different order of disparity obtains under rules for determining a voter's intent that have been applied (and could continue to be applied) to identical types of ballots used in identical brands of machines and exhibiting identical physical characteristics (such as "hanging" or "dimpled" chads). *** I can conceive of no legitimate state interest served by these differing treatments of the expressions of voters' fundamental rights. The differences appear wholly arbitrary. *** I would *** remand the case to the courts of Florida with instructions to establish uniform standards. ***

JUSTICES BREYER, STEVENS, GINSBURG, and SOUTER dissented concerning the Court's remedy as follows:

*** [T]here is no justification for the majority's remedy, which is to *** halt the recount entirely. An appropriate remedy would be, instead, to remand this case with instructions that, even at this late date, would permit the Florida Supreme Court to require recounting *all* undercounted votes in Florida, ***

whether or not previously recounted prior to the end of the protest period, and to do so in accordance with a single-uniform substandard. *** Of course, it is too late for any such recount to take place by December 12, the date by which election disputes must be decided if a State is to take advantage of the safe harbor provisions of 3 U.S.C.§ 5. Whether there is time to conduct a recount prior to December 18, when the electors are scheduled to meet, is a matter for the state courts to determine. ***

IX-4. By permission of Mike Luckovich and Creators Syndicate, Inc.

Notes

1. **Rational Basis or Strict Scrutiny?** What is the Court's level of scrutiny for equal treatment of the votes to be recounted in *Bush v. Gore*? If it is "strict" or "middle-tier" scrutiny, is the theory that there was discriminatory treatment of a protected class? Or elevated scrutiny based on a fundamental interest? The per curiam opinion avoids these matter-of-fact equal protection fundamentals. Here are some issues such considerations might have raised:

 • If rational basis is the standard, isn't it rational for the Florida Supreme Court to respond to Gore's strategy of seeking to recount votes only in heavily Democratic counties by ordering a statewide recount? Wasn't it rational for the court to rely on a broad general standard ("intent of the voter") supplemented by a statewide process supervised by a single ultimate decision-maker (Judge Lewis)? Isn't it rational to recount "undervotes" but not "overvotes," when "undervote" ballots are more readily identifiable?

 • The strongest case for heightened scrutiny of the statewide recount would be if racial minorities (or majorities) or gender minorities (or majorities) were adversely treated. Claims of racial exclusion (disparate treatment at the polls) or disparate impact (minorities disproportionately lived in counties using less accurate voting machinery) were considered and rejected on other post-election proceedings.

• It has been many years since the Court has used heightened scrutiny based on a "fundamental interest," such as voting rights. On an "original intent" basis, it is arguable that the Fourteenth Amendment was not intended to apply to voting at all. Since the Supreme Court has rejected that argument, however, it is appropriate to look for how far the cases go in providing elevated scrutiny in voting cases. Though prior caselaw did not concern application of strict scrutiny to vote counting (or recounting), such an application is not much of a stretch: if one can win elections either at the polls or through vote counting after the polls, equal protection voting standards might well apply to vote counts and recounts. But the cases relied upon by the Court have facts very different from those of *Bush v. Gore*. Equal protection invalidation of voting restrictions adversely affecting poor citizens (at a time prior to *Rodriguez*) is weak precedent for invalidation of recounts that have no economic bias. Similarly, cases denying political majorities their fair say, when the courts were the only institution that could open up the political process, seem inapposite when other institutions (the Florida Legislature and Congress) could have resolved this election contest.

2.   **The Holding of *Bush v. Gore*.** On September 15, 2003, a Ninth Circuit panel postponed California's recall of Governor Gray Davis because the claim "presents almost precisely the same issue as the Court considered in *Bush*, that is, whether unequal methods of counting votes among counties constitutes a violation of the Equal Protection Clause. *** [U]sing error-prone voting equipment in some counties, but not in others will result in votes being counted differently among the counties." Reversing, and thus allowing the recall to proceed on October 7, as scheduled, an en banc panel held that "the plaintiffs have not established a clear probability of success on the merits of their equal protection claim." *Southwest Voter Registration Education Project v. Shelley*, 344 F.3d 882 (Sept. 15, 2003), rev'd 344 F.3d 914 (Sept. 23, 2003) (en banc). Which court read *Bush* correctly? Why?

3.   **Rationale Versus Remedy?** What is significant, for equal protection purposes, about the December 12, 2000 cutoff date? For equal protection purposes, is it important that the state legislature wished to avail itself of the "safe harbor" provision of Title 3? Did the per curiam opinion essentially adopt the analysis of the concurring opinion in refusing to remand for another effort by the Florida Supreme Court?

4.   **State Court, State Law, Federal Court, Federal Law.** Are the "Warren Court" era (1954-68) cases cited by the per curiam opinion regarding civil rights infractions in the Jim Crow South relevant in rejecting the Florida Supreme Court's method for counting votes cast for the presidency? What awakened the U.S. Supreme Court's latent "fundamental rights equal protection" jurisprudence to strike down the Florida Supreme Court's statewide standard?

5.   **Standing.** Did Bush have standing to raise an equal protection challenge to the recount process in the several Florida counties? What injury-in-fact did Governor Bush experience that would satisfy the standing doctrine set forth in *Friends of the Earth v. Laidlaw*, supra Ch. II?

6. **Review Questions and Comments:**

a. Judicial function. Below are two hypothetical comments criticizing and supporting the U.S. Supreme Court and the Florida Supreme Court for the manner in which they conducted themselves in the post-election period follow. Consider the extent to which you agree or disagree with each.

1. "The justices of the U.S. Supreme Court allowed political considerations to dictate how they approached and resolved this case. The Court had already made up its mind to craft an opinion that would halt the recount proceedings in Florida and deliver the Presidency to Governor Bush. The best way to describe the per curiam's equal protection analysis is that it was contrived to justify the outcome. In language at the outset of the opinion, the Court desperately tries to limit the application of the broadest equal protection decision in decades. The refusal to remand the case and accept the final date for purposes of Title 3's 'safe harbor' provision cannot be justified on any grounds. Moreover, the Court resolved the election when that function was left to Congress, not the Court."

2. "The justices of the U.S. Supreme Court were confronted with a scenario in which the Florida Supreme Court was willing to go to any lengths necessary to deliver the election to Vice-President Gore. Faced with an openly defiant state supreme court, remanding the case for further consideration would have been futile. Why let the Florida Supreme Court bend the State's pre-existing election law again, with further recounts and additional political chaos? The per curiam opinion is sound and is appropriately limited to the unique set of facts that were before the Court. In any event, the concurring opinion's analysis of Article II requirements forcefully supports the need to end the recount process. The justices did the best they could with unclear constitutional provisions and precedents to prevent the will of the state legislature from being thwarted."

b. Separation of powers. Some constitutional scholars are concerned with the propensity of the Rehnquist Court to resolve what might have been considered political questions under *Baker v. Carr*, 369 U.S. 186. The text of Article II, § 1, cl. 2 specifically delegates to state legislatures the power to select the manner in which a state's slate of electors will be chosen to participate in the Electoral College. If no candidate is successful in garnering a majority of electoral votes, the outcome of the Presidential election is decided by the U.S. House of Representatives. Title 3, on which both the per curiam and concurring opinions place a great deal of emphasis, calls for Congress, not the courts, to be the final arbiter in settling disputes regarding competing slates of electors from a given state. Given the statutory and constitutional provisions delegating authority over various aspects of the presidential election process to Congress and the state legislatures (not the federal courts), did *Bush v. Gore* raise a political question calling for abstention rather than intervention?

c. Federalism. What is the appropriate scope of state judicial review of determinations made by the state legislature as to the manner in which electors will be appointed? CHIEF JUSTICE REHNQUIST's concurring opinion indicates that a large deviation from the electoral scheme enacted by the state legislature raises a federal question, which then allows the federal judiciary to take on an independent review of State law. In other words, the federal judiciary can intervene in a presidential election to preserve the appropriate balance of Article II power enjoyed by the state legislature and the state judiciary, ensuring that proper deference is paid to determinations made by the state legislature. The thrust of JUSTICE STEVENS' dissenting opinion is that Article II of the U.S. Constitution does not create state legislatures, "it takes them as they come," subject to state constitutional constraints even in the exercise of powers conferred by Article II. Gore's attorneys argued that the Florida State Constitution was the product of the state legislature. Does Title 3 impose any affirmative duties upon the States to appoint electors and take part in the Electoral College? If not, why do both the per curiam and concurring opinions place so much emphasis on this statute? Indeed, why do these opinions focus only on section five of the statute, when section fifteen (3 U.S.C. §15) specifically calls for Congress to resolve disputes that stem from competing slates of electors or other disputes relating to the process of appointing presidential electors?

E. RATIONAL BASIS AND HYBRID REVIEW

Now it is time to look at two cases that do not fit neatly in the categories of race, gender, or fundamental rights, but likewise do not quite fit into the rational basis methodology treated in the first section of this chapter.

CITY OF CLEBURNE v. CLEBURNE LIVING CENTER
473 U.S. 432 (1985)

JUSTICE WHITE delivered the opinion of the Court.

A Texas city denied a special use permit for the operation of a group home for the mentally retarded, acting pursuant to a municipal zoning ordinance requiring permits for such homes. The Court of Appeals for the Fifth Circuit held that mental retardation is a "quasi-suspect" classification and that the ordinance violated the Equal Protection Clause because it did not substantially further an important governmental purpose. We hold that a lesser standard of scrutiny is appropriate, but conclude that under that standard the ordinance is invalid as applied in this case.

In July 1980, respondent Jan Hannah purchased a building *** in the city of Cleburne, Texas, with the intention of leasing it to Cleburne Living Center, Inc. (CLC), for the operation of a group home for the mentally retarded. It was anticipated that the home would house 13 retarded men and women *** under the constant supervision of CLC staff members. *** The city informed CLC that a special use permit would be required for the operation of a group home at the site, and CLC accordingly submitted a permit application. In response to a subsequent inquiry from CLC, the city explained that under the zoning regulations applicable to the site, a special use permit, renewable annually, was required for the construction of "[h]ospitals for the insane or feeble-minded, or alcoholic [sic] or drug addicts, or penal or correctional institutions." The city had determined that the proposed group home should be classified as a "hospital for the feebleminded." After holding a public hearing on CLC's application, the City Council voted 3 to 1 to deny a special use permit.

CLC then filed suit in Federal District Court against the city and a number of its officials, alleging, *inter alia*, that the zoning ordinance was invalid on its face and as applied because it discriminated against the mentally retarded in violation of the equal protection rights of CLC and its potential residents. ***

The Equal Protection Clause of the Fourteenth Amendment commands that no State shall "deny to any person within its jurisdiction the equal protection of the laws," which is essentially a direction that all persons similarly situated should be treated alike. *Plyler v. Doe.* *** The general rule is that legislation is presumed to be valid and will be sustained if the classification drawn by the statute is rationally related to a legitimate state interest. *** When social or economic legislation is at issue, the Equal Protection Clause allows the States wide latitude, and the Constitution presumes that even improvident decisions will eventually be rectified by the democratic processes.

The general rule gives way, however, when a statute classifies by race, alienage, or national origin. These factors are so seldom relevant to the achievement of any legitimate state interest that laws grounded in such considerations are deemed to reflect prejudice and antipathy—a view that those in the burdened class are not as worthy or deserving as others. For these reasons and because such discrimination is unlikely to be soon rectified by legislative means, these laws are subjected to strict scrutiny and will be sustained only if they are suitably tailored to serve a compelling state interest. Similar oversight by the courts is due when state laws impinge on personal rights protected by the Constitution. ***

We have declined, however, to extend heightened review to differential treatment based on age: "While the treatment of the aged in this Nation has not been wholly free of discrimination, such persons, unlike, say, those who have been discriminated against on the basis of race or national origin, have not experienced a 'history of purposeful unequal treatment' or been subjected to unique disabilities on the basis of stereotyped characteristics not truly indicative of their abilities." *Massachusetts Board of Retirement v. Murgia*, 427 U.S. 307, 313 (1976).

The lesson of *Murgia* is that where individuals in the group affected by a law have distinguishing characteristics relevant to interests the State has the authority to implement, the courts have been very reluctant, as they should be in our federal system and with our respect for the separation of powers, to closely scrutinize legislative choices as to whether, how, and to what extent those interests should be pursued. In such cases, the Equal Protection Clause requires only a rational means to serve a legitimate end.

Against this background, we conclude for several reasons that the Court of Appeals erred in holding mental retardation a quasi-suspect classification calling for a more exacting standard of judicial review than is normally accorded economic and social legislation. First, it is undeniable, and it is not argued otherwise here, that those who are mentally retarded have a reduced ability to cope with and function in the everyday world. Nor are they all cut from the same pattern: as the testimony in this record indicates, they range from those whose disability is not immediately evident to those who must be constantly cared for. They are thus different, immutably so, in relevant respects, and the States' interest in dealing with and providing for them is plainly a legitimate one. How this large and diversified group is to be treated under the law is a difficult and often a technical matter, very much a task for legislators guided by qualified professionals and not by the perhaps ill-informed opinions of the judiciary. ***

Second, the distinctive legislative response, both national and state, to the plight of those who are mentally retarded demonstrates not only that they have unique problems, but also that the lawmakers have been addressing their difficulties in a manner that belies a continuing antipathy or prejudice and a corresponding need for more intrusive oversight by the judiciary. *** Such legislation thus singling out the retarded for special treatment reflects the real and undeniable differences between the retarded and others. That a civilized and decent society expects and approves such legislation indicates that governmental consideration of those differences in the vast majority of situations is not only legitimate but also desirable. It may be, as CLC contends, that legislation designed to benefit, rather than disadvantage, the retarded would generally withstand examination under a test of heightened scrutiny. The relevant inquiry, however, is whether heightened scrutiny is constitutionally mandated in the first instance. ***

Third, the legislative response, which could hardly have occurred and survived without public support, negates any claim that the mentally retarded are politically powerless in the sense that they have no ability to attract the attention of the lawmakers. Any minority can be said to be powerless to assert direct control over the legislature, but if that were a criterion for higher level scrutiny by the courts, much economic and social legislation would now be suspect.

Fourth, if the large and amorphous class of the mentally retarded were deemed quasi-suspect for the reasons given by the Court of Appeals, it would be difficult to find a principled way to distinguish a variety of other groups who have perhaps immutable disabilities setting them off from others, who cannot themselves mandate the desired legislative responses, and who can claim some degree of prejudice from at least part of the public at large. One need mention in this respect only the aging, the disabled, the mentally ill, and the infirm. *** Our refusal to recognize the retarded as a quasi-suspect class does not leave them entirely unprotected from invidious discrimination. To withstand equal protection review, legislation that distinguishes between the mentally retarded and others must be rationally related to a legitimate governmental purpose. This standard, we believe, affords government the latitude necessary both to pursue policies designed to assist the retarded in realizing their full potential, and to freely and efficiently engage in activities that burden the retarded in what is essentially an incidental manner. ***

*** It is true, as already pointed out, that the mentally retarded as a group are indeed different from others not sharing their misfortune, and in this respect they may be different from those who would occupy other facilities that would be permitted. *** But this difference is largely irrelevant unless the *** home and those who would occupy it would threaten legitimate interests of the city in a way that other permitted uses such as boarding houses and hospitals would not. ***

The District Court found that the City Council's insistence on the permit rested on several factors. *** [T]he Council was concerned with the negative attitude of the majority of property owners located within 200 feet of the *** facility, as well as with the fears of elderly residents of the neighborhood. But mere negative attitudes, or fear, unsubstantiated by factors which are properly cognizable in a zoning proceeding, are not permissible bases for treating a home for the mentally retarded differently from apartment houses, multiple dwellings, and the like. It is plain that the electorate as a whole *** could not order city action violative of the Equal Protection Clause, and the City may not avoid the strictures of that Clause by deferring to the wishes or objections of some fraction of the body politic. "Private biases may be outside the reach of the law, but the law cannot, directly or indirectly, give them effect." *Palmore v. Sidoti*, 466 U.S. 429, 433 (1984).

*** [T]he Council had two objections to the location of the facility. It was concerned that the facility was across the street from a junior high school, and it feared that the students might harass the occupants of the *** home. But the school itself is attended by about 30 mentally retarded students, and denying a permit based on such vague, undifferentiated fears is again permitting some portion of the community to validate what would otherwise be an equal protection violation. The other objection to the home's location was that it was located on "a five hundred year flood plain." This concern with the possibility of a flood, however, can hardly be based on a distinction between the *** home and, for example, nursing homes, homes for convalescents or the aged, or sanitariums or hospitals, any of which could be located on the *** site without obtaining a special use permit. The same may be said of another concern of the Council—doubts about the legal responsibility for actions which the mentally retarded might take. If there is no concern about legal responsibility with respect to other uses that would be permitted in the area, such as boarding and fraternity houses, it is difficult to believe that the groups of mildly or moderately mentally retarded individuals who would live at [the home] would present any different or special hazard. *** [The] Council was concerned with the size of the home and the number of people that would occupy it. *** [However,] there would be no restrictions on the number of people who could occupy this home as a boarding house, nursing home, family dwelling, fraternity house, or dormitory. *** The short of it is that requiring the permit in this case appears to us to rest on an irrational prejudice against the mentally retarded, including those who would occupy the *** facility and who would live under the closely supervised and highly regulated conditions expressly provided for by state and federal law. ***

JUSTICE STEVENS, with whom *** CHIEF JUSTICE BURGER joins, concurring.

*** [Our] cases reflect a continuum of judgmental responses to differing classifications which have been explained in opinions by terms ranging from "strict scrutiny" at one extreme to "rational basis" at the other. I have never been persuaded that these so-called "standards" adequately explain the decisional process. Cases involving classifications based on alienage, illegal residency, illegitimacy, gender, age, or—as in this case—mental retardation, do not fit well into sharply defined classifications. *** In my own approach to these cases, I have always asked myself whether I could find a "rational basis" for the classification at issue. The term "rational," of course, includes a requirement that an impartial lawmaker could logically believe that the classification would serve a legitimate public purpose that transcends the harm to the members of the disadvantaged class. Thus, the word "rational"— for me at least—includes elements of legitimacy and neutrality that must always characterize the performance of the sovereign's duty to govern impartially.

The rational-basis test, properly understood, adequately explains why a law that deprives a person of the right to vote because his skin has a different pigmentation than that of other voters violates the Equal Protection Clause. It would be utterly irrational to limit the franchise on the basis of height or weight; it is equally invalid to limit it on the basis of skin color. None of these attributes has any bearing at all on the citizen's willingness or ability to exercise that civil right. We do not need to apply a special standard, or to apply "strict scrutiny," or even "heightened scrutiny," to decide such cases.

In every equal protection case, we have to ask certain basic questions. What class is harmed by the legislation, and has it been subjected to a "tradition of disfavor" by our laws? What is the public purpose that is being served by the law? What is the characteristic of the disadvantaged class that justifies the disparate treatment? In most cases the answer to these questions will tell us whether the statute has a "rational basis." *** [The] Court of Appeals correctly observed that through ignorance and prejudice the mentally retarded "have been subjected to a history of unfair and often grotesque mistreatment." The discrimination against the mentally retarded that is at issue in this case is the city's decision to require an annual special use permit before property in an apartment house district may be used as a group home for persons who are mildly retarded. The record convinces me that this permit was required because of the irrational fears of neighboring property owners, rather than for the protection of the mentally retarded persons who would reside in respondent's home. ***

JUSTICE MARSHALL, with whom JUSTICE BRENNAN and JUSTICE BLACKMUN join, concurring in the judgment in part and dissenting in part.

The Court holds that all retarded individuals cannot be grouped together as the "feebleminded" and deemed presumptively unfit to live in a community. Underlying this holding is the principle that mental retardation *per se* cannot be a proxy for depriving retarded people of their rights and interests without regard to variations in individual ability. With this holding and principle I agree. The Equal Protection Clause requires attention to the capacities and needs of retarded people as individuals.

I cannot agree, however, with the way in which the Court reaches its result or with the narrow, as-applied remedy it provides for the city of Cleburne's equal protection violation. The Court holds the ordinance invalid on rational-basis grounds and disclaims that anything special, in the form of heightened scrutiny, is taking place. Yet Cleburne's ordinance surely would be valid under the traditional rational-basis test applicable to economic and commercial regulation. *** [T]he Court's heightened-scrutiny discussion is even more puzzling given that Cleburne's ordinance is invalidated only after being subjected to precisely the sort of probing inquiry associated with heightened scrutiny. To be sure, the Court does not label its handiwork heightened scrutiny, and perhaps the method employed must hereafter be called "second order" rational-basis review rather than "heightened scrutiny." But however labeled, the rational basis test invoked today is most assuredly not the rational-basis test of *Williamson v. Lee Optical of Oklahoma, Inc.*, 348 U.S. 483 (1955), and [its] progeny.

The Court, for example, concludes that legitimate concerns for fire hazards or the serenity of the neighborhood do not justify singling out respondents to bear the burdens of these concerns, for analogous permitted uses appear to pose similar threats. Yet under the traditional and most minimal version of the rational-basis test, "reform may take one step at a time, addressing itself to the phase of the problem which seems most acute to the legislative mind." *Williamson v. Lee Optical of Oklahoma, Inc.*, 348 U.S., at 489. The "record" is said not to support the ordinance's classifications, but under the traditional standard we do not sift through the record to determine whether policy decisions are squarely supported by a firm factual foundation. Finally, the Court further finds it "difficult to believe" that the retarded present different or special hazards inapplicable to other groups. In normal circumstances, the burden is not on the legislature to convince the Court that the lines it has drawn are sensible; legislation is presumptively constitutional, and a State "is not required to resort to close distinctions or to maintain a precise, scientific uniformity with reference" to its goals.

I share the Court's criticisms of the overly broad lines that Cleburne's zoning ordinance has drawn. But if the ordinance is to be invalidated for its imprecise classifications, it must be pursuant to more powerful scrutiny than the minimal rational-basis test used to review classifications affecting only economic and commercial matters. The same imprecision in a similar ordinance that required opticians but not optometrists to be licensed to practice, or that excluded new but not old businesses from parts of a community, would hardly be fatal to the statutory scheme.

*** [T]he mentally retarded have been subject to a "lengthy and tragic history" of segregation and discrimination that can only be called grotesque. *** By the latter part of the [19th] century and during the first decades of the new one, however, social views of the retarded underwent a radical transformation. Fueled by the rising tide of Social Darwinism *** and the extreme xenophobia of those years, leading medical authorities and others began to portray the "feeble-minded" as a "menace to society and civilization *** responsible in a large degree for many, if not all, of our social problems." A regime of state-mandated segregation and degradation soon emerged that in its virulence and bigotry rivaled, and indeed paralleled, the worst excesses of Jim Crow. *** Prejudice, once let loose, is not easily cabined. *** As of 1979, most States still categorically disqualified "idiots" from voting, without regard to individual capacity and with discretion to exclude left in the hands of low-level election officials. Not until Congress enacted the Education of the Handicapped Act were "the door[s] of public education" opened wide to handicapped children. But most important, lengthy and continuing isolation of the retarded has perpetuated the ignorance, irrational fears, and stereotyping that long have plagued them.

In light of the importance of the interest at stake and the history of discrimination the retarded have suffered, the Equal Protection Clause requires us to do more than review the distinctions drawn by Cleburne's zoning ordinance as if they appeared in a taxing statute or in economic or commercial legislation. The searching scrutiny I would give to restrictions on the ability of the retarded to establish community group homes leads me to conclude that Cleburne's vague generalizations for classifying the "feeble-minded" with drug addicts, alcoholics, and the insane, and excluding them where the elderly, the ill, the boarder, and the transient are allowed, are not substantial or important enough to overcome the suspicion that the ordinance rests on impermissible assumptions or outmoded and perhaps invidious stereotypes.

*** With respect to a liberty so valued as the right to establish a home in the community, and so likely to be denied on the basis of irrational fears and outright hostility, heightened scrutiny is surely appropriate.

In light of the scrutiny that should be applied here, Cleburne's ordinance sweeps too broadly to dispel the suspicion that it rests on a bare desire to treat the retarded as outsiders, pariahs who do not belong in the community. *** I must dissent from the novel proposition that "the preferred course of adjudication" is to leave standing a legislative Act resting on "irrational prejudice", thereby forcing individuals in the group discriminated against to continue to run the Act's gauntlet. *** In my view, the Court's remedial approach is both unprecedented in the equal protection area and unwise. *** [I]n focusing obsessively on the appropriate label to give its standard of review, the Court fails to identify the interests at stake or to articulate the principle that classifications based on mental retardation must be carefully examined to assure they do not rest on impermissible assumptions or false stereotypes regarding individual ability and need. *** I would *** strike down on its face the provision at issue. I therefore concur in the judgment in part and dissent in part.

Notes

1. *Cleburne* **and Equal Protection Theory.** Why does the Court find it necessary or appropriate to discuss "the plight of the mentally retarded"? Remember that in *Rodriguez*, the Court refused to premise its analysis on "the

plight of the poor," and in *Massachusetts Board of Retirement v. Murgia*, the Court refused to elevate the level of scrutiny because of "the plight of the aged." Should the Court have cited *Plyler* more forcefully, saying the retarded were a blameless disadvantaged group (like children of immigrants) and that the city's zoning totally deprived them of housing (like exclusion from schools)?

2. **Irrationality, Prejudice, and Close Scrutiny.** Equal protection inquiry focuses on the "who," not the "what," of the city's special use permit denial. Perhaps the city's reasons were based on "vague, undifferentiated fears" masking "irrational prejudice." But ferreting out prejudice requires careful evidentiary assessments more common in strict than rational basis scrutiny. *See Yick Wo v. Hopkins*, supra. The Court in *Village of Willowbrook v. Olech*, 528 U.S. 1073 (2000), held, per curiam, that one person (a "class of one") may show an equal protection violation from "irrational and wholly arbitrary" official behavior "quite apart from *** subjective motivation." JUSTICE BREYER concurred, but opined that "vindictive action," "illegitimate animus," or "ill will" is needed to avoid "transforming run-of-the-mill zoning cases into cases of constitutional right." Should courts defer equally to elected officals' rule applications and their rule-making?

ROMER v. EVANS
517 U.S. 620 (1996)

JUSTICE KENNEDY delivered the opinion of the Court.

*** The enactment challenged in this case is an amendment to the Constitution of the State of Colorado, adopted in a 1992 statewide referendum. *** Amendment 2 repeals [various local] ordinances to the extent they prohibit discrimination on the basis of "homosexual, lesbian or bisexual orientation, conduct, practices or relationships." Yet Amendment 2, in explicit terms, does more than repeal or rescind these provisions. It prohibits all legislative, executive or judicial action at any level of state or local government designed to protect the named class, a class we shall refer to as homosexual persons or gays and lesbians. ***

The State's principal argument in defense of Amendment 2 is that it puts gays and lesbians in the same position as all other persons. So, the State says, the measure does no more than deny homosexuals special rights. This reading of the amendment's language is implausible. We rely not upon our own interpretation of the amendment but upon the authoritative construction of Colorado's Supreme Court [which said] "The immediate objective of Amendment 2 is, at a minimum, to repeal existing statutes, regulations, ordinances, and policies of state and local entities that barred discrimination based on sexual orientation. *** The 'ultimate effect' of Amendment 2 is to prohibit any governmental entity from adopting similar, or more protective statutes, regulations, ordinances, or policies in the future unless the state constitution is first amended to permit such measures."

Sweeping and comprehensive is the change in legal status effected by this law. *** Homosexuals, by state decree, are put in a solitary class with respect to transactions and relations in both the private and governmental spheres. The amendment withdraws from homosexuals, but no others, specific legal protection from the injuries caused by discrimination, and it forbids reinstatement of these laws and policies.

The change that Amendment 2 works in the legal status of gays and lesbians in the private sphere is far-reaching, both on its own terms and when considered in light of the structure and operation of modern anti-discrimination laws. That structure is well illustrated by contemporary statutes and ordinances prohibiting discrimination by providers of public accommodations. *** Colorado's state and municipal laws typify this emerging tradition of statutory protection and follow a consistent pattern. The laws first enumerate the persons or entities subject to a duty not to discriminate. The list goes well beyond the entities covered by the common law. The Boulder ordinance, for example, has a comprehensive definition of entities deemed places of "public accommodation." They include "any place of business engaged in any sales to the general public and any place that offers services, facilities, privileges, or advantages to the general public or that receives financial support through solicitation of the general public or through governmental subsidy of any kind." The Denver ordinance is of similar breadth, applying, for example, to hotels, restaurants, hospitals, dental clinics, theaters, banks, common carriers, travel and insurance agencies, and "shops and stores dealing with goods or services of any kind."

These statutes and ordinances also depart from the common law by enumerating the groups or persons within their ambit of protection. Enumeration is the essential device used to make the duty not to discriminate concrete and to provide guidance for those who must comply. In following this approach, Colorado's state and local governments have not limited anti-discrimination laws to groups that have so far been given the protection of heightened equal protection scrutiny under our cases. Rather, they set forth an extensive catalogue of traits which cannot be the basis for discrimination, including age, military status, marital status, pregnancy, parenthood, custody of a minor child, political affiliation, physical or mental disability of an individual or of his or her associates——and, in recent times, sexual orientation.

Amendment 2 bars homosexuals from securing protection against the injuries that these public-accommodations laws address. That in itself is a severe consequence, but there is more. Amendment 2, in addition, nullifies specific legal protections for this targeted class in all transactions in housing, sale of real estate, insurance, health and welfare services, private education, and employment.

Not confined to the private sphere, Amendment 2 also operates to repeal and forbid all laws or policies providing specific protection for gays or lesbians from discrimination by every level of Colorado government. The State Supreme Court cited two examples of protections in the governmental sphere that are now rescinded and may not be reintroduced. The first is Colorado Executive Order D0035 (1990), which forbids employment discrimination against "'all state employees, classified and exempt' on the basis of sexual orientation." Also repealed, and now forbidden, are "various provisions prohibiting discrimination based on sexual orientation at state colleges." The repeal of these measures and the prohibition against their future reenactment demonstrates that Amendment 2 has the same force and effect in Colorado's governmental sector as it does elsewhere and that it applies to policies as well as ordinary legislation.

Amendment 2's reach may not be limited to specific laws passed for the benefit of gays and lesbians. It is a fair, if not necessary, inference from the broad language of the amendment that it deprives gays and lesbians even of the protection of general laws and policies that prohibit arbitrary discrimination in governmental and private settings. At some point in the systematic administration of these laws, an official must determine whether homosexuality is an arbitrary and thus forbidden basis for decision. Yet a decision to that effect would itself amount to a policy prohibiting discrimination on the basis of homosexuality, and so would appear to be no more valid under Amendment 2 than the specific prohibitions against discrimination the state court held invalid.

If this consequence follows from Amendment 2, as its broad language suggests, it would compound the constitutional difficulties the law creates. The state court did not decide whether the amendment has this effect, however, and neither need we. *** In any event, even if, as we doubt, homosexuals could find some safe harbor in laws of general application, we cannot accept the view that Amendment 2's prohibition on specific legal protections does no more than deprive homosexuals of special rights. To the contrary, the amendment imposes a special disability upon those persons alone. Homosexuals are forbidden the safeguards that others enjoy or may seek without constraint. They can obtain specific protection against discrimination only by enlisting the citizenry of Colorado to amend the State Constitution or perhaps, on the State's view, by trying to pass helpful laws of general applicability. This is so no matter how local or discrete the harm, no matter how public and widespread the injury. We find nothing special in the protections Amendment 2 withholds. These are protections taken for granted by most people either because they already have them or do not need them; these are protections against exclusion from an almost limitless number of transactions and endeavors that constitute ordinary civic life in a free society.

The Fourteenth Amendment's promise that no person shall be denied the equal protection of the laws must co-exist with the practical necessity that most legislation classifies for one purpose or another, with resulting disadvantage to various groups or persons. We have attempted to reconcile the principle with the reality by stating that, if a law neither burdens a fundamental right nor targets a suspect class, we will uphold the legislative classification so long as it bears a rational relation to some legitimate end.

Amendment 2 fails, indeed defies, even this conventional inquiry. First, the amendment has the peculiar property of imposing a broad and undifferentiated disability on a single named group, an exceptional and, as we shall explain, invalid form of legislation. Second, its sheer breadth is so discontinuous with the reasons offered for it that the amendment seems inexplicable by anything but animus toward the class that it affects; it lacks a rational relationship to legitimate state interests.

Taking the first point, even in the ordinary equal protection case calling for the most deferential of standards, we insist on knowing the relation between the classification adopted and the object to be attained. The search for the link between classification and objective gives substance to the Equal Protection Clause; it provides guidance and discipline for the legislature, which is entitled to know what sorts of laws it can pass; and it marks the limits of our own authority. In the ordinary case, a law will be sustained if it can be said to advance a legitimate government interest, even if the law seems unwise or works to the disadvantage of a particular group, or if the rationale for it seems tenuous. See *** *Williamson v. Lee Optical of Okla., Inc.*, 348 U.S. 483 (1955) (assumed health concerns justified law favoring optometrists over opticians); *Railway Express Agency, Inc. v. New York*, 336 U.S. 106 (1949) (potential traffic hazards justified exemption of vehicles advertising the owner's products from general advertising ban); *Kotch v. Board of River Port Pilot Comm'rs for Port of New Orleans*, 330 U.S. 552 (1947) (licensing scheme that disfavored persons unrelated to current river boat pilots justified by possible efficiency and safety benefits of a closely knit pilotage system). The laws challenged in the cases just cited were narrow enough in scope and grounded in a sufficient factual context for us to ascertain that there existed some relation between the classification and the purpose it served. By requiring that the classification bear a rational relationship to an independent and legitimate legislative end, we ensure that classifications are not drawn for the purpose of disadvantaging the group burdened by the law.

Amendment 2 confounds this normal process of judicial review. It is at once too narrow and too broad. It identifies persons by a single trait and then denies them protection across the board. The resulting disqualification of a class of persons from the right to seek specific protection from the law is unprecedented in our jurisprudence. The absence of precedent for Amendment 2 is itself instructive; "[d]iscriminations of an unusual character especially suggest careful consideration to determine whether they are obnoxious to the constitutional provision."

It is not within our constitutional tradition to enact laws of this sort. *** "A law declaring that in general it shall be more difficult for one group of citizens than for all others to seek aid from the government is itself a denial of equal protection of the laws in the most literal sense. "The guaranty of 'equal protection of the laws is a pledge of the protection of equal laws.'" *Skinner v. Oklahoma*, 316 U.S. 535 (1942) (quoting *Yick Wo v. Hopkins*, 118 U.S. 356 (1886)).

Davis v. Beason, 133 U.S. 333 (1890), not cited by the parties but relied upon by the dissent, is not evidence that Amendment 2 is within our constitutional tradition, and any reliance upon it as authority for sustaining the amendment is misplaced. In *Davis*, the Court approved an Idaho territorial statute denying Mormons, polygamists, and advocates of polygamy the right to vote and to hold office because, as the Court construed the statute, it "simply excludes from the privilege of voting, or of holding any office of honor, trust or profit, those who have been convicted of certain offences, and those who advocate a practical resistance to the laws of the Territory and justify and approve the commission of crimes forbidden by it." To the extent *Davis* held that persons advocating a certain practice may be denied the right to vote, it is no longer good law. To the extent it held that the groups designated in the statute may be deprived of the right to vote because of their status, its ruling could not stand without surviving strict scrutiny, a most doubtful outcome. To the extent *Davis* held that a convicted felon may be denied the right to vote, its holding is not implicated by our decision and is unexceptionable.

A second and related point is that laws of the kind now before us raise the inevitable inference that the disadvantage imposed is born of animosity toward the class of persons affected. "[I]f the constitutional conception of 'equal protection of the laws' means anything, it must at the very least mean that a bare *** desire to harm a politically unpopular group cannot constitute a *legitimate* governmental interest." Even laws enacted for broad and ambitious purposes often can be explained by reference to legitimate public policies which justify the incidental disadvantages they impose on certain persons. Amendment 2, however, in making a general announcement that gays and lesbians shall not have any particular protections from the law, inflicts on them immediate, continuing, and real injuries that outrun and belie any legitimate justifications that may be claimed for it. We conclude that, in addition to the far-reaching deficiencies of Amendment 2 that we have noted, the principles it offends, in another sense, are conventional and venerable; a law must bear a rational relationship to a legitimate governmental purpose, and Amendment 2 does not.

The primary rationale the State offers for Amendment 2 is respect for other citizens' freedom of association, and in particular the liberties of landlords or employers who have personal or religious objections to homosexuality. Colorado also cites its interest in conserving resources to fight discrimination against other groups. The breadth of the amendment is so far removed from these particular justifications that we find it impossible to credit them. We cannot say that Amendment 2 is directed to any identifiable legitimate purpose or discrete objective. It is a status-based enactment divorced from any factual context from which we could discern a relationship to legitimate state interests; it is a classification of persons undertaken for its own sake, something the Equal Protection Clause does not permit. "[C]lass legislation *** [is] obnoxious to the prohibitions of the Fourteenth Amendment. *** Amendment 2 classifies homosexuals not to further a proper legislative end but to make them unequal to everyone else. This Colorado cannot do. A State cannot so deem a class of persons a stranger to its laws. Amendment 2 violates the Equal Protection Clause. ***

JUSTICE SCALIA, with whom THE CHIEF JUSTICE and JUSTICE THOMAS join, dissenting.

The Court has mistaken a Kulturkampf for a fit of spite. The constitutional amendment before us here is not the manifestation of a "'bare *** desire to harm'" homosexuals, but is rather a modest attempt by seemingly tolerant Coloradans to preserve traditional sexual mores against the efforts of a politically powerful minority to revise those mores through use of the laws. That objective, and the means chosen to achieve it, are not only unimpeachable under any constitutional doctrine hitherto pronounced (hence the opinion's heavy reliance upon principles of righteousness rather than judicial holdings); they have been specifically approved by the Congress of the United States and by this Court.

In holding that homosexuality cannot be singled out for disfavorable treatment, the Court contradicts a decision, unchallenged here, pronounced only 10 years ago, see *Bowers v. Hardwick*, 478 U.S. 186 (1986), and places the prestige of this institution behind the proposition that opposition to homosexuality is as reprehensible as racial or religious bias. *** Since the Constitution of the United States says nothing about this subject, it is left to be resolved by normal democratic means, including the democratic adoption of provisions in state constitutions. ***

[The Court rejects] the State's arguments that Amendment 2 "puts gays and lesbians in the same position as all other persons," and "does no more than deny homosexuals special rights". *** The amendment prohibits *special treatment* of homosexuals, and nothing more. *** They may not obtain *preferential* treatment without amending the State Constitution. That is to say, the principle underlying the Court's opinion is that one who is accorded equal treatment under the laws, but cannot as readily as others obtain *preferential* treatment under the laws, has been denied equal protection of the laws. If merely stating this alleged "equal protection" violation does not suffice to refute it, our constitutional jurisprudence has achieved terminal silliness.

The central thesis of the Court's reasoning is that any group is denied equal protection when, to obtain advantage (or, presumably, to avoid disadvantage), it must have recourse to a more general and hence more difficult level of political decisionmaking than others. The world has never heard of such a principle, which is why the Court's opinion is so long on emotive utterance and so short on relevant legal citation. And it seems to me most unlikely that any multilevel democracy can function under such a principle. For *whenever* a disadvantage is imposed, or conferral of a benefit is prohibited, at one of the higher levels of democratic decisionmaking (i.e., by the state legislature rather than local government, or by the people at large in the state constitution rather than the legislature), the affected group has (under this theory) been denied equal protection. ***

I turn next to whether there was a legitimate rational basis for the substance of the constitutional amendment—for the prohibition of special protection for homosexuals.[1] *** [T]he answer is so obviously yes. *** In *Bowers v. Hardwick* we held that the Constitution does not prohibit what virtually all States had done from the founding of the Republic until very

---

[1] The Court evidently agrees that "rational basis"—the normal test for compliance with the Equal Protection Clause—is the governing standard. *** And the Court implicitly rejects the Supreme Court of Colorado's holding that Amendment 2 infringes upon a "fundamental right" of "independently identifiable class[es]" to "participate equally in the political process."

recent years—making homosexual conduct a crime. *** If it is constitutionally permissible for a State to make homosexual conduct criminal, surely it is constitutionally permissible for a State to enact other laws merely *disfavoring* homosexual conduct. *** And *a fortiori* it is constitutionally permissible for a State to adopt a provision *not even* disfavoring homosexual conduct, but merely prohibiting all levels of state government from bestowing *special protections* upon homosexual conduct. *** If it is rational to criminalize the conduct, surely it is rational to deny special favor and protection to those with a self-avowed tendency or desire to engage in the conduct. ***

Moreover, even if the provision regarding homosexual "orientation" were invalid, respondents' challenge to Amendment 2—which is a facial challenge—must fail. *** Some individuals of homosexual "orientation" who do not engage in homosexual acts might successfully bring an as-applied challenge to Amendment 2, but so far as the record indicates, none of the respondents is such a person. *** What [Colorado] has done is not only unprohibited, but eminently reasonable, with close, congressionally approved precedent in earlier constitutional practice.

First, as to its eminent reasonableness. The Court's opinion contains grim, disapproving hints that Coloradans have been guilty of "animus" or "animosity" toward homosexuality, as though that has been established as un–American. Of course it is our moral heritage that one should not hate any human being or class of human beings. But I had thought that one could consider certain conduct reprehensible—murder, for example, or polygamy, or cruelty to animals—and could exhibit even "animus" toward such conduct. Surely that is the only sort of "animus" at issue here: moral disapproval of homosexual conduct, the same sort of moral disapproval that produced the centuries-old criminal laws that we held constitutional in *Bowers*. The Colorado amendment does not, to speak entirely precisely, prohibit giving favored status to people who are *homosexuals*; they can be favored for many reasons—for example, because they are senior citizens or members of racial minorities. But it prohibits giving them favored status *because of their homosexual conduct*—that is, it prohibits favored status for *homosexuality*. ***

Amendment 2 *** sought to counter both the geographic concentration and the disproportionate political power of homosexuals by (1) resolving the controversy at the statewide level, and (2) making the election a single-issue contest for both sides. *** The Court today asserts that this most democratic of procedures is unconstitutional. *** What the Court says is even demonstrably false at the constitutional level. The Eighteenth Amendment to the Federal Constitution, for example, deprived those who drank alcohol not only of the power to alter the policy of prohibition *locally* or through *state legislation*, but even of the power to alter it through *state constitutional amendment* or *federal legislation*. The Establishment Clause of the First Amendment prevents theocrats from having their way by converting their fellow citizens at the local, state, or federal statutory level; as does the Republican Form of Government Clause prevent monarchists.

But there is a much closer analogy, one that involves precisely the effort by the majority of citizens to preserve its view of sexual morality statewide, against the efforts of a geographically concentrated and politically powerful minority to undermine it. The constitutions of the States of Arizona, Idaho, New Mexico, Oklahoma, and Utah to this day contain provisions stating that polygamy is "forever prohibited." Polygamists, and those who have a polygamous "orientation," have been "singled out" by these provisions for much more severe treatment than merely denial of favored status; and that treatment can only be changed by achieving amendment of the state constitutions. *** The United States Congress *** *required* the inclusion of these antipolygamy provisions in the constitutions of Arizona, New Mexico, Oklahoma, and Utah, as a condition of their admission to statehood. *** [T]his Court *** approved a territorial statutory provision that went even further, depriving polygamists of the ability even to achieve a constitutional amendment, by depriving them of the power to vote. *Davis v. Beason*, 133 U.S. 333 (1890) *** [T]he proposition that polygamy can be criminalized, and those engaging in that crime deprived of the vote, remains good law. *Beason* rejected the argument that "such discrimination is a denial of the equal protection of the laws." *** Has the Court concluded that the perceived social harm of polygamy is a "legitimate concern of government," and the perceived social harm of homosexuality is not?

I strongly suspect that the answer to the last question is yes, which leads me to the last point I wish to make *** When the Court takes sides in the culture wars, it tends to be with *** the views and values of the lawyer class from which the Court's Members are drawn. How that class feels about homosexuality will be evident to anyone who wishes to interview job applicants at virtually any of the Nation's law schools. The interviewer may refuse to offer a job because the applicant is a Republican; because he is an adulterer; because he went to the wrong prep school or belongs to the wrong country club; because he eats snails; because he is a womanizer; because she wears real-animal fur; or even because he hates the Chicago Cubs. But if the interviewer should wish not to be an associate or partner of an applicant because he disapproves of the applicant's homosexuality, *then* he will have violated the pledge which the Association of American Law Schools requires all its member-schools to exact from job interviewers: "assurance of the employer's willingness" to hire homosexuals. This law-school view of what "prejudices" must be stamped out may be contrasted with the more plebeian attitudes that apparently still prevail in the United States Congress, which has been unresponsive to repeated attempts to extend to homosexuals the protections of federal civil rights laws. ***

Today's opinion has no foundation in American constitutional law, and barely pretends to. The people of Colorado have adopted an entirely reasonable provision which does not even disfavor homosexuals in any substantive sense, but merely denies them preferential treatment. Amendment 2 is designed to prevent piecemeal deterioration of the sexual morality favored by a majority of Coloradans, and is not only an appropriate means to that legitimate end, but a means that Americans have employed before. Striking it down is an act, not of judicial judgment, but of political will. I dissent.

Notes

1. **Hearts and Heads.** "Since *Romer* came down, I have had many conversations about it with law professors and law students across the country. The initial consensus seems to be that while JUSTICE KENNEDY's language soared, JUSTICE SCALIA's logic held. JUSTICE KENNEDY won their hearts; JUSTICE SCALIA, their heads." Amar, *Attainder and Amendment 2: Romer's Rightness,* 95 MICH. L. REV. 203, 204 (1996). Do you agree with the "consensus"? Amar argues that Colorado's Amendment 2 is unconstitutional in light of the Attainder Clause of Article I, Section 9, which he calls "an early forebear of the Equal Protection Clause." It is unconstitutional as "legal and social outlawry in cowboy country—a targeting of outsiders, a badge of second-class citizenship, a tainting of queers, a scarlet Q." For a skeptical response by one of Amar's students, *see Hills, Is Amendment 2 Really a Bill of Attainder? Some Questions About Professor Amar's Analysis of Romer*, 95 MICH. L. REV. 236 (1996).

2. **Rational Basis Review.** Some argue that this may be merely one of several cases in which the Court says one thing (rational basis standard) and does something different (heightened scrutiny). Do you think *Romer* is explicable as (1) an early step towards elevating sexual orientation to protected class status or (2) an anomaly caused by the breadth of Amendment 2 to deny homosexuals protection against discrimination regardless of the context?

3. **Question.** Assume a city amends its charter to include this language: "no special class status may be granted based upon sexual orientation, conduct or relationships." Accordingly, the city may not enact, adopt, enforce, or administer any ordinance, regulation, rule, or policy which provides that homosexual, lesbian, or bisexual orientation, status, conduct, or relationship constitutes, entitles, or otherwise provides a person with the basis to have any claim of minority or protected status, quota preference, or other preferential treatment. The amendment also includes language that makes all previous city programs designed to give preferential treatment to homosexuals "null and void." Does it violate the Equal Protection Clause of the Fourteenth Amendment? *See Equality Foundation of Greater Cincinnati, Inc. v. City of Cincinnati*, 128 F.3d 289 (6th Cir. 1997), *cert. denied*, 525 U.S. 943 (1998) (no).

UNITED STATES v. WINDSOR
133 S. Ct. 2675 (2013)

JUSTICE KENNEDY delivered the opinion of the Court.

When at first Windsor and Spyer longed to marry, neither New York nor any other State granted them that right. *** For marriage between a man and a woman no doubt had been thought of by most people as essential to the very definition of that term and to its role and function throughout the history of civilization. *** [Recently, however,] some States concluded that same-sex marriage ought to be given recognition and validity in the law for those same-sex couples who wish to define themselves by their commitment to each other. *** Slowly at first and then in rapid course, the laws of New York *** recognized same-sex marriages performed elsewhere; and then it later amended its own marriage laws to permit same-sex marriage. *** By history and tradition the definition and regulation of marriage ***has been treated as being within the authority and realm of the separate States. Yet it is further established that Congress, in enacting discrete statutes, can make determinations that bear on marital rights and privileges. ***

In addressing the interaction of state domestic relations and federal immigration law Congress determined that marriages "entered into for the purpose of procuring an alien's admission [to the United States] as an immigrant" will not qualify the noncitizen for that status, even if the noncitizen's marriage is valid and proper for state-law purposes. And in establishing income-based criteria for Social Security benefits, Congress decided that although state law would determine in general who qualifies as an applicant's spouse, common-law marriages also should be recognized, *** Though these discrete examples establish the constitutionality of limited federal laws that regulate the meaning of marriage in order to further federal policy, [the Federal Defense of Marriage Act] DOMA has a far greater reach; for it enacts a directive applicable to over 1,000 federal statutes and the whole realm of federal regulations. *** In order to assess the validity of that intervention it is necessary to discuss the extent of the state power and authority over marriage as a matter of history and tradition. State laws defining and regulating marriage, of course, must respect the constitutional rights of persons, but, subject to those guarantees, "regulation of domestic relations" is "an area that has long been regarded as a virtually exclusive province of the States." *** The definition of marriage is the foundation of the State's broader authority to regulate the subject of domestic relations with respect to the "[p]rotection of offspring, property interests, and the enforcement of marital responsibilities." "[T]he states, at the time of the adoption of the Constitution, possessed full power over the subject of marriage and divorce ... [and] the Constitution delegated no authority to the Government of the United States on the subject of marriage and divorce" [and] the Federal Government, through our history, has deferred to state-law policy decisions with respect to domestic relations. ***

Against this background DOMA rejects the long-established precept that the incidents, benefits, and obligations of marriage are uniform for all married couples within each State, though they may vary, subject to constitutional guarantees, from one State to the next. Despite these considerations, it is unnecessary to decide whether this federal intrusion on state power is a violation of the Constitution because it disrupts the federal balance. The State's power in defining the marital relation is of central relevance in this case quite apart from principles of federalism. Here the State's decision to give this class of persons the right to marry conferred upon them a dignity and status of immense import. When the State used its historic and essential authority to define the marital relation in this way, its role and its power in making the decision enhanced the recognition, dignity, and protection of the class in their own community. DOMA, because of its reach and extent, departs from this history and tradition of reliance on state law to define marriage. *** The Federal Government uses this state-defined class for the opposite purpose—to impose restrictions and disabilities. That result requires this Court now to address whether the resulting injury and indignity is a deprivation of an essential part of the liberty protected by the Fifth Amendment. What the State of New York treats as alike the federal law deems unlike by a law designed to injure the same class the State seeks to protect. ***

DOMA seeks to injure the very class New York seeks to protect. By doing so it violates basic due process and equal protection principles applicable to the Federal Government. The Constitution's guarantee of equality "must at the very least mean that a bare congressional desire to harm a politically unpopular group cannot" justify disparate treatment of that group. In determining whether a law is motived by an improper animus or purpose, " '[d]iscriminations of an unusual character' " especially require careful consideration. DOMA cannot survive under these principles. The responsibility of the States for the regulation of domestic relations is an important indicator of the substantial societal impact the State's classifications have in the daily lives and customs of its people. DOMA's unusual deviation from the usual tradition of recognizing and accepting state definitions of marriage here operates to deprive same-sex couples of the benefits and responsibilities that come with the federal recognition of their marriages. This is strong evidence of a law having the purpose and effect of disapproval of that class. The avowed purpose and practical effect of the law here in question are to impose a disadvantage, a separate status, and so a stigma upon all who enter into same-sex marriages made lawful by the unquestioned authority of the States.

The history of DOMA's enactment and its own text demonstrate that interference with the equal dignity of same-sex marriages, a dignity conferred by the States in the exercise of their sovereign power, was more than an incidental effect of the federal statute. It was its essence. The House Report announced its conclusion that "it is both appropriate and necessary for Congress to do what it can to defend the institution of traditional heterosexual marriage.... H.R. 3396 is appropriately entitled the 'Defense of Marriage Act.' The effort to redefine 'marriage' to extend to homosexual couples is a truly radical proposal that would fundamentally alter the institution of marriage." The House concluded that DOMA expresses "both moral disapproval of homosexuality, and a moral conviction that heterosexuality better comports with traditional (especially Judeo–Christian) morality." The stated purpose of the law was to promote an "interest in protecting the traditional moral teachings reflected in heterosexual-only marriage laws." Were there any doubt of this far-reaching purpose, the title of the Act confirms it: The Defense of Marriage. *** The congressional goal was "to put a thumb on the scales and influence a state's decision as to how to shape its own marriage laws." The Act's demonstrated purpose is to ensure that if any State decides to recognize same-sex marriages, those unions will be treated as second-class marriages for purposes of federal law. This raises a most serious question under the Constitution's Fifth Amendment.

DOMA's operation in practice confirms this purpose. When New York adopted a law to permit same-sex marriage, it sought to eliminate inequality;

but DOMA frustrates that objective through a system-wide enactment with no identified connection to any particular area of federal law. DOMA writes inequality into the entire United States Code. The particular case at hand concerns the estate tax, but DOMA is more than a simple determination of what should or should not be allowed as an estate tax refund. Among the over 1,000 statutes and numerous federal regulations that DOMA controls are laws pertaining to Social Security, housing, taxes, criminal sanctions, copyright, and veterans' benefits.

DOMA's principal effect is to identify a subset of state-sanctioned marriages and make them unequal. The principal purpose is to impose inequality, not for other reasons like governmental efficiency. Responsibilities, as well as rights, enhance the dignity and integrity of the person. And DOMA contrives to deprive some couples married under the laws of their State, but not other couples, of both rights and responsibilities. By creating two contradictory marriage regimes within the same State, DOMA forces same-sex couples to live as married for the purpose of state law but unmarried for the purpose of federal law, thus diminishing the stability and predictability of basic personal relations the State has found it proper to acknowledge and protect. By this dynamic DOMA undermines both the public and private significance of state-sanctioned same-sex marriages; for it tells those couples, and all the world, that their otherwise valid marriages are unworthy of federal recognition. This places same-sex couples in an unstable position of being in a second-tier marriage. The differentiation demeans the couple, whose moral and sexual choices the Constitution protects, and whose relationship the State has sought to dignify. And it humiliates tens of thousands of children now being raised by same-sex couples. The law in question makes it even more difficult for the children to understand the integrity and closeness of their own family and its concord with other families in their community and in their daily lives.

Under DOMA, same-sex married couples have their lives burdened, by reason of government decree, in visible and public ways. By its great reach, DOMA touches many aspects of married and family life, from the mundane to the profound. It prevents same-sex married couples from obtaining government healthcare benefits they would otherwise receive. It deprives them of the Bankruptcy Code's special protections for domestic-support obligations. It forces them to follow a complicated procedure to file their state and federal taxes jointly. It prohibits them from being buried together in veterans' cemeteries. ***

What has been explained to this point should more than suffice to establish that the principal purpose and the necessary effect of this law are to demean those persons who are in a lawful same-sex marriage. This requires the Court to hold, as it now does, that DOMA is unconstitutional as a deprivation of the liberty of the person protected by the Fifth Amendment of the Constitution.

The liberty protected by the Fifth Amendment's Due Process Clause contains within it the prohibition against denying to any person the equal protection of the laws. While the Fifth Amendment itself withdraws from

Government the power to degrade or demean in the way this law does, the equal protection guarantee of the Fourteenth Amendment makes that Fifth Amendment right all the more specific and all the better understood and preserved.

The class to which DOMA directs its restrictions and restraints are those persons who are joined in same-sex marriages made lawful by the State. DOMA singles out a class of persons deemed by a State entitled to recognition and protection to enhance their own liberty. It imposes a disability on the class by refusing to acknowledge a status the State finds to be dignified and proper. DOMA instructs all federal officials, and indeed all persons with whom same-sex couples interact, including their own children, that their marriage is less worthy than the marriages of others. The federal statute is invalid, for no legitimate purpose overcomes the purpose and effect to disparage and to injure those whom the State, by its marriage laws, sought to protect in personhood and dignity. By seeking to displace this protection and treating those persons as living in marriages less respected than others, the federal statute is in violation of the Fifth Amendment. This opinion and its holding are confined to those lawful marriages. ***

CHIEF JUSTICE ROBERTS, dissenting.

*** Interests in uniformity and stability amply justified Congress's decision to retain the definition of marriage that, at that point, had been adopted by every State in our Nation, and every nation in the world. *** That the Federal Government treated this fundamental question differently than it treated variations over consanguinity or minimum age is hardly surprising—and hardly enough to support a conclusion that the "principal purpose," of the 342 Representatives and 85 Senators who voted for it, and the President who signed it, was a bare desire to harm. Nor do the snippets of legislative history and the banal title of the Act to which the majority points suffice to make such a showing. *** I would not tar the political branches with the brush of bigotry.

But while I disagree with the result to which the majority's analysis leads it in this case, I think it more important to point out that its analysis leads no further. The Court does not have before it, and the logic of its opinion does not decide, the distinct question whether the States, in the exercise of their "historic and essential authority to define the marital relation," may continue to utilize the traditional definition of marriage. *** The majority emphasizes that DOMA was a "systemwide enactment with no identified connection to any particular area of federal law," but a State's definition of marriage "is the foundation of the State's broader authority to regulate the subject of domestic relations with respect to the '[p]rotection of offspring, property interests, and the enforcement of marital responsibilities.' "And the federal decision undermined (in the majority's view) the "dignity [already] conferred by the States in the exercise of their sovereign power," whereas a State's decision whether to expand the definition of marriage from its traditional contours involves no similar concern.

We may in the future have to resolve challenges to state marriage definitions affecting same-sex couples. That issue, however, is not before us in this case ***

JUSTICE SCALIA, with whom JUSTICE THOMAS joins.

*** There are many remarkable things about the majority's merits holding. The first is how rootless and shifting its justifications are. For example, the opinion starts with *** the traditional power of States to define domestic relations—initially fooling many readers, I am sure, into thinking that this is a federalism opinion. But we are eventually told that "it is unnecessary to decide whether this federal intrusion on state power is a violation of the Constitution," and that "[t]he State's power in defining the marital relation is of central relevance in this case quite apart from principles of federalism" because "the State's decision to give this class of persons the right to marry conferred upon them a dignity and status of immense import." But no one questions the power of the States to define marriage (with the concomitant conferral of dignity and status), so what is the point of devoting seven pages to describing how long and well established that power is? Even after the opinion has formally disclaimed reliance upon principles of federalism, mentions of "the usual tradition of recognizing and accepting state definitions of marriage" continue. What to make of this? The opinion never explains. My guess is that the majority, while reluctant to suggest that defining the meaning of "marriage" in federal statutes is unsupported by any of the Federal Government's enumerated powers,[4] nonetheless needs some rhetorical basis to support its pretense that today's prohibition of laws excluding same-sex marriage is confined to the Federal Government (leaving the second, state-law shoe to be dropped later, maybe next Term). But I am only guessing.

Equally perplexing are the opinion's references to "the Constitution's guarantee of equality." Near the end of the opinion, we are told that although the "equal protection guarantee of the Fourteenth Amendment makes [the] Fifth Amendment [due process] right all the more specific and all the better understood and preserved"—what can *that* mean?—"the Fifth Amendment itself withdraws from Government the power to degrade or demean in the way this law does." The only possible interpretation of this statement is that the Equal Protection Clause, even the Equal Protection Clause as incorporated in the Due Process Clause, is not the basis for today's holding. But the portion of the majority opinion that explains why DOMA is unconstitutional begins by citing *Bolling v. Sharpe,* 347 U.S. 497 (1954), *Department of Agriculture v. Moreno,* 413 U.S. 528 (1973), and *Romer v. Evans* 517 U.S. 620, (1996)—*all* of which are equal-protection cases. And those three cases are the *only* authorities that the Court cites *** about the Constitution's meaning, except for its citation of *Lawrence v. Texas* (not an

---

[4] Such a suggestion would be impossible, given the Federal Government's long history of making pronouncements regarding marriage—for example, conditioning Utah's entry into the Union upon its prohibition of polygamy. ***

equal-protection case) to support its passing assertion that the Constitution protects the "moral and sexual choices" of same-sex couples.

Moreover, if this is meant to be an equal-protection opinion, it is a confusing one. The opinion does not resolve and indeed does not even mention what had been the central question in this litigation: whether, under the Equal Protection Clause, laws restricting marriage to a man and a woman are reviewed for more than mere rationality. *** But the Court certainly does not *apply* anything that resembles that deferential framework.

The majority opinion need not get into the strict-vs.-rational-basis scrutiny question, and need not justify its holding under either, because it says that DOMA is unconstitutional as "a deprivation of the liberty of the person protected by the Fifth Amendment of the Constitution"; that it violates "basic due process" principles; and that it inflicts an "injury and indignity" of a kind that denies "an essential part of the liberty protected by the Fifth Amendment." The majority never utters the dread words "substantive due process," perhaps sensing the disrepute into which that doctrine has fallen, but that is what those statements mean. Yet the opinion does not argue that same-sex marriage is "deeply rooted in this Nation's history and tradition," *Washington v. Glucksberg,* a claim that would of course be quite absurd. *** The sum of all the Court's nonspecific hand-waving is that this law is invalid (maybe on equal-protection grounds, maybe on substantive-due-process grounds, and perhaps with some amorphous federalism component playing a role) because it is motivated by a "bare ... desire to harm" couples in same-sex marriages. It is this proposition with which I will therefore engage.

As I have observed before, the Constitution does not forbid the government to enforce traditional moral and sexual norms. See *Lawrence v. Texas* (SCALIA, J., dissenting). *** However, even setting aside traditional moral disapproval of same-sex marriage (or indeed same-sex sex), there are many perfectly valid—indeed, downright boring—justifying rationales for this legislation. Their existence ought to be the end of this case. For they give the lie to the Court's conclusion that only those with hateful hearts could have voted "aye" on this Act. *** To choose just one of these defenders' arguments, DOMA avoids difficult choice-of-law issues that will now arise absent a uniform federal definition of marriage. *** That is a classic purpose for a definitional provision.

Further, DOMA preserves the intended effects of prior legislation against then-unforeseen changes in circumstance. When Congress provided (for example) that a special estate-tax exemption would exist for spouses, this exemption reached only *opposite-sex* spouses—those being the only sort that were recognized in *any* State at the time of DOMA's passage. When it became clear that changes in state law might one day alter that balance, DOMA's definitional section was enacted to ensure that state-level experimentation did not automatically alter the basic operation of federal law, unless and until Congress made the further judgment to do so on its own. That is not animus—just stabilizing prudence. *** The Court *** says that the motivation for DOMA was to "demean"; to "impose inequality"; to "impose ...

a stigma"; to deny people "equal dignity".; to brand gay people as "unworthy"; and to "*humiliat[e]*" their children. *** But to defend traditional marriage is not to condemn, demean, or humiliate those who would prefer other arrangements, any more than to defend the Constitution of the United States is to condemn, demean, or humiliate other constitutions. To hurl such accusations so casually demeans *this institution*. ***

The penultimate sentence of the majority's opinion is a naked declaration that "[t]his opinion and its holding are confined" to those couples "joined in same-sex marriages made lawful by the State." I have heard such "bald, unreasoned disclaimer[s]" before. *Lawrence*. When the Court declared a constitutional right to homosexual sodomy, we were assured that the case had nothing, nothing at all to do with "whether the government must give formal recognition to any relationship that homosexual persons seek to enter." Now we are told that DOMA is invalid because it "demeans the couple, whose moral and sexual choices the Constitution protects,"—with an accompanying citation of *Lawrence*. It takes real cheek for today's majority to assure us, as it is going out the door, that a constitutional requirement to give formal recognition to same-sex marriage is not at issue here—when what has preceded that assurance is a lecture on how superior the majority's moral judgment in favor of same-sex marriage is to the Congress's hateful moral judgment against it. I promise you this: The only thing that will "confine" the Court's holding is its sense of what it can get away with. *** In my opinion, however, the view that *this* Court will take of state prohibition of same-sex marriage is indicated beyond mistaking by today's opinion. As I have said, the real rationale of today's opinion, whatever disappearing trail of its legalistic argle-bargle one chooses to follow, is that DOMA is motivated by " 'bare ... desire to harm' " couples in same-sex marriages. How easy it is, indeed how inevitable, to reach the same conclusion with regard to state laws denying same-sex couples marital status. *** By formally declaring anyone opposed to same-sex marriage an enemy of human decency, the majority arms well every challenger to a state law restricting marriage to its traditional definition. *** The result will be a judicial distortion of our society's debate over marriage—a debate that can seem in need of our clumsy "help" only to a member of this institution.

As to that debate: Few public controversies touch an institution so central to the lives of so many, and few inspire such attendant passion by good people on all sides. Few public controversies will ever demonstrate so vividly the beauty of what our Framers gave us, a gift the Court pawns today to buy its stolen moment in the spotlight: a system of government that permits us to rule *ourselves*. Since DOMA's passage, citizens on all sides of the question have seen victories and they have seen defeats. There have been plebiscites, legislation, persuasion, and loud voices—in other words, democracy. Victories in one place for some are offset by victories in other places for others. *** In the majority's telling, this story is black-and-white: Hate your neighbor or come along with us. The truth is more complicated. It is hard to admit that one's political opponents are not monsters, especially in a struggle like this one, and the challenge in the end proves more than today's Court can handle. Too bad. A reminder that disagreement over something so fundamental as marriage can still be politically legitimate would have been a fit task for what in earlier times was called the judicial temperament. We might have covered ourselves with honor today, by promising all sides of this debate that it was theirs to settle and that we would respect their resolution. We might have let the People decide. *** But the Court has cheated both sides, robbing the winners of an honest victory, and the losers of the peace that comes from a fair defeat. We owed both of them better. I dissent.

JUSTICE ALITO dissenting, with whom JUSTICE THOMAS concurs.

*** Same-sex marriage presents a highly emotional and important question of public policy—but not a difficult question of constitutional law. The Constitution does not guarantee the right to enter into a same-sex marriage. Indeed, no provision of the Constitution speaks to the issue. *** The Court has sometimes found the Due Process Clauses to have a substantive component *** But it is well established that any "substantive" component to the Due Process Clause protects only "those fundamental rights and liberties which are, objectively, "deeply rooted in this Nation's history and tradition," *** It is beyond dispute that the right to same-sex marriage is not deeply rooted in this Nation's history and tradition. *** What Windsor and the United States seek, therefore, is not the protection of a deeply rooted right but the recognition of a very new right, and they seek this innovation not from a legislative body elected by the people, but from unelected judges. ***

At present, no one—including social scientists, philosophers, and historians—can predict with any certainty what the long-term ramifications of widespread acceptance of same-sex marriage will be. And judges are certainly not equipped to make such an assessment. *** In our system of government, ultimate sovereignty rests with the people, and the people have the right to control their own destiny. Any change on a question so fundamental should be made by the people through their elected officials.

Perhaps because they cannot show that same-sex marriage is a fundamental right under our Constitution, Windsor and the United States couch their arguments in equal protection terms. They argue that § 3 of DOMA discriminates on the basis of sexual orientation, that classifications based on sexual orientation should trigger a form of "heightened" scrutiny, and that § 3 cannot survive such scrutiny. *** Our equal protection framework, upon which Windsor and the United States rely, is a judicial construct that provides a useful mechanism for analyzing a certain universe of equal protection cases. But that framework is ill suited for use in evaluating the constitutionality of laws based on the traditional understanding of marriage, which fundamentally turn on what marriage is. *** In asking the Court to determine that § 3 of DOMA is subject to and violates heightened scrutiny, Windsor and the United States thus ask us to rule that the presence of two members of the opposite sex is as rationally related to marriage as white skin is to voting or a Y-chromosome is to the ability to administer an estate. *** By asking the Court to strike down DOMA as not satisfying some form of heightened scrutiny, Windsor and the United States are really seeking to have the Court resolve a debate between two competing views of marriage.

The first and older view, which I will call the "traditional" or "conjugal" view, sees marriage as an intrinsically opposite-sex institution. *** They argue that marriage is essentially the solemnizing of a comprehensive, exclusive, permanent union that is intrinsically ordered to producing new life, even if it does not always do so. ***The other, newer view is what I will call the "consent-based" vision of marriage, a vision that primarily defines marriage as the solemnization of mutual commitment—marked by strong emotional attachment and sexual attraction—between two persons. ***

The Constitution does not codify either of these views of marriage (although I suspect it would have been hard at the time of the adoption of the Constitution or the Fifth Amendment to find Americans who did not take the traditional view for granted). The silence of the Constitution on this question should be enough to end the matter as far as the judiciary is concerned. *** Legislatures, however, have little choice but to decide between the two views. We have long made clear that neither the political branches of the Federal Government nor state governments are required to be neutral between competing visions of the good, provided that the vision of the good that they adopt is not countermanded by the Constitution. Accordingly, both Congress and the States are entitled to enact laws recognizing either of the two understandings of marriage. ***

To the extent that the Court takes the position that the question of same-sex marriage should be resolved primarily at the state level, I wholeheartedly agree. I hope that the Court will ultimately permit the people of each State to decide this question for themselves. *** In any event, § 3 of DOMA, in my view, does not encroach on the prerogatives of the States, assuming of course that the many federal statutes affected by DOMA have not already done so. Section 3 does not prevent any State from recognizing same-sex marriage or from extending to same-sex couples any right, privilege, benefit, or obligation stemming from state law. All that § 3 does is to define a class of persons to whom federal law extends certain special benefits and upon whom federal law imposes certain special burdens. In these provisions, Congress used marital status as a way of defining this class—in part, I assume, because it viewed marriage as a valuable institution to be fostered and in part because it viewed married couples as comprising a unique type of economic unit that merits special regulatory treatment. Assuming that Congress has the power under the Constitution to enact the laws affected by § 3, Congress has the power to define the category of persons to whom those laws apply. *** I would hold that § 3 of DOMA does not violate the Fifth Amendment. ***

Notes

1. **Marriage Equality Paradigms**. Which is the correct paradigm for marriage: (a) the right of each adult to marry one partner at a time or (b) the right of each adult to marry one partner of the opposite sex at a time? The formulations embody different notions of equality. The first is functional for all adults, focusing on the fulfillment of one's bonding with "the one you love." The second is formally equal for all adults, but is functional only for heterosexuals, who are not restricted by the "opposite sex" caveat.

2. **Prejudice Theory and Evidence.** Justice Kennedy's majority opinion says DOMA was premised on prejudice against homosexuals. Do you agree? Does this strengthen or weaken the decision as a "same sex rights" opinion? What about DOMA shows this prejudice: (1) the title? (2) statements in a committee report to that effect (House report, Senate report, or joint conference committee report)? (3) Floor statements by individual legislators, including legislators who sponsored DOMA? The votes were 342-67 in favor of passing in the House and 85-14 in favor of passing in the Senate. What do such overwhelming votes say about Justice Kennedy's "prejudice" was the "but for" prerequisite for DOMA?

3. **What Interpretive Approach Does *Windsor* Use?** Which interpretive approach do you think best describes the Majority opinion: originalist, purposivist, or realist? The Majority opinion does not rest on any singular constitutional theory (i.e., federalism, equal protection, due process). Do you think this is a strength or weakness of the majority opinion?

4. **Due Process and Equal Protection.** Are the same rights "fundamental" for substantive due process analysis and equal protection analysis? Beyond that, and the "synergy" Justice Kennedy notes between the two concepts embodied in Section 1 of the Fourteenth Amendment, are there any reasons that *Obergefell* is primarily a due process case and *Windsor* is primarily an equal protection case?

5. **Justice Kennedy's America?** Justice Kennedy wrote the majority opinions in all the major Supreme Court gay rights cases (*Romer, Lawrence, Obergefell* and *Windsor*). Have his views evolved? Has the Court changed?

6.   **State and Federal Constitutions**. Though they may contain identical phrases (like equal protection and due process) state constitutions differ from the federal constitution in several ways. First, each applies in one state, not fifty. Second, they are easier to amend. For example, Alabama has amended its 1901 constitution almost 600 times.   Third, state constitutions sometimes contain slightly different words or unique traditions not applicable to the United States Constitution. Should interpretations of state constitutions affect the Supreme Court's construction of implied fundamental rights under the Fourteenth Amendment (or vice versa)?

7.   **International Trends**. The Netherlands, Belgium, Canada, and Spain have recently recognized same-sex marriages or civil unions. Is this relevant to interpreting the Fourteenth and Fifth Amendments?

8. **Congressional Power, Federalism, and Marriage**. As *Windsor* notes, DOMA is limited to defining marriage for purposes of dealing with federal interests. Congress "has never purported to lay down a general code defining marriage or purporting to bind the states to such a regime." Could it? Consider whether the Commerce Clause and other powers you have studied would support a federal "general code" of marriage. Then proceed to Chapter X, which examines Congress's power to enforce the Fourteenth Amendment, including the equal protection and due process clauses.

X

THE POWER TO ENFORCE
THE RECONSTRUCTION AMENDMENTS

The question here is not whether the statute is appropriate remedial legislation to cure an established violation of a constitutional command, but whether there has in fact been an infringement of that constitutional command ***. That question is one for the judicial branch ultimately to determine. Were the rule otherwise, Congress would be able to qualify this Court's constitutional decisions under the Fourteenth and Fifteenth Amendments ***

—JUSTICE HARLAN (dissenting)
Katzenbach v. Morgan (1966)

You now have a fairly extensive understanding of § 1 of the Fourteenth Amendment, its state action requirement and the three grand protections listed therein: Privileges and Immunities, Due Process, and Equal Protection. You are knowledgeable about judicial interpretation of § 1, including the history and current content of substantive due process, application of the Bill of Rights to state and local governments through incorporation, the levels of scrutiny and their application under the equal protection clause, and so forth.

This final chapter covers the reach of Congress's power under § 5 of the Fourteenth Amendment: "The Congress shall have power to enforce, by appropriate legislation, the provisions of this article." What does it mean to "enforce" the guarantees of Section 1? Can Congress provide protection broader (or narrower) than the due process and equal protection rights accorded to persons by the Court? Is there any limit to the remedies Congress can provide when the alleged violator is a state that would otherwise have immunity under the Eleventh Amendment? Is Congress's power greater for race discrimination (strict scrutiny under the equal protection clause) than for sex discrimination (intermediate scrutiny under the equal protection clause) or other discrimination (where rational basis has been the equal protection mantra, even when the Court demands more than simple rationality)?

The cases that follow explore these questions. The two cases in Part A provide the framework established by the Court for assessing the §5 power of Congress. The cases in Part B examine specific problems of applying § 5 in the areas of disability and sex discrimination, revealing deep divides within the Court concerning the appropriate relationship between itself and Congress. These cases also provide ample opportunity for review and reflection on the themes of judicial and congressional power, federal and state authority and immunity, government power and individual rights. In short, they draw together the themes that pervade this book.

A. THE FRAMEWORK FOR ENFORCING THE FOURTEENTH AMENDMENT

The Supreme Court held, in *Lassiter v. Northampton County Bd. of Elections*, 360 U.S. 45 (1959) that it was not unconstitutional for a state to require English literacy as a prerequisite to vote, so long as the requirement was applied equally to all citizens of the state regardless of race. Shortly thereafter, Congress passed the Voting Rights Act of 1965, one provision of which was examined in the following decision.

KATZENBACH v. MORGAN
384 U.S. 641 (1966)

MR. JUSTICE BRENNAN delivered the opinion of the Court.

These cases concern the constitutionality of § 4(e) of the Voting Rights Act of 1965. That law, in the respects pertinent in these cases, provides that no person who has successfully completed the sixth primary grade in a public school in, or a private school accredited by, the Commonwealth of Puerto Rico in which the language of instruction was other than English shall be denied the right to vote in any election because of his inability to read or write English. Appellees, registered voters in New York City, brought this suit to challenge the constitutionality of § 4(e) insofar as it pro tanto prohibits the enforcement of the election laws of New York requiring an ability to read and write English as a condition of voting. Under these laws many of the several hundred thousand New York City residents who have migrated there from the Commonwealth of Puerto Rico had previously been denied the right to vote, and appellees attack § 4(e) insofar as it would enable many of these citizens to vote.[3] *** The [District] court held that in enacting § 4(e) Congress exceeded the powers granted to it by the Constitution and therefore usurped powers reserved to the States by the Tenth Amendment. Appeals were taken directly to this Court. We reverse. We hold that, in the application challenged in these cases, § 4(e) is a proper exercise of the powers granted to Congress by § 5 of the Fourteenth Amendment[5] and that by force of the Supremacy

---

[3] *** The Solicitor General informs us in his brief to this Court, that in all probability the practical effect of § 4(e) will be limited to enfranchising those educated in Puerto Rican schools. He advises us that, aside from the schools in the Commonwealth of Puerto Rico, there are no public or parochial schools in the territorial limits of the United States in which the predominant language of instruction is other than English and which would have generally been attended by persons who are otherwise qualified to vote save for their lack of literacy in English.

[5] *** [We need not] consider whether § 4(e) could be sustained as an exercise of power under the Territorial Clause, Art. IV, § 3; or as a measure to discharge certain treaty obligations of the United States. Nor need we consider whether § 4(e) could be sustained insofar as it relates to the election of federal officers as an exercise of congressional power under Art. I, § 4; nor whether § 4(e) could be sustained, insofar as it relates to the election of state officers, as an exercise of congressional power to enforce the clause guaranteeing to each State a republican form of government.

Clause, Article VI, the New York English literacy requirement cannot be enforced to the extent that it is inconsistent with § 4(e). ***

The Attorney General of the State of New York argues that an exercise of congressional power under § 5 of the Fourteenth Amendment that prohibits the enforcement of a state law can only be sustained if the judicial branch determines that the state law is prohibited by the provisions of the Amendment that Congress sought to enforce. More specifically, he urges that § 4(e) cannot be sustained as appropriate legislation to enforce the Equal Protection Clause unless the judiciary decides—even with the guidance of a congressional judgment—that the application of the English literacy requirement prohibited by § 4(e) is forbidden by the Equal Protection Clause itself.

We disagree. *** A construction of § 5 that would require a judicial determination that the enforcement of the state law precluded by Congress violated the Amendment, as a condition of sustaining the congressional enactment, would depreciate both congressional resourcefulness and congressional responsibility for implementing the Amendment. It would confine the legislative power in this context to the insignificant role of abrogating only those state laws that the judicial branch was prepared to adjudge unconstitutional, or of merely informing the judgment of the judiciary by particularizing the "majestic generalities" of § 1 of the Amendment.

Thus our task in this case is not to determine whether the New York English literacy requirement as applied to deny the right to vote to a person who successfully completed the sixth grade in a Puerto Rican school violates the Equal Protection Clause. *** [The] question before us here [is]: Without regard to whether the judiciary would find that the Equal Protection Clause itself nullifies New York's English literacy requirement as so applied, could Congress prohibit the enforcement of the state law by legislating under § 5 of the Fourteenth Amendment? In answering this question, our task is limited to determining whether such legislation is, as required by § 5, appropriate legislation to enforce the Equal Protection Clause.

By including § 5 the draftsmen sought to grant to Congress, by a specific provision applicable to the Fourteenth Amendment, the same broad powers expressed in the Necessary and Proper Clause, Art. I, § 8, cl. 18. *** Correctly viewed, § 5 is a positive grant of legislative power authorizing Congress to exercise its discretion in determining whether and what legislation is needed to secure the guarantees of the Fourteenth Amendment.

We therefore proceed to the consideration whether § 4(e) is "appropriate legislation" to enforce the Equal Protection Clause, that is, under the *McCulloch v. Maryland* standard, whether § 4(e) may be regarded as an enactment to enforce the Equal Protection Clause, whether it is "plainly adapted to that end" and whether it is not prohibited by but is consistent with "the letter and spirit of the constitution."[10]

There can be no doubt that § 4(e) may be regarded as an enactment to enforce the Equal Protection Clause. Congress explicitly declared that it enacted § 4(e) "to secure the rights under the fourteenth amendment of persons educated in American-flag schools in which the predominant classroom language was other than English." The persons referred to include those who have migrated from the Commonwealth of Puerto Rico to New York and who have been denied the right to vote because of their inability to read and write English, and the Fourteenth Amendment rights referred to include those emanating from the Equal Protection Clause. More specifically, § 4(e) may be viewed as a measure to secure for the Puerto Rican community residing in New York nondiscriminatory treatment by government—both in the imposition of voting qualifications and the provision or administration of governmental services, such as public schools, public housing and law enforcement.

Section 4(e) may be readily seen as "plainly adapted" to furthering these aims of the Equal Protection Clause. The practical effect of § 4(e) is to prohibit New York from denying the right to vote to large segments of its Puerto Rican community. Congress has thus prohibited the State from denying to that community the right that is "preservative of all rights." *** Section 4(e) *** was well within congressional authority to say that this need of the Puerto Rican minority for the vote warranted federal intrusion upon any state interests served by the English literacy requirement. It was for Congress, as the branch that made this judgment, to assess and weigh the various conflicting considerations—the risk or pervasiveness of the discrimination in governmental services, the effectiveness of eliminating the state restriction on the right to vote as a means of dealing with the evil, the adequacy or availability of alternative remedies, and the nature and significance of the state interests that would be affected by the nullification of the English literacy requirement as applied to residents who have successfully completed the sixth grade in a Puerto Rican school. It is not for us to review the congressional resolution of these factors. *** [I]t is enough that we perceive a basis upon which Congress might predicate a judgment that the application of New York's English literacy requirement to deny the right to vote to a person with a sixth grade education in Puerto Rican schools in which the language of instruction was other than English constituted an invidious discrimination in violation of the Equal Protection Clause.

There remains the question whether the congressional remedies adopted in § 4(e) constitute means which are not prohibited by, but are consistent

---

[10] *** § 5 does not grant Congress power to exercise discretion in the other direction and to enact "statutes so as in effect to dilute equal protection and due process decisions of this Court." We emphasize that Congress' power under § 5 is limited to adopting measures to enforce the guarantees of the Amendment; § 5 grants Congress no power to restrict, abrogate, or dilute these guarantees. Thus, for example, an enactment authorizing the States to establish racially segregated systems of education would not be—as required by § 5—a measure "to enforce" the Equal Protection Clause since that clause of its own force prohibits such state laws.

"with the letter and spirit of the constitution." The only respect in which appellees contend that § 4(e) fails in this regard is that the section itself works an invidious discrimination in violation of the Fifth Amendment by prohibiting the enforcement of the English literacy requirement only for those educated in American-flag schools (schools located within United States jurisdiction) in which the language of instruction was other than English, and not for those educated in schools beyond the territorial limits of the United States in which the language of instruction was also other than English. This is not a complaint that Congress, in enacting § 4(e), has unconstitutionally denied or diluted anyone's right to vote but rather that Congress violated the Constitution by not extending the relief effected in § 4(e) to those educated in non-American-flag schools. *** [This] argument fails ***.

MR. JUSTICE DOUGLAS joins the Court's opinion [except for whether the congressional remedies are constitutional, on which he reserves judgment].

MR. JUSTICE HARLAN, whom MR. JUSTICE STEWART joins, dissenting.

*** The Court declares that since § 5 of the Fourteenth Amendment gives to the Congress power to "enforce" the prohibitions of the Amendment by "appropriate" legislation, the test for judicial review of any congressional determination in this area is simply one of rationality; that is, in effect, was Congress acting rationally in declaring that the New York statute is irrational? *** I believe the Court has confused the issue of how much enforcement power Congress possesses under § 5 with the distinct issue of what questions are appropriate for congressional determination and what questions are essentially judicial in nature.

When recognized state violations of federal constitutional standards have occurred, Congress is of course empowered by § 5 to take appropriate remedial measures to redress and prevent the wrongs. But it is a judicial question whether the condition with which Congress has thus sought to deal is in truth an infringement of the Constitution, something that is the necessary prerequisite to bringing the § 5 power into play at all. *** Section 4(e), however, presents a significantly different type of congressional enactment. The question here is not whether the statute is appropriate remedial legislation to cure an established violation of a constitutional command, but whether there has in fact been an infringement of that constitutional command, that is, whether a particular state practice or, as here, a statute is so arbitrary or irrational as to offend the command of the Equal Protection Clause of the Fourteenth Amendment. That question is one for the judicial branch ultimately to determine. *** In view of this Court's holding in *Lassiter v. Northampton County Bd. of Elections*, 360 U.S. 45 (1959), that an English literacy test is a permissible exercise of state supervision over its franchise, I do not think it is open to Congress to limit the effect of that decision as it has undertaken to do by § 4(e). In effect the Court reads § 5 of the Fourteenth Amendment as giving Congress the power to define the substantive scope of the Amendment. If that indeed be the true reach of § 5, then I do not see why Congress should not be able as well to exercise its § 5 "discretion" by enacting statutes so as in effect to dilute equal protection and due process decisions of this Court. In all such cases there is room for reasonable men to differ as to whether or not a denial of equal protection or due process has occurred, and the final decision is one of judgment. Until today this judgment has always been one for the judiciary to resolve.

I do not mean to suggest in what has been said that a legislative judgment of the type incorporated in § 4(e) is without any force whatsoever. Decisions on questions of equal protection and due process are based not on abstract logic, but on empirical foundations. To the extent "legislative facts" are relevant to a judicial determination, Congress is well equipped to investigate them, and such determinations are of course entitled to due respect. *** But no such factual data provide a legislative record supporting § 4(e) by way of showing that Spanish-speaking citizens are fully as capable of making informed decisions in a New York election as are English-speaking citizens. Nor was there any showing whatever to support the Court's alternative argument that § 4(e) should be viewed as but a remedial measure designed to cure or assure against unconstitutional discrimination of other varieties, e.g., in "public schools, public housing and law enforcement" to which Puerto Rican minorities might be subject in such communities as New York. There is simply no legislative record supporting such hypothesized discrimination of the sort we have hitherto insisted upon when congressional power is brought to bear on constitutionally reserved state concerns.

Thus, we have here not a matter of giving deference to a congressional estimate, based on its determination of legislative facts, bearing upon the validity vel non of a statute, but rather what can at most be called a legislative announcement that Congress believes a state law to entail an unconstitutional deprivation of equal protection. *** Federal authority, legislative no less than judicial, does not intrude unless there has been a denial by state action of Fourteenth Amendment limitations, in this instance a denial of equal protection. ***

To deny the effectiveness of this congressional enactment is not of course to disparage Congress' exertion of authority in the field of civil rights; it is simply to recognize that the Legislative Branch like the other branches of federal authority is subject to the governmental boundaries set by the Constitution. To hold, on this record, that § 4(e) overrides the New York literacy requirement seems to me tantamount to allowing the Fourteenth Amendment to swallow the State's constitutionally ordained primary authority in this field. ***

Notes

1. **Logic of *Katzenbach v. Morgan.*** The Fourteenth Amendment's first sentence creates a new notion of national citizenship that enhances the abolition of slavery in the Thirteenth Amendment. The second sentence, however, begins with the phrase "No State shall." Is Congress' § 5 authority to enforce the Fourteenth Amendment's protections contained in this second sentence limited to preventing states from violating "privileges or immunities," "equal protection," and "due process"? How can Congress enact § 4(e) to "eliminat[e] an invidious discrimination in establishing voter qualifications" when New York's literacy

requirement had been held constitutional? Is the scope of § 5 limited to judicial notions of what is encompassed by the concepts set forth in § 1?

2. **Scope of *Katzenbach v. Morgan*.** In *Oregon v. Mitchell*, 400 U.S. 112 (1970), the Supreme Court considered the constitutionality of a federal statute that lowered the voting age in both state and federal elections from 21 to 18. The Court upheld the age reduction for federal elections but found the state age reduction unconstitutional. JUSTICE BLACK's opinion, which provided the swing vote on both issues, stressed three limitations on Congress' § 5 Power: (1) there can be no legislative repeal of the Constitution, (2) the power was not intended to "strip the States of their power to govern themselves or to convert our national government of enumerated powers into a central government of unrestrained authority," and (3) the "appropriate legislation" language forbids Congress from undercutting "personal equality and freedom from discrimination" [citing *Katzenbach*] or undermining the Bill of Rights (which the Court by then, for the most part, had made applicable to the States). Can you square this case with *Katzenbach v. Morgan*? Incidentally, the Twenty-sixth Amendment (ratified in 1971) overturned *Oregon v. Mitchell*, providing that the right to vote of citizens 18 or older "shall not be denied or abridged by the United States or by any State on account of age."

CITY OF BOERNE v. FLORES
521 U.S. 507 (1997)

KENNEDY, J.

A decision by local zoning authorities to deny a church a building permit was challenged under the Religious Freedom Restoration Act of 1993 (RFRA). The case calls into question the authority of Congress to enact RFRA. *** Situated on a hill in the city of Boerne, Texas, some 28 miles northwest of San Antonio, is St. Peter Catholic Church. Built in 1923, the church's structure replicates the mission style of the region's earlier history. The church seats about 230 worshippers, a number too small for its growing parish. *** [T]he Archbishop applied for a building permit so construction to enlarge the church could proceed. City authorities, relying on [its] ordinance and the designation of a historic district (which, they argued, included the church), denied the application. The Archbishop brought this suit challenging the permit denial [based in part on RFRA]. ***

Congress enacted RFRA in direct response to the Court's decision in *Employment Div., Dept. of Human Resources of Oregon v. Smith*, 494 U.S. 872 (1990). There we considered a Free Exercise Clause claim brought by members of the Native American Church who were denied unemployment benefits when they lost their jobs because they had used peyote. Their practice was to ingest peyote for sacramental purposes, and they challenged an Oregon statute of general applicability which made use of the drug criminal. In evaluating the claim, we declined to apply the balancing test set forth in *Sherbert v. Verner*, 374 U.S. 398 (1963), under which we would have asked whether Oregon's prohibition substantially burdened a religious practice and, if it did, whether the burden was justified by a compelling government interest. We stated:

[G]overnment's ability to enforce generally applicable prohibitions of socially harmful conduct *** cannot depend on measuring the effects of a governmental action on a religious objector's spiritual development. To make an individual's obligation to obey such a law contingent upon the law's coincidence with his religious beliefs, except where the State's interest is "compelling" *** contradicts both constitutional tradition and common sense.

The application of the *Sherbert* test, the *Smith* decision explained, would have produced an anomaly in the law, a constitutional right to ignore neutral laws of general applicability. The anomaly would have been accentuated, the Court reasoned, by the difficulty of determining whether a particular practice was central to an individual's religion. *** *Smith* held that neutral, generally applicable laws may be applied to religious practices even when not supported by a compelling governmental interest.

Four Members of the Court *** argued the law placed a substantial burden on the Native American Church members so that it could be upheld only if the law served a compelling state interest and was narrowly tailored to achieve that end. *** Many criticized the Court's reasoning, and this disagreement resulted in the passage of RFRA. Congress announced:

" ***"(2) laws 'neutral' toward religion may burden religious exercise as surely as laws intended to interfere with religious exercise;

"(3) governments should not substantially burden religious exercise without compelling justification;

"(4) in *Employment Division v. Smith*, 494 U.S. 872 (1990), the Supreme Court virtually eliminated the requirement that the government justify burdens on religious exercise imposed by laws neutral toward religion; and

"(5) the compelling interest test as set forth in prior Federal court rulings is a workable test for striking sensible balances between religious liberty and competing prior governmental interests." ***

RFRA prohibits "[g]overnment" from "substantially burden[ing]" a person's exercise of religion even if the burden results from a rule of general applicability unless the government can demonstrate the burden "(1) is in furtherance of a compelling governmental interest; and (2) is the least restrictive means of furthering that compelling governmental interest." *** RFRA "applies to all Federal and State law, and the implementation of that law, whether statutory or otherwise, and whether adopted before or after [RFRA's enactment]." In accordance with RFRA's usage of the term, we shall use "state law" to include local and municipal ordinances.

*** The parties disagree over whether RFRA is a proper exercise of Congress' § 5 power "to enforce" by "appropriate legislation" the constitutional guarantee that no State shall deprive any person of "life, liberty, or property, without due process of law" nor deny any person "equal protection of the laws."

In defense of the Act respondent contends, with support from the United States as amicus, that RFRA is permissible enforcement legislation. Congress, it is said, is only protecting by legislation one of the liberties guaranteed by the Fourteenth Amendment's Due Process Clause, the free exercise of religion, beyond what is necessary under *Smith*. It is said the congressional decision to dispense with proof of deliberate or overt discrimination and instead concentrate on a law's effects accords with the settled understanding that § 5 includes the power to enact legislation designed to prevent as well as remedy constitutional violations. It is further contended that Congress' § 5 power is not limited to remedial or preventive legislation. ***

Legislation which deters or remedies constitutional violations can fall within the sweep of Congress' enforcement power even if in the process it prohibits conduct which is not itself unconstitutional and intrudes into "legislative spheres of autonomy previously reserved to the States." *** [M]easures protecting voting rights are within Congress' power to enforce the Fourteenth and Fifteenth Amendments, despite the burdens those measures placed on the States. *** In assessing the breadth of § 5's enforcement power, we begin with its text. Congress has been given the power "to enforce" the "provisions of this article." We agree with respondent, of course, that Congress can enact legislation under § 5 enforcing the constitutional right to the free exercise of religion. *** Congress' power under § 5, however, extends only to "enforc[ing]" the provisions of the Fourteenth Amendment. The Court has described this power as "remedial." The design of the Amendment and the text of § 5 are inconsistent with the suggestion that Congress has the power to decree the substance of the Fourteenth Amendment's restrictions on the States. Legislation which alters the meaning of the Free Exercise Clause cannot be said to be enforcing the Clause. Congress does not enforce a constitutional right by changing what the right is. It has been given the power "to enforce," not the power to determine what constitutes a constitutional violation. Were it not so, what Congress would be enforcing would no longer be, in any meaningful sense, the "provisions of [the Fourteenth Amendment]."

While the line between measures that remedy or prevent unconstitutional actions and measures that make a substantive change in the governing law is not easy to discern, and Congress must have wide latitude in determining where it lies, the distinction exists and must be observed. There must be a congruence and proportionality between the injury to be prevented or remedied and the means adopted to that end. Lacking such a connection, legislation may become substantive in operation and effect. History and our case law support drawing the distinction, one apparent from the text of the Amendment.

The Fourteenth Amendment's history confirms the remedial, rather than substantive, nature of the Enforcement Clause. *** Republican Representative John Bingham of Ohio reported the following draft amendment to the House of Representatives on behalf of the Joint Committee:

> The Congress shall have power to make all laws which shall be necessary and proper to secure to the citizens of each State all privileges and immunities of citizens in the several States, and to all persons in the several States equal protection in the rights of life, liberty, and property.

*** Members of Congress from across the political spectrum criticized the Amendment, and the criticisms had a common theme: The proposed Amendment gave Congress too much legislative power at the expense of the existing constitutional structure. *** As a result of these objections ***, the House voted to table the proposal [which] was seen as marking the defeat of the proposal. ***

Section 1 of the new draft Amendment imposed self-executing limits on the States. Section 5 prescribed that "[t]he Congress shall have power to enforce, by appropriate legislation, the provisions of this article." Under the revised Amendment, Congress' power was no longer plenary but remedial. Congress was granted the power to make the substantive constitutional prohibitions against the States effective. *** After revisions not relevant here, the new measure passed both Houses and was ratified in July 1868 as the Fourteenth Amendment.

The significance of the defeat of the Bingham proposal was apparent even then. During the debates over the Ku Klux Klan Act only a few years after the Amendment's ratification, Representative James Garfield argued there were limits on Congress' enforcement power, saying "unless we ignore both the history and the language of these clauses we cannot, by any reasonable interpretation, give to [§ 5] *** the force and effect of the rejected [Bingham] clause." Scholars of successive generations have agreed with this assessment.

The design of the Fourteenth Amendment has proved significant also in maintaining the traditional separation of powers between Congress and the Judiciary. The first eight Amendments to the Constitution set forth self-executing prohibitions on governmental action, and this Court has had primary authority to interpret those prohibitions. The Bingham draft, some thought, departed from that tradition by vesting in Congress primary power to interpret and elaborate on the meaning of the new Amendment through legislation. *** As enacted, the Fourteenth Amendment confers substantive rights against the States which, like the provisions of the Bill of Rights, are self-executing. The power to interpret the Constitution in a case or controversy remains in the Judiciary.

The remedial and preventive nature of Congress' enforcement power, and the limitation inherent in the power, were confirmed in our earliest cases on the Fourteenth Amendment. In the *Civil Rights Cases*, 109 U.S. 3 (1883), the Court invalidated sections of the Civil Rights Act of 1875 which prescribed criminal penalties for denying to any person "the full enjoyment of" public accommodations and conveyances, on the grounds that it exceeded Congress' power by seeking to regulate private conduct. The Enforcement Clause, the

Court said, did not authorize Congress to pass "general legislation upon the rights of the citizen." ***

Recent cases have continued to revolve around the question of whether § 5 legislation can be considered remedial. In *South Carolina v. Katzenbach*, we emphasized that "[t]he constitutional propriety of [legislation adopted under the Enforcement Clause] must be judged with reference to the historical experience *** [T]he Act's new remedies *** were deemed necessary given the ineffectiveness of the existing voting rights laws, and the slow costly character of case-by-case litigation." *** Any suggestion that Congress has a substantive, non-remedial power under the Fourteenth Amendment is not supported by our case law. In *Oregon v. Mitchell*, a majority of the Court concluded Congress had exceeded its enforcement powers by enacting legislation lowering the minimum age of voters from 21 to 18 in state and local elections. ***

If Congress could define its own powers by altering the Fourteenth Amendment's meaning, no longer would the Constitution be "superior paramount law, unchangeable by ordinary means." It would be "on a level with ordinary legislative acts, and, like other acts, *** alterable when the legislature shall please to alter it." *Marbury v. Madison*. Under this approach, it is difficult to conceive of a principle that would limit congressional power. Shifting legislative majorities could change the Constitution and effectively circumvent the difficult and detailed amendment process contained in Article V.

We now turn to consider whether RFRA can be considered enforcement legislation under § 5 of the Fourteenth Amendment.

Respondent contends that RFRA is a proper exercise of Congress' remedial or preventive power. The Act, it is said, is a reasonable means of protecting the free exercise of religion as defined by *Smith*. It prevents and remedies laws which are enacted with the unconstitutional object of targeting religious beliefs and practices. To avoid the difficulty of proving such violations, it is said, Congress can simply invalidate any law which imposes a substantial burden on a religious practice unless it is justified by a compelling interest and is the least restrictive means of accomplishing that interest. If Congress can prohibit laws with discriminatory effects in order to prevent racial discrimination in violation of the Equal Protection Clause, then it can do the same, respondent argues, to promote religious liberty.

While preventive rules are sometimes appropriate remedial measures, there must be a congruence between the means used and the ends to be achieved. The appropriateness of remedial measures must be considered in light of the evil presented. Strong measures appropriate to address one harm may be an unwarranted response to another, lesser one.

A comparison between RFRA and the Voting Rights Act is instructive. In contrast to the record which confronted Congress and the judiciary in the voting rights cases, RFRA's legislative record lacks examples of modern instances of generally applicable laws passed because of religious bigotry. *** This lack of support in the legislative record, however, is not RFRA's most serious shortcoming. *** Regardless of the state of the legislative record, RFRA cannot be considered remedial, preventive legislation, if those terms are to have any meaning. RFRA is so out of proportion to a supposed remedial or preventive object that it cannot be understood as responsive to, or designed to prevent, unconstitutional behavior. It appears, instead, to attempt a substantive change in constitutional protections. Preventive measures prohibiting certain types of laws may be appropriate when there is reason to believe that many of the laws affected by the congressional enactment have a significant likelihood of being unconstitutional. Remedial legislation under § 5 "should be adapted to the mischief and wrong which the [Fourteenth] [A]mendment was intended to provide against." *Civil Rights Cases*.

RFRA is not so confined. Sweeping coverage ensures its intrusion at every level of government, displacing laws and prohibiting official actions of almost every description and regardless of subject matter. RFRA's restrictions apply to every agency and official of the Federal, State, and local Governments. RFRA applies to all federal and state law, statutory or otherwise, whether adopted before or after its enactment. RFRA has no termination date or termination mechanism. Any law is subject to challenge at any time by any individual who alleges a substantial burden on his or her free exercise of religion. *** The stringent test RFRA demands of state laws reflects a lack of proportionality or congruence between the means adopted and the legitimate end to be achieved. If an objector can show a substantial burden on his free exercise, the State must demonstrate a compelling governmental interest and show that the law is the least restrictive means of furthering its interest. *** [This test] would open the prospect of constitutionally required religious exemptions from civic obligations of almost every conceivable kind." Laws valid under *Smith* would fall under RFRA without regard to whether they had the object of stifling or punishing free exercise. *** This is a considerable congressional intrusion into the States' traditional prerogatives and general authority to regulate for the health and welfare of their citizens.

The substantial costs RFRA exacts, both in practical terms of imposing a heavy litigation burden on the States and in terms of curtailing their traditional general regulatory power, far exceed any pattern or practice of unconstitutional conduct under the Free Exercise Clause as interpreted in *Smith*. Simply put, RFRA is not designed to identify and counteract state laws likely to be unconstitutional because of their treatment of religion. In most cases, the state laws to which RFRA applies are not ones which will have been motivated by religious bigotry. If a state law disproportionately burdened a particular class of religious observers, this circumstance might be evidence of an impermissible legislative motive. *Cf. Washington v. Davis*, 426 U.S. 229 (1976). RFRA's substantial burden test, however, is not even a discriminatory effects or disparate impact test. It is a reality of the modern regulatory state that numerous state laws, such as the zoning regulations at issue here, impose a substantial burden on a large class of individuals. When the exercise of religion has been burdened in an incidental way by a law of general application, it does not follow that the persons affected have been burdened any more than other citizens, let alone burdened because of their religious beliefs. In addition, the Act imposes in every case a least restrictive means requirement—a requirement that was not used in the pre-*Smith* jurisprudence RFRA purported to codify—which also indicates that the legislation is broader than is appropriate if the goal is to prevent and remedy constitutional violations. ***

Our national experience teaches that the Constitution is preserved best when each part of the government respects both the Constitution and the proper actions and determinations of the other branches. *** RFRA was designed to control cases and controversies, such as the one before us; but as the provisions of the federal statute here invoked are beyond congressional authority, it is this Court's precedent, not RFRA, which must control. *** It is for Congress in the first instance to "determin[e] whether and what legislation is needed to secure the guarantees of the Fourteenth Amendment," and its conclusions are entitled to much deference. *Katzenbach v. Morgan*. Congress' discretion is not unlimited, however, and the courts retain the power, as they have since *Marbury v. Madison*, to determine if Congress has exceeded its authority under the Constitution. *** RFRA contradicts vital principles necessary to maintain separation of powers and the federal balance. ***

JUSTICE STEVENS, concurring.

RFRA is a "law respecting an establishment of religion" that violates the First Amendment to the Constitution. ***

JUSTICE O'CONNOR, whom JUSTICE BREYER joins, dissenting.

*** *Smith* was wrongly decided, and I would use this case to reexamine the Court's holding there. ***

Notes

1. **Other RFRA Issues.** Could RFRA be reenacted under Congress' Commerce Clause power? Consider this question in light of *Seminole Tribe* and reconsider *Alden*, supra Chapter V. Could Congress reenact RFRA but make it applicable only to the federal government, not the states? Seven states have enacted state legislation modeled on RFRA. Do you see any constitutional problems with state mini-RFRAs?

2. **Other Statutes at Risk?** Does this decision have any bearing on the constitutionality of statutes in which Congress has defined discrimination to include practices having a "disparate impact" as unlawful, even though such practices are not unlawful under § 1 of the Fourteenth Amendment? *See Washington v. Davis*, supra.

3. **Remedial, Not Substantive.** Is the Court's distinction between remedial and substantive power coherent? The law professor who argued the case for the losing side wrote: "The ordinary meaning of "remedial" would be legislation that provides a remedy for a judicially determined violation. *** The ordinary meaning of "substantive" would be legislation that defines a statutory violation in some way different from the Court's definition of a constitutional violation. But a

vast range of possible legislation is substantive in this sense." Laycock, *Conceptual Gulfs in City of Boerne v. Flores*, 39 WM. & MARY L. REV. 743 (1998).

4.   **Congruence and Proportionality.** Is the Court's test of "congruence and proportionality" consistent with usual notions of judicial deference to Congress and with the necessary and proper clause? Is that clause relevant when Congress uses its § 5 power?

5.   **Religious Accommodation**. May a state employee sue her state employer for failing to reasonably accommodate her "religious observances and practices," as § 701 (j) of Title VII of the Civil Rights Act of 1964 requires? Is § 701(j) appropriate legislation to "enforce" the equal protection clause? Does the provision pass the "congruence and proportionality" test? Is it important that (1) there was little Civil Rights Act legislative history about religious discrimination, (2) religion was considered an aspect of race when the Fourteenth Amendment was ratified, and (3) anti-Jewish, anti-Catholic, anti-Mormon, and anti-Muslim sentiments have been widespread at various times in American history? See *Endres v. Indiana State Police*, 334 F. 3d 618 (7th Cir. 2003).

SHELBY COUNTY, ALABAMA v. HOLDER
133 S. Ct. 2612 (2013)

CHIEF JUSTICE ROBERTS delivered the opinion of the Court.

The Voting Rights Act of 1965 employed extraordinary measures to address an extraordinary problem. Section 5 of the Act required States to obtain federal permission before enacting any law related to voting—a drastic departure from basic principles of federalism. And § 4 of the Act applied that requirement only to some States—an equally dramatic departure from the principle that all States enjoy equal sovereignty. This was strong medicine, but Congress determined it was needed to address entrenched racial discrimination in voting, "an insidious and pervasive evil which had been perpetuated in certain parts of our country through unremitting and ingenious defiance of the Constitution." As we explained in upholding the law, "exceptional conditions can justify legislative measures not otherwise appropriate." Reflecting the unprecedented nature of these measures, they were scheduled to expire after five years.

Nearly 50 years later, they are still in effect; indeed, they have been made more stringent, and are now scheduled to last until 2031. There is no denying, however, that the conditions that originally justified these measures no longer characterize voting in the covered jurisdictions. By 2009, "the racial gap in voter registration and turnout [was] lower in the States originally covered by § 5 than it [was] nationwide." Since that time, Census Bureau data indicate that African–American voter turnout has come to exceed white voter turnout in five of the six States originally covered by § 5, with a gap in the sixth State of less than one half of one percent.

At the same time, voting discrimination still exists; no one doubts that. The question is whether the Act's extraordinary measures, including its disparate treatment of the States, continue to satisfy constitutional requirements. *** The Fifteenth Amendment was ratified in 1870, in the wake of the Civil War. It provides that "[t]he right of citizens of the United States to vote shall not be denied or abridged by the United States or by any State on account of race, color, or previous condition of servitude," and it gives Congress the "power to enforce this article by appropriate legislation." *** Inspired to action by the civil rights movement, Congress responded in 1965 with the Voting Rights Act. Section 2 was enacted to forbid, in all 50 States, any "standard, practice, or procedure ... imposed or applied ... to deny or abridge the right of any citizen of the United States to vote on account of race or color." *** Section 2 is permanent, applies nationwide, and is not at issue in this case.

Other sections targeted only some parts of the country. At the time of the Act's passage, these "covered" jurisdictions were those States or political subdivisions that had maintained a test or device as a prerequisite to voting as of November 1, 1964, and had less than 50 percent voter registration or turnout in the 1964 Presidential election. *** A covered jurisdiction could "bail out" of coverage if it had not used a test or device in the preceding five years "for the purpose or with the effect of denying or abridging the right to vote on account of race or color." In 1965, the covered States included Alabama, Georgia, Louisiana, Mississippi, South Carolina, and Virginia. The additional covered subdivisions included 39 counties in North Carolina and one in Arizona.

In those jurisdictions, § 4 of the Act banned all such tests or devices. Section 5 provided that no change in voting procedures could take effect until it was approved by federal authorities in Washington, D.C.—either the Attorney General or a court of three judges. A jurisdiction could obtain such "preclearance" only by proving that the change had neither "the purpose [nor] the effect of denying or abridging the right to vote on account of race or color."

Sections 4 and 5 were intended to be temporary; they were set to expire after five years. *** In 1970, Congress reauthorized the Act for another five years, and extended the coverage formula in § 4(b) to jurisdictions that had a voting test and less than 50 percent voter registration or turnout as of 1968. *** In 1975, Congress reauthorized the Act for seven more years, and extended its coverage to jurisdictions that had a voting test and less than 50 percent voter registration or turnout as of 1972. *** As a result of these amendments, the States of Alaska, Arizona, and Texas, as well as several counties in California, Florida, Michigan, New York, North Carolina, and South Dakota, became covered jurisdictions. *** In 1982, Congress reauthorized the Act for 25 years, but did not alter its coverage formula. *** We upheld each of these reauthorizations against constitutional challenge.

In 2006, Congress again reauthorized the Voting Rights Act for 25 years, again without change to its coverage formula. Congress also amended § 5 to prohibit more conduct than before. Section 5 now forbids voting changes with "any discriminatory purpose" as well as voting changes that diminish the ability of citizens, on account of race, color, or language minority status, "to elect their preferred candidates of choice." ***

Shelby County is located in Alabama, a covered jurisdiction. It has not sought bailout ***. Instead, in 2010, the county sued the Attorney General in Federal District Court in Washington, D.C., seeking a declaratory judgment that sections 4(b) and 5 of the Voting Rights Act are facially unconstitutional, as well as a permanent injunction against their enforcement. ***

Outside the strictures of the Supremacy Clause, States retain broad autonomy in structuring their governments and pursuing legislative objectives. Indeed, the Constitution provides that all powers not specifically granted to the Federal Government are reserved to the States or citizens. *** Not only do States retain sovereignty under the Constitution, there is also a "fundamental principle of *equal* sovereignty" among the States. *** The Voting Rights Act sharply departs from these basic principles. It suspends "*all* changes to state election law—however innocuous—until they have been precleared by federal authorities in Washington, D.C." States must beseech the Federal Government for permission to implement laws that they would otherwise have the right to enact and execute on their own, subject of course to any injunction in a § 2 action. ***

And despite the tradition of equal sovereignty, the Act applies to only nine States (and several additional counties). While one State waits months or years and expends funds to implement a validly enacted law, its neighbor can typically put the same law into effect immediately, through the normal legislative process. Even if a noncovered jurisdiction is sued, there are important differences between those proceedings and preclearance proceedings; the preclearance proceeding "not only switches the burden of proof to the supplicant jurisdiction, but also applies substantive standards quite different from those governing the rest of the nation." ***

Congress *** when it reauthorized the Act in 2006 [wrote] that "[s]ignificant progress has been made in eliminating first generation barriers experienced by minority voters, including increased numbers of registered minority voters, minority voter turnout, and minority representation in Congress, State legislatures, and local elected offices." *** The preclearance statistics are also illuminating. In the first decade after enactment of § 5, the Attorney General objected to 14.2 percent of proposed voting changes. In the last decade before reenactment, the Attorney General objected to a mere 0.16 percent.

There is no doubt that these improvements are in large part *because of* the Voting Rights Act. *** Yet the Act has not eased the restrictions in § 5 or narrowed the scope of the coverage formula in § 4(b) along the way. *** We now consider whether that coverage formula is constitutional in light of current conditions. *** Coverage today is based on decades-old data and eradicated practices. *** The Government's defense of the formula is limited. First, the Government contends that the formula is "reverse-engineered": Congress identified the jurisdictions to be covered and *then* came up with criteria to describe them. Under that reasoning, there need not be any logical relationship between the criteria in the formula and the reason for coverage; all that is necessary is that the formula happen to capture the jurisdictions Congress wanted to single out. ***

The Government falls back to the argument that because the formula was relevant in 1965, its continued use is permissible so long as any discrimination remains in the States Congress identified back then— regardless of how that discrimination compares to discrimination in States unburdened by coverage. *** But history did not end in 1965. By the time the Act was reauthorized in 2006, there had been 40 more years of it. In assessing the "current need[ ]" for a preclearance system that treats States differently from one another today, that history cannot be ignored. During that time, largely because of the Voting Rights Act, voting tests were abolished, disparities in voter registration and turnout due to race were erased, and African–Americans attained political office in record numbers. And yet the coverage formula that Congress reauthorized in 2006 ignores these developments, keeping the focus on decades-old data relevant to decades-old problems, rather than current data reflecting current needs.

The Fifteenth Amendment commands that the right to vote shall not be denied or abridged on account of race or color, and it gives Congress the power to enforce that command. The Amendment is not designed to punish for the past; its purpose is to ensure a better future. To serve that purpose, Congress—if it is to divide the States—must identify those jurisdictions to be singled out on a basis that makes sense in light of current conditions. It cannot rely simply on the past. *** There is no valid reason to insulate the coverage formula from review merely because it was previously enacted 40 years ago. *** Congress could have updated the coverage formula at that time, but did not do so. Its failure to act leaves us today with no choice but to declare § 4(b) unconstitutional. ***

JUSTICE THOMAS, concurring.

I join the Court's opinion in full but *** would find § 5 of the Voting Rights Act unconstitutional as well. *** "Section 5 now forbids voting changes with 'any discriminatory purpose' as well as voting changes that diminish the ability of citizens, on account of race, color, or language minority status, 'to elect their preferred candidates of choice.' " While the pre–2006 version of the Act went well beyond protection guaranteed under the Constitution, it now goes even further. *** However one aggregates the data compiled by Congress, it cannot justify the considerable burdens created by § 5. ***

JUSTICE GINSBURG, with whom JUSTICE BREYER, JUSTICE SOTOMAYOR, and JUSTICE KAGAN join, dissenting.

In the Court's view, the very success of § 5 of the Voting Rights Act demands its dormancy. Congress was of another mind. *** Until today, in considering the constitutionality of the VRA, the Court has accorded Congress the full measure of respect its judgments in this domain should garner. *** For three reasons, legislation *re*authorizing an existing statute is especially likely to satisfy the minimal requirements of the rational-basis test. First, when reauthorization is at issue, Congress has already assembled a legislative record justifying the initial legislation. *** Second, the very fact that reauthorization is necessary arises because Congress has built a temporal limitation into the Act. *** Third, a reviewing court should expect the record supporting reauthorization to be less stark than the record originally made. Demand for a record of violations equivalent to the one earlier made would expose Congress to a catch–22. If the statute was working, there would be less evidence of discrimination, so opponents might argue that Congress should not be allowed to renew the statute. In contrast, if the statute was not working, there would be plenty of evidence of discrimination, but scant reason to renew a failed regulatory regime.

This is not to suggest that congressional power in this area is limitless. It is this Court's responsibility to ensure that Congress has used appropriate means. *** The 2006 reauthorization of the Voting Rights Act fully satisfies the standard stated in *McCulloch*: Congress may choose any means "appropriate" and "plainly adapted to" a legitimate constitutional end. ***

The surest way to evaluate whether that remedy remains in order is to see if preclearance is still effectively preventing discriminatory changes to voting laws. *** All told, between 1982 and 2006, DOJ objections blocked over 700 voting changes based on a determination that the changes were discriminatory. Congress found that the majority of DOJ objections included findings of discriminatory intent, and that the changes blocked by preclearance were "calculated decisions to keep minority voters from fully participating in the political process." On top of that, over the same time period the DOJ and private plaintiffs succeeded in more than 100 actions to enforce the § 5 preclearance requirements. *** Congress [also] received evidence that more than 800 proposed changes were altered or withdrawn since the last reauthorization in 1982. *** There is no question, moreover, that the covered jurisdictions have a unique history of problems with racial discrimination in voting. *** Although covered jurisdictions account for less than 25 percent of the country's population, *** they accounted for 56 percent of successful § 2 litigation since 1982. Controlling for population, there were nearly *four* times as many successful § 2 cases in covered jurisdictions as there were in noncovered jurisdictions. *** The evidence before Congress, furthermore, indicated that voting in the covered jurisdictions was more racially polarized than elsewhere in the country. ***

The Court stops any application of § 5 by holding that § 4(b)'s coverage formula is unconstitutional. It pins this result, in large measure, to "the fundamental principle of equal sovereignty." In *Katzenbach,* however, the Court held, in no uncertain terms, that the principle "*applies only to the terms upon which States are admitted to the Union,* and not to the remedies for local evils which have subsequently appeared." *** Today's unprecedented extension of the equal sovereignty principle outside its proper domain—the admission of new States—is capable of much mischief. Federal statutes that treat States disparately are hardly novelties. *** Do such provisions remain safe given the Court's expansion of equal sovereignty's sway? ***

Notes

1. Reauthorization and the Coverage Formula. The Majority cites the fact that the 2006 reauthorization used the same coverage formula for Section 4(b) as the 1975 reauthorization. Would the outcome have been different if Congress more carefully revisited the coverage issue in 2006? How would Congress have demonstrated reconsideration if the states had remained the same post-2006? Has the Court started "grading Congress' homework"?

2. VRA Section 5. If Congress does not update the formula for the Voting Rights Act, isn't it likely that Section 5 is unenforceable? Could this explain JUSTICE GINSBURG's emphasis on Section 5 of the Voting Rights Act in her dissent and JUSTICE THOMAS' emphasis on that section in his concurrence?

3. Two Views of Intent. The Majority emphasizes access to the ballot, whereas JUSTICE GINSBURG emphasizes voting dilution. Who has the better argument about the primary intent of the Voting Rights Act?

4. Precedent and CHIEF JUSTICE ROBERTS' "Long Game." Both the majority and dissent reference an earlier 7-1 decision, *Northwest Austin*, which noted in dicta that there was a problem with treating states differently under federal legislation. Why do you think that some of the dissenters in Shelby County agreed to these parts of Northwest Austin? Linda Greenhouse, in THE NEW YORK TIMES, cites this as an example of CHIEF JUSTICE ROBERTS playing a "long game" of restraint to get majority support now on narrow grounds then build on the earlier decision to establish a more fundamental conservative proposition. Can you apply this insight about CHIEF JUSTICE ROBERTS in other important cases (e.g. *NFIB v. Sibelius, Fisher, Windsor,* and *Hollingsworth*)?

B. SECTION 5 POWER APPLICATIONS: DISABILITY AND SEX DISCRIMINATION

UNIVERSITY OF ALABAMA v. GARRETT
531 U.S. 356 (2001)

CHIEF JUSTICE REHNQUIST delivered the opinion of the Court.

We decide here whether employees of the State of Alabama may recover money damages by reason of the State's failure to comply with the provisions of Title I of the Americans with Disabilities Act of 1990 (ADA or Act). ***

The ADA prohibits certain employers, including the States, from "discriminat[ing] against a qualified individual with a disability ***." To this end, the Act requires employers to "mak[e] reasonable accommodations to the known physical or mental limitations of an otherwise qualified individual with a disability who is an applicant or employee, unless [the employer] can demonstrate that the accommodation would impose an undue hardship on the operation of the [employer's] business." *** [T]he ADA can apply to the States only to the extent that the statute is appropriate § 5 legislation. *** § 5 legislation reaching beyond the scope of § 1's actual guarantees must exhibit "congruence and proportionality between the injury to be prevented or remedied and the means adopted to that end."

The first step in applying these now familiar principles is to identify with some precision the scope of the constitutional right at issue. Here, that inquiry requires us to examine the limitations § 1 of the Fourteenth Amendment places upon States' treatment of the disabled. *** In *Cleburne v.*

Cleburne Living Center, 473 U.S. 432 (1985), we considered *** whether *** mental retardation qualified as a "quasi-suspect" classification under our equal protection jurisprudence. We [concluded] *** that such legislation incurs only the minimum "rational-basis" review applicable to general social and economic legislation. *** Thus, the result of *Cleburne* is that States are not required by the Fourteenth Amendment to make special accommodations for the disabled, so long as their actions towards such individuals are rational. ***

Once we have determined the metes and bounds of the constitutional right in question, we examine whether Congress identified a history and pattern of unconstitutional employment discrimination by the States against the disabled. *** The legislative record of the ADA, however, simply fails to show that Congress did in fact identify a pattern of irrational state discrimination in employment against the disabled.

Respondents contend that the inquiry as to unconstitutional discrimination should extend not only to States themselves, but to units of local governments, such as cities and counties. All of these, they say, are "state actors" for purposes of the Fourteenth Amendment. This is quite true, but the Eleventh Amendment does not extend its immunity to units of local government. These entities are subject to private claims for damages under the ADA without Congress' ever having to rely on § 5 of the Fourteenth Amendment to render them so. It would make no sense to consider constitutional violations on their part, as well as by the States themselves, when only the States are the beneficiaries of the Eleventh Amendment. ***

Respondents in their brief cite half a dozen examples from the record that did involve States. *** Several of these incidents undoubtedly evidence an unwillingness on the part of state officials to make the sort of accommodations for the disabled required by the ADA. *** But even if it were to be determined that each incident upon fuller examination showed unconstitutional action on the part of the State, these incidents taken together fall far short of even suggesting the pattern of unconstitutional discrimination on which § 5 legislation must be based. See *Kimel*; *City of Boerne*. Congress, in enacting the ADA, found that "some 43,000,000 Americans have one or more physical or mental disabilities." In 1990, the States alone employed more than 4.5 million people. It is telling, we think, that given these large numbers, Congress assembled only such minimal evidence of unconstitutional state discrimination in employment against the disabled. ***

Even were it possible to squeeze out of these examples a pattern of unconstitutional discrimination by the States, the rights and remedies created by the ADA against the States would raise the same sort of concerns as to congruence and proportionality as were found in *City of Boerne*. For example, whereas it would be entirely rational (and therefore constitutional) for a state employer to conserve scarce financial resources by hiring employees who are able to use existing facilities, the ADA requires employers to "mak[e] existing facilities used by employees readily accessible to and usable by individuals with disabilities." The ADA does except employers from the "reasonable accommodatio[n]" requirement where the employer "can demonstrate that the accommodation would impose an undue hardship on the operation of the business of such covered entity." However, even with this exception, the accommodation duty far exceeds what is constitutionally required in that it makes unlawful a range of alternate responses that would be reasonable but would fall short of imposing an "undue burden" upon the employer. The Act also makes it the employer's duty to prove that it would suffer such a burden, instead of requiring (as the Constitution does) that the complaining party negate reasonable bases for the employer's decision.

The ADA also forbids "utilizing standards, criteria, or methods of administration" that disparately impact the disabled, without regard to whether such conduct has a rational basis. Although disparate impact may be relevant evidence of racial discrimination, such evidence alone is insufficient even where the Fourteenth Amendment subjects state action to strict scrutiny. *** Congressional enactment of the ADA represents its judgment that there should be a "comprehensive national mandate for the elimination of discrimination against individuals with disabilities." Congress is the final authority as to desirable public policy, but in order to authorize private individuals to recover money damages against the States, there must be a pattern of discrimination by the States which violates the Fourteenth Amendment, and the remedy imposed by Congress must be congruent and proportional to the targeted violation. Those requirements are not met here, and to uphold the Act's application to the States would allow Congress to rewrite the Fourteenth Amendment law laid down by this Court in *Cleburne*. Section 5 does not so broadly enlarge congressional authority. ***

JUSTICE KENNEDY, with whom JUSTICE O'CONNOR joins, concurring.

*** If the States had been transgressing the Fourteenth Amendment by their mistreatment or lack of concern for those with impairments, one would have expected to find in decisions of the courts of the States and also the courts of the United States extensive litigation and discussion of the constitutional violations. This confirming judicial documentation does not exist. *** It must be noted, moreover, that what is in question is not whether the Congress, acting pursuant to a power granted to it by the Constitution, can compel the States to act. What is involved is only the question whether the States can be subjected to liability in suits brought not by the Federal Government, but by private persons seeking to collect moneys from the state treasury without the consent of the State. ***

JUSTICE BREYER, with whom JUSTICE STEVENS, JUSTICE SOUTER and JUSTICE GINSBURG join, dissenting.

Reviewing the congressional record as if it were an administrative agency record, the Court holds the statutory provision before us unconstitutional. The Court concludes that Congress assembled insufficient evidence of unconstitutional discrimination, that Congress improperly attempted to "re-write" the law we established in *Cleburne v. Cleburne Living Center, Inc.*, and that the law is not sufficiently tailored to address unconstitutional discrimination. *** In my view, Congress reasonably could have concluded that the remedy before us constitutes an "appropriate" way to enforce this basic equal protection requirement.   And that is all the Constitution requires.*** The powerful evidence of discriminatory treatment throughout society in general, including discrimination by private persons and local governments, implicates state governments as well, for state agencies form part of that same larger society. *** In any event, there is no need to rest solely upon evidence of discrimination by local governments or general societal discrimination. There are roughly 300 examples of discrimination by state governments themselves in the legislative record. *** Congress could have reasonably believed that these examples represented signs of a widespread problem of unconstitutional discrimination.

The Court's failure to find sufficient evidentiary support may well rest upon its decision to hold Congress to a strict, judicially created evidentiary standard, particularly in respect to lack of justification. *** Unlike courts, Congress can readily gather facts from across the Nation, assess the magnitude of a problem, and more easily find an appropriate remedy. Unlike courts, Congress directly reflects public attitudes and beliefs, enabling Congress better to understand where, and to what extent, refusals to accommodate a disability amount to behavior that is callous or unreasonable to the point of lacking constitutional justification. Unlike judges, Members of Congress can directly obtain information from constituents who have firsthand experience with discrimination and related issues.

The Court argues in the alternative that the statute's damage remedy is not "congruent" with and "proportional" to the equal protection problem that Congress found.   The Court suggests that the Act's "reasonable accommodation" requirement, and disparate-impact standard, "far excee[d] what is constitutionally required." But we have upheld disparate-impact standards in contexts where they were not "constitutionally required."

And what is wrong with a remedy that, in response to unreasonable employer behavior, requires an employer to make accommodations that are reasonable? *** Nothing in the words "reasonable accommodation" suggests that the requirement has no "tend[ency] to enforce" the Equal Protection Clause that it is an irrational way to achieve the objective, that it would fall outside the scope of the Necessary and Proper Clause, or that it somehow otherwise exceeds the bounds of the "appropriate." ***

The Court's harsh review of Congress' use of its § 5 power is reminiscent of the similar (now-discredited) limitation that it once imposed upon Congress' Commerce Clause power. *** [I]t is difficult to understand why the Court, which applies "minimum 'rational-basis' review" to statutes that *burden* persons with disabilities, subjects to far stricter scrutiny a statute that seeks to *help* those same individuals. *** The Court, through its evidentiary demands, its non-deferential review, and its failure to distinguish between judicial and legislative constitutional competencies, improperly invades a power that the Constitution assigns to Congress.   Its decision saps § 5 of independent force, effectively "confin[ing] the legislative power *** to the insignificant role of abrogating only those state laws that the judicial branch [is] prepared to adjudge unconstitutional." Whether the Commerce Clause does or does not enable Congress to enact this provision, in my view, § 5 gives Congress the necessary authority. ***

Notes

1. **Adequate Legislative Record.** With respect to state actions that would be subjected to "rational basis" review, states are not required to articulate their reasons for enacting legislation or regulations prior to passage. This is a primary difference between rational basis review on the one hand, and the Court's intermediate scrutiny standard for gender distinctions and strict scrutiny standard for racial distinctions on the other. *See* Chapter IX. The Court has also required discriminatory intent for governmental action to run afoul of the equal protection clause—disparate impact that results from the challenged state action is not sufficient. The majority in *Garrett* found the lack of a legislative record demonstrating a pattern of unconstitutional discrimination by the States fatal to the ADA's application to the States as an "appropriate" exercise of Congress's § 5 power. Since the State does not need to articulate its reasoning before enacting legislation that disadvantages disabled individuals, and that intent to discriminate must be proven for a violation of § 1 of the Fourteenth Amendment to lie, how could Congress ever assemble a legislative record that would allow the ADA to apply to the States?

2. **"State" in the Eleventh and Fourteenth Amendments.** Respondents claimed that local government discrimination against the disabled should be considered in assessing whether a pattern of discrimination supported passage of the ADA. In rejecting that argument, CHIEF JUSTICE REHNQUIST recognized that the term "State" in the Fourteenth Amendment encompasses local governments, but noted that "the Eleventh Amendment does not extend its immunity to units of local government. *** These entities are subject to private claims for damages under the ADA without Congress ever having to rely on § 5 of the Fourteenth Amendment to render them so. It would make no sense to consider constitutional violations on their part, as well as by the States themselves, when only the states are the beneficiaries of the Eleventh Amendment." To make sure you understand this statement, consider the following:

- Congress can use Article I powers against local governments without being limited by the Eleventh Amendment. Congress is also not required to show that § 5 is the only grant of legislative authority supporting particular legislation. Application of the ADA to local government is supported by the Commerce Clause power, can't it also be supported by the § 5 power?

- The Court says that aggregating state and local government discrimination in making a legislative record is not appropriate when Congress passes legislation limiting state sovereignty. Could that be because local government discrimination is (a) contrary to state law or (b) without the knowledge of the state government? If so, it will be very hard for Congress to amass a record that is adequate: state governments can avoid suits under federal laws by delegating broad authority to local government.

- Perhaps it would have been better to leave the aggregation point out of the analysis if the real concern was that individual acts of discrimination by local officials are simply not sufficiently numerous and notorious to support imposition of federal restrictions on state-level actors. Must Congress be more careful in articulating the local-state ties when it passes legislation applicable to state as well as local entities?

3. **Level of Scrutiny and Factual Predicate.** In *Katzenbach v. Morgan*, 384 U.S. 641 (1966) the Supreme Court noted that "[I]t is enough that we perceive a basis upon which Congress *might* predicate a judgment that the application of New York's English literacy requirement to deny the right to vote to a person with a sixth grade education in Puerto Rican schools in which the language of instruction was other than English constituted an invidious discrimination in violation of the Equal Protection Clause." (emphasis added). Though racial classifications by the States are subjected to the most stringent of constitutional tests, the Supreme Court clearly states with respect to the legislative record in *Morgan* that "it need only perceive a basis" for congressional action under § 5. Compare this with the heightened scrutiny the legislative records in *Garrett* when Congress sought to combat age or disability discrimination on the part of the states—classifications subjected to only rational basis review. Yet, in these cases, the Supreme Court insisted upon a showing of a pattern and history of pervasive discrimination committed by the States at the state level and found the ADA lacking in this regard. Does this suggest that there is an inverse relationship between the Court's level of constitutional scrutiny of State classifications and the Court's scrutiny of congressional findings supportive of § 5 legislation? Is it paradoxical that Congressional findings amassed in support of remedial legislation dealing with racial classifications would be subjected to more lenient level of scrutiny than similar findings compiled by Congress in support of statutes similar to the ADA? Or is this simply a tool the Court uses to keep Congress from expanding its power under § 5 excessively?

4. **Congruence and Proportionality in *Garrett*.** If the necessary history and pattern of discrimination existed, could Congress cure the remaining constitutional defect by making the ADA less demanding on employers? If government subsidized costs of access above a certain amount, would that make otherwise identical legislation congruent and proportional? Would legislation be congruent and proportional if the undue burden standard required only "reasonable" alternative responses? If you have difficulty answering these questions consider JUSTICE SCALIA's dissent in *Tennessee v. Lane*, 541 U.S. 509 (2004) ("The 'congruence and proportionality' standard, like all such flabby tests, is a standing invitation to judicial arbitrariness and policy-driven decisionmaking. Worse still, it casts this Court in the role of Congress's taskmaster. *** [W]hat § 5 does *not* authorize is so-called 'prophylactic' measures, prohibiting primary conduct that is itself not forbidden by the Fourteenth Amendment.").

5. **Public Accommodations**. Title II of the ADA requires that public "services, programs or activities" be accessible to people with disabilities" and allows private monetary damages for state violations of this requirement. Responding to Title II suits by a wheelchair-impaired plaintiff who had to crawl up two flights of stairs at a county courthouse to make a required court appearance, and a disabled court reporter who could not gain access to several courthouses where she had been hired to record proceedings, state defendants argue the suits are barred by sovereign immunity. Are these cases controlled by *Garrett*? *See Tennessee v. Lane*, 541 U.S. 509 (2004) (To the extent that ADA

Title II enforces constitutional right of access to courts and court proceedings, and only requires the states to make "reasonable modifications" to remove barriers to accessibility, it is a congruent and proportional exercise of the § 5 power.) The Court in *Lane* noted the legislative finding of persistent disability discrimination in areas of public services (including court access), the "sheer volume" of evidence underlying that finding, and previous unsuccessful legislative attempts to remedy the problem.

6. **Non-Judicial Public Venues.** How would you advise a wheelchair-impaired client who finds no access to a public park, a federal wilderness area, a state hospital, or a public school? What if the area of the park is a "speaker's corner" where individuals regularly present their views on matters of public policy to small gatherings (sometimes accompanied by media coverage)?

7. **Constitutional and Statutory Violations.** In *United States v. Georgia*, 546 U.S. 151 (2006), a paraplegic prisoner alleged that prison conduct violated Title II and the Eighth Amendment prohibition on cruel and unusual punishment. The Court unanimously remanded the case so the lower court could sort out conduct that violated the constitution; actual violations of Section 1 may be enforced against the states without any Eleventh Amendment bar. More cryptically, the Court told the lower courts to determine, "insofar as such misconduct violated Title II but did not violate the Fourteenth Amendment, whether Congress's purported abrogation of sovereign immunity as to that class of conduct is nevertheless valid."

NEVADA DEP'T OF HUMAN RESOURCES v. HIBBS
538 U.S. 721 (2003)

CHIEF JUSTICE REHNQUIST delivered the opinion of the Court.

The Family and Medical Leave Act of 1993 (FMLA or Act) entitles eligible employees to take up to 12 work weeks of unpaid leave annually for any of several reasons, including the onset of a "serious health condition" in an employee's spouse, child, or parent. The Act creates a private right of action to seek both equitable relief and money damages "against any employer (including a public agency) in any Federal or State court of competent jurisdiction," should that employer "interfere with, restrain, or deny the exercise of" FMLA rights. We hold that employees of the State of Nevada may recover money damages in the event of the State's failure to comply with the family-care provision of the Act. ***

The FMLA aims to protect the right to be free from gender-based discrimination in the workplace. We have held that statutory classifications that distinguish between males and females are subject to heightened scrutiny. For a gender-based classification to withstand such scrutiny, it must "serv[e] important governmental objectives," and "the discriminatory means employed [must be] substantially related to the achievement of those objectives." The State's justification for such a classification "must not rely on overbroad generalizations about the different talents, capacities, or preferences of males and females." We now inquire whether Congress had evidence of a pattern of constitutional violations on the part of the States in this area.

The history of the many state laws limiting women's employment opportunities is chronicled in–and, until relatively recently, was sanctioned by–this Court's own opinions. *** Congress responded to this history of discrimination by abrogating States' sovereign immunity in Title VII of the Civil Rights Act of 1964. *** But state gender discrimination did not cease. *** According to evidence that was before Congress when it enacted the FMLA, States continue to rely on invalid gender stereotypes in the employment context, specifically in the administration of leave benefits. ***

As the FMLA's legislative record reflects, a 1990 Bureau of Labor Statistics (BLS) survey stated that 37 percent of surveyed private-sector employees were covered by maternity leave policies, while only 18 percent were covered by paternity leave policies. *** This and other differential leave policies were not attributable to any differential physical needs of men and women, but rather to the pervasive sex-role stereotype that caring for family members is women's work.

Finally, Congress had evidence that, even where state laws and policies were not facially discriminatory, they were applied in discriminatory ways. It was aware of the "serious problems with the discretionary nature of family leave," because when "the authority to grant leave and to arrange the length of that leave rests with individual supervisors," it leaves "employees open to discretionary and possibly unequal treatment." Testimony supported that conclusion, explaining that "[t]he lack of uniform parental and medical leave policies in the work place has created an environment where [sex] discrimination is rampant." *** Against the above backdrop of limited state leave policies, *** Congress was justified in enacting the FMLA as remedial legislation.[10]

In sum, the States' record of unconstitutional participation in, and fostering of, gender-based discrimination in the administration of leave benefits is weighty enough to justify the enactment of prophylactic § 5 legislation.

We reached the opposite conclusion in *Garrett* and *Kimel*. In those cases, the § 5 legislation under review responded to a purported tendency of state officials to make age- or disability-based distinctions. Under our equal protection case law, discrimination on the basis of such characteristics is not judged under a heightened review standard, and passes muster if there is "a rational basis for doing so at a class-based level, even if it 'is probably not true' that those reasons are valid in the majority of cases." *Kimel*, 528 U.S., at 86. Thus, in order to impugn the constitutionality of state discrimination against the disabled or the elderly, Congress must identify, not just the existence of age- or disability-based state decisions, but a "widespread pattern" of irrational reliance on such criteria. ***

---

10 *** The FMLA is not a "substantive entitlement program"; Congress did not create a particular leave policy for its own sake. Rather, Congress sought to adjust family leave policies in order to eliminate their reliance on and perpetuation of invalid stereotypes, and thereby dismantle persisting gender-based barriers to the hiring, retention, and promotion of women in the workplace. ***

Here, however, Congress directed its attention to state gender discrimination, which triggers a heightened level of scrutiny. Because the standard for demonstrating the constitutionality of a gender-based classification is more difficult to meet than our rational-basis test–it must "serv[e] important governmental objectives" and be "substantially related to the achievement of those objectives,"–it was easier for Congress to show a pattern of state constitutional violations. *** Stereotypes about women's domestic roles are reinforced by parallel stereotypes presuming a lack of domestic responsibilities for men. Because employers continued to regard the family as the woman's domain, they often denied men similar accommodations or discouraged them from taking leave. ***

We believe that Congress' chosen remedy, the family-care leave provision of the FMLA, is "congruent and proportional to the targeted violation." Congress had already tried unsuccessfully to address this problem through Title VII and the amendment of Title VII by the Pregnancy Discrimination Act. *** By setting a minimum standard of family leave for *all* eligible employees, irrespective of gender, the FMLA attacks the formerly state-sanctioned stereotype that only women are responsible for family caregiving, thereby reducing employers' incentives to engage in discrimination by basing hiring and promotion decisions on stereotypes. ***

Indeed, in light of the evidence before Congress, a statute mirroring Title VII, that simply mandated gender equality in the administration of leave benefits, would not have achieved Congress' remedial object. Such a law would allow States to provide for no family leave at all. Where "[t]wo-thirds of the nonprofessional caregivers for older, chronically ill, or disabled persons are working women," and state practices continue to reinforce the stereotype of women as caregivers, such a policy would exclude far more women than men from the workplace.

Unlike the statutes at issue in *City of Boerne*, *Kimel*, and *Garrett*, which applied broadly to every aspect of state employers' operations, the FMLA is narrowly targeted at the fault line between work and family–precisely where sex-based overgeneralization has been and remains strongest–and affects only one aspect of the employment relationship. *** We also find significant the many other limitations that Congress placed on the scope of this measure. The FMLA requires only unpaid leave, and applies only to employees who have worked for the employer for at least one year and provided 1,250 hours of service within the last 12 months. *** [O]f particular importance to the States, the FMLA expressly excludes from coverage state elected officials, their staffs, and appointed policymakers. *** In choosing 12 weeks as the appropriate leave floor, Congress chose "a middle ground, a period long enough to serve 'the needs of families' but not so long that it would upset 'the legitimate interests of employers.'" Moreover, the cause of action under the FMLA is a restricted one: The damages recoverable are strictly defined and measured by actual monetary losses, and the accrual period for backpay is limited by the Act's 2-year statute of limitations. ***

For the above reasons, we conclude that [the FMLA] is congruent and proportional to its remedial object, and can be understood as responsive to, or designed to prevent, unconstitutional behavior.

JUSTICE SCALIA, dissenting.

*** The constitutional violation that is a prerequisite to "prophylactic" congressional action to "enforce" the Fourteenth Amendment is a violation *by the State against which the enforcement action is taken.* *** Today's opinion for the Court does not even attempt to demonstrate that each one of the 50 States covered *** was in violation of the Fourteenth Amendment. It treats "the States" as some sort of collective entity which is guilty or innocent as a body. *** This will not do. Prophylaxis in the sense of extending the remedy beyond the violation is one thing; prophylaxis in the sense of extending the remedy beyond the violator is something else. ***

JUSTICE KENNEDY, with whom JUSTICE SCALIA and JUSTICE THOMAS join, dissenting.

*** In examining whether Congress was addressing a demonstrated "pattern of unconstitutional employment discrimination by the States," the Court gives superficial treatment to the requirement that we "identify with some precision the scope of the constitutional right at issue." *** All would agree that women historically have been subjected to conditions in which their employment opportunities are more limited than those available to men. As the Court acknowledges, however, Congress responded to this problem by abrogating States' sovereign immunity in Title VII of the Civil Rights Act of 1964. The provision now before us has a different aim than Title VII. It seeks to ensure that eligible employees, irrespective of gender, can take a minimum amount of leave time to care for an ill relative. *** The question is not whether the family leave provision is a congruent and proportional response to general gender-based stereotypes in employment which "ha[ve] historically produced discrimination in the hiring and promotion of women;" the question is whether it is a proper remedy to an alleged pattern of unconstitutional discrimination by States in the grant of family leave. *** The paucity of evidence to support the case the Court tries to make demonstrates that Congress was not responding with a congruent and proportional remedy to a perceived course of unconstitutional conduct. Instead, it enacted a substantive entitlement program of its own. If Congress had been concerned about different treatment of men and women with respect to family leave, a congruent remedy would have sought to ensure the benefits of any leave program enacted by a State are available to men and women on an equal basis. Instead, the Act imposes, across the board, a requirement that States grant a minimum of 12 weeks of leave per year. *** [T]he abrogation of state sovereign immunity pursuant to Title VII was a legitimate congressional response to a pattern of gender-based discrimination in employment. The family leave benefit conferred by the Act is, by contrast, a substantive benefit Congress chose to confer upon state employees. *** [State] immunity cannot be abrogated without documentation of a pattern of unconstitutional acts by the States, and only then by a congruent and proportional remedy. ***

Notes

1. **How Will Congress Know if an Act is Constitutional?** You have now read two modern cases – *Garrett* and *Hibbs* – where the Court reached opposite conclusions regarding whether particular federal legislation was a valid exercise of Congress' § 5 enforcement power. Is the Court's reasoning in these outcomes consistent? Could these opinions, together, be used to determine when an Act will be upheld or struck down? Both cases point to several general factors that should be considered, such as: whether the "state action" is one of the state government or other smaller government units (such as a cities or municipalities); whether the federal legislation appears to "enforce," versus "rewrite," § 1 of the Fourteenth Amendment; whether the right or principal at issue is core concern of the Fourteenth Amendment; and the likely result of applying the congruence and proportionality test when considering both the breadth of the legislation and the legislative findings.

2. **Gender and Race v. Age and Disability?** How much, if at all, does the "type" of classification or discrimination play a role in the Court's decision in *Hibbs*? Is the level of scrutiny given under § 1 the key to the intensity of scrutiny given to congressional evidence and findings when the Court assesses whether Congress legitimately engaged in its § 5 enforcement authority? Would JUSTICE REHNQUIST'S rationale in *Hibbs* allow Congress to mandate caretaker leave for women but not men? *Hibbs* does not explain how the FMLA differs from the VAWA (see *Morrison*) in terms of Congress' § 5 enforcement power. Are these two sex discrimination statutes distinguishable?

3. **Title VII Ramifications?** Do all members of the Court concede that Title VII was a proportional and congruent exercise of enforcement power? Are the parts of Title VII that concern religious and national origin discrimination more vulnerable than the race and sex discrimination prohibitions? May Congress use its § 5 enforcement power to prohibit otherwise permissible (but not required) race-based affirmative action in state university admissions processes? Title VII makes it unlawful for employers to engage in practices having a "disparate impact" by race or sex where the practices are not justified by "business necessity." Is this portion of Title VII within Congress' powers?

4. **§ 5 Power and the Content of § 1.** Consider the following hypotheticals in light of the cases in this chapter:

   • Assume the Supreme Court has held that equal payment of male and female state employees who occupy *different* jobs of "comparable worth" is not required by the Equal Protection Clause. Could Congress nevertheless require "comparable worth" pay based on its § 5 Power?

   • Would a federal statute denying students the "in-state" tuition rate until the student had lived in the state for one year be a proper exercise of § 5 power?

   • Would a federal statute making false and misleading advertising unlawful be within the § 5 power?

5. **Contrasting Commerce Clause and § 5 Power.** Could § 5 serve as a basis for any of the legislation suggested in the Chapter IV B problems?

COLEMAN v. COURT OF APPEALS OF MARYLAND
132 S. Ct. 1327 (2012)

JUSTICE KENNEDY announced the judgment of the Court and delivered an opinion, in which THE CHIEF JUSTICE, JUSTICE THOMAS, and JUSTICE ALITO joined.

*** The Family and Medical Leave Act of 1993 (FMLA or Act) entitles eligible employees to take up to 12 work weeks of unpaid leave per year. An employee may take leave under the FMLA for: *** (D) the employee's own serious health condition when the condition interferes with the employee's ability to perform at work. The Act creates a private right of action to seek both equitable relief and money damages "against any employer (including a public agency) in any Federal or State court of competent jurisdiction." *** This Court considered subparagraph (C) in [*Hibbs*] *** [and] held that Congress could subject the States to suit for violations of subparagraph (C). That holding rested on evidence that States had family-leave policies that differentiated on the basis of sex and that States administered even neutral family-leave policies in ways that discriminated on the basis of sex. Subparagraph (D), the self-care provision, was not at issue in *Hibbs*. *** When Coleman requested sick leave, he was informed he would be terminated if he did not resign. Coleman then sued the state court. ***

A foundational premise of the federal system is that States, as sovereigns, are immune from suits for damages, save as they elect to waive that defense. As an exception to this principle, Congress may abrogate the States' immunity from suit pursuant to its powers under § 5 of the Fourteenth Amendment. *** The question then becomes whether the self-care provision and its attempt to abrogate the States' immunity are a valid exercise of congressional power under § 5 of the Fourteenth Amendment. *** [This] requires an assessment of both the "'evil' or 'wrong' that Congress intended to remedy," and the means Congress adopted to address that evil. Legislation enacted under § 5 must be targeted at "conduct transgressing the Fourteenth Amendment's substantive provisions." And "[t]here must be a congruence and proportionality between the injury to be prevented or remedied and the means adopted to that end." *** *Hibbs* concluded that requiring state employers to give all employees the opportunity to take family-care leave was "narrowly targeted at the faultline between work and family—precisely where sex-based overgeneralization has been and remains strongest."

The same cannot be said for requiring the States to give all employees the opportunity to take self-care leave. *** [W]hat the family-care provisions have to support them, the self-care provision lacks, namely evidence of a pattern of state constitutional violations accompanied by a remedy drawn in narrow terms to address or prevent those violations. *** The evidence did not suggest States had facially discriminatory self-care leave policies or that they administered neutral self-care leave policies in a discriminatory way. *** Congress considered evidence that "men and women are out on medical leave approximately equally." *** The legislative history of the self-care provision reveals a concern for the economic burdens on the employee and the employee's family resulting from illness-related job loss and a concern for discrimination on the basis of illness, not sex. ***

It is true the self-care provision offers some women a benefit by allowing them to take leave for pregnancy-related illnesses; but as a remedy, the provision is not congruent and proportional to any identified constitutional violations. *** It follows that abrogating the States' immunity from suits for damages for failure to give self-care leave is not a congruent and proportional remedy if the existing state leave policies would have sufficed.

As an alternative justification for the self-care provision, it has been suggested that the provision is a necessary adjunct to the family-care provisions. *** The fact that self-care leave could have this effect does not mean that it would. *** Congress made no findings, and received no specific testimony, to suggest the availability of self-care leave equalizes the expected amount of FMLA leave men and women will take. ***

In addition petitioner's first defense of the self-care provision contradicts his second defense of the provision. In the first defense, the Court is told employers assume women take more self-care leave than men. In the second defense, the Court is told the self-care provision provides an incentive to hire women that will counteract the incentives created by the family-care provisions because employers assume women take more family-care leave than men. But if the first defense is correct, the second defense is wrong. In other words, if employers assume women take self-care leave more often than men (the first defense), a self-care provision will not provide an incentive to hire women. To the contrary, the self-care provision would provide an incentive to discriminate against women. ***

The petitioner's last defense of the self-care provision is that the provision helps single parents retain their jobs when they become ill. This, however, does not explain how the provision remedies or prevents constitutional violations. The fact that most single parents happen to be women, demonstrates, at most, that the self-care provision was directed at remedying employers' neutral leave restrictions which have a disparate effect on women. "Although disparate impact may be relevant evidence of ... discrimination ... such evidence alone is insufficient [to prove a constitutional violation] even where the Fourteenth Amendment subjects state action to strict scrutiny." [*Washington v. Davis*] To the extent, then, that the self-care provision addresses neutral leave policies with a disparate impact on women, it is not directed at a pattern of constitutional violations. Because, moreover, it is "unlikely that many of the [neutral leave policies] ... affected by" the self-care provision are unconstitutional, "the scope of the [self-care provision is] out of proportion to its supposed remedial or preventive objectives." *** To abrogate the States' immunity from suits for damages under § 5, Congress must identify a pattern of constitutional violations and tailor a remedy congruent and proportional to the documented violations. It failed to do so when it allowed employees to sue States for violations of the FMLA's self-care provision.

JUSTICE THOMAS, concurring.

*** *Hibbs* was wrongly decided because the family-care provision is not sufficiently linked to a demonstrated pattern of unconstitutional discrimination by the States. The self-care provision at issue in this case is even further removed from any such pattern.

JUSTICE SCALIA, concurring in the judgment.

The plurality's opinion seems to me a faithful application of our "congruence and proportionality" jurisprudence. So does the opinion of the dissent. That is because the varying outcomes we have arrived at under the "congruence and proportionality" test make no sense. *** This grading of Congress's homework is a task we are ill suited to perform and ill advised to undertake. *** [W]e should instead adopt an approach that is properly tied to the text of § 5, which grants Congress the power "to *enforce,* by appropriate legislation," the other provisions of the Fourteenth Amendment. *** [O]utside of the context of racial discrimination (which is different for *stare decisis* reasons), I would limit Congress's § 5 power to the regulation of conduct that *itself* violates the Fourteenth Amendment. Failing to grant state employees leave for the purpose of self-care—or any other purpose, for that matter—does not come close. ***

JUSTICE GINSBURG, with whom JUSTICE BREYER, JUSTICE SOTOMAYOR and JUSTICE KAGAN join *** dissenting.

*** [T]he plurality undervalues the language, purpose, and history of the FMLA, and the self-care provision's important role in the statutory scheme. As well, the plurality underplays the main theme of our decision in *Hibbs*: "The FMLA aims to protect the right to be free from gender-based discrimination in the workplace." *** "[A] state's refusal to provide pregnancy leave to its employees," Maryland responds, is "not unconstitutional." *** First, "[a]s an abstract statement," it is "simply false" that "a classification based on pregnancy is gender-neutral." *** Second, pregnancy provided a central justification for the historic discrimination against women this Court chronicled in *Hibbs*. In sum, childbearing is not only a biological function unique to women. It is also inextricably intertwined with employers' "stereotypical views about women's commitment to work and their value as employees." [The disssenters would overturn Geduldig v. Aiello, which held "pregnancy" was not "sex" for EP purposes.]***

Boerne's third step requires "a congruence and proportionality between the injury to be prevented or remedied and the means adopted to that end." *** It would make scant sense to provide job-protected leave for a woman to care for a newborn, but not for her recovery from delivery, a miscarriage, or the birth of a stillborn baby. And allowing States to provide no pregnancy-disability leave at all, given that only women can become pregnant, would obviously "exclude far more women than men from the workplace." ***

Finally, as in *Hibbs,* it is important to note the moderate cast of the FMLA[.] *** FMLA leave is unpaid. It is limited to employees who have worked at least one year for the employer and at least 1,250 hours during the past year. High-ranking employees, including state elected officials and their staffs, are not within the Act's compass. Employees must provide advance notice of foreseeable leaves. Employers may require a doctor's certification of a serious health condition. And, if an employer violates the FMLA, the employees' recoverable damages are "strictly defined and measured by actual monetary losses." The self-care provision, I would therefore hold, is congruent and proportional to the injury to be prevented. ***

Congress [also] had good reason to conclude that the self-care provision—which men no doubt would use—would counter employers' impressions that the FMLA would otherwise install female leave. Providing for self-care would thus reduce employers' corresponding incentive to discriminate against women in hiring and promotion. *** The plurality pays scant attention to the overarching aim of the FMLA: to make it feasible for women to work while sustaining family life. *** The self-care provision is a key part of that endeavor, and *** a valid exercise of congressional power under § 5 of the Fourteenth Amendment. ***

Notes

1. **Statute and Constitution**. The plurality and dissent see congressional intent to the to self-care provisions differently. Does this determine the outcome of the Section 5 inquiry? Or is the case a more fundamental pushback against *Hibbs*, perhaps because of Chief Justice Rehnquist's replacement by Chief Justice Roberts?

2. **Concurrence**. Justice Scalia's concurrence says the Court should only allow Congress to regulate actions violating the Fourteenth Amendment except in the area of race discrimination. Does the plurality opinion endorse this view? Does this case further limit congressional regulation under Section 5?

3. **Regulating Unconscious Bias**. Disagreements between the plurality and dissent in *Coleman* can be read as a disagreement over how much unconscious bias by employers can be regulated under employment discrimination law. Michael Waterstone, *Last Thoughts on Coleman*, PrawfsBlog. The plurality notes "[t]here is nothing in particular about self-care leave, as opposed to leave for any personal reason, that connects it to gender discrimination." Justice Ginsburg's dissent points out that the law addresses gender discrimination by countering impressions that might otherwise exist concerning leaves for female employees.

Appendix A

THE ARTICLES OF CONFEDERATION

Agreed to by Congress November 15, 1777; ratified and in force, March 1, 1781.

Preamble. *** Whereas the Delegates of the United States of America in Congress assembled did *** agree to certain articles of Confederation and perpetual Union between the States of New Hampshire, Massachusetts bay, Rhode Island and Providence Plantations, Connecticut, New York, New Jersey, Pennsylvania, Delaware, Maryland, Virginia, North Carolina, South Carolina and Georgia ***.

Article I. The Style of this confederacy shall be "The United States of America."

Article II. Each state retains its sovereignty, freedom and independence, and every power, jurisdiction and right, which is not by this Confederation expressly delegated to the United States, in Congress assembled.

Article III. The said States hereby severally enter into a firm league of friendship with each other, for their common defence, the security of their liberties, and their mutual and general welfare, binding themselves to assist each other, against all force offered to, or attacks made upon them, or any of them, on account of religion, sovereignty, trade, or any other pretence whatever.

Article IV. The better to secure and perpetuate mutual friendship and intercourse among the people of the different States in this Union, the free inhabitants of each of these States, paupers, vagabonds and fugitives from justice excepted, shall be entitled to all privileges and immunities of free citizens in the several States; and the people of each state shall have free ingress and regress to and from any other State, and shall enjoy therein all the privileges of trade and commerce, subject to the same duties, impositions and restrictions as the inhabitants thereof respectively, provided that such restriction shall not extend so far as to prevent the removal of property imported into any state, to any other state of which the Owner is an inhabitant; provided also that no imposition, duties or restriction shall be laid by any state, on the property of the United States, or either of them.

If any person guilty of or charged with treason, felony, or other high misdemeanor in any state, shall flee from Justice, and be found in any of the United States, he shall upon demand of the governor or executive power of the state from which he fled, be delivered up and removed to the State having jurisdiction of his offence.

Full faith and credit shall be given in each of these States to the records, acts and judicial proceedings of the courts and magistrates of every other state.

Article V. For the more convenient management of the general interests of the United States, delegates shall be annually appointed in such manner as the legislature of each state shall direct *** No state shall be represented in Congress by less than two, nor by more than seven Members; and no person shall be capable of being a delegate for more than three years in any term of six years; nor shall any person, being a delegate, be capable of holding any office under the United States, for which he, or another for his benefit receives any salary, fees or emolument of any kind. *** In determining questions in the United States, in Congress assembled, each State shall have one vote.

Freedom of speech and debate in Congress shall not be impeached or questioned in any Court, or place out of Congress, and the members of Congress shall be protected in their persons from arrests and imprisonments, during the time of their going to and from, and attendance on Congress, except for treason, felony, or breach of the peace.

Article VI. No state without the Consent of the United States in Congress assembled, shall send any embassy to, or receive any embassy from, or enter into any conference, agreement, or alliance or treaty with any king, prince or state; nor shall any person holding any office of profit or trust under the United States, or any of them, accept of any present, emolument, office or title of any kind whatever from any king, prince or foreign state; nor shall the United States in Congress assembled, or any of them, grant any title of nobility.

limitations

No two or more States shall enter into any treaty, confederation or alliance whatever between them, without the consent of the United States in Congress assembled, specifying accurately the purposes for which the same is to be entered into, and how long it shall continue.

No state shall lay any imposts or duties, which may interfere with any stipulations in treaties, entered into by the United States in Congress assembled, with any king, prince or state, in pursuance of any treaties already proposed by Congress, to the courts of France and Spain.

No vessels of war shall be kept up in time of peace by any State, except such number only, as shall be deemed necessary by the United States in Congress assembled, for the defence of such State or its trade; nor shall any body of forces be kept up by any State, in time of peace, except such number only, as in the judgment of the United States in Congress assembled, shall be deemed requisite to garrison the forts necessary for the defence of such State; but every State shall always keep up a well regulated and disciplined militia, sufficiently armed and accoutered, and shall provide and constantly have ready for use, in public stores, a due number of field pieces and tents, and a proper quantity of arms, ammunition and camp equipage.

No state shall engage in any war without the consent of the United States in Congress assembled, unless such state be actually invaded by enemies, or shall have received certain advice of a resolution being formed by some nation of Indians to invade such State, and the danger is so imminent as not to admit of a delay, till the United States in Congress assembled can be consulted: nor shall any state grant commissions to any ships or vessels of war, nor letters of marque or reprisal, except it be after a declaration of war by the United States in Congress assembled, and then only against the kingdom or State and the subjects thereof, against which war has been so declared, and under such regulations as shall be established by the United States in Congress assembled, unless such state be infested by pirates, in which case vessels of war may be fitted out for that occasion, and kept so long as the danger shall continue, or until the United States in Congress assembled shall determine otherwise.

Article VII. When land forces are raised by any state for the common defence, all officers of or under the rank of colonel, shall be appointed by the legislature of each state respectively by whom such forces shall be raised, or in such manner as such state shall direct, and all vacancies shall be filled up by the state which first made the appointment.

Article VIII. All charges of war, and all other expenses that shall be incurred for the common defence or general welfare, and allowed by the United States in Congress assembled, shall be defrayed out of a common treasury, which shall be supplied by the several States, in proportion to the value of all land within each state, granted to or surveyed for any person, as such land and the buildings and improvements thereon shall be estimated according to such mode as the United States in Congress assembled, shall from time to time direct and appoint. The taxes for paying that proportion shall be laid and levied by the authority and direction of the legislatures of the several States within the time agreed upon by the United States in Congress assembled.

power

Article IX. The United States in Congress assembled, shall have the sole and exclusive right and power of determining on peace and war, except in the cases mentioned in the sixth article-of sending and receiving ambassadors-entering into treaties and alliances, provided that no treaty of commerce shall be made whereby the legislative power of the respective States shall be restrained from imposing such imposts and duties on foreigners, as their own people are subjected to, or from prohibiting the exportation or importation of any species of goods or commodities whatsoever-of establishing rules for deciding in all cases, what captures on land or water shall be legal, and in what manner prizes taken by land or naval forces in the service of the United States shall be divided or appropriated-of granting letters of marque and reprisal in times of peace-appointing courts for the trial of piracies and felonies committed on the high seas and establishing courts for receiving and determining finally appeals in all cases of captures, provided that no member of Congress shall be appointed a judge of any of the said courts.

The United States in Congress assembled shall also be the last resort on appeal in all disputes and differences now subsisting or that hereafter may arise between two or more States concerning boundary, jurisdiction or any other cause whatever *** provided also that no State shall be deprived of territory for the benefit of the United States.

All controversies concerning the private right of soil claimed under different grants of two or more States, *** shall on the petition of either party to the Congress of the United States, be finally determined as near as may be in the same manner as is before prescribed for deciding disputes respecting territorial jurisdiction between different States.

The United States in Congress assembled shall also have the sole and exclusive right and power of regulating the alloy and value of coin struck by their own authority, or by that of the respective States-fixing the standard of weights and measures throughout the United States.-regulating the trade and managing all affairs with the Indians, not members of any of the States, provided that the legislative right of any state within its own limits be not infringed or violated-establishing and regulating post offices from one State to another, throughout all the United States, and exacting such postage on the papers passing through the same as may be requisite to defray the expenses of the said office-appointing all officers of the land forces, in the service of the United States, excepting regimental officers-appointing all the officers of the naval forces, and commissioning all officers whatever in the service of the United States-making rules for the government and regulation of the said land and naval forces, and directing their operations.

The United States in Congress assembled shall have authority to appoint a committee, to sit in the recess of Congress, to be denominated "A Committee of the States," and to consist of one delegate from each state; and to appoint such other committees and civil officers as may be necessary for managing the general affairs of the United States under their direction-to appoint one of their number to preside, provided that no person be allowed to serve in the office of president more than one year in any term of three years; to ascertain the necessary sums of Money to be raised for the service of the United States, and to appropriate and apply the same for defraying the public expenses-to borrow money, or emit bills on the credit of the United States, transmitting every half year to the respective States an account of the sums of money so borrowed or emitted,-to build and equip a navy-to agree upon the number of land forces, and to make requisitions from each state for its quota, in proportion to the number of white inhabitants in such state; ***.

The United States in Congress assembled shall never engage in a war, nor grant letters of marque and reprisal in time of peace, nor enter into any treaties or alliances, nor coin money, nor regulate the value thereof, nor ascertain the sums and expenses necessary for the defence and welfare of the United States, or any of them, nor emit bills, nor borrow money on the credit of the United States, nor appropriate money, nor agree upon the number of vessels of war, to be built or purchased, or the number of land or sea forces to be raised, nor appoint a commander-in-chief of the army or navy, unless nine States assent to the same: nor shall a question on any other point, except for adjourning from day to day be determined, unless by the votes of a majority of the United States in Congress assembled.

The Congress of the United States shall have power to adjourn to any time within the year, and to any place within the United States, so that no period of adjournment be for a longer duration than the space of six months, and shall publish the journal of their proceedings monthly, except such parts thereof relating to treaties, alliances or military operations as in their judgment require secrecy; and the yeas and nays of the delegates of each state on any question shall be entered on the journal, when it is desired by any delegate; and the delegates of a State, or any of them, at his or their request shall be furnished with a transcript of the said journal, except such parts as are above excepted, to lay before the legislatures of the several States.

Article X. The Committee of the States, or any nine of them, shall be authorized to execute, in the recess of Congress, such of the powers of Congress as the United States in Congress assembled, by the consent of nine States, shall from time to time think expedient to vest them with; provided that no power be delegated to the said Committee, for the exercise of which, by the Articles of Confederation, the voice of nine States in the Congress of the United States assembled is requisite.

Article XI. Canada acceding to this Confederation, and joining in the measures of the United States, shall be admitted into, and entitled to all the advantages of this Union: but no other colony shall be admitted into the same, unless such admission be agreed to by nine States.

Article XII. All bills of credit emitted, monies borrowed and debts contracted by, or under the authority of Congress, before the assembling of the United States, in pursuance of the present Confederation, shall be deemed and considered as a charge against the United States, for payment and satisfaction whereof the said United States, and the public faith are hereby solemnly pledged.

Article XIII. Every State shall abide by the determinations of the United States in Congress assembled, on all questions which by this Confederation are submitted to them. And the Articles of this Confederation shall be inviolably observed by every state, and the union shall be perpetual; nor shall any alteration at any time hereafter be made in any of them; unless such alteration be agreed to in a Congress of the United States, and be afterwards confirmed by the legislatures of every State.

And whereas it hath pleased the Great Governor of the World to incline the hearts of the legislatures we respectively represent in Congress, to approve of, and to authorize us to ratify the said Articles of Confederation and perpetual Union, KNOW YE that we the undersigned delegates, by virtue of the power and authority to us given for that purpose, do by these presents, in the name and in behalf of our respective constituents, fully and entirely ratify and confirm each and every of the said Articles of Confederation and perpetual Union, ***. And that the Articles thereof shall be inviolably observed by the States we respectively represent, and that the Union shall be perpetual. ***

Appendix B

JAMES MADISON'S SPEECH TO THE HOUSE OF REPRESENTATIVES PRESENTING THE PROPOSED BILL OF RIGHTS, JUNE 8, 1789

(from Gales & Seaton's HISTORY OF DEBATES IN CONGRESS, pp.448–459)

Mr. Madison.– [I move] that a select committee be appointed to consider and report such amendments as are proper for Congress to propose to the Legislatures of the several States, conformably to the fifth article of the constitution. *** Government by eleven of the thirteen United States, in some cases unanimously, in others by large majorities; *** the great mass of the people who opposed it, disliked it because it did not contain effectual provisions against the encroachments on particular rights, *** nor ought we to consider them safe, while a great number of our fellow-citizens think these securities necessary. *** The amendments which have occurred to me, proper to be recommended by Congress to the State Legislatures, are these:

First. That there be prefixed to the constitution a declaration, that all power is originally vested in, and consequently derived from, the people.

That Government is instituted and ought to be exercised for the benefit of the people; which consists in the enjoyment of life and liberty, with the right of acquiring and using property, and generally of pursuing and obtaining happiness and safety.

That the people have an indubitable, unalienable, and indefeasible right to reform or change their Government, whenever it be found adverse or inadequate to the purposes of its institution.

Secondly. That in article 1st, section 2, clause 3, these words be struck out, to wit: "The number of Representatives shall not exceed one for ever thirty thousand, but each State shall have at least one Representative, and until such enumeration shall be made," and that in place thereof inserted these words, to wit: "After the first actual enumeration, there shall be on Representative for every thirty thousand until the number amounts to _____, after which the proportion shall be so regulated by Congress, that the number shall never be less than, nor more than _____, but each State shall, after the first enumeration, have at least two Representatives; and prior thereto."

Thirdly. That in article 1st, section 6, clause 1, there be added to the end of the first sentence, these words, to wit: "But no law varying the compensation last ascertained shall operate before the next ensuing election of Representatives."

Fourthly. That in article 1st, section 9, between clauses 3 and 4, be inserted these clauses, to wit: The civil rights of none shall be abridged on account of religious belief or worship, nor shall any national religion be established, nor shall the full and equal rights of conscience be in any manner, or on any pretext, infringed.

The people shall not be deprived or abridged of their right to speak, to write, or to publish their sentiments; and the freedom of the press, as one of the great bulwarks of liberty, shall be inviolable.

The people shall not be restrained from peaceably assembling and consulting for their common good; nor from applying to the Legislature by petitions, or remonstrances, for redress of their grievances.

The right of the people to keep and bear arms shall not be infringed; a well armed and well regulated militia being the best security of a free country: but no person religiously scrupulous of bearing arms shall be compelled to render military service in person.

No soldier shall in time of peace be quartered in any house without the consent of the owner; nor at any time, but in a manner warranted by law.

No person shall be subject, except in cases of impeachment, to more than one punishment or one trial for the same offence; nor shall be compelled to be a witness against himself; nor be deprived of life, liberty, or property without due process of law; nor be obliged to relinquish his property, where it may be necessary for public use, without a just compensation.

Excessive bail shall not be required, nor excessive fines imposed, nor cruel and unusual punishments inflicted.

The rights of the people to be secured in their persons, their houses, their papers, and their other property, from all unreasonable searches and seizures, shall not be violated by warrants issued without probable cause, supported by oath or affirmation, or not particularly describing the places to be searched, or the persons or things to be seized.

In all criminal prosecutions, the accused shall enjoy the right to a speedy and public trial, to be informed of the cause and nature of the accusation, to be confronted with his accusers, and the witnesses against him; to have a compulsory process for obtaining witnesses in his favor; and to have the assistance of counsel for his defence.

The exceptions here or elsewhere in the constitution, made in favor of particular rights, shall not be so construed as to diminish the just importance of other rights retained by the people, or as to enlarge the powers delegated by the constitution; but either as actual limitations of such powers, or as inserted merely for greater caution.

Fifthly. That in article 1st, section 10, between clauses 1 and 2, be inserted this clause, to wit:

No State shall violate the equal rights of conscience, or the freedom of the press, or the trial by jury in criminal cases.

Sixthly. That, in article 3d, section 2, be annexed to the end of clause 2d, these words, to wit:

But no appeal to such court shall be allowed where the value in controversy shall not amount to _____ dollars; nor shall any fact triable by jury, according to the course of common law, be otherwise re-examinable than may consist with the principles of common law.

Seventhly. That in article 3d, section 2, the third clause be struck out, and in its place be inserted the clauses following, to wit:

The trial of all crimes (except in cases of impeachments, and cases arising in the land or naval forces, or the militia when on actual service, in time of war or public danger) shall be by an impartial jury of freeholders of vicinage, with the requisite of unanimity for conviction, of the right of challenge, and other accustomed requisites; and in all crimes punishable with loss of life or member, presentment or indictment by a grand jury shall be an essential preliminary, provided that in cases of crimes committed within any county which may be in possession of an enemy, or in which a general insurrection may prevail, the trial may by law be authorized in some other county of the same State, as near as may be to the seat of the offence.

In cases of crimes committed not within any county, the trial may by law be in such county as the laws shall have prescribed. In suits at common law, between man and man, the trial by jury, as one of the best securities to the rights of the people, ought to remain inviolate.

Eighthly. That immediately after article 6th, be inserted as article 7th, the clauses following, to wit:

The powers delegated by this constitution are appropriated to the departments to which they are respectively distributed: so that the legislative department shall never exercise powers vested in the executive or judicial, nor the executive exercise powers vested in the legislative or judicial, nor the judicial exercise the powers vested in the legislative or executive departments.

The powers not delegated by this constitution, nor prohibited by it to the States, are reserved to the States respectively.

Ninthly. That article 7th be numbered as article 8th. ***

The people of many States have thought it necessary to raise barriers against power in all forms and departments of Government, and I am inclined to believe, if once bills of rights are established in all the States as well as the federal constitution, we shall find, that, although some of them are rather unimportant, yet, upon the whole, they will have a salutary tendency. *** In some instances they assert those rights which are exercised by the people in forming and establishing a plan of Government. In other instances, they specify those rights which are retained when particular powers are given up to be exercised by the Legislature. In other instances, they specify positive rights, which may seem to result from the nature of the compact. *** In other instances, they lay down dogmatic maxims with respect to the construction of the government; declaring that the legislative, executive, and judicial branches shall be kept separate and distinct. Perhaps the best way of securing this in practice is to provide such checks as will prevent the encroachment of the one upon the other. *** But I confess that I do conceive, that in a Government modified like this of the United States, the great danger lies rather in the abuse of the community than in the Legislative body. The prescriptions in favor of liberty ought to be levelled against that quarter where the greatest danger lies, namely, that which possesses the highest prerogative of power. But this is not found in either the executive or legislative departments of Government, but in the body of the people, operating by the majority against the minority. ***

It has been said, that in the Federal Government they are unnecessary, because the powers are enumerated, and it follows, that all that are not granted are retained; that the constitution is a bill of powers, the great residuum being the rights of the people; and, therefore, a bill of rights cannot be so necessary as if the residuum was thrown into the hands of the Government. I admit that these arguments are not entirely without foundation; but they are not conclusive to the extent which has been supposed. It is true, the powers of the General Government are circumscribed, they are directed to particular objects; but even if Government keeps within these limits, it has certain discretionary powers with respect to the means, which may admit of abuse to a certain extent, in the same manner as the powers of the State Governments under their constitutions may to an indefinite extent; because in the constitution of the United States, there is a clause granting to Congress the power to make all laws which shall be necessary and proper for carrying into execution all the powers vest in the Government of the United States, or in any department or officer thereof; this enables them to fulfil every purpose for which the Government was established. Now, may not laws be considered necessary and proper by Congress, for it is for them to judge of the necessity and propriety to accomplish those special purposes which they may have in contemplation, which laws in themselves are neither necessary nor proper; as well as improper laws could be enacted by the State Legislatures, for fulfilling the more extended objects of those Governments? I will state an instance, which I think in point, that proves that this might be the case. The General Government has a right to pass all laws which shall be necessary to collect its revenue; the means for enforcing the collection are within the direction of the Legislature: may not general warrants be considered necessary for this purpose, as well as for some purposes which it was supposed at the framing of their constitutions the State Governments had in view? If there was reason for restraining the State Governments from exercising this power, there is like reason for restraining the Federal Government.

It may be said, indeed it has been said, that a bill of rights is not necessary, because the establishment of this Government has not repealed those declarations of rights which are added to the several State constitutions; that those rights of the people which had been established by the most solemn act, could not be annihilated by a subsequent act of that people, who meant and declared at the head of the instrument, that they ordained and established a new system, for the express purpose of securing to themselves and posterity the liberties they had gained by an arduous conflict.

I admit the force of this observation, but I do not look upon it to be conclusive. In the first place, it is too uncertain ground to leave this provision upon, if a provision is at all necessary to secure rights so important as many of those I have mentioned are conceived to be, by the public in general, as well as those in particular who opposed the adoption of this constitution. Besides, some States have no bills of rights, there are others provided with very defective ones, and there are others whose bills of rights are not only defective, but absolutely improper; instead of securing some in the full extent which republican principles would require, they limit them too much to agree with the common ideas of liberty.

It has been objected also against a bill of rights, that, by enumerating particular exceptions to the grant of power, it would disparage those rights which were not placed in that enumeration; and it might follow by implication, that those rights which were not singled out, were intended to be assigned into the hands of the General Government, and were consequently insecure. This is one of the most plausible arguments I have ever heard urged against the admission of a bill of rights into this system; but, I conceive, that it may be guarded against. I have attempted it, as gentlemen may see by turning to the last clause of the fourth resolution.

It has been said, that it is unnecessary to load the constitution with this provision, because it was not found effectual in the constitution of the particular States. It is true, there are a few particular States in which some of the most valuable articles have not, at one time or other, been violated; but it does not follow but they may have to a certain degree, a salutary effect against the abuse of power. If they are incorporated into the constitution, independent tribunals of justice will consider themselves in a peculiar manner the guardians of those rights; they will be in an impenetrable bulwark against every assumption of power in the Legislative or Executive; they will be naturally led to resist every encroachment upon rights expressly stipulated for the constitution by the declaration of rights. Besides this security, there is a great probability that such a declaration in the federal system would be enforced; because the State Legislatures will jealously and closely watch the operations of this Government, and be able to resist with more effect every assumption of power, than any other power on earth can do; and the greatest opponents to a Federal Government admit the State Legislatures to be sure guardians of the people's liberty. ***

I wish, also, in revising the constitution, we may throw into that section, which interdicts the abuse of certain powers in the State Legislatures, some other provisions of equal, if not greater importance than those already made. *** I should, therefore, wish to extend to extend this interdiction, and add, as I have stated in the 5th resolution, that no State shall violate the equal right of conscience, freedom of the press, or trial by jury in criminal cases; because it is proper that every Government should be disarmed of powers which trench upon those particular rights. ***

Appendix C

REVIEW PROBLEMS

Chapter III:

1. Dissolution of a prominent investment banking institution and collapse of the home mortgage market in 2008 led to extensive emergency efforts by the Treasury Department and the Federal Reserve Board (an independent agency which regulates the money supply), to avoid a complete meltdown of the American economy. More than a trillion taxpayer dollars later, and after the economy finally returned to a somewhat normal state in 2010, Congress and the President turned their attention to legislation designed to prevent future occurrences of such financial crises.

There was not, however, a consensus among economists about the causes of the crisis of 2008. Various economists focused on (1) the development of new financial instruments called "derivatives," (2) aggressive marketing of subprime mortgages encouraged by Congress, (3) the lax regulatory framework prior to the collapse, or (4) the excessive size of banks that had grown "too big to fail." Furthermore, there were deep divides among policy-makers about what the proper fixes should be, a problem aggravated by different approaches by the Democratic Party and the Republican Party concerning potential legislative fixes. What Congress could agree upon, across party lines, was that a regulatory body with technical expertise in macroeconomics and finance should be given broad authority to take preventive actions in this field. Eventually, the following legislation passed which President Obama reluctantly signed.

The Financial Regulation Act (FRA)

§1. Findings:

(a) The United States of America cannot afford another financial crisis like the crisis of 2008, which led to the Great Recession of 2009.

(b) To prevent further such financial disasters, an oversight system is needed to regulate complex financial instruments, reduce risk in markets central to the economic health of the country.

(c) The regulatory body charged with avoiding systemic risk in the economy must be comprised of professionals insulated from partisan political pressures.

§2. Therefore:

(a) An independent agency, the Financial Alert and Remediation Trust (FART) is hereby established.

(b) The FART shall have the power to investigate lending and investment practices at both commercial and investment banks, to promulgate regulations designed to reduce the risk of systemic financial market failures, and to prosecute violations of these rules.

(c) The FART shall consist of a Chair and four Trustees who, by majority vote, shall be empowered to promulgate the regulations to reduce systemic financial risks and a General Counsel, who shall prosecute violations of FART regulations. Each of these individuals shall be appointed for a term of five years.

(d) The Chair of the FART shall be appointed by the Federal Reserve Board, the four Trustees shall be appointed by the Secretary of the Treasury, and the General Counsel shall be appointed by the Attorney General.

(e) The FART Chair and Commissioners may be removed only as follows: The Senate Banking Committee, by majority vote, may commence removal proceedings. If proceedings are so initiated, a hearing shall be conducted and the final decision shall be made by the most junior Justice of the United States Supreme Court. The FART General Counsel may be removed only by a majority vote of the Federal Reserve Board.

Explain whether the provisions of FRA violate separation of powers principles (including appointment and removal principles).

2.   Congress recently enacted a foreign aid bill that provides for grants to dozens of countries around the world. Because of concern with the problem of terrorism directed at the United States, Congress included a provision in the legislation that requires the President to determine whether countries that receive foreign aid from the United States are terrorist nations. The legislation defines a terrorist nation as "a nation that supports, harbors, or encourages persons or organizations that use or support the use of violence against citizens of the United States." The foreign aid legislation authorizes (but does not require) the President to cancel foreign aid that would otherwise go to a nation that the President determines is a terrorist nation.

The legislation further provides that before a cancellation takes effect, the President must inform the chairs of the foreign affairs committees of the Senate and the House of Representatives of his or her intent to cancel. Cancellation does not take effect until two months after this notification. During the two-month interval, Congress may enact legislation (through the usual legislative process) reauthorizing the foreign aid and exempting it from presidential cancellation. If no legislation is enacted within two months, the presidential cancellation takes effect.

President Powell believes international narcotics trafficking poses as great a threat to the United States as international terrorism and "fosters violent crime in the United States." Accordingly, he issues an Executive Order canceling foreign aid to nations that harbor or support individuals who smuggle narcotics into the United States. With regard to these cancellations, the Executive Order sets out the same procedures that the foreign aid legislation provides for terrorist nations: informing the foreign affairs committee chairs of intent to cancel the expenditure and waiting two months before actual cancellation.

a.   Does the terrorist nation cancellation provision violate the separation of powers?

b.   Does President Powell have the authority to cancel foreign aid to nations that harbor or support drug traffickers?

3. As the presidential election campaign heated up in the summer of 2012, President Obama began to turn from criticizing Congress for gridlock to vigorously pressing his agenda through unilateral executive action.

When Congress seemed reluctant to intervene in Syria to protect civilians, President Obama provided humanitarian aid, then weaponry, and finally military advisors to Syrian rebels who had been violently attacked by the forces of Syrian President Bashar Assad. Critics in Congress decried this "foreign adventurism," and predicted further disasters like the costly and undeclared wars in Afghanistan and Iraq, both of which seemed to rapidly be sinking into civil wars after the drawdown of American troops.

Next, President Obama began to press a domestic agenda in response to being called a "do-nothing" president by Republican foes. For example, President Obama granted waivers of drilling permits, approved construction of liquefied natural gas terminals to ship natural gas overseas, and pushed the Nuclear Regulatory Commission to approve several new nuclear power plants. These actions inflamed environmentalists, who called the President's actions "a signal betrayal of everything sacred to us." President Obama also took strong steps to enhance enforcement of the Internal Revenue Code. The Internal Revenue Service (IRS) is part of the Department of the Treasury, which is an agency in the executive branch. President Obama directed the IRS to pursue criminal penalties in any case in which the IRS determined there was a shortfall of $1 million or more from any individual or corporation. These actions led to protests by a coalition of Republicans who said he was engaging in "class warfare" and by civil libertarians who were appalled at the aggressive actions of the IRS.

President Obama won reelection in November 2012, but substantial Republican majorities were elected to both the Senate and the House. To show the president where his authority ended and congressional authority began, Congress passed the Congressional Reassertion of Authority over the President (CRAP) Act of 2013. When, as expected, the CRAP Act was vetoed, Congress overrode the veto. The relevant text of the Act appears below:

Congressional Reassertion of Authority over President Act (CRAP)

Section 1. The Constitution provides that the legislative power of the United States resides in Congress rather than the President. Presidents have increasingly ignored that constitutional principle, necessitating that Congress reassert its legislative supremacy.

Section 2. With regard to any executive orders, the following procedure shall be followed:
(a) At least two weeks prior to the proposed effective date of any executive order, the President shall provide to Congress a copy of such proposed executive order;
(b) A joint conference committee of Representatives and Senators appointed by the Speaker of the House of Representatives and the Majority Leader of the Senate shall consider such proposed executive order and accept it, reject it, or propose changes in it;

(c) If the joint committee accepts the proposed executive order or if the President makes the proposed changes, then the order will take effect;

(d) However, if the joint committee rejects the proposed executive order or if the President refuses to accept the proposed changes, then the proposed executive order shall not take effect.

Section 3. There is created in the Internal Revenue Service the office of Taxpayer Advocate.

(a) The Taxpayer Advocate shall be appointed by the Secretary of the Treasury, subject to confirmation by the Senate. Other than by impeachment, the Taxpayer Advocate may be removed from office only by the Secretary of the Treasury and only for good cause. The Internal Revenue Service, without the approval of the Taxpayer Advocate, may undertake no revenue collection measure.

(b) The decisions of the Taxpayer Advocate may be reviewed solely through suit in the Federal District Court of the District of Columbia, whose decision shall be final and subject to no further appeal by the taxpayer, the Internal Revenue Service, or the Taxpayer Advocate.

You are the head of the Office of Legal Counsel, the unit of the Department of Justice charged with providing constitutional law advice to the executive branch. The President has asked your advice concerning whether the CRAP Act violates constitutional separation of powers principles. Please provide this advice in a memo to the President, using appropriate references to the Constitution and Supreme Court case law.

4. After Hillary Clinton was elected President in 2016, she negotiated a new treaty with Iran, which was approved by the necessary ⅔ Senate vote in early 2017. Under the treaty, Iran committed to give inspectors immediate access to its nuclear facilities. In exchange, the United States committed to give Iran a monopoly over its domestic Persian rug trade. Congress thereafter considered legislation to implement the treaty provision giving Iran a monopoly over the Persian rug trade in the United States, but such legislation was never enacted.

In late 2017, Clinton issued this Executive Order:

EO1. There is hereby created an executive branch agency, the Iran Treaty Implementation Agency (ITIA) with power to adopt regulations implementing the U.S.-Iran Treaty of 2017.

EO2. The ITIA shall consist of three members: the Senate Majority Leader, the Speaker of the House, and a member appointed by the President. The third member shall serve a four-year term and may not be removed except by impeachment.

Though Clinton had tried to please Congress by putting its leaders atop the ITIA, the new Congress elected in 2018 rebelled and passed this statute over her veto:

§ 101.   The validity of any regulation promulgated by any treaty-implementing agency may be challenged directly in the Supreme Court.

President Clinton appointed her husband Bill as the third ITIA member, and the Agency adopted this regulation:

R1. All states shall identify Persian rug merchants not licensed by Iran, and impose a penalty of $1 million on each violator of the treaty.

R2. Persian rug merchants licensed by Iran may sue any non-complying state in federal court to recover such penalties.

By a 60% vote in each House, an angry Congress passed this two-House ("concurrent") resolution:

CR1.   The Iranian Treaty-Implementing Agency is hereby abolished.

President Clinton and the ITIA, ignoring CR1, sent the regulations to all the state governors. New York seeks to challenge ITIA and its regulations. As a summer intern working for the New York Attorney General, you are asked to advise her **(1) how strong New York's structural constitutional law challenges to the ITIA and its regulations are and (2) whether New York can bring these challenges in the Supreme Court. (Ignore whether the regulations violate any rights: other interns are working on that question.)**

5. The Black Lives Matter movement, which started in Ferguson, Missouri, focused national attention on use of disproportionate force by police officers when dealing with minority group members. Demonstrations in various American cities led to changes in police protocols and training as well as some prosecutions of individual officers charged with excessive use of force.

Subsequently, a substantial increase in shootings of police officers in metropolitan areas around the United States occurred, as did elevated levels of violent crime in urban areas. This led to the "Blue Lives Matter" movement, which advocated supporting the authority of law enforcement and restraining violence directed against police officers.

Senator Joe Friday, a Blue Lives Matter leader, introduced legislation to "Protect our embattled police, whose low numbers and tough jobs place them in tension and sometimes conflict with citizens. Their uniforms and badges make them sitting ducks for well-armed criminals." As part of comprehensive legislation meant to strengthen state and local law enforcement, the following legislation making violence against police officers punishable as federal crimes passed the Senate and House and was signed by the President:

THE BLUE LIVES MATTER ACT OF 2016

Section 1. Findings.
   (a) There has been a nationwide increase in violent crimes targeting police officers, including police officers from minority groups;
   (b) There has been a nationwide reduction in the ability of the police to keep citizens safe, especially in urban minority areas;

(c) State and local efforts have not stemmed violence against police officers;

(d) Violence against police officers interferes with interstate commerce and hinders economic development, especially in urban minority areas; and

(e) Weapons used in crimes against the police usually come from states other than the states in which they were used.

Section 2. Therefore:

(a) Whoever causes unjustified bodily injury or death to any person because of the actual or perceived status of the person as a police officer, shall be imprisoned for the terms of years provided for other federal hate crimes or, if the officer dies, for life;

(b) If the perpetrator is a different race from the victim, the sentence under section 2(a) shall be enhanced by five (5) additional years of imprisonment by the trial court or, if the officer dies, by a sentence of death; and

(c) All government entities employing police officers shall provide such officers with Kevlar body armor and institute procedures to encourage use of this body armor.

(a) Does Congress have the power, (1) under the Commerce Clause and (2) under Section 5 of the Fourteenth Amendment, to enact the provisions of the Blue Lives Matter Act of 2016? (60 minutes)

*****

In 2017, President Trump issued an executive order providing that his administration would not prosecute cases under the Blue Lives Matter Act of 2016 involving state or local police officers but would fully prosecute cases of violence against federal border patrol agents "as provided in the Blue lives Matter Act." At the press conference announcing this executive order, President Trump said: "It is not the federal government's job to deal with state and local police matters, but it is the job of the federal government to protect our borders. This order is a necessary and proper response to increased violence along the border, including a recent incident in which a border patrol agent was killed by a Mexican national who tunneled under a recently-completed section of our wall on the border." Finally, referring to the color of border patrol agent uniforms, President Trump closed his press conference by saying "Olive green lives matter also."

(b) Does President Trump's executive order violate separation of powers principles? (30 minutes)

Chapter IV:

1. The shooting at Virginia Tech of 32 students in April 2007 by a mentally disturbed student led to extensive discussions nation-wide about what could be done to prevent such tragedies from happening in the future. Some colleges implemented additional security measures such as installation of sirens and text-message warning systems and some states modified components of their systems for reporting persons with serious mental illnesses to data-bases used in checking on purchases of firearms, Systematic reforms, however, proved elusive until a bipartisan coalition of Senators running for President agreed on a federal statutory reform. Sponsored by Senators Thompson, Obama, McCain,, the following legislation passed both houses of Congress and was signed by a lame duck President Bush in late 2007.

The Campus Security Act of 2007 ("CSA 2007")

§ 1. Findings:

a. The Virginia Tech shootings indicate a grave lack of attention to campus security measures by college administrators and state and local authorities.

b. Large state universities are more vulnerable to such incidents than private colleges and universities.

c. The sale of weapons and ammunition to a mentally deranged Korean immigrant responsible for the Virginia Tech massacre demonstrates systemic problems with enforcement of the Brady Handgun Violence Prevention Act of 1993.

d. Fear of future campus violence has caused some parents to withdraw their sons and daughters from state universities, particularly universities located in states remote from the parents' homes.

e. The post-Virginia Tech educational fear factor burdens interstate commerce and has increased incidents of discrimination against Korean immigrants and persons with mental illnesses, including discrimination in admissions and hiring by state universities.

§ 2. Therefore:

a. Every state university president shall provide to the Secretary of Homeland Security proof that the university has an operable campus-wide siren warning system, an operable text-messaging system for broadcasting warnings of threats of violence to students, staff, and faculty, and an adequate system for random checks of firearms on campus on or before December 31, 2008.

b. In addition to other punishments that exist under state or federal law, any student or employee found with a firearm on a state university campus shall be expelled or discharged from the university.

c. All federal student loan guarantees and research funding shall terminate at any state university that fails to comply with the provisions of § 2a and 2b.

d. All state and local mental health authorities shall post to an online database, updated weekly and in readily searchable form, the names of each individual who, in their professional judgment, would be a risk to self or others if sold a firearm.

e. Each state shall administer a mental fitness check to resident aliens within its jurisdiction to identify those who would be a threat to themselves or others. The mental fitness check shall be first applied to immigrants from Korea so the people of the United States will no longer be fearful of or discriminate against such individuals.

       f. No university may discriminate in its admissions decisions against any applicant with a history of mental illness, where such mental illness is not of a type associated with a risk of violence.

       1. Does Congress have the power under Article I of the Constitution to enact the provisions of the CSA 2007?

       2. Does Congress have the power under § 5 of the 14th Amendment to enact the provisions of the CSA 2007? (After reading Chapter X)

2. Naturism (also known as nudism) is a cultural and political movement and lifestyle choice based on a belief in the benefits of social nudity in both public and private venues. Naturists believe that "clothes-free" living promotes the values of equality, freedom, healthy living, respect for individuals, and respect for the environment.

    Throughout the first decade of the 21st Century, the so-called "Naturist Parenting" movement steadily grew in popularity. Particularly after the publication of <u>Naturism at School, Home, Work, and Play</u>, which remained on the *New York Times* nonfiction bestseller list for a remarkable 73 weeks, many young, affluent professionals joined the Naturist Union Democracy Institute for Education (NUDIE) and sought to harmonize their lives with their naturist philosophies. In 2002, billionaire naturist Dabny T. Agart endowed the NUDIE Foundation "for the purpose of funding the construction and operation of clothing-optional schools, resorts, housing complexes, and sports facilities that cater to naturist families." By 2010, nearly 50 such institutions were in operation across the U.S. serving thousands of families.

    Congressman Knute Ringich was an early and frequent critic of the naturist movement. When the NUDIE Foundation announced the Agart gift, Rep. Ringich stated, "If God had wanted us to stay naked . . . we wouldn't have department stores!" He introduced "The Anti-Body and Morality Preservation Act" to combat what he viewed as "the slow slide into degeneracy that the nudie movement represents." In response, NUDIE issued a position paper citing several recent academic studies which suggested that the practice of family, social, and school nudity increases students' standardized test scores and leads to improved body image and psychological well-being among both children and adults. After holding lengthy hearings and compiling a substantial record, Congress passed and the President signed the following legislation:

THE ANTI-BODY AND MORALITY PRESERVATION ACT (ABMPA)

§ 1. Findings:
    (1) Social and familial nudism is a dangerous trend that threatens the moral and social   order of the Nation.

(2)   There are currently thousands of nudist families; this number is likely to grow unless swift and decisive action is taken against it.

(3) It is harmful to children to teach them that parading the naked body is an alternative "lifestyle choice" to wearing clothing.

(4)   Children older than four are likely to be psychologically damaged by purposeful and extended viewing of their parents' and others' unclothed bodies.

(5) So-called "clothing optional" schooling is distracting to students and leads to suboptimal educational outcomes, which in turn has substantial detrimental effects on the national economy.

(6) Minors have a right of privacy and autonomy that includes the right to be clothed in public and private.   NUDIE parents may coerce or brainwash their children into a lifestyle that the children would otherwise reject.

(7) Clothing is a multibillion dollar industry critical to the nation's economy.

§ 2. Therefore:

(1)   It shall be a violation of this Act for any Place of Education of Minors, as defined in § 3(1) of this Act, to permit any child or adult therein at any time to be   Unclothed, as defined in § 3(2) of this Act, in the presence of any other person. Violations shall be punishable by civil fines of up to $10,000 per violation.

(2)   Any person who intentionally exposes his or her Unclothed body to any child   aged four years or older, including the person's own child, shall be guilty of a misdemeanor   punishable by up to six (6) months in prison and a fine of up to $10,000. Any   parent   who intentionally causes his or her own child aged four years or older to appear Unclothed in the presence of any person other than such parent shall be guilty of the same offense and subject to the same punishment.

§ 3. Definitions:

(1)   "Place of Education of Minors" as used in this Act means any home, building,   school, or institution of any kind that engages in formal education of children under 18, including but not limited to public, religious, secular, charter, and home-school education.

(2) "Unclothed" as used in this Act means having any part of the person's nude buttocks or genitals visible. A person is not "Unclothed" if he or she is a minor person changing his or her clothes in order to engage in physical education activity who is briefly without clothing in the presence only of minors of the same sex and age of such minor person.

(A) Does Congress have the power to enact the ABMPA under the Commerce Clause?

(B) Does the ABMPA violate the Due Process Clause?

Where appropriate, address the constitutionality of different provisions of the statute separately (i.e. one provision may be constitutional whereas another is not).

Chapter VI:

1.   Medical technology allows doctors to transplant human organs, such as lungs, kidneys, and livers.   The organs are "harvested" from people after death and transplanted into recipients whose own organs are improperly functioning. The transplants must generally take place within a short period of time following death of the donor.   The need for transplanted organs greatly exceeds the supply, and many people die while awaiting transplants. Consent for transplant must be obtained in advance from the potential donor or from that person's family after his or her death. Many organs suitable for transplant are not transplanted because the potential donor fails to consent in advance, family cannot be located in time, and family may be reluctant to consent.   To address these problems, the State General Assembly recently enacted this legislation:

STATE ORGAN DONATION ACT

§ 1. **Findings**:

(a)   The State should strongly encourage potential donors to consent in advance to transplant and encourage families to consent to transplant following the death of a potential donor;

(b)   It is fair and appropriate for State citizens to benefit from the State's expenditures to encourage its citizens to become organ donors;

(c)   Organ donations are more likely to be successful if there is the shortest time possible between harvesting and transplanting organs into recipients. When organs are removed in-state, transplantation will likely be quicker if the recipient is a State citizen; and

(d)   Organ donations are more likely to be successful if the donor and recipient have a similar genetic make up. It may be time-consuming to perform a comprehensive genetic screening of potential organ donors and potential organ recipients.   People of the same races or ethnic backgrounds are more likely to have a similar genetic make up.

§ 2. **Therefore**:

(a) $10 million is appropriated for a public education campaign to encourage State citizens to become organ donors.

(b)   To further encourage organ donations, the State shall pay $1000 to the family of any person who dies in the State, if the person consents in advance to become an organ donor.

(c)   All organs harvested in the State must be transplanted in accordance   with a "recipient priority" list created by the State Health Department   and it shall be unlawful to transplant organs harvested in the State except in accordance with this list.

(d)   In determining the "recipient priority" list, the State Health Department shall give preference to citizens of the State.

Assume that the Federal Government does not regulate organ transplants. **Does the State Organ Donation Act violate the:**

a.   **Dormant Commerce Clause?**
b.   **Article IV Privileges and Immunities Clause?**

2.   In the wake of news reports of sexual predators stalking their victims using the internet, Congress became concerned about the use of the internet by sexual predators.   Congress held hearings on the problem, focusing especially on the conduct of people who have been convicted under state law of various sexual crimes.   Based on the hearings, members of Congress concluded that states currently closely track people in the state who have been released from prison after having been convicted of sex crimes in that state.   However, members of Congress concluded that the tracking of people convicted of sexual crimes becomes much more difficult when the people move to a different state.   Based on these concerns Congress enacted and the President signed the following federal statute.

INTERSTATE INTERNET PREDATION PROTECTION ACT (IIPPA)

§1. Findings:

    (a) Sexual predators and the fear of sexual predators cause people to stay at home and not undertake business and travel, thus imposing substantial costs on the economy.

    (b) Sexual predators use the internet to locate future victims.

    (c) Knowledge that sexual predators use the internet to locate victims increases fear of sexual crimes.

    (d) Knowledge that sexual predators use the internet to locate victims inhibits people from using the internet for personal or business activities.

§2. Therefore:

    (a) For purposes of this statute, any person who moves to a new state after being convicted in a state court of a state crime of sexual violence shall be designated as an "Interstate Sexual Predator."

    (b) For the five years following their release from prison (or for five years following their conviction if no prison time is served), Interstate Sexual Predators shall not access the internet by any means.

    (c) Violation of section 2(b) of this Act is a federal crime punishable by up to ten years in prison.

    (d) To assist in enforcement of this Act, all states must inform the United States Department of Justice (a) when any person in the state is convicted of a state crime of sexual violence and (b) when any person who has been convicted of a state crime of sexual violence is released from prison.

Discuss whether Congress has the power to enact IIPPA. Answer this question <u>without considering</u> Congress' powers under section 5 of the Fourteenth Amendment.

3.   The Florida Everglades extends from Lake Okeechobee on the north to Florida Bay on the south and was once bordered by Big Cypress Swamp on the west and the Atlantic Coastal Ridge on the east. Called the "River of Grass" because of the slow flow of water from Okeechobee southward and the predominance of sawgrass, some 50% of the original Everglades has been lost to agriculture. Most of the rest is now protected as a state and national treasure in park, wildlife refuge, and water conservation areas.

The Everglades faces an ongoing threat from the melaleuca tree, a plant in the myrtle family native to Australia. The thirsty melaleuca tree was introduced to the Everglades in the 1950's to absorb water and make the "land" of the Everglades suitable for development. The melaleuca tree species is highly invasive, difficult to eradicate, and threatens the ecology of the Everglades. It drains water, crowds out native plants and, because the oils in the trees are flammable, leads to increased danger from wildfires. Oil extracted from the melaleuca tree (sometimes called "tea tree oil") is a valuable and highly-effective topical antibacterial and antifungal. Many products containing this oil are manufactured, advertised, and sold in the United States.

Florida owns several hundred thousand acres of land in the state, over 100,000 of which have melaleuca trees growing on them. Florida has passed a statute, the Melaleuca Control Act ("MCA"), which reads as follows:

(a) No person may bring melaleuca seeds, seedlings, or trees into the State of Florida.

(b) Melaleuca trees that are already in the State of Florida may be cultivated for their oils.

(c) Melaleuca trees on land owned by the State of Florida shall be cultivated and harvested exclusively by citizens of the State of Florida.

(d) All oils extracted from melaleuca trees on land owned by the State of Florida shall be processed by Florida Melaleuca, Inc., a company owned by the State of Florida which employs Florida citizens exclusively.

Discuss whether the MCA violates Dormant Commerce Clause principles.

4. State legislators in Oregon were concerned by widespread reports of obesity and poor nutrition in children and young adults. The legislators decided to begin by addressing the food that high school students eat in school. Public high schools in Oregon typically provide a food court in which private vendors sell food to students. These private vendors pay rent to the state of Oregon for the space in the public school food courts.

When the state legislature was debating various options relating to healthy eating, Senator Sam Spud recommended increasing the consumption of locally produced food as a means to promote healthy eating. Spud stated, "People worldwide are rediscovering the benefits of buying local food. It is fresher than other food. Because it is fresh, it does not require harmful preservatives or processing. In addition, local food is more nutritious because foods tend to lose nutrients in the time between harvesting and consumption. Buying local is good for the environment because less energy is used in transporting the food. Buying local also helps to support local farmers."

The Oregon legislature enacted the Healthy High Act (HHA). Under the provisions of the HHA, the state may only rent space in high school food courts to food vendors that agree to buy more than fifty percent (50%) of their food supplies from local farms. Under the HHA, "local" is defined as a farm located no more than fifty (50) miles from the high school where the food is sold.

Sprouts, a national chain of health food restaurants, specializes in salads and vegetable dishes. Sprouts grows all its food on farms near its corporate headquarters in San Jose, California. Sprouts would like to rent space in Oregon high school food courts to sell its food. However, because all of Sprouts' food supplies would come from California, rather than from "local" sources, Sprouts is barred by the HHA from renting space in public high school food courts in Oregon. Sprouts brings suit challenging the HHA.

Analyze whether the HHA violates Sprouts' Dormant Commerce Clause and/or Article IV Privileges and Immunities Clause rights.

5. Motivated by a mix of state's rights, libertarianism, and liberalism, Congress and President Obama reached agreement to take marijuana off the federal controlled substance list. This repeal left states free to experiment with marijuana regulation. Following repeal, President Obama said on his weekly radio show "we want the citizens of each state to have the freedom to choose whether marijuana will be legal. This is not about imposing drug use on any non-consenting state." A few states passed statutes allowing purchase and use of marijuana for medical or recreational purposes, some adopted laws allowing marijuana purchase and use for medical purposes, and many states continued to criminalize marijuana possession and use.

Colorado adopted a statute allowing adults to purchase marijuana for medical and recreational purposes. It allows state residents to purchase one ounce of marijuana at a time; out-of-state visitors may purchase one-quarter of an ounce of marijuana at a time. Colorado's reasons for this differential were to "discourage the diversion of legally-purchased marijuana out of Colorado, reduce the likelihood of federal scrutiny of Colorado's adult-use marijuana industry, and support harmonious relationships with Colorado's neighboring states." Colorado's limit on "marijuana tourism" generally worked as intended, keeping marijuana purchases by out-of-staters fairly low.

Alice B. Toklas and Timothy Leary are residents of the anti-marijuana neighboring state of Wyoming. Alice has glaucoma and a cancerous tumor. There is some scientific evidence that marijuana consumption reduces the pain and perhaps slows the development of both conditions. Timothy is a recreational marijuana user whose mantra is "turn on, tune in, and drop out."

Alice and Timothy wish to sue Colorado for discriminating against them. **Advise them whether Colorado's law violates (1) constitutional privileges and immunities concepts and (2) dormant commerce clause concepts.**

Chapter VIII:

1.   New Hope is a state in the United States. The New Hope Health Department recently issued a report entitled "Sex-Selection Abortion in New Hope," which stated that abortions were being used in New Hope to decrease the number of female babies born. Normally, 105 male babies are born for every 100 female babies. However, the report found that in New Hope, the number of male babies per female babies has been rising and that 115 male babies are now born for every 100 female babies. According to the Report, the cause for this deviation from normal gender balance is sex-selection abortion, since no pre-conception technology exists to increase the chance of having a male fetus. The Report further noted that many men prefer having boys rather than girls, that women generally have no systematic preference for male or female children, and that, in other societies, an increase in the male-to-female ratio has led to increased violence and social instability. In response to this report, the New Hope legislature enacted the following statute:

SEX-SELECTION ABORTION PREVENTION ACT ("SAPA")

(a)   Before a fetus is viable, no medical professional may reveal its probable gender to anyone except the mother of the fetus.

(b)   No medical professional may reveal the probable gender of the pre-viable fetus unless the mother executes a sworn affidavit asserting (1) that she will not seek to have the fetus aborted and (2) that she understands it is a crime for her to thereafter seek an abortion.

(c)   Every medical professional who reveals the gender of a pre-viable fetus to the mother must submit a Gender Disclosure Report to the state verifying that the gender has been revealed and the provisions of Section 2 of this Act have been satisfied.

(d)   No one may perform an abortion unless the mother of the fetus signs an affidavit stating that she did not learn the gender of the fetus. The abortion provider must ensure that no Gender Disclosure Report has been filed concerning the fetus whose abortion is sought.

(e)   After fetal viability, no abortion may be performed unless it is necessary to preserve the life or health of the mother.

(f)   Violation of this act is a felony punishable by up to 10 years in prison.

Suits challenging SAPA have been filed by two New Hope residents, Paula Pound and Lori Lasker. Paula, excited when she became pregnant with her third child, asked for the fetus's gender and executed the SAPA affidavit. She knew that, under SAPA, she would no longer be able to abort her fetus. Early in her pregnancy, following several personal and professional calamities, Paula now wishes to abort her not-yet-viable fetus. Meanwhile, Lori Lasker and her husband have four daughters and want a son. Lori is pregnant and wishes to know the gender of her fetus. However, she wants to keep the option of aborting the fetus before viability, and knows that once she learns the gender of her fetus, SAPA will prohibit her from having an abortion.

Does SAPA violate the Due Process rights of Paula Pound and Lori Lasker?

2. Gambrell is a fictional state in the U.S. in which same-sex unions are legal and carry all the rights and responsibilities of heterosexual marriage. There is no applicable federal legislation on point.

As part of a family law reform initiative, the Gambrell legislature held extensive hearings on adoption policy and practice in the state. During the hearings, several professional and community organizations presented studies to the effect that failure to match adoptees with proper adoptive families leads to negative outcomes for children. A sociologist testified that, ideally, adoptions will involve stable heterosexual couples, but that most lesbian couples and a small number of gay male couples are also able to provide positive outcomes for adoptees. A psychologist testified that, above all else, it s important that, when only one person adopts a child, that person should be female, for nurturing influences are particularly important to orphans. There was also professional testimony critical of the methodology and conclusions of these studies. Following hearings and debate, the following legislation was duly enacted:

CHILD ADOPTION REFORM ACT (CARA)

§ 1. Findings:
    (a) Every child deserves to grow up in a loving and stable home.
    (b) Children, including adopted children, are more likely to thrive when raised by male-female couples.
    (c) It is more important for a child to be raised by a mother than a father, and usually harmful for a child to be raised without a mother.

§ 2. Therefore:
    (a) If the Georgia Child Placement Agency (GCPA) places a child for adoption with a family other than a male-female couple, such adoption shall remain provisional for a period of two years. Within this provisional time period, if a more suitable family becomes eligible to adopt the child, the GCPA shall revoke the provisional placement and place the child with such suitable family unless the provisional family demonstrates by clear and convincing evidence that this removal would cause severe and permanent emotional damage to the child.
  (b) In the case of two or more otherwise eligible adoptive families for a child, the GCPA shall preferentially place the child as follows: first, with a family consisting of a legally married mother and father; second, with a family consisting of a mother only; third, with a family consisting of two mothers in a legal same-sex union. If none of these placements is available, the child shall remain on the adoption waiting list.

Matthew Sanders, a heterosexual single man, wishes to adopt a nine-year-old child, Allison, whom he has cared for as a foster parent for four years. Pursuant to CARA, the GCPA has determined that Sanders is not eligible to adopt Allison although he is a fit and loving caregiver and no eligible adoptive family wishes to adopt Allison. Sanders challenges the constitutionality of CARA and GCPA's decision. He has asked your advice.

Assume Sanders has standing to challenge the constitutionality of CARA and the actions of GCPA pursuant to CARA and that Sanders, before becoming Allison's foster parent, underwent a sex change surgical procedure, was given hormone therapy, and commenced to dress as a woman. With these changes, Matthew Sanders also took on a new name, Melissa Sanders. **Analyze Sanders's claims under the Fourteenth Amendment.**

3. Local juvenile curfews were advocated by both Bill Clinton and Bob Dole during the 1996 presidential campaign, and numerous towns across America adopted a variety of such curfews. It was not until 2006, however, that warring Democrats and Republicans in Congress agreed to the following legislation to adopt juvenile curfews nationwide.

THE JUVENILE CURFEW ACT

§ 1. **Findings**:

(a) Juvenile delinquency, including petty theft, burglary, drug and alcohol abuse, and premarital sex, occurs primarily between the hours of 11 p.m. and 6 a.m.;

(b) Juvenile victims of crime suffer most assaults, thefts, rapes, and homicides between the hours of 11 p.m. and 6 a.m.; and

(c) Juvenile delinquency adversely affects school attendance, school performance, and the work reliability of juveniles.

§ 2. **Therefore**:

(a) It shall be unlawful for any juvenile to remain, idle, wander, stroll or play in any public place or establishment away from home during curfew hours unless the juvenile is:

  (1) Performing an emergency errand;
  (2) Accompanying a parent, guardian, custodian, or other adult person having custody or control of such juvenile;
  (3) Engaging in a specific activity directed or permitted by such parent, guardian, custodian, or other adult person; or
  (4) Attending or returning from a special function or event sponsored by any religious institution, school, club, or other organization.

(b) Police officers must issue citations to violators, take violators to the police station, and fine violators not more than $100 per violation.

(c) In this legislation, the term "juvenile" shall mean any individual under age 18 and "curfew hours" shall mean the hours of 11 p.m. to 6 a.m.

Nora Nightowl and Jason Moonshine, 17-year-old residents of Smalltown, were apprehended by the Smalltown police while conversing at midnight on a park bench located roughly midway between their homes. They were taken to the police station, issued a citation, and fined $50 apiece. Their parents were then contacted to pick them up at the station. Mortified and angered, Nora and Jason ask you, an attorney for the Anti-Curfew League of America, to challenge the Juvenile Curfew Act of 2006 ("JCA").

a. Does Congress have the power under the Commerce Clause to enact the JCA?

b. Does the JCA violate the Fifth Amendment's due process guarantee?

4. Angelica and Bernice, both female, are a married couple who live in North Carolina. They would like to become parents and they discuss various options. They want their child to be genetically related to both of them and are thus delighted when Angelica's brother, Caleb, offers to act as a sperm donor. They plan to artificially inseminate Bernice's egg with Caleb's sperm and have the resulting embryo implanted into Angelica's uterus for gestation and birth. In this way, the child would be genetically related to Bernice through her egg and to Angelica through her biological brother's sperm. However, when they present this plan to their fertility doctor, she informs them it would violate the following North Carolina statute:

INFERTILITY CESSATION TABOO (INCEST) ACT OF 2016

Preamble: Technology has the potential to enable a range of unnatural and immoral reproductive results, contrary to the values and traditions of the People of North Carolina.

Section 1: It shall be unlawful for any male knowingly to serve as a sperm donor where (a) his sperm would fertilize the ovum of any female relative where it would be unlawful for the male to marry that female under the laws of the State, or (b) his sperm would create an embryo implanted and gestated by any female relative where it would be unlawful for the male to marry that gestating female under North Carolina law.

Section 2: Violation of Section 1 shall be punishable by two years imprisonment.

As their doctor explains to the couple, North Carolina law prohibits marriage between siblings, whether related by blood, half-blood, or adoption. Therefore, under the INCEST ACT, if Angelica carried an embryo created with her brother's sperm and her spouse Bernice's egg, Caleb would be guilty of a criminal offense.

Sexual intercourse between people prohibited from marrying under state law has long been criminalized, in North Carolina and most other states, though the specific rules have changed somewhat over time (for example, marrying a second cousin was legal in North Carolina in 1850, illegal in 1920, and legal since 1960.) Indeed, taboos and prohibitions against sexual relations between siblings have existed to some extent in all known human societies and are thought to be driven by the so-called "Westermark effect." Scientists believe this effect, present in many animal species, keeps individuals raised together in close proximity from experiencing sexual attraction for one another, helps maintain genetic diversity, and tends to prevent genetic diseases and defects.

When the North Carolina legislature in 1960 altered its laws regarding marriage of relatives, proponents asserted there was no scientific basis for banning second degree and more distant cousins from marrying or reproducing because the increased risk of birth defects was negligible. They also argued there was no basis for banning consensual intercourse between adult siblings or first cousins not related by blood but rather by adoption or marriage. Opponents of the amendments responded that all such intimate relations were immoral and improper, regardless of genetics or science and apart from any risk of birth defects in offspring. The change in the 1960 law to allow second degree cousins to marry, but leave in place other restrictions, resulted from an eleventh-hour compromise between these legislative factions.

The INCEST ACT of 2016 was enacted amid national debate around marriage equality. Led by Donald Cruise, the Act's sponsors stated in a joint press conference: "It is immoral and just plain yucky for a woman to carry a baby conceived with her brother's sperm. That means his sperm is sort of like inside his sister's body, and that's just gross no matter how it got there. If it's her egg, well, that's even worse." Asked whether women involved in such acts should also be punished, Cruise stated, "well, of course they should be. They should go to jail." However, after an aide whispered something in his ear, he said, "I mean no, of course not, only the man should be punished. Women don't need to be punished because they have common sense and will realize it is immoral and disgusting, but men sometimes just want to spread their sperm around, so we need a law to make them stop."

Angelica, Bernice, and Caleb, wishing to challenge the INCEST Act, consult the law firm where you are a summer associate. A partner sends you this email: "**Analyze the constitutionality of the INCEST Act of 2016 under the Fourteenth Amendment. Avoid other issues, as other associates are working on them.**" Do so.

5. The Boston Marathon bombing of April 15, 2013, which killed three people and wounded scores more, occurred just as Congress was considering the most wide-ranging immigration reform in a generation.

The bombers, labeled "terrorists" by President Obama, were two brothers who immigrated to the United States from the Chechen region of Russia in 2002. The older brother, Tamerlan Tsarnaev, a lawful resident of the United States, had spent three months in the Chechen region of Russia a year prior to the bombings. Though he allegedly went to visit relatives, Tamerlan became radicalized by a Chechen Islamic affiliate of al Qaeda while in Russia. The younger brother, 19-year-old Dzhokhar Tsarnaev, was a naturalized American citizen. To radicalize and train his younger brother, Tamerlan used Islamic jihadist indoctrination videos and bomb making instructions obtained from the internet.

The comprehensive immigration reform bill generally reflected the view that immigration, despite this tragedy, was good for the country. However, in exchange for their support of the bill, a group of Senators successfully demanded that a group of homeland security protections be inserted, citing data showing that all virtually all terrorism threats in the past decade were from radicalized Islamists. Referred to as the Save the Homeland from

Immigrant Terrorists (SHIT) provisions by detractors, these provisions were enacted by Congress as part of the broader bill. President Obama signed the bill despite these provisions, three of which follow:

§ 1300. Blood samples shall be drawn from all Islamic immigrants immediately after entry to the United States. The biometric data from such samples shall be entered into the National Biometric Database (NBD). [The NBD currently contains only data from persons arrested in the United States]

§ 1301. Each high school principal shall certify to the Secretary of Homeland Security, for each Islamic immigrant student graduating from the school, that the student has demonstrated his or her loyalty to the United States and has renounced terrorism. Certification shall be provided only after such student has successfully completed a course, Values in American Democracy (VAD). The curriculum for VAD shall be provided in regulations issued by the Secretary of Education, with the consent of the Speaker of the House of Representatives, not more than six months following passage of this Act. The federal district courts shall order deportation of each Islamic immigrant student who has graduated from high school without being so certified.

Using the concepts and cases you have studied in Constitutional Law, answer the following questions:

(1) Does § 1300 violate Fifth Amendment rights of Muslim immigrants not to be "deprived of life, liberty, or property, without due process of law"?

(2) Does § 1301 violate separation of powers and federalism concepts?

Chapter IX:

1.   Justin Travis had felt uncomfortable "inhabiting a male body" ever since he was in junior high school. After attending college and beginning a career in California, Justin decided he would convert his body to match his psyche.

In 1999, Travis changed his name to Julienne Travis, began taking female hormones, and commenced to dress and groom as a female. In 2001, Travis had breast implants and began using women's restrooms. Finally, in early 2003, after saving diligently for the procedure over many months, Travis was prepared to take the final step to femininity: surgical conversion of his genitals from those of a male to those of a female. The very day that Travis made a down payment on the $10,000 operation, he was driving home listening to California Public Radio when he heard a news story that almost caused him to crash. A transcript of the story follows:

> Today, the culture wars reached a new level of combat. Governor Ashcrafty signed legislation making it a felony for any physician, clinic or hospital in the State of California to perform 'any surgical procedure converting the genitals of a male to those of a female.' The Governor noted that over 100 California males had such operations in the past year, that no comparable surgical procedure has been developed for converting females to

males, and that the legislation would also prevent such tragedies as the one that befell a famous singer who died last year from complications arising out of such an operation. The Governor's statement also mentioned the widespread belief among most Californians that such legislation would keep mentally unstable individuals from being mutilated by predatory clinics and would reaffirm God's plan 'to divide the human species into two sexes, inalterably distinguishable, from birth to death.' Challenges to the legislation are expected, says Northern California law professor Larry Tribal.

Deciding (s)he would rather fight than run, Travis has teamed up with the "Be What You Wanna Be" Clinic, the site of the scheduled operation. **Travis and the Clinic have asked your advice concerning their chances of overturning the new legislation on either substantive Due Process or Equal Protection grounds.** They have asked for advice of another specialist as to whether the legislation is vulnerable on other grounds (such as the First Amendment), so you need not worry about those issues. You may also assume that the Governor Ashcrafty's statement that there is no comparable surgical procedure for female to male operations is accurate.

2. The fiftieth anniversary of *Brown v. Board of Education* generated many public and private discussions about the education of racial minorities in the United States, as well as a large number of academic studies concerning that topic. As a result, Congress held hearings on the topic and passed the following legislation, which was signed by the President:

THE PROMISE OF BROWN EDUCATION ACT

§ 1. **Findings**:

(a) *Brown v. Board of Education* in 1954 properly removed state-imposed barriers to the education of African-American students wishing to attend public elementary and secondary schools with White students;

(b) Congress provided federal financial support in the Civil Rights Act of 1964 for racially integrated public schools and denied such support for single-race or segregated public schools;

(c) Despite the foregoing decision and statute, African-American students continue to receive educational opportunities inferior to the educational opportunities of White students;

(d) Educational experts are overwhelmingly of the opinion that there are two causes for this educational disparity: (1) unequal funding for predominantly African-American public schools compared to predominantly White public schools; and (2) preferential treatment of White students in mixed race classrooms; and

(e) The courts have failed to adequately address the inequality of funding, and virtually no lawsuits have been filed challenging the inequality of classroom treatment.

§ 2. **Remediation**: To remedy the continuing problems of educational inequity in the United States, Congress hereby provides as follows:

(a) The states are hereby required to create, in any urban area exceeding a population of more than 500,000 persons, magnet elementary schools for African-American students who choose to enroll in such schools.

(b) Funds are hereby appropriated to equalize funding of any public elementary school attended predominantly by African-American students, including the magnet schools mandated by Section 2(a) of this Act, so that the per-pupil funds available to such school are equal to the per-pupil funds available to the best-funded predominately White public elementary school in the state.

Does the Promise of Brown Education Act of 2005 ("PBEA") violate the constitutional guarantee of Equal Protection?

3. The Council on Higher Education issued a report noting that women currently constitute 20% of the graduate students in engineering, 30% of the graduate students in the physical sciences, and 35% of the graduate students in mathematics. The report stated that the underrepresentation of women reflected many factors, including the lack of female role models in these areas (attributable in part to past discrimination against female applicants in these fields) and social pressures for women to seek other fields. The report asserted that the relatively small number of women interfered with the education of all graduate students in these fields, that scientists are playing an increasingly important role in public policy, and that women must not be excluded from these leadership roles. In response to the report, many universities sought to enroll more women in their engineering, math, and science graduate programs. Many universities gave preferences to women applying to graduate programs in engineering, math, and science.

The Education Committee of the United States Senate held hearings focusing both on the number of women in graduate engineering, math, and science programs and on the adoption of preferential admissions for female applicants in these fields. The testimony included the following statement from Larry Winter, the President of Crimson University:

> What's responsible for the small number of leading women in engineering, math, and science fields is the general clash between people's legitimate family desires and employers' current desire for high power and high intensity. In science, math, and engineering, there are also issues of intrinsic sex-linked aptitudes.

As a result of these hearings, Congress passed and the President signed the following legislation:

EQUAL GRADUATE SCIENCE ACT

§ 1. **Findings**:

(a) Public and private educational institutions have a history of pervasive and pernicious discrimination based on gender in their graduate programs in engineering, mathematics, and science;

(b) Discrimination based on gender in graduate admissions programs denies equal protection to those who are rejected because of the discrimination and stigmatizes all admitted students of the favored gender;

(c) The relative representation of genders in various graduate programs today reflects voluntary career choices and innate abilities; and

(d) Maintaining the highest standards of excellence in engineering, math, and science is essential to the health of the nation's economy.

§ 2. **Therefore**:

(a) With respect to graduate programs in engineering, math, and science, no educational institution may set limits on the number of admitted students of any gender.

(b) With respect to graduate programs in engineering, math, and science, no educational institution may give any preference in admissions based on gender.

(c) To help ensure compliance with this Act, all educational institutions offering graduate programs in engineering, math, and science, shall submit a report on an annual basis to the United States Department of Education containing the following information on each applicant: the applicant's gender, the applicant's test scores on the Graduate Record Exam or similar standardized test, and whether the applicant was offered admission.

Is the Equal Graduate Science Act ("EGSA") a valid exercise of Congress' power to enforce the Equal Protection Clause of the Fourteenth Amendment?

4. Following several highly publicized crimes by repeat sex offenders in several states, United States House and Senate committees held hearings on sex crime recidivism. The evidence presented to the committee included scientific studies showing that, if a man commits a sexual offense, the probability is very high that he will commit another sexual offense in the future. The evidence before the committees also included testimony by a geneticist at Emory University who stated that certain genetic markers located on the "Y" chromosome (present only in males) indicate a high likelihood of committing violent sex crimes. Some states have sex offender registries, which alert local police to potential dangers. However, sex offenders move frequently and often do not register in their new locations.

Representatives and Senators considered several possible responses. The proposals included mandatory chemical castration of sex offenders through the injection of certain chemicals and also mandatory surgical castration. Chemical and surgical castration reduce a man's urge to commit sexual offenses, though surgical castration results in a greater reduction. Chemical castration is temporary; surgical castration is permanent. Surgical castration also makes a man incapable of becoming a biological parent.

Members of Congress also debated whether female offenders should be subject to analogous chemical or surgical procedures. However, the sponsor of the bill, herself a victim of a sex offense, declared, "The reality is that women have enough problems, taking care of children and helping to support families. We should not impose additional hassles on them without very good reason." Following the hearings and debates, this legislation was enacted into law:

SEX OFFENSE PREVENTION ACT (SOPA)

1. **Findings**:
   (a) Sex offenders present a great threat to the safety and security of American families.
   (b) Sex offenses and the fear of sex offenses make people less willing to leave their homes and their offices to engage in business activity, serving as barriers to interstate travel and imposing large costs on the economy.
   (c) Male sex offenders have a very high rate of committing future sex crimes. Female sex offenders have a very low rate of recidivism.
   (d) Scientific studies have identified genetic markers that indicate a very high likelihood that certain men will commit a sex offense. Surgical castration greatly reduces the chances that genetically predisposed men will commit sex offenses.
   (e) The incidence of sex crimes can be greatly reduced if police authorities are aware of the names and locations of sex offenders within their jurisdictions.
   (f) It is difficult for individual States to track Sex offenders, who often evade surveillance by moving between States and within a single State.

2. **Therefore**:
   (a) <u>Definition:</u> For purposes of this Act, "sex offender" means a man convicted under the law of any State for a crime that includes sexual contact with the victim. Such crimes include, but are not limited to, rape and child molestation.
   (b) <u>State Sex Offender Registry Program</u>
       (1) Each State shall establish a sex offender registry program, under which sex offenders are required to provide to the State their names, current addresses, and current employer and the employer's address.
       (2) Each State shall transmit sex offender information, including any updates in that information, to the United States Department of Justice, within 10 days of the State's receiving the information.
   (c) <u>Federal Crime of Failure to Register or Update</u>
       (1) A sex offender must register with the State sex offender registry within 30 days of moving to a State.
       (2) A sex offender must provide updated information to a State sex offender registry within 30 days of buying or renting a house, apartment, or other dwelling place in the State, or accepting new employment in the State.
       (3) It shall be a federal crime, punishable by up to 10 years in prison, for a sex offender to violate the registration or updating requirements of (c)(1) and (c)(2).

(d) <u>Funding for Zero Strike Program</u>

     (1) All States receiving federal health care funds shall establish a program

        (i) to identify men genetically predisposed to commit sexual offenses, and

        (ii) to castrate such men.

     (2) If a State fails to implement subsection (d)(1) of this section, the State shall forfeit 10 per cent of the federal health care funds it otherwise would receive.

(1) Does SOPA violate federalism principles?

(2) Is section 2(c) of SOPA a valid exercise of Congress's power under the commerce clause?

(3) Does SOPA violate equal protection principles?

(4) Does section 2(d) of SOPA violate due process principles?

5. The Virginia Women's Prison, a state-run facility for women convicted of felonies involving injury to persons or property and drug offenses, has long had a rule against sex among inmates, whether coerced or consensual. The warden, Baba Vawa, says such a rule is common to all prisons in Virginia, whether they hold male or female inmates. The rule is "primarily to prevent violence and the spread of disease," but Vawa acknowledged that "prison is punishment, and prohibition on sexual activity is part of punishment." The sole exception is that prisons for white-collar prisoners (those convicted of tax evasion and similar non-violent crimes) allow conjugal visits (including sexual relations) once a month in special "motel-like" units. Conjugal visits are permitted only for "one man, one woman" state-licensed marriages entered into prior to incarceration. The Virginia Women's Prison houses no white-collar prisoners and has no such units, and conjugal visits are not allowed.

About a year ago, under Warden Vawa's leadership, the Virginia Women's Prison conducted a study which revealed that, despite the standard rule against sexual relationships, a number of female inmates were involved in sexual relationships with other inmates. To terminate these relationships, the warden ordered that masculine-looking inmates be systematically relocated to a separate wing of the prison to break up relationships with more feminine inmates. The determination as to who would be moved was based on whether the inmate had "loose-fitting clothes, short hair, or otherwise masculine looks."

Warden Vawa acknowledged in an interview with the *Gay Times*, a local newspaper, that she knew this solution to prison sex was not a "complete cure," because some sexually active inmates were not as easily identified as those moved to what she called the "butch wing." "We probably solved 80% of the problem," said Vawa, "and are seeking to solve the other 20% with selective changes of cellmates as we discover relationships having a sexual component." Vawa also acknowledged that a few women moved may not have been lesbians, but said "There is no better way to identify them."

One inmate moved to the separate wing, Summer Triola, said she "had never been so humiliated." "I have been a lesbian my whole life, and until now did not feel stigmatized. But when the guards told me I was being transferred to the 'butch wing,' I was mortified." Triola acknowledged that the cells in the separate wing of the prison are identical to the other cells, but noted that prisoners in this wing are taken to meals and outdoor exercise breaks on schedules preventing contact with other inmates. Both Triola and her former cellmate, Winter Biola, say the change has been a real hardship. "I miss her so much," said each inmate. Warden Vawa acknowledged that "with female prisoners, relationships are very important," but that "they should have thought of that before they started dealing drugs."

You are a lawyer with the Lawyers for More Humane Prison Conditions Project. Analyze whether the above prison practices violate Triola's rights under the Equal Protection Clause of the Fourteenth Amendment.

Chapter X:

1. In the wake of several highly publicized incidents in which gays and lesbians were the targets of violent acts, Congress held hearings on the problem of crime motivated by anti-gay and -lesbian bias. At the hearings, several witnesses testified that state and local police forces did not provide adequate protection for gays and lesbians. The witnesses suggested that the police officers, themselves, often had anti-gay and anti-lesbian feelings and that because of these feelings, the police officers did not adequately patrol areas prone to anti-gay and -lesbian violence and did not adequately investigate violent acts against gays and lesbians. After the hearings, Congress enacted and the President signed the following legislation:

EQUAL POLICE PROTECTION ACT

§ 1. Findings:

(a) Gays and lesbians are disproportionately the targets of violent crime;

(b) Because of bias against gays and lesbians, state and local police forces often do not provide adequate protection for gays and lesbians; and

(c) Violent crime against gays and lesbians interferes with their ability to work, shop, transact business and otherwise engage in commerce, including interstate commerce.

§ 2. Therefore:

(a) In performing their law enforcement functions, including crime-prevention activity and criminal investigation, state and local police forces shall not discriminate based on the sexual orientation of the victim or intended victim of the crime.

(b) Any person who suffers injury because a state or local police force violates Section 2(a) of this Act shall have a cause of action for damages not to exceed $250,000 against that state or locality.

(c) In any action brought to enforce this Act, the state or locality may not assert a defense of sovereign immunity.

New Hope is a state in the United States. The National Gay and Lesbian Coalition ("NGLC") organized a weekend symposium at Woody Hollow, a state park in New Hope, for March 17, 2000. The New Hope State Police are the police with jurisdiction over Woody Hollow. A week before the symposium, the NGLC notified the New Hope State Police that it had received threats that anti-gay and anti-lesbian violence might occur at the symposium. The NGLC also notified the New Hope State Police that some of NGLC's prior events have been disrupted by violent attacks.

The New Hope State Police generally provide police protection for events at state parks. However, no police protection was provided for the NGLC symposium. The symposium events were disrupted by violent anti-gay and lesbian protests, and several of the participants were severely injured. A seminar participant who was injured has threatened to sue NGLC and the symposium organizer. Invoking the Equal Police Protection Act ("EPPA"), the symposium organizer files suit against New Hope in state court seeking compensatory damages of $250,000.

> **a.   Is the EPPA a valid exercise of Congress's powers: (i) To regulate interstate commerce; or (ii) To enforce the Equal Protection Clause of the Fourteenth Amendment?**
>
> **b.   Do (i) standing or (ii) sovereign immunity bar the suit?**

2.   Assume that police officers may make investigative stops of vehicles that arouse their suspicion, even without any evidence of criminal activity, may search the vehicle if they have reasonable suspicion of criminal activity. Police officers may not actually arrest the driver or any other occupants of the car unless the police discover actual evidence of criminal activity.

* * *

News reports alleged that police target African Americans and other racial minorities for such investigative stops disproportionately. They, emphasized the large number of African American drivers stopped, but not arrested, as evidence of police bias. Congress held hearings to investigate these allegations of racial bias and debated various legislative proposals. One of the concerns expressed in these debates was that a future President might not fully enforce the provisions of the legislation. Ultimately, Congress enacted and the President signed the following legislation, effective in December, 2002:

DRIVING WITHOUT DISCRIMINATION ACT

§ 1. **Findings**:

> (a) The vast majority of law enforcement agents nationwide discharge their duties professionally, without bias, and protect the safety of their communities;
>
> (b) Statistical evidence demonstrates that racial profiling (police officers' use of race or ethnicity in deciding which drivers should be subject to investigative stops) is a real and measurable phenomenon;

(c) A Department of Justice report found that, although African-American and Hispanic motorists were more likely to be stopped and searched, they were less likely to be in possession of contraband than white drivers; and

(d) Racial profiling violates the guarantee of equal protection and may discourage individuals from driving freely, impairing both interstate and intrastate commerce.

§ 2. **Therefore**:

(a)   No state or local law enforcement officer shall stop a driver based on the driver's race or ethnicity.

(b)   Every state and local police department shall keep a record of all investigative traffic stops, including the race and ethnicity of the driver and whether an arrest was made. By February 1 of each year, every state and local police department shall transmit the investigative stop record for the preceding calendar year to the United States Department of Justice.

(c)   In a given calendar year, no state or local police department shall stop but not arrest drivers of one race or ethnicity in a substantially greater percentage than their proportion of the drivers in that state or locality. Substantially greater percentage shall mean more than 10 percentage points.

(d)   If a state or local police department violates section 2(c) of this Act, such police department shall be subject to suit for damages by any driver who (i) was stopped but not arrested by that police department during the calendar year and (ii) is a member of a racial or ethnic group subject to substantially greater percentage stops without arrests by that police department during that calendar year. If such a suit is successful, the plaintiff shall be entitled to liquidated damages in the amount of $10,000 and reasonable attorneys' fees.

(e)   There shall be created, in the United States Department of Justice, an official known as the Racial Justice Coordinator ("RJC"). The United States Supreme Court shall appoint the RJC, and the appointment must be confirmed by a majority of the Senate. The RJC may not be removed except by impeachment and shall have the authority to seek an injunction against any state or local police force to enforce the provisions of this Act.

A New Jersey State Police officer stopped Janice Joiner, an African American from Princeton, New Jersey, in February, 2003, while she was driving to visit her father in a nearby New Jersey town. The officer checked her driver's license, which was valid. He then told her that he thought he smelled marijuana. He searched her car. When the police officer found no contraband, he allowed Janice to continue on her way. The stop lasted approximately 30 minutes, and Janice had to wait on the side of the highway while the car was searched.

The February 1, 2004 investigative stop record required by Section 2(b) of the Driving Without Discrimination Act ("DWDA") revealed that, during 2003, thirty percent (30%) of the drivers stopped but not arrested by the New

Jersey State Police were African-American. It is undisputed that African Americans constituted only ten percent (10%) of the drivers in New Jersey. It is thus undisputed that the New Jersey State Police violated Section 2(c) of the DWDA.

Invoking the DWDA, Janice files suit against the New Jersey State Police in New Jersey state court seeking liquidated damages of $10,000 for the inconvenience and embarrassment of the stop plus attorneys' fees.

a. Is the DWDA a valid exercise of Congress's powers (i) To regulate interstate commerce; or (ii) To enforce the provisions of the 14th Amendment equal protection clause?

b. Does DWDA Section 2(e) violate the separation of powers?

3. The Georgia legislature approved funding for a public high school intended to serve the "special needs of the State's gay, lesbian, bisexual, and transgender teens." At a news conference, Governor Frank Barney stated, "these students have a hard time in the regular schools. They get harassed. Studies show that gay teens have a high rate of depression and suicide. They need a place where they can feel safe and secure so that they can learn. Every young person – gay and straight – deserves an equal educational opportunity in this great State." The Georgia Learning Brings Transformation (GLBT) High School opened with an initial enrollment of 100 students. The school's facilities, staff, and materials were excellent.

Sally Student was an eighth-grade student who attended an inner-city Georgia middle school infamous for its run-down facilities, lack of adequate materials, and large class sizes. Sally's parents submitted an application for Sally, a heterosexual female, to attend GLBT High. Despite her excellent academic performance, Sally was rejected. The principal of GLBT High wrote to Sally and her parents that the school "reserves its few spaces for gay, lesbian, bisexual, and transgender students." Sally's parents sued Georgia, claiming that GLBT High violates the Equal Protection Clause.

GLBT High proved extremely controversial. Many local and national leaders protested that the school gave "special treatment" to homosexuals and "promoted a homosexual lifestyle." After legislatures in several other states opened schools similar to GLBT High, Congress passed, and the President signed, this statute:

VALUES IN EDUCATION ACT ("VEA")

§ 1. **Findings and Purpose**:

  (a) Heterosexuality, a tradition of our nation, should be fostered by public schools;
  (b) Children and teens respond to suggestion and pressure about lifestyle choices;
  (c) Schools based on sexual preference injure educational performance, harm the national economy, and undermine the nation's commitment to equality; and

(d) The psychological health of children and teens requires exposure to diverse views on the morality of homosexuality, not insulation in segregated schools.

§ 2. **Therefore**:

(a) No public school shall employ a student's sexual preference or orientation as a factor in admission.

(b) No federal school funding shall be provided to any state that employs a student's sexual preference or orientation as a factor for admission to any public school.

a. Did Gambrell violate the Equal Protection Clause of the 14th Amendment when it funded GLBT High?

b. Did Congress have the power to enact the Values in Education Act under the: (i) Commerce Clause; (ii) Spending Clause; or (iii) 14th Amendment?

4. Sally Smart is a United States Senator from the State of New Hope. On her way to the office one morning, she heard the following story on the radio:

> State legislators in the State of Bessland just passed legislation establishing two single-sex state colleges. Currently Bessland has no public single-sex colleges. The sponsor of the legislation, state senator Brenda Bright, commented, 'Social science evidence proves that some students of both genders perform better in college in a single-sex environment. Those students should have the option of a public, single-sex college education.' It appears that other states may well follow the lead of Bessland. Legislation to establish single-sex colleges is currently pending in the legislatures of 30 other states.

Senator Smart arrived at her office enraged. She called in her chief legislative counsel and declared, "I have a Ph.D. in sociology. I know those studies claiming that students perform better in single-sex colleges, and those studies are a load of rubbish. Single-sex colleges are a return to the old days when women went to finishing schools to learn flower arranging and men went to all-male colleges to get their fancy education without the need to compete against well-qualified women. We have to stop that from happening again."

Senator Smart, who chairs the Senate Education Committee, held hearings about single-sex education. About 20 education scholars testified. Fifteen of the education scholars testified that no reliable, social scientific data proves that any students perform better in single-sex colleges. These fifteen scholars further testified that the most reliable studies showed that both men and women perform better in mixed-gender (that is, coeducational) colleges. By contrast, the five other scholars testified that they believed that reliable social scientific studies, such as those studies relied on by the Bessland legislature, did prove that some men and women perform better in single-sex colleges. In addition, about 10 historians appeared before the committee, and all testified that in the past, the great majority of public and private colleges were single-sex, the women's colleges had much less funding, and that the prior system of single-sex colleges interfered with the ability of women to receive an education equal to men.

Following the hearings, Senator Smart introduced the following legislation, which passed both houses of Congress and was signed by President Rumsfeld:

EQUAL ACCESS TO COLLEGE ACT

§ 1. **Findings**:

(a) Single-sex colleges in the past have interfered with the educational opportunities of women;

(b) Social scientific evidence demonstrates that single-sex colleges do not enhance the educational opportunities of men or women;

(c) Mixed-gender educational environments are essential for men and women to learn to function together in society;

(d) Providing the best possible educational environment is essential for the economic welfare of the United States; and

(e) Single-gender education impairs interstate commerce and violates the guarantee of equal protection.

§ 2. **Therefore**:

(a) No state college may deny admission to any student on the basis of gender.

(b) To ensure proper enforcement of this Act, every state college shall prepare a report on an annual basis containing the following information on each applicant: the applicant's gender, the applicant's test scores on the SAT, ACT or similar standardized test, and whether the applicant was admitted.

(c) Violation of any provision of this Act shall constitute a misdemeanor, for which the state college may be fined up to $10,000.

***

a. Is the Equal Access to College Act a valid exercise of Congress's powers to regulate interstate commerce?

b. Is the Equal Access to College Act a valid exercise of Congress's powers to enforce the provisions of the Equal Protection Clause of the Fourteenth Amendment?

***

At the signing ceremony for the Equal Access to College Act, President Rumsfeld held a news conference at which he said: "I am four-square behind the intent of this legislation. In Iraq, men and women fought together. It is essential that they learn to work together in civilian life as well." Shortly thereafter, President Rumsfeld issued an executive order specifying steps the Executive Branch would take to "further the goals of the Equal Access to College Act." This order provided that military recruiters would not visit any public or private single-sex college, that no graduate of such a college would be eligible to be an officer in the military, and that no government contracts would be awarded to any college having less than a 20% representation of either gender among its student body.

c. Is President Rumsfeld's order constitutional?

5, Paul Beebe and Jesse Sanford, members of the White Nazi Party of America (WNPA) and part-time firemen in Page, Oklahoma, assaulted and tied up a developmentally disabled Native American man in the firehouse. The two men then branded their victim with a swastika and the words "Property WNPA." Beebe and Sanford were indicted for violating the Hate Crimes Prevention Act (HCPA), which makes it a crime to "willfully cause bodily injury to any person because of the actual or perceived race, color, religion, national origin, or disability of any person." Violation of HCPA involves criminal punishment of up to life in prison. When it passed the Hate Crimes Prevention Act, Congress explicitly premised its authority on both the Thirteenth and Fourteenth Amendments. Legislative history shows that Congress was concerned about hate crimes against all persons, and documented numerous instances of hate crimes against gays and African-Americans in the decades prior to the passage of the HCPA.

Before trial, defendants moved to dismiss the indictments on the theory that HCPA exceeds Congress's Thirteenth and Fourteenth Amendment enforcement powers. Advise the judge how she should rule, using concepts and cases from your constitutional law course.

6. As genetic manipulation techniques became more advanced, some fertility clinics and obstetricians began to promote a range of "designer baby" services to wealthy prospective parents. For example, after a study showed that height in males was positively correlated with academic, social, financial, and romantic success, as well as increased happiness, some clinics added "male fetus height selection" to their menus of services. These clinics claimed to predict as early as eight weeks after conception whether a fetus would be above average in height. Other services included selection for attractiveness (facial symmetry), intelligence, and mental health.

In the fictional state of Gambrell, state employees receive generous health care benefits including contraception, fertility treatment, and abortion services. Recently, a number of Gambrell employees have accessed "designer baby" clinic services and Gambrell has paid for such services.

The Congressional Pro-Life Caucus (CPLC) is a group of United States Representatives and Senators opposed to abortion. At weekly prayer breakfasts, they discuss strategies to overturn or undermine *Roe v. Wade*. At one of these breakfasts, the Caucus discussed "the increasing use of height-selective abortion by rich liberal yuppie blue-state anti-lifers," and other "designer baby abominations." Following this meeting, several CPLC members sponsored the following legislation, which passed Congress, was vetoed by President Obama, and was then enacted over presidential veto by an overwhelming vote of both Houses:

THE ALL FETUSES ARE PRECIOUS (AFAP) ACT

§ 1 Findings:

(a) Selective abortion is increasingly being used to terminate pregnancies based on projected height, intelligence, attractiveness, or physical and mental disability.

(b) A Designer Baby Boutique (DBB) is any person or entity that provides abortions described in § 1(a). DBBs are a multibillion-dollar industry, particularly in New York, California, and Gambrell, to which women frequently travel to obtain such abortions.

(c) Recent studies by the American College of Obstetricians show fetuses experience more pain and higher cognitive functions than previously understood.

§ 2 Therefore:

(a) It shall be a violation of this Act to knowingly (i) counsel or perform an abortion, at any time in a pregnancy, knowing that such abortion is sought based on the projected height, intelligence, attractiveness, physical disability, or mental disability of the child; or (ii) cross state lines or transport a woman across state lines for the purpose of securing such an abortion.

b) Counseling or abortion that otherwise would violate §2(a) is permitted where necessary to preserve the mother's life, except in New York, California, and Gambrell, where lax regulations and enforcement have encouraged DBBs to falsely assert maternal life exceptions to circumvent federal abortion regulation.

(c) No employer may reimburse, cover the cost of, or provide insurance for any services performed by DBBs, regardless of whether those services include selective abortion based on the projected height, intelligence, attractiveness, or physical or mental disability of the child.

(1) Does Congress have the power to enact the AFAP Act (or any parts of it) under (a) the Commerce Clause or (b) § 5 of the Fourteenth Amendment?

(2) Does the AFAP Act (or any parts of it) violate due process?

Index

References are to Pages

T

U

V

W